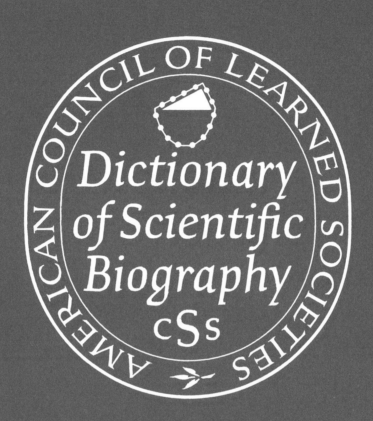

AMERICAN COUNCIL OF LEARNED SOCIETIES

Dictionary
of Scientific
Biography

cSs

DICTIONARY
OF
SCIENTIFIC BIOGRAPHY

PUBLISHED UNDER THE AUSPICES OF
THE AMERICAN COUNCIL OF LEARNED SOCIETIES

The American Council of Learned Societies, organized in 1919 for the purpose of advancing the study of the humanities and of the humanistic aspects of the social sciences, is a nonprofit federation comprising forty-one national scholarly groups. The Council represents the humanities in the United States in the International Union of Academies, provides fellowships and grants-in-aid, supports research-and-planning conferences and symposia, and sponsors special projects and scholarly publications.

MEMBER ORGANIZATIONS

AMERICAN PHILOSOPHICAL SOCIETY, 1743

AMERICAN ACADEMY OF ARTS AND SCIENCES, 1780

AMERICAN ANTIQUARIAN SOCIETY, 1812

AMERICAN ORIENTAL SOCIETY, 1842

AMERICAN NUMISMATIC SOCIETY, 1858

AMERICAN PHILOLOGICAL ASSOCIATION, 1869

ARCHAEOLOGICAL INSTITUTE OF AMERICA, 1879

SOCIETY OF BIBLICAL LITERATURE, 1880

MODERN LANGUAGE ASSOCIATION OF AMERICA, 1883

AMERICAN HISTORICAL ASSOCIATION, 1884

AMERICAN ECONOMIC ASSOCIATION, 1885

AMERICAN FOLKLORE SOCIETY, 1888

AMERICAN DIALECT SOCIETY, 1889

AMERICAN PSYCHOLOGICAL ASSOCIATION, 1892

ASSOCIATION OF AMERICAN LAW SCHOOLS, 1900

AMERICAN PHILOSOPHICAL ASSOCIATION, 1901

AMERICAN ANTHROPOLOGICAL ASSOCIATION, 1902

AMERICAN POLITICAL SCIENCE ASSOCIATION, 1903

BIBLIOGRAPHICAL SOCIETY OF AMERICA, 1904

ASSOCIATION OF AMERICAN GEOGRAPHERS, 1904

HISPANIC SOCIETY OF AMERICA, 1904

AMERICAN SOCIOLOGICAL ASSOCIATION, 1905

AMERICAN SOCIETY OF INTERNATIONAL LAW, 1906

ORGANIZATION OF AMERICAN HISTORIANS, 1907

COLLEGE ART ASSOCIATION OF AMERICA, 1912

HISTORY OF SCIENCE SOCIETY, 1924

LINGUISTIC SOCIETY OF AMERICA, 1924

MEDIAEVAL ACADEMY OF AMERICA, 1925

AMERICAN MUSICOLOGICAL SOCIETY, 1934

SOCIETY OF ARCHITECTURAL HISTORIANS, 1940

ECONOMIC HISTORY ASSOCIATION, 1940

ASSOCIATION FOR ASIAN STUDIES, 1941

AMERICAN SOCIETY FOR AESTHETICS, 1942

METAPHYSICAL SOCIETY OF AMERICA, 1950

AMERICAN STUDIES ASSOCIATION, 1950

RENAISSANCE SOCIETY OF AMERICA, 1954

SOCIETY FOR ETHNOMUSICOLOGY, 1955

AMERICAN SOCIETY FOR LEGAL HISTORY, 1956

AMERICAN SOCIETY FOR THEATRE RESEARCH, 1956

SOCIETY FOR THE HISTORY OF TECHNOLOGY, 1958

AMERICAN COMPARATIVE LITERATURE ASSOCIATION, 1960

DICTIONARY

OF

SCIENTIFIC BIOGRAPHY

CHARLES COULSTON GILLISPIE

Princeton University

EDITOR IN CHIEF

Volume XII

IBN RUSHD — JEAN-SERVAIS STAS

CHARLES SCRIBNER'S SONS · NEW YORK

Editorial Staff

Panel of Consultants

Contributors to Volume XII

The following are the contributors to Volume XII. Each author's name is followed by the institutional affiliation at the time of publication and the names of the articles written for this volume. The symbol†
means that an author is deceased.

HANS AARSLEFF
Princeton University
SPRAT

GIORGIO ABETTI
Osservatorio Astrofisico di Arcetri
SCHIAPARELLI; SECCHI

FREDERIC J. AGATE, JR.
Columbia University
P. E. SMITH

GARLAND ALLEN
Washington University
SHULL

PIETRO AMBROSIONI
University of Bologna
SANARELLI

ADEL ANBOUBA
Institut Moderne de Liban
AL-SAMAW'AL

TOBY A. APPEL
Johns Hopkins University
SOULEYET

WILBUR APPLEBAUM
Illinois Institute of Technology
SCHICKARD

ROGER ARNALDEZ
IBN RUSHD

RICHARD P. AULIE
Loyola University
E. J. RUSSELL

OLIVER L. AUSTIN, JR.
University of Florida
SCLATER

ROBERT AYCOCK
North Carolina State University
E. F. SMITH

VASSILY BABKOFF
Academy of Sciences of the U.S.S.R.
SAKHAROV

LAWRENCE BADASH
University of California, Santa Barbara
E. RUTHERFORD

LUIGI BELLONI
University of Milan
SACCO

ENRIQUE BELTRÁN
*Mexican Institute for the Conservation of
Natural Resources*
SIEDLECKI; SIGÜENZA Y GÓNGORA

RICHARD BERENDZEN
The American University
V. M. SLIPHER

WALTER L. BERG
SHALER

MICHAEL BERNKOPF
Pace University
E. SCHMIDT

P. W. BISHOP
Smithsonian Institution
STANTON

A. BLAAUW
European Southern Observatory, Hamburg
DE SITTER

L. J. BLACHER
Academy of Sciences of the U.S.S.R.
SCHMALGAUSEN

HERMANN BOERNER
University of Göttingen
SCHUR; SCHWARZ

UNO BOKLUND
Royal Pharmaceutical Institute, Stockholm
SCHEELE

MARTIN BOPP
University of Heidelberg
SACHS

FRANCK BOURDIER
École Pratique des Hautes Études
SERRES DE MESPLÈS

GERT H. BRIEGER
Duke University
SABIN

T. A. A. BROADBENT †
B. A. W. RUSSELL; SHANKS

HARCOURT BROWN
SALLO

K. E. BULLEN
University of Auckland
SEZAWA

IVOR BULMER-THOMAS
SERENUS

WERNER BURAU
University of Hamburg
SCHEFFERS; SCHROETER; SCHUBERT;
SCHWEIKART

JOHANN JAKOB BURCKHARDT
University of Zurich
SCHLÄFLI

JOHN G. BURKE
University of California, Los Angeles
SOHNCKE

WILLIAM F. BYNUM
University College London
H. W. SMITH

W. A. CAMPBELL
University of Newcastle Upon Tyne
SOLVAY

KENNETH L. CANEVA
University of Utah
SCHWEIGGER

MILIČ ČAPEK
Boston University
STALLO

ALBERT V. CAROZZI
University of Illinois at Urbana-Champaign
H. B. DE SAUSSURE; SCHLUMBERGER

CARLO CASTELLANI
University of Parma
SALVIANI

JAMES F. CHALLEY
Vassar College
M. SEGUIN

ALLAN CHAPMAN
University of Oxford
SHAKERLEY

CARLETON B. CHAPMAN
The Commonwealth Fund, New York City
E. SMITH; STARLING

ROBERT A. CHIPMAN
University of Toledo
C. W. SIEMENS

F. A. L. CLOWES
University of Oxford
SHARROCK

BRUCE C. COGAN
Johns Hopkins University
H. N. RUSSELL

EDWIN H. COLBERT
Museum of Northern Arizona
W. B. SCOTT

ALBERT B. COSTA
Duquesne University
H. J. SCHIFF

J. K. CRELLIN
*Wellcome Institute of the History of
Medicine*
SCHULZE

JOHN F. DALY, S. J.
Saint Louis University
SACROBOSCO

GLYN DANIEL
University of Cambridge
SCHLIEMANN

UMBERTO MARIA D'ANTINI
SARPI

CONTRIBUTORS TO VOLUME XII

GAVIN DE BEER †
SLOANE

ALLEN G. DEBUS
University of Chicago
SEVERINUS

ALBERT DELAUNAY
Institut Pasteur, Paris
SERGENT

R. G. C. DESMOND
India Office Library of Records, London
SPRUCE

SALLY H. DIEKE
Johns Hopkins University
SCHWARZSCHILD; SEARES

HÂMIT DILGAN
Istanbul University
AL-SAMARQANDĪ

YVONNE DOLD-SAMPLONIUS
AL-SIJZĪ; SINĀN IBN THĀBIT IBN QURRA

CLAUDE E. DOLMAN
University of British Columbia
T. SMITH; SPALLANZANI

HAROLD DORN
Stevens Institute of Technology
SMEATON

SIGALIA DOSTROVSKY
Barnard College
SAGNAC; J. SAUVEUR; SAVART

J. M. EDMONDS
University of Oxford Museum
SOLLAS

VASILIY A. ESAKOV
Academy of Sciences of the U.S.S.R.
SARYCHEV

D. G. EVANS
National Institute for Biological Standards and Control, London
W. SMITH

JOSEPH EWAN
Tulane University
SETCHELL

JOAN M. EYLES
W. SMITH; SOWERBY

W. V. FARRAR
University of Manchester
SCHUNK

SISTER MAUREEN FARRELL, F.C.J.
University of Manchester
SCHUMACHER; SCHWABE; SOLDNER

VERA N. FEDCHINA
Academy of Sciences of the U.S.S.R.
SEDOV; SEMYONOV-TYAN-SHANSKY

JEAN FELDMANN
Pierre and Marie Curie University
SAUVAGEAU

MARTIN FICHMAN
Glendon College, York University
SIGORGNE

WALTHER FISCHER
SÉNARMONT

MARCEL FLORKIN
University of Liège
SCHWANN; SLUSE; STAS

PAUL FORMAN
Smithsonian Institution
SMEKAL; SOMMERFELD

PIETRO FRANCESCHINI
University of Florence
SCARPA

EUGENE FRANKEL
Trinity College, Hartford
SEEBECK

F. FRAUNBERGER
SCHUMANN

ARTHUR H. FRAZIER
SAXTON

H.-CHRIST. FREIESLEBEN
B. V. SCHMIDT; J. F. J. SCHMIDT; SEIDEL; SPOERER

HANS FREUDENTHAL
State University of Utrecht
SCHOENFLIES; SCHOTTKY

B. VON FREYBERG
University of Erlangen-Nuremberg
SCHLOTHEIM

DAVID J. FURLEY
Princeton University
SEXTUS EMPIRICUS

ELIZABETH B. GASKING †
A. E. R. A. SERRES

GERALD L. GEISON
Princeton University
SCHULTZE

A. GEUS
University of Marburg
SCHMIDEL; SIEBOLD

OWEN GINGERICH
Smithsonian Astrophysical Observatory
SHAPLEY

THOMAS F. GLICK
Boston University
SANCHEZ

J. B. GOUGH
Washington State University
SIGAUD DE LAFOND

I. GRATTAN-GUINNESS
Middlesex Polytechnic of Enfield
STÄCKEL

JOHN C. GREENE
University of Connecticut
B. SILLIMAN

A. T. GRIGORIAN
Academy of Sciences of the U.S.S.R.
SEGNER; SHATUNOVSKY; SOMOV

N. A. GRIGORIAN
Academy of Sciences of the U.S.S.R.
SAMOYLOV

M. D. GRMEK
Archives Internationales d'Histoire des Sciences
SANTORIO

J. GRUNOW †
SPRUNG

HENRY GUERLAC
Cornell University
SAGE

FRANCISCO GUERRA
SAINT-HILAIRE

JOHN S. HALL
Lowell Observatory, Flagstaff
E. C. SLIPHER

MARIE BOAS HALL
Imperial College
P. SHAW

THOMAS M. HARRIS
University of Reading
SEWARD

RICHARD HART
National Academy of Sciences
V. M. SLIPHER

MELVILLE H. HATCH
University of Washington
SCUDDER

THOMAS HAWKINS
Boston University
SAKS

KARL HEINIG
University of Berlin
SCHORLEMMER

ARMIN HERMANN
University of Stuttgart
SCHRÖDINGER; SOMMERFELD; STARK

H. M. HINE
University of Oxford
SENECA

ERICH HINTZSCHE
University of Bern
SOEMMERRING

E. DORRIT HOFFLEIT
Yale University
SCHLESINGER

J. E. HOFMANN †
SAINT VINCENT; SCHOOTEN

ZDENĚK HORNOF
ŠKODA

WŁODZIMIERZ HUBICKI
Marie Curie-Skłodowska University
SENDIVOGIUS

CONTRIBUTORS TO VOLUME XII

THOMAS PARKE HUGHES
University of Pennsylvania
E. W. VON SIEMENS; SPERRY

G. L. HUXLEY
Queen's University of Belfast
SOSIGENES

ALBERT Z. ISKANDER
Wellcome Institute for the History of Medicine
IBN RUSHD

JEAN ITARD
Lycée Henri IV
SAINT-VENANT

DANIEL P. JONES
Oregon State University
SMITHSON

GISELA KANGRO
SALA

HANS KANGRO
University of Hamburg
SENNERT

ROBERT H. KARGON
Johns Hopkins University
SCHUSTER; R. A. SMITH

ALEX G. KELLER
University of Leicester
G. SCHOTT; O. DE SERRES

DANIEL J. KEVLES
California Institute of Technology
W. C. W. SABINE

DAVID A. KING
Smithsonian Institution Project in Medieval Islamic Astronomy
IBN AL-SHĀṬIR

LAWRENCE J. KING
State University of New York at Geneseo
C. K. SPRENGEL

LESTER S. KING
American Medical Association
STAHL

MARC KLEIN †
SCHLEIDEN

DAVID KNIGHT
University of Durham
SCHONLAND

H. KOBAYASHI
Shimane University
SATŌ FAMILY

AKIRO KOBORI
SEKI

ZDENĚK KOPAL
University of Manchester
SPENCER JONES

SHELDON J. KOPPERL
Grand Valley State Colleges
SCHRÖTTER; SERULLAS

HANS-GÜNTHER KÖRBER
Zentralbibliothek des Meteorologischen Dienstes der DDR, Potsdam
O. F. SCHOTT; SIEDENTOPF

EDNA E. KRAMER
Polytechnic Institute of New York
SOMMERVILLE

P. G. KULIKOVSKY
Moscow University
SHARONOV; SHAYN; SHIRAKATSÍ

KAZIMIERZ KURATOWSKI
Polish Academy of Sciences
SIERPIŃSKI

G. D. KUROCHKIN
Academy of Sciences of the U.S.S.R.
SEVERGIN

GISELA KUTZBACH
University of Wisconsin
W. N. SHAW

BENGT-OLOF LANDIN
University of Lund
SCHÖNHERR

M. G. LAROSHEVSKY
Academy of Sciences of the U.S.S.R.
SECHENOV

CHAUNCEY D. LEAKE
University of California, San Francisco
SANTORINI

HENRY M. LEICESTER
University of the Pacific
SØRENSEN

MARTIN LEVEY †
AL-SAMARQANDĪ

G. A. LINDEBOOM
Free University, Amsterdam
RUYSCH; SPIEGEL

MADELEINE LY-TIO-FANE
Sugar Industry Research Institute, Mauritius
SONNERAT

A. J. McCONNELL
University of Dublin
SALMON

WILLIAM McGUCKEN
University of Akron
J. SCHEINER

DUNCAN McKIE
University of Cambridge
L. J. SPENCER

ROGERS McVAUGH
University of Michigan Herbarium
SESSÉ Y LACASTA

KARL MÄGDEFRAU
University of Munich
SANIO

MICHAEL S. MAHONEY
Princeton University
SAURIN; STAMPIOEN

CLIFFORD L. MAIER
Wayne State University
RYDBERG

CARLTON MALEY
Wayne State University
P. E. SABINE

ERNST M. MANASSE
North Carolina Central University
SPEUSIPPUS

BRIAN G. MARSDEN
Smithsonian Astrophysical Observatory
ST. JOHN

KIRTLEY F. MATHER
Harvard University
SALISBURY

ERNST MAYR
Harvard University
SARS; SEMPER

KURT MENDELSSOHN
University of Oxford
SIMON

ROBERT K. MERTON
Columbia University
SARTON

MARKWART MICHLER
University of Giessen
SORANUS OF EPHESUS

WYNDHAM D. MILES
National Institutes of Health
E. F. SMITH

E. MIRZOYAN
Academy of Sciences of the U.S.S.R.
SEVERTSOF

A. M. MONNIER
University of Paris
A. SABATIER

EDGAR W. MORSE
California State College, Sonoma
R. SMITH

LETTIE S. MULTHAUF
SAMPSON; SCHRÖTER

SHIGERU NAKAYAMA
University of Tokyo
SHIBUKAWA; SHIZUKI

CLIFFORD M. NELSON
University of California, Berkeley
RÜTIMEYER

AXEL V. NIELSEN †
SCHJELLERUP

ALBERT NIJENHUIS
University of Pennsylvania
SCHOUTEN

CALVERT E. NORLAND
San Diego State College
SANDERSON

CONTRIBUTORS TO VOLUME XII

J. D. NORTH
University of Oxford
H. C. RUSSELL; H. J. S. SMITH

MARY JO NYE
University of Oklahoma
P. SABATIER

HERBERT OETTEL
SKOLEM

LEROY E. PAGE
Kansas State University
SCROPE

ELIZABETH C. PATTERSON
Albertus Magnus College
SOMERVILLE

J. D. Y. PEEL
University of Liverpool
H. SPENCER

STUART PIERSON
Memorial University of Newfoundland
A. SÉGUIN

VICENTE R. PILAPIL
California State University, Los Angeles
SERVETUS

P. E. PILET
University of Lausanne
N.-T. DE SAUSSURE; SCHEUCHZER;
SCHOPFER; SENEBIER

DAVID PINGREE
Brown University
ŚATĀNANDA; SPHUJIDHVAJA; ŚRĪDHARA;
ŚRĪPATI

A. F. PLAKHOTNIK
Academy of Sciences of the U.S.S.R.
SHOKALSKY; SHTOKMAN

EMMANUEL POULLE
École Nationale des Chartes
SIMON DE PHARES

VARADARAJA V. RAMAN
Rochester Institute of Technology
SAHA

P. RAMDOHR
University of Heidelberg
SCHNEIDERHÖHN

RHODA RAPPAPORT
Vassar College
SOULAVIE

ROY A. RAUSCHENBERG
Ohio University
SOLANDER

NATHAN REINGOLD
Smithsonian Institution
RUTHERFURD; E. SABINE; C. A. SCHOTT

P. W. RICHARDS
University College of North Wales
W. P. SCHIMPER

GUENTER B. RISSE
University of Wisconsin-Madison
SCHAUDINN; M. SCHIFF; SEMMELWEIS;
K. P. J. SPRENGEL

GLORIA ROBINSON
Yale University
SCHNEIDER; SCHÖNLEIN

FRANCESCO RODOLICO
University of Florence
SCILLA; SOLDANI

PAUL LAWRENCE ROSE
University of Cambridge
SCALIGER

EDWARD ROSEN
City University of New York
SCHÖNER

SIDNEY ROSS
Rensselaer Polytechnic Institute
SPRING

K. E. ROTHSCHUH
University of Münster/Westphalia
STANNIUS

M. J. S. RUDWICK
Free University, Amsterdam
SEDGWICK

DAVID RYNIN
University of California, Berkeley
SCHLICK

MORRIS H. SAFFRON
New Jersey College of Medicine and Dentistry
SALERNITAN ANATOMISTS

A. P. M. SANDERS
State University, Utrecht
A. F. W. SCHIMPER; SCHOUW;
SCHWENDENER; SPIX

EBERHARD SCHMAUDERER
SERTÜRNER

F. SCHMEIDLER
University of Munich Observatory
SCHÖNFELD; SEELIGER

CHARLES B. SCHMITT
Warburg Institute
SCHEGK; SEVERINO

RONALD SCHORN
SEE

E. L. SCOTT
Stamford High School, Lincolnshire
D. RUTHERFORD

BENIAMINO SEGRE
Academia Nazionale dei Lincei
SEVERI

EDITH SELOW
SCHELLING

WILLIAM R. SHEA
McGill University
C. SCHEINER

N. P. SHIKHOBALOVA
Academy of Sciences of the U.S.S.R.
SKRYABIN

ELIZABETH NOBLE SHOR
Scripps Institution of Oceanography
SAY; SCHOOLCRAFT

DIANA M. SIMPKINS
Polytechnic of North London
J. E. SMITH; S. I. SMITH

NATHAN SIVIN
Massachusetts Institute of Technology
SHEN KUA

W. A. SMEATON
University College London
SENAC

CYRIL STANLEY SMITH
Massachusetts Institute of Technology
A. SAUVEUR; SORBY

IAN N. SNEDDON
University of Glasgow
SIMSON

H. A. M. SNELDERS
State University, Utrecht
SCHÖNBEIN; SCHROEDER VAN DER
KOLK; SMITS

E. SNORRASON
Rigshospitalet, Copenhagen
SALOMONSEN

Y. I. SOLOVIEV
Academy of Sciences of the U.S.S.R.
SHILOV

PIERRE SPEZIALI
University of Geneva
SEGRE

NILS SPJELDNAES
University of Aarhus
E. J. SCHMIDT; SCHREIBERS

F. STOCKMANS
University of Brussels
SAPORTA

D. J. STRUIK
Massachusetts Institute of Technology
SACCHERI; SCHOUTE; SERRET; SNEL

ROGER H. STUEWER
University of Minnesota
G. C. N. SCHMIDT

L. E. SUTTON
University of Oxford
SIDGWICK

JUDITH P. SWAZEY
Boston University
SHERRINGTON

CONTRIBUTORS TO VOLUME XII

MANFRED E. SZABO
Concordia University
SPORUS OF NICAEA

RENÉ TATON
École Pratique des Hautes Études
SERVOIS

DOUGLASS W. TAYLOR
University of Otago Medical School
SHARPEY; SHARPEY-SCHÄFER

M. TEICH
University of Cambridge
SKRAUP

ANDRZEJ A. TESKE †
SMOLUCHOWSKI

ARNOLD THACKRAY
University of Pennsylvania
SARTON

K. BRYN THOMAS
Royal Berkshire Hospital
SNOW

ELIZABETH H. THOMSON
Yale University
B. SILLIMAN, JR.

VICTOR E. THOREN
Indiana University
SEVERIN

V. V. TIKHOMIROV
Academy of Sciences of the U.S.S.R.
SOKOLOV

HEINZ TOBIEN
University of Mainz
K. F. SCHIMPER

CAROLYN TOROSIAN
University of California, Berkeley
SHERARD

THADDEUS J. TRENN
University of Regensburg
SMITHELLS; SODDY

G. L'E. TURNER
University of Oxford
SHORT; SOLEIL

G. UBAGHS
University of Liège
SCHMERLING

GEORG USCHMANN
Deutsche Akademie der Naturforscher Leopoldina
SEMON

F. VAN STEENBERGHEN
University of Louvain
SIGER OF BRABANT

G. VERBEKE
University of Louvain
SIMPLICIUS

C. H. WADDINGTON
University of Edinburgh
SPEMANN

WILLIAM A. WALLACE, O.P.
Catholic University of America
SOTO

P. J. WALLIS
University of Newcastle Upon Tyne
SIMPSON

ANTHONY A. WALSH
Dickinson College
SPURZHEIM

C. W. WARDLAW
D. H. SCOTT

DEBORAH JEAN WARNER
Smithsonian Institution
SCHAEBERLE; SMYTH; SOUTH

DIEDRICH WATTENBERG
Archenhold Observatory
C. A. VON SCHMIDT

EUGENE WEGMANN
SCHARDT; SEDERHOLM

RONALD S. WILKINSON
Library of Congress
STARKEY

C. GORDON WINDER
University of Western Ontario
SELWYN

MARY P. WINSOR
University of Toronto
SAVIGNY

HANS WUSSING
Karl Marx University
SCHRÖDER

ELLIS L. YOCHELSON
SCHUCHERT

L. D. G. YOUNG
SEE

A. A. YOUSCHKEVITCH
Academy of Sciences of the U.S.S.R.
SLUTSKY

A. P. YOUSCHKEVITCH
Academy of Sciences of the U.S.S.R.
SEGNER; SHATUNOVSKY; SHNIRELMAN; SOKHOTSKY; SONIN

BRUNO ZANOBIO
University of Pavia
SERTOLI

DICTIONARY
OF
SCIENTIFIC BIOGRAPHY

DICTIONARY OF SCIENTIFIC BIOGRAPHY

IBN RUSHD, ABŪ'L-WALĪD MUḤAMMAD IBN AHMAD IBN MUḤAMMAD, also known as **Aver-roës** (*b.* Cordoba, Spain, 1126; *d.* Marrakech, Morocco, 10 December 1198), *astronomy, philosophy, medicine.*

Ibn Rushd, who was called the Commentator in the Latin Middle Ages, came from an important family of jurists. His grandfather (who bore the same name as he, for which reason the philosopher is called the Grandson [*al-Ḥafīd*]) had been cadi (religious judge) and imam of the great mosque of Cordoba; he was also the author of a famous treatise on Malikite law, the *Kitāb al-Muqad dimāt al-mumahhidāt,* in which he set forth its principles with a view to facilitating its study. His father was also cadi. In this milieu the young Ibn Rushd received a very good Muslim education. His training was especially thorough in law, in which field his teacher was al-Ḥāfiẓ Abū Muḥammad ibn Rizq. He learned by heart the *Muwaṭṭa'* of the Imam Mālik. He was also initiated into the science of the traditions, but he was less interested in it than in the principles of law. In theology he worked through the Ashʿarite kalam, which, in Sunnite thought, represents a system of the *juste milieu* and of equilibrium between the extreme doctrines; it could not easily be defended except with dialectical arguments, which were inspired by controversies and often led to intellectually unsatisfactory compromises. Ibn Rushd later turned against this theology, attacking the most famous proponent of Ashʿarism, al-Ghazālī. Ibn Rushd was certainly well acquainted with the Muʿtazilite kalam, which sought to be more rational, and if he included it in his condemnation of the speculative methods of all the mutakallimun, he was not indifferent to the problems that occupied this school. But it is evident from his own works that he favored primarily the type of reasoning used by the jurists, which seemed to him much more solid than theological reasoning and, in the areas in which it finds application, much more in harmony with the requirements of pure logic.

Ibn Rushd studied medicine under Abū Jaʿfar Hārūn al-Tajālī (originally from Trujillo), a noted figure in Seville who was versed in the works of Aristotle and the ancient physicians. Thoroughly familiar with the principles (*uṣūl*) and various branches (*furūʿ*) of medical science, he was an excellent practitioner, and his cures were frequently successful. He was in the service of Abū Yaʿqūb Yūsuf (1163–1184), the father of al-Manṣūr Yaʿqūb ibn Yūsuf (1184–1199). This prince, during his stay in Seville, surrounded himself with philosophers, physicians, and poets. He patronized meetings of scientists, which were attended by men like Ibn Ṭufayl, Ibn Zuhr (Avenzoar), and Ibn Rushd himself. It is likely therefore that Abū Jaʿfar played an important role in the life of his student, teaching him not only medicine but also Aristotelian philosophy. It is worth noting, for a better understanding of Ibn Rushd's intellectual development, that he studied the Stagirite during his medical training. This explains why, later, while viewing Aristotle as the master of logic (*Ṣāḥib al-Manṭiq*) and the first *falāsifa*, he was particularly interested in the natural sciences and physics, which occupy such a prominent place in the thought of the Greek philosopher.

Ibn al-Abbār, a historian born in Valencia in the year following the Commentator's death, gives in his *Takmila* the name of another physician—a man of the first rank in the practice of his art—who was one of Ibn Rushd's teachers: Abū Marwān ibn Jurrayūl.

The biographers make no mention of Ibn Rushd's philosophical studies. Ibn Abī Uṣaibiʿa confirms that it was under Abū Jaʿfar that Ibn Rushd became interested in the philosophical sciences, and Ibn al-Abbār notes simply that he "inclined towards the sciences of the Ancients." These meager data are sufficient to substantiate the idea

1

that he approached philosophical problems with a scientific outlook, though without forgetting his early instruction in legal reasoning. To an important degree, therefore, it was his scientific and legal training that gave Ibn Rushd's thinking its particular cast.

It was still science that occupied Ibn Rushd's attention when he was in Marrakech, where, according to Renan, he supported the views of the Almohad ruler ʿAbd al-Muʾmin "in the erection of colleges that he was founding at this moment" (1153). We know, in fact, from his commentary on *De caelo* that Ibn Rushd conducted astronomical observations at Marrakech. He was undoubtedly referring to this period when he recalls, in the commentary on a book of the *Metaphysics*, his penchant for the study of astronomy in his younger years. It is possible that as early as this period he met Ibn Ṭufayl, who was to play a major role in his philosophical career by introducing him to Abū Yaʿqūb Yūsuf. Now, Abū Bakr ibn Ṭufayl (Abubacer) was a philosopher, but also an astronomer. F. J. Carmody, in the introduction to his edition of al-Biṭrūjī's *De motibus celorum*, reports an interesting remark by the author of this work:

> You know, brother, that Abū Bakr ibn Ṭufayl, may God bless him, told us that he had been inspired with an astronomical system and with principles of motion other than those postulated by Ptolemy; these avoid use of eccentrics or epicycles. And he explained by this system all movements; and nothing impossible arose from this. He also promised to write on this matter; and his place in science is not unknown.

This declaration can explain the numerous similarities between the ideas of al-Biṭrūjī and those of Ibn Rushd, if it is assumed that they derived from a common source in the thought of Ibn Ṭufayl. More directly, perhaps, than medicine, astronomy posed metaphysical problems. This fact is brought out by the account of a meeting that Marrākushī, who reports it in his *Muʿjib*, had from the lips of one of Ibn Rushd's disciples. It concerns an encounter between Abū Yaʿqūb, Ibn Ṭufayl, and Ibn Rushd. The prince asked if heaven is a substance that has always existed and will continue to exist throughout eternity, or if it has a beginning. Ibn Rushd, who was at first troubled, became more confident and took part brilliantly in the discussion. Henceforth he enjoyed the favor of the prince. This episode reveals the close relationship that existed at this time between the problems of astronomy and those of metaphysics.

Abū Yaʿqūb, complaining of the obscurity of Aristotle's texts, asked Ibn Ṭufayl to make commentaries on them. The latter, thinking himself too old and too busy, may in turn have asked Ibn Rushd to undertake the project. This is perhaps what prevented him from pursuing the research and astronomical observations to which he would have preferred to devote his time.

Ibn Rushd remained in high favor throughout the reign of Abū Yaʿqūb Yūsuf (1163–1184). In 1169 the philosopher became cadi of Seville, but he continued to work on his commentaries and paraphrases. In the latter year he completed his paraphrase of the *Parts of Animals*, and in the fourth book he stated that his task was made much more difficult by his official duties and by the absence of his books, which were still in Cordoba. He returned to Cordoba in 1171, still holding the office of cadi. Despite his many responsibilities, he managed to find even more time to devote to his commentaries. Between 1169 and 1179 he traveled through the Almohad empire, in particular to Seville, where he dated several of his works. In 1182 he went to Marrakech to replace Ibn Ṭufayl as chief physician to Abū Yaʿqūb Yūsuf. He was then honored with an appointment as grand cadi of Cordoba.

During the reign of Yaʿqūb al-Manṣūr Ibn Rushd enjoyed the prince's favor for ten years. It was only in 1195 that he fell into disgrace. It is possible, and even probable, that the Malikite *fuqahāʾ* — doctors of the law who in Spain were always the intransigent guardians of a legalistic form of Islam — had regained influence as a result of the struggles against the Christians. They may have then inspired a hardening of the attitude of the government toward all positions that could be suspected of weakening, at first doctrinally and then politically, the bastion of religion. Ibn Rushd was banished to Lucena, near Cordoba, and subsequently appeared before a high court of Cordoban notables who anathematized his doctrines. Edicts were issued ordering the burning of philosophy books and forbidding the study of philosophy.

When al-Manṣūr returned to Marrakech, to a Berber milieu, he canceled all these edicts and recalled the philosopher. But Ibn Rushd did not have long to enjoy his return to favor; he died at the end of 1198. He was buried in Marrakech near the Taghzut gate. Later his body was brought back to Cordoba. The mystic Ibn ʿArabī, who was still young, attended his funeral. He is supposed to have said, upon seeing the Commentator's remains placed on one side of the base of a monument and the books he had written placed on the other, that all these philosophical works were equal to no more than a corpse. Although another anecdote recounts a meeting between Ibn Rushd and Ibn ʿArabī, in which the old philosopher supposedly recognized the young man's genius, it is certain that Averroism in no way leads to mysticism, unlike Avicennism. Seen in this light, Ibn ʿArabī's judgment assumes its full significance. Moreover, in the anecdote in question, when Ibn ʿArabī finds himself in the presence of Ibn Rushd, he first says "yes": yes, no doubt, to the philosopher's intentions; then he says "no": no to the method, no to a system in which the immobile prime mover closes the universe in upon itself, leaving no prospect at all for a mystical life.

Astronomy. In his commentary on Aristotle's *Metaphysics*, Ibn Rushd wrote:

> In my youth I hoped it would be possible for me to bring this research [in astronomy] to a successful conclusion. Now, in my old age, I have lost hope, for several obstacles have stood in my way. But what I say about it will perhaps attract the attention of future researchers. The astronomical science of our days surely offers nothing from which one can derive an existing reality. The model that has been developed in the times in which we live accords with the computations, not with existence.

These lines express the essence of Ibn Rushd's thinking on astronomy. He was interested in the subject and acquainted with the history of its theories. Capable of explaining what Aristotle said about the systems of Eudoxus and Callippus, he was just as well informed about the work of Ptolemy, and, through the latter, he had some knowledge of the ideas of the ancients who preceded Hipparchus. He also knew the writings of the Arab astronomers. In this connection, it should be recalled that whereas scientists like al-Battānī (Albategnius) and Ibn Yūnus remained faithful to Ptolemy, others, such as Farghānī, Zarqālī, and Biṭrūjī (who lived slightly later than Ibn Rushd, but whose conceptions are, in several respects, similar) altered more or less thoroughly the Ptolemaic explanations.

Certain authors returned to the vision of a world composed of homocentric spheres, while others took up again a theory that goes back to Thābit ibn Qurra, that of trepidations, or approach and recession (*al-iqbāl wa'l-idbār*), which Ibn Rushd briefly explains in his commentary. In this situation Ibn Rushd aligned himself with those astronomers who advocated a return to Aristotle, but in order to sort out his own ideas, he took into account the whole of the history of the subject that separates him from the Greek philosopher. In fact, the abundance and the weakness of the contending theories left him very perplexed. Although he treated the scientific aspects of these problems as an expert, he hesitated to offer definitive solutions.

Ibn Rushd was certainly influenced by the "moderns," but he did not follow them blindly. He remarked that if one considers the plurality of the planetary motions, one can distinguish three kinds: (1) those accessible to the naked eye; (2) those that can be detected only with the use of observational instruments—which sometimes take place over periods exceeding the lifetime of an individual and sometimes over shorter periods; and finally, (3) those whose existence is established only by reasoning. The first movements pose no problems, but their description is far from sufficient for astronomical investigation. The second kind require the continuous collaboration of several generations, during which time it is evident that the instruments used can undergo improvement. As for the movements postulated on the basis of reasoning, one cannot always be sure that they correspond to physical realities, although it is possible to criticize a hypothesis by appealing either to new observational data or to the requirements of physical principles. These considerations are responsible for the caution Ibn Rushd displays when judging theories based on a given state in the development of the science (for example, those concerning the number of planetary movements, or the theory of the spiral movements [*harakāt lawlabiyya*]). On the other hand, they account for his rigor when principles are at stake.

Widely varying figures had been proposed for the number of the planetary motions. Aristotle himself had counted fifty-five of them, which he reduced to forty-seven. Ibn Rushd relates that in his time the astronomers fixed this number at fifty, including the motions of the starry sphere. He himself admits forty-five: thirty-eight for the sphere of the fixed stars and the planets and seven for the diurnal motions of the planetary spheres. All the same, he wrote, "As to a profound examination of what is necessarily and really involved in this question, we leave it to those who devote themselves more completely to this art, those who dedicate themselves entirely to it and who concern themselves with nothing else." He expressed the same reserve regarding the spiral motions. They result from contrary motions, but they must be executed around different poles; for contrary motions around a single pole cancel themselves. It may be objected that if the sphere that carries the celestial body is situated between two spheres moved in opposite directions, its resultant motion will be a violent one (*haraka qasriyya*), an impossibility for such a body. The best recourse is to suppose that these spiral movements arise from contrary movements about different poles. On this supposition, the body is able to move sometimes directly and sometimes with a retrograde motion, sometimes more rapidly and sometimes less rapidly; and there can be differences of latitude with respect to the zodiacal sphere. This explanatory principle leads to no absurdity: the spiral motion is that which occurs in the heavens by the combination of the diurnal movement of the sphere of the planet with the movement of the planet in its oblique sphere (*al-falak al-mā'il*). Understood in this sense, spiral motions can be admitted.

Ibn Rushd found the system of eccentrics and epicycles, adopted and developed by Ptolemy, completely unacceptable. From the time of Plato the task of astronomy had been to save the phenomena by providing a rational account of the irregular apparent motions of the planets. The burden of Ibn Rushd's criticism of this type of explanation is that it is mathematical and not physical. Physics explains, and metaphysics confirms, that the motion of the celestial bodies should be uniform, contrary to what it appears to be to the sight. It is, therefore, necessary to construct a model (*hay'a*) of a planetary configuration in such a fashion that it yields the visible phenomena, without at the same time entailing physical impossibilities. Posed in this manner, the problem has only two conceivable solutions. But only one of them fulfills all the conditions: the one that furnishes a model corresponding to a physical reality and that considers the apparent motion as composed of several motions. In this conception the planet is moved by the motion of the sphere and thereby participates in the universal motion; but it also has its own peculiar motions within its sphere. Ibn Rushd gives the example of the government of a just city (*medīna fādila*, an expression borrowed from al-Fārābī); it is unique, and its unity is preserved to the degree that the various chiefs imitate the monarch in serving him. Each one has his own function, just like the monarch who has his function and whose activity is the noblest. Another example is the subordination of the arts and sciences, which aid each other in the execution of a single work. This is the case of the auxiliary arts of the science of equitation, such as the art of bridling a horse.

The second solution is to posit the existence of spheres the centers of which are exterior to the center of the world, the eccentrics (*al-aflāk al-khārijat al-marākiz*), as well as of epicycles having their centers on the deferent (called in Arabic *aflāk al-tadāwīr*). This option involves various kinds of constructions, a circumstance that explains the disagreement of the astronomers over the number of the movements of the heavenly bodies. Regarding the zodiacal anomaly (that is to say, the fact that the planets traverse equal arcs in unequal times), Ibn Rushd shows how the astronomer is led to multiply the movements: "When one calculates the movements of the heavenly bodies, the calculation requires that they be in definite places on the sphere of the zodiac. Now, observing them with instruments, one discovers them in other places, which requires the introduction of a new movement for the body in question." It was in this way that Ptolemy introduced new movements for the moon and the other planets. But it was impossible for him to base these upon a *hay'a*, a term designating a configuration that, according to Ibn Rushd, should not be a simple theoretical model, but a physical reality. Ibn Rushd raised particularly strong objections to the hypothesis of the equant (*circulus aequans*), to which he alludes in these terms: "The same is true regarding what he believed, that is to say, that the uniform movements of the planets on their eccentric spheres take place [in a uniform manner] with respect to centers other than those of the eccentric spheres."

It is clear that the center of the equant and the equant itself, on which absolutely nothing actually turns, are pure mathematical fictions without the least physical reality. The Ptolemaic theory does not accord with the nature of things. The existence of the epicycle is fundamentally impossible, for "the body that moves in a circle moves about the center of the universe and not exterior to it, since it is the movable body moved along a circle that determines the center." Thus, in contradistinction to geometry, in which a circle is defined with respect to its center, the physical method starts from the reality of the circular movement, which is what entails the position of a center, the earth. If, therefore, there were an eccentric, there would be another earth exterior to our own. Now, that is physically impossible; if there existed numerous centers other than the earth, heavy bodies would fall toward these centers out of their natural places. Moreover, these hypotheses imply the existence in the heavens of superfluous bodies (*fadl*) with no utility "except that of producing a filling (*ḥashw*), as occurs, it is thought, in the body of animals." Elsewhere, concerning the theory of Eudoxus, Ibn Rushd writes: "There is no need to assume two movements of two celestial bodies [the second and third sphere for the moon and the sun]; for what their natures (*ṭabā'i*) can accomplish with a single instrument, they do not do with two."

At the end of these criticisms Ibn Rushd comes over to the opinions of the ancients: "They are exact," he asserts,

> . . . by virtue [of their conformity to] the principles of nature; they are established, according to me, on [the basis of] the movement of a sphere unique in itself, about a center unique in itself, with different poles, two or more, as a function of what is required by an application corresponding to the apparent motions; for it may happen accidentally that such motions will be more or less rapid, direct, or retrograde.

Ibn Rushd remained loyal to Aristotle because he considered the master's thought a coherent system that must be taken as a whole. Undoubtedly, metaphysics was not for Ibn Rushd a sovereign science that imposes its conceptions on the other sciences. On the contrary, it is to a certain degree tributary to the others; it draws its knowledge of mobile substances, whether corruptible or eternal, from physics; and from astronomy it derives everything that it knows concerning the motions of the heavens. Nevertheless, celestial phenomena can be understood only within the framework of a general theory of substance. The celestial bodies have only a single motion, eternal circular translation in space. Since motion has a contrary—rest— these bodies preserve in themselves the possibility of rest (*imkān fī an taskana*). Aristotle showed that this possibility remains in them a pure possibility that can never be realized. But the result is, that while this motion is eternal, it is not established as such in the celestial bodies themselves. Thus arises the necessity of a first mover, immaterial and immobile, which moves bodies "*as* the loved one moves the lover." There exists, among the heavenly bodies, a hierarchical order (*tartīb*): as the motor of all the rest, the first heaven is obviously anterior "by nature, by the place it occupies, and by its size," as well as by the great number of its stars and the rapidity of its movement. The order of the planets follows the order of their spheres with regard to position (*makān*), but for the velocities this order is inverted; those closest to the earth have the most rapid motion, whether because of the "nobility" of their motors or the smallness of their bodies (*ajrām*).

Ibn Rushd rejected the hypothesis of the "moderns" postulating a ninth sphere anterior to the first heaven. According to him, the reasoning that led to this doctrine was inspired by the Neoplatonic axiom that out of primary substance, which is one and simple, there can only proceed a being that is itself one. Now, what depends immediately on the prime mover is both the first heaven itself and the motor of the sphere that follows it. This, accordingly, is not a simple effect, and there must exist an anterior cause of this complexity. For Ibn Rushd this reasoning was pure fantasy; there is, at the level of the prime mover, neither procession, nor necessary dependence, nor action, since it moves while remaining immobile. Just as, for example, one and the same intelligible entity can be grasped by several knowing subjects from different points of view, the unique prime mover can be the end toward which several different mobile entities tend. The motive force that the first heaven receives from the prime mover is strictly analogous to the motive force that the sphere of Saturn receives from this same prime mover. "That is to say, the perfection of each sphere is given in the representation of the cause that is proper to it together with the first cause." It is in this manner that one must understand the motions of each of the heavenly bodies; they tend to a unique motion, which is that of the body itself, and which, in other terms, is their resultant. Similarly, the motions of the spheres tend toward the motion of the starry sphere, in the sense that they derive their perfection from the diurnal motion of the first heaven under the effect of the motion of the prime mover. Thus, the rejection of the Neoplatonic axiom allows the astronomer to unify the motions of the universe while justifying their diversity and plurality, above all at the level of the planets.

Philosophy. The philosophical writings of Ibn Rushd are divided into two groups, the commentaries on the works of Aristotle, and the personal writings, which are entitled *Faṣl al-Maqāl, Kitāb al-Kashf*, and *Tahāfut al-Tahāfut*.

As a commentator on Aristotle, Ibn Rushd attempted to restore the Stagirite's own thought, and to supplant the Neoplatonic interpretations of al-Fārābī and Ibn Sīnā. Ibn Rushd regarded Aristotelianism as the truth, inasmuch as truth is accessible to the human mind. Referring to a passage of the *Metaphysics*—which in the Arabic version reads, "The difficulty of metaphysics is shown by the fact that it has not been possible to grasp either the truth as a whole or one of its important parts"— Ibn Rushd wrote:

> Aristotle means that this [grasping of truth] has been impossible from the earliest times to his own age; it is as if he were hinting that he himself has grasped the truth, or at least most of the truth, and that what his predecessors grasped was very little in comparison, whether it be the whole or the most important part. The best thing is to assume that he comprehended the entire truth, and by the whole of the truth I mean that quantity which human nature—insofar as it is human—is capable of grasping [*Tafsīr mā ba'd at-Tabī'at*, Bouyges, ed., I, p. 7, 6g].

The implication of this declaration should be carefully noted: Aristotle not only greatly advanced human knowledge, he brought it to the highest possible state of perfection. He enunciated all the truth that is accessible to man, that is to say, all that can be established by demonstrative proof (*burhān*).

Although Ibn Rushd had a more complete knowledge of the *corpus Aristotelicum* and analyzed it more carefully and more accurately than did his predecessors al-Fārābī and Ibn Sīnā, he continued to view Aristotle essentially as the master of logic (*Ṣāhib al-Manṭiq*), and it was the logical rigor of the demonstrations in the Stagirite's philosophical and scientific writings that produced the greatest impression on him.

Ibn Rushd made an important qualification in his evaluation of Aristotle, however; he cautioned that while the Greek philosopher possessed the totality of the truth available to man, he did not possess the Truth itself. In other words, man is confronted with questions that cannot be answered by the strict application of logical reasoning. While following Aristotle in all his demonstrations, Ibn Rushd nevertheless allowed for faith in revealed truths. When the Koran touches on the same subject as philosophy, it is philosophy that must be heeded, and the sacred text must be interpreted so that it will agree with the requirements of demonstrative reason. But in those cases where philosophy is silent, then instruction must come from the word of God.

The obscurity of many Aristotelian texts permitted wide latitude in their interpretation. The Commentator (as Ibn Rushd was called in the Latin West) naturally did not always give the correct explanation, especially since he often had to work with defective and even incomprehensible translations. In any case, it is clear that he always inter-preted the texts in such a way as to accomplish two things: emphasis on the opposition between Aristotle and Plato, and criticism and correction of the positions advanced by Ibn Sīnā. Ibn Rushd rejected the view of metaphysics as the universal science that gives to all the other sciences their goals and principles, as well as the corollary to this view, that all human knowledge can, in principle at least, be deduced from metaphysics. At the same time, he opposed a cosmology that claimed to deduce, by the process of emanation, the celestial world of the Intelligences and of the spheres from the existence of the First Principle (*al-Awwal*) or Necessary Being. Nor did Ibn Rushd accept the idea that the last of the Intelligences, that of the sphere of the moon (also called the Active Intellect), is the *dator formarum* (*wāhib al-ṣuwar*), which gives form to the material beings of the sublunary world. In short, he rejected the Avicennian world view that explained the universe as having started from above and as having then proceeded downward, moving from the superior to the inferior. In Ibn Rushd's eyes this was Platonism. Faithful in this regard to Aristotle, he considered that beings become what they are as a consequence of a movement of desire toward the First Unmoved Mover, which causes them to pass from a potential state to an active state. This movement is, therefore, from below to above. Similarly, metaphysics is not a primal science that abides in a region beyond physics, whence it projects its light on both thought and matter. Metaphysics is instead the keystone that supports the edifice of physics; but it is a keystone set into place only after the latter has been constructed. For Ibn Rushd, it is not metaphysics that gives physical science its subject: changeable substance. Without the study of physics, the human mind would lack even the idea of change or movement. Further, contrary to Ibn Sīnā's erroneous interpretation of a passage of the *Posterior Analytics* (I, 2, 72a), it is metaphysics that, far from supplying the answer to everything, presses physics with its own questions (*yuṣā-diru*). In discussing the main subject of metaphysics, being as being, Ibn Rushd stated that "being" is, first of all, a word that the metaphysician studies according to its different applications in order to show that it refers, first of all, to substance: "The nine categories relate to existence by the fact that their existence is in a real existent (*al-mawjūd al-haqīqī*), which is substance." The metaphysician also investigates the word "being" from different points of view. "Aristotle noted these different points of view concerning such words [the analogues] in order to show that what is true of substance and the nine categories is also true of the word 'being' (*mawjūd*)." Thus, like Aristotle, Ibn Rushd accorded primacy to substance in his theory of being. This led him, in commenting on the *Metaphysics*, to hold that metaphysics in its entirety is a study of substance, corruptible or incorruptible, changeable or unchangeable. Such a study, of course, was not based on the fact that substance is qualified in this way, but rather on the fact that with these qualifications it is being. That is to say, metaphysics always considers substance under the aspect of being. Physics, on the other hand, studies substance as changeable, but it is, in any case, led to conceive of an unchanging substance. Thus the subject of this particular science is the same as that of metaphysics, but it is not examined from the point of view of being. Conversely, metaphysics is not unconcerned with the substances of our world or of the celestial world. It deals with the same substances discussed in Aristotle's *Physics* and *De caelo*, although it treats them from the point of view of being as being. Consequently, being as being is not a separate subject, distinct from all the others, and reserved to metaphysics in the way that, for example, changeable substance is the subject of physics and of no other science. Metaphysics studies being as being not in itself (that is impossible since it has no concept), but in all beings, and particularly in substance in all its forms.

Ibn Rushd propounded a theory of the intellect that is important both in itself and for its influence on the Latin Middle Ages. In order to understand it properly, one must constantly bear in mind that Ibn Rushd's main goal was to explain intellection without appealing to such separate intelligible entities as the Platonic Ideas. He observed, first, that man thinks by abstracting forms (called material forms) from the objects of perception. Apprehended by a process of abstraction, they are not intelligible entities perpetually *in actu*; rather, they are at first intelligible potentially, and only later actually. Thus, they are capable of being generated and of being destroyed; abstraction is not sufficient to prove that they exist separately. In fact, they are separable only in thought. Moreover, they consist of two elements, one of which plays the role of matter and the other that of form. This can be seen in the case of the concept "snub-nosed," in which concave is, as it were, the form, and the nose is the matter. Similarly, with the concept of man: it contains a quiddity that corresponds to its definition — this is the formal aspect; but there can be no man without flesh and bones — this is the material aspect

(cf. Aristotle, *De anima*, III, 4, 429b, 10 ff.). Consequently, in the intelligibles that we abstract there is a part that is liable to disappear (*fan*^in) and a part that subsists (*baq*^in). The latter resembles a purely immaterial "speculative intelligible" (*ma'qūl nazarī*). But such an intelligible is absolutely identical with the intellect that apprehends it. This being so, the material intelligibles that arise in us require an activating agent and a subject. Since it is evident that they are abstracted from perceived objects and, more immediately, from images of the imagination, it is permissible to suppose that in this faculty there is a disposition (*isti'dād*) to produce and receive these intelligibles when they become actual. For Ibn Rushd, the forms of the imagination are, above all, the activating elements in the process. They are not subjects, except by virtue of the fact that the intelligibles are in them potentially, but not to the extent that they are *in actu*. Otherwise, there would be a mixture of the forms of the imagination and of the intelligible forms. Now, in order for it to be able to think all things, the intellect must be without mixture (cf. *De anima*, III, 4, 429a, 19). Ibn Rushd gives the name "first material intellect" to this "disposition to receive the intelligibles that are in the forms of the imagination." But this intellect cannot be the true subject; it can be generated and it can be destroyed, since the imagination is inseparable from the corporeal structure.

It is therefore necessary to introduce a second subject, the receptacle of the intelligible forms *in actu*. This is the material intellect (but not the first material intellect), also called the intellect *in potentia* (*al-'aql bi'l-quwwa*). It stands in the same relation to the intelligibles as the prime matter does to the perceptible forms. It is eternal (*azalī*), and it is called material because it plays a role analogous to that of prime matter. Like the latter, it cannot be generated and cannot be destroyed. As pure potentiality, it must receive from an intellect *in actu* the intelligibles *in actu*, without which it is nothing. But the individual human being, who, by his faculty of reason, not only conceives and apprehends but also exercises judgment (*hukm, tasdiq*), participates personally in these operations. The intelligibles that existed potentially in the forms of his imagination and are received in the material intellect common to all men constitute a kind of stockpile for each individual, to which he has free access whenever he wishes (*matā shā'a*). Thus arises the habitual intellect or intellect *en habitus* (*al-'aql bi'l-malaka*). An example of the knowledge it contains is that possessed by a professor at a time when he is not teaching, but which he can make actual at will when he begins to teach. Since this habitual intellect depends on the individual's decision, it appears that it is particular to each man and represents his personal store of intelligibles among all those that are received or can be received *in actu* in the common material intellect.

If the imagination plays an activating role in this process, then the agent upon which everything depends is an intellect perpetually in an active state, and is called, for this reason, the active intellect (*al-'aql al-fa''āl*). It bestows being upon the material intellect in the way that what is actual bestows being on what is potential. In order to accomplish this, it actualizes the disposition in the imagination by acting on the imaginative forms — which are potentially intelligible entities — causing them to pass into a state of actuality. But it is not only agent: in itself it is form, intellect perpetually *in actu*; and it is absolutely identical with the intelligible entity that it apprehends. It is this intelligible that is called speculative. It was seen above that by their formal aspect the material intelligibles we grasp are like speculative intelligibles. On this level, man can be said to think with a speculative intellect. "One may therefore suppose," wrote Ibn Rushd, "that it is possible for us to apprehend the active intellect." In this case we will have reached an intelligible that is itself eternal and that, in contradistinction to the material intelligibles, is not dependent for its existence on the act by which we conceive it. Man thus arrives at a state that is called conjunction (*ittiṣāl*) or union (*ittiḥād*). This is the path that the sufis sought to travel. But, according to Ibn Rushd, they did not really succeed. Turning to Ibn Bājja's theory on this subject, Ibn Rushd subjected it to thorough criticism, asking if such a state of union will be natural or divine. If it is divine, how could it be an ultimate perfection of nature? If it is natural, how could nature manage to produce a state in which she negates herself? If this conjunction does not occur as a result of natural perfection, then it must itself be a perfection in the sense that the separate forms are a perfection for the celestial bodies endowed with circular motion, which in itself is a perfect motion. "In short, it is a separate perfection for a natural relation of perfection that is in matter." The divine perfection exists only in the relationship (*iḍāfa*); that is to say, it is not there through a substantial presence. In conclusion, Ibn Rushd stated: "It is on account of this relationship [*nisba*] that the active intellect is called the acquired intellect [*al-'aql al-mustafād*].

It is evident, therefore, that while Ibn Rushd employed the notion of an intellect common to all men, he did not infer from it that human immortality — which it alone can assure — is impersonal. He studiously modified Ibn Bājja's ideas so that they did not in fact lead to such a doctrine. If Ibn Rushd's conclusion is far from being clear and definite, it is owing to the difficulty of the problem. Moreover, the obscurity of even Aristotle on this very point is proof that the problem admits of no perfectly cogent demonstration. Under these conditions, one may let faith settle the issue.

In his personal writings Ibn Rushd sets forth his positions on the religious problems of his time, notably on the agreement between reason and faith and on the interpretation and speculative use that can be made of the verses of the Koran. A philosopher but also a believer, Ibn Rushd accepted the reality of Revelation. He maintained that the Koran and *ḥadith* encourage the study of nature. But the divine message takes into account the diversity of human capacities. All men are not equally responsive to rational demonstrations, and thus it is necessary to resort to dialectical or even rhetorical arguments. Whatever the means employed, it is our duty to understand both nature and the meaning of the language of Revelation. The role of the philosopher is either to furnish a demonstrative argument where it is appropriate but has not yet been formulated, or else to give the unsuitable literal meaning a metaphorical meaning (*majāz*) through a commentary containing figurative language (*ta'wīt*). The theologians (*al-mutakallimūn*) err in seeking to defend surface meanings that have no value as they stand with arguments that can only be dialectical if not sophistical. On the other hand, Ibn Rushd often appeals to the juridical reasoning of the *fuqahā'*. These methodological questions form the subject of Ibn Rushd's *Decisive Treatise and Exposition of the Convergence of the Religious Law and Philosophy.*

Ibn Rushd also wrote *Kitāb al-Kashf*, the full title of which may be rendered as *Exposition of the Methods of Demonstration Relative to the Religious Dogmas and to the Definition of the Equivocal Meanings and Innovations Encountered in the Process of Interpretation and which Alter the Truth and Lead to Error.* In this work Ibn Rushd examined the theories of the major theological sects, particularly the demonstrations of the existence of God, of His unicity, and of His attributes, and conceptions about the origin of the universe and the infinite chain of causation, as well as about predestination and human freedom. This treatise, too, is primarily methodological, but in it Ibn

Rushd stated his position on a number of issues, correcting errors based on false arguments and offering demonstrative proof wherever he can. Thus, on the subject of causes, he shows that God exercises an actual causality through his commandment (*amr*), and that it is not necessary to traverse in thought an infinite time to discover his creative act at the beginning of time. The question of human freedom, however, remains difficult to settle philosophically. One must trust in the Koran and accept its teaching of the existence of both divine omnipotence and human initiative, thus holding — as Bossuet was later to say — the two ends of the chain without knowing how they are joined. Finally, Ibn Rushd upholds the reality of a future life, stating that the dogma is not contrary to reason, even though reason cannot specify modalities of such an existence.

After the *Kashf*, which prepared the way for it, the *Tahāfut al-Tahāfut* may be considered the most complete exposition of Ibn Rushd's personal thought. It takes the form of a critique of the *Tahāfut al-Falāsifa*, in which the theologian al-Ghazāli refutes Ibn Sīnā in the name of religious dogma, using arguments that Ibn Rushd attacks because they are not demonstrative. While he considers al-Ghazāli's refutation worthless, he nevertheless thinks that Ibn Sīnā's ideas should be combated, and marshals a number of demonstrative proofs against the major themes of Avicennian thought. In the process, Ibn Rushd presents virtually an entire philosophical treatise. On the whole, he sought to replace Arab Neoplatonism with what he thought were Aristotle's real views, at the same time taking into account the demands of religious faith. Thus, while upholding the doctrine of the eternity of the creation, he explained that the First Mover moves the world not by a sort of attraction, but by his commandment (*amr*), like a king seated on his throne who has no need himself of moving in order to act. Offering an interpretation of what the Koran calls divine will, Ibn Rushd stated that it is the mode of action *ad extra* of a being perfectly transcendent to his own action and who thus can create a multiplicity of beings (contrary to the Neoplatonic doctrine, adopted by Ibn Sīnā, that the one can come only out of the one). In this perspective, Ibn Rushd demonstrated that God knows particular things in themselves and not in the universal — in this sense, that God's knowledge, which is creative, is closer to the knowledge we have of particulars than to our knowledge of the universal. With regard to the soul's destiny, Ibn Rushd, referring to Aristotle's *Nicomachean Ethics*, observed that the soul acquires not only the comtemplative virtues linked to the apprehension of the intelligible entities common to all men who think, but also personal moral virtues that it may preserve. A personal immortality is therefore possible.

Medicine. The philosophical, religious, and legal works of Ibn Rushd have been studied more thoroughly than his medical books, since he was primarily a theologian-philosopher and scholar of the Koranic sciences. Among his teachers in medicine were ʿAlī Abū Jaʿfar ibn Hārūn al-Tarrajānī (from Tarragona) and Abū Marwān ibn Jurrayūl (or Ḥazbūl, according to al-Ṣafadī). Ibn Rushd's major work in medicine, *al-Kulliyyāt* ("Generalities"), was written between 1153 and 1169. Its subject matter leans heavily on Galen, and occasionally Hippocrates' name is mentioned. It is subdivided into seven books: *Tashrīḥ al-aʿḍāʾ* ("Anatomy of Organs"), *al-Ṣiḥḥa* ("Health"), *al-Maraḍ* ("Sickness"), *al-ʿAlāmāt* ("Symptoms"), *al-Adwiya wa 'l-aghdhiya* ("Drugs and Foods"), *Ḥifẓ al-ṣiḥḥa* ("Hygiene"), and *Shifāʾ al-amrāḍ* ("Therapy"). Ibn Rushd requested his close friend Ibn Zuhr to write a book on *al-Umūr al-juzʾiyya* (particularities, i.e., the treatment of head-to-toe diseases), which he did, and called his book *al-Taisīr fī 'l-mudāwāt wa 'l-tadbīr* ("An Aid to Therapy and Regimen"). Ibn Rushd's *al-Kulliyyāt* and Ibn Zuhr's *al-Taisīr* were meant to constitute a comprehensive medical textbook (hence certain printed Latin editions present these two books together), possibly to serve instead of Ibn Sīnā's *al-Qānūn*, which was not well received in Andalusia by Abu 'l-ʿAlāʾ Zuhr ibn ʿAbd al-Malik ibn Marwān ibn Zuhr (Ibn Zuhr's grandfather). Two Hebrew versions of *al-Kulliyyāt* are known, one by an unidentified translator, another by Solomon ben Abraham ben David. The Latin translation, *Colliget*, was made in Padua in 1255 by a Jew, Bonacosa, and the first edition was printed in Venice in 1482, followed by many other editions. Ibn Rushd wrote a *talkhīṣ* (abstract) of Galen's works, parts of which are preserved in Arabic manuscripts. He showed interest in Ibn Sīnā's *Urjūza fī 'l-ṭibb* ("Poem on Medicine," *Canticum de medicina* . . .), on which he wrote a commentary, *Sharḥ Urjūzat Ibn Sīnā*. It was translated into Hebrew prose by Moses ben Tibbon in 1260; a translation into Hebrew verse was completed at Béziers (France) in 1261 by Solomon ben Ayyub ben Joseph of Granada. Further, a Latin translation of the same work was made by Armengaud, son of Blaise, in 1280 or 1284, and a printed edition was published at Venice in 1484.

Another revised Latin translation was made by Andrea Alpago, who translated Ibn Rushd's *Maqāla fi 'l-Tiryāq* ("Treatise on Theriac," *Tractatus de theriaca*).

So far, no evidence has been provided to support, or refute, the claim that Ibn Rushd is quoted as saying, "He who is occupied with the science of anatomy will have more faith in God." In 1182, he succeeded Ibn Ṭufayl, who retired on account of his advanced age from the post of court physician to the caliph Abū Yaʿqūb Yūsuf, and continued to be favored by his son and successor al-Manṣūr Yaʿqūb ibn Yūsuf until the year when Ibn Rushd fell out of favor and his philosophical works (but not his medical and other strictly scientific books) were banned or burned. In the East, the writings of al-Ghazālī against the principles of Greek philosophy probably led to changes in the medical curriculum, whereby Greek philosophy was gradually supplanted by Islamic theology, which included some aspects of philosophy, and particularly logic. Furthermore, the massacre of Herāt in 1222 and the Mongol invasion that led to the eradication of the eastern caliphate in 1258, and (in the West) the period that followed Ibn Rushd's unsuccessful attempts to defend philosophers against theologians paved the way for a decline in Arabic medicine. The great image of the *ḥakīm* (physician-philosopher), which culminated in the persons of al-Rāzī and Ibn Sīnā, has been superseded by that of *faqīh mushārik fi 'l-ʿulūm* (a jurist who participates in sciences), among whom were physician-jurists and theologian-physicians.

BIBLIOGRAPHY

I. ORIGINAL WORKS. *Incipit translatio Canticor. Avic. cum commento Averrhoys facta ab Arabico in Latinum a mag. Armegando blassi de Montepesulano* (Venice, 1484); *Abhomeron Abynzohar Colliget Averroys* (containing the *Taisīr* and *Antidotarium* of Avenzoar and the *al-Kuliyyāt* of Ibn Rushd, edited by Hieronymus Surianus) (Venice, 1496); *Collectaneorum de Re Medica Averrhoi philosophi . . . Sectiones tres. I. De sanitatis functionibus, ex Aristot. et Galeno. II. De sanitate tuenda, ex Galeno. III. De curandis morbis, a J. Bruyerino Campegio . . . nunc primum Latinitate donatae* (Lyons, 1537); *Quitab el culiat. Libro de las generalidades* (Publ. del Inst. Gen. Franco para la investigación hispano-árabe) (Larache, 1939), in Arabic, published by manuscript photo-reproduction; *Talkhīṣ k. al-ḥummayāt* (Abstract of the book: "Fevers," Escurial, MS 884, i.); *Talkhīṣ k. al-ʿilal wa al-aʿrāḍ* (Abstract of the book: "Diseases and Symptoms," Escurial, MS 884, iii.); *Talkhīṣ k. al-mizāj* (Abstract of the book: "Tempera-

ment," Escurial, MS 881, ii.); *Talkhīṣ k. al-quwā al-ṭabīʿiyya* (Abstract of the book: "Natural Faculties," Escurial, MSS 881, iii.; 884, ii.); *Talkhīṣ k. al-usṭuqussāt* (Abstract of the book: "Elements," Escurial, MS 881, i.); *Sharḥ urjūzat Ibn Sīnā fī al-ṭibb* (Commentary on Ibn Sīnā's "Poem on Medicine," Dār al-Kutub al-Miṣriyya Ṭibb 1239; Yale University Library, Landberg Collection, MS 157, n. 1513).

The Mediaeval Academy of America has begun publication of a critical ed. of the collected commentaries (medieval Latin and Hebrew trans.), H. A. Wolfson, et al., eds., in the series Corpus Commentariorum Averrois in Aristotelem (Cambridge, Mass., 1949–   ); see H. A. Wolfson, "Revised Plan for the Publication of a *Corpus Commentariorum* . . .," in *Speculum*, **38** (1963), 88–104, which includes detailed bibliographical information. E. I. J. Rosenthal, *Averroes' Commentary on Plato's Republic*, 2nd ed., rev. (Cambridge, 1966), is based on a Hebrew trans. of the lost Arabic original.

For bibliographical details of Ibn Rushd's works, see also C. Brockelmann, *Geschichte der arabischen Literatur*, I (Leiden, 1943), 604–606, and supp. I (Leiden, 1937), 833–836; G. Sarton, *Introduction to the History of Science*, II, pt. 2 (Baltimore, 1931), 355–360; and M. Steinschneider, *Die hebräischen Übersetzungen des Mittelalters und die Juden als Dolmetscher* (Berlin, 1893; repr. Graz, 1956). M. J. Müller, ed., *Philosophie und Theologie des Averroes*, 2 vols. (Munich, 1859–1875), is a basic work.

II. SECONDARY LITERATURE. L. Leclerc, *Histoire de la médecine arabe*, II (Paris, 1876), 97–109; Ibn Abī ʾUṣaybiʿa's *ʿUyūn al-anbāʾ fī ṭabaqāt al-aṭibbāʾ*, A. Müller ed., II (Cairo-Königsberg, 1882–1884), 75–78; *The Encyclopaedia of Islam*, II (Leiden-London, 1913–1938), 410–413; new ed., III (Leiden-London, 1960–   ), 909–920; al-Yāfiʿī's *Mirʾāt al-janān*, III (Hyderabad, 1918–1920), 479; P. M. Bouyges, "Inventaire des textes arabes d'Averroés," in *Mélanges de l'Université Saint-Joseph*, **8**, 1 (1922), 3–54; *ibid.*, **9**, 2 (1924), 43–48 (additions and corrections to note V. 1); D. Campbell, *Arabian Medicine and Its Influence on the Middle Ages*, I (London, 1926), 92–96; G. Sarton, *Introduction to the History of Science*, II, pt. 1 (Baltimore, 1927–1948), 355–361; Y. A. Sarkīs, *Muʿjam al-maṭbūʿāt al-ʿarabiyya wa al-muʿarraba . . . .* I (Cairo. 1928–1931), 108–109; H. Ritter and S. Dedering, eds., *Das biographische Lexikon des Ṣalāhaddīn Halīl Ibn Aibak aṣ-Ṣafadī*, II (Istanbul-Damascus, 1931–1970), 114–115; Ibn al-ʿImād's *Shadharāt al-dhahab fī akhbār man dhahab . . . ,* IV (Cairo, 1931–1932), 320; C. Brockelmann, *Geschichte der arabischen Litteratur* (Leiden, 1943–1949), supplement I (Leiden, 1937–1942), 604, 833; H. P. J. Renaud, *Les manuscrits arabes de l'Escurial, décrits d'après les notes de H. Derenbourg*, II (Paris, 1941); *Publications de l'École Nationale des Langues Orientales Vivantes*, 5th ser., 91–92; 94–95; ʿA. M. al-ʿAqqād, *Nawābigh al-fikr al-ʿarabī, Ibn Rushd: Ibn Rushd al-ṭabīb*, Dār al-Maʿārif, ed. (Cairo, 1953), 96–112; *Kh. al-Ziriklī, al-Aʿlām . . . ,* 2nd ed., VI

(Cairo, 1954–1959), 212–213; L. Nemoy, "Arabic Manuscripts in the Yale University Library," in *Transactions of the Connecticut Academy of Arts and Sciences*, XL (New Haven, 1956), 160 (n. 1513); F. X. Rodríguez Molero, "Averroes, médico y filósofo," in *Archivo Ibéro Americano de Historia de la Medicina*, **8** (1956), 187–190; S. Muntner, "Averrhoes (Abu-el-Walid ibn Ahmed ibn Rushd). Le médecin dans la littérature hébraique," in *Imprensa Médica* **21**, 4 (1957), 203–208: ʿU. R. Kaḥḥāla, *Muʿjam al-muʾallifīn . . .* , VIII (Damascus, 1957–1961), 313; Ṣ. el-Munajjed, "Maṣādir jadīda ʿan tārīkh al-ṭibb ʿind al-ʿarab," in *Majallat Maʿhad al-Makhṭūṭāt al-ʿArabiyya*, **5**, 2 (1959), 257 (ns. 66–68); R. Walzer, *Greek into Arabic. Essays on Islamic Philosophy*, Oriental Studies, I (Oxford, 1962), 26–28; S. Hamarneh, "Bibliography on Medicine and Pharmacy in Medieval Islam. Mit einer Einführung Arabismus in der Geschichte der Pharmazie von Rudolf Schmitz," in *Veröffentlichungen der Internationalen Gesellschaft für Geschichte der Pharmazie*, e.V., n. s., **25** (1964), 92; S. Hamarneh, *Index of Manuscripts on Medicine, Pharmacy, and Allied Sciences in the Ẓāhiriyya Library* (Damascus, 1969), 175–178; A. Dietrich, "Medicinalia Arabica. Studien über arabische medizinische Handschriften in türkischen und syrischen Bibliotheken," in *Abhandlungen der Akademie der Wissenschaften zu Göttingen*, 3rd series, no. 66 (1966), 99–100 (n. 39); J. C. Bürgel, "Averroes, 'Contra Galenum.' Das Kapitel von der Atmung im Colliget des Averroes als ein Zeugnis mittelalterlich-islamischer Kritik an Galen, eingeleitet, arabisch herausgegeben und übersetzt," in *Nachrichten der Akademie der Wissenschaften in Göttingen*, I (1967), 9, 263–340; A. Z. Iskandar, *A Catalogue of Arabic Manuscripts on Medicine and Science in the Wellcome Historical Medical Library* (London, 1967), 37; B. S. Eastwood, "Averroes' View of the Retina—a Reappraisal," in *Journal of the History of Medicine*, **24** (1969), 77–82; A. Amerio, "Spunti di rinascimento scientifico negli averroisti latini del XIII secola," in *Med. Secoli*, **7** (1970), 13–18, refs.; M. Ullmann, *Die Medizin im Islam*, Handbuch der Orientalistik, supp. 6 (Leiden-Cologne, 1970), 166–167; R. Y. Ebied, *Bibliography of Mediaeval Arabic and Jewish Medicine and Allied Sciences*, Wellcome Institute of the History of Medicine (London, 1971), 107–108.

On Ibn Rushd's life and philosophical thought, see the following: L. Gauthier, *La théorie d'Ibn Rochd (Averroès) sur les rapports de la religion et de la philosophie* (Paris, 1909), with bibliography; and *Ibn Rochd (Averroès)* (Paris, 1948); M. Grabmann, *Der lateinische Averroismus des 13. Jahrhunderts und seine Stellung zur Christlichen Weltanschauung* (Munich, 1931); R. de Mendizábal Allende, *Averroes, un andaluz para Europa* (Madrid, 1971); F. W. Muller, *Der Rosenroman und der lateinische Averroismus des 13. Jahrhunderts* (Frankfurt, 1947); S. Münk, *Mélanges de philosophie juive et arabe* (Paris, 1859), 418–458; G. Quadri, *La filosofia degli arabi nel suo fiore*, II (Florence, 1939); and *La philosophie arabe dans l'Europe médiévale* (Paris, 1947),

198–340; E. Renan, *Averroès et l'averroïsme* (Paris, 1852; repr. 1949); and K. Werner, *Der Averroismus in der Christlich-peripatetischen Psychologie des späteren Mittelalters*, new ed., (Amsterdam, 1964).

ROGER ARNALDEZ
ALBERT Z. ISKANDAR

RUSSELL, BERTRAND ARTHUR WILLIAM (*b.* Trelleck, Monmouthshire, England, 18 May 1872; *d.* Plas Penrhyn, near Penrhyndeudraeth, Wales, 2 February 1970), *mathematical logic.*

The Russell family has played a prominent part in the social, intellectual, and political life of Great Britain since the time of the Tudors; Russells were usually to be found on the Whig side of politics, with a firm belief in civil and religious liberty, as that phrase was interpreted by the Whigs. Lord John Russell (later first earl Russell), the third son of the sixth duke of Bedford, was an important figure in nineteenth-century politics: He was a leader in the struggle to establish the great Reform Act of 1832, held several high offices of state, and was twice prime minister in Whig and Whig-Liberal administrations. His eldest son, known by the courtesy title of Viscount Amberley, married Katherine Stanley, of another famous English family, the Stanleys of Alderley. The young couple were highly intelligent and were in strong sympathy with most of the reforming and progressive movements of their time, a stance that made them far from popular with the conservative section of the aristocracy. Unhappily, neither enjoyed good health; the wife died in 1874 and the husband in 1876. There were two children, Frank and Bertrand, the latter the younger by about seven years.

The Russell family did not approve of the arrangements made by Viscount Amberley for the upbringing of the two children in the event of his death. When this occurred, the boys were made wards in chancery and placed in the care of Earl Russell and his wife, who were then living at Pembroke Lodge in Richmond Park, a house in the gift of the Crown. Bertrand's grandfather died in 1878, but his grandmother lived until 1898 and had a strong influence on his early life.

Like many Victorian children of the upper class, the boy was educated at home by a succession of tutors, so that when he entered Trinity College, Cambridge, as a scholar in 1890, he had had no experience of communal life in an educational establishment save for a few months in a "cramming" school in London. At Trinity he was welcomed into a society that for intellectual brilliance could hardly have been bettered anywhere at that time. He obtained a first class in the mathematical tripos and in the moral sciences tripos, although the formality of examinations seems not to have appealed to him. He remarks in his autobiography that the university teachers "contributed little to my enjoyment of Cambridge," and that "I derived no benefits from lectures."

A great stimulus to Russell's development was his election in 1892 to the Apostles. This was a small, informal society, founded about 1820, that regarded itself—not without some justification—as composed of the intellectual cream of the university; its main object was the completely unfettered discussion of any subject whatsoever. One member was A. N. Whitehead, then a mathematical lecturer at Cambridge, who had read Russell's papers in the scholarship examination and had in consequence formed a high opinion of his ability. Through the society Russell acquired a circle of gifted friends: the philosophers G. E. Moore and Ellis McTaggart, the historian G. M. Trevelyan and his poet brother R. C. Trevelyan, the brilliant brothers Crompton and Theodore Llewelyn Davies, and later the economist J. M. Keynes and the essayist Lytton Strachey.

In the latter part of the nineteenth century, progressive opinion at Cambridge had begun to maintain that university dons should regard research as a primary activity, rather than as a secondary pursuit for leisure hours after teaching duties had been performed. This opinion was particularly strong in Trinity, where A. R. Forsyth, W. W. Rouse Ball, and Whitehead encouraged the researches of younger men such as E. W. Barnes, G. H. Hardy, J. H. Jeans, E. T. Whittaker, and Russell; these themselves exercised a great influence on the next generation, the remarkable set of Trinity mathematicians of the period 1900–1914.

One mode of encouragement was the establishment of prize fellowships, awarded for original dissertations; such a fellowship lasted for six years and involved no special duties, the object being to give a young man an unhindered opportunity for intellectual development. Russell was elected in 1895, on the strength of a dissertation on the foundations of geometry, published in 1897. During the later part of his tenure and after it lapsed, he was not in residence; but in 1910 the college appointed him to a special lectureship in logic and the philosophy of mathematics.

During World War I pacifism excited emotions much more bitter than was the case in World War II. Russell's strongly held views made him unpopular in high places; and when in 1916 he published a leaflet protesting against the harsh treatment of a conscientious objector, he was prosecuted on a charge of making statements likely to prejudice recruiting for and discipline in the armed services, and fined £100. The Council, the governing body of Trinity, then dismissed him from his lectureship, and Russell broke all connection with the college by removing his name from the books. In 1918 another article of his was judged seditious, and he was sentenced to imprisonment for six months. The sentence was carried out with sufficient leniency to enable him to write his very useful *Introduction to Mathematical Philosophy* in Brixton Prison.

Many members of Trinity felt that the Council's action in dismissing Russell in 1916 was excessively harsh. After the war the breach was healed: in 1925 the college invited Russell to give the Tarner lectures, later published under the title *The Analysis of Matter*; and from 1944 until his death he was again a fellow of the college.

In the prologue to his *Autobiography* Russell tells us that three strong passions have governed his life: "the longing for love, the search for happiness, and unbearable pity for the suffering of mankind." His writings and his actions testify to the perseverance with which he pursued his aims from youth to extreme old age, undeterred by opposition and regardless of obloquy. Russell's perseverance did not necessarily imply obstinacy, for his mind was never closed; and if his acute sense of logic revealed to him a fallacy in his argument, he would not cling to a logically indefensible view but would rethink his position, on the basis of his three strong principles. But it was also his devotion to logic that led him frequently to reject the compromises so often forced on the practical politician.

Russell—not surprisingly, in view of his ancestry—was always ready to campaign for "progressive" causes. About 1907 he fought hard for women's suffrage, a cause that provoked more opposition and rowdyism in the United Kingdom than any other political question during this century—even more than the pacifism for which Russell was prosecuted in World War I. After the war Russell continued his search for a genuine democracy, in which freedom for the individual should be compatible with the common good; his experiments in education were designed to contribute to this end. Never insular, he would expose what he saw as the faults of his own country or of the English-speaking nations as caustically as he would those of the totalitarian regimes; but that the growth of the latter could be met only by war was a conclusion to which he came very reluctantly. At the close of World War II, his vision of humanity inevitably destroying itself through the potency of nuclear weapons caused him to lead a long campaign for nuclear disarmament.

A long list of books bears witness to Russell's endeavor to encourage human beings to think clearly, to understand the new scientific discoveries and to realize some of their implications, and to abhor injustice, violence, and war. *The Impact of Science on Society, History of Western Philosophy, Common Sense and Nuclear Warfare, Marriage and Morals, Freedom and Organisation,* and *Prospects of Industrial Civilisation,* to name only a few, show how earnestly he sought to promote his ideals. All were written in an English that was always clear and precise, and often beautiful. Critics might disagree with his opinions but seldom could misunderstand them. An occasional didactic arrogance might offend, but it could be forgiven in view of the author's manifest sincerity.

A few of Russell's many honors were fellowship of the Royal Society in 1908, the Order of Merit in 1949, and the Nobel Prize for literature in 1950.

Russell has told us in his autobiography how he began the study of geometry, with his elder brother as tutor, at the age of eleven. Like almost every other English boy of his time, he began on Euclid; unlike almost every other English boy, he was entranced, for he had not known that the world contained anything so delicious. His brother told him that the fifth proposition of book I, the notorious *pons asinorum,* was generally considered difficult; but Russell found it no trouble. Having been told, however, that Euclid proved things, he was disappointed at having to begin by assimilating an array of axioms and would not accept this necessity until his brother told him that unless he did so, his study of geometry could not proceed, thus extorting a reluctant acceptance. The anecdote is not irrelevant; Russell's mathematical work, which occupied him until he was over forty, was almost entirely concerned with probing and testing the foundations of mathematics, in order that the superstructure might be firmly established.

Russell's fellowship thesis was revised for publication in 1897 as *An Essay on the Foundations of Geometry.* Its basic theme was an examination of the status assigned to geometry by Kant in his doctrine of synthetic a priori judgments. Analytic propositions are propositions of pure logic; but synthetic propositions, such as "New York is a large city," cannot be obtained by purely logical processes. Thus all propositions that are known through experience are synthetic; but Kant would not accept the converse, that only such propositions are synthetic. An empirical proposition is derived from experience; but an a priori proposition, however derived, is eventually recognized to have a basis other than experience.

Kant's problem was to determine how synthetic a priori judgments or propositions are possible. He held that Euclidean geometry falls into this category, for geometry is concerned with what we perceive and thus is conditioned by our perceptions. This argument becomes dubious when the full implication of the existence of non-Euclidean geometries is appreciated; but although these geometries were discovered about 1830, the philosophical implications had hardly been fully grasped by the end of the nineteenth century. One considerable step was taken by Hilbert when he constructed his formal and abstract system based on his epigram that in geometry it must be possible to replace the words "points," "lines," and "planes" by the words "tables," "chairs," and "beer mugs"; but his *Grundlagen der Geometrie* was not published until 1899.

To Russell, non-Euclidean spaces were possible, in the philosophical sense that they are not condemned by any a priori argument as to the necessity of space for experience. His examination of fundamentals led him to conclude that for metrical geometry three axioms are a priori: (1) the axiom of free mobility, or congruence: shapes do not in any way depend on absolute position in space; (2) the axiom of dimensions: space must have a finite integral number of dimensions; (3) the axiom of distance: every point must have to every other point one and only one relation independent of the rest of space, this relation being the distance between the two points.

For projective geometry the a priori axioms are (1) as in metrical geometry; (2) space is continuous and infinitely divisible, the zero of extension being a point; (3) two points determine a unique figure, the straight line. For metrical geometry an empirical element enters into the concept of distance, but the two sets are otherwise equivalent. In the light of modern views on the nature of a geometry, these investigations must be regarded as meaningless or at least as devoted to the wrong kind of question. What remains of interest in the *Foundations of Geometry* is the surgical skill with which Russell can dissect a corpus of thought, and his command of an easy yet precise English style.

Following the publication of the *Foundations of Geometry,* Russell settled down to the composition of a comprehensive treatise on the principles of mathematics, to expound his belief that pure mathematics deals entirely with concepts that can be discussed on a basis of a small number of fundamental logical concepts, deducing all its propositions by means of a small number of fundamental logical principles. He was not satisfied with his first drafts, but in July 1900 he went to Paris with Whitehead to attend an International Congress of Philosophy. Here his meeting with Peano brought about, in his own phrase, "a turning point in my intellectual life." Until then he had had only a vague acquaintance with Peano's work, but the extraordinary skill and precision of Peano's contributions to discussions convinced Russell that such mastery must be to a large extent due to Peano's knowledge of mathematical logic and its symbolic language.

The work of Boole, Peirce, and Schröder had constructed a symbolic calculus of logic; and their success contributed to Peano's systematic attempt to place the whole of mathematics on a purely formal and abstract basis, for which purpose he utilized a symbolism of his own creation. This enabled him and his disciples to clarify distinctions hitherto obscured by the ambiguities of ordinary language, and to analyze the logic, basis, and structure of such mathematical concepts as the positive integers. The apparently trivial symbolism that replaces "The entity x is a member of the class A" with "$x \,\epsilon\, A$" leads not only to brevity but, more importantly, to a precision free from the ambiguities lurking in the statement "x is A." One result of Peano's work was to dispose of Kant's synthetic a priori judgments.

Russell rapidly mastered Peano's symbolism and ideas, and then resumed the writing of his book on principles; the whole of the first volume was completed within a few months of his meeting with Peano. Some sections were subjected to a thorough rewriting, however; and volume I of *Principles of Mathematics* was not published until 1903. The second edition (1937) is perhaps more valuable for the study of the development of Russell's ideas, for it both reprints the first edition and contains a new introduction in which Russell gives his own opinion on those points on which his views had changed since 1903; but in spite of Hilbert and Brouwer, he is still firm in his belief that mathematics and logic are identical.

The second volume of the *Principles,* to be written in cooperation with Whitehead, never appeared

because it was replaced by the later *Principia Mathematica.* It was to have been a completely symbolic account of the assimilation of mathematics to logic, of which a descriptive version appears in volume I. The main sections of volume I treat indefinables of mathematics (including a description of Peano's symbolic logic), number, quantity, order, infinity and continuity, space, and matter and motion. On all these topics Russell's clarity of thought contributed to the establishment of precision; thus his analysis of the words "some," "any," "every," for instance, is very searching. In two places, at least, he was able to throw light on familiar but vexed topics of mathematical definition and technique.

That the positive integer 2 represents some property possessed by all couples may be intuitively acceptable but does not supply a precise definition, since neither existence nor uniqueness is guaranteed in this way. Russell's definition of a number uses a technique of equivalence that has had many further applications. The definition had already been given by Frege, but his work was not then known to Russell;[1] indeed, it was known to hardly any mathematician of the time, since Frege's style and symbolism are somewhat obscure. Two classes, A and B, are said to be similar ($A \sim B$) if each element of either class can be uniquely mated to one element of the other class; clearly A is similar to itself. Similarity is a transitive and symmetrical relation; that is, if $A \sim B$ and $B \sim C$, then $A \sim C$, and if $A \sim B$, then $B \sim A$. The (cardinal) number of a class A is, then, the class consisting of all classes similar to A. Thus every class has a cardinal number, and similar classes have the same cardinal number. The null class φ is such that $x \,\epsilon\, \varphi$ is universally false, and its cardinal is denoted by 0. A unit class contains some term x and is such that if y is a member of this class, then $x = y$; its cardinal is denoted by 1. The operations of addition and multiplication are then readily constructed. We thus have a workable definition with no difficulties about existence or uniqueness; but—and this is a considerable concession—the concept of "class" must be acceptable.

A similar clarification of the notion of a real number was also given by Russell. Various methods of definition were known, one of the most popular being that of Dedekind. Suppose that p and q are two mutually exclusive properties, such that every rational number possesses one or the other. Further, suppose that every rational possessing property p is less than any rational possessing property q. This process defines a section of the rationals, giving a lower class L and an upper class R. If L has a greatest member, or if R has a least member, the section corresponds to this rational number. But if L has no greatest and R no least member, the section does not determine a rational. (The case in which L has a greatest and R has a least member cannot arise, since the rationals are dense.) Of the two possible cases, to say that the section in one case corresponds to a rational number and in the other it corresponds to or represents an irrational number is—if instinctive—not to define the irrational number, for the language is imprecise. Russell surmounts this difficulty by simply defining a real number to be a lower section L of the rationals. If L has a greatest member or R a least member, then this real number is rational; in the other case, this real number is irrational.

These are two of the outstanding points in the *Principles*. But the concept of "class" is evidently deeply involved, and the "contradiction of the greatest cardinal" caused Russell to probe the consequences of the acceptance of the class concept more profoundly, particularly in view of Cantor's work on infinite numbers. Cantor proved that the number of subclasses that can be formed out of a given class is greater than the number of members of the class, and thus it follows that there is no greatest cardinal number.

Yet if the class of all objects that can be counted is formed, this class must have a cardinal number that is the greatest possible. From this contradiction Russell was led to formulate a notorious antinomy: A class may or may not be a member of itself. Thus, the class of men, mankind, is not a man and is not a member of itself; on the other hand, the class consisting of the number 5 is the number 5, that is, it is a member of itself. Now let W denote the class of all classes not members of themselves. If W is not a member of itself, then by definition it belongs to W—that is, it is a member of itself. If W is a member of W, then by definition it is not a member of itself—that is, it is not a member of W. In the main text this contradiction is discussed but not resolved. In an appendix, however, there is a brief anticipation of an attempt to eliminate it by means of what Russell called the "theory of types," dealt with more fully in *Principia Mathematica*.

A commonsense reaction to this contradiction might well be a feeling that a class of objects is in a category different from that of the objects themselves, and so cannot reasonably be regarded as a member of itself. If x is a member of a class A, such that the definition of x depends on A, the definition is said to be impredicative; it has the appearance of circularity, since what is defined is part of its own definition. Poincaré suggested that the various antinomies were generated by accepting impredicative definitions,[2] and Russell enunciated the "vicious circle principle" that no class can contain entities definable only in terms of that class. This recourse, however, while ostracizing the antinomies, would also cast doubt on the validity of certain important processes in mathematical analysis; thus the definition of the exact upper bound is impredicative.

To meet the difficulty, Russell devised his theory of types. Very crudely outlined, it starts with primary individuals; these are of one type, say type 0. Properties of primary individuals are of type 1, properties of properties of individuals are of type 2, and so on. All admitted properties must belong to some type. Within a type, other than type 0, there are orders. In type 1, properties defined without using any totality belong to order 0; properties defined by means of a totality of properties of a given order belong to the next higher order. Then, finally, to exclude troubles arising from impredicative definitions, Russell introduced his axiom of reducibility: for any property of order other than 0, there is a property over precisely the same range that is of order 0; that is, in a given type any impredicative definition is logically equivalent to some predicative definition.

Whitehead and Russell themselves declared that they were not entirely happy about this new axiom. Even if an axiom may well be arbitrary, it should, so one feels, at least be plausible. Among the other axioms this appears as anomalous as, for instance, the notorious axiom of parallels seems to be in Euclidean geometry.

F. P. Ramsey showed that the antinomies could be separated into two kinds: those which are "logical," such as Russell's, and those which are "semantical," such as that involved in the assertion "I am lying."[3] The first class can then be eliminated by the simpler theory of types, in which the further classification into orders is not required. But even so, Ramsey did not regard this reconstruction of the Whitehead-Russell position as altogether satisfactory. Weyl pointed out that one might just as well accept the simpler axiomatic set theory of Zermelo and Fraenkel as a foundation, and remarked that a return to the standpoint of Whitehead and Russell was unthinkable.[4]

Before leaving the *Principles*, some other matters are worthy of note. First, the important calculus of relations, hinted at by De Morgan and explored by C. S. Peirce, is examined in detail.[5] Second, Russell was not concerned merely with foundations; he took the whole mathematical world as his parish. There is thus a long examination of the nature of space and of the characteristics of projective, descriptive, and metrical geometries. Third, there is an analysis of philosophical views on the nature of matter and motion. Finally, he draws, possibly for the first time, a clear distinction between a proposition, which must be true or false, and a propositional function, which becomes a proposition, with a truth value, only when the argument is given a determinate value; the propositional function "x is a prime number" becomes a proposition, which may be true or false, when x is specified.

In the three volumes of *Principia Mathematica* (1910–1913) Whitehead and Russell took up the task, attempted in Russell's uncompleted *Principles,* of constructing the whole body of mathematical doctrine by logical deduction from the basis of a small number of primitive ideas and a small number of primitive principles of logical inference, using a symbolism derived from that of Peano but considerably extended and systematized.

Associated with elementary propositions p, q, the primitive concepts are (1) negation, the contradictory of p, not-p, denoted by $\sim p$; (2) disjunction, or logical sum, asserting that at least one of p and q is true, denoted by $p \vee q$; (3) conjunction, or logical product, asserting that both p and q are true, denoted by $p \cdot q$; (4) implication, p implies q, denoted by $p \supset q$; (5) equivalence, p implies q and q implies p, denoted by $p \equiv q$. If a proposition is merely to be considered, it may be denoted simply by p; but if it is to be asserted, this is denoted by $\vdash p$, so that $\vdash$ may be read as "It is true that. . . ." The assertion of a propositional function for some undetermined value of the argument is denoted by $\exists$, which may be read as "There exists a . . . such that. . . ."

Dots are used systematically in place of brackets; the rule of operation is that the more dots, the stronger their effect. An example will show the way in which the dots are used. The proposition "if either p or q is true, and either p or 'q implies r' is true, then either p or r is true" may be written as

$$\vdash : \cdot p \vee q : p \cdot \vee \cdot q \supset r : \supset \cdot p \vee r.$$

The five concepts listed above are not independent. In the *Principia* negation and disjunction are taken as fundamental, and the other three are then defined in terms of these two. Thus conjunction, $p \cdot q$, is defined as $\sim (\sim p \vee \sim q)$; implication,

$p \supset q$, as $\sim p \vee q$; and equivalence, $p \equiv q$, as $(p \supset q) \cdot (q \supset p)$, which can of course now be expressed entirely in terms of the symbols $\sim$ and $\vee$. Another elementary function of two propositions is incompatibility; p is incompatible with q if either or both of p and q are false, that is, if they are not both true; the symbolic notation is p/q. Negation and disjunction are then definable in terms of incompatibility:

$$\sim p = p/p, p \vee q = p/ \sim q.$$

Thus the five concepts (1) – (5) are all definable in terms of the single concept of incompatibility; for instance, $p \supset q = p/(q/q)$. This reduction was given by H. M. Sheffer in 1913,[6] although Willard Quine points out that Peirce recognized the possibility about 1880.

The primitive propositions first require two general principles of deduction—anything implied by a true proposition is true, and an analogous statement for propositional functions: when $\phi(x)$ and "$\phi(x)$ implies $\psi(x)$" can be asserted, then $\psi(x)$ can be asserted. There are then five primitive propositions of symbolic logic:

(1) Tautology. If either p is true or p is true, then p is true:

$$\vdash : p \vee p \cdot \supset \cdot p.$$

(2) Addition. If q is true, then "p or q" is true:

$$\vdash : q \cdot \supset \cdot p \vee q.$$

(3) Permutation. "p or q" implies "q or p":

$$\vdash : p \vee q \cdot \supset \cdot q \vee p.$$

(4) Association. If either p is true or "q or r" is true, then either q is true or "p or r" is true:

$$\vdash : p \vee (q \vee r) \cdot \supset \cdot q \vee (p \vee r).$$

(5) Summation. If q implies r, then "p or q" implies "p or r":

$$\vdash : \cdot q \supset r \cdot \supset : p \vee q \cdot \supset \cdot p \vee r.$$

Following up Sheffer's use of incompatibility as the single primitive concept, Nicod showed that the primitive propositions could be replaced by a single primitive proposition of the form

$$p \cdot \supset \cdot q \cdot r : \supset \cdot t \supset t \cdot s/q \supset p/s,$$

which, since $p \supset q = p/(q/q)$, can be expressed entirely in terms of the stroke symbol for incompatibility.[7]

The second edition of the *Principia* (1925–1927) was mainly a reprint of the first, with small errors corrected; but its worth to the student is considerably increased by the addition of a new introduction, of some thirty-four pages, in which the authors give an account of modifications and improvements rendered possible by work on the logical bases of mathematics following the appearance of the first edition—for instance, the researches of Sheffer and Nicod just mentioned. The authors are mildly apologetic about the notorious axiom of reducibility; they are not content with it, but are prepared to accept it until something better turns up. In particular, they refer to the work of Chwistek and of Wittgenstein, without, however, being able to give wholehearted approval.[8] Much of the introduction is devoted to Wittgenstein's theory and its consequences. Here they show that the results of volume I of the *Principia* stand, although proofs have to be revised; but they cannot, on Wittgenstein's theory, reestablish the important Dedekindian doctrine of the real number, nor Cantor's theorem that $2^n > n$, save for the case of n finite. The introduction was also much influenced by the views of Ramsey, whose death in 1930, at the age of twenty-seven, deprived Cambridge of a brilliant philosopher.

The publication of the *Principia* gave a marked impulse to the study of mathematical logic. The deft handling of a complicated but precise symbolism encouraged workers to use this powerful technique and thus avoid the ambiguities lurking in the earlier employment of ordinary language. The awkwardness and inadequacy of the theory of types and the axiom of reducibility led not only to further investigations of the Whitehead-Russell doctrine but also to an increased interest in rival theories, particularly Hilbert's formalism and Brouwer's intuitionism. Perhaps because none of these three competitors can be regarded as finally satisfactory, research on the foundations of mathematics has produced new results and opened up new problems the very existence of which could hardly have been foreseen in the early years of this century. Whitehead and Russell may have failed in their valiant attempt to place mathematics once and for all on an unassailable logical basis, but their failure may have contributed more to the development of mathematical logic than complete success would have done.

The *Introduction to Mathematical Philosophy* (1919), written while Russell was serving a sentence in Brixton Prison, is a genuine introduction but certainly is not "philosophy without tears"; it may perhaps best be described as *une oeuvre de haute vulgarisation*. The aim is to expound work done in this field, particularly by Whitehead and Russell, without using the complex symbolism of *Principia Mathematica*. Russell's mastery of clear and precise English stood him in good stead for such a task, and many young students in the decade 1920–1930 were first drawn to mathematical logic by a study of this efficient and readable volume.

To explain the arrangement of the book, Russell remarks, "The most obvious and easy things in mathematics are not those that come logically at the beginning: they are things that, from the point of view of logical deduction, come somewhere near the middle." Taking such things as a starting point, a close analysis should lead back to general ideas and principles, from which the starting point can then be deduced or defined. This starting point is here taken to be the familiar set of positive integers; the theory of these, as shown by Peano, depends on the three primitive ideas of zero, number, and successor, and on five primitive propositions, one of which is the principle of mathematical induction. The integers themselves are then defined by the Frege-Russell method, using the class of all similar classes, and the relation between finiteness and mathematical induction is established. Order and relations are studied next, to enable rational, real, and complex numbers to be defined, after which the deeper topics of infinite cardinals and infinite ordinals can be broached. It is then possible to look at certain topics in analysis, such as limit processes and continuity.

The definition of multiplication when the number of factors may be infinite presents a subtle difficulty. If a class A has m members and a class B has n members, the product $m \times n$ can be defined as the number of ordered couples that can be formed by choosing the first term of the couple from A and the second from B. Here m or n or both may be infinite, and the definition may readily be generalized further to the situation in which there is a finite number of classes, $A, B, \cdots, K$. But if the number of classes is infinite, then in defect of a rule of selection, we are confronted with the impossible task of making an infinite number of arbitrary acts of choice.

To turn this obstacle, recourse must be had to the multiplicative axiom, or axiom of selection: given a class of mutually exclusive classes (none being null), there is at least one class that has exactly one term in common with each of the given classes. This is equivalent to Zermelo's axiom that every class can be well-ordered, that is, can be arranged in a series in which each subclass (not being null) has a first term.[9] This matter is dealt with in *Principia Mathematica*, but here Russell offers a pleasant illustration provided by the arithmetical perplexity of the millionaire who buys a pair of socks whenever he buys a pair of boots, ultimately purchasing an infinity of each. In dealing with the number of boots, the axiom is not required, since we can choose, say, the right boot (or the left) from every pair. But no such distinction is available in counting the socks, however, and here the axiom is needed.

The last six chapters of the *Introduction* are concerned with the theory of deduction and the general logical bases of mathematics, including an analysis of the use and nature of classes and the need, in Russell's theory, for a doctrine of types.

Among the essays collected in *Mysticism and Logic* (1921) are some that deal, in popular style, with Russell's views on mathematics and its logical foundations. One of these, "Mathematics and the Metaphysicians," written in 1901, had appeared in *International Monthly*. The editor had asked Russell to make the article "as romantic as possible," and hence it contains a number of quips, some now famous, in which the air of paradox masks a substantial degree of truth. To say that pure mathematics was discovered by George Boole in 1854 is merely Russell's way of stating that Boole was one of the first to recognize the identity of formal logic with mathematics, a point of view firmly held by Russell. In emphasizing that pure mathematics is made up of logical steps of the form "If p, then q" —that is, if such and such a proposition is true of anything, then such and such another proposition is true of that thing—Russell remarks that it is essential not to discuss whether the first proposition is really true, and not to mention what the anything is, of which it is supposed to be true. He is thus led to his oft-quoted description of mathematics as "the subject in which we never know what we are talking about, nor whether what we are saying is true." He comments that many people may find comfort in agreeing that the description is accurate.

Russell's gifts as a popularizer of knowledge are shown in a number of his other books, such as *The Analysis of Matter* and *The ABC of Relativity*, in which problems arising from contemporary physics are discussed. He never wholly divorced mathematics from its applications; and even his first book, on the foundations of geometry, had its origin in his wish to establish the concept of motion and the laws of dynamics on a secure logical basis.

In these later books his critical skill is exercised on the mathematical foundations of physics and occasionally is used to provide alternatives to suggested theories.

For instance, the advent of relativity, bringing in the notion of an event as a point in the space-time continuum, had encouraged Whitehead to deal with the definition of points and events by the application of his principle of extensive abstraction, discussed in detail in his *An Enquiry Concerning the Principles of Natural Knowledge* (1919). This principle has a certain affinity with the Frege-Russell definition of the number of a class as the class of all similar classes. To state the application very crudely, a point is defined as the set of all volumes that enclose that point; Whitehead is of course careful to frame the principle in such a way as to avoid the circularity suggested in this crude statement. This idea is then used to define an event. In *The Analysis of Matter,* Russell argues that while logically flawless, this definition, in the case of an event, does not seem genuinely to correspond to the nature of events as they occur in the physical world, and that it makes the large assumption that there is no minimum and no maximum to the time extent of an event. He develops an alternative theory involving an ingenious application of Hausdorff's axioms for a topological space.[10]

Whatever the final verdict on Russell's work in symbolic logic may be, his place among the outstanding leaders in this field in the present century must be secure.

NOTES

1. G. Frege, *Die Grundlagen der Arithmetik* (Breslau, 1884), also in English (Oxford, 1953); *Grundgesetze der Arithmetik, begriffsschriftlich abgeleitet,* 2 vols. (Jena, 1893–1903), vol. I also in English (Berkeley–Los Angeles, 1964).
2. H. Poincaré, "La logique de l'infini," in *Scientia,* **12** (1912).
3. F. P. Ramsey, "The Foundations of Mathematics," in *Proceedings of the London Mathematical Society,* 2nd ser., **25** (1926).
4. H. Weyl, "Mathematics and Logic," in *American Mathematical Monthly,* **53** (1946); and "David Hilbert and His Mathematical Work," in *Bulletin of the American Mathematical Society,* **50** (1944).
5. A. De Morgan, "On the Logic of Relations," in *Transactions of the Cambridge Philosophical Society,* **10** (1864); C. S. Peirce, "On the Algebra of Logic," in *American Journal of Mathematics,* **3** (1880).
6. H. M. Sheffer, "A Set of Five Independent Postulates of Boolean Algebra," in *Transactions of the American Mathematical Society,* **14** (1913).
7. Jean Nicod, "A Reduction in the Number of the Primitive Propositions of Logic," in *Proceedings of the Cambridge Philosophical Society. Mathematical and Physical Sciences,* **19** (1919).
8. Leon Chwistek, "The Theory of Constructive Types," in

Annales de la Société mathématique de Pologne (1924); L. Wittgenstein, *Tractatus Logico-Philosophicus* (London, 1922).

9. E. Zermelo, "Beweis, dass jede Menge wohlgeordnet werden kann," in *Mathematische Annalen,* **59** (1904); see also *ibid.,* **65** (1908).

10. F. Hausdorff, *Grundzüge der Mengenlehre* (Leipzig, 1914).

BIBLIOGRAPHY

I. ORIGINAL WORKS. Russell's contributions to mathematical logic are best studied through *An Essay on the Foundations of Geometry* (London, 1897); *The Principles of Mathematics,* I (London, 1903; 2nd ed. with new intro., 1937); *Principia Mathematica,* 3 vols. (London, 1910–1913; 2nd ed., with new intro., 1925–1927), written with A. N. Whitehead; and *Introduction to Mathematical Philosophy* (London, 1919).

The Autobiography of Bertrand Russell, 3 vols. (London, 1967–1969), contains a nontechnical account of his mathematical work in vol. I and early chs. of vol. II. *Mysticism and Logic* (London, 1917) contains some essays of a popular nature.

II. SECONDARY LITERATURE. The primary authority for Russell's life in his *Autobiography,* cited above. G. H. Hardy, *Bertrand Russell and Trinity* (London, 1970), clears away some misconceptions concerning Russell's relations with the college. An able and witty criticism of Russell's logical ideas is presented by P. E. B. Jourdain, given in *The Philosophy of Mr. B*rtr*nd R*ss*ll* (London, 1918).

For useful surveys of the doctrine of *Principia Mathematica,* see S. K. Langer, *An Introduction to Symbolic Logic* (New York, 1937); S. C. Kleene, *Introduction to Metamathematics* (New York, 1952), which has a valuable selected bibliography; and, by F. P. Ramsey, several items in *The Foundations of Mathematics and Other Logical Essays* (London, 1931). *The Philosophy of Bertrand Russell,* P. A. Schilpp, ed. (Chicago, 1944), contains a section by Gödel on Russell's mathematical logic.

To trace the many publications related directly or indirectly to Russell's work, see A. Church, "A Bibliography of Symbolic Logic," in *Journal of Symbolic Logic,* **1** (1936) and **3** (1938); it is also available as a separate volume. For the literature since 1935, the reader is advised to consult the volumes and index parts of the *Journal of Symbolic Logic.*

T. A. A. BROADBENT

RUSSELL, EDWARD JOHN (*b.* Frampton-on-Severn, Gloucestershire, England, 31 October 1872; *d.* Goring-on-Thames, Oxfordshire, England, 12 July 1965), *agricultural chemistry, agronomy.*

For a complete study of his life and work, see Supplement.

RUSSELL, HENRY CHAMBERLAINE (*b.* West Maitland, New South Wales, Australia, 17 March 1836; *d.* Sydney, Australia, 22 February 1907), *astronomy, meteorology.*

For a complete study of his life and work, see Supplement.

RUSSELL, HENRY NORRIS (*b.* Oyster Bay, New York, 25 October 1877; *d.* Princeton, New Jersey, 18 February 1957), *astrophysics, spectroscopy.*

Russell was educated at home until the age of twelve before attending a preparatory school in Princeton, the home of his maternal grandparents. His father, Alexander Russell, a Scottish-Canadian immigrant to the United States, was a Presbyterian minister in Oyster Bay. Both Russell's mother and maternal grandmother had had some advanced formal education and an outstanding gift for mathematics—a trait especially strong in Russell himself. He graduated *insigne cum laude* from Princeton University in 1897 and remained there to obtain his doctorate (1900). His dissertation was entitled "The General Perturbations of the Major Axis of *Eros,* by the Action of *Mars.*"

After completing graduate work, Russell suffered a serious breakdown of his health and spent much of the following year at Oyster Bay. In the fall of 1901 he returned to Princeton and the following autumn began a three-year stay at Cambridge University. During the first year he was a student at King's College and also worked at the Cavendish Laboratory. The last two years were spent at the Cambridge observatory as a research assistant supported by the Carnegie Institution of Washington. There he worked in association with Arthur Hinks on a program of determining stellar parallaxes by photographic means. In September 1904 Russell was again taken seriously ill, and in his absence the remaining observations were made by Hinks.

In 1905 Russell accepted a post as instructor in astronomy at Princeton. In 1911 he was appointed professor of astronomy and, in 1912, director of the observatory, positions he held until his retirement in 1947. From June 1918 to early 1919 he was a consulting and experimental engineer in the Bureau of Aircraft Production of the Army Aviation Service. His chief responsibility was a study of problems in aircraft navigation, which included making observations in open aircraft at altitudes of up to 16,000 feet.

In 1921 Russell began his association with the Mt. Wilson Observatory, where he was a research associate until his retirement. In this capacity he usually spent two months of each year at the California observatory. Following his retirement he held research appointments at Lick and Harvard observatories.

Russell was a member of the American Astronomical Society (president, 1934–1937), the American Philosophical Society (president, 1931–1932), the National Academy of Sciences, the American Association for the Advancement of Science (president, 1933); an associate of the Royal Astronomical Society; a foreign member of the Royal Society; and a correspondent of the academies in Paris, Brussels, and Rome. He was president of the commissions of the International Astronomical Union on stellar spectroscopy and on the constitution of stars. Russell was awarded the Draper, Bruce, Rumford, Franklin, Janssen, and Royal Astronomical Society gold medals, and the Lalande Prize. In 1946 the American Astronomical Society established the annual Henry Norris Russell lectureship in his honor.

In the course of nearly sixty years of research, Russell concerned himself with most of the major problems of astrophysics. His principal contributions, however, can be summarized into four general categories. First, Russell presented (in 1912) the earliest systematic analysis of the variation of the light received from eclipsing binary stars; he later pointed out the importance of the motion of the periastron of the orbit in providing information about the internal structure of the component stars. Second, on the basis of his parallax studies, Russell developed a theory of stellar evolution that at the time was in good agreement with the known data. This work stimulated other astrophysicists, especially Arthur Eddington, and was the original context in which he introduced the Hertzsprung-Russell diagram. Third, in the 1920's Russell began a series of quantitative investigations of the absorption-line spectrum of the sun that resulted in a reliable determination of the abundance of various chemical elements in the solar atmosphere. This work provided clear evidence of the predominance of hydrogen in the sun and, by inference, in most stars. Fourth, Russell carried out, with various co-workers, extensive analyses of the spectra of a number of elements, those of calcium, tita-

nium, and iron being the more important. In this work he developed empirical rules for the relative strengths of lines of a given multiplet, and with F. A. Saunders he devised the theory of L-S coupling to explain spectra produced by atoms with more than one valence electron.

Russell's first research papers were published while he was a student at Princeton. Several of them, and most notably his dissertation, dealt with problems in celestial mechanics and orbit determinations. In light of his later work, however, the most interesting of these early studies was a short paper (1899) that showed how an upper limit to the densities of Algol-variable stars could be obtained. At this time the idea that these were binary stars, the components of which eclipsed each other, was not universally accepted. Only in a few particular cases had orbits been derived from the light variation. Recognizing that an upper limit to the sum of the diameters of the two stars (relative to the size of the orbit) could be determined from the duration of the eclipse, Russell derived limits for the mean densities of seventeen systems. After considering the possible systematic errors in his method, he concluded that Algol-variables were, as a class, much less dense than the sun—a determination that became important in his later work on stellar evolution.

At Cambridge, Russell learned about astrometric methods from Hinks, and in 1903 they embarked upon a program of photographically determining stellar parallaxes. Their two main objectives were to find the most suitable compromise between the amount of work done and the accuracy achieved, and to eliminate all known sources of systematic error. Because photographic techniques in astrometry were still plagued with difficulties and were generally considered inferior to visual observations, Hinks and Russell found it desirable to reconsider the entire observing procedure. The technique they developed was similar to that devised at about the same time by Frank Schlesinger in the United States and was one of the first modern parallax programs.

Russell completed the work of measuring all of the photographic plates and reducing the data in 1910. To him the most interesting result was the correlation between the spectral types and absolute magnitudes of different stars. For those of known parallax, the absolute magnitude decreased systematically from type B to type M—that is, from stars of high surface temperature to those of low surface temperature. This conclusion seemed contrary to the general opinion that many cool, red stars were at great distances and thus were of high luminosity. Russell pointed out that such stars were systematically excluded from parallax studies (since the parallax was undetectably small) and that all the known data could be accounted for under the assumption of two distinct groups of red stars.

To explain the existence of these two types of red stars, Russell adapted a theory of stellar evolution proposed by August Ritter and modified by Sir Norman Lockyer. According to this theory the stars first appeared as highly luminous cool objects that contracted and grew hotter until the high density of the gas caused a significant reduction in the compressibility. Thereafter the star decreased in brightness and in surface temperature. Thus the two kinds of red stars were representatives of the first and last stages of stellar evolution. This finding was in striking contrast with the prevalent view that stars evolved continuously from class B to class M.

To support his ideas, Russell returned to the study of binary stars. In several short papers presented at meetings of the American Astronomical Society between 1910 and 1912, he provided observational evidence that the basic distinguishing feature of the two groups of red stars was their density—as his theory demanded. He also saw other evidence for the correctness of his theory in the orbits of binary stars. Developing the ideas of G. H. Darwin (whose lectures he had attended at Cambridge) on the formation of binary stars from the fission of a single, rapidly rotating star (1910), Russell argued that the youngest stars were single and that binary stars with short orbital periods did not form until the density of the contracting star had become fairly high. The empirical evidence was that bright red stars were rarely members of binary systems and that when hot type-B stars were members of such systems the orbital periods were quite short. Thus Darwin's picture of the development of binary systems agreed quite satisfactorily with Russell's theory of the evolution of the individual stars.

The complete account of his theory of stellar evolution that Russell gave in December 1913 served to make his work more widely known. In this lecture he presented graphs plotting absolute magnitudes of stars against their spectral types (now known as Hertzsprung-Russell diagrams), which he used to illustrate the empirical evidence for his theory. It was also at this time that the terms "giant" and "dwarf" came into use, largely through his papers, to describe the two groups of

stars, although it is not clear who actually coined them.

While developing his ideas on evolution, Russell began a systematic study of the interpretation of the variations in intensity of the light from eclipsing binary systems. In the decade since he had written his paper on the densities of Algol-variables, two developments had made such a study desirable: the availability of data of much greater precision and completeness—primarily from the observations of Raymond S. Dugan at Princeton and from the photoelectric observations of Joel Stebbins at the University of Illinois—and Russell's need for the densities of individual stars as further supporting evidence for his theory of stellar evolution. These densities could be obtained only by detailed analysis of eclipsing binaries.

In the first of four papers (1912) on the subject, Russell stated his objective of determining both the orbital elements of the system and the dimensions and brightnesses of the component stars from the observed light curve. The problem was first reduced to one of the simplest cases—two spherical stars, seen as uniformly illuminated disks, moving in a circular orbit. Russell then showed under what circumstances a complete solution could be obtained and gave tabular values for the special functions that were required. His solution emphasized the importance of accurate observations of the binary system at all phases, not only at the primary eclipse.

The remaining papers showed how the basic solution could be extended to more realistic representations of the binary system. In the second paper Russell introduced the refinements of elliptical orbits of small eccentricity and of stars distorted into ellipsoids by their mutual gravitational attraction. Russell handled the latter effect by what he called "rectification"—a transformation of the observed light curve to remove the effects of ellipticity and to reduce the problem to the previously studied case of spherical stars.

At the end of this paper Russell briefly outlined a means of handling the problem of limb darkening—the decrease in brightness of the stellar disk near its apparent edge. The extensive calculations for this part of the theory were assigned to Harlow Shapley, who had recently arrived at Princeton as a graduate student. The results of their collective efforts were presented in the third and fourth papers of the series, in which the systematic treatment of eclipsing binaries was extended to those with limb-darkened components. Under Russell's direction Shapley later applied the new techniques to ninety eclipsing binaries, thereby providing a large number of new density determinations.

For nearly thirty years the standard techniques of dealing with eclipsing binary systems were essentially those introduced by Russell, and much of his nomenclature and notation became a permanent part of the subject. The wide acceptance of this work can in part be attributed to the very practical manner in which the analysis was presented. There were references to how much time certain calculations required and comments that certain refinements were not worth the work. Indeed, this was a characteristic feature of many of Russell's papers, in which a balance was struck between ease of computation and precision of results.

From 1914 to 1921 Russell worked on various subjects, some of which were a continuation of his study of stellar evolution. He published several papers on the orbits of visual binaries and the determination of the masses of the component stars. He continued a project on the photographic determination of the position of the moon, carried out jointly by the Harvard, Yale, and Princeton observatories. A review of the determination of the albedoes and magnitudes of planets and satellites was also conducted. In 1921 Russell showed that the age of the earth's crust was about 4×10^9 years, basing his statement on the radioactive decay of uranium and the abundance of its end products, lead and thorium.

Two developments in 1921 marked a major shift in Russell's career. The first was the publication of M. N. Saha's theory of the ionization of atoms in stellar atmospheres; the second was Russell's appointment as a research associate at the Mt. Wilson observatory, which brought him into close association with Walter S. Adams and other astronomers and spectroscopists in California.

During his first visit to Mt. Wilson, in the summer of 1921, Russell investigated the application of Saha's formula to the sun. To do so it was necessary to generalize Saha's original theory, which described a gas composed of a single atomic species. Russell pointed out that in a mixed gas, such as the sun's atmosphere, the ionization relationships were more complex because one of the products of the ionization process, the free electron, was common to the ionization reactions of all atoms. Thus the equilibrium state of ions and electrons could be determined only for all elements simultaneously. The result of this analysis was that the degree of ionization of an atom depended not only upon the pressure and temperature of the gas and the ionization potential of the atom, but also upon the relative abundances of other atomic species and their ionization potentials.

Russell undertook a critical test of the expanded theory by comparing the spectrum of the normal solar photosphere with that of sunspots. Since the temperatures of both the photosphere and the sunspots were well known and the pressures, although not well determined, were assumed to be equal, the relative strengths of absorption lines in the two spectra provided the desired comparison of theory and observation.

The most exact comparisons were for the alkali metals, since their ionization potentials were known. In particular Saha had predicted that the lines of neutral potassium would be stronger in the spot spectrum and that lines of neutral rubidium would be faintly visible in the sunspots, although they had not been detected in the normal solar spectrum. Russell's examination of spectra taken at Mt. Wilson confirmed these predictions and, in general, supported the Saha theory.

This success made Russell keenly aware of the tremendous possibilities that the new theory offered. The spectra of stars could now be used to give quantitative information about the state of the atmosphere where the lines were formed. In concluding his paper he wrote:

> The possibilities of the new method appear to be very great. To utilize it fully, years of work will be required to study the behavior of [the alkali earths, scandium, titanium, vanadium, manganese, and iron] and of others, in the stars, in laboratory spectra, and by direct measurement of ionization, but the prospect of our knowledge, both of atoms and of stars, as a result of such researches, makes it urgently desirable that they should be carried out ["Theory of Ionization," pp. 143–144].

Although he continued to investigate problems relating directly to the atmospheres of stars, such as the theoretical determination of the pressure at the solar photosphere (carried out jointly with John Q. Stewart), Russell soon turned to the determination of atomic structure through the study of spectra. His first major effort in this direction was a study, in collaboration with the Harvard spectroscopist F. A. Saunders, of the spectra of the alkali earths—calcium, scandium, and barium (1925). In 1923, when this work was being carried out, atomic theory was unable to explain "complex" spectra—the spectra of elements other than hydrogen, helium, and the alkali metals. Of the remaining elements, the spectra of the alkali earths were partially understood in terms of the Bohr atom; but it was clear that energy levels existed that did not fit into the regular series of terms.

Russell and Saunders had found several groups of lines in the ultraviolet spectrum of calcium that led to the identification of three new "anomalous" triplet terms for this element. With the additional data they were able to find some systematic relationships among the anomalous terms. The most important discovery was that the energies of some of these terms were greater than the ionization potential of the atom, a fact also recognized by Gregor Wentzel at about the same time. They interpreted this result as evidence that the anomalous terms were produced by an excitation of both optical electrons. This idea explained not only why an atom can absorb energy greater than its ionization potential, but also why the alkali metals — which have only one valence electron — do not have any anomalous terms.

From this basic concept of excitation of more than one electron (which had also occurred to Bohr), Russell and Saunders proceeded to extend Alfred Landé's vector model to account for the quantum numbers and energies of the anomalous terms. Landé's model identified the azimuthal quantum number with the orbital angular momentum of the electron, the multiplicity of the spectroscopic term with the angular momentum of the rest of the atom (the *Rumpf*), and the inner quantum number with the vectoral sum of the two. Russell and Saunders assumed that the quantized angular momentum of the individual excited electrons could be combined first, and the resultant combined with that of the *Rumpf*. This technique of handling complex spectra, which later became known as L-S coupling, proved quite successful in predicting both the energy levels for the anomalous terms and the observed transitions to those levels resulting from the excitation of only a single electron.

The final section of Russell's and Saunders' paper is of some interest in the history of spectroscopy for its attempt to introduce uniformity into the chaotic state of spectroscopic notation. The proposed system became the basis for the modern notation, although it was later refined by Russell, Allen G. Shenstone, and L. A. Turner (1929).

Russell subsequently turned to the problem of finding formulas that could represent the relative intensities of the spectral lines of a particular atom (1926). He accomplished this for the lines of a given multiplet, that is, all the lines arising from transitions between the various levels of two spectroscopic terms. (It is an indication of the vigorous

activity in this field in 1926 that two other spectroscopists, R. Kronig and Sommerfeld, derived similar formulas at the same time.) Determined without any detailed theory of atomic structure, the intensity formula was based upon Bohr's correspondence principle and a rule for the sum of the intensities of the lines having a given initial or final level. Thus, this work was carried out entirely within the framework of the "old" quantum mechanics, as was essentially all of Russell's spectroscopic work.

The motivation for these spectroscopic studies was, as Russell had indicated in 1921, not only atomic but also astrophysical. By 1928 he was able, in collaboration with Walter Adams and Charlotte Moore, to bring this new knowledge to bear on stellar spectra. The first problem to be solved was one of calibration: how could one deduce the number of atoms in the solar atmosphere that were responsible for producing a particular absorption line? Two methods appeared possible — a measurement of contours of the lines, followed by a theoretical interpretation in terms of atomic physics, or a direct calibration of the empirical Rowland intensity scale of spectral lines in terms of numbers of atoms. The latter method was chosen. Russell, Adams, and Moore assumed that the intensity of the lines, as derived from Russell's multiplet formulas, was proportional to the number of atoms acting to produce the line. The problem then reduced to that of calibrating the Rowland scale in terms of the theoretical one. Since the Mt. Wilson observatory was then revising Rowland's table of absorption lines in the solar spectrum, abundant information was available. A comparison of these data with the multiplet intensity formulas gave a relative scale of intensities — relative in the sense that although the shape of the curve was determined, the zero point was not; the zero point, in fact, proved to be different for each multiplet.

Yet even this relative calibration was of considerable interest. Adams and Russell used the results in conjunction with the Saha-Boltzmann relationship to compare the atmospheres of different stars (1928). Using the sun as a standard, they analyzed seven stars on the basis of high-dispersion spectra taken with the 100-inch telescope. In calculating the relative populations of excited states of atoms in different stars, they found — as expected — that in hotter stars the population of higher states was greater. In the cooler stars, however, the dependence on excitation potential was not what was expected (the Adams-Russell effect), leading them to believe that the atmospheres of cool stars were not in thermodynamic equilibrium. Their temperature determinations of these stars were in substantial agreement with the results of other methods, and the values they found for the partial pressure of free electrons emphasized the extremely low densities in red giant stars.

Russell continued this analysis in 1929 with the help of Albrecht Unsöld's measurements of line profiles. Unsöld's work provided an absolute calibration of the number of atoms involved in producing an absorption line. Because of the amount of work involved in his procedure, only a relatively small number of lines had been so analyzed. Using this work to provide the zero point for his own scale, Russell developed an absolute calibration scale for the Rowland intensities. He then showed that the total abundances of elements in the sun could be calculated by taking into account the atoms in various states of excitation and ionization. In this manner Russell determined the abundances of fifty-five elements and several molecules in the solar atmosphere. In many instances the abundance ratios between elements was similar to that in the earth's crust—with one notable exception. Hydrogen proved to be by far the most abundant element. This discovery was not completely unexpected, for Cecilia Payne had earlier found high abundances of hydrogen in giant stars but had dismissed the numerical values as "spurious." Russell's analysis had proceeded on more solid footing, however, and he was also able to show that the high abundance of hydrogen actually removed several other apparent difficulties in the analysis of the sun. Thus, there was clear evidence of the dominant abundance of hydrogen in the sun and, therefore, in most stars. It is difficult to overestimate the importance of this result in the development of astrophysics, since much of the subsequent progress has depended upon recognizing the predominant role of hydrogen in astrophysical processes.

Although this discussion of Russell's work in the 1920's might suggest that he proceeded singlemindedly toward the goal of a quantitative analysis of stellar spectra, Russell also investigated related matters. In atomic spectroscopy he carried out detailed analyses of several elements (most notably titanium, iron, and scandium); and on the basis of Friedrich Hund's theory of complex spectra, he found systematic similarities in the spectra of the elements of the iron group (those in the periodic table from potassium through zinc).

Eddington's discovery (1924) that the ideal gas law was applicable to the interiors of stars on the main sequence led Russell back to his old theory of stellar evolution, which had now been rendered untenable. Recognizing the chief problem to be the source of energy, he postulated highly temperature-sensitive processes of transforming matter to energy (1925). Thus, as a star contracted and grew hotter, the energy source would become activated and contraction would cease. The main sequence and giant branch were thus interpreted as stages in which different processes were active. As one of these processes proceeded, mass was converted into energy and the total mass of the star decreased. With the decrease, the temperature and luminosity changed as, consequently, did the position of the star in the Hertzsprung-Russell diagram. The main sequence and giant branches were again seen to be the evolutionary paths taken by stars. This theory was challenged by James Jeans, who claimed that Russell's stars would be unstable and who preferred an energy source the rate of which was independent of temperature or pressure. No substantial progress in unraveling the complexities of stellar evolution occurred, however, until the identification, fifteen years later, of the particular nuclear reactions occurring inside stars.

Russell also contributed to the theory of stellar structure. He suggested that instead of calculating models with a specific opacity formula or equation of state, an attempt should be made to postulate only very general principles and to search for distinctive relationships among stars (1931). The most important result of this approach, now known as the Vogt-Russell theorem, was that on very general grounds the properties of a star can be expected to be completely determined by its mass and chemical composition. Heinrich Vogt had derived a similar result, but apparently his work was not well known in England and the United States, where most of the research in stellar structure was being conducted.

Eddington's work had made the question of mass distribution inside a star an important one, and Russell realized that there was an empirical method of estimating the ratio of the mean density to the central density of a star (1928). In close binary systems the interaction of the distorted stars would result in an advance of the periastron of the orbit, and this advance could be detected from the light curve of an eclipsing binary system. Although Russell's initial results were not very satisfactory, his method was sound; and later investigators were able to derive better results.

During the 1930's and 1940's, Russell continued to work on most of the subjects that had occupied him in the previous twenty years. He made detailed analyses of the spectra of several more elements. His study of the orbits of visual binary stars and the masses derived therefrom led to the publication, with Charlotte Moore, of a monograph on the subject (1940). Russell enlarged his work on the chemical composition of the sun to include a study of molecular abundances (1933). He also returned to the analysis of eclipsing binary systems, extending his methods to more complicated systems and considering further the effects of the internal structure of the stars upon the advance of the periastron (1939, 1942).

While Russell continued to make significant contributions to astrophysical research during the latter part of his career, his role as an adviser and consultant to other astronomers became increasingly important. His yearly trips from Princeton to Mt. Wilson afforded many opportunities to visit other American observatories; and because his own interests covered such a wide range, he was often quite familiar with the problems on which others were working.

Russell's role as a critic and reviewer of contemporary research began at least as early as 1919, when, at the request of the National Academy of Sciences, he wrote a comprehensive review of current research in sidereal astronomy that pointed out to his colleagues some of the most important problems to be solved. Another indication of his interest in analyzing the work of others is his review of the dispute between Jeans and Eddington over the mass-luminosity relation for stars (1925). By placing their arguments within the framework of a more general theory, Russell resolved the apparent discrepancy between their results.

Russell's interest in teaching began fairly early in his career. By 1911 he had started a revision of the general astronomy textbook written by his predecessor at Princeton, Charles A. Young, but other work delayed its completion. With the collaboration of his Princeton colleagues Raymond Dugan and John Q. Stewart, it was finally published in 1926. The first volume was the originally projected revision of Young's book; the second contained largely new material, most of it written by Russell. This textbook was widely used for thirty years, and many American astronomers trained in this period were introduced to the subject through studying it.

After 1930 especially, Russell gave a number of lectures in which he reviewed the progress in various areas of astrophysics. Although new results were rarely presented in these talks, they did serve the important function of summarizing and organizing recent work.

These lectures, and even his textbook, were aimed principally at the scientist or potential scientist. To reach a larger, more general audience, Russell wrote a monthly article in *Scientific American*. Beginning in 1900 as a column describing the appearance of the evening sky for the coming month, the articles soon included information on recent research in astronomy. By 1911 Russell was regularly including a short essay on some astronomical subject, and this section of the article soon came to be the dominant feature. By 1943, when the last one appeared, he had written 500 short articles discussing all phases of astronomy.

Although in the vast majority of his writings Russell kept strictly to scientific matters, he did on several occasions discuss his ideas concerning science and religion. The fullest exposition was in a series of lectures given at Yale University in 1925 and published two years later as *Fate and Freedom*. The title reflects one of his central concerns: the conflict between the concept of a deterministic universe and the belief in free will. Although Russell concluded that the universe was completely mechanistic, he felt that the observed behavior of men should be considered a kind of statistical phenomenon and that consequently free will was as real as (to use his analogy) statistical phenomena in physics, such as the pressure of a gas. These ideas were formulated prior to the introduction into quantum mechanics of the uncertainty principle, which Russell in his later writings does not seem to have considered of central philosophical importance.

Over a period of fifty years Russell's work showed a continuous effort to provide a clear understanding of the physics of stars. Early in his career he focused on stellar evolution and the related problems of determining masses, radii, temperatures, luminosities, and densities of stars. A result of this effort was his series of investigations of eclipsing binary systems. His interest later turned to stellar atmospheres, the problems of determining pressures and temperatures, and the quantitative measurement of chemical abundances. An outgrowth of this work was his extensive work in the theory of atomic spectra.

BIBLIOGRAPHY

I. ORIGINAL WORKS. Bibliographies of Russell's published writings are in Poggendorff, V, 1081–1082, and VI, 2249–2250, and at the end of the biographical essays by Shapley and Seaton (see below). The most extensive is that following Shapley's article, although it does not include abstracts of certain papers presented at meetings of the American Astronomical Society or Russell's articles in *Scientific American.*

Russell's principal publications include "The Densities of the Variable Stars of the Algol Type," in *Astrophysical Journal,* **10** (1899), 315–318; "The General Perturbations of the Major Axis of *Eros,* by the Action of *Mars,*" in *Astronomical Journal,* **21** (1900), 25–28; "On the Origin of Binary Stars," in *Astrophysical Journal,* **31** (1910), 185–207; *Determinations of Stellar Parallax* (Washington, D.C., 1911); "On the Determination of the Orbital Elements of Eclipsing Variable Stars," in *Astrophysical Journal,* **35** (1912), 315–340, and **36** (1912), 54–74; "On Darkening at the Limb in Eclipsing Variables," *ibid.,* **36** (1912), 239–254, 385–408, written with H. Shapley; "Relations Between the Spectra and Other Characteristics of the Stars," in *Nature,* **93** (1914), 227–230, 252–258, 281–286; and "Some Problems of Sidereal Astronomy," in *Proceedings of the National Academy of Sciences of the United States of America,* **5** (1919), 391–416.

See also "A Superior Limit to the Age of the Earth's Crust," in *Proceedings of the Royal Society,* **99A** (1921), 84–86; "The Theory of Ionization and the Sun-Spot Spectrum," in *Astrophysical Journal,* **55** (1922), 119–144; "New Regularities in the Spectra of the Alkaline Earths," *ibid.,* **61** (1925), 38–69, written with F. A. Saunders; "The Intensities of Lines in Multiplets," in *Proceedings of the National Academy of Sciences,* **11** (1925), 314–328; "Note on the Relations Between the Mass, Temperature, and Luminosity of a Gaseous Star," in *Monthly Notices of the Royal Astronomical Society,* **85** (1925), 935–939; *Astronomy, a Revision of Young's Manual of Astronomy,* 2 vols. (Boston, 1926–1927), written with R. S. Dugan and J. Q. Stewart; *Fate and Freedom* (New Haven, 1927); "On the Advance of Periastron in Eclipsing Binaries," in *Monthly Notices of the Royal Astronomical Society,* **88** (1928), 641–643; "A Calibration of Rowland's Scale of Intensities for Solar Lines," in *Astrophysical Journal,* **68** (1928), 1–8, written with W. S. Adams and C. E. Moore; "Preliminary Results of a New Method for the Analysis of Stellar Spectra," *ibid.,* 9–36, written with W. S. Adams; "On the Composition of the Sun's Atmosphere," in *Astrophysical Journal,* **70** (1929), 11–82; "Notes on the Constitution of the Stars," in *Monthly Notices of the Royal Astronomical Society,* **91** (1931), 951–966, and **92** (1931), 146; *The Solar System and Its Origin* (New York, 1935); and *The Masses of the Stars, With a General Catalog of Dynamical Parallaxes* (Chicago, 1940), written with C. E. Moore.

II. SECONDARY LITERATURE. The most extensive biographical essays are those by F. J. M. Stratton in *Biographical Memoirs of Fellows of the Royal Society,* **3** (1957), 173–191; and by Harlow Shapley in *Biographical Memoirs. National Academy of Sciences,* **32** (1958), 354–378. Obituary notices include those by

Donald H. Menzel in *Yearbook. American Philosophical Society* (1958), 139–143; and Otto Struve, in *Publications of the Astronomical Society of the Pacific,* **69** (1957), 223–226. See also Axel V. Nielsen, "Contributions to the History of the Hertzsprung-Russell Diagram," in *Centaurus,* **9** (1964), 219–253; and the following articles in *Vistas in Astronomy,* **12** (1970): Katherine G. Kron, "Henry Norris Russell (1877–1957): Some Recollections," 3–6; Bancroft W. Sitterly, "Changing Interpretations of the Hertzsprung-Russell Diagram, 1910–1940: A Historical Note," 357–366; and R. Szafraniec, "Henry Norris Russell's Contribution to the Study of Eclipsing Variables," 7–20.

BRUCE C. COGAN

RUTHERFORD, DANIEL (*b.* Edinburgh, Scotland, 3 November 1749; *d.* Edinburgh, 15 December 1819), *chemistry.*

An uncle of Sir Walter Scott's, Rutherford is mentioned frequently in works devoted to the life and letters of the famous novelist; his place in the history of chemistry depends solely on his discovery of nitrogen. He was a son of John Rutherford, professor of medicine at the University of Edinburgh from 1726 to 1765, and his second wife, Anne Mackay; Scott's mother was Daniel Rutherford's stepsister.

A pupil of William Cullen and Joseph Black at Edinburgh, Rutherford traveled in Europe for about three years after obtaining his M.D. and before beginning practice at Edinburgh in 1775. Shortly afterward he became a member of the Philosophical Society of Edinburgh (later the Royal Society of Edinburgh), and in 1786 succeeded John Hope, father of Thomas Charles Hope, as regius professor of botany at the university. In the same year he married Harriet Mitchelson; they had two sons and three daughters.

Rutherford's M.D. dissertation, dated 12 September 1772, was devoted mainly to the discoveries regarding the gas that Black had called "fixed air" (carbon dioxide), but which Rutherford preferred to call "mephitic air." About two-thirds of the way through the work he wrote that, having dealt with the air from calcareous bodies, he would say something of the air rendered malignant by animal respiration. He noted the contraction of air in which animals had been confined, and said that by their respiration good air became in part "mephitic" but also suffered a further change: the separation of the mephitic air by means of a caustic alkaline solution did not render the remaining air wholesome. Although it gave no precipitate with limewater, it nonetheless extinguished flame and life.

This is the earliest published account of the awareness of a gas (nitrogen) that, although unable to support life and combustion, was clearly not Black's "fixed air." There can be little doubt about Rutherford's priority of publication, but priority of discovery seems attributable to Cavendish, Priestley, or Scheele. Cavendish, in a manuscript published thirty years after his death by W. V. Harcourt (*Report of the British Association for the Advancement of Science, 1839* [1840], 64–65), wrote: "Air which has passed thro' a charcoal fire contains a great deal of fixed air . . . but . . . consists principally of common air, which has suffered a change in its nature from the fire." He removed fixed air from air in which charcoal had been burned and found the remaining air unfit for combustion and of a density slightly less than that of common air.

The paper was undated but was marked "communicated to Dr. Priestley." The latter gave an inaccurate account of it in his classical paper "Observations on Different Kinds of Air," read (over four meetings) to the Royal Society in March 1772 (*Philosophical Transactions of the Royal Society,* **62** [1772], 147–252, see 225; the volume was not published until 1773). A few pages earlier in the same paper Priestley described how, in one of his own experiments, air in which moist iron filings and sulfur had been confined had decreased in volume by approximately a quarter; the remaining air gave no precipitate with limewater and was less dense than common air. Scheele's observation that air consisted of two gases, his names for which are usually translated as "vitiated air" (nitrogen) and "fire air" (oxygen), was not published until 1777 but may have been made as early as 1771.

BIBLIOGRAPHY

I. ORIGINAL WORKS. Rutherford's *Dissertatio inauguralis de aere fixo dicto, aut mephitico* (Edinburgh, 1772) is his only work of importance. An English translation by A. Crum Brown (communicated by L. Dobbin) is "Daniel Rutherford's Inaugural Dissertation," in *Journal of Chemical Education,* **12** (1935), 370–375. Rutherford also published a short account of a maximum and minimum thermometer, the design of which has been attributed to him but which he clearly attributes to his father, in "A Description of an Improved Thermometer," in *Transactions of the Royal Society of Edinburgh,* **3** (1794), 247–249. The authorship of two works ascribed to Rutherford by M. E. Weeks is uncertain.

II. SECONDARY LITERATURE. M. E. Weeks, "Daniel Rutherford and the Discovery of Nitrogen," in *Journal of Chemical Education,* **11** (1935), 101–107, repr. with additions in M. E. Weeks and H. M. Leicester, *Discovery of the Elements,* 7th ed. (Easton, Pa., 1968), 191–205, gives numerous references to Rutherford in the literature about Sir Walter Scott. D. McKie, "Daniel Rutherford and the Discovery of Nitrogen," in *Science Progress,* **29** (1935), 650–660, gives a translation of the relevant sections of the dissertation.

E. L. SCOTT

RUTHERFORD, ERNEST (*b.* between the settlements of Brightwater and Spring Grove, near Nelson, New Zealand, 30 August 1871; *d.* Cambridge, England, 19 October 1937), *physics, chemistry.*

Both of Rutherford's parents were taken as youngsters to New Zealand in the mid-nineteenth century. His father, James, from Perth, Scotland, acquired the skills of his wheelwright father and brought this technological inclination to his work: flax farming and processing, railroad-tie cutting, bridge construction, and small-scale farming. Although he was moderately successful in this range of endeavors, his family of a dozen children necessarily learned hard work and thrift. Rutherford's mother, Martha Thompson, accompanied her widowed mother to New Zealand from Hornchurch, Essex, England, and a few years later took over her mother's teaching post when she remarried. One need look no further than his parents for the source of Rutherford's characteristic traits of simplicity, directness, economy, energy, enthusiasm, and reverence for education.

Success in the local schools brought Rutherford a scholarship to Nelson College, a nearby secondary school. Until this time he had tinkered with clocks, made models of the waterwheels his father used in his mills, and at the age of ten had a copy of Balfour Stewart's science textbook; but he had not exhibited intellectual precocity or a predilection for a scientific career. At Nelson he excelled in nearly every subject, particularly mathematics, in which he was given a solid grounding by W. S. Littlejohn. Another scholarship took Rutherford in 1889 to Canterbury College, Christchurch, where he came under the influence of A. W. Bickerton, a man of contagious scientific enthusiasm whose cosmological theories were never taken seriously, and C. H. H. Cook, a rigorous and orthodox mathematician. At the conclusion of the three-year course Rutherford received his B.A. and a mathematical scholarship that enabled him to remain for another year. For his postgraduate work he obtained the M.A. in 1893, with double first-class honors in mathematics and mathematical physics and in physical science.

By this time Rutherford's special talents must have been apparent, for he was encouraged to stay at Canterbury for yet another year, during which he began research on the magnetization of iron by high-frequency discharges, work that earned him the B.Sc. in 1894. His activities until mid-1895 are not known for certain; but he seems to have continued this line of research under Bickerton, taught briefly at a boys' school, and fallen in love with his future wife, Mary Newton, the daughter of the woman in whose house he lodged.

In this first research Rutherford examined the magnetization of iron by a rapidly alternating electric current, such as the oscillatory discharge of a Leyden jar, and showed it to occur even with frequencies of over 10^8 cycles per second. Heinrich Hertz, less than a decade before, had caused a sensation by detecting the radio waves predicted by Maxwell's electromagnetic theory; and Rutherford, always interested in the latest scientific advances, probably was drawn to his own investigation involving high frequencies by Hertz's work. More important than Rutherford's initial observation—Joseph Henry had discovered the effect half a century earlier—was his finding that the alternating field diminished the magnetization of a needle that was already magnetized. This discovery enabled him to devise a detector of wireless signals before Marconi began his experiments, and during the next year or two Rutherford endeavored to increase the range and sensitivity of his device.

In 1895 Rutherford was awarded a scholarship established with the profits from the famous 1851 Exhibition in London. The terms of this award required attendance at another institution, and Rutherford chose Cambridge University's Cavendish Laboratory, of which the director, J. J. Thomson, was the leading authority on electromagnetic phenomena. The university had just altered its rules to admit graduates of other schools, thereby enabling Rutherford to become the laboratory's first research student. He brought with him to England his wireless wave detector and soon was able to receive signals from sources up to half a mile away. This work so impressed a number of Cambridge dons, J. J. Thomson included, that Rutherford quickly made a name for himself. Upon the discovery of X rays, Thomson asked Rutherford in early 1896 to join him in studying the effect of this radiation upon the discharge of electricity in gases.

Although he might have hesitated, for Rutherford was anxious to earn enough to marry his fiancée in New Zealand and saw a limited use for his detector in lighthouse or lighthouse-to-shore communication, he could not refuse the honor of Thomson's offer or the opportunity to investigate the most recently discovered physical phenomenon.

Out of this collaboration came a joint paper famous for its statement of a theory of ionization. The idea—that the X rays created an equal number of positive and negative carriers of electricity, or "ions," in the gas molecules—presumably was Thomson's, while much of the experimentation that placed this formerly descriptive subject on a quantitative basis was Rutherford's. The latter continued this work through 1897, measuring ionic velocities, rates of recombination, absorption of energy by gases, and the electrification of different gases while Thomson independently determined the existence of the particle later called the electron. Rutherford logically next examined the discharge of electricity by ultraviolet light, then conducted a similar study of the effects of uranium radiation. Again his inclination to pursue the most recent—and significant—problems led to a more detailed study of radioactivity. This was his field of endeavor for the next forty years; his work and that of his students was to make this the most significant area of physical science as radioactivity evolved into atomic physics and then into nuclear physics.

Radioactivity had been chanced upon in 1896 by Henri Becquerel, had enjoyed a brief period of moderate attention, and had then been abandoned even by its discoverer because it seemed relatively uninteresting among the numerous radiations being studied at the end of the nineteenth century. In early 1898 interest was somewhat revived when G. C. Schmidt and Marie Curie independently showed that not only uranium, but also thorium, exhibited this property. When Pierre and Marie Curie, with Gustave Bémont, announced later in 1898 the discovery of two new radioactive elements, polonium and radium, world scientific attention finally crystallized. Rutherford did not jump on this bandwagon, for his investigations had begun earlier, even before the discovery of thorium's activity. It is likely, in fact, that his own work alone would have served the same purpose as radium in creating the science of radioactivity, if somewhat more slowly; for within a short time Rutherford, not Becquerel or the Curies, was the dominant figure in the field.

He began by examining the Becquerel rays from

uranium. Indeed, until about 1904 the emissions received far more attention than the emitters. Passage of the radiation through foils revealed one type that was easily absorbed and another with greater penetrating ability; these Rutherford named alpha and beta, "for simplicity." While this work was in progress, Rutherford was seriously considering his future prospects. A lectureship or, even better, a fellowship at Trinity College would allow him to marry. But either a Trinity regulation about length of residence or, as he felt, the prevailing Cambridge snobbery toward those who had been undergraduates elsewhere, especially in the colonies, prevented the offer of a fellowship. With little hope of success, for older men with far greater teaching experience had also applied, Rutherford entered the competition for the professorship of physics at McGill University. The Montreal authorities, however, were looking for someone to direct work in their well-equipped laboratory and were convinced by Thomson's testimonial: "I have never had a student with more enthusiasm or ability for original research than Mr. Rutherford."

Arriving at McGill in September 1898, Rutherford found a warm welcome; perhaps the best laboratory in the western hemisphere (it was financed by a tobacco millionaire who considered smoking a disgusting habit); widespread skepticism that he would measure up in research ability to his predecessor, H. L. Callendar; and a department chairman, John Cox, who soon voluntarily assumed some of Rutherford's teaching duties when he recognized his colleague's genius. While in Cambridge, Rutherford's work in radioactivity had been solely with uranium minerals; in Montreal his first inclination was to examine thorium substances, since the activity of this element had been noticed only half a year earlier. When a colleague obtained erratic ionization measurements, Rutherford succeeded in tracing the irregularity to a gaseous radioactive product escaping from the thorium; and because he was uncertain of the nature of this product, in 1900 he gave it the deliberately vague name "emanation." Within a short time the emanations from radium and actinium also were found, by Ernst Dorn and F. Giesel, respectively.

The number of known radioelements was increasing. Rutherford added several more to the list, the next being thorium active deposit, which in time was resolved into thorium A, B, C, and so on. The active deposit, or excited activity, which was laid down on surfaces touched by the decaying emanation, was found by Rutherford because of the apparent breakdown of good insulators and

was described in *Philosophical Magazine* just one month after his announcement of the emanation. A curious feature he immediately noticed was that, unlike uranium, thorium, and radium, such materials as thorium emanation, radium emanation, their active deposits, and polonium lost their activities over periods of time. Moreover, the rate of this decrease was unique for each radioelement and thus an ideal identifying label. This meant that an exponential curve could be plotted for the half-life of each radioelement with a discernible decay period, and theory could thereby be compared with experiment.

Sir William Crookes, among others, doubted that uranium and thorium were intrinsically active; he believed, rather, that the active materials were only entrained with the atoms of these long-known elements. In 1900 he succeeded, through repeated dissolution and recrystallization of uranium nitrate, in preparing uranium that left no image on a photographic plate and in isolating the active constituent, called uranium X. But the confidence thereby generated in the stability of uranium was shaken little more than a year later, when Becquerel reexamined his materials, prepared by Crookes's method, and found that his uranium X was inactive, while his uranium had regained its activity. By this time Rutherford had recognized the need for skilled chemical assistance in his radioactivity investigations and had secured the services of a young chemistry demonstrator at McGill, Frederick Soddy. Together they removed most of the activity from a thorium compound, calling the active matter thorium X; but they too found that the X product lost its activity and that the thorium recovered its original level in a few weeks. Had Becquerel's similar finding for uranium not been immediately at hand, they might have searched for errors in their work. In early 1902, however, they began to plot the activities as a function of time, seeing evidence of a fundamental relationship in the equality of the time for thorium X to decay to half value and thorium to double in activity.

This work led directly to Rutherford's greatest achievement at McGill, for with Soddy he advanced the still-accepted explanation of radioactivity. Becquerel for several years had considered the phenomenon a form of long-lived phosphorescence, although by the first years of the twentieth century he spoke vaguely of a "molecular transformation." Crookes, in the British tradition of visualized mechanical models, had suggested a modified Maxwell demon sitting on each uranium atom and extracting the excess energy from faster-moving air molecules, this energy then appearing as uranium radiation. The Curies had considered several possibilities but inclined strongly toward the concept of an unknown ethereal radiation the existence of which is manifested only through its action on the heaviest elements, which then emit alpha, beta, and gamma rays as secondary radiations. Perhaps the most prescient idea was offered by Elster and Geitel—that the energy exhibited by radioactive substances comes not from external sources but from within the atoms themselves— but it was left to Rutherford and Soddy to add quantitative evidence to such speculation.

Their iconoclastic theory, variously called transformation, transmutation, and disintegration, first appeared in 1902 and was refined in the following year. Although alchemy had long been exorcised from scientific chemistry, they declared that "radioactivity is at once an atomic phenomenon and the accompaniment of a chemical change in which new kinds of matter are produced." The radioactive atoms decay, they argued, each decay signifying the transmutation of a parent into a daughter element, and each type of atom undergoing its transformation in a characteristic period. This insight set the course for their next several years of research, for the task was then to order all the known radioelements into decay series and to search for additional members of these families.

The theory also explained the experimental decay and rise curves as a measure of a radioelement's quantity and half-life. At equilibrium the same number of atoms of a parent transform as the number of atoms of its daughter and its granddaughter, and so on until a stable end product is obtained. But when a chemical process separates members of a series, the parent must regain its former activity as it produces additional daughters while its own numbers are maintained constant, unless it is the very first member of the family— whose numbers can only decrease. The daughter side of a chemical separation, however, is destined only to decay, for there is no means of replenishing its stock of transformed atoms.

Rutherford and Soddy saw that the apparently constant activities of uranium, thorium, and radium were due to half-lives that are long compared with human lives. This understanding overcame the puzzle at the core of all previous theories; for if the total radioactivity in the universe was growing smaller and tending to disappear, the law of conservation of energy would not be violated. They considered radioactivity a fundamental property of nature, fit to join the select group of electricity,

magnetism, light, and gravity. Not the least remarkable thing about this theory which proclaimed that the atom was not indestructible was the uncontroversial way in which it was accepted. Aside from the elderly and unalterable Lord Kelvin and the constantly contentious Henry Armstrong, the transformation theory encountered little opposition. Chemists, especially, although it violated views about the unchangeability of atoms that they "absorbed with their mothers' milk," could not refute the evidence and at most could adopt a wait-and-see attitude.

To a large degree Rutherford spent the next years mining this rich vein of interpretation. Working with Soddy and using the new liquid-air machine given to McGill by its wealthy benefactor, he condensed emanation at low temperatures, proving that it is a gas. Other tests convinced them that emanation belonged to the family of inert gases found not long before by Sir William Ramsay. Soddy then left Montreal in 1903 for London, where he and Ramsay proved spectroscopically that helium is produced during transformations from radium emanation. Such work was highly important, for there were numerous radioelements of which the chemical identity and place in the decay series were uncertain.

Helium, while not a radioelement, was of particular interest because of Rutherford's certainty that, as a positive ion, it was identical with the alpha particle. And the alpha particle, being of ponderable mass, he saw as the key in the change from an element of one atomic weight to an element of another. It fascinated Rutherford also because he could appreciate the enormous speed and energy with which it is ejected from a decaying atom. In 1903 he was able to deflect it in electric and magnetic fields, thereby showing its positive charge, but his charge-to-mass ratio measurement lacked the precision required to distinguish between a helium atom with two charges and a hydrogen atom with one charge. The proof of the particle's identity awaited Rutherford's transfer to Manchester, although he determined many useful facts about the alpha particle, such as the number emitted per second from one gram of radium, a constant that is the basis for several other important quantities, including the half-life of radium, and in 1906 made another assault upon the e/m ratio.

Halfway between Soddy's departure in 1903 and Otto Hahn's arrival at McGill in 1905, Rutherford found another chemist of comparable skill upon whom he could rely. This was Bertram Boltwood, who had proved circumstantially that uranium and radium are related, thus linking two previously separate decay series, and who in 1907 discovered ionium, the immediate parent of radium, which went far in proving the uranium-radium connection directly. Since Boltwood remained in New Haven, Connecticut, his collaboration with Rutherford was conducted through the mails. This work extended from determination of the quantity of radium present per gram of uranium in minerals to Rutherford's suggestion that, if quantity and rate of formation of a series' end product were known, it would be possible to calculate the age of the mineral. R. J. Strutt in England followed up this idea, using the helium found in radioactive substances; but the variable amount of this gas that escaped permitted only minimum age determinations. Boltwood showed the universal occurrence of lead with uranium minerals; considered this the series' final product; and, using Rutherford's value for radium's half-life and their figure for the amount of radium in a gram of uranium, was able to calculate the rate of formation for lead. The ages of some of his rock samples were over a billion years, furnishing for the first time quantitative proof of the antiquity of the earth.

Many other problems in radioactivity were pursued by Rutherford, sometimes alone, sometimes with one of the research students in the strong school he established. Among the projects in his laboratory were measurements of radiation energy, studies of beta- and gamma-ray properties, attempts to change rates of decay by extreme conditions of temperature, efforts to place actinium in a decay series, and investigations of the radioactivity of the earth and atmosphere. Few advances in this science throughout the world failed to be reflected in the work at McGill. Nor, single-minded though he was, did Rutherford entirely abandon other areas of science; radio, the conduction of electricity in gases, and N rays received some attention.

Rutherford's nine years at McGill, filled with the great work that brought him the Nobel Prize for chemistry in 1908, were no less replete with other professional activities. He was in great demand as a speaker and traveled frequently to distant parts of the United States and to England, to give a lecture, a series of talks, or a summer-session course. While he could not be expected to refuse the honor of speaking at the Royal Institution, the Bakerian lecture to the Royal Society (1904), or the Silliman lectures at Yale University (1905), some well-wishers urged him to limit his outside engagements. His time was also consumed in writing *Radio-Activity*, the first textbook on the subject

and recognized as a classic at its publication in 1904. So fast did the science progress, however, that Rutherford prepared a second edition the following year that was 50 percent larger. No sooner was this done than he faced the task of fashioning the Silliman lectures into a book. Small wonder that he confined his writing to journals for the next several years.

A veritable fallout of honors began to descend upon him, continuing for the rest of his life. Rutherford thoroughly enjoyed this recognition, for, while not vain, he was fully aware of his own worth. The Royal Society offered him fellowship in 1903 and the Rumford Medal the next year, while various universities presented both honorary degrees and job offers. While he was happy at McGill, Rutherford desired to return to England, where he would be closer to the world's leading scientific centers. Thus when Arthur Schuster offered to resign from his chair at the University of Manchester on the condition that Rutherford succeed him, the post and the laboratory were sufficiently attractive for Rutherford to make the move in 1907.

If the Cavendish, under Thomson, was the premier physics laboratory in England, Manchester, under Rutherford, was easily the second. Schuster had built a fine structure less than a decade earlier and bequeathed to his successor a strong research department, his assistant, Hans Geiger, and a personally endowed readership in mathematical physics, filled in turn by Harry Bateman, C. G. Darwin, and Niels Bohr. Rutherford's great and growing fame attracted to Manchester (and later to Cambridge) an extraordinarily talented group of research students who made profound contributions to physics and chemistry.

On his return to England, Rutherford had only a few milligrams of radioactive materials, a quantity insufficient for even his own research. In a generous gesture the Austrian Academy of Sciences sent, from the Joachimsthal uranium mines under its control, about 350 milligrams of radium chloride, as a joint loan to Rutherford and Ramsay. Unfortunately, Ramsay wished to retain possession indefinitely, while both saw the wisdom of leaving the supply undivided; so until the Vienna authorities sent another comparable radium supply for Rutherford's exclusive use, he was limited to work with the "draw" of emanation that Ramsay sent periodically from London. To a degree this determined most of Rutherford's initial investigations at Manchester, an extensive study of radium emanation; but he always found emanation and its active deposit decay products more convenient sources than radium itself.

The emanation could easily be purified in liquid air, and Rutherford soon determined the volume of this gas in equilibrium with one gram of radium. This corrected earlier results by Ramsay and A. T. Cameron, and, by confirming his calculated amount, removed some doubt cast on the accuracy of radioactive data and theory. With the spectroscopist Thomas Royds, Rutherford next photographed the spectrum of emanation, not examined since Ramsay and Collie's visual observations in 1904. Such work involved him in scientific controversy, which he usually sought to avoid; but after Soddy left Ramsay's laboratory, the latter's contributions to radioactivity were noted for their almost uniform incorrectness. Although an expert at handling minute quantities of rare gases, Ramsay never took the trouble to learn well the techniques of radioactivity. His imprecise work, coupled with a strong desire to gain priority, led him to publish quickly numerous results that Rutherford and others in this field felt compelled to correct. Further contributions to emanation studies included Rutherford's examination in 1909 of its vapor pressure at different low temperatures, and, with Harold Robinson in 1913, measurement of its heating effect.

Never one to limit the scope of his investigations—he preferred to advance across radioactivity in a wide path—Rutherford pursued "his" alpha particles in 1908. These were his favorites; the beta particles were too small and, being electrons, too common. The alphas, however, were massive, of atomic dimension; and he could clearly visualize them hurtling out of their parent atoms with enormous speed and energy. Certainly these would be the key to the physicist's classic goal: an understanding of the nature of matter. Until that time nothing had changed Rutherford's early conviction that the alpha particle was a doubly charged helium atom, but he had not succeeded in proving that belief. In 1908 he and Geiger were able to fire alpha particles into an evacuated tube containing a central, charged wire and to record single events. Ionization by collision, a process studied by Rutherford's former colleague at Cambridge, J. S. E. Townsend, caused a magnification of the single particle's charge sufficient to give the electrometer a measurable "kick." By this means they were able to count, for the first time accurately and directly, the number of alpha particles emitted per second from a gram of radium.

This experiment enabled Rutherford and Geiger to confirm that every alpha particle causes a faint but discrete flash when it strikes a luminescent zinc sulfide screen, and thus led directly to the widespread method of scintillation counting. It was also the origin of the electrical and electronic methods of particle counting in which Geiger later pioneered. But at this time the scintillation technique, now proved reliable, was more convenient. This counting work also led Rutherford and Geiger to the most accurate value of the fundamental electric charge e before Millikan performed his oildrop experiment. They measured the total charge from a radium source and divided it by the number of alphas counted to obtain the charge per particle. Since this figure was about twice the previous values of e, they concluded that the alpha was indeed helium with a double charge. But Rutherford still desired decisive, direct proof; and here his skilled glassblower came to his aid. Otto Baumbach in 1908 was able to construct glass tubes thin enough to be transparent to the rapidly moving alpha particles yet capable of containing a gas. Such a tube was filled with emanation and was placed within a larger tube made of thicker glass. In time, alpha particles from the decaying emanation penetrated into and were trapped in the space between inner and outer tubes; and when Royds sparked the material in this space, they saw the spectrum of helium.

As in Montreal, Rutherford found chemical help in Manchester of the highest quality. Boltwood spent a year with him, during which time they redetermined more accurately the rate of production of helium by radium. By combining these results with those from the counting experiments mentioned above, they obtained Avogadro's number more directly than ever before. There were new researchers too—Alexander Russell, Kasimir Fajans, and Georg von Hevesy—fitting radioelements into the periodic table, generating information and ideas on which displacement laws and concept of isotopy would be based, and working on branching of the decay series, periods of the short-lived elements, and other radiochemical problems.

Rutherford's greatest discovery at Manchester—in fact, of his career—was of the nuclear structure of the atom. In retrospect, its origins can be seen in the slight evidences of alpha particle scattering in thin metal foils or sheets of mica, which he noticed while at McGill, and in similar scattering by air molecules in his later electrical counting experiments with Geiger. With a view to learning more about this scattering, both because it introduced experimental difficulties leading to less precise results and because it bore upon the perplexing question of the nature of alpha and beta absorption in matter, Geiger made a quantitative study of the phenomenon. Counting the scintillations produced by scattered alphas, he found that they increased with the atomic weight of the target foil and, until the particles could no longer penetrate the foil, with its thickness. Only very small angular deflections from the beam were measured and, as expected, fewer particles were bent through the larger angles.

In 1909 Rutherford and Geiger decided that Ernest Marsden, who had not yet taken his bachelor's degree, was ready for a real research problem. Much has been said of Rutherford's great insight in suggesting that Marsden look for large-angle alpha particle scattering; but, inspired though it was, it came logically from knowledge of the "diffuse" scattering still interfering with Geiger's measurement of small-angle scattering. On the other hand, Rutherford was aware that the alpha particle, being very fast and massive, was not likely to be scattered backward by the accumulated effect of a number of small deflections. His urging the experiment upon Marsden may well have been an example of his characteristic willingness to try "any damn fool experiment" on the chance that it might work. This one worked magnificently. Geiger then joined Marsden, and the two measured the exceedingly small number of particles that were deflected not only through ninety degrees, but more. Rutherford's reaction on learning of this — rather embellished over the years — has become a classic: "It was almost as incredible as if you fired a fifteen-inch shell at a piece of tissue paper and it came back and hit you."

Rutherford pondered long over the implications of this experiment, for it was early 1911 before he announced that he knew what the atom looked like. The small deflections investigated by Geiger could be reasonably explained by the theory of multiple scattering then current. This was based on the "plum pudding" model of the atom — a sphere of positive electrification in which electrons (plums) were regularly positioned — proposed by Lord Kelvin and highly refined by Thomson. The alpha particle was believed to suffer numerous collisions with the atoms of the target foil, each collision resulting in a small deflection; and a probability distribution for each angle could be calculated to compare with experiment. But for large angles the comparison failed; multiple scattering theory predicted virtually no deflections, while Geiger and Marsden found a measurable few.

Thomson's multiple-scattering theory, moreover, was challenged regarding beta particle encounters, its area of special competence: John Madsen, in Australia, obtained data on beta deflections that suggested that this type of scattering was done in a single collision. Other experiments, conducted at Manchester by William Wilson, showed that beta particles suffered inelastic collisions in their passage through matter; like the alpha particles, therefore, they gradually lost their energy, and it was possible to think that both particles experienced the same type of encounters.

By the end of 1910, Rutherford began tying these several factors into a new atomic model and theory of scattering. The alpha projectile, he said, changed course in a single encounter with a target atom. But for this to occur, the forces of electrical repulsion (or attraction — it made no difference for the mathematics) had to be concentrated in a region of 10^{-13} centimeters, whereas the atom was known to measure 10^{-8} centimeters. This meant that the atom consisted largely of empty space, with a very tiny and very dense charged nucleus at the center and opposite charges somehow placed in the surrounding void. Rutherford next calculated the probability of such single scattering at a given angle and found his predictions confirmed experimentally by Geiger and Marsden. The scientific community, however, was not impressed; this novel theory of the atom was not opposed, but largely ignored.

There were some, though, whose scientific orientation made them more likely than Rutherford to see the implications of a nuclear atom. One was Niels Bohr, who first met Rutherford in 1911 and later spent extended periods at Manchester. To Bohr it was apparent that radioactivity must be a phenomenon of the nucleus, while an element's chemical and physical properties were influenced by the electrons about this core. He brilliantly fitted chemical, radioactive, and spectroscopic data into the nuclear atom. His success in 1913 in applying quantum considerations to the orbital electron of hydrogen, thereby explaining its optical spectrum, eventually drew deserved attention to Rutherford's model of the atom. Bohr also treated heavier elements, and his attention to their electron arrangements brought the nuclear atom into chemistry.

H. G. J. Moseley was another of Rutherford's students whose work showed the fertility of the nuclear concept. In 1913, immediately after Max von Laue proved the wave nature of X rays and Rutherford's good friend at Leeds, W. H. Bragg, and his son, W. L. Bragg, who succeeded Rutherford at both Manchester and Cambridge, showed how to measure X-ray wavelengths by reflecting them from crystals, Moseley determined the wavelength of a particular line in the X-ray spectra of a large number of elements. When he organized his data according to each element's place in the periodic table, the wavelength (or frequency) of each line varied in regular steps. Only one thing, Moseley said, could change by such a constant amount: the positive charge on the atom's nucleus. Previously the organization of elements by atomic weights into the periodic table was seen by some as nothing more than fortuitous and by others as signifying a profound law of nature. It was Moseley's contribution to show that the profundity lay in the ordering of elements not by their weights but by their atomic numbers or nuclear charges, for it was precisely these charges that determined the number of orbital electrons and, hence, the chemical nature of the atom.

More was yet to come from Rutherford's school concerning the nucleus. Fajans and Soddy, both "alumni," and Russell, still at Manchester, each proposed a scheme to place the numerous radioelements into the periodic table. Russell's suggestion, a few months before Moseley's work mentioned above, and the more accurate versions that followed from the other two, stated simply that the daughter of an alpha-emitting element was two places to the left of the parent in the table, while the daughter of a beta-emitter was one place to the right. Moseley's work, showing that each place in the periodic table corresponds to a change of one nuclear charge, allowed further insight to these displacement laws, for the alpha particle bore a charge of +2 and the beta particle a charge of −1. That an alpha decay followed by two beta decays would lead back to the same place in the periodic table but, with a loss of about four atomic weight units, soon indicated the concept of isotopy.

Other important work was accomplished at Manchester, such as the Geiger-Nuttall rule connecting the range of an alpha particle with the average lifetime of the parent atom, beta- and gamma-ray spectroscopy, and the measurement by Rutherford and E. N. da C. Andrade in 1914 of gamma-ray wavelengths by the crystal technique. In all of these investigations Rutherford either played a direct part or kept closely abreast of developments during his daily rounds of the laboratory. At Manchester these rounds were possible, for Rutherford was largely spared time-consuming administrative duties and other chores. But he was

increasingly busy, and service on the Council of the Royal Society, the presidency of Section A of the British Association for the Advancement of Science in 1909, attendance at several overseas conferences, and his numerous lectures took him more and more away from the Midlands.

The outbreak of World War I caught Rutherford in Australia at a meeting of the British Association for the Advancement of Science. On his return to England, he found his laboratory virtually empty, for before governments found scientists useful in wartime and before conscription was introduced, many young scientists felt it was their duty to enlist for action. Rutherford himself was called upon to serve as a civilian member of the Admiralty's Board of Invention and Research committee dealing with submarine problems.

As the war progressed and hydrophone research became centralized at a naval base, Rutherford found time to return to his more customary line of investigation. A few years before, Marsden had noticed scintillations on a screen placed far beyond the range of alpha particles when these particles were allowed to bombard hydrogen. Rutherford repeated the experiment and showed that the scintillations were caused by hydrogen nuclei or protons. This was easily understood, but when he substituted nitrogen for the hydrogen, he saw the same proton flashes. The explanation he gave in 1919 stands beside the transformation theory of radioactivity and the nuclear atom as one of Rutherford's most important discoveries. This, he said, was a case of artificial disintegration of an element. Unstable, or radioactive, atoms disintegrated spontaneously; but here a stable nucleus was disrupted by the alpha particle, and a proton was one of the pieces broken off.

This line of work was to be the major theme for the remainder of Rutherford's career, which he spent at Cambridge from 1919. In that year Thomson was appointed master of Trinity College and decided to resign as director of the Cavendish Laboratory. The postwar period saw great activity in the game of professorial "musical chairs," but to no one's surprise Rutherford was elected as Thomson's successor. With him came James Chadwick, a former research student at Manchester who had spent the war years interned in Germany; he was to become Rutherford's closest collaborator. During the 1920's they determined that a number of light elements could be disintegrated by bombardment with swift alpha particles; as a corollary, they measured the distance of closest approach between projectile and target to ascertain both the size of the nucleus and that the inverse-square force law applied at this small distance.

There was no doubt that the alpha particle caused such elements as nitrogen, boron, fluorine, sodium, aluminum, and phosphorus to disintegrate. But did the alpha merely bounce off the target nucleus, which then emitted a proton, or did it combine with this nucleus? While these two reactions would form different elements, the number of atoms was too small for chemical tests. C. T. R. Wilson, who still worked independently in the Cavendish Laboratory, had perfected a cloud chamber before the war that was an ideal instrument to resolve this problem. If the alpha bounced off its target, there would be three tracks diverging from the collision point: the alpha, the proton, and the recoil nucleus. If, on the other hand, the alpha and the target formed a compound nucleus, there would be only two trails: the proton and the compound nucleus. From the photographs of some 400,000 alpha-particle tracks, P. M. S. Blackett in 1925 showed that it was the latter process which occurred, for he found eight doubly branched tracks from nuclear collisions. Later work at the Cavendish by Blackett and G. P. S. Occhialini, with cosmic rays triggering coincidence counters and thus photographing themselves in a cloud chamber, confirmed the discovery of the positron, made shortly before by Carl D. Anderson in California.

With its charge of +2, the alpha particle was too strongly repelled by the large numbers of positive charges on the nuclei of the heavier elements to cause disintegrations. To overcome this potential barrier, Rutherford recognized that projectiles might be accelerated but disregarded the alpha and proton because electrical engineers in the 1920's could not furnish the voltage required even to match the energy of alphas from natural radioactive sources. Instead, he inclined toward the idea of electron acceleration, with the thought that this projectile, once past the orbital electrons of similar charge, would be attracted to the nucleus. In the last few years of the 1920's, T. E. Allibone, one of a growing number at the Cavendish with engineering training—a new trend in physics—attempted disintegrations with accelerated electrons, but without success. George Gamow, on one of his several visits to Cambridge, then pointed out that the new wave mechanics predicted that a small number of particles of relatively low energy could tunnel through the potential barrier around a nucleus instead of climbing over it. This put the matter of effecting disintegrations by accelerated particles

of positive charge (and with more mass than the electron) back into the range of laboratory possibilities.

John Cockcroft and E. T. S. Walton built an apparatus capable of accelerating protons through several hundred thousand volts, with which, in 1932, they succeeded in bombarding lithium and producing alpha particles. By measuring the energy of these products, they further offered experimental proof of Einstein's famous relationship $E = mc^2$. The mass values were furnished with great accuracy by another long-time Cavendish member, F. W. Aston, who, like C. T. R. Wilson, worked to a large degree independently. In 1919 Rutherford had produced artificial disintegrations by natural means, that is, by alphas from naturally decaying radioactive materials. The Cockcroft-Walton work of 1932, artificial disintegrations by artificial means—that is, by accelerated particles—made Rutherford a believer in the quantum mechanics on which it was based. Although he was not generally interested in highly mathematical physical theories, especially ones difficult to visualize, these new ideas of the late 1920's worked—and that was Rutherford's criterion.

An instance of his willingness to use, if not fully understand, quantum mechanics was Rutherford's construction with Marcus Oliphant of a special discharge tube that generated a far more copious supply of protons than the Cockcroft-Walton apparatus and at lower voltages. His faith in the ability of these protons to tunnel through the potential barrier at these lower energies was rewarded with a number of disintegrations. But the heavier elements still resisted such bombardments; and it was clear that, for them, projectiles of greater energy were required. Ernest Lawrence, in California, had built the cyclotron a few years before and generously shared his plans with Rutherford. A new high-voltage laboratory was also planned for the Cavendish, to house a two-million-volt, commercially built apparatus; but neither of these heralds of the new age of "big science and big money" was in significant use by the time of Rutherford's death in 1937.

There were other important activities at the Cavendish, some with direct connections to Rutherford's main interest in disintegrations and others with no connection at all. Among the latter were the work of G. I. Taylor on problems in classical physics, E. V. Appleton on radio waves, and Peter Kapitza on phenomena in intense magnetic fields and at low temperatures. More in the mainstream of the laboratory's orientation was the long series of investigations by C. D. Ellis on beta- and gamma-ray spectra. Since these rays, as well as the alpha, come from the decaying nucleus, they offered a view of the energy levels in this nucleus and, hence, an insight to nuclear structure.

Not long after the discovery of heavy water in the United States, Rutherford obtained a small quantity of this precious fluid and in 1934, with Oliphant and Paul Harteck, bombarded deuterium with deuterons. This reaction was notable for the first achievement of what is now called fusion, as well as for the production of tritium. Another major advance at the Cavendish, the significance of which is not sufficiently appreciated, was the application by C. E. Wynn-Williams of Heinrich Greinacher's ideas for electronic amplification of ionization. With the Geiger-Müller tube, which was based on a different principle, and especially with Wynn-Williams' tubes and associated electronics, research workers in the laboratory were able to count particles at much higher rates than with scintillations and with other benefits.

Rutherford recognized the value to his experimentalists of contact with theoretical physicists and encouraged their presence in the laboratory. Some, such as Gamow, came as visitors for a period. The Cambridge theoreticians, however, were by administrative fiat in the mathematics department and were somewhat isolated from the Cavendish. A notable exception was Ralph Fowler, Rutherford's son-in-law, whose advice was eagerly sought during the nearly two decades that Rutherford directed the laboratory. Along with the Cockcroft-Walton experiment, the most important discovery during this period by one of Rutherford's colleagues was Chadwick's proof, in 1932, of the existence of the neutron. Rutherford had long considered the neutron a possibility and in his 1920 Bakerian lecture to the Royal Society had predicted its likely properties. Chadwick made several attempts to detect the neutral particle, but none was successful until he learned of experiments by the Joliot-Curies in Paris, in which, they said, extremely penetrating gamma rays were emitted. As he suspected, Chadwick found the rays were not gammas but neutrons; and not long afterward Norman Feather, also at the Cavendish, showed that neutrons were capable of causing nuclear disintegrations.

Even by the beginning of Rutherford's second period at Cambridge, he was a public figure. Increasingly beset with outside calls upon his time, he had less and less opportunity for his own research and for keeping abreast of his students'

work. Yet, with the tradition of enthusiasm for research that he had established earlier, his still frequent rounds to "ginger up" his "boys," and Chadwick's invaluable assistance, the laboratory's output remained far more than respectable.

From 1921, when he succeeded Thomson, until his death, Rutherford was professor of natural philosophy at the Royal Institution in London, a post that entailed several lectures each year. There were numerous other public lectures to which great honor was attached, such as his presidential address to the British Association for the Advancement of Science in 1923. Between 1925 and 1930 he was president of the Royal Society, and following this he became chairman of the advisory council to the British government's Department of Scientific and Industrial Research. Both posts involved many public appearances, such as opening conferences and new laboratories, in addition to administrative and policy-making chores. Although liberal-minded, Rutherford customarily side-stepped political issues. Yet he felt he could not remain idle when Nazi Germany expelled hundreds of Jewish scholars; and from 1933 he was president of the Academic Assistance Council, which sought to obtain positions and financial aid for these refugees.

In work that may be characterized as radioactivity at McGill, atomic physics at Manchester, and nuclear physics at Cambridge, Rutherford, more than any other, formed the views now held concerning the nature of matter. It is to be expected that numerous honors would come to such a man, called the greatest experimental physicist of his day and often compared with Faraday. In 1922 he received the Copley Medal, the highest award given by the Royal Society. Dozens of universities and scientific societies awarded him honorary degrees and memberships. For the fame Rutherford brought to the British Empire—not for his relatively minor services to his government—he was made a knight in 1914 and a peer (Baron Rutherford of Nelson) in 1931. King George V personally honored him in 1925 by conferring on him the Order of Merit, which is limited to a handful of the most distinguished living Englishmen.

BIBLIOGRAPHY

I. ORIGINAL WORKS. Approximately two dozen boxes of Rutherford's correspondence and miscellaneous papers are preserved in the Cambridge University Library. Most of his published papers have been reprinted, under the scientific direction of Sir James Chadwick, in *Collected Papers of Lord Rutherford of Nelson*, 3 vols. (London, 1962–1965). Rutherford's books are *Radio-Activity* (Cambridge, 1904; 2nd ed., 1905); *Radioactive Transformations* (London, 1906); *Radioactive Substances and Their Radiations* (Cambridge, 1913); *Radiations From Radioactive Substances* (Cambridge, 1930), written with J. Chadwick and C. D. Ellis; and *The Newer Alchemy* (Cambridge, 1937). A portion of his correspondence is reproduced in Lawrence Badash, ed., *Rutherford and Boltwood, Letters on Radioactivity* (New Haven, 1969). Badash has also compiled the *Rutherford Correspondence Catalog* (New York, 1974).

II. SECONDARY LITERATURE. There are three biographies written by Rutherford's former students: A. S. Eve, *Rutherford* (Cambridge, 1939); Norman Feather, *Lord Rutherford* (London, 1940); and E. N. da C. Andrade, *Rutherford and the Nature of the Atom* (London, 1964). Other biographies and partial biographies include Ivor Evans, *Man of Power, the Life Story of Baron Rutherford of Nelson, O.M., F.R.S.* (London, 1939); John Rowland, *Ernest Rutherford, Atom Pioneer* (London, 1955); Robin McKown, *Giant of the Atom, Ernest Rutherford* (New York, 1962); John Rowland, *Ernest Rutherford, Master of the Atom* (London, 1964); D. Danin, *Rutherford* (Moscow, 1966), in Russian; O. A. Staroselskaya-Nikitina, *Ernest Rutherford, 1871–1937* (Moscow, 1967), in Russian; E. S. Shire, *Rutherford and the Nuclear Atom* (London, 1972); and, especially valuable for personal information, Mark Oliphant, *Rutherford, Recollections of the Cambridge Days* (Amsterdam, 1972).

Collections of articles about Rutherford include *Rutherford by Those Who Knew Him*, which is the first five Rutherford lectures of the Physical Society, by H. R. Robinson, J. D. Cockcroft, M. L. Oliphant, E. Marsden, and A. S. Russell, reprinted from *Proceedings of the Physical Society*, 1943–1951; a series of Rutherford memorial lectures, by J. D. Cockcroft, J. Chadwick, E. Marsden, C. Darwin, E. N. da C. Andrade, P. M. S. Blackett, T. E. Allibone, and G. P. Thomson, in *Proceedings of the Royal Society*, from 1953 on; J. B. Birks, ed., *Rutherford at Manchester* (London, 1962); Albert Parry, ed., *Peter Kapitsa on Life and Science* (New York, 1968); *Notes and Records of the Royal Society*, 27 (Aug. 1972), an issue devoted to Rutherford, with articles by M. L. Oliphant, H. Massey, N. Feather, P. M. S. Blackett, W. B. Lewis, N. Mott, P. P. O'Shea, and J. B. Adams; P. L. Kapitza, ed., *Rutherford—Scholar and Teacher, On the Hundredth Anniversary of his Birth* (Moscow, 1973), which is in Russian.

Among the wide range of articles written about Rutherford during his lifetime, obituary notices, recollections, and historical studies are the following: A. S. Eve, "Some Scientific Centres. VIII. The Macdonald Physics Building, McGill University, Montreal," in *Nature*, 74 (1906), 272–275; J. A. Harker, "Some Scientific Centres. XI. The Physical Laboratories of Manchester University," in *Nature*, 76 (1907), 640–642; "The Ex-

tension of the Physical and Electrotechnical Laboratories of the University of Manchester," in *Nature*, 89 (1912), 46; N. Bohr, "Sir Ernest Rutherford, O.M., P.R.S.," in *Nature Supplement*, 118 (1926), 51–52; O. Hahn and L. Meitner, "Lord Rutherford zum Sechzigsten Geburtstag," in *Die Naturwissenschaften*, 19 (1931), 729; M. de Broglie, "Scientific Worthies: The Right Hon. Lord Rutherford of Nelson, O.M., F.R.S.," in *Nature*, 129 (1932), 665–669; and J. G. Crowther, "Lord Rutherford, O.M., F.R.S.," in *Great Contemporaries* (London, 1935), pp. 359–370.

Obituary notices are in the *Times* (London) 20, 21, 22, and 26 Oct. 1937; *New York Times*, 20 Oct. 1937 and 21 Jan. 1938; *Nature*, 140 (1937), 717, 746–755, 1047–1054; and 141 (1938), 841–842.

See also A. S. Russell, "More About Lord Rutherford," in *The Listener*, 18 (1937), 966; A. N. Shaw, "Rutherford at McGill," in the *McGill News* (Winter 1937), no pagination; C. M. Focken, "Lord Rutherford of Nelson, a Tribute to New Zealand's Greatest Scientist," a 19-page brochure (privately printed in New Zealand, n.d., but *ca.* 1938); the obituary notice by R. A. Millikan, in *Yearbook of the American Philosophical Society for 1938*, 386–388; F. R. Terroux, "The Rutherford Collection of Apparatus at McGill University," in *Transactions of the Royal Society of Canada*, 32 (1938), 9–16; the obituary notice by E. F. Burton, in *University of Toronto Quarterly*, 7 (1938), 329–338; A. George, "Lord Rutherford ou l'Alchimiste," in *La Revue de France*, (1938), 525–533; the obituary notice by G. Guében, in *Revue des Questions Scientifiques*, 113 (1938), 5–19; the obituary notice by A. S. Eve and J. Chadwick, in *Obituary Notices of the Royal Society of London*, 2 (1938), 395–423; H. Geiger, "Memories of Rutherford in Manchester," in *Nature*, 141 (1938), 244; H. Geiger, "Das Lebenswerk von Lord Rutherford of Nelson," in *Die Naturwissenschaften*, 26 (1938), 161–164; and obituary notices in *Proceedings of the Physical Society*, 50 (1938), 441–466.

Other articles are an obituary notice by E. Marsden, in *Transactions and Proceedings of the Royal Society of New Zealand*, 68 (1938), 4–16, to which is appended a partial bibliography compiled by C. M. Focken, pp. 17–25; "51 Years as Laboratory Steward," an interview with W. Kay, in the *Manchester Guardian*, 27 Dec. 1945; H. Tizard, "The Rutherford Memorial Lecture," in *Journal of the Chemical Society* (1946), 980–986; "Rutherford Commemoration, Paris, 7 and 8 November 1947," in *Notes and Records of the Royal Society*, 6 (1948), 67–68; H. Dale, "Some Personal Memories of Lord Rutherford of Nelson," in *Cawthron Lecture Series*, no. 25 (1950); P. M. S. Blackett, "Rutherford and After," in the *Manchester Guardian Weekly*, 63 (14 Dec. 1950), 13; E. N. da C. Andrade, "The Birth of the Nuclear Atom," in *Scientific American*, 195 (1956), 93–104; C. P. Snow, "The Age of Rutherford," in *Atlantic Monthly*, 202 (Nov. 1958), 76–81; C. D. Ellis, "Rutherford; One Aspect of a Complex Character," in *Trinity Review* (Lent 1960), 13–15; J. E. Geake, "Rutherford in

Manchester," in *Contemporary Physics*, **3** (1961), 155–158; "The Jubilee of the Nuclear Atom," in *Endeavour*, **21** (1962), 3–4; N. Feather, an essay-review of volume one of Rutherford's collected papers, in *Contemporary Physics,* **4** (1962), 73–76; W. A. Kay, "Recollections of Rutherford. Being the Personal Reminiscences of Lord Rutherford's Laboratory Assistant, Here Published for the First Time. Recorded and Annotated by Samuel Devons," in *The Natural Philosopher*, **1** (1963), 127–155; W. E. Burcham, "Rutherford at Manchester, 1907–1919," in *Contemporary Physics*, **5** (1964), 304–308; T. H. Osgood and H. S. Hirst, "Rutherford and His Alpha Particles," in *American Journal of Physics,* **32** (1964), 681–686; P. L. Kapitza, "Recollections of Lord Rutherford," in *Proceedings of the Royal Society,* **A294** (1966), 123–137; M. L. Oliphant, "The Two Ernests" [Rutherford and Lawrence], in *Physics Today,* **19** (Sept. 1966), 35–49, (Oct. 1966), 41–51; L. Badash, "How the 'Newer Alchemy' Was Received," in *Scientific American,* **215** (1966), 88–95; L. Badash, "Rutherford, Boltwood, and the Age of the Earth: The Origin of Radioactive Dating Techniques," in *Proceedings of the American Philosophical Society,* **112** (1968), 157–169; J. L. Heilbron, "The Scattering of α and β Particles and Rutherford's Atom," in *Archive for History of Exact Sciences,* **4** (1968), 247–307; L. Badash, "The Importance of Being Ernest Rutherford," in *Science,* **173** (1971), 873; T. Trenn, "Rutherford and Soddy: From a Search for Radioactive Constituents to the Disintegration Theory of Radioactivity," in *RETE Strukturgeschichte der Naturwissenschaften,* **1** (1971), 51–70; and T. Trenn, "The Geiger-Marsden Scattering Results and Rutherford's Atom, July 1912 to July 1913: The Shifting Significance of Scientific Evidence," in *Isis,* **65** (1974), 74–82.

For information about some of Rutherford's colleagues, see the various articles in the *DSB* and Albert Parry, ed., *Peter Kapitsa on Life and Science* (New York, 1968); *Sir Ernest Marsden. 80th Birthday Book* (Wellington, New Zealand, 1969); and Robert Reid, *Marie Curie* (New York, 1974).

Various aspects of the history of radioactivity may be found in the following selections: T. W. Chalmers, *A Short History of Radio-Activity* (London, 1951); Alfred Romer, *The Restless Atom* (Garden City, New York, 1960); A. Romer, ed., *The Discovery of Radioactivity and Transmutation* (New York, 1964); L. Badash, *The Early Developments in Radioactivity, With Emphasis on Contributions From the United States* (Ph.D. diss., Yale University, 1964); L. Badash, "Radioactivity Before the Curies," in *American Journal of Physics,* **33** (1965), 128–135; L. Badash, "Chance Favors the Prepared Mind: Henri Becquerel and the Discovery of Radioactivity," in *Archives Internationales d'Histoire des Sciences,* **18** (1965), 55–66; L. Badash, "The Discovery of Thorium's Radioactivity," in *Journal of Chemical Education,* **43** (1966), 219–220; L. Badash, "Becquerel's 'Unexposed' Photographic Plates," in *Isis,* **57** (1966), 267–269; L. Badash, "An Elster and Geitel Failure:

Magnetic Deflection of Beta Rays," in *Centaurus,* **11** (1966), 236–240; A. Romer, ed., *Radiochemistry and the Discovery of Isotopes* (New York, 1970); Marjorie Malley, "The Discovery of the Beta Particle," in *American Journal of Physics,* **39** (1971), 1454–1460; and Thaddeus J. Trenn, *The Rise and Early Development of the Disintegration Theory of Radioactivity* (Ph.D. diss., University of Wisconsin, 1971).

Lawrence Badash

RUTHERFURD, LEWIS MORRIS (*b.* New York, N.Y., 25 November 1816; *d.* Tranquility, New Jersey, 30 May 1892), *astrophysics.*

As early as his student days at Williams College, Rutherfurd displayed an interest in science, assisting in the chemistry course. Initially he was destined for the law and studied with William H. Seward. He came from a prominent family and his independent means, subsequently augmented by marriage into the wealthy Stuyvesant family, must have made him seem like a few other members of what was an emerging American patriciate, a dilettantish amateur. Samuel Ward and J. P. Morgan the elder, for example, both gave up youthful interests in mathematics for more lucrative careers. The Rutherfurd who was on the yacht *America* during its challenge of the British must have appeared to superficial observers an unpromising candidate for honors in astrophysics. But he had already published his first scientific paper.

Freed from the need to practice law by his marriage, Rutherfurd traveled abroad for seven years, partly because of his wife's health. In Florence he associated with Amici, who was known for his work in both microscopy and optical astronomy. When Rutherfurd returned to the United States, he had an observatory constructed in 1856 on the Stuyvesant family estate, in what is now New York City's Lower East Side. Here he worked on astronomical photography and spectroscopy. Rutherfurd sometimes made his own instruments, work at which he was very skilled; more frequently the instruments were constructed by others according to his specifications.

In 1858 Rutherfurd started working on astronomical photography, using an 11.5-inch achromatic refracting telescope made by Henry Fitz. Although placing the plates at the actinic focus produced fine lunar photographs as well as images of Jupiter, Saturn, the sun, and stars of the fifth magnitude, Rutherfurd tried various expedients to obtain better photographs before he completely omitted the visual element from the telescope. Starting in December 1864 he employed a new 11.5-inch objective lens useful solely for photography. The resulting pictures of the moon were widely admired. In 1865 Rutherfurd began to photograph star clusters in order to map the heavens. His friend Benjamin Apthorp Gould collaborated in reducing the data for the Pleiades and the Praesepe. Rutherfurd also devised a micrometer for measuring the stellar photographs. When doubts were expressed concerning the stability of the photographic plates, particularly in connection with the proposed observations of the transits of Venus, Rutherfurd published results of tests of albuminized glass plates with wet collodion film (1872). After 1868 Rutherfurd used a thirteen-inch refractor with an exterior photographic corrective lens.

In 1861 O. W. Gibbs called Rutherfurd's attention to the spectroscopic work of Bunsen and Kirchhoff. By the next year Rutherfurd had made spectroscopic studies of the sun, moon, Jupiter, Mars, and sixteen fixed stars. From the last he independently gave a stellar spectra classification quite similar to Secchi's. Rutherfurd also used the spectroscope for color correction of telescope lenses.

His first spectroscopic observations used a cylindrical lens between a prism and the objective of the 11.25-inch Fitz telescope. In the winter of 1862–1863, Rutherfurd developed a spectroscope using glass prisms filled with carbon disulfide and ingenious devices for maintaining equal density of the disulfide and for adjusting the prisms. At the January 1864 meeting of the National Academy of Sciences, Rutherfurd displayed a never-published photograph of the solar spectrum 15 centimeters wide and 78.7 centimeters between lines H and F (according to Gould), with three times the lines given by Bunsen and Kirchhoff.

Encouraged by Gibbs and Ogden Rood of Columbia University, who were also working in this area, Rutherfurd turned in 1863 to diffraction gratings. An early ruling engine proved inadequate; in 1867 Rutherfurd devised another, in which a screw, rather than levers, powered by a turbine run by tap water, moved the plate. The gratings he produced were superior to the best then made (by Nobert), and by 1877 they were available with up to 17,296 lines to the inch. The earliest gratings were on glass; later ones had rulings on speculum metal. Rutherfurd freely and widely distributed his gratings, which were unsurpassed until the work of Rowland.

When his health began to fail in 1877, Rutherfurd started to dismantle his observatory, making his last observations in 1878. The growth of the city, in any event, made precision work at that location extremely difficult. A trustee of Columbia University, in 1881 Rutherfurd helped the university found its department of geodesy and practical astronomy; and in 1883 he donated the equipment of his observatory. In 1890 he transferred twenty volumes of plate measures and a large collection of his photographic plates that provided intellectual employment for the university observatory, named in his honor, for many years.

BIBLIOGRAPHY

I. ORIGINAL WORKS. Rutherfurd's writings include "Observations During the Lunar Eclipse, 12 September 1848," in *American Journal of Science,* n.s. **6** (1848), 435–437; "Astronomical Observations With the Spectroscope," *ibid.,* n.s. **35** (1863), 71–77; "Letter on a Companion to Sirius, Stellar Spectra, and the Spectroscope," *ibid.,* 407–409; "Observations on Stellar Spectra," *ibid.,* n.s. **36** (1863), 154–157; "On the Construction of the Spectroscope," *ibid.,* n.s. **39** (1865), 129–132; "Astronomical Photography," *ibid.,* 304–309; "On the Stability of the Collodion Film," *ibid.,* 3rd ser., **6** (1872), 430–433; "A Glass Circle for the Measurement of Angles," *ibid.,* 3rd ser., **12** (1876), 112–113. See also the correspondence of O. W. Gibbs at the Franklin Institute, Philadelphia, and the Ogden Rood correspondence at the Columbia University Library, New York City.

II. SECONDARY LITERATURE. The recent and enlightening article by Deborah Jean Warner, "Lewis M. Rutherfurd: Pioneer Astronomical Photographer and Spectroscopist," in *Technology and Culture,* **12** (1971), 180–216, is the best introduction to his work. Still useful are Benjamin Apthorp Gould, "Memoir of Lewis Morris Rutherfurd," in *Biographical Memoirs. National Academy of Sciences,* **3** (1895), 417–441; and John K. Rees, "Lewis Morris Rutherfurd," in *Astronomy and Astro-Physics,* **11** (1892), 689–697. The results of the work of the Columbia University's Rutherfurd Observatory on the materials presented by Rutherfurd are in John K. Rees, Harold Jacoby, Herman S. Davis, and Frank Schlesinger, *Lewis Morris Rutherfurd, a Brief Account of His Life and Work . . . ,* 2 vols. (New York, 1898–1919).

NATHAN REINGOLD

RÜTIMEYER, KARL LUDWIG (*b.* Biglen, Bern Canton, Switzerland, 26 February 1825; *d.* Basel, Switzerland, 25 November 1895), *vertebrate paleozoology, geography.*

The scion of an ancient cantonal family, Rütimeyer was intended for the ministry. His parents, Albrecht Rütimeyer, a pastor in Biglen, and Marie Margaretha Küpfer, subsequently moved to Bern, where Rütimeyer studied theology and then medicine at the University of Bern. His early interests in natural history and geology were stimulated under the fascinating influence of Studer, who taught geology at the university. Rütimeyer's field studies in the 1840's of the Bernese Oberland and of the Solothurn Jura, as well as his correspondence with Murchison, led to his dissertation on the Swiss nummulitic terrain. In 1850 he received the doctorate in medicine.

Following three lively years of geological, zoological, and clinical study and experience in Paris, London, Leiden, and Italy, Rütimeyer accepted (1853) an extraordinary professorship in comparative anatomy at the university in Bern. Apparently his reception at Bern was somewhat mixed — perhaps because of his stance during the Sonderbund. He subsequently resigned from this post and spent part of 1854 with Murchison in London, where a Himalayan expedition reached the planning stages. Late in 1855 he was named ordinary professor of zoology and comparative anatomy at the University of Basel, thus beginning a distinguished teaching and research career that spanned almost four decades. He was later named rector (1865) and then professor in the medical and philosophical faculties, having received in 1874 a doctorate in philosophy *honoris causa.*

Rütimeyer made significant contributions to the natural history and evolutionary paleontology of ungulate mammals, especially the artiodactyls. His comparative odontography of ungulates (1863) was perhaps the first serious attempt after Darwin's *Origin* to interpret fossil mammals as parts of evolutionary lineages by showing the gradual change in dentitions. Rütimeyer discovered that ungulate milk teeth are conservative and thus closer in character to those of their nearest known ancestors than to permanent dentitions that are dissimilar in series. The significance that Rütimeyer attached to dental characters for phylogenetic interpretations preceded the more explicit series of horses and other ungulates proposed in the 1870's by Huxley, Kovalevsky, and Marsh.

A cautious developmentalist, Rütimeyer did not accept the Darwinian explanation of natural selection. It was likely too mechanistic a concept for a theologically trained biologist who held the widest view of natural history and whose writings reflect early influences of Humboldt's *Kosmos,* vertebrate

body plans, and something of Karl von Baer's *Naturphilosophie.*

Rütimeyer's work advanced the study of mammalian evolution and biogeography. His investigation of the fauna of the Swiss lake dwellings (1862) appears to have been as significant for his subsequent researches as Darwin's interest in variation under domestication was for his ideas of transmutation of species. Rütimeyer's researches into the natural history, comparative osteology, evolutionary patterns, and paleozoogeography of perissodactyls, suids, and ruminants, as well as his studies of the diverse Eocene fauna of Egerkingen and of fossil turtles, earned him world renown. Many of his findings were used by Karl von Zittel in the latter's contemporary, general paleontological treatises.

In 1869 Rütimeyer published a significant analysis of Swiss valley and lake origin. To the earlier fluvialist explanations of Hutton and Lyell, he added an actualistic concept of valley development by headward stream erosion. Rütimeyer emphasized that varying rates of erosion, acting over long time intervals on differing geographies and rock types along stream courses, will produce diverse landforms. These forms might then be classified by relative age, a concept foreshadowing the Davisian tradition in geomorphology.

Rütimeyer traveled extensively in Europe during the 1870's and 1880's, adding to his experience and collections. In Basel he actively and influentially promoted and served both national and civic academic, natural history, paleontological, anthropological, and mountaineering societies and museums. With the brothers Sarasin, he aided Swiss conservation efforts. Rütimeyer retired from the university faculty late in 1893, but he retained his membership in the public libraries commission of Basel and also his directorship of its natural history museums. He continued his researches until his death. Rütimeyer was survived by his wife, Charlotte Laura Fankhauser, whom he had married in 1855, and their only child, Ludwig Leopold, who later became extraordinary professor of anthropology at Basel.

BIBLIOGRAPHY

I. ORIGINAL SOURCES. Rütimeyer's autobiographical sketch is in *Gesammelte Kleine Schriften allgemeinen Inhalts aus dem Gebiete der Naturwissenschaft . . . ,* Hans Georg Stehlin, ed., I (Basel, 1898), in which several of his zoological papers are reprinted. Vol. II contains four of his earlier physiographical works, a quartet of memorials, and a bibliography. The Staatsarchiv in Basel contains complete correspondence between Rütimeyer and the cantonal government concerning his position as university professor and head of the Vergleichend-anatomische Sammlungen in the Museum of Natural History.

The Archiv also holds correspondence between Rütimeyer and Felix, Paul, and Fritz Sarasin, and Rudolf Staehelin-Stockmeyer. Most of his important letters, which are held by his granddaughter Dr. Elizabeth Rütimeyer and others of the family, are in *Brief von Ludwig Rütimeyer (1825–1895) als Manuscript gedruckt* (Basel, 1902) and "Ludwig Rütimeyer: Brief und Tagebuchblätter," both edited by L. L. Rütimeyer; the latter was published in L. E. Iselin and P. Sarasin, *Einleitung: Lebens- und Charakterbild Rütimeyers* (Frauenfeld, 1906), The University of Basel library holds a few letters and student notes from several of Rütimeyer's courses.

Rütimeyer's paleontological and zoological writings are cited in Alfred Sherwood Romer, *et al.*, *Bibliography of Fossil Vertebrates Exclusive of North America, 1509–1927. II, L-Z*, which is *Memoirs. Geological Society of America*, **87** (1962), 782, 1191–1193. Major works include: "Die fauna der Pfahlbauten der Schweiz," in *Neue Denkschriften der Allgemeinen Schweizerischen Gesellschaft der gesammten Naturwissenschaften*, **19**, no. 1 (1862); "Eocaene Saugethier aus dem Gebiet des schweizerischen Jura," *ibid.*, **19**, no. 3 (1862); "Beiträge zur Kenntniss der fossilen Pferd und zur vergleichenden Odontographie der Hufthiere überhaupt," in *Verhandlungen der Naturforschenden Gesellschaft in Basel*, **3** (1863 [1862]), 558–696, pls. I–IV; *Die Grenzen der Thierwelt. Eine Betrachtung zu Darwin's Lehre* (Basel, 1868), dedicated to Karl von Baer; *Ueber die Art des Fortschrittes in den organischen Geschöpfen* (Basel, 1876); "Ueber einige Beziehungen zwischen den Säugetierstämmen alter und neuer Welt. Erster Nachtrag . . . Egerkingen," in *Abhandlungen der Schweizerischen Paläontologischen Gesellschaft*, **15** (1888), 1–63, pl. 1; "Uebersicht der eocaenen Fauna von Egerkingen. Nebst einer Erwiderung von Prof. E. D. Cope. Zweiter Nachtrag . . . Egerkingen (1862)," in *Verhandlungen der Naturforschenden Gesellschaft in Basel*, **9** (1890), 331–362; and, "Die eocaenen Säugethierwelt von Egerkingen. Gesammtdarstellung und dritter Nachtrag . . . 'Eocaenen Säugethieren . . . (1862),'" *op. cit.*, **18** (1891), 153 p., 8 pls.

Rütimeyer's writings in other fields are *Vom Meer bis nach den Alpen. Schilderungen von Bau, Form und Farbe unseres Continentes auf einem Durchschnitt von England bis Sicilien* (Basel, 1854), also published as *Van de Zee tot de Alpen* (Doesburgh, 1857); *Ueber Thal- und Seebildung. Beiträge zum Verständniss der Oberfläche der Schweiz* (Basel, 1869); "Ein Blick auf die Geschichte der Gletscherstudien in der Schweiz," in *Jahrbuch der Schweizer Alpenclub*, **16** (1881), 377–418; and *Entstehung und Verlauf der Vermessung des Rhonegletschers* (Basel, 1896).

Rütimeyer's verse is collected in *Gedichte von Ludwig Rütimeyer*, L. L. Rütimeyer, ed. (Basel, 1901).

II. SECONDARY LITERATURE. An evaluation of Rütimeyer's papers is Antoine Wahl, *L'Oeuvre géographique de L. Rütimeyer. Une analyse critique* (Fribourg, 1927). Of the ten memorials and obituaries listed in *Gesammelte Kleine Schriften*, II, the most extensive are L. E. Iselin, "Carl Ludwig Rütimeyer," in *Basler Jahrbuch 1897* (1897), 1–47; and Carl Schmidt, "Ludwig Rütimeyer," in *Basler Nachrichten*, 3–7 December 1895, repr. with modifications in *Verhandlungen der Schweizerischen Naturforschenden Gesellschaft, 78 Jahresversammlung . . . 1895* (1896), 213–256.

Brief sketches and evaluations are Eduard His, "Karl Ludwig Rütimeyer 1825–1895," in His, ed., *Basler Gelehrte des 19. Jahrhunderts* (Basel, 1941), 202–212; Adolf Portmann, "Ludwig Rütimeyer 1825–1895 . . . ," in Andrew Staehlin, ed., *Professoren der Universität Basel aus fünf Jahrhunderten. Bildnisse und Würdigungen . . .* (Basel, 1960), 160–161; H. G. Stehlin, "Karl Ludwig Rütimeyer aus Bern, 1825–1895," in Eduard Fueter, ed., *Grosse Schweizer Forscher . . .* (Zurich, 1941), 270–271; and Ewald Wust, "Ludwig Rütimeyer (1825–1895) als Begründer der historischen Paläontologie," in *Palaeontologische Zeitschrift*, **8**, no. 1/2 (1927), 34–39.

CLIFFORD M. NELSON

RUYSCH, FREDERIK (*b.* The Hague, Netherlands, 23 March 1638; *d.* Amsterdam, Netherlands, 22 February 1731), *botany, obstetrics, anatomy, medicine.*

Ruysch was descended from an old and notable family whose members held posts in various city governments, including those of Utrecht and Amsterdam. His great-great-grandfather was councillor to the bishop of Liège; his great-grandfather was councillor to the duke of Arensberg and, later, pensionary of Amsterdam; and his grandfather was secretary of the audit office. The Dutch war with Spain seems to have brought a change in 1576 in the fortunes of the family.

Ruysch was the son of Hendrik Ruysch, a secretary in the service of the state, and Anna van Berchem. Probably he attended the grammar school in The Hague. The early death of his father may explain Frederik's apprenticeship as a boy in an apothecary's shop. In 1661, even though not yet admitted to the apothecaries' guild, he prepared drugs and opened a shop in The Hague. The board of the guild ordered him to close the shop and forbade him to sell remedies to anyone until he had successfully passed the necessary examination, as he did on 16 and 17 June 1661. He was then admitted *confrater* in the guild and quickly reopened his shop. In the same year he married Maria Post, daughter of Pieter Post, the well-known architect of Frederik Henry, prince of Orange. Of this marriage many (perhaps twelve) children were born; but only two are known: Hendrik and Rachel, who married the painter Jurriaan Pool and was herself a well-known painter. Her works were bought by Johann Wilhelm, the elector palatinate. Rachel helped her father make anatomical preparations in his old age.

In his youth Ruysch had a passion for anatomy; and he himself told how he would ask grave diggers to open graves so that he could make anatomical investigations. Soon after his marriage, he began his medical studies at Leiden. To attend the lectures there, he had to travel from The Hague, where he lived and managed a chemist's shop. His teachers included Johannes van Horne, who was professor of anatomy and surgery, and Franciscus Sylvius, who taught practical medicine. On 28 July 1664 he received the M.D. at Leiden (not, as is sometimes reported, at Franeker) for his thesis *De pleuritide,* which was written under van Horne's guidance. He then established a medical practice in The Hague and almost immediately was overwhelmed with plague victims. During this time, he also conducted serious anatomical studies and continued them in his spare time. But he remained somewhat aloof from the experiments on live dogs that were then being carried out by de Graaf and Swammerdam (and attended by Steno) in the Leiden laboratories.

In 1665 Ruysch settled a dispute between van Horne and Louis de Bils, a self-taught, unqualified anatomist who claimed to be able to preserve corpses for years, when the latter cited van Horne's name in his fantastic theory on the course of the lymph in the lymph vessels. Although Bils firmly denied the existence of valves in these vessels, Ruysch succeeded in demonstrating their presence. His research, published as *Dilucidatio valvularum in vasis lymphaticis et lacteis* (1665), ended the controversy.

On 29 December 1666 Ruysch was named praelector of anatomy for the surgeon's guild in Amsterdam. He attended the session of the guild on 12 January 1667 and soon moved to Amsterdam. Ruysch held this post until his death in 1731. He was annoyed when, in 1727, at the age of eighty-nine, the burgomasters appointed Willem Roëll as his assistant without consulting him. As *praelector anatomiae,* Ruysch taught anatomy to the surgeons and performed the public dissections in the winter months. In this role he was painted twice with the masters of the guild: in 1670 by Adriaan Backer and in 1683 by Johan van Neck. The latter painted Ruysch dissecting a child while his son Hendrik (then about age twenty) is pictured as a boy holding the skeleton of a child. Also, Pool twice made a portrait of Ruysch. In 1672, after the death of Hendrik von Roonhuyse, Ruysch was also appointed city obstetrician. Thus he contributed to the education of midwives, giving one lesson a month and four demonstrations a year on female corpses. Ruysch held this post for forty years; in 1712 he retired in favor of his son Hendrik.

In 1679 Ruysch was appointed doctor of the court of justice. He reported on persons wounded or killed in robberies or quarrels—rather frequent occurrences in the great port of Amsterdam. Ruysch thus gathered extensive experience in forensic medicine. On 24 March 1685 he was appointed professor of botany at the Athenaeum Illustre and thus became supervisor of the botanical garden. He delivered three botanical lectures a week: to the surgeons, to the apothecaries' apprentices, and to the apothecaries. From 1692 he was assisted at the garden by Petrus Hotton and, later, by Caspar Commelin, who lectured on exotic plants. With F. Kiggelaar, Ruysch wrote a description of the rare plants in the garden.

Although Ruysch ably fulfilled these varied responsibilities for many years, he considered himself primarily an anatomist. He gave private courses in anatomy to foreign students and devoted himself throughout his life to making anatomical preparations. His skill in this art remains unsurpassed. The technique of injecting had already been used by Swammerdam and de Graaf during his student years at Leiden. De Graaf had invented a special syringe for this purpose, but Ruysch developed his own method and was thus able to prepare various organs (for example, the liver and the kidneys) and to preserve entire corpses for years. In the summer of 1696 he announced the dissection of bodies "which appear still to be alive but which have been dead for about two years."

Ruysch himself never disclosed the composition of the fluids he used, but in 1743 J. C. Rieger revealed that he used a mixture of talc, white wax, and cinnabar for injecting vessels, whereas his embalming fluid (liquor balsamicus) consisted of alcohol (prepared from wine or corn) to which some black pepper was added. Ruysch drew on his art not only for strict medical science but also for flights of fancy. He often made up preparations in a rather romantic, dramatic way. He prepared the corpse of a child as if it were alive so that Peter the Great was inclined to kiss it. A hydrocephalic child was prepared, seated on a cushion and with a placenta in its hands.

Ruysch displayed these preparations in several small rented houses in Amsterdam, and this "cabinet" became a major attraction for foreign visitors. He frequently added appropriate inscriptions referring to the brevity of life. Ruysch wrote a description (in both Dutch and Latin) of his collection in a series of ten books: *Thesaurus anatomicus primus* through *Thesaurus anatomicus decimus*. In 1715 he announced the sale of his collection. But no buyers presented themselves before 1717, when Peter the Great bought it for 30,000 guilders. It was carefully packed and transported by boat to Russia. The tale that the collection was destroyed by the sailors drinking the embalming fluid seems not to be true, or at least only partly so. Several pieces of the collection (for example, skeletons of children) are held by the Museum of the Academy of Sciences in Leningrad; the collection originally contained 935 items. Immediately after the sale, the energetic Ruysch, age seventy-nine, began to set up a new collection, which, after his death, was sold publicly. The greater part of it went to the king of Poland, John Sobieski, who entrusted it to the University of Wittenberg.

Ruysch had many friends and admirers, but also several critics with whom he became involved in scientific polemics—namely, G. Bidloo, J. J. Rau, and R. Vieussens. Boerhaave, his junior by thirty years, was a close friend. Ruysch visited Boerhaave at Leiden, and the latter seems to have passed several summer holidays with Ruysch. The friends' opinions diverged on some points of anatomy, including the structure of the glands. Ruysch rejected the view of Malpighi that the liver contains glandular tissue (parenchyma). Boerhaave supposed that Ruysch was misled by injecting the embalming fluid under too great a pressure. In 1721 the two friends published together two letters on the subject—*Opusculum anatomicum de fabrica glandularum.*

In addition to the valves in the lymph vessels, Ruysch described, independently of others, the arteria bronchialis. He also studied the eye and described a thin layer behind the retina (formerly called tunica Ruyschiana), as well as a circular muscle in the fundus uteri.

Foreign honors came relatively late to Ruysch. In 1705 he became a member of the Academia Leopoldo-Carolina. He was also elected to the Royal Society of London (1720) and to the Acadé-mie des Sciences (1727) in Newton's place. At the end of his life Ruysch suffered a fracture of the collum femoris. The site of his grave is not known.

BIBLIOGRAPHY

I. ORIGINAL WORKS. Ruysch's major works are *Disputatio medica inauguralis de pleuritide* (Leiden, 1664); *Dilucidatio valvularum in vasis lymphaticis et lacteis* (The Hague, 1665; Leiden, 1667; Amsterdam, 1720, 2nd ed. 1742); a facs. of the 1665 ed., with intro. by A. M. Luyendijk-Elshout, appeared in Dutch Classics on the History of Science, no. 11 (Nieuwkoop, 1964); *Epistolae anatomicae problematicae*, 14 vols. (Amsterdam, 1696–1701); *Museum anatomicum Ruyschianum, sive catalogus rariorum quae in Authoris aedibus asservantur* (Amsterdam, 1691; 2nd ed., 1721; 3rd ed. 1737); *Thesaurus anatomicus . . . ,* 10 vols. (Amsterdam, 1701–1716), all with Dutch trans.; *Curae posteriores seu thesaurus anatomicus omnium precedentium maximus* (Amsterdam, 1724); and *Curae renovatae seu thesaurus anatomicus post curas posteriores novus* (Amsterdam, 1733).

Other writings are *Observationum anatomico-chirurgicarum centuria* (Amsterdam, 1691; 2nd ed., 1721; 3rd ed., 1737); *Thesaurus animalium primus* (Amsterdam, 1728); *Responsio ad Godefridi Bidloi libellum cui nomen vindicias inscripsit* (Amsterdam, 1697; 2nd ed., 1738); *Adversariorum anatomico-medico-chirurgicorum decas prima* (Amsterdam, 1717; 2nd ed., 1729), *decas secunda* (1720), *decas tertia* (1728); *Opusculum anatomicum de fabrica glandularum in corpore humano* (Leiden, 1722; Amsterdam, 1733), written with Boerhaave; *Tractatio anatomica de musculo in fundo uteri* (Amsterdam, 1723), with Dutch trans. by A. Lambrechts as *Over de baarmoeder-, of de ronde spier van de lijfmoeder* (Amsterdam, 1726; 2nd ed., 1731); *Opera omnia,* 4 vols. (Amsterdam, 1721); *Opera omnia anatomico-medico-chirurgica huc usque edita,* 5 vols. (Amsterdam, 1737); *Alle de ontleed- genees- en heelkundige werken van Fr. Ruysch* (Amsterdam, 1744), Dutch trans. by Y. G. Arlebout; and *Horti medici Amstelodamensis rariorum descriptio . . .* (Amsterdam, 1697), written with F. Kiggelaar.

II. SECONDARY LITERATURE. On Ruysch and his work, see Bernard Fontenelle, "Éloge de M. Ruysch," in *Histoire de l'Académie royale des sciences pour l'année 1731 avec les mémoires de mathématique et physique pour la même année, tirés des registres de cette Académie;* N. T. Hazen, "Johnson's Life of Frederic Ruysch," in *Bulletin of the History of Medicine,* **7** (1939), 324; J. G. de Lint, "Frederik Ruysch," in *Nieuw Nederlandsch Biographisch Woordenboek,* III, 1108–1109; A. M. Luyendijk-Elshout's intro. to the facs. ed. of the *Dilucidatio valvularum* (see above); P. Scheltema, "Het leven van Frederik Ruysch" (M.D. diss., Univ. of

Leiden, 1886); and V. F. Schreiber's intro. to the *Opera omnia* (see above), also in the Dutch translation.

G. A. LINDEBOOM

RYDBERG, JOHANNES (JANNE) ROBERT (*b.* Halmstad, Sweden, 8 November 1854; *d.* Lund, Sweden, 28 December 1919), *mathematics, physics.*

Rydberg was the son of Sven R. and Maria Anderson Rydberg. After completing the Gymnasium at Halmstad in 1873, he entered the University of Lund, from which he received a bachelor's degree in philosophy in 1875. He continued his studies at Lund and was granted a doctorate in mathematics in 1879 after defending a dissertation on the construction of conic sections. In 1880 Rydberg was appointed a lecturer in mathematics. After some work on frictional electricity, he was named lecturer in physics in 1882 and was promoted to assistant at the Physics Institute in 1892. Rydberg married Lydia E. M. Carlsson in 1886; they had two daughters and a son. After provisionally occupying the professorship in physics at Lund from 1897, he was granted the appointment permanently in March 1901 and held it until November 1919. He was elected a foreign member of the Royal Society in 1919.

Rydberg's most significant scientific contributions were to spectroscopy; but his involvement with spectra had its origin in his interest in the periodic system of the elements, an interest that endured throughout his professional life. His earliest published papers in physics dealt with the periodic table. In the introduction to his major work on spectra (1890), he stated that he considered it only a part of a broader investigation, the goal of which was to achieve a more exact knowledge of the nature and constitution of the chemical and physical properties of the elements. He held that the effective force between atoms must be a periodic function of their atomic weights and that the periodic motions of the atoms, which presumably gave rise to the spectral lines and were dependent on the effective force, thus might be a fruitful study leading to a better knowledge of the mechanics, nature, and structure of atoms and molecules and to a deeper understanding of the periodic system of the other physical and chemical properties of the elements. In line with contemporary conceptions, Rydberg's view was that each individual line spectrum was the product of a single fundamental system of vibrations.

His major spectral work, "Recherches sur la constitution des spectres d'émission des éléments chimiques," published in 1890, mapped out Rydberg's total approach with remarkable clarity. He conceived of the spectrum of an element as composed of the superposition of three different types of series—one in which the lines were comparatively sharp, one in which the lines were more diffuse, and a third that he called principal series even though they consisted mostly of lines in the ultraviolet. The first lines were located in the visible spectrum and were usually the most intense. The members of each series might be single, double, triple, or of higher multiplicity. Any particular elementary spectrum might contain any number (even zero) of series of each of the basic types.

While Rydberg observed and measured some spectral lines on his own, he was not particularly noted as an experimental physicist and did not publish any of his experimental investigations or spectroscopic measurements. Most of the data he needed were already available in the voluminous literature. While T. R. Thalén and Bernhard Hasselberg, Rydberg's major Swedish contemporaries in spectral studies, concentrated upon accurate measurements of the spectra of the elements, Rydberg's major spectral contributions were to theory and mathematical form, and those to form were the ones of enduring value.

Unlike most others, Rydberg used wave numbers (the number of waves per unit length) instead of a correlated reciprocal, the directly measured wavelengths. This enabled him to manipulate his final formula into a particularly useful form.

Rydberg concluded that each series could be expressed approximately by an equation of the form

$$n = n_0 - \frac{N_0}{(m+\mu)^2},$$

where n was the wave number of a line; $N_0 = 109,721.6$, a constant common to all series and to all elements; n_0 and μ constants peculiar to the series; and m any positive integer (the number of the term). The lines of a series were generated by allowing m to take on integer values sequentially; n_0 defined the limit of the series that the wave number n approached when m became very large.

Just when he became occupied with confirming this relationship, Rydberg learned about Balmer's formula, which represented the observed lines of the hydrogen spectrum with extraordinary accuracy. He arranged Balmer's formula into its wave-number form and noted that, with appropriately selected constants, it was then a special form of his own more general formula. He felt that the success of Balmer's formula strengthened the justification of his own form. Thus encouraged, Rydberg proceeded to use the latter with sufficient success to propose it as the general formula for all series in all elementary line spectra, and to conclude that N_0 was indeed a universal constant, which has since become known as Rydberg's constant.

Spectroscopy had been a major developed field of physical study for several decades, but its most pressing need near the end of the nineteenth century was for the organization of its vast amount of data into some mathematically ordered form that theoreticians might find useful in their attempts to understand the underlying significance of spectra. Rydberg's general formula was the most important presentation of this type. Many others groped in the same general direction, mostly with ephemeral results. Rydberg's most significant competitors in this regard were Heinrich Kayser and Carl Runge, but their general formulas were of significantly different form.

The scope and structure of Rydberg's formula allowed him to note some important relationships. For example, he found not only that certain series with different values of μ exhibited the same value of n_0 but also that the value of the constant term n_0 in any series coincided with a member of the sequence of variable terms in some other series of the element. In particular, he discovered that the difference between the common limit of the diffuse and sharp series and the limit of the corresponding principal series gave the wave number of the common first-member term of the sharp and principal series, a relationship independently noted by Arthur Schuster and commonly known as the Rydberg-Schuster law.

Along this same line, Rydberg speculatively suggested as a comprehensive formula for every line of an element the relationship

$$\pm n = \frac{N_0}{(m_1 + \mu_1)^2} - \frac{N_0}{(m_2 + \mu_2)^2},$$

with which he hoped to represent a series according to whether he assumed either m_1 or m_2 to be variable. Thus, he viewed every spectral series as a set of differences between two terms of the type $N_0/(m + \mu)^2$ — that is, every spectral line would be expressed as $n = T_1 - T_2$, where T_1 and T_2 are two members of a set of terms characteristic of the element. This aspect, little appreciated at the time,

was stated independently in 1908 by Walther Ritz and is commonly known as the Ritz combination principle.

The combination principle revealed several significant features about spectra. First, the wave number of each line could be conveniently represented as the difference between two numbers, called terms. Second, the terms could be naturally grouped into ordered sequences — the terms of each sequence converging toward zero. Third, the terms could be combined in various ways to give the wave numbers of the spectral lines. Fourth, a series of lines all having similar character resulted from the combination of all terms of one sequence taken in succession with a fixed term of another sequence. Thus, fifth, a large number of spectral lines could be expressed as the differences of a much smaller number of terms that in some way were characteristic of the atom and therefore, from a theoretical perspective, were more important than the lines themselves when speculating on atomic structure. Now it was these terms, rather than the lines, for which a direct physical interpretation should be found. This last point was widely overlooked by most contemporary physicists, including Rydberg.

As deeply as the notion of the existence of some fundamental mechanism might be stimulated by them, all the regularities noted by Rydberg were in themselves only empirical generalizations. His own theoretical concepts on atomic structure were still based on an analogy to acoustics. Therefore, Rydberg did not reach the final goal he had set for his work: an adequate insight into the nature and structure of the atom. His work did, however, provide a basis for the later development of successful ideas on atomic structure.

Some radically new ideas concerning the structure of the atom resulted from the development of other lines of evidence. In 1913 Niels Bohr proposed his theory of atomic structure based on Ernest Rutherford's nuclear atomic model and on Max Planck's quantum theory of radiation. These conceptions led to the first reasonably successful theoretical account of spectral data.

Bohr's view provided an immediate interpretation of the combination principle by identifying each Rydberg spectral term multiplied by hc (Planck's constant times the speed of light) with the energy of an allowable stationary state of the atom. The difference between two such states equaled the energy in the light quantum emitted in the transition from a higher allowable atomic-energy state to a lower one.

On this basis, spectral series were used to determine the excitation energies and ionization potentials of atoms. The further elaboration of these views led to a classification of the states of electron binding in a shell structure of the atoms that accounted for the periodic relationships of the properties of the elements, thereby fully justifying Rydberg's earlier faith that spectral studies could assist in attaining this goal. Rydberg played no role in this elaboration, however.

But earlier, along similar lines, Rydberg's study of the periodic properties of the elements led him in 1897 to suggest that certain characteristics of the elements could be more simply organized by using an atomic number instead of the atomic weights. This atomic number was to be identified with the ordinal index of the element in the periodic table. In 1906 Rydberg stated for the first time that 2, 8, and 18 (that is, $2n^2$, where $n = 1,2,3$) represented the number of elements in the early periods of the system. In 1913 he went further, correcting an earlier error about the number of rare earths from 36 to 32, thus allowing the $n = 4$ group to be included in the pattern.

Rydberg presented a spiral graph arrangement of the periodic table in which earlier holes in his system were corrected so that atomic numbers from helium on were two greater than at present. He maintained that there were two elements, nebulium and coronium, between hydrogen and helium in the system, supporting their existence by evidence from both spectra and graphical symmetry.

In 1913, H. G. J. Moseley published his paper based on researches on the characteristic X-ray spectra of the elements that strongly supported the fundamental importance of atomic numbers and Rydberg's basic expectations about the lengths of the periods of the periodic table. The physical reality that underlay Rydberg's atomic-number proposal was later interpreted as the positive charge on the atomic nucleus expressed in elementary units of charge.

Rydberg received a copy of Moseley's paper in manuscript form before publication. In a note written in 1914, he expressed satisfaction at the confirmation of his ideas on atomic numbers and the details of the periodic system, but he still maintained his conviction of the existence of the two elements between hydrogen and helium and the resulting difference of two in most atomic numbers. Later the nebulium spectrum was attributed to ionized oxygen and nitrogen, and the coronium lines to highly ionized iron.

Rydberg's health did not permit him to follow subsequent developments. In 1914 he became seriously ill. He went on an extended leave of absence that lasted until his formal retirement in 1919, a month before his death.

BIBLIOGRAPHY

I. ORIGINAL WORKS. Rydberg's most important spectral publication was "Recherches sur la constitution des spectres d'émission des éléments chimiques," in *Kungliga Svenska vetenskapsakademiens handlingar*, n.s. **23**, no. 11 (1890). Some of his other spectral works of significance are "On the Structure of the Line-Spectra of the Chemical Elements," in *Philosophical Magazine*, 5th ser., **29** (1890), 331–337; "Contributions à la connaissance des spectres linéaires," in *Ofversigt af K. Vetenskapsakademiens förhandlingar*, **50** (1893), 505–520, 677–691; "The New Elements of Cleveite Gas," in *Astrophysical Journal*, **4** (1896), 91–96; "The New Series in the Spectrum of Hydrogen," *ibid.*, **6** (1897), 233–238; "On the Constitution of the Red Spectrum of Argon," *ibid.*, 338–348; and "La distribution des raies spectrales," in *Rapports présentés au Congrès international de physique, Paris*, II (1900), 200–224.

Concerning his other work related to the periodic table, significant articles are "Die Gesetze der Atomgewichtszahlen," in *Bihang till K. Svenska vetenskapsakademiens handlingar*, **11**, no. 13 (1886); "Studien über die Atomgewichtszahlen," in *Zeitschrift für anorganische Chemie*, **14** (1897), 66–102; *Elektron der erste Grundstoff* (Berlin, 1906); "Untersuchungen über das System der Grundstoffe," in *Acta Universitatis lundensis*, Avd. 2, n.s. **9**, no. 18 (1913); and "The Ordinals of the Elements and the High-Frequency Spectra," in *Philosophical Magazine*, 6th ser., **28** (1914), 144–148.

II. SECONDARY LITERATURE. A short biography of value is Manne Siegbahn, in *Swedish Men of Science 1650–1950*, Sten Lindroth, ed., Burnett Anderson, trans. (Stockholm, 1952), 214–218. Siegbahn was a student at the University of Lund from 1906 to 1911 and an assistant at the Physics Institute from 1911 to 1914 while Rydberg was there. In the autumn of 1915 Siegbahn was appointed to fulfill Rydberg's duties while the latter went on an extended leave. In early 1920 Siegbahn permanently succeeded Rydberg in the chair of physics at Lund.

On the centenary of Rydberg's birth, an important collection of papers was presented at Lund: "Proceedings of the Rydberg Centennial Conference on Atomic Spectroscopy," in *Acta Universitatis lundensis*, Avd. 2, n.s. **50**, no. 21 (1954). Biographically, the two most significant articles are Niels Bohr, "Rydberg's Discovery of the Spectral Laws," 15–21; and Wolfgang Pauli, "Rydberg and the Periodic System of the Elements," 22–26.

Another biographical essay of merit is Sister St. John Nepomucene, "Rydberg: The Man and the Constant," in *Chymia*, **6** (1960), 127–145. Two brief biographical obituaries are in *Physikalische Zeitschrift,* **21** (1920), 113; and *Nature,* **105** (1920), 525.

C. L. MAIER

SABATIER, ARMAND (*b.* Ganges, Hérault, France, 14 January 1834; *d.* Montpellier, Hérault, France, 22 December 1910), *comparative anatomy, philosophy.*

Sabatier's parents were dedicated Protestants. They closely supervised Armand's early education in the schools of his native town. Later he was admitted to the study of medicine at the nearby University of Montpellier, where the Faculty of Medicine was one of the oldest in Europe. His early interest in anatomy continued throughout his life.

In 1855 Sabatier was appointed assistant in anatomy at Montpellier. In 1858 he obtained an internship in Lyons. He subsequently returned to Montpellier to present his doctoral thesis. He worked in the department of anatomy and in 1869 was made associate professor. During the Franco-Prussian war, he served with distinction in command of a field ambulance. In 1873 he was associate professor and in 1876 professor of zoology in the Faculty of Sciences at Montpellier.

Sabatier's book on the heart and circulation in vertebrates (1873) immediately established his reputation as an anatomist. He made a detailed investigation of the cardiac morphology and physiology of amphibians and reptiles and from this research established the general laws that govern the functional evolution of the heart from fishes to mammals. He showed that these laws apply not only to the zoological series but also to the developing embryo. But he insisted that such parallelism between phylogenesis and ontogenesis should not be viewed too strictly. He did not intend the eventual deviation from this parallelism as evidence against the evolutionary doctrine.

Sabatier also compared the thoracic and pelvic girdles in the vertebrate series. He based this comparison on muscle insertions, which appear to be similar along the vertebrate series and to exhibit a certain similarity among bony structures. This work resolved several lengthy debates, including that on the significance in man of the coracoid process. He demonstrated that this structure is analogous to the pubis of the pelvic girdle.

Throughout his life Sabatier was interested in comparative osteology. He was also an excellent zoologist and cytologist. In such a commonplace mollusk as the mussel, he elucidated many unknown features of the circulatory system. He also investigated egg and sperm formations in various invertebrate groups and in the lower vertebrates. Although some of his conclusions have been challenged, many of his observations remain valid, and in some cases might (with modern techniques) be the starting point of fertile investigations.

In 1879 Sabatier founded one of the earliest marine laboratories—the Station Zoologique de Sète, which he installed for some years in the modest surroundings of a fisherman's cabin. Public support of marine stations was difficult to obtain in those days, but Sabatier's persistent efforts to win funds succeeded seventeen years later, when the station was finally given a well-equipped laboratory. But even when its facilities were modest, the laboratory was an active institution, and Sabatier trained many young marine biologists there.

Sabatier's mind inclined toward philosophy. He was a Christian of firm beliefs and a biologist of equally firm adherence to evolutionary doctrines. In two important books he brilliantly defended the compatibility of these two positions. In his *Philosophie de l'effort . . .* he maintained that man's striving toward a saintly or simply moral life furthers the survival of the species.

BIBLIOGRAPHY

I. ORIGINAL WORKS. Sabatier's works include *Études sur le coeur et la circulation centrale dans la série des vertébrés. Anatomie, physiologie comparée, philosophie naturelle* (Paris–Montpellier, 1873); "Sur quelques points de l'anatomie de la Moule commune," in *Comptes rendus hebdomadaires des séances de l'Académie des sciences,* **79** (1874), 581–584; "Sur les cils musculoïdes de la Moule commune," *ibid.,* **81** (1875), 1060–1063; "Études sur la Moule commune (Mytilus edulis)," in *Mémoires de l'Académie de Montpellier, section des sciences,* **8** (1879), 413–506; "Comparaison des ceintures et des membres antérieurs et postérieurs dans la série des vertébrés," *ibid.,* **9** (1878), 277–336, **9** (1879), 337–709; "Appareil respiratoire des ampullaires," in *Comptes rendus hebdomadaires des séances de l'Académie des sciences,* **88** (1879), 1325–1328; "Formation du blastoderme chez les aranéides," *ibid.,* **92** (1881), 200–204; "La spermatogénèse chez les Annélides et les vertébrés," *ibid.,* **94** (1882), 172–175; "De la spermatogénèse chez les plagiostomes et les amphibiens," *ibid.,* **94** (1882), 1097–1100; "De l'ovogénèse chez les ascidiens," *ibid.,* **96** (1883), 799–802; "Sur les cellules du follicule de l'oeuf et sur la nature de la sexualité," *ibid.,* **96** (1883), 1804–1807; "Sur le noyau vitellin des aranéides," *ibid.,* **97** (1883), 1570–1573.

Later writings are "Sur la spermatogenèse des crustacés décapodes," in *Comptes rendus hebdomadaires des séances de l'Académie des sciences,* **100** (1885), "Sur la morphologie de l'ovaire chez les insectes," *ibid.,* **102** (1886), 61–64; "Recherches sur l'oeuf des ascidiens," in *Mémoires de l'Académie de Montpellier, section des sciences,* **10** (1885), 429–480; "Recueil de mémoires sur la morphologie des éléments sexuels et sur la nature de la sexualité," in *Travaux du laboratoire de zoologie de la Faculté des sciences de Montpellier et de la station zoologique de Sète,* **5** (1886), 1–271; "Sur les formes de spermatozoïdes de l'elédone musquée," in *Comptes rendus hebdomadaires des séances de l'Académie des sciences,* **106** (1888), 954–957; "Sur la station zoologique de Sète," *ibid.,* **109** (1889), 388–391; "La Spermatogenèse chez les locustides," *ibid.,* **111** (1890), 797–800; and "Sur quelques points de la spermatogenèse chez les sélaciens," *ibid.,* **120** (1895), 47–50.

See also "De la spermatogenèse chez les poissons sélaciens," in *Mémoires de l'Académie de Montpellier, section des sciences,* **2** (1896), 53–237; "Morphologie des membres des poissons osseux," in *Comptes rendus hebdomadaires des séances de l'Académie des sciences,* **122** (1896), 121–124; "Morphologie du sternum et des clavicules," *ibid.,* **124** (1897), 805–808; *ibid.,* 932–935; "Sur la signification morphologique des os en chevrons des vertébres caudales," *ibid.,* 932–935, written with Ducamp and Petit; "Etude des huîtres de Sète au point de vue des microbes pathogènes," *ibid.,* **125** (1897), 685–688, written with Ducamp and Petit; "Sur la genèse des épithéliums," *ibid.,* **127** (1898), 704–707, written with M. E. de Rouville; "Morphologie des ceintures et des membres pairs et impairs des sélaciens," *ibid.,* 928–932; "Morphologie de la ceinture pelvienne des amphibiens," *ibid.,* **130** (1900), 633–637; "Sur les mains scapulaires et pelviennes des poissons," *ibid.,* **137** (1903), 893–894; "Sur les mains scapulaires et pelviennes chez les poissons chondroptérygiens," *ibid.,* 1216–1220; and "Sur les mains scapulaires et pelviennes des poissons holocéphales et dipneustes," *ibid.,* **138** (1904), 249–253.

Sabatier's philosophical works are *Essai sur l'immortalité au point du vue de naturalisme évolutionniste,* (Paris, 1895); and *Philosophie de l'effort. Essais philosophiques d'un naturaliste* (Paris, 1903).

A. M. MONNIER

SABATIER, PAUL (*b.* Carcassonne, France, 5 November 1854; *d.* Toulouse, France, 14 August 1941), *chemistry.*

Sabatier achieved scientific distinction for his pioneering work in catalysis. From a family of modest means, he had his secondary education at Carcassonne and then at Toulouse. Admitted to the École Normale Supérieure in 1874, he received the *agrégé* in the physical sciences in 1877 and was first in his class. He taught briefly at the *lycée* of Nîmes, then, encouraged by Berthelot, entered the latter's laboratory at the Collège de France in 1878 and received his doctorate in the physical sciences in 1880. After a year at Bordeaux, Sabatier taught at Toulouse, where he was named to the chair of chemistry in 1884, when he was thirty, the minimum age for the post.

In 1907 Sabatier was offered Moissan's chair at the Sorbonne and that of Berthelot at the Collège de France. Although he realized that all candidates for the Académie des Sciences were required to be residents of Paris, he nevertheless chose to remain at Toulouse. In 1912 he shared the Nobel prize in chemistry with Victor Grignard, and in 1913 he became the first scientist elected to one of six chairs newly created by the Academy for provincial members. At this time Sabatier also was dean of the Faculty of Sciences at Toulouse, a post he held officially from 1905 to 1929. He was instrumental in founding three schools of applied science at Toulouse—in chemistry, electrical engineering, and agriculture. Both by personal example and by administrative action, Sabatier was throughout his life an important influence in steps toward the decentralization of scientific institutions in France.

Sabatier's initial researches were inorganic studies within the thermochemical tradition of Berthelot's laboratory. They included analyses of metallic and alkaline-earth sulfides and of chlorides, the preparation of hydrogen disulfide by vacuum distillation, the isolation of selenides of boron and silicon, the definition of basic cupric salts containing four copper atoms, and preparations of the deep blue nitrosodisulfonic acid and the basic mixed argentocupric salts. He studied the partition of a base between two acids, using the spectrophotometric change of coloration of chromates and dichromates as an indicator of acidity, and analyzed the velocity of transformation of metaphosphoric acid. In 1895 Sabatier had begun the preparation of metals by reduction of their oxides with hydrogen, when he noted with interest British chemists' preparation of nickel carbonyl by the direct action of carbon monoxide on finely divided nickel. Wondering if other unsaturated gaseous molecules might behave analogously to carbon monoxide, he succeeded in 1896 in fixing nitrogen peroxide on copper, cobalt, nickel, and iron.

Sabatier then learned that Moissan and Charles Moureu had failed to achieve a similar result with acetylene. Assured that they did not intend to pursue the experiment, he repeated it with the less violent hydrocarbon ethylene, heating an oxide of nickel to 300°C. in a current of hydrogen gas and then directing a current of ethylene upon the slivers of reduced nickel. He found that the resulting gaseous product was not hydrogen, as Moissan had assumed, but mostly ethane resulting from the hydrogenation of ethylene. Sabatier then succeeded in oxidizing acetylene to ethylene and ethane, and in 1901 attempted the transformation of benzene into cyclohexane. Berthelot had failed to do this with a hydriodic-acid hydrogenation agent, but Sabatier succeeded with benzene vapors and hydrogen over reduced nickel at 200°C.

In the next years Sabatier continued this work on hydrogenating organic compounds in the presence of finely disintegrated metals, for which he was awarded the 1912 Nobel Prize. Assisted by his student J. B. Senderens, Sabatier demonstrated the general applicability of his method to the hydrogenation of nonsaturated and aromatic carbides, ketones, aldehydes, phenols, nitriles, and nitrate derivatives. He synthesized methane from carbon monoxide, and demonstrated that at higher temperatures his hydrogenation procedures would lead to dehydrogenation, applying this principle to the production of aldehydes and ketones from their corresponding primary and secondary alcohols. Sabatier established that certain metallic oxides, particularly manganous oxide, behave analogously to metals in hydrogenation and dehydrogenation, although at slower rates; and that powdered oxides such as thoria, alumina, and silica possess hydration and dehydration properties. For example, reduced copper acts as a catalyst for splitting alcohol vapors into hydrogen and aldehyde, whereas replacing copper with alumina results in a division of alcohol into water and ethylene.

Sabatier's *La catalyse en chimie organique* first appeared in 1913, its utility enhanced by a principally empirical and analogical approach. His theory of catalytic mechanism, later termed "chemisorption," strongly opposed that of most nineteenth-century chemists. Berzelius, Ostwald, and others had assumed that known catalyzed reactions—such as the effect of platinum on the combustion of hydrogen and oxygen—resulted from an absorption of gases in the cavities of the porous metal, where compression and local temperature elevation led to chemical combination.

In contrast, Sabatier believed that in both homogeneous and heterogeneous systems, a temporary, unstable intermediary between the catalyst and one of the reactants forms on the surface of the catalyst. The intermediary's combination with the second reactant regenerates the catalyst. Like his predecessors' theory, Sabatier's view implied that the activity of a catalyst increases with its granular surface area; he thus also accounted for poisoning of a catalyst by impurities and for fatigue by surface modifications. But unlike his predecessors, Sabatier indicated that the course of a reaction would depend upon the chemical as well as the physical nature of the catalyst, a contention supported by his ability to manipulate the products of a reaction by substituting one catalyst for another (an oxide for a metal, for example). His view also predicted the empirically verified facts that a catalyst of hydrogenation will be equally one of dehydrogenation, and that promoters of catalysis are often the same types of material as inhibitors or poisons.

Although his work laid the foundation for many of the giant industries of the twentieth century, Sabatier paid little or no attention to the practical applications of his discoveries. He had no interest in liquid-phase hydrogenation and avoided high-pressure hydrogenation techniques. He obtained a few French patents, including one of 1909, which envisioned means of cracking heavy fractions of petroleum on a metal catalyst and then hydrogenating the volatile products.

BIBLIOGRAPHY

I. ORIGINAL WORKS. Sabatier's most important publication was *La catalyse en chimie organique* (Paris, 1913; 2nd ed., 1920). E. Emmet Reid's translation, *Catalysis in Organic Chemistry* (New York, 1923), has been revised and reprinted in *Catalysis Then and Now* (Palisades Park, N.J., 1965), which contains numerous references to Sabatier's papers on catalysis. His two other major publications were his thesis, *Recherches thermiques sur les sulfures* (Paris, 1880) and *Leçons élémentaires de chimie agricole* (Paris, 1890). His 1926 address before the American Chemical Society in Cincinnati, Ohio, records his recollections about his work: "How I Have Been Led to the Direct Hydrogenation Method by Metallic Catalysts," in *Industrial and Engineering Chemistry*, **18** (Oct. 1926), 1005–1008.

II. SECONDARY LITERATURE. There is no biography of Sabatier other than Lucien Babonneau's "Paul Sabatier," in *Génies occitans de la science* (Toulouse, 1947), 167–189. Other discussions of his life and work are in Gabriel Bertrand, Charles Camichel, *et al.*, *Cérémonies du centenaire de la naissance de Paul Sabatier à Toulouse* (Hendaye, 1954); Charles Camichel, Gaston Dupouy *et al.*, *Centenaire Paul Sabatier. Prix Nobel. Membre de l'Institut. 1854–1954* (Toulouse, 1956); and J. R. Partington, "Paul Sabatier," in *Nature*, **174** (1954), 859–860.

MARY JO NYE

SABIN, FLORENCE RENA (*b*. Central City, Colorado, 9 November 1871; *d*. Denver, Colorado, 3 October 1953), *anatomy, immunology*.

The second daughter of Serena M. and George K. Sabin, who had given up the study of medicine to work in the Colorado mines, Florence Sabin attended schools in Denver and Vermont. She followed her sister Mary to Smith College and concentrated on mathematics and science, receiving the B.S. degree in 1893. While at Smith she became interested in women's rights and also decided to study medicine. The year she received her Smith degree, the Johns Hopkins Medical School opened with the financial help of a group of Baltimore women who stipulated that women be admitted on the same basis as men. Sabin taught mathematics for two years in Denver and zoology for a year at Smith to earn sufficient money to continue her education. She then matriculated at Johns Hopkins Medical School in the fall of 1896.

Sabin began her career in medical research under the stimulus and guidance of Franklin P. Mall, professor of anatomy at the Johns Hopkins Medical School. While still a student she undertook to construct a three-dimensional model of the mid- and lower brain. Her work was published as *An Atlas of the Medulla and Midbrain* in 1901 and quickly became a popular text. Also in 1901, a year after receiving the M.D. degree, she was appointed to a fellowship in anatomy after completion of an internship. She thus began a twenty-five-year academic association with Johns Hopkins. When she became an assistant in anatomy in 1902, Sabin had the distinction of becoming the first woman faculty member at the school. She was the first woman to achieve professorial rank at the Hopkins Medical School when she was promoted to professor of histology in 1917. Three similar distinctions occurred in 1924–1925, when she became the first woman elected president of the American Association of Anatomists, the first woman elected to the National Academy of Sciences, and the first woman to become a full member of the Rockefeller Institute.

In her early Johns Hopkins years, Sabin worked on the origins of blood cells and the lymphatics. Understanding of the anatomy of the lymph channels was vague at the time. Particularly under debate were the relationship of the smallest lymphatics to the tissue spaces and the embryonic origins of the lymph vessels. One theory held that the lymphatics arose from the tissue spaces and grew toward the veins. The opposing view was that they arose from the veins directly, by a series of small endothelial buds. Using small pig embryos rather than the larger ones used by earlier investigators, Sabin was able to show that the latter view was the correct one.

On numerous summer trips to German laboratories, Sabin learned and brought back techniques. One of the most important of these was supravital staining, the staining of living cells. She used this method in studies on the cellular reaction in tuberculosis and work on the site of antibody production. In 1925 Sabin left her teaching position in Baltimore to establish a laboratory at the Rockefeller Institute in New York that was devoted to the cellular aspects of the immune response. She worked especially with the large mononuclear white blood cells (monocytes), showing their role in the antigen-antibody reaction, a subject not yet fully understood fifty years later.

After thirteen years as a member of the Rockefeller Institute, Sabin became emeritus in 1938 and retired to Denver. She remained active on several national boards; but not until 1944, when she was asked to head a subcommittee on health for the governor's Post War Planning Committee, did she again work with her usual vigor and efficiency. Colorado had long prided itself as a health resort, and thus it came as a shock when the Sabin Committee began to publicize its findings. The state health department was an ineffective, politically controlled body, and its lack of efficiency and power was reflected in some of the worst health statistics of any state in the nation. Sabin worked tirelessly for the passage of new health laws. In 1947, the year of their passage, she was appointed chairman of the Interim Board of Health and Hospitals of Denver, a post she held until 1951, her eightieth year.

BIBLIOGRAPHY

I. ORIGINAL WORKS. Sabin's numerous scientific papers appeared for the most part in anatomical journals, *Science,* and publications of the institutions where she worked. Besides *An Atlas of the Medulla and Midbrain* (Baltimore, 1901), she contributed a widely cited chapter on the lymphatics to Franz Keibel and Franklin P. Mall's *Manual of Human Embryology,* II (Philadelphia, 1912), 709–745, that also appeared as *The Origin and Development of the Lymphatic System* (Baltimore, 1913). *Franklin Paine Mall, the Story of a Mind* (Baltimore, 1934) is the standard biography of Mall and reveals much about Sabin's attitudes as well.

II. SECONDARY LITERATURE. The most complete book about Sabin is Elinor Bluemel's *Florence Sabin, Colorado Woman of the Century* (Boulder, Colo.,

1959). Mary K. Phelan, *Probing the Unknown* (New York, 1969), is for younger readers. The best treatment of Sabin's scientific contributions is Philip D. McMaster and Michael Heidelberger, "Florence Rena Sabin," in *Biographical Memoirs. National Academy of Sciences,* **34** (1960), 271–305. See also Vincent T. Andriole, "Florence Rena Sabin—Teacher, Scientist, Citizen," in *Journal of the History of Medicine and Allied Sciences,* **14** (1959), 320–350; George W. Corner, *A History of the Rockefeller Institute 1901–1953* (New York, 1964), 238–239; Lawrence S. Kubie, "Florence Rena Sabin, 1871–1953," in *Perspectives in Biology and Medicine,* **4** (1961), 306–315; John H. Talbott, *A Biographical History of Medicine* (New York, 1970), 1181–1183; and Edna Yost, *American Women of Science* (Philadelphia, 1943), 62–79.

GERT H. BRIEGER

SABINE, EDWARD (*b.* Dublin, Ireland, 14 October 1788; *d.* Richmond, Surrey, England, 26 June 1883), *geophysics.*

An artillery officer, Sabine was a graduate of the Royal Military Academy, Woolwich. While retaining his commission—Sabine eventually reached the rank of general—he started scientific work at the close of the Napoleonic Wars. On the recommendation of the Royal Society, he accompanied John Ross on an expedition to seek the Northwest Passage in 1818 and was with William Edward Parry on his 1819–1820 Arctic expedition. From the latter voyage, he said, came the idea of a great shipborne expedition of "physical discovery" to the southern hemisphere.

The Royal Society next sent Sabine on a pendulum expedition in 1821–1822 around the Atlantic to determine the true figure of the earth, a project that brought him the Copley Medal. A pattern was developing in his work, clearly of a Humboldtian nature—the gathering and analysis of geophysical data on a large, even global, scale. While the range of Sabine's interests was wide, terrestrial magnetism attracted most of his attention. In 1826 he and Babbage worked jointly on the subject in the British Isles, an ironic collaboration in view of subsequent events. In the 1830's Sabine, Humphrey Lloyd, James Clark Ross, and others completed the magnetic survey of the British Isles; Sabine repeated the survey in 1858–1861.

Sabine was distinguished from his many contemporaries who collected similar data by his successful promotion and administration of a world-wide effort to gather terrestrial magnetism observations, designated the "magnetic fever" or the "magnetic crusade" by observers. Basic to an understanding of his accomplishments are the scientific viewpoints he embodied and the strategic position he came to occupy in the politics of British science for nearly four decades.

As a follower of Christopher Hansteen, in contradiction to Gauss's later theories on terrestrial magnetism, Sabine believed in the existence of two magnetic poles in each hemisphere and that terrestrial magnetism was essentially the same as, or closely related to, atmospheric phenomena; the latter view was widely held in the first third of the nineteenth century. Humboldt and Arago, for example, assumed a connection between the earth's central heat, volcanic eruptions, and atmospheric electricity. Seebeck's work on thermoelectricity reinforced the belief in the relationship to meteorological phenomena. Sir John Herschel and Charles Babbage assumed that the atmospheric electricity arose from a thermoelectric interaction of sky and earth that, in turn, produced terrestrial magnetism by a kind of induction. Gauss (1839) flatly limited the origins of terrestrial magnetism to the surface or interior of the planet, much to Sabine's dismay. Yet when Faraday published a theory similar to Herschel's (1851), Sabine informed him that the data gathered in the "crusade" disclosed none of the predicted correlations. Sabine ruefully admitted to Faraday that he had consulted William Thomson, who verified Gauss's mathematics. Yet Gauss's views did not dampen Sabine's interest in atmospheric phenomena or stop his search for extraterrestrial effects.

Sabine was infuriated by the confusion of his scientific aims with what he considered the lesser goal of geographic discovery. His was the widely shared tradition of viewing the earth as a heavenly body, the physical processes of which required study with the spirit and precision devoted to other astronomical phenomena. In tacit opposition were other views challenging both Sabine's methods and his order of priorities. In the early years of the British Association, for example, the study of "magnetism" was included in the stated scopes of two separate committees, one on the chemical sciences and the other dominated by astronomy and meteorology.

The distinction was, thus, between experimental and observational sciences. When the Royal Society launched the "magnetic crusade," it had two committees (physics and meteorology) combined under the direction of Sir John Herschel. Faraday accidentally came to one subcommittee meeting on instrumentation for the magnetic observations but thereafter was conspicuously absent from its deliberations. Herschel dealt with the distinction between observational and experimental fields in the *Preliminary Discourse on the Study of Natural Philosophy*, giving preference to the former because they lacked the opportunity of simply recreating an artificial situation. Herschel further elevated geophysical problems above astronomical problems because the former were not simply cyclical but undergoing complex secular changes. A missed observation might be literally unrepeatable. Sabine was in complete agreement.

In 1839 the British dispatched an expedition to the southern hemisphere and established a network of magnetic and meteorological observatories. Sabine had a key role in both the origins and the consequences of these events. The "magnetic crusade" did not originate, as is sometimes stated, in an 1836 suggestion of Humboldt's or in a desire to test Gauss's *Allgemeine Theorie des Erdmagnetismus*. As early as 1805, on his return from the Americas, Humboldt disclosed the important fact that the intensity of terrestrial magnetism varied at different points on the earth, thereby stimulating further interest in what many regarded as the great remaining physical mystery since Newton's work on gravitation. In 1828 Humboldt suggested a worldwide system of observations, and by 1830 a rather rickety one existed, stretching from Germany to Peking. Although Gauss's interest in the subject went back many years, the 1833 announcement of the first method of obtaining an absolute measurement of magnetic intensity brought him into prominence among British magneticians. By 1835, at least, Gauss and Weber were in contact with G. B. Airy, Humphrey Lloyd, and Sabine. The last two were aware as early as 1837 that Gauss was working on a general theory; it appeared early in 1839, in volume III of the *Resultate aus den Beobachtungen des Magnetischen Vereins*, in time to add testing of the theory to the goals of the worldwide effort. Of greater impact were the new method and the fact that by 1836–1838 Gauss and Weber's Magnetische Verein had a sixteen-station net of observatories stretching from Dublin to St. Petersburg from east to west and from Uppsala to Catania in the north-south axis.

Both intellectual curiosity and nationalistic zeal motivated Sabine and his associates. They looked back to Halley's work for precedent and spoke frankly about a great scientific prize slipping into foreign hands. In 1834 Arago, clearly Humboldtian in his views, wrote to the British Association,

suggesting a British global effort, apparently unaware of Gauss's work. Having learned soon afterward of Gauss's method and the work of the Magnetische Verein, Sabine and others hesitated about siding with Gauss. His precise, large equipment was unsuitable for magnetic mapping of the oceans or the uses of scientific travelers. Sabine was also critical of the lack of observations of dip and inclination in the Gauss system. Unlike Herschel and Gauss, he was as interested in these aspects as in the intensity. Unlike Gauss and Herschel, Sabine believed that the routine periodic variations were as important as the readings for magnetic storms.

Originally an outsider to the British Association, Sabine was now very active there; and at the Dublin meeting of 1835 a resolution was passed calling on the government to send an expedition to the southern hemisphere and to open magnetic and meteorological observatories in the colonies. When this proved to no avail, Sabine convinced Humboldt in 1836 to write a letter to the duke of Sussex, the president of the Royal Society, calling for British action. For two years little happened outwardly, the Royal Society apparently being as unsuccessful as the British Association. From the surviving correspondence of participants, this was a period of intense politicking. Sabine was particularly anxious to avoid all pressures limiting the venture either to a voyage of discovery or to a series of fixed observatories. James Clark Ross was to head the former, and Humphrey Lloyd was to have charge of the theoretical work. Fellow artillery officers would staff the fixed observatories. From a scientific standpoint Sabine's most notable move was the publication of known intensity observations in the world (1837), which enabled Gauss to do the requisite calculations for the *Allgemeine Theorie*.

Yet the venture remained dormant in the Royal Society until John Herschel's return from South Africa in 1838. Although he once admitted to never having taken a magnetic reading, Herschel was generally interested in terrestrial magnetism. More important, he and Sabine were in complete agreement on the desirability of seizing this occasion to advance meteorology. Temperature and pressure readings were necessary, because they were sometimes responsible for greater effects on the compass needle than the earth's magnetism. Herschel also had great popular esteem and much influence with members of the government. At the British Association meeting at Newcastle-on-Tyne in 1838, he deftly swayed the crowd. Lloyd and Sabine went that year to Göttingen and Berlin to coordinate their coming venture with Gauss and Humboldt. On cue from Sabine and Herschel, Humboldt wrote a final letter to British officials, assuring the "crusade's" launching.

Originally the magnetic crusade was for three years, but Sabine very adroitly manipulated British and foreign opinion to get two successive three-year renewals. But disenchantment soon spread among former supporters. As early as 1839 Sabine aroused Lloyd's ire by taking over processing of the data, causing the latter to withdraw. Although the Royal Society at first refused to recognize Sabine's role, from 1841 to 1861 he maintained a staff at Woolwich for data reduction. Sabine's ambitions next clashed with Herschel's beliefs. The King's Observatory at Kew had been unused since Rigaud's death in 1839. Sabine wanted the facility to be the basic geophysical observatory for the empire, providing standard data and equipment for the colonial observatories. Neither Airy's Greenwich nor Lloyd's Dublin observatory would do. For three years the issue remained before the Royal Society while Sabine unsuccessfully tempted Herschel, who had long favored the founding of a facility combining geophysical observations, determination of standards, and physical experimentation. By 1842 the Royal Society had declined the offer of Kew because Herschel saw it as a limited observatory too narrowly tied to a particular venture. Sabine took the proposal to the British Association, which acquired the site in 1842 and managed the observatory until its 1871 transfer to the Royal Society. Sabine was very active in the management of Kew, which became a leading center for work in geophysics. From 1849 he was on the Kew Observatory Committee of the British Association, being particularly close to John Gassiot in its work.

Herschel early took exception to Sabine's seemingly endless compilation of data. The production of charts showing "lines of iso-x" aroused Herschel's ire; chartism, he called it. Not all facts were equally important, he insisted; and the data were not the ends, but merely the preliminaries to theory. Sabine, however, relished facts and was dubious of theoreticians' speculations.[1] In his view, the magnetic work was following the precedent of astronomy, a Baconian science in which accumulations of facts yielded sound theory. When the data from around the globe did not wholly validate Gauss, Sabine undoubtedly was pleased. Even more impressive was his discovery in 1851 of the relation between Schwabe's sunspot cycle and the periodicity of magnetic storms, even

though it was marred by a priority squabble with Johann von Lamont. It was a vindication of a long-held belief. In the same year Sabine announced his important finding that the daily magnetic variation consists of two superimposed variations, one deriving from within and the other from outside the earth.

Much of science in Victorian Britain, not merely geomagnetism and related topics, is explicable in terms of Sabine's career. He was the artful dodger of the British scientific establishment. Bright, energetic, shrewd, he could have been the very model of Gilbert and Sullivan's modern major general. Although his publications are properly specialized, Sabine's range of interests was quite broad, as is evident from his association with Gassiot and the work at Kew of Francis Ronalds, John Welsh, and Balfour Stewart. He even published pieces on Arctic ornithology and Eskimos. As a proper Humboldtian or even a Herschelian, Sabine considered geomagnetism an aspect of an interconnected nature. Such a man commanded respect, loyalty, and even affection. Yet his enthusiasm, verging on the fanatic, and his intellectual limitations became increasingly tyrannical as the climate of ideas changed and aging took its toll.

Quite early, Sabine disclosed a talent for influencing the influentials and slipping into strategic positions. This talent produced the greatest embarrassment of his career. A member of the Royal Society Council in 1828, he was named an adviser to the Admiralty, an appointment that aroused Babbage's ire. Two years later Babbage, in *Reflections on the Decline of Science in England,* accused Sabine of falsifying data. If we are to believe his anonymous necrologist, Sabine was at least guilty of great naïveté in handling numbers, hardly an auspicious start for a career involving vast quantities of worldwide data. Babbage's attack also placed Sabine in the awkward position of being seemingly outside the wave of the future in the politics of British science — in the camp of the old guard.

Ever resilient, Sabine became active in Babbage's creation, the British Association, when furthering terrestrial magnetism called for that move; and soon he was an officer. The pattern was fixed and quite simple. Sabine became entrenched in both the Royal Society and the British Association, shifting programs adroitly from one to another to gain objectives, as in the cases of the magnetic crusade and the Kew observatory. Obstacles were evaded or removed. One suspects that more than coincidence was involved in Sabine's election as one of the general secretaries of the British Association at Newcastle in 1838 and the simultaneous resignation of Babbage as a trustee. Sabine remained a general secretary until 1859 with the exception of 1852, when he was president of the British Association. At various times in that period (1841–1861), in addition to Council membership, Sabine was foreign secretary, vice-president, and treasurer of the Royal Society. From 1861 until 1871 he was its president.

His unpublished correspondence discloses that Sabine, distressed by the disputes over reforming the Royal Society, viewed the magnetic crusade as a happy opportunity for the scientific community to present a united front. Abhorring divisions in the ranks of science, he and Grove tried to have the scientific societies unite when Burlington House became available. In the late 1840's Sabine, again with Grove, played a leading role in carrying out the reforms of the Royal Society that largely answered the earlier complaints of Davy and Babbage about the election of fellows.

Relying upon the support of the like-minded, Sabine quietly ensured that his intellectual interests received the lion's share of British Association funds. This is evident from its annual reports through the time of his resignation from the presidency of the Royal Society. Kew Observatory was the largest single recipient, but the number of grants to geophysical and related areas is notable. A suspicion arises that Sabine backed the move for the £1,000 parliamentary grant partly to quiet criticism from relatively neglected disciplines. Even allowing for his sincerity and for the general quality of the research, this allocation of resources was dubious, especially in the face of developments in Germany.

In time, Sabine's became a dead hand at the tiller, frozen on an old course. When Faraday reported his experimental demonstration of the relationship of light and magnetism in 1845, Sabine argued against giving him the Rumford Medal. James Clark Ross in 1834, Sabine asserted, had already described the effect as naturally observed on an Arctic voyage. Sabine was overruled.[2] When Grove was proposed for the Copley Medal in 1871, Sabine trotted out procedural quibbles to deny the honor.[3] It was Sabine who in 1863 answered the clamor of the younger naturalists for awarding the Copley Medal to Darwin by seeing that Adam Sedgwick was chosen.[4] (Note how well Sabine's later actions accorded with Babbage's earlier complaints about the Royal Society's distribution of awards.) Accused by Tyndall of neglecting natural history, the octogenarian oligarch resigned the Royal Society presidency in 1871 when he realized the days of artful dodging were over.[5]

NOTES

1. Sabine to Tyndall, 24 Apr. [1855], vol. IV, 1307 of Tyndall Papers, Royal Institution: "I notice that he [Secchi] gives me credit for abstaining from all such attempts at combining facts and hypothetical connections or views. I have adhered to this quite as a duty—but have made my writings far less *interesting* than they might have been otherwise, thereby. For to many men speculations are far more attractive than facts."
2. Royal Society, *Minutes of Council*, printed ser., I, 512–513, 530–531. In Royal Society Library.
3. Gassiot, recommendation of Copley Medal for Grove, 18 Oct. 1871 (copy), with undated note by Grove on the events in the Royal Society Council: "My chance never recurred." Grove Papers, Royal Institution.
4. Sabine to John Phillips, 12 Nov. 1863, Miscellaneous MSS Collection, Library of the American Philosophical Society.
5. J. P. Gassiot, *Remarks on the Resignation of Sir Edward Sabine, K.C.B., of the Presidency of the Royal Society* (London, 1871).

BIBLIOGRAPHY

I. PRIMARY SOURCES. This account is largely derived from unpublished sources. The best collection of Sabine documents is in the archives of the Meteorological Office, Bracknell, Berkshire, as part of the records of the Kew Observatory. A smaller but valuable body of Sabine letters is in the library of the Royal Society, which also contains the papers of John Herschel, an essential source. The papers of Humphrey Lloyd, Sabine's colleague, are divided between the Royal Society and the archives of the Royal Greenwich Observatory. Unfortunately, few records of James Clark Ross survive: some are included in the two bodies of Sabine papers, and there is a smaller batch on sunspots at the Royal Greenwich Observatory. The Airy Papers at Greenwich are useful in presenting the views of an opponent of Sabine. Particularly valuable are the correspondence and minutes of the Royal Society's Committee on Physics (Including Meteorology) and its predecessors, in the archives of the Society. The Grove and Tyndall collections at the Royal Institution are very pertinent. Of the non-British collections, the Hansteen MSS at the University of Oslo are a rich, still largely unexplored source. The few items in the Gauss *Nachlass* at Göttingen are useful; the Quetelet Papers in the Académie Royale de Belgique are an extensive, rich source. Sabine materials at the American Philosophical Society and in the correspondence of Sabine's American friends A. D. Bache and Joseph Henry are also valuable.

Sabine's numerous articles (more than 100) are well covered in the Royal Society *Catalogue of Scientific*

Papers, V, 351–354; VIII, 805–806; XI, 251. In addition, see the following: *Remarks on the Account of the Late Voyage of Discovery to Baffin's Bay, Published by Captain J[ohn] Ross* (London, 1819) and the rejoinder by Ross, *An Explanation of Captain Sabine's Remarks on the Late Voyage of Discovery to Baffin Bay* (London, 1819); *North Georgia Gazette and Winter Chronicle* (1821); *An Account of Experiments to Determine the Figure of the Earth . . .* (London, 1825); the article on magnetism in the three eds. of the Admiralty's *A Manual of Scientific Enquiry . . .;* Sabine edited the 3rd ed. (London, 1859); *Observations on the Days of Unusual Magnetic Disturbances Made at the British Colonial Magnetic Observatories,* 2 vols. (London, 1843–1851); and 10 vols. of observations at the observatories. Sabine helped prepare the translations of Gauss and Weber's "Results of the Observations Made by the Magnetic Association in the Year 1836," in Taylor's *Scientific Memoirs,* **2** (1841), 20–25. Under his "superintendence," his wife, Elizabeth Julian Sabine, translated works by Humboldt and Arago.

II. SECONDARY SOURCES. See the following, arranged chronologically: John Ross, *A Voyage of Discovery in H. M. Ships Isabella and Alexander* (London, 1819); William Edward Parry, *Journal of a Voyage for the Discovery of a North-West Passage* (London, 1821); C. Babbage, *Reflections on the Decline of Science in England* (London, 1830); "Memoir of General Sir Edward Sabine, F.R.S., K.C.B.," in *Proceedings of the Royal Artillery,* **12** (1883), 381–396, unsigned, but obviously written by a military associate in the magnetic work; S. Chapman and J. Bartels, *Geomagnetism,* 2 vols. (Oxford, 1940); Johannes Georgi, "Edward Sabine, ein grosser Geophysiker des 19 Jahrhunderts," in *Deutsche hydrographische Zeitschrift,* **11** (1959), 225–239; and Nathan Reingold, "Babbage and Moll on the State of Science in Great Britain . . .," in *British Journal for the History of Science,* **4** (1968), 58–64.

NATHAN REINGOLD

SABINE, PAUL EARLS (*b.* Albion, Illinois, 22 January 1879; *d.* Colorado Springs, Colorado, 28 December 1958), *acoustics.*

Sabine was the son of a Methodist minister. After graduating from McKendree College in 1899 he went to Harvard University, where his cousin, Wallace Clement Sabine, was on the physics faculty. At Harvard he earned the baccalaureate (1903), the master's (1911), and the doctorate in physics (1915). Sabine taught at Worcester Academy (1903–1910), served as assistant in physics at Harvard (1915–1916), and was an assistant professor at Case School of Applied Science in Cleveland (1916–1918). In 1919 he became director of acoustical research at the Wallace Clement Sabine Laboratory of Acoustics, better known as the Riverbank Laboratory, in Geneva, Illinois. He remained there until his retirement in 1947, except for a period of war work at the Harvard Underwater Sound Laboratory (1942–1945). Sabine was a charter member of the Acoustical Society of America (1929), served as its fourth president (1935–1937), and was elected to honorary membership in 1954. After his retirement, while continuing to be active as a consultant, he turned his thoughts to the reconciliation of Christianity with the results of modern physical science and psychology. Sabine published his conclusions in *Atoms, Men and God,* his second book.

The bulk of Sabine's scientific work followed directly from Wallace Sabine's recognition of the reverberation time as the most significant variable affecting the acoustical quality of listening rooms and his subsequent discovery of the empirical relationship between reverberation time and total absorption. Total absorption was a summation of the sound-absorbing power of the various constituents of the room, a quantity that Wallace Sabine defined and showed how to measure. The Riverbank Laboratory was built for Wallace Sabine's use in determining the sound-absorptive properties of architectural materials as well as the sound absorption and transmission characteristics of architectural elements and types of construction. Wallace Sabine died just as the Riverbank Laboratory was completed, and Paul Sabine was appointed to carry out the research program that would make it possible to design acoustical environments on a scientific basis. The results of this research were incorporated in his textbook on acoustical design, *Acoustics and Architecture* (1932).

Sabine was also active as an acoustical consultant to architects. He was consulted in the design of the Radio City Music Hall in New York and of the Fels Planetarium in Philadelphia. He was most proud, however, of his work in the planning of the remodeling of the House and Senate Chambers of the United States Capitol Building after World War II. The acoustical design of the remodeled chambers was a notable success.

BIBLIOGRAPHY

Sabine's books are *Acoustics and Architecture* (New York–London, 1932) and *Atoms, Men and God* (New York, 1953). His scientific papers may be located through the cumulative indexes of the *Journal of the*

Acoustical Society of America and through the citations in *Acoustics and Architecture.* Several of his papers, as well as extensive sections of *Acoustics and Architecture,* offer retrospectives of the development of architectural acoustics as it grew from the work of Wallace Sabine.

CARLTON MALEY

SABINE, WALLACE CLEMENT WARE (*b.* Richwood, Ohio, 13 June 1868; *d.* Cambridge, Massachusetts, 10 January 1919), *physics.*

Sabine's parents, Hylas Sabine and Anna Ware, were both college-educated and had a strong interest in literature and science. His father, at one time a member of the Ohio State Senate and state commissioner of railways and telegraphs, was a farmer and landowner who lost most of his holdings in the panic of 1873. His mother, eager to see her two children do better, raised them both under a stern moral and educational regimen. The elder Sabines were practicing Protestants, but as an adult Wallace belonged to no church and professed no religious faith.

After earning an A.B. at Ohio State University in 1886, Sabine went to Harvard, where in 1888 he was awarded an M.A. in physics and in 1890 appointed to an instructorship. Neglecting to take a Ph.D., he devoted himself to teaching, and his courses were among the most popular in the department. A full professor in 1905, he was instrumental in the creation of the Harvard graduate school of applied science, which he administered as dean from 1906, the year of its founding, until 1915.

Following the United States's declaration of war in 1917, Sabine held various administrative posts in what became the Army Air Service. In June 1918 he became director of the Department of Technical Information of the Bureau of Aircraft Production, and that September he was appointed to the National Advisory Committee for Aeronautics by President Woodrow Wilson. At his death Sabine was a member of the American Physical Society and the National Academy of Sciences and a fellow of the American Academy of Arts and Sciences and the American Association for the Advancement of Science. He was married in 1900 to Jane Downes Kelly, a physician of Cambridge, Massachusetts.

As a research physicist Sabine is known for having turned architectural acoustics from a qualitative, rule-of-thumb practice into a quantitative engineering science. He started work in this field in 1895, when Charles William Eliot, the president of Harvard, asked him to do something about the very poor acoustics of the lecture hall in the university's new Fogg Art Museum. Measuring the time during which a given sound reverberated within the hall, Sabine found that a single syllable of speech persisted long enough to overlap confusingly with those that followed it. By hanging sonically absorptive materials on the walls, he reduced the reverberation time and, hence, improved the acoustical quality of the room.

In 1898, at Eliot's urging, the architectural firm of McKim, Mead, and White turned to Sabine for advice on the design of Symphony Hall in Boston. Using the raw data from his Fogg Museum experiments, Sabine managed, with the ingenious use of graphs, to derive an acoustical law of general applicability. He showed that the product of the reverberation time and the summed absorptive power of the walls, furnishings, and materials of appointment equaled a constant; and that this constant was directly proportional to the volume of the room. The formula enabled Sabine to predict the acoustical properties of an auditorium in advance of construction. The practical value of his law was confirmed by the acoustical success of Symphony Hall, and its essential scientific validity was demonstrated by a later analysis of reverberation that employed statistical methods from the kinetic theory of gases.

In 1900, in a comprehensive paper on reverberation, Sabine set down what have since been accepted as the three basic criteria for good acoustical quality in any auditorium: sufficient loudness, minimal distortion, and maximum distinctness. In subsequent years Sabine, who made his expertise available free to numerous architects, investigated how interference and resonance affect acoustics and the best way of sonically insulating a room. In honor of Sabine's seminal significance in architectural acoustics, the unit of sound-absorbing power is called the sabin.

BIBLIOGRAPHY

Sabine's *Collected Papers on Acoustics* (Cambridge, Mass., 1922) contains almost all of his important articles. A useful introduction to his life and work is Edwin H. Hall, "Wallace Clement Sabine," in *Biographical Memoirs. National Academy of Sciences,* **11,** no. 13 (1926), 1–19. William Dana Orcutt, *Wallace Clement Sabine: A Study in Achievement* (Norwood, Mass., 1933), apparently was commissioned by his widow and emphasizes Sabine's personal life and character.

DANIEL J. KEVLES

SACCHERI, (GIOVANNI) GIROLAMO (*b.* San Remo, Italy, 5 September 1667; *d.* Milan, Italy, 25 October 1733), *mathematics.*

Saccheri is sometimes confused with his Dominican namesake (1821–1894), a librarian at the Bibliotheca Casanatense of Rome. In 1685 Saccheri entered the Jesuit novitiate in Genoa and after two years taught at the Jesuit college in that city until 1690. Sent to Milan, he studied philosophy and theology at the Jesuit College of the Brera, and in March 1694 he was ordained a priest at Como. In the same year he was sent to teach philosophy first at Turin and, in 1697, at the Jesuit College of Pavia. In 1699 he began teaching philosophy at the university, where until his death he occupied the chair of mathematics.

One of Saccheri's teachers at the Brera was Tommaso Ceva, best known as a poet but also well versed in mathematics and mechanics. Through him Saccheri met his brother Giovanni, a mathematician living at the Gonzaga court in Mantua. This Ceva is known for his theorem in the geometry of triangles (1678). Under Ceva's influence Saccheri published his first book, *Quaesita geometrica* (1693), in which he solved a number of problems in elementary and coordinate geometry. Ceva sent this book to Vincenzo Viviani, one of the last surviving pupils of Galileo, who in 1692 (*Acta eruditorum,* 274–275) had challenged the learned world with the problem in analysis known as the window of Viviani. Although it had been solved by Leibniz and others, Viviani published his own solution and sent it to Saccheri in exchange for the *Quaesita.* Two letters from Saccheri to Viviani (1694) are preserved, one containing Saccheri's own solution (without proof).

While in Turin, Saccheri wrote *Logica demonstrativa* (1697), important because it treats questions relating to the compatibility of definitions. During his years at Pavia he wrote the *Neo-statica* (1708), inspired by and partly a polemic against T. Ceva's *De natura gravium* (Milan, 1669). This book seems of little importance now, being well within the bounds of Peripatetic statics. *Euclides ab omni naevo vindicatus* (1733), also written at Pavia, contains the classic text that made Saccheri a precursor of the discoverers of non-Euclidean geometry.

Saccheri's two most important books, the *Logica* and the *Euclides,* were virtually forgotten until they were rescued from oblivion—the *Euclides* by E. Beltrami in 1889 and the *Logica* by G. Vailati in 1903. They show that Euclid's fifth postulate (equivalent to the parallel axiom) intrigued Sac-

cheri throughout his life. In the *Logica* it led him to investigate the nature of definitions and in the *Euclides* to an attempt to apply his logic to prove the correctness of the fifth postulate. Although the fallacy in this attempt is now apparent, much of Saccheri's logical and mathematical reasoning has become part of mathematical logic and non-Euclidean geometry.

The *Logica demonstrativa* is divided into four parts corresponding to Aristotle's *Analytica priora, Analytica posteriora, Topica,* and *De sophisticis Elenchis.* It is an attempt, probably the first in print, to explain the principles of logic *more geometrico.* Stress is placed on the distinction between *definitiones quid nominis* (nominal definitions), which simply define a concept, and *definitiones quid res* (real definitions), which are nominal definitions to which a postulate of existence is attached. But when we are concerned with existence, the question arises whether one part of the definition is compatible with another part. This may be the case in what Saccheri called complex definitions. In these discussions he was deeply influenced by Euclid's *Elements,* notably by the definition of parallelism of two lines. He warned against the definition, given by G. A. Borelli (*Euclides restitutus* [Pisa, 1658]), of parallels as equidistant straight lines. Thus Saccheri was one of the first to draw explicit attention to the question of consistency and compatibility of axioms.

To test whether a valid proposition is included in a definition, Saccheri proposed reasoning seemingly analogous to the classical *reductio ad absurdum,* using for his example *Elements* IX, 12: if $1, a_1, a_2, \cdots, a_n$ form a geometric progression and a_n has a prime factor p, then a_1 also contains this factor. There was a difference in Saccheri's proposal, however: his demonstration resulted from the fact that, reasoning from the negation, we obtain exactly the proposition to be proved, so that this proposition appears as the consequence of its own negation (an example of his reasoning is seen below). As Vailati observed, Saccheri's reasoning had much in common with that of Leibniz (see L. Couturat, *Opuscules et fragments inédits de Leibniz* [Paris, 1903]); but whereas Leibniz's primary inspiration came from algebra and the calculus, Saccheri's came from geometry.

In the *Euclides* Saccheri applied his logical principle to three "blemishes" in the *Elements.* By far the most important was his application of his type of *reductio ad absurdum* to Euclid's parallel axiom. He took as true Euclid's first twenty-six propositions and then assumed that the fifth postulate was false. Among the consequences of this hypothesis he sought a proposition to test the postulate itself. He found it in what is now called the quadri-

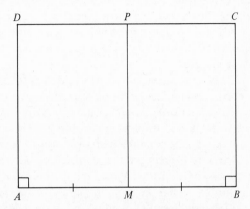

lateral of Saccheri, an isosceles birectangular quadrilateral consisting of a side AB and two sides of equal length, AD and BC at right angles to AB. Then without the fifth postulate it cannot be proved that the angles at C and D are right. One can prove that they are equal, since if a line MP is drawn through the midpoint M of AB perpendicular to AB, it intersects DC at its midpoint P. Thus there are three possibilities, giving rise to three hypotheses:

1. that of the right angle: $\angle C = \angle D = 1$ right angle;

2. that of the obtuse angle: $\angle C = \angle D > 1$ right angle;

3. that of the acute angle: $\angle C = \angle D < 1$ right angle.

Saccheri proceeded to prove that when each of these hypotheses is true in only one case, it is true in every other case. Thus in the first case the sum of the angles of a triangle is equal to, in the second it is greater than, and in the third case it is less than, two right angles.

For the proofs Saccheri needed the axiom of Archimedes and the principle of continuity. Then came the crucial point: he proved that for both the hypothesis of the right angle and that of the obtuse angle the fifth postulate holds. But the fifth postulate implies the hypothesis of the right angle; hence the hypothesis of the obtuse angle is false. (This argument is not now cogent because in the case of the obtuse angle the existence of the finite length of lines is accepted.) He could not dispose of the hypothesis of the acute angle in this way, but he was able to show that it leads to the existence of asymptotic straight lines, which, he concluded, was repugnant to the nature of the straight line. Saccheri thus thought that he had established the truth

of the hypothesis of the right angle and, hence, of the fifth postulate and of Euclidean geometry as a whole.

Several other theorems resulted from Saccheri's three hypotheses, some of which are now established as part of non-Euclidean geometry. The three types of quadrangles had already been studied by al-Khayyāmī and Nasīr-al-Dīn al-Tūsī; the latter was cited by John Wallis (1693) in a book known to Saccheri.

Saccheri's *Euclides,* although it had little direct influence on the subsequent discovery of non-Euclidean geometry, was not so forgotten as is sometimes believed. (See Segre, below.)

BIBLIOGRAPHY

I. ORIGINAL WORKS. Saccheri's writings include *Quaesita geometrica a comite Rugerio De Vigintimilliis* . . . (Milan, 1693), included in *Sphinx geometra, seu quesita geometrica proposita et solida* . . . (Parma, 1694); *Logica demonstrativa quam una cum thesibus ex tota philosophiae decerptis defendendam proposuit J. F. Caselette Graveriarum Comes* (Turin, 1697), 2nd ed. entitled *Logica demonstrativa auctore Hieronym. Saccherio Societatis Jesu* . . . (Pavia, 1701), 3rd ed. entitled *Logica demonstrativa, theologicis, philosophicis et mathematicis disciplinis accomodata* . . . (Cologne, 1735); *Neo-statica* . . . (Milan, 1708); and *Euclides ab omni naevo vindicatus: Sive conatus geometricus quo stabiliuntur prima ipsa universae geometriae principia* . . . (Milan, 1733). Theological works are listed in P. C. Sommervogel, *Bibliothèque des écrivains de la Compagnie de Jésus, VII* (Brussels–Paris, 1897), 360.

Letters by Saccheri to Viviani, Ceva, and Grandi are in A. Favaro, "Due lettere inedite del P. Girolamo Saccheri d. C. d. G. a Vincenzo Viviani," in *Rivista di fisica, matematica e scienze naturali,* 4 (1903), 424–434; A. Pascal, "Sopra una lettera inedita di G. Saccheri," in *Atti del R. Istituto Veneto di scienze, lettere ed arti,* 74 (1914–1915), 813–820; and A. Agostini, "Due lettere inedite di G. Saccheri," in *Memorie della R. Academia d'Italia,* Cl. di Scienze Matematiche e Naturale, 2, no. 7 (1931), 31–48.

II. SECONDARY LITERATURE. The full text of the *Logica demonstrativa,* with English trans., is in A. F. Emch, "The *Logica demonstrativa* of Girolamo Saccheri" (Ph.D. diss., Harvard, 1933), with a life of Saccheri by F. Gambarana from a MS at the Biblioteca Estense in Modena. The *Logica* is discussed by Emch in articles of the same title as his dissertation in *Scripta mathematica,* 3 (1935–1936), 51–60, 143–152, 221–233. On the *Logica,* see also G. Vailati, "Di un' opera dimenticata del P. Gerolamo Saccheri," in *Rivista filosofica,* 4 (1903), 528–540; with other papers on the book, it is also in *Scritti di G. Vailati (1863–1909)* (Leipzig–Florence, 1911), 477–484, see also 449–453.

Also of value is F. Enriques. *Per la storia della logica* (Bologna, 1922), 94–99, also available in French, German, and English.

The *Euclides ab omni naevo vindicatus* has been partially translated (only bk. I with the discussion of the parallel axiom) by P. Stäckel and F. Engel in *Die Theorie der Parallellinien von Euclid bis auf Gauss* (Leipzig, 1895), 31–136, and into English by G. B. Halsted in *Girolamo Saccheri's Euclides vindicatus* (Chicago–London, 1920). See also ten articles by Halsted on non-Euclidean geometry in *American Mathematical Monthly,* **1** (1894), see index, p. 447. There is an unsatisfactory Italian trans. by G. Boccardini, *L'Euclide emendato . . .* (Milan, 1904). Further literature on the *Euclides* (listed chronologically) includes E. Beltrami, "Un precursore italiano di Legendre e di Lobatschewsky," in *Atti della Reale Accademia Lincei, Rendiconti,* 4th ser., **5**, no. 1 (1889), 441–448, also in Beltrami's *Opere,* IV (Milan, 1920), 348–355; P. Mansion, "Analyse des recherches du P. Saccheri S.J. sur le postulatum d'Euclide," in *Annales de la Société scientifique de Bruxelles,* **14** (1889–1890), pt. 2, 46–59, also in *Mathesis,* 2nd ser., **1** (1891), supp. 15–29; C. Segre, "Congettare informo all'influenza di Girolamo Saccheri sulla formazione della geometrica non-euclidea," in *Atti dell'Accademia delle scienze* (Turin), **38** (1902–1903), 535–547; A. Pascal, "Girolamo Saccheri nella vita e nelle opere," in *Giornale di matematica di Battaglini,* **52** (1914), 229–251; and H. Bosmans, "Le géomètre Jérome Saccheri S. J.," in *Revue des questions scientifiques,* 4th ser., **7** (1925), 401–430.

Saccheri's contribution to non-Euclidean geometry is discussed in R. Bonola, *La geometria non-euclidea* (Bologna, 1906), also in English (Chicago, 1911; repr. 1955) and in German (Berlin, 1908). See also article on Saccheri by E. Carruccio, *Enciclopedia italiana di scienze, lettere ed arte,* **30** (Rome, 1936), 389–390.

D. J. STRUIK

SACCO, LUIGI (*b.* Varese, Lombardy, Italy, 9 March 1769; *d.* Milan, Italy, 26 December 1836), *medicine.*

Sacco obtained his degree in medicine and surgery in 1792 at the University of Pavia, where he was a pupil of Johann Peter Frank, the founder of social medicine. Sacco subsequently established a medical practice in Milan, where he became a friend of the physician Pietro Moscati. In 1778 Moscati had given the first public demonstrations in Milan of smallpox inoculation. He later became one of the foremost political personalities in Jacobinic and Napoleonic Milan.

Following Jenner's publication (1798) of his work on cowpox inoculation, Sacco had the good fortune, in September 1800, to find a spontaneous cowpox stock in the neighborhood of Varese. He used this stock to inoculate first himself and then a group of children on the farm where he was staying. From these and numerous other inoculations, he recognized the advantages of inoculating cowpox rather than human smallpox. He decided to publicize this new prophylactic practice, and he realized the importance of giving his work a social and political flavor in accordance with the new times.

Sacco persuaded the government of the Cisalpine Republic to set up a general vaccination department, which was entrusted to him. This department allowed Sacco to extend his work to many other regions of Italy besides Lombardy. By 1809 he had succeeded in reaching "a million and a half vaccinated people, five hundred thousand of whom I have had the satisfaction of vaccinating myself." In the same year he left his post as general director of vaccination and gave to the press his *Trattato di vaccinazione.* Shortly afterward this treatise was translated into French and German, thus presenting the important conclusions that he had been able to draw from his ample statistics. Sacco became a major advocate of cowpox vaccination, and his stock from Lombardy was sent to Jean de Carro in Vienna. The latter sent it in 1802 to Baghdad, and it was with this stock that the first vaccinations were given in the East Indies.

Sacco subscribed to the theory of *contagium vivum,* but he believed that the leukocytes in pus were the *animalcula* that caused disease and transmitted it from one individual to another by contagion. From 1803 he was chief physician at the Ospedale Maggiore in Milan and for several years served as director.

BIBLIOGRAPHY

I. ORIGINAL WORKS. Sacco's major works are *Osservazioni pratiche sull'uso del vajuolo vaccino, come preservativo del vajuolo umano* (Milan, 1801); *Omelia sopra il Vangelo della XIII. Domenica dopo la Pentecoste, in cui si parla dell'utile scoperta dell'innesto del vajuolo vaccino, recitata dal Vescovo di Goldstat, dalla Tedesca nell'Italiana lingua transportata* (Brescia, 1802; Parma, 1805; Pistoia, 1805); *Memoria sul vaccino unico mezzo per estirpare radicalmente il vajuolo umano diretta ai Governi che amano la prosperità delle loro nazioni* (Milan, 1803); and *Trattato di vaccinazione con osservazioni sul giavardo e sul vajuolo pecorino* (Milan, 1809), with French and German trans. as *Traité de vaccination . . . ,* Joseph Daquin, trans. (Chambéry, 1811), and *Neue Entdeckungen über die Kuhpocken . . . ,* Wilhelm Sprengel, trans. (Leipzig, 1812), respectively.

II. SECONDARY LITERATURE. On Sacco and his work, see Luigi Belloni, "L'innesto del vaccino," in *Storia di Milano*, XVI (1962), 960–971, with full bibliography; "Una ricerca del contagio vivo agli albori dell'Ottocento," in *Gesnerus*, 8 (1951), 15–31; and "Per la storia dell'innesto del vaiuolo a Milano," in *Physis*, 2 (Florence, 1960), 213–222.

LUIGI BELLONI

SACHS, JULIUS VON (*b.* Breslau, Silesia [now Wrocław, Poland], Germany, 2 October 1832; *d.* Würzburg, Germany, 29 May 1897), *botany, plant physiology.*

Sachs was the eighth of nine children of Christian Gottlieb Sachs, an engraver, and the former Maria-Theresia Hofbauer, who were quite poor. From 1840 to 1845 the gifted boy attended the poorly run seminary school in Breslau and, from 1845 to 1850, the Gymnasium, where he frequently was first in his class. After the deaths of his father (1848) and mother (1849), he had no means of support and was forced to leave school. Sachs had met the physiologist Purkyně, who took him to Prague as his personal assistant, where his principal duties were those of draftsman. In Prague, Sachs took his final secondary school examination (1851), after which he studied at the University of Prague until 1856. The most lasting intellectual influence upon him in this period was that of the philosopher Zimmermann. The botany and zoology lectures failed to hold his interest, but research that he conducted on his own led to eighteen publications on botanical and zoological topics in this period. These papers, general treatments designed for a popular audience, were translated into Czech and published in Purkyně's journal *Živa*.

Sachs received the Ph.D. in 1856; and in the same year he attended a scientific congress at Vienna, where he met many prominent botanists. The next year he qualified at Prague—although the faculty did not wish the new subject to be taught— as a lecturer in plant physiology. Thus, Sachs, who later became the leader in the field, was the first to teach a whole course of the subject at a German university. At this time plant physiology encompassed the whole of botany except systematics.

In 1859 Sachs became assistant in plant physiology at the Agricultural and Forestry College in Tharandt, near Dresden. With Wilhelm Hofmeister, he began to edit the *Handbuch der physiologischen Botanik* in 1860; and the following year he became a botany teacher at the Agricultural College in Poppelsdorf, near Bonn. During these extremely productive years at Poppelsdorf he laid the foundations of all his later scientific work. Sachs succeeded Anton de Bary as professor at Freiburg im Breisgau in 1867 but left the following year to become full professor of botany at Würzburg, a post he held for the rest of his life. Except for a trip to Norway and several visits to Italy, Sachs never left Würzburg. He refused offers that followed in rapid succession from Jena (1869), Heidelberg (1872), Vienna (1873), and Berlin (1877), as well as later ones from the Agricultural College of Berlin, from Bonn, and finally one from Munich (1891) to succeed Naegeli.

A brilliant lecturer and a highly imaginative experimenter, Sachs won fellow scientists to his views through the persuasive logic of his arguments. These talents, joined with his position as leader of the rapidly developing science of plant physiology, earned him an international reputation.

Sachs received many honors. The University of Würzburg elected him rector in 1871, and in 1877 he was named privy councillor and awarded the Order of Maximilian and the Order of the Bavarian Crown. This was accompanied by a grant of personal nobility, entitling Sachs to place "von" before his name. He also received honorary doctorates from the universities of Bonn, Bologna, and London. He was, in addition, a member or honorary member of many scientific societies and academies, including those of Frankfurt, Munich, Turin, and Amsterdam, as well as the Linnean Society of London and the Royal Society. Many important scientists were his students or worked for a time in his institute: Francis Darwin, Goebel, Klebs, F. Noll, Pfeffer, Stahl, De Vries, S. H. Vines, and Appel.

Throughout his life Sachs displayed an enormous appetite for work. Unfortunately, the intense inner restlessness that constantly drove him to new efforts and achievements also severely damaged his health, to such an extent that the letters from the last fifteen years of his life constitute one protracted health report (Goebel). He suffered from nervous disorders and excruciating pains—probably neuralgic—accompanied by insomnia and aggravated by extensive damage to his liver and kidneys.

Like many other outstanding scientists, Sachs was often overbearing and unfair. In scientific controversies and in many letters he occasionally adopted a harsh and implacable tone—which, to be sure, was not unusual in scholarly disputes of the nineteenth century. He was extremely reserved toward those around him, including most of his students, and had close ties with only a few people.

When Sachs began his scientific research, plant physiology was a totally neglected field; it became developed only through his work, which extended to nearly all branches of the subject. Even Sachs's earliest independent investigations aroused general admiration and are still of value. In the course of this research on the metabolism of stored nutrients during the germination of seeds (1858–1859), he discovered the transformation of oil into starch in *Ricinus* seeds. His work was characterized by a combination of microscopic and microchemical methods, by means of which he provided a clear picture of the catabolism and transport of stored nutrients. Another early investigation dealt with the culture of plants in pure nutrient solution (1860).

Pursuing research begun by Liebig, Sachs solved both practical and theoretically important problems regarding the mineral requirements of plants. In this connection he discovered the corrosive action of roots on marble slabs, indicating their ability to sequester minerals (1860) and the toxicity of solutions containing a single salt. He studied the influence of temperature on life processes (1860), especially the effects of freezing. He discovered the law of "cardinal points," according to which each vital process has a minimum, an optimum, and a maximum temperature that are mutually related.

Particularly important was Sachs's demonstration, beginning in 1861, that the starch in the chloroplasts is the first visible product of assimilation and that carbon dioxide assimilation (photosynthesis) actually occurs in chloroplasts. These discoveries, like many others that he made, are cornerstones of modern plant physiology.

Further experiments dealt with the effect of light and, above all, with the origins of etiolation (1862) and the formation of flowers and roots (from 1865). His highly significant studies of growth and its mechanisms in roots (from 1872) and shoots led to the discovery of the "great period of growth." Sachs also demonstrated that the formation of plants depends more on processes of cell enlargement than on those of cell division in the meristem. From about 1873 Sachs devoted increasing attention to the physiology of stimuli: geotropism, "heliotropism" (phototropism), and hydrotropism.

In his later investigations and theoretical papers, which lacked much of the experimental ardor of the earlier ones, Sachs sought evidence for his theory of "specific organ-forming substances." This theory took as its starting point the fact that although plants can grow in the dark, they cannot form flowers there (1865). From this, he contended, it follows that specific substances necessary for the formation of flowers are produced in the leaves and that these substances are essential for this development. Sachs claimed that similar substances cause differentiation in the shoots and roots. In his last publications he gave a detailed account of this theory of "matter and form," which was simultaneously a challenge to idealistic morphology as advocated by Alexander Braun.

Although modern plant physiology would be inconceivable without Sachs's contributions in these areas, he was, however, less successful in dealing with certain other questions, especially those concerning the transport of nutrients and water. He stubbornly held to the theory—not original with him—that water is conducted in the cell walls of wood (imbibition theory). Insisting that the sieve tubes play no role in transporting carbohydrates, he maintained instead that the latter are transported in the form of "wandering starch." Moreover, his great authority long delayed discovery of the real answers to these questions. Equally untenable were the attacks he made in the last years of his life against the mechanisms proposed by Darwin in his theory of evolution and against other writings of Darwin.

Sachs's skill in experimentation was astonishing, especially in view of the rudimentary methods available when he began his research. He was constantly concerned to point out the independence of physiology from physics and chemistry: "More and more I find that physiology achieves its most important results when it goes its own way entirely, without concerning itself very much with physics and chemistry" (letter of 15 May 1879). This is not to imply that Sachs did not use chemical and physical knowledge in his research. That he did so can be clearly seen, for example, in the number of microchemical demonstration methods he used, many of which he himself devised. Further examples are his proof of the existence of starch in the whole leaf by the iodine test, still used as a lecture experiment, and the gas bubble method for demonstrating the formation of oxygen in photosynthesis, also still used in laboratory classes.

Sachs invented or at least substantially improved many of the devices that were long prominent in botany laboratories: the hanging sieve, for demonstrating hydrotropism; the root box, for making visible the growth and branching of roots; the auxanometer, for automatically recording the processes of growth; a hand spectroscope, for measuring the light absorbed through the leaves; the clinostat, for compensating for gravity; centrifuges, for experiments involving centrifugal force; and thermostats and boxes for unilateral illumination. Although much of this apparatus now appears simple, even primitive, it was revolutionary in Sachs's day, when scarcely any apparatus other than the microscope was used. Sachs also was responsible for innovations in experimental technique, having introduced, for example, the use of seedlings in order to obtain a large number of uniform plants.

Many of the experimental papers written by Sachs and his students were published in *Arbeiten des Botanischen Instituts in Würzburg*. The most important were collected as *Gesammelte Abhandlungen über Pflanzenphysiologie*.

Sachs also exerted a major influence through his books. In *Geschichte der Botanik vom 16. Jahrhundert bis 1860* he went far beyond a dry historical description, presenting with great skill the basis of his own scientific work. This masterful presentation records all the fundamental elements upon which Sachs built his many theories. His immense contribution to the subject is most clearly apparent in *Lehrbuch der Botanik* (which went through four editions) and in *Vorlesungen über Pflanzenphysiologie* (which appeared in two editions). The *Vorlesungen* in particular, by virtue of the freer style permitted by the lecture form, illustrates Sachs's achievements in an especially vivid manner. The material it contains, much of which Sachs himself had elaborated, meshes harmoniously with contemporary knowledge in related branches of science and with it forms a unified whole.

Sachs's books were long the definitive works in plant physiology. Through them the results both of his own research and of that of many contemporaries, such as Hofmeister and Naegeli, became widely known. In fact, so complete was this process that it is frequently difficult to isolate Sachs's personal contributions. The numerous illustrations in these books, the majority of which derived from Sachs's drawings, often were incorporated, without his knowledge, in the textbooks of other authors, and this practice was continued until quite recent times.

In reviewing Sachs's work it becomes clear that he was little interested in making narrow observations or in answering highly specific questions. He always sought major laws of universal applicability. Even when he failed to solve a problem he attempted to outline a comprehensive framework which might lead to the relevant physiological aspects. To the extent permitted by contemporary knowledge, he was highly successful in this endeavor.

BIBLIOGRAPHY

I. ORIGINAL WORKS. Sachs's writings include *Handbuch der Experimentalphysiologie der Pflanzen*, which is vol. IV of *Handbuch der physiologischen Botanik*, W. Hofmeister, A. de Bary, T. Irmisch, N. Pringsheim, and J. Sachs, eds. (Leipzig, 1865); *Lehrbuch der Botanik* (Leipzig, 1868, 1870, 1872, 1874); *Geschichte der Botanik vom 16. Jahrhundert bis 1860* (Munich, 1875); *Vorlesungen über Pflanzenphysiologie* (Leipzig, 1882, 1887); and *Gesammelte Abhandlungen über Pflanzenphysiologie*, 2 vols. (Leipzig, 1892–1893). Sachs also edited *Arbeiten des Botanischen Instituts in Würzburg*, **1–3** (1871–1888).

II. SECONDARY LITERATURE. See K. Goebel, "Julius Sachs," in *Flora*, **84** (1897), 101–130; R. B. Harvey, "Julius von Sachs," in *Plant Physiology*, **4** (1929), 155–157; P. Hauptfleisch, "Julius von Sachs," in *Münchener medizinische Wochenschrift*, **26** (1897); F. Noll, "Julius v. Sachs," in *Naturwissenschaftliche Rundschau*, **12** (1897), 495–496; E. G. Pringsheim, *Julius Sachs der Begründer der neuen Pflanzenphysiologie 1832–1897* (Jena, 1932); W. Ruhland, "Julius Sachs," in *Handwörterbuch der Naturwissenschaften*, VIII (Jena, 1913), 529; and S. H. Vines, obituary in *Proceedings of the Royal Society*, **62** (1897–1898), xxiv–xxix.

MARTIN BOPP

SACROBOSCO, JOHANNES DE (or **JOHN OF HOLYWOOD**) (*b.* Holywood, Yorkshire, England, end of twelfth century; *d.* Paris, France, 1256 [1244?]), *astronomy*.

Sacrobosco (also called John or Johannes Halifax, Holyfax, Holywalde, Sacroboscus, Sacrobuschus, de Sacro Bosco, or de Sacro Busto) has been called a Scot, an Irishman, a Frenchman, a Brabançon, a Catalan, and a Jewish convert—all unfounded attributions. Some put his birthplace at Holywood near Dublin, or even at Nithsdale, Scotland. Very little is known of his life. English biographies maintain, and it is commonly held, that he was educated at Oxford.

After his studies Sacrobosco entered into orders and became a canon regular of the Order of St. Augustine at the famous monastery of Holywood in Nithsdale. About 1220 he went to Paris, where he spent most of his life and where he was admitted as a member of the university, on 5 June 1221, under the syndics of the Scottish nation. Elected professor of mathematics soon afterward, he won wide and enduring renown and was among the first exponents in the thirteenth century of the Arab arithmetic and algebra. By 1231 he was the outstanding mathematician and astronomer. He died in either 1244 or 1256 and was buried in the cloisters of the Fathers of Mercy, convent of St. Mathurin, in Paris.

The ambiguity of the year of Sacrobosco's death comes from the epitaph engraved on his tombstone in the convent cloisters: "M. Christi bis C. quarto deno quater anno De Sacro Bosco discrevit tempora ramus Gratia cui dederat nomen divina Joannes." If *quater* modifies only *deno*, then four times ten equals forty, plus four gives forty-four. If *quater* modifies *quarto deno*, then *quarto deno* is fourteen, and four times fourteen is fifty-six. The second interpretation is preferred by Johannes Fabricius, Christopher Saxius, Montucla, Bossut, and G. J. Vossius. An astrolabe decorates the stone, identifying the science to which he was most dedicated.

Sacrobosco's chief extant works are elementary textbooks on mathematics and astronomy: *De algorismo, De computo,* and *De sphaera.* All three are frequently found in the same manuscript, or at least bound together, and may be his only extant books. Prosdocimo de Beldemandis, however, wrote in his fifteenth-century commentary on the *De sphaera* that there were "many other works that it would take too long to enumerate here." A second arithmetic on fractions, *Algorismus de minutiis,* is attributed to Sacrobosco by Prosdocimo, but the opening words are those commonly occurring in a treatise usually ascribed to a Richard of England. Other works dubiously ascribed to him are a brief tract on physical or philosophical (that is, sexagesimal or astronomical) rather than common fractions, two tracts on the quadrant (one of which is more often ascribed to Campanus of Novara), an *Arithmetica communis,* and perhaps some commentaries on Aristotle.

Sacrobosco's fame rests firmly on his *De sphaera,* a small work based on Ptolemy and his Arabic commentators, published about 1220 and antedating the *De sphaera* of Grosseteste. It was quite generally adopted as the fundamental astronomy text, for often it was so clear that it needed little or no explanation. It was first used at the University of Paris.

There are only four chapters to the work. Chapter one defines a sphere, explains its divisions, including the four elements, and also comments on the heavens and their movements. The revolutions of the heavens are from east to west and their shape is spherical. The earth is a sphere, acting as the middle (or center) of the firmament; it is a mere point in relation to the total firmament and is immobile. Its measurements are also included.

Chapter two treats the various circles and their names—the celestial circle; the equinoctial; the movement of the *primum mobile* with its two parts, the north and south poles; the zodiac; the ecliptic; the colures; the meridian and the horizon; and the arctic and antarctic circles. It closes with an explanation of the five zones.

Chapter three explains the cosmic, chronic, and heliacal risings and settings of the signs and also their right and oblique ascensions. Explanations are furnished for the variations in the length of days in different global zones, namely, the equator, and in zones extending from the equator to the two poles. A discussion of the seven climes ends the chapter.

The movement of the sun and other planets and the causes of lunar and solar eclipses form the brief fourth chapter.

During the Middle Ages the *De sphaera* enjoyed great renown, and from the middle of the thirteenth century it was taught in all the schools of Europe. In the sixteenth century it gained the attention of mathematicians, including Clavius. As late as the seventeenth century it was used as a basic astronomy text, but after 1700 it was completely forgotten.

After Manilius' *Astronomica, The Sphere* was the first printed book on astronomy (Ferrara, 1472). Twenty-four more editions appeared in the following twenty-eight years, and more than forty editions from 1500 to 1547, the last being issued at Leiden. For eighty years after Barocius in 1570 had pointed out some eighty-four errors, *The Sphere* was still studied, and in the seventeenth century it served as a manual of astronomy in some German and Low Countries schools. Often it appeared with commentaries by the most distinguished scholars of the time. There were three Italian editions: by Maurus (Florence, 1550); by Dante de'Rinaldi (Florence, 1571), and by Francesco Pifferi at Sienna in 1537, 1550, 1572, 1579, 1604. Two French editions, by Martin Perer and Guillaume Desbordes, were printed at Paris in 1546 and 1576.

Some claim that *The Sphere* merely paraphrases the elementary ideas of Ptolemy and the Arab astronomers al-Battānī and al-Farghānī, but this is a great exaggeration. Sacrobosco's *Sphere* is far superior in structure and order to that of al-Farghānī. Resemblances should not be surprising, however, since both writers summarized the *Almagest*. Actually Sacrobosco omitted much of what is found in al-Farghānī, condensed what little he did use of it, and restated and rearranged the matter into a more effective plan. Indications are equally strong for his using Macrobius' *Commentary on the Dream of Scipio* as for al-Farghānī's *Elements*, although Macrobius is rarely mentioned.

Commentaries on *The Sphere* were written by Michael Scot between 1230 and 1235; by John Pecham, a Franciscan, sometime before 1279; by the Dominican Bernard of Le Treille between 1263 and 1266; and by Campanus of Novara between 1265 and 1292. Robertus Anglicus gave a course of lectures on Sacrobosco's *Sphere* at either the University of Paris or the University of Montpellier in 1271, which helps to date his own commentary. He stated that for the most part *The Sphere* was so clear it needed no further explanation.

Cecco d'Ascoli was the earliest of the fourteenth-century commentators on *The Sphere* (probably before 1324). The Dominican Ugo de Castello (Ugo di Città di Castello) wrote a commentary on *The Sphere* that was begun at Paris and finished at Florence in 1337. On 19 October 1346, at Ghent, Henry of Sinrenberg, an Augustinian friar, completed a commentary on *The Sphere*, in which he addressed friends and fellow Augustinians in the *studium* of the monastery of Milan. This indicates the wide geographical spread of the use of *The Sphere*, beyond universities to convent schools. Blasius of Parma commented on *The Sphere* in the late fourteenth century.

Fifteenth-century commentators included Prosdocimo de Beldemandis in 1418 and Franciscus Capuanus de Manfredonia about 1475. Their works are quite detailed and concern any subject that might be even remotely connected with *The Sphere*. Other commentators of this period were Jacques Lefèvre d'Étaples, Wenceslaus Faber of Budweis, and Pedro Ciruelo of Daroca (his commentary was published in February 1498). Incunabula editions of Sacrobosco's *Sphere* were brought out by Gasparino Borro (*d.* 1498), a Servite; and by George of Montferrat. Fausto Andrelini, the Italian humanist, lectured on *The Sphere* while at the University of Paris in 1496.

Sixteenth- and seventeenth-century commentators included Joannes Baptista Capuanus, Bartolomaeus Vespuccius, Erasmus Oswald (Schreckenfuchs), Maurus Florentinus, and Christoph Clavius, the Jesuit astronomer whose huge commentary was held in high regard.

Although the university curriculum of the time was based heavily on logic, Sacrobosco's *Sphere* was required reading, and properly so, first at Paris. The Faculty of Arts at Vienna in 1389 made *The Sphere* and the *De algorismo* required for the A.B. degree. At Erfurt in 1420 the matter of the quadrivium consisted solely of *The Sphere*. At Bourges in the fifteenth century, Euclid, various works of Aristotle, and *The Sphere* were required for the licentiate. In 1409 at Oxford it was required for the A.B. degree. At Bologna the Faculty of Arts required the *De algorismo* in the first year of their premedical course and *The Sphere* in the second year.

The *De computo ecclesiastico* or *De anni ratione*, written about 1232 and probably after *The Sphere*, points out the increasing error in the Julian calendar and suggests a remedy markedly similar to the one actually used under Gregory XIII, some 350 years later, in the revision of the calendar. It was printed at Paris in 1538(?), 1550, and 1572, and at Antwerp in 1547 and 1566.

Sacrobosco's *De computo ecclesiastico* deals with the division of time—marked out by the movements of the sun and moon and their interrelationship—into days and years. A discussion of the sun and its influence on the lengths of days, months, and years forms the first half of the work. In the second half, similar considerations are applied to the moon. The solar and lunar years, the solar and lunar cycles, intercalary days, and the movable feasts are examined.

De algorismo discusses the art of calculating with nonnegative integers. The work contains eleven chapters and examines numeration, addition, subtraction, mediation, duplication, multiplication, division, progression, and extraction of both the square and cube roots of numbers. Mediation is the halving of a given number, and duplication is the doubling of a number. Six rules of multiplication are included, depending on what combination of digits and articles are to be multiplied. Natural progression begins with the number one and the difference between adjacent numbers is one. Broken progression begins with the number two and the difference between adjacent terms of the progression is two. Two rules are given for finding the sum of terms in a natural progression, depending on whether the last term is an odd or even number. In the section on extracting roots, lineal, superficial, and solid numbers are first defined and their properties listed. Lastly, methods of extracting the square and cubic roots of a number are discussed.

Throughout the work examples of various arithmetic processes are included, and diagrams are supplied to facilitate understanding the method.

The *De algorismo* or *De arte numerandi* was first printed without date or place (1490[?]). It was later printed at Vienna by Hieronymus Vietor in 1517, at Cracow in 1521 or 1522, at Venice in 1523, and on occasion printed with *The Sphere*. It was the most widely used manual of arithmetic in the Middle Ages. Copies abound in manuscript form: some forty-three are in the Vatican holdings alone. Peter Philomenus of Dacia wrote a commentary on *De algorismo* toward the close of the thirteenth century, a copy of which is included in Holliwell's *Rara mathematica* of 1841.

BIBLIOGRAPHY

I. ORIGINAL WORKS. Maximilian Curtze's ed. of Sacrobosco's *Algorismus vulgaris*, with the commentary of Peter Philomenus of Dacia, is *Petri Philomeni de Dacia in Algorismus vulgarem Johannis de Sacrobosco commentarius una cum Algorismo ipso* (Copenhagen, 1897). Robert R. Steele translated Sacrobosco's *De arte numerandi* as "The Art of Nombryng," in R. Steele, ed., *The Earliest Arithmetics in English*, Early English Text Society Extra Ser. no. 118 (London, 1922), 33–51. MSS are McGill University MS 134, fols. 1r–20v; Vaticana Latina 3114, fols. 28–33; and Vaticana Rossi 732, fols. 76–80.

II. SECONDARY LITERATURE. See Pierre Duhem, *Le système du monde*, 5 vols. (Paris, 1913–1917); J. O. Halliwell-Phillips, *Rara arithmetica* (London, 1839; 2nd ed., 1841); *Histoire littéraire de la France*, XIX (1838), 1–4; and Lynn Thorndike, *History of Magic and Experimental Science*, IV (1941), 560; and *The Sphere of Sacrobosco and Its Commentators* (Chicago, 1949).

JOHN F. DALY, S.J.

AL-ṢADAFĪ. See Ibn Yūnus, Abu'l-Ḥasan ᶜAlī ibn ᶜAbd al-Raḥmān ibn Aḥmad ibn Yūnus al-Ṣadafī.

SAGE, BALTHAZAR-GEORGES (*b*. Paris, France, 7 May 1740; *d*. Paris, 9 September 1824), *metallurgy, assaying, chemistry*.

Except as founder of the Paris École des Mines,

there is little reason to rate Sage as an important scientific figure. He published extensively, often hurriedly, and—toward the dismal end of his life—usually for self-serving purposes. The chief modern study of Sage describes his scientific work as totally without value.[1] Another historian has called him a "faux savant."[2] Partington, on the whole, is somewhat more charitable.[3]

The younger son of a Paris pharmacist of limited means (who was the son of a notary of St.-Jean-de-Maurienne in Savoy named Sapienti), Sage was sent as a day student to the famous Collège des Quatre Nations.[4] His interest aroused in science, he became an accredited pharmacist and attended the public lectures on experimental physics of the Abbé Nollet and the chemical lectures of G. F. Rouelle, whose experiments he repeated in a small laboratory he was able to equip. In 1760 Sage opened at the family pharmacy a public course of lectures in chemistry and the techniques of assaying. Here, too, he housed the beginnings of an extensive mineralogical collection. In 1769 he published his first work, *Examen chymique de différentes substances minérales*.[5]

Skilled at finding and bemusing powerful patrons, Sage made connections at court and obtained the direct support of Louis XV, who put pressure on the Academy of Sciences (even sending his orders by special courier) to admit Sage, even if it meant installing him above the lowest rank.[6] The Academy evidently compromised, for it elected Sage in 1770 but ranked and promoted him according to its established procedures. At the death of Rouelle in that year, Sage replaced Cadet de Gassicourt as *adjoint,* when Cadet was promoted to *associé.* In 1777 Cadet became *pensionnaire,* and Sage succeeded him as *associé.*[7]

Sage's dubious qualifications as a chemist were soon evident. In his *Examen chymique* and his more successful *Élémens de minéralogie docimastique* (1772), Sage had claimed that a white lead ore found at the famous mine of Poullaouen in Brittany was a compound of lead and marine acid (hydrochloric acid), even asserting in the latter book that the ore contained twenty percent by weight of marine acid. Late in 1772 a master apothecary of Paris, one Laborie, reported to the Academy of Sciences an analysis of this ore which controverted Sage's results; accordingly, a committee composed of the other chemists in the Academy carried out experiments in Baumé's laboratory to decide between the contestants. They concluded unanimously that the ore contained no trace of marine acid.[8] It is perhaps significant that while both Laborie and Sage were invited to observe the experiments, only Laborie accepted the invitation.

Yet in these early years Sage took an active part in the Academy's proceedings, often joining other chemists, among them Lavoisier, on special investigating committees. In 1774, for example, Sage, Brisson, and Lavoisier demonstrated that the rival preparations of mercuric oxide (mercure précipité per se) by Baumé and Cadet were identical and—this was to play a part in the earliest preparation of oxygen gas in France—were reducible without the addition of substances supposed to contain phlogiston.[9] In 1778 Sage joined Macquer and Lavoisier in analyzing a sample of water from the Dead Sea.[10] He also was appointed one of the commissioners to award a prize in 1778 for the best method of increasing the production of saltpeter in the kingdom; and, with Macquer, Lavoisier, Baumé, and d'Arcy, he helped assemble the *Recueil de mémoires et d'observations sur la formation & sur la fabrication du salpêtre* (1776).[11] Later he contributed rare mineral specimens and precious stones from his collection for Lavoisier's experiments on the effect of intense heat produced by combustion with oxygen.[12]

The verdict on Sage as a chemist is almost universally negative. Partington, to be sure, ascribes to him a small number of minor chemical discoveries: the preparation, independently of Guyton de Morveau, of solid potassium ferrocyanide; the discovery of hypophosphoric acid; the demonstration (1776) that silver chloride can be reduced by iron and that phosphorus can reduce metallic salts to metals.[13]

If Lavoisier often cited Sage, it was not infrequently to correct his manifest errors. Perhaps the most notorious of Sage's stubborn mistakes was his report that he had obtained substantial amounts of gold from ashes. Others were unable to duplicate his results. The chemists of the Academy carried out a careful analysis and found that the amount of gold was not only infinitely small, but was derived from the minium used in treating the ashes.[14] Polemics on this matter shook the Academy, taking on the dimensions of a scandal. Indeed, according to one observer, censure of Sage by his colleagues was avoided only by personal antagonisms within the Academy.[15]

Most contemporaries viewed Sage as a successful teacher, esteemed by his students, but as a very poor chemist. This judgment was common well before he expressed his opposition to Lavoisier's new chemistry. In 1772 Turgot wrote to Condorcet that it was foolishness (*sottise*) for the Academy to have passed over the younger Rouelle and Jean Darcet and to elect Sage.[16] On 28 March 1775, Macquer—the dean of French chemists—wrote to Bergman that Sage

 . . . totally lacks a gift for chemistry [*n'a point du tout l'espirit de la chimie*] and does not understand that science at all. This is what makes him so bold in making hasty inferences from the slightest evidence [*les moindres apparences*]. In the end, he will seriously damage himself with the real chemists. But since he has as much confidence as he has little knowledge, many people who know no more than he, think of him as a remarkable discoverer, and these are highly-placed persons [*grands personnages*] and very numerous.[17]

A recent history of chemical mineralogy has little to say on Sage's behalf, describing his analytical technique as "most unsatisfactory" except when he was using traditional methods in assaying metallic ores. Because of his peculiar theories "he became hopelessly entangled whenever he attempted to use 'wet' methods of analysis."[18] In the light of his dubious competence and Macquer's opinion of him, it is ironic that Sage was promoted to *pensionnaire* in the Academy upon the latter's death in 1784.

Two years after his promotion Sage's *Analyse chimique et concordance des trois règnes* was published (1786). Fulsomely dedicated to Louis XVI, to whom he owed "tout ce que je suis," Sage described it as the result of twenty-five years of work. Here, as well as in his *Mémoires historiques et physiques* (1817), he set forth the doctrine that formed the basis of his teaching. Sage could not deny the experimental demonstration by his contemporaries that air is a mixture of gases. Yet he continued to believe not only in the reality of phlogiston but also in what he called *l'acide igné,* a substance imagined to be "the essence of the different aeriform fluids."[19] From the union of this acid with phlogiston arose the different sorts of air, notably oxygen, as well as electricity, oils, and the "principle" of metallicity. Acids were derived from this *acide igné élémentaire*, which was combined in compound bodies (*corps organisés*) with different amounts of phlogiston, earth, and water. In his *Analyse chimique* Sage noted that two celebrated scientists (Lavoisier and Laplace) had advanced the view that water is composed of inflammable air (hydrogen) and dephlogisticated air (oxygen). A series of ingenious experiments seemed to support their theory, but to Sage such experiments merely proved that water is one of the constituents of the different sorts of aeriform fluids.[20]

In 1787 there appeared, with the sanction of the Academy of Sciences, the famous *Nomenclature chimique*, the work of Guyton de Morveau, Lavoisier, Berthollet, and Fourcroy. To appraise this work, the Academy appointed a committee consisting of Baumé, Cadet de Gassicourt, Darcet, and Sage. The *rapporteurs* recognized without hesitation that a new theory of chemistry was implicitly being arrayed against the old.[21] They gave high praise to the authors of this radical work, pointed out some of its advantages, and raised certain doubts (about, among other matters, the conclusions drawn from the synthesis of water). Not only was it difficult, they wrote, to abandon all the principles of one's chemical education, but it was even more difficult suddenly to admit that a host of substances, which analogy suggested must be compound, should henceforth be regarded as simple substances. And they concluded:

> We therefore believe that one must submit this new theory, as well as its nomenclature, to the test of time, to the impact of experiments, to the consequent weighing of opinions; finally to the judgment of the public as the only tribunal by which it ought or can be judged.[22]

Although Sage's opposition was muted by the views of his more discreet coauthors, he never abandoned his idiosyncratic position. As late as 1810 he expressed his disapproval of the new chemistry and the new nomenclature by publishing his *Exposé des effets de la contagion nomenclative et réfutation des paradoxes qui dénaturent la physique*. When Sage published his *Mémoires historiques et physiques* in 1817 he still praised the old theory of Johann Friedrich Meyer and rejected Joseph Black's demonstration of some sixty years earlier that chalk is composed of quicklime and "fixed air" (carbon dioxide). Instead, Sage wrote, *terre calcaire* (calcium carbonate) is a salt composed of his cherished *acide igné* (obviously a descendant of Meyer's *acidum pingue*) with a specific earth, some oleaginous matter, and water. Yet, he continued, Black's erroneous theory (he described Black as a *chimiste anglais*!) had been adopted by the "secte lavoisienne" as if it were a demonstrated truth.[23]

The creation of the Paris École des Mines is Sage's major claim to distinction. The idea of such a school had first occurred to Daniel Trudaine, the *intendant des finances* who had founded in 1747 the École des Ponts et Chaussées. Yet it did not seem feasible at that time, in view of the primitive state of the French mining industry, to establish a parallel school of mines. Instead, on the advice of Jean Hellot, chief assayer at the mint, Trudaine reserved a few places at the Ponts et Chaussées for young persons recommended by the directors and owners of mines. Their professional instruction was to be completed by a course in chemistry and practical experience at one of the better-managed mines. In this fashion were trained the earliest inspectors and advisors to the mining industry, notably Gabriel Jars and J. P. F. Guillot-Duhamel (1730–1816).[24]

The first steps toward the creation of the École des Mines were taken under the auspices of Henri-Léonard-Jean-Baptiste Bertin. A protégé of Mme de Pompadour, he had served as *contrôleur-général des finances* from 1759 to 1763. On leaving that office, he retained the title of minister and secretary of state and put together a catch-all department, responsible for several diverse activities. Among these, and of particular interest to him, were the mines of France.[25]

Soon after taking over his new post, Bertin received memoirs proposing the creation of two schools of mines in the provinces. Consulted by Bertin, Antoine Monnet, recently appointed to the post of inspector general of mines, strongly opposed this suggestion and urged instead that courses in mineralogy and metallurgy be established at the Jardin des Plantes and that students, after being examined on these subjects (as well as on chemistry and mathematics), should complete their training at one of the better-run mines. Soon after, Monnet's colleague Jourdan, together with Sage, who then held the post of supervisor of assaying at the mint, urged Bertin to create a school of mines at Paris, to be supported by a tax levied on the mine owners. Monnet opposed this project with enthusiasm enhanced by his dislike of Sage.[26]

Yet Sage gained at least a partial victory. By letters patent of 11 June 1778 a chair of mineralogy and docimastic metallurgy was established at the mint. Sage received the royal appointment with a stipend of 2,000 livres per annum and with Guillot-Duhamel as his assistant. He installed his already substantial collection of minerals in the great hall of the building recently taken over for the mint and completely redesigned by the architect Jacques-Denis Antoine (1733–1801). Here Sage taught mineralogy, in what he later called his first École des Mines, to students among whom, we are told, were Chaptal (the future industrial chemist), the crystallographer Romé de l'Isle, and the surgeon

Jean Demeste (1743–1783), who described Sage as the most distinguished chemist in France.[27]

When Bertin left the government in 1780, the special department was abolished and the Service des Mines was put under four *intendants de commerce*. On 21 May 1781 the supervisory administration for the mines was further modified by the creation of a special *intendant* for the mines, Douet de La Boullaye. Under Douet, despite the predictable opposition of Monnet, three decrees (*arrêts*) dated 19 March 1783 were issued, one of which established a full-fledged school of mines, modeled after the highly successful École des Ponts et Chaussées. After stressing the backwardness of France's exploitation of its mineral resources and the difficulty of finding qualified personnel, this *arrêt* provided for the establishment of two professorships, one for mineralogy and assaying (*la chimie docimastique*) and the other for the practical aspects of mining (*l'exploitation des mines*). The school was to be located at the Hôtel de la Monnaie on the Quai de Conti; and the chair of mineralogy and assaying was filled by Sage, who was also to serve as director. The other professorship went to Guillot-Duhamel. Secondary posts were established for the teaching of mathematics (Prud'homme), drawing (Miché), and foreign languages (the Abbé Pierre-Romain Clouet). At least for a brief time Jean-Henri Hassenfratz, who in 1785 became a deputy inspector of mines, taught physics at the school, as did J. A. Charles.[28] Lesser staff included a curator of the mineralogical cabinet, the core of which was Sage's collection, ceded to the king in exchange for a lifetime annuity (*rente viagère*) of 5,000 livres.[29]

To be admitted to the École des Mines, a student had to be sixteen years old; the course of studies, in principle at least, lasted three years; and lectures were delivered from November to June. The number of students was never large: eight were admitted in 1783, and the entering class of 1786 numbered twenty-one. Of these, twelve were called *élèves titulaires* or *stipendiés,* for they received a government scholarship of 200 livres.[30] No new students were admitted after 1787.

Sage served as director and professor for at least seven years. The audience for his lectures may have been substantial, since besides those registered in the École des Mines, students of the École des Ponts et Chaussées were expected to attend his lectures on chemistry and mineralogy. His teaching, if the content can be judged from his *Analyse chimique des trois règnes,* was probably not very scientific or profound. He taught mineralogy, remarked Aguillon, as a simple display of minerals and rocks distinguished by inadequate and superficial characters, with no trace of the classification made possible by recent advances in chemistry and by the new crystallography of Haüy, both of which he totally ignored.[31]

The school, although small, was elegantly housed in the mint. Sage records that he received a substantial gratuity from the king for having salvaged gold worth some 440,000 francs from gilded decorations (*vieilles dorures*), and had received permission to apply his *gratification* of 40,000 francs to decorating the school's quarters according to the plans of the architect Antoine.[32] With the onset of the Revolution, and the increasingly desperate state of French finances, this extravagance was held against Sage and the institution he had founded.

Reporting in 1790 for the finance committee of the Constituent Assembly, Charles-François Lebrun, the future duke of Piacenza, concluded that the budget of the École des Mines was better suited to a country like Sweden, where mining was a major source of the national income, than to an agricultural country like France. The small size of the school, moreover, did not justify the sums expended. In June of the same year, Lebrun set forth a proposal of the finance committee that the Corps des Mines and its school should be amalgamated with the Corps des Ponts et Chaussées and its famous school.[33] This proposal fitted well with a plan for the reorganization of the Jardin des Plantes, which included the recommendation that the mineralogical collection of the mint should be transferred there and that its professor of chemistry should give a course in metallurgy. Neither proposal was implemented.[34] Indeed, the Constituent Assembly disbanded without having legislated any reorganization of the Corps des Mines and its school.

As a teaching institution the École des Mines continued a tenuous existence; its collections, although sought by various rival bodies, remained undisturbed. A law of 1792 continued the salaries of the mine inspectors, the teachers, and the students. Sage had played a major part in defending his school, but his much-vaunted contacts with the court came more and more to endanger his position. In 1793–1794 he was arrested and imprisoned, regaining his freedom only upon payment of a substantial fine.[35]

In 1794 the Committee of Public Safety, now

reformed but weakened in authority, created the Agence des Mines, to be composed of three members selected by the Committee.[36] Of the three appointees, two had been members of the first class at the École des Mines; all three continued to dominate mining affairs until the basic reorganization in 1810.[37]

Sage was simply ignored during these changes. The Agence des Mines established a new school, in the Hôtel de Mouchy in the rue de l'Université, and courses began there in November 1794. The school had a library, an assaying laboratory, and its own mineralogical collection (the core of which was Guettard's cabinet). The scientific level of the teaching staff was markedly raised: Vauquelin taught what had been Sage's course in assaying, mineralogy and physical geography were taught by Hassenfratz, and crystallography by Haüy. Two of Sage's original associates were retained: practical mining was again taught by Guillot-Duhamel, and the Abbé Clouet gave his course in German.[38]

In all this Sage played no part; but in 1797 the Directory put him once again in charge of his collections at the mint with a stipend of 6,000 francs. In 1801 he was elected a full member of the Institut de France.[39] A few years later, however, he became totally blind and soon after was deprived of his pension. His last years were spent in penury, in attempts to win back public favor, and in writing pamphlets protesting his ill treatment and enumerating his real and imaginary achievements. He died in his eighty-fifth year, an unregenerate royalist, a scientific fossil, and a pathetic hangover of the *ancien régime*.

NOTES

1. Paul Dorveaux, "Apothicaires membres de l'Académie royale des sciences, XI, Balthazar-Georges Sage," in *Revue d'histoire de la pharmacie,* **23** (1935), 152–166, 216–232. For this evaluation, see p. 232.
2. Arthur Birembaut, "L'enseignement de la minéralogie et des techniques minières," in René Taton, ed., *Enseignement et diffusion des sciences en France au XVIIIe siècle* (Paris, 1964), 387 and n. 2. Édouard Grimaux describes Sage as "expérimentateur maladroit, imagination fantaisiste, qui a beaucoup publié, beaucoup écrit, entassé erreurs sur erreurs, et n'a pas laissé dans la science un seul fait bien observé." See his *Lavoisier,* 2nd ed. (Paris, 1896), 122.
3. J. R. Partington, *A History of Chemistry,* III (1962), 97–98.
4. "Sage," in Didot-Hoefer, *Biographie générale.* The biographical sketch in John Ferguson, *Bibliotheca chemica,* II (Glasgow, 1906), 312–313, appears to draw uncritically upon the *Biographie générale.*
5. A copy of this work is cited in Denis I. Duveen, *Bibliotheca alchemica et chemica* (London, 1949); 523.
6. Dorveaux, *op. cit.,* 155–159.
7. The article in the *Biographie générale* errs in stating that in 1768, at the age of twenty-eight, Sage replaced Rouelle in the Academy of Sciences. This error reappears in Ferguson, *op. cit.,* p. 312. A reliable source is the *Index biographique des membres et correspondants de l'Académie des sciences* (Paris, 1939, and later eds.).
8. An account of this episode is given by Leslie J. M. Coleby in *Chemical Studies of P. J. Macquer* (London, 1938), 78–79. See *Oeuvres de Lavoisier,* IV (1868), 159–175. For his later admission of this error, see Sage, *Analyse chimique et concordance des trois règnes,* I, "Préface," v. Here, too, he admits his mistake in stating that manganese ore (pyrolusite) contains zinc; but he adds that he corrected himself by repeating the experiments of Gahn, Bergman, and Scheele. *Ibid.,* p. vi.
9. "Rapport sur une contestation entre MM. Cadet et Baumé sur le précipité per se," in *Oeuvres de Lavoisier,* IV (1868), 188–190.
10. "Analyse de l'eau du lac asphaltite,"*ibid.,* II (1862), 234–237.
11. *Oeuvres de Lavoisier,* V (1892), 464, 481.
12. *Ibid.,* II (1862), 445–446, 473.
13. Partington, *op. cit.,* p. 97. This last discovery was cited with approval by Lavoisier in his important "Mémoire sur l'affinité du principe oxygine," in *Oeuvres de Lavoisier,* II, 554.
14. Coleby, *op. cit.,* pp. 114–115.
15. Arthur Birembaut, "L'Académie royale des sciences en 1780 vue par l'astronome suédois Lexell (1740–1784)," in *Revue d'histoire des sciences et de leurs applications,* **10** (1957), 156, 163–164.
16. Charles Henry, *Correspondance inédite de Condorcet et de Turgot* (Paris, 1883), 123.
17. *Torbern Bergman's Foreign Correspondence,* Göte Carlid and Johan Nordström, eds., I (Stockholm, 1965), 246. For similar skeptical allusions by Guyton de Morveau and by the Irish chemist Kirwan, see *ibid.,* pp. 112, 188. During a visit to Paris in 1781–1782, Alessandro Volta followed a course in chemistry given by Sage, probably the course at the mint. See *Epistolario di Alessandro Volta,* II (Bologna, 1951), 79.
18. David Roger Oldroyd, "From Paracelsus to Haüy: The Development of Mineralogy in Its Relation to Chemistry" (Ph.D. diss., Univ. of New South Wales, 1974). I owe this reference to Professor Seymour Mauskopf of Duke University.
19. Sage, *Analyse chimique,* I, "Préface," i–ii.
20. *Ibid.,* p. 29.
21. *Méthode de nomenclature chimique, proposé par MM. de Morveau, Lavoisier, Bertholet [sic], & de Fourcroy* (Paris, 1787), 244–249.
22. *Ibid.,* p. 251. Sage's open attack on the new nomenclature appeared in a series of letters published in Rozier's *Journal de physique* (1788, 1789). See Dorveaux, *op. cit.,* p. 223, n. 30.
23. Sage, *Mémoires historiques et physiques,* 50–51.
24. Aguillon, "L'École des mines . . .," 441–443, and Rouff, *Les mines de charbon,* 481. On Guillot-Duhamel, see H. Guerlac, "Some French Antecedents of the Chemical Revolution," in *Chymia,* **5** (1959); 93; and Alfred Lacroix, *Figures des savants,* I (Paris, 1932), 19–23.
25. Aguillon, *op. cit.,* p. 446. In 1766 Bertin officially commissioned Guettard to continue, under government sponsorship, his work on a mineralogical atlas of France, a project with which Lavoisier, and later Monnet, were closely associated.
26. On Jourdan, also called Jourdan de Montplaisir, who was an inspector of mines based at Lyons, see Aguillon, *op. cit.,* pp. 447–448. On Monnet see Rhoda Rappaport, "Guettard, Lavoisier, and Monnet: Geologists in the Service of

the French Monarchy" (Ph.D. diss., Cornell Univ., 1964), and her short article in this *Dictionary* with an excellent bibliography. According to Sage, Monnet was not the only influential opponent of his schemes. He charges Buffon with delaying his nomination to the chair for a year, hoping to have it awarded to his disciple Daubenton at the Jardin des Plantes. See Sage, *Mémoires historiques et physiques*, p. 73.

27. Aguillon, *op. cit.*, pp. 449–451. Partington, *op. cit.*, III, 65, describes Demeste as "a Liège surgeon who made chemistry a hobby." Sage deserves credit for his support of Romé de l'Isle, a distinguished crystallographer whose *Essai de cristallographie* first appeared in 1772. In turn Romé de l'Isle, in his *L'action du feu central bannie de la surface du globe* (2nd ed., 1781) quotes from Sage's experiments.

28. On Hassenfratz and Charles as teachers of physics in the early École des Mines, see Aguillon, *op. cit.*, p. 463. The *Almanach Royal* for 1789 lists only Sage, "Professeur de Minéralogie Docimastique, Directeur Général des Etudes, & Commissaire du Conseil pour les Essais des Mines"; Guillot-Duhamel, "Professeur de Géométrie Souterraine, et Démonstrateur de Toutes les Machines Servant à l'Exploitation des Mines"; the Abbé Clouet, "Professeur de Langues Étrangères"; and "M. de Voselles, Secrétaire Général & Garde du Cabinet du Roi." The same names appear in the *Almanach* through 1792. According to the *Rapport du Comité des finances–Département des Mines. Par M. Le Brun*, p. 4, the chair of foreign languages and the chair of physics were established in 1785. This and other related pamphlets can be consulted in the French Revolution collection of Cornell University.

29. In 1784 Sage published his *Description méthodique du cabinet de l'École royale des mines*.

30. In his *Fondation de l'École royale des mines*, 6, Sage writes that the twelve *élèves stipendiés* were paid 500 francs as their *traitements* and 200 francs for their travel, presumably to visit mines.

31. Aguillon, *op. cit.*, pp. 461–462, who adds that "en chimie et docimasie [Sage gave only] l'indication des recettes alors connues dans les laboratoires sans aucune véritable théorie scientifique pour les expliquer et les relier entre elles."

32. Sage, *Fondation de l'École royale des mines*, 7.

33. Aguillon, *op. cit.*, pp. 465–466.

34. Sage fought both proposals. In reply to Lebrun he published *Remarques de M. Sage, directeur de l'École royale des mines, sur l'extrait raisonné des rapports du Comité des finances de l'Assemblée nationale* (Paris, n.d. [probably 1790]). See also his *Observations sur un écrit qui a pour titre, vues sur le Jardin royal des plantes et le cabinet d'histoire naturelle; à Paris, chez Baudouin, imprimeur de l'Assemblée nationale, 1789* (Paris, 1790). Both pamphlets can be consulted in the Lavoisier Collection at Cornell University. In his *Mémoires historiques et physiques* Sage accused Lebrun of abolishing the 2,000 francs that was his stipend as professor of *minéralogie docimastique* at the mint.

35. Sage rather absurdly blamed his arrest and imprisonment on Guyton de Morveau and Fourcroy, who, while members of the Committee of Public Safety, "se vengèrent du ridicule que j'avais répandu sur leur vocabulisme insignifiant et sans euphonie, et de ce que j'avais prouvé que la nouvelle doctrine lavoisienne était une métachimie . . . ." *Mémoires historiques et physiques*, 74.

36. Aguillon, *op. cit.*, pp. 471–473.

37. The two who had studied at the École des Mines were Lelièvre and Lefebvre d'Hellancourt. Both were among those commissioned (*brevetés*) after a single year of study.

38. Aguillon, *op. cit.*, pp. 482–484.

39. According to the *Index biographique des membres et correspondants de l'Académie des sciences*, Sage had been elected *associé non-résident* of the section of natural history and mineralogy of the Première Classe of the Institut on 5 March 1796.

BIBLIOGRAPHY

I. ORIGINAL WORKS. The following list, with no pretense at completeness, may give some idea of the range of Sage's interests. *Examen chymique de différentes substances minérales* (Paris, 1769) would seem to be his earliest publication. It was followed by *Élémens de minéralogie docimastique* (Paris, 1772; 2nd ed., 2 vols., 1777). *Mémoires de chimie* (Paris, 1773) contains, besides other papers, memoirs read to the Academy of Sciences from 1766 to 1772, many of them describing mineral analyses. These works were followed by *Analyse des blés, et expériences propres à faire connaître la qualité du froment* (Paris, 1776); and *Observations nouvelles sur les propriétés de l'alkali fluor ammoniacal* (Paris, 1778). His *L'art d'essayer l'or et l'argent* (Paris, 1780) contains his first description of the production of potassium ferrocyanide in solid form. This was followed by his ambitious *Analyse chimique et concordance des trois règnes de la nature*, 3 vols. (Paris, 1786). After the Revolution and in his later years he published various speculative works on electricity and natural philosophy, as well as his attack on Lavoisier's chemistry and the new chemical nomenclature: *Exposé des effets de la contagion nomenclative et la réfutation des paradoxes qui dénaturent la physique* (Paris, 1810). Of autobiographical interest are his *Mémoires historiques et physiques* (Paris, 1817); *Fondation de l'Ecole royale des mines à la monnaie* (Paris, 1817); and *Notice autobiographique* (Paris, 1818). Other of Sage's publications are cited in the notes and still others are listed in the catalog of printed books of the Bibliothèque Nationale.

II. SECONDARY LITERATURE. Although a member of the Paris Academy of Sciences and (at the time of his death) of the Première Classe of the Institut de France, Sage was never accorded the customary honor of an *éloge* composed by the perpetual secretary. There is a passable, if not always accurate, sketch by E. M. [Ernest Mézières?] in the Didot-Hoefer *Nouvelle biographie générale*, based largely on Sage's autobiographical writings and an obituary notice in the *Journal de la librairie* of 1824. Sage is judged by E. M. as "ayant crée la docimasie en France," which would seem to be an exaggeration. The best modern evaluation is the two-part study by Paul Dorveaux (see Note 1). Sage's work in chemical metallurgy is briefly mentioned by Hermann Kopp in his *Geschichte der Chemie*, 2 vols. in 4 pts. (Brunswick, 1843), pt. II, 87–88, but is not discussed in F. Hoefer's *Histoire de la chimie*, 2 vols. (Paris, 1866). The most favorable account of Sage's chemical work (perhaps too favorable) is by J. R. Partington in his *History of Chemistry*, III (1962), 97–98. On the Paris École des Mines and Sage's role as its founder and first director, see Louis Aguillon, "L'École des mines de Paris—notice historique," in *Annales de mines*, 8th ser., **15** (1889); 433–686; and Marcel Rouff, *Les mines de charbon en France au XVIIIe siècle, 1744–1791* (Paris, 1922), 480–488.

HENRY GUERLAC

SAGNAC, GEORGES M. M. (*b*. Périgueux, France, 14 October 1869; *d*. Meudon, France, 26 February 1928), *physics*.

Sagnac studied mainly the radiation produced by X rays and the optics of interference. He is remembered today primarily for his design of a rotating interferometer and for the experimental results it provided. He was very interested in the theoretical analysis of optics of moving systems; his approach was classical, and he interpreted the results of his optical experiments as contradicting Einstein's theory of relativity.

Sagnac came from an old bourgeois family. His father was a lawyer who directed the Assurances Générales, and his mother was the daughter of a notary. From 1889 to 1894 Sagnac studied at the École Normale Supérieure and at the University of Paris. In 1894 he received his *agrégé* and became an assistant in physics at the university. In 1900 he was awarded the *docteur ès sciences* degree and became professor of physics at the University of Lille. From 1911 he was professor of physics at the University of Paris. He was twice a candidate for the physics section of the Academy, and he received the Pierson-Perrin, the Wilde, and the Lacaze prizes.

Sagnac's earliest research (and the subject of his dissertation) was motivated by the newly observed X rays.[1] From 1896, the year following Röntgen's discovery, to 1900 Sagnac studied the radiations produced by X rays. He observed that secondary radiation is produced when X rays fall on heavier metals. He showed that this radiation contained secondary X rays (of lower frequency than the original X rays) and negatively charged rays. He suggested that it was through the action of the negative rays that X rays produce ionization in air.

Sagnac next worked on the propagation of light in moving systems (he was particularly interested in the Fizeau effect) and with the optics of interference. From about 1910 he was especially concerned with designing and using a rotating interferometer. In this instrument all the components—light source, mirrors, and photographic plate—are on a disk that can be rotated at various velocities.

Light travels around the disk along a polygonal circuit determined by successive reflections from four mirrors placed around it. Light from the source is split into two beams that travel around the disk in opposite directions and, on recombination, produce interference fringes on the photographic plate. In 1913 Sagnac measured the shift in the position of the fringes when the direction of rotation was reversed.

Sagnac interpreted the shift in the position of the interference fringes in terms of an "ether wind" that gave the light beams traveling in opposite directions different velocities. He was convinced that the phenomenon observed with the rotating interferometer demonstrated the existence of an immobile ether. Sagnac later tried to develop a theory of electrodynamics that would retain classical ideas of space, time, and ether by analyzing the propagation of energy statistically and separately from the propagation of motion. He retained a lifelong dislike for relativity, and in 1923 he interpreted some observations of stellar color shift as being due to an ether wind, rather than as supporting the general theory of relativity.

The results of Sagnac's interferometer experiments were used by some scientists in France as an argument against the theory of relativity. As late as 1937 Dufour and Prunier repeated the experiment in a modified form for that purpose.[2] The experiment does not contradict relativity theory in any way, however, and in 1921 and 1937 Langevin responded with an explanation of how it should be interpreted.[3]

As Langevin explained it, the experiment can be understood equally well in terms of both classical and relativistic theories (the phenomenon involves only a first-order effect in v/c). The fringe shift is produced by the difference in optical path for light beams traveling in opposite directions around the rotating disk. In fact, the experiment provides a neat way to demonstrate the rotation of a system without reference to anything external to it. As Pauli observed, "It is essentially the optical analogue of the Foucault pendulum."[4] In terms of general relativity the experiment can be understood by thinking of the light in the coordinate system of the disk as being subjected to a gravitational field directed away from the center.

An analysis of the rotating interferometer experiment existed in Germany even before Sagnac performed it. Max von Laue discussed the theory of the experiment in 1911 in response to Michelson's suggestion that it be used to demonstrate the earth's motion with respect to the ether.[5] He showed that both relativity theory and ether theory predicted the same result for the experiment. Laue discussed Sagnac's experiment explicitly in 1919 and the similar experiment of F. Harress in 1920.[6]

NOTES

1. *De l'optique des rayons de Röntgen et des rayons secondaires qui en dérivent* (Paris, 1900).
2. A. Dufour and F. Prunier, "Sur l'observation du phénomène de Sagnac par un observateur non entraîné," in *Comptes rendus hebdomadaires des séances de l'Académie des sciences,* **204** (1937), 1925–1927.
3. Paul Langevin, "Sur la théorie de relativité et l'expérience de M. Sagnac" and "Sur l'expérience de M. Sagnac," in his *Oeuvres scientifiques* (Paris, 1950), 467–472.
4. W. Pauli, *Theory of Relativity* (New York, 1958), 19.
5. Max von Laue, "Über einem Versuch zur Optik der bewegten Körper," in his *Gesammelte Schriften und Vorträge,* I (Brunswick, 1961), 154–161.
6. Max von Laue, *Das Relativitätsprinzip,* 3rd ed. (Leipzig, 1919); and "Zum Versuch von F. Harress," in his *Gesammelte Schriften,* I. 526–541.

BIBLIOGRAPHY

I. ORIGINAL WORKS. Sagnac's papers include "Sur la transformation des rayons X par la matière," in *Éclairage électrique,* **18** (1899), 41–48; "Théorie nouvelle des phénomènes optiques d'entraînement de l'éther par la matière," in *Comptes rendus hebdomadaires des séances de l'Académie des sciences,* **129** (1899), 818–821; "Electrisation negative des rayons secondaires issus de la transformation des rayons X," in *Journal de physique théorique et appliquée,* 4th ser., **1** (1902), 13–21, with P. Curie; "Sur la propagation de la lumière dans un système en translation et sur l'aberration des étoiles," in *Comptes rendus hebdomadaires des séances de l'Académie des sciences,* **141** (1905), 1220–1223; "Sur les interférences de deux faisceaux superposés en sens inverses le long d'un circuit optique de grandes dimensions," *ibid.,* **150** (1910), 1302–1305; "Les systèmes optiques en mouvement et la translation de la terre," *ibid.,* **152** (1911), 310–313; "L'éther lumineux demontré par l'effet du vent relatif d'éther dans un interféromètre en rotation uniforme," *ibid.,* **157** (1913), 708–710; "Effet tourbillonnaire optique. La circulation de l'éther lumineux dans un interférographe tournant," in *Journal de physique théorique et appliquée,* 5th ser., **4** (1914), 177–195; "Les deux mécaniques simultanées et leurs liaisons réelles," in *Comptes rendus hebdomadaires des séances de l'Académie des sciences,* **171** (1920), 99–102; and "Sur le spectre variable périodique des étoiles doubles: Incompatibilité des phénomènes observés avec la théorie de la relativité générale," *ibid.,* **176** (1923), 161–173.

II. SECONDARY LITERATURE. Sagnac's scientific work was summarized in connection with the Academy's award of the Pierson-Perrin Prize in *Comptes rendus*

hebdomadaires des séances de l'Académie des sciences, **169** (1919), 1227–1232. See also Sagnac's *Notice sur les titres et travaux scientifiques de M. Georges Sagnac* (Paris, 1920). For discussions of Sagnac's rotating interferometer experiment, see the works by Langevin, Pauli, and Laue listed in the notes and André Metz, "Les problèmes relatifs à la rotation dans la théorie de la relativité," in *Journal de physique et le radium,* 8th ser., **13** (1952), 224–238.

SIGALIA DOSTROVSKY

SAHA, MEGHNAD (*b.* Scoratali, Dacca district, India [now Bangladesh], 6 October 1894; *d.* New Delhi, India, 16 February 1956), *theoretical physics.*

Saha was the fifth child of Jagannath Saha, a small shopkeeper, and Bhubaneswari Debi. The family lived in modest circumstances, and Saha was able to go to primary school through the kindness of a local patron. He entered the Government Collegiate School on a scholarship when he was eleven, but was soon expelled for participating in a political demonstration; he then attended a private school and, in 1911, enrolled in the Calcutta Presidency College. He received the M.A. in applied mathematics in 1915 and, in the following year, was appointed lecturer in mathematics on the all-Indian faculty of the University College of Science, which had just been founded by Sir Astosh Mukherjee.

A personality conflict with the chairman of the mathematics department soon led Saha to transfer to the department of physics, where he taught and did research. He received the D.Sc. in 1918. In the meantime, he had become interested in astrophysics, and had begun a systematic study of twenty-five years of the *Monthly Notices of the Royal Astronomical Society.* Since he was also teaching thermodynamics on the graduate level (although he had not previously studied the subject in depth), he often considered the relationship between thermodynamics and astrophysics. Thus, when he read J. Eggert's paper "Über den Dissoziationzustand der Fixsterngase," published in *Physikalische Zeitschrift* in 1919, Saha was prepared to begin the work on thermal ionization that won him a permanent place in the history of science.

By boldly applying thermodynamics and quantum theory to stellar matter and by drawing an analogy between chemical dissociation and atomic ionization, Saha derived a formula by which the degree of ionization in a very hot gas could be expressed in terms of its temperature and electron pressure. He set out his results in a paper entitled "On Ionization in the Solar Chromosphere," published in *Philosophical Magazine* in 1920. There is some dispute concerning where this paper was written, since Saha left India in September 1919 on a scholarship that permitted him to visit both A. Fowler's laboratory at Imperial College, London, and later Nernst's laboratory in Berlin. At any rate, in London Saha worked not only with Fowler but with E. A. Milne, who developed important extensions of Saha's theory; while in Berlin he met Planck, Einstein, Laue, and Sommerfeld and set up experiments to confirm his theory, of which he gave an account in an article, "Versuch einer Theorie der physikalischen Erscheinungen bei höhen Temperaturen . . .," published in *Zeitschrift für Physik* in 1921.

Saha's theory may be considered to be the starting point of modern astrophysics. The long-noted absence of rubidium and cesium in the solar spectrum could be understood for the first time, since it follows from Saha's formula that the degree of ionization increases with temperature and decreases with pressure, and is therefore smaller for elements with lower ionization potentials. It is thus possible to predict whether or not the spectrum of an element may be expected in a region with a given temperature and pressure if its ionization potential is known. It was also soon confirmed that other lines existed in the cooler regions of the solar atmosphere, as the theory predicted, and H. N. Russell was thereby able to identify rubidium in the spectra of sunspots. (It must be noted, however, that in the years immediately following the publication of Saha's theory, enthusiasm led some astrophysicists to apply the equation rather rashly, and some significant errors were made.) But in general, important knowledge of stellar atmospheres could be obtained by an analysis of their spectra through Saha's theory.

Saha returned to India in 1921 to accept a professorship at the University of Calcutta, but lack of funds and encouragement prompted him to look for a position elsewhere. In 1923 he went to the University of Allahabad, where he taught for the next fifteen years. As confirmations and extensions of his theory brought him fame he received a number of honors. He was elected president of the physics section of the Indian Science Congress Association in 1925, and two years later he was named a member of the Royal Society. In 1938 he left the University of Allahabad to become professor of physics at the University of Calcutta, where he worked to create an institute of nuclear physics

(which was officially opened by Irène Joliot-Curie, and is now named in Saha's honor). He also initiated researches on cosmic rays, the ionosphere, and geophysics, and traveled widely in connection with his increasing organizational responsibilities. He was directly or indirectly responsible for the establishment of a number of scientific bodies and institutions, including the United Provinces Academy of Sciences (later the National Academy of Sciences), the Indian Science News Association, and the National Institute of Sciences.

Saha was further active in planning scientific and industrial projects for India. In particular he was involved in river valley projects (the result of having in his youth witnessed devastating floods), calendar reform, and geophysical explorations. In 1935 he founded the influential socioscientific journal *Science and Culture;* but although he was interested in the social implications of science, and although he was sympathetic to the Indian struggle for independence, he remained aloof from politics in general. He was opposed to the *khadi* movement of Ghandi and his followers because he thought that it would impede Indian industrialization. Following India's political independence, Saha devoted more time to social, political, and economic problems, and in 1951 he was elected, as an independent, to Parliament. He died during a trip to New Delhi to discuss some matters pertaining to the administration of his nuclear physics institute.

BIBLIOGRAPHY

A complete bibliography of Saha's works may be found in S. N. Sen, ed. (see below).

For further details on the life and works of Saha, consult S. N. Sen, ed., *Professor Meghnad Saha, His Life, Work and Philosophy* (1954); *Science and Culture,* **19** (1954), 442; *Science and Culture,* **22** (1956), a complete issue devoted to Saha; D. S. Kothari, "Meghnad Saha," in *Biographical Memoirs of Fellows of the Royal Society,* **4**, 217–236; and an obituary by F. J. M. Stratton in *Nature,* **177** (1956), 917.

For discussions of Saha's theory of thermal ionization, any work on astrophysics may be consulted. In particular, a nonmathematical treatment of the ideas as they stood in the early years of the theory may be found in H. Dingle, *Modern Astrophysics* (New York, 1924), 197–217. See also Giorgio Abetti, *The Sun,* J. B. Sidgwick, trans. (London, 1955), ch. 5. For a more technical discussion, see, A. Unsöld, *Physik der Sternatmosphären,* 2nd ed. (Berlin, 1955), 40–48; and S. Rosseland, *Theoretical Astrophysics* (Oxford, 1936), 170–183.

V. V. RAMAN

IBN AL-ṢĀ'IGH. See Ibn Bājja, Abū Bakr Muḥammad ibn Yaḥyā ibn al-Ṣā'igh.

SAINTE-MESME, MARQUIS DE. See L'Hospital (L'Hôpital), Guillaume-François-Antoine de.

SAINT-HILAIRE, AUGUSTIN FRANÇOIS CÉSAR PROUVENÇAL (usually known as **AUGUSTE DE)** (*b.* Orléans, France, 4 October 1779; *d.* La Turpinière, near Sennely, Loiret, France, 30 September 1853), *natural history.*

Saint-Hilaire was interested in entomology and botany from an early age; and despite his appointment as accountant in the civil service, in 1816 left for Rio de Janeiro, accompanying M. de Luxembourg, the French ambassador. He intensively surveyed the flora and fauna of Brazil from Jequitinhonha to the Río de la Plata for six years. In August 1822 Saint-Hilaire returned to Paris with 24,000 plants, 2,000 birds, 16,000 insects, 135 quadrupeds, and many reptiles, fishes, and minerals that he intended to classify. He fell seriously ill, however, lost his voice, and almost lost his sight while preparing the publication of the Brazilian flora. Under the care of Michel Dunal and Claude Lallemand at Montpellier, he recovered.

In 1830 Saint-Hilaire was elected a member of the Academy of Sciences and became professor at the Faculty of Sciences in Paris. On all his travels he made interesting anthropological, botanical, and pharmacognostic observations. His work on Brazilian botany, however, was superseded by that of Martius.

BIBLIOGRAPHY

Saint-Hilaire's first works appeared in the *Bulletin des sciences physiques, médicales, et d'agriculture d'Orléans.* Shortly after his return from Brazil he published "Aperçu d'un voyage dans l'intérieur du Brésil, la province cisplatine et les missions dites du Paraguay," in *Mémoires du Muséum d'histoire naturelle,* **9** (1822), 307–380. *Histoire des plantes les plus remarquables du Brésil et du Paraguay* (Paris, 1824) and *Plantes usuelles des brasiliens* (Paris, 1824) were followed by his most important work, *Flora Brasiliae meridionalis,* 3 vols. (Paris, 1825–1833), written with A. de Jussieu and J. Cambessèdes. Saint-Hilaire published the diaries of his travels in Brazil as *Voyage dans les provinces de Rio de Janeiro et de Minas Geraes* (Paris, 1830); *Voyage dans le district des diamants et sur le littoral du Brésil* (Paris, 1833); *Voyage aux sources du Rio de S. Francisco et dans la province de Goyaz,* 2 vols. (Paris, 1847–1848); and *Voyage dans les provinces de Saint Paul et de Sainte Cather-*

ine (Paris, 1851). Saint-Hilaire's *Voyage à Rio Grande do Sul (Brésil)* (Orléans, 1887) was published posthumously, edited by R. de Dreuzy.

Anna Eliza Jenkins wrote an introductory essay to Saint-Hilaire's "Esquisse de mes voyages au Brésil et Paraguay," in *Chronica botanica,* **10** (1946), 1–62, with an interesting biographical study.

FRANCISCO GUERRA

ST. JOHN, CHARLES EDWARD (*b.* Allen, Michigan, 15 March 1857; *d.* Pasadena, California, 26 April 1935), *astronomy.*

The youngest in the family of Hiram Abiff St. John, a millwright, and Lois Amanda Bacon, St. John graduated from the Michigan Normal School in 1876. Overwork had weakened his health, however, and he could not resume work until 1885, when he became an instructor of physics at the normal school. He received the B.S. degree from Michigan Agricultural College in 1887; and after graduate study at the University of Michigan and at Harvard, including also a stay in Berlin and Heidelberg, he was awarded the Ph.D. by Harvard in 1896. After a year as an instructor at the University of Michigan, St. John was appointed associate professor of physics and astronomy at Oberlin College, becoming professor in 1899 and dean of the College of Arts and Sciences in 1906. Beginning in 1898, he spent several summer vacations working at the Yerkes Observatory. His association there with George Ellery Hale led him, in 1908, to resign his post at Oberlin and to join the staff of the Mount Wilson Observatory; after his retirement in 1930 he was appointed a research associate there.

St. John's research was mainly in solar physics. One of his earliest investigations (1910–1911) was of the H and K lines of ionized calcium in the solar spectrum. After measuring the absolute wavelengths of these lines in terrestrial sources, he compared them with those of the corresponding emission and absorption lines observed in the solar spectrum, making a particular study of the spectral lines over sunspots and flocculi. In 1913 St. John confirmed John Evershed's discovery concerning the displacement of Fraunhofer lines in the spectra of the penumbras of sunspots, and he made a detailed examination of the flow of gases in the spots. He concluded that ionized calcium exists at the highest level in the solar atmosphere, followed by hydrogen, with the metals and rare elements confined to the lower regions; his analysis of the flash spectrum obtained by S. A. Mitchell during the

1905 eclipse reinforced this conclusion. At the same time St. John refuted W. H. Julius' idea that the displacements in the spectral lines were due to anomalous dispersion in the solar atmosphere.

St. John's principal contribution was his revision of Rowland's table of the wavelengths in the solar spectrum. In collaboration with Charlotte Moore, Louise Ware, Edward Adams, and Harold Babcock, he produced this monumental work in 1928. Two independent series of measurements were made, one with the Mount Wilson tower spectrographs and the other with an interferometer; the differences rarely exceeded 0.002 Å. From the violet limit of 2,975 Å, the lines listed ranged beyond Rowland's extreme of 7,330 Å to about 10,200 Å. The revision listed the intensities of the spectral lines in spots as well as in the disk, and the lines were classified according to their furnace spectra and behavior under pressure; excitation potentials were also provided. In connection with this work St. John served for a time as president of the International Astronomical Union commission devoted to wavelength standards, and he was also president of the solar physics commission.

St. John paid particular attention to the problem of measuring the relativistic deflection of the lines in the solar spectrum. An initial study (1917), based on some forty lines, gave a negative result. By 1923, however, he was satisfied that the effect, which at the center of the sun amounts to about 0.01 Å, was detectable; and his final publication on the subject (1928), using 1,537 lines, illustrated it quite convincingly. Although St. John regarded this as his most important work, the motion of the perihelion of Mercury and the systematic displacement observed beyond the limb of the sun are generally regarded as more definitive tests of relativity.

In collaboration with Walter Adams and Seth Nicholson, St. John made spectroscopic observations of Mars and Venus, mainly in the hope of detecting the presence of oxygen and water vapor in their atmospheres.

BIBLIOGRAPHY

I. Original Works. St. John's *Revision of Rowland's Preliminary Table of Solar Spectrum Wavelengths, With an Extension to the Present Limit of the Infra-Red,* written with C. E. Moore, L. M. Ware, E. F. Adams, and H. D. Babcock, is Carnegie Institution of Washington Publication no. 396 (Washington, D.C., 1928) and *Papers of the Mount Wilson Solar Observatory,* 3 (1928). Most of his other publications appeared in *Astrophysical Journal* and were reprinted as *Contribu-*

tions from the Mount Wilson Solar Observatory. They include "The Absolute Wave-Lengths of the H and K Lines of Calcium in Some Terrestrial Sources," in *Astrophysical Journal,* **31** (1910), 143–156; "The General Circulation of the Mean and High-Level Calcium Vapor in the Solar Atmosphere," *ibid.,* **32** (1910), 36–82; "Motion and Condition of Calcium Vapor Over Sun-Spots and Other Special Regions," *ibid.,* **34** (1911), 57–78, 131–153; "Radial Motions in Sun-Spots," *ibid.,* **37** (1913), 322–353, and **38** (1913), 341–391; "On the Distribution of the Elements in the Solar Atmosphere as Given by Flash Spectra," *ibid.,* **40** (1914), 356–376; "The Accuracy Obtainable in the Measured Separation of Close Solar Lines: Systematic Errors in the Rowland Table for Such Lines," *ibid.,* **44** (1916), 15–38, written with L. W. Ware; "The Elimination of Pole-Effect From the Source for Secondary Standards of Wave-Length," *ibid.,* **46** (1917), 138–166, written with H. D. Babcock; "On Systematic Displacements of Lines in Spectra of Venus," *ibid.,* **53** (1921), 380–391, written with S. B. Nicholson; "Evidence for the Gravitational Displacement of Lines in the Solar Spectrum Predicted by Einstein's Theory," *ibid.,* **67** (1928), 195–239; "Elements Unidentified or Doubtful in the Sun: Suggested Observations," *ibid.,* **70** (1929), 160–174; and "Excitation Potential in Solar Phenomena," *ibid.,* 319–330.

II. Secondary Literature. Obituary notices appeared in *Astrophysical Journal,* **82** (1935), 273–283; *Publications of the Astronomical Society of the Pacific,* **47** (1935), 115–120; and *Popular Astronomy,* **43** (1935), 611–617. See also Walter S. Adams' notice in *Biographical Memoirs. National Academy of Sciences,* **18,** no. 12 (1938), 285–304, with bibliography of St. John's works.

Brian G. Marsden

SAINT-VENANT, ADHÉMAR JEAN CLAUDE BARRÉ DE (*b.* Villiers-en-Bière, Seine et-Marne, France, 23 August 1797; *d.* St.-Ouen, Loir-et-Cher, France, 6 January 1886), *mechanics, geometry.*

Saint-Venant entered the École Polytechnique in 1813. Upon graduating he joined the Service des Poudres et Salpêtres and in 1823 transferred to the Service des Ponts et Chaussées, where he served for twenty years. He devoted the remainder of his life to teaching and, especially, to scientific research. In 1868 he was elected to the mechanics section of the Académie des Sciences, succeeding Poncelet.

Saint-Venant's investigations deal chiefly with the mechanics of solid bodies, elasticity, hydrostatics, and hydrodynamics. Closely related to engineering, they frequently had immediate applications to road- and bridge-building, to the control of streams, and to agriculture. On the basis of his work on the torsion of prisms or cylinders of any base and on the equilibrium of elastic beams, Saint-Venant presented a memoir to the Académie des Sciences in 1844 dealing with gauche curves. In it he introduced the term "binormal," which is still used: "This line is, in effect, normal to two consecutive elements at the same time."

In "Mémoire sur les sommes et les différences géométriques et sur leur usage pour simplifier la mécanique" (1845), Saint-Venant set forth a vector calculus displaying certain analogies with the conceptions of H. G. Grassmann. In a subsequent priority dispute Saint-Venant asserted in a letter to Grassmann, written in 1847, that his ideas dated from 1832.

Saint-Venant used this vector calculus in his lectures at the Institut Agronomique, which were published in 1851 as *Principes de mécanique fondés sur la cinématique*. In this book Saint-Venant, a convinced atomist, presented forces as divorced from the metaphysical concept of cause and from the physiological concept of muscular effort, both of which, in his opinion, obscured force as a kinematic concept accessible to the calculus. Although his atomistic conceptions did not prevail, his use of vector calculus was adopted in the French school system.

BIBLIOGRAPHY

I. ORIGINAL WORKS. The Royal Society *Catalogue of Scientific Papers*, I, 189–191; VIII, 812–814; and XI, 262, lists 111 works by Saint-Venant and four of which he was coauthor. Among his some 170 published writings are *Leçons de mécanique appliquée faites à l'École des ponts et chaussées* (Paris, 1838); "Mémoire et expériences sur l'écoulement de l'air," in *Journal de l'École polytechnique*, 16 (1839), 85–122, written with Laurent Wantzel: "Mémoire sur les courbes non planes," *ibid.*, 18 (1845), 1–76; "Mémoire sur les sommes et les différences géométriques et sur leur usage pour simplifier la mécanique," in *Comptes rendus . . . de l'Académie des sciences*, 21 (1845), 620–625; *Principes de mécanique fondés sur la cinématique* (Paris, 1851); "De l'interprétation géométrique des clefs algébriques et des déterminants," in *Comptes rendus . . . de l'Académie des sciences*, 36 (1853), 582–585; *Mécanique appliquée de Navier, annotée par Saint-Venant* (Paris, 1858); "Deux leçons sur la théorie générale de l'élasticité," in Chanoine Moigno, *Stratique* (Paris, 1868), lessons 21 and 22; R. Clebsch, *Theorie de l'élasticité des corps solides*, translated by Saint-Venant and Alfred Flamant, with notes by Saint-Venant (Paris, 1883), and "Resistance des fluides: Considérations historiques phy-

siques et pratiques relatives au probléme de l'action dynamique mutuelle d'un fluide et d'un solide, spécialemente dans l'état de permanence supposé acquis dans leurs mouvements," in *Mémoires de l'Académie des sciences*, 44 (1888), 1–192, 271–273.

II. SECONDARY LITERATURE. See J. Boussinesq and A. Flamant, "Notice sur la vie et les travaux de M. de Saint-Venant," in *Annales des ponts et chaussées*, 6th ser., 12 (1886), 557–595, which includes a very comprehensive bibliography; Michel Chasles, *Rapport sur les progrès de la géométrie* (Paris, 1870), 197–199; Michael J. Crowe, *A History of Vector Analysis* (Notre Dame, Ind., 1967), 81–85; René Dugas, *Histoire de la mécanique* (Paris, 1950), 421–422; and E. Phillips, "Notice sur M. de Saint-Venant," in *Comptes rendus . . . de l'Académie des sciences*, 102 (1886), 141–147.

JEAN ITARD

ST. VICTOR, HUGH OF. See **Hugh of St. Victor.**

SAINT VINCENT, GREGORIUS (*b.* Bruges, Belgium, 8 September 1584; *d.* Ghent, Belgium, 27 January 1667), *mathematics, astronomy.*

Nothing is known of Gregorius' origins. He entered the Jesuit *collège* of Bruges in 1595 and from 1601 studied philosophy and mathematics at Douai. In 1605 he became a Jesuit novice at Rome and in 1607 was received into the order. His teacher Christoph Clavius recognized Gregorius' talents and arranged for him to remain in Rome to study philosophy, mathematics, and theology. When Galileo compared his telescope with those of the Jesuits in 1611, Gregorius hinted that he had doubts about the geocentric system, thereby displeasing the scholastically oriented philosophers.

After Clavius died in 1612, Gregorius went to Louvain to complete his theological studies, and in 1613 he was ordained priest. After being assigned to teach Greek for several years, first in Brussels, then in Bois-le-Duc ('s Hertogenbosch, Netherlands [1614]), and in Courtrai (1615), he served for a year as chaplain with the Spanish troops stationed in Belgium. He then became lecturer in mathematics at the Jesuit college in Antwerp, succeeding François d'Aguilon (*d.* 1617). Gregorius' *Theses de cometis* (Louvain, 1619) and *Theses mechanicae* (Antwerp, 1620) were defended by his student Jean Charles de la Faille, who later made them the basis of his highly regarded *Theoremata de centro gravitatis* (1632).

Established as a mathematician at Louvain in 1621, Gregorius elaborated the theory of conic sections on the basis of Commandino's editions of Archimedes (1558), Apollonius (1566), and Pappus (1588). He also developed a fruitful method of infinitesimals. His students Gualterus van Aelst and Johann Ciermans defended his *Theoremata mathematica scientiae staticae* (Louvain, 1624); and two other students, Guillaume Boelmans and Ignaz Derkennis, aided him in preparing the *Problema Austriacum,* a quadrature of the circle, which Gregorius regarded as his most important result. He requested permission from Rome to print his manuscript, but the general of the order, Mutio Vitelleschi, hesitated to grant it. Vitelleschi's doubts were strengthened by the opinion that Christoph Grienberger (Clavius' successor) rendered on the basis of preliminary material sent from Louvain.

Gregorius was called to Rome in 1625 to modify his manuscript but returned to Belgium in 1627 with the matter still unsettled. In 1628 he went to Prague, where he suffered a stroke. Following his recovery, his superiors granted his request that a former student, Theodor Moret, be made his assistant. His poor health forced Gregorius to decline an offer from the Madrid Academy in 1630. The following year he fled to Vienna just ahead of the advancing Swedes, but he was obliged to leave behind his scientific papers, including an extensive work on statics. A colleague, Rodrigo de Arriaga, rescued the studies on the conic sections and on methods of quadrature. Gregorius, who meanwhile had become a mathematician in Ghent (1632), did not receive his papers until 1641. He published them at Antwerp in 1647 as *Opus geometricum quadraturae circuli et sectionum coni.* His *Opus geometricum posthumum ad mesolabium* (Ghent, 1668) is an unimportant work, the first part of which had been printed at the time of his death.

Gregorius' major work is the *Opus geometricum* of 1647, misleadingly entitled *Problema Austriacum;* it is over 1,250 folio pages long and badly organized. It treats of four main subjects. Book I contains various introductory theorems on the circle and on triangles as well as geometrically clothed algebraic transformations. Book II includes the sums of geometric series obtained by means of transformation to the differences of the terms. Among the applications presented in this book is the step-by-step approximation of the trisection of an angle through continuous bisection, corresponding to the relationship $1/2 - 1/4 + 1/8 \mp \cdots = 1/3$. Another is the skillful treatment of Zeno of Elea's paradox of Achilles and the tortoise. In book VIII it is shown that if the horn an-

gle is conceived as a quantity, the axiom of the whole and the parts no longer holds.

Books III–VI are devoted to the circle, ellipse, parabola, and hyperbola, and to the correspondence between the parabola and the Archimedean spiral (today expressed as $x = r$, $y = r\phi$). These books contain various propositions concerning the metric and projective properties of conic sections. Their scope far exceeds that found in older treatments, but their presentation is unsystematic. Common properties are based on the figure of the conic section pencil $y^2 = 2px - (1 - \epsilon^2)x^2$, where ϵ is the parameter. (This figure had appeared in 1604 in a work by Kepler.) By inscribing and circumscribing rectangles in a geometric series in and about a hyperbola, Gregorius developed a quadrature of a segment bound by two asymptotes, a line parallel to one of them, and the portion of the curve contained between the two parallels. The relation between this procedure and logarithms was first noted by Alfonso Antonio de Sarasa (1649).

Book VII contains Gregorius' remarkable quadrature method. It is a summation procedure— the so-called *ductus plani in planum*—related to the method of indivisibles developed by Bonaventura Cavalieri, although the two are mutually independent. Gregorius' method, however, is somewhat better founded. In modern terms it amounts to the geometric interpretation of cubatures of the form $\int y(x) \cdot z(x) \cdot dx$. It touches on considerations related to the then-unknown *Method* of Archimedes, considerations that, in book IX, are applied to bodies of simple generation. A section of book VII deals with "virtual" parabolas, expressible in modern notation as $y = \sqrt{ax + b} + \sqrt{cx + d}$.

Book X is devoted to the quadrature of the circle, which here is based on cubatures of the following type:

$$X_1 = 2a \int_{x-c}^{x+c} \sqrt{a^2 - t^2} dt, \quad X_2 = \int_{x-c}^{x+c} (a^2 - t^2) dt,$$

$$X_3 = \int_{x-c}^{x+c} (a^2 - t^2)^2 dt / 4a^2$$

$$Y_1 = 2a \int_{y-c}^{y+c} \sqrt{a^2 - t^2} dt, \quad Y_2 = \int_{y-c}^{y+c} (a^2 - t^2) dt,$$

$$Y_3 = \int_{y-c}^{y+c} (a^2 - t^2)^2 dt / 4a^2,$$

given that $x \neq y$ and $0 \leq x - c < x + c \leq a$ and $0 \leq y - c < y + c \leq a$. The crucial element of the argument is the false assertion that from $X_2/Y_2 = (X_1/Y_1)^n$ it follows that $X_3/Y_3 = (X_2/Y_2)^n$. The result is the appearance in the calculations of an error of integration, first detected by Huygens (1651). The error arose from the geometric presentation of the argument, which made it extraordinarily difficult to get an overall grasp of the problem. This error considerably damaged Gregorius' reputation among mathematicians of the following generation. But their reaction was unfair, for his other results show that he was a creative mathematician with a broad command of the knowledge of his age. Although Gregorius basically despised algebraic terminology, he was, as his students recognized, one of the great pioneers in infinitesimal analysis.

BIBLIOGRAPHY

I. Original Works. Gregorius' unprinted posthumous papers are in the Bibliothèque Royale Albert Ier, nos. 5770–5793. Nos. 5770–5772, which are partially illustrated with remarkable figures, are discussed in E. Sauvenier-Goffin, "Les manuscrits de Saint-Vincent," in *Bulletin de la Société r. des sciences de Liège,* **20** (1951), 413–436, 563–590, 711–737. See also P. Bockstaele, "Four Letters from Gregorius a S. Vincentio to Christophe Grienberger," in *Janus,* **56** (1969), 191–202. A portrait of Gregorius is in *Opus geometricum posthumum* (1668).

II. Secondary Literature. For a biography of Gregorius, see H. Bosmans, "Saint Vincent (Grégoire de)," in *Biographie nationale belge,* XXI, cols. 141–171, which contains an extensive bibliography.

For a discussion of Gregorius' work on conic sections, see K. Bopp, "Die Kegelschnitte des Gregorius a S. Vincentio," in *Abhandlungen zur Geschichte der Mathematik,* no. 20 (1907), 83–314.

Gregorius' work on infinitesimal analysis and its influence on other mathematicians is discussed in J. E. Hofmann, "Das *Opus geometricum* des Gregorius a S. Vincentio und seine Einwirkung auf Leibniz," in *Abhandlungen der Preussischen Akademie der Wissenschaften,* Math. Naturwiss. Kl. (1941), no. 13.

On the debate over the quadrature of the circle, see A. A. de Sarasa, *Solutio problematis a M. Mersenno propositi* (Antwerp, 1649); C. Huygens, *Exetasis cyclometriae Gregorii a S. Vincentio,* which was appended to *Theoremata de quadratura hyperboles, ellipsis et circuli ex dato portionum gravitatis centro* (Leiden, 1651), repr. in Huygens' *Oeuvres complètes,* XI (The Hague, 1908), 315–337; and *Ad. Fr. X. Ainscom epistola* (The Hague, 1656), repr. in his *Oeuvres complètes,* XII (1910), 263–277; Alexius Sylvius, *Lunae circulares periodi . . ., adjunctum quoque est examen quarundam propositionum quadraturae circuli Gregorii a S. Vincentio* (Lesna, 1651), 374–418; Gottfried Alois Kinner von Löwenthurn, *Elucidatio geometrica problematis Austriaci* (Prague, 1653); Vincent Léotaud, *Examen circuli quadraturae . . .* (Lyons, 1654); and *Cyclomathia . . .* (Lyons, 1663), I, *Quadraturae examen confirmatur ac promovetur;* Marcus Meibom, *De proportionibus dialo-*
gus (Copenhagen, 1655); and Franz X. Aynscom, *Expositio ac deductio geometrica quadraturarum circuli Gregorii a S. Vincentio* (Antwerp, 1656).

J. E. Hofmann

SAKHAROV, VLADIMIR VLADIMIROVICH (*b.* Simbirsk [now Ulyanovsk], Russia, 28 February 1902; *d.* Moscow, U.S.S.R., 9 January 1969), *genetics.*

Sakharov's research was basically in experimental chemical mutagenesis, polyploids, radiation genetics, and human genetics. His father, Vladimir Matveevich Sakharov, was an agronomist; his mother, Maria Antonovna Ponyatovskaya, was the daughter of a Moscow physician and taught French in the Simbirsk Gymnasium.

In 1919 the family moved to Moscow, and in 1920 Sakharov entered the Pedagogical Faculty of the Second Moscow State University, from which he graduated in 1926, defending as dissertations two works done at the Institute of Experimental Biology (IEB) from 1922 to 1924: "Novaya mutatsia u drozofily" ("New Mutation in Drosophila") and "Razbor muzykalnykh genealogy" ("Analysis of Musical Genealogies"). From 1925 through 1929 he taught soil science in a Moscow school.

In 1929 Sakharov entered the IEB, where he worked until 1948 under the immediate direction of its organizer and director, N. K. Koltsov. During the 1930's and early 1940's Sakharov did research on experimental mutagenesis. In 1932 he showed for the first time the mutagenic action of chemical agents (iodine, methylcholanthrene). Continuing this line of work, Sakharov formulated the idea of the "specific action of mutagenic factors" and showed the difference in the nature of spontaneous and induced chemical and physical factors in mutations. This research was completed with the discovery of the role of factors inherent in the mutational process (the aging of sperm, hibernation, inbreeding, and hybridization). At the beginning of the 1930's Sakharov also studied medical anthropogenesis, for instance, the distribution and character of inherited endemic goiter and of blood types in Uzbekistan (1929 and 1930).

In 1941 Sakharov began research on polyploids. With S. L. Frolova and V. V. Mansurova, he obtained by the colchicine method a highly fertile variety of tetraploid buckwheat, which by 1948 successfully competed with the best diploid variety. Sakharov continued to combine research with teaching in the department of general biology (headed by V. F. Natali of the Moscow Pedagogical Institute).

In 1950–1956 Sakharov worked at the Moscow Pharmaceutical Institute in the department of botany, which was headed by A. P. Zhebrak. Besides lecturing on plant genetics, he continued his research on polyploids (now on medicinal plants) and began experiments on chemical mutagenesis in plants. With B. M. Griner he created a botanical garden of medicinal plants. In 1956 he organized a section of genetics at the Moscow Society of Experimenters with Nature, which became the basis of the Vavilov All-Union Society of Geneticists and Selectionists, created in 1965.

In 1956 Sakharov moved to the Laboratory of Radiation Genetics of the Institute of Biophysics of the Soviet Academy of Sciences, where he headed a group for the study of polyploids; in 1966–1967 he headed the Laboratory of Polyploids of the Institute of General Genetics of the Soviet Academy of Sciences. In 1967 he moved his laboratory to the Institute of Biology of Development of the Soviet Academy. From 1956, combining his research on mutagenesis and polyploids, Sakharov began a comparative study of sensitivity of diploid and autotetraploid forms to the action of radiation and chemical mutagenesis (for example, on buckwheat and meadow brown butterflies), discovering the physiological protection of polyploids against the influence of mutagenesis. This work led Sakharov to pose the question and prove the possibility of selection for radiation-resistance on a theoretical level, and later in direct experiments on diploid and tetraploid buckwheat. At the end of the 1960's he became professor at the Timiryazev Institute of Plant Physiology, where he lectured on genetics.

Sakharov was a scientist with a broad general biological and philosophical viewpoint, as well as an author who both posed problems and indicated the means for solving them in an original way. His scientific credo was stated in a small book, *Organizm i sreda* ("Organism and Environment," 1968). Besides his personal scientific contribution, he played a large role in the development of genetics in the Soviet Union through his scientific administration and teaching and through propaganda for genetic knowledge, especially in the periods of conflict over genetics and its restoration.

BIBLIOGRAPHY

I. ORIGINAL WORKS. Sakharov's writings include "Novye mutatsii *Drosophila melanogaster*" ("New Mutations of *Drosophila melanogaster*"), in *Zhurnal eksperimentalnoi biologii i meditsiny*, ser. A, **1**, nos. 1–2 (1925), 75–91, written with A. S. Serebrovsky; "Yod kak khimichesky faktor deystvuyushchii na mutatsionny protsess u *Drosophila melanogaster*," in *Biologicheskii zhurnal*, **1**, nos. 3–4 (1932), 1–8, with German summary, "Erregung des Mutationprozesses bei *Drosophila melanogaster* durch Jodbehandlung," 7–8; "Jod als chemischer Faktor, der auf dem Mutationprozess von *Drosophila melanogaster wirkt*," in *Genetica* (The Hague), **18**, nos. 3–4 (1936), 193–216; "Spetsifichnost deystvia mutatsionnykh faktorov," in *Biologicheskii zhurnal*, **7**, no. 3 (1938), 595–618, with English summary, "The Specificity of the Action of the Factors of Mutation," 617–618; and "Vlianie inbridinga i gibridizatsii na temp mutatsionnogo protsessa," in *Zhurnal obshchei biologii*, **3**, nos. 1–2 (1942), 99–123, written with K. V. Magrzhikovskaya, with an English summary, "Effect of Inbreeding and Hybridization on the Mutation Rate," 120–123.

See also "Tetraploidy in Cultivated Buckwheat (*Fagopyrum esculentum*)," in *Doklady Akademii nauk SSSR*, **43**, no. 5 (1944), 213–216, written with S. L. Frolova and V. V. Mansurova; "Cytological Basis of High Fertility in Autotetraploid Buckwheat," in *Nature*, **158**, no. 4015 (1945), 520, written with S. L. Frolova and V. V. Mansurova; "Chuvstvitelnost diploidnykh i autotetraploidnykh rastenii k gamma-izlucheniyu," in *Botanicheskii zhurnal SSSR*, **43**, no. 7 (1958), 989–997, written with V. V. Mansurova and V. V. Khvostova, with English summary, "The Sensitivity of Diploid and Autotetraploid Plants to Gamma Radiation," 997; "Otbor na radioustoichivost diploidnykh i autotetraploidnykh form grechiki posevnoi (*Fagopyrum esculentum* Moënh)" ("Selection for Radio-Resistance in Diploid and Autotetraploid Forms of Buckwheat"), in *Radiobiologia*, **2**, no. 4 (1962), 595–600, written with R. N. Platonova; and *Organizm i sreda* ("Organism and Environment"; Moscow, 1968).

II. SECONDARY LITERATURE. See B. L. Astaurov, A. A. Malinovsky, and V. S. Andreev, "Vladimir Vladimirovich Sakharov," in *Genetika* (Moscow), **5**, no. 2 (1969), 177–182, with a bibliography of 84 titles; and Y. I. Polansky, "Vladimir Vladimirovich Sakharov (1902–1969)," in *Citologia*, **2**, no. 3 (1969), 398–400.

VASSILY BABKOFF

SAKS, STANISŁAW (*b.* Warsaw, Poland, 30 December 1897; *d.* Warsaw, November 1942), *mathematics.*

Saks was a member of the Polish school of mathematics that flourished between the two world wars. The son of Philip and Ann Łabedz Saks, he received his secondary education in Warsaw. In the autumn of 1915 Saks entered the newly established Polish University of Warsaw, from which he received his doctorate in 1921 with a dissertation in topology. From 1921 to 1939 he was an assistant at the Warsaw Technical University and, from 1926 to 1939, he also lectured at the University of Warsaw. In 1942 he was arrested by the Nazi authorities and killed, allegedly while attempting to escape from prison.

Most of Saks's research involved the theory of real functions, such as problems on the differentiability of functions and the properties of Denjoy-Perron integrals. His work also touched upon questions in such related fields as topology and functional analysis. The two mathematicians at the University of Warsaw who exerted the greatest influence upon Saks were the topologist Stefan Mazurkiewicz, from whom Saks acquired a sensitivity to topological problems and methods, and Wacław Sierpiński. Saks, in turn, considerably influenced the development of real analysis within the Polish school.

Saks's contributions to mathematics included two important books. The first, *Théorie de l'intégrale* (1933), grew out of his lectures at the University of Warsaw and appeared as the second volume in the series Monografie Matematyczne. A thoroughly revised English edition was published in 1937 as the seventh volume of the series. In this highly original work Saks systematically developed the theory of integration and differentiation from the standpoint of countably additive set functions. Widely read outside Poland, it is now considered a still useful classic. In 1938 Saks collaborated with Antoni Zygmund to produce the ninth volume of Monografie Matematyczne, *Funkcje analityczne,* which received the prize of the Polish Academy of Sciences that year. An English edition, published by Zygmund in 1952, helped make its contents known to a larger audience, for whom it has become a standard reference work on complex analysis.

BIBLIOGRAPHY

I. ORIGINAL WORKS. Saks's papers have not been published in collected form, but many appeared in *Fundamenta mathematicae* and, to a lesser extent, in *Studia mathematica*. His books are *Zarys teorii całki* (Warsaw, 1930); *Théorie de l'intégrale* (Warsaw, 1933), rev. as *Theory of the Integral,* L. C. Young, trans. (Warsaw–Lvov–New York, 1937; repr. New York, 1964); and *Funkcje analityczne* (Warsaw, 1938), written with A. Zygmund, rev. as *Analytic Functions,* E. J. Scott, trans. (Warsaw, 1952; 2nd English ed., 1965).

II. SECONDARY LITERATURE. Apparently nothing has

been written on Saks. (The author is indebted to Professor A. Zygmund of the University of Chicago for much helpful information.) For further references concerning the Polish school of mathematics, see M. G. Kuzawa, *Modern Mathematics: The Genesis of a School in Poland* (New Haven, 1968).

THOMAS HAWKINS

SALA, ANGELO (Angelus) (*b.* Vicenza, Italy [?], 1576; *d.* Bützow, Germany, 2 October 1637), *pharmaceutics, chemistry, medicine.*

Sala was the son of Bernhardino Sala, a spinner; nothing is known about his mother. After Sala's grandfather, Angelo Sala, immigrated to Geneva, Sala followed him (at an unknown date), as did his brother Domenico. There the family converted to Calvinism. Sala probably had already begun his "chymical" studies in northern Italy (1593), perhaps during his years in Vicenza, which was close to Padua and Venice, then the centers of the manufacture and sale of medicines.

The years from 1602 to about 1612 were Sala's *Wanderjahre*. He is reported working as a physician in a number of cities, including Dresden (1602), Sondrio and Ponte (1604), Nuremberg (1606), Frauenfeld (1607), and Geneva (1609). In 1610 he served as physician to the Protestant troops under the command of Prince Johann of Nassau in the Upper Palatinate (for example, in Amberg and Neumark). Finally, in 1612, he settled in The Hague, the Netherlands, where for five years he practiced medicine and gave instruction in chemistry to medical students from various countries. He had already published two early works, *De variis tum chymicorum, tum galenistarum erroribus . . .* (n.p., 1608) and the famous *Anatomia vitrioli* (Geneva, 1609), but in The Hague he engaged in much more scientific research, which is reflected in a number of new works he published during this period.

From 1617 to 1620 he worked as physician in ordinary to Count Anton Günther of Oldenburg, living partly in the city of Oldenburg and partly in Jever. In addition, he supervised all the pharmacies in the count's territory. In Oldenburg, Sala met Anton Günther Billich, who became his student and an enthusiastic proponent of his chemical theories. In 1625 Billich married Sala's only daughter, Maria. (It is not known when Sala married his wife, Katherine von Brockdorf, who survived him.)

Sala continued to publish books while at Oldenburg and also at his next place of residence, Hamburg (1620–1625). Beginning in this period he wrote mainly in German (although he continued to give most of his works Latin titles). He made this decision after joining, in 1617, the Fruchtbringende Gesellschaft in Weimar, which promoted the use of the German language. In Hamburg, where he served as *Chymiater*, Sala published for the first time a list of the medications that he had prepared (Wandsbek [now part of Hamburg], 1624).

At the recommendation of the Landgrave Moritz of Hesse (Kassel), Sala transferred to the service of the rulers of Mecklenburg. Very active henceforth as both a physician (principally in connection with the use of drugs) and a researcher, he lived in Güstrow until 1636 and then, for the rest of his life, in Bützow. To be sure, during the troubles caused by the Thirty Years' War, he was obliged to move around several times, spending the years from 1628 to 1631 in Bernburg and Harzgerode in Anhalt. On his return trip he spent several days in Lübeck as a guest of the physician Hermann Westhoff. As early as 1622 Westhoff had reported on Sala's medicinal preparations to his friend Joachim Jungius (also from Lübeck) and had himself brought samples of them to Rostock. In his own theoretical research Jungius therefore drew indirectly on Sala's chemical studies and perhaps also met him.

Sala recorded his original chemical observations chiefly in his later works, notably those written after about 1620. Of his nineteen books, only a few have attracted the attention of historians. There exists no direct evidence concerning his medical practice. Early in his career, from about 1608, he followed the teachings of Paracelsus and agreed with the principle that "similia similibus curantur." From about 1625, he prescribed medicines in conformity with the basic principle "that they have a force . . . that resists the disease"; and he adopted a skeptical attitude toward the followers of Paracelsus, as previously he had done toward the Galenic physicians. Frequently attacked by representatives of both these medical traditions, Sala said that none of them was willing "to deviate a hair's breadth from his opinions, no matter whether he was right or wrong."[1]

Sala's chemical ideas proved to be historically influential. He performed the earliest known experiment in which a synthesis was confirmed by analysis ("anatomia"). Sala wished to establish "what blue *vitriolum* is, and out of what kind of pieces or materials it is composed or put together by nature."[2] As proof that this *vitriolum* consists of "copper ore, sulfur fumes, and water," Sala observed that out of it one can distill, successively, water and "sulfur-bearing vapor" ("schweffelischen Dampff," that is to say, sulfuric acid), with the result that there remains "a reddish-brown substance similar to burned copper" (cupric oxide). Going beyond this qualitative analysis, Sala made quantitative observations, notably that these three substances can "exist in combination only in their appropriate proportion." He further remarked that after distillation of the water, the remainder "cannot weigh more than two-thirds with respect to the previous weight of the raw vitriol." This weight is now determined to be 64 percent; thus Sala was not yet able to arrive at exact results.[3]

Closely connected with Sala's conception of the constitution of vitriol out of constituent parts is his notion that the possibility of *reductio* (that is to say, of a return to the earlier state) is proof that no genuine *transmutatio* has occurred. Although Sala thought that the theory of transmutation was valid for salts in general, he did not think it applied to vitriol, since he did not consider it to be a salt. Another example of *reductio*, he thought, was the precipitation of copper by means of iron. Iron draws (*attrahit*) copper out of copper or blue vitriol solution (copper sulfate) but not out of iron vitriol solution or out of sulfuric acid. The *reductio* consists, according to Sala, of a joining together of the copper particles dispersed in the blue vitriol solution. Previously, in 1603, Nicolas Guibert had also interpreted *praecipitatio* as a process of *attractio*, but not from a corpuscular point of view. Both authors went beyond Libau, who still accepted the concept of *transmutatio*. Still, they did not perceive, as did van Helmont in 1624, that the iron goes into solution. Nor did they realize, as did Jungius in 1630, that an exact exchange of the two metals takes place, both at the metallic precipitate and in the substance in solution.[4]

Sala did not succeed in carrying out the *Anatomia antimonii* (that is, of antimony [V] sulfide).[5] It was too difficult at that time to distinguish between synthesis and analysis.[6] In the case of sal ammoniac, the synthesis was successful but not the analysis.[7] Sala considered sulfur to be a *compositum*, because he perceived corrosive "smoke" being liberated from it in the process of burning. It should be remembered that for the pharmacists of the period, preparation, and therefore synthesis, was of primary interest. Accordingly, Sala's attempts to conduct analyses are all the more praiseworthy. It is worth noting that in 1614 Sala reported the blackening of silver nitrate by sunlight.[8]

Considering his work as a whole, it is evident

that Sala was above all a practitioner. In his view, demonstrations could be carried out only through manual operations (*inventionibus manualibus*), that is to say, only with the aid of experimental examples, which he clearly distinguished from argumentation. For him, chemistry was still a handicraft (*ars*).

NOTES

1. R. Capobus, *Angelus Sala* (Berlin, 1933), 46.
2. A. Sala, *De natura, proprietatibus et usu spiritus vitrioli fundamentalis dissertatio. Oder Gründliche Beschreibung, was Spiritus Vitrioli eigentlich sey* (Hamburg, 1625), 4–5.
3. R. Hooykaas, *Het begrip element in zijn historisch-wijsgeerige ontwikkeling* (Utrecht. 1933), 150.
4. On the history of metallic precipitates, see H. Kangro, *Joachim Jungius' Experimente und Gedanken zur Begründung der Chemie als Wissenschaft* (Wiesbaden, 1968), 159–173.
5. Hooykaas (1933), 158.
6. Hooykaas, "The Experimental Origin of Chemical Atomic and Molecular Theory Before Boyle," in *Chymia*, **2** (1949), 72–73; H. Kangro, "Ein allgemeines Prinzip, mit dessen Hilfe im 17. Jahrhundert chemische Reaktionen ohne quantitative Analyse gedeutet worden sind," in *Beiträge zum XIII. Internationalen Kongress für Geschichte der Wissenschaft* (Moscow, 1974), 7th section, 225–231.
7. R. P. Multhauf, *The Origins of Chemistry* (London, 1966), 333.
8. J. R. Partington, *A History of Chemistry*, II (London, 1961), 278; Multhauf, *op. cit.*, 330.

BIBLIOGRAPHY

I. Original Works. A complete bibliography is in Robert Capobus, *Angelus Sala* (Berlin, 1933), 53–55, although the titles are abbreviated and not always exact. Part of Sala's work is listed in the *Catalogue of the British Museum* and in the *Catalogue général des livres imprimés de la Bibliothèque Nationale* (Paris). Sala's Latin *Opera medico-chymica* appeared at Frankfurt am Main (1647), then at Rouen (1650), and again at Frankfurt am Main (1682).

Single works besides the two early works mentioned in the article and the work in n. 2 are *Septem planetarum terrestrium spagirica recensio* (Amsterdam, 1614); *Emetologia, ou enarration du naturel et usage des vomitoires* (Delft, 1613); *Opiologia* (The Hague, 1614); *Ternarius Bezoarticorum, ou trois souverains medicaments Bezoardiques* (Leiden, 1616); *Anatomia antimonii* (Leiden, 1617); *Anatomia vitrioli*, enlarged by the famous *Brevis demonstratio, quid sit vitriolum . . .* (Leiden, 1617); *Traicté de la peste* (Leiden, 1617); *Aphorismorum chymiatricorum synopsis* (Bremen, 1620); *Descriptio brevis antidoti pretiosi* (Marburg, 1620); *Chrysologia, seu examen auri chymicum* (Hamburg, 1622); *Von etlichen kräfftigen vnd hochbewerthen Medicamenten* (Wandesbeck, 1624); *De natura . . .* (Hamburg, 1625; see n. 2); and *Processus de auro potabili* (Strasbourg, 1630).

See also *Essentiarum vegetabilium anatome, darinnen von den fürtrefflichsten Nutzbarkeiten der Vegetabilischen Essentzen in der Artzney . . . gelehret vnnd gehandelt wird* (Rostock, 1630); *Tartarologia. Das ist: Von der Natur vnd Eigenschafft des Weinsteins* (Rostock, 1632); *Hydrelaeologia. Darinnen, wie man allerley Wasser, Oliteten vnd brennende Spiritus der Vegetabilischen Dingen, durch gewisse Chymische Regeln, vnd manualia destilliren vnd rectificiren soll . . . gehandelt wird* (Rostock, 1633); *Spagyrische Schatzkammer, Darinnen von unterschiedlichen, erbrechenmachenden . . . spagyrischen Medicamenten . . . treulich erwiesen vnd gelehret wird* (Rostock, 1634); *Saccharalogia. Darinnen erstlich von der Natur, qualiteten, nützlichem Gebrauch, vnd schädlichem Missbrauch des Zuckers: Darnach, wie von demselben ein Weinmässiger starker Getrank, Brandwein vnd Essig, als auch medicamenten . . . können bereitet werden . . . angezeiget wird* (Rostock, 1637). The last ed. of a work of Sala is the *Tractatus II de variis tum chymicorum, tum Galenistarum erroribus* (Frankfurt am Main, 1702).

II. Secondary Literature. Apart from the literature mentioned in notes 3, 6, 7, and 8 there can only be recommended G. F. A. Blanck, *Angelus Sala, sein Leben und seine Werke* (Schwerin, 1883); and a short biographical sketch in *Die Mecklenburgischen Ärzte von den ältesten Zeiten bis zur Gegenwart* (Schwerin, 1929), 83.

Gisela Kangro

SALERNITAN ANATOMISTS (*fl.* eleventh to thirteenth centuries, Salerno, Italy), *anatomy*.

In order to assess the contribution made by the school of anatomists at Salerno to the revival of their science in the West, it is essential to review briefly the arid millennium in the history of anatomy that began after the death of Galen (A.D. 199/200). Even during the latter's lifetime, dissection of the human body was no longer permitted at Alexandria; and the early Christian aversion to such studies is clearly shown by the opprobrium heaped on the memory of Herophilus by Tertullian, who castigated the great anatomist as "more of a butcher than a physician." Although Galen based many of his studies on the Barbary ape and rhesus monkey, he frequently made use of the pig (among other domestic animals), not only because of its ready availability but also because the internal organs were thought to show a remarkable similarity to those of man. Indeed, it was while vivisecting a pig that Galen discovered the function of the recurrent laryngeal nerve in voice production.

Although the written records do not say so, there is reason to believe that during the Dark Ages an occasional intrepid soul investigated the interior of the human body. A recent find in a fourth-century Roman catacomb shows a rather apathetic-looking group of master and pupils observing the dissection of a male corpse. Cassiodorus (sixth century) stated that human dissection was strictly forbidden by law and added a warning—presumably for the more intrepid—about cemetery guards and the harsh penalties for grave desecration. The various barbarian legal codes also contained sections on the violation of sepulchers. Some three centuries later George Teofano (d. 818) related that some Greek soldiers stationed in Bulgaria turned over a condemned prisoner to the physicians before consigning his body to the flames.

It is generally held that none of the anatomical works of Hippocrates, Aristotle, or Galen were in use in Europe before the end of the eleventh century. The meager anatomical literature available at Salerno before the arrival of the Constantinian translations included the *Schema anatomica* of Vindicianus (late fourth century), which survives in a solitary fragment written in the Benedictine script used at Salerno; the book on anatomical terminology in the *Differentiae* and the *Origines* of Isidore of Seville (*ca.* 560–636); and the anatomical chapters—derived ultimately from Celsus and Galen—in the *Epitome* of Paul of Aegina (seventh century). This situation changed radically with the arrival at Salerno of Constantine the African (d. 1087), translator of numerous works from the Arabic. Most important from an anatomical viewpoint was the *Kitāb al-Mālikī* of Haly Abbas (ᶜAlī ibn al-ᶜAbbās, d. 994), titled *Pantechne* by Constantine, who rendered parts of it into Latin and claimed it as his own original work. The *Kitāb al-Mālikī* was later (1127) translated in its entirety by Stephen of Antioch as the *Liber regalis*. The two chapters on anatomy in this book, although derived entirely from Galen and showing no evidence of direct observation, exerted a strong influence on the later anatomical writings produced at Salerno.

By the mid-eleventh century Salerno was rapidly approaching its zenith as the undisputed center of medical teaching in the Western world. The earliest writings of the school, such as the *Passionarius* of Gariopontus and the *Practica petrocelli,* were compiled for students and practitioners from late Greek and Byzantine works and contain little of anatomical interest. Yet there is every reason to believe that before the end of the century an annual public demonstration of porcine anatomy had become a traditional occurrence in the *civitas Hippocratica,* as Salerno came to be known.

The text that is considered to give the earliest account of such a dissection has for many centuries been attributed—although without any definite proof—to a Master Copho (*fl. ca.* 1080–1115), the author of *De modo medemdi* and other writings. The most primitive version of the *Anatomia porci,* as it is now called, treats only the neck, chest, and abdomen; the brief sections on the uterus and brain seem to have been added later, possibly by Stephen of Antioch, who called himself a pupil of Copho. In the cervical region the author identified the larynx, trachea, esophagus, epiglottis, and thyroid, and demonstrated to his pupils the function of the recurrent laryngeal nerve. He then proceeded to the contents of the thorax, identifying the pleura, pericardium, heart, and diaphragm as well as demonstrating the hollowness of the lung. He also described the course of the *vena concava* from the liver (as he thought) through the diaphragm into the inferior (right) auricle, where it becomes the artery "from which all other arteries arise." In the abdomen he enumerated eight subdivisions of the gastrointestinal tract, described the five-lobed liver, spleen, chylous vein, kidneys, ureters, omentum, and peritoneum. In the description of the uterus, allusion is made to seven cells or chambers that accommodate the fetuses, and to the placenta and membranes (secundines).

Throughout this brief tract (it contains less than a thousand words) the demonstrator speaks with assurance and clarity; his terminology has been described as transitional but is, in fact, almost entirely Greco-Latin or late Latin; and the three words of Arabic derivation may well have been interpolated during a revision. One recent student, noting that the order of dissection differs from the *de capite ad calcem* of Vindicianus and Isidore, suggests the influence of Celsus and Aristotle, although the means of transmission of the latter remains unclear. Certainly there is an agreement between the description of the large vessels of the heart in the *Historia animalium* and the *Anatomia porci.* The author seems to have been unfamiliar with the Galenic concept of blood passing from right to left ventricle through pores in the interventricular septum and depended on the earlier tradition (common to all twelfth-century Salernitan anatomies) that had the superior vena cava entering directly into the aorta.

Summing up the evidence for dating the earliest version of the *Anatomia porci,* I would suggest a year between 1080 and 1090, the decade just before the Constantinian translations had begun to circulate freely in Salerno.

Regardless of its antecedents and meagerness of content, the value of the *Anatomia porci* to the historian of science cannot be denied. Any eleventh-century investigation at which students from all over Europe could observe their master verify or criticize statements of other authorities must have had more than ordinary significance as marking the beginning of a new era. The text itself has survived in at least five manuscripts; it also has a remarkable printing history, having served as a working tool in book form from 1502 to 1655. Few works in the history of medicine can claim use over more than five centuries; long after the works of Mondino de' Luzzi and Vesalius were freely available, students continued to memorize the ancient text "as a preparatory exercise to the noble art of anatomy." Indeed, Mondino himself must have known and relied on this earlier work, since he continued to describe the human liver as five-lobed and the human uterus as bicornuate and multichambered.

The exact number of anatomies attributed to Salerno has varied with authorities, but Sudhoff and Corner agree on four. The second pig dissection, the *Demonstratio anatomica*, is related to the first as far as basic anatomical facts are concerned but differs greatly in style, methodology, and terminology. This work is approximately five times as long as the *Anatomia porci* and can best be described as an elaborate, polemic, early Scholastic commentary on the short primitive text. The author frequently wandered from descriptive anatomy to elaborate discussions of humoral physiology and made repeated references to the teleological concepts of Galen. Apparently this master had fallen completely under Arabic influence, and he made no attempt to conceal his indebtedness to Constantine. Indeed, he mentioned the latter by name on eight occasions, but only in reference to the terminology of various subdivisions of the gastrointestinal tract. Corner has clearly shown that vocabulary, phrases, and even entire paragraphs have been lifted almost verbatim from the *Pantechne*.

This second demonstration lacks the spontaneity of the first, and because of its prolixity never gained a student following. Since the author referred, somewhat pompously, to his own commentaries on several texts of the still-growing *Articella*, I have tentatively identified him with Master Bartholomaeus (*fl.* first half of the twelfth century), who is now known to have written precisely such commentaries as well as an *Anatomia* (all still unpublished). In his occasionally critical side remarks, the author confirmed the tradition of an annual dissection at Salerno; emphasized to his students the importance of committing his remarks to memory; and described the professional rivalry and competition for students in the still loosely organized school. He refused flatly to accept the *lateralia* "described in a recent booklet"—probably a revision of the *Anatomia porci*—because he "had never discovered these in animals," nor would he admit the usage of the term *faringes* proposed by a predecessor, because he had "not found it written in any book or heard it from any teacher." On the other hand, he did not hesitate to describe the human liver (which he obviously had never studied) as being five-lobed, "since certainly the same number [as in the pig] occurs in man."

The authorship of the third dissection, or *Anatomia mauri*, which has survived in four manuscripts (two of which explicitly name the author) has been attributed to Master Maurus, the *optimus physicus* of the school, who flourished in the latter half of the twelfth century and is known to have died in 1214. Although this brief tract shows familiarity with Arabic terminology, the descriptions are not so obviously dependent on the *Pantechne* as those of the second demonstration; and the author seems deliberately to have followed the *Anatomia porci* in format and method. In addition to the two hypochondria below the diaphragm mentioned by earlier authors, Maurus postulated, for teaching purposes, the existence of two superior hypochondria, one containing the lung and the other the heart. In his description of the circulation Maurus was somewhat more explicit than his predecessors: "Then you will see the cover of the heart and the heart itself and that *vena concava* which rises from the convexity of the liver through the diaphragm to the right auricle of the heart and then emerges through the left, where from the substance of the heart it acquires another coat and is thus transformed into an artery which is called the aorta, the name given to the Chief of all arteries." Again there is no mention of the interventricular pores. For the Latin term *peritoneum* Maurus also used the Arabic *siphac* and the Greek *epigasunta hymenon*, thus recalling the multilingual character of the Salernitan medical milieu. Nevertheless, the text in general is rather unoriginal and, aside from some changes in terminology, offers little improvement on its predecessors.

The fourth and last surviving porcine anatomy that can definitely be related to Salerno was discovered by Sudhoff and attributed by him to Urso of Calabria, a contemporary of Maurus, who fell entirely under the spell of the "new" Aristotelian logic. Basically a theoretician and philosopher rather than a physician, Urso was concerned only vaguely with morphological data; and the Scholastic method and terminology that dominated his work exclude any practical approach to the subject. Urso provided one historical note: he recalled that in his youth he had witnessed several dissections performed by his master, Matthaeus Platearius (*d. ca.* 1150).

In 1224 Frederick II issued a decree that surgeons must study anatomy for a year and be examined in that subject before they could practice; whether this involved actual dissection of the human body or simple observation is not known, nor has it ever been definitely proved whether a further edict of 1231, ordering that a human cadaver be publicly dissected at least once every five years in the presence of all practicing physicians and surgeons, was ever carried out. The political turmoil that threatened the latter years of Frederick's reign makes this unlikely.

For the sake of completeness we mention briefly an anatomy attributed to a Ricardus Salernitanus (*d.* 1252). He had undoubtedly studied at Salerno, for he mentioned many of its masters and reverentially compared Bartholomaeus with Hippocrates. He seems, however, to have taught at Montpellier; and his anatomy, not of the pig but of the human body, is thoroughly pseudo-Galenic and unoriginal. The work of Ricardus was edited and enlarged by a pupil, and the *Anatomia nicolai* is simply an elaboration of his master's text. Neither of these works can be considered as directly related to Salerno.

The earliest Salernitan anatomical demonstration had some influence on disciplines other than medicine. This is particularly evident in the writings of the philosopher-mystic Hugh of St. Victor (*d.* 1141), the great rival of Abelard at Paris. Three of Hugh's writings—"De bestiis et aliis rebus," "De hominis membris ac partibus," and "De natura hominis"—bear witness to the pervasive influence of the small but provocative *Anatomia porci* on the intellectual life of Europe.

BIBLIOGRAPHY

See George W. Corner, *Anatomical Texts of the Earlier Middle Ages* (Washington, D.C., 1927); Salvatore De Renzi, *Storia documentata della scuola di medicina di Salerno,* 2nd ed. (Naples, 1857), 254–255, 334–335; Thomas Haviland, " 'Anatomia porci,' a Twelfth Century Anatomy of the Pig Used in Teaching Human Anatomy," in *Wiener tierärztliche Monatsschrift,* Festschrift (1960), 246–265; Ynez Violé O'Neill, "William of Conches and the Cerebral Membranes," in *Clio Medica,* **2** (1967), 13–21; and "Another Look at the 'Anatomia porci,' " in *Viator,* **1** (1970), 115–124; Werner L. H. Ploss, ed., *Anatomia mauri* (Leipzig, 1921); Morris H. Saffron, *Maurus of Salerno* (Philadelphia, 1972), 13, 62; and Karl Sudhoff, "Die erste Tieranatomie von Salerno und ein neuer Salernitanischer Anatomietext," in *Archiv für Geschichte der Mathematik, der Naturwissenschaften und der Technik,* **10** (1927), 137–154; "Die vierte Salernitaner Anatomie," in *Archiv für Geschichte der Medizin,* **20** (1928), 33–50; and "Codex Fritz Paneth," in *Archiv für Geschichte der Mathematik, der Naturwissenschaften und der Technik,* **12** (1929), 2.

MORRIS H. SAFFRON

SALISBURY, ROLLIN DANIEL (*b.* Spring Prairie, Wisconsin, 17 August 1858; *d.* Chicago, Illinois, 15 August 1922), *geology, physical geography.*

Salisbury is best known for his collaboration with T. C. Chamberlin in the writing of geological textbooks that profoundly influenced the growth of the earth sciences during the first third of the twentieth century. His field studies, especially in Wisconsin, New Jersey, and Greenland, contributed notably to the then new science of glaciology.

Salisbury had come to Chamberlin's attention as a student at Beloit College, where Chamberlin was a part-time professor of geology. When he withdrew from that assignment to give full time to other duties, Salisbury was selected to succeed him, becoming professor of geology in 1884, only three years after receiving his bachelor's degree. His work at Beloit was interrupted for a year (1887–1888) by a trip to Europe, where he studied under Rosenbusch at Heidelberg and traced a previously unidentified belt of glacial moraines from Denmark to Russia. Chamberlin had employed him earlier in the glacial division of the United States Geological Survey, and his first important scientific contribution was their joint paper published in 1885. In 1891, four years after Chamberlin had become president of the University of Wisconsin, Salisbury resigned his post at Beloit to become professor of geology at the larger institution. Only a year later, however, Chamberlin accepted an invitation to organize the department of geology at the new University of Chicago and took Salisbury with him as professor of geographic geology. Both men remained at Chicago for the rest of their lives.

From 1899 until his death in 1922, Salisbury was dean of the Ogden Graduate School of Science at the University of Chicago, devoting much of his time to the manifold duties of that office. In addition, when the burgeoning program in geography was separated from that in geology to form a new department in 1903, he became its head. In 1918, when Chamberlin retired, Salisbury succeeded him as head of the department of geology, leaving the administration of the geography department to others. During his thirty years at the University of Chicago, Salisbury also assumed much of the editorial responsibility for the *Journal of Geology,* founded at Chicago during his first year there.

Salisbury never married. All his energy and devotion were concentrated on his students, his administrative responsibilities, and his science. He had a reputation for being brusque in speech and gruff in manner, but beneath the mask was a warm and kindly heart.

BIBLIOGRAPHY

I. ORIGINAL WORKS. Salisbury's writings include "Preliminary Paper on the Driftless Area of the Upper Mississippi Valley," in *Report of the United States Geological Survey,* **6** (1885), 205–322, written with T. C. Chamberlin; "On the Relationship of the Pleistocene to the Pre-Pleistocene Formations of Crowley's Ridge and Adjacent Areas South of the Limit of Glaciation," in *Report of the Arkansas Geological Survey* (for 1889), **2** (1891), 224–248; "The Drift of the North German Lowland," in *American Geologist,* **9** (1892), 294–318; "Distinct Glacial Epochs and the Criteria for Their Recognition," in *Journal of Geology,* **1** (1893), 61–84; "Salient Points Concerning the Glacial Geology of North Greenland," *ibid.,* **4** (1896), 769–810; *The Physical Geography of New Jersey,* vol. IV of *Final Report of the* [*New Jersey*] *State Geologist* (Trenton, 1898); "The Geography of the Region About Devil's Lake and the Dalles of the Wisconsin," in *Bulletin of the Wisconsin Geological and Natural History Survey,* no. 5 (1900), 1–151, written with W. W. Atwood; *Geology,* 3 vols. (New York, 1904–1906), written with T. C. Chamberlin; *Physiography* (New York, 1907; 3rd ed., 1919); *Elements of Geography* (New York, 1912), written with H. H. Barrows and W. S. Tower; and *Introductory Geology* (New York, 1914), written with T. C. Chamberlin.

II. SECONDARY LITERATURE. See the memorial by R. T. Chamberlin, in *Bulletin of the Geological Society of America,* **42** (1931), 126–138, with bibliography of 95 titles; and T. C. Chamberlin's obituary in *Journal of Geology,* **30** (1922), 480–481.

KIRTLEY F. MATHER

SALLO, DENYS DE (*b.* Paris, France, 1626; *d.* Paris, 14 May 1669), *scientific journalism.*

Denys de Sallo, Seigneur de la Coudraye, was the son of Jacques de Sallo, conseiller of the grand-chambre of the Parlement of Paris. He was educated at the Collège des Grassins, winning awards in Greek and Latin, before studying law. Admitted to the Paris bar in 1652, he won respect for his solid judgment, intelligence, and wit. In 1655 he married Elisabeth Mesnardeau, daughter of a colleague; they had one son and four daughters, the latter entering religious orders. Details of Sallo's life are extremely scarce; in 1657 he was in Frankfurt for the preliminaries to the election of a successor to Ferdinand III. E. Bigot records at this time that Sallo carried books from J. Boecler of Strasbourg to Paris for the astronomer Bouillaud.[1] During his last years Sallo was unable to walk, a condition attributed to his constant reading; although competent analysis of recorded symptoms now suggests a diabetic condition, then undiagnosed. In 1664 he began preparing the first scholarly periodical, *Journal des sçavans.* His 4,000 books and 200 manuscripts were sold after his death for 6,000 francs.

A *privilège* for the printing of the *Journal des sçavans* for twenty years was granted to Sallo on 8 August 1664; it was ceded on 30 December to Jean Cusson, printer and publisher; and on 5 January 1665 the first number was put on sale, priced at five sous. Thirteen weekly issues were published under Sallo's editorship; after the last, that of 30 March, there was a nine-month gap before resumption under Jean Gallois on 4 January 1666. A member of Sallo's household, Gallois was competent in languages and mathematics, and probably was one of three or four unidentified persons actively engaged in writing for the *Journal des sçavans* from the beginning.

Even before publication started, the *Journal des sçavans* had been actively promoted: by J. Chapelain, poet, critic, and correspondent of many French and foreign scholars; by Henri Justel, acquainted with innumerable travelers and men of letters; and by Éméric Bigot, well-known in foreign centers of learning. These and others had assured the *Journal* of a favorable reception abroad. Henry Oldenburg, secretary of the Royal Society, and Christiaan Huygens promised their assistance, which is apparent in the early issues. Sallo's active collaborators, apart from Gallois, for whom circumstantial evidence is persuasive, cannot be identified with assurance. Amable Bourzeis, the novelist Martin Le Roy de Gomberville, and Chapelain have been named on the basis of a rumor repeated by Gui Patin, who was not a friend of the circle in which the *Journal des sçavans* had originated. Of these only Chapelain probably was involved.

The *Journal des sçavans* responded to several aspects of contemporary life. Scientists, historians, philosophers, and others were finding that new facts, theories, and techniques posed issues that changed the basis of their thought. A rising skepticism about traditional views was transforming all disciplines, and the usual methods of exchanging information by letter were inadequate to the challenge. The *Gazette*, founded at Paris in 1631 by Théophraste Renaudot, reported competently on politics and military affairs; and it was logical that a similar periodical should chronicle events of intellectual interest. François de Mézeray, author of a comprehensive history of France and aware of the need for a record of cultural events as a basis for future histories of the sciences and arts, drafted a program (in the form of a *privilège*), outlining the aims of such a journal.[2] Mézeray lived in the same house in Paris as Sallo, a coincidence that cannot be passed over.

Mézeray's project emphasized the need for a record of discoveries and inventions, with only secondary attention to publications; as finally realized, the *Journal des sçavans* was a record of new books, a readable and critical account of current writings, and a marketable production in which the hand of the publisher is evident. The prospectus in the first pages of the first number resembles the program that Mézeray had outlined; but the accent was now on utility to the reader, whom the *Journal des sçavans* would inform of the content and value of the books reviewed.

In its first three months some eighty publications were discussed, sometimes at length. Almost all were in French or Latin, four in Italian or Spanish, and one in English—the first issue of the *Philosophical Transactions*, listed because of the repute of the newly founded Royal Society. A capable translator had been found who promised reviews of books in English. The *Journal des sçavans* was international from the outset: about half the books reviewed were published in Paris, while the rest came from London, Amsterdam, Rome, and other French and German cities. A quarter of the space was devoted to scientific material, some identified as trivial. Several important works were reviewed with insight: Thomas Willis' *Cerebri anatome*, at length; Steno's *De musculis et glandulis*, also in detail; G. Campani's work on his new lenses and telescopes; Clerselier's edition of Descartes's *De l'homme;* and G. Huret on the geometry of columns, treated with sharp criticism.

In addition there were reports of current scientific and technological developments: William Pet-

ty's double-hulled vessel and Robert Holmes's use of Huygens' clocks on Atlantic voyages. The most important scientific article offered an account[3] of a learned conference on comets held at the college of the Jesuits, followed by a detailed report on Adrien Auzout's calculation of the path of the comet then visible, with predictions for following weeks. While the views set forth before the distinguished audience at the conference were treated with formal respect, a discreet emphasis showed that traditional lore on the causes and nature of comets was not significant in comparison with accurate observation and sound mathematics, which demonstrated that the course followed by comets was much more regular than the lecturers, including Roberval, had asserted.

Various reasons have been given for the interruption of the *Journal des sçavans*. Sallo had offended certain persons of importance who were unaccustomed to seeing their work criticized in public print; the editor had commented critically on papal policy and the decrees of the Congregation of the Index concerning French publications; and the ironical view toward traditional attitudes in science and philosophy had indicated a leaning to excessive freedom of thought. The fact that the weekly numbers of the *Journal des sçavans* were not submitted in page proof for official approval was given as the cause of suppression; and Sallo, who could not tolerate constraints on speech and thought, was glad to turn his work over to others, although he seems to have acted as an intermediary for Gallois in dealing with Oldenburg in London. There is no record of his association with the *Journal des sçavans* after early 1668.

NOTES

1. Leonard E. Doucette, *Emery Bigot: Seventeenth-Century French Humanist* (Toronto, 1970), 11.
2. The papers of François Eudes de Mézeray in the Bibliothèque Nationale contain a leaf on which is drafted a *privilège* for a "Journal littéraire général" (Fonds français 20792, between ff. 112 and 113). This undated document was first published by the critic C. A. Sainte Beuve in 1853 (reprinted in *Causeries de lundi*, VIII, 183–184) and again from the original text by W. H. Evans in *L'Historien Mézeray et la conception de l'histoire en France au dix-septième siècle* (Paris, 1930), pp. 63–64.
3. *Journal des sçavans*, "du Lundy, 26 janvier, M.DC.LXV."

BIBLIOGRAPHY

A Paris *thèse de l'université* by Betty Trebell Morgan, *Histoire du Journal des Savants depuis 1665 jusqu'en 1701* (Paris, 1928), offers a rapid summary of the available information on De Sallo and his periodical; the book contains a full bibliography of earlier material. See also R. Birn, "Le *Journal des Savants* sous l'ancien régime," in *Journal des Savants* (1965), 15–35; Harcourt Brown, *Scientific Organizations in Seventeenth-Century France* (Baltimore, 1934; New York, 1967), 185–207; and "History and the Learned Journal," in *Journal of the History of Ideas*, 33, no. 2 (1972), 365–378. For De Sallo, see Louis Moreri, *Le grand dictionaire* [sic] *historique ou le Mélange curieux de l'histoire sacrée et profane*, IV (Paris, 1699), 392. The fullest article on De Sallo is Dugast-Matifeux, "Débuts du journalisme littéraire en France: Denis de Sallo, fondateur du Journal des Savants," in *Annales de la Société d'Emulation de la Vendée (1883)*.

HARCOURT BROWN

SALMON, GEORGE (*b.* Cork, Ireland, 25 September 1819; *d.* Dublin, Ireland, 22 January 1904), *mathematics*.

Salmon's father, Michael Salmon, was a linen merchant; his mother, Helen, was the daughter of the Reverend Edward Weekes. After early schooling in Cork he entered Trinity College, Dublin, in 1833 to read classics and mathematics. He graduated in 1838 as first mathematical moderator. He was elected a fellow of Trinity College in 1841 and, as required by college statutes, took Holy Orders in the Church of Ireland. In 1844 he married Frances Anne, the daughter of the Reverend J. L. Salvador; they had four sons and two daughters.

The main burden of teaching in Trinity College was then borne by the fellows, and Salmon spent twenty-five years as a lecturer and tutor—mainly in the mathematical school, but also to a lesser extent in the divinity school. During this period he published some forty papers in various mathematical journals and wrote four important textbooks.

Over the years Salmon became frustrated by the heavy load of tutoring and lecturing, much of it of an elementary kind, and was disillusioned because he was not made a professor, a promotion that would have relieved him of most of this load and given him more time for his research. It must have been this which influenced him, in about 1860, to turn away from mathematics toward the theological studies in which he had always been interested—and which appeared to offer better prospects of promotion. In fact, in 1866 he was appointed regius professor of divinity and head of the divinity school, a post that he held for twenty-two years. During this period he published four more

books; they earned him a reputation as a theologian that was as great as the one he already had as a mathematician.

In 1888 Salmon was appointed provost of Trinity College. He remained an administrator for the rest of his life. He was a good and much-loved head of his college, although he had become a strong conservative in his old age, so that his provostship was a period of consolidation in the college rather than one of reform.

When Salmon joined the staff of Trinity College in 1841, its mathematical school was already internationally known and his colleagues included the well-known scholars Rowan Hamilton, James MacCullagh, Charles Graves, and Humphrey Lloyd. There was a strong bias toward synthetic geometry in the school, and it was in this field that Salmon began his research work, although he shortly became interested in the algebraic theories that were then being developed by Cayley and Sylvester in England and by Hermite and later Clebsch on the Continent. Salmon soon joined their number, and played an important part in the applications of the theory of invariants and covariants of algebraic forms to the geometry of curves and surfaces. He became a close friend of both Cayley and Sylvester and exchanged a voluminous mathematical correspondence with them for many years. His chief fame as a mathematician, however, rests on the series of textbooks that appeared between 1848 and 1862. These four treatises on conic sections, higher plane curves, modern higher algebra, and the geometry of three dimensions not only gave a comprehensive treatment of their respective fields but also were written with a clarity of expression and an elegance of style that made them models of what a textbook should be. They were translated into every western European language and ran into many editions (each incorporating the latest developments); they remained for many years the standard advanced textbooks in their respective subjects.

Salmon's own most important contributions to mathematics included his discovery (with Cayley) of the twenty-seven straight lines on the cubic surface, his classification of algebraic curves in space, his investigations of the singularities of the ruled surface generated by a line meeting three given directing curves, his solution of the problem of the degree of a surface reciprocal to a given surface, his researches in connection with families of surfaces subjected to restricted conditions, his conditions for repeated roots of an algebraic equation, and his theorem of the equianharmonic ratio of the four tangents to a plane cubic curve from a variable point on it.

When his investigations called for it, Salmon was an indefatigable calculator. The most famous example of this was his calculation of the invariant E of the binary sextic, which he published in the second edition (1866) of his treatise on modern higher algebra and which occupied thirteen pages of text.

BIBLIOGRAPHY

I. ORIGINAL WORKS. The Royal Society *Catalogue of Scientific Papers*, V, 381–382; VII, 819, lists forty-one memoirs by Salmon published between 1844 and 1872. His mathematical textbooks are *A Treatise on Conic Sections* (Dublin, 1848); *A Treatise on the Higher Plane Curves: Intended as a Sequel to a Treatise on Conic Sections* (Dublin, 1852); *Lessons Introductory to the Modern Higher Algebra* (Dublin, 1859); and *A Treatise on the Analytic Geometry of Three Dimensions* (Dublin, 1862).

His most important theological writings are *A Historical Introduction to the Study of the Books of the New Testament* (London, 1885); *The Infallibility of the Church* (London, 1888); *Some Thoughts on the Textual Criticism of the New Testament* (London, 1897); and *The Human Element in the Gospels*, N. J. D. White, ed. (London, 1907), posthumously published.

II. SECONDARY LITERATURE. On Salmon and his work, see the obituary by J. H. Bernard in *Proceedings of the British Academy*, 1 (1903–1904), 311–315; by R. S. Ball in *Proceedings of the London Mathematical Society*, 2nd ser., 1 (1903–1904), xxii–xxviii; the unsigned obituary in *Nature*, 69 (1903–1904), 324–326; and the obituary by C. J. Joly in *Proceedings of the Royal Society*, 75 (1905), 347–355. See also *The Times* (London) (23 Jan. 1904), 13; and *Dictionary of National Biography*.

A. J. McCONNELL

SALOMONSEN, CARL JULIUS (*b.* Copenhagen, Denmark, 6 December 1847; *d.* Copenhagen, 14 November 1924), *medicine, bacteriology.*

The only child of a wealthy and cultured family, Salomonsen obtained an excellent education in both the sciences and the classics. He was the son of Martin Salomonsen, a physician who had published scientific works on epidemiologic problems, and Eva Henriques, whose family included many eminent physicians in Denmark.

After undergraduate work at the Metropolitan school in Copenhagen, Salomonsen received the M.D. (1871) at the University of Copenhagen. He also took a great interest there in zoological studies, which later inspired his works in experimental pathology and parasitology. Through his father's friendships with the archaeologist Worsaae and the physiologist Peter Panum, Salomonsen met Virchow and became his private secretary, assisting him in his Copenhagen measurements of ancient skulls (1869).

During his first years as a physician, Salomonsen shared a large practice with his father. He also worked as an assistant in the pathology department of the Almindelig Hospital and, later, at the Kommunehospital, where Fritz Valdemar Rasmussen and Panum inspired his interest in the relationship between bacteria, which had recently been discovered, and pyemic processes. Pasteur and Koch had recently investigated this problem, and Panum had published his investigations concerning the putrefaction of blood and the role of microbes in the fermentative effects of putrefaction.

In 1877 Salomonsen defended his thesis "Studier over Blodets Forraadnelse"—some opponents finding it a book more of botanical than of medical interest. Nevertheless, it became the fundamental starting point for the study of bacteriology in Denmark. He showed that the colorshift in putrid blood at 5–10°C is produced by microbes that have begun to putrefy. With the aid of long capillary tubes he isolated live microbes and developed a method for growing them in pure cultures. (This method of cultivation was soon surpassed by Koch's use of transparent solidifiable media.) In his thesis Salomonsen suggested dyeing bacteria in diluted fuchsine solutions to preserve the form of the microbes better than was possible with the more complicated dyeing in hardened preparations. His thesis also gave effective support to the school of Ferdinand Cohn, who maintained that the bacteria were distinct species, against the school of Billroth, who considered them different forms of a single species of coccobacteria septica.

After defending his thesis, Salomonsen traveled to Germany and Paris for half a year. In Breslau (now Wrocław) he worked with Julius Cohnheim; and together they demonstrated the specificity of tuberculosis. That was in 1878, four years before Koch's discovery of the tubercle bacillus. They used an aseptic method of inoculating fresh tuberculous material into the camera anterior bulbi of rabbits. In Breslau Salomonsen also met many scientists, including Weigert, Welch, Neisser, Koch, and Ehrlich. In Paris he met Pasteur—an encounter that later proved of great significance for young Danish bacteriologists. On his return to Copenhagen, Salomonsen was appointed prosector at the

Copenhagen Municipal Hospital. He also lectured privately, and thus began his lifelong interest in education.

In 1878 Salomonsen published "Notits om Forekomsten af Bakterier i metastatiske Pusansamlinger hos Levende," an investigation of bacteria from pus accumulations in live human beings. He identified streptococci from various suppurations and, by inoculating pyogenic material in rabbits, developed a fatal peritonitis with streptococci in pure cultivation.

In 1883 Salomonsen was named lecturer in medical bacteriology at Copenhagen. His was the first such chair in Europe. In the cellar of the Botanical Museum of Copenhagen he assembled a circle of physicians and veterinarians who diligently followed his demonstrations and lectures. Among this group were the physicians Vilhelm Jensen; Thorvald Madsen, later director of the State Serum Institute; J. Christmas; and the veterinary surgeons Bernhard Bang and C. O. Jensen. In 1885 Salomonsen published his important textbook *Ledetraad i Bakteriologisk Teknik,* which was translated into English, French, and Spanish.

In 1893 Salomonsen was named professor of pathology at the University of Copenhagen and for nearly two decades used the new chemistry and physiology laboratory facilities that had been installed in a building in Ny Vestergade. In 1910 he moved to the Rigshospital, where a special building had been constructed for him.

During these years, Salomonsen published his investigations on immunity (1880), diphtheria (1891), and anthrax (1899). In 1884 he published, with Christmas, his studies on pseudoinfection and the ophthalmia produced by the jequirity. In this work he demonstrated that the jequirity microbe is nonvirulent: the venom promoted a morbid predisposition in test animals that enabled the microbes to develop in the blood, thus producing a pseudoinfection. When serum therapy was developed, Salomonsen quickly acknowledged both its practical and its scientific value; and in Ny Vestergade he built up a small department for the production of antidiphtheric serum. Because of the widespread use of this serum, both in hospitals and in research on immunity, the department soon sought better facilities, and Salomonsen proposed (1896, 1899) the construction of an independent serum institute. Despite political difficulties and economic restrictions, he succeeded with his plans and the institute was inaugurated in 1902. He had hoped to have it affiliated with the university, but it was taken over by the Ministry of Health. Denmark being a small country, the institute has been able to sponsor many centralized investigations on immunity serum reactions in infectious diseases. These surveys have made its research world famous.

Salomonsen was director of the State Serum Institute until 1909, when Madsen, his collaborator, succeeded him. They investigated antitoxin formation in horses that were diphtheria-immunized (1896) and demonstrated the fluctuating progress that led to studies of the basis of antitoxin formation. They showed that the cells of an organism that is actively immunized have the unique ability to produce antitoxins. They also observed a constant formation and destruction of such substances and identified the stability of the antitoxin quantity by bleeding the animals and replacing the evacuated blood with transfusions of fresh blood (1897). Because of his interest in hygienic problems, Salomonsen made certain that vaccination procedures in Denmark were reformed; only animal vaccine from healthy calves was used—human vaccine was prohibited.

With Georges Dreyer, Salomonsen demonstrated the physiological effects of radium on amoebas and trypanosomes. He also showed (1904) that radium produces severe hemolysis. Besides his inspiring work as a bacteriologist, Salomonsen was interested in the improvement of education. In 1917 he proposed the construction of a tuition-free college for needy students—an idea that was realized shortly before his death. His many addresses on science, biography, university education, and the history of medicine were published in 1917.

Salomonsen was a cofounder (1907) of the Danish Museum for the History of Medicine and from 1917 president of the Danish Society for the History of Medicine. As dean of the University of Copenhagen, he published (1910) a historical essay on epidemiologic theories during the first half of the nineteenth century; and he wrote (1914) on the sanctuary of Asclepius on Cos. In 1921 he published a book of silhouettes of many outstanding scientists of his time, taken from his personal collection. He also published two polemics on dysmorphism in art, believing that art forms produced just after World War I reflected a deranged state of mind.

In 1891 Salomonsen was elected to the Royal Danish Academy of Sciences. He was made honorary doctor of medicine in 1905 by Victoria University of Manchester and in 1911 by the University of Christiania (Oslo). In 1880 he married Ellen Henriques. His last years were complicated by crippling rheumatoid arthritis and the death of his wife and only daughter.

BIBLIOGRAPHY

I. ORIGINAL WORKS. Salomonsen's major works are *Studier over Blodets Forraadnelse* (Copenhagen, 1877), his M.D. diss.; "Notits om Forekomsten af Bakterier i metastatiske Pusansamlinger hos Levende," in *Nordiskt medicinskt archiv*, **10** (1878), 1–10; "Versuche über künstliche Tuberculose," in *Jahresberichte der Schlesischen Gesellschaft für vaterländische Kultur*, **56** (1878), 222–223, written with J. Cohnheim; "Om Indpodning af Tuberculose i Kaniners Iris," in *Nordiskt medicinskt archiv*, **11**, no. 12 (1879), 1–29, and no. 19, 1–38; "Eine einfache Methode zur Reinkultur verschiedener Fäulniss bacterien," in *Botanische Zeitung*, **38** (1880), 481–489; "Nyeste experimentelle Undersøgelser over Immunitet," in *Hospitalstidende*, **71** (1880), 861–872, 881–894; "Uber die Aetiologie des Jequerity-ophtalmie," in *Fortschritte der Medizin*, **2** (1884), 78–87, written with J. Christmas; "Ueber Pseudo-Infektion bei Fröschen," *ibid.*, 617–631; *Ledetraad for Medicinere i Bakteriologisk Teknik* (Copenhagen, 1885); and *Bakteriologisk Teknik for Medicinere* (Copenhagen, 1889; 4th ed., 1906); with French trans. by R. Durand-Fardel, *Technique élémentaire de bactériologique à l'usage des médecins* (Paris, 1891), and English trans., *Bacteriological Technology for Physicians* (New York, 1891).

Later works include "Difterilaerens nuvaerende Standpunkt," in *Ugeskrift for Laeger*, **24** (1891), 63–79; "Redegørelse for Virksomheden ved den serumtherapeutiske Anstalt," in *Hospitalstidende*, **4**, no. 1 (1896), 225–226; "Studier over Antitoxindannelse," in *Nordiskt medicinskt archiv*, **30** (1897), 1–21, written with T. Madsen; "Forslag om Oprettelse af et Seruminstitut," *ibid.*, **7**, no. 4 (1899), 142; "The Rise and Growth of the State Serum Institute," in the *Festskrift ved Indvielsen af Statens Seruminstitut* (Copenhagen, 1902), 1–20; "Recherches sur les effets physiologiques du radium," in *Comptes rendus hebdomadaires des séances de l'Académie des sciences*, **138** (1904), 1543–1545, written with G. Dreyer; *Erindringsord og Notesbog for Deltagere i de medicinskbakteriologiske Øvelser ved Københavns Universitet* (Copenhagen, 1906; 2nd ed., 1911); and *Epidemiologiske Teorier i den første Halvdel af det 19. Aarhundrede* (Copenhagen, 1910).

See also *Erindringsord og Notesbog for Deltagere i de experimental-pathologiske Øvelser ved Københavns Universitet* (Copenhagen, 1912; 2nd ed., 1919); *Menneskets Snyltere* (Copenhagen, 1913), with atlas (1913); *Asklepios' Helligdom på Kos* (Copenhagen, 1914); *Maa-Arbejder* (Copenhagen, 1917); *Smitsomme Sindslidelser for og nu med Henblik paa de nyeste Kunstretninger* (Copenhagen, 1919); *Om Dysmorfismens syge-* *lige Natur* (Copenhagen, 1920); and *Medicinske Silhouetter* (Copenhagen, 1921).

II. SECONDARY LITERATURE. On Salomonsen and his work, see E. Gotfredsen, *Medicinens Historie*, 3rd ed. (Copenhagen, 1973), *passim;* T. Madsen, "Carl Julius Salomonsen," in *Oversigt over glet Kd Danske Videnskabernes Selskabs Forhandlinger* (1925), 59–75; and Oluf Thomsen, "Carl Julius Salomonsen," in *Copenhagen University Program* (Nov. 1925), 75–81.

E. SNORRASON

SALVIANI, IPPOLITO (*b.* Citta di Castello [?], Italy, 1514; *d.* 1572), *medicine, natural history.*

Little is known of Salviani's life: according to some, he was born in Rome, to others, in Citta di Castello. The latter is more likely since Pope Julius III, by a *motu proprio,* made him a Roman citizen—a pointless action if he had been born in Rome.

It is certain that Salviani studied medicine and was closely connected with the Vatican. He was personal physician to Julius III, Paul IV, and Cardinal Cervini, who later became Pope Marcellus II. It is also known that he was a professor of practical medicine, from 1551 until at least 1568, at the Sapienza, the Roman university of the Renaissance. The Vatican gave him many honors: in 1564 the cardinal in charge sent Salviani in his place to supervise the degree sessions in medicine; he was made principal physician of the medical college of Rome; and in 1565 he was nominated *conservatore* ("registrar") of Rome, which was more an administrative than a medical post. As *conservatore* he arranged for the transportation to the Campidoglio of the two famous statues of Caesar Augustus and Julius Caesar, which until then had been in the keeping of Alessandro Ruffini, bishop of Melfi.

Salviani enjoyed considerable renown, probably because of his privileged position as papal physician; he also had many rich clients and, in time, became very wealthy.

Salviani published only one medical work, *De crisibus ad Galeni censuram* (1556). Its success is evident from a second edition that was published only two years later. He is better known, however, for his monumental work on natural science, *De piscibus tomi duo,* the publication date of which is uncertain; it has been conjectured by various biographers to be 1554, 1555, or 1558.

The work had been encouraged and supported financially by Cardinal Cervini. It describes, in two folio volumes, the fishes of the Mediterranean and is accompanied by beautiful copper engravings by various contemporary artists. Despite Aldrovandi's unconditional praise for the illustrations, more recent critics have pointed out that their merits are artistic rather than scientific. Many species of fishes are so approximately represented that they cannot be identified with precision.

The work was dedicated not to Cardinal Cervini, as Salviani had intended, but to the new pope, Paul IV; Cervini died before publication was complete. A slight bibliographical controversy has ensued from this alteration. Polidorus Vergilius, who is never very reliable, went so far as to reproduce the dedication that Salviani would have written for Cervini. But no such dedication has been found in any copy of the work, the one to Pope Paul IV being the only known dedication.

Salviani's *De piscibus tomi duo* was reprinted in Venice in 1600–1602, but with the title changed to *De aquatilium animalium . . . formis,* which led some biographers to believe that it was a different book. Salviani also wrote poetry and a play, *La ruffiana.* The latter was popular during his life and went through several editions, but it is completely ignored by modern literary critics.

BIBLIOGRAPHY

Salviani's two scientific works are *De crisibus ad Galeni censuram liber* (Rome, 1558), and *De piscibus tomi duo, cum eorumdem figuris aere incisis* [Rome, 1554], reprinted as *De aquatilium animalium curandorum formis* (Venice, 1600–1602). His play was entitled *La ruffiana* (Rome, 1554).

On Salviani and his work, see Polidorus Vergilius, *De inventoribus rerum* (Basel, 1563); G. Marini, *Degli archiatri pontifici,* 2 vols. (Rome, 1784), I, 402–405; II, 306–307, 314–317; and G. Tiraboschi, *Biblioteca Modenese,* VII, pt. 2 (Modena, 1781–1786), 119.

CARLO CASTELLANI

AL-SAMARQANDĪ, NAJĪB AL-DĪN ABŪ ḤAMID MUḤAMMAD IBN ʿALĪ IBN ʿUMAR (*d.* Herat, Afghanistan, 1222), *medicine, materia medica.*

Al-Samarqandī, who flourished at the time of the philosopher Fakhr al-Dīn al-Rāzī (*d.* 1210), died during the pillage of Herat by the Mongols. Ibn Abī Uṣaybiʿa states that al-Samarqandī was a famous physician and gives his name as Najīb al-Dīn Abū Ḥamid Muḥammad ibn ʿAlī ibn ʿUmar al-Samarqandī. Nothing more is known of his life.

The most important of his medical works is *al-*

Asbāb wa'l-ʿalāmāt ("Etiology and Symptoms [of Diseases]"). It is described in the work of Nafīs ibn ʿIwaḍ al-Kirmānī (*d.* 1449), who wrote *Sharḥ al-asbāb wa'l-ʿalāmāt* ("Commentary on Etiology and Symptoms"). According to Ibn Abī Uṣaybiʿa, al-Samarqandī also wrote a book on the treatment of diseases by diet and two medical formularies. The treatise *Uṣūl tarkīb [al-adwiya]* ("On the Principles of Compounding Drugs") also is ascribed to him.

Works still extant are *al-Adwiya al-mufrada* ("Simple Drugs"), *Aghdhiyat al-marḍā* ("Diet for the Ill"), *al-Aghdhiya wa'l-ashriba wa-mā yattaṣil bihā* ("Food and Drink and What Relates to Them"), *Fī mudāwāt wajaʿ al-mafāṣil* ("On the Cure of Pain in the Joints"), *Fi 'l-ṭibb* ("On Medicine"), *Fī kayfiyyat tarkīb ṭabaqāt al-ʿayn* ("On the Mode of Composition of the Layers of the Eyes"), *Tractatus de medicamentis repertu facilibus, Aqrābādhīn* ("Medical Formulary"), *Fī ʿilāj man suqiya 'l-sumūm aw nahashahu 'l-hawāmm waghayruhā* ("On the Treatment for One Who Has Been Poisoned or Has Had a Poisonous Bite, and Similar Cases"), *Ghāyat al-gharaḍ fī muʿālajat al-amrād* ("The Last Word on Treating the Ill"), *Fī ittikhādh māʾ al-jubn wamanāfi ʿihi wakayfiyyat isti ʿmālihi* ("On Administration of Water of Cheese, Its Benefits, and Its Various Uses"), and *Fi 'l-adwiya al-mustaʿmala ʿinda 'l-sayādila* ("On Drugs Prepared by Pharmacists").

It is significant that al-Samarqandī did not rely entirely on the old humoral pathology. In fact, he displayed originality in not considering the theory of humors of decisive importance in therapeutics. He dealt with the many "accidents" of drugs and conditions of the body in the much broader framework of medicine and the prescribing of drugs.

BIBLIOGRAPHY

Nafīs' *Commentary* on al-Samarqandī's *al-Asbāb wa'l-ʿalāmāt* was published by Mawlawi ʿAbd al-Majīd (Calcutta, 1836). The *Ṭibb-i Akbarī* of Muḥammad Arzānī, completed in 1700–1701, includes a Persian translation of this *Commentary.* Printed and lithograph eds. of the *Ṭibb-i Akbarī* are listed in G. Sarton, *Introduction to the History of Science,* II (Baltimore, 1962), 661.

See also G. M. Anawati, *Drogues et médicaments* (Cairo, 1959), 117–118, text in Arabic; Carl Brockelmann, *Geschichte der arabischen Literatur,* I² (Leiden, 1943), 491, and supp. I (Leiden, 1937), 895–896; S. Hamarneh and G. Sonnedecker, *A Pharmaceutical View of Abulcasis* (Leiden, 1963); L. Leclerc, *Histoire de la médecine arabe,* II (Paris, 1876), 128–129; Martin Levey, *Chemistry and Chemical Technology in Ancient Mesopotamia* (Amsterdam, 1959), introduction; *The Medical Formulary or Aqrābadhīn of Al-Kindī* (Madison, Wis., 1966); *Medieval Arabic Toxicology* (Philadelphia, 1966); and *The Medical Formulary of al-Samarqandī and the Relation of Early Arabic Simples to Those Found in the Indigenous Medicine of the Near East and India* (Philadelphia, 1967); P. Sbath and C. D. Averinos, *Deux traités médicaux* (Cairo, 1953); and Ibn Abī Uṣaybiᶜa, *Kitāb ᶜuyūn al-anbā' fī ṭabaqāt al-aṭibbā'*, A. Müller, ed., II (Cairo, 1882), 31; and (Beirut, 1950), pt. 2, 47–48.

MARTIN LEVEY

AL-SAMARQANDĪ, SHAMS AL-DĪN MUḤAM-MAD IBN ASHRAF AL-ḤUSAYNĪ (*b.* Samarkand, Uzbekistan, Russia, *fl.* 1276), *mathematics, logic, astronomy.*

Al-Samarqandī was a contemporary of Naṣīr al-Dīn al-Ṭūsī (1201–1274) and Quṭb al-Dīn al-Shīrāzī (1236–1311). Al-Samarqandī was not among the scientists associated with al-Ṭūsī at the observatory at Marāgha. A noted logician, al-Samarqandī was best known to mathematicians for his famous tract *Kitāb Ashkāl al-taᵓsīs* ("Book on the Fundamental Theorems"). This work of twenty pages, probably composed around 1276, summarizes with their abridged demonstrations thirty-five fundamental propositions of Euclid's geometry. To write this short work, Samarqandī consulted the writings of Ibn al-Haytham, ᶜUmar al-Khayyāmī, al-Jawharī, Naṣīr al-Dīn al-Ṭūsī, and Athīr al-Dīn al-Abharī. Several mathematicians, notably Qāḍī Zāda, commented on this work by al-Samarqandī.

It was chiefly with his book on dialectics that al-Samarqandī became famous. This valuable work, entitled *Risāla fī ādāb al-baḥth* ("Tract on the Methods of Enquiry"), was the subject of several commentaries. Two other works on logic by al-Samarqandī are known: *Mīzān al-Qusṭās* and *Kitāb ᶜAyn al-naẓar fīᶜilm al-jadal*. Al-Samarqandī was also interested in astronomy. He wrote *Al-Tadhkira fī 'l-hay'a* ("Synopsis of Astronomy") and a star calendar for 1276–1277. His *Ṣaḥā'if al-ilāhiyya* and his *ᶜAqā'id* are two works on dogmatic theology.

BIBLIOGRAPHY

MSS of the works of al-Samarqandī are listed in C. Brockelmann, *Geschichte der arabischen Literatur*, I (Weimar, 1898), 486; and *ibid.*, supp. 1 (Leiden, 1937), 860. See also H. Suter, *Die Mathematiker und Astrono-men der Araber* (Leipzig, 1900), 157; and "Nachträge und Berichtigungen zu 'Die Mathematiker . . .,'" in *Abhandlungen zur Geschichte der Mathematik*, **14** (1902), 176.

Also helpful are Ḥājjī Khalīfa's *Kashf al-ẓunūn*, G. Flügel, ed. (Leipzig, 1835–1855), I, 322; Carra de Vaux's article "Baḥth," in *Encyclopaedia of Islam*, 1st ed., I (1911), 587; and G. Sarton, *Introduction to the History of Science*, II (Baltimore, 1962), 1020–1021.

For a demonstration of Euclid's fifth postulate attributed to al-Samarqandī, see H. Dilgan, "Démonstration du Vᵉ postulat d'Euclide par Shams-ed-Dīn Samarkandī," in *Revue d'histoire des sciences et de leurs applications*, **13** (1960), 191–196. For the attribution of this demonstration to Athīr al-Dīn al-Abharī, see A. I. Sabra, "Thābit ibn Qurra on Euclid's Parallels Postulate," in *Journal of the Warburg and Courtauld Institutes*, **31** (1968), 14, note 9.

HÂMIT DILGAN

AL-SAMAWᵓAL, IBN YAḤYĀ AL-MAGHRIBĪ (*b.* Baghdad, Iraq; *d.* Marāgha, Iran [?], *ca.* 1180), *mathematics, medicine.*

Al-Samawᵓal was the son of Yehuda ben Abun (or Abu'l-ᶜAbbās Yaḥyā al-Maghribī), a Jew learned in religion and Hebrew literature who had emigrated from Fez (Morocco) and settled in Baghdad. His mother was Anna Isaac Levi, an educated woman who was originally from Baṣra (Iraq). Al-Samawᵓal thus grew up in a cultivated milieu; a maternal uncle was a physician, and after studying Hebrew and the Torah the boy was encouraged, when he was thirteen, to take up the study of medicine and the exact sciences. He then began to study medicine with Abu'l-Barakāt, while taking the opportunity to observe his uncle's practice. At the same time he started to learn mathematics, beginning with Hindu computational methods, *zījes* (astronomical tables), arithmetic, and *misāḥa* (practical techniques for determining measure, for use in surveying), then progressing to algebra and geometry.

Since scientific study had declined in Baghdad, al-Samawᵓal was unable to find a teacher to instruct him beyond the first books of Euclid's *Elements* and was therefore obliged to study independently. He finished Euclid, then went on to the *Algebra* of Abū Kāmil, the *al-Badīᶜ* of al-Karajī, and the *Arithmetic* of al-Wasīṭī (most probably Maymūn ibn Najīb al-Wasīṭī, who collaborated in making astronomical observations with ᶜUmar al-Khayyāmī between 1072 and 1092). By the time he was eighteen, al-Samawᵓal had read for himself all of the works fundamental to the study of mathematics and had developed his own mode of mathematical thinking.

In science, this independence of thought led al-Samaw'al to point out deficiencies in the work of al-Karajī (whom he admired) and to challenge the arrangement of the *Elements*; in religion he was similarly inclined to test the validity of the claims of the various creeds and came to accept those of Islam, although he postponed his conversion for a number of years to avoid distressing his father. His autobiography states that he reached his decision at Marāgha on 8 November 1163 as a result of a dream; four years later he wrote to his father, setting out the reasons for which he had changed his religion, and his father immediately set out to Aleppo to see him, dying en route. Al-Samaw'al himself spent the rest of his life as an itinerant physician in and around Marāgha. His earlier travels had taken him throughout Iraq, Syria, Kūhistān, and Ādharbayjān.

His biographers record that al-Samaw'al was a successful physician, and had emirs among his patients. In his autobiography al-Samaw'al recorded that he had compounded several new medicines, including an almost miraculous theriac, but no other account of them has survived. His only extant medical work is his *Nuzhat al-aṣḥāb* (usually translated as "The Companions' Promenade in the Garden of Love"), which is essentially a treatise on sexology and a collection of erotic stories. The medical content of the first and longer section of the book lies chiefly in descriptions of diseases and sexual deficiencies; the second, more strictly medical, part includes a discussion of states of virile debility and an account of diseases of the uterus and their treatment. This part is marked by al-Samaw'al's acute observation and his interest in the psychological aspects of disease; he provides a detailed description of the condition of being in love without recognizing it, and gives a general prescription for the anguished and melancholic that comprises well-lighted houses, the sight of running water and verdure, warm baths, and music.

It is, however, chiefly as a mathematician that al-Samaw'al merits a place in the history of science. His extant book on algebra, *Al-bāhir* ("The Dazzling"), written when he was nineteen years old, represents a remarkable development of the work of his predecessors. In it al-Samaw'al brought together the algebraic rules formulated by, in particular, al-Karajī and, to a lesser extent, Ibn Aslam and other authors, including al-Sijzī, Ibn al-Haytham, Qusṭā ibn Lūqā, and al-Ḥarīrī. The work consists of four parts, of which the first provides an account of operations on polynomials in one un-

known with rational coefficients; the second deals essentially with second-degree equations, indeterminate analysis, and summations; the third concerns irrational quantities; and the fourth, and last, section presents the application of algebraic principles to a number of problems.

It is apparent in the first section of this work that al-Samaw'al was the first Arab algebraist to undertake the study of relative numbers. He chose to treat them as if they possessed an identity proper to themselves, although he did not recognize the significance of this choice. He was thus able, in a truly bold stroke, to subtract from zero, writing that

> If we subtract an additive [positive] number from an empty power $(0 \cdot x^n - a \cdot x^n)$, the same subtractive [negative] number remains; if we subtract the subtractive number from an empty power, the same additive number remains $(0 \cdot x^n - [-ax^n] = ax^n)$. . . . If we subtract an additive number from a subtractive number, the remainder is their subtractive sum: $(-ax^n) - (bx^n) = -(a + b) x^n$; if we subtract a subtractive number from a greater subtractive number, the result is their subtractive difference; if the number from which one subtracts is smaller than the number subtracted, the result is their additive difference.

These rules appear in the later European work of Chuquet (1484), Pacioli (1494), Stifel (1544), and Cardano (1545); it is likely that al-Samaw'al reached them by considering the extraction of the square root of a polynomial.

Al-Karajī had conceived the algorithm of extraction, but did not succeed in applying it to the case in which the coefficients are subtractive. His failure may have stimulated al-Samaw'al's abilities, since the problem in which these rules are stated in the *Al-bāhir* is that of the extraction of the square root of

$$25x^6 + 9x^4 + 84x^2 + 64 + 100(1/x^2) + 64(1/x^4)$$
$$- 30x^5 - 40x^3 - 116x - 48(1/x) - 96(1/x^3).$$

Since al-Karajī's algebra lacked symbols, so that the numbers had to be spelled out in letters, this operation would have presented an insurmountable obstacle. Al-Samaw'al was able to overcome this trial of memory and imagination by using a visualization in which he assigned to each power of x a place in a table in which a polynomial was represented by the sequence of its coefficients, written in Hindu numerals. This technique, a major step in the development of symbolism, was requisite to the progress of algebra because of the increasing complexity of mathematical computations.

Al-Samaw'al's rules of subtraction were also

important in the division of polynomials; in the interest of obtaining better approximations he pursued division up to negative powers of x, and thereby approached the technique of development in series (although he overlooked the opportunity of unifying the various cases of the second-degree equation and of computation by double error). He computed the quotient of $20x^2 + 30x$ by $6x^2 + 12$, for example, to obtain the result $3\ 1/3 + 5(1/x) - 6\ 2/3(1/x^2) - 10(1/x^3) + 13\ 1/3(1/x^4) + 20(1/x^5) - 26\ 2/3(1/x^6) - 40(1/x^7)$. He then recognized that he could apply the law of the formation of coefficients $a_{n+2} = -2a_n$, which allowed him to write out the terms of the quotient directly up to $54{,}613 \cdot 1/3$ $(1/x^{28})$.

Al-Samaw[>]al further applied the rules of subtraction to the multiplication and division of the powers of x, which he placed in a single line on both sides of the number 1, to which he assigned the rank zero. The other powers and other constants are displayed on each side of zero, in ascending and descending order:

...	4	3	2	1	0	1	2	3	4	...
	x^4	x^3	x^2	x	1	$\frac{1}{x}$	$\frac{1}{x^2}$	$\frac{1}{x^3}$	$\frac{1}{x^4}$	

The rules of multiplication and division that al-Samaw[>]al enunciated are, except for their notation, those still in use.

The second part of the *Al-bāhir* contains the six classical equations ($ax = b$, $ax^2 + bx = c$, and so forth) that were set out by al-Khwārizmī. Interestingly, however, al-Samaw[>]al gave only geometrical demonstrations of the equations, although their algebraic solutions were known to his predecessor al-Karajī, who dedicated a monograph, ^c*Ilal ḥisāb al-jabr wa 'l-muqābala*, to them. Al-Samaw[>]al then presented a remarkable calculation of the coefficients of $(a + b)^n$, which al-Karajī discovered after 1007 (for the dating of this and other of al-Karajī's works, see A. Anbouba, ed., *L'algèbre al-Badī^c d'al-Karagi* [Beirut, 1964], p. 12). Since al-Karajī's original computation has been lost, al-Samaw[>]al's work is of particular interest in having preserved it; these coefficients are arranged in the triangular table that much later became known in the west as Tartaglia's or Pascal's triangle.

A further, and equally important, part of the second section of the book deals with number theory. This chapter contains about forty propositions, including that among n consecutive integers there is one divisible by n; that

$$1 \cdot 2 + 3 \cdot 4 + \cdots + (2n-1)\,2n = 1 + 3 + \cdots + (2n-1) + 1^2 + 3^2 + \cdots + (2n-1)^2;$$

and that $1^2 + 2^2 + \cdots + n^2 = n(n+1)(2n+1)/6$. Al-Samaw[>]al was especially proud of having established the last, since neither Ibn Aslam nor al-Karajī had been successful in doing so.

The chief importance of the second part of the *Al-bāhir* lies, however, in al-Samaw[>]al's use of recursive reasoning, which appears in such equations as

$$(n-1)\sum_1^n i = (n+1)\sum_1^{n-1} i \text{ and}$$
$$(n-1)\sum_1^n i = (n-1)\sum_1^{n-3} i + 3(n-1)^2.$$

The third part of *Al-bāhir* is chiefly concerned with the classification of irrationals found in Book X of the *Elements*. Al-Samaw[>]al's account is complete and clear, but contains nothing new or noteworthy except his rationalization of $\sqrt{30} : \sqrt{2} + \sqrt{5} + \sqrt{6}$, which had eluded al-Karajī.

The final section of the work contains a classification of problems by the number of their known solutions, a device used by earlier writers. Al-Samaw[>]al was led by this procedure to solve a varied group of these problems and to master a prodigious system of 210 equations in ten unknowns, a result of his having undertaken the determination of ten numbers of which are given their sums, taken six at a time. He further elucidated the 504 conditions necessary to the compatibility of the system. He overcame the lack of symbolic representation by the expedient of designating the unknown quantities 1, 2, 3, $\cdots$, 10, and was then able to draw up a table that started from

$$123456 \cdots 65$$
$$123457 \cdots 70$$
$$123458 \cdots 75$$
$$123459 \cdots 80.$$

Al-Samaw[>]al's intention in writing the *Al-bāhir* was to compensate for the deficiencies that he found in al-Karajī's work and to provide for algebra the same sort of systematization that the *Elements* gave to geometry. He wrote the book when he was young, then allowed it to remain unpublished for several years; it seems quite possible that he reworked it a number of times. It is difficult to ascertain the importance of the book to the development of algebra in the Arab world, but an indirect and restricted influence may be seen in the *Miftaḥ-al-ḥisab* ("Key of Arithmetic") of al-Kāshī, published in 1427. The book was apparently altogether unknown in the west.

The mathematical counterpart of the *Al-bāhir*,

the *Al-zāhir* ("The Flourishing"), has been lost, and of al-Samawʾal's mathematical writings only two almost identical elementary treatises remain. These are the *Al-tabṣira* ("Brief Survey") and *Al-mūjiz* ("Summary"). The influence of the Arabic language is seen in their classification of fractions as deaf, Arab, or genitive, and both contain sections on ratios that are clearly derived from the work of al-Karajī. The ratio 80:3·7·9·10, for example, is expressed as a sum of fractions with numerator 1 and the respective denominators 3·10, 3·7·9, and 3·9·10; this use of the sexagesimal system reflects the continuing importance of the concerns of the commercial and administrative community of Baghdad, since this system was still favored by merchants and public servants. In his account of division, al-Samawʾal noted the periodicity of the quotient 5:11, also calculated in the sexagesimal system. The last section of *Al-mūjiz* exists only in mutilated form, but what remains would indicate that it contained interesting material on abacuses.

In an additional work related to his mathematics al-Samawʾal again demonstrated the independence of his thinking. In this, the *Kashf ʾuwār al-munaj-jimīn* ("The Exposure of the Errors of the Astrologers"), he refuted the pronouncements of scientific astrology by pointing out the multiple contradictions in its interpretation of sidereal data, as well as the errors of measurement that he found in astrological observations. He then, for the sake of argument, assumed astrology to be valid, but showed that the astrologer could scarcely hope to make a valid prediction since, by al-Samawʾal's count, he would have to take into simultaneous consideration 6,817 celestial indicators, a computation that would surely exceed his abilities.

BIBLIOGRAPHY

I. Original Works. Al-Samawʾal wrote at least eighty-five works, of which most have been lost. (It must be remembered, however, that the word *kitāb* may be used to designate either a brief note or a full volume.) A brief autobiographical writing may be found in *Ifḥām ṭā ʾifat al-yahūd*, Cairo MS (Cat. F. Sayyid, I, p. 65), fols. 25–26, and in *Al-ajwiba al fākhira raddan ʿala'l milla 'l-kāfira*, Paris MS 1456, fols. 64–65.

His mathematical works that have been preserved include *Al-bāhir* ("The Dazzling"), Istanbul MS Aya Sofya 2718, 115 ff., and Esat Ef. 3155; extracts are in A. Anbouba, "Mukhtārāt min Kitāb al-Bāhir," in *al-Mashriq* (Jan.-Feb. 1961), 61–108, while a complete modern ed., with notes, a detailed analysis, and French introduction is S. Ahmad and R. Rashed, eds., *Al-bāhir en algèbre*

d'as-Samawʾal (Damascus, 1972). *Al-ṭabsira fi'l ḥisāb* ("Brief Survey") is Berlin MS 5962, 29 ff., Bodleian (Oxford) I, 194, and Ambrosiana (Milan) C. 211 ii; *Al-mūjiz al-mūḍawī* [?] *fi'l ḥisāb* ("Summary") is Istanbul MS Fatih 3439, 15 (consisting of thirty-three pages of thirty-five lines each); and *Kashf ʿuwār al-munajjimīn wa ghalaṭihim fī akthar al-aʿmāl wa'l-aḥkām* ("The Exposure of the Errors of the Astrologers") is Leiden MS Cod. Or 98, 100 ff., and Bodleian I, 964, and II, 603, while its preface has been translated into English by F. Rosenthal, "Al-Asṭurlābī and al-Samawʾal on Scientific Progress," in *Osiris,* 9 (1950), 555–564.

Al-Samawʾal's only surviving medical work, *Nuzhat al-aṣḥāb fī muʿāsharat al-aḥbāb* ("The Companions' Promenade in the Garden of Love"), is preserved in Berlin MS 6381, Paris MS 3054, Gotha MS 2045, Istanbul MS Aya Sofya 2121, and Escorial MS 1830. His other extant works are apologetics, and include *Ifḥām ṭā'ifat al-yahūd* ("Confutation of the Jews"), Cairo MS Cat. F. Sayyid, I, p. 65, Cairo MS VI, ii, and Teheran MS I, 184, and II, 593, of which the text and an English trans. with an interesting introduction by M. Perlmann are *Proceedings of the American Academy for Jewish Research.* 32 (1964); and *Ghāyat al-maqṣūd fī 'l-radd ʿala 'l-naṣārā wa 'l-yahūd* ("Decisive Refutation of the Christians and the Jews"), Istanbul MS As'ad 3153 and Asir 545. A last MS, *Badhl al-majhūd fī iqnāʿ al-yahūd* ("The Effort to Persuade the Jews"), formerly in Berlin, has been lost since World War II. See also Perlmann (above), pp. 25–28, 127).

II. Secondary Literature. Recent editions of Arabic sources on al-Samawʾal and his work include Ibn Abī Uṣaybiʿa, *ʿUyūn al anbāʾ*, II (Cairo, 1882), 30–31; Ḥājjī Khalīfa, *Kashf al-ẓunūn*, I (Istanbul, 1941), col. 664, and II (1943), col. 1377; Ibn al ʿIbrī [Barhebraeus], *Taʾrīkh mukhtaṣar al-duwal* (Beirut, 1958), 217; Ibn al-Qifṭī, *Ikhbār al-ʿulama* (Cairo, 1908), 142; Ibn Ṣāʿid al-Akfānī, *Irshād al-Qāṣid* (Beirut, 1904), 123, 125, 127; and Tash Kupri Zadeh, *Miftāḥ al-Saʿāda*, I (Hyderabad, 1910), 327, 329.

Works by later authors include A. Anbouba, "Al-Karajī," in *Al-Dirāsāt al-Adabiyya* (Beirut, 1959); and "Mukhtārāt min Kitāb al-Bāhir," in *al-Mashriq* (Jan.-Feb. 1961), 61–108; C. Brockelmann, *Geschichte der arabischen Literatur,* I² (Leiden, 1943), 643, and Supp. I (Leiden, 1937), 892; H. Hirschfeld, "Al-Samawʾal," in *Jewish Encyclopedia,* I (New York–London, 1901), 37–38; Lucien Leclerc, *Histoire de la médecine arabe,* II (Paris, 1876), 12–17; S. Perez, *Biografías de los mathematicos arabos que florecieron en España* (Madrid, 1921), 137; F. Rosenthal, "Al-Asṭurlābī and al-Samawʾal on Scientific Progress," in *Osiris,* 9 (1950), 555–564; G. Sarton, *Introduction to the History of Science,* II (Baltimore, 1953), 401, and III (1953), 418, 596; M. Steinschneider, *Mathematik bei den Juden* (Hildesheim, 1964), 96; and H. Suter, *Die Mathematiker und Astronomen der Araber und ihre Werke* (Leipzig, 1900), biography, 24.

See also introductions and notes in S. Ahmad and

R. Rashed, eds., *Al-bāhir en algèbre d'as-Samawɔal* (Damascus, 1971); and in A. Anbouba, ed., *L'algèbre al-Badīc d'al-Karagi* (Beirut, 1964).

ADEL ANBOUBA

SAMOYLOV, ALEKSANDR FILIPPOVICH (*b.* Odessa, Ukraine, Russia, 7 April 1867; *d.* Kazan, U.S.S.R., 22 July 1930), *physiology, electrophysiology, electrocardiography.*

After early education at the Gymnasium in Odessa, Samoylov studied for two years in the natural history section of the faculty of physics and mathematics of Novorossysk University. In 1891 he graduated from the medical faculty of the University of Dorpat, where he conducted his first experimental research under the guidance of the well-known pharmacologist E. R. Kobert. His dissertation for the M.D. degree was entitled "O sudbe zheleza v zhivotnom organizme" ("On the Fate of Iron in the Living Organism"; 1891).

From 1892 to 1894 Samoylov worked with Pavlov in the physiology section of the Institute of Experimental Medicine; and from 1894 to 1903 he was I. M. Sechenov's assistant and docent in the department of physiology of the Moscow University. Samoylov worked in the laboratories of Ludimar Hermann in Königsberg, Wilhelm Nagel in Berlin, and Johannes von Kries in Freiburg im Breisgau. On 3 October 1903 he became professor of physiology of Kazan University, where he remained until his death. In 1924 he became chairman of the department of physiology of Moscow University.

Samoylov conducted more than 120 original experimental and theoretical investigations in electrophysiology, electrocardiography, the physiology of sense organs, clinical physiology, and the history of science. His methodological research was important in the development and training of specialists in electrophysiology. His improvements in methods of string galvanometry include a special compensator and string indicator, and a special form of immersed electrodes. He was generally recognized as a leading electrophysiologist, and among his students at Kazan were I. S. Beritov, M. A. Kiselev, V. V. Parin, and M. N. Livanov. With Einthoven, Samoylov laid the foundations for clinical and theoretical electrocardiography.

In 1924 he published his hypothesis of the chemical nature of the transfer of nerve excitation in "O perekhode vozbuzhdenia s dvigatelnogo nerva na myshtsu" ("On the Transfer of Excitation From the Motor Nerve to the Muscle"). He also carried out electrophysiological research on the central nervous system and on the mechanisms of coordination of complex reflex actions. He added to the theory of reflexes new concepts of the existence of circular forms of excitation, and closed reflex arcs. This research was published in "Koltsevoy ritm vozbuzhdenia" ("The Circular Rhythm of Excitation"; 1930).

A gifted scientific administrator, Samoylov received the Lenin Prize in 1930 and for several years was a deputy of the Tatar Republic.

BIBLIOGRAPHY

Samoylov's major works are collected in *Izbrannye stati i rechi* ("Selected Articles and Speeches"; Moscow–Leningrad, 1946), with a bibliography of Samoylov's works, pp. 308–313; and *Izbrannye trudy* ("Selected Works"; Moscow, 1967).

On Samoylov and his work, see N. A. Grigorian, *Aleksandr Filippovich Samoylov* (Moscow, 1963).

N. A. GRIGORIAN

SAMPSON, RALPH ALLEN (*b.* Skull, County Cork, Ireland, 25 June 1866; *d.* Bath, England, 7 November 1939), *astronomy.*

Sampson studied at St. John's College, Cambridge, and in 1888 graduated third wrangler in the mathematical tripos. In 1891 he received the first Isaac Newton studentship in astronomy and physical optics at Cambridge, where he studied astronomical spectroscopy with Newall. In 1893 Sampson published "On the Rotation and Mechanical State of the Sun," in which he discussed the distribution of temperature by radiation and absorption. In the same year he was elected professor of mathematics at the University of Durham and also started his great work on the four large satellites of Jupiter.

The advent of the Harvard photometric eclipse observations of the satellites of Jupiter stimulated Sampson to reexamine previous observations, and as a result he published in 1909 "A Discussion of the Eclipses of Jupiter's Satellites 1878–1903." He developed a new theory for the motions of the four satellites and in 1910 published *Tables of the Four Great Satellites of Jupiter.* (Sampson's tables have since formed the basis for computing the phenomena for the national ephemerides.) The new theory itself was not published until 1921 in "Theory of the Four Great Satellites of Jupiter."

In 1910 Sampson was appointed astronomer

royal for Scotland and professor of astronomy at the University of Edinburgh, where he interested himself in problems concerning the determination of time. He encouraged the development of the Shortt free-pendulum clock, which became standard equipment in many observatories. Sampson also carried out photometric research and introduced the concept of spectrophotometric gradients. He retired from the observatory in 1937.

BIBLIOGRAPHY

I. ORIGINAL WORKS. Sampson's major works are "On the Rotation and Mechanical State of the Sun," in *Memoirs of the Royal Astronomical Society,* **51** (1893), 123–183; "Description of Adam's Manuscripts on the Perturbation of Uranus," *ibid.,* **54** (1901), 143–170; "A Discussion of the Eclipses of Jupiter's Satellites 1878–1903," in *Annals of Harvard College Observatory,* **52** (1909), 149–343; "The Old Observations of the Eclipses of Jupiter's Satellites," in *Memoirs of the Royal Astronomical Society,* **59** (1909), 199–256; *Tables of the Four Great Satellites of Jupiter* (London, 1910); *The Sun* (Cambridge–New York, 1914); "A Census of the Sky," in *Observatory,* **38** (1915), 415–426; and "Theory of the Four Great Satellites of Jupiter," *Memoirs of the Royal Astronomical Society,* **63** (1921).

Sampson also edited the unpublished MSS of John C. Adams in *Scientific Papers of John Couch Adams,* II, pt. 1 (Cambridge, 1896–1900).

II. SECONDARY LITERATURE. On Sampson and his work, see W. M. H. Greaves, "Ralph Allen Sampson," in *Monthly Notices of the Royal Astronomical Society,* **100** (1940), 258–263.

LETTIE S. MULTHAUF

SANARELLI, GIUSEPPE (*b.* Monte San Savino, Italy, 24 April 1864; *d.* Rome, Italy, 6 April 1940), *hygiene.*

Sanarelli obtained his degree in medicine and surgery at the University of Siena in 1889. He then studied under Pasteur at the Institut Pasteur in Paris. In 1893 he received the chair of hygiene at the University of Siena but two years later went to Uruguay, at the invitation of the government, to set up an institute of experimental hygiene at the University of Montevideo. In 1898 he returned to Italy and became professor of hygiene at the University of Bologna and then at the University of Rome, where he remained until 1935, serving as vice-chancellor in 1922–1923.

Sanarelli was made doctor *honoris causae* of the universities of Paris and Toulouse; and he was a member of the Académie des Sciences, the Medical Academy of Paris, and the Royal Medical Academy of Belgium.

In 1892–1894 Sanarelli published his research on the pathogenesis of typhoid fever: he was the first to propose the theory of general infection with a secondary, localized infection in the intestine. (In 1925 he extended this theory to paratyphoid infections and to bacillary dysentery.) In a series of papers that appeared between 1916 and 1924, and as a book in 1931, Sanarelli discussed his investigations on the pathogenesis of cholera, demonstrating that the bacillus of cholera has a marked gastric enterotropism. He then studied (1924–1925) the so-called hematic carbuncle in the intestine and showed that cholera is hematogenetic rather than enteric.

From his studies on cholera, and especially those on the pathogenesis of choleraic algidity, Sanarelli discovered (1916) the hemorrhagic allergy, or "Sanarelli's phenomenon." He was also the first to propose the concept of hereditary immunity to tuberculosis, thus opposing the traditional concept of a hereditary predisposition to the disease. In Montevideo, Sanarelli had the opportunity to investigate the cause of yellow fever. From his research on diseased patients and corpses, he was able to isolate *Bacterium icteroides,* the earliest discovered (1897) human exit-paratyphoid.

In 1898 Sanarelli discovered the myxomatosis virus of the rabbit, the first known tumor disease in animals caused by a filterable virus. He was also the first to use the method of ultrafiltration through colloidal membranes. This method enabled him to study (1930) the germination and development of the tubercular ultravirus. In other important studies he showed that spirillum and fusiform associations of bacteria are not real microbic associations, but are, instead, a single germ, which can appear as either a rod or a spiral according to the environmental conditions. He called this microorganism *Heliconema vincenti.* Sanarelli was also a pioneer in the field of nasal vaccination (1924).

BIBLIOGRAPHY

I. ORIGINAL WORKS. Sanarelli's major works are "Die Ursachen der natürlichen Immunität gegen den Milzbrand," in *Zentralblatt für Bakteriologie und Parasitenkunde,* **9** (1891), 467; "Études sur la fièvre typhoïde expérimentale," in *Annales de l'Institut Pasteur,* **6** (1892), 721; **8** (1894), 193, 353; *Etiologia e patogenesi della febbre gialla* (Turin, 1897); *Etiología y patogenia de la fiebre amarilla* (Montevideo, 1897); "Das myxomatogene virus," in *Zentralblatt für Bakteriologie und Parasitenkunde*, **23** (1898), 865; *Tubercolosi ed evoluzione sociale* (Milan, 1913); *Manuel d'igiene generale e coloniale* (Florence, 1914); "La patogenesi del colera. Nota preventiva," in *Annali d'igiene sperimentale*, **26** (1916), 685; and "Pathogénie du choléra," in *Comptes rendus hebdomadaires des séances de l'Académie des sciences*, **163** (1916), 538. Later writings are "Le gastro-entérotropisme des vibrions," *ibid.*, **168** (1919), 578, repr. in *Annali d'igiene sperimentale*, **29** (1919), 129; **31** (1921), 1; "De la pathogénie du choléra . . . Voies de pénétration et de sortie des vibrions cholériques dans l'organisme animal," in *Annales de l'Institut Pasteur*, **37** (1923), 364, repr. in *Annali d'igiene sperimentale*, **33** (1923), 457; "L'algidité cholérique," in *Annales de l'Institut Pasteur*, **37** (1923), 806, repr. *Annali d'igiene sperimentale*, **34** (1924), 1; "Sulle vaccinazioni per via nasale," in *Annali d'igiene sperimentale*, **34** (1924); 861; "Sur le charbon dit 'intestinal,' " in *Comptes rendus hebdomadaires des séances de l'Académie des sciences*, **179** (1924), 937; *Nuove vedute sulle infezioni dell'apparato digerente* (Rome, 1925); and "Sulla patogenesi del carbonchio detto 'interno' o 'spontaneo,' " in *Annali d'igiene sperimentale*, **35** (1925), 273, repr. *Annales de l'Institut Pasteur*, **39** (1925), 209.

See also "Identité entre spirochètes et bacilles fusiformes. Les Héliconèmes 'vincenti,' " in *Annales de l'Institut Pasteur*, **41** (1927), 679; "Dimostrazione in vivo e in vitro delle forme filtranti del virus tubercolare," in *Annali d'igiene sperimentale*, **40** (1930), 589, written with A. Alessandrini; "Il fattore ereditario nella tubercolosi," in *Romana medica* (Rome, 1930); and *Il colera* (Milan, 1931).

PIETRO AMBROSIONI

SANCHEZ (or **SANCHES**), **FRANCISCO** (*b.* diocese of Braga, Portugal, 1550 or 1551; *d.* Toulouse, France, November 1623), *philosophy, medicine.*

An exponent of an extreme nominalist skepticism, Sanchez was probably born near Valença, Portugal, and was probably of Jewish descent. In 1562 his family immigrated to Bordeaux, a frequent refuge for fleeing *conversos*. In Bordeaux, Sanchez studied at the reformist Collège de Guyenne; but in 1569 he departed for Rome to study anatomy. In 1574 he completed his doctorate in medicine at the University of Montpellier. The following year, in order to avoid religious strife in heavily Protestant Montpellier, he settled in Toulouse.

In Toulouse, Sanchez held a variety of posts: professor of philosophy from 1585 and of medicine from 1612; rector of the university; and, for thirty years, director of the Hospital of Saint Jacques,

where he is said to have sequestered himself at night in order to study cadavers. His first writings were nevertheless on mathematics. In 1575 he wrote a letter to Clavius, who the previous year had published an edition of Euclid's *Elements*, questioning the certainty of geometrical proofs. In Sanchez' view, mathematics deals with ideal, rather than real, objects and therefore can say nothing certain about actual experience.

In 1576, at the age of twenty-six, Sanchez composed his major philosophical work, *Quod nihil scitur*. Beginning with a rigorously nominalist critique of scholastic epistemology, Sanchez attacked, first, the Aristotelian concept of science as concentrating too much on abstract categories rather than on real objects, and, second, the syllogistic method of doing science as self-fulfilling: anything can be proved by starting with the correct premises. He concluded that Aristotelian science was not science at all, since one cannot reach certitude through definitions nor in the endless search for causes. True science, according to Sanchez, must be the study of particulars, but is in fact, even with this limitation, beyond man's reach because of the imperfection of his senses. In order to replace scholastic methodology, Sanchez proposed a commonsensical, empirical approach, which would not seek vainly to gain knowledge, but would entertain the more circumscribed aim of dealing realistically with experience.

The very next year (1577) Sanchez extended his skeptical critique into the realm of astrology, in a long, versified comment on the hysterical reactions to the comet of that year. In the poem he ridiculed the beliefs of astrologers such as Francesco Giuntini, who asserted that all comets must be evaluated as the source of prognostication. Sanchez wrote that such beliefs were untenable philosophically because they seemed to limit man's free will and practically because such predictions were based on inconsistent correlations between the appearance of comets and human events. (In a later treatise he condemned, in a similar vein, the practice of divination through dreams.)

The practice of medicine was Sanchez' lifelong occupation and primary source of income. He was a shrewd clinical observer in the Hippocratic tradition, although he was careful to point out errors in the works of past medical writers. In his anatomical works, the influence of Colombo, Vesalius, and Falloppio is explicit. Moreover, his diagnostic experience, convincing him of the limitations of the human senses, played an important role in the formulation of his skeptical philosophy.

BIBLIOGRAPHY

I. ORIGINAL WORKS. See *Quod nihil scitur* (Lyons, 1581; 2nd ed., Frankfurt, 1618); Spanish trans., *Que nada se sabe,* with an intro. by Marcelino Menéndez y Pelayo (Buenos Aires, 1944). This major work, along with three shorter treatises *(De longitudine et brevitate vitae, In lib. Aristotelis physiognomicon commentarius,* and *De divinatione per somnum ad Aristotelem),* is also included in Sanchez' collected works: *Opera medica* (see below) and *Tractatus philosophici* (Rotterdam, 1649). Modern eds. are *Opera philosophica,* Joaquim de Carvalho, ed. (Coimbra, 1955); and *Tratados filosóficos,* A. Moreira de Sá, ed., 2 vols. (Lisbon, 1955).

The *Carmen de cometa* was originally published in Lyons (1578); a recent ed. is *O cometa do ano de 1577,* A. Moreira de Sá, ed. (Lisbon, 1950). The letter to Clavius, which originally circulated in MS, was first published by J. Iriarte, "Francisco Sánchez el Escéptico disfrazado de Carneades en discusión epistolar con Christóbal Clavio," in *Gregorianum,* **21** (1940), 413–451; for a Portuguese trans., see *Revista portuguesa de filósofia,* **1** (1945), 295–305.

His medical works are in *Opera medica* (Toulouse, 1636), a posthumous compilation of his classroom notes. The most representative treatises are *De morbis internis, Observationes in praxi,* and a *Summa anatomica.*

II. SECONDARY LITERATURE. For Sanchez' contributions to the philosophy of science, see João Cruz Costa, *Ensaio sôbre a vida e a obra do filósofo Francisco Sanchez* (São Paulo, 1942); J. Iriarte, "Francisco Sanchez . . . a la luz de muy recientes estudios," in *Razón y Fe,* **110** (1936), 23–42, 157–181; Evaristo de Moraes Filho, *Francisco Sanches na renasença portuguesa* (Rio de Janeiro, 1953); Artur Moreira de Sá, *Francisco Sanchez, filósofo e matemático,* 2 vols. (Lisbon, 1947); and Emilien Senchet, *Essai sur la méthode de Francisco Sanchez* (Paris, 1904).

General works setting Sanchez in historical perspective are John Owen, *The Skeptics of the French Renaissance* (London, 1893), and Richard H. Popkin, *The History of Scepticism From Erasmus to Descartes,* 2nd ed. (Assen, Netherlands–New York, 1963).

On the medical works of Sanchez, see Luis de Pina, "Francisco Sanches, médico," in *Revista portuguesa de filósofia,* **7** (1951), 156–191.

THOMAS F. GLICK

SANCTORIUS. See **Santorio, Santorio.**

SANDERSON, EZRA DWIGHT (*b.* Clio, Michigan, 25 September 1878; *d.* Ithaca, New York, 27 September 1944), *entomology, rural sociology.*

Sanderson was the son of John P. and Alice Sanderson. He attended Michigan Agriculture College, receiving the B.S. degree in 1897 and, a year later, the same degree in agriculture from Cornell University. His first position was that of assistant entomologist at Maryland Agricultural College, a post he held until the summer of 1899, when he accepted an assistantship with the federal Division of Entomology. During this year he married Anna Cecilia Blanford, by whom he had a daughter.

In the fall of 1899 Sanderson became entomologist for the Delaware Agricultural Experiment Station at Newark and associate professor of zoology at Delaware College, where he remained until 1902. He then accepted the post of state entomologist of Texas and professor of entomology at Texas Agricultural and Mechanical College, where he remained for two years. He was subsequently appointed professor of zoology at New Hampshire College and, three years later, director of the agricultural experiment station of that institution. In the autumn of 1910 he became dean of the College of Agriculture at West Virginia University and from 1912 to 1915 was director of its agricultural experiment station. He resigned from this position in order to pursue graduate studies in sociology at the University of Chicago, from which he received the Ph.D. in 1921.

In 1918 Sanderson became head of the Rural Social Organization at Cornell, an institution that furthered the cause of rural sociology. He attracted many graduate students to this new discipline, and their joint efforts resulted in the provision of guidelines for ameliorating the plight of many rural communities. Sanderson's entire attention from 1918 until his retirement in 1943 was directed to these sociological activities.

Sanderson's active career falls into three fairly definite categories: economic entomology, academic administration, and rural sociology. Although he attained real distinction in each area, his enduring scientific reputation probably will rest on his earlier entomological contributions. The results of these fundamental and pioneering researches appeared in the early issues of the *Journal of Economic Entomology,* which has become the most important periodical dealing with applied entomology. Sanderson was influential in establishing it, as well as its parent sponsoring agent, the American Association of Economic Entomologists. His research articles are considered landmarks in the development of the recent discipline of insect ecology. Sanderson early realized the value of applying statistical analysis to the problems of applied entomology, an area to which he also contributed through his participation in establishing the standardization of insecticides, work that culminated in the Federal Insecticide Act of 1910. In many respects Sanderson was an "ideas" man who stimulated original thinking in entomology, and his early departure from the field was a distinct loss.

The central concept in Sanderson's approach to rural sociology appears to have been the building of the natural rural community, in which the centralized school became a major factor in community unification.

BIBLIOGRAPHY

Sanderson's entomological writings include *Insects Injurious to Staple Crops* (New York, 1902); *A Statistical Study of the Decrease in the Texas Cotton Crop Due to the Mexican Cotton Boll Weevil . . .* (Austin, Tex., 1905); "The Relation of Temperature to the Hibernation of Insects," in *Journal of Economic Entomology*, **1** (1908), 56–65; "The Influence of Minimum Temperatures in Limiting the Northern Distribution of Insects," *ibid.*, 245–262; "The Relation of Temperature to the Growth of Insects," *ibid.*, **3** (1910), 113–140; and *Insect Pests of the Farm, Garden, and Orchard* (New York, 1912; 3rd ed., rev. and enl. by L. M. Peairs, 1931).

His sociological works include *The Farmer and His Community* (New York, 1922); *The Rural Community; the Natural History of a Sociological Group* (New York, 1932), which contains ecological considerations far ahead of its time; *Rural Community Organization* (New York–London, 1939); and *Rural Sociology and Rural Social Organization* (New York–London, 1942).

An obituary is E. F. Phillips, "Dwight Sanderson, 1878–1944," in *Journal of Economic Entomology*, **37** (1944), 858–859.

C. E. NORLAND

SANDERSON, JOHN S. B. See **Burdon-Sanderson, John Scott.**

SANIO, KARL GUSTAV (*b.* Lyck, East Prussia [now Elk, Poland], 5 December 1832; *d.* Lyck, 28 January 1891), *botany.*

The son of Johann Sanio, a landowner, Sanio began studying the flora and fauna around Lyck while attending the Gymnasium. After passing the final secondary school examination in 1852, he studied science and medicine at the University of Königsberg and, from 1855 to 1857, at the University of Berlin, where his teachers were Alexander Braun and Nathanael Pringsheim. In the fall of 1857 Sanio returned to Königsberg, where he earned the

Ph.D. for the dissertation "Florula Lyccensis" in 1858. In the same year Sanio qualified as lecturer in botany with an essay entitled "Untersuchungen über die Epidermis und die Spaltöffnungen der Equisetaceen." The university administration objected to his manner of living, however, and he was ultimately compelled to give up teaching. He returned to his family in Lyck, where he conducted botanical research for the rest of his life.

Although Sanio's floristic examination of the region around Lyck essentially ended with his dissertation, he occasionally returned to floristics and systematics. He was mainly concerned, however, with other areas of botany, including the ferns, the Characae, and, above all, the moss genus *Drepanocladus* (*Harpidium*).

Sanio had begun microscopic studies of plant anatomy as a student, and his first publication was on the development of the spores of *Equisetum*. He recognized that the spiral bands (haptera) arise in the outer layer of the spore wall and exhibit an oblique structure on the exterior. Sanio was the first to point out that the stomata of *Equisetum* are composed of two pairs of cells: an external, upper pair and an inner, lower one with thickening stripes. The upper pair lies either at the same level as the epidermis or deeper. On the basis of this finding, Julius Milde later (1865) divided the genus *Equisetum* into two groups of species, *Equiseta phaneropora* and *Equiseta cryptopora*.

Sanio made his most important contributions in the anatomy of wood, a subject that had attracted his attention when he was a student. In his first studies on this topic, he dealt with the wood parenchyma, which is found in almost all woody plants. He found that it consists of rows of cells that are joined into a spindle-shaped unit and that arise from a fiber cell through oblique division. In autumn the wood parenchyma contains starch, which is dissolved in the spring.

Sanio explained the structure and development of cork so completely that later writers could add nothing essential to his account. He showed that every radial row of cork cells is derived from the action of a single cambium cell, which divides only centripetally or carries out one or two divisions in a centrifugal direction and then divides uninterruptedly only in a centripetal sequence. In the first case only cork is produced; in the second, a thin phelloderm is generated on the inside at the start of the process. The formation of cork occurs either in the epidermis or in the uppermost cortical layers, rarely in deeper tissue.

Sanio thoroughly examined 166 European and

exotic trees and shrubs. Through this research he resolved many uncertainties concerning the terminology and origin of various types of cells. He also explained the formation of annual rings and established the first table for identifying woods on the basis of anatomical features (1863).

Sanio's last works were devoted to the anatomy of the wood of the Scotch pine (*Pinus silvestris*). He showed that the cells of the wood (tracheids) in trunks and branches grow in length and breadth from the inside toward the outside for a number of annual rings, until a final size is reached. Sanio refuted Hartig's view that every radial row of wood and phloem cells derives from two mother cells, one of which transmits only wood cells toward the inside, while the other yields only phloem cells that move toward the outside. He demonstrated that each radial wood and phloem cell row in the cambium derives from only a single mother cell, which alternately sends wood cells toward the inside and phloem cells toward the outside.

Sanio owed the success of his scientific works to outstanding skill in preparing anatomical thin sections (with a razor he could produce series of sections of .03 mm) and to his great care in observation and drawing. His work also benefited from his critical attitude toward the literature and from examination of the greatest possible number of genera and families, which prevented hasty conclusions based on a few samples.

Sanio's findings and his precise terminology became widely known through their inclusion in H. A. de Bary's *Vergleichende Anatomie der Vegetationsorgane der Phanerogamen und Farne* (1877). Almost all the terms that he coined are still in use.

BIBLIOGRAPHY

I. ORIGINAL WORKS. Sanio's writings include "Über die Entwickelung der Sporen von *Equisetum*," in *Botanische Zeitung*, 14 (1856), 175–185, 193–200; "Untersuchungen über diejenigen Zellen des Holzkörpers, welche im Winter assimilierte Stoffe führen," in *Linnaea*, 29 (1857), 111–168; "Florula Lyccensis," *ibid.*, 169–264; "Untersuchungen über die Epidermis und die Spaltöffnungen der Equisetaceen," *ibid.*, 385–416; "Vergleichende Untersuchungen über den Bau und die Entwickelung des Korkes," in *Jahrbücher für wissenschaftliche Botanik*, 2 (1860), 39–108; "Vergleichende Untersuchungen über die Elementarorgane des Holzkörpers," in *Botanische Zeitung*, 21 (1863), 85–91, 93–98, 101–111, 113–118, 121–128; "Vergleichende Untersuchungen über die Zusammensetzung des Holzkörpers," *ibid.*, 357–363, 369–375, 377–385, 389–399, 401–412; "Uber die Grösse der Holzzellen

bei der gemeinen Kiefer (*Pinus silvestris*)," in *Jahrbücher für wissenschaftliche Botanik*, 8 (1872), 401–420; and "Anatomie der gemeinen Kiefer (*Pinus silvestris*)," *ibid.*, 9 (1873), 50–126.

II. SECONDARY LITERATURE. A detailed obituary is by P. Ascherson, in *Verhandlungen des Botanischen Vereins der Provinz Brandenburg*, 34 (1893), xli–xlix. Shorter biographies are J. T. Ratzeburg, *Forstwissenschaftliches Schriftsteller-Lexikon* (Berlin, 1872), 449–450; and *Allgemeine deutsche Biographie*, LIII (1907), 709–711. Sanio's work is discussed in H. A. de Bary, *Vergleichende Anatomie der Vegetationsorgane der Phanerogamen und Farne* (Leipzig, 1877); K. Mägdefrau, *Geschichte der Botanik* (Stuttgart, 1973); Julius Sachs, *Geschichte der Botanik* (Munich, 1875); and T. Schmucker and G. Linnemann, "Geschichte der Anatomie des Holzes," in H. Freund, ed., *Handbuch der Mikroskopie in der Technik*, V, pt. 1 (Frankfurt, 1951), 1–78.

KARL MÄGDEFRAU

SANTORINI, GIOVANNI DOMENICO (*b.* Venice, Italy, 6 June 1681; *d.* Venice, 7 May 1737), *medicine, anatomy.*

The son of an apothecary, Santorini studied medicine at Bologna, Padua, and Pisa, receiving the doctorate in 1701. He began anatomical dissection in 1703 and was demonstrator in anatomy at Venice from 1706 to 1728, when he became physician to the Spedaletto in that city.

Santorini was generally acknowledged as the outstanding anatomist of his time, carefully dissecting and delineating many difficult and complex gross features of the human body, such as facial muscles involved in emotional expression, accessory pancreatic ducts, and duodenal papillae. His name has been given to some of these structures, such as the arytenoid cartilages (1724), the risorius muscle, and the *plexus pudendalis venosus*.

Santorini's contributions began with *Opuscula medica de structura* (1705). His most important work was *Observationes anatomicae* (1724), a valuable exposition of details of human anatomy that contains "De musculis facies," "De aure exteriore," "De cerebro," "De naso," "De larynge," "De iis," "De abdominae," "De virorum naturalibus," and "De mulierum partis procreationes datis." Santorini was a popular teacher and a pioneer in teaching obstetrics.

BIBLIOGRAPHY

See *Opuscula medica de structura* (Venice, 1705; Rotterdam, 1718), later repr. in Georgius Baglivi, *Opera*

(Leiden, 1710); *Observationes anatomicae* (Venice, 1724; Leiden, 1739), his most important work; *Istoria d'un feto* (Venice, 1727); *Istruzioni intorno alla febbre* (Venice, 1734, 1751), and his *Opera* (Parma, 1773). His *Opuscula quatuor: De structura et motu fibrae, De nutritione animali, de haemorrhoidibus,* and *De catameniis* appeared in Baglivi's *Opera omnia medico-practica et anatomica* (Leiden, 1745).

CHAUNCEY D. LEAKE

SANTORIO, SANTORIO, also known as **Sanctorius** (*b.* Justinopolis, Venetian Republic [now Koper, Yugoslavia], 29 March 1561; *d.* Venice, Italy, 6 March 1636), *medicine, physiology, invention of measuring instruments.*

Santorio was the son of Antonio Santorio, a nobleman from Friuli who had come to Justinopolis (also named Capraria and Capodistria) as a high official of the Venetian Republic. While serving there, he married Elisabetta Cordonia, the heiress of a local noble family.

Santorio, the eldest of four children, received at his baptism his family name as his given name — a practice fashionable at that time in Istria. He was educated at Justinopolis and Venice, where his father's friendship with an illustrious nobleman, Morosini, enabled Santorio to share the same tutors as Morosini's sons, Paolo and Andrea. (The latter became a famous historian and a reformer of the University of Padua.) Thus Santorio acquired a thorough knowledge of classical languages and literature.

In 1575 Santorio enrolled at the Archilyceum of Padua, where he followed the traditional sequence of studying philosophy and then medicine. He obtained his doctor's degree in 1582. At the very beginning of his medical practice, Santorio carried out a systematic study of the changes in weight that occurred in his own body following the ingestion of food and the elimination of excrement.

Most biographers assert that, following an invitation from King Maximilian, Santorio lived for a long time in Poland. The only document supporting this statement is late testimony quoting a copy of a letter written by Nicolò Galerio, vicar of the University of Padua. In 1587 an important person requested a qualified physician from the medical faculty at Padua; the faculty replied through Galerio that Santorio — the most suitable choice because of his learning, his loyalty, and his zeal — was ready to undertake the journey. It is claimed that Galerio's response was addressed to the king of Poland, but this is an unproved conjecture. The original

document has disappeared. Capello was Santorio's only biographer to have seen the draft (also lost) of Galerio's letter, which, according to Capello's testimony, was written "for a certain Polish prince." Therefore, it can be assumed that the draft did not bear the name of the intended recipient. The Polish archives contain no material indicating that Santorio ever stayed in Poland, but there are several pieces of evidence attesting his presence in Croatia, particularly in Karlovac, during the last decade of the sixteenth century. The invitation of 1587 would thus seem to have come from a leading Croatian nobleman, probably Count Zrinski. From 1587 to 1599 Santorio spent most of his time, not in Poland, but among the South Slavs. It was on the Adriatic coast, at or near Senj, that Santorio made the first trials with both his wind gauge and a new apparatus designed to measure the force of water currents.

Santorio often returned to his native city and maintained cordial relations with the scientists of Venice and Padua. In 1599 he finally left Croatia and established a medical practice in Venice. One reason for his departure was perhaps a desire to escape the plague that in 1598 began to ravage the valley of the Sava River. Also, he was attracted by the exchange of new ideas and the intellectual fervor that Venice was then enjoying. The home of the Morosinis had become a true meeting place for the proponents of the new science: Santorio met Galileo and became friendly with Paolo Sarpi, Girolamo Fabrici, Giambattista Della Porta, and Francesco Sagredo, among others. In 1607 Santorio treated Sarpi after the latter had been wounded during an attempted political assassination.

Santorio's first book appeared in 1602, *Methodi vitandorum errorum omnium qui in arte medica contingunt.* It is a comprehensive study on the method to be followed in order to avoid making errors in the art of healing. Without breaking with the Galenic tradition, Santorio ventured certain criticisms of classical physiology and expressed ideas that prefigured the mechanistic explanations of the iatrophysical school. According to Santorio, the properties of the living body do not depend only on the four elementary qualities, nor even on the secondary and tertiary qualities, as they were defined by Galen, but also on "number, position, form, and other accidental factors." Santorio employed the analogy (later used by Descartes) between an organism and a clock, the movements of which depend on the number, the form, and the disposition of its parts. Nevertheless, he remained faithful to traditional humoral pathology and tried to explain all internal diseases as particular cases of humoral dyscrasia.

Although Santorio accepted the ancient scheme that attributed diseases to a bad mixture of the four humors, he modified it profoundly by some quantitative attributions. In the pathology of Hippocrates and Galen there is no discontinuity between eucrasia and the innumerable possible pathological deviations. Santorio, starting from certain remarks of Galen on the "degrees" of dyscrasia, defined the discontinuity of morbid states and proposed to make known, by mathematical deduction, all the possible diseases. (According to his calculations, their total number was about 80,000.) In *Methodi vitandorum errorum,* Santorio mentioned a few measuring instruments (the scale and the "pulsilogium") but did not seem to attach special importance to them. It should be emphasized, however, that theoretical considerations form only the background to this medical textbook, which is of an eminently practical orientation. The book contains several good descriptions of diseases and offers model cases of differential diagnostics, for example, the clinical distinction between an abscess of the mesentery and intestinal ulcerations.

On 6 October 1611 Santorio was appointed professor of theoretical medicine at the University of Padua. He owed his appointment to the success of his book, to his growing reputation as a practitioner, and to the support of his friends in the upper Venetian nobility. Originally he was supposed to have held the position for six years; but at the end of that period, in 1617, the Venetian Senate extended his contract for six more years and granted him an exceptionally high salary. Santorio's talents as an orator, the originality of his ideas, and his demonstrations of new methods of clinical examination made his courses very popular. As professor of theoretical medicine, Santorio was required to present and comment upon the *Ars parva* of Galen, the *Aphorisms* of Hippocrates, and the first book of the *Canon* of Ibn Sīnā. This obligation led him to publish most of his own views in the restricted form of scholarly commentaries on these three works. Cautious and introverted, Santorio preferred to express himself through allusions and to envelop his bold and original ideas in a thick layer of conventional erudition. Still, as early as 1602, he clearly set forth his personal creed: "One must believe first in one's own senses and in experience, then in reasoning, and only in the third place in the authority of Hippocrates, of Galen, of Aristotle, and of other excellent philosophers" (*Methodi vitandorum errorum,* 215).

In 1612 Santorio published *Commentaria in artem medicinalem Galeni,* a large volume of commentaries on Galen that contains the first printed mention of the air thermometer. In 1614 he published *De statica medicina,* a short work on the variation in weight experienced by the human body as a result of ingestion and excretion. The latter work made him famous. Filled with incisive and elliptic aphorisms, *De statica medicina* dazzled his contemporaries, although its style is rather irritating to modern readers. The book briefly describes the results of a long series of experiments that Santorio conducted with a scale and other measuring instruments. Its success stemmed chiefly from the simplicity and apparent precision of the methods by which he promised to preserve health and to direct all therapeutic measures.

On 9 February 1615 Santorio sent a copy of *De statica medicina* to Galileo. In an accompanying letter he explained that his work was based on two principles: first, Hippocrates' view that medicine is essentially the addition of what is lacking and the removal of what is superfluous; and second, experimentation. The origin of "static medicine" was, in fact, the Hippocratic conception that health consists in the harmony of the humors. One expression of this harmony is the equilibrium between the substances consumed by the organism and those rejected by it. According to this view, pathological conditions should be accompanied by a quantitative disequilibrium of the exchanges between the living body and its surroundings. To verify this supposition, Santorio turned to quantitative experimentation. With the aid of a chair scale, he systematically observed the daily variations in the weight of his body and showed that a large part of excretion takes place invisibly through the skin and lungs (*perspiratio insensibilis*). Moreover, he sought to determine the magnitude of this invisible excretion; its relationship to visible excretion; and its dependence on various factors, including the state of the atmosphere, diet, sleep, exercise, sexual activity, and age. Thus he invented instruments to measure ambient humidity and temperature. From this research he concluded (1) that *perspiratio insensibilis,* which had been known since Erasistratus but which was considered imponderable, could be determined by systematic weighing; (2) that it is, in itself, greater than all forms of sensible bodily excretions combined; and (3) that it is not constant but varies considerably as a function of several internal and external factors; for example, cold and sleep lessen it and fever increases it.

The invention of the thermometer gave rise to a

priority dispute between Santorio, Galileo, Sagredo, and several other scientists. It seems probable that Galileo invented the first open-air thermoscope. Santorio built a similar device, and whether or not he knew of Galileo's, he was the first to add a scale, thereby transforming the thermoscope into the thermometer. The exact date of this invention is unknown, but it falls between 1602 and 1612. The fixed reference points that Santorio employed to create a thermometric scale—namely, the temperature of snow and the temperature of a candle flame—are mentioned in his commentaries on Galen, although not in the first edition of that work. Galileo made no use at all of the thermoscope. In contrast, Santorio attempted to measure body temperature in health and illness and employed his thermometer in physiological experiments and in medical practice. It is not possible to estimate the accuracy of the figures that Santorio obtained with his apparatus. In any case, the instrument did have the great drawback of being subject to variations in barometric pressure, a factor that was still unknown.

Santorio also invented other measuring instruments and medical devices, including a hygrometer, a pendulum for measuring the pulse rate, a trocar, a special syringe for extracting bladder stones, and a bathing bed. He spoke of these inventions in his lectures and demonstrated their uses. For example, he publicly used the trocar for abdominal and thoracic paracentesis and even for a tracheotomy. Although Santorio promised to reveal the methods of construction of his apparatus in a book entitled *De instrumentis medicis,* the work never appeared.

Santorio was an advocate of the Copernican system and a fierce opponent of astrology. These stands involved him in difficulties with certain of his colleagues, who accused him, among other things, of neglecting his professional duties. An adept of the occult sciences, Ippolito Obizzi, professor at Ferrara, violently attacked *De statica medicina*; and Santorio felt himself obliged to respond in a new edition of his book. Many of the criticisms were justified (Santorio had attributed to static medicine a practical significance that proved to be grossly exaggerated), but Obizzi was wrong in attacking Santorio's experimental method.

In 1624, at the end of his second term as professor at Padua, Santorio wished to retire from his post. His request was granted by the Venetian Senate, which, as a sign of its regard for his services, also awarded him an annual pension and the permanent title of professor. Subsequently Santorio

declined offers from the universities of Bologna, Pavia, and Messina and returned to Venice.

In 1625 he published there his commentaries on Ibn Sīnā's *Canon (Commentaria in primam fen primi libri Canonis Avicennae).* The chief value of this work lies in its revelation (still quite hesitant, although accompanied by diagrams for the first time) of the principles of construction of various instruments. In 1630 Santorio was given the task of organizing measures against an epidemic of plague in Venice. In the same year he was elected president of the Venetian College of Physicians.

A misogynist, Santorio never married. Although frugal and little concerned with personal comfort, he was eager for gain and in fact assembled a considerable fortune. He was restrained and prudent, but his style occasionally ran to incisive irony. Above all, Santorio was endowed with a highly critical intelligence. He quickly accepted the ideas of Galileo on mechanics and on the nature of the celestial bodies as well as those of Kepler on optics. Curiously, despite his penchant for mechanistic explanations, he did not grasp the significance of Harvey's discovery of the circulation of the blood.

Santorio died from a disease of the urinary tract. He was buried in the Church of the Servi in Venice, but his skeleton was removed when the church was demolished in 1812. His skull is now at the museum of the University of Padua.

Throughout the seventeenth century and the first half of the eighteenth, physicians sympathetic with the doctrines of iatrophysics praised Santorio as one of the greatest innovators in physiology and practical medicine. Many scientists agreed with Baglivi that the new medicine was based on two pillars: Santorio's statics and Harvey's discovery of the circulation of the blood. Boerhaave wrote of *De statica medicina* that "no medical book has attained this perfection." The exaggerated praise accorded to Santorio's little book detracted from its author's reputation in the nineteenth century, by which time scientists had rejected as illusory the medical content of his teaching, namely, the claim that knowledge of the quantity of *perspiratio insensibilis* provides essential information for hygiene, diagnostics, and therapeutics. Although static medicine is no longer a viable medical doctrine, the method through which it emerged is no less fruitful on that account. Santorio's great achievement was the introduction of quantitative experimentation into biological science. Undoubtedly inspired by the ideas of Galileo, Santorio opened the way to a mathematical and experimental analysis of physiological and pathological phenomena.

BIBLIOGRAPHY

I. ORIGINAL WORKS. Santorio's most famous work is *Ars de statica medicina sectionibus aphorismorum septem comprehensa* (Venice, 1614); the second, greatly revised ed. is *De medicina statica libri octo* (Venice, 1615). This second ed. was reprinted about forty times, either by itself or with commentaries by M. Lister, Baglivi, J. Gorter, D. L. Rüdiger, or A. C. Lorry. It was also translated into English (1676), Italian (1704), French (1722), and German (1736).

Santorio's other writings are *Methodi vitandorum errorum omnium qui in arte medica contingunt* (Venice, 1602); *Commentaria in artem medicinalem Galeni* (Venice, 1612); *Commentaria in primam fen primi libri Canonis Avicennae* (Venice, 1625); and *Liber de remediorum inventione* (Venice, 1629). These works are contained in his *Opera omnia quatuor tomis distincta* (Venice, 1660).

II. SECONDARY LITERATURE. The most helpful old biographies are A. Capello, *De vita cl. viri Sanctorii Sanctorii* (Venice, 1750); and J. Grandi, *De laudibus Sanctorii* (Venice, 1671). Further details can be found in M. Del Gaizo, *Ricerche storiche intorno a Santorio Santorio ed alla medicina statica* (Naples, 1889) and *Alcune conoscenze di Santorio intorno ai fenomeni della visione ed il testamento di lui* (Naples, 1891); and in P. Stancovich, *Biografie degli uomini illustri dell'Istria*, II (Trieste, 1829).

More recent studies of Santorio's life and work include A. Castiglioni, *La vita e l'opera di Santorio Santorio Capodistriano* (Bologna–Trieste, 1920), with English trans. by E. Recht in *Medical Life*, **38** (1931), 729–785; M. D. Grmek, *Istarski liječnik Santorio Santorio i njegovi aparati i instrumenti* (Zagreb, 1952); and R. H. Major, "Santorio Santorio," in *Annals of Medical History*, n.s. **10** (1938), 369–381.

For an appraisal of Santorio's role in the history of science, see M. D. Grmek, *L'Introduction de l'expérience quantitative dans les sciences biologiques* (Paris, 1962) and H. Miessen, *Die Verdienste Sanctorii Sanctorii um die Einführung physikalischer Methoden in die Heilkunde* (Düsseldorf, 1940). On static medicine see E. T. Renbourn, "The Natural History of Insensible Perspiration," in *Medical History*, **4** (1960), 135–152. The best work on the invention of the thermometer is W. E. K. Middleton, *A History of the Thermometer and Its Use in Meteorology* (Baltimore, 1966).

M. D. GRMEK

SAPORTA, LOUIS CHARLES JOSEPH GASTON DE (*b.* St. Zacharie, France, 28 July 1823; *d.* St. Zacharie, 26 January 1896), *paleobotany.*

Saporta's ancestors came from Zaragoza, Spain, and included physicians, botanists, and entomologists. He himself was at first more inclined toward literature, but following the death of his wife in 1850, when he was twenty-seven, he sought diversion in botany. His interest in paleobotany developed after he had by accident found some plant fossils from a nearby gypsum mine in an antique shop in Aix. He related this discovery to Adolphe Brongniart, a friend of his grandfather's, and Brongniart encouraged him to make a systematic study of the deposits around Aix.

Saporta devoted his initial research to the Tertiary flora of France, on which he published a number of monographs, illustrated with detailed drawings that he executed directly from nature. These included a study of a sequence of local floras separated by short intervals that he discovered in lacustrian formations from the Upper Eocene to the Lower Miocene. The remarkable state of preservation of the fossils that he studied allowed him to examine the outlines and rib networks of leaves and to make more exact determinations of species than are usually possible.

Saporta next turned his attention to the Mesozoic. Among his publications dealing with that period was an extensive examination of Jurassic flora that comprised four volumes each of text and illustrations. This work brought his services into demand, and he was invited to Belgium (to collaborate with A. F. Marion in a work on the Gelinden flora), to Portugal (to study Lower Cretaceous and Cretaceous floras), to Greece (to study the Miocene flora of Koumi), and to the United States (to assist Lesquereux in his work on the Cretaceous flora of the Dakotas). He published other major works, including *Le monde des plantes avant l'apparition de l'homme* (Paris, 1879), which represented revised versions of articles that Saporta had already brought out in nontechnical journals, *L'évolution du règne végétal* (Paris, 1881–1885), written with Marion, and *Origine paléontologique des arbres cultivés ou utilisés par l'homme* (Paris, 1888). The first of these gave a synoptic view of the stages through which vegetation on earth had passed, while the last two were more specialized treatments of the same subject.

In his work in general Saporta was a patient and meticulous researcher who attempted both to give a precise description of a species and to relate it to historical developments so as to clarify its origin. He was particularly concerned with elucidating the climatic conditions of an era and wrote a number of works on historic climate. He emphasized the difficulty of determining species, and advised caution; while he has been accused of erroneously increasing the number of species, such accusations are unjustified, and recent studies have frequently served to confirm his general views, although with some qualifications.

Saporta's scientific reputation was widespread. He was elected to the Académie d'Aix in 1866, and served as its president on several occasions; from 1886 he was permanent secretary of its science section. In 1872 he was admitted to the Académie de Marseille, and in 1876 he became a corresponding member of the Académie des Sciences. He was also an associate foreign member of the Royal Academy of Belgium and of the Madrid Academy of Science. In addition to his paleontological research, Saporta was interested in history. He wrote *La famille de Madame de Sévigné en Provence,* of which the first chapter served as his last presidential address to the Académie d'Aix.

BIBLIOGRAPHY

I. ORIGINAL WORKS. In addition to the works cited, see Saporta's own *Notice sur les travaux scientifiques* (Paris, 1875); Poggendorff lists a selection of his articles in periodicals, and R. Zeiller, cited below, gives a further bibliography. His book on the history of Provence is *La famille de Madame de Sévigné en Provence* (Paris, 1889).

II. SECONDARY LITERATURE. On Saporta and his work, see J. A. Henriques, "Luiz Carlos José Gaston, Marquez de Saporta," in *Boletim da Sociedade Broteriana,* **13** (1896), 1–10; A. Pons, "Contribution palynologique à l'étude de la flore et de la végétation pliocènes de la région Rhodanienne," in *Annales des sciences naturelles,* Botanique, 12th ser., **5** (1964), 499–722; R. Zeiller, "Le marquis G. de Saporta. Sa vie et ses travaux," in *Revue générale de botanique,* 7 (1895), 353–388, with bibliography; and Y. Conry, *Correspondance entre Charles Darwin et Gaston de Saporta* (Paris, 1972).

F. STOCKMANS

SARPI, PAOLO (*b.* Venice, Italy, 14 August 1552; *d.* Venice, 16 January 1623), *natural philosophy, theology.*

Sarpi was the son of Francesco Sarpi and Isabella Morelli. The financial straits of the family, after the death of his father, shifted the responsibility for Sarpi's education to his uncle, Ambrogio Morelli, the head titular priest of St. Hermangora. Impressed with the boy's precocity, Don Ambrogio

placed him under the tutelage of the Servite friar Giammaria Capella, who instructed him in philosophy, theology, and logic, and was influential in his entry into the Servite Order at the age of fourteen. At the end of his novitiate, in 1570, Sarpi displayed such argumentative skill in publicly defending 318 philosophical and theological theses that the duke of Mantua, Guglielmo Gonzaga, appointed him court theologian and professor of positive theology.

In 1574, as a bachelor in theology, Sarpi worked with Cardinal Carlo Borromeo in Milan and, later that year, returned to Venice to teach philosophy in the Servite monastery. In 1578 he was awarded the degree of doctor of theology by the University of Padua and the following year was elected provincial of his order. As procurator general from 1585 to 1588, Sarpi resided in Rome, where he enjoyed the friendship of Pope Sixtus V, the Jesuit theologian Robert Bellarmine, and Giambattista Della Porta. He was appointed state theologian by the Venetian Senate in 1606 and counseled defiance of the bull of interdict and excommunication launched against Venice by Paul V. Having failed to appear before the Roman Inquisition to answer charges of heresy, he was excommunicated in January 1607. The reconciliation between the papacy and the Republic of Venice did not lessen the hostility harbored in Rome against Sarpi, and on 5 October 1607 he was the object of an attempted assassination that he accused the Roman Curia of engineering.

As adviser to the Venetian Senate, an office he continued to hold until his death sixteen years later, Sarpi arbitrated the dispute between Galileo and Baldassar Capra, who had claimed the invention of the proportional compass as his own. In July 1609, when offered the opportunity to purchase one of the earliest telescopes, the Senate referred the matter to Sarpi for his opinion. Sarpi, who as early as November 1608 had been the first in Italy to learn of the invention of the Flemish spectacle-maker Hans Lippershey, recommended that the offer be refused, confident that his friend Galileo could construct an instrument of comparable if not superior quality. This Galileo did, and presented it to the government as a gift in August 1609, in return for which he received a lifetime appointment to the University of Padua.

Chiefly remembered now for his highly biased *Istoria del Concilio Tridentino* (1619), Sarpi was well versed in the works of all the Scholastic philosophers, especially Ockham, whom he held in great esteem. His *Arte di ben pensare,* in which he distinguishes between sensation and reflection, and examines the relationship of the senses to cognition, has been credited with anticipating Locke's *Essay Concerning Human Understanding.*

Although Sarpi was highly praised for his mathematical and speculative abilities by such contemporaries as Galileo, Della Porta, and Acquapendente, all that remains by which one can judge the originality of his scientific thought are some letters and the notebooks containing his philosophical, physical, and mathematical thoughts. Extant are reliable copies of the originals that perished in a fire in 1769. They consist of more than 600 numbered paragraphs, which were written over a period of three decades but date chiefly from 1578 to 1597. Rather than forming a consistent philosophical system, the notebooks are a collage of disparate thoughts about the nature of the physical world—a chronicle of the intellectual evolution of a man in the mainstream of the scientific developments of his age. In Venice, Sarpi religiously frequented the *ridotto* at the home of the historian Andrea Morosini; while in Padua he regularly attended colloquiums sponsored by Giovanni Vincenzio Pinelli and, in Rome, at the Accademia dei Lincei. There he met and exchanged views with some of the most celebrated scientists of the day and, it appears, recorded in his notebooks their ideas in addition to his own.

The entries, chronologically annotated, touch upon every aspect of contemporary science, from a discussion of the corpuscular nature of light and a refutation of the Peripatetic denial of its passage through a vacuum, to an enumeration of the properties of conic sections. Of particular interest are Sarpi's ideas on optical relativity, his negation of the concept of absolute rest, and his refutation of the Aristotelian doctrine of an essential difference between natural and violent motion together with its corollary—that the two types of motion cannot be simultaneously operative in the same body. In anatomy, to which he devoted himself from 1582 to 1585, Sarpi has been credited with correctly interpreting the function of the venous valves and the discovery of the circulation of the blood, for which Harvey later provided experimental proof. The subject of magnetism is one in which the notebooks reflect a constant interest. Several entries suggest (as, a decade later, did William Gilbert, whom Sarpi knew) that all bodies fall to earth not because it is their nature to do so but because they are drawn to it "as iron is to a magnet." Other entries deal with the reflection of light by curved mirrors, centers of gravity, the relative weights of bodies immersed in water, speeds of descent of freely falling bodies, the motion of projectiles, cause and effect, and a short discussion of the inconclusiveness of the arguments marshaled by opponents of the Copernican system.

BIBLIOGRAPHY

I. ORIGINAL WORKS. See F. Griselini, ed., *Opere di F. Paolo Sarpi Servita,* 8 vols. (Verona, 1761–1768). R. Amerio, *Pensieri naturali, metafisici e matematici del Padre Maestro Paolo Sarpi Servita* (Bari, 1951), consists of excerpts from the notebooks, including the *Arte di ben pensare.* Copies of the notebooks made by Configlio Capra in 1740 are in the Marciana Library in Venice, MSS Ital. Cl.II, no. 129 (Provenienza Giacomo Morelli), Collocazione 1914: "Opuscoli e frammenti del Padre M.ro Paola Servita, in varie materie filosofiche, volume primo, an. 1740, Pensieri naturali, metafisici e matematici, opusc. I," 1–142; *Arte di ben pensare,* 275–292. G. Gambarin edited *Istoria del Concilio Tridentino,* 3 vols. (Bari, 1935; repr. Florence, 1966).

II. SECONDARY LITERATURE. See G. Abetti, *Amici e nemici di Galileo* (Milan, 1945); D. Bertolini, ed., *Enciclopedia italiana,* XXX (1949), 877–879; A. G. Campbell, *The Life of Fra Paolo Sarpi* (London, 1869); P. Cassani, *Paolo Sarpi e le scienze matematiche e naturali* (Venice, 1882); A. Favaro, "Fra Paolo Sarpi, fisico e matematico, secondo i nuovi studi del prof. P. Cassani," in *Atti del R. Istituto veneto di scienze, lettere ed arti,* 6th ser., **1** (1882–1883), 893–911; G. Getto, *Paolo Sarpi* (Florence, 1967); Fulgenzio Micanzio, *Vita del Padre Paolo del Ordine dei Servi* (Leiden, 1646), also in English (London, 1651); A. Robertson, *Fra Paolo Sarpi the Greatest of the Venetians* (London, 1894); and T. A. Trollope, *Paul the Pope and Paul the Friar* (London, 1861).

UMBERTO MARIA D'ANTINI

SARS, MICHAEL (*b.* Bergen, Norway, 30 August 1805; *d.* Christiania [Oslo], Norway, 22 October 1869), *marine biology.*

Sars's father, for whom he was named, was born in Bremen but later settled in Bergen, as sea captain and merchant. The ancestors of his mother, Divert Henriche Heilmann, came from Narva, Estonia.

Sars's early enthusiasm for natural history was much encouraged by his teachers. He studied theology and received the candidate's degree in 1828. From 1828 to 1854 he served as teacher, vicar, and later rector of seashore communities in western Norway, often traveling by boat to visit parishioners and devoting much of his time to zoological studies. Some of his most important work was done in this period. Following his appointment on 7 August 1854, Sars was professor extraordinarius of zoology at the University of Christiania (Oslo) until his death; but his excessive concern with details of morphology made him neither a successful nor a popular teacher.

His marriage in 1831 to Maren Welhaven produced twelve children, one of whom, Georg Ossian, became a noted zoologist.

Sars traveled widely in his younger years, beginning with a journey to the northern seas of Norway. A large grant supported a six-month natural history trip in 1837 to Holland, France, Germany, Prague, Denmark, and Sweden. Sars often visited the Mediterranean, the Adriatic in 1851, and Naples and Messina in the winter of 1852–1853. These study trips not only greatly increased his knowledge but also brought him in contact with the leading zoologists of Europe.

One of the fathers of marine zoology, Sars from 1830 to 1860 made what is perhaps the greatest single contribution to the elucidation of the life cycles of marine invertebrates. His findings on the alternation of generations in coelenterates were among the most important evidence for Steenstrup's classical work on *Generationswechsel* (1842). Because the larval stages of most marine organisms are so different from the adults, their connection cannot be discovered until a series of intermediate stages is established; it was Sars who discovered many of them. Simultaneously with the Swedish zoologist Sven Lovén he found and described the first trochophore larvae (annelid). Likewise, Sars was the first to describe the veliger larvae of the mollusks (1837, 1840) and the bipinnaria larva (1835), which he later (1844, 1846) identified as a stage in the development of starfish.

From 1830 on, Sars used the dredge invented by O. F. Müller in his collecting. His numerous discoveries of deep-sea organisms by dredging were a sensation in his day because—until he proved otherwise—it had been universally assumed that the depths of the ocean where light did not penetrate were without life. In 1864 his son Georg, who participated in the collecting, dredged up from a depth of 300 fathoms (near Lofoten) the first living stalked crinoids (sea lilies), a group of organisms then known only from fossils and thought to have been extinct since the Mesozoic. The description of *Rhizocrinus lofotensis* (1864) was followed by intensified work at greater ocean depths, and in 1868 Sars published a memoir on 427 species of invertebrates collected off Norway at depths of from more than 200 to 450 fathoms. These exciting results induced him to promote deep-sea expeditions and thus led to the conception and organization of the *Challenger* expedition.

Although a competent taxonomist and morphologist, Sars was interested mainly in life cycles, larval stages, parental care through brood pouches, seasons of reproduction, cyclic phenomena, and migrations of marine organisms. His own research yielded major contributions to knowledge of annelids, ascidians, coelenterates, crustaceans, echinoderms, and mollusks. Actively interested in fossils, he also published a number of contributions to paleontology.

Sars published ninety-five papers (six posthumous). He was an honorary or corresponding member of more than twenty foreign academies and societies and was awarded honorary doctorates from the universities of Zurich (1846) and Berlin (1860). Most of his original publications appeared in Norwegian; but some were subsequently republished, at least in abstract, in French, English, or German.

BIBLIOGRAPHY

I. ORIGINAL WORKS. A complete bibliography of Sars's works is found in Økland (below); they include *Beskrivelser og iagttagelser over nogle . . . ved den Bergenske kyst levende dyr* (Bergen, 1835), French abstract in *Annales d'anatomie et de physiologie*, **2** (1838), 81–90; "Beitrag zur Entwicklungsgeschichte der Mollusken und Zoophyten," in *Archiv für Naturgeschichte*, **3** (1837), 402–407; **6** (1840), 196–219; "Mémoire pour servir à la connaissance des crinoïdes vivants," in University Program, first semester 1867 (Christiania, 1868); and "On Some Remarkable Forms of Animal Life From the Great Deeps of the Norwegian Coast I," *ibid.*, first semester 1869 (Christiania, 1872), written with G. O. Sars.

II. SECONDARY LITERATURE. Information on Sars's life and work is in Fridthjof Økland, *Michael Sars et Minneskrift* (Oslo, 1955), which has a full bibliography; the obituary by Gwynn Jeffreys in Nature, **1** (1870), 265–266; and J. J. S. Steenstrup, *Ueber den Generationswechsel* (Copenhagen, 1842).

ERNST MAYR

SARTON, GEORGE ALFRED LÉON (*b.* Ghent, Belgium, 31 August 1884; *d.* Cambridge, Massachusetts, 22 March 1956), *history of science*.

Sarton was the only child of Alfred Sarton, a chief engineer and director of the Belgian State

Railways. His mother, Léonie Van Halmé, died when he was a few months old. An isolated child, surrounded by servants, George had a prosperous but lonely upbringing.

Secure in a setting as bourgeois as a Balzac novel, Sarton followed a course of schooling that normally led to the study of philosophy at the University of Ghent. But he soon abandoned philosophy in disgust for the natural sciences. He studied chemistry (for which he won a gold medal), crystallography, and then mathematics. His 1911 D.Sc. dissertation on "Les principes de la mécanique de Newton" provided an early indication of the direction his interests were taking under the philosophical influence of Comte, Duhem, and Tannery. A visit to London at this time led to the systematic exploration of the works of Wells, Shaw, and the Fabians, whose ideas Sarton experienced as a refreshing contrast to the doctrinaire Marxism that he and his friends youthfully espoused. Socialism rather than communism thus came to seem the necessary and inevitable prelude to the final achievement of benevolent anarchism.

Sarton graduated from the university in 1911. In May of the same year he married Eleanor Mabel Elwes of London, who had experienced a similar lonely childhood, after being boarded out when her parents (her father was a civil and mining engineer) traveled abroad. Among other similarities in their backgrounds, her father was a Fabian and agnostic, while his was liberal, anticlerical, and a Mason. The small private income Sarton enjoyed was not enough to sustain a family, while all the assets of his wife's father had been lost in speculative mining stocks. Sarton thus found it necessary to seek employment. A 1910 note in his diary had already indicated his intention—before trying to get a post at the university—to "become the pupil, if I prove worthy, of Henri Poincaré: the most intelligent man of our time." He continued, in a passage both prophetic and revealing:

> It is almost certain that I shall devote a great part of my life to the study of "natural philosophy." There is great work to be accomplished in that direction. And—from that point of view—*living* history, the passionate history of the physical and mathematical sciences is still to be written. Isn't that really what history is, the evolution of human *greatness,* as well as its weakness?

This liberal and characteristically enlightened faith was to guide most of the remaining forty-six years of his life. The transition from a dawning conviction of the importance of a passionate history of the physical sciences to the systematic work of equipping a new discipline with tools and standards, and more especially the transition to paid employment in an as-yet-nonexistent profession, was to prove slow and complex.

Using the proceeds from the sale of his deceased father's wine cellar (the sale itself was a typically outrageous act of the confident and iconoclastic young man), Sarton bought a pleasant country house in Wondelgem, near Ghent. Here his only surviving child, May Sarton, was born in May 1912. At about this time Sarton made the bold decision to found *Isis,* his "*Revue consacrée á l'histoire de la science.*" Displaying the single-minded and disinterested opportunism that marks the actions of a man wholly convinced of his mission, he recruited a distinguished editorial board. By September 1912 he had secured the patronage of his idol Poincaré and Arrhenius, Durkheim, Heath, Jacques Loeb, Ostwald, Ramsay, and David Eugene Smith. Sarton's methodical placing of these names in categories shows he was already convinced that the history of science subsumed under its wider heading the histories of mathematics, technology, chemistry, medicine, biology, physics, and astronomy and required besides the expert advice of scientists, historians, sociologists, and historians of philosophy. The methodical division of his field also displays Sarton's passion for tidiness and classificatory order. This passion was to inform all his efforts and may in part explain his attraction to the work of Comte, just as it lay behind his particular admiration for Linnaeus among men of science.

The decision to found a journal was crucial. In retrospect we can see how *Isis* provided Sarton with the first of the institutional tools he needed, if a long-continued but still incoherent area of inquiry was to be transformed under his leadership into an articulated discipline, with agreed critical standards and a definitive cognitive identity. Sarton himself conceived of *Isis* as having far wider aims. His overarching vision and evangelical belief were announced to the world in a series of explanatory passages in the early numbers of the journal. As he pointed out, it was not the chosen domain of activity which made *Isis* unique, but the fact that no other journal would systematically and holistically connect methodological, sociological, and philosophical perspectives with the purely historical and thus allow historical inquiry to "attain its full significance."

Sarton always insisted that the history of science was by nature an encyclopedic discipline, that is, a discipline devoted to summation, comparison, and synthesis. Indeed his own interest in the history of science was "dominated . . . by a philosophical conception." As he wrote to a correspondent in 1927, "I am anxious to prove inductively the unity of knowledge and the unity of mankind." The immensity of the task did not daunt him. Rather it provided the rationale for a lifetime pursuit of difficult linguistic skills and wide-ranging historical and scientific knowledge. He eventually mastered fourteen languages.

Sarton was above all a man of the nineteenth century. He was culturally oriented toward universal history and the progressivist philosophies that found their basis in positive science and their end in the imminent and universal brotherhood of man. Yet in his thinking he was indebted to Condorcet as well as to Comte. The lines of English thought that led from Spencer to the Webbs and Shaw were also important in defining his developed view of the goals to be served by that new synthesis of knowledge to which the history of science was the essential key. High theory and a rigorous consistency were less urgent to him than sustained, appropriate action. Thus throughout his life, Sarton enjoyed the role of propagandist. His evangelizing on behalf of his chosen subject inevitably calls to mind the way Francis Bacon served as apostle for the field of science itself. And, like Bacon, Sarton had his most enduring impact in this vital, although little-acknowledged capacity. Other roles were more nearly central to his mission. With a discipline to be created, a world to be won, the provision of tools, techniques, methodologies, and intellectual orientations lay uppermost in his mind and at the forefront of his actions. A cognitive identity for his new discipline was the primary goal, and his own pattern of work was the self-exemplifying model of appropriate scholarship. Sarton was also well aware of the real, if less immediate, need for professional as well as cognitive identity, without which his field of learning could never be secure let alone accepted as crucial to man's intellectual quest. Appropriate exhortations poured from his pen. The need for career positions and institutes for the history of science were matters to which he often returned. Once again, Sarton provided the self-exemplifying models. He was to "invent" for himself both a research institute and a full-time career, when the discipline barely possessed a cognitive, let alone a professional identity.

While he would on occasion write in an avowedly pragmatic and relativist vein, it was the heritage from positivism, progressivism, and utopian so-

cialism that more often controlled Sarton's argument and guided his actions. He would repeatedly present a "theorem on the history of science," which ran as follows:

> *Definition.* Science is systematized positive knowledge, or what has been taken as such at different ages and in different places. *Theorem.* The acquisition and systematization of positive knowledge are the only human activities which are truly cumulative and progressive. *Corollary.* The history of science is the only history which can illustrate the progress of mankind.

The scholar who until his last years largely devoted himself to critical bibliography could also say that "The quest for truth and beauty is indeed man's glory. This is certainly the highest moral certainty which history allows. . . . History itself is of no concern to us. . . . To build up [the] future, to make it beautiful [is rather the aim]." Whatever the contradictions and gaps between words and deeds, the fundamental belief was the one expressed in some words from the first volume of his monumental *Introduction* to the discipline. "The history of science is the history of mankind's unity, of its sublime purpose, of its gradual redemption."

In these statements we may perceive some reasons behind a paradox in Sarton's career. From one perspective his major achievement was that of the discipline builder: providing a key journal; establishing an identity for a field; encouraging the formation of a discipline-based learned society with its potential for sanction and reward (the History of Science Society, 1924); locating and mobilizing scarce resources of men and money in pursuit of crucial scholarly objectives; and seeking to furnish reference works, general surveys, advanced monographs, and teaching manuals. To create the necessary infrastructure for a coherent discipline was a task that demanded a lifetime of devotion.

To Sarton himself such work was only preliminary and minor compared with achieving the "new humanism," the holistic and all-embracing synthesis which would be based on a just appreciation of science in history. The yearning for this synthesis made his contributions to his new subject less than complete. Partly because his vision was so catholic, he could not communicate to others that sense of either the problematics or the conceptual and analytic *schema* necessary if his chosen field were to become a coherent, fully articulated discipline. The paradox is acute. Ambitious for the total vision, it is rather for bibliography, documentation, and the establishment of historical standards and facts that Sarton is most readily remembered.

In the early days of *Isis* all these matters, of course, lay in an unknown and surely unforeseen future. But the events that would crack, erode, and finally destroy the progressive, bourgeois confidence of which Sarton was such a supreme exemplar were already under way. The German invasion of Belgium in August 1914 immediately and dramatically rendered Sarton's private world precarious. Abandoning Wondelgem, his library, and his notes (which he buried in the garden), he fled to London with his family. For the next four years he lived a life of great uncertainty and occasional despair as he sought to find a context in which to pursue his ideals, and his as yet uninvented discipline. Prospects of an English position proved deceptive. Early in 1915 Sarton sailed to the United States, temporarily leaving his family behind. His hopes lay with the greater range and diversity of American institutions, with the progressive spirit, and with Robert S. Woodward.

Woodward was the second president and successful organizer of the Carnegie Institution of Washington. He was also a man with a personal interest in the history of science, and Sarton was in touch with him even before the forced retreat from Belgium. Woodward was initially unsympathetic but slowly softened. The universities in the United States provided sustenance both more immediate and more limited. When Sarton landed, the history of science was actually well established as an activity, although far from being an intellectual discipline and almost unthought of as a profession. A 1915 review article in *Science* makes this plain. It details no fewer than 162 courses in the history of particular sciences as well as fourteen general courses in the history of science, spread among 113 institutions.

Through the help of friends and acquaintances, Sarton managed to arrange a frenetic but sustaining round of guest lectures, seminars, and temporary appointments in American universities. One of those most involved in the promotion of the history of science as a new area of pedagogy was L. J. Henderson, a polymathic biological chemist and junior but influential member of the Harvard faculty. Since 1911 Henderson had himself been teaching at Harvard a regular course on the history of science. He was no doubt early aware of Sarton's program, of which he was to become such a willing supporter. As a member of the inner circle, he was in a position to advance the institutionalization of the field at Harvard and in the process to have a profound effect on Sarton's life. By 3 May 1916 Henderson was able to write his new friend with the glad news that "from several different sources we have been able to put together $2,000 for your first year [at Harvard]. The second year is not fully arranged, but I have not much doubt that we shall be successful." On the strength of this encouraging letter, Sarton understandably wrote Woodward the optimistic interpretation that "I have been appointed lecturer on the history of science at Harvard University for two years. A new chair has been endowed for the purpose." As it turned out, Sarton was first featured as "lecturer in philosophy," with the bulk of his teaching being listed under the auspices of the department of philosophy. Partly because of the financial problems Harvard faced as a result of the entry of the United States into World War I (but perhaps also partly because his courses did not draw many students), his two-year appointment was not extended.

At this juncture, Woodward's informed aid was to prove decisive. In response to Sarton's renewed appeals and with the help of Andrew Dickson White, historian of the warfare between science and theology and a trustee of the Carnegie Institution, an appointment was created as research associate in the history of science, initially for two years from 1 July 1918.

Thus began an association with the Carnegie Institution that endured throughout Sarton's professional life. Although employed on a full-time basis from Washington, he remained in Cambridge, pleading the uncertainty of war and the great value of a study in the then-new Widener Library. When the end of his Harvard appointment raised the prospect of eviction from Widener, Woodward's solicited intervention proved crucial in allowing him to remain unmolested. The unexpected end of the war allowed Sarton to plan an expedition to Wondelgem to recover his library and notes in the summer of 1919. Following this journey he was supposed to settle in Washington. Instead he quickly returned to Cambridge. There, through the good offices of Henderson, he once more secured a room in Widener Library on the basis of an annual unpaid appointment at Harvard as lecturer in the history of science.

Secure in one of the world's great libraries, with his salary guaranteed by Carnegie, and with no specific duties other than those he fashioned for himself, Sarton was at last free to develop his own mission and his own life-style. It was against this background that the idea of an *Introduction to the History of Science* gradually matured. Aside from *Isis*, Sarton's immediate plans were often vague and shifting during the precarious years between 1912 and 1920. In 1915 he expressed the intention to sail for China and Japan. By 1918, when he had been at Harvard twenty months, his interests had somewhat changed. In reply to Woodward's request for specific information on the work he was undertaking, Sarton mentioned a study of Leonardo da Vinci's scientific manuscripts, which would take "about six months" to finish, and a book on *The Teaching of the History of Science*, which would take a further six months. A little later he was confiding to Woodward that throughout his life he planned "to carry on simultaneously research on ancient science and on XIXth century science." This same letter referred specifically to "my book on XIXth century physics."

In further exchanges Sarton set out one of those ambitious overarching programs that continually recurred in his thinking. The plan was "to lay the foundation of an empirical philosophy of science, to evidence the unity of science." The means included *Isis*; an annual series of studies in the history and method of science to be jointly edited with Charles Singer of Oxford; a "General History of Science and Civilization, to be written on an extensive scale by a large group of scholars"; a history of physics in the nineteenth century; a complete account of the [ancient] beginnings of science; facsimile copies of scientific books and manuscripts; a Chinese encyclopedia; an exhibition of the progress of science; and a catalogue of scientific instruments down to 1900. In all this, the cooperation of Charles Singer was described as essential; and if he could be brought to Washington (where Sarton still intended to go), the city would become an international center for the history of science.

The work on Leonardo gradually made Sarton aware of his own historical naiveté and lack of training. In common with all founders of disciplines, he was perforce an autodidact. His very anxiety to escape from dilettantism and to establish critical standards also protracted his work. Another reason for slow progress was Sarton's incurable tendency to project and begin several studies at once. His first annual report to the Carnegie Institution refers to the Leonardo studies, the accumulation of materials for a history of physics in the nineteenth century, "activity in behalf of the new humanism," and plans for a retrospective survey on the occasion of the twenty-fifth anniversary of the Carnegie Institution. Characteristically, this last would "consider the Institution not as an isolated unit, but as part of the scientific organization of the world."

As if these activities were not enough, early the next year Sarton was planning a general history of science. The work was to be edited jointly with Singer, written by the scholars best qualified, and published in ten or twelve volumes over the next decade by the Oxford University Press. As late as 1934 Sarton was still projecting what had by then become *The Harvard History of Science* in eight illustrated volumes "comparable to the Cambridge Medieval History and other Cambridge and Oxford standard collections." All this was in addition to his published plans for a research institute in the history of science, an incessant round of travel and public lecturing, the detailed personal editing and directing of *Isis,* and, throughout, work on the *Introduction* itself. This vast labyrinth of labor left no time for a private social life (although an hour of classical music remained a daily anodyne). And only by heroic effort could Sarton keep track of his many commitments and produce that controlled order he loved and which his critical bibliographies exemplify.

Sarton's tendency to project programs in the history of science had ramified intellectual roots. Never having been trained for historical work, he long underestimated its difficulty and slow-moving character, until hard-won experience taught him otherwise. Then again he was burdened with a sense of how many different things wanted doing, and all quickly, if the history of science were to become an academically reputable subject. Journals, teaching manuals, standard histories, source books, and, above all, critical bibliographies of what already existed and was being produced— each was desperately needed and would, if necessary, be produced by Sarton himself. In thinking so, he was of course displaying his emerging orientation as a visionary, almost solipsistic scholar rather than as administrative entrepreneur. But beyond such reasons, Sarton embraced global projects because he passionately believed in the unity of knowledge, in the integrity of experience, and in the need for a holistic philosophy that embraced art and science. "The moral failure which the [First World] War implied" made this philosophy all the more urgent. Only what he came to call "the new humanism" could afford the necessary "mixing of the historical with the scientific spirit, of life with knowledge, or beauty with truth." Specialization everywhere threatened such broader insight and reinforced Sarton's belief in "the necessity of synthetic or encyclopedic studies, to keep alive the pure spirit of science." In holding these views he manifested one French-language response to Cassirer and other neo-Kantian cultural generalists, just as Sarton's own idols had earlier reacted to the then-ruling German Kantians and Hegelians.

It was out of this complex background that Sarton's most ambitious and significant work gradually took shape. The essential impulse came in 1919, when he returned to Belgium and retrieved his private notes. With these notes at last safely ensconced in Widener Library, his second annual report to the Carnegie Institution was able to reintroduce what he described as "an old design." It was "the writing of an introduction to the history and philosophy of science, a sort of compendium of the sources of information to which the student . . . may have to refer." By January 1921 the project had grown greatly in scope. The work was now to be in two parts, dealing with the history and philosophy of science as a whole and the history and philosophy of special sciences and their branches. The fundamental aim remained that of establishing the history of science as an independent discipline, with its own tools and methods. The project continued to grow and develop in Sarton's mind. By 1927, with the appearance of the first volume of what was by then to be a multivolume *Introduction to the History of Science,* Sarton envisaged the project as containing "A purely chronological survey . . . which will require seven or eight more volumes," "Surveys of different types of civilization, e.g. Jewish, Muslim, Chinese . . . [in] seven or eight volumes," and a "Survey of the evolution of special sciences . . . [in] some eight or nine volumes."

Sarton was forty-three years of age, with ample time, he felt, to finish the first series down through the eighteenth century, write parts of the Semitic and Far Eastern volumes for the second, and write the whole of the physical sciences volume for the third series. In actuality, work on the *Introduction* progressed far more slowly than his optimism allowed. It was to be 1948 before the third (and final) volume of this magisterial work appeared. Even then its contents reached only as far as A.D. 1400.

The public events of the 1930's and 1940's, together with the growing realization of the immensity of the task he had undertaken, served to erode the beliefs that lay behind Sarton's *Introduction.* As he wrote many times, "the day of Munich was

the nadir of my life." Another blow from quite a different direction was the decision of the Carnegie Institution in 1941 "not to continue the work on the history of science after I am gone." The failure of Harvard to support his plans for an institute was equally hard to accept. J. B. Conant did, however, show his sympathy for the man, if not his ambitious plans, in 1940. In his capacity as Harvard president he arranged Sarton's transfer from lecturer on annual appointment to professor with tenure. Even after this new arrangement, Sarton still drew the major part of his salary from the Carnegie Institution. Yet he was moved to write Conant that "I hope that the day may come when I would serve only Harvard, which appreciates the humanities, including the humanities of science, and not the Carnegie Institution, which considers them 'irrelevant.' " But Conant preferred to have Carnegie continue to pay.

After all, Sarton was, in the special calculus of Harvard, a marginal although illustrious man. In 1940 he had still to produce his first successful Ph.D. candidate, his undergraduate courses remained small, and he almost completely avoided all committee service and routine academic administration. The difference in attitude of the research scholar and the budget-conscious university president was highlighted in Conant's politely negative response to one of Sarton's articles on an institute for the history of science: "I can sum up my point of view by saying that I feel Macaulay was necessary in the development of scholarly and reputable political history, although I understand that now he is not considered as being at all scholarly and hardly reputable. I feel the history of science badly needs a Macaulay, indeed several of them."

Sarton was manifestly no Macaulay, and his enduring monument lies not in narrative accounts that have shaped the thinking of a generation, nor in lectures and students. It lies rather in the creation of tools, standards, and critical self-awareness in a discipline. The *Introduction* was foremost among these tools. In form somewhat like an "inspired dictionary" (as Singer was to label it), the *Introduction* deals with the emergence and growth of positive knowledge by means of contemporaneous surveys across all disciplines, races, and cultures, and by systematic division into half-century time units. Critical bibliography was another essential basis of the work. Hence the deliberate cross-linking of information in the *Introduction* with that contained in *Isis* (and its later occasional fellow-journal *Osiris*). As Sarton himself expressed it in retrospective summary:

The materials contained in the *Introduction, Isis* and *Osiris* are integrated by means of thousands of cross references. Thus we may say that volume 1 [of the *Introduction*] was built on a foundation of 8 volumes; volume 2, on a foundation of 15; volume 3 on a foundation of 42. . . . the *Introduction* is the most elaborate work of its kind, and by far, in world literature. This statement can be made without falling under the suspicion of boasting, for it is objective, controllable, and obviously correct.

Besides such heroic achievement, Sarton's many other publications appear almost lighthearted. In his later years, especially, he occupied named lectureships at a number of American universities. From them came such studies as *The History of Science and the New Humanism* (New York, 1931) and *Appreciation of Ancient and Medieval Science During the Renaissance* (Philadelphia, 1955). The same desire to make his message known and his discipline accessible lay behind a bibliographic venture like *Horus: A Guide to the History of Science* (Waltham, Massachusetts, 1952). His last years were largely devoted to work on the projected eight-volume *History of Science,* from antiquity to the present, which was to emerge from his lectures at Harvard from 1916 to 1951. He lived to complete two volumes: *Ancient Science Through the Golden Age of Greece* (Cambridge, Massachusetts, 1952) and the posthumously published *Hellenistic Science and Culture in the Last Three Centuries B.C.* (Cambridge, Massachusetts, 1959).

In what amounted to his last testament, Sarton continued to express his faith that "the only road to intellectual progress was scientific research." Yet paradoxically, as various historians of science in antiquity observed in their reviews, these readable volumes, rich in factual detail and lacking in the synthesis of ideas, were primarily devoted to cultural history rather than narrowly scientific development.

George Sarton came to epitomize the history of science to both European and American audiences. In the years immediately after World War II, when the first small cluster of teaching positions in the discipline were appearing in the United States, he automatically served as the central reference point—the continuing propagandist for, and the ideal type of, the historian of science as researcher, scholar, and teacher. The international and the intensely personal aspects of his achievement also won increasing recognition. He was honored with a rich variety of awards, including the Charles Homer Haskins Medal of the Mediae-

val Academy of America (1949) and the George Sarton Medal of the History of Science Society (1955). In 1934 he was elected to the American Philosophical Society.

Sarton's immediate influence in the postwar years was that of the catalyst rather than that of the reactant. He had only a limited intellectual impact on the discipline he did so much to create. His holistic concerns, his ambition for full comprehension, and his emphasis on the moral virtues of historical inquiry all ran counter to the preference for depth, particularity of pertinent detail, and detached analysis that have increasingly characterized historical scholarship (not just the history of science) over the last half-century. The positivistic cast of his thought ("I have tried to name the people who were first to do this or that; to take the first step in the right direction. . . .") and his belief in the uniqueness of science were antithetical to the idealistic, intuitionistic, and relativistic currents so powerful in recent Western thought. Finally, his emphasis on historical approaches through biography and bibliography, necessary and useful as they are, could not capture the imagination of scholars or provide a powerful technique of analysis around which a research school could form.

Instead Sarton opened the way for Koyré to have a major impact on the first generation of American "professional" historians of science, when shifts in the larger society created a demand for university teachers of this new discipline in the later 1950's and early 1960's. Equipped with a growing range of reference aids and a profound sense of the importance of their task, they could not find in Sarton's work coherent general ideas or theoretically derived, finite problems and techniques of investigation.

Sarton's influence on the discipline he labored so faithfully to create has thus been further obscured. His monument is also of its nature becoming progressively less visible to newcomers to the field. In founding a journal, in emphasizing critical bibliography, in essaying broad surveys, and above all in writing the *Introduction,* he was creating elements required by the discipline, not methods to be emulated or finished products for display. Yet as all those who turn to his work are aware, he also possessed, preached, and put into practice a range of insights that reveal a mind of remarkable range, catholicity, and tenacity. And of course his presence at Harvard was crucial to the later creation and legitimation of a department that is now one of the world's major centers of the history of science.

The limits of Sarton's influence on the history of

science reveal by default how the cognitive identity of a discipline is a matter of theoretical orientation and worldview as well as tools and techniques. His inability to engineer the careers and train the disciples who would create a professional identity for his subject also demonstrates how much this latter aspect of discipline-building depends on factors beyond the control of any individual. The history of science is now a firmly institutionalized field of learning. At first glance it shows little trace of Sarton's influence. Yet he not only created and assembled the necessary building materials through heroic feats of labor, but he also saw himself as—and he was—the first deliberate architect of the history of science as an independent and organized discipline.

BIBLIOGRAPHY

Sarton wrote 15 books and over 300 articles and notes, besides editing *Isis* for almost 40 years and personally producing 79 critical bibliographies of the history of science (containing perhaps 100,000 of his brief analyses). For a complete bibliography of his publications, with a number of illuminating essays by colleagues, pupils, and friends, see the memorial issue of *Isis,* **49** (1957). There are many other obituary notices in scholarly journals.

More immediately helpful as a source for the study of Sarton's achievements is his daughter's delightful "Sketches for an Autobiography," in May Sarton, *I Knew a Phoenix* (New York, 1969). She has also written "An Informal Portrait of George Sarton," in *Texas Quarterly,* **5** (1962), 101–112. For a sampling of Sarton's varied writings, see Dorothy Stimson, ed., *Sarton on the History of Science* (Cambridge, Mass., 1962). The most recent study of his work is Arnold Thackray and Robert K. Merton, "On Discipline-Building: the Paradoxes of George Sarton," in *Isis,* **63** (1972), 673–695. Sarton's university education is treated by J. Gillis, "Paul Mansion en George Sarton," in *Mededelingen van der Koninklijke Academie . . . van België, Klasse der Wetenschappen,* **35** (1973), 3–21.

Some of Sarton's correspondence now preserved in Belgium is in Paul Van Oye, *George Sarton, de Mens en zijn Werk uit Brieven aan Vrienden en Kennissen* (Brussels, 1965). Most of the letters are in French or English and date from his youth. The commentary is in Flemish. Further letters of this period (in French) are in Suzanne Delorme, "La naissance d'*Isis*," in *Actes du XIe Congrès international d'histoire des sciences,* **2** (Warsaw, 1967), 223–232. Lynn Thorndike's contribution to the memorial issue of *Isis* also includes some of his and Sarton's correspondence over the years.

Much Sarton correspondence undoubtedly exists in other private archives. Several collections of his letters are publicly available. Somewhere between 20,000 and 30,000 letters from 2,108 and to 788 correspondents are preserved and indexed in the Houghton Library of Harvard University. Small but important collections are at California Institute of Technology (George Ellery Hale papers) and Columbia University (David Eugene Smith papers). An unknown number of letters (perhaps 500 to 1,000) to and from the president of the Carnegie Institution of Washington are also available in an uncatalogued state in the Institution library. Sarton's work for and in relation to the Carnegie Institution over the years may be followed in his reports, published annually in the Institution *Yearbook* from 1919 to 1949.

ARNOLD THACKRAY
ROBERT K. MERTON

SARYCHEV, GAVRIIL ANDREEVICH (*b.* St. Petersburg, Russia, 1763; *d.* St. Petersburg, 11 August 1831), *hydrography.*

In 1775 Sarychev entered the Naval Cadet Corps in Kronstadt, and was commissioned in 1781. From 1785 to 1793 he and Joseph Billings participated in an extensive surveying expedition to northeastern Siberia, the Aleutian Islands, and the shores of North America, the most important research on the northern Pacific and its shores by Russian scientists since the Bering-Chirikov expedition. The results of the expedition were described in *Puteshestvie flota kapitana Sarycheva . . .* ("The Journey of the Fleet of Captain Sarychev . . .," 1802) and in Billings' account of his trip along the Chukchi Peninsula (1811).

Beginning in 1802 Sarychev spent many years on surveying expeditions to the Baltic Sea. An atlas (1812) and *Lotsia . . .* ("Sailing Directions," 1817) for this sea were published under his direction. His handbook on surveying shores and on compiling marine charts (1804) played an important role in the development of methods of marine surveying from sail- and oar-powered vessels. Sarychev's methods of describing ocean shores, compiling charts, and writing up the results of expeditions served as models for many researchers. In 1808, as hydrographer-general, he directed the hydrographical service in Russia; and in 1829 he became an admiral.

Sarychev initiated and led many hydrographic expeditions during the first third of the nineteenth century and was teacher and guide of a large group of Russian seafaring scientists (F. P. Litke, M. F. Reyneke, A. E. Kolodkin, E. P. Manganeri, P. F. Anjou, F. P. Wrangel). No expedition was sent without his knowledge and supervision, either to inland seas or to the Far East and America. His great achievement was *Atlas severnoy chasti Vostochnogo okeana* ("Atlas of the Northern Part of the Eastern Ocean," 1826), compiled under his direction. Sarychev was elected an honorary member of the Academy of Sciences and of many university and scientific societies.

BIBLIOGRAPHY

I. ORIGINAL WORKS: Sarychev's writings include *Puteshestvie flota kapitana Sarycheva po severo-vostochnoy chasti Sibiri, Ledovitomu moryu i Vostochnomu okeanu . . .* ("The Journey of the Fleet of Captain Sarychev Through the Northeastern part of Siberia, the Arctic Sea and the Eastern Ocean . . ."), 2 vols. (St. Petersburg, 1802; 2nd ed., Moscow, 1952), with atlas and drawings; *Pravila, prinadlezhashchie k Morskoy Geodezii . . .* ("Rules Appropriate for Ocean Geodesy . . ."; St. Petersburg, 1804; 2nd ed., 1825); *Dnevnye zapiski plavania . . . Gavrily Sarycheva po Baltyskomu moryu i Finskomu zalivu v 1802, 1803, 1804 godakh. . . .* ("Daily Notes on the Voyage of . . . Sarychev on the Baltic Sea and the Gulf of Finland in 1802, 1803, and 1804. . . ."; St. Petersburg, 1808); *Puteshestvie kapitana Billingsa cherez Chukotskuyu zemlyu ot Beringova proliva do Nizhnekolymskogo ostroga . . .* ("Voyage of Captain Billings Across the Chukchi Peninsula From the Bering Strait to the Lower Kolyma Fortress . . ."; St. Petersburg, 1811); *Morskoy atlas vsego Baltyskogo morya s Finskim zalivom i Kattegotom . . .* ("Marine Atlas of the Entire Baltic Sea With the Gulf of Finland and Kattegat . . ."; St. Petersburg, 1812); *Lotsia ili Puteukazanie k bezopasnomu korablevozhdeniyu po Finskomu zalivu, Baltyskomu moryu i Kattegat* ("Sailing Directions or Voyage Instructions for Safely Piloting Ships in the Gulf of Finland, the Baltic Sea and Kattegat"; St. Petersburg, 1817); and *Atlas severnoy chasti Vostochnogo okeana . . .* ("Atlas of the Northern Part of the Eastern Ocean . . ."; St. Petersburg, 1826).

II. SECONDARY LITERATURE. See the following, listed chronologically: A. P. Sokolov, *Russkaya morskaya biblioteka. 1701–1851* ("Russian Marine Library. 1701–1851"), 2nd ed. (1883), which contains a biography of Sarychev and annotations to his work; N. N. Zubov, *Otechestvennye moreplavateli-issledovateli morey i okeanov* ("Native Sailors and Investigators of the Seas and Oceans"; Moscow, 1954), 123–131; M. I. Belov, *Arkticheskoe moreplavanie s drevneyshikh vremen do serediny XIX veka* ("Arctic Sea Voyages From Ancient Times to the Middle of the Nineteenth Century"; Moscow, 1956); E. E. Shvede; "G. A. Sarychev," in *Otechestvennye fiziko-geografy i puteshestvenniki* ("Native Physical Geographers and Travelers"; Moscow, 1959), 116–125; V. A. Esakov, A. F. Plakhotnik, and A. I. Alekseev, *Russkie okeanicheskie i morskie issledovania v XIX–nachale XX v* ("Russian Oceanic and Marine Research in the Nineteenth and Beginning of the Twentieth Centuries"; Moscow, 1964); and A. I. Alekseev, *Gavriil Andreevich Sarychev* (Moscow, 1966).

VASILIY A. ESAKOV

ŚATĀNANDA (*fl.* India, 1099), *astronomy.*

The only certain biographical data concerning Śatānanda are that he was the son of Śaṅkara and Sarasvatī and that he wrote the *Bhāsvatī* in 1099 on the basis of Varāhamihira's (*fl. ca.* 505) summary in the *Pañcasiddhāntikā* (I, 14; IX; X; XI [?]; and XVI) of Lāṭadeva's (*fl.* 505) recension of the *Sūryasiddhānta* according to the Ārdharātrikapakṣa (see essay in Supplement) of Āryabhaṭa I (*b.* 473). The last verse of the *Bhāsvatī*, it is true, refers to the divine utterance of Puruṣottama, and some have mistakenly concluded therefrom that Śatānanda lived at Puruṣottama or Puri, in Orissa; but the only Indian locality referred to by Śatānanda is Ujjayinī. In any case, the *Bhāsvatī*, containing only eighty-one verses, was instrumental in spreading this version of the *Sūryasiddhānta* throughout northern and, especially, eastern India, as can be seen from the existence of numerous manuscripts (nearly a hundred), commentaries, and editions. The commentators include the following:

1. Aniruddha (*b.* 1463), who wrote a *ṭīkā* in Benares in 1495 (see D. Pingree, *Census of the Exact Sciences in Sanskrit*, ser. A, I [Philadelphia, 1970], 43b).

2. Acyuta (*fl.* 1505–1534), who wrote a *Bhāsvatīratnadīpikā* in Bengal (see D. Pingree, *op. cit.*, I, 36a–36b).

3. Gaṇapati Bhaṭṭa (*fl.* 1512), who wrote a *vivṛti* in Bengal (see D. Pingree, *op. cit.*, vol. II [Philadelphia, 1971], 89a).

4. Mādhava Miśra (*fl.* 1525), who wrote a *vivaraṇa* at Kanauj.

5. Balabhadra (*b.* 1495), who wrote a *Bālabodhinī* in 1543 in Bengal.

6. Kuvera Miśra (*fl.* 1685), who wrote a *ṭīkā*, probably in Bengal (see D. Pingree, *op. cit.*, II, 47b).

7. Gaṅgādhara (*fl.* 1685), who wrote a *ṭīkā*, probably in Rājasthān (see D. Pingree, *op. cit.*, II, 85a).

8. Rāmakṛṣṇa (*fl.* 1738), who wrote a *Tattvaprakāśikā.*

9. Kamalanayana (*fl.* 1740?), who wrote an *udāharaṇa* in Mithilā (see D. Pingree, *op. cit.*, II, 20a).

10. Yogīndra (*fl.* 1742), who wrote an *udāharaṇa*, probably in Mithilā.

Those commentators who cannot be dated include Cakravartin *(Bhāsvatīpaddhati)*; Cakravipradāsa *(ṭīkā)*; Dharmāditya *(Bhāsvatītilaka)*; Gopāla *(vivaraṇa;* see D. Pingree, *op. cit.,* II, 130b); Gopīnātha Sudhī *(Bhāsvatīprakāśikā;* see D. Pingree, *op. cit.,* II, 132b); Govinda Miśra *(ṭīkā;* see D. Pingree, *op. cit.,* II, 137a); Keśava (?) *(udāharaṇa;* see D. Pingree, *op. cit.,* II, 64a); Madhusūdana *(Subodhinī)*; Rāmeśvara *(ṭīkā)*; Vanamālin (Hindī *ṭīkā)*; Viśveśvaranātha *(vyākhyā)*; and Vṛndāvana *(udāharaṇa).*

BIBLIOGRAPHY

The *Bhāsvatī* has been published several times: at the Akhavāra Press (Benares, 1854); with *vivaraṇa* of Mādhava Miśra in *Aruṇodaya,* I (1890–1891); with his own Sanskrit *ṭīkā, Chātrabodhinī,* and his own Hindī explanation by Mātṛprasāda Pāṇḍeya (Benares, 1917); and with his own *ṭīkā, Manoramā,* and several appendices by Ṭīkārāma Dhanañjaya (Vārāṇasī, N.D.).

There are short biographical notices on Śatānanda in S. Dvivedin, *Gaṇakataraṅgiṇī* (Benares, 1933), 33–34, repr. from *The Pandit,* n.s. **14** (1892); and in Ś. B. Dīkṣita, *Bhāratīya Jyotiḥśāstra* (Poona, 1896, repr. Poona, 1931), 243–245.

DAVID PINGREE

SATŌ NOBUHIRO (*b.* Ugo [now Akita] prefecture, Japan, 1769; *d.* Edo [now Tokyo], Japan, 6 January 1850); **SATŌ NOBUKAGE** (*b.* Nishimonai, 1674; *d.* Nishimonai, 1732); **SATŌ NOBUSUE** (*b.* 1724; *d.* 1784), *mining, agriculture, economics.*

The Satō family served the feudal lords of Ugo (now Akita) prefecture as physicians. Of the five generations so employed, there is little information about the first two, Satō I, Nobukuni (whose pen name was Kan'an) and Satō II, Nobutaka (Gen'an), save that they were father and son. Of Satō Nobutaka's son Satō Nobukage (Fumaiken) it is known that while originally a physician, he studied agricultural administration, natural history, and natural science in order to find a means of helping farmers who had experienced crop failures. He spent the years 1688 to 1703 on the island of Yesso (now Hokkaido) and drew upon his experiences there to compose the twelve-volume *New Theory of Developing the Country.* He also wrote a five-volume work entitled *Features of the Soil,* and a shorter, two-volume book called *Secrets of the Mountain Phase* and managed the Matsuoka mine in Ugo with notable success.

Satō IV, Nobusue (Genmeika), was, like his father Satō Nobukage, a physician. He also studied agricultural management and economics and wrote a work entitled *How to Preserve Fishermen's Villages* and another, in four volumes, called *Illustration of the Secret of the Mountain Phase.* His son, Satō V, was Satō Nobuhiro (Yūsai), who in 1782 accompanied him to Yesso, where he remained for a year. Satō Nobuhiro was present when his father died at the Ashio mine; he obeyed his last wish, and went to Edo to study science under Genzui Udagawa and Gentaku Ōtsuki. He there learned astronomy, mensuration, geography, and surveying. In 1787 he traveled to Kyushu and through western Honshu. In 1808 he studied literature with Atsutane Hirata and about 1839 he became closely associated with the leading members of Bansha, the Association of Foreign Learning. These included Watanabe Kazan, a painter and minister of the Tawara clan, and the physician Takano Chōei; Satō Nobuhiro was imprisoned with them in the same year, when Bansha was suppressed through the efforts of conservative scholars, but he was soon released. During the Tempo reformation (1841–1843) he acted as adviser to prime minister Mizuno Tadakuni.

The accomplishments of the elder Satōs can be understood only in the context of the secrecy in which science and technology were held in feudal Japan. Knowledge was jealously guarded and, for the most part, passed on orally from father to son. Even when a formal school existed (and it may be assumed that the works of the earlier Satōs were composed for such a school), its members were sworn to hold what they had learned in confidence. Even Satō Nobuhiro notes this tradition in his book *Laws of the Mine,* reminding his patron that "Although the laws of the mine are essentially the most precious secret of our family, I will transmit them to you, not revealing that fact even to the staff of my school, since I was impressed by your enthusiasm and patriotism. In consequence, you must not show this work even to your parents or your brother."

The knowledge accumulated by the Satō family and published by Satō Nobuhiro was concerned with politics, agricultural administration, economics, natural history, natural science, mining techniques, metallurgy, the exploration of ore deposits, mine management, geography, education, law, and military science. Satō Nobukage and Satō Nobusue both wished to alleviate the lot of the farmers, which they had observed in their travels; Satō Nobuhiro, in addition, had in his youth experienced the severe famine of the Temmei era (in

1782) and later observed the great famine of the Tempo period (in 1836). Since all the Satōs served a feudal lord, their concern with agricultural subjects was doubly legitimate.

The deep interest of the Satō family in mining was in part the result of the changing economic conditions of Japan in the seventeenth and eighteenth centuries. As trade developed rapidly, a merchant class rose to power and the warrior aristocracy, the samurai class, correspondingly declined. As Japan gradually began to emerge from feudalism, it became necessary for the feudal lords to find an economic basis other than agriculture, and some of them began to develop a mining industry; by the beginning of the eighteenth century the Ugo district, the seat of the Satōs, produced more copper than any other part of Japan. The interest of the Satōs in mining was therefore predictable.

Indeed, Satō Nobuhiro's best-known work concerns mining. Part of his *Secret of the Mountain Phase* is devoted to describing a method for predicting the presence of ores. The method given was, however, an unscientific one, based on the shape of the mountain that might contain the ores, together with the characteristics of the "spirit," or moisture, that evaporates from the ore body. A large part of the rest of the book describes methods for refining gold, silver, copper, lead, tin, iron, mercury, and sulfur ores, and discusses the management of mines, with particular emphasis on the well-being of miners. Satō Nobuhiro set out a system for the division of the operations of a mine into departments, and considered the role of each department, as well as its physical location at the site of a mine. His discussion includes the daily supply of food and other necessary goods, as well as the need for a recreation area for the miners and the part to be played by religion in their lives.

Satō Nobuhiro also presented a system for the management of the whole civil state in his *Elements of Economics* and *Government and Reactionism*. He designed an authoritarian, ideal state in which the class distinctions between the samurai, farmers, manufacturers, merchants, and peasants would be abolished and all Japan would be united under a single ruler. All land and all the means for production would be owned by the state, and the state would administer all commerce and foreign trade. Satō Nobuhiro's plan also included a system of free education, up to and including the university level.

In drawing up his scheme of government, Satō Nobuhiro was influenced by western political science and science, taking from them in particular the notion of the equality of men. He was a popularizer of western thought (as a young man he had attempted to learn Dutch, since the Dutch were the only westerners permitted in Japan at that time) and wrote the first Japanese works on western science and history. He spent much of his later life composing such studies and died in retirement.

H. KOBAYASHI

SAURIN, JOSEPH (*b*. Courthézon, Vaucluse, France, 1 September 1659; *d*. Paris, France, 29 December 1737), *mathematics, mechanics, cosmology.*

The youngest son of Pierre Saurin, a Calvinist minister of Grenoble, Saurin was educated at home and in 1684 entered the ministry as curate of Eure. Outspoken in the pulpit, he soon had to take refuge in Switzerland, where he became pastor of Bercher, Yverdon. No less combative in exile, he refused at first to sign the *Consensus* of Geneva (1685). The pressure brought to bear on him as a result apparently weakened his Calvinist persuasion; after discussions with elders in Holland, he had an audience with Bishop Bossuet in France and shortly thereafter, on 21 September 1690, embraced Roman Catholicism. After an adventurous[1] return to Switzerland to fetch his wife, the daughter of a wealthy family named de Crouzas, Saurin settled in Paris for the rest of his life.

Forced to find a new career, Saurin turned to mathematics, which he studied and then taught. By 1702, as mathematics editor for the *Journal des sçavans*, he was again involved in dispute, most notably with Rolle, over the infinitesimal calculus. Failing to get a satisfactory response from Rolle, Saurin appealed to the Academy of Sciences, of which Rolle was a member. The Academy avoided a direct decision in favor of an outsider by naming Saurin an *élève géomètre* on 10 March 1707 and a full *pensionnaire géomètre* on 13 May 1707.

Even this rise to prominence could not keep Saurin out of trouble. Accused by the poet Jean-Baptiste Rousseau of having written libelous poems against him, Saurin spent six months in jail before an *arrêt* of Parlement (7 April 1712) exonerated him and sent Rousseau into exile. Thereafter, Saurin appears to have retired to his scientific research, working all night and sleeping all day.[2] His active career ended with his being named a *vétéran* of the Academy in 1731. He died of le-

117

thargic fever in 1737, leaving at least one son, Bernard-Joseph (1706–1781), who earned some fame as a dramatic poet.

Saurin made no original contributions to mathematics. Rather, firmly committed to the new infinitesimal calculus, he explored the limits and possibilities of its methods and defended it against criticism based on lack of understanding. Rolle, for example, assumed that the new method of tangents could not handle singularities of multivalued curves where dy/dx took the form 0/0. In reply (1702, 1703, 1716), Saurin explicated the nature and treatment of such indeterminate expressions on the basis of L'Hospital's theorem (*Analyse des infiniment petits* [1969], section 9, article 163), by which, for a $f(x) = g(x)/h(x)$ of the form 0/0 at $x = a$, one determines $f(a)$ by differentiating $g(x)$ and $h(x)$ simultaneously until one of them is nonzero at $x = a$. His further study of multivalued curves (1723, 1725) became the basis for correcting Guisnée's and Crousaz's misunderstanding of the nature of extreme values and of their expression in the new calculus.

Saurin's two papers (1709) on curves of quickest descent represent a solution of a problem first posed by Jakob I Bernoulli—to find which of the infinitely many cycloids linking a given point as origin to a given line is the curve of quickest descent from the point to the line—and then an extension of the problem to any family of similar curves. Saurin followed the differential methods of Johann I Bernoulli, although he studiously avoided taking a position in the brothers' famous quarrel.[3]

Combining his command of infinitesimal methods with a firm understanding of the new dynamics, Saurin offered (1722) a sensitive and subtle explanation of why the infinitesimal path of a simple pendulum must be approximated by the arc of a cycloid rather than by the chord subtending the arc of the circle. Thus he defended Huygens' theory of the pendulum against the attacks of Antoine Parent and the Chevalier de Liouville. Saurin had already provided (1703) rather neat algebraic demonstrations of Huygens' theorems on centrifugal force and the cycloidal path and had done an experimental and theoretical study (1720) of the damping and driving effects of the escapement and weight in a pendulum clock.

Huygens himself became the target of Saurin's rebuttals on the issue of Descartes's vortex theory of gravity. Saurin's first effort (1703)—to explain how a terrestrial vortex with lines of force parallel to the equatorial plane could cause bodies to fall toward the center of the earth—was patently clumsy. In 1709, however, to counter Huygens' objection that the necessarily greater speed of the vortex would sweep objects off the earth, Saurin proposed an attenuated ether that, on the basis of Mariotte's experimental findings on the force of moving fluids, made the ether all but nonresisting while still accounting for gravity by its greater speed of rotation. In Johann I Bernoulli's opinion, it was the best theory of gravity devised up to that time. Although, as Aiton points out,[4] it offered the chance for a reconciliation of Cartesian and Newtonian cosmology, Saurin himself felt that Newtonianism threatened a return to "the ancient shadows of Peripateticism" (*Mémoires de mathématique et physique* [1709], 148).

NOTES

1. The biographical note in Didot speaks of an outstanding charge of theft, while other notices recount the dangers of religious persecution only.
2. Fontenelle, "Éloge de M. Saurin," 120, makes this point and then adds that Saurin had few friends.
3. Saurin did, however, sarcastically reject Johann's claims of priority over L'Hospital in the matter of indeterminate expressions; cf. his 1716 paper and Joseph E. Hofmann, *Geschichte der Mathematik*, III (Berlin, 1957), 11.
4. *Vortex Theory of Planetary Motion*, 176. On Bernoulli's judgment, *ibid.*, 188.

BIBLIOGRAPHY

I. ORIGINAL WORKS. Saurin's works include "Démonstration des théorèmes que M. Hu(y)gens a proposés dans son Traité de la Pendule sur la force centrifuge des corps mûs circulairement," in *Mémoires pour servir à l'histoire des sciences et des beaux-arts (Mémoires de Trevoux)*, 1702 (Addition pour . . . Novembre et Decembre), 27–60; "Réponse à l'écrit de M. Rolle de l'Académie Royale des Sciences inséré dans le Journal du 13. Avril 1702, sous le titre de Règles et Remarques pour le Problème général des Tangentes par M. Saurin," in *Journal des sçavans* (Amsterdam ed.), **30** (3 Aug. 1702), 831–861; "Solution de la principale difficulté proposée par M. Hu(y)gens contre le système de M. Descartes, sur la cause de la pesanteur," *ibid.*, **31** (8 Jan. 1703), 36–47; "Remarques sur les courbes des deux premiers exemples proposés par M. Rolle dans le Journal du jeudi 13. Avril 1702," *ibid.* (15 Jan. 1703), 65–73, (22 Jan. 1703), 78–84; and "Manière aisée de démontrer l'égalité des temps dans les chutes d'un corps tombant par une cycloide de plus ou de moins haut, et de trouver le rapport du temps de la chute par la cycloide au temps de la chute perpendiculaire par son axe," *ibid.* (4 June 1703), 563–570.

In the *Mémoires de mathématique et physique* of the Paris Academy of Sciences, see "Solutions et analyses de quelques problèmes appartenants aux nouvelles méthodes" (1709), 26–33; "Examen d'une difficulté considérable proposée par M. Hu(y)ghens contre le système cartésien sur la cause de la pesanteur" (1709), 131–148; "Solution générale du problème, où parmi une infinité de courbes semblables décrites sur un plan verticale, et ayant un même axe et un même point d'origine, il s'agit de déterminer celle dont l'arc compris entre le point d'origine et une ligne donnée de position, est parcouru dans le plus court temps possible" (1709), 257–266, with addendum in 1710, pp. 208–214; "Remarques sur un cas singulier du problème général des tangentes" (1716), 59–79, 275–289; and "Problème" (1718), 89–92.

In the same journal, see "Démonstration d'une proposition avancée dans un des mémoires de 1709. Avec l'examen de quelques endroits de la *Recherche de la vérité*, qui se trouvent dans la dernière edition, et qui ont rapport à ce mémoire" (1718), 191–199; "Démonstration de l'impossibilité de la quadrature indéfinie du cercle. Avec une manière simple de trouver une suite de droites qui approchent de plus en plus d'un arc de cercle proposé, tant en dessus qu'en dessous" (1720), 15–19; "Remarques sur les horloges à pendule" (1720), 208–230; "Éclaircissement sur une difficulté proposé aux mathématiciens par M. le Chevalier de Liouville" (1722), 70–95; "Sur les figures inscrites et circonscrites au cercle" (1723), 10–11; "Dernières remarques sur un cas singulier du problème des tangentes" (1723), 222–250; "Observations sur la question des plus grandes et des plus petites quantités" (1725), 238–260; and "Recherches sur la rectification des baromètres" (1727), 282–296.

II. Secondary Literature. Bernard Fontenelle's "Éloge de M. Saurin," in *Histoire de l'Académie royale des sciences . . .* (1737), 110–120, is the basis for the account in Joseph Bertrand's *L'Académie des sciences et les académiciens de 1666 à 1793* (Paris, 1869), 242–247. The entry in the Didot *Nouvelle biographie générale* provides some additional details from Swiss sources. Saurin earns only passing mention in histories of mathematics, but his vortex theory of gravity receives considerable attention from Eric J. Aiton in *The Vortex Theory of Planetary Motions* (London–New York, 1972), 172–176 and *passim*.

Michael S. Mahoney

SAUSSURE, HORACE BÉNÉDICT DE (*b.* near Geneva [Conches], 17 February 1740; *d.* Geneva, 22 January 1799), *geology, meteorology, botany, education.*

Saussure's ancestors emigrated to Geneva from France and Italy to escape the religious persecutions of the sixteenth century. (The name "Saulxures" is still to be found in several villages in Lorraine.) The family contained a number of writers and scientists. Saussure may have inherited his early interest in botany from his father, the agricultural author Nicolas de Saussure; from his mother, an invalid, he inherited an ability to endure hardship, a philosophical turn of mind, and a delicate constitution. He was sent to the *Collège* of Geneva when he was six and entered the university there when he was fourteen. During his early years he also took long walking trips in the vicinity of Geneva and in the Salève, the Voirons, and the Jura, and was strongly influenced by two naturalists, his uncle Charles Bonnet and the physician and botanist Albrecht von Haller.

Saussure completed a degree in philosophy in 1759 with a dissertation on the transmission of heat from the rays of the sun. In 1760 he made the first of a number of trips to Chamonix, on this occasion for the specific purpose of collecting plant specimens for Haller. He wrote a lyrical description of the mountains and glaciers of the area and climbed the Brévent with Pierre Simon, who served as his guide on a number of subsequent occasions. In addition, Saussure placed a notice in each of the surrounding parishes, offering a handsome reward to the first person to climb Mont Blanc.

In 1761 Saussure was a candidate for the chair of mathematics at the Academy of Geneva, but he was not elected; he therefore turned for consolation to the classical authors and continued his botanical investigations. His treatise *Observations sur l'écorce des feuilles et des pétales,* published in 1762, was dedicated to Haller. He presented this, together with a philosophical thesis entitled "Principal Causes of Errors Arising from the Qualities of the Mind" and a work "On Rainbows, Haloes, and Parhelia," when the chair of philosophy at the Academy became vacant in the same year. Haller strongly supported his candidacy, and he was elected. He lectured in French on physics and natural history and in Latin on metaphysics in alternate years.

Saussure made another trip to Chamonix in March 1764, and at about this time he began to concentrate on geology, although he did not abandon botany completely. In the following year he married Albertine Amélie Boissier, who brought him a considerable fortune and a beautiful house in Geneva. His passion for mountains (he had decided both to climb Mont Blanc and to take an annual alpine tour) nevertheless remained unabated and was to become a source of anxiety to his family. In July 1767 he completed a tour of Mont Blanc, where he carried out experiments on heat and cold, on the weight of the atmosphere, and on electricity and magnetism. In these he employed what was probably the first electrometer, an instrument that he himself had developed. He returned to Geneva for the birth of his son, Nicolas-Théodore, in October.

Saussure held liberal views that set him apart from most of his fellow patricians and professors, and in 1768 presented as a private citizen a plan for reform that advocated both a more democratic constitution and popular education. It was not accepted, and he thereupon decided to escape recurrent political crises between the aristocracy and the people of Geneva by immediately going on a "grand tour" with his wife. He spent some time in Paris, where he met Buffon (their dislike was mutual) and held discussions with a number of French geologists, including a long dialogue on the basalts of the Auvergne with Desmarest and Guettard. He also took every opportunity to attend plays. Saussure was in England by mid-summer of the same year, and visited coal, tin, and lead mines, as well as quarries, from the Midlands to Cornwall. In London he met with members of the Royal Society and discussed electricity with Benjamin Franklin. He and his wife returned to Geneva in February 1769, and Saussure refused any participation in local politics, although strongly sympathetic to the popular parties.

In the summer of 1771 Saussure made an expedition to study the lakes and flora of northern Italy; on his return trip through the Great St. Bernard he felt the first symptoms of a serious gastric illness, and by the fall of the following year his health had so declined that he was advised to spend the winter in a warmer climate. He therefore returned to Italy, where he investigated the iron mines of Elba, then proceeded to Rome and to Naples, where Sir William Hamilton acted as his guide on a visit to Vesuvius and the Campi Phlegraei. Saussure then went on to Sicily and on 5 June 1773 climbed Mt. Etna. He found his health improved and was enthusiastic about the attractions that Italy offered to the naturalist, although he published only a few papers on it instead of the larger work that he considered.

Returning to Geneva, Saussure was appointed rector of the university, in which post he served for two years, from 1774 until 1776. He took advantage of this position to present a series of proposals for the reform of the Geneva Collège; sensitive to the popular unrest that was enveloping all Europe, Saussure felt that its effects might be dissipated by more adequate public education. His proposals led to a violent controversy, with political overtones, particularly since he had drawn on some of the ideas set out in Rousseau's Émile, a work recently condemned at Geneva. Since his proposed reforms were not to be put into effect, Saussure tried another approach, founding the Société des Arts, in which different social classes and professions were to meet to apply the arts and sciences to industry. In 1776 Saussure served as the society's first president.

At the same time, Saussure also began to make the extensive alpine investigations that he described in the four volumes of his Voyages dans les Alpes, précédés d'un essai sur l'histoire naturelle des environs de Genève, published between 1779 and 1796. Although he resigned his professorship in January 1786, citing ill health, the years from 1774 through 1789 marked the period of his most strenuous alpine activity. This period also coincides with an increasing involvement of Saussure in local politics. Until 1781, his proposals for political and educational reforms were personal endeavors; after that date his sense of civic duty led him to accept numerous public offices. They ranged from his election to several councils of the patrician governing system before the revolution to membership in numerous committees involved in successive changes of the form of government in Geneva and in foreign affairs immediately before, during, and after the revolution, until his voluntary withdrawal from public life in 1794 after the famous Massacre of the Bastions.

In the summer of 1787 Saussure climbed Mont Blanc, a feat that had been accomplished for the first time only in the preceding August, by Jacques Balmat and Michel Gabriel Paccard. On his own ascent, Saussure was accompanied by eighteen guides and carried a number of scientific instruments, many of them of his own design and construction, with which he undertook appropriate experiments during the four and one-half hours that he spent at the summit. The great elevation also allowed him to observe directly a number of geological features about which he had previously only been able to speculate. The success of his expedition caught the popular imagination (at one point it was even suggested that the mountain be renamed in his honor) and won Saussure an international reputation. He was elected a fellow of the Royal Society of London in April 1788, under the sponsorship of Hamilton, and in 1791 he became one of the eight foreign members of the French Academy of Sciences.

Since Saussure had had only limited time on top of Mont Blanc, he sought further opportunities to perform high-altitude experiments and observations. In July 1788, with his son, Nicolas-Théodore, he camped for fifteen days at a base 11,000 feet high on the Col du Géant. Despite precarious conditions, the two men completed a full series of observations of the daily variations of winds and other meteorological phenomena. Saussure was also able to observe geological and topographical details during the hours of dawn and sunset, the conditions under which structure is most apparent.

In July 1789, again in the company of his son, Saussure set out to measure the height of Monte Rosa and to investigate its geological structure. He made a series of observations that confirmed his neptunist ideas about the formation of granite and was greatly impressed by the sight of the Matterhorn, which he decided to measure next. While he was on this expedition, Saussure received news of the fall of the Bastille. His letters show that he maintained his liberal attitudes—indeed, he had taken part in drafting legislation designed to alleviate in Geneva the unrest similar to that which produced events in France—but he was unfortunately too optimistic about the fate of the French securities in which most of his money was invested.

Saussure continued his scientific work as the French Revolution began to make itself felt in Geneva. In August 1792, during a short period of political calm, he returned with his son to the Matterhorn to measure its altitude. This was the last trip that he recorded in his *Voyages*. He returned to Geneva to learn that he had lost most of his fortune and that his wife's income had been drastically reduced. As the revolution spread to Geneva in the fall, many patrician families fled the country; Saussure remained, however, and participated in several committees that were attempting to draw up a new revolutionary constitution. In 1793 he took the voluntary oath to Liberty, Equality, and Fraternity.

Saussure once again took the opportunity to present a project for national public education, but his health had again begun to fail. He had a series of seizures that left him partially paralyzed in March 1794, yet he continued under the necessity of finding a position that would increase his income. In particular, Saussure hoped to find a professorship at a French university, perhaps combined with an inspectorship of mines, but no such position was offered him. He also considered the universities of Göttingen, Berlin, and St. Petersburg, and even an exile in the United States, where Thomas Jefferson was looking for a faculty for the new university he was organizing at Charlottesville, Virginia

(Jefferson had suggested to Washington that some of the professors at the University of Geneva, especially Saussure, might be glad to find refuge and employment in America). Nonetheless, no offer was actually made to him, and Saussure remained in Geneva until his death in 1799. By 1796, when the third and fourth volumes of his *Voyages* were published, largely under the direction of his son, he had been entirely incapacitated by a second stroke.

Although the *Voyages* are a record of Saussure's expeditions between 1774 and 1787, he did not set out the descriptions of his travels in chronological order. Rather, he abstracted and grouped the results of his journeys into three sections, of which one concerned his work in the area of Mont Blanc, another his trips through the Mont Cenis pass to the Italian and French Rivieras and his return through Provence, and the last his numerous expeditions to the area of the Gries, the St. Gotthard, and the Italian lakes. Subjects not subsumed under these general headings were given specific chapters, arranged chronologically. His book incorporated the observations that Saussure made on the spot, which he recorded instantly, then wrote up in a more finished draft within twenty-four hours. The work also reflects his method of exploration, whereby he returned to an area several times in order to complete and verify his observations.

The *Voyages* demonstrate Saussure's approach toward a theory of the earth, to which end he collected data tirelessly. He had arrived at a tentative theory as early as 1774, when he had investigated only a few alpine passes. In the same year he delivered a lecture on mountain structure; although the lecture itself is not preserved, an abstract of it appears in the *Voyages*.

As Saussure originally conceived of the structure of the Alps, the primitive and central chain of the mountains consist of vertical strata, while the marginal or secondary mountains adjacent to the primitive mountains consist of steeply inclined beds. These progressively approach the horizontal as they reach the margins of the chain, where they are partially surrounded by tertiary mountains that are composed of the debris of all earlier deposits. It was therefore apparent to Saussure that both the primitive and secondary mountains of the chain must consist of distinct strata that display a transition in both their composition and their structure.

Saussure had accepted the notion that the secondary mountains had been formed on the bottom of the sea; he therefore drew upon the similarities between the primitive and secondary mountains to argue that the primitive mountains were also deposited on the ocean floor. The earth must therefore have been covered by a universal sea, which through crystallizations and successive deposits generated first the primitive mountains, then, around them in a series of concentric shells, the secondary ranges. The fire—or other "elastic fluids"—enclosed within the earth later lifted and ruptured the entire crust of the earth; in this process, the primitive mountains were lifted up, while the secondary ones became tilted against them. The waters of the universal ocean then rushed into the fissures left along the margins of the Alps, transporting for great distances huge boulders that were eventually scattered across the plains. Following the retreat of the waters, the germs of plants and animals, made fecund by their exposure to the air, began to develop on the newly exposed ground and in the residual water that remained in depressions of the earth.

Although Saussure stated specifically that he had arrived at his ideas without giving any thought to any particular system, it is easy to recognize in his approach the neptunist ideas associated with the contemporary school of Werner, as well as a plutonist idea of vertical movements as the result of internal fire of Cartesian origin. The concept of the universal waters rushing away from the Alps prevented Saussure from understanding the systems of frontal moraines that he observed on both sides of the mountains, although he had actually seen the recent fluctuations of glaciers in the valley of Chamonix.

After some thirteen years of accurate observations and thinking, and particularly after having studied the St. Gotthard area, Saussure concluded that the dislocation, distortion, and even overturning of the alpine rocks had been caused by processes of horizontal compression, as well as by uplifting by internal explosions. He thus came close to an accurate understanding of the structure of the Alps.

Despite his early formulation of a theory of the earth, and despite his further work toward emending this theory, Saussure never presented his material in a final, synthetic form. Why he did not do so remains a matter of some controversy. Although Cuvier, in his *Éloge* of Saussure, suggested that Saussure deliberately refrained from developing any theory, an analysis of the *Voyages* indicates that, on the contrary, Saussure fully intended to write such a synthesis until the time that he became physically disabled. It must not be forgotten that Saussure became incapacitated when he was

only fifty-four; having completed his travels, he must have anticipated ten or twenty years in which he could put his data into order. Since his illness did not permit him to do so, he substituted, in the last volume of the *Voyages,* an "Agenda or General Compendium of the Results of the Observations and Investigations Which Are to Serve as a Basis for the Theory of the Earth," which he characterized as a list of the problems to be solved by his followers. He thereby placed in the hands of his successors the fruits of his thirty-six years of travel and work, and left to them the task of reaching a general theory.

Saussure envisioned a theory of the earth that was to be based on uniformitarian principles, in which the present state of the earth would be carefully studied both to elucidate its past history and to predict its future. He proposed that such a theory should begin with a thorough review of the results of all previous workers and a description of the character of the various rocks (including their fossils) that compose mountain ranges. A discussion of all the fundamental laws, both physical and chemical, that affect the atmospheric envelope of the earth and play a significant role in shaping its features should then follow; finally, the successive stages of the evolution of the crust of the earth through geological time should be demonstrated by relating observations to laws.

Whether or not Saussure himself could have constructed an adequate theory within this outline remains open to question. It seems as if he was perhaps too timid in drawing conclusions and in discarding the theories of others when they were in conflict with his own observations. It is also the case that the structure of the Alps, his chief concern, was simply too complicated to be understood in the light of the geological knowledge available to the eighteenth century. Saussure himself seems to have known this intuitively, since at the end of the *Voyages* he noted that the only constant feature of the Alps was their variety.

Nonetheless, Saussure's dedicated work was of great importance in the development of geology, since, among other things, it provided James Hutton with fundamental documentation. In addition, Saussure devised a number of useful instruments, among them a hair hygrometer that utilized a degreased human hair to measure humidity, and he also performed some experiments on the fusion of granites and porphyries that entitled him to be considered the first experimental petrologist. Finally, he popularized the very term "geology," which replaced "geognosy" in the 1770's and 1780's.

BIBLIOGRAPHY

I. ORIGINAL WORKS. Saussure's major work is *Voyages dans les Alpes, précédés d'un essai sur l'histoire naturelle des environs de Genève*, 4 vols. (Neuchâtel–Geneva, 1779–1796, and later eds.), repr. in facsimile (Bologna, 1969).

See also *Dissertatio physica de igne* (Geneva, 1758); *Observations sur l'écorce des feuilles et des pétales des plantes* (Geneva, 1762); "Description des effets du tonnerre, observés à Naples dans la maison de Mylord Tilney," in *Observations sur la physique*, **1** (1773), 442–450; *Projet de réforme pour le Collège de Genève* (Geneva, 1774); *Eclaircissemens sur le projet de réforme pour le collège de Genève* (Geneva, 1774); *Essais sur l'hygrométrie* (Neuchâtel, 1783); "Lettre à Son Excellence M. le Chevalier Hamilton . . . sur la géographie physique de l'Italie," in *Observations sur la physique*, **7** (1776), 19–38; "Lettre de M. de Saussure à M. Faujas de Saint-Fond," in Faujas de Saint-Fond, *Description des expériences de la machine aérostatique de M. M. de Montgolfier*, II (Paris, 1784), 112–127; "Lettre de M. de Saussure à M. l'Abbé J. A. Mongez le jeune, sur l'usage du chalumeau," in *Observations sur la physique*, **26** (1785), 409–413; *Relation abrégée d'un voyage à la cîme du Mont-Blanc* (Geneva, 1787); "Défense de l'hygromètre à cheveu," in *Observations sur la physique*, **32** (1788), 24–45, 98–107, and repr. separately (Geneva, 1788); "Description d'un cyanomètre ou d'un appareil destiné à mesurer la transparence de l'air," in *Memorie della R. Accademia delle scienze di Torino*, **4** (1788–1789), 409–424; and "Description d'un diaphanomètre ou d'un appareil destiné à mesurer l'intensité de la couleur bleue du ciel," *ibid.*, 425–453.

See further "De la constitution physique de l'Italie," in J. J. F. de Lalande, *Voyage en Italie . . .*, I (Geneva, 1790), 45–48; "Description de deux nouvelles espèces de trémelles douées d'un mouvement spontané," in *Observations sur la physique*, **37** (1790), 401–409; *Éloge historique de Charles Bonnet* (Geneva, 1793); *Rapport et projet de loi du Comité d'Instruction Publique. Lu à l'Assemblée Nationale le 9 août 1793 par les citoyens Dessaussure et Bourrit fils* (Geneva, 1793); "Sur les collines volcaniques du Brisgau," in *Journal de physique*, **1** (1794), 325–362; "Notice sur la mine de fer de Saint-George en Maurienne," in *Journal des mines*, **1**, no. 4 (1794), 56–61; "Agenda ou tableau général des observations et des recherches dont les résultats doivent servir de base à la théorie de la terre," *ibid.*, **4**, no. 20 (1796), 2–70, and repr. in last vol. of *Voyages* and separately as *Agenda du voyageur géologue tiré du 4ème volume des "Voyages dans les Alpes"* (Geneva, 1796); "Mémoire sur les variations de hauteur et de température de l'Arve," in *Journal de physique*, **4** (1798), 50–55; and *Voyages dans les Alpes, partie pittoresque des ouvrages de H. B. Saussure*, with intro. by A. Sayous (Geneva-Paris, 1834).

Saussure's letters to his wife have been published as *Lettres de H. B. Saussure à sa femme*, annotated by E. Galliard and H. F. Montagnier (Chambéry, 1937).

II. SECONDARY LITERATURE. On Saussure and his work, see Georges Cuvier, "Éloges historiques de Charles Bonnet et H. B. de Saussure," in *Recueil des éloges historiques lus dans les séances publiques de l'Institut Royal de France*, II (Strasbourg-Paris, 1819), 383–430; Douglas W. Freshfield and H. F. Montagnier, *The Life of Horace Bénédict de Saussure* (London, 1920); and Jean Senebier, *Mémoire historique sur la vie et les écrits de Horace Bénédict de Saussure, pour servir d'introduction à la lecture de ses ouvrages* (Geneva, 1801).

ALBERT V. CAROZZI

SAUSSURE, NICOLAS-THÉODORE DE (*b.* Geneva, Switzerland, 14 October 1767; *d.* Geneva, 18 April 1845), *chemistry, plant physiology.*

Saussure was the son of the scientist Horace-Bénédict de Saussure (1740–1799) and Albertine-Amélie Boissier. His father supervised his initial studies and Saussure aided his father in his research. During the famous ascent of Mont Blanc on 3 August 1787, Nicolas was assigned by his father to make all the meteorological and barometric observations. In 1788 Nicolas accompanied his father on the expedition to the Col du Géant. They remained for seventeen days and nights in the snow fields.

During other expeditions, Saussure made observations on the composition of the atmosphere, the density of the air, and the geodesic features of the area around Geneva. In July 1789 he climbed Monte Rosa, where he pursued his experiments on the weight of the air. Using new techniques, he corroborated, with great precision, the observations of Mariotte, which had given rise to the Boyle-Mariotte law.

At this time Saussure became passionately interested in chemistry and in plant physiology, and he accumulated original observations, particularly on the mineral nutrition of plants. He later published this work. When the Revolution broke out, Saussure left Geneva for England. He returned in 1802 to occupy a promised chair in plant physiology at the Geneva Academy. Instead, he was named honorary professor of mineralogy and geology, a title he held until 1835. Disappointed at not being able to teach plant chemistry, the subject that had absorbed his attention since his first publication in 1797, he requested a leave of absence several days after his nomination. He never gave a course at the Academy.

In 1797, in *Annales de Chimie*, Saussure published three remarkable articles on carbonic acid and its formation in plant tissues. These works, followed in 1800 by an important study of the role of soil in the development of plants, brought him the recognition of his fellow scientists.

Saussure published his *Recherches chimiques sur la végétation* in Paris in 1804. An immediate success, it was translated into German in 1805 by F. S. Voigt and went through many editions. This work, which took seven years to write, laid the foundations of a new science, phytochemistry. Saussure examined the chief active components of plants, their synthesis, and their decomposition. He specified the relationships between vegetation and the environment and here, too, did pioneering work in what became the fields of pedology and ecology.

Starting in 1808, Saussure published a series of important articles, most of them devoted to a rigorous analysis of biochemical reactions occurring in the plant cell. The first dealt with the phosphorus content of seeds (1808). Then came two works on the conversion of starch into sugars by the action of air and water (1814 and 1819). These were followed by a study of the oil stored in fruits (1820). Saussure also investigated the biochemical processes that take place during the maturation of fruits (1821) and flowers (1822). Later he turned to the chemistry of germination and was the first to note the influence of desiccation on several food grains (1826). He then examined the formation of sugar during the germination of wheat (1833) and compared germination to fermentation reactions (1833). Several of the publications in which he reported his analysis of fermentation were regarded highly by Pasteur.

Saussure next studied the action of fermentation on the oxygen and hydrogen of air (1839) and also alcoholic fermentation (1841). Toward the end of his life, he took up again his research on plant nutrition (1841). His last paper was on the germination of oilseeds (1842).

Saussure received many honors. He was named a corresponding member of the Institut de France (1805), member of the Conseil Représentatif de Genève (1814), and was a founding member of the Société Helvétique des Sciences Naturelles (1815). By 1825 he was an associate member of virtually all the great European academies, and in 1842 he was elected president of the Congrès Scientifique of Lyons. In 1837 A. P. de Candolle named a genus of composite flower *Saussurea* and a section of the genus *Theodora*.

BIBLIOGRAPHY

I. ORIGINAL WORKS. Saussure's works include "Essai sur cette question: La formation de l'acide carbonique est-elle essentielle à la végétation?" in *Annales de chimie*, **24** (1797), 135–149, 227–228, 336–337; *Recherches chimiques sur la végétation* (Paris, 1804); "Sur le phosphore que les graines fournissent par la distillation et sur la décomposition des phosphates alcalins par le carbone," in *Annales de chimie*, **65** (1808), 189–201; "Observations sur la décomposition de l'amidon à la température atmosphérique par l'action de l'air et de l'eau," *ibid.*, **11** (1819), 379–408; "Observations sur la combinaison de l'essence de citron avec l'acide muriatique et sur quelques substances huileuses," in *Archives des sciences physiques et naturelles*, **13** (1820), 20–42, 112–135; "De l'influence des fruits verts sur l'air avant leur maturité," in *Mémoires de la Société de physique et d'histoire naturelle de Genève*, **1** (1821), 245–287; "De l'action des fleurs sur l'air, et de leur chaleur propre," in *Annales de chimie et de physique*, **21** (1822), 279–304; "De l'influence du dessèchement sur la germination de plusieurs graines alimentaires," in *Mémoires de la Société de physique et d'histoire naturelle de Genève*, **3** (1826), 1–28; "De la formation du sucre dans la germination du froment," *ibid.*, **6** (1841), 239–256; "Faits relatifs à la fermentation vineuses," in *Archives des sciences physiques et naturelles*, **32** (1841), 180–256; and "Sur la nutrition des végétaux," *ibid.*, **36** (1841), 340–355.

II. SECONDARY LITERATURE. On Saussure and his work, see C. Borgeaud, *Histoire de l'Université de Genève*, II (Geneva, 1909), 83; J. Briquet, "Biographies des botanistes à Genève de 1500 à 1931," in *Bericht der Schweizerischen botanischen Gesellschaft*, **50** (1940), 425–428; M. Macaire, "Notice sur la vie et les écrits de Théodore de Saussure," in *Bibliothèque universelle de Genève, Nouvelle série*, **57** (1845).

P. E. PILET

SAUVAGEAU, CAMILLE-FRANÇOIS (*b.* Angers, Maine-et-Loire, France, 12 May 1861; *d.* Vitrac [near Sarlat], Dordogne, France, 5 August 1936), *botany.*

Sauvageau came from a family of landowners and lawyers that had been established for several centuries in Anjou. After completing his secondary education at a *collège libre* in Angers, he entered the University of Montpellier. He obtained his *licence ès sciences physiques* and *licence ès sciences naturelles* in 1884 and immediately became an assistant to Charles Flahault, who held the chair of botany at the university.

Having successfully passed the *agrégation*, in 1888 Sauvageau was named professor at the *lycée* in Bordeaux. He left this post the following year to prepare a dissertation at the Muséum National d'Histoire Naturelle in Paris. He worked in the laboratory of P. van Tieghem, who encouraged most of his students to investigate problems in plant anatomy. Thus it is not surprising that Sauvageau's thesis (1891) was entitled "Sur les feuilles de quelques Monocotylédones aquatiques." In this work Sauvageau emphasized marine species; and because his research had taken this direction, Flahault introduced him to Édouard Bornet. The latter started him on the study of marine algae, and Sauvageau soon gave up his anatomical research to concentrate on this group.

Shortly after earning his doctorate, Sauvageau was appointed *maître de conférences* at Lyons and then professor at the Faculty of Sciences of Dijon. In 1901 he became professor at the Faculty of Sciences of Bordeaux, a post that he held until his retirement in 1932. Sauvageau was married to Marie-Louise Michelot, by whom he had one daughter.

Sauvageau's scientific work brought him many honors. He was elected corresponding member of the Académie des Sciences (1918), and he was a member of numerous foreign scientific academies and societies.

In his initial research, Sauvageau studied the anatomy of aquatic monocotyledons, mycology, phytopathology, and, particularly, diseases of the grape. But the bulk of his work was devoted to marine algae and in fact was concentrated almost exclusively on the study of Phaeophyceae. The few papers that were not concerned with this group dealt with the marine flora of the Gulf of Gascony, the coloration of oysters by the blue diatom, gelose (agar), the commercial uses of marine algae, and the iodine-containing cells (*ioduques*) of Bonnemaisoniaceae.

Sauvageau's first research was concerned with Ectocarpaceae. He showed in particular the great variety of their reproductive organs (1892–1897). He observed the isogamous and anisogamous copulation of certain flagellate cells produced by these organs and also noted the frequency with which they develop parthenogenetically.

He then studied Myrionemaceae (1898) and Cutleriaceae (1899). In the course of this research he confirmed and extended the observations of Johannes Reinke and Paul Falkenberg on the heteromorphic life-cycle of Cutleriaceae and demonstrated that the alternation of generations of *Cutleria-Aglaozonia* is not absolutely constant.

In "Remarques sur les Sphacelariacées" (1900–

1914), a series of papers totaling more than six hundred pages, Sauvageau described the complex anatomical structure of the various genera of this family, discussed their reproduction and development, and established a classification for them. Also, he published works on the various forms of *Fucus* and on the *Cystoseira* of the Mediterranean and the Atlantic (1913); these works are model systematic and ecological studies.

It was known that some certain Phaeophyceae produce only unilocular organs and appear to be deprived of sexuality because their zoospores are incapable of copulation. This condition is the case of the Laminariaceae, whose mode of reproduction was still unknown as late as 1915. In that year Sauvageau announced that the zoospores of *Saccorhiza bulbosa* give rise to filamentous microscopic plantlets. He further stated that some of these plantlets produce antherozoids while others produce oospheres, and he concluded that the plantlets are actually forms of prothallia. He then extended his investigations to other Laminariaceae found on the coasts of France and showed that this family, type of the order of Laminariales, is characterized by a type of alternation of generations that was previously unknown among the Phaeophyceae but is comparable to that encountered among the ferns.

Sauvageau also showed that this type of alternation of generations is exhibited by other Phaeophyceae, namely, *Dictyosiphon* (in which the prothallium produces isogamous gametes) and *Carpomitra* (in which the female prothallium is regularly apogamic). These two genera became the model types of two new orders: Dictyosiphonales and Sporochnales.

Sauvageau showed that among other types of Phaeophyceae, the discoid or filamentous microscopic plantlets emerging from the developing zoospores are not sexed. Thus he concluded that this stage of development, which he called adelophyceae in contrast to that of macroscopic plants (delophyceae), is not that of a prothallium. Instead, this stage produces numerous zoospores that, if placed in culture, are capable of reproducing several generations of microscopic plantlets before reaching (under favorable conditions) the delophycean stage. Sauvageau gave the name *plethysmothalli* to these microscopic plantlets, which have no analogues among the other plants.

Sauvageau's discoveries, which were made with simple culture techniques, greatly elucidated the extremely complex cycles of the brown algae.

More concerned with facts than with theories, Sauvageau did not attempt to derive general conclusions from his many discoveries. Yet, these discoveries form the basis of all our present knowledge concerning Phaeophyceae—its classification and the evolution of its reproductive cycles.

BIBLIOGRAPHY

I. Original Works. Among Sauvageau's works are "Remarques sur la reproduction des Phéosporées et en particulier des *Ectocarpus*," in *Annales des sciences naturelles*, 8th ser., **2** (1896); "Sur quelques Myrionémacées (premier mémoire)," *ibid.*, **5** (1898); "Les Cutlériacées et leur alternance de générations," *ibid.*, **10** (1899); 265–362; *Remarques sur les Sphacélariacées*, published in parts in *Journal de botanique*, **14–18** (1900–1904) and separately (Bordeaux, 1904, 1914); "A propos de *Cystoseira* de Banyuls at de Guethary," *Bulletin de la Station biologique d'Arcachon*, **14** (1912); "Recherches sur les Laminaires des côtes de France," *Mémoires de l'Académie des sciences*, **56** (1918); and *Utilisation des Algues marines* (Paris, 1920). A large number of papers was published in *Bulletin de la Station biologique d'Arcachon* from 1905 to 1936.

II. Secondary Literature. See the obituary by P. Dangeard in *Bulletin. Société botanique de France*, **84** (1937), 13–18; and *Bulletin de la Station biologique d'Arcachon*, **34** (1937), 5–59; and J. Feldmann, "L'oeuvre de C. Sauvageau (1892–1936)," in *Histoire de la botanique en France* (Paris–Nice, 1954), 212–217.

Jean Feldmann

SAUVEUR, ALBERT (*b.* Louvain, Belgium, 21 June 1863; *d.* Cambridge, Massachusetts, 26 January 1939), *metallurgy, metallography.*

Sauveur was the son of Lambert and Hortense Franquin Sauveur. He was educated at the Athénée Royale, Brussels (where his father was *préfet*), and at the École de Mines in Liège (1881–1886). Sauveur came to the United States in 1887 and enrolled as an advanced student at the Massachusetts Institute of Technology, where he graduated in 1889 with a thesis on copper smelting. For a year and a half he worked for the Pennsylvania Steel Company at an undemanding job as an analyst, which left him time to study the metallurgy of steel on his own.

In 1891 Sauveur married Mary Prince Jones, by whom he had three children. In the same year he went to the Illinois Steel Company in order to set up a laboratory, and he became the first in the United States effectively to study the microscopy of steel. Sauveur showed how grain-size was affected by mechanical and thermal treatment, and how, in turn, the properties of steel depend on grain-size. In an 1896 paper Sauveur critically summarized all the diverse current theories of steel-hardening mechanisms. He attributed the hardness of quenched steel to a fine dispersion of carbide (Fe_3C) particles. This paper attracted international notice and led to a debate at a meeting of the American Institute of Mining Engineers that occupied a hundred printed pages (*Transactions,* **27** [1898], 846–944). Using quantitative methods for the first time in metallography, he related the grain-size and the volume-fraction of the principal microconstituents in steel (ferrite, cementite, austenite and its decomposition products, martensite and pearlite) to the carbon content and to the temperature of quenching. In the same year, the laboratory of the steel works was disbanded; Sauveur returned to Massachusetts, where he established a commercial testing laboratory and began a consulting practice that continued throughout his life.

In 1898 Sauveur founded a quarterly journal, *Metallographist,* which he edited until its failure in 1906; in 1904 the title was changed to the *Iron and Steel Magazine.* Published in the most active period of metallographic discovery, the journal is a prime (if not always a primary) source for metallurgical history and contains biographies by Sauveur of all the principal workers in metallography of the time. In association with H. M. Boylston, Sauveur started a correspondence course in metallography, which was followed by 1,500 students and did much to spread knowledge of the new techniques throughout American industry. Sauveur joined the Harvard faculty as instructor in metallurgy in 1899, became professor in 1905, and remained there until his death.

With his lucid book, *The Metallography and Heat Treatment of Iron and Steel* (1912), and as an urbane man of the world with wide international contacts in both scientific and industrial spheres, Sauveur had a great influence on metallurgical institutions and received many honors. Nevertheless, he made few important scientific discoveries after joining Harvard, and he had few eminent research students. His main contribution after 1896 was that of a gifted advocate and interpreter of the work of others.

BIBLIOGRAPHY

I. ORIGINAL WORKS. A list of Sauveur's 160 papers is in R. A. Daly, in *Biographical Memoirs. National Academy of Sciences,* **21** (1943), 26–33. Sauveur's most important papers are "The Microstructure of Steel," in *Transactions of the American Institute of Mining Engineers,* **22** (1893), 546–557; "The Microstructure of Steel and the Current Theories of Hardening," *ibid.,* **26** (1896), 863–906, with German trans. by Hanno von Juptner (Leipzig, 1898); and "Current Theories of Hardening Steel, Thirty Years Later," in *Transactions of the American Institute of Mining and Metallurgical Engineers,* **73** (1926), 859–908. Sauveur was editor of *Metallographist,* **1–6** (1898–1904); and its successor, *Iron and Steel Magazine,* **7–11** (1904–1906).

Sauveur's books include *Laboratory Experiments in Metallurgy* (Cambridge, Mass., 1908); *The Metallography of Iron and Steel* (Cambridge, Mass., 1912; 2nd ed., retitled *The Metallography and Heat Treatment of Iron and Steel,* Cambridge, Mass.–New York, 1916, 1918, 1920; 3rd ed., 1926; 4th ed. 1935). Sauveur also wrote two political pamphlets: *Germany and the European War* (Boston, 1914), and *Germany's Holy War* (Cambridge, Mass., 1915); and a brief autobiography, *Metallurgical Dialogue* (Cleveland, Ohio, 1935), reissued as *Metallurgical Reminiscences* (New York, 1937).

II. SECONDARY LITERATURE. On Sauveur and his work, see R. A. Daly, "Albert Sauveur," in *Biographical Memoirs. National Academy of Sciences,* **22** (1943), 121–133; and Cyril S. Smith, *A History of Metallography* (Chicago, 1960), ch. 16.

CYRIL STANLEY SMITH

SAUVEUR, JOSEPH (*b.* La Flèche, France, 24 March 1653; *d.* Paris, France, 9 July 1716), *physics.*

Sauveur worked on early problems in the physics of sound, especially beats, harmonics, and the determination of absolute frequency; and he was influential as a teacher of practical mathematics.

Sauveur was the son of Louis Sauveur, a notary, and Renée des Hayes. Born with a voice defect, he did not begin to speak until the age of seven and retained a lifelong difficulty with his speech. He first attended the famous Jesuit school of La Flèche, where arithmetic intrigued him. Hoping to learn science, Sauveur went to Paris in 1670, where he studied mathematics and medicine and attended the physics lectures of Jacques Rohault. Despite his speech problem, Sauveur became well known as a good teacher and was a tutor at the court of Louis XIV. Interested primarily in practical mathematics, he prepared tables for simplifying calculations and for converting weights and measures. He also worked on problems of engineering and in 1681 conducted hydraulic experiments with Mariotte at Chantilly. In 1691 he visited the town of Mons while it was under active siege, in connection with his plan to write a treatise on fortification. In 1703 he replaced Vauban as examiner for the Engineering Corps. When he obtained the chair of mathematics at the Collège Royal in 1686, Sauveur was sufficiently well known that he dared to read the required public speech (earlier, he had dropped a plan to apply for the post because the speech seemed too difficult for him). In 1696 he became a member of the Paris Academy of Sciences.

Like Mersenne and others in the seventeenth century, Sauveur used musical experience to obtain information on sound and vibration. According to Fontenelle, Sauveur was fascinated by music, even though he had no ear for it, and consulted frequently with musicians. Despite the musical foundation of his work, Sauveur proposed the development of a new subject, which he named *acoustique,*[1] dealing with sound in general rather than with the *son agréable* of music.

Sauveur began his work in acoustics by developing a method of classifying temperaments of the musical scale. He divided the octave into forty-three equal intervals, or *merides,* each of which was divided into seven *eptamerides.*[2] Sauveur's intention was to indicate the size of any musical interval, at least to a reasonable approximation with respect to the ability of the ear to discriminate pitch, in terms of an integral number of *eptamerides.* These divisions made it simple to describe and compare different tuning systems. For example, the fifths and thirds given by an integral number of *merides* approximate those of the one-fifth comma meantone tuning used in the sixteenth and seventeenth centuries.[3]

Sauveur's first work on the physics of vibration, originally presented to the Paris Academy in 1700, concerned the determination of absolute frequency. The problem of pitch standardization was a natural successor to the problem of temperament standardization. Sauveur wanted to use a *son fixe* of 100 cycles per second. Pitch had been identified with frequency early in the seventeenth century, and the ratio of the frequencies of a pair of tones was known, ultimately, from the inverse relative string lengths.[4] Sauveur was the first to use beats to determine the frequency difference and was therefore able to calculate the absolute frequencies. Since he correctly interpreted beats, it appears that Sauveur may have been the first to have an understanding of superposition.

To determine absolute frequency, Sauveur used a pair of organ pipes a small half-tone apart in just intonation (frequency ratio 25:24). This interval is sufficiently small that the beats can be counted, for low pitches. Furthermore, the interval can be obtained accurately by tuning through thirds and perfect fifths (for example, by tuning up two major thirds and then down a fifth). As a result of experiments done with Deslandes, an organ builder, Sauveur found that the frequency of an open organ pipe five Paris feet long was between 100 and 102 cps. Sauveur claimed to have obtained consistent results from experiments done with other pipes. Newton made a rough check of Sauveur's results: knowing that the velocity of sound is the product of frequency and wavelength, he knew the wavelength of a tone of 100 cps to be just over twice the length of Sauveur's pipe.[5] Since the exact dimensions of the pipe are not known, there is no way to determine how accurate Sauveur was in his determination of its frequency. However, its pitch was an A of the time, in agreement with a later determination of the frequency of an eighteenth-century Paris tuning fork.[6] If each of the three tunings made in the process of obtaining the small half-tone is accurate to within half a cent (1/200 of an equal tempered semitone), it would be possible, in principle, to find the absolute frequency to within 2.5 percent.

Later, in work presented in 1713, Sauveur derived the frequency of a string theoretically. He treated the string, stretched horizontally and hanging in a curve because of the gravitational field, as a compound pendulum and he found the frequency of the swinging motion, assumed to have small amplitude. His result agrees with the modern one except for a factor of $\sqrt{10/\pi}$.

In 1701, at a lively meeting of the Paris Academy, Sauveur explained the basic properties of harmonics. Harmonics had seemed paradoxical ever since the early seventeenth century, when the identification of pitch with frequency had implied the seemingly impossible phenomenon of a single object vibrating simultaneously at several frequencies. Sauveur argued that a string can vibrate at additional, higher frequencies, which he called *sons harmoniques*, by dividing up into the appropriate number of equal shorter lengths separated by stationary points, which he called *noeuds*. Sauveur apparently did not know of the paper rider

demonstration, reported by Wallis (1677)[7] and Robartes (1692),[8] that nodes are associated with higher modes. However, Wallis' paper was mentioned by a member of the audience, and Sauveur's argument for the existence of nodes culminated with Wallis' demonstration. In a discussion of the organ, presented in 1702, Sauveur stated explicitly (he was the first to do so) that harmonics are components of all musical sound and that they affect the timbre of a tone.

Among Sauveur's interests, the subject of harmonics proved the most important for later developments—in mathematics, physics, and music. In the eighteenth century, analysis of the vibrating string was inspired, in part, by knowledge of the higher vibrational modes. The composer and theorist Rameau used harmonics to provide a physical basis for his theory of harmony, and a century later Helmholtz emphasized the effect of harmonics on timbre. It was through Sauveur and the Paris Academy that ideas about harmonics became well known in the early eighteenth century.[9] Sauveur's terminology, including "harmonics" and "node," was adopted and is still current.

NOTES

1. The word had already been used occasionally in connection with sound.
2. Other systems of multiple division were already in use; the most important, developed by Huygens, was the division of the octave into 31 intervals.
3. J. Murray Barbour, *Tuning and Temperament, an Historical Survey* (East Lansing, Mich., 1953), 122.
4. Mersenne made the first known estimate of vibrational frequency by extrapolating from the countable vibrations of a long string to the frequency of a short section of it; see *Harmonie universelle* (Paris, 1636; facs. ed., 1963), I, Bk. 3, Prop. VI, 169–170.
5. In the 2nd and 3rd eds. of the *Principia*, Bk. 2, Prop. L; cf. Isaac Newton, *Mathematical Principles of Natural Philosophy*, F. Cajori, ed. (Berkeley, Calif., 1962), I, 383–384.
6. Alexander J. Ellis, "On the History of Musical Pitch," in *Journal of the Society of Arts*, **28** (1879–1880), 318, col. 1.
7. John Wallis, "On the Trembling of Consonant Strings, a New Musical Discovery," in *Philosophical Transactions of the Royal Society*, **12** (1677), 839–842.
8. Francis Robartes, "A Discourse Concerning the Musical Notes of the Trumpet, and the Trumpet Marine, and of Defects of the Same," *ibid.*, **17** (1692), 559–563.
9. In 1809, when Chladni's experimental demonstration of nodal lines inspired the Academy competition for theoretical analysis of vibrating surfaces, Prony remarked that Sauveur's work had led to important research on the vibrating string; see *Procès-verbaux de l'Académie des sciences*, IV (Hendaye, 1913), 175.

BIBLIOGRAPHY

Sauveur's papers include "Système général des intervalles des sons," in *Mémoires de l'Académie royale des sciences,* 1701 (Paris, 1704), 297–460; "Application des sons harmoniques à la composition des jeux d'orgues," *ibid.,* 1702 (Paris, 1704), 308–328; "Rapport des sons des cordes d'instruments de musique aux flèches des cordes; et nouvelle détermination des sons fixes," *ibid.,* 1713 (Paris, 1716), 324–348.

Fontenelle is the main source of information on Sauveur's life and the reception of his work. His *éloge* is in *Histoire de l'Académie royale des sciences,* 1716 (Paris, 1718), 79–87. His discussions of Sauveur's work include "Sur la détermination d'un son fixe," *ibid.,* 1700 (Paris, 1703), 131–140; "Sur un nouveau système de musique," *ibid.,* 1701 (Paris, 1704), 123–139; "Sur l'application des sons harmoniques aux jeux d'orgues," *ibid.,* 1702 (Paris, 1704), 90–92; and "Sur les cordes sonores, et sur une nouvelle détermination du son fixe," *ibid.,* 1713 (Paris, 1716), 68–75.

See also Léon Auger, "Les apports de J. Sauveur (1653–1716) à la création de l'acoustique," in *Revue d'histoire des sciences et de leurs applications,* 1 (1948), 323–336; and the article on Sauveur by F. Winckel in F. Blume, ed., *Die Musik in Geschichte und Gegenwart,* XI (Kassel, 1963), cols. 1437–1438.

SIGALIA DOSTROVSKY

SAVART, FÉLIX (*b.* Mézières, France, 30 June 1791; *d.* Paris, France, 16 March 1841), *physics.*

Savart made experimental studies of many phenomena involving vibration. With Biot he showed that the magnetic field produced by the current in a long, straight wire is inversely proportional to the distance from the wire. In most of his vibrational studies Savart observed the nodal lines of vibrating surfaces and solids, and he thereby obtained information on vibrational modes and elastic properties.

Savart was the son of Gérard Savart, an engineer at the military school of Metz. His brother, Nicolas, who studied at the École Polytechnique and was an officer in the engineering corps, also did work on vibration. Savart studied medicine, first at the military hospital at Metz and then at the University of Strasbourg, where he received his medical degree in 1816. At this time Savart presumably was already interested in the physics of the violin, for he built an experimental instrument in 1817 and in 1819 presented a memoir on the subject to the Paris Academy of Sciences. Biot, one of Savart's first contacts in Paris, was interested in his work and helped him to find a position teaching physics there. In 1827, Savart replaced Fresnel as a member of the Paris Academy; and in 1828 he became a professor of experimental physics at the Collège de France, where he taught acoustics.

In 1820, a few months after Oersted's discovery of the magnetic field produced by a current, Biot and Savart determined the relative strength of the field by observing the rate of oscillation of a magnetic dipole suspended at various distances from a long, straight wire. In some measurements the earth's field was canceled by an appropriately placed magnet, while in others the apparatus was oriented so that the field produced at the dipole by the current was in the magnetic north-south direction.

In his earliest work Savart gave the first explanation of the function of certain parts of the violin. To learn how vibrations are transmitted from the strings to the rest of the instrument, he induced vibrations in a free wood plate by passing a vibrating string over a bridge at its center; he also used Chladni's sand-pattern technique to observe the resulting nodal lines. Savart showed that the bridge transmits the string's vibrations; that the plate can be made to vibrate at any frequency; and that the corresponding mode is a modification of an unforced mode. He demonstrated that the sound post also serves to transmit vibrations, and he explained that it therefore should not be placed under a nodal line. Thinking that symmetry and regularity would produce the best tone, Savart built a trapezoidal violin with rectangular sound holes. When the instrument was played before a committee that included Biot, the composer Cherubini, and other members of the Academy of Sciences and the Académie des Beaux-Arts, its tone was judged as extremely clear and even, but somewhat subdued.

Over a period of twenty years, Savart performed numerous experiments in acoustics and vibration. He generalized his work on the violin to analyze the vibrations of coupled systems. He also greatly extended Chladni's observations of the modes of plates: adding a dye to the sand, he made prints of the nodal patterns for brass plates in the shapes of circles, ellipses, and polygons. Savart was able to locate directly the nodes of a vibrating air column by lowering a light membrane covered with sand into a vertical pipe.

On the basis of his experience observing vibrational modes, Savart introduced a new way to learn about the structure of materials. The variation of nodal patterns for laminae cut along different planes of a nonisotropic material indicated the orientational dependence of the material's elasticity. Savart sought the axes of elasticity of various substances, including certain crystalline ones. His papers on this subject were translated and reprinted.

Savart also studied aspects of the voice and of hearing. In connection with determining the lower frequency limit of hearing, he devised and used the rotating toothed wheel for producing sound of any frequency. Savart was highly regarded as an experimenter, and his results were relevant for the contemporary analyses of vibration and elasticity made by Poisson, Cauchy, and Lamé.

BIBLIOGRAPHY

I. ORIGINAL WORKS. Savart's published works include *Mémoire sur la construction des instruments à chordes et à archet* (Paris, 1819); "Mémoire sur la communication des mouvements vibratoires entre les corps solides," in *Annales de chimie et de physique,* 2nd ser., **14** (1820), 113–172; "Note sur le magnétisme de la pile de Volta," *ibid.,* **15** (1820), 222–223, written with J. B. Biot; "Recherches sur les vibrations de l'air," *ibid.,* **24** (1823), 56–88; "Mémoire sur les vibrations des corps solides, considérées en général," *ibid.,* **25** (1824), 12–50, 138–178, 225–269; "Recherches sur l'élasticité des corps qui cristallisent regulièrement," *ibid.,* **40** (1829), 5–30, 113–137; "Recherches sur la structure des métaux," *ibid.,* **41** (1829), 61–75; and "Sur les modes de division des plaques vibrantes," *ibid.,* **73** (1840), 225–273. More of Savart's papers are listed in the Royal Society *Catalogue of Scientific Papers,* V (London, 1871), 419–420.

Savart began a book on acoustics but did not complete it. See *Comptes rendus . . . de l'Académie des sciences,* **12** (1841), 651–652.

II. SECONDARY LITERATURE. There are brief biographies of Savart in Michaud's *Biographie universelle,* XXXVIII, 104–105; and in *Nouvelle biographie générale* (Paris, 1969), 387–389. The report of the committee that studied Savart's *mémoire* on the violin is in *Annales de chimie et de physique,* 2nd ser., **12** (1819), 225–255. The determination of the Biot-Savart law is discussed in detail by J. B. Biot in *Précis élémentaire de physique,* 3rd ed., II (Paris, 1824), 707–723; this section is translated by O. M. Blunn in R. A. R. Tricker, *Early Electrodynamics* (Oxford, 1965), 119–139. Some of Savart's work on vibration and elasticity is discussed by I. Todhunter in *A History of the Theory of Elasticity,* K. Pearson, ed. (New York, 1960), 167–183.

SIGALIA DOSTROVSKY

SAVASORDA. See **Abraham bar Ḥiyya ha-Nasi.**

SAVIGNY, MARIE-JULES-CÉSAR LELORGNE DE (*b.* Provins, Brie, France, 5 April 1777; *d.* Versailles, France, 5 October 1851), *biology.*

Savigny used his full name only on legal documents. His parents, Jean-Jacques Lelorgne de Savigny and Françoise Josèphe de Barbaud, had one other child, Amable Eléanore Louise Josèphe. Savigny studied at the local Collège des Oratoriens; his education there was supplemented by visits to the Génovéfains de Saint-Jacques. Besides classical languages, he was introduced to botany, the use of the microscope, and tales of travel. He was studying chemistry and botany with a local apothecary when, in 1793, he was chosen by a government commission to study in Paris. He enrolled at the École de Santé, attended lectures at the Muséum d'Histoire Naturelle, and became known to Lamarck, Daubenton, Cuvier, and Étienne Geoffroy Saint-Hilaire. Savigny's mother, widowed and impoverished, joined him in Paris and died when he was twenty.

Savigny was about to begin a teaching career in botany when Cuvier urged him to join Napoleon's expedition to Egypt as a zoologist: he would study invertebrates while Geoffroy Saint-Hilaire studied vertebrates. With many other scholars, they remained in Egypt from June 1798 until January 1802. Savigny then returned to France and spent the rest of his life in Paris and Versailles, with the exception of an excursion to Italy between February and November of 1822. (Pallary first put this trip during the period 1817–1822 ["Vie," 45] but later found letters that show the visit to have been briefer ["Documents," 90, 101].) Beginning about 1817, Savigny suffered from a severe nervous affliction (not blindness) that made visual work, and even thought, impossible. His life as a scientist had virtually ended by the time he was elected to the Académie des Sciences in 1821. When the commission responsible for publishing the results of the Egyptian expedition finally despaired of receiving his promised descriptions, they corresponded with Savigny's devoted mistress, Agathe-Olympe Letellier de Sainteville. She seems to have helped effect a compromise; plates drawn under Savigny's supervision were eventually published in *Description de l'Égypte,* with notes written by Victor Audouin.

Savigny's *Mémoires sur les animaux sans vertèbres* (1816) deeply impressed his contemporaries and was cited as a model of fine zoology for the next fifty years. By example rather than by precept, he demonstrated the value of comparative morphology. Presumably it was his botanical training that led him to seek, in the insects and crustacea collected in Egypt, "perfectly Linnaean characters, that is, where the same organs are always disposed in the same order, and can be compared without interruption" (*Mémoires sur les animaux sans vertèbres*, iii).

Just as flowers were analyzed into calyx, corolla, stigma, and style, so Savigny analyzed insect mouthparts into labrum, mandibles, maxillae, and labium. Previous zoologists had distinguished Lepidoptera, for example, by the absence of regular mouthparts and the presence of a two-part coiled tubule. Savigny interpreted the tubule as a highly modified pair of maxillae and said that the other mouthparts, however minute, were present. Savigny extended his comparison to the appendages of crustacea and other arthropods, to the point of seeing the mouthparts of the horseshoe crab as homologous to the legs of insects. In the second part of the *Mémoires*, he compared the anatomy of solitary ascidians with that of various zoophytes, demonstrating that the latter should be regarded as colonial ascidians. He even suggested some homologies between ascidians and salps.

While Savigny was showing unsuspected homologies among these invertebrates, Geoffroy Saint-Hilaire was doing the same with the bones of reptiles and fish. Savigny's work encouraged Geoffroy Saint-Hilaire to search for homologies between vertebrates and arthropods. Savigny did not discuss principles or suggest a "unity of plan," but his work became a model for the morphological zoology that flourished in the nineteenth century.

BIBLIOGRAPHY

I. ORIGINAL WORKS. Savigny's principal works are *L'histoire naturelle et mythologique de l'ibis* (Paris, 1805); *Mémoires sur les animaux sans vertèbres* (Paris, 1816); *Description de l'Égypte, publiée par les ordres de sa majesté l'Empereur Napoléon-le-Grand. Histoire naturelle* (Paris, 1809–[1826]), which includes "Système des oiseaux de l'Égypte et de la Syrie" (1809), "Système des annélides, principalement de celles des côtes de l'Égypte et de la Syrie" (1820), and reprs. of his already published material on the ibis and on ascidians; and "Remarques sur certain phénomènes dont le principe est dans l'organe de la vue, ou fragments du journal d'un observateur atteint d'une maladie des yeux," in *Mémoires de l'Académie des sciences de l'Institut de France*, **18** (1842), 385–416.

II. SECONDARY LITERATURE. On his life and work, see Paul Pallary, "Marie Jules-César Savigny: sa Vie et son Oeuvre: la Vie de Savigny," in *Mémoires. Institut d'Égypte*, **17** (1931), 1–111; "L'oeuvre de Savigny," *ibid.*, **20** (1932), 1–112, with bibliography, 88–92; and "Documents," *ibid.*, **23** (1934), 1–203.

MARY P. WINSOR

SAXTON, JOSEPH (*b.* Huntingdon, Pennsylvania, 22 March 1799; *d.* Washington, D.C., 26 October 1873), *scientific instrumentation.*

Saxton was the son of James Saxton and Hannah Ashbaugh. After leaving school at the age of twelve and working at his father's nail factory in Huntingdon, he became apprenticed to a local watchmaker, David Newingham, from whom he apparently acquired his taste for precision craftsmanship. Newingham died soon afterward and in 1818 Saxton went to Philadelphia, in the hope of using his talents for precision work.

His earliest major achievement in Philadelphia was a clock with a unique temperature-compensating pendulum and an oil-less escapement. The Franklin Institute awarded him a silver medal for it in 1824. He also invented a device for shaping clock gear teeth into the ideal (epicycloidal) configuration and a "reflecting pyrometer and comparator" for checking the precision of pendulums; the city of Philadelphia awarded him the John Scott legacy medal for this device on 11 November 1841. He also made a cane gun in 1824; it was not muzzle-loaded but employed a metal-jacketed cartridge.

Saxton's ingenuity led Isaiah Lukens, a leading mechanic and tower clockmaker in Philadelphia, to make him an associate. Together they built the clock that occupied the steeple of Independence Hall from 1828 until 1876, when it was moved to the town hall in Germantown, where it is still in operation. All of Saxton's innovations had been installed in this particular clock.

In 1829 Saxton moved to London, where he built many of the permanent exhibits for the newly constructed Adelaide Gallery. An early visitor was Michael Faraday, whose electromagnetic discoveries inspired Saxton to build a highly regarded electric generator and electric motor. Other visitors included the physicist Charles Wheatstone and William Cubitt and Thomas Telford, two of London's best-known engineers. Saxton built a water-current meter for Cubitt and the apparatus that Wheatstone used for determining the speed of current electricity. He also built the apparatus that Telford and his assistant John Macneill used to study water resistance, at various speeds, of canal boats.

In January of 1835 Franklin Peale commissioned Saxton to build a precision assay balance for the Philadelphia Mint. When it was completed he returned to Philadelphia to take charge of the construction and maintenance of the balance scales at the mint. He occupied this post from 1837 until 1844. One of his balances is still on exhibit there.

In Philadelphia, Saxton pioneered in daguerreotype photography (1839) with a view of the state arsenal and the old Central High School. He also engraved a diffraction grating that enabled John William Draper to make the first photograph (a daguerreotype) of the diffraction spectrum (1844).

From 28 February 1844 until his death, Saxton was director of the U.S. Coast Survey Office of Weights and Measures, the forerunner of the National Bureau of Standards. Every state that had not previously been furnished with sets of federally approved weights, measures, and balance scales was supplied with sets built, checked, and in many instances personally installed at the various state capitals by Saxton. His skill in making precision balances reached its zenith during these years. A set of them, exhibited at the 1851 Great Exhibition in London, brought him a gold medal—the highest award.

Saxton designed and built for the Coast Survey a gauge for recording tide levels, a current meter like the one he had made in London, a unique hydrometer, and a maximum-minimum thermometer for deep-sea observations. Each of these instruments was the first of its kind manufactured in America.

For engraving degrees on a circle, he and William Wurdemann devised an automatic dividing engine that eliminated the errors caused by the body temperature of the operator.

Saxton married Mary H. Abercrombie in 1850. He was a member of the American Philosophical Society, the Franklin Institute, and a charter member (1863) of the National Academy of Sciences.

BIBLIOGRAPHY

I. ORIGINAL WORKS. Saxton's patents are Great Britain, 6351 (1832) and 6682 (1834); U.S., 3806, 22982, 23046, and 44460. See also National Archives Patent No. 5446X (1829). For descriptions of his exhibits, see the quarterly catalogs of the Society for the Illustration and Encouragement of Practical Science, Adelaide Gallery (London, 1832–1835); and the Society's *Magazine of Popular Science and Journal of the Useful Arts,* **1–4** (1836–1840), which contains material on Saxton's work, some probably written by him.

See also "Notice of Electro-Magnetic Experiments," in *Journal of the Franklin Institute,* **14** (1832), 66–72; "Description of a Revolving Keeper Magnet for Producing Electrical Currents," *ibid.,* **17** (1834), 155–156; and "On the Application of the Rotating Mirror to the Aneroid Barometer," in *Proceedings of the American Association for the Advancement of Science,* **12** (1858), 40–42.

A MS scrapbook and diary of his life in London are in the Smithsonian Institution archives; letters are in the U.S. National Archives, Record Gp. 104. A MS letter (2 Oct. 1825) is in Proctor papers, University of Virginia library.

Saxton's daguerreotype of the state arsenal and the old Central High School is at the Historical Society of Pennsylvania, Philadelphia. The Historical Society of York County, York, Pennsylvania, has a ruling machine of his construction.

II. SECONDARY LITERATURE. On Saxton and his work, see Joseph Henry's notice in *Biographical Memoirs. National Academy of Sciences,* **1** (1877), 287–316; J. Saxton Pendleton, *Joseph Saxton, 1799–1873* (Reading, Pa., 1935); C. W. Mitman, in *Dictionary of American Biography,* XVI (New York, 1943), 400; and Thomas Coulson, in *Journal of the Franklin Institute,* **259** (1955), 277–291.

ARTHUR H. FRAZIER

SAY, THOMAS (*b.* Philadelphia, Pennsylvania, 27 July 1787; *d.* New Harmony, Indiana, 10 October 1834), *entomology, conchology.*

One of the generation of self-taught naturalists, Say was an indifferent scholar in the Quaker boarding school he attended until the age of fifteen. His father, Benjamin Say, and his grandfather, Thomas Say, had both been physician-apothecaries, public-spirited philanthropists, and founders of hospitals; they were also noted as "fighting Quakers" for the colonial cause. Say's mother, Anna Bonsall Say, died when he was six years old. She was a granddaughter of John Bartram, and through this relationship Say became acquainted with the beetle and butterfly collections of William Bartram, for whom he collected specimens.

Say's father tried to discourage his son's early interest in natural history but inadvertently opened the door wider by putting him into partnership in the apothecary business with John Speakman. The partners' lack of business acumen soon brought the shop to failure; but the meetings of a congenial group of friends, occasionally in the back of the shop, led to the founding (1812) of the Academy of Natural Sciences of Philadelphia, with Say among the charter members. His father having died, Say lived frugally in the Academy building, tended the small museum, and studied his own collections. Here his friendship developed with William Maclure, president of the Academy from 1817.

In 1818, with Maclure, George Ord, and T. R. Peale, Say went on an expedition to the Sea Islands of Georgia and Spanish Florida, where they were thwarted by hostile Indians. The next year Say became chief zoologist on Major Stephen H. Long's exploration of the tributaries of the Missouri River, and in 1823 he was zoologist on Long's trip to the headwaters of the Mississippi River. Say declined the offer to be the expedition historian, but in addition to the many hitherto unknown animals he collected, he also gathered a great many plants. The explorers concluded that the treeless expanse between the Mississippi and Missouri rivers offered no possibilities for future settlement and would indefinitely remain the home of numberless bison and a few Indians.

Maclure persuaded Say to accompany him to New Harmony, Indiana, in 1825. This idealistic community, the dream of Scottish industrialist Robert Owen, had been established as an escape from the harshness of clamoring cities and as a proof that beauty, culture, and science could flourish where all worked willingly together. It failed. Say was among its victims, for, although hopeless at financial matters, he stayed as Maclure's agent after the latter's departure; and the malarial climate on the Wabash River contributed to Say's early death.

Say effectively did scientific work at New Harmony, and there he continued the study of mollusks that he had begun in Philadelphia. In 1816 he had published the first paper on American shells by an American. At New Harmony he completed and printed *American Conchology*. He also produced the third volume of *American Entomology*, which had been well under way. These works were illustrated by Charles-Alexandre Lesueur and by the talented Lucy Way Sistaire, whom Say had married at New Harmony. He also published descriptions of more than a thousand new species of insects.

New Harmony attracted the attention of scientists throughout the world, many of whom visited the community. Say's reputation led to his becoming a foreign member of the Linnean Society of London and the Zoological Society of London, and

a correspondent of the Société Philomathique of Paris.

Say's studies of insects, on which he spent the greater time, had few predecessors in the United States. The first book on American insects appeared in 1797, based on notes of John Abbot, and studies of individual insects or groups went back as far as Paul Dudley's account of bees in 1723 and Moses Bartram's work on the seventeen-year cicada in 1767. The emphasis was on economic insects, as evidenced by Thomas Jefferson's participation on a committee to study the Hessian fly in 1792. Amateurs in the United States customarily sent specimens to Europe for identification, especially after the impetus given to the subject by Réaumur in the six-volume *History of Insects* (1734–1742). Say's entry into entomology changed that, for his published descriptions were accurate and readily usable by others. Although entirely too trustful of others and excessively modest, he had a delightful personality, and he readily identified specimens for a growing list of American collectors. He was familiar with American and European literature on insects and was a natural taxonomist, showing excellent judgment in selecting the significant features of each species so that his descriptions did not leave taxonomic confusion. Say described many important economic insects, which bear his name. Although he urged others to study also the habits of insects, he did little of that himself.

Unfortunately, after his death, Say's collection of insects was long neglected before it was finally established at the Academy of Natural Sciences and many of the type specimens were hopelessly damaged by dermestids.

BIBLIOGRAPHY

I. ORIGINAL WORKS. Say's two major works were *American Conchology*, 6 vols. (New Harmony, 1830–1834), and *American Entomology; or Descriptions of the Insects of North America*, 3 vols. (Philadelphia, 1817–1828); both are classics in their fields. His first publication of shells (the first by an American) was "Conchology," in *Nicholson's British Encyclopedia*, American ed. (1816–1817). Say's papers on insects were gathered into *The Complete Writings of Thomas Say on the Entomology of North America*, John L. LeConte, ed., 2 vols. (New York, 1859), with biography by George Ord. Some of Say's descriptions of specimens and some of his narratives are included in the reports of Long's two expeditions.

II. SECONDARY LITERATURE. For accounts of Say's prominence in early American science, see William J.

Youmans, *Pioneers of Science in America* (New York, 1896), 215–222; and Bernard Jaffe, *Men of Science in America* (New York, 1944), 130–153. See also William H. Dall, "Some American Conchologists," in *Proceedings of the Biological Society of Washington,* **4** (1888), 98–102; and E. O. Essig, *A History of Entomology* (New York, 1931), 750–756.

ELIZABETH NOBLE SHOR

SCALIGER (BORDONIUS), JULIUS CAESAR (*b.* Padua, Italy, 23/24 April 1484; *d.* Agen, France, 21 October 1558), *natural philosophy, medicine, botany.*

An evident desire to claim noble descent led Julius Caesar Bordonius (later called Scaliger) and his son, the great classical scholar Joseph Justus Scaliger, to trace their origins to the della Scala family, sometime rulers of Verona. Conveniently for the Scaliger claim, Julius Caesar's family died out around 1512, which thus made it difficult for contemporaries to verify the alleged genealogy. Although the Scaliger account has been widely accepted, recent research has exposed the elaborate camouflage surrounding Julius Caesar's birth and early life.

According to the Scaligers' version, Julius Caesar was born at Riva on Lake Garda on 23/24 April 1484. The parents were held to be Benedetto and Berenice Scaliger (della Scala). Julius was named Caesar at the insistence of Paul of Middelburg, the noted astronomer and astrologer, who had cast the infant's horoscope. Styling himself Count of Burden, Julius Caesar fought in the Imperial army against the Venetians, hereditary enemies of the della Scala. Afterward he toyed with monastic life at Bologna in the hope of becoming pope and of regaining the family property but, disillusioned, quit the monastery for the University of Bologna, where he studied Aristotelian philosophy and physics, before reentering the army. During his second tour, Julius Caesar studied medicine and collected medicinal herbs in northern Italy. Following his second military retirement, Scaliger in 1524 accompanied, as personal physician, Bishop Antonio della Rovere to Agen in southern France.

After the departure for Agen in 1524, the details of Scaliger's life are not in dispute, but the account of the period before 1524 is open to doubt. Although Scaliger was probably born in 1484, it was not at Riva but at Padua. His father was Benedetto Bordon, an expert illuminator of manuscripts and a

graphic artist, and also an astronomer and geographer who had perhaps known Paul of Middelburg, when the latter was teaching at Padua in 1479. The Bordon family was of Paduan, not Veronese, stock, although it is possible that Scaliger's father held dual Paduan and Veronese citizenship. Certainly there is no possibility that Scaliger was a true descendant of the della Scala.

Scaliger seems to have grown up in his father's household at nearby Venice and may have entered a Franciscan convent there. It is conceivable that he knew the architect and mathematician Fra Giovanni Giocondo, also a Franciscan, who was at Venice after 1506. If Scaliger's tales of military service are largely true, then he was fighting from 1509 to 1515 and may, as he says, have fought at the great battle of Ravenna in 1512. After leaving the army, Scaliger did not go to the University of Bologna but to the University of Padua, where, as "Giulio, son of Benedetto Bordon," he received the doctorate in arts in 1519 and the following year seems to have been appointed lecturer in logic, a post that he did not accept. The refusal of the appointment may have been due to his pursuit of a doctorate in medicine, although there is no proof of Scaliger's medical degree. There is evidence, however, that Scaliger was working at Venice (1521–1524) on a translation of Plutarch that was published there in 1525. Interestingly, Joseph Justus Scaliger implied that his father had studied at Padua (despite his banishment from the city as a della Scala), when he said that his father had been taught mathematics by Pomponazzi as well as by Luca Gaurico. Scaliger himself claimed that his instructors in philosophy had included Marc'Antonio Zimara, Nifo, and Pomponazzi, all of whom were teachers at Padua.

After his arrival at Agen in 1524, Scaliger entered a new life as "Julius Caesar de l'Escale de Bordons." He became a well-known and respected physician and in March 1528 was naturalized as a French citizen. In April 1529 he married Andiette de la Roque Lobejac, who bore him fifteen children and was reckoned a restraining influence on Scaliger's combativeness. Active in civic life, Scaliger served as consul of Agen (1532–1533). In 1538, as a Huguenot sympathizer, he was summoned before the Inquisition but was acquitted. (Scaliger's *Poetics* and his commentaries on Theophrastus were later placed on the *Index of Prohibited Books.*) The Huguenot historian Théodore de Bèze regarded Scaliger's career as a paradigm of the relation between enlightened intellectual views and Protestantism. After prolonged attacks of gout, Scaliger died at Agen in 1558, possessed of a European reputation.

Scaliger first established his fame by a savage literary attack (Paris, 1531) on the satire of Erasmus against the Ciceronian stylists (1528). Later Scaliger wrote the more lasting *Poetics*, which represents a reworking of Aristotelian aesthetics in order to form an important early statement of neoclassicism. Among Scaliger's literary friends were Pierre de Ronsard, François Rabelais (for a time), and George Buchanan. (Scaliger's *De causis linguae Latinae* [1540] has been termed the first modern scientific attempt at a Latin grammar.)

The creative approach to classical thought is manifest in Scaliger's writings on botany. Scaliger sought to advance botany and simples by his admirable editions of three ancient treatises: the *De plantis* of pseudo-Aristotle (Nicolaus of Damascus) and the two works of Theophrastus on plants. All three works benefit from the editor's knowledge of actual specimens. The dedication of the pseudo-Aristotelian treatise (all were published posthumously) remarks that seasonal and regional variations make it difficult to identify European plants with classical descriptions, many of the regional variations also being vague or erroneous. Scaliger tried to effect a new and more consistent classification of plants but feared that ignorant physicians would continue to adhere to the older descriptions. Elsewhere he remarked: "It is necessary to submit everything to examination [and] not to embrace anything with servile adulation. The ancients must not put a brake on us."

In medicine Scaliger considered himself an empirical Averroist, who relied upon observation and experience rather than system. "I should like men of learning to become un-complex again and no longer consider themselves members of systematic schools." Scaliger's medical skills secured his appointment as physician to the king of Navarre (1548–1549). On account of Scaliger's reputation, many students eager for instruction, including Nostradamus and Rabelais, were attracted to Agen. The relationship between Scaliger and Rabelais was exacerbated by their conceit and by Rabelais's preference for systematic "ancient" medicine. Although Rabelais left Agen in 1530 to study under Scaliger's rival at Montpellier, the Rabelais-Scaliger hostility continued for decades. Rabelais's lampoon of "entelechy" and "endelechy" in *Gargantua and Pantagruel* (book V, chapter 19) seems directed at his former mentor's proneness to philosophize.

Scaliger was proud of his disputatious nature. In the *Exotericarum exercitationum* (1557) he wrote: "Vives maintains that silent meditation is more profitable than dispute. This is not true. Truth is brought forth by a collision of minds, as fire by a collision of stones. Unless I discover an antagonist, I can do nothing successfully." As Scaliger made his reputation by an attack on Erasmus, so he confirmed it with a spirited critique of Cardano's *De subtilitate libri XXI*. The *Exotericarum exercitationum* runs to well over 1,200 pages. When Cardano failed to reply immediately, Scaliger, believing a false rumor that Cardano had died, was stricken with remorse and wrote a funeral oration in which he repented for the onslaught on his late opponent. Ironically, Cardano published his reply two years after Scaliger's death.

Scaliger based his critique on a reprint (Lyons, 1554) of the first edition of *De subtilitate*, rather than the revised second edition (Basel, 1554) (perhaps because of difficulty of access to the latter). The full title of the *Exotericarum exercitationum* implies that the critique is merely the fifteenth book of Scaliger's philosophical exercises (the first fourteen remained unpublished). Following its target, the work ranges over the whole of natural philosophy. In astronomy Scaliger ridiculed Cardano's stress on the astrological significance of comets; and he denied that the world's decay is proven because the apse of the sun was thirty-one semidiameters nearer the earth than in Ptolemy's time. Scaliger also rejected several of Cardano's beliefs in natural history: that the swan sings at its death; that gems have occult virtues ("a flea has more virtue than all the gems"); that there exist corporeal spirits that eat; that the bear forms its cub by licking; and that the peacock is ashamed of its ugly legs. Like Cardano, Scaliger was aware that lead and tin gain in weight during calcination, although he preferred to explain the increase as a result of the addition of particles of fire to the metal.

In order to refute Cardano's theory of the origin of mountain springs, Scaliger used the strange argument that the sea is not in its natural place, since earth should be nearer than water to the center of the earth. Consequently, seawater presses upward, emerging sometimes through superior earth as a mountain spring. This view, of course, failed to account for the difference in salinity between sea and mountain water.

Scaliger casts aside Cardano's Aristotelian view that the medium is a motive force. This view is refuted experimentally when a thin wooden disk, cut from a plank, is set to spin within the plank. According to Scaliger, the air between the disk and the surrounding plank is insufficient to act as a motive force, as postulated by the Aristotelians. Instead, as an admirer of Parisian dynamics, Scaliger preferred to use the impetus theory (which he called *motio*). Following Albert of Saxony and Jean Buridan, Scaliger stated that accelerated motion is a result of a persisting gravity within the moving body. This gravity generates from instant to instant a new impetus, which, intensifying, produces acceleration. The impetus, although evanescent, is an efficient cause, and as such need not be coterminous with the effect.

The *Exotericarum exercitationum* won a celebrity that survived its author's death. Lipsius, Bacon, and Leibniz were among its later admirers; and Kepler, who read it as a young man, accepted its Averroist doctrine of attributing the movement of each star to a particular intelligence.

BIBLIOGRAPHY

I. ORIGINAL WORKS. Scaliger's works and commentaries include *Hippocratis liber de somniis cum J. C. Scaligeri commentariis* (Lyons, 1539, 1561, 1610, 1659); *In libros duos, qui inscribuntur de plantis, Aristotele autore, libri duo* (Paris, 1556; Geneva, 1566; Marburg, 1598); *Exotericarum exercitationum liber XV. De subtilitate ad Hieronymum Cardanum* (Paris, 1557); *Commentarii et animadversiones in sex libros de causis plantarum Theophrasti* (Geneva, 1566); *M. Manilii astronomicon cum commentariis J. C. Scaligeri* (Paris, 1579, 1590, 1599, 1600, 1655); *Animadversiones in Theophrasti historias plantarum* (Lyons, 1584, 1644); and *Aristotelis de animalibus historia J. C. Scaligeri interprete cum eiusdem commentariis* (Toulouse, 1619).

The funeral oration for Cardano is in *Epistolae aliquot nunc primum vulgatae*, Joseph Justus Scaliger, ed. (Toulouse, 1620–1621), 63–66. Other writings of Scaliger are in *Epistolae et orationes*, F. Donsa, ed. (Leiden, 1600). Autograph codices by Scaliger in the Bibliothèque Universitaire, Leiden, include MSS Scaligerani 18 (Galen in Greek); 27 (Latin miscellany); 34 (Aristotle, *De animalibus*, dated 17 Dec. 1538); and MS Graecus 44 (autographed letters). For the Scaligerani from the collection of Joseph Justus, see *Bibliotheca Universitatis Leidensis: codices manuscripti. II, codices Scaligerani* (Leiden, 1910). Cardano's reply to Scaliger, "Actio prima in calumniatorem librorum de subtilitate," was first published in *De subtilitate*, 3rd ed. (Basel, 1560), 1265–1426; cf. Girolamo Cardano, *De vita propria*, (Paris, 1643), ch. 48.

II. SECONDARY LITERATURE. On Scaliger and his work, see Joseph Justus Scaliger, *Epistolae* (Leiden, 1627), which includes the misleading life of Julius Caesar; and V. Hall, Jr., "The Life of Julius Caesar Scaliger (1484–1558)," in *Transactions of the American Philosophical Society*, n.s. **40** (1950), 85–170. The Scaliger version is refuted by P. O. Kristeller, in his review of Hall in *American Historical Review*, **107** (1952), 394–396; and by J. F. C. Richards, "The Elysium of Julius Caesar Bordonius (Scaliger)," in *Studies in the Renaissance*, 9 (1962), 195–217. Much new material appears in Myriam Billanovich, "Benedetto Bordon e Giulio Cesare Scaligero," in *Italia medioevale e umanistica*, **11** (1968), 187–256. For the botanical commentaries, see Charles B. Schmitt, "Theophrastus," in *Catalogus Translationum: Mediaeval and Renaissance Latin Commentaries and Translations*, P. O. Kristeller and F. Edward Cranz, eds., II (Washington, D.C., 1971), 239–322, 269–271, 274–275. Remarks on Scaliger's natural philosophy appear in Pierre Duhem, *Études sur Léonard de Vinci*, 3 vols. (Paris, 1906–1913), esp. I, 240–244; III, 198–204.

PAUL LAWRENCE ROSE

SCARPA, ANTONIO (*b.* Motta di Livenza, near Treviso, Italy, 19 May 1752; *d.* Pavia, Italy, 31 October 1832), *anatomy, neurology.*

Scarpa was an eminent anatomist, a skilled surgeon, and one of the powerful teachers at Pavia University during its period of greatest renown. The child of Giuseppe Scarpa, a boatman, and Francesca Corder, he was taught by his paternal uncle, Canon Paolo Scarpa. It was only with great financial difficulty that in 1766 he entered the University of Padua, where he became a favorite of Morgagni. After graduating on 31 May 1770, he assisted Morgagni until his death in December 1771. Scarpa was next helped by Girolamo Vandelli, physician to the duke of Modena; and by October 1772 he had been appointed professor of anatomy at Modena University and chief surgeon of the military hospital in that city. He worked at Modena for eleven years, the happiest of his academic life; it was there that he laid the foundations for his major work, which was carried out at Pavia. Highly esteemed for his brilliance, Scarpa had a true anatomical amphitheater built at Modena (it is still in existence); and in 1781 he obtained permission and funds for a study trip to Paris and London. In Paris he met the anatomist Félix Vicq d'Azyr and J. A. von Brambilla (1728–1800), surgeon-superintendent of the Imperial Austrian army; in London, the brothers William and John Hunter.

In 1783, through the assistance of Brambilla, Scarpa was named to the chair of anatomy at Pavia, where he gave his inaugural lecture on 25 November 1783, "Oratio de promovendis anatomicarum administrationum rationibus." At Pavia, Scarpa was responsible for the construction of a new, enlarged anatomical amphitheater. To show his gratitude to Brambilla, Scarpa, accompanied by Volta, went in the summer of 1784 to Vienna, where he performed some anatomical demonstrations and repeated his blood-transfusion experiments on sheep. From 1787 to 1812 he was in charge of teaching clinical surgery; in 1803, after thirty years, he gave up the teaching of anatomy. His fame was so great that in 1805 he was personally complimented by Napoleon; and in 1815 the restored Austrian government appointed him director of the medical school at Pavia, a post he held until 1818.

Scarpa also wrote and edited many works; from 1772 to 1825 he spent much of the money earned from his profession on the printing of his works. He retained an admirable clearness of mind even at a very advanced age, as is shown in his two letters *De gangliis* (1831) to Ernst Heinrich Weber. Possessor of the highest honors (he was a member of the Paris Academy, the Leopoldina, and the Royal Society), he died, unmarried, in his own home and was buried in the basilica of San Michele in Pavia.

All of Scarpa's work bears the unmistakable mark of his exacting personality. In his description of surgical procedures (amputation, the removal of cataracts, perineal cutting for the urinary calculi), the technique is always related to precise and very detailed anatomical description. In his monumental atlas on hernia (1809), he masterfully described the exact structure of the inguinal canal ("Memoria prima," sections 2–10) and of the crural ring ("Memoria terza," sections 2–4), as well as the disposition of the parts today known as the "triangle of Scarpa." His essay (1784) on freemartins was a pioneer study of hermaphroditism. His pathological works on diseases of the eye and on aneurysm were remarkable. Scarpa's greatest works, however—those that established him as a scientist—were in descriptive anatomy. His great skill in the use of the microscope is shown in his microscopical observations on nerve ganglia (1799) and on bones (1799). But above all he was a fine dissector and made his own anatomical drawings, which were engraved in copper by Faustino Anderloni.

Scarpa began his scientific activity with comparative investigation of the ear, suggested to him by Morgagni, *De structura fenestrae rotundae auris, et de tympano secundario . . .* (1772); for man and for the hen and pig he gave a more accurate and complete description of the osseous labyrinth and demonstrated the true function of the round window. In 1789 Scarpa made his historic observations on the membrane labyrinth, which he discov-

ered together with its endolymph (the perilymph had been discovered in 1761 by Domenico Cotugno). He also discovered the vestibule, which is admirably depicted by Anderloni in the 1794 edition of *Anatomicae disquisitiones de auditu . . . .* Scarpa precisely described the membrane semicircular canals with their ampullae and the utricle, and discovered the vestibular nerve and its ganglion (named for him [Herrick, 1928]). He was even able to observe the microscopical structure of the ampullae and identify the origin of the fibers of the vestibular nerve. Probably Scarpa had also observed the neurosensorial structure of the otolithic membrane. He accurately illustrated the course of the human acoustic nerve from the cochlea to the rhombencephalon. Enthusiasm for his own discoveries, however, led Scarpa to the mistaken affirmation that the semicircular canals are the organ of hearing. As early as 1672 Thomas Willis had correctly stated that the cochlea is the essential organ of hearing.

At about the same time Scarpa conducted research on the olfactory apparatus. His *De organo olfactus praecipuo . . .* (1785) presented the first illustration of the human olfactory nerves, olfactory bulbs, and olfactory tracts, as well as of the sphenopalatine ganglion (described by Johann Meckel the elder in 1748) and of the interior nasal nerves. He also documented his discovery of the human nasopalatine nerve. Scarpa was the first to provide a clear comparative anatomical illustration of the olfactory apparatus in the dogfish, reptiles, birds, and mammals.

These classic works on the auditory and olfactory apparatus were part of a broad plan of research on the nervous system, the premise of which had been set forth in Scarpa's *De nervorum gangliis et plexubus* (1779), the first accurate analysis of these nerve structures. Scarpa also was the first to distinguish the spinal (*ganglia simplicia*) from the sympathetic ganglia (*ganglia composita*) and to demonstrate that the spinal ganglia are formed only on the dorsal roots of the spinal nerves. Further, he stated that the ganglia of thoracic-lumbar sympathetic nerves are connected to the ventral roots of the spinal nerves only.

By 1779 Scarpa had established the foundation upon which he developed his great neurological work. In 1787 he studied the connection between the vagus nerve and its accessory, as acknowledged by Claude Bernard. According to Willis, the accessory nerve originated from the cervical spinal cord only, but Scarpa was the first to demonstrate that the accessory is also formed by fibers arising from the medulla oblongata. Scarpa's masterpiece was his *Tabulae . . . neurologicae* (1794), with seven life-size plates engraved in copper by Anderloni that illustrate the human glossopharyngeal, vagus, and hypoglossal nerves. Of particular interest are the two plates on the cardiac nerves, which were also a reply to arbitrary statements made by the physician Johann Bernard Behrends, who supported the views of Albrecht von Haller on the "irritability" of the heart. The latter was considered to be an autonomous contractile property and hence independent of sensibility; contractility and irritability were, in Haller's opinion, identical. This view formed one of the points of disagreement for Felice Fontana, who published his *De irritabilitatis legibus* in 1767. But Behrends also denied the existence of cardiac nerves and in 1792 published a book to show that the heart lacks nerves. In his plates Scarpa very accurately demonstrated the number, origin, and course of cardiac nerves. He also stated that the heart is richly supplied with its own nerve structures, that all of its nerves have ganglia, and that the terminal ramifications of the cardiac nerves are directly connected to cardiac muscular fibers. Scarpa thus decisively first demonstrated cardiac innervation.

BIBLIOGRAPHY

I. ORIGINAL WORKS. Earlier writings by Scarpa are *De structura fenestrae rotundae auris, et de tympano secundario anatomicae observationes* (Modena, 1772); *Anatomicarum annotationum liber primus. De nervorum gangliis et plexubus* (Modena, 1779); "Osservazione anatomica sopra un vitello-vacca detto dagli Inglesi Freemartin," in *Memorie di matematica e di fisica della Società italiana delle scienze*, **2**, pt. 2 (1784), 846–852; *Anatomicarum annotationum liber secundus. De Organo olfactus praecipuo deque nervis nasalibus interioribus e pari quinto nervorum cerebri* (Pavia, 1785); "Abhandlung über den zum achten Paar der Gehirnnerven hinlaufenden Beynerven der Rückgräte," in *Abhandlungen der K. K. Medizinisch-chirurgischen Josephs-Akademie*, **1** (1787), 15–45, translated into Italian by Albrecht von Schoenberg as *Trattato sopra il nervo accessorio decorrente all'ottavo paio de' nervi cerebrali* (Naples, 1817); *Anatomicae disquisitiones de auditu et olfactu* (Pavia, 1789; Milan, 1794); *Tabulae ad illustrandam historiam anatomicam cardiacorum nervorum, noni nervorum cerebri, glossopharyngaei et pharyngaei ex octavo cerebri* (Pavia, 1794); and *De penitiori ossium structura commentarius* (Leipzig, 1799), repr. as *De anatome et pathologia ossium commentarii* (Pavia, 1827).

Later works are *Saggio di osservazioni e di esperienze sulle principali malattie degli occhi* (Pavia, 1801), 5th ed., enl., repr. as *Trattato delle principali malattie degli occhi*, 2 vols. (Pavia, 1816); *Memoria chirurgica sui piedi torti congeniti dei fanciulli e sulla maniera di correggere questa deformità* (Pavia, 1803; 2nd ed., enl., Pavia, 1806); *Osservazioni anatomico-chirurgiche sull'aneurisma* (Pavia, 1804), translated into English by John Henry Wishart as *A Treatise on the Anatomy, Pathology and Surgical Treatment of Aneurism* (Edinburgh, 1808); *Memorie anatomico-chirurgiche sulle ernie* (Milan, 1809; Pavia, 1819), translated into French, German, and English; *Elogio storico di Leon Battista Carcano 1536–1606 professore di notomia nella Università di Pavia* (Milan, 1813); *Memoria sulla legatura delle principali arterie degli arti* (Pavia, 1817); *Sull'ernia del perineo* (Pavia, 1821); *Memoria sull'idrocele del cordone spermatico* (Pavia, 1823); *Memoria sulla gravidanza susseguita da ascite* (Pavia, 1825); *Osservazioni sul taglio retto-vescicale per l'estrazione della pietra della vescica orinaria* (Milan, 1826); *De gangliis nervorum deque origine et essentia nervi intercostalis ad illustrem virum Henricum Weber anatomicum Lipsiensem epistola* (Pavia, 1831); *De gangliis deque utriusque ordinis nervorum per universum corpus distributione ad illustrem virum Henricum Weber anatomicum Lipsiensem epistola altera* (Pavia, 1831); and *Opuscoli di chirurgia*, 3 vols. (Pavia, 1825–1832), reprint of all his minor surgical notes.

Posthumously published works are *Opere del Cavaliere Antonio Scarpa*, Pietro Vannoni, ed., 5 pts. in 2 vols. (Florence, 1836–1838); *Atlante di tutte le opere del Professore Antonio Scarpa*, (Florence, 1839); and *Epistolario: 1772–1832* (Pavia, 1938), which contains Scarpa's autobiography and a collection of his 659 letters, reprinted in their original text.

Portraits of Antonio Scarpa are in his *Opere* (1836) and *Epistolario*; and in Favaro, *Antonio Scarpa*; Franceschini; Ovio; Politzer; and Putti.

II. SECONDARY LITERATURE. See J. B. Behrends, *Dissertatio anatomico-physiologica qua demonstratur cor nervis carere* (Mainz, 1792); Claude Bernard, *Leçons sur la physiologie et la pathologie du système nerveux*, II (Paris, 1858), 271; M. Brazier, "Felice Fontana," in *Essays on the History of Italian Neurology. International Symposium on the History of Neurology . . .* (Milan, 1963), 107–116; P. Capparoni, *Spallanzani* (Turin, 1941), 101–114; G. Chiarugi, "Triangolo femorale dello Scarpa," in his *Istituzioni di anatomia dell'uomo*, II (Milan, 1924), 226–228; G. Favaro, "Antonio Scarpa e l'Università di Padova," in *Atti del Istituto veneto di scienze, lettere ed arti*, **91** (1931), 1–22; "Antonio Scarpa e i Caldani," *ibid.* 23–37; "Il 'Publicum doctoratus privilegium' di Antonio Scarpa," in *Rivista di storia delle scienze mediche e naturali*, **23** (1932), 193–204; "Antonio Scarpa e Michele Girardi," in *Valsalva*, **8** (1932), 742–748; *Antonio Scarpa e l'Università di Modena* (Modena, 1932); "I primi periodi della vita e della carriera di Antonio Scarpa descritti da un suo curriculum autografo," in *Bollettino dell'Istituto storico italiano dell'arte sanitaria*, **13** (1933), 29–32;

and "Antonio Scarpa nella storia dell'anatomia," in *Monitore zoologico italiano,* **43** (1933), supp., 29–43; P. Franceschini, *L'opera nevrologica di Antonio Scarpa* (Florence, 1962); C. J. Herrick, *An Introduction to Neurology* (Philadelphia, 1928), 399; G. Levi, *I gangli cerebrospinali* (Florence, 1908); G. Ovio, *L'oculistica di Antonio Scarpa e due secoli di storia,* 2 vols. (Naples, 1936); A. Politzer, "Antonio Scarpa," in his *Geschichte der Ohrenheilkunde,* I (Stuttgart, 1907), 260–271; and V. Putti, "Opere dello Scarpa riguardanti argomenti di anatomia e chirurgia dell'apparato motore," in *Biografie di chirurghi del XVI e XIX secolo* (Bologna, 1941), 24–28.

PIETRO FRANCESCHINI

SCHAEBERLE, JOHN MARTIN (*b.* Württemberg, Germany, 10 January 1853; *d.* Ann Arbor, Michigan, 17 September 1924), *practical astronomy.*

Schaeberle's most important work was with astronomical instruments. He devised new apparatus, particularly for astronomical photography; he figured mirrors and constructed telescopes; he investigated instrumental errors and atmospheric conditions; and he used instruments to good advantage. For this he was well trained, first as a machinist's apprentice and later as a civil engineer at the University of Michigan. Following graduation in 1876, Schaeberle spent twelve years at the university observatory before moving to Mt. Hamilton, California, as one of the original staff members of the Lick Observatory. For a brief period in 1897 Schaeberle served as acting director of Lick; then, after traveling around the world, he retired to Ann Arbor.

Schaeberle's early studies of comets included computations of their orbits and, with the aid of reflecting telescopes of his own construction, the discovery of two comets in 1880 and 1881. At Lick, Schaeberle turned to photography of stars, planets, nebulae, and solar eclipses. His visual observations led to his discovery in 1896 of the thirteenth-magnitude companion of Procyon.

During four eclipses—in California in 1889; at Cayenne, French Guiana, in 1889; at Mina Bronces, Chile, in 1893; and in Japan in 1896—Schaeberle took excellent large-scale photographs. From these he developed a mechanical theory of the solar corona (as opposed to the magnetic theories then widely discussed), according to which ejection of matter from the sun and its subsequent movement in a conic section accounted for the apparent structure of the corona.

Other theories expounded by Schaeberle, with perhaps more vigor than reason, concerned the history of the earth. He argued, for instance, that the inherent heat of the earth, not of the sun, controls the temperature of the earth, and that the sun is the parent body of the sidereal as well as of the solar system.

BIBLIOGRAPHY

The most extensive list of Schaeberle's published articles is in the Royal Society *Catalogue of Scientific Papers,* XI, 297; XVIII, 477–479.

Secondary literature includes W. J. Hussey, "John Martin Schaeberle," in *Publications, Astronomical Society of the Pacific,* **36** (1924), 309–312; a biography in *Dictionary of American Biography,* XVI, 412; and John A. Eddy, "The Schaeberle 40-ft. Eclipse Camera of Lick Observatory," in *Journal for the History of Astronomy,* **2** (1971), 1–22.

DEBORAH JEAN WARNER

SCHAFER. See **Sharpey-Schäfer, Edward Albert.**

SCHARDT, HANS (*b.* Basel, Switzerland, 18 June 1858; *d.* Zurich, Switzerland, 3 February 1931), *geology.*

Schardt was interested in natural history from the time he was a schoolboy in Basel. He entered the University of Lausanne to prepare himself for a career in pharmacy, but during his practical training at Yverdon (Vaud) he became acquainted with Édouard Desor and Auguste Jaccard, professors of geology at the University of Neuchâtel, who diverted his attention to the earth sciences. The structure and stratigraphy of the nearby Jura mountains provided Schardt with an excellent field for his researches, so that by the time he returned to Lausanne, geology had begun to become an increasingly important part of his studies. He received the diploma in both pharmacy and science in 1883, then, in the following year, presented at the University of Geneva a thesis entitled "Étude géologique sur le Pays-d'Enhaut Vaudois," for which he was awarded the D.Sc. He then took a job as science master at the *collège* at Montreux, which was admirably situated to allow him to continue his study of the Prealps. Schardt won four academic prizes between 1879 and 1891, the year in which he became a lecturer in geology at the University of Lausanne. In order to increase his knowledge of the subject, he undertook further studies, in 1892–1893, at the University of Heidelberg, where his teachers included Harry Rosenbusch.

In 1897 Schardt was called to the University of Neuchâtel to succeed Léon du Pasquier as professor of geology and paleontology. He was given only modest means with which to create a department, and devoted a considerable amount of his time to this task, spending Sundays and holidays on field trips. He soon began to take an active part in Neuchâtel scientific circles, and published a number of his observations in the series Mélanges Géologiques, edited by the Société Neuchâteloise des Sciences Naturelles. In 1911 Schardt left Neuchâtel for Zurich, where he had accepted an appointment as professor at both the Swiss Federal Polytechnical Institute and at the university. He also served as director of the university geological collections and, for several years, was concerned in organizing a department of geology and supervising the construction of new buildings to house it. He remained at Zurich for seventeen years; upon his retirement in 1928 he was succeeded by Rudolf Staub. He continued to do field research and to climb mountains until the year before he died of a stroke at the age of seventy-three.

Schardt's research encompassed tectonics, hydrology, stratigraphy, and engineering geology. His most important work, however, lay in his discovery of the older, rootless exotic complexes of the Alps, which, floating on younger series, led him to the hypothesis concerning the great alpine mass displacements that became known as the nappe theory.

Schardt's early research had made him familiar with the puzzling problem of the Prealps in which, from the Stockhorn in the east to the Chablais in the west, the Mesozoic series exhibits quite different facies from those of the surrounding mountains, so that it is obvious that they cannot have been laid down in the same basin. He made the complex flysch series of this region, which contains exotic blocks, the subject of his 1891 prize paper "Versuch einer Bahnbrechung zur Lösung der Flyschfrage und zur Entdeckung der Herkunft der exotischen Blöcke im Flysch."

In 1891–1893 Schardt, drawing upon his extensive knowledge of the geology of the area and influenced by the ideas of Marcel Bertrand, became convinced that the stratigraphical series of the Prealps had been deposited in basins far to the south, and had slid into their present position. This view was at a considerable variance with the geological thought of his contemporaries, and was greeted with, at best, condescension. The nappe theory found greater acceptance around 1903, when it had been developed and extended by Lugeon. It is interesting to note that it was not Schardt's original sliding theory (nappes du charriage) that then gained currency, but rather the thrusting theory (tectonique de poussée); Schardt's own hypothesis, as he himself had predicted, was fully accepted only after a number of years. In the meantime, Argand drew upon Schardt's studies of Jurassic folding, thrusting, and strike-slip faults for his own theory of cover folds (nappes de récouvrement).

Schardt did other important work in the exploration of the Simplon area, where he advised on the construction of the Simplon tunnel. He made observations of the recumbent folds of this metamorphosed area and described the springs that the tunnelers encountered, showing that these waters circulated in a highly complex manner, since both hot and cold springs can simultaneously flow from the same fissure. He applied his structural knowledge and analytical methods to a number of other hydrological problems, and he distinguished a number of modes of water circulation. He was particularly interested in karst hydrology and subterranean exsolution, and acted as consultant to a number of European countries on improving their water supplies. Schardt further demonstrated his expertise in both hydrology and engineering geology by advising on dam sites, landslides, and related phenomena; he was also concerned with discovering the correlations among geological structure, lithology, and the regime and chemical qualities of waters.

Schardt was vigorous and tenacious, a combination that allowed him to weather the disappointing years in which his nappe theory was scorned. His students were impressed by the force of his will and by his unfailing optimism; if he had decided to take them on a field trip, it was never postponed on account of bad weather. Schardt instead looked doggedly for a rift in the clouds, and, in deepening darkness, sought fossils by the light of matches. While reserved indoors, in the field Schardt became warm and even enthusiastic. He influenced his students by his toughness and capacity for hard work; he taught in both French and German, and supervised some sixty theses. He retained his early interest in plants and their properties, probably a relic of his pharmacological studies, and although not overly fond of alcoholic beverages nevertheless liked the bitter spirits prepared from the roots of the yellow gentian plant.

BIBLIOGRAPHY

I. ORIGINAL WORKS. Schardt published almost 200 papers and nine major geological maps. His most important writings include "Théorie des plis déjetés et couchés des Dents du Midi et des Tours Saillères," in *Bulletin de la Société neuchâteloise des sciences naturelles* (1890); "Sur la géologie du massif du Simplon," *ibid.,* **27** (1891); "L'origine des Alpes du Chablais et du Stockhorn, en Savoie et en Suisse," in *Comptes rendus hebdomadaires des séances de l'Académie des sciences,* **117** (1893); "Compte rendu de l'excursion au travers des Alpes de la Suisse occidentale," in *Comptes rendus du VIᵉ Congrès géologique international à Zurich* (1896); "L'origine des régions exotiques et des Klippes du versant N. des Alpes suisses et leurs relations avec les blocs exotiques et les brèches du Flysch," in *Archives des sciences physiques et naturelles de Genève* (1897); "Note sur le profil géologique et la tectonique du massif du Simplon, comparés aux travaux antérieurs," in *Eclogae geologicae helvetiae,* **8** (1904); "Les causes du plissement et des chauvements dans le Jura," *ibid.,* **10,** no. 4 (1908); "Neue Gesichtspunkte der Geologie. Antrittsrede als Professor der Geologie an der Universität Zurich," in *Mitteilungen der Naturforschenden Gesellschaft in Winterthur,* **9** (1911); "Unsere heutigen Kenntnisse vom Bau und von der Entstehung der Alpen. (Autorreferat)," in *Sitzungsberichte der Naturforschenden Gesellschaft in Zürich,* **71** (1926); and "Zur Kritik der Wegenerschen Theorie der Kontinentenverschiebung. (Autorreferat)," *ibid.* (1928).

II. SECONDARY LITERATURE. On Schardt and his works, see J. Leuba, "Le professeur Hans Schardt," in *Bulletin de la Société neuchâteloise des sciences naturelles,* n.s. **56** (1932), 103–119; and Hans Suter, "Professor Dr. Hans Schardt zu seinem 70. Geburtstag am 18 Juni, 1928," in *Vierteljahrsschrift der Naturforschenden Gesellschaft in Zürich,* **73** (1928), 375–388; and "Prof. Dr. Hans Schardt," in *Verhandlungen der Schweizerischen naturforschenden Gesellschaft,* **112** (1931), 411–422. All contain portraits and bibliographies, and the last contains a complete list of Schardt's works.

EUGENE WEGMANN

SCHAUDINN, FRITZ RICHARD (*b.* Röseningken, Germany, 19 September 1871; *d.* Hamburg, Germany, 22 June 1906), *zoology, medicine.*

Schaudinn's brief but highly successful career in the late nineteenth century and early twentieth century revealed the growing importance of protozoology for an understanding of various contemporary medical problems. His research on the etiologic agents of malaria and amebiasis was precise and accurate. The culmination of Schaudinn's investigations was the discovery of the microorganism responsible for venereal syphilis, first named *Spirochaeta pallida,* later *Treponema pallidum* or Schaudinn's bacillus. This important accomplishment greatly facilitated the subsequent development of an effective method of treating the disease.

The only son of an old East Prussian family of farmers, Schaudinn demonstrated in early childhood an interest in the natural world around him by systematically collecting plants, insects, and small animals. During his education in the cities of Insterburg (now Chernyakhovsk, U.S.S.R.) and Gumbinnen (now Gusev, U.S.S.R.), he showed considerable affection for both physics and chemistry. Schaudinn was a voracious reader with broad interests, especially in German philology, which led him to matriculate in philosophy at the University of Berlin in 1890. Soon he shifted his attention to the natural sciences, especially zoology; and under the direction of Schulze, he concentrated on the study of protozoa.

In 1894, after receiving a doctorate in the natural sciences from the university (he wrote a dissertation on a new genus of Foraminifera), Schaudinn participated in a highly successful expedition to Bergen, Norway, to study Arctic fauna. Upon his return he was appointed assistant at the Zoological Institute of the University of Berlin, where he intensified his protozoological studies. During the next four years, he published a number of papers dealing with the reproductive cycles of lower organisms such as the Coccidia and Haemosporidia.

In 1898 Schaudinn successfully defended his *Habilitationsschrift,* which was concerned with the importance of protozoological research on the cell theory, and he became a *Privatdozent* at the University of Berlin. In the same year he made another expedition to the Arctic. Unlike France, which had the Pasteur Institute, and Italy, with a Malaria Society, the zoologists, pathologists, and physicians of Germany worked in relative isolation from one another. Schaudinn vigorously promoted contacts between his discipline and medicine. He also stressed the importance of certain protozoa both as parasites of the human organism and as etiologic agents for certain diseases.

As a result of this interest, in 1901 Schaudinn was appointed director of a German-Austrian zoological station located in the town of Rovigno (now Rovinj, Yugoslavia) on the Dalmatian coast. The assignment was the most productive period in Schaudinn's life. He conducted several field studies on malaria in the nearby village of San Michele di Leme, observing the entrance of the sporozoite into the red blood cell. Moreover, Schaudinn clearly revealed the amoebic nature of tropical dysentery. His distinction between the harmless *Entamoeba coli* and the disease-producing *Entamoeba histolytica* was achieved by experimental self-infection with these organisms. Other studies carried out on the trypanosomes and Coccidia led in 1903 to Schaudinn's receiving the Tiedemann Award, although he had published only short abstracts on his findings. In the same year he was joined at Rovigno by Prowazek.

In 1904 Schaudinn was called to Berlin in order to assume the direction of the newly established Institute for Protozoology at the Imperial Ministry of Health. His first assignment was a study of the hookworm disease that affected German miners, and he was one of the first to confirm that the larvae of the parasite gained entrance to the body by actively penetrating the skin of the feet or legs.

During the spring of 1905, Schaudinn was given the task of verifying some experimental work on syphilis carried out by John Siegel under the direction of his former mentor Schulze. The conclusions of this rather dubious research pointed toward a common etiologic agent *(cytorrhyctes luis)* for scarlet fever, smallpox, hoof-and-mouth disease, and syphilis. The joint clinical and parasitological investigation of syphilis was conducted with the help of the dermatology clinic at the Charité Hospital in Berlin. The dermatologist Erich Hoffmann became Schaudinn's clinical consultant and the bacteriologist Fred Neufeld, his assistant.

Soon thereafter, Schaudinn detected a pale-looking spiral-shaped rod among a myriad of other microorganisms contained in a fresh microscopical preparation derived from the fluid of an eroded syphilitic papule. Schaudinn was excited about his finding, although he believed that the organism, named *Spirochaeta pallida,* was probably a saprophyte. Other types of spirochetes were found in subsequent preparations of nonsyphilitic lesions such as condylomas.

Thus, the first report of Schaudinn and Hoffmann dated 10 March 1905 merely pointed out the existence of *Spirochaeta pallida* in syphilitic lesions without ascribing to it any importance as a possible causal factor for the disease in question. Sometime later, Schaudinn was able to differentiate between the coarse and fine spirochetes and observe the *Spirochaeta pallida* in Giemsa-stained microscopical preparations obtained from syphilitic lymph nodes. These more significant findings, reported 17 May 1905 to the Berlin Medical Society, more clearly implicated the microorganism as the etiologic agent of syphilis, since it had been observed in both primary and secondary syphilitic lesions.

Schaudinn remained extremely cautious and, although he was confident of the causal relationship between the *Spirochaeta pallida* and syphilis, he was unconvincing in his presentation of his findings to the Berlin Medical Society on 17 and 25 May. He faced strong opposition from Schulze's followers, and the presiding officer's closing remarks at the meeting reflected the deep skepticism with which Schaudinn's discovery was greeted. The distinguished surgeon Ernst von Bergmann declared the session adjourned "until another agent responsible for syphilis engages our interest."

Soon various investigators in other countries were able to verify the repeated and exclusive presence of the *Spirochaeta pallida* in syphilitic lesions, but no pure cultures of the microorganism could be obtained immediately. Schaudinn received a series of offers to work and teach abroad, notably at the universities of London and Cambridge, but he finally took a leave of absence from his post with the Ministry of Health in order to work in the new protozoology laboratory of the Research Institute for Naval and Tropical Diseases at Hamburg.

The post was confirmed by the senate of Hamburg in early 1906, but Schaudinn's career at the new location was short-lived. From 1904 onward he had suffered from furunculosis, which caused an anal fistula. He died of a rectal abscess and general sepsis shortly after returning from the International Medical Congress in Portugal. Among the honors bestowed upon him were corresponding memberships in the Senckenbergische Naturforschende Gesellschaft (1903), the Imperial Academy of Sciences in St. Petersburg (1905), and the Berlin Society of Internal Medicine (1906).

BIBLIOGRAPHY

I. ORIGINAL WORKS. Schaudinn's most important articles, in a number of journals, have been collected in *Fritz Schaudinns Arbeiten* (Hamburg–Leipzig, 1911), published under the auspices of the Hamburgische Wissenschaftliche Stiftung; with biographical sketch by S. von Prowazek and with a list of all the material that Schaudinn published in his short career. Schaudinn's first paper on the discovery of *Spirochaeta pallida* was dated April 1905 and appeared as "Vorläufiger Bericht über das Vorkommen von Spirochaeten in syphilitischen Krankheitsprodukten und bei Papillomen," in *Arbeiten an das K. Gesundheitsamte,* **22,** no. 2 (1905), 527–534.

The article was shortly thereafter published with the same title in book form (Berlin, 1905). A second paper, also co-authored by Erich Hoffman, reported the findings of *Spirochaeta pallida* in syphilitic lymph nodes: "Ueber Spirochaetenbefunde im Lymphdrüsensaft Syphilitischer," in *Deutsche medizinische Wochenschrift*, **31**, no. 18 (1905), 711–714. See also Schaudinn's report to the Berlin Medical Society, "Ueber Spirochaeta pallida bei Syphilis und die Unterschiede dieser Form gegenüber anderer Arten dieser Gattung," in *Berliner klinische Wochenschrift*, **42**, no. 22 (29 May 1905), 673–675; no. 23 (5 June 1905), 726.

II. Secondary Literature. The best biographical account is Christel Kuhn, *Aus dem Leben Fritz Richard Schaudinns* (Stuttgart, 1949). Although brief, the work is based on extensive archival material and personal interviews with Schaudinn's widow and sister; it contains a small bibliography of secondary sources on Schaudinn and his work.

Shorter biographical sketches are in two obituaries: W. Loewenthal, in *Medizinische Klinik*, **2**, no. 26 (1906), 693–694; and S. von Prowazek, in *Wiener klinische Wochenschrift*, **19** (1906), 880–882. On the occasion of the 25th anniversary of Schaudinn's discovery, the personal recollections of one of his assistants appeared: F. Neufeld, "Zum 25 jährigen Gedenktage der Entdekkung des Syphiliserregers," in *Deutsche medizinische Wochenschrift*, **56** (1930), 710–712. Similar source material is in Erich Hoffmann, *Vorträge und Urkunden zur 25 jährigen Wiederkehr der Entdeckung des Syphiliserregers* (Berlin, 1930), and in A. Schuberg and H. Schlossberger, "Zum 25 Jahrestag der Entdeckung der Spirochaeta Pallida," in *Klinische Wochenschrift*, **9** (1930), 582–586.

See also O. T. Schultz, "Fritz Schaudinn, a Review of His Work," in *Johns Hopkins Hospital Bulletin*, **19** (1908), 169–173; J. H. Stokes, "Schaudinn, a Biographical Appreciation," in *Science*, **74** (1931), 502–506; and a short biographical sketch "Fritz Richard Schaudinn (1871–1906)," in John H. Talbott, ed., *A Biographical History of Medicine* (New York, 1970), 796–798.

Guenter B. Risse

SCHEELE, CARL WILHELM (*b.* Stralsund, Swedish Pomerania, 19 December 1742; *d.* Köping, Sweden, 21 May 1786), *pharmacy, chemistry.*

Scheele was the seventh of eleven children of Jochim Christian Scheel(e) and Margaretha Eleonora Warnekros. Like his oldest brother, Johan Martin, he became interested in pharmacy at an early age and chose it as his career. It is said that while still a boy he was taught how to read prescriptions and to write chemical symbols by two friends of the family in Stralsund, a physician named Schütte and a pharmacist named Cornelius.

After finishing school, which did not include a Gymnasium course, Scheele went to Göteborg in 1757 and began his training in the pharmacy of Martin Bauch, where his brother also had been an apprentice.

Bauch's great influence on Scheele's development has been confirmed by previously unused source material and is supported by the general reputation for competence that Bauch enjoyed among contemporaries as knowledgeable as Linnaeus. Although Bauch was sixty-three years old when Scheele came to him, he was by no means set on outdated alchemical theories—on the contrary, he was aware of new developments in his profession.

Scheele remained with Bauch beyond his six years of apprenticeship, until the pharmacy was sold in 1765. Then he left Göteborg and for the next ten years traveled as a journeyman. In Malmö he found work in a pharmacy run by Peter Magnus Kjellström, who fully understood Scheele's preference for experimental work and allowed him to work in the laboratory of the pharmacy. His stay in Malmö was especially important because of its proximity to the university city of Lund. It gave Scheele his first contact with the academic world through his friendship with Anders Retzius, lecturer in chemistry at the university and the same age as Scheele. The proximity of Copenhagen, a center of culture and trade, made it possible to buy recently published chemical literature.

Scheele remained in Malmö for three years, until tempted by the better facilities available in Stockholm: the Royal Swedish Academy of Sciences was located there, and Uppsala with its famous university was nearby. In the spring of 1768 he found a position in a Stockholm pharmacy run by Johan Scharenberg, but was allowed only to prepare prescriptions. Since this was hardly to his liking, in the summer of 1770 he moved to the establishment of Christian Ludwig Lokk in Uppsala. There he had a workbench in the laboratory, was soon recognized as an able chemist, and met Johan Gottlieb Gahn. Gahn was then an assistant to Torbern Bergman, and he soon brought together the unusually capable apprentice experimenter and the outstanding theorist. This contact eventually developed into a lifelong friendship.

Scheele made important discoveries during his five years in Uppsala. On 4 February 1775, still a *studiosus pharmaciae*, he was elected a member of the Swedish Academy of Sciences and began to publish in its *Handlingar* ("Transactions"). Also while in Uppsala he began his major work: to combine the many and varied experiments with fire and air made during the previous years into an integrated book.

Since after fulfilling his apprenticeship Scheele had for thirteen years contented himself with subordinate positions offering limited possibilities for experimental research, it is not surprising that he was eager to seize an opportunity that held the promise of independence. Sara Margaretha Sonneman, the daughter of a councilman in Köping, had married a pharmacist named Herman Pohl in 1772. He died in 1775, and now she was looking for someone to carry on the pharmacy privilege that she had inherited. In the summer of that year Scheele reached an agreement with the widow that he would manage the pharmacy independently for one year and that after nine months he could negotiate for its purchase. This agreement nearly fell through when another prospective buyer secretly rented the pharmacy. In less than a year, however, Scheele had become so popular and respected that the citizens of the province demanded that he continue to be the city's pharmacist. He remained in the small town until his death, disregarding all offers to leave it, including that to succeed Marggraf at Berlin.

Scheele left Köping only once, for a few days. After the dispute about the ownership of the pharmacy had been settled, he traveled to Stockholm, where he took his long-postponed pharmacy examination and swore the pharmacist's oath on 11 November 1777. Two weeks earlier he had finally taken his seat as a member of the Royal Swedish Academy of Sciences, to which he had been elected in 1775. On 23 November Scheele returned to Köping. On 18 May 1786, on his deathbed, he married the widow Pohl and made her his heiress.

The earlier periods of Scheele's scientific career have not yet been elucidated; but from the extant letters of his employers Bauch and Kjellström, as well as from statements of his co-workers in Göteborg, it is clear that his curiosity was as boundless as his persistence. A surviving inventory of 1755 shows that the two most famous chemical handbooks of the time, Kunckel's *Laboratorium chymicum* and Caspar Neumann's *Praelectiones chemicae*, were available in Bauch's pharmacy; and Scheele undertook to repeat the numerous experiments in these books. The critical mind that Scheele had developed in his teens soon led him to conclude that in many instances he knew better than the authorities of his time. This belief explains his boldness in declaring his opposition to an important detail of the phlogiston theory. According

to this theory all combustible material contained a special substance, phlogiston, that escaped as the material burned. Scheele, however, thought that the phlogiston went into the heat that was formed, so that it could be liberated from the heat or fire. Thus, while denying that fire was an element, he simultaneously changed the phlogiston theory by stating that some reductions can occur without the addition of the reducing medium, phlogiston, but solely by providing heat. As a demonstration he cited the reduction of silver nitrate to metallic silver by heating it to redness (in which case the necessary phlogiston was provided by the fire).

Scheele's refusal to accept phlogiston as an element of combustibility, regardless of what the leading authorities said, showed an unusual instinct for research in a teen-ager; and one could expect that such exceptional abilities would soon produce written results, perhaps as laboratory notes. Among the extant papers of this kind, however, nothing can be ascribed with certainty to the early years in Göteborg. For the last several years there has been a renewed attempt in Sweden to make an inventory and a more thorough examination of Scheele's manuscripts, and it is anticipated that this effort will lead to a more precise dating. The preserved laboratory notes are quite detailed but difficult to interpret, for they are jotted down in an ungrammatical Old German and in a script that is extremely hard to read. The words are often so abbreviated as to be incomprehensible and the text filled with variations of now obsolete chemical symbols, or with their Latin equivalents.

The first to try to decipher Scheele's manuscripts was the mineralogist and polar scientist Adolf Erik Nordenskiöld, who, in connection with the commemoration of the 150th anniversary of Scheele's birth (1892), published a selection of Scheele's correspondence with excerpts from his laboratory notes. Nordenskiöld himself described this as a pioneering work and pointed out that through the publication of Scheele's manuscripts it would be possible to learn more of his development, evolution of ideas, and work habits. The ambitious plan, however, yielded to an aim that seemed more in harmony with the patriotic feelings of the time: to secure Scheele's priority for the discovery of oxygen. When Nordenskiöld had accomplished this task, he abruptly halted deciphering of the manuscripts.

In 1942, in connection with the festivities held on the bicentennial of Scheele's birth, a new edition of the laboratory notes from which Nordenskiöld had presented excerpts was published. The work, edited by the physicist C. W. Oseen, still did not satisfy the demand for clear, scientific interpretation; and the dating was rejected by experts. Neither Nordenskiöld nor Oseen had exhausted the existing manuscript material, however. Therefore the chemist and historian of science Uno Boklund has undertaken the publication of all available laboratory notes and Scheele's correspondence, complete with commentary.

Among the items of Scheele's correspondence published by Nordenskiöld in 1892 are several letters to contemporary lecturers in chemistry at the University of Lund. Anders Retzius was a correspondent between 1 December 1767 and 26 April 1768. These letters are the oldest dated documents written by Scheele that have so far been found. The contents are concerned entirely with chemistry and thus are of great value in following the course of thought that led to Scheele's opposition to the leading theories and to his discovery of oxygen. It would be almost impossible to obtain a thorough understanding of Scheele and his work without an intimate knowledge of these temperamental and stimulating letters. They reveal a number of experiments on nitrous acid, which Scheele named "volatile acid of niter," which for that time were outstanding scientific achievements.

As is so often the case, Scheele's great experimental abilities were overlooked by scholars because of insufficient understanding of eighteenth-century chemistry. They did not realize that the young apprentice was facing a serious conflict, having reached a point in his research where the evidence of his experiments no longer agreed with the classic phlogiston theory. Relying on his experiments, he felt compelled to speak out, a course of action that led not only to the formulation of his theories of combustion and calcination but also to the discovery of oxygen. By comparing his experimental results with reports to Retzius of the same period, it can be seen that in connection with experiments with the volatile nitrous acid, Scheele had already observed that saltpeter becoming red-hot in a crucible seemed to "boil" and that above the crucible sparks flamed up and burned with a vivid brilliance. He did not know that this was caused by a gas emanating from the saltpeter that was identical with a component of the air, but his comments concerning the experiments are noteworthy:

> I realized the necessity to learn about fire. . . . But I soon realized that it was not possible to form an opinion on the phenomena of fire as long as one did not understand air. And after I had made a certain number of experiments, I . . . saw that the air penetrated into the burning material and constituted a component of flames and sparks.

This marked a milestone in the development of Scheele's thought, for if air penetrated into the burning material, fire could not be an element; it must be a compound.

It is not known how and when Scheele completed his research on the phenomena of combustion. According to Retzius, in 1768–1770, while in Stockholm, Scheele undertook a series of experiments that laid the basis for his book on air and fire. No attempt has ever been made to find out what these experiments signified, but a manuscript dating from the time before his stay in Stockholm shows that Scheele was already occupied with highly advanced gas experiments. It is of importance, but has gone unnoticed, that his experiments often had a physiological background. He examined how plants react to gases and gas mixtures and had already perfected a technique to isolate and collect in ox bladders the air he wanted to examine. It is especially interesting that he began to examine exhaled air and understood that lime removes *aer fixus* (carbon dioxide) from it and, thus, that air is separated into its various components through physiological processes. On the whole the above-mentioned manuscripts support Retzius' statements and, in combination with other known facts, give validity to the assumption that it was in Stockholm that Scheele definitively rejected the theory of air as an element.

Among the many problems that occupied Scheele in the 1760's, his examinations of volatile nitrous acid are undoubtedly the most interesting for tracing the evolution of his thought. But in letters to Retzius he mentions the excellent results of his work with Prussian blue, which many years later led to the discovery of prussic acid, and also of a long series of experiments with boric acid and the first experiments with hydrogen sulfide. The isolation of tartaric acid also was part of this early work; but Scheele's account of it, sent to the Academy of Sciences, went unnoticed. Retzius, who in the fall of 1768 had come to Stockholm, enlarged it with some additional experiments and published it in the *Handlingar* of the Academy in 1770, with due acknowledgment of Scheele's priority. While in Stockholm, Scheele also undertook research on the chemical reactions of light on silver salts and discovered that different parts of the solar spectrum reduce with different strength. According to

Retzius it was also in Stockholm that Scheele found that *aer fixus* was an acid.

The fields of interest mentioned so far reveal the youthful Scheele's imposing versatility, but they are greatly overshadowed by the veritable catalog of important chemical observations and discoveries that appeared under the heading "P. M. hördt af Herr Scheele. År 1770 om Våhren" ("Memorandum Heard from Herr Scheele. Spring 1770"). This document, preserved in the Scheele archives of the library of the Academy of Sciences in Stockholm, was written in Swedish by Johan Gottlieb Gahn.

By way of introduction this memorandum presents Scheele's observations concerning the chemical composition of *terra animalis* (bone ash), which later, after Gahn had proved the presence of phosphorus, led to Scheele's method of producing phosphorus from animal bones instead of from urine (as had been customary until then). Other observations concern tartaric acid, pyrotartaric and pyruvic acids, oxalic acid, gallic and pyrogallic acids, and citric acid. A number of notes about gases deal with the production of ammonia gas and its combustibility, with hydrochloric acid gas, and with *aer fixus*. One experiment concerns the change of water into earth, and there are many observations about different chemical compounds. Of the greatest interest are some notes on the solution of iron in acid, for they make it clear that Scheele already knew about the different oxidation grades of iron.

This detailed memorandum covering Scheele's earliest years at Uppsala sheds no light on the research in minerals that then attracted his interest. His work with fluorspar led to the discovery of a new mineral acid, hydrofluoric acid (mixed with hydrofluosilicic acid). The discovery of "the Swedish acid" attracted great attention and was the subject of Scheele's first independent contribution to the *Handlingar* of the Academy (1771). In a letter of 10 April 1772 Macquer wrote about it to Torbern Bergman and requested more information.

When the experiments on fluorspar were finished, Bergman suggested that Scheele study the chemistry of pyrolusite. Although chemists had been interested in the mineral for many years, they had discovered little more than properties necessary to differentiate it from other minerals. By contrast, Scheele began his examination by determining the solubility of pyrolusite, under various conditions, in all the known acids. Thus he was able to show that it has a very strong attraction for phlogiston (in modern terms, it is a strong oxidizing

agent) and could place it in a phlogistic reducing system, which gave him the key to many of the mineral's properties that were not then understood.

The most important result of these experiments, however, was Scheele's discovery of chlorine, which occurred in connection with the attempts to dissolve pyrolusite in hydrochloric acid. In a communication to Gahn of 28 March 1773, Scheele said that by dissolving pyrolusite, hydrochloric acid loses its phlogiston and becomes a yellowish gas that smells like aqua regia and can dissolve gold but is barely soluble in water. In a subsequent letter he reported additional properties of the new gas, among them the observation that it reacts as a bleach with textile dyes, becoming hydrochloric acid in the process, and that the original colors cannot be restored.

From the same communication to Gahn it is clear that Scheele, after the successful dephlogistication of hydrochloric acid that resulted in the discovery of chlorine, conceived the idea of placing arsenic in a hypothetical phlogistic reducing system. In an article on arsenic, published in 1775, he says that shortly after he had discovered the phlogiston content of arsenic and that it could be dephlogisticated (oxidized), he decided to investigate arsenic without phlogiston and found that it contained an acid (arsenic acid). The detailed article describes more than 100 experiments and contains the first mention of the later famous "Scheele's green." Before the article was published, Scheele added a short note concerning a newly discovered material, "earth of heavy spar," which was later renamed baryta. A separate article about this earth was published in 1779.

Scheele's experimental activity in Uppsala was quite extensive. In a letter of 1 March 1773 he stated that he was the first to discover that gases are absorbed by recently ignited charcoal, and, in another letter, that he had analyzed *sal microcosmicum*, which could be isolated from urine, and found it to be sodium ammonium phosphate. In addition, he had worked out a method to produce *sal benzoes* by keeping it wet. This communication was read to the Academy of Sciences in 1774 and was later printed in the *Handlingar*. Another pharmaceutical preparation discussed in these letters was rhubarb with mercurous chloride.

Further studies of Scheele's correspondence from this period show that he began to make notes on still greater discoveries. Ironically, in foreign countries, especially in France, he and his work were much better known than in Sweden. Thus, when Lavoisier published his *Opuscules physiques et chymiques* at the beginning of January 1774 and sent a copy to the Academy of Sciences in Stockholm, he showed his great respect for Scheele's scientific work by stating that he would forward an additional copy to him.

In a letter to Lavoisier of 30 September 1774 Scheele freely disclosed his discovery of oxygen and, to demonstrate his gratitude for the book, gave him instructions on how to make pure oxygen. Until then no chemist who had produced or released it had been aware that it was a completely new gas or had been fully familiar with all its properties. Scheele demonstrated his superiority over his scientific contemporaries by giving Lavoisier information on both the chemical and the physiological properties of oxygen. This letter from Scheele is the earliest known written description of the detailed method of producing oxygen, together with complete information on its chemical nature and physiological properties. It was discovered among Lavoisier's papers by his biographer Édouard Grimaux, who published the letter in a way that clearly showed his awareness of its importance; as part of a communication entitled "Une lettre inédite de Scheele à Lavoisier," it adorns the first page of the initial issue, dated 15 January 1890, of the *Revue générale des sciences pures et appliquées*. The important content of the letter was not understood, however; it was ignored in the research on the chemical revolution and was not even reprinted by Grimaux. This letter has not been included in the most recent French edition of Lavoisier's correspondence.

In a letter of 2 August 1774 from Scheele to the secretary of the Stockholm Academy, Per Wargentin, in which he said that he had studied air and fire for many years, Scheele mentioned that until recently he had thought he was the only one to know of certain phenomena but that "some Englishman had gone very far in his researches." It is conceivable that this realization that he had rivals impelled him to summarize his own results, for the manuscript of *Chemische Abhandlung von der Luft und dem Feuer* was ready for the printer on 22 December 1775. In it, with the assistance of numerous elegant experiments, Scheele proved that air liberated from aerial acid (carbon dioxide) and water vapor consists of two gases: fire air (oxygen), which can support combustion, and vitiated, foul air (nitrogen), which cannot.

The printing of the book was delayed for two years, partly because Torbern Bergman did not deliver his promised preface until 1 July 1777; the work appeared the following month. By then oxy-

gen was already known, and some of the observations in the book had been published by others. Priestley, during a visit to Paris in October 1774, informed Lavoisier, Le Roy, and many other scientists of his discovery of a new remarkable gas on 1 August 1774; and that date was long accepted as the "birthday" of oxygen. Now it is known from Scheele's laboratory notes that the discovery was made at least two years before Priestley's. Even the notion that Priestley should have published it earlier is negated when it is noted (Partington) that Bergman had published a summary of Scheele's discovery of oxygen and of his theory of heat in *Nova acta Regiae societatis scientiarum upsaliensis* many months before Priestley revealed his discovery.

In the last chapter of *Luft und Feuer*, Scheele wrote about his experiments with "fetid sulfurous air" (hydrogen sulfide), the first correct description of its properties; he was also the first to record a synthesis of the gas through the heating of sulfur in hydrogen. Scheele's view that this gas consisted of sulfur, heat, and phlogiston was correct, since he thought that hydrogen was a combination of heat and phlogiston. Further, Scheele provided the first description of hydrogen polysulfides, which he had already mentioned in a letter to Retzius in 1768.

The minerals plumbago (graphite) and molybdena (molybdenite, MoS_2) are so similar in appearance and physical properties that they are often confused. In an effort to differentiate them, Scheele thickened and boiled molybdenite with all known acids, but even arsenic and nitric acids had no effect. But the oxidizing nitric acid eventually yielded a white powder that was soluble in water and gave an acid reaction. Scheele named it *terra molybdaenae* (MoO_3) and observed that "the earth" gave a blue solution with concentrated sulfuric acid, a reaction that led him to consider it "not reluctant to attract phlogiston" – in other words, it could be reduced. Since Scheele did not possess a furnace that could reduce the earth to metal, he asked his friend Peter Jacob Hjelm, a mineralogist, to do this for him. In 1781, with improved ovens, Helm produced the metal and suggested the name molybdenum.

In 1770–1771 Scheele had examined plumbago (manuscript no. 2 in the *Brown Book*) but had obtained no definite results. He now took up the problem again and showed that the end product obtained by detonation with saltpeter or heating with arsenic acid was aerial acid (carbon dioxide). From this he concluded that graphite is carbon dioxide combined with a great amount of phlogiston—that carbon is a reduction product of carbon dioxide. In a letter to Bergman of 18 August 1780, Scheele discussed his thorough study of tungsten (*lapis ponderosus*, now called scheelite, $CaWO_4$). He had found that it consists of lime and a new acid, tungstic acid; but his efforts to reduce it to metal failed.

Scheele's contributions to inorganic chemistry should not overshadow his research in organic chemistry, which may be considered more imposing, since he had no precedent. In his preliminary attempts to isolate from plants or animals the delicate materials he planned to examine, he had to avoid the destructive methods (calcination, distilling until dry) common in inorganic chemistry and to proceed with greater caution, working with lower temperatures and learning to extract with water or some other solvent. Scheele was especially successful in his method of isolating organic acids by precipitating the acid as an insoluble calcium salt or potassium ferrocyanide and then separating it with diluted sulfuric acid.

Scheele had obtained excellent results in inorganic chemistry by oxidation, and the same methods in organic chemistry led to the discovery of many new acids. When this work is added to his researches in protein and fat, it is clear that Partington's judgment that Scheele's influence in organic chemistry was fundamental was fully justified.

Scheele had isolated tartaric acid during his stay in Malmö and had discussed its property of forming both acid and neutral salts. Later he observed the formation of pyrotartaric acid. Scheele documented his interest in plant acids in his first known letter (1 December 1767), in which he wrote to Retzius: "So far as the essential salts [acids] of plants are concerned, I have crystallized the juices of *Aconitum, Stramonium* and *Mentha crispa*." In manuscript no. 1 of the *Brown Book* he began to examine "rhubarb earth," which he thought consisted of citric acid bound with lime (also in manuscript no. 2). About 1770 he changed his mind and thought it was phosphoric acid, then finally found that "rhubarb earth" was the calcium salt of acid of sorrel. Until then no chemist had been able to prepare free acid of sorrel. At the beginning of 1776 Scheele had succeeded in isolating it through the use of baryta, but it was not absolutely pure. In 1784 he obtained the pure acid by precipitating it out with potassium ferrocyanide and then changing it with a calculated amount of sulfuric acid. At the same time he learned that the pure acid of sorrel was identical with acid of sugar that he had discov-

ered earlier and had produced through the oxidation of sugar with nitric acid. Both acids were later called oxalic acid.

Scheele's outstanding experimental ability also led to his solution of the difficult problem of obtaining pure crystallized citric acid from lemon juice. If he could do so, he could determine the properties of the acid and also compare it with acids of other fruits and berries. Scheele investigated twenty-one kinds of fruit and berries, as well as fifteen other materials of vegetable origin and some animal material (glue, egg white, egg yolk, blood), all of which were analyzed after oxidation with nitric acid. He finally found an organic acid (which he named malic acid) in the apple. The same process with milk sugar had already yielded yet another new acid, *acidum sacchari lactis*, later called mucic acid.

Valentine, Paracelsus, and Helmont had tried without success to analyze urinary calculi, and their successors had not fared any better. Scheele attempted to solve the problem in a different manner, and in 1776 he reported that he had separated from both kidney stones and urine the acid of calculus (uric acid). He added that it could be recognized by the red spots it produced on the skin after being dusted with nitric acid.

According to one of his letters to Retzius, Scheele's work with the coloring principle of Prussian blue dated from 1765. This intricate problem was one of the most difficult of Scheele's career, and it took eighteen years for him to reach his goal: the discovery of prussic acid. He reported that this *acidum berolinense* (hydrocyanic acid) had "a peculiar but not disagreeable smell, a taste somewhat approaching sweet, and warm in the mouth, at the same time exciting a cough." It is difficult, says Partington, to understand how he escaped with his life.

The capstones of Scheele's gigantic chemical edifice were his discovery of glycerol and of the art of preserving vinegar by heating the vessel containing it in a kettle with boiling water—pasteurization a century before Pasteur. He also found that vinegar is an oxidation product of alcohol and that "an ether of exquisite smell" (acetaldehyde) is an intermediate product during the oxidation.

The list of Scheele's discoveries does not tell the whole story of his work. For this, more thorough source studies are needed, especially editions of Scheele's collected manuscripts with expert commentary. When such material is available, it will be possible to consider his work as that of an indefatigable seeker after truth who was driven to test and retest the validity of contemporary answers to the great chemical controversies of the time, without regard for theoretical attitudes. Scheele's thousands of experiments seem to be random, but closer examination reveals that they are ordered into groups, each of which has a characteristic background that connects it to central theoretical chemical questions: the concept of phlogiston, the value concept, the concepts of elements, the concepts of alkali and acid, and the controversy over *acidum pingue*.

Also needed is a study of the dissemination of Scheele's ideas and experimental findings to other countries and their influence on the development of chemistry. It is therefore important to examine his foreign correspondence. Since Scheele informed Torbern Bergman in great detail of his discoveries, it is no less vital to determine the ways in which Bergman disseminated these chemical reports, which were given to him without any request for secrecy.

BIBLIOGRAPHY

I. ORIGINAL WORKS. MSS in the Library of the Royal Academy of Sciences in Stockholm are *Scheele's Brown Book*, a collection described as extremely difficult to decipher, that includes laboratory notes, drafts of papers, and drafts of letters (the draft of Scheele's letter to Lavoisier among them); a collection of laboratory notes, difficult to read, on sheets of paper of different shapes and sizes; and part of Scheele's extensive correspondence.

MSS in the library of the University of Uppsala are mainly Scheele's important letters to Torbern Bergman.

A selection of the above material has been published in the following editions: A. E. Nordenskiöld, ed., *Carl Wilhelm Scheele. Efterlemnade bref och anteckningar* (Stockholm, 1892), also in *Carl Wilhelm Scheele. Nachgelassene Briefe und Aufzeichnungen* (Berlin, 1893); C. W. Oseen, ed., *Carl Wilhelm Scheele, Manuskript 1756–1777* (Uppsala, 1942); and a selection of these MSS deciphered by C. W. Oseen, also published as *Carl Wilhelm Scheele, Manuskript 1756–1777* (Uppsala, 1942); Otto Zekert, ed., *Carl Wilhelm Scheele. Sein Leben und seine Werke*, 7 vols. (Mittenwald, 1931–1935).

None of these eds., however, offers exact deciphering and critical clarity. Nordenskiöld arbitrarily modernizes Scheele's seventeenth-century German and omits important letters, such as the correspondence with J. C. Wilcke, secretary of the Academy of Sciences. (These letters can be found in J. C. Oseen, *Johan Carl Wilcke. Experimentalfysiker* [Uppsala, 1939], 312–341). Oseen's ed. of . . . *Scheele, Manuskript 1756–1777* must be used with great care, since the work abounds with mis-takes due to incorrect reading of the text and his dating of the MSS is extremely questionable. Johan Nordström's review, "En edition av Scheeles efterlämnade manuskript" ("An Edition of Scheele's Remaining Manuscripts"), in *Lychnos* (1942), 254–277, is recommended for its detailed and clear criticism. It is a thorough examination of Oseen's work and also severely criticizes Zekert's mistakes in his work on Scheele.

A new ed. of Scheele's work has now been started, supported by the Bank of Sweden Tercentenary Fund and other foundations. It is complete, with commentary on all his laboratory notes, letters to and from him, and English trans. of all of the material: *Carl Wilhelm Scheele. His Work and Life*, Uno Boklund, ed., 8 vols. Thus far 2 vols. have appeared: I–II, *The Brown Book* (Stockholm, 1969). In preparation are III–IV, *Laboratory Notes*, facs. ed. with intro., decipherment, English trans., and commentary; V, *Correspondence 1767–1777*, with intro. and parallel English trans.; VI–VII, *Correspondence 1778–1786*, with parallel English trans., commentary, and index; and VIII, which will cover Scheele's life and scientific achievements, his influence on contemporary European chemistry, and his role in the chemical revolution, plus a bibliography and general index.

A complete bibliography of Scheele's numerous printed works is in Nordenskiöld, *op. cit.*, xxxii–xxxviii. Partington includes a list of Scheele's most important works in his *A History of Chemistry*, III (London, 1962), 210–211.

II. SECONDARY LITERATURE. There is no standard biography of Scheele; but since the first obituary was published by Lorenz von Crell in *Chemische Annalen*, 1 (1787), 175–192, many works of varying reliability have appeared. Nordenskiöld, who published an interesting description of Scheele's life (*op. cit.*, vii–xxxi) gives a list of the most important biographies (pp. xli–cl). An indispensable guide for the study of the abundant literature about Scheele is Bengt Hildebrand, "Scheeleforskning och Scheelelitteratur," in *Lychnos* (1936), 76–102. An American contribution is Georg Urdang, *The Apothecary Chemist Carl Wilhelm Scheele, A Pictorial Biography* (Madison, Wis., 1942; 2nd ed., 1958). Important for questions of priority is J. R. Partington, "The Discovery of Oxygen," in *Journal of Chemical Education*, 39 (1962), 123–125.

Among the Swedish contributions are the following, listed chronologically: J. Nordström, "Några bortglömda brev och tidskriftsbidrag av Carl Wilhelm Scheele" ("Some Forgotten Letters and Journal Contributions by Carl Wilhelm Scheele"), in *Lychnos* (1942); and "Två notiser till Scheeles biografi" ("Two Notes to Scheele's Biography"), *ibid.*, 280–284; Uno Boklund, "A Lost Letter From Scheele to Lavoisier," *ibid.* (1957–1958), 39–62; *Carl Wilhelm Scheele. Bruna Boken. Utgiven i faksimil med deschiffrering och innehållsanalys jämte inledning och kommentar* ("Carl Wilhelm Scheele. The Brown Book. Published in Facsimile With Deciphering and an Analysis of the Contents With an Introduction and Commentary"; Stockholm, 1961); "Varför Scheele måste börja tala engelska" ("Why Scheele Had to Begin Speaking English"), in *Svensk farmaceutisk tidskrift*, **68** (1964), 967–979; and "Die Rolle Carl Wilhelm Scheeles in der chemischen Revolution des 18. Jahrhunderts," in *Ruperto-Carola*, **18** (1966), 306–317; and Hugo Olsson, *Kemiens historia i Sverige intill år 1800* ("The History of Sweden Until the Year 1800"; Uppsala, 1971), 136–151, 221–234, 282–297, and *passim*.

UNO BOKLUND

SCHEFFERS, GEORG (*b.* Altendorf, near Holzminden, Germany, 21 November 1866; *d.* Berlin, Germany, 12 August 1945), *mathematics*.

Scheffers studied mathematics and physics from 1884 to 1888 at the University of Leipzig, where his father was professor at the Academy of Art. He received the doctorate from Leipzig in 1890 and qualified as a lecturer there the following year. In 1896 he became extraordinary professor at the Technische Hochschule in Darmstadt, and in 1900 he was promoted to full professor. In 1907 he succeeded Guido Hauck as full professor at the Technische Hochschule in Charlottenburg, where he remained until his retirement in 1935.

As a student Scheffers was greatly influenced by Sophus Lie, who was professor at the University of Leipzig from 1886 to 1898. He followed Lie's suggestions in choosing topics for both his doctoral dissertation and his *Habilitationsschrift*, which dealt respectively with plane contact transformations and complex number systems. Scheffers' most important independent research inspired by Lie was his 1903 paper on Abel's theorem and translation surfaces.

In later years Scheffers' reputation was based largely on his own books. These writings, which grew out of his wide-ranging activities at technical colleges, were directed at a broader audience than the books he edited with Lie; and they all went through several editions. Scheffers' two-volume *Anwendung der Differential- und Integralrechnung auf Geometrie* (1901–1902) was a popular textbook of differential geometry. Also widely used was his revision of Serret's *Lehrbuch der Differential- und Integralrechnung*, the last edition of which appeared in 1924; subsequently it was superseded by books written in a more modern style. Scheffers also published *Lehrbuch der darstellenden Geometrie* and, in 1903, an article entitled "Besondere transzendente Kurven" in the *Encyklopädie der mathematischen Wissenschaften*.

Scheffers' favorite field of study was geometry and, more specifically, the differential geometry of intuitive space. In this area he was a master at discovering many properties of particular curves and surfaces and their representation; he also possessed a gift for giving an easily understandable account of them—although in a much wordier style than is now customary. His exceptional talent for vividly communicating material is also apparent in a later work on the grids used in topographic maps and stellar charts.

BIBLIOGRAPHY

Scheffers' original works are as follows: "Bestimmung einer Klasse von Berührungstransformationsgruppen," in *Acta mathematica*, **14** (1891), 117–178; *Zurückführung komplexer Zahlensysteme auf typische Formen* (Leipzig, 1891); *Anwendung der Differential- und Integralrechnung auf Geometrie*, 2 vols. (Leipzig, 1901–1902; 3rd ed., 1922–1923); "Das Abelsche Theorem und das Lie'sche Theorem über Translationsflächen," in *Acta mathematica*, **28** (1902), 65–91; "Besondere transzendente Kurven," in *Encyklopädie der mathematischen Wissenschaften*, III, pt. 3 (Leipzig, 1903), 185–268; *Lehrbuch der darstellenden Geometrie*, 2 vols. (Berlin, 1919–1920; 2nd ed., 1922–1927); and *Wie findet und zeichnet man Gradnetze von Land- und Sternkarten?* (Leipzig–Berlin, 1934).

Scheffers edited the following volumes by Lie: *Vorlesungen über Differentialgleichungen mit bekannten infinitesimalen Transformationen* (Leipzig, 1891); *Vorlesungen über kontinuierliche Gruppen mit geometrischen und anderen Anwendungen* (Leipzig, 1893); and collaborated with Lie on *Geometrie der Berührungstransformationen*, I (Leipzig, 1896). He also revised J. A. Serret's *Lehrbuch der Differential- und Integralrechnung*, A. Harnack, trans., 5th ed., 3 vols. (Leipzig, 1906–1914; I, 8th ed., 1924; II, 7th ed., 1921; III, 6th ed., 1924).

WERNER BURAU

SCHEGK, JAKOB (in Latin, **Jacobus Schegkius** *or* **Scheggius**; also sometimes called **Jakob Degen**) ((*b.* Schorndorf, Germany, 7 June 1511; *d.* Tübingen, Germany, 9 May 1587), *medicine, natural philosophy, methodology of science*.

Schegk was the son of a well-to-do burgher, Bernhard Degen; it is not known why he changed his name to Schegk. As a boy he was taught Latin, Greek, Hebrew, and rhetoric by Johann Thomas, a student of Johann Reuchlin's, before entering the University of Tübingen in 1527 to study philosophy. A year later he received the baccalaureate and, in 1530, a master's degree. He also studied theology and medicine, taking a doctorate in the latter in 1539, and taught philosophy, logic, and medicine at Tübingen for forty-five years before retiring in 1577. During five decades Schegk published more than thirty works, including many very long ones, on philosophy, theology, and medicine. He was generally Aristotelian in orientation and wrote numerous commentaries and treatises on Aristotle's works, in addition to becoming involved in polemics with Theodore Beza, Petrus Ramus, and Simone Simoni. Besides many compendia of natural philosophy, he wrote *De demonstratione libri XV* (1564), in which he attempted to reassert the validity of Aristotle's scientific methodology, and in *De plastica seminis facultate libri tres* (1580) he argued in behalf of the Peripatetic doctrine of the formative power of the semen.

One of the most prominent sixteenth-century spokesmen for German Scholasticism, Schegk approached natural philosophy through a strong emphasis on a return to a study of the Greek text of Aristotle. Thus he followed in large measure the humanistic tradition of Renaissance Aristotelianism.

BIBLIOGRAPHY

I. ORIGINAL WORKS. Schegk's writings include *De demonstratione libri XV* (Basel, 1564); and *De plastica seminis facultate libri tres* (Strasbourg, 1580). The most complete list of his works is in the article by Sigwart (below). See also C. Sigwart, "Ein Collegium logicum im XVI. Jahrhundert," *Tübinger Universitätsschriften* for 1889–1890 (1890).

II. SECONDARY LITERATURE. The basic source for information on Schegk's life is Georg Liebler, *Oratio de vita . . . Jacobi Schegki . . .* (Tübingen, 1587). See also N. W. Gilbert, *Renaissance Concepts of Method* (New York, 1960), 158–162; W. Pagel, "William Harvey Revisited, Part II," in *History of Science*, **9** (1970), 1–41, esp. 26–30; P. Petersen, *Geschichte der Aristotelischen Philosophie im protestantischen Deutschland* (Leipzig, 1921; repr. Stuttgart–Bad Canstatt, 1964); C. Sigwart, "Jakob Schegk, Professor der Philosophie und Medizin," in his *Kleine Schriften*, I (Freiburg im Breisgau, 1889), 256–291, the best general survey; and C. Vasoli, *La dialettica e la retorica dell'umanesimo* (Milan, 1968), *passim*.

CHARLES B. SCHMITT

SCHEINER, CHRISTOPH (*b.* Wald, near Mindelheim, Swabia, Germany, 25 July 1573; *d.* Neisse, Silesia [now Nysa, Poland], 18 June 1650), *astronomy*.

Scheiner attended the Jesuit Latin school at Augsburg and the Jesuit College at Landsberg before he joined the Society of Jesus in 1595. In 1600 he was sent to Ingolstadt, where he studied philosophy and, especially, mathematics under Johann Lanz. From 1603 to 1605 he spent his "magisterium," or period of training as a teacher, at Dillingen, where he taught humanities in the Gymnasium and mathematics in the neighboring academy. During this period he invented the pantograph, an instrument for copying plans on any scale; and his results were published several years later in the *Pantographice, seu ars delineandi* (1631). He returned to Ingolstadt to study theology, and after completing his second novitiate or "third year" at Edersberg, he was appointed professor of Hebrew and mathematics at Ingolstadt in 1610.

The following year Scheiner constructed a telescope with which he began to make astronomical observations, and in March 1611 he detected the presence of spots on the sun. His religious superiors did not wish him to publish under his own name, lest he be mistaken and bring discredit on the Society of Jesus; but he communicated his discovery to his friend Marc Welser in Augsburg. In 1612 Welser had Scheiner's letters printed under the title *Tres epistolae de maculis solaribus*, and he sent copies abroad, notably to Galileo and Kepler. Scheiner believed that the spots were small planets circling the sun; and in a second series of letters, which Welser published in the same year as *De maculis solaribus . . . accuratior disquisitio*, Scheiner discussed the individual motion of the spots, their period of revolution, and the appearance of brighter patches or *faculae* on the surface of the sun. Having observed the lower conjunction of Venus with the sun, Scheiner concluded that Venus and Mercury revolve around the sun.

Welser had concealed Scheiner's identity under the pseudonym of *Apelles latens post tabulam*. Galileo, however, identified Scheiner as a Jesuit and took him to task in three letters addressed to Welser and published in Rome in 1613. Galileo claimed priority in the discovery of the sunspots and hinted darkly that Scheiner had been apprised of his achievement and was guilty of plagiarism. This criticism was unfair, for the sunspots were observed independently not only by Galileo in Florence and Scheiner in Ingolstadt, but also by Thomas Harriot in Oxford, Johann Fabricius in Wittenberg, and Domenico Passignani in Rome.

151

In Ingolstadt, Scheiner trained young mathematicians and organized public debates on current issues in astronomy. Two of these "disputations" were subsequently published. In the first, the *Disquisitiones mathematicae de controversis et novitatibus astronomicis,* Scheiner upheld the traditional view that the earth is at rest at the center of the universe but praised Galileo for his discovery of the phases of Venus and the satellites of Jupiter. In the second, *Exegeses fundamentorum gnomonicorum,* Scheiner discussed the theory behind sundials and explained their construction. In the *Sol ellipticus* (1615) and the *Refractiones caelestes* (1617), which he dedicated to Maximilian, the archduke of Tirol, Scheiner also called attention to the elliptical form of the sun near the horizon, and he explained the form as the effect of refraction.

In 1616 Scheiner accepted an invitation from Maximilian and took up residence at the court in Innsbruck. The following year he was ordained to the priesthood. He performed several experiments on the physiology of the eye. In the *Oculus, hoc est: fundamentum opticum* (1619) he showed that the retina is the seat of vision.

In 1620 the University of Freiburg im Breisgau was entrusted to the Jesuits; Scheiner was one of the first seven Jesuits to be assigned to the university, but the following year he was recalled to Innsbruck. In 1622 he accompanied the Archduke Charles, the bishop of Neisse, to that city; and in 1623 Scheiner was appointed superior of the Jesuit College to be erected there. In 1624 he left with the Archduke Charles on a journey to Spain; but they parted ways at Genoa, and Scheiner proceeded to Rome to settle matters concerning the foundation of the college. He was detained in Rome until March 1633. When not occupied with administrative problems, he busied himself with astronomical observations and the writing of his major work, the *Rosa ursina sive sol,* which was printed at Bracciano between 1626 and 1630. In the *Rosa ursina,* Scheiner confirmed his method and criticized Galileo for failing to mention the inclination of the axis of rotation of the sunspots to the plane of the ecliptic, which Scheiner determined as 7° 30' (modern value 7° 15').

Scheiner does not appear to have played an active role in the trial and condemnation of Galileo, and his refutation of the Copernican system, *Prodromus de sole mobili et stabili terra contra Galilaeum,* was published only posthumously in 1651.

From 1633 to 1639 Scheiner lived in Vienna and then in Neisse, where he was active in pastoral work until his death in 1650.

BIBLIOGRAPHY

I. ORIGINAL WORKS. Scheiner's works include *Tres epistolae de maculis solaribus scriptae ad Marcum Velserum . . .* (Augsburg, 1612) and *De maculis solaribus et stellis circa Jovem errantibus, accuratior disquisitio . . .* (Augsburg, 1612), which were reedited as an appendix to Galileo Galilei, *Istoria e dimostrazioni intorno alle macchie solari . . .* (Rome, 1613).

See also *Disquisitiones mathematicae de controversis et novitatibus astronomicis* (Ingolstadt, 1614), written with his pupil Johann Georg Locher; *Sol ellipticus; hoc est novum et perpetuum solis contrahi soliti phaenomenon* (Augsburg, 1615); *Exegeses fundamentorum gnomonicorum* (Ingolstadt, 1615), written with his pupil Johann Georg Schoenberg; *Refractiones caelestes, sive solis elliptici phaenomenon illustratum* (Ingolstadt, 1617); *Oculus, hoc est: fundamentum opticum . . .* (Innsbruck, 1619; 2nd ed., Freiburg im Breisgau, 1621; 3rd ed., London, 1652); *Rosa ursina sive sol ex admirando facularum et macularum suarum phaenomeno varius necnon circa centrum suum et axem fixum, ab occasu in ortum annua, circaque alium axem mobilem ab ortu in occasum conversione quasi menstrua, super polos proprios, libris quatuor mobilis ostensus* (Bracciano, 1626–1630); and *Pantographice, seu ars delineandi res quaslibet . . .* (Rome, 1631; Italian eds: Padua, 1637; Bologna, 1653).

Two sets of lecture notes are preserved in the Bayerische Stadtsbibliothek in Munich: *Commentarius in Aristotelis libros de caelo et de meteorologicis. 1614–1615,* Pg. 128 (*Catal. MSS latin. Monach.,* n. 11878); and *Euclidis liber V dictatus an. 1615* (*ibid.,* n. 12425). There are also unpublished letters of Scheiner in the Bibliothèque Nationale in Paris.

II. SECONDARY LITERATURE. On Scheiner and his work, see Augustin and Alois de Backer, *Bibliothèque de la Compagnie de Jésus,* VIII (Louvain, 1960), cols. 734–740; Anton von Braunmuehl, *Christoph Scheiner als Mathematiker, Physiker und Astronom* (Bamberg, 1891); Bellino Carrara, *"L'unicuique suum" a Galileo, Fabricius e Scheiner nella scoperta delle macchie solari* (Rome, 1900); Stillman Drake, *Galileo Studies* (Ann Arbor, 1970); Antonio Favaro, "Oppositori di Galileo. III. Cristoforo Scheiner," in *Atti del R. Istituto veneto di scienze, lettere ed arte,* 78 (1919), 1–107; Johann Schreiber, "P. Christoph Scheiner, S.J. und seine Sonnebeobachtungen," in *Natur und Offenbarung,* 48 (1902), 1–20, 78–98, 145–158, 209–221; and William R. Shea, "Galileo, Scheiner, and the Interpretation of Sunspots," in *Isis,* 61 (1970), 498–519.

WILLIAM R. SHEA

SCHEINER, JULIUS (*b.* Cologne, Germany, 25 November 1858; *d.* Potsdam, Germany, 20 December 1913), *astrophysics, astronomy.*

Scheiner was the son of Jacob Scheiner, a painter of landscapes and architectural subjects. In 1878 he entered the University of Bonn to read mathematics and natural science. While there he developed an interest in astronomy, which led to his becoming an assistant at the Bonn observatory. In 1882 he obtained the doctorate with a dissertation on the observations of Algol made by E. Schonfeld, then director of the observatory. Scheiner continued to work at the observatory until moving, early in 1887, to the Royal Astrophysical Observatory at Potsdam, where he remained for the rest of his life, rising from assistant to permanent assistant to senior observer (1900). In 1894 Scheiner was appointed extraordinary professor of astrophysics at the University of Berlin.

While at the Bonn observatory Scheiner was engaged primarily in assisting in zone observations. On moving to Potsdam he immediately set to work in astrophysics, the latest, and flourishing, branch of astronomy. He collaborated closely with Potsdam's director, Hermann Vogel, in applying the new instrument that Vogel had designed and named the spectrograph. Together they inaugurated the era of accurate measurement of stellar radial velocities. Their average probable error was only 2.6 kilometers per second, an improvement over earlier results by a factor of ten.

From the early 1890's Scheiner was also much occupied with celestial photography and with the preparation of the international astrographic chart. In connection with the latter he represented the Potsdam observatory at meetings in Paris in 1891, 1896, and 1900, and supervised the publication of six large volumes during the period 1899–1912. Work on the chart also benefited in several respects from Scheiner's considerable practical and experimental skills. For example, he tested the previously employed law of photographic photometry and showed it to be incorrect.

Around the turn of the century the close relations between Scheiner and Vogel became impaired, and afterward Scheiner worked in collaboration with J. Wilsing. Among other things they made a photometric determination of the relative intensities of the three principal lines in the nebular spectra and measured visually the radial velocities of nine of the brighter gaseous nebulae. Availing themselves of recent advances in the study of blackbody radiation, they also made determinations of the temperatures of more than 100 stars.

Scheiner's strengths lay in the experimental and practical areas of research. Drawing on his rich knowledge of both laboratory and workshop, he could quickly devise an experiment for settling a debated point. Scheiner was also an excellent teacher and enjoyed giving numerous popular accounts of astrophysical matters, both in lectures and in writing.

BIBLIOGRAPHY

I. ORIGINAL WORKS. Scheiner's more important books are *Die Spectralanalyse der Gestirne* (Leipzig, 1890), translated into English by E. B. Frost (Boston, 1890), a textbook on stellar physics; *Photographie der Gestirne* (Leipzig, 1897), at the time considered indispensable to those interested in any branch of the subject; *Strahlung und Temperatur der Sonne* (Leipzig, 1899), valuable for discussion of the temperature of the sun, in light of contemporary studies of blackbody radiation; *Populäre Astrophysik* (Leipzig–Berlin, 1908), Scheiner's 1906 lectures at Berlin; and *Spectralanalytische und photometrische Theorien* (Leipzig, 1909), meant for those with a general interest in astrophysics.

Scheiner's more important papers are discussed by J. Wilsing (see below).

II. SECONDARY LITERATURE. See E. B. Frost, "Julius Scheiner," in *Astrophysical Journal*, **41** (1915), 1–9; Hector Macpherson, Jr., *Astronomers of Today and Their Work* (London, 1905), 234–239; and J. Wilsing, "Julius Scheiner," in *Vierteljahrsschrift der Astronomischen Gesellschaft*, **49** (1914), 22–36.

WILLIAM McGUCKEN

SCHELLING, FREDERICK WILHELM JOSEPH (later **von Schelling**) (*b.* Leonberg, Württemberg, Germany, 27 January 1775; *d.* Bad Ragaz, Switzerland, 20 August 1854), *philosophy.*

Schelling was the son of Joseph Friedrich Schelling (1737–1812), a deacon, preacher, and theological writer, and the former Gottliebin Maria Cless. Both parents were the children of pastors. Schelling early displayed extraordinary gifts, and in 1790, at age fifteen, he entered the Protestant theological foundation at the University of Tübingen. There he studied theology and philosophy and was friends with Hegel and Hölderlin. Like most of his fellow students, he embraced the ideas of the French Revolution. Consequently, he forfeited the patronage of Duke Karl of Württemberg.

In 1791 Schelling began an intensive study of the works of Kant and of Fichte, whose importance for the further development of the Kantian philosophy he immediately recognized. In 1792 he obtained a master's degree in philosophy for a paper dealing with biblical subjects and, in 1795, a master's degree in theology. At this time (1794–1795) he wrote several essays on philosophy and theology.

After finishing his studies, Schelling took a post as a tutor, traveling with two aristocratic pupils to Leipzig in 1796. In his two years there he studied natural science and medicine and published several works on philosophy, which attracted the attention of Fichte and Goethe. At their suggestion, Schelling, in 1798, was offered a position as extraordinary professor at Jena, then a center of German cultural life. Around this time he spent several weeks in Dresden, where he was introduced into the circle of the Romantic school, notably to the brothers August Wilhelm and Friedrich Schlegel and their wives, and to Novalis and Tieck. At Jena, Schelling lectured primarily on Kant's transcendental idealism and Fichte's theory of science (*Wissenschaftstheorie*), but soon he began to develop his own ideas on the philosophy of nature (*Naturphilosophie*). In 1803 the Bavarian government invited him to Würzburg as a full professor. As at Jena, the first part of his stay was successful, but then he encountered increasing opposition, in this case from both Catholics and "dogmatic Kantians." He was accused of materialism, atheism, obscurantism, and mysticism.

Schelling left Würzburg in 1806 and moved to Munich. For the next thirty-five years he remained in the service of the Bavarian state, becoming a member of the Bavarian Academy of Sciences and general secretary of the Academy of Fine Arts. Granted a leave of absence from 1820 to 1827, Schelling went to Erlangen, where he gave private lectures on philosophy, mythology, and the history of philosophy. At Erlangen he enjoyed the respect and admiration of a circle of sympathetic friends.

In 1827 Schelling returned to Munich. The University had been moved from Landshut to the Bavarian capital, and King Ludwig I had made a great effort to attract outstanding faculty members. Schelling was appointed head curator of the scientific collections and president of the Academy of Sciences. He also made a major contribution to a project for reforming the Bavarian school system, but the project was abandoned after a reactionary turn in government policy.

Meanwhile, Hegel's philosophy had triumphed in Prussia, and it appeared that the schools of thought growing out of his teaching would soon be dominated by materialistic and antimonarchical ideas. Looking to Schelling to achieve the "destruction of the dragon's teeth" of materialism, King Friedrich Wilhelm IV of Prussia, encouraged

by the Humboldt brothers, offered the philosopher a post in Berlin. Despite his advanced age, Schelling accepted the offer, for he viewed it as an obligatory mission. He taught in Berlin for only a short time (1841–1846). After vehement disputes with one of his opponents, Heinrich Eberhard Gottlob Paulus, Schelling gave up his lectures, which initially had been very popular but then attracted fewer and fewer listeners. He withdrew increasingly from public life and devoted himself exclusively to perfecting his philosophy. He lived long enough to witness the victory of Hegelian philosophy and the rise of materialism.

Schelling's first marriage was to Dorothea Caroline Michaelis, daughter of the famous Orientalist Johann David Michaelis. Schelling met her in Dresden while she was still married to A. W. Schlegel. Extremely intelligent and witty, she had led a very eventful life. Her early death left Schelling deeply shaken. Although it may not have been the reason that he virtually ceased to publish (and even withdrew works already printed), the two events occurred at about the same time. In 1812 Schelling married Pauline Gotter, the daughter of a friend of his late wife. They enjoyed a harmonious marriage and had three sons and three daughters.

Unlike Kant or Hegel, Schelling left behind no finished, logically constructed system. While still young, he published a number of brilliant works, and whenever he embarked on a new subject, he aroused the highest expectations, which, however, he was not able to fulfill. Curious, enthusiastic, and receptive to a broad range of influences, he grasped at new ideas, reworked them, and integrated them into his own philosophy. He repeatedly started over from the beginning, used new terminology, invented new schemata, ignored or altered previous statements, and gave new content to earlier concepts. Most of his early writings were derived from or were composed at the same time as his lectures, often under pressure of time; consequently the writings contain material that is immature or insufficiently thought out. Journals that he founded in order to publish essays soon went out of existence. Much in his late philosophy is difficult to understand and is even difficult to enter into at all, laden as it is with mythological notions.

Earlier historians of philosophy distinguished definite stages in the development of Schelling's thinking. Recent research (especially that of Horst Fuhrmans and Manfred Schröter) has shown that, viewed from the standpoint of his late philosophy, Schelling's work as a whole developed organically and without breaks and that certain fundamental concepts and images are evident throughout. For the sake of convenience, Schelling's philosophy can be presented—with little violence to its contents—in a strictly chronological order: philosophy of nature and transcendental philosophy, philosophy of identity, and philosophy of religion.

Schelling attentively followed the discoveries of the great scientists of his time: Galvani, Volta, Lavoisier, John Brown, and Kielmeyer. Like Goethe, Schelling was temperamentally opposed to a purely mechanistic conception of nature. He viewed nature as a living organism, an active force. He was, however, just as little a vitalist as he was a mechanist, for he rejected the notion of an autonomous life-force. Rather he supposed that nature contains the organic within itself, inorganic matter being matter that has ceased to live.

In his treatment of Fichte's *Wissenschaftslehre*, Schelling expressed dissatisfaction with its assignment of a passive role to nature as the nonego (*Nicht-Ich*). In order to balance Fichte's primarily ethical concerns, he sought to create a "speculative physics." His starting point was Kant's concept of natural purpose as developed in the *Critique of Judgment* and Fichte's theory of the unconscious creative ego. In a work of 1797 Schelling developed Kant's idealism in accord with Fichte's position, in that he wished to make no distinction between the thing as represented and the actual thing. According to Schelling, nature institutes in the faculty of intuition a dynamic process based on attraction and repulsion, and it is this process that appears in the intuition as an object, recognizable as such and accessible to the understanding.

In order that the individual products of nature can come to exist as enduring objects at all, the perpetually active nature-force must be opposed by an obstructing or checking force. These mutually opposed forces, the formative drive (*Bildungstrieb*) and the obstructing force, arise through the spontaneous division of the original force (*Urkraft*) of nature. The entire realm of natural occurrences is permeated by polarity (a universal principle to which the more modern term "differentiation" may be given) and dualism (conflict of forces). Their effectiveness is determined by quantity (in the mechanical natural process) or quality (in the chemical natural process). In the dead body the opposing forces are neutralized; in the chemical process the equilibrium of the forces is destroyed; and in the life process these forces are engaged in a perpetual struggle.

Out of the original forces of attraction and repulsion there emerges the primary phenomenon (*Urphänomen*) of light as the duplexity of ether (repulsive) and oxygen (attractive). Just as in magnetism, which Schelling considered the primary phenomenon of polarity, a north and a south pole stand opposed to each other; in electricity, a negative and a positive pole; and in chemistry, acids and bases—so, too, he thought, the dynamic natural process consists, universally, in the unification of the opposites on a higher plane. Accordingly, the world Soul, the organizing principle of the entire universe, is a unity of mutually conflicting forces. Its existence explains the progress observable from the lowest to the highest forms.

In his *Naturphilosophie* Schelling dealt with all the important physical, chemical, and biological phenomena and processes that occupied the scientists of his day: ether, light, weight, heat, air, gravitation, the atom (which he conceived of as a center of force), matter, combustion, electricity, magnetism, and evolution. To Kant's mechanistic theory of the formation of the cosmos, Schelling opposed an organic theory according to which the universe came into being through the expansion and contraction of the primary matter (*Urmaterie*).

Schelling's philosophy of nature was well received not only by the poets and writers of the Romantic school, but also by L. Oken, H. Steffens, K. E. von Baer, and Karl Friedrich von Burdach. The physicians of the Brownian school, who viewed man as the unity of body and soul, also welcomed Schelling's ideas. In 1802 the faculty of medicine of the University of Landshut awarded Schelling an honorary doctorate of medicine.

In his transcendental philosophy, which is partly a reworking and partly a major revision of Fichte's *Wissenschaftslehre*, Schelling treated the problem of nature from the point of view of consciousness. With the philosophy of nature, it completed the theoretical part of his doctrines. In the practical part, Schelling took up questions concerning the freedom of the will, the moral law and natural law, and the philosophy of history. The latter field, he asserted, displays the realization of the unity of necessity and freedom. For Schelling, the summit of subjective activity is attained, not in morality, as Kant and Fichte held, but in the free creative act of the artist. He alone is capable of representing the infinite in the finite, for he brings the identity of the real and the ideal, toward which philosophy aspires, to concrete representation in the work of art.

With the philosophy of identity, Schelling went one step further: real and ideal, and nature and mind are seen to be identical when conceived with sufficient understanding. Mind, and life as the bearer of mind, can be understood only on the assumption that nature is not a conglobation of dead matter, but rather, in its essence, a living primary force, capable of infinite activity. The secret of the unity of nature and mind in the Absolute, however, can ultimately be grasped only in the completion of the creative act, which leads to the product of nature. This occurs in intellectual intuition, which, according to Schelling, affords an immediate, concrete, intuitive apprehension of the Absolute. (Kant, on the other hand, reserved this intuition to the divine intellect.) Such intuition cannot be taught, but it becomes immediately evident in the contemplation of art.

Schelling was a natural philosopher, not a scientist. His philosophy of nature must be assessed in terms of the historical situation in which it was created. Along with Fichte and Hegel, he propounded an epistemological idealism the starting-point of which was the philosophy of Kant. Schelling shared a number of traits with the literary figures, scientists, and philosophers who had embraced Romanticism in reaction against the rationalism of the Enlightenment: a sense of historical development and an emphasis on feeling, the irrational, fantasy, the creative individual, and intuition. All the same, Schelling—in contradistinction to many of his followers—retained a modicum of sobriety and openness to empirical findings. Even considering that the experimental basis of the science of his time was relatively narrow, Schelling applied his concepts to nature without sufficient regard for scientific rigor and thereby brought the speculative philosophy of nature into discredit. (To be sure, some of his disciples were even less disciplined in this respect.) In Schelling's own lifetime, readers found it difficult to follow his expositions because of his penchant for esoteric formulations. The problem was especially acute for those not intimately familiar with the history of philosophy, in which Schelling had immersed himself with characteristic enthusiasm. Not surprisingly, contemporary scientists and philosophers who favored mechanistic explanations were repelled by Schelling's notions, particularly since his notions were heavily burdened with analogies. Their skeptical attitude undoubtedly hardened in response to the new knowledge steadily accumulating in all fields of biology, chemistry, and physics as a result of intensive exact research and the application of more refined methods.

Although critics were correct in denouncing Schelling's all too facile use of concepts and images, they forgot the magnitude and profundity of Schelling's project and its fruitful stimuli to further thinking. A good example of the latter is the notion of a basic type (*Bauplan*), which appears in nature in limitless variations. Another is the concept of biological evolution, although Schelling's formulation of it is closer to the Romantic ideas of evolution as a product of the creative, active force in nature than it is to Darwin's origin of species.

The impact of Schelling's *Naturphilosophie* was very great. Aside from the direct influence that his theory of nature had on such scientists as L. Oken, H. Steffens, G. H. Schubert, and Franz von Baader, its fundamental ideas entered into the thinking of the age and became the common property of educated men. Traces of them can be found in Johannes Müller, K. E. von Baer, and C. G. Carus. Only this pervasiveness can account for the violent reaction of leading scientists like Virchow, Helmholtz, and du Bois-Reymond against speculative philosophy of nature at a time when idealism and Romanticism had long ceased to be vital intellectual movements and when scientists believed that all change in nature could be explained causally through reduction to mechanics.

Beginning in 1806 Schelling occupied himself increasingly with the philosophy of religion. His own thinking on this subject was stimulated by his encounter with the ideas of Jacob Boehme, which had been brought to his attention by Franz von Baader. Schelling's conceptions, which he termed "positive" philosophy, were frequently misunderstood and vigorously attacked as a form of gnostic theosophy. Schelling himself was partially responsible for this, since he refused to publish the themes he treated in his lectures (at Munich, Erlangen, Stuttgart, and Berlin). (Some works did reach the printer, but Schelling always recalled them at the last minute to make further revisions.) Many thousands of pages of handwritten manuscripts attest to this decades-long struggle with the ultimate problems of God, freedom, and the universe. Overcoming the impasse of Romanticism, and freeing himself, in this domain, from the thinking of his age, he arrived at a new realism—that of struggling, suffering man, the fundamental concept of existentialism. A direct line can be drawn from this formulation to the work of Kierkegaard, the founder of this new philosophy and for a time Schelling's student at Berlin. It has rightly been remarked (at a congress celebrating the hundredth anniversary of Schelling's death) that Schelling's philosophy of religion held more of the future within it than of the past.

The entire corpus of Schelling's manuscripts, which were preserved at the Bavarian State Library in Munich, was destroyed during World War II. Fortunately, in 1943 H. Fuhrmans encouraged M. Schröter to examine this material. Schröter either analyzed or in some cases copied portions of the "Weltalter," which he later published. The studies undertaken in connection with or in the wake of this project have given a new impetus to research on Schelling.

BIBLIOGRAPHY

I. ORIGINAL WORKS. Schelling's collected works were edited by K. F. A. von Schelling (his second eldest son) as *Sämtliche Werke* (Stuttgart–Augsburg, 1856–1861); they appeared in two sections: the first, in 10 vols., was published between 1856 and 1861; the second, which is made up of 4 vols. taken from the posthumous MSS, appeared between 1856 and 1858. Sec. 1, vol. I (writings from 1792 to 1797) contains the following works: Schelling's master's diss. on the origin of evil, based on Genesis 3. The full Latin title is "Antiquissimi de prima malorum humanorum origine philosophematis Genesis III explicandi tentamen criticum et philosophicum" (1792). Other writings are *Über Mythen, historische Sagen und Philosopheme der ältesten Welt* (1793); *Uber die Möglichkeit einer Form der Philosophie überhaupt* (1794), Schelling's first purely philosophical work, which is a criticism of Kant in accord with Fichte's *Wissenschaftslehre*, and which sets forth the task of his future work; diss. for his theology degree, *Marcion* (1795), a study in the history of religion; a commentary on the *Wissenschaftslehre vom Ich als Prinzip der Philosophie, oder über das Unbedingte im menschlichen Wissen* (1795; repr., 1809), which shows the influence of Spinoza, whose absolute substance becomes, in Schelling, the active ego; *Philosophische Briefe über Dogmatismus und Kriticismus* (1795; repr., 1809), which first appeared anonymously, is directed against the dogmatic Kantians and exhibits the influence of Spinoza (Schelling develops Kantian doctrines in accord with Fichte's views); *Neue Deduktion des Naturrechts*, first published in *Philosophisches Journal*, **4** (1796), but completed in 1795 (it leads into the subject of practical philosophy); and *Abhandlungen zur Erläuterung des Idealismus der Wissenschaftslehre* (1796–1797; repr., 1809), an apology of Fichte's views, appeared in *Philosophisches Journal* as "Allgemeine Übersicht der neuesten philosophischen Literatur."

Vol. II, which has Schelling's first writings on the philosophy of nature, contains *Ideen zu einer Philosophie der natur* (1797), with subtitle in 2nd ed. of *Als Einleitung in das Studium dieser Wissenschaft* (here Schelling extends the *Wissenschaftslehre* into the speculative theory of nature); *Von der Weltseele, eine Hypothese der höheren Physik zur Erklärung des allgemeinen Organismus* (1798), preceded in the 2nd ed. (1806) by an essay "Über das Verhältniss des Realen und Idealen in der Natur oder Entwicklung der ersten Grundsätze der Naturphilosophie an den Principien der Schwere und des Lichts."

Schelling's first systematic works are in vol. III: *Erster Entwurf eines Systems der Naturphilosophie* (1799), with additions from Schelling's MSS; *Einleitung zu dem Entwurf eines Systems der Naturphilosophie oder über den Begriff der speculativen Physik und der inneren Organisation eines Systems der Wissenschaft* (1799); and *System des tranzendentalen Idealismus* (1800), an attempt to unite philosophy of nature, transcendental philosophy, and ethics.

Vol. IV contains *Allgemeine Deduction des dynamischen Processes oder der Kategorien der Physik* (1800), an essay on the boundary between philosophy of nature and the doctrine of identity, which originally appeared in *Zeitschrift für spekulative Physik*, **1** (1800); *Uber den wahren Begriff der Naturphilosophie und die richtige Art ihre Probleme anzufassen* (1801); *Darstellung meines Systems der Philosophie* (1801) (Philosophy of nature is Plato's theory of ideas. This work is a fragment, only first part of the theory of nature, directed at Fichte); *Bruno oder über das göttliche und natürliche Prinzip der Dinge* (1802; 2nd, unaltered ed., 1842), a dialogue in which Bruno—named for Giordano Bruno—upholds Schelling's position and convinces Lucian (Fichte) of the validity of his position; and *Fernere Darstellungen aus dem System der Philosophie* (1802).

Vol. V is *Vorlesungen über die Methode des akademischen Studiums* (1803), a literary work, which includes Schelling's farewell offering to Würzburg and also a unified account of his worldview: philosophy is the doctrine of ideas (*Ideenlehre*); the 2nd ed. (1803) has additions of the *Ideen*.

Vol. VI contains *Immanuel Kant* (1804), an obituary, which, according to the editor, was unearthed from "an obscure journal" following up an allusion made by Schelling; *Philosophie und Religion* (1804), in which philosophy is coordinated with, and even subordinated to, religion; this work shows the influence of Neoplatonism and mysticism; *Propaedeutic to Philosophy* (ca. 1804), taken from the posthumous MSS; and *System der gesammten Philosophie und der Naturphilosophie insbesondere* (1804), a development of the first three potencies of the ideal side—taken from the posthumous MSS.

Vol. VII includes the following works: *Darlegung des wahren Verhältnisses der Naturphilosophie zu der verbesserten Fichteschen Lehre, eine Erläuterungsschrift der ersten* (1806), which marks Schelling's settling with and break from Fichte; various essays in the *Jahrbücher der Medicin als Wissenschaft* (1806–1807), including "Aphorismen zur Einleitung in die Naturphilosophie," "Aphorismen über die Naturphilosophie," "Kritische Fragmente," and "Vorläufige Bezeichnung des Standpunktes der Medicin nach Grundsätzen der Naturphilosophie"; *Uber das Verhältnis der bildenden Künste zu der Natur* (1807), a lecture before the Academy of Sciences at Munich on the occasion of the birthday (12 Oct. 1807) of the Bavarian king; *Philosophische Untersuchungen über das Wesen der menschlichen Freiheit und die damit zusammenhängenden Gegenstände* (1809), taken from the posthumous MSS, still borders on the philosophy of nature but goes beyond both it and the theory of identity. In the winter of 1809–1810, following the death of Caroline, Schelling was in Stuttgart, where at the request of several friends he gave private lectures. In them he anticipated his later work in the field of the philosophy of religion. Other works in vol. VII are essays and book reviews (1807–1809) from *Jenaer, Erlanger Literaturzeitung,* and *Morgenblatt; Die Weltalter* (1814–1815), which, according to the editor, is from the posthumous MSS composed in 1814 or 1815, and which is the most complete of several existing versions of the work, which was to include three books, one each on the past, the present, and the future; *Uber die Gottheiten von Samothrake* (1815), a lecture that is a supp. to the *Weltalter,* was delivered at a public session of the Bavarian Academy of Sciences on the king's name day in 1815; and short essays (1811) from the posthumous MSS (one of them was on "weather-shooting," that is, on the influence that cannon shots, for example, might have upon the weather [thunderstorms, hail]).

Vol. IX includes *Über den Zusammenhang der Natur mit der Geisterwelt* (ca. 1816–1817), a dialogue taken from the posthumous MSS; lectures delivered (1821–1825) at Erlangen, from the posthumous MSS; Schelling's first lecture in Munich (1827); and various lectures, addresses, and speeches given from 1828 to 1841 at the Academy of Sciences or at the University.

Works in vol. X are *Vorrede zu einer philosophischen Schrift des Herrn Cousin (Fragments philosophiques),* 2nd ed. (Paris, 1833), which contains an attack on Hegel; *Darstellung des philosophischen Empirismus* (1836), from the posthumous MSS of the introductory lectures on philosophy delivered at Munich for the last time in 1836; *Anthropologisches Schema* (no date), a brief outline, written at Munich and devoted to psychological and characterological questions; Schelling's first lecture at Berlin (1841); *Darstellung des Naturprozesses* (1843–1844), a fragment of the posthumous MSS of a lecture held at Berlin on the principles of philosophy; and *Vorwort zu Henrik Steffens nachgelassenen Schriften* (1845), from a public lecture—with a few additions in Steffen's memory—held on 24 April 1845.

In the preface of sec. 2, vol. I (1856), the editor K. F. A. von Schelling explains that he undertook to prepare this edition with the assistance of his brothers at the explicit request of his father, and that he was especially aided in the first volume by his younger brother Her-

mann Schelling. Part 1, vol. I, with a historical-critical introduction and lectures 1–10, contains a philosophical criticism of the possible ways of elucidating mythology. Revised by Schelling during his last years at Munich and again at Berlin from 1842 to 1845, pt. 1 was printed 30 years previously but was never published. Part 2 of vol I, with a philosophical introduction and lectures 11–24 (Schelling's last work), is an account of rational (negative) philosophy, which is presented, however, in the form he gave to it after he had fully developed his positive philosophy.

Philosophie der Mythologie, II (1857), which includes "Buch. Der Monotheismus" and "Buch. Die Mythologie" (these works were compiled by Schelling's son after his death); *Philosophie der Offenbarung,* III (1858), which consists of "Stellung der Aufgabe, nämlich der philosophischen Religion," "Lösung der Aufgabe," and a 3rd part, which includes "Einleitung in die Philosophie der Offenbarung, 1.–8. Vorlesung," "Der Philosophie der Offenbarung erster Teil," and "Der Philosophie der Offenbarung zweiter Teil."

Other editions of Schelling's works are *Werke,* M. Schröter, ed., 6 vols. (Munich, 1927–1928), with a supp. vol. containing the original versions of the *Weltalter* (1946); and *Werke,* Otto Weiss, ed., 3 vols. (Leipzig, 1907), with a foreword by A. Drews. See also *Clara oder Zusammenhang der Natur mit der Geisterwelt,* 2nd ed. (Stuttgart, 1862), and an expanded ed. prepared by M. Schröter (Munich, 1948). For Schelling's correspondence, see *Aus Schellings Leben in Briefen, 1775–1803,* I (Leipzig, 1869), II, III (Leipzig, 1870); "Briefwechsel," in *Maximillian II, König von Bayern und Schelling,* L. Trost and F. Leist, eds. (Stuttgart, 1891); and *Caroline, Briefe* (to her brothers and sisters, her daughter Auguste, the Gotter family, F. L. W. Meyer, A. W. and F. Schlegel, and J. Schelling), G. Waitz, ed. (Schelling's son-in-law).

II. SECONDARY LITERATURE. On Schelling and his work, see Kuno Fischer, "Geschichte der neueren Philosophie," in *Schellings Leben und Lehre,* 4th ed., VII (Heidelberg, 1923), with an appendix that contains H. Falkenheim's thorough list of literature on Schelling up to 1922; Horst Fuhrmans, *Schellings Philosophie der Weltalter. Schellings Philosophie in den Jahren 1806–1821. Zum Problem des Schellingschen Idealismus* (Düsseldorf, 1954); Eduard von Hartmann, *Schellings philosophisches System* (Leipzig, 1897); Hinrich Knittermeyer, *Schelling und die romantische Schule* (Munich, 1928); Wolfgang Pfeiffer-Belli, "Schelling und seine Weltalter," in *Philosophisches Jahrbuch,* **58,** pt. 1 (1948), 65–68; G. Schneeberger, *F. W. J. von Schelling* (Berne, 1954); Manfred Schröter, *Kritische Studien. Über Schelling und zur Kulturphilosophie* (Munich, 1971); and Wilhelm Szilasi, *Philosophie und Naturwissenschaft* (Berne, 1961).

See also Bernhard Taureck, *Mathematische und transzendentale Identität* (Vienna–Munich, 1973); Friedrich Ueberweg, *Grundriss der Geschichte der Philosophie* (Tübingen, 1951), 35–67; John Watson, *Schelling's*

Transcendental Idealism (Chicago, 1882); Wolfgang Wieland, "Schellings Lehre von der Zeit," in *Grundlagen und Voraussetzungen der Weltalterphilosophie* (Hamburg, 1956).

Schelling founded or cofounded the following periodicals: *Zeitschrift für speculative Physik*, 2 vols. (1800–1801), followed by *Neue Zeitschrift für speculative Physik*, pt. 1 (1802); *Kritisches Journal der Philosophie* (1802–1803), edited with Hegel; and *Jahrbücher der Medizin als Wissenschaft* (1806–1808), edited with A. F. Marcus.

EDITH SELOW

SCHEUCHZER, JOHANN JAKOB (*b.* Zurich, Switzerland, 2 August 1672; *d.* Zurich, 23 June 1733), *medicine, natural history, mathematics, geology, geophysics.*

A diligent pupil at the age of three, Scheuchzer later became a brilliant student at the Carolinum in Zurich. Devoted to the natural sciences, he decided to study medicine and, having won a scholarship in 1691, was able to enroll in both science and medicine courses at the Altdorf Academy, near Nuremberg. He remained there for two years, then went to Utrecht, where he was awarded the doctorate in 1694. The fossil collection that he began assembling in 1690 soon became famous and brought Scheuchzer to the attention of the scholarly world. In 1694 he returned to Zurich and began systematic exploration of the Alps. His first writings for the Collegium der Wohlgesinnten (1695) were a scientific study of the Helvetic Alps. Scheuchzer then went to Nuremberg, where he studied for a diploma in mathematics, intending to teach this subject. But he was recalled to Zurich to become assistant municipal physician and medical supervisor of the orphanage. A few years later he became head of the Bibliothèque des Bourgeois, a post that he occupied while serving as director of the Museum of Natural History (then called the Kunsthammer).

By the age of thirty Scheuchzer had become prominent in Zurich and was carrying on a voluminous correspondence with many European scholars that has become of great interest to historians of science. A grant from the Zurich government in 1702 enabled him to resume his Alpine excursions, which provided the subject for numerous communications on geology, geophysics, natural sciences, and medicine. The results of his annual excursions to the Alps are presented in *Helvetiae stoicheiographia* (1716–1718), his greatest work in natural history and geophysics. In 1716 he became profes-

sor of mathematics at the Carolinum, and a few months before his death he was named *premier médecin* of Zurich, professor of physics at the Academy, and *Chorherr.*

Scheuchzer left the municipal library of Zurich more than 260 folio volumes, which he wrote in less than forty years. The moving force in the establishment of paleontology in Switzerland, he is also considered the founder of paleobotany and his *Herbarium diluvianum* remained a standard through the nineteenth century. His work on a great variety of fossils and notably on *Homo diluvii testis* of Oensingen (1726) makes him generally considered the founder of European paleontology. Scheuchzer became famous for his medical studies on the effects of altitude, published a remarkable topographic map of Switzerland, and took an active part in the military life of his canton as an army doctor.

In addition to his scientific accomplishments, Scheuchzer compiled a twenty-nine-volume *Histoire suisse* and a critical collection of deeds and other documents, entitled *Diploma Helvetiae.*

BIBLIOGRAPHY

I. ORIGINAL WORKS. A complete bibliography of Scheuchzer is in the Steiger article (below) with a list of his correspondence. Among his works are his medical diss., *De surdo audiento* (Zurich, 1694); "De generatione conchitarum," in *Miscellanea curiosa Academiae naturae curiosorum*, IV (Zurich, 1697); *Helvetiae stoicheiographia, orographia et oreographia* (Zurich, 1716); *Homo diluvii testis* (1726); and *Physica sacra*, 3 vols. (Zurich, 1731–1733).

II. SECONDARY LITERATURE. The most complete account of Scheuchzer is R. Steiger, "Johann Jakob Scheuchzer (1672–1733)," in *Beiblatt zur Vierteljahrsschrift der Naturforschenden Gesellschaft in Zurich*, **21** (1933), 1–75, with a complete bibliography. See also C. Walkmeister, "J. J. Scheuchzer und seiner Zeit," in *Bericht der St. Gallischen naturwissenschaft Gesellschaft* (1896), 364–401; F. X. Hoeherl, "J. J. Scheuchzer, der Begrunder der physischen Geographie des Hochgebirges" (diss., University of Munich, 1901); and B. Peyer, "J. J. Scheuchzer im europaischen Geistleben seiner Zeit," in *Gesnerus*, **2** (1945), 23–33.

P. E. PILET

SCHIAPARELLI, GIOVANNI VIRGINIO (*b.* Savigliano, Cuneo province, Italy, 14 March 1835; *d.* Milan, Italy, 4 July 1910), *astronomy.*

After receiving his degree in civil engineering at Turin in 1854, Schiaparelli taught mathematics and studied modern languages and astronomy at the University of Turin. As a result of his increasing interest in astronomy, in 1857 he was sent by the Piedmont government to continue advanced studies at the observatories of Berlin and Pulkovo. On his return to Italy in 1860. Schiaparelli was appointed astronomer at the Brera Observatory in Milan; and in 1862, when his work had already brought him a certain renown, he succeeded Francesco Carlini as director. He retired voluntarily in 1900 and spent the rest of his life in Milan. In 1889 Schiaparelli became senator of the kingdom of Italy; he also was a member of the Lincei and of many other Italian and foreign academies. He received gold medals from the governments of Italy, England, and Germany, and twice won the Lalande Prize of the Institut de France.

At the beginning of his observations at Brera, Schiaparelli, using primitive instruments, discovered the asteroid Hesperia. In 1860 he became interested in comets and undertook a theoretical study on the initial direction of their tails in which he demonstrated the existence of a repulsive force that tends to pull parts of the tail away from the part opposite the sun. This force, combined with gravity, generates in the tail a parabola, similar to that described by terrestrial projectiles.

The appearance of the bright comet of 1862 stimulated Schiaparelli's interest in these celestial objects; and while observing it, he reflected on the forces that determine the features of comets in general. His accurate study of the shape and position of the tails of comets led him to new theories on the repulsive action exerted by the sun and to classify the tails according to this action.

Schiaparelli assiduously continued his observations of physical position and calculations of the orbits of comets while developing the idea that comets give rise to meteors. It was discovered that Biela's comet, when it appeared in 1845, had split in two; and on its next appearance, in August 1852, Secchi found its larger fragment. The smaller fragment was discovered about a month later at a far greater distance from the first than had previously been calculated. It became clear that the comet was disintegrating as it approached the sun. In April 1862, still using the modest instruments available at Brera, Schiaparelli observed the large comet of that year and saw that the nucleus—the luminous head of the comet followed by a long tail—was emitting a luminous jet that rapidly increased in size and assumed the shape of a clearly outlined pear. Its mass was much greater than the nucleus proper; the form was that of a small cloud

in which, over a clear background, more luminous points flared at intervals, like small stars visible in the field of a telescope.

The hypothesis had been advanced that meteor showers, observed over the centuries as originating from a well-defined point in the sky, could be related to the disintegration of comets. Schiaparelli's hypothesis was based chiefly on his observations of the meteor swarms of August 1866. He stated the hypothesis more definitely in five letters to Secchi "concerning the course and probable origin of the meteoric stars." Secchi published the letters in *Bullettino meteorologico dell'Osservatorio del Collegio romano* in 1866. To confirm his hypothesis Schiaparelli had to prove that if meteors are subject to the attraction of the sun, they must move in elliptical or parabolic orbits around it and that these orbits must be identical with or similar to those of the comets that cause meteor swarms. The latter become visible when the earth, in its course around the sun, meets either of the swarms that extend along its orbit. In the second letter Schiaparelli stated that in the planetary spaces the meteors must form a multitude of continuous currents that, on meeting the earth in its orbit, become visible in the form of luminous showers falling from a determined direction of the celestial sphere. Secchi accurately observed these directions (the "radiants") and proved that the orbit of the periodic stars of August is practically identical to that of the large comet of 1862.

Schiaparelli published a complete elaboration of his theory as *Entwurf einer astronomischen Theorie der Sternschnuppen* (1871). Following the extraordinary meteor shower of 27 November 1872, he explained the phenomena and the theory behind them in three letters. In the third letter he stated:

> The meteor showers are the product of the dissolution of the comets and consist of very minute particles that they . . . have abandoned along their orbit because of the disintegrating force that the sun and the planets exert on the very fine matter of which they are composed.

Schiaparelli's hypothesis on the origin of meteors, elaborated in depth and with elegance, has been fully confirmed in the several cases listed: these include the relation he discovered between the Perseids of 10 August and the great comet of 1862; C. H. F. Peters' observations concerning the November Leonids in relation to the comet of 1866; and Galle's and Weiss's studies of the first comet of 1861 and the meteor shower of 20 April. A fourth case deals with Biela's comet, the relations of which to certain previously observed meteors had been noted as early as 1867 by d'Arrest and Weiss and were confirmed by the meteor shower of 27 November 1872. The meteor showers of 1933 and 1946 are related to the Giacobini-Zinner comet; the swarm of the Taurids, to Encke's comet. Thus, Schiaparelli's theory was confirmed.

In 1877, using a Merz refractor far superior to the antiquated instruments he had previously used, Schiaparelli turned his attention to the study of Mars. This exceptional instrument, with an objective aperture of twenty-two centimeters, revealed "a large quantity of minute objects, which in the earlier oppositions had been overlooked by the gigantic telescopes in which foreign countries justly take pride." During the great opposition of Mars in 1877 Schiaparelli observed the planet thoroughly, detecting even the smallest surface features. He began to determine the orientation of Mars in the sky, publishing a first memoir in *Astronomische Nachrichten*: "Sur l'axe de rotation et sur la tâche polaire australe de Mars." It was followed by *Osservazioni astronomiche e fisiche sull'asse di rotazione e sulla topografia del pianeta Marte durante l'opposizione del 1877.*

In drawing a complete picture of the areographic positions of the fundamental points for the construction of an accurate map, Schiaparelli stated that the interpretation of the phenomena observed on Mars was still largely hypothetical, varying among observers even when they saw the same details. He was the first to classify the features as "seas" and "continents"; the term "canal" had been used by Secchi in his observations of 1859. Schiaparelli's was an original nomenclature, and he observed that "the names I adopted will in no way harm the cold and rigorous observations of facts." Although he understood that the features he observed on Mars were stable, like their terrestrial counterparts, he was cautious in drawing conclusions on the nature of the surface and atmosphere until he could establish that the seas, continents, and canals were identifiable with analogous terrestrial formations.

During the opposition of 1879–1880 Schiaparelli continued his observations, from which he prepared a catalog of the positions of all visible topographical features. In it he sought to provide a less geometric interpretation than that of his first map of 1877–1878. Schiaparelli noted that because Mars was moving away from the earth, its diameter gradually decreased during subsequent oppositions. In 1879 he had observed that certain canals seemed to be splitting into two parts. In the 1881–1882 opposition he noted the increasing clarity of the geminations of canals, which he thought would greatly change current opinions on the physical constitution of the planet. His areographic map of this opposition apparently is a more geometric representation, perhaps in order to stress the gemination of the canals, which also appeared in the 1883–1884 oppositions. In the latter nearly all of them were split.

In his observations of the 1886 opposition, Schiaparelli used a new refractor with an aperture of fifty centimeters, among the largest at that time. The disk of the planet then measured only ten seconds in diameter and Schiaparelli, continuing to make increasingly geometric drawings, marked only one large gemination: the Nilus-Hydrae Fons. In the 1888 opposition, which occurred under good atmospheric conditions, he found it impossible to represent adequately all the detailed features and their colors. Observing the geminations that had been absent from the preceding opposition, Schiaparelli thought that their reappearance constituted a strictly periodic phenomenon related to the solar year of Mars, and that it was necessary to follow it closely in successive, and more favorable, oppositions. He noted that the split canals appeared and remained visible for a few days or weeks before again becoming simple canals or disappearing entirely.

Schiaparelli's observations of Mars ended with the 1890 opposition. This cycle included seven oppositions that present all conceivable varieties of inclinations of the axis, of the apparent diameter, and of geocentric declination, and it occurred at points along the zodiac almost equidistant from each other. Schiaparelli recalled that three astronomers of the Lick observatory, using the refractor with a ninety-two-centimeter aperture, insisted they saw the same details differently through the same telescope and, one might say, at the same instant. Other observers, using less powerful instruments, saw a thick web of lines (the canals proper) so clearly that they could be recognized with good telescopes having an aperture of only ten centimeters. The last areographic map, which Schiaparelli drew at the conclusion of his observations, is the most geometric of all and depicts most of the canals as split. E. Antoniadi, another well-known observer of Mars, using a telescope with an eighty-three-centimeter aperture at the Meudon (Paris) observatory, noted in 1930 that Schiaparelli, with instruments of equal power, had surpassed everyone with his numerous observations.

Schiaparelli also observed Saturn and, for eight years, the few dark spots visible on Mercury in the form of shadowy bands, difficult to recognize in full daylight. He concluded that Mercury revolves about the sun in the same manner that the moon does around the earth and Iapetus around Saturn—with the same side always turned to the sun. He also tried to solve the problem of the rotation of Venus on its axis. In outlining the history of the subject, which also concerned Jean-Dominique Cassini, he recalled the observations made at Rome in 1726 by Francesco Bianchini. On the basis of the diffused and indefinite shadows visible on the surface, Bianchini had concluded that it completed one rotation on its axis in about twenty-four days and eight hours. Schiaparelli observed Venus in 1877 and 1878, noting luminous oval spots that were quite visible but transitory, perhaps resulting from variations in the planet's atmosphere. He concluded that the rotation of Venus was "very slow . . . , much slower than Bianchini had supposed." From observations of well-defined spots, he obtained as a very probable result that the rotation occurs in 224.7 days, a period exactly equal to that of the sidereal revolution of the planet around an axis almost coincident with the perpendicular to the plane of the orbit.

Schiaparelli also made numerous observations of double stars. For many of the more interesting binaries, the measurements were continued for several years, in order to deduce the orbital elements of the systems.

Schiaparelli's work in the history of astronomy was noteworthy. The orientalist C. A. Nallino was sent by the Brera Observatory to the Escorial to copy and translate into Latin the only existing Arab text of al-Battānī's *Opus astronomicum*. Schiaparelli collaborated with Nallino to complete the translation, which was published by the Brera Observatory between 1899 and 1907. He also contributed many explanatory notes to several chapters. He noted that much more was known about Arab astronomy as a result of the translation of this vast work, which is not limited to the works of al-Battānī. A comparison between the *Opus astronomicum* and Ptolemy's *Almagest*, with which there are many points of similarity, is of special value to an understanding of the development of astronomy in the Arab world.

Schiaparelli had intended to compile a major work on the history of ancient astronomy, In preparation for it he read the original texts of the He-brews, Assyrians, Greeks, and Romans. During his lifetime he published several monographs on the subject. These and many similar works that Schiaparelli was not able to complete were published by his pupil Luigi Gabba in 1925–1927.

The first volume deals with the astronomy of Babylonia, of the Old Testament lands, and of Greece. In the second volume he treats later Greek astronomy: the homocentric spheres of Eudoxus of Cnidus, Callippus, and Aristotle. Schiaparelli next considers the origin of the Greek heliocentric planetary system with Aristarchus of Samos, who, as Schiaparelli demonstrates, must have developed the system through the hypothesis proposed centuries later by Tycho Brahe. According to Schiaparelli's research, the Tychonic system was known to the Greeks at the time of Heraclides Ponticus (fourth century B.C.). The second volume ends with minor writings on "parapegmata," the astrometeorological calendars of the ancients. The third volume contains writings designed to integrate the history of ancient astronomy: his studies on the calendar of the ancient Egyptians; on the observations and ephemerides of the Babylonians; on the phenomena of Venus, according to the discoveries made in the ruins of Nineveh; on the discovery of the precession of the equinoxes; and on the astronomy of Hipparchus. These three volumes, even though they may not contain all that Schiaparelli had wanted to include in the project, nevertheless provide data and information of inestimable value on the history of ancient astronomy.

BIBLIOGRAPHY

I. ORIGINAL WORKS. Schiaparelli's writings have been brought together in *Le opere di G. V. Schiaparelli*, 11 vols. (Milan, 1929–1943); and *Scritti sulla storia della astronomia antica*, Luigi Gabba, ed., 3 vols. (Bologna, 1925–1927).

II. SECONDARY LITERATURE. See G. Abetti, *Storia della astronomia* (Florence, 1963), 224–228; and the obituary by E. Millosevich, in *Memorie della Società degli spettroscopisti italiani*, **39** (1910), 138–140, with photograph.

GIORGIO ABETTI

SCHICKARD, WILHELM (*b*. Herrenberg, Germany, 22 April 1592; *d*. Tübingen, Germany, 23 October 1635), *astronomy, mathematics, natural philosophy*.

Schickard, a brilliant student, received the B.A.

in 1609 and the M.A. in 1611 from the University of Tübingen, where he continued with the study of theology and oriental languages until 1613. He then served as deacon or pastor in several nearby towns. In 1617 he befriended Kepler, who reawakened in him an interest in mathematics and astronomy and with whom he maintained an active correspondence for several years. In 1619 he was named professor of Hebrew at the University of Tübingen. Upon the death in 1631 of his former teacher, Michael Mästlin, Schickard succeeded to the chair of astronomy but continued to lecture on Hebrew.

Schickard was a polymath who knew several Near Eastern languages, some of which he taught himself. He was a skilled mechanic, cartographer, and engraver in wood and copperplate; and he wrote treatises on Semitic studies, mathematics, astronomy, optics, meteorology, and cartography. He invented and built a working model of the first modern mechanical calculator and proposed to Kepler the development of a mechanical means of calculating ephemerides. Schickard's works on astronomy include a lunar ephemeris, observations of the comets of 1618, and descriptions of unusual solar phenomena (meteors and the transit of Mercury in 1631). He also constructed and described a teaching device consisting of a hollow sphere in three segments with the heavens represented on the inside.

Schickard was an early supporter of Kepler's theories; his treatise on the 1631 transit of Mercury called attention to some of Kepler's ideas and works and to the superiority of the *Rudolphine Tables*. Schickard also mentioned Kepler's first two laws of planetary motion; the second law, however, was given only in the inverse-distance, rather than in the correct, equal-areas formulation.

BIBLIOGRAPHY

I. ORIGINAL WORKS. Schickard's unpublished MSS are in the Österreichische Nationalbibliothek of Vienna and in the Württembergische Landesbibliothek in Stuttgart. His chief works (all published in Tübingen) are *Astroscopium pro facillima stellarum cognitione noviter excogitatum* (1623); *Ignis versicolor e coelo sereno delapsus et Tubingae spectatus* (1623); *Weiterer Bericht von der Fliegenden Liecht-Kugel* (1624); *Anemographia, seu discursus philosophicus de ventis* (1631); *Contemplatio physica de origine animae rationalis* (1631); and *Pars responsi ad epistolas P. Gassendi . . . de mercurio sub sole viso et alijs novitatibus uranicis* (1632). Useful collections of his correspondence are in *Epistolae W. Schickarti et M. Berneggeri mutuae* (Strasbourg, 1673); *Johannes Kepler Gesammelte Werke*, **17–18**, Max Caspar, ed. (Munich, 1955, 1959); and the appendix to Schnurrer's biography (see below), pp. 249–274.

II. SECONDARY LITERATURE. The standard biographies remain Johann C. Speidel, in his ed. of Schickard's *Nova et plenior grammatica Hebraica* (Tübingen, 1731) and Christian F. Schnurrer, in *Biographische und litterarische Nachrichten von ehmaligen Lehrern der hebräischen Litteratur in Tübingen* (Ulm, 1792), 160–225. Recent accounts of Schickard's invention of the calculating machine are Franz Hammer, "Nicht Pascal, sondern der Tübinger Professor Wilhelm Schickard erfand die Rechenmaschine," in *Büromarkt-Bibliothek*, **13** (1958), 1023–1025; and René Taton, "Sur l'invention de la machine arithmétique," in *Revue d'histoire des sciences et de leurs applications*, **16** (1963), 139–160.

WILBUR APPLEBAUM

SCHIFF, HUGO JOSEF (*b.* Frankfurt, Germany, 26 April 1834; *d.* Florence, Italy, 8 September 1915), *chemistry.*

Schiff, the last surviving representative of the Karlsruhe Congress (1860), was the brother of the distinguished physiologist Moritz Schiff. He studied under Wöhler at Göttingen and was awarded the doctorate in 1857. Shortly thereafter he left Germany because of his strong liberal views and became *Privatdozent* at the University of Bern. In 1863 the physicist Carlo Matteucci invited Schiff to Florence. He taught chemistry at the Museo di Storia Naturale until 1876, when he became professor of general chemistry at the University of Turin. In 1879 he returned to Florence to assume the chair of chemistry at the Istituto di Studi Superiori, remaining there for the rest of his life.

In addition to his prolific research, Schiff devoted himself to disseminating chemical knowledge and to continuing the tradition represented by Berzelius and Wöhler, on whose teaching methods he modeled his own. At Florence he transformed the chemistry laboratory into one of the best in Europe. In 1871, with Cannizzaro and Francesco Selmi, he founded the journal *Gazzetta chimica italiana*. Schiff wrote the widely used *Introduzione allo studio della chimica* (1876) and also contributed many articles to Francesco Selmi's *Enciclopedia di chimica* (1868–1883). A man of many interests, he also published writings in history and literary criticism.

Schiff's chemical studies were predominantly in organic chemistry. His earliest noteworthy work was his isolation and investigation in 1857 of thionyl chloride from the action of sulfur dioxide on phosphorus pentachloride. In 1864 he discovered the condensation products of aldehydes and amines, later known as "Schiff bases." In 1866 Schiff introduced the fuchsine test for aldehydes, in which decolorized fuchsine regains its color in the presence of aldehydes, the color reaction being specific for aldehydes and serving to distinguish them from ketones. His studies on the color bases derived from furfural led to his discovery of the sensitive xylidine-acetic acid reagent for furfural.

Schiff published many papers on the constitution of natural glucosides, examining esculin, amygdalin, arbutin, helicin, and phlorizin. By fusing salicin with benzoic anhydride, he synthesized populin, a glucoside present in the bark and leaves of aspen trees. Other researches dealt with metal-ammonium compounds, the biuret reaction, esters of boric acid, and the constitution of tannins. A resourceful experimentalist, Schiff in 1866 devised the nitrometer that bears his name, an improved version of the Dumas method for the determination of nitrogen.

Before Emil Fischer, Schiff attempted to obtain high-molecular-weight polymers of amino acids having the properties of proteins. By condensing aspartic acid molecules, he prepared tetraaspartic and octoaspartic acids. His formulas did not, however, include the peptide linkages that Fischer later proposed to explain how amino acid molecules were joined in proteins.

BIBLIOGRAPHY

I. ORIGINAL WORKS. Schiff's books include *Untersuchungen über metallhaltige Anilinderivate und über die Bildung des Anilinroths* (Berlin, 1864); *Introduzione allo studio della chimica* (Turin, 1876); and *Empirismo e metodo nell'applicazione di chimica alle scienze naturale e biologiche* (Turin, 1877). The more important of his almost 300 published papers include "Über die Einwirkung des Phosphorsuperchlorids auf einige anorganische Säuren," in *Justus Liebigs Annalen der Chemie,* **102** (1857), 111–118; "Eine neue Reihe organischer Basen," *ibid.,* **131** (1864), 118–119; "Eine neue Reihe organischer Diamine," *ibid.,* **140** (1866), 92–137; "Zur Azotometrie," in *Zeitschrift für analytische Chemie,* **7** (1868), 430–432; "Untersuchungen über Salicinderivate," in *Justus Liebigs Annalen der Chemie,* **150** (1869), 193–200; and **154** (1870), 1–39; "Zur Stickstoffbestimmung," in *Berichte der Deutschen chemischen Gesellschaft,* **13** (1880), 885–887; "Über Polyaspartsäuren," *ibid.,* **30** (1897), 2449–2459; and "Intorno a composti poliaspartici," in *Gazzetta chimica italiana,* **28**, pt. 1 (1898), 49–64; **29**, pt. 1 (1899), 319–340; and **30**, pt. 1 (1900), 8–25.

II. SECONDARY LITERATURE. For accounts of Schiff's life and work, see M. Betti, in *Berichte der Deutschen chemischen Gesellschaft,* **48** (1915), 1566–1567; and *Journal of the Chemical Society,* **109** (1916), 424–428; I. Guareschi, in *Atti dell' Accademia delle scienze* (Turin), **52** (1917), 333–351; and William McPherson, in *Science,* **43** (1916), 921–922.

ALBERT B. COSTA

SCHIFF, MORITZ (*b*. Frankfurt, Germany, 28 January 1823; *d*. Geneva, Switzerland, 6 October 1896), *zoology, physiology.*

Schiff was one of the eminent biologists who pioneered the experimental method in the new science of physiology. Following in the steps of his teacher Magendie, he approached the subject matter from a biological point of view instead of carrying out reductionist physicochemical studies like those of du Bois-Reymond and Helmholtz. Schiff's often controversial vivisections uncovered details in spinal cord physiology, clarified the role of the autonomic nervous system, and revealed the importance of certain internal secretions.

Schiff was descended from a family of Jewish merchants. His interest in the natural sciences emerged in early childhood, during which he established in his attic a veritable museum of small animals. Following the family tradition, Schiff was sent to study the textile business, but his utter incompetence convinced his father that his talents lay elsewhere.

Thus, in the late 1830's Schiff began to study the natural sciences at the Senckenberg Institute, transferring to Heidelberg in 1840 in order to pursue a career in medicine. After some anatomical work with Friedrich Tiedemann, Schiff moved to Berlin, where he studied morphology with Johannes Müller. Finally, in 1843, he went to Göttingen as a student of Rudolf Wagner and received his medical degree there a year later.

After his graduation Schiff traveled to Paris in order to conduct zoological research at the museum of the Jardin des Plantes. He also visited local hospitals and studied experimental techniques with Magendie and served briefly as a research assistant to both François Longet and Carlo Matteucci, who were studying the physiology of the nervous system.

In 1845 Schiff returned to Frankfurt to practice medicine. Instead of seeing many patients, he spent most of his time in a small homemade laboratory, where he conducted physiological experiments. In 1846 he was appointed a member of the ornithology section of the Senckenberg Museum, where he cataloged South American birds.

Schiff's early research dealt with cardiac contraction and its possible relation to nerve-mediated action. By 1849 he had concluded that the diastole was a reflection of nervous exhaustion. Following studies on digestion and the influence of neural centers on bodily heat, Schiff received the Montyon Prize of the French Academy in 1854 for his work on bone physiology.

A year later Schiff decided to begin his academic career at Göttingen, but his petition to become *Privatdozent* in zoology was rejected by the university authorities without explanation. The true reasons for the decision were Schiff's Jewish ancestry and his past membership in the revolutionary medical corps during the 1848 uprising in Baden. Undaunted, Schiff accepted an appointment in 1856 as assistant professor of comparative anatomy and zoology at the University of Bern. In 1859, after rejecting an offer to teach physiology at Jena, he was appointed professor of physiology at the Istituto di Studii Superiori of the University of Florence in 1862. During the ensuing years, the most productive of his scientific career, he studied the pathways of pain and touch in the spinal cord.

In 1874 Schiff made a comparative study of the two anesthetic agents then in vogue, chloroform and ether. He succeeded in proving the toxicity of the former and branded its use dangerous. A systematic campaign aimed at his vivisection experiments forced Schiff to leave Florence in 1876, and he returned to Switzerland to assume the chair of physiology at the University of Geneva. Before his death from diabetes, Schiff studied primarily the functions of the thyroid, establishing the foundations for the surgical removal of goiters. He was a corresponding member of the Royal Academy of Rome and Paris Academy of Medicine, and a coeditor of the *Schweizerische Zeitschrift für Heilkunde.*

Schiff pioneered research on the vasomotor functions of the autonomic nervous system and especially the innervation of the heart. He also studied thyroid function, artificially inducing myxedema through the surgical removal of the gland and reversing that condition through thyroid transplants in dogs. Schiff wrote on the formation of glycogen in the liver in experimentally induced diabetes, using Claude Bernard's puncture of the fourth ventricle in the brain.

BIBLIOGRAPHY

I. Original Works. Schiff's collected papers in German and French were published as *Moritz Schiff's gesammelte Beiträge zur Physiologie,* 4 vols. (Lausanne, 1894–1898). In vol. I Schiff himself rearranged some of his articles on the centers in the nervous system that are related to respiration. The papers are arranged by topic and then presented chronologically. Vol. IV was edited by Alexandre Herzen and Émile Levier.

Schiff's earlier books include *Untersuchungen zur Physiologie des Nervensystems mit Berücksichtigung der Pathologie* (Frankfurt, 1855); and *Untersuchungen über die Zuckerbildung in der Leber, und den Einfluss des Nervensystems auf die Erzeugung der Diabetes* (Würzburg, 1859). He began a textbook of physiology, completing the first volume on muscle physiology and neurophysiology: *Lehrbuch der Physiologie des Menschen* (Lahr, 1858–1859).

Several of his Italian lectures were translated into French by R. Guichard de Choisity as *Contribution à la physiologie: De l'inflammation et de la circulation* (Paris, 1873). Two works written in Italian are *Lezioni di fisiologia sperimentale sul sistema nervoso encefalico,* compiled by P. Marchi (Florence, 1865); and *La pupilla come estesiometro* (Florence, 1875).

II. Secondary Literature. Among the short biographical sketches of Schiff is an obituary note by Arthur Biedl in *Wiener klinische Wochenschrift,* 9, no. 44 (1896), 1008–1010; the article by J. R. Ewald in *Allgemeine deutsche Biographie,* LIV, 8–11; and the entry in August Hirsch, ed., *Biographisches Lexikon der hervorragenden Ärzter,* 2nd ed., V, 72–73. More recent is P. Riedo, "Der Physiologe Moritz Schiff (1823–1896) und die Innervation des Herzens," *Zürcher medizingeschichtliche Abhandlungen,* n.s. no. 85 (1970).

Schiff's formal application for an academic position at the University of Göttingen has been published together with some biographical details by H. Friedenwald, "Notes on Moritz Schiff (1823–1896)," in *Bulletin of the Institute of the History of Medicine,* 5 (1937), 589–602; the document furnishes a chronological account of Schiff's physiological research before 1855. A recent brief editorial containing some paragraphs of Schiff's articles in English translation is "Moritz Schiff (1823–1896), Experimental Physiologist," in *Journal of the American Medical Association,* 203 (1968), 1133–1134.

Guenter B. Risse

SCHIMPER, ANDREAS FRANZ WILHELM (*b.* Strasbourg, France, 12 May 1856; *d.* Basel, Switzerland, 9 September 1901), *botany.*

Schimper was the son of Wilhelm Philipp Schimper, professor of natural history and geology at the University of Strasbourg and director of the city's museum of natural history. From 1864 to 1874 he attended the Strasbourg Gymnasium. His father allowed him to take part in the excursions he conducted for his students. His mother, Adèle Besson, who was greatly interested in her husband's botanical activities, stimulated the boy's interest in natural history.

In 1874 Schimper entered the University of Strasbourg, where he came under the influence of Anton de Bary. He received the doctorate in natural philosophy in November 1878. While at Strasbourg he studied the origin and development of starch grains. Following the death in 1880 of his father, whose assistant he had been, the trustees of the museum of natural history elected him director. De Bary opposed the appointment, although he acknowledged Schimper as one of his best students. As a result, Schimper accepted a post at the Lyons botanical garden but soon returned to Germany to work with Julius Sachs at Würzburg.

In the autumn of 1880 Schimper was appointed a fellow of the Johns Hopkins University in Baltimore. The results of his further observations on the growth of starch grains induced him to abandon Naegeli's intussusception theory. In the spring of 1881 he went to Florida and, the following winter, to the West Indies. These trips awakened Schimper's interest in plant geography. During the summer he visited the zoological summer laboratory at Annisquam, Massachusetts, where he studied insectivorous plants. Schimper returned to Germany in January 1882 and worked in the laboratory of Eduard Strasburger at Bonn until 1898. Strasburger, who ranked Schimper as one of his outstanding students, was instrumental in keeping him in Germany when an attractive post in the United States was offered to him in 1889.

From December 1882 to August 1883 Schimper traveled in Barbados, Trinidad, Venezuela, and Dominica, studying the morphology and biology of the epiphytes. On 16 November 1883 he was appointed lecturer in physiological botany at the University of Bonn. He lectured on plant geography, historical and geographical distribution of important cultivated plants, and, after 1885, on medicinal plants, pharmacognosy, and microscopic research on drugs and food products. He also made botanical excursions with his students. On 12 February 1886 he was named extraordinary professor.

During these years Schimper wrote very important medicopharmaceutical books. In August 1886 he traveled to Brazil, where he studied the mangrove vegetation. In both the West Indies and Brazil he made observations and physiological experiments to determine the influence of high salt con-

centrations on the marine littoral vegetation. To study the vegetation of tropical beaches Schimper visited Ceylon and Java in 1889–1890. During this voyage he visited the Buitenzorg (now Bogor) botanic garden, near Batavia (now Jakarta) and made excursions to several volcanoes with solfataras and halophytic vegetation.

In July 1898 Schimper joined the important German marine expedition on board the *Valdivia*, during which he studied the oceanic plankton flora and the vegetation of the Canary Islands, Kerguelen, the Seychelles, Cameroon, the Congo and eastern Africa, Sumatra, and the Cape of Good Hope. In October, near Cameroon, he suffered a severe attack of malaria, from the effects of which he never recovered.

In June 1898 Schimper had been appointed professor of botany at the University of Basel, where he took up his duties in April 1899. The following February he delivered his inaugural oration on marine plankton but his deteriorating health (he had suffered from diabetes since 1899) prevented him from carrying out his duties for long.

Schimper, who was able to penetrate quickly to the core of scientific problems, preferred to work independently. Not physically strong, he had enormous energy and enthusiasm, and a very deep love for nature. He was greatly interested in literature and the arts. Schimper did not care for large groups, preferring to spend the evenings with a few close friends. Although solid and accurate in his research, he was impulsive in thought and speech.

BIBLIOGRAPHY

The most important of Schimper's 27 books and articles are *Untersuchungen über die Proteinkrystalloide der Pflanzen* (Strasbourg, 1878), his dissertation; "Untersuchungen über die Entstehung der Stärkekörner," in *Botanische Zeitung,* **38** (1880), 881–902, in English in *Quarterly Journal of Microscopical Science,* **21** (1881), 291–306; "Untersuchungen über das Wachsthum der Stärkekörner," in *Botanische Zeitung,* **39** (1881), 185–194, 201–211, 217–228; "The Growth of Starch Grains," abstract, in *American Naturalist,* **15** (1881), 556–558; "Die Vegetationsorgane von *Prosopanche burmeisteri,*" in *Abhandlungen der Naturforschenden Gesellschaft zu Halle,* **15** (1882), 21–47; *Anleitung zur mikroskopischen Untersuchung der Nahrungs- und Genussmittel* (Jena, 1886); *Taschenbuch der medicinisch-pharmaceutischen Botanik und pflanzlichen Drogenkunde* (Strasbourg, 1886); *Schimper's botanische Mittheilungen aus den Tropen,* 3 vols. (Jena, 1888–1891): I, *Die Wechselbeziehungen zwischen Pflanzen und Ameisen im tropischen Amerika;* II, *Die epiphy-*

tische Vegetation Amerikas; III, *Die indomalayische Strandflora;* "Ueber Schutzmittel des Laubes gegen Transpiration, besonders in der Flora Java's," in *Sitzungsberichte der Preussischen Akademie der Wissenschaften zu Berlin,* Phys.-math. Kl., **40** (1890), 1045–1062; and *Pflanzengeographie auf physiologischer Grundlage* (Jena, 1898), trans. as *Plant Geography Upon a Physiological Basis* (Oxford, 1903).

A good biography, with complete bibliography, is H. Schenk, "A. F. W. Schimper," in *Berichte der Deutschen botanischen Gesellschaft, XIX, Generalversammlungsheft,* **1** (1901), 54–70.

A. P. M. SANDERS

SCHIMPER, KARL FRIEDRICH (*b.* Mannheim, Germany, 15 February 1803; *d.* Schwetzingen, near Heidelberg, Germany, 21 December 1867), *botany, geology, zoology, meteorology.*

Schimper's father was a mathematics teacher and later a government engineer; his mother, Meta, Baroness Furtenbach, came from a noble family of Nuremberg. Their uncongenial marriage ended in divorce. Schimper and his younger brother thus had an unhappy childhood, all the more so since their father had a very modest income. Schimper gained such a broad knowledge of plants during his school days in Mannheim that his teacher, F. W. L. Succow, asked him to collaborate on his *Flora Manhemiensis.* In 1822 Schimper began to study theology at the University of Heidelberg because it was the only subject for which he could obtain a scholarship. In 1826 he turned to the study of medicine and became friends with Alexander Braun and Louis Agassiz. The three continued their studies at Munich in 1827–1828, and in 1829 they received their doctorates. Braun and Agassiz returned home, but Schimper remained in Munich until 1841.

Schimper hoped to embark on an academic career in Munich but was unable to obtain a post. After a short stay in Zweibrücken (Rhenish Palatinate) he returned, disappointed and poor, to Mannheim. His situation did not improve until 1845, when the grand duke of the Rhenish Palatinate awarded him a small annuity. He also encountered difficulties in Mannheim, and in 1849 he moved to nearby Schwetzingen, where he spent the rest of his life. Lacking a permanent position and a regular income, he was constantly in financial difficulties. This period was interrupted only by a stay at Jena in 1854–1855. In 1856 Schimper's friends and admirers sought unsuccessfully to procure a professorship of botany for him. He died

of dropsy in 1867, following months of confinement to bed. He was engaged twice, the second time to a sister of Alexander Braun. Neither engagement led to marriage.

In botany Schimper's principal concern was to formulate a theory of phyllotaxy. He pointed out that leaves that grow in spiral formations are arranged in regular, cyclic patterns and that each species has a characteristic pattern. He also dealt with the unequal, eccentric growth in thickness of branches of deciduous and coniferous trees (epinasty and hyponasty), with the morphology and physiology of plant roots, with the heterophylly of certain aquatic plants (variation in the forms of the leaves, depending on the depth of the water), and with water transport in mosses. Since his school days Schimper had had a good knowledge of floristics and systematics. Besides the Mannheim flora, he collaborated on the *Flora Friburgensis* with F. C. L. Spenner. A catalog of the mosses of Baden that Schimper planned to publish in the last years of his life never appeared, as was the case with many of his projects.

Since his days in Munich, Schimper had been interested in prehistoric animals. He did not, however, undertake specific research on particular groups of fossils, desiring instead to formulate an overall view. In "Eintheilung und Succession der Organismen" he proposed the existence of a succession of different faunas. They, and the floras that accompanied them, were related to each other; but phases of development *(Belebungen)* were, he held, separated by periods of desolation *(Verödungen).* Schimper expressed his ideas, which contradicted Cuvier's catastrophist theory, in a schema similar to a genealogical tree. Much of this account was similar to the theory of evolution, but Schimper completely rejected the theory of natural selection later formulated by Darwin.

In geology Schimper was especially interested in the traces of Pleistocene glaciers that he detected in the northern Alpine foothills, notably in Bavaria, Switzerland, and the Black Forest. This study led him to the concept of the "Ice Age," which he discussed in a paper presented in 1837 to the congress of Swiss scientists held at Neuchâtel. The paper gave rise to an unpleasant priority dispute with Louis Agassiz that was not decided in Schimper's favor until much later. Through his investigations in the Bavarian Calcareous Alps, Schimper recognized in 1840 that the Alps had not been raised by a force acting from below but had emerged as the result of horizontal pressure—in the same way that a range of folded mountains is created. The pressure was generated, he speculated, by the shrinking of the earth's core. These views anticipated the contraction theory proposed by Suess in 1875.

In 1843 Schimper presented a paper on prehistoric climatic conditions and postulated an alternation of warm and cold periods in the earth's history. Accordingly, his Ice Age was preceded by warmer weather. Further, he interpreted desiccation cracks and raindrop impressions in the Triassic of southern Germany as evidence of the existence, during a given period, of a dry or a moist climate. From the evidence of postglacial calcareous tuffs in Upper Bavaria and the annual rings in Triassic silicified trees, Schimper deduced the existence of change of seasons in the period he studied. Finally, he contended that the snails occurring in the Pleistocene loess indicated their emergence in a cool climate.

In hydrology and meteorology Schimper made a series of new and stimulating observations for which he proposed ingenious explanations. Among the topics he treated were the refraction and reflection of light in inland waters and their effect on plant life, the attenuation of the reflection of light from the surface of bodies of water because of the presence of pollen, and the formation of ice on rivers.

Schimper expressed many of his scientific ideas in poems. Several hundred of these are known, and they encompass the most varied verse forms. Their artistic merit has been quite variously judged. Schimper was an extraordinarily versatile scientist, but almost all of his publications have a preliminary or fragmentary character. He frequently planned to publish large-scale works but never carried out his intentions. Consequently, many of his results fell into neglect or were taken over and developed by others, with their origin often forgotten. This circumstance, together with his volcanic temperament and a certain lack of objectivity and of consideration for his colleagues, surely contributed to the difficulties that marked Schimper's personal life.

BIBLIOGRAPHY

I. ORIGINAL WORKS. Schimper's writings include "Vorträge über die Möglichkeit eines Verständnisses der Blattstellung," in *Flora*, **18**, no. 1 (1835), 145–192; "Vortrag über Blattstellungstheorie," in *Verhandlungen der Versammlung der Schweizerischen naturfor-* *schenden Gesellschaft*, **22** (1836), 114–117; "Auszug aus dem Schreiben des Herrn Dr. Schimper über die Eiszeit . . .," *ibid.*, **23** (1837), 38–51; *Gedichte* (Erlangen, 1840); "Über den Bau der bayerischen Kalkalpen," in *Amtlicher Bericht über die 18. Versammlung der Gesellschaft deutscher Naturforscher und Ärzte zu Erlangen* (1841), 93–100; *Über die Witterungsphasen der Vorwelt, Entwurf zu einem Vortrage bei Gelegenheit der zehnten Stiftungsfeier und Generalversammlung des Mannheimer Vereins für Naturkunde* (Mannheim, 1843); *Gedichte 1840–1846* (Mannheim, 1847); "Über hyponastische, epinastische und diplonastische Gewächse . . .," in *Amtlicher Bericht über die Versammlung deutscher Naturforscher und Ärzte zu Göttingen* (1854), 87–88; *Natursonette . . . eine Weihnachtsgabe für Gebildete* (Jena, 1854); "Nützliches Allerlei von der ganzen Pflanze; Auswahl förderlichster Thatsachen aus der Morphologie," in *Amtlicher Bericht über die Versammlung deutscher Naturforscher und Ärzte zu Bonn* (1857), 129–132, 137–138; "Wasser und Sonnenschein oder die Durchsichtigkeit und der Glanz der Gewässer betrachtet nach ihrem Einfluss auf die Entwickelungen organischer und geologischer Art am Äussern des Erdballs," in *Festschrift der Naturforschenden Gesellschaft zu Emden* (Emden, 1865), 37–66; and "Uber Eintheilung und Succession der Organismen," L. Eyrich, ed., in *Jahresbericht des Mannheimer Vereins für Naturkunde* for 1878–1882 (1882), 1–36.

II. SECONDARY LITERATURE. See L. Eyrich, "Nachrede zum Vortrage von Dr. K. F. Schimper . . .," in *Jahresbericht des Mannheimer Vereins für Naturkunde* for 1878–1882 (1882), 37–64, with biographical data, poems, and bibliography; R. Lauterborn, "Karl Friedrich Schimper, Leben und Schaffen eines deutschen Naturforschers," in "Der Rhein. Naturgeschichte eines deutschen Stromes," in *Berichte der Naturforschenden Gesellschaft in Freiburg i. Br.*, **33** (1934), 269–324, with bibliographical data and portrait; and G. H. O. Volger, *Leben und Leistungen des Naturforschers K. Schimper* (Frankfurt, 1889).

HEINZ TOBIEN

SCHIMPER, WILHELM PHILIPP (GUILLAUME PHILIPPE) (*b.* Dossenheim, Alsace, France, 12 January 1808; *d.* Strasbourg, France [then part of Germany], 20 March 1880), *botany.*

Schimper, the cousin of two notable botanists, Karl Friedrich (1803–1867) and Wilhelm Schimper (1804–1878), and father of the plant geographer A. F. W. Schimper, was the son of Franz Schimper, Lutheran pastor of Offweiler. From 1826 to 1833 he studied at Strasbourg University, first philosophy, philology, and mathematics, and later, to please his father, theology. But from an early age he had been attracted to the study of natural history, in which he was encouraged by his cousins, the elder of whom often visited Offweiler. Soon after graduating, Schimper decided to devote his life to science and made a long journey in the Alps, studying plants and especially mosses, in which his interest was stimulated by the apothecary Philipp Bruch (1781–1847) of Zweibrücken. In 1835 Schimper was appointed assistant in the geological section of the Strasbourg Natural History Museum. He remained with this institution in various capacities throughout his life and eventually became its director.

In 1845 Schimper received a degree in natural sciences and in 1848 obtained a doctorate for his *Recherches anatomiques sur les mousses*. In 1849 he married Adèle B. Besson, of Swiss origin; they had two daughters and one son. The even course of his busy life was temporarily disrupted by the Franco-Prussian War, as a result of which Alsace was ceded to Germany. Faced with the painful choice of leaving his native province for a post in Paris or staying in Strasbourg, he decided to remain at the museum and to accept the chair of geology and paleontology at the reorganized German university.

With Bruch, Schimper in 1836 began publication of the *Bryologia Europaea*, his most famous work, which set a new standard in the description and delineation of mosses. Publication of this work (which appeared in parts) was continued by Schimper after Bruch's death, for a time with the assistance of Theodor Gümbel. Among Schimper's other publications on mosses, his study of the structure and development of the sphagna is particularly valuable. Although best known as a botanist, he also worked and wrote on zoology and geology. He made important contributions to paleobotany, especially on the Triassic flora of the Vosges. His work covered a vast field, but he was a supremely competent observer and describer rather than an originator of new ideas.

Schimper traveled extensively throughout his life and visited many European countries; one of his most productive journeys was to the Sierra Nevada in Spain (1847), from which he brought back specimens of a previously undescribed species of ibex as well as many interesting plants.

Schimper's many-sided activity, maintained almost to the end of his life, was made possible by powers of physical endurance hardly suggested by his tall, emaciated figure and delicate appearance.

BIBLIOGRAPHY

I. Original Works. Schimper's principal writings are *Bryologia Europaea seu genera muscorum Europaeorum monographice illustrata*, 6 vols. (Stuttgart, 1836–1855), also *Corollarium* (1856) and *Supplementum*, 2 vols. (1864–1866), written with P. Bruch and T. Gümbel, reprinted and rearranged in 3 vols. with intro. by P. A. Florschütz and W. D. Margadant (Amsterdam, 1971); *Monographie des plantes fossiles du Grès Bigarré de la chaine des Vosges* (Leipzig, 1844); *Recherches anatomiques sur les mousses* (Strasbourg, 1848), reissued in *Mémoires de la Société d'histoire naturelle de Strasbourg*, **4**, no. 1 (1850), 1–69; *Mémoire pour servir à l'histoire naturelle des sphaignes (Sphagnum L.)* (Paris, 1857), reissued in *Mémoires présentés par divers savants*, Cl. sci. math. et phys., **15** (1858), 1–97, also published as *Versuch einer Entwicklungsgeschichte der Torfmoose (Sphagnum) und einer Monographie der in Europa vorkommenden Arten dieser Gattung* (Stuttgart, 1858); *Synopsis muscorum Europaeorum praemissa introductione de elementis bryologici tractante* (Strasbourg, 1860; 2nd ed., Stuttgart, 1876); *Traité de palaeontologie végétale ou la flore du monde primitif dans ses rapports avec les formations géologiques et la flore du monde actuel*, 3 vols. and atlas (Paris, 1869–1874); and *Palaeophytologie*, vol. II of K. A. von Zittel, ed., *Handbuch der Palaeontologie* (Munich–Leipzig, 1879), completed by A. Schenk.

II. Secondary Literature. See "dBy" (Anton de Bary), "Wilhelm Philip Schimper," in *Botanische Zeitung*, **38**, no. 26 (1880), 443–450; E. Desor, "Philipp Wilhelm Schimper," in *Neues Jahrbuch für Mineralogie, Geologie und Palaeontologie*, **2** (1880), 1–7; C. Grad, "Guillaume-Philippe Schimper, sa vie et ses travaux, 1808–1880," in *Bulletin de la Société d'histoire naturelle de Colmar*, **20–21** (1880), 351–392; T. Gümbel, "Dr. Philipp Wilhelm Schimper," in *Allgemeine deutsche Biographie*, XXXI (1890), 277–279; S. O. Lindberg, "W. Ph. Schimper," in *Meddelanden af Societas pro fauna et flora fennica*, **6** (1881), 268; and W. D. Margadant and P. Florschütz, introduction to repr. of *Bryologia Europaea* (above).

P. W. Richards

SCHJELLERUP, HANS CARL FREDERIK CHRISTIAN (*b.* Odense, Denmark, 8 February 1827; *d.* Copenhagen, Denmark, 13 November 1887), *astronomy*.

Schjellerup was trained as a watchmaker, but through the interest and help of H. C. Oersted he was admitted to the Polytechnic School of Copenhagen, where he passed the final examination in applied mathematics and mechanics. In 1851 he was appointed senior astronomer at the Copenhagen observatory, a post he held until his death. In 1857 he received the doctorate at Jena with a dissertation deriving the orbit of the comet of 1580 by means of Tycho Brahe's observations.

In 1861–1863 Schjellerup observed 10,000 positions of faint stars in declinations between −15° and +15° using the new Pistor-Martin meridian circle. A catalog, inspired by Bessel's zone observing about forty years earlier, was published in 1864 by the Royal Danish Academy. Schjellerup's catalog, outstanding at the time for its completeness and accuracy, was used as recently as 1952 for determining the constant of precession.

Schjellerup compiled two catalogs of colored stars (1866, 1874); the second, an extension of the first, contains 400 stars. During the same period several astronomers started a survey of the spectra of such stars, and Schjellerup's compilations appeared in time to be used in this work.

Schjellerup also made a signal contribution to the history of astronomy. At an advanced age he studied oriental languages, especially Arabic and Chinese. He had access to a pair of Arabic manuscripts, one in the Royal Library at Copenhagen and the other in the Imperial Library at St. Petersburg, which contain a description of the sky elaborated about 950 by the Persian astronomer al-Ṣūfī. Al-Ṣūfī had made a careful comparison between Ptolemy's catalog from about A.D. 150, which contains the positions and magnitudes of about 1,000 stars, and the sky itself; his specifications of relative magnitudes are the only series of this kind of observation that remains from the years between antiquity and modern times. Schjellerup's French translation was published in 1874 by the Academy of St. Petersburg.

Another result of his rare combination of linguistic and scientific ability was Schjellerup's control of different moon tables of his time, taking into account three solar eclipses from 708, 600, and 548 B.C. that he found mentioned in ancient Chinese literature.

BIBLIOGRAPHY

I. ORIGINAL WORKS. Schjellerup's writings include "Tycho Brahes Original-Observationer, benyttede til Banebestemmelse af Cometen 1580," in *Kongelige Danske Videnskabernes Selskabs Skrifter*, Naturv.-math. Afd., 5th ser., **4** (1856), 1–39; *Stjernefortegnelse indeholdende 10000 Positioner af teleskopiske Fixstjerner imellem −15 og +15 Graders Deklination* (Copenhagen, 1864); "Catalog der rothen, isolirten Sterne, welche bis zum Jahre 1866 bekannt geworden sind," in *Astronomische Nachrichten*, **67** (1866), 97–112; "Eine Uranometrie aus dem zehnten Jahrhundert," *ibid.*, **74** (1869), 97–104; "Bidrag til Bedømmelsen af de moderne Maaneelementers Paalidelighed," in *Oversigt over det K. Danske Videnskabernes Selskabs Forhandlinger* (1874), 64–95; *Description des étoiles fixes composée au milieu du dixième siècle de notre ère par l'astronome persan Abd-al-Rahman al-Sūfi* (St. Petersburg, 1874); "Zweiter Catalog der rothen, isolierten Sterne, vervollständigt und fortgeführt bis zum Schluss des Jahres 1874," in *Vierteljahrsschrift der Astronomischen Gesellschaft*, **9** (1874), 252–287; and "Recherches sur l'astronomie des anciens," in *Copernicus* (Dublin), **1** (1881), 25–39, 41–47, 223–236.

II. SECONDARY LITERATURE. Obituaries are J. L. E. Dreyer, in *Monthly Notices of the Royal Astronomical Society*, **48** (1888), 171–174; V. Hjort, in *Tidsskrift for Mathematik*, 5th ser., **5** (1887), 148–153; and J. Holetschek, in *Deutsche Rundschau für Geographie*, **10** (1888), 381–382; and in *Sirius*, **21** (1888), 161–163. See also J. E. Gordon, "Derivation of the Constant of Precession From a Comparison of the Catalogues of Schjellerup (1865.0) and Morin-Kondratiev (1900.0)," in *Izvestiya Glavnoi astronomicheskoi observatorii v Pulkove*, **19**, pt. 1(1952), 72–121.

AXEL V. NIELSEN

SCHLÄFLI, LUDWIG (*b*. Grasswil, Bern, Switzerland, 15 January 1814; *d*. Bern, Switzerland, 20 March 1895), *mathematics*.

Schläfli, the son of Johann Ludwig Schläfli, a citizen of Burgdorf, and Magdalena Aebi, attended primary school in Burgdorf. With the aid of a scholarship he was able to study at the Gymnasium in Bern, where he displayed a gift for mathematics. He enrolled in the theological faculty at Bern but, not wishing to pursue an ecclesiastical career, decided to accept a post as teacher of mathematics and science at the *Burgerschule* in Thun. He taught there for ten years, using his few free hours to study higher mathematics. In the autumn of 1843 Jakob Steiner, who was traveling to Rome with Jacobi, Dirichlet, and Borchardt, proposed that they take Schläfli with them as interpreter. Schläfli thus had an opportunity to learn from the leading mathematicians of his time. Dirichlet instructed him daily in number theory, and Schläfli's later works on quadratic forms bear the mark of this early training. During this period Schläfli translated two works by Steiner and two by Jacobi into Italian.

In 1848 Schläfli became a *Privatdozent* at Bern, where, as he expressed it, he was "confined to a stipend of Fr. 400 and, in the literal sense of the word, had to do without (*darben musste*)." His nomination as extraordinary professor in 1853 did not much improve his situation, and it was not until he became a full professor in 1868 that he was freed from financial concerns. Schläfli's scientific achievements gained recognition only slowly. In 1863 he received an honorary doctorate from the University of Bern; in 1868 he became a corresponding member of the Istituto Lombardo di Scienze e Lettere in Milan and was later accorded the same honor by the Akademie der Wissenschaften in Göttingen (1871) and the Accademia dei Lincei (1883). He won the Jakob Steiner Prize for his geometric works in 1870.

While at Bern, Schläfli was concerned with two major problems, one in elimination theory and the other in *n*-dimensional geometry, and he brought his results together in two extensive works. The first problem is discussed in "Ueber die Resultante eines Systems mehrerer algebraischer Gleichungen. Ein Beitrag zur Theorie der Elimination" (published in *Denkschriften der Akademie der Wissenschaften*, **4**). Schläfli summarized the first part of this work in a letter to Steiner:

> For a given system of *n* equations of higher degree with *n* unknowns, I take a linear equation with literal (undetermined) coefficients *a*, *b*, *c*, $\cdots$ and show how one can thus obtain true resultants without burdening the calculation with extraneous factors. If everything else is given numerically, then the resultant must be decomposable into factors all of which are linear with respect to *a*, *b*, *c*, $\cdots$. In the case of each of these linear polynomials the coefficients of *a*, *b*, *c*, $\cdots$ are then values of the unknowns belonging to a *single* solution.

Drawing on the works of Hesse, Jacobi, and Cayley, Schläfli presented applications to special cases. He then developed the fundamental theorems on class and degree of an algebraic manifold, theorems that attracted the interest of the Italian school of geometers. The work concluded with an examination of the class equation of third-degree curves. Through this publication Schläfli became acquainted with Arthur Cayley, whose paper "Sur un théorème de M. Schläfli" begins: "In §13 of a very interesting memoir by M. Schläfli one finds a very beautiful theorem on resultants." The acquaintance led to an extensive correspondence and opened the way for Schläfli to publish in English journals. In his obituary of Schläfli, F. Brioschi wrote:

> While rereading this important work recently it occurred to me that it displays the outstanding characteristics of Schläfli's work as a whole. These are, first, deep and firsthand knowledge of the writings of other authors; next, a desire and ability to generalize results; and, finally, great penetration in investigating problems from very different points of view.

The second of the two major works, "Theorie der vielfachen Kontinuität," was rejected by the academies of Vienna and Berlin because of its great length and was not published until 1901 (in *Neue Denkschriften der Schweizerischen naturforschenden Gesellschaft*). For many years only sections of it appeared in print—in the journals of Crelle and Liouville and in the *Quarterly Journal of Mathematics*. The core of this work consisted of the detailed theory of regular bodies in Euclidean space R_n of *n* dimensions and the associated problems of the regular subdivision of the higher-dimensional spheres. Schläfli based his investigation of regular polytopes on his discovery that such objects can be characterized by certain symbols now known as Schläfli symbols. His definition was recursive: $\{k_1\}$ is the symbol of the plane regular k_1-gon. $\{k_1, \cdots, k_{n-1}\}$ is the Schläfli symbol of that regular polytope the boundary polytopes of which have the symbol $k_1, \cdots, k_{n-2}$ and the vertex polytopes of which have the symbol $\{k_2, \cdots, k_{n-1}\}$.

Schläfli discovered a way of finding all regular polytopes by calculating the numbers $k_1, \cdots, k_{n-1}$ in the following manner: In the plane, for every k_1 there exists a $\{k_1\}$. In considering *n*-space he started from Euler's theorem on polyhedrons, which he formulated and proved for R_n: assume a polytope with a_0 vertexes, a_1 edges, a_2 faces and so on in higher dimensions until a_{n-1} boundary polytopes of dimension $n-1$, and $a_n = 1$. Then it is true that

$$a_0 - a_1 + a_2 - \cdots (-1)^{n-1} a_{n-1} + (-1)^n a_n = 1.$$

For $n = 3$ the Euler theorem on polyhedrons becomes $a_0 - a_1 + a_2 = 2$. Since, further, for $\{k_1, k_2\}$ it is true that $k_2 \cdot a_0 = 2a_1 = k_1 \cdot a_2$, it follows that

$$a_0 : a_1 : a_2 : 1 = 4k_1 : 2k_1 k_2 : 4k_2 : [4 - (k_1 - 2)(k_2 - 2)].$$

The nature of the problem requires a positive value for $[4 - (k_1 - 2)(k_2 - 2)]$; therefore $(k_1 - 2)(k_2 - 2)$ can take only the values 1,2,3. This yields the following possibilities: $\{3,3\}$ tetrahedron, $\{3,4\}$ octahedron, $\{3,5\}$ icosahedron, $\{4,3\}$ cube, and $\{5,3\}$ dodecahedron. For $n = 4$ the Euler equation $a_0 - a_1 + a_2 - a_3 = 0$ becomes homogeneous and yields only the ratios of the a_i. Schläfli therefore determined the radius of the circumscribed sphere of a $\{k_1, k_2, k_3\}$ of edge length 1. If this radius is to be real, then it must be true that $\sin \frac{\pi}{k_1} \cdot \sin \frac{\pi}{k_3} >$ $\cos \frac{\pi}{k_2}$. This condition yields the six bodies {3,3,3}, {4,3,3}, {3,3,4}, {3,4,3}, {5,3,3}, and {3,3,5}. Schläfli proved further that in every R_n with $n > 4$ there are only three regular solids: {3, 3, · · ·, 3}, regular simplex; {4, 3, · · ·, 3}, n-dimensional cube; and {3, 3, · · ·, 3, 4}, regular n-dimensional octahedron.

Schläfli achieved another beautiful result by considering the unit sphere in R_n and n hyperplanes through the origin (1) = 0, · · ·, (n) = 0. Specifically, he found that the inequalities (1) ≥ 0, · · ·, (n) ≥ 0 determine a spherical simplex with surface S_n. Schläfli proved $dS_n = \frac{1}{n-2} \{\Sigma S_{n-2} \, d\lambda\}$, where S_{n-2} is the surface of a boundary simplex of two dimensions less and λ is a suitable angle between two such simplexes, and the summation extends over all such boundary simplexes. Let O_n be the surface of the sphere; then the Schläfli function f_n is defined by $S_n = \frac{1}{2^n} O_n f_n$. It can be proved that $f_{2m+1} = a_0 \Sigma f_{2m} - a_1 \Sigma f_{2m-2} + \cdots$, where a_k is proportional to the $k + 1$ Bernoulli number B_k. This equation states that the Schläfli function in a space of odd dimension can be reduced to Schläfli functions in spaces of even dimension. Concerning this discovery Schläfli wrote to Steiner: "I believe I am not overestimating the importance of this general theorem if I set it beside the most beautiful results that have been achieved in geometry."

Besides the theory of Schläfli functions the second section of the paper included a detailed treatment of the decomposition of an arbitrary spherical simplex into right-angled simplexes. The section concluded with a theorem on the sum of the squares of the projections of a ray on the vertex rays of a regular polytope, a question that has interested researchers in recent times.

The third section, headed "Verschiedene Anwendungen der Theorie der vielfachen Kontinuität, welche das Gebiet der linearen und sphärischen übersteigen," contains both applications of theorems of Binet, Monge, Chasles, and Dupin to quadratic continua in R_n and Schläfli's own discoveries. After first determining the midpoint, major axes, and conjugate diameters for a quadratic continuum, he demonstrates the law of inertia of the quadratic forms by means of continuity considerations. Among other results presented is a generalization of a theorem of Binet for a system of conjugate radii: the sum of the squares of all m-

fold parallelepipeds constructed out of the conjugate radii of a system is equal to the sum obtained when the system is formed from the major axes. Schläfli then divided the quadratic continua into two classes and generalized Monge's theorem on the director circle, or great circle, of a central conic section. He also examined confocal systems and showed that in R_3 their determination depends on a third-order linear differential equation.

After "Theorie der vielfachen Kontinuität" had appeared in its entirety, P. H. Schoute wrote in 1902:

This treatise surpasses in scientific value a good portion of everything that has been published up to the present day in the field of multidimensional geometry. The author experienced the sad misfortune of those who are ahead of their time: the fruits of his most mature studies cannot bring him fame. And in this case the success of the division of the cubic surfaces was only a small compensation; for, in my opinion, this achievement, however valuable it might be, is far from conveying the genius expressed in the theory of manifold continuity.

Steiner communicated to Schläfli Cayley's discovery of the twenty-seven straight lines on the third-degree surface. Schläfli thereupon found the thirty-six "doubles sixes" on this surface and then the division of the cubic surface into twenty-two species according to the nature of the singularities. Schläfli also solved problems posed by the Italian school of geometers. He gave a condition under which a manifold has constant curvature: its geodesic lines must appear as straight lines in a suitable coordinate system. He also investigated the space of least dimension in which a manifold can be imbedded; his conjecture on this question was demonstrated by M. Janet and E. Cartan (1926–1927). Schläfli's work on the division of third-order surfaces led him to assert the one-sidedness of the projective plane in a letter to Felix Klein in 1874.

Schläfli wrote a work on the composition theory of quadratic forms in which he sought to provide the proof of the associative law that was lacking in Gauss's treatment of the subject. Schläfli's posthumous papers contain extensive tables for the class number of quadratic forms of both positive and negative determinants.

Schläfli's geometric and arithmetical studies were equaled in significance by his work in function theory. Stimulated by C. G. Neumann's investigations (1867) and following up the representation of the gamma function by a line integral, Schläfli gave the integral representation of the Bessel function $J_n(z)$ for arbitrary n, even where n is not integral. He also wrote an outstanding work on elliptic modular functions (1870) that gave rise to the designation "Schläfli modular equation." An examination of his posthumous manuscripts reveals that in 1867, ten years before Dedekind, Schläfli discovered the domain of discontinuity of the modular group and used it to make a careful analysis of the Hermite modular functions from the analytic, number theoretic, and geometric points of view. As early as 1868, moreover, Schläfli employed means that Weber discovered only twenty years later and termed f-functions or class invariants.

Besides his mathematical achievements, Schläfli was an expert on the flora of the canton of Bern and an accomplished student at languages. He possessed a profound knowledge of the *Veda,* and his posthumous manuscripts include ninety notebooks of Sanskrit and commentary on the *Rig-Veda.*

BIBLIOGRAPHY

I. ORIGINAL WORKS. Schläfli's writings were brought together as *Gesammelte mathematische Abhandlungen,* 3 vols. (Basel, 1950–1956). His correspondence with Steiner is in *Mitteilungen der Naturforschenden Gesellschaft in Bern* for 1896 (1897), 61–264. That with Cayley is in J. H. Graf, ed., *Briefwechsel von Ludwig Schläfli mit Arthur Cayley* (Bern, 1905); and that with Borchardt (1856–1877) is in *Mitteilungen der Naturforschenden Gesellschaft in Bern* for 1915 (1916), 50–69. Graf also edited the following: "Lettres de D. Chelini à L. Schläfli," in *Bullettino di bibliografia e di storia delle scienze matematiche e fisiche,* **17** (1915), 36–40; "Correspondance entre E. Beltrami et L. Schläfli," *ibid.,* 81–86, 113–122; and "Correspondance entre Luigi Cremona et Ludwig Schläfli," *ibid.,* **18** (1916), 21–35, 49–64, 81–83, 113–121, and **19** (1917), 9–14. Two letters from Schläfli to P. Tardy (1865) are in G. Loria, "Commemorazione del socio Prof. Placido Tardy," in *Atti dell'Accademia nazionale dei Lincei. Rendiconti,* Cl. fis., **24** (1915), 519–531.

II. SECONDARY LITERATURE. See J. J. Burckhardt, "Der mathematische Nachlass von Ludwig Schläfli, mit einem Anhang: Ueber Schläflis nachgelassene Manuskripte zur Theorie der quadratischen Formen," in *Mitteilungen der Naturforschenden Gesellschaft in Bern* for 1941 (1942), 1–22; and "Ludwig Schläfli," supp. no. 4 of *Elemente der Mathematik* (1948); J. H. Graf, "Ludwig Schläfli," in *Mitteilungen der Naturforschenden Gesellschaft in Bern* for 1895 (1896), 120–203; A. Häusermann, *Ueber die Berechnung singulärer Moduln bei Ludwig Schläfli* (inaugural diss., Zurich, 1943); W. Rytz, "Prof. Ludwig Schläfli als Botaniker," in *Mitteilungen der Naturforschenden Gesellschaft in Bern* for 1918 (1919), 213–220; and O. Schlaginhaufen, "Der Schädel des Mathematikers Ludwig Schläfli," *ibid.* for 1930 (1931), 35–66.

JOHANN JAKOB BURCKHARDT

SCHLEIDEN, JACOB MATHIAS (*b.* Hamburg, Germany, 5 April 1804; *d.* Frankfurt am Main, Germany, 23 June 1881), *botany, natural science, scientific popularization.*

Schleiden came from a well-to-do family; his father was municipal physician of Hamburg. After legal studies, culminating in a doctorate, at the University of Heidelberg (1824–1827), Schleiden established a legal practice in Hamburg. He was dissatisfied, however, and, after a period of deep depression, he abandoned this profession. In 1833 he began to study natural science at Göttingen and then transferred to Berlin. He devoted himself enthusiastically to the subject of botany, in which he was encouraged by his botanist uncle, Johann Horkel, to whom he remained forever grateful. During these years Alexander von Humboldt and Robert Brown were resident at Berlin. Schleiden worked in the laboratory of the celebrated physiologist Johannes Müller, and there he met Theodor Schwann. In this inspiring milieu, Schleiden worked intensively and produced noteworthy publications. He obtained his doctorate in 1839 at Jena and was then able to give free reign to his pedagogical fervor. He lectured and wrote both technical and popular scientific works on the widest range of topics.

Schleiden's lectures drew enthusiastic, overflow audiences; his numerous articles appeared in highly respected journals, or in collections that were often reprinted and translated. He declined an offer from the University of Giessen in 1846, but in 1850 he accepted nomination as titular professor of botany at Jena. He also received many honors from learned societies. In spite of his success, Schleiden decided to leave Jena. His combative personality probably contributed to this decision: he was often involved in polemics with leading figures of the day. Also, he had an insatiable desire to study problems going beyond the confines of botany and natural history. He soon became a highly regarded popular lecturer and writer; indeed, he was one of the most successful popularizers of the age—no small achievement at a time when scientists like Virchow, Helmholtz, Liebig, Moleschott, Alexander von Humboldt, and Ludwig Büchner, among others, were addressing the general public. Following his departure from Jena in 1862 and a stay at Dresden, Schleiden became professor of anthropology at Dorpat. Even though he soon left Dorpat, the Russian government granted him a pension. He became a *Privatgelehrter* and thereafter frequently moved from one city to another.

In 1838 Schleiden published "Beiträge zur Phytogenesis" in *Müller's Archiv*, one of the most respected journals of the time. This article, which was immediately translated into French and English, fixed his name in the history of biology. According to a well-known tradition, the cell theory was conceived in a conversation between Schleiden and Schwann on the subject of phytogenesis. In fact, however, historical investigation has shown that Schleiden's article, like Schwann's book, represents only one stage—although admittedly an important one—in the evolution of the search for the elementary unit common to the animal and plant kingdoms. (On this subject see the publications of Studnička, Klein, Baker, and Florkin; the biographies in this Dictionary of Mohl, Oken, Raspail, and Schwann, among others, should also be consulted.)

Schleiden reprinted the article in a collection of studies and dealt at length with its contents in his textbook on botany. In the article, which evoked wide interest and sparked violent debates, Schleiden starts from Robert Brown's discovery of the cell nucleus (1832), which Schleiden called the cytoblast, and then indicates its role in the formation of cells. According to Schleiden, as soon as the cytoblast reaches its final size, a fine, transparent vesicle forms around it: this is the new cell. The cell then crystallizes within a formative liquid. The best statement of this interpretation can be found in his botany textbook, *Grundzüge der wissenschaftlichen Botanik* (1842): "Since the elementary organic cells present a marked individualization and since they are the most general expression of the concept of the plant, it is necessary, first of all, to study this cell as the foundation of the vegetable world. We have therefore produced a study of the vegetable cell." This clearly announced the advent of plant cytology. This subject became the starting point of all subsequent botany textbooks. As Schleiden stated, the cells can form only in a liquid containing sugar, gum, and mucus (cytoblastema). This phenomenon occurs in the following manner: the mucous portion condenses into more or less round corpuscles (cytoblastus). On its surface, a part of the liquid is transformed into jelly, a relatively insoluble substance; thus there is created a closed gelatinous vesicle that is penetrated by the external liquid. . . . During the progressive expansion of the vesicle, the jelly of the wall is generally transformed into a membranous substance and the formation of the cell (cellula) is completed.

Schleiden's interpretation merits careful attention. The idea that cells are crystallized inside an amorphous primary substance is as old as the study of the cell itself. The idea can be traced back to the writings of Grew (1675), who compared the process with the fermentation of a paste or liquid. It appears again, independently, in Raspail, as a vesicular crystallization. Mohl observed cell division but was undecided in his views on the existence of "the free formation of cells," as this type of process was long called. Despite increasing evidence of nuclear activity during division, and despite Virchow's definitive aphorism, "omnis cellula a cellula," the notion of the formative blastema long survived, owing mainly to the support of Charles Robin. An eminent figure in the development of the subject of microscopic anatomy, Robin remained faithful to the notion, granting the cell a position of no special distinction among the anatomical elements of the higher organisms (see Klein, 1936; 1960).

From the start of his career, Schleiden showed a predilection for the microscope, and he contributed greatly to its introduction in biological research. He engaged in long and sometimes bitter disputes with Amici, one of the outstanding micrographers and opticians of the period. Schleiden is thought to have played an active role in the establishment of the Zeiss optical works in Jena.

Schleiden based his description of cytogenesis on an examination of the pollen tube. Ironically, his interpretation of this tube was fundamentally wrong, both morphologically and biologically: he considered it a female reproductive element in the plant. This error, like the one concerning the free genesis of cells, gave rise to much further research and to violent controversies; but one may truly call both these mistakes fruitful.

Schleiden's botany textbook merits an extensive methodological discussion, but we shall restrict our comments to a few essential points. A number of Schleiden's articles contain virulent criticism of the botanists of the first half of the nineteenth century, many of whom still upheld the ideas of nature philosophy, against which his textbook was a frontal attack. More important, however, it introduced new pedagogical standards that were to dominate the teaching of botany for years. Beginning with the second edition, the work bore the subtitle *Botanik als inductive Wissenschaft.*

Schleiden considered the inductive method the only valid one in biology, and the first part of his book constitutes an important document for the study of the methodology of natural history. He declared himself an enemy of all philosophical speculation, while at the same time adhering to the views of Kant and rejecting the label of materialist. He completed his attacks against the philosophers with a brief polemical monograph against the philosophy of Schelling and of Hegel. The entire structure of Schleiden's textbook was fundamentally new. The lengthy work begins with a study of the material elements of the plant. Next there is a large section on plant cytology, and then a treatment of morphology and organology. The book, which established the teaching of botany on a completely new basis, was often reprinted and appeared in various translations and adaptations. To appreciate the enthusiasm it aroused and its influence in turning young men to the study of botany, it is necessary to read the testimony of contemporaries, particularly of Julius Sachs, a famous botanist and author of a well-known history of botany.

Schleiden's pedagogical genius manifested itself in other publications as well. From the time of its founding in 1857, Schleiden was an assiduous contributor to Westermann's *Monatshefte*, a periodical that maintained high literary and scientific standards. His lectures, delivered to vast audiences, were occasionally published in book form and met with great success. Among the best known of these collections was *Die Pflanze und ihr Leben*, which was handsomely reproduced and reprinted many times. Another, somewhat more difficult series, *Wissenschafiliche Studien*, covered a wide range of topics in natural history. Later, Schleiden devoted entire monographs to subjects of apparently limited scope—for example, one to the rose and another to salt, in which he discussed its history, symbolism, and economic and social importance to human life. In other writings he dealt with the Isthmus of Suez and with anthropological questions. Among his last publications were scholarly studies on the fate of the Jews in the Middle Ages, on their martyrdom, and on their importance in transmitting knowledge to the Occident. These works, which were reprinted and translated, stimulated much interest; they also testify to the liberality of Schleiden's thinking in a period that witnessed the first anti-Semitic campaigns in the universities of Wilhelmine Germany.

This very liberality, however, joined with his combative nature, constantly involved Schleiden in debates and harsh polemics with the most eminent scientists and thinkers of the age, among whom were Amici, Fechner, Liebig, Mohl, Nees von Esenbeck, and Schelling. A few words may be said about his controversy with Fechner. The celebrated founder of modern psychophysiology, convinced of the existence of a soul in all living creatures, had published a work entitled *Nanna or the Soul of the Plants.* Schleiden violently attacked it, and Fechner responded with a book that is still delightful to read, *Professor Schleiden and the Moon.* But it should be noted that Schleiden often cut polemics short by the simple expedient of silence.

One of his early biographers, L. Errera, has a neat epitome of his career: "As a popularizer he was a model, as a scientist an initiator."

BIBLIOGRAPHY

I. ORIGINAL WORKS. A list of Schleiden's writings is given by Möbius (see below). The following works are cited in the text: "Beiträge zur Phytogenesis," in *Archiv für Anatomie, Physiologie und wissenschaftliche Medicin* (1838), 137–176, with French trans. in *Annales des sciences naturelles. Botanique,* **11** (1839), 242–252, 362–370, and English trans. in *Scientific Memoirs,* **2** (1841), 281–312; *Grundzüge der wissenschaftlichen Botanik,* 2 vols. (Leipzig, 1842–1843), 2nd ed., *Die Botanik als inductive Wissenschaft behandelt* (Leipzig, 1845–1846), 3rd ed., *Die Botanik als inductive Wissenschaft. Grundzüge der wissenschaftlichen Botanik nebst einer Einleitung als Anleitung zum Studium der Pflanzen* (Leipzig, 1849): vol. I, *Methodologische Grundlage. Vegetabilische Stofflehre. Die Lehre von der Pflanzenzellen,* vol. II, *Morphologie, Organologie,* with 153 figs. and 4 plates, 4th ed. (Leipzig, 1861); English trans. by E. Lankester as *Principles of Scientific Botany as an Inductive Science* (London, 1849; 2nd ed., 1868), facs. ed. by Lorch (see below).

See also *Beiträge zur Botanik. Gesammelte Aufsätze* (Leipzig, 1844); *Schelling's und Hegel's Verhältniss zur Naturwissenschaft* (Leipzig, 1844); *Die Pflanze und ihr Leben. Populäre Vorträge* (Leipzig, 1848; 5th ed., 1858), also translated into English (1848), French (1859), and Dutch (1873); *Studien. Populäre Vorträge* (Leipzig, 1855; 2nd ed., 1857); "Über den Materialismus unserer Zeit: Zerstreute Gedanken," in *Westermanns Monatshefte,* **1** (1857), 37–45; "Die Landenge von Suez und der Auszug der Isräeliten aus Egypten," *ibid.,* **4** (1858), 262–273; "Ueber die Anthropologie als Grundlage für alle übrigen Wissenschaften, wie überhaupt der Menschenbildung," *ibid.,* **11** (1862), 49–58; *Das Salz. Seine Geschichte. Seine Symbolik und seine Bedeutung im Menschenleben. Eine monographische Skizze* (Leipzig,

1875); "Die Bedeutung der Juden für Erhaltung und Wiederbelebung der Wissenschaften im Mittelalter," in *Westermanns Monatshefte*, **41** (1877), 52–60, 156–169; and "Die Romantik des Martyriums bei den Juden im Mittelalter," *ibid.*, **44** (1878), 62–79, 166–178.

II. SECONDARY LITERATURE. On Schleiden and his work, see J. R. Baker, "The Cell Theory, a Restatement. History and Critique," in *Quarterly Journal of Microscopical Science*, **89** (1948), 103–125; **90** (1949), 87–108, 331; **93** (1952), 157–190; **94** (1953), 407–440; **96** (1955), 449–481; L. Errera, "J. M. Schleiden," in *Revue scientifique de la France et de l'étranger*, 3rd ser., **2** (1882), 289–298; G. T. Fechner, *Professor Schleiden und der Mond* (Leipzig, 1856); M. Florkin, *Naissance et déviation de la théorie cellulaire dans l'oeuvre de Théodore Schwann* (Paris, 1960), 57, 62; E. Hallier, "Mathias Jacob Schleiden. Seine Bedeutung für das wissenschaftliche Leben der Gegenwart geschildert," in *Westermanns Monatshefte*, **51** (1882), 348–358; M. Klein, *Histoire des origines de la théorie cellulaire* (Paris, 1936), 36–39; *A la recherche de l'unité élémentaire des organismes vivants. Histoire de la théorie cellulaire* (Paris, 1960), 18; J. Lorch, *Introduction to Principles of Botany as an Inductive Science by Mathias Jacob Schleiden*, Sources of Science, no. 40 (New York–London, 1969), i–xxxiv, a facs. ed. of the London 1849 ed.; M. Möbius, *Mathias Jacob Schleiden* (Leipzig, 1904); E. Nordenskjöld, *Die Geschichte der Biologie* (Jena, 1926), 396–401; C. Robin, *Anatomie et Physiologie cellulaires* (Paris, 1873), 565 ff.; J. Sachs, *Geschichte der Botanik* (Munich, 1875), 202–207, 349; F. L. Studnička, "Mathias Jacob Schleiden und die Zelltheorie von Theodor Schwann," in *Anatomischer Anzeiger*, **76** (1933), 80–95; and A. Wartenberg, "Mathias Jacob Schleiden," H. Freund and A. Berg, eds., in *Geschichte der Mikroskopie*, **1** (1963), 299–302.

MARC KLEIN

SCHLESINGER, FRANK (*b.* New York, N.Y., 11 May 1871; *d.* Lyme, Connecticut, 10 July 1943), *astronomy.*

Schlesinger was the youngest of seven children of William Joseph Schlesinger and Mary Wagner, both of whom were German immigrants. He was first educated in the public schools of New York City. He graduated in 1890 from the City College of New York and was awarded the Ph.D. from Columbia University in 1898. His dissertation, which was based on measurements of star positions on plates photographed many years before by Lewis Rutherfurd, was a forerunner in his distinguished career in astrometry.

During this era, determinations of stellar parallaxes (which are inversely proportional to the distances of the stars) were carried out largely by the visual methods of Bessel. Experimentation with photographic techniques was progressing, and Schlesinger was eager to test the performance of the Yerkes forty-inch refractor for photographic parallax work. The parallax of a star is defined as the angle at the star subtended by the radius of the earth's orbit. It is manifested by an apparent slight change in the direction of the star observed at intervals of six months, during which the earth moves in its orbit from one side to the other of the sun. In practice these parallactic displacements are measured relative to very distant faint stars, the motions of which are negligibly small. The uncertainties of the measurements are reduced photographically when there is a minimum disparity in the sizes of the images of the parallax star and the faint comparison stars. In order to achieve that, Schlesinger designed a rotating sector to occult the image of the bright star intermittently, while the faint stars were exposed continuously; this technique is still used extensively. By devising his time-saving "method of dependences," Schlesinger also improved and simplified the mathematical and numerical procedures for the reductions of the measurements.

After two years at Yerkes Observatory (1903–1905), Schlesinger was called to the Allegheny Observatory in Pittsburgh as its director. Here he expended considerable effort on spectroscopic studies of eclipsing and spectroscopic binary stars, and also on the improvement of instrumentation for parallax work. In addition, he began his first investigations for the preparation of "zone catalogues" to provide accurate positions and proper motions (that is, apparent changes in position) of many thousands of stars to the ninth and fainter magnitudes. These early beginnings he pursued vigorously at the Yale University Observatory, where he was director from 1920 until his retirement in 1941. With the enthusiastic collaboration of Ida Barney, Schlesinger published ten volumes of zone catalogues, including some 150,000 stars, between declinations −30° and +30° of declination.

At Yale he extended his work on parallaxes to the southern hemisphere, where the Yale-Columbia Southern Station began operation in Johannesburg, South Africa, in 1925. Before Schlesinger began his investigations of stellar parallaxes, only a few hundred were known; during his lifetime, and primarily owing to his direct influence, the number grew to four thousand.

In 1908 E. C. Pickering, director of the Harvard Observatory, had published his "Revised Harvard Photometry," giving the positions, magnitudes, and spectral classes of all stars of magnitude 6.5 and brighter. Using this as a basis, Schlesinger in 1924 published his first edition of the "Bright Star Catalogue," vastly extending its usefulness by adding proper motions, radial velocities, and other relevant data. The second edition, published with Louise Jenkins in 1940, became probably the most widely used of all astronomical catalogues.

BIBLIOGRAPHY

A list of 262 of Schlesinger's papers is in Dirk Brouwer, "Biographical Memoir of Frank Schlesinger," in *Biographical Memoirs. National Academy of Sciences,* **24** (1945), 105–144. These works by Schlesinger include "Photographic Determinations of Stellar Parallaxes," in *Probleme der Astronomie: Festschrift für Hugo v. Seeliger* (1924), 422–437; "Some Aspects of Astronomical Photography of Precision," in *Monthly Notices of the Royal Astronomical Society,* **87** (1927), 506–523, which is the first George Darwin Lecture; and *General Catalogue of Stellar Parallaxes,* 2nd ed. (New Haven, 1935), compiled with Louise Jenkins.

E. DORRIT HOFFLEIT

SCHLICK, (FRIEDRICH ALBERT) MORITZ (*b.* Berlin, Germany, 14 April 1882; *d.* Vienna, Austria, 22 June 1936), *theory of knowledge, philosophy of science.*

Schlick, the son of Albert Schlick and Agnes Arndt, studied at Heidelberg and Lausanne, and took his doctorate under Max Planck at Berlin in 1904 with a dissertation on the physics of light. An early and abiding interest in philosophy (he published his *Lebensweisheit* at the age of twenty-six) led him to abandon science in favor of a philosophical career; and in due course, following the necessary preparation, he entered academic life as a teacher of philosophy, first at Rostock and then at Kiel. After the publication of his *Allgemeine Erkenntnislehre* (1918), he was called to the chair of the philosophy of the inductive sciences at the University of Vienna (1922), formerly held by such eminent philosopher-scientists as Ernst Mach and Ludwig Boltzmann. Apart from two visits to the United States, where he held visiting professorships at Stanford University and the University of California at Berkeley, he retained this post until he was murdered by a deranged former student.

At Vienna, Schlick soon became the center of a group of thinkers with predominantly scientific and mathematical backgrounds, who were devoted to the cultivation and development of a scientific philosophy, as opposed to the then prevailing metaphysical orientation of Continental, and especially German, philosophy. The group came to be known as the Vienna Circle and later, in England and the United States, as the logical positivists. In addition to producing much solid philosophical work, published for the most part in the journal *Erkenntnis,* the Vienna Circle engaged in a fair amount of antimetaphysical crusading, earning enthusiastic support from younger philosophical "radicals" and at least as much hatred from the conservative representatives of "academic" philosophy.

Schlick, although the leading figure of the circle, was far from being a typical exponent of some of the views generally held to be representative of the group. While he shared their interest in logic as a tool of philosophical analysis and their repudiation of metaphysics as a viable discipline, as well as their rejection of synthetic a priori propositions, he was much more sympathetic than some members to the great figures of the Western philosophical tradition, despite strong criticism of what he considered to be their errors. Honoring science as man's highest intellectual achievement, he nevertheless deemed the problems of culture and of life to be of far greater significance. Like Wittgenstein, who greatly influenced him in his Vienna period, Schlick saw philosophical activity as meaning clarification, and as no less important for conduct and enlightening life's goals than in preparing the way for scientific ascertainment. In his ethical and related writings—*Lebensweisheit*, *Vom Sinn des Lebens* (a pamphlet of 1927), and *Fragen der Ethik* (1930)—his profound understanding of life often finds expression in the elevated language of the poet or the philosopher as man of wisdom. His main reputation will, however, probably rest on his work in theory of knowledge and philosophy of science.

Schlick's first work in this area was a brief expository, interpretive book (one of the earliest) on Einstein's theory of relativity, published in German in 1917 and in English translation as *Space and Time in Contemporary Physics* (1920). In it he stresses the profound philosophical implications of Einstein's work, to which, in his later writings, he frequently refers as a paradigm of philosophical activity conceived as meaning clarification—Einstein's main achievement having been his clarification of the hitherto vague concept of simultaneity at a distance.

Allgemeine Erkenntnislehre (1918), his major work, examines a very wide range of problems and concepts relating to scientific knowledge. Schlick begins with the all-important concept of knowledge itself, the analysis of which sets the tone and determines the special character of the work as a whole. Despite the half century since its appearance, the work remains perhaps the most comprehensive and valuable treatment of the general theory of knowledge. Schlick's central idea is that knowledge is discursive, not intuitive: it yields true descriptions of the object to be known as a special case of something already known; it is not simply awareness of something confronting us. In German the point can be made perspicuous by distinguishing between *Erkenntnis* (recognition, knowledge) and *Kenntnis* (cognition, in the narrow sense of acquaintance with something; experience of it). The whole of Schlick's epistemology is permeated and affected by this distinction. In its simplest terms the work may be seen as a polemic against Kant, who denied that we can have knowledge of what lies beyond the phenomenal, and against Hume and his modern followers, who tended to deny meaning to talk of the transcendent and identify reality with the immediately given. The latter view is sometimes expressed by the slogan "Only the given exists" and is closely connected with the view that what cannot be sensed cannot be known.

Since knowledge is not simple acquaintance with or awareness of some datum but, rather, true description of class membership, causal connections, or governing laws of objects to be known, knowledge is in no way restricted to what can be sensed. The relatively few electrical phenomena accessible to the senses do not give us knowledge of electricity but only furnish occasions for inquiring into their causes and consequences and, ultimately, for investigating the laws governing electrical events; for the true concern of knowledge is with laws, not things or appearances. Knowledge in its higher levels seeks ever more general laws from which can be derived those on lower levels. The ideal of knowledge would be maximum descriptive power using a minimum of concepts; then our picture of the universe would be of a single tightly knit system in which each thing (event) stood in some known relationship to all others. The business of science is not simply to report sense data, but to formulate and test hypotheses that have consequences ascertainable in the given.

Schlick brought this conception of knowledge to bear on the errors of traditional metaphysics, which he located in the vain effort to capture and express in language the immediate quality of life and experience—a task for which it is wholly unfit.

Only form or structure is expressible, communicable—can enter into knowledge. The immediate is ineffable, to be enjoyed or experienced (*erlebt*), a matter of feeling, while knowledge is a matter of intellect, of thought; the two are incommensurable.

Schlick's broad conception of science by no means excluded systematic knowledge relating to questions of life and values. He was, in fact, most deeply concerned with the meaning of life and the path to happiness. In his *Lebensweisheit* he explores the pleasure-happiness value of the senses, the instincts, and of personal and social relations and institutions, and he returned to this topic in the unfinished work *Natur und Kultur*. The richest source of happiness ultimately proves to be the social instincts and love. This theme plays a central role in Schlick's *Fragen der Ethik*, where it culminates in the view that in the long run virtue (moral conduct) and happiness go hand in hand, a fact which explains why man acts morally. Such explanation is the explicit topic of the book as a whole, which however also contains much rich psychological material bearing on human conduct and happiness, as well as passages of profound wisdom and eloquence. In *Lebensweisheit* Schlick develops Schiller's theme of man's finding his highest vocation in "play"—free, joyous activity pursued for its own sake; and in answer to the question "What is the meaning of life?" he answers "Youth!" "Preserve the spirit of youth," he urges, "for it is the meaning of life!" Youth alone makes sense of life, so that for the youthful spirit the question of the meaning of life does not arise.

BIBLIOGRAPHY

I. ORIGINAL WORKS. Schlick's early works are *Lebensweisheit* (Munich, 1908); "Das Grundproblem der Ästhetik in entwicklungsgeschichtlicher Beleuchtung," in *Archiv für die gesamte Psychologie*, **14** (1909), 102–132; "Die Grenze der naturwissenschaftlichen und philosophischen Begriffsbildung," in *Vierteljahrsschrift für wissenschaftliche Philosophie und Soziologie*, **34** (1910), 121–142; "Das Wesen der Wahrheit nach der modernen Logik," *ibid.*, 386–477; "Gibt es intuitive Erkenntnis?" *ibid.*, **37** (1913), 472–488; "Die philosophische Bedeutung des Relativitätsprinzips," in *Zeitschrift für Philosophie und philosophische Kritik*, **159** (1915), 129–175; "Idealität des Raumes, Introjektion und psychophysisches Problem," in *Vierteljahrsschrift für wissenschaftliche Philosophie und Soziologie*, **40** (1916), 230–254; *Raum und Zeit in der gegenwärtigen Physik* (Berlin, 1917; 4th ed., 1922), English trans. by H. L. Brose as *Space and Time in Contemporary Physics*

(Oxford, 1920); and *Allgemeine Erkenntnislehre* (Berlin, 1918; 2nd ed., 1925).

Subsequent works include "Naturphilosophische Betrachtungen über das Kausalprinzip," in *Naturwissenschaften*, **8** (1920), 461–474; "Naturphilosophie," in M. Dessoir, ed., *Lehrbuch der Philosophie*, II (Berlin, 1925), 397–492; "Erleben, Erkennen, Metaphysik," in *Kantstudien*, **31** (1926), 146–158; *Vom Sinn des Lebens* (Berlin, 1927); "Erkenntnistheorie und moderne Physik," in *Scientia*, **45** (May 1929), 307–316; *Fragen der Ethik* (Vienna, 1930), English trans. by D. Rynin as *Problems of Ethics* (New York, 1939; repr., New York, 1962); "Die Kausalität in der gegenwärtigen Physik," in *Naturwissenschaften*, **19** (1931), 145–162, English trans. by D. Rynin as "Causality in Contemporary Physics," in *British Journal for the Philosophy of Science*, **12** (1961–1962), 177–193, 281–298; and "Positivismus und Realismus," in *Erkenntnis*, **3** (1932), 1–31, English trans. by D. Rynin as "Positivism and Realism," in A. J. Ayer, ed., *Logical Positivism* (Glencoe, Ill., 1959), and in *Synthèse*, **7** (1948–1949), 478–505.

Later works include "Über das Fundament der Erkenntnis," in *Erkenntnis*, **4** (1934), 79–99, English trans. by D. Rynin as "The Foundation of Knowledge," in A. J. Ayer, ed., *Logical Positivism* (Glencoe, Ill., 1959); "Philosophie und Naturwissenschaft," in *Erkenntnis*, **4** (1934), 379–396; "Facts and Propositions," in *Analysis*, **2** (1935), 65–70; "Sind die Naturgesetze Konventionen?" in *Actes du congrès international de philosophie scientifique, Paris, 1935* (Paris, 1936), 8–17, English trans. by H. Feigl as "Are Natural Laws Conventions?" in H. Feigl and M. Brodbeck, eds., *Readings in the Philosophy of Science* (New York, 1953), 181–188; "Meaning and Verification," in *Philosophical Review*, **45** (1936), 339–369; "Quantentheorie und Erkennbarkeit der Natur," in *Erkenntnis*, **6** (1937), 317–326; "L'école de Vienne et la philosophie traditionnelle," in *Travaux du 9ᵉ congrès international de philosophie* (Paris, 1937); and "Über die Beziehung zwischen den psychologischen und den physikalischen Begriffen," in Schlick's *Gesammelte Aufsätze* (Vienna, 1938; repr. Hildesheim, 1969), English trans. by W. Sellars as "On the Relation Between Psychological and Physical Concepts," in H. Feigl and W. Sellars, ed., *Readings in Philosophical Analysis* (New York, 1949), and in French trans. by J. Haendler as "De la relation entre les notions psychologiques et les notions physiques," in *Revue de synthèse*, **10** (1935), 5–26—both the English and German versions have dropped lines.

Miscellaneous works are *Grundzüge der Naturphilosophie*, W. Hollitscher and J. Rauscher, eds. (Vienna, 1948), a version of his lectures at the University of Vienna on the philosophy of culture; *Natur und Kultur*, J. Rauscher, ed. (Vienna–Stuttgart, 1952), an unfinished work on the philosophy of nature; and *Aphorismen*, B. H. Schlick, ed. (Vienna, 1962), a privately printed selection of philosophic reflections and aphorisms taken from Schlick's writings.

II. SECONDARY LITERATURE. V. Kraft, *Der Wiener Kreis* (Vienna, 1950), English trans. by A. Pap as *The Vienna Circle* (New York, 1953, 1969), has numerous references to, and comments on, Schlick's views during the last decade of his life. Biographical information together with impressions of Schlick as man, teacher, and philosopher may be found in the obituary articles by H. Reichenbach, in *Erkenntnis*, **6** (1936), 141–142; and H. Feigl, *ibid.*, **7** (1937), 393–419; and in F. Waisman's intro. to Schlick's *Gesammelte Aufsätze*.

See also Béla Juhos, "Moritz Schlick," in *Encyclopedia of Philosophy*, VII (New York, 1967), 319–324; and D. Rynin, "Moritz Schlick," in *International Encyclopedia of the Social Sciences*, XIV (New York, 1968), 52–56.

For critical evaluations, see comments in K. R. Popper, *The Logic of Scientific Discovery* (London–New York, 1959); and the critical discussion by D. Rynin prefixed to his trans. of "Positivism and Realism," in *Synthèse*, **7** (1948–1949), 466–477.

DAVID RYNIN

SCHLIEMANN, HEINRICH (*b.* Neu Buckow, Mecklenburg-Schwerin, Germany, 6 January 1822; *d.* Naples, Italy, 26 December 1890), *archaeology.*

Schliemann was the son of a poor Protestant minister, who encouraged his interest in classical antiquity. A picture of Troy in flames, in a copy of Jerrer's *Universal History* that his father had given him as a Christmas present, captured his imagination and fortified his belief in the reality of the events described by Homer; the picture remained in his memory throughout his youth and during his later career in business. Unable to continue his education past the age of fourteen, Schliemann became an apprentice to a grocer in 1836; in 1841 he decided to immigrate to America, and signed on as cabin boy on a ship that was wrecked shortly thereafter. He then settled in Amsterdam, and was employed by a Dutch business firm for five years, during which he learned almost all the European languages. In 1846 he was sent to St. Petersburg as the firm's agent there, but he soon started his own business, dealing chiefly in indigo, and became rich from it. In 1850 he was in California; his business continued to prosper, and he became an American citizen. He then returned to Russia, where he married, and, at the age of thirty-six, retired from business to devote his time and his great fortune to the study of prehistoric archaeology, and especially to finding the remains of Troy.

To this end, Schliemann studied ancient and modern Greek, traveled extensively in Europe, Egypt, Syria, and Greece, and studied archaeology in Paris. In 1864 he traveled around the world, then in 1868 visited archaeological sites in Greece and Asia Minor. In 1869 he published *Ithaka, der Peloponnes und Troja*, based upon his own excavations at Ithaca and Mycenae, in which he argued that the tombs of Agamemnon and Clytemnestra were to be sought in the citadel of Mycenae, rather than in the treasuries in the lower town. Troy, he went on to state, was not a myth, nor was it located, as some had claimed, at Burnarbashi; rather, it was to be found in the mound of Hissarlik, the site of historic Ilion, and there Schliemann decided to dig.

Some isolated discoveries concerning prehistoric Greek archaeology had been made before Schliemann began to dig at Troy. Chief among these was F. Fouqué's 1862 excavation of painted pottery and frescoed walls at Santorin; since these artifacts were covered by twenty-six feet of pumice deposited by the volcanic eruption of about 2000 B.C., there could be little doubt that they indicated a prehistoric Aegean culture. Schliemann's goal was specific—he wished to prove, through archaeology, the truth of Homer—but he in fact achieved much more; his work at Hissarlik led him to discover the archaeological record of centuries of pre-Homeric, prehistoric, and pre-Hellenic culture.

With his young Greek second wife, Sophia Engastromenos, whom he had married following his divorce, Schliemann began to dig at Hissarlik in 1871. Within the mound he found evidence of seven heavily fortified settlements, which he designated Troy and distinguished by Roman numerals, the deepest being Troy I. Troy II held the greatest interest for him; he found fortress walls, evidence of violent overthrow, and indications that the city had traded in gold, silver, ivory, amber, and jade. Because Troy II had been totally destroyed by fire, Schliemann called it the "burnt layer"; it was succeeded by the small villages of Troy III, Troy IV, and Troy V, and then by the grand Mycenaean city Troy VI. Since a considerable interval must have elapsed between Troy II and Troy VI, it was clear to Schliemann that Troy II must have existed well before the first Olympiad of 776 B.C., traditionally the earliest date in Greek history. He identified Troy II as Homeric Troy, "the citadel of Priam," and, the day before he finished the dig in 1873, found "Priam's treasure," a magnificent cache of gold objects that he hastily smuggled out of Turkey.

Schliemann's attempt to keep the treasure together, against the claims of the Ottoman government to a share of it, precluded his immediate return to Hissarlik. He prepared his *Trojanische Altertümer* for publication in 1874 (his long business experience had made him assiduous in publishing his work immediately), then returned to Mycenae, where he dug for the tombs of Clytemnestra and Agamemnon at the site of his earlier prediction. Excavating within a circle of stones inside the Lion Gate of the citadel, he found the tombs he was looking for—the now-famous shaft graves. The contents of these graves (Schliemann discovered five, and a sixth was unearthed after he left the site) far surpassed "Priam's treasure" in richness, and included gold and silver vases, inlaid swords of gold, silver, copper, and bronze, gold ornaments for the clothing of the dead, and gold masks. In addition to his work within the citadel, Schliemann excavated two tholoi, the treasury of Atreus (or Agamemnon), and the treasury of Clytemnestra.

Schliemann's *Mycenae*, published in 1877, was written in eight weeks and represented a daily record of his excavations. Like the rest of his books, it was written in German and almost immediately translated into French and English. This book, together with the Mycenaean treasure itself (established in the National Museum in Athens), brought Schliemann considerable fame; the English translation carried a preface by W. E. Gladstone, himself a Homeric scholar as well as a statesman.

Following a short and not very productive visit to Ithaca, Schliemann, in 1879, returned to Hissarlik. He was assisted in this new series of digs by a classical archaeologist, Émile Burnouf, and by Rudolf Virchow, the founder of the Berlin Society for Anthropology, Ethnology, and Prehistory, and organizer of the Berlin Museum für Volkerkunde. The results of this expedition, including new evidence to identify Hissarlik with ancient Troy, are set out in *Ilios* (1881). In 1880 Schliemann went to Orchomenus, where he excavated the treasury of Minyas, a structure similar to the treasuries of Agamemnon and Clytemnestra at Mycenae. His book on the subject, *Orchomenos*, was also published in 1881. He returned to Hissarlik the following year, accompanied by Wilhelm Dörpfeld, who gave him expert assistance on an extensive dig that lasted until 1883. Dörpfeld, a practical architect who had worked with Ernst Curtius at Olympia, brought to the work at Troy the systematization and efficiency of the new German archaeology; he was able to expose the stratigraphy of Hissarlik with precision, and he revolutionized Schliemann's technique.

In 1884 Schliemann went to Tiryns, where he

uncovered the royal palace. In 1886 he traveled to Egypt with Virchow and visited the excavations being conducted by William Petrie (who characterized Schliemann as "dogmatic but always ready for facts"). During the next two years Schliemann also worked at Cythera and Pylos, then, in 1889, returned with Dörpfeld to Hissarlik. He was, throughout these last few years of his life, greatly afflicted by an ear ailment, and made a number of trips to Europe seeking a cure; it was on one such that he collapsed and died while in Naples.

Dörpfeld continued to work at Troy until 1894. Three years after Schliemann's death, he identified Troy VI, rather than Troy II, as the Homeric city, and established that the treasure that Schliemann had found at Troy II predated Priam's time. In his work at Mycenae, Orchomenus, and Tiryns, Schliemann also attributed to the Homeric Greeks artifacts of a much older civilization. The Greeks themselves had always regarded Mycenae and Tiryns as Homeric sites, but the scholarly world was deeply divided over the nature of Schliemann's discoveries. Some scholars willingly accepted his claims, while others argued that the artifacts were Byzantine in origin, or perhaps the work of Celts, Goths, Avars, Huns, or unspecified "orientals." Nonetheless, a number of Schliemann's contemporaries were certain that the Mycenaean civilization that Schliemann had found was not Homeric, but pre-Homeric, as is now known to be the case—what Schliemann had in fact discovered, in both Greece and western Anatolia, was the great pre-Hellenic civilization of the eastern Mediterranean, and this marks his chief contribution to prehistoric archaeology.

Schliemann's contribution to the development of archaeological technique and method has also been vigorously disputed. Stanley Carson, for example, called him (in *The Discovery of Man*, p. 221) the inventor of "a proper archaeological method which could be followed in any land," and added that Schliemann's techniques "constituted an innovation of the first order of importance in the study of the antiquity of man by archaeological methods." A. Michaelis, on the other hand, characterized Schliemann as "a complete stranger to every scientific method of treatment of his subject" and accused him of having "no idea that a method and a well-defined technique existed" (*A Century of Archaeological Discoveries*, p. 217).

It is, however, certain that Schliemann's excavation of Hissarlik was the first such operation conducted upon a tell and was, as Sir John Myres wrote, "the first large-scale dissection of a dryland settlement unguided by the remains of great monuments such as simplified the task in Babylon and Nineveh" (*The Cretan Labyrinth*, p. 273). Schliemann's discovery of seven occupation levels at Troy further gave a considerable impetus to the application of the principles of stratigraphy to archaeology, although it is necessary to note that he himself understood the stratigraphy of Hissarlik only slowly and with the assistance of Dörpfeld. (Indeed, he came to recognize the strata only slowly, thinking at one time that the whole mound covered Priam's city; and for a while the recurrence of stone tools puzzled him, so that he wrote that he could not understand "how it is that I am unearthing stone implements throughout the length of my excavations.")

Schliemann's archaeological work was of interest to the non-scientific world as well. He kept the public informed of his discoveries through his books and through his dispatches to the London *Times* and *Daily Telegraph*, as well as a number of other newspapers, so that, as A. T. White wrote, "every person of culture and education lived through the drama of discovering Troy" (*Lost Worlds*, p. 27). His readers were excited by the romance of his undertaking and rejoiced in Schliemann's incredible good luck in finding exactly what he had set out to find—the physical evidence of Homer's Troy, and a buried hoard of golden treasure. Schliemann also provided inspiration to a whole generation of professional archaeologists and ancient historians; although Emil Ludwig described him as "monomaniacal" and as perhaps of "a mythomaniacal nature which at times overstepped the limits of the normal," Sir John Myres wrote that upon the news of Schliemann's death it seemed to many that "the spring had gone out of the year" (*The Cretan Labyrinth*, p. 272).

BIBLIOGRAPHY

I. ORIGINAL WORKS. Schliemann's writings include *Ithaka, der Peloponnes und Troja* (1869); *Trojanische Altertümer* (1874); *Troja und seine Ruinen* (1875); *Mycenae* (1877); *Ilios* (1880); *Orchomenos* (1881); *Troja* (1884); and his autobiography, edited by his wife Sophia, *Selbstbiographie bis zu seinem Tode vervollständigt* (Leipzig, 1892; 9th ed., Wiesbaden, 1961).

II. SECONDARY LITERATURE. On Schliemann and his work, see Stanley Casson, *The Discovery of Man* (London, 1939); Emil Ludwig, *Schliemann: The Story of a Gold-Seeker* (London, 1931); Sir John Myres, *The Cretan Labyrinth* (London, 1933); Sir John Sandys, *A History of Classical Scholarship* (Cambridge, 1908);

and Carl Schuchardt, *Schliemann's Excavations and Archaeological and Historical Studies* (London, 1891).

GLYN DANIEL

SCHLOTHEIM, ERNST FRIEDRICH, BARON VON (*b.* Almenhausen, Thuringia, Germany, 2 April 1765; *d.* Gotha, Germany, 28 March 1832), *geology, paleontology.*

Schlotheim was the son of Ernst Ludwig von Schlotheim and Friederike Eberhardine von Stange. After receiving his basic education at home from a tutor, he attended the Gymnasium in Gotha from 1779 to 1781. He then studied public administration, and the natural sciences under Blumenbach, at Göttingen. Since he was especially interested in the geological sciences, he next went to Freiberg to study under Werner; he also became a friend of Alexander von Humboldt. In 1792 Schlotheim entered the Gotha civil service as an assessor, rising to minister and lord high marshal by 1828.

From 1822 Schlotheim also served as superintendent of the ducal art, natural history, coin, and book collections in Gotha. At an early age Schlotheim had started his own geological and especially paleontological collections; and he now began to publish his observations of the countryside. Reporting on the stratigraphy of the calcareous tufa at Gräfentonna, in which a complete fossil elephant skeleton had been found in 1695, Schlotheim recognized that in addition to indigenous stones, it contained other field stones, predominantly granite. He was the first to trace this combination to Scandinavia.

Schlotheim's later investigations were concerned primarily with paleontology. He studied the plants found in the bituminous schists of the Lower Permian in Thuringia and realized (1801, 1804) that they belonged to extinct species and could not be given—as had been customary—contemporary names. He also concluded that during the Lower Permian epoch Thuringia must have had a warmer climate. In his article of 1813 Schlotheim was the first to insist that the species of the fossils must be determined in order to distinguish the various formations. He called for the establishment of a nomenclature in paleontology analogous to that provided by Linnaeus for existing organisms. Paleontology would thereby become a tool for determining the age of strata—a principle advocated independently by William Smith (1816). Schlotheim's article also presented primarily a survey of fossils according to geological formations. His *Petrafaktenkunde* (1820) employed the binomial nomenclature systematically and thus put the science of paleontology onto a rigorous basis. It was the first major advance in that science since 1762, when J. G. Walch had comprehensively classified fossils within the zoological system; and it marked the beginning of an era of rapid and important growth.

Schlotheim also realized that the distribution of fossils, their association, their degree of preservation, the facies of the neighboring rock, and the mixture of marine with terrestrial forms made it possible to draw important inferences concerning the history of the earth. The study of these factors was not taken up systematically until a century later, as biostratinomy. Schlotheim was also critical of catastrophism, which was challenged for the first time in 1822 by his friend K. E. A. von Hoff, an early uniformitarian.

BIBLIOGRAPHY

I. ORIGINAL WORKS. Schlotheim's most important works are "Mineralogische Beschreibung der unteren Herrschaft Tonna," in J. C. W. Voigt, *Mineralogische und bergmännische Abhandlungen,* III (Leipzig, 1791), 182–200; "Beiträge zur nähern Kenntniss einzelner Fossilien," in *Magazin für die gesamte Mineralogie, Geognosie und mineralogischer Erdschreibung,* **1** (1801), 143–172; "Über die Kräuterabdrücke im Schieferton und Sandstein der Steinkohlenformation," *ibid.; Beschreibung merkwürdiger Kräuterabdrücke und Pflanzenversteinerungen* (Gotha, 1804); "Beiträge zur Naturgeschichte der Versteinerungen in geognostischer Hinsicht," in *Taschenbuch für die gesammte Mineralogie,* **7** (1813), 3–134; "Die Versteinerungen im Höhlenkalkstein von Glücksbrunn," in *Magazin für die neuesten Entdeckungen in der gesammten Naturkunde,* **7** (1816), 156–158; "Beiträge zur Naturgeschichte der Versteinerungen in geognostischer Hinsicht," in *Denkschriften der K. Akademie der Wissenschaften zu München,* **6** (1816–1817), 13–36; "Der Kalktuff als Glied der aufgeschwemmten Gebirgsformation," in *Taschenbuch für die gesammte Mineralogie,* **12** (1818), 315–345; *Die Petrafaktenkunde auf ihrem jetzigen Standpunkte* (Gotha, 1820; supps., 1822, 1823); and *Der thüringische Flözmuschelkalkstein in besonderer Beziehung auf seine Versteinerungen* (Gotha, 1823).

II. SECONDARY LITERATURE. See C. Credner, "Ernst Friedrich von Schlotheim," in *Neuer Nekrolog der Deutschen,* **10**, no. 1 (1832), 246–250; B. von Freyberg, "Ernst Friedrich Baron von Schlotheim," in "Aus der Heimat," *Naturwissenschaftliche Zeitschrift,* **45**, no. 10 (1932); and *Die geologische Erforschung Thüringens in* *älterer Zeit* (Berlin, 1932); W. von Gümbel, "Ernst Friedrich Freiherr von Schlotheim," in *Allgemeine deutsche Biographie*, XXXI, 550–551; and K. A. von Zittel, *Geschichte der Geologie und Paläontologie* (Munich–Leipzig, 1899).

          B. von Freyberg

SCHLUMBERGER, CHARLES (*b.* Mulhouse, France, 29 September 1825; *d.* Paris, France, 13 July 1905), *micropaleontology.*

 After completing his education at the École Polytechnique, Schlumberger joined the navy corps of engineers at Toulon in 1849. His transfer in 1855, to Nancy, where he was in charge of purchasing timber, enabled him to make many field trips and to develop an interest in natural history, which dated from his youth. The collecting of fossils, combined with his acquaintance with Olry Terquem, led to his career as a micropaleontologist specializing in Foraminifera.

 In 1879 Schlumberger went to Paris; and although he was promoted a few years later to the rank of chief engineer, he requested early retirement and became a guest scientist at the laboratory of paleontology of the Muséum d'Histoire Naturelle and later at the École des Mines. About 1882 he began his collaboration with E. Munier-Chalmas, who had just recognized dimorphism in *Nummulitids.* By means of a new thin-section technique developed by Schlumberger, both men were able to discover the same character among Miliolidae, as well as important features pertaining to their apertures.

 By 1894 dimorphism in Foraminifera had been recognized by many as an extremely widespread character and had been explained by alternating phases of sexual and asexual reproduction. Unfortunately, Schlumberger was not active in this final development and interpretation of some of his original discoveries because Munier-Chalmas's reluctance to write papers in final form had gradually brought their collaboration to a standstill. Consequently Schlumberger continued his research on other groups of Foraminifera alone. He wrote in particular a series of important papers on the stratigraphic distribution of *Orbitoids.* After the death of Munier-Chalmas and during the last years of his life, he resumed his studies on Miliolidae.

 Despite his lack of formal scientific training, Schlumberger contributed in a fundamental manner to the solution of one of the most puzzling problems of micropaleontology.

BIBLIOGRAPHY

 Schlumberger's writings include "Note sur les Foraminifères," in *Feuille des jeunes naturalistes,* **12** (1882), 83–112; "Nouvelles observations sur le dimorphisme des Foraminifères," in *Comptes rendus . . . de l'Académie des sciences,* **96** (1883), 862–866, 1598–1601, written with E. Munier-Chalmas, also in English as "New Observations on the Dimorphism of the Foraminifera," in *Annals and Magazine of Natural History,* 5th ser., **11** (1883), 336–340; "Sur les Miliolidées trématophorées, lère partie," in *Bulletin de la Société géologique de France,* 3rd ser., **13** (1885), 273–323; "Révision des Biloculines des grands fonds, expéditions du *Travailleur* et du *Talisman*," in *Mémoires de la Société zoologique de France,* **4** (1891), 155–191; "Monographie des Miliolidées du golfe de Marseille," *ibid.,* **6** (1893), 199–222; "Première note sur les Orbitoïdes (*Orbitoides,* s. str.)," in *Bulletin de la Société géologique de France,* 4th ser., **1** (1901), 459–467; "Deuxième note sur les Orbitoïdes (*Orbitoides,* s. str.)," *ibid.,* **2** (1902), 255–261; "Troisième note sur les Orbitoïdes (*Orthophragmina* discoïdes)," *ibid.,* **3** (1903), 273–289; "Quatrième note sur les Orbitoïdes (*Orthophragmina* étoilés)," *ibid.,* **4** (1904), 119–135; and "Deuxième note sur les Miliolidées trématophorées," *ibid.,* **5** (1905), 115–134.

 A complete list of Schlumberger's publications is in H. Douvillé, "Charles Schlumberger, notice nécrologique," in *Bulletin de la Société géologique de France,* 4th ser., **6** (1906), 340–350.

         Albert V. Carozzi

SCHMERLING, PHILIPPE-CHARLES (*b.* Delft, Netherlands, 24 February 1791; *d.* Liège, Belgium, 6 November 1836), *paleontology.*

 Schmerling's paternal ancestors came from Austria. After completing his secondary education in Delft, he studied medicine at Leiden for two years and then went to The Hague. Appointed a health officer in 1812 and a military physician the following year, he left the army in 1816 in order to establish a civilian practice. In 1821 he married Sara Henriette Caroline Douglas, a descendant of a noble Scots family, one branch of which had immigrated to the Netherlands. A few months later Schmerling and his wife moved to Liège, where he continued his medical studies and, after receiving the doctorate in 1825, began to practice.

 Schmerling became a paleontologist by chance. In 1829 he went to Chokier, a small village near Liège, to treat a poor quarry worker. He was amazed to see the man's children playing with very unusual bones that had been unearthed at a nearby quarry. Stimulated by this find, the first known excavation of fossil bones in Belgium, Schmerling traveled extensively in the region and within less than four years located more than forty similar sites. He collected the remains of some sixty animal species. Those that made him famous were human bones in an indisputably fossil state.

Following a carefully formulated plan, Schmerling studied first the caves, then the animal remains they contained, and finally the human bones. He observed that the stalagmitic floors covered deposits containing the remains of extinct species, such as the mammoth, and of apparently contemporaneous species still in existence, such as the wolf and the boar. He noted that the human remains were in the same state of preservation as the animal bones unearthed with them. They were of the same color, were dispersed in similar patterns, and sometimes were so abraded and scattered that the hypothesis of their deliberate burial in the caves had to be excluded. Therefore, Schmerling asserted, the human bones had undoubtedly been buried at the same time and by the same causes as the bones of the extinct species. He also discovered chipped stones and carved bones in the same conditions; their very presence, he asserted, demonstrated the existence of man during the "antediluvian period."

The most famous of the caves that Schmerling explored was that of Engis, located on the left bank of the Meuse about fifteen kilometers upstream from Liège. There, in 1830, he exhumed two skulls at different levels. One, of a child (today called Engis I), was lying at the base of the deposits, next to a mammoth's tooth; the other, of an adult (Engis II), was found at a somewhat higher level in a hole containing rhinoceros teeth and the bones of horses, reindeer, and several ruminants. (It was later shown that Engis I was of the Neanderthal type—the first such example ever found, whereas Engis II belonged to a variety of Cro-Magnon man.) Others before Schmerling (E. J. C. Esper in 1771 and Buckland in 1823) and at about the same time (P. Tournal) had discovered human bones associated with the remains of extinct animals, but Schmerling was the first to demonstrate the existence of fossil man by means of irrefutable stratigraphic arguments.

Schmerling's medical training led to his interest in the pathological lesions on the Quaternary mammalian bones found in the Belgian caves, and his 1836 memoir on paleopathology was one of the first of its kind. His recognition of the importance of this discipline is a further indication of both the originality and the scope of his thought.

Although Schmerling's five published works on paleontology (1832–1836) were characterized by exemplary scientific rigor, they generated little enthusiasm (except for the last one, on paleopathology, which stimulated much discussion in Germany). Indeed, his work fell into such neglect that many copies of his principal study (1833–1834) were destroyed after his death. Lyell visited Schmerling in 1834 and cited his discoveries in the third edition of *Principles of Geology* (1834, p. 161); but he did not grasp their importance until much later, as he himself admitted (1863). Schmerling's contemporaries were not, however, completely unaware of his scientific ability. He was elected a corresponding member of the Royal Academy of Brussels (1834) and a corresponding member of the Royal Institute of the Low Countries (1836).

BIBLIOGRAPHY

I. ORIGINAL WORKS. In addition to his doctoral dissertation (1825) and a note on dyeing with colchicum (1832), Schmerling published five works on paleontology. The two principal ones are *Recherches sur les ossements fossiles découverts dans les cavernes de la province de Liège*, 2 vols. and 2 vols. of plates (Liège, 1833–1834), translated or analyzed in Italy, France, Germany, Russia, England, and the United States, and containing the description of the Engis men; and "Notice sur quelques os de pachydermes découverts dans le terrain meuble près du village de Chokier," in *Bulletin de l'Académie royale des sciences et belles-lettres de Bruxelles*. Classe de sciences, **3** (1836), 82–87, his contribution to paleopathology.

II. SECONDARY LITERATURE. See the following, listed chronologically: C. Morren, "Notice sur la vie et les travaux de Philippe Charles Schmerling," in *Annuaire de l'Académie royale des sciences et belles-lettres de Bruxelles*, **4** (1838), 130–150; A. Le Roy, *L'Université de Liège depuis sa fondation* (Liège, 1869), 550; C. Lyell, *The Geological Evidences of the Antiquity of Man*, 1st ed. (London, 1863), 70–71; R. L. Moodie, *Paleopathology. An Introduction to the Study of Ancient Evidence of Disease* (Urbana, Ill., 1923), 64–65; C. Fraipont, "Les hommes fossiles d'Engis," *Archives de l'Institut de paléontologie humaine*, no. 16 (1936); and K. P. Oakley, "The Problem of Man's Antiquity. An Historical Survey," in *Bulletin of the British Museum (Natural History)*, Geology, **9**, no. 5 (1964), 91–93.

G. UBAGHS

SCHMIDEL (or **Schmiedel**), **CASIMIR CHRIS-
TOPH** (*b.* Bayreuth, Germany, 21 November
1718; *d.* Ansbach, Germany, 18 December 1792),
medicine, natural history.

Schmidel was the son of Georg Cornelius
Schmidel, a Brandenburg financial councillor and
physician-in-ordinary to the margrave in Bayreuth.
Schmidel was best known for his studies of the
morphology of the cryptogams and for his editing
of Konrad Gesner's posthumous botanical publications. He also lectured and wrote many essays on
general medicine and anatomy.

Following the early death of his parents, Schmidel left Bayreuth in 1728, going first to Arnstadt
and then, in 1733, to Gera. He began medical
studies at Jena in 1735 and continued them a year
later at Halle, where he attended the lectures of
Friedrich Hoffmann and Johann Heinrich Schulze.
He returned to Jena in 1739 and on 17 February
1742 received the M.D. for his *Dissertatio inauguralis de exulceratione pericardii et cordis exemplo illustrata.* His teachers included Georg Erhard
Hamberger, Simon Paul Hilscher, Karl Friedrich
Kaltschmied, Hermann Friedrich Teichmeyer,
Johann Adolph Wedel, and Johann Bernhard
Wiedeburg. Schmidel learned natural history on his
own and in the company of other amateurs.

After completing his studies, Schmidel became
professor of pharmacology at the newly opened
Friedrichs-Akademie and simultaneously established a medical practice in Bayreuth. When the
university was moved the following year from
Bayreuth to Erlangen, Schmidel assumed the second professorship of medicine at its new quarters.
He was also appointed the first dean of the medical
faculty. In 1745 he was named Brandenburg court
councillor, and in 1750 he became a member of
the Kaiserliche Akademie der Naturforscher in
Halle. He took the cognomen Oribasius II.

From 1756 to 1758 Schmidel studied botany and
geology in Saxony, Holland, and Switzerland. In
1760 Schmidel obtained the post of first full professor at Erlangen, a position left vacant by the
death of Johann Friedrich Weismann. Schmidel's
teaching responsibilities were chiefly in the fields
of physiology, where he drew on Boerhaave's *Institutiones medicae,* and natural history, where he
followed Linnaeus' *Systema naturae.* He also lectured on anatomy, surgery, dietetics, pathology,
semiotics, therapeutics, and legal medicine. Because of scientific disagreements with his colleague
Heinrich Friedrich von Delius, Schmidel left Erlangen and in 1763 went to Ansbach to serve as physi-

cian-in-ordinary to Margrave Carl Alexander. A
few years later he had temporarily to give up this
appointment because of a dispute with the sovereign. Thus he was left with sufficient leisure both to
conduct extensive research in botany and to enjoy
a career as a respected physician. In recognition of
his services, Carl Alexander made him a privy
councillor and president of the board of health.

In 1773 and 1774 Schmidel accompanied the ailing daughter of Margrave Friedrich of Bayreuth on
a journey to Lausanne, where she consulted Si-
mone-André Tissot, and then to Dieppe, in Nor-
mandy. (Schmidel's account of the trip was first
published in 1794 in an edition prepared by Johann
Christian Daniel Schreber.) Shortly thereafter,
Friedrich requested that Schmidel serve as physician on a tour through France and Italy in 1775–
1776. On 16 July 1783 Schmidel was awarded an
honorary M.D. by the philosophy faculty of the
University of Erlangen. During the last four years
of his life, Schmidel suffered from mental disorders.

BIBLIOGRAPHY

I. ORIGINAL WORKS. Schmidel's works include *Dissertatio inauguralis de exulceratione pericardii et cordis
exemplo illustrata* (Jena, 1742), his diss., "Anmerkungen
über die bisherige Eintheilung der Schwämme, besonders nach ihren Arten," in *Erlangische gelehrte Anzeigen,* **19** (1746), 145–152; *Icones plantarum et analyses
partium aeri incisae atque viuis coloribus insignitae,
adjectis indicibus nominum necessariis, figurarum expli-
cationibus et breuibus animaduersionibus* (Nuremberg,
1747); "Von der Grösse und Einrichtung der erschaffe-
nen Erde," in *Fränkische Sammlungen von Anmerkungen aus der Naturlehre, Arzneygelahrtheit, Oekonomie,*
23 (1761), 195–208; *Demonstratio vteri praegnantis
mulieris e foetu ad partum maturo in tabulis sex ad naturae magnitudinem post dissectionem depictis et ea
methodo dispositis . . .* (Nuremberg, 1761); *Fossilium
metalla et res metallicas concernentium, glebae suis
coloribus expressae* (Nuremburg, 1762); "Beschreibung
eines Seesterns mit rosenförmigen Verzierungen," in
Der Naturforscher, **16** (1781), 1–7; *Vorstellung einiger
merkwürdigen Versteinerungen mit kurzen Anmerkungen versehen* (Nuremberg, 1781); and *Descriptio itineris
per Heluetiam, Galliam et Germaniae partem 1773 et
1774 instituti, mineralogici, botanici et historici argumenti* (Erlangen, 1794), Johann Christian Daniel Schreber, ed.

Schmidel also edited *Conradi Gessneri opera botanica, per duo secula desiderata, quorum pars prima pro-
dromi loco figuras continet vltra 400 minoris formae,
partim ligno excisas, partim aeri insculptas omnia. Ex*

bibliotheca D. Ch. Jac. Trew nunc primum in lucem edidit et praefatus est (Nuremberg, 1753); *Conradi Gessneri historiae plantarum fasciculus quam ex bibliotheca D. Ch. Jac. Trew edidit et illustravit* (Nuremberg, 1759); and *Conradi Gessneri opera botanica,* 2 vols. (Nuremberg, 1764–1771).

II. SECONDARY LITERATURE. On Schmidel and his work, see G. W. A. Fickenscher, *Gelehrtes Fürstenthum Baireut* (Nuremberg, 1804), 7, 112–127; W. Hess, "Kasimir Christoph Schmidel," in *Allgemeine Deutsche Biographie* (Berlin, 1890), 31, 700; H. Krauss, *Die Leibärzte der Ansbacher Markgrafen* (Neustadt an der Aisch, 1941); F. Leydig, "Kasimir Christoph Schmidel, Naturforscher und Arzt 1716–1792," in *Abhandlungen der Naturhistorischen Gesellschaft zu Nürnberg,* 15 (1905), 325–355; J. A. Vocke, *Geburts- und Todten-Almanach Ansbachischer Gelehrten, Schriftsteller und Künstler* (Augsburg, 1797), 2, 326–329; and T. Wohnhaas, "Miscellanea anatomica zu Kasimir Christoph Schmidel," in *Sitzungsberichte der Physikalisch-medizinischen Sozietät in Erlangen,* 82 (1963), 27–32.

A. GEUS

SCHMIDT, BERNHARD VOLDEMAR (*b.* Naissaar, Estonia [now Estonian S.S.R.], 30 March 1879; *d.* Hamburg, Germany, 1 December 1935), *optics.*

Schmidt studied in Göteborg, Sweden, and then engineering in Mittweida, Saxony, where he established a small workshop for the manufacture of astronomical mirrors (up to about twenty centimeters in diameter). Their perfection was much appreciated. In 1905 Schmidt constructed for the Potsdam Astrophysical Observatory the first reflector with an aperture of forty centimeters and with a focal length of about one meter. Schmidt already had used for Cassegrain reflectors a spherical mirror that corrected spherical aberration by an adequate deformation of the second mirror.

In addition to the construction of astronomical instruments, Schmidt also improved and himself used some of the great objectives (for example, at the Hamburg observatory, Bergedorf). In 1909 he constructed for his own small observatory at Mittweida a new horizontal reflector, later on named "Uranostat," which consisted of a parabolic mirror of forty-centimeter aperture and of eleven-meter focal length. The reflector was mounted so that the axis was in the north-south direction and caught the light of the object to be observed from two plane mirrors rotatable around two perpendicular axes.

Later Schmidt constructed two similar arrangements of several mirrors for the Bergedorf and Breslau observatories. In 1926 Schmidt moved to Bergedorf, where with the first arrangement he himself made excellent photographs of Jupiter, Saturn, and the moon.

Schmidt always was an odd man, who neither married nor was willing to lead a normal life. He once said that he got his best ideas on awaking slowly after some days of complete intoxication. Drink was certainly the cause of his early death. At the Bergedorf observatory he had no regular duties and was free of economic worries, receiving generous aid from R. Schorr, the director of the observatory. Schmidt thus had the time and the resources to carry out his most famous work—the construction of a reflector without coma. He used a correction plate shaped as a very small curved circular torus, which compensates for spherical aberration and coma. Photographs could now be taken which yielded undistorted star images over a large field: formerly only objects near the optical axis could be delineated.

Schmidt had lost his right arm in an accident in his youth, but he nevertheless did all of his work alone and unaided. He polished his mirrors by hand, using glass instead of metal disks.

Schmidt spent the last year of his life in a mental hospital and died there.

BIBLIOGRAPHY

Schmidt's only work is "Ein lichtstarkes komafreies Spiegelsystem," in *Zentralzeitung für Optik und Mechanik, Elektrotechnik,* 52 (1931), 25–26. For works on Schmidt and his work, see B. Strömgren, "Das Schmidt'sche Spiegelteleskop," in *Vierteljahrsschrift der Astronomischen Gesellschaft,* 70 (1935), 65–86; and A. A. Wachmann, "From the Life of Bernhard Schmidt," in *Sky and Telescope,* 15 (1959), 4–9.

H.-CHRIST. FREIESLEBEN

SCHMIDT, CARL AUGUST VON (*b.* Diefenbach, Württemberg, Germany, 1 January 1840; *d.* Stuttgart, Germany, 21 March 1929), *geophysics, astrophysics.*

Schmidt, the son of a schoolteacher, studied Protestant theology at the seminary in Tübingen from 1858 to 1862. In 1863 he obtained a doctorate in philosophy from the University of Tübingen, where during the same year he studied mathematics and natural science. From 1864 to 1866 he studied chemistry in Paris and then in Stuttgart at the polytechnic school until 1868. At this time he also took the examination to qualify for teaching mathematics and science in secondary school.

From 1868 to 1871 Schmidt was a student-teacher and from 1872 to 1904, professor at the Realgymnasium in Stuttgart, where he taught chemistry, physics, and mathematics. In addition, in 1896 he was appointed a full member of the Württemberg office of statistics and director of the central weather bureau in Stuttgart, which he headed until 1912. From 1902 to 1912 he served on the board of directors of the earthquake research center in Strasbourg and from 1906 to 1912, on the board of the weather station on Lake Constance. The latter institution, founded by H. Hergesell, employed kites in its meteorological research.

One of Schmidt's notable works (most of which dealt with geophysics and astrophysics) was his "Wellenbewegung und Erdbeben" (1888), in which he demonstrated that seismic waves do not spread rectilinearly from the focus of an earthquake but in curved paths. This phenomenon partly arises from Snell's law of refraction, and partly because the quotient of density to modulus of elasticity is not constant over the entire surface of the earth. Schmidt also established the law, named for him, concerning the turning point in the apparent propagation velocity of seismic waves; and he introduced the time-distance curve into seismology. In order to measure the vertical movement of the earth he devised the bifilar or trifilar gravimeter.

In 1886, in Württemberg, Schmidt made the first seismic measurements, and in 1892 he and K. Mack established an earthquake observatory in Hohenheim. As early as 1894 he pointed out the separation of seismic waves into longitudinal and transverse components, thus anticipating the subsequent findings of Wiechert. In 1896 Schmidt became director of the entire earthquake bureau in Württemberg, a position he held until 1912. During this period the geomagnetic survey of Württemberg, which Schmidt had promoted, was completed by K. G. F. Haussmann; Schmidt wrote the preface to the publication of the results of the survey. He also reported on the results in a separate work, as well as on the geomagnetic measurement of the Riesen Gebirge (1906)—a region in which current research indicates the presence of an impact crater of a large meteorite.

In other works Schmidt treated terrestrial magnetism and the shape of the earth (1895), the displacement of the terrestrial poles (1896), continental tides (1897), and plumb-line deflection (1898). He contributed to meteorology through works on the application of thermodynamics and the kinetic theory of gases to the study of the atmosphere (1889), on the fostering of aerological observations at the kite station on Lake Constance, and on the discussion of problems of climatology. Furthermore, he introduced the concept of barometric tendency into weather forecasting and investigated the mechanism of thunderstorms (1895).

Schmidt directed his astronomical research to questions of refraction in the solar atmosphere and chromosphere (beginning in 1891), and also to general problems of solar physics (rotation of the sun, sources of solar energy, the spectrum of the chromosphere, and solar flares). He also investigated phenomena on the planet Mars (1893) and commented on the stability of the rings of Saturn (1894).

Schmidt's importance lay in the breadth of his interests and in his knowledge of the interrelated aspects of geophysics and astrophysics.

BIBLIOGRAPHY

A list of Schmidt's works is in Poggendorff, III (1898), 1200; IV (1904), 1335–1336; and in *Beiträge zur Geophysik,* **22** (1929), 235–238.

On Schmidt and his work, see K. Kleinschmidt, *ibid.,* **22** (1929), 233–235; in *Meteorologische Zeitschrift,* **64** (1929), 265–267; and in *Unterrichtsblätter für Mathematik und Naturwissenschaften,* **35** (1929), 129.

Diedrich Wattenberg

SCHMIDT, ERHARD (*b*. Dorpat, Germany [now Tartu, E.S.S.R.], 13 January 1876; *d*. Berlin, Germany, 6 December 1959), *mathematics.*

Schmidt's most significant contributions to mathematics were in integral equations and in the founding of Hilbert space theory. Specifically, he simplified and extended David Hilbert's results in the theory of integral equations; and he formalized Hilbert's distinct ideas on integral equations into the single concept of a Hilbert space, in the process introducing many geometrical terms. In addition, he made contributions in the fields of partial differential equations and geometry. The most important of these discoveries were the extensions of the isoperimetric inequality, first to *n*-dimensional Euclidean space and then to multidimensional hyperbolic and spherical spaces. Although his methods were classical rather than abstractionist, nevertheless he must be considered a founder of modern functional analysis.

The son of Alexander Schmidt, a medical biologist, Erhard studied at Dorpat, Berlin, and finally at Göttingen, where he was a doctoral candidate under Hilbert. His degree was awarded in 1905 after the presentation of his thesis, "Entwicklung willkürlicher Funktionen nach Systemen forgeschriebener." After short periods as a teacher in Bonn, Zurich, Erlangen, and Breslau (now Wrocław), in 1917 he went to the University of Berlin, where he was to remain the rest of his life. In 1946 he became the first director of the Research Institute for Mathematics of the German Academy of Sciences, a post he held until 1958. He was also one of the founders and first editors of *Mathematische Nachrichten* (1948).

The integral equation on which Schmidt's reputation is based has the form

$$f(s) = \phi(s) - \lambda \int_a^b K(s, t)\,\phi(t)\,dt. \qquad (1)$$

In (1), $K(s, t)$—called the kernel—and $f(s)$ are known functions and ϕ is an unknown function that is to be found. This equation has a long history. Interest in it stemmed from its many applications; for example, if (1) can be solved, then the partial differential equation $\Delta u = \partial^2 u/\partial x^2 + \partial^2 u/\partial y^2 = 0$ with the prescribed condition $u(x, y) = b(s)$ of arc length s on the boundary of a given region of the plane can also be solved. This differential equation arises in many problems of physics.

From the early nineteenth century on, there were many attempts to solve equation (1), but only partial results were obtained until 1903. In that year Ivar Fredholm was able to present a complete solution to (1), although in his theory the parameter λ plays no significant role. Fredholm showed that for a fixed λ and K either (1) has a unique solution for every function f, or the associated homogeneous equation

$$\phi(s) - \lambda \int_0^1 K(s, t)\phi(t)\,dt = 0 \qquad (2)$$

has a finite number of linearly independent solutions; in this case (1) has a solution ϕ only for those f that satisfy certain orthogonality conditions.

In 1904 Hilbert continued the study. He first used a complicated limiting process involving infinite matrices to show that for the fixed but symmetric kernel K ($K(s, t) = K(t, s)$), there would always be values of λ—all real—for which (2) had nontrivial solutions. These λ's he called the *eigenvalues* associated with K, and the solutions he called *eigenfunctions*. He also proved that if f is such that there exists g continuous on [0, 1] with

$$f(s) = \int_a^b K(s, t)g(t)\,dt,$$

then $f(s)$ can be expanded in a series in eigenfunctions of K, that is,

$$f(s) = \sum_{p=1}^{\infty} a_p \phi_p$$

where $\{\phi_p\}$ is an orthonormal[1] set of eigenfunctions of K.

A year later Hilbert introduced the concept of infinite bilinear forms into both the theory of integral equations and the related topic of infinite matrices. He discovered the concept of complete continuity[2] for such forms and then showed that if $\{a_{ij} : i, j = 1, 2, \cdots\}$ are the coefficients of a completely continuous form, then the infinite system of linear equations

$$x_i + \sum_{j=1}^{\infty} a_{ij}x_j = a_i, \qquad i = 1, 2, \cdots \qquad (3)$$

either has a unique square summable[3] solution $\{x_i : i = 1, 2, \cdots\}$ for every square summable sequence $\{a_i\}$ or the associated homogeneous system $x_i + \Sigma\, a_{ij}x_j = 0$ has a finite number of linearly independent solutions. In the latter case, (3) will have solutions only for those sequences $\{a_i\}$ that satisfy certain orthogonality conditions. Hilbert then went on to prove again Fredholm's result converting equation (1) to equation (3) by using Fourier coefficients.

Schmidt's paper on integral equation (1) appeared in two parts in 1907. He began by reproving Hilbert's earlier results concerning symmetric kernels. He was able to simplify the proofs and also to show that Hilbert's theorems were valid under less restrictive conditions. Included in this part of the work is the well-known Gram-Schmidt process for the construction of a set of orthonormal functions from a given set of linearly independent functions.

Schmidt then went on to consider the case of (1) in which the kernel $K(s, t)$ is no longer symmetric. He showed that in this case, too, there always will be eigenvalues that are real. The eigenfunctions, however, now occur in adjoint pairs; that is, ϕ and ψ are adjoint eigenfunctions belonging to λ if ϕ satisfies

$$\phi(s) = \lambda \int_a^b K(t, s)\psi(t)\,dt,$$

which is called an eigenfunction of the first kind, and ψ satisfies

$$\psi(s) = \lambda \int_a^b K(s, t)\phi(t)\,dt,$$

an eigenfunction of the second kind. Moreover, if $\phi = \phi_1 + i\phi_2$, $\psi = \psi_1 + i\psi_2$, then ϕ_1 and ψ_1 are an adjoint pair of eigenfunctions, as are ϕ_2 and ψ_2. Thus, it is only necessary to consider real pairs of eigenfunctions.

Other extensions of the symmetric to the unsymmetric case were also developed by Schmidt. As a broadening of Hilbert's result, Schmidt proved (Hilbert-Schmidt theorem) that if f is such that there is a function g continuous on $[a, b]$ with

$$f(s) = \int_a^b K(s, t) g(t) dt,$$

then f can be represented by an orthonormal series of the eigenfunctions of the first kind of K; and if

$$f(s) = \int_a^b K(t, s) g(t) dt,$$

then f has a representation in a series of the second kind of eigenfunctions. He also proved a type of diagonalization theorem: If $x(s)$ and $y(s)$ are continuous on $[a, b]$, then

$$\int_a^b \int_a^b K(s, t) x(s) y(s) ds dt =$$

$$\sum_v \frac{1}{\lambda_v} \int_a^b x(s) \phi_v(s) ds \int y(t) \psi_v(t) dt$$

where $\{\phi_p\}$ and $\{\psi_p\}$ are orthonormal sets of eigenfunctions of the first or second kinds and λ_v are the associated eigenvalues.

The idea behind Schmidt's work is extremely simple. From the kernel $K(s, t)$ of equation (1) he constructed two new kernels:

$$\overline{K}(s, t) = \int_a^b K(s, r) K(t, r) dr$$

and

$$\underline{K}(s, t) = \int_a^b K(r, s) K(r, t) dr,$$

which are both symmetric. Then ϕ and ψ are an adjoint pair of eigenfunctions belonging to λ if and only if

$$\phi(s) = \lambda^2 \int_a^b \overline{K}(s, t)\, \phi\,(t)\, dt,$$

and

$$\psi(t) = \lambda^2 \int_a^b \underline{K}(s, t) \psi(t) dt;$$

that is, ϕ is an eigenfunction belonging to λ^2 of $\overline{K}$ and ψ is an eigenfunction belonging to λ^2 of $\underline{K}$. Thus Schmidt could then apply much of the earlier theory of symmetric kernels.

Schmidt's contributions to Hilbert space theory stem from Hilbert himself. Before Hilbert there had been some attempts to develop a general theory of infinite linear equations, but by the turn of the twentieth century only a few partial results had been obtained. Hilbert focused the attention of mathematicians on the connections among infinite linear systems, square summable sequences, and matrices of which the entries define completely continuous bilinear forms. These equations were of importance since their applications were useful not only in integral equations but also in differential equations and continued fractions.

In 1908 Schmidt published his study on the solution of infinitely many linear equations with infinitely many unknowns. Although his paper is in one sense a definitive work on the subject, its chief importance was the explicit development of the concept of a Hilbert space and also the geometry of such space—ideas that were only latent in Hilbert's own work.

A vector or point z of Schmidt's space H was a square summable sequence of complex numbers, $\{z_n\}$. The inner product of two vectors z and w—denoted by (z, w)—was given by the formula

$$(z, w) = \sum_{p=1}^\infty z_p w_p$$

and a norm—denoted by $\|z\|$—was defined by $\|z\| = \sqrt{(z, \bar{z})}$. The vectors z and w were defined to be perpendicular or orthogonal if $(z, w) = 0$, and Schmidt showed that any set of mutually orthogonal vectors must be linearly independent. The Gram-Schmidt orthogonalization process was then developed for linearly independent sets, and from this procedure necessary and sufficient conditions for a set to be linearly independent were derived.

Schmidt then considered convergence. If $\{z^n\}$ is a sequence of vectors of H, then $\{z^n\}$ is defined to converge strongly in H to z if $\lim_{h \to \infty} \|z^n - z\| = 0$, and $\{z^n\}$ is said to be a strong Cauchy sequence if $\lim \|z^p - z^n\| = 0$ independently in p and n. He then showed that every strong Cauchy sequence in H converges strongly to some element of H. Then the nontrivial concept of a closed subspace A of H was introduced. Schmidt showed how such subspaces could be constructed and then proved the projection theorem: If z is a vector H and A is a closed subspace of H, then z has a unique representation $z = a + w$ where a is in A and w is orthogonal to every vector in A. Furthermore, $\|w\| = \min \|z - y\|$ where y is any element of A, and this minimum is actually assumed only for $y = a$. Finally, these results were used to establish necessary and sufficient conditions under which the infinite system of equations

$$\sum_{p=1}^\infty a_{np} z_p = c_n$$

has a square summable solution $\{z_p\}$ where $\{c_n\}$ is a square summable sequence and, for each n, $\{a_{np}\}$ is also square summable. He then obtained specific representations for the solutions.

Schmidt's work on Hilbert space represents a long step toward modern mathematics. He was one of the earliest mathematicians to demonstrate that the ordinary experience of Euclidean concepts can be extended meaningfully beyond geometry into the idealized constructions of more complex abstract mathematics.

NOTES

1. The set $\{\phi_p\}$ is orthonormal if

$$\int_a^b (\phi_p(s))^2 \, ds = 1 \quad (p = 1, 2, \cdots)$$

and

$$\int_a^b \phi_p(s)\phi_q(s) \, ds = 0 \quad (p \neq q).$$

2. The form $K(x, x)$ is completely continuous at a if

$$\lim_{h \to \infty} \epsilon_i^{(h)} \to 0 \quad (i = 1, 2, \cdots)$$

implies that

$$\lim_{h \to \infty} K(a + \epsilon^{(h)}, a + \epsilon^{(h)}) = K(a, a)$$

where $a = (a_1, a_2, \cdots)$ and $\epsilon^{(h)} = (\epsilon_1^{(h)}, \epsilon_2^{(h)}, \cdots)$. In a Hilbert space this is stronger than ordinary continuity (in the norm topology).

3. The sequence of (complex) numbers $\{b_n\}$ is square summable if

$$\sum_{n=1}^{\infty} |b_n|^2 < \infty.$$

BIBLIOGRAPHY

I. Original Works. A complete bibliography of Schmidt's works can be found in the obituary by Kurt Schröder in *Mathematische Nachrichten,* **25** (1963), 1–3. Particular attention is drawn to "Zur Theorie der linearen und nichtlinearen Integralgleichungen. I," in *Mathematische Annalen,* **63** (1907), 433–476; "Zur Theorie . . . II," *ibid.,* **64** (1907), 161–174; and "Über die Auflösung linearen Gleichungen mit unendlich vielen Unbekannten," in *Rendiconti del Circolo matematico di Palermo,* **25** (1908), 53–77.

II. Secondary Literature. On Schmidt and his work, see Ernst Hellinger and Otto Toeplitz, "Integralgleichungen und Gleichungen mit unendlichvielen Unbekannten," in *Encyklopädie der Mathematischen Wissenschaften,* IIC, 13 (Leipzig, 1923–1927), 1335–1602. This article, also published under separate cover, is an excellent general treatise, and specifically shows the relationship between integral equation theory and the theory of infinite linear systems.

Michael Bernkopf

SCHMIDT, ERNST JOHANNES (*b.* Copenhagen, Denmark, 2 January 1877; *d.* Copenhagen, 21 February 1933), *marine biology.*

Schmidt was the son of Ernst Schmidt, an estate inspector, and Camilla Ellen Sophie Johanne Kjeldahl. His father died when he was seven. Schmidt eventually entered the University of Copenhagen to study botany and in 1898 received the M.Sc. and in 1903 the Ph.D. for a paper on the prop roots of the mangrove. From 1899 to 1909 he was attached to the Botanical Institute of the university, and from 1910 he served as director of the Carlsberg Physiological Laboratory in Copenhagen. Schmidt published numerous botanical papers, particularly on tropical faunas and marine plants; and with F. Weis he wrote a textbook on bacteria.

From 1899 Schmidt was a member of the Danish Commission for the Investigation of the Sea. He went on several marine biological expeditions in the North Atlantic, and his fame rests chiefly on his research there. Schmidt's interest soon turned to the larval development of fishes, and his first paper on this subject was published in 1904. In the same year he investigated eel larvae and was led into the study of the breeding of eels.

At that time the life cycle of eels was a complete mystery. The larvae until only recently had been described as a separate species; and the breeding grounds were unknown. From his research in the North Atlantic and in the Mediterranean (1908–1910), Schmidt hypothesized that the European eel has a common breeding ground in the Atlantic and that it belongs to a single population. To prove this theory, Schmidt led an expedition to the North Atlantic from 1920 to 1922. By tracing the area where the youngest larvae were found, he eventually located the breeding grounds in the Sargasso Sea. He was able to show that adult eels from all of western Europe and the Mediterranean migrate to this place and die after spawning. The larvae then migrate to their parents' adult habitats. (He showed also that American eels have a similar pattern and a nearby breeding ground.) This peculiar pattern had profound implications not only in biology but also in the discussion of continental drift.

To extend his theory to all eels, Schmidt received a grant from the Carlsberg Foundation to lead an expedition around the world (1928–1930). During this time, he collected material on other species of fishes as well, especially deepwater fishes.

Schmidt also studied the eel-like *Zoarces viviparus.* He showed that this species breeds locally and identified differences between the various populations. Later he extended these observations to other species and made a number of important studies of environmental effects on the size and shape of many populations. Schmidt's biometric findings contributed to the concept of the inter-breeding populations as a fundamental unit. Since most of this research was done on economically important species of fishes, his work was also of great value to fisheries.

Schmidt's research was highly appreciated during his lifetime, and he received many academic and public honors. He also took an active role in several international organizations concerned with the sea, especially the International Permanent Council for the Study of the Sea, which had its seat in Copenhagen.

In 1903 Schmidt married Ingeborg Kühle, daughter of the director of the Old Carlsberg Breweries. Their home was both a social and scientific center.

BIBLIOGRAPHY

I. ORIGINAL WORKS. A complete list of Schmidt's scientific publications is in Regan (see below). His major works are *Bakterierne. Naturhistorisk Grundlag for det baktereologiske Studium* (Copenhagen, 1899–1901), written with F. Weis, German ed., M. Porsild, trans. (Jena, 1902); "Danish Researches in the Atlantic and Mediterranean on the Life-History of the Fresh-Water Eel (*Anguilla vulgaris*)," in *Internationale Revue der gesamten Hydrobiologie u Hydrographie*, **5** (1912), 317–342; and "The Breeding Places of the Eel," in *Philosophical Transactions of the Royal Society*, **205** (1922), 179–208.

II. SECONDARY LITERATURE. The best biography is C. Tate Regan, "Johannes Schmidt," in *Journal du Conseil*, **8** (1933), 145–160, with complete bibliography.

NILS SPJELDNAES

SCHMIDT, GERHARD CARL NATHANIEL (*b.* London, England, 5 July 1865; *d.* Münster, Germany, 16 October 1949), *physical chemistry.*

Although born in England, Schmidt was of German ancestry. From 1886 he obtained his higher education at Tübingen, Berlin, Strasbourg, Greifswald, and Basel. In 1891, under Georg Kahlbaum's guidance, he received the Ph.D. at Basel. Schmidt's subsequent work on solutions, mixtures, and adsorption led to a lifelong interest in physical chemistry. In 1895 he received a *Dozentur* in Eilhard Wiedemann's small but exceptionally lively institute at the University of Erlangen. Schmidt often worked closely with Wiedemann himself; he studied luminescence, phosphorescence, and photoelectric phenomena. During a brief

excursion into another area in late 1897 or early 1898, he made the discovery for which he is most famous—the radioactivity of thorium. (Marie Curie soon made the same discovery independently.)

Schmidt made this discovery while examining "many elements and compounds" in an effort to determine whether any of the rays that were emitted bore a resemblance to those that Henri Becquerel had found emerging from uranium and uranium compounds. He located only one such element, thorium, and immediately conducted absorption, ionization, reflection, refraction, and polarization studies to determine the characteristics of its rays. Having combined a misinterpretation of Becquerel's with one of his own, Schmidt concluded that thorium rays most resembled Röntgen rays—a conclusion that soon required revision in view of the researches of Marie Curie and Ernest Rutherford.

In 1900 Schmidt became professor ordinarius of physics at the Forstakademie in Eberswalde but soon moved to Erlangen as professor extraordinarius (1901–1904). He then went to Königsberg as professor ordinarius and director of the physical institute (1904–1908) and finally to Münster, where he occupied the chair once held by Hittorf, whom Schmidt admired and commemorated in several addresses. Schmidt retired from this post in 1935.

During these years, Schmidt studied canal-ray and cathode-ray phenomena, the electrical conductivity of salt vapors, solid electrolytes, adsorption, passivity, and luminescence. He was unusually vigorous and healthy until the last year of his life, when he fractured his hipbone and was hospitalized. Shortly after he was released, he suffered a stroke and died.

BIBLIOGRAPHY

I. ORIGINAL WORKS. Schmidt's writings include "Ueber die von den Thorverbindungen und einigen anderen Substanzen ausgehende Strahlung," in *Annalen der Physik*, **65** (1898), 141–151; "Wilhelm Hittorf," *Schriften der Gesellschaft zur Förderung der Westfälischen Wilhelms-Universität zu Münster*, no. 4 (1924); and "Eilhard Wiedemann," in *Physikalische Zeitschrift*, **29** (1928), 185–190.

II. SECONDARY LITERATURE. On Schmidt and his work, see Lawrence Badash, "The Discovery of Thorium's Radioactivity," in *Journal of Chemical Education*, **43** (1966), 219–220. For obituary notices see A. Kratzer, *Physikalische Blätter*, **6** (1950), 30; and K. Kuhn,

Naturwissenschaftliche Rundschau, **4** (1951), 41. Schmidt's portrait is in J. A. Barth, *Deutsche Senioren der Physik* (Leipzig, 1936).

ROGER H. STUEWER

SCHMIDT, JOHANN FRIEDRICH JULIUS (*b.* Eutin, Germany, 26 October 1825; *d.* Athens, Greece, 7 February 1884), *astronomy, geophysics.*

Schmidt was the son of Carl Friedrich Schmidt, a glazier, and Maria Elisabeth Quirling. He received his early education in Eutin and Hamburg, where his interest in the sciences and his aptitude for drawing were encouraged. From 1842 he studied practical astronomy under Carl Rümker at the Hamburg observatory. Then, in 1845, he went to Benzenberg's private observatory in Bilk, near Düsseldorf. The following year, he assisted Argelander at the latter's observatory in Bonn, where he became an accomplished astronomer.

With Argelander's recommendation, Schmidt was named observator at the observatory of the canon and provost E. von Unkrechtsberg in Olmütz (now Olomouc), where he remained from 1853 to 1858. He was then named director (1858) of the new observatory founded by Baron Sica in Athens. Schmidt worked there until his death. He continued the observations that he had begun in Olmütz and also observed comets, variable stars, nebulae, sunspots, and the zodiacal light. He later studied volcanic and seismic phenomena but is known chiefly for his selenographic observations.

Although Schmidt's research was voluminous, he lacked the means to publish it. But through the intervention of the German ambassador to Greece, this work was placed in the Potsdam observatory.

Schmidt never married. He was well liked and respected at the Greek court; and the evening before his death, he attended the usual social gathering at the German Embassy in Athens. Schmidt received many honors and in 1868 was awarded the Ph.D. *honoris causa* by the University of Bonn.

BIBLIOGRAPHY

Schmidt's major works are *Das Zodiakallicht* (Brunswick, 1856); *Resultate aus 11-jährigen Beobachtungen der Sonnenflecken* (Vienna, 1857); *Physikalische Geographie von Griechenland* (Athens, 1869); *Vulkanstudien* (Leipzig, 1874); *Studien über Erdbeben* (Leipzig, 1875; 2nd ed., 1879); *Karte der Gebirge der Mondes nach eigenen Beobachtungen 1840–1874* (Berlin, 1878); and *Erläuterungsband* (Berlin, 1874).

The only useful secondary source is A. Krueger's obituary in *Astronomische Nachrichten,* **108** (1884), 129.

H.-CHRIST. FREIESLEBEN

SCHMIEDEL. See Schmidel, Casimir Christoph.

SCHNEIDER, FRIEDRICH ANTON (*b.* Zeitz, Germany, 13 July 1831; *d.* Breslau, Germany [now Wrocław, Poland], 30 May 1890), *zoology, comparative anatomy, cytology.*

Schneider's zoological interests were in morphology and systematization. After years of studying the roundworms and flatworms, he reported in an 1873 paper his various laboratory observations of the life history of the Platyhelminthes. The paper contains the first description of the process of cell division and the visible changes during its successive stages—a detailed account of Schneider's microscopic investigations, with drawings of the nucleus and the chromosomal strands as he had seen them in the flatworm *Mesostomum ehrenbergii.* Following Schneider's discovery, the phenomena of division were independently observed and reported on by Fol and Bütschli. Hertwig saw the fusion of the maternal and paternal nuclei in fertilization, and over the next years there developed a new understanding of the cell, the process and significance of fertilization, and the role of the chromosomes in inheritance.

Schneider was the son of Karl Friedrich Schneider, a merchant, and Friederike Wilhelmine Müller. He was frail and occasionally ill, and his schooling at the small Gymnasium at Zeitz was somewhat irregular. His mother died when he was young, and his father remarried. Schneider's father often took him on business trips and imbued his son with his own lively interest in literature and the arts. Country visits intensified the youth's love of nature, and at home there was a well-rounded library.

At the age of eighteen Schneider entered the University of Bonn, where he concentrated at first in mathematics and the natural sciences, but he increasingly leaned toward zoology, stimulated by the lectures he heard in that field. In 1851 he continued his studies at Berlin, where he came under the influence of a great teacher, Johannes Müller, whose laboratory provided a formative experience for so many students. In 1854 Schneider received the doctorate in philosophy at the University of

Berlin, but much of the next year was spent in Zeitz. His father had died and he had to assume family responsibilities.

Müller often took his students on field trips, and in 1855 Schneider accompanied him to Norway via Copenhagen. During the return voyage, their ship sank after a collision and explosion. The two were rescued, but another student of Müller's was drowned. Schneider visited Italy in 1856–1857; Naples and Messina provided unique opportunities for marine biological studies. In 1859 he habilitated at the University of Berlin and then taught as *Privatdozent*. He also served as a custodian in the zoological museum, where he worked especially on the nematode collections. He made many friends among his colleagues at the university and became well acquainted with Nathaniel Pringsheim, while both were working with the small marine forms in Helgoland, in the North Sea.

Schneider succeeded Leuckart as professor at the University of Giessen in 1869. He truly enjoyed lecturing and teaching, and he filled his laboratory with freshwater specimens from the nearby lakes and streams. Students gathered about him, and he also gave a number of lectures on various topics at meetings of the local scientific society, the Oberhessische Gesellschaft für Natur- und Heilkunde. In the society's *Bericht* appeared Schneider's "Untersuchungen über Plathelminthen," with the observations of cell division. Although he may not then have fully realized the implications of his studies of cell division, Schneider did recognize, even in 1873, that the phenomena he was describing were significant and that they opened up a new understanding of the cell.

The years he spent at Giessen were full. He even volunteered to care for the sick during the Franco-Prussian War and actually spent some time in France. He was rector of the university until 1881, when he was appointed professor of zoology and comparative anatomy at the University of Breslau. He became rector at Breslau in 1886, and it was also there that he married. Schneider founded the *Zoologische Beiträge*, directed the zoological institute, and taught actively until his death in 1890.

Schneider's major contribution grew out of his work on the flatworm *Mesostomum*, an ideal subject because of its transparency. He not only followed the life cycle of the living specimen, but using acetic acid to fix his microscopic sections he rendered the changes in the nucleus and chromosomes visible. Staining with carmine, for which the chromosomes showed an affinity, made them still more visible. The earliest mention of his using this stain is 1880, but how much earlier he had employed it is unknown.

Using acetic acid, Schneider saw that, contrary to accepted belief, the outline of the nucleus did not disappear. He saw the nucleolus disappear and a mass of filaments take form; the filaments arranged themselves on the equatorial plane of the cell, seemed to thicken and increase, and then—in an orderly and typical arrangement—one part of the filaments went to one pole; the other part, to the other pole. The cell was divided, and each of the two new cells again exhibited a fluid-filled nucleus and a nucleolus. Schneider then suggested that the nucleus might persist similarly in other forms in which it had been thought to disappear during division, and that the transitions of the chromosomes might be quite general in occurrence. He concluded that cell division might take place with or without these "metamorphoses."

Schneider's observations of mitosis remain outstanding, and he made some lasting contributions to morphology; but his intuitive conclusions were sometimes less sure. A friend later recalled that Schneider preferred the spoken to the written word; and he was known to like working out problems in his head. He eschewed writing whenever possible, and the various papers he did publish provide an incomplete view of the extent of his work and record errors that he later corrected.

In the years after his description of division, Schneider seemed to his colleagues to oppose the very advances in the understanding of the cell and its life processes that he had foretold. The priority of his 1873 observations was acknowledged, but he had received little notice then because he published his results in a paper on observations of the flatworm and systematics, in a journal that was not widely read. Then, as new researches clarified the process of fertilization and the division stages that Schneider had seen in the summer eggs of *Mesostomum*, he persisted in his own interpretations. Schneider thought that the spermatozoon breaks up or disappears after its entrance into the ovum; thus he did not agree with Hertwig that fertilization signifies a fusion of nuclei. The implications for the understanding of heredity of the view Schneider expressed are apparent, and his contemporaries in cytological investigation felt his concept to be regressive. Schneider in turn took on other investigations, and it is not known whether he ever changed his mind.

He left an important monograph on the nematodes, papers on a range of zoological subjects in the area of morphology, and numerous descriptions that were cited by other comparative anatomists who followed him.

BIBLIOGRAPHY

I. ORIGINAL WORKS. Schneider's most important writings are "Untersuchungen über Plathelminthen," in *Bericht der Oberhessischen Gesellschaft für Natur- und Heilkunde*, **14** (1873), 69–140; see esp. 113–116 and pl. V, fig. 5, a–f, for description of cleavage as Schneider saw it in the summer eggs of *Mesostomum*. See also "Über Befruchtung," in *Zoologischer Anzeiger*, **3** (1880), 252–257; "Über Befruchtung der thierischen Eier," *ibid.*, 426–427; *Das Ei und seine Befruchtung* (Breslau, 1883); and *Monographie der Nematoden* (Berlin, 1866; Farnborough, Hampshire, England, 1968).

II. SECONDARY LITERATURE. On Schneider and his work, see the following articles by Wulf Emmo Ankel: "Anton Schneider, 1831–1890," in Hugo Freund and Alexander Berg, eds., *Geschichte der Mikroskopie, Leben und Werk Grosser Forscher*, I (Frankfurt am Main, 1963), 303–311; "Anton Schneider, ein Bild und ein Nachruf," in *Bericht der Oberhessischen Gesellschaft für Natur- und Heilkunde zu Giessen, naturwissenschaftliche Abteilung*, n.s. **28** (1957), 163–185; and "Zur Geschichte der wissenschaftliche Biologie in Giessen," in *Ludwigs-Universität Justus Liebig Hochschule 1607–1957 . . . Giessen, Festschrift zur 350 Jahrfeier* (Giessen, 1957), 327–328.

Friedrich Keller, "Anton Schneider und die Geschichte der Karyokinese" (inaugural M.D. diss., Freiburg im Breisgau: Albert-Ludwigs University, 1926), presents biographical material and describes Schneider's studies and the conclusions other investigators were reaching meanwhile on cell division. For an evaluation of Schneider's work by a contemporary whose own researches were basic to cytology, see Oskar Hertwig, *Dokumente zur Geschichte der Zeugungslehre. Eine historische Studie als Abschluss eigener Forschung* (Bonn, 1918), 7–8, 58–59; see p. 9 for reproductions of Schneider's figures of division in *Mesostomum*. M. J. Sirks, "The Earliest Illustrations of Chromosomes," in *Genetica*, **26** (1952), 65–76, shows the chromosomes as they appeared to nineteenth-century investigators, and it discusses Schneider's observations in this context, including the above-cited drawings of egg cleavage and those of spermatocyte division. Schneider's contribution is assessed also in John R. Baker, "The Cell Theory: A Restatement, History and Critique, Part V, the Multiplication of Nuclei," in *Quarterly Journal of Microscopical Science*, 3rd ser., **96** (1955), 463; John A. Moore, *Heredity and Development* (New York, 1963), 22–23; (the last two sources have Schneider's landmark illustrations); and William Coleman, "Cell, Nucleus, and Inheritance: An Historical Study," in *Proceedings of the American Philosophical Society*, **109** (1965), 131.

GLORIA ROBINSON

SCHNEIDERHÖHN, HANS (*b.* Mainz, Germany, 2 June 1887; *d.* Sölden, near Freiburg im Breisgau, Germany, 5 August 1962), *geology.*

Schneiderhöhn possessed great knowledge of ore deposits and, with Joseph Murdoch and Rudolf Willem van der Veen, was one of the classical authors on ore microscopy. After graduating from the Gymnasium in Mainz, he studied geology and mineralogy at Freiburg, Munich, and especially Giessen, under the petrologist Erich Kaiser. After receiving his doctorate and spending a short time as an assistant to Kaiser, he was for several years the assistant to Theodor Liebisch, then professor of mineralogy at the University of Berlin. In 1913 Schneiderhöhn became the mineralogist for the Tsumeb mine in South-West Africa, which was then working the boundary between the spectacular oxidation zone and the enriched and primary sulfides. Forced by the war to remain in South-West Africa from 1914 to 1918, he began his major works on ore microscopy. He had only extremely primitive equipment, but the difficulties he experienced made him familiar with many technical and theoretical problems.

Schneiderhöhn made very careful studies of the primary mineral content of the Tsumeb deposit and its relations to the secondary enrichment. While doing this he discovered "Rosa Erz," now known as germanite, and made important observations of the unusual oxidation minerals of Tsumeb, as well as of the karst phenomena and the petrology of Otavi highlands. In addition, he explored other parts of South-West Africa, working with Ernst Reuning, and gained a profound knowledge of the extremely varied types of ore deposits.

In 1919 Schneiderhöhn was appointed to the chair of mineralogy at Giessen, and five years later he succeeded F. Klockmann at Aachen. In 1926 he accepted the chair of mineralogy at Freiburg im Breisgau, where he taught and worked until his retirement in 1955. He later moved to Sölden, in the Black Forest, where he continued his scientific work.

Schneiderhöhn examined many deposits in Europe, Africa, North America, and Turkey. His experience, memory, knowledge of the literature, and sharp and critical intellect gave him an intuitive sense of similarities, differences, and weak points in earlier opinions. He sometimes offered his interpretations and opinions—and published them—after a very short time, perhaps a visit of one or two days. Mistakes and oversimplifications were unavoidable; but generally, and especially in the most important cases (such as the Northern Rhodesian [now Zambian] copper deposits) he was right and his statements were later confirmed.

Friendships with Paul Niggli and (since his Berlin years) with Max Berek, who made major contributions to the optics of reflected light, were very fruitful for all concerned. Niggli's *Versuch einer natürlichen Klassifikation der im weiteren Sinne magmatischen Erzlagerstätten* was greatly influenced by discussions with Schneiderhöhn, and Berek's papers often dealt with topics suggested by Schneiderhöhn.

Careful study of the Manfeld copper shale convinced Schneiderhöhn that it was of sedimentary origin and had been formed in a manner similar to that of all black shales. The tiny globules of framboidal form were explained as "mineralized bacteria." This idea gave rise to strong discussion; but whether "bacteria" or other primitive organisms, the globules are surely organic. His discussion of these "Schwefelkreislauf" became a basic idea of geology.

Schneiderhöhn gradually became convinced that the purist magmatic ideas, such as those of Niggli and Louis Caryl Graton, were untenable in many cases where undoubtedly "hydrothermal" deposits could not be connected with magmatism. He suggested that such deposits could be derived from superficial waters, heated by some means, from much older deposits. This idea explains many enigmatic deposits—in northern Algeria, Tunisia, and Morocco, and lead-zinc-silver veins surrounding the much older Broken Hill—but probably fails elsewhere.

Schneiderhöhn presented his experience and tremendous knowledge of the literature in many books. *Die Lagerstätten der magmatischen Abfolge*, the first volume of his *Lehrbuch der Erzlagerstätten*, appeared in 1941 but had a very limited circulation; most of the stock, still in the publisher's office, was destroyed by the first bombing of Berlin. He then prepared *Erzlagerstätten Kurzvorlesungen*, a comprehensive introduction to the science of ore deposits. It appeared in several editions in German and has been translated into English and other languages. In the 1950's Schneiderhöhn began *Die Erzlagerstätten der Erde*, of which the first volume, *Die Erzlagerstätten der Frühkristallisation*, appeared in 1958. It contains excellent and critical descriptions and comparisons. The second volume, *Die Pegmatite*, appeared soon after his death. Much data had also been collected for the four remaining volumes that he had planned.

BIBLIOGRAPHY

Schneiderhöhn's works are *Lehrbuch der Erzlagerstättenkunde*, I (Jena, 1941); *Erzlagerstätten Kurzvorlesungen zur Einführung und zur Wiederholung* (Jena, 1944); *Die Erzlagerstätten der Fruhkristallisation* (Stuttgart, 1958); and *Die Erzlagerstätten der Erde*, II (Stuttgart, 1961).

On Schneiderhöhn and his work, see K. F. Chudoba, "Prof. Dr. phil. Hans Schneiderhöhn," in *Aufschluss*, **14** (1963), 106–107; D. Di Colbertaldo, "Nachruf für das Mitglied auf Lebenszeit Hans Schneiderhöhn," in *Rendiconti della Società mineralogica italiana*. **20**, 51–54; K. R. Mennert, "In Memoriam Hans Schneiderhöhn," in *Neues Jahrbuch für Mineralogie. Monatshefte* (1962), 245–246; and "Festband Hans Schneiderhöhn zum 70. Geburtstag," in *Neues Jahrbuch für Mineralogie. Abhandlungen*, **91** (1957).

P. RAMDOHR

SCHOENFLIES, ARTHUR MORITZ (*b.* Landsberg an der Warthe, Germany [now Gorzów, Poland], 17 April 1853; *d.* Frankfurt am Main, Germany, 27 May 1928), *mathematics, crystallography*.

Schoenflies studied with Kummer at the University of Berlin from 1870 to 1875 and received the Ph.D. in 1877. From 1878 he taught at a Gymnasium in Berlin and then, from 1880, in Colmar, Alsace. In 1884 he earned his *Habilitation* as *Privatdozent* at the University of Göttingen, where, in 1892, he was named professor extraordinarius and was given the chair of applied mathematics. (This chair had been created thanks to Felix Klein's initiative.) In 1899 Schoenflies was appointed professor ordinarius at the University of Königsberg and then, in 1911, at the Academy for Social and Commercial Sciences in Frankfurt am Main; this school became a university in 1914. He was later professor ordinarius (1914–1922) at the University of Frankfurt and in 1920–1921 served as rector of the university.

Schoenflies produced an extensive mathematical *oeuvre* consisting of about ninety papers and many reports and books. He started his scientific work with rather traditional geometry and kinematics. This research was published in 1886 (1) and was later translated into French (1*a*). In the same year, under Klein's influence, Schoenflies turned to Euclidean motion groups and regular space divisions. His investigations culminated in 1891 in his magnum opus (2). The result of this book, the 230 crystallographic groups, was at the same time obtained independently by E. S. Fedorov. During the last phase of this research, Schoenflies corresponded with Fedorov and was thus able to correct some minor errors that he had originally made in his classification. In 1923 Schoenflies reedited his 1891 publication under another title (2a). He also wrote a textbook on crystallography (9).

In the mid-1890's Schoenflies, by then in his forties, turned to topology and set theory. In 1898 he published an article (5) on this subject in the *Encyklopädie der mathematischen Wissenschaften*. He also published extensive reports in *Deutsche Mathematiker-Vereinigung*, which appeared in 1900 and 1908 (6) and were reedited in 1913 (6a). These reports were totally eclipsed by Hausdorff's *Grundzüge der Mengenlehre* (1914). The greater part of Schoenflies' original contributions to topology is contained in three papers (7) and is devoted to plane topology. He proved the topological invariance of the dimension of the square, and he invented the notions and theorems that are connected with the characterization of the simple closed curve in the plane by its dividing the plane into two domains of which it is the everywhere attainable boundary. There are numerous gaps and wrong statements in this part of Schoenflies' work, and these errors led L. Brouwer to some of his startling discoveries.

Schoenflies published four articles in the *Encyklopädie der mathematischen Wissenschaften* (on set theory, kinematics, crystallography, and projective geometry), in part with others (5). With W. Nernst, he wrote a textbook (1895) on calculus (3) that went through at least eleven editions and two Russian translations. He also wrote textbooks on descriptive geometry (8) and analytic geometry (10). In 1895 he edited the work of Julius Plücker (4). Schoenflies was elected a fellow of the Bayerische Akademie der Wissenschaften in 1918.

BIBLIOGRAPHY

I. ORIGINAL WORKS. Schoenflies' works are the following:

(1) *Geometrie der Bewegung in synthetischer Darstellung* (Leipzig, 1886), with French trans. by C. Speckel as (1a) *La géométrie du mouvement—exposé synthétique* (Paris, 1893);

(2) *Kristallsysteme und Kristallstruktur* (Leipzig, 1891); the 2nd ed. appeared as (2a) *Theorie der Kristallstruktur* (Berlin, 1923);

(3) *Einführung in die mathematische Behandlung der Naturwissenschaften—Kurzgefasstes Lehrbuch der Differential- und Integralrechnung* (Munich, 1895; 11th ed., 1931), written with W. Nernst;

(4) Julius Plücker, *Gesammelte Mathematische Abhandlungen*, Schoenflies, ed. (Leipzig, 1895);

(5) "Mengenlehre," in *Encyklopaedie der mathematischen Wissenschaften*, 184–207; "Kinematik," *ibid.*, IV, 190–278, written with M. Grübler; "Kristallographie," *ibid.*, V, pt. 7, 391–492, written with T. Liebisch and O. Mügge; "Projektive Geometrie," *ibid.*, III, pt. 5, 389–480;

(6) "Die Entwicklung der Lehre von den Punktmannigfaltigkeiten. I," in *Jahresbericht der Deutschen Mathematiker-Vereinigung*, 8 (1900). 1–250; "Die Entwicklung . . . II," supp. 2 (1908), 1–331;

(6a) *Entwicklung der Mengenlehre und ihrer Anwendungen* (Leipzig, 1913), written with H. Hahn;

(7) "Beiträge zur Theorie der Punktmengen," in *Mathematische Annalen*, **58** (1903), 195–234; **59** (1904), 152–160; **62** (1906), 286–326;

(8) *Einführung in die Hauptgesetze der zeichnerischen Darstellungsmethoden* (Leipzig, 1908);

(9) *Einführung in die Kristallstruktur—ein Lehrbuch* (Berlin, 1923);

(10) *Einführung in die analytische Geometrie der Ebene und des Raumes*, Grundlehren der Mathematischen Wissenschaften no. 21 (Leipzig, 1925), with 2nd ed. by M. Dehn (Leipzig, 1931).

II. SECONDARY LITERATURE. On Schoenflies and his work, see L. Bieberbach, "Arthur Schoenflies," in *Jahresbericht der Deutschen Mathematiker-Vereinigung*, **32** (1923), 1–6; J. J. Burckhardt, "Zur Entdeckung der 230 Raumgruppen," in *Archives for History of Exact Sciences*, **4** (1967), 235–246; "Der Briefwechsel von E. S. Fedorow mit A. Schoenflies, 1889–1908," *ibid.*, **7** (1971), 91–141; R. von Mises, "Schoenflies," in *Zeitschrift für angewandte Mathematik und Mechanik*, **3** (1923), 157–158; A. Sommerfeld, "A. Schoenflies," in *Jahrbuch der bayerischen Akademie der Wissenschaften* (1928–1929), 86–87; and K. Spangenberg, "A. Schönflies," in *Handwörterbuch der Naturwissenschaften*, 2nd ed., VIII (1933), 1108–1109.

HANS FREUDENTHAL

SCHÖNBEIN, CHRISTIAN FRIEDRICH (*b.* Metzingen, Swabia [now West Germany], 18 October 1799; *d.* Sauersberg, near Baden-Baden, Germany, 29 August 1868), *physical chemistry.*

His family's financial condition would not permit any advanced schooling, and at the age of fourteen Schönbein became an apprentice in a chemical and pharmaceutical factory in Böblingen. He acquired a profound knowledge of theoretical and applied chemistry, and he also privately studied Latin, French, English, philosophy, and mathematics.

In April 1820 Schönbein obtained a post at the chemical factory of J. G. Dingler in Augsburg, where he assisted Dingler in making German translations of French publications for the new *Dinglers polytechnisches Journal*. In his spare time Schönbein studied chemistry and later, in 1820, accepted a post in the chemical factory of J. N. Adam in Hemhofen, near Erlangen. He frequently visited the University of Erlangen, where he met the philosopher Schelling; J. W. A. Pfaff, professor of physics and mathematics; and G. H. Schubert, the *Naturphilosoph* and professor of zoology. He remained friends with Schelling until the latter's death in 1854. After a semester, Schönbein moved to Tübingen but in February 1823 returned to Erlangen.

Although largely a self-educated chemist, Schönbein taught (1823) chemistry, physics, and mineralogy at Friedrich Froebel's institute in Keilhau, a small town near Rudolfstadt, in Thuringia. In 1826 he was in England, where he taught mathematics and natural philosophy at a boys' school in Epsom (1826), and in 1827 he went to France, where he attended the lectures of Gay-Lussac, Ampère, César Despretz, and Thenard. In 1828 Schönbein moved to Basel. He received the Ph.D. *honoris causa* from the faculty of philosophy there and also lectured on physics and chemistry. In 1835 he was appointed professor of physics and chemistry at the University of Basel, where he remained until his death. In 1852, when the professorship was divided, Schönbein retained the chair of chemistry. From 1848 he was a member of the Basel parliament.

Schönbein was also interested in philosophy. The influence of *Naturphilosophie* (he was also a friend of Lorenz Oken) is evident in all of Schönbein's work, especially in his speculative views that lack a sufficient experimental basis. Schönbein published more than 350 works, mostly qualitative, covering a wide range of research—but especially ozone, autoxidation, induced reactions, guncotton, electrochemistry, and passive iron. Schönbein's speculative bent is evident even in his early studies (from 1835 on) on the passivity of iron. He started from the well-known fact that iron reacts with dilute nitric acid but not with concentrated nitric acid. He sought to explain this phenomenon as a type of polymerism (he himself spoke always of isomerism) and thus disagreed with Faraday's explanation of a layer of oxide on the iron. Schönbein assumed that a conversion of the metallic iron takes place. Thus he agreed with Friedrich Fischer, professor of philosophy at Basel, who accounted for the passivity of iron by means of polarization, through which the pure attracting chemical affinity is changed into attraction and repulsion.

Schönbein thought that the iron particles possessed two "poles," one that attracts and one that repels (1838). But under certain conditions the poles that attract oxygen are directed to the inside of the metallic iron while those that repel oxygen are directed to the outside, thus producing passive iron. To account for this passivity Schönbein assumed that iron in the passive state possesses on its surface the properties of a "noble" metal. Consequently, he questioned the status of iron as an element: if iron can be converted into a noble metal, would all other metals possess the same property? He claimed that too little is known about the nature of matter and the workable forces in it to give definitive answers to these questions. Schönbein's reasoning was based on the analogies he drew from his 1835 lecture on isomerism, in which he stated that all known examples of isomerism (for example, tartaric and racemic acids, fulminic and cyanic acids) are dimorphic, with the exception of sulfur. He concluded that all dimorphic substances must be composite, and that sulfur is a compound.

Schönbein is known primarily for his work on ozone. While conducting experiments on the decomposition of water (autumn 1839), he noticed that the oxygen obtained in the process had a peculiar odor similar to that produced when a large electrical machine is operating—a similarity first noted by the Dutch chemist van Marum (1785). Schönbein recognized that the substance is a gas, that it is produced at the anode, and that it resembles chlorine and bromine in its chemical and electric properties. He studied extensively the properties of this gas and found (1844) that it is produced when phosphorus glows in air. He also discovered that it bleaches litmus, frees iodine from potassium iodide, and changes potassium ferrocyanide into ferricyanide.

Schönbein's ideas concerning the nature of ozone were rather confused. At first, he thought that nitrogen is composed of ozone and hydrogen. But phosphorus cannot decompose nitrogen ("ozone-hydrogen") unless another substance is present that can combine with the hydrogen. That substance is oxygen. Thus nitrogen is decomposed by phosphorus only in the presence of oxygen. The hydrogen in the nitrogen reacts with the oxygen of the water and ozone partly liberates and partly is bound with the phosphorus to "ozone-phosphorus." Like phosphorus trichloride, "ozone-phosphorus" is decomposed by water, namely into phosphorous acid and nitrogen. Schönbein saw a strong analogy between ozone and the halogens chlorine and bromine. Because the electrical, chemical, and physiological reactions of ozone closely resemble those of chlorine and bromine, he concluded that ozone also forms a salt and that its chemical affinity must place it directly after chlorine.

In 1845 Marignac and Auguste Arthur de la Rive proved independently that ozone is formed by an electric spark in pure, dry oxygen. They regarded ozone as oxygen in a particular state of chemical affinity. Although Schönbein persisted in his belief that ozone is a compound, he held that its oxidation state is higher than that of hydrogen, or even more likely, that it is a particular compound of water and oxygen. He suggested that there are three forms of oxygen: ozone, antozone, and ordinary oxygen, the last being a neutralization product of the first two. Similarly, Schönbein concluded that chlorine is a compound. Only in 1851 did he declare that, in all probability, ozone is an allotropic form of oxygen.

In the field of physical chemistry Schönbein studied the phenomenon of autoxidation: the spontaneous oxidation of a substance by atmospheric oxygen, part of which combines with the substance while a second part is converted into ozone or "antozone" (hydrogen peroxide) or combines with another substance. From various reactions, he concluded that ordinary oxygen is converted into ozone and antozone. Oxidation of phosphorus yields ozone; oxidation of metals in the presence of water yields antozone. Schönbein also studied induced reactions. To investigate this phenomenon he first used compounds of sodium sulfite and sodium arsenite; only the former is oxidized when exposed to air. But both sulfite and arsenite are oxidized when mixed and exposed to air. Thus he stated (1858) that the oxidation of sulfite "induces" that of arsenite.

From 1836 on, Schönbein's publications on voltaic current attributed the origin of this form of electricity to chemical action. His 1838 tendency theory stated that the tendency of two substances to combine with each other is sufficient to disturb their chemical equilibrium and to produce an electric current.

At the 11 March 1846 meeting of the Naturforschende Gesellschaft in Basel, Schönbein announced his discovery of guncotton. He also discovered collodion, a solution of guncotton in ether, which early found applications in medicine and photography. Schönbein produced guncotton by dipping cotton-wool in a mixture of fuming nitric and sulfuric acids and then washing and drying the product. His method of preparation remained a secret until it was discovered independently in 1846 by Böttger and Friedrich Julius Otto. Schönbein was also interested in the rise of dissolved materials from filter paper. His technique of capillary chromatography was based on the specific low rate of individual substances in nonimpregnated slips of paper. The height of ascent under standardized conditions and the time required for the ascent were recognized as characteristics of each individual substance present in the mixture under investigation. Schönbein's pupil Friedrich Goppelsroeder greatly extended the knowledge of the technique of capillary analysis.

Schönbein's general ideas on chemistry, and particularly on the phenomenon of catalysis, are discussed in *Beiträge zur physikalischen Chemie* (1844). His dynamical ideas are also emphasized. Schönbein was opposed to the atomic theory: he rejected the explanation of chemical combination as the basis for the formation of chemical substances. He thought that the qualitative changes in the formation of chemical substances indicated that every particle of a chemical element is a system of continuously working molecular forces. Schönbein sent a copy of his *Beiträge* to Faraday; and in a covering letter he pointed out that for years he had doubted the validity of the atomic theory and that he considered the molecule of a compound to be the "centre of physical forces."

Although Schelling's influence is clearly evident in the work of Schönbein, he was not strictly a *Naturphilosoph*. More than once he expressed himself against the views of Schelling and Oken and he passionately denounced Hegel and his school. Nevertheless, Schönbein's work is filled with speculative remarks lacking an adequate experimental basis and with excessive recourse to analogy.

BIBLIOGRAPHY

I. ORIGINAL WORKS. Schönbein's works include "Ueber das Verhalten des Zinns und des Eisens gegen Salpetersäure," in *Annalen der Physik und Chemie*, 2nd ser., **37** (1836), 390–399; "Ueber das Verhalten des Eisens zum Sauerstoff," *ibid.,* **38** (1836), 492–497; *Das Verhalten des Eisens zum Sauerstoff. Ein Beitrag zur Erweiterung electro-chemischer Kenntnisse* (Basel, 1837); "Further Experiments on the Current Electricity Excited by Chemical Tendencies, Independent of Ordinary Chemical Action," in *London and Edinburgh Philosophical Magazine and Journal of Science*, **12** (1838), 311–317; "Beobachtungen über das electromotorische Verhalten einiger Metallhyperoxyde des Platins und des Eisens," in *Annalen der Physik und Chemie*, 2nd ser., **43** (1838), 89–102; "Notiz über die Passivität des Eisens," *ibid.*, 103–104; and "Beobachtungen über den bei der Electrolyse des Wassers und dem Ausströmen der gewöhnlichen Electricität sich entwickelnden Geruch," *ibid.*, **50** (1840), 616–635.

Later writings are *Ueber die Häufigkeit der Berührungswirkungen auf dem Gebiete der Chemie* (Basel, 1843); *Beiträge zur physikalischen Chemie* (Basel, 1844); *Ueber die Erzeugung des Ozons auf chemischen Wege* (Basel, 1844); "On the Nature of Ozone," in *London, Edinburgh, and Dublin Philosophical Magazine and Journal of Science*, **27** (1845), 386–389; "Einige Bemerkungen über die Anwesenheit des Ozons in der atmosphärischen Luft und die Rolle, welche es bei langsamen Oxidationen spielen dürfte," in *Annalen der Physik und Chemie*, 3rd ser., **65** (1845), 161–172; *Chemische Beobachtungen über die langsame und rasche Verbrennung der Körper in atmosphärischer Luft* (Basel, 1845); *Denkschrift über das Ozon* (Basel, 1849); *Ueber den Einfluss des Sonnenlichtes auf die chemische Thätigkeit des Sauerstoffs und den Ursprung der Wolken-electricität und des Gewitters* (Basel, 1850); and *Ueber den Zusammenhang der katalytischen Erscheinungen mit der Allotropie* (Basel, 1856).

Schönbein's letters are collected in *Letters of Faraday and Schönbein, 1836–1862*, G. W. A. Kahlbaum and F. V. Darbishire, eds. (Basel–London, 1899); *Letters of Jöns Jacob Berzelius and Christian Friedrich Schönbein, 1836–1847*, G. W. A. Kahlbaum, ed., trans. by F. V. Darbishire and N. V. Sidgwick (London, 1900); and *Justus von Liebig und Christian Friedrich Schönbein. Briefwechsel 1853–1868*, G. W. A. Kahlbaum and E. Thon, eds. (Leipzig, 1900).

II. SECONDARY LITERATURE. The best study of the life and work of Schönbein is G. W. A. Kahlbaum and E. Schaer, *Christian Friedrich Schönbein, 1799–1868, Ein Blatt zur Geschichte des 19. Jahrhunderts*, 2 vols. (Leipzig, 1899–1901). See also E. Färber, "Christian Friedrich Schönbeins Werk," in *Prometheus*, **29** (1918), 413–416; E. Hagenbach, *Christian Friedrich Schönbein* (Basel, 1868); R. E. Oesper, "Christian Friedrich Schönbein," in *Journal of Chemical Education*, **6** (1929), 432–440, 677–685; and the chap. on Schönbein in W. Prandtl, *Deutsche Chemiker in der ersten Hälfte des neunzehnten Jahrhunderts* (Weinheim, 1956), 193–241.

H. A. M. SNELDERS

SCHÖNER, JOHANNES (*b.* Karlstadt, Germany, 16 January 1477; *d.* Nuremberg, Germany, 16 January 1547), *astronomy, geography.*

On or after 18 October 1494, Schöner paid the full fee when he enrolled in the University of Erfurt,[1] where he studied theology. He left the university before he took a degree, was ordained a Roman Catholic priest, and served in Bamberg, where an astrological tract was addressed to him in October 1506. In 1509 he bought manuscript ephemerides for the years 1464–1484, and on 20 March 1518 he was paid for binding a book for his bishop.

Schöner assembled a printing shop in his house in Bamberg. He himself set the type, carved the woodblocks for the illustrations, and bound the finished product. He also made his own globes. His earliest terrestrial globe named the recently discovered continental mass "America," the first printed globe to do so. This globe was issued with his *Luculentissima quaedam terrae totius descriptio* (Nuremberg, 1515), which Schöner dedicated to his bishop on 24 March 1515. He likewise dedicated to the bishop his *Solidi et sphaerici corporis sive globi astronomici canones usum et expeditam praxim ejusdem exprimentes* (Nuremberg, 1517). In 1521, again using his own press in Bamberg, Schöner published his *Aequatorium astronomicum*, with movable disks to represent the motions of the planets. Having neglected to celebrate mass, Schöner was relegated to officiate at early mass in Kirchehrenbach. In this small village near Forchheim he printed on his own press his *De nuper . . . repertis insulis ac regionibus*, with the gores (triangular segments) for his globe of 1523. On 24 April 1525 he finished the last of his Kirchehrenbach books, his correction of a faulty Latin translation of a work by al-Zarqālī. The threat of the rebellious peasants to kill all Roman Catholic clergymen ended Schöner's career as a priest in 1525.

Fortunately, in 1526 Nuremberg opened the Melanchthon Gymnasium, where Schöner taught mathematics for two decades. He turned Lutheran and married Anna Zelerin on 7 August 1527.[2] The appearance of a comet in August 1531 impelled him to publish Regiomontanus' *De cometae magnitudine . . . problemata XVI* (Nuremberg, 1531). Thus began Schöner's valuable editions of many previously unpublished works by the greatest astronomer of the fifteenth century. As a zealous defender of astrology against its critics, Schöner printed on his own press his *Horoscopium generale, omni regioni accomodum* (Nuremberg, 1535).

After Schöner's death his mathematical works, all of which had been placed on the *Index of Prohibited Books*, were published by his son Andreas, with a portrait of the father at the age of sixty-nine (*Opera mathematica* [Nuremberg, 1551; 2nd edition, revised and enlarged, 1561], signature B4v).

NOTES

1. H. J. C. Weissenborn, ed., *Acten der Erfurter Universität,* which is Geschichtsquellen der Provinz Sachsen und angrenzender Gebiete, vol. 8, II (Halle, 1881–1899), 185, left column, line 10.
2. Karl Schornbaum, *Ehebuch von St. Sebald in Nürnberg 1524–1543* (Nuremberg, 1949), 91, no. 3043. Our "Johann Schöner" was confused with a Hanns Schonner, who married on 15 May 1537 (Schornbaum, 80, no. 2617); see Johannes Kist, *Die Matrikel der Geistlichkeit des Bistums Bamberg 1400–1556* (Würzburg, 1955–1960), 367, no. 5585; Veröffentlichungen der Gesellschaft für fränkische Geschichte, IV. Reihe; Matrikeln fränkischer Schulen und Stände, 7.

BIBLIOGRAPHY

There is no full-length biographical study of Schöner. His astronomical publications are listed in Ernst Zinner, *Geschichte und Bibliographie der astronomischen Literatur in Deutschland zur Zeit der Renaissance,* 2nd ed. (Stuttgart, 1964). For the works that Schöner printed on his own press in Bamberg, Kirchehrenbach, and Nuremberg, see Karl Schottenloher, "Johann Schöner und seine Hausdruckerei," in *Zentralblatt für Bibliothekswesen,* **24** (1907), 145–155; and Henry Stevens, *Johann Schöner,* Charles H. Coote, ed. (London, 1888), 149–170, with the Latin text of Schöner's *De nuper . . . repertis insulis ac regionibus,* pp. 47–55, and an English trans., pp. 91–99. The Latin text of this letter was printed also by Franz Wieser; see "Der verschollene Globus des Johannes Schöner von 1523," in *Sitzungsberichte der philosophisch-historischen Classe der k. Akademie der Wissenschaften in Wien,* **117,** no. 5 (1888), 15–18. Wieser's *Magalhâes-Strasse und Austral-Continent auf den Globen des Johannes Schöner* (Innsbruck, 1881) was recently reprinted (Amsterdam, 1967). Frederik Caspar Wieder, *Monumenta cartographica,* I (The Hague, 1925), 1–4, deals with Schöner; and the book was reviewed by George E. Nunn, "The Lost Globe Gores of Johann Schöner, 1523–1524," in *Geographical Review,* **17** (1927), 476–480.

EDWARD ROSEN

SCHÖNFELD, EDUARD (*b.* Hildburghausen, Germany, 22 December 1828; *d.* Bonn, Germany, 1 May 1891), *astronomy.*

Schönfeld was educated at the Gymnasium in Hildburghausen. He then attended the Technische Hochschule at Hannover, from which he was expelled in 1849 because of his involvement in the political unrest of 1848. Schönfeld continued his technical studies at Kassel but found them unsatisfactory and began to study chemistry and astronomy at Marburg University in the autumn of 1849. In 1852 he went to Bonn University, where he was introduced to Argelander and became his assistant in 1853; the following year Schönfeld received his doctorate. In 1859 he was appointed director of the observatory at Mannheim. When Argelander died in 1875, Schönfeld succeeded him as director of the Bonn observatory and as professor of astronomy at the university. An active member of the Astronomische Gesellschaft, he served as secretary from 1875 until his death.

Schönfeld's name is very closely connected with the *Bonner Durchmusterung,* a catalog of all stars down to the ninth magnitude begun by Argelander. Schönfeld was one of his most enthusiastic collaborators and made a great many of the necessary observations using a telescope having an aperture of not more than about three inches. Schönfeld also performed most of the preparatory work for the publication of the results. After Argelander's death, he started work to expand the *Durchmusterung* to include more southern declinations; within ten years he completed the *Schönfeld-Durchmusterung,* which extended Argelander's *Durchmusterung* from declination −2° down to −23°. All observations for this work were made by Schönfeld himself. The great importance of these *Durchmusterungen* is best shown by the fact that in 1967, almost a century later, they were completely reprinted.

Schönfeld also observed nebulae, variable stars, and comets. He published the results of his observations of nebulae at Mannheim in two catalogs that appeared in 1862 and 1875.

BIBLIOGRAPHY

Schönfeld collaborated with Argelander and A. Krüger on "Bonner Sternverzeichnis," *Astronomische Beobachtungen auf der Sternwarte zu Bonn,* **3** (1859); **4** (1861); and **5** (1862). He was sole author of "Bonner Sternverzeichnis," *ibid.,* **8** (1886).

See also E. von der Pahlen, *Lehrbuch der Stellarstatistik* (Leipzig, 1937), 182, 341.

F. SCHMEIDLER

SCHÖNHERR, CARL JOHAN (*b.* Stockholm, Sweden, 10 June 1772; *d.* Sparresäter, near Skara, Sweden, 28 March 1848), *entomology.*

Schönherr was completely self-taught. From his father he inherited a silk factory in Stockholm, but after a few years he gave it up to settle on his estate, Sparresäter. There he was in convenient proximity to his entomological teacher, Leonhard Gyllenhaal, and their close collaboration was important.

At the age of twelve Schönherr began an insect collection, which soon developed into an ardent hobby; and he taught himself Latin in order to understand entomological literature. He was an extremely systematic person, who wanted order and reason in everything, including entomological synonyms and nomenclature. He was obliged to undertake these topics in order to clear up the chaos that long held sway in the field, and between 1806 and 1817 he published *Synonymia insectorum*, concerning beetles. This series was continued later (1833–1845) under the same title with another work on the weevils, Curculionidae. The work ran to eight volumes.

Schönherr intended to work on the whole insect class, but like other similar projects, the result was the publication of an intensive and penetrating treatment of a single group: the beetles. Schönherr was especially interested in the large family of weevils, and his exemplary descriptions of the genera, and the analyses of synonyms and explanations of nomenclature have remained of lasting value. Besides Gyllenhaal, he also collaborated with C. H. Boheman and other experts.

Schönherr's private library was one of the greatest entomological book collections of his time and was also an unusually beautiful collection (now preserved in the library of the Royal Swedish Academy of Sciences). His insect collection was as rich; it is said to have included some 13,500 species in about 37,700 specimens. By his will, the collections were transferred to the Naturhistoriska Riksmuseet in Stockholm.

BIBLIOGRAPHY

Schönherr's works are *Synonymia insectorum oder Versuch einer Synonymie aller bisher bekannten Insecten nach Fabricius Syst. Eleutheratorum geordnet, mit Berichtigungen und Anmerkungen, wie auch Beschreibungen neuer Arten und illuminirten Kupfern,* 3 vols. and appendix (Stockholm–Skara, 1806–1817); "Entomologiska Anmärkningar och beskrifningar på några för Svenska Faunan nya Insekter," in *Kungliga Svenska vetenskapsakademiens handlingar,* **30** (1809), 48–58; "Pulex segnis, ny Svensk species," *ibid.,* **31** (1811), 98–102; *Curculionidum dispositio methodica cum generum characteribus, descriptionibus atque observationibus variis, seu prodromus ad Synonymiae insectorum Partem IV* (Leipzig, 1826); and *Synonymia insectorum oder Versuch einer Synonymie aller von mir bisher bekannten*

Insecten, mit Berichtigungen und Anmerkungen, wie auch mit Beschreibung neuer Arten, 8 vols. (Paris, 1833–1845).

BENGT-OLOF LANDIN

SCHONLAND, BASIL FERDINAND JAMIESON
(*b.* Grahamstown, South Africa, 5 February 1896; *d.* Winchester, England, 24 November 1972), *atmospheric electricity, scientific administration.*

Schonland's father received the Ph.D. from the University of Kiel and was the first professor of botany at Rhodes University, Grahamstown. His mother was the daughter of a botanist. Schonland was the eldest of three sons. After graduating at Grahamstown, he failed to win a Rhodes scholarship to Oxford, and thus, in 1915, went instead to Gonville and Caius College, Cambridge. He interrupted his studies there to serve in World War I, working on signals. In 1919 he returned to Cambridge and after graduating in 1920, registered for the Ph.D. at the Cavendish Laboratory. At Cambridge he met Isabel Marion Craib, a fellow South African, whom he married when he returned to South Africa in 1923. They had a son and two daughters. In 1927–1928 he returned to Cambridge.

From 1922 to 1936 Schonland taught physics at the University of Cape Town and from 1937 to 1954 at the University of Witwatersrand. He also served as deputy director of the Atomic Energy Research Establishment at Harwell (1954–1958) and from 1958 to 1960 was its director. He was elected a fellow of the Royal Society of London in 1938 and in 1960 was knighted.

At the Cavendish, Schonland studied cathode rays; but after returning to South Africa, he investigated thunderstorms. He designed apparatus to photograph lightning discharges and confirmed Charles Wilson's theory that positive ions are carried to the top rather than to the bottom of the thundercloud. Schonland described this work in *Atmospheric Electricity* (1932); *The Flight of Thunderbolts* (1950), a popularized account; and in numerous papers.

In 1938 Cockcroft invited Schonland to join a group of scientists investigating radar. During World War II, he continued this work, ultimately becoming scientific adviser to General Montgomery. In 1945 Schonland returned to South Africa to direct the Council for Scientific and Industrial Research; but after the 1948 elections he found South Africa less congenial. He resigned the post in 1950 and in 1954 returned to England.

BIBLIOGRAPHY

Schonland's writings include *Atmospheric Electricity* (London, 1932; 2nd ed., 1953); *The Flight of Thunderbolts* (Oxford, 1950; 2nd ed., 1964); and *The Atomists, 1805–1933* (Oxford, 1968).

On Schonland and his work, see T. E. Allibone, "Sir Basil Schonland," in *Biographical Memoirs of Fellows of the Royal Society*, **14** (1973), 629–653, with portrait and full bibliography.

DAVID KNIGHT

SCHÖNLEIN, JOHANN LUCAS (*b.* Bamberg, Germany, 30 November 1793; *d.* Bamberg, 23 January 1864), *medicine.*

Schönlein was his country's leading clinician, and his methods and teaching gave a new direction to German medicine. His brief paper on favus, which recognized for the first time a fungus parasite as the cause of a disease in man, contributed importantly to the understanding of contagious disease.

Schönlein was the only child of Thomas Schönlein, a successful ropemaker, and Margaretha Hümmer, who intended him at first to follow in his father's occupation. But his scholarly interests soon became apparent and, largely through his mother's intercession, he attended the local Gymnasium and proceeded to university studies.

A lifelong collector, Schönlein received early encouragement from a Gymnasium teacher as he amassed specimens ranging from stones to insects. During visits to the country, he gathered plants. He had a continuing interest in paleobotany and collected fossil plants while touring Switzerland on vacations. In his reading on botany he especially admired Linnaeus and Linnaeus' system of classification of plants. Zoology, too, drew Schönlein's curiosity, and independently he dissected frogs and lizards.

Schönlein first studied the natural sciences in 1811 at the University of Landshut but later undertook the study of medicine. Tiedemann was his teacher of comparative anatomy. In 1813 he transferred to Würzburg, where, as at Landshut, *Naturphilosophie* still exerted an influence. But Döllinger, professor of anatomy and physiology, who provided Schönlein with a wealth of material illustrating developmental anatomy, stressed observation. Schönlein's dissertation on the metamorphosis of the brain, "Von der Hirnmetamorphose" (1816), reflected both approaches. After visits to Göttingen and Jena and after an interval during which he practiced medicine, Schönlein became

Privatdozent (1817) at Würzburg, lecturing in pathological anatomy.

In 1819 Schönlein was named provisional head of the medical clinic at the Julius Hospital in Würzburg. By 1824 he had been appointed ordinary professor of special pathology and therapy and was director of the clinic. He soon attracted students from throughout Europe. At the clinic percussion and auscultation, which had been introduced in France, were first routinely used in Germany as diagnostic aids. Blood, urine, and various secretions were examined under the microscope and chemical reagents were utilized; autopsies provided still further information. Schönlein's bedside teaching emphasized direct observation and careful reasoning. Each student followed the patients' symptoms and the courses of their diseases.

Schönlein's respect for the systems of classification used in the natural sciences led him to develop his "natural historical school." He distinguished his approach from the "natural philosophical school," and set forth his own "system." He was convinced that, in much the same way that botanists and zoologists applied their systems, he could classify pathological conditions according to their characteristics and symptoms and thus establish their relationships: three classes—morphae, haematoses, and neuroses—were subdivided into families, then groups.

At Würzburg, Schönlein married Theresa Heffner in 1827. Although he had been made an honorary citizen of Würzburg, he was forced to leave because of his liberal beliefs and associations. His academic appointment was rescinded in 1832. Having refused a post at Passau, he established a medical practice in Frankfurt but again had to leave.

In 1833 Schönlein became professor of medicine at Zurich, where a new hospital was built, providing him with fine facilities, and his fame grew. At Zurich he wrote two papers, which, besides his thesis, were his only publications. (His lectures were published by his pupils.) The first paper, on crystals in the urine of typhoid fever patients, was of little moment; but the second, a letter to Johannes Müller, occupying only a page in Müller's *Archiv* for 1839, described the cause of *porrigo lupinosa*, or favus: a minute parasitic fungus.

Schönlein's paper related the sources of his interest in favus, a disease typified by crusts that form on the scalp. Following Bassi's discovery, confirmed by Audouin, that the silkworm disease *muscardine* is caused by a microscopic parasitic fungus (Bassi suggested that certain diseases in man might be similarly caused), Schönlein examined infected silkworms, again confirming Bassi's findings. Schönlein also noted the botanist Franz Unger's *Die Exantheme der Pflanzen* (1833), where Unger described plant diseases in which fungi are present and suggested a parallel between plant exanthems "and like diseases of the animal organism." In this connection Schönlein recalled his view "of the plant nature of many an impetigo," and his examination of fragments of the "pustules" of favus obtained from his own patients revealed "the fungous nature" of the disease. His communication implicated a living parasitic plant organism as the cause of a disease in man, an important step toward the understanding of contagious disease; but he never published on the further investigations he promised. Henle noted Schönlein's finding in 1840 in his paper "Von den Miasmen und Contagien und von den miasmatisch-contagiösen Krankheiten" but pointed out that it had not yet been shown whether the fungus actually caused the pustules or merely grew on them.

Meanwhile, Schönlein had left Zurich in 1839 for political and personal reasons—he had not been made a citizen there because he was a Catholic. In 1840 he became professor of medicine at Berlin and director of the clinic at the Charité. His assistant, Robert Remak, who in 1837 had seen the organism that caused favus but had not then recognized it as a fungus, carried on the experiments and later named it *Achorion schoenleinii*. Gruby also discovered it independently, not knowing at first of Schönlein's 1839 paper.

At Berlin, Schönlein's lectures and clinical work made him a guiding influence in medicine. His many distinguished students had included Schwann at Würzburg; Billroth and Virchow were among his students at Berlin.

Schönlein left Berlin in 1859 to retire with his daughters in Bamberg; his only son had died the previous year on a botanical expedition, and his wife had died in 1846. At Bamberg he devoted time to his books and collections. Although he was interested in ethnology and other subjects, his fine collection of writings on epidemiology is evidence of his lasting concern with contagious disease.

BIBLIOGRAPHY

I. ORIGINAL WORKS. Schönlein's works are "Ueber Crystalle im Darmcanal bei Typhus abdominalis," in *Archiv für Anatomie, Physiologie und wissenschaftliche Medicin* (1836), 258–261; "Zur Pathogenie der Impetigines," *ibid.* (1839), 82, on favus.

II. SECONDARY LITERATURE. Schönlein's lectures, published by his pupils, appear in various eds., some noted in the sources below (see also the catalogs of the Library of the Surgeon General); they include *Allgemeine und specielle Pathologie und Therapie*, 4th ed. (St. Gallen, 1839). Rudolf Virchow, *Gedächtnissrede auf Joh. Lucas Schönlein* (Berlin, 1865), is a comprehensive biography and appreciation; he added notes in "Aus Schönlein's Leben," in *Archiv für pathologische Anatomie und Physiologie und für klinische Medicin,* 33 (1865), 170–174. A. Göschen, "Johann Lucas Schönlein," in *Deutsche Klinik,* 17 (1865), 29–32; and W. Griesinger, "Zum Gedächtnisse an J. L. Schönlein," in *Aerztliches Intelligenz-Blatt,* 11 (1864), 445–451 and in *Berliner klinische Wochenschrift,* 1 (1864), 276–279, stress his contributions as a clinician. J. Pagel, "Johann Lucas Schoenlein," in *Biographisches Lexikon hervorragenden Ärzte des neunzehnten Jahrhunderts,* J. Pagel, ed. (Berlin–Vienna, 1901), 1522–1524, and his "Johann Lucas Schoenlein," in *Allgemeine deutsche Biographie.* XXXII (Leipzig, 1891), 315–319, are general accounts.

Erwin H. Ackerknecht, "Johan Lucas Schoenlein, 1793–1864," in *Journal of the History of Medicine and Allied Sciences,* 19 (1964), 131–138, has a facs. of the paper on favus with a trans.

See also Walther Koerting, "Zum hundertjährigen Todestag von Johann Lukas Schoenlein," in *Bayerisches Ärzteblatt,* 19 (1964), 58–60; and W. Löffler's detailed study, "Johann Lucas Schönlein (1793–1864, Zürich 1833–1839) und die Medizin seiner Zeit," in *Zürcher Spitalgeschichte,* Regierungsrat des Kantons Zürich, II (Zurich, 1951), 2–89; Friedrich von Müller, "Johann Lukas Schönlein, Professor der Medezin, 1793–1864," in *Lebensläufe aus Franken,* Gesellschaft für Frankische Geschichte (Erlangen, 1936), 332–339; and Henry E. Sigerist, *The Great Doctors,* trans. by Eden and Cedar Paul (New York, 1958), 295–299, 336. W. Schönfeld, "Aus der Frühzeit der Pilzerkrankungen des Menschen, Jean Victor Audouin (1797–1839), Agostino Bassi (1773–1856), Franz Unger (1800–1870)," in *Deutsche medizinische Wochenschrift,* 82, pt. 2 (1957), 1235–1237, reviews the background of the investigation of favus. For Schönlein's description of peliosis rheumatica, or Schönlein's disease, see R. H. Major, *Classic Descriptions of Disease,* 3rd ed. (Springfield, Ill., 1945), 225–227, which is taken from the lectures published in 1841.

GLORIA ROBINSON

SCHOOLCRAFT, HENRY ROWE (*b.* Albany County, now Guilderland, New York, 28 March 1793; *d.* Washington, D.C., 10 December 1864), *ethnology.*

Schoolcraft's father, Lawrence Schoolcraft, a descendant of English settlers in Canada and New York, was a glass manufacturer, who served in the

Revolutionary War and the War of 1812. Schoolcraft's mother was Margaret Ann Barbara Rowe Schoolcraft, who was of English descent. Schoolcraft was a natural scholar, who quite young gathered a small library of good books. He collected rocks and minerals, painted, and wrote poems and essays that were locally published. With private instruction he prepared for Union College, and attended it for a time. He later studied informally under Frederick Hall at Middlebury College, Vermont.

Devoted to his father, Schoolcraft readily joined him in the manufacture of glass in 1809; both men superintended factories at several localities in New York and New England. Under the influx of cheaper foreign imports, all of these businesses collapsed soon after the War of 1812.

In 1818 Schoolcraft set out westward to tour the lead mines of Missouri, where he hoped to become superintendent by federal appointment. His six-thousand-mile tour of the Mississippi valley, the Ozark Mountains, and the lead district, published in 1819 as *A View of the Lead Mines of Missouri*, brought him to the attention of Secretary of War John C. Calhoun, who in 1820 assigned Schoolcraft as naturalist on the Lewis Cass expedition from Detroit to the source of the Mississippi River. The expedition turned back before reaching its goal, but twelve years later, at the request of Cass, who was by then secretary of war, Schoolcraft continued the search to Lake Itasca, considered the river's source by the accompanying Indian guides.

Schoolcraft's major scientific accomplishment resulted from his appointment as Indian agent in 1822 at Sault Ste. Marie, Michigan Territory. The first and only agent in that post, for nineteen years he gathered notes on the Indian tribes, especially the Chippewa and their customs, languages, myths, songs, and history. In this work Schoolcraft was greatly aided by his wife, Jane Johnston Schoolcraft, granddaughter of an Ojibwa chief; her father, a cultured fur trader, also provided valuable help. From 1836 Schoolcraft was also acting superintendent of Indian affairs for the northwest. He negotiated a number of treaties on land and mineral rights, and, devoutly religious himself, encouraged missionaries and their Indian schools.

In 1841 Schoolcraft left Michigan for New York in order to supervise his many publications. In 1847 he returned to the Office of Indian Affairs in Washington to compile information on all American Indian tribes. For over ten years he edited the six-volume *Historical and Statistical Information Respecting the History, Condition and Prospects of the Indian Tribes of the United States*, an unassorted, lavishly illustrated compendium of material gathered by agents and staff of the Office of Indian Affairs and by himself. His second wife, Mary Howard Schoolcraft, helped him considerably in continuing the work despite his increasing paralysis. These books and Schoolcraft's other publications on American Indian lore were Longfellow's major reference sources for *The Song of Hiawatha*.

Schoolcraft was elected to the Lyceum of Natural History of New York and to the New-York Historical Society in 1820, upon the publication of his report on the lead district. He was a founder of the American Ethnological Society in 1842 and was awarded the LL.D. by the University of Geneva in 1846.

Schoolcraft's reports on mineral occurrences in both the Missouri and the Lake Superior region were among the earliest descriptions of mineral resources in the United States. He presented assays of lead ore, descriptions of the Missouri mines, distribution of outcrops, local geography, and notes on other resources. From his first report in 1819, privately published, he learned the value of publication. Henceforth he prodigiously contributed notes, observations, poems, and articles to newspapers, magazines of his own founding, and established journals; he also published books and government reports. He often repeated material, and he made little effort to organize his observations. His name became widely known, and he developed correspondences with distinguished scientists, including Benjamin Silliman (1779–1864), and with literary figures. His extended reports on the two upper Mississippi expeditions considerably influenced new settlement into Michigan Territory.

Almost the only predecessor of Schoolcraft in making ethnological notes on American Indians was Governor Lewis Cass of Michigan Territory, who provided the agents in his area with questionnaires on Indian observations, and who undoubtedly sparked Schoolcraft's interest. The latter's own fondness for poetry led him to record especially the American Indian songs, myths, and legends. His contributions to ethnology resulted chiefly from his having been an early observer in the field and his presenting widespread, written results from which later workers could synthesize, after the westward expansion and conflict made observations less reliable.

BIBLIOGRAPHY

I. ORIGINAL WORKS. Schoolcraft's monument to early ethnology is *Historical and Statistical Information . . . of the Indian Tribes of the United States,* I–V (Washington, D.C., 1851–1855), VI (Philadelphia, 1857), to which Frances S. Nichols compiled an index, which is *Bulletin of the Bureau of American Ethnology,* **152** (1954). In addition to Schoolcraft's numerous shorter works, many of his observations of American Indians were also included in *Personal Memories of a Residence of Thirty Years With the Indian Tribes on the American Frontiers* (Philadelphia, 1851). *Algic Researches,* 2 vols. (New York, 1839), includes Indian oral legends, compiled over many years. For the state of New York, Schoolcraft compiled *Notes on the Iroquois* (New York, 1846).

The descriptive accounts of his Mississippi River and Missouri trips are in *A View of the Lead Mines of Missouri* (New York, 1819), *Narrative Journal of Travels Through the Northwestern Regions of the United States . . . to the Sources of the Mississippi River* (New York, 1821), and *Narrative of an Expedition Through the Upper Mississippi to Itasca Lake the Actual Source of the Mississippi* (New York, 1834).

II. SECONDARY LITERATURE. For an effusive biography of Schoolcraft, a long list of shorter biographical sources, and an extensive bibliography of his writings, see Chase S. Osborn and Stellanova Osborn, *Schoolcraft-Longfellow-Hiawatha* (Lancaster, Pa., 1942).

ELIZABETH NOBLE SHOR

SCHOOTEN, FRANS VAN (*b.* Leiden, Netherlands, *ca.* 1615; *d.* Leiden, 29 May 1660), *mathematics.*

Schooten's father, Frans van Schooten the Elder, succeeded Ludolph van Ceulen at the engineering school in Leiden. The younger Schooten enrolled at the University of Leiden in 1631 and was carefully trained in the tradition of the Dutch school of algebra. In early youth he studied Michael Stifel's edition of Christoph Rudolff's German *Coss.* He was also acquainted with the Dutch and French editions of the works of Simon Stevin, with van Ceulen's *Arithmetische en geometrische Fondamenten,* and with Albert Girard's *Invention nouvelle en l'algèbre.* Schooten studied Girard's edition of the mathematical works of Samuel Marolois and his edition of Stevin's *Arithmétique.* He was of course familiar with Commandino's editions of Archimedes, Apollonius, and Pappus, and with Cavalieri's geometry of indivisibles.

It was probably through his teacher, the Arabist and mathematician Jakob Gool, that Schooten met Descartes, who had just come to Leiden from Utrecht to supervise the printing of the *Discours de la méthode* (1637). Schooten saw the proofs of the *Géométrie* (the third supplement to the *Discours*) by the summer of 1637 at the latest. He recognized the utility of the new notation, but he had difficulty in mastering the contents of the work. He therefore undertook a more intensive study of literature on the subject and sought to discuss the work with colleagues.

Armed with letters of introduction from Descartes, Schooten went to Paris. Although he was a convinced Arminian, he received an extremely cordial welcome from the Minimite friar Marin Mersenne and his circle. In Paris, Schooten was able to read manuscripts of Viète and Fermat; and, on a commission from the Leiden printing firm of Elzevier, he gathered all the printed works of Viète that he could find. He went next to England, where he met the leading algebraists of the day, and finally to Ireland.

Schooten returned home in 1643 and served as his father's lecture assistant, introducing a number of young people—including Jan de Witt—to mathematics. He also prepared a collected edition of the mathematical writings of Viète (1646). Although Schooten generally followed the original texts closely, he did change the notation in several places to simplify the mathematical statements and to make the material more accessible, for Viète's idiosyncratic presentation and the large number of Greek technical terms rendered the originals quite difficult to read. Unfortunately, because he misunderstood a remark that Viète made concerning the unsuccessful edition of his *Canon mathematicus* (1579), Schooten omitted this work and the interesting explanatory remarks that accompanied it from his edition. Schooten had also brought back copies of Fermat's papers, but he was unable to convince Elzevier to publish them, especially since Descartes had expressed an unfavorable opinion of Fermat's work.

In 1645 Christiaan Huygens and his elder brother Constantijn began to study law at Leiden. They attended Schooten's general introductory course (published by Erasmus Bartholin in 1651), and in advanced private instruction became acquainted with many interesting questions in mathematics. A close friendship developed between Schooten and Christiaan Huygens, as their voluminous correspondence attests. The letters reveal how quickly Huygens outgrew the solicitous guidance of his teacher to become the leading mathematician and physicist of his time.

Schooten's first independent work was a study of the kinematic generation of conic sections (1646). In an appendix he treated the reduction of higher-order binomial irrationals $\sqrt[n]{a} + \sqrt{b}$ to the form $x + \sqrt{y}$ in cases where this is possible, using a development of a procedure of Stifel's. An interesting problem that Schooten considered was how to construct a cyclic quadrilateral of given sides, one of which is to be the diameter—a problem that Newton later treated in the lectures on *Arithmetica universalis* (*Mathematical Papers*, V, 162–181).

After the death of his father in 1645, Schooten took over his academic duties. He also worked on a Latin translation of Descartes's *Géométrie*. Although Descartes was not completely satisfied with Schooten's version (1649), it found a broad and receptive audience by virtue of its more carefully executed figures and its full commentary. It was from Schooten's edition of the *Géométrie* that contemporary mathematicians lacking proficiency in French first learned Cartesian mathematics. In this mathematics they encountered a systematic presentation of the material, not the customary, more classificatory approach that essentially listed single propositions, for the most part in unconnected parallel. Further, in the Cartesian scheme the central position was occupied by algebra, which Descartes considered to be the only "precise form of mathematics."

The great success of Schooten's edition led him to prepare a second, much enlarged one in two volumes (1659–1661), which became the standard mathematical work of the period. A third edition appeared in 1683, and an appendix to the fourth edition (1695) contained interesting remarks by Jakob Bernoulli. In the second edition Schooten not only greatly expanded his commentary, but also added new material including an example of Fermat's extreme value and tangent method (with a reference to Hérigone's *Cursus mathematicus* [*Supplementum*, 1642]) and a peculiar procedure for determining the center of gravity of parabolic segments. Since Fermat was not mentioned in the latter connection, it is likely that Schooten came upon the procedure independently, for he usually cited his sources very conscientiously.

In the first edition (1649) Schooten inserted Debeaune's rather insignificant *Notae breves* to the *Géométrie*. The commentary of the second edition contained valuable contributions by Huygens dealing with the intersections of a parabola with a circle and certain corollaries, as well as on an improved method of constructing tangents to the conchoid. Schooten also included longer contributions by his students: Jan Hudde's studies on equations and the rule of extreme values and Hendrik van Heuraet's rectification method.

Volume II of the second edition of the *Geometria* (1661) commences with a reprinting of Schooten's introductory lectures. This material is followed by Debeaune's work on the limits of roots of equations and then by de Witt's excellent tract on conic sections. The volume concludes with a paper by Schooten's younger half brother Pieter on the algebraic discussion of Descartes's data. This edition shows the great effort Schooten devoted to the training of his students and to the dissemination of their findings. This effort can be seen even more clearly in his wide-ranging correspondence, most of which is reprinted in Huygens' *Oeuvres complètes*. (Unfortunately, not all of Schooten's correspondence has been located.)

Schooten made an original contribution to mathematics with his *Exercitationes mathematicae* (1657). Book I contains elementary arithmetic and geometry problems similar to those found in van Ceulen's collection. Book II is devoted to constructions using straight lines only and Book III to the reconstruction of Apollonius' *Plane Loci* on the basis of hints given by Pappus. Book IV is a revised version of Schooten's treatment of the kinematic generation of conic sections, and Book V offers a collection of interesting individual problems. Worth noting, in particular, is the restatement of Hudde's method for the step-by-step building-up of equations for angular section and the determination of the girth of the folium of Descartes: $x^3 + y^3 = 3\,axy$. Also noteworthy is the determination of Heronian triangles of equal perimeter and equal area (Roberval's problem) according to Descartes's method (1633). As an appendix Schooten printed Huygens' *De ratiociniis in aleae ludo*, which was extremely important in the development of the theory of probability.

Schooten possessed an excellent knowledge of the mathematics of both his own time and earlier periods. Besides being an extraordinarily industrious and conscientious scholar, a skillful commentator, and an inspiring teacher, he was a man of rare unselfishness. He recognized his own limitations and did not seek to overstep them. Fascinated by the personality and ideas of Descartes, he worked hard to popularize the new mathematics; his highly successful efforts assured its triumph.

BIBLIOGRAPHY

I. ORIGINAL WORKS. Schooten's writings include his ed. of Viète's *Opera mathematica* (Leiden, 1646); *De organica conicarum sectionum in plano descriptione* (Leiden, 1646); *Geometria a Renato Descartes anno 1637 gallice edita, nunc autem . . . in linguam latinam versa* (Leiden, 1649; 2nd ed., 2 vols., Amsterdam, 1659–1661; 3rd ed., 1683; 4th ed., Frankfurt, 1695): *Principia matheseos universalis*, E. Bartholin, ed. (Leiden, 1651), also included in the 2nd ed. of *Geometria; Exercitationum mathematicarum libri quinque* (Leiden, 1657), also in Flemish as *Mathematische Oefeningen* (Amsterdam, 1660); and "Tractatus de concinnandis demonstrationibus geometricis ex calculo algebraico," Pieter van Schooten, ed., in the 2nd ed. of *Geometria*.

II. SECONDARY LITERATURE. See J. E. Hofmann, "Frans van Schooten der Jüngere," in *Boethius*, II (Wiesbaden, 1962), with portrait; and C. de Waard, "Schooten, Frans van," in *Nieuw Nederlandsch biographisch woordenboeck*, VII (1927), 1110–1114.

J. E. HOFMANN

SCHOPFER, WILLIAM-HENRI (*b*. Yverdon, Switzerland, 8 May 1900; *d*. Geneva, Switzerland, 19 June 1962), *biology, microbiology, biochemistry*.

Schopfer received all of his higher education in Geneva and was awarded two *licences* in the natural sciences, one in 1923 and another in 1925. He won the Prix Davy for his first works, which were concerned essentially with parasitology and protozoology and dealt particularly with the molecular concentration of the juices of parasites (trematodes and cestodes). While working in the general botany laboratory, Schopfer prepared a dissertation under the direction of Robert Chodat. In 1928 he received his doctorate from the University of Geneva after presenting his remarkable work on the sexuality of mushrooms, in which he treated a completely new problem, the comparative biochemistry of sexual reproduction. Schopfer studied abroad on several occasions, notably at the Pasteur Institute in Paris, at the biological station at Roscoff, and in Berlin (1929–1930), where he worked with Hans Kniep, an outstanding specialist in the sexuality of microorganisms.

Schopfer advanced quickly in his academic career. In 1929 he was a *Privatdozent* in general physiology at the Faculty of Sciences of Geneva, and in 1933 he accepted the chair of botany and general biology at the University of Bern. In the same year he became director of the university botanical institute and garden. He remained there until his death, occupying the post of dean of the Faculty of Sciences in 1941–1942 and that of rector in 1948–1949. Schopfer was president of the Swiss Society of Microbiology (1942–1943) and of the Swiss Society for the History of Medicine and Natural Sciences (from 1946), and vice-president of the International Union of the History and Philosophy of Science. In addition he was actively involved with the scientific journals *Archiv für Mikrobiologie, Enzymologia, Excerpta medica*, and *Internationale Zeitschrift für Vitaminforschung*. Schopfer was awarded honorary doctorates by the Paris Faculty of Pharmacy (1949), the Nancy Faculty of Pharmacy (1950), the Lyons Faculty of Sciences (1950), and the Besançon Faculty of Sciences (1956). Between 1923 and 1962 he published 299 scientific works and directed twenty-two doctoral dissertations.

It was in 1927 that Schopfer, after about twenty works devoted primarily to protozoology, published his first memoir on the sexuality of the Mucoraceae. Henceforth the path of his research was clearly marked. All of Schopfer's works and the majority of those by his students were devoted to the study of the role of organic factors controlling the growth of microorganisms. Schopfer opened the immense area of research on microbial vitamins, in which plant and animal biochemists and physiologists met.

In 1930 he inaugurated a series of experiments, which became classics, on the mold *Phycomyces blakesleeanus*. Following an apparently fortuitous observation, in 1931 Schopfer made a series of studies that were decisive for the new science of vitaminology. This *Phycomyces* cannot grow on a synthetic medium containing purified maltose, but it will grow if unpurified maltose is used. Schopfer then demonstrated that the impurity, linked to maltose, was vitamin B_1. In this way it was demonstrated for the first time that an animal vitamin was necessary to the growth of a fungus. In many subsequent papers Schopfer demonstrated the roles of riboflavin, biotin, and mesoinositol—to cite only the well-known compounds—in the growth of microorganisms. To the classic distinction between autotrophic and heterotrophic individuals, Schopfer added that between auxoautotrophic species, capable of producing the vitamins necessary for their growth, and the auxoheterotrophic species incapable of synthesizing them. He devoted a series of studies to what he called artificial symbiosis. He showed, for example, that certain mushrooms that need only one of the constituents of the vitamin B complex, such as *Rhodotorula rubra*, the growth of which requires pyrimidine, and *Mucor ramanninanus*, which needs thiazole, are able to live in association without these substances.

But Schopfer employed mainly *Phycomyces* as a biological test of the quantitative dosage of vitamin B₁, and it permitted him to determine precisely a group of questions concerning the biosynthesis of vitamins, their role in the soil, and their importance for the higher organisms. Schopfer also concentrated on the mechanisms of action of these vitamins and demonstrated the effects of structurally similar substances that behave as antagonists, which he called antivitamins. All the investigation of vitamins conducted by Schopfer and his students were joined with those of other scientists in a remarkable work published in 1939, then reworked and completed in English as *Plants and Vitamins* (1943). Schopfer also conducted research on nitrogen metabolism, the in vitro culture of plant organs, graftings, and morphogenesis.

In addition to research, Schopfer was greatly interested in the history of science; and his studies in the history of biology are valuable for the abundance of their documentation and for his critical analysis of the facts discussed. Among his writings in this field are "L'histoire des théories relatives à la génération au 18me et au 19me siècle" (1944), *La recherche de l'unité en biologie* (1948), and a study of the work of Jules Raulin (1949). He also produced *Situation de la biologie dans le système des sciences* (1951), *L'évolution de la méthode en biologie du point de vue de l'histoire des sciences* (1952), and an edition of the letters of Leeuwenhoek (1955).

BIBLIOGRAPHY

I. ORIGINAL WORKS. A list of 299 scientific papers by Schopfer was published in *Mitteilungen der Naturforschenden Gesellschaft in Bern*, **20** (1964), 86–102. They include "Vitamine und Wachstumsfaktoren bei den Mikroorganismen, mit besonderer Berücksichtigung des Vitamins B₁," in *Ergebnisse der Biologie*, **16** (1939), 1–172; revised and enlarged as *Plants and Vitamins*, N. N. Noecker, trans. (Waltham, Mass., 1943; 2nd ed., 1949); "Les vitamines, facteurs de croissance pour les microorganismes," in *Schweizerische Zeitschrift für Pathologie und Bakteriologie*, **7** (1944), 303–345; "L'histoire des théories relatives à la génération au 18me et au 19me siècle," in *Actes de la Société helvétique des sciences naturelles* (1944), 192–193; "Les tests microbiologiques pour la détermination des vitamines," in *Experientia*, **1** (1945), 183–194, 219–229; *La recherche de l'unité en biologie* (Bern, 1948); *Les répercussions hors de France de l'oeuvre de Jules Raulin relative au zinc* (Lyons, 1948); "Remarque bibliographique sur l'histoire du terme Cambium," in *Archives internationales d'histoire des sciences*, **28** (1949), 457–458; "Situation de la biologie dans le systeme des sciences; les relations de la biologie avec les autres sciences," in *Actes de la Société helvétique des sciences naturelles* (1951), 68–80; "Le méso-inositol en biologie," in *Bulletin de la Société de chimie biologique*, **83** (1951), 1113–1146; "L'évolution de la méthode en biologie du point de vue de l'histoire des sciences," in *Actes scientifiques et industrielles Herrman*, **8** (1952), 117–125; "Les cultures d'organes et leurs applications en physiologie végétale," in *Actes de la Société helvétique des sciences naturelles* (1952), 61–73; "La botanique et le bien-être humain," in *Actes du 8me congrès international botanique, 1954* (1959), 53–57; and "Recherches sur le role du méso-inositol dans la biologie cellulaire de *Schizosaccharomyces pombe* Lindner," in *Archiv fur Mikrobiologie*, **44** (1962), 113–151, his last work.

II. SECONDARY LITERATURE. See K. H. Erismann, "William-Henri Schopfer (1900–1962)," in *Verhandlungen der Schweizerischen naturforschenden Gesellschaft*, **142**, pt. 1 (1962), 252–258; and "Die wissenschaftlichen Arbeiten von Prof. Dr. W.-H. Schopfer: Chronologisch geordner von 1923 bis 1962," in *Mitteilungen der Naturforschenden Gesellschaft in Bern*, n.s. **20** (1963), 86–102; and A. Tronchet, "Rapport sur l'attribution du Dr. H. C. de l'Université de Besançon à M. le professeur Schopfer," in *Annales scientifiques de l'Université de Besançon*, 2nd ser., **2** (1958), 1–4.

P. E. PILET

SCHORLEMMER, CARL (*b.* Darmstadt, Germany, 30 September 1834; *d.* Manchester, England, 27 June 1892), *organic chemistry, history of chemistry.*

Schorlemmer was the son of Johann Schorlemmer, a master carpenter. After attending the *Volksschule* and the *Realschule*, he enrolled at what is now the Technische Universität of Darmstadt. In 1853 he became an apprentice pharmacist in Umstadt (Hesse) and then an assistant pharmacist in Heidelberg. In the latter city Schorlemmer attended Bunsen's lectures, gave up pharmacy, and began to study chemistry. In 1858 he enrolled at the University of Giessen, where he studied chemistry for a semester under Heinrich Will and Hermann Kopp. On the advice of his friend William Dittmar he went to Manchester the following year. He began as a private assistant to H. E. Roscoe at Owens College, became an assistant instructor in 1861, lecturer in 1872, and in 1874, on Roscoe's recommendation, England's first professor of organic chemistry, at Owens College.

In the years before he became a professor, Schorlemmer experimented with simple hydrocarbons. During this period he made important contributions to the development of modern organic chemistry, including investigations of the compounds "methyl" (CH_3-CH_3) and "ethyl hydride" (C_2H_5H), which he recognized as equivalent (that is, ethane) and not isomeric, as had been suggested. Industrial research on coal tar distillate and American petroleum (naphtha) constituted the first petrochemical investigations.

Kopp's influence can be seen in Schorlemmer's experimental investigations, especially his studies on the relations between boiling point and chemical constitution, and it is unmistakable in Schorlemmer's works on the history of chemistry. A close friend of Friedrich Engels and Karl Marx, Schorlemmer became a member of the International Workingmen's Association and of the German Social Democratic party. A believer in scientific socialism, and in dialectical and historical materialism, Schorlemmer presented the history of chemistry from a sociological point of view and discovered important relations between chemistry, economics, and philosophy.

Schorlemmer was a member of many scientific societies and academies. The technical college at Merseburg, German Democratic Republic, is named for him.

BIBLIOGRAPHY

I. ORIGINAL WORKS. Schorlemmer's writings include *Lehrbuch der Kohlenstoffverbindungen* (Brunswick, 1874), also in English, *A Manual of the Chemistry of the Carbon Compounds or Organic Chemistry* (London, 1874); *Treatise of Chemistry* (London, 1877), also in German, *Ausführliches Lehrbuch der Chemie* (Brunswick, 1877), written with H. E. Roscoe; and *The Rise and Development of Organic Chemistry* (Manchester, 1879; 2nd ed., London, 1895), also in German, *Der Ursprung und die Entwicklung der organischen Chemie* (Brunswick, 1889).

Schorlemmer also translated two works by H. E. Roscoe: *Kurzes Lehrbuch der Chemie* (Brunswick, 1868) and *Die Spektralanalyse* (Brunswick, 1870).

II. SECONDARY LITERATURE. Appreciations and obituaries are in *Berichte der Deutschen chemischen Gesellschaft*, **25** (1892), 1106 ff.; *Festschrift der Technische Hochschule für Chemie "Carl Schorlemmer"* (Merseburg, 1964), 12 ff.; *Journal of the Chemical Society. Transactions*, **63** (1893), 756–763, with a complete bibliography of Schorlemmer's papers; *Nature*, **46**, no.

1191 (25 Aug. 1892), 394–395; and "Vorwärts 3.7. 1892," in Karl Marx and Friedrich Engels, *Werke*, XXII (Berlin, 1963), 313–315. See also Karl Heinig, "Carl Schorlemmer—der erste marxistische Chemiker. Darstellung seines wissenschaftlichen und gesellschaftlichen Wirkens" (Ph.D. diss., Humboldt University, Berlin, 1968); and *Carl Schorlemmer—Chemiker und Kommunist ersten Ranges* (Leipzig, 1974), with bibliography of Schorlemmer's works and secondary literature.

KARL HEINIG

SCHOTT, CHARLES ANTHONY (*b.* Mannheim, Germany, 7 August 1826; *d.* Washington, D.C., 31 July 1901), *geophysics.*

Schott studied for six years at the Technische Hochschule in Karlsruhe, graduating as a civil engineer. The revolution of 1848, in which he participated briefly, and poor career prospects led him to emigrate to the United States in that year. On 8 December 1848 he received an appointment in the U.S. Coast Survey and remained in its service until his death. His initial post was in the agency's computing division; in 1855 he became its chief, relinquishing the title in 1899.

Although Schott had various field assignments, his career was principally in the Washington office. His division was responsible for processing the data gathered by Survey parties. Before the age of electronic computers these calculations were arduous, if not tedious, often requiring great ingenuity in devising shortcuts and methods of approximation. But Schott's importance in the Coast Survey far transcended his industry and cleverness in computing. On him, perhaps more than any other individual, depended the precision and the theoretical adequacy of the Survey's work. This involved not only the study of the instruments, observational techniques, and data but also appraisals of proposed innovations, including theoretical changes.

Evaluating Schott's role is awkward, since the Coast Survey was a team effort and its publications often did not identify particular contributors. Yet his bibliography and the esteem accorded by informed contemporaries are clues to his stature. Before John F. Hayford, Schott was the leading geodesist in the Survey. His work on the great triangulation across the continent was a high point in the older style of determining the figure of the earth, yielding results falling between those of Bessel and Alexander Ross Clarke. Like others in the Coast Survey, Schott was greatly interested in terrestrial magnetism and was responsible for several studies in this area. When the French Academy awarded him the Wilde Prize in 1898 for his contributions, it was recognition for nearly fifty years of collecting and reducing data, constructing new apparatus, studying the influence of the aurora, and investigating the relations of sunspots and magnetic storms.

Schott was also well-known for his climatological studies. The principal evidence of his scientific competence remains unpublished and unstudied in the records of the Coast and Geodetic Survey in the United States National Archives, which contain nearly 150 volumes of his reports on scientific topics, as well as similar documents dispersed in many of the agency's series of records.

BIBLIOGRAPHY

Cleveland Abbe's memoir of Schott in *Biographical Memoirs. National Academy of Sciences,* **8** (1915), 87–133, contains a very good bibliography of Schott's writings but is not very enlightening on his life. The greatest source is Record Group 23 of the U.S. National Archives, the Records of the Coast and Geodetic Survey. They are described by N. Reingold, in *Preliminary Inventory of the National Archives,* no. 105 (Washington, D.C., 1958). Of particular relevance are the Computing Division Reports (entry 45) and Geodetic Reports (entry 83).

NATHAN REINGOLD

SCHOTT, GASPAR (*b.* Königshofen, near Würzburg, Germany, 5 February 1608; *d.* Würzburg, 22 May 1666), *mathematics, physics, technology.*

Apart from the place and date of his birth, nothing is known of Schott's origins; almost the only childhood recollection in his works is of a suction pump bursting at Paderborn in 1620, which suggests an early interest in machinery. In 1627 he entered the Society of Jesus and was sent to Würzburg University, where he studied philosophy under Athanasius Kircher. The Swedish invasion of the Palatinate in 1631 forced teacher and pupils to flee. Schott may have first accompanied Kircher to France, for he mentions his travels in that country; but he certainly completed his studies in theology, philosophy, and mathematics at Palermo. He remained in Sicily for twenty years, mostly teaching at Palermo, although he spent two years at Trapani. Nevertheless he was anxious to satisfy a strong thirst for knowledge and to resume his connection with Kircher, whom he always revered as his master. Schott was able to satisfy his desire in 1652, when he was sent to Rome, where for three years he collaborated with Kircher on his researches. Schott decided that since Kircher did not have time to publish all that he knew and all the information communicated to him by Jesuits abroad, he himself would do so. While compiling this material, he returned to Germany in the summer of 1655, first to Mainz and then to Würzburg, where he taught mathematics and physics.

Schott first published what had originally been intended as a brief guide to the hydraulic and pneumatic instruments in Kircher's Roman museum, expanding it into the first version of his *Mechanica hydraulico-pneumatica.* But he added as an appendix a detailed account of Guericke's experiments on vacuums, the earliest published report of this work. This supplement contributed greatly to the success of Schott's compendium; and as a result he became the center of a network of correspondence as other Jesuits, as well as lay experimenters and mechanicians, wrote to inform him of their inventions and discoveries. Schott exchanged several letters with Guericke, seeking to draw him out by suggesting new problems, and published his later investigations. He also corresponded with Huygens and was the first to make Boyle's work on the air pump widely known in Germany. Schott repeated Guericke's experiments, and later those of Boyle, at Würzburg, as well as some medical experiments on the effects of intravenous injections. He does not, however, seem to have attempted any original investigations.

During the last years of his life, Schott was engaged in publishing this mass of material, besides what he had brought with him from Rome, adding his own commentaries and footnotes: he produced some eleven titles over eight years (1658–1666). But although his industry was impressive, these books consist largely of extracts from communications he had received or from books he had used. Schott was so determined to include all possible arguments on every side that it is often hard to discover what he himself thought. While he maintained that the experiments of Guericke, Torricelli, Boyle, and others had not produced a true vacuum, the space exhausted of air being filled with "aether," he accepted the assumption that the phenomena previously attributed to the effects of *horror vacui* were really due to atmospheric pressure or to the elasticity of the air. In a treatise on the then very popular theme of the origin of springs, his own opinion, when finally expressed, amounted to saying that everyone was right: some springs are due to precipitation, some to underground condensation, and some are connected directly to the sea.

Schott's chief works, the *Magia universalis* and the two companion volumes, *Physica curiosa* and *Technica curiosa,* are huge, uncritical collections, mines of quaint information in which significant nuggets must be extracted from a great deal of dross. Like many of his time, Schott believed that the principles of nature and art are best revealed in their exceptions. This makes him a useful source on the history of scientific instruments and mechanical technology; a treatise on "chronometric marvels" (which may be his own, since it is ascribed to "a friend" and often quotes his earlier writings) contains the first description of a universal joint to translate motion and a classification of gear teeth. Although the "natural curiosities" include some useful matter (such as on South American mammals), his syncretic attitude and taste for the abnormal made him far readier than most of his contemporaries to credit tales of ghosts, demons, and centaurs. All this writing about magic, both natural and supernatural, involved him in slight difficulties with the censors.

Schott apparently yearned for the intellectual delights of Rome, and after twenty-five years in Italy he suffered from German winters and had to have his own hypocaust installed. He visited Rome in 1661, and in 1664 he applied for a post to teach mathematics at the Jesuits' Roman college; this was rejected, and instead he was offered the headship of the college at Heiligenstadt, which he rejected, feeling himself unsuited to administration. Exhausted, it was said, by overwork on his books, he died in 1666.

Undoubtedly Schott was extraordinarily productive. But his contribution was essentially that of an editor who prepared the researches of others for the press without adding much of consequence. Still, he did much to popularize the achievements of contemporary physicists, especially—but not exclusively—in Catholic Germany.

BIBLIOGRAPHY

I. ORIGINAL WORKS. Schott's most important writings are *Mechanica hydraulico-pneumatica* (Würzburg, 1657); *Magia universalis,* 4 vols. (Würzburg, 1657–1659); *Physica curiosa,* 2 vols. (Würzburg, 1662); *Anatomia physico-hydrostatica fontium ac fluminum* (Würzburg, 1663); and *Technica curiosa* (Würzburg, 1664).

II. SECONDARY LITERATURE. All later articles are based on N. Southwell [N. Bacon], *Bibliotheca scriptorum Societatis Jesu* (Rome, 1682), 282; and A. de Backer, in *Bibliothèque des écrivains de la Compagnie de Jésus,* K. Sommervogel, ed., VII (Paris, 1896), 904–912. The only later biographer to add further information is G. Duhr, *Geschichte der Jesuiten in den Ländern deutscher Zunge,* III (Munich–Regensburg, 1923), 587–592.

A. G. KELLER

SCHOTT, OTTO FRIEDRICH (*b.* Witten, Germany, 17 December 1851; *d.* Jena, Germany, 27 August 1935), *glass chemistry, glass manufacture.*

A leading pioneer in glass chemistry, Schott created new types of glass of outstanding quality for use in optics, in the laboratory, and in industry. He came from a family of glassmakers: his father, a master in the making of window glass, became co-owner of a glassworks in Westphalia in 1853. Schott attended the *Realschule* in Witten and the trade school in Hagen. In 1869 he volunteered for service in chemical factories in Haspe and abroad. From 1870 to 1873 he studied chemistry and chemical technology at the technical college in Aachen and at the universities of Würzburg and Leipzig. He received his doctorate from the University of Jena in 1875 for a work on defects in window glass manufacturing. He then returned to Haspe as an industrial chemist and made study trips to England and France. In 1877–1878 he established an iodine and saltpeter factory in Oviedo, Spain, and in 1880 was responsible for the renovation of two Spanish glassworks.

In May 1879 Schott sent a sample of his newly smelted lithium glass to Ernst Abbe, requesting him to test its optical properties. The ensuing close collaboration between the two researchers led Schott to move to Jena in 1882. Glasses with high refractive power had always possessed high dispersive power and consequently could not satisfy the theoretical requirements for optical systems that Abbe had set forth. But the glass samples that Schott smelted finally made possible "a large variety in the gradation of optical characteristics," as Abbe wrote in 1881, and far surpassed the existing types of glass.

Putting to use his energy and talent for the technical application of knowledge, Schott, along with his associates Abbe, Carl Zeiss, and the latter's son Roderich, founded a glass technology laboratory in 1883 and, in 1884, the Glastechnische Versuchsanstalt at Jena. The latter, which subsequently became the Jena glassworks of Schott and Associates, soon achieved world fame for its Jena standard glass 16 III (thermometer glass, 1884), the laboratory glasses (beginning in 1892), Supraxglass

(1890's), uviol glass (1903), and apparatus glass 20 (1920). Schott directed the factory—which in 1919 became part of the Carl Zeiss Foundation—until 1927 and was the recipient of many honors.

BIBLIOGRAPHY

I. ORIGINAL WORKS. Schott's writings and patents include *Beiträge zur Theorie und Praxis der Glasfabrikation* (Jena, 1875), his dissertation; "Chemische Vorgänge beim Schmelzen des Glassatzes," in *Dinglers polytechnisches Journal,* **215** (1875), 529–538; "Ueber Abkühlung des Glases und vom sogenannten Hartglase," *ibid.,* **216** (1875), 75–78, 288; "Ueber die Constitution des Glases," *ibid.,* 346–353; "Ueber Krystallisations-Produkte im gewöhnlichen Glase," in *Annalen der Physik und Chemie,* **155** (1875), 422–442, also in *Dinglers polytechnisches Journal,* **218** (1875), 151–165; "Gewinnung des Schwefels aus Gyps und Glaubersalz bei der Glasfabrikation," *ibid.,* **221** (1876), 142–146 (Prussian patent of 3 Dec. 1875); "Studien über die Härtung des Glases," in *Verhandlungen des Vereins zur Beförderung des Gewerbefleisses,* **58** (1879), 273–305; "Lithiumglas," *ibid.,* **59** (1880), 130–135; *Beiträge zur Kenntniss der unorganischen Schmelzverbindungen* (Brunswick, 1881); "Über Glasschmelzerei für optische und andere wissenschaftliche Zwecke," in *Verhandlungsberichte des Vereins zur Beförderung des Gewerbefleisses,* **67** (1888), 162–180; and "Verfahren zur Herstellung von Verbund-Hartglas," *Patentschrift* no. 51, 578, Kl. 82, Glas, issued 11 Mar. 1892 (German patent issued 5 Apr. 1891). His scientific papers on the physical properties of new glasses written with A. Winkelmann were published in *Annalen der Physik und Chemie,* n.s. **51** (1894), 698–720, 730–746; **61** (1897), 105–141; and "Über elektrisches Kapillarlicht," *ibid.,* **59** (1896), 768–772.

Scientific correspondence includes *Der Briefwechsel zwischen Otto Schott und Ernst Abbe über das optische Glas 1879–1881,* H. Kühnert, ed. (Jena, 1946), with bibliography of Schott's scientific papers on p. xxxv; and *Briefe und Dokumente zur Geschichte des VEB Optik Jenaer Glaswerk Schott & Genossen,* I, *Die wissenschaftliche Grundlegung (Glastechnisches Laboratorium und Versuchsglashütte) 1882–1884,* H. Kühnert, ed. (Jena, 1953), with bibliography of Schott's scientific papers on pp. lxxix–lxxxi.

There are also bibliographies in Poggendorff, III, 1209; IV, 1346; and VI, 2364.

II. SECONDARY LITERATURE. Obituaries and other biographical notes are listed in Poggendorff, VIIa, 240. See especially E. Berger, in *Zeitschrift für technische Physik,* **17** (1936), 6–11; G. Keppler, in *Glastechnische Berichte,* **14** (1936), 49–54; H. Kühnert, in *Zeitschrift für technische Physik,* **17** (1936), 1–6; H. Schimank, in *Glastechnische Berichte,* **25** (1952), 18–24; A. Silverman, in *Bulletin of the American Ceramics Society,* **15** (1936), 169–175; and W. E. S. Turner, in *Journal of the Society of Glass Technology,* **20** (1936), 84–94.

Other literature is E. Berger, "50 Jahre Jenaer Glas," in *Zeiss Nachrichten,* no. 8 (Jan. 1935), 1–7; H. Kühnert, *Urkundenbuch zur Thüringischen Glashüttengeschichte* (Jena, 1934), 271–281; and *Otto Schott. Eine Studie über seine Wittener Zeit bis zur Gründung des Jenaer Glaswerkes* (Witten, 1940); M. von Rohr, "Zu Otto Schotts siebzigsten Geburtstag (17. Dez.)," in *Naturwissenschaften,* **9** (1921), 999–1010; and "Die Entwicklungsjahre der Kunst, optisches Glas zu schmelzen," *ibid.,* **12** (1924), 781–797; and E. Zschimmer, *Die Glasindustrie in Jena—ein Werk von Schott und Abbe,* 2nd ed. (Jena, 1923).

Also see E. Abbe, *Gesammelte Abhandlungen,* IV, pt. 1, *Arbeiten zum Glaswerk zwischen 1882 und 1885. Die Entstehung des Glaswerkes Schott & Gen.,* M. von Rohr. ed. (Jena, 1928); F. Auerbach, *Ernst Abbe* (Leipzig, 1918); and N. Günther, "Ernst Abbe," in *Dictionary of Scientific Biography,* I, 6–9.

HANS-GÜNTHER KÖRBER

SCHOTTKY, FRIEDRICH HERMANN (*b.* Breslau, Germany [now Wrocław, Poland], 24 July 1851; *d.* Berlin, Germany, 12 August 1935), *mathematics.*

After attending the Humanistisches Gymnasium St. Magdalenen in Breslau, Schottky studied mathematics and physics at Breslau University from 1870 to 1874 and continued his studies at Berlin with Weierstrass and Helmholtz. He received the Ph.D. in 1875, was admitted as a *Privatdozent* at Berlin in 1878, and in 1882 was appointed a professor at Zurich—at the university, according to one source, and at the Eidgenössische Technische Hochschule, according to another. In 1892 Schottky was appointed to a chair at Marburg University and in 1902 to one at Berlin, where he remained until 1922. In 1902 he was elected a fellow of the Preussische Akademie der Wissenschaften and, in 1911, a corresponding member of the Akademie der Wissenschaften in Göttingen.

Schottky's thesis [1,3] was an important contribution to the conformal mapping of multiply connected plane domains and was the origin of the famous mapping of a domain bounded by three disjoint circles, which, continued by mirror images, provides an example of an automorphic function with a Cantor set boundary. The dissertation also dealt with the conformal mapping of domains bounded by circular and conic arcs.

A contribution to the realm of Picard's theorem, known as Schottky's theorem [5], is an absolute estimation $C(f(0), |z|)$ for functions $f(z)$ defined in

$|z| < 1$ and omitting the values 0,1. Schottky also initiated the study of the oscillation, at the boundary, of regular functions defined in the unit circle [4].

The greater part of Schottky's work concerned elliptic, Abelian, and theta functions, a subject on which he wrote a book [2]. He published some fifty-five papers, most of them in *Journal für die reine und angewandte Mathematik, Mathematische Annalen,* and *Sitzungsberichte der Preussischen Akademie der Wissenschaften zu Berlin.* His work is difficult to read. Although he was a student of Weierstrass, his approach to function theory was Riemannian in spirit, combined with Weierstrassian rigor.

BIBLIOGRAPHY

I. ORIGINAL WORKS. Schottky's writings include [1] "Ueber die conforme Abbildung mehrfach zusammenhängender ebener Flächen," in *Journal für die reine und angewandte Mathematik,* **83** (1877), 300–351, his dissertation; [2] *Abriss einer Theorie der Abel'schen Functionen von drei Variablen* (Leipzig, 1880); [3] "Ueber eine specielle Function, welche bei einer bestimmten linearen Transformation ihres Arguments unverändert bleibt," in *Journal für die reine und angewandte Mathematik,* **101** (1887), 227–272; [4] "Ueber die Werteschwankungen der harmonischen Functionen," *ibid.,* **117** (1897), 225–253; [5] "Ueber den Picardschen Satz und die Borelschen Ungleichungen," in *Sitzungsberichte der Preussischen Akademie der Wissenschaften zu Berlin* (1904), 1244–1262; and "Bemerkungen zu meiner Mitteilung . . . ," *ibid.* (1906), 32–36.

II. SECONDARY LITERATURE. See [6] L. Bieberbach, "Friedrich Schottky zum 80. Geburtstage," in *Forschungen und Fortschritte,* **7** (1931), 300; and [7] "Gedächtnisrede auf Friedrich Schottky," in *Sitzungsberichte der Preussischen Akademie der Wissenschaften zu Berlin,* Math.-phys. Kl. (1936), cv–cvi; and the [8] obituary in *Nachrichten von der Gesellschaft der Wissenschaften zu Göttingen* (1935–1936), 6–7.

Portraits of Schottky are in *Acta mathematica 1882–1913, Table générale des tomes 1–35* (Uppsala, 1913), 168; and *Journal für die reine und angewandte Mathematik,* **165** (1931), frontispiece.

HANS FREUDENTHAL

SCHOUTE, PIETER HENDRIK (*b.* Wormerveer, Netherlands, 21 January 1846; *d.* Groningen, Netherlands, 18 April 1923), *mathematics.*

Schoute, whose family were industrialists on the Zaan near Amsterdam, studied at the Polytechnical School at Delft, from which he graduated in 1867 as a civil engineer. He continued his study of mathematics at Leiden, where he received his Ph.D. in 1870 with the dissertation "Homography Applied to the Theory of Quadric Surfaces." While teaching at high schools in Nijmegen (1871–1874) and The Hague (1874–1881), he published two textbooks on cosmography. From 1881 until his death he was professor of mathematics at the University of Groningen.

Schoute was a typical geometer. In his early work he investigated quadrics, algebraic curves, complexes, and congruences in the spirit of nineteenth-century projective, metrical, and enumerative geometry. From 1891 he turned to geometry in Euclidean spaces of more than three dimensions, then a field in which little work had been done. He did extensive research on regular polytopes (generalizations of regular polyhedrons). Some of his almost thirty papers in this field were written in collaboration with Alice Boole Stott (1860–1940), daughter of the logician George Boole.

Schoute was an editor of the *Revue semestrielle des publications mathématiques* from its founding in 1893, and in 1898 he became an editor of the *Nieuw archief voor wiskunde.* He held both positions until his death. In 1886 he became a member of the Royal Netherlands Academy of Sciences.

BIBLIOGRAPHY

I. ORIGINAL WORKS. Much of Schoute's work appeared in *Verhandelingen der Koninklyke nederlandsche akademie van wetenschappen,* Afdeeling Natuurkunde, 1st section; see esp. "Regelmässige Schnitte und Projektionen des Hundertzwanzigzelles und des Sechshundertzelles im vierdimensionalen Raume," **2,** no. 7 (1894); and **9,** no. 4 (1907). Writings on other polytopes are in **2,** no. 2 and 4 (1894), which deal with the 8-cell, the 16-cell, and the 24-cell. See also "Het vierdimensionale prismoïde," **5,** no. 2 (1896); and "Les hyperquadratiques dans l'espace à quatre dimensions," **7,** no. 4 (1900). Several articles appeared in *Archives néerlandaises des sciences exactes et naturelles,* 2nd ser. **5–9** (1896–1904). Many of Schoute's results were collected in his *Mehrdimensionale Geometrie,* 2 vols. (Leipzig, 1902–1905).

II. SECONDARY LITERATURE. See H. S. M. Coxeter, *Regular Polytopes* (New York–London, 1948; 2nd ed., 1963), *passim;* and D. J. Korteweg, "P. H. Schoute," in *Zittingsverslagen der Koninklyke nederlandsche akademie van wetenschappen,* **21** (1912–1913), 1396–1400. Also: H. Fehr, *Enseignement mathématique,* **35** (1913), 256–257.

D. J. STRUIK

SCHOUTEN, JAN ARNOLDUS (*b*. Nieuweramstel [now part of Amsterdam], Netherlands, 28 August 1883; *d*. Epe, Netherlands, 20 January 1971), *tensor analysis*.

A descendant of a prominent family of shipbuilders, Schouten grew up in comfortable surroundings. He became not only one of the founders of the "Ricci calculus" but also an efficient organizer (he was a founder of the Mathematical Center at Amsterdam in 1946) and an astute investor. A meticulous lecturer and painfully accurate author, he instilled the same standards in his pupils.

After studying electrical engineering at what is now the Technische Hogeschool at Delft, Schouten practiced this profession for a few years and then returned to study in Leiden when an inheritance gave him the necessary independence. Upon completion of his doctoral dissertation in 1914, his first contribution to the foundations of tensor analysis, he was appointed professor at Delft. In 1943 Schouten resigned the post, divorced his wife, and remarried. From then on, he lived in semiseclusion at Epe. Although he was a professor at the University of Amsterdam from 1948 to 1953, the Mathematical Center had replaced teaching as his first commitment. He served the Center until 1968 and was its director for about five years.

Schouten attained numerous distinctions during his lifetime, including membership in the Royal Netherlands Academy of Sciences, the rotating position of *rector magnificus* at Delft, the presidency of the 1954 International Congress of Mathematicians at Amsterdam, several terms as president of the Wiskundig Genootschap (the society of Netherlands mathematicians), and a royal decoration.

Schouten's scientific contributions comprise some 180 papers and six books, virtually all related to tensor analysis and its applications to differential geometry, Lie groups, relativity, unified field theory, and Pfaffian systems of differential equations. Having entered the field when it was in its infancy, he helped develop and perfect the basic techniques of local differential geometry and applied them in numerous ways. He discovered connections ("geodesic displacements") in Riemannian manifolds in 1919, independently of, although later than, Levi-Civita; and he also discovered basic properties of Kähler manifolds in 1931, two years before Kähler. Under the influence of Weyl and Eddington he was led to general linear connections and investigated affine, projective, and conformal manifolds.

Schouten's approach to differential geometry was strongly influenced by Felix Klein's "Erlanger Programm" (1872), which viewed each geometry as the theory of invariants of a particular group. This approach led him to a point of view that handled geometric problems more formally than most other prominent differential geometers of his time, notably Levi-Civita, E. Cartan, Veblen, Eisenhart, and Blaschke. This same point of view underlies his "kernel-index method," a notation of great precision, which he and his pupils used masterfully, but which gained favor elsewhere only in less extreme forms.

Schouten inspired numerous co-workers, including D. J. Struik, D. van Dantzig, J. Haantjes, E. R. van Kampen, V. Hlavaty, S. Gołab, Kentaro Yano, E. J. Post, and A. Nijenhuis. His influence extended as far as Russia and Japan.

BIBLIOGRAPHY

I. ORIGINAL WORKS. Most of Schouten's work on tensor analysis and differential geometry can be found or is referred to in *Der Ricci Kalkül* (Berlin, 1924); *Einführung in die neueren Methoden der Differentialgeometrie*, 2 vols. (Groningen, 1934–1938), I, *Uebertragungslehre*, by Schouten, II, *Geometrie*, by D. J. Struik, also translated into Russian (Moscow, 1939, 1948); and *Pfaff's Problem and Its Generalisations* (Oxford, 1948), written with W. van der Kulk. *Ricci Calculus* (Berlin, 1954), the 2nd ed. of *Der Ricci Kalkül*, is completely rewritten and contains all that Schouten considered relevant in differential geometry at the end of his career. *Tensor Analysis for Physicists* (Oxford, 1951) is an attempt to spread to sophisticated physicists the subtleties of tensor analysis and its implications for field theory and elasticity.

A collection of Schouten's papers and correspondence has been deposited at the library of the Mathematical Center in Amsterdam.

II. SECONDARY LITERATURE. A short biographical article, concentrating on Schouten's scientific work, is D. J. Struik's *Levensbericht* on Schouten, in *Jaarboek der K. Nederlandsche akademie van wetenschappen* for 1971, pp. 94–100, with portrait. A. Nijenhuis, "J. A. Schouten: A Master at Tensors," in *Nieuw archief voor wiskunde*, 3rd ser., **20** (1972), 1–19, contains a complete list of publications.

ALBERT NIJENHUIS

SCHOUW, JOAKIM FREDERIK (*b*. Copenhagen, Denmark, 7 February 1789; *d*. Copenhagen, 28 April 1852), *plant geography*, *climatology*.

Schouw was the eldest of seven children born to Poul Schouw, a wine merchant, and Sara Georgia Liebenberg. Since he had to work at his father's business, he was educated by a tutor. His interest in botany began while he was attending the lectures on cryptogamic botany given in the winter of 1803–1804 by Martin Vahl, who assisted him in making a herbarium. Because working in his father's wine cellar had undermined his weak health, Schouw became a clerk in a lawyer's office in 1804; seven years later he passed the examination for the candidate's degree in law.

In 1812 Schouw took part in a botanical expedition to Norway headed by the Norwegian botanist Christian Smith and was strongly impressed by the conspicuous division of the vegetation into zones. After his return Schouw obtained a civil-service post in 1813. He pursued his interest in botany by studying all the available literature on plant geography, especially the works of Humboldt and Wahlenberg.

In 1816 Schouw received the Ph.D., along with a grant and a three-year leave to make a botanical trip to Italy, where he visited the Alps, the Apennines, and Sicily. On his return trip he visited P. de Candolle in Geneva and Adrien de Jussieu and Humboldt in Paris. Schouw returned to Copenhagen in 1820, where he was appointed extraordinary professor of botany, especially phytogeography, at Copenhagen University. During 1823–1824 Schouw had meteorological observations made in several Danish towns, the results of which he published in *Tidsskrift for Naturvidenskaberne*. In 1829, en route to Italy to complete his observations, he met Martius, Joseph Gerhard Zuccarini, and Mohl in Munich. Schouw was greatly interested in popularizing science and in improving the teaching of natural history. From 1831 he was editor of *Dansk Ugeskrift*, in which many of his popular-science lectures were printed. Through this work he became well known, and during the summer of 1839 he was invited to take part in the preparations for the meeting of Scandinavian naturalists at Göteborg.

In 1841 Schouw was appointed curator of the botanical gardens of Copenhagen, and four years later he became a full professor. During his last years his health deteriorated, and on 1 April 1853 he resigned.

While in Italy in 1817, Schouw met Susette Dalgas. They were married in 1827 and had a son and a daughter.

BIBLIOGRAPHY

I. ORIGINAL WORKS. Schouw's writings include *Dissertatio de sedibus plantarum originariis. Sectio prima.*

De pluribus cujusvis speciei individuis originariis statuendis (Copenhagen, 1816), his dissertation; "Einige Bemerkungen über zwei, die Pflanzengeographie betreffende Werke des Herrn von Humboldt," in *Jahrbücher der Gewächskunde*, **1** (1818), 6–56, unsigned; *Grundtraek til en almindelig Plantegeographie* (Copenhagen, 1822), translated by Schouw into German as *Grundzüge einer allgemeinen Pflanzengeographie* (Berlin, 1823), one of his principal works on plant geography; *Skildring af Vejrligets Tilstand i Danmark* (Copenhagen, 1826), his major work on climatology; *Specimen geographiae physicae comparativae . . .* (Copenhagen, 1828); and *Europa, En letfattelig Naturskildring* (Copenhagen, 1832).

Collections of his popular lectures are *Natur-Skildringer. En Raekke af almeenfattelige Forelaesniger* (Copenhagen, 1837, 1845) and *Naturskildringer. En Raekke populaere Foredrag. Ny foroget Udgave. Med Forfatterens Biographie* (Copenhagen, 1856).

Many of Schouw's letters are in the library of the botanical gardens, Copenhagen, and in the Royal Library, Copenhagen.

II. SECONDARY LITERATURE. Detailed biographies, in Danish, are Carl Christensen, "Joachim Frederik Schouw," in *Botanisk Tidsskrift*, **38**, no. 1 (1923), 1–56; and *Den Danske Botanisk Historie*, I, pt. 1 (Copenhagen, 1924), 253–276; with a bibliography of Schouw's works, II (1926), 165–179.

A. P. M. SANDERS

SCHREIBERS, KARL (or CARL) FRANZ ANTON VON (*b.* Pressburg, Hungary [now Bratislava, Czechoslovakia], 15 August 1775; *d.* Vienna, Austria, 21 May 1852), *zoology*.

Schreibers came from a noble family that had supplied numerous civil servants and scientists to the Austrian Empire. His father, Joseph Ludwig von Schreibers, was in the military administration; and the family moved to Vienna when Schreibers was a boy. After graduating from the Gymnasium, he entered the University of Vienna and was soon attracted to natural science and medicine. In 1793 he published a two-volume work on mollusks. Five years later he received the M.D. degree and began to practice medicine with his uncle, Johann Ludwig von Schreibers.

Although Schreibers used and campaigned for inoculation against smallpox, he did not remain in the medical profession for long. He made an extensive study tour through most of western Europe; and in 1800 he was named professor at the University of Vienna, becoming director of both the zoological and the mineralogical museums there in 1806. Schreibers proved to be an effective museum organizer, improving the museums and enlarging the collections, partly through expeditions, notably to Brazil (1817–1822). In 1809 he was put in charge of removing the Vienna treasury and archives from the reach of the advancing French army, and in 1815 he led the Austrian commission to retrieve the art treasures confiscated by the French during the Napoleonic Wars.

The author of many scientific papers and a large general work on meteorites, Schreibers was active mainly in zoology. Especially in his younger days he readily adopted new ideas and put them to effective use. He was the first to teach Cuvier's system of comparative anatomy in German, and even after he had left the University of Vienna he remained an important teacher and adviser to younger scientists. Schreibers made notable contributions to ornithology and entomology, and was an expert on arachnids. His main field, however, was reptiles and amphibians, and he considerably extended the knowledge of the central European faunas. Schreibers' best-known work in this field was his description of the salamander *Proteus anguinus*, a blind white amphibian that lives only in dark caves. Schreibers understood the biological importance of the find, which was the introduction to a long series of studies on cave faunas and their development and distribution.

In 1848 the zoological and mineralogical museums caught fire during a thunderstorm; and Schreibers, who lived in the museum buildings, lost not only the collections and the library, but also his private library, manuscripts, and other belongings. He tried to rebuild the museums, but his age prevented it. He was obliged to retire and died shortly afterward. Schreibers was a highly respected scientist who received a number of titles and decorations, both for his work with the museums and for his scientific achievements. His most lasting works are the large monographs on the fauna of Austria and his investigations of *Proteus*.

BIBLIOGRAPHY

I. ORIGINAL WORKS. Schreibers' writings include *Versuch einer vollständigen Conchylienkenntniss nach Linne's System*, 2 vols. (Vienna, 1793); "A Historical and Anatomical Description of a Doubtful Amphibious Animal of Germany Called by Laurenti *Proteus anguinus*," in *Philosophical Transactions of the Royal Society* (1801), 241–264; *Nachrichten von den Kaiserlichen Naturforschern in Brasilien*, 2 vols. (Brünn [Brno], 1818–1820); and *Beiträge zur Geschichte und Kenntniss meteorische Stein- und Metalmassen* (Vienna, 1820).

II. SECONDARY LITERATURE. See A. F. G. Marshall, "Nekrolog des K. K. Hofrathes Carl, Ritter von Schreibers," in *Verhandlungen der Zoologisch-botanischen Gesellschaft in Wien*, **2** (1852), 46–51; and C. von Wurzbach, "Carl Franz Anton, Ritter von Schreibers," in *Biographisches Lexicon der Kaiserthum Osterreich*, XXXI (Vienna, 1876), 283–287.

NILS SPJELDNAES

SCHRÖDER, FRIEDRICH WILHELM KARL ERNST (*b.* Mannheim, Germany, 25 November 1841; *d.* Karlsruhe, Germany, 16 June 1902), *mathematics.*

Schröder was the son of Heinrich Schröder, who did much to foster the teaching of science in secondary and college-level schools and also strongly influenced his son to choose a scientific career. Schröder's mother, the former Karoline Walter, was the daughter of a minister. Her father tutored Ernst until he was fifteen, providing him with an excellent basic education, especially in Latin. In 1856 Schröder enrolled at the lyceum in Mannheim, from which he graduated in 1860.

Schröder then attended the University of Heidelberg, where he studied under Hesse, Kirchhoff, and Bunsen. He passed his doctoral examination in 1862 and spent the next two years studying mathematics and physics at the University of Königsberg under Franz Neumann and F. J. Richelot. Soon afterward, at Karlsruhe, he took the examination to qualify for teaching in secondary schools. He then went to the Eidgenössische Polytechnikum in Zurich, where he qualified as a lecturer in mathematics in 1865 and taught for a time. In 1874, after teaching at Karlsruhe, Pforzheim, and Baden-Baden, Schröder was offered, on the basis of his mathematical publications, a full professorship at the Technische Hochschule in Darmstadt. In 1876 he accepted a post at the Technische Hochschule in Karlsruhe, of which he became director in 1890. He most often lectured on arithmetic, trigonometry, and advanced analysis.

Schröder was described as kind and modest. A lifelong bachelor, he was an ardent mountain climber and cyclist, and learned to ski when he was sixty years old.

Schröder published more than forty mathematical works, including seven separately printed essays and books. They deal almost exclusively with the foundations of mathematics, notably with combinatorial analysis; the theory of functions of a real variable; and mathematical logic. Particularly noteworthy was his early support of Cantor's ideas

216

on set theory, which he was one of the first to accept.

Through his writings on theoretical algebra and symbolic logic, especially *Algebra der Logik*, Schröder participated in the development of mathematical logic as an independent discipline in the second half of the nineteenth century. This is his real achievement, although his contribution was not recognized until the beginning of the twentieth century. Three factors accounted for the delay; the immature state of the field during his lifetime; a certain prolixity in his style; and, above all, the isolation imposed by his teaching in technical colleges. As a result he was an outsider, at a disadvantage in choosing terminology, in outlining his argumentation, and in judging what mathematical logic could accomplish.

Despite Schröder's relative isolation, his work was in the mainstream of the conceptual development of mathematical logic, the chief figures in which were Boole, de Morgan, and C. S. Peirce. Other new ideas that Schröder adopted and elaborated were Peano's formulation of the postulates of arithmetic (1889) and the abstract conception of mathematical operations vigorously set forth by Grassmann and Hankel. With respect to the philosophical problems raised in the formation of mathematical logic, Schröder was guided primarily by Lotze and Wundt, who closely followed Aristotle in questions of logic.

The terminology and contents of Schröder's "logical calculus" are now primarily of historical interest. His ideas, however, furnished the fundamental notion of mathematical logic: the partition of objects into classes. His work constituted a transitional stage that helped to prepare the way for the development of mathematical logic in the twentieth century.

BIBLIOGRAPHY

I. ORIGINAL WORKS. Schröder's writings are listed in Poggendorff, III, 1212–1213; IV, 1353–1354; V, 1131–1132. They include *Lehrbuch der Arithmetik und Algebra* (Leipzig, 1872); *Formale Elemente der absoluten Algebra* (Baden-Baden–Stuttgart, 1874); *Operationskreis des Logikkalküls* (Stuttgart, 1877); *Vorlesungen über die Algebra der Logik*, 3 vols. in 4 pts. (Leipzig, 1890–1905; 2nd ed., New York, 1966), II, pt. 2, edited by E. Müller; *Uber das Zeichen. Festrede bei dem Direktoratswechsel an der Technischen Hochschule zu Karlsruhe am 22. November 1890* (Karlsruhe, 1890); and *Abriss der Algebra der Logik*: pt. 1, *Elementarlehre* (Leipzig, 1909), and pt. 2, *Aussagentheorie, Funktionen,*

Gleichungen und Ungleichungen (Leipzig, 1910), both parts edited by E. Müller.

II. SECONDARY LITERATURE. See J. Lüroth, "Nekrolog auf Ernst Schröder," in *Jahresbericht der Deutschen Mathematiker-Vereinigung,* **12** (1903), 249–265, with portrait and bibliography; and Lüroth's obituary and bibliography in Schröder's *Vorlesungen über die Algebra der Logik,* II, pt. 2 (1905), iii–xix.

H. WUSSING

SCHRÖDINGER, ERWIN (*b.* Vienna, Austria, 12 August 1887; *d.* Alpbach, Austria, 4 January 1961), *theoretical physics.*

Schrödinger's father, Rudolf Schrödinger, inherited an oilcloth factory, which, although run in an old-fashioned manner, was successful enough to free him of financial worries. After studying chemistry he turned to his real interests—painting and, later, botany—and published a series of scientific papers in the *Abhandlungen* and *Verhandlungen der Zoologisch-botanischen Gesellschaft in Wien.* He married the daughter of Alexander Bauer, professor of chemistry at the Technische Hochschule in Vienna; Erwin was their only child.

Schrödinger attended public elementary school only once, for a few weeks in Innsbruck, while his parents were on vacation. In Vienna an elementary school teacher came to his home twice a week to tutor him; but, in Schrödinger's opinion, his "friend, teacher, and tireless partner in conversation" was his father. In the fall of 1898 Schrödinger entered the highly regarded academic Gymnasium in Vienna. As was then customary, the curriculum emphasized Latin and Greek, the sciences being somewhat neglected. Schrödinger wrote: "I was a good student, regardless of the subject. I liked mathematics and physics, but also the rigorous logic of the ancient grammars. I hated only memorizing 'chance' historical and biographical dates and facts. I liked the German poets, especially the dramatists, but hated the scholastic dissection of their works."

As a student Schrödinger regularly attended the theater in Vienna and was a passionate admirer of Franz Grillparzer. He kept an album containing programs of the performances he had seen and made extensive annotations on them. He did not, however, neglect his studies. In 1907, during his third semester at the University of Vienna, he began to attend lectures in theoretical physics, which had just been resumed after a nearly two-year interruption following the death of Boltzmann. Friedrich Hasenöhrl's brilliant inaugural lecture on the work of his predecessor made a powerful impression on Schrödinger.

Schrödinger highly esteemed Hasenöhrl and attended his lectures on theoretical physics five days a week for eight successive semesters. He also was present at the mathematics lectures of Wilhelm Wirtinger and those on experimental physics of Franz Exner, whose laboratory assistant he later became.

In 1910 Schrödinger received the doctorate under Hasenöhrl, and the following year he became assistant to Exner at the university's Second Physics Institute, where he remained until the outbreak of war. During these years Egon von Schweidler was *Privatdozent* at the university; Schrödinger learned a great deal from him and called him his teacher, second only to Hasenöhrl and Exner. Schrödinger was obliged to supervise the large physics laboratory courses, a duty for which he was very thankful all his life because it taught him "through direct observation what measuring means."

Schrödinger served in World War I as an officer in the fortress artillery; and in the isolated areas where he was stationed, he often had time to study physics. In 1916, while at Prosecco, he learned the fundamentals of Einstein's general theory of relativity, which he at first found quite difficult to understand. Soon, however, he was able to follow Einstein's train of thought and the relevant calculations; he found much in the initial presentation of the theory that was "unnecessarily complicated."

As early as 1918 Schrödinger had a sure prospect of obtaining a position; he was to succeed Josef Geitler as extraordinary professor of theoretical physics at the University of Czernowitz (now Chernovtsy, Ukraine). "I intended to lecture there honorably on theoretical physics, at first on the model of the splendid lectures of my beloved teacher, fallen in the war, Fritz Hasenöhrl, and beyond this to study philosophy, deeply immersed as I then was in the writings of Spinoza, Schopenhauer, Mach, Richard Semon, and Richard Avenarius." The collapse of the Austro-Hungarian monarchy prevented this plan, and after the war he worked again at the Second Physics Institute in Vienna. As a result, Schrödinger's first scientific papers were in the experimental field. In 1913, at the summer home of Egon von Schweidler at Seeham, Schrödinger collaborated with K. W. F. Kohlrausch on a work that was awarded the Haitinger Prize of the Imperial Academy of Sciences and that was published as "Radium-A-Gehalt der Atmosphäre in Seeham 1913." At Seeham, Schrö-

dinger met Annemarie Bertel, whom he married on 6 April 1920.

Shortly after his marriage Schrödinger moved to Jena, where he was an assistant to Max Wien in the experimental physics laboratory. He left Jena after only four months, in order to accept an extraordinary professorship at the Technische Hochschule in Stuttgart. He remained there for only one semester; in the meantime he had received three offers of full professorships—from Kiel, Breslau, and Vienna. He would have preferred to succeed Hasenöhrl at Vienna, but the working conditions for university professors in Austria were then so poor that this alternative was unacceptable. Instead he went to Breslau, where a few weeks after his arrival he received and accepted an offer to assume the chair formerly held by Einstein and Max von Laue at Zurich.

While at Zurich, Schrödinger worked chiefly on problems related to the statistical theory of heat. He wrote papers on gas and reaction kinetics, oscillation problems, and the thermodynamics of lattice vibrations and their contribution to internal energy; in other works he elucidated aspects of mathematical statistics. In an article on the theory of specific heats and in a monograph on statistical thermodynamics he gave a comprehensive account of the latter subject.

Although Schrödinger published several contributions to the old quantum theory, he did not pursue that topic systematically. His first papers on relativity pointed to a second major field of interest. In addition to these works, and his early papers on relativity, Schrödinger made a detailed study, through both measurement and computation, of the metric of color space and the theory of color vision. The main results of his efforts were an article in J. H. J. Müller and C. S. M. Pouillet's *Lehrbuch der Physik* and the acceptance by physiologists of his interpretation of the relationship between the frequency of red-green color blindness and that of the blue-yellow type.

In the meantime, on 25 November 1924, Louis de Broglie defended his dissertation before the examining committee at the Sorbonne: "Recherche sur la théorie des quanta." The contents of the dissertation first became known through a direct communication from Paul Langevin to Einstein and then, more generally, through publication in the *Annales de physique*. At first no physicist—except Einstein—was willing to believe in the reality of the Broglie waves.

As in his first quantum papers, of 1905, Einstein at the end of 1924 again hypothesized "a far-reaching formal relationship between radiation and gas"; but by the latter year he was concerned primarily with the properties of the gas. Basing his analysis on what is today known as Einstein-Bose statistics, he obtained expression for the fluctuation in number of molecules that hinted at interference effects.

Schrödinger, who in 1925 was also investigating problems of quantum statistics, was "suddenly confronted with the importance of de Broglie's ideas" in reading Einstein's "Quantentheorie des einatomigen idealen Gases. 2. Abhandlung," which appeared on 9 February 1925 in *Sitzungsberichte der Preussischen Akademie der Wissenschaften zu Berlin*. He recognized that Einstein had introduced a fundamental new approach, but he sought "to recast it in a more pleasing form, to liberate it from Bose's statistics," which he deeply disliked.

Shortly before the middle of December, Schrödinger completed a paper on this topic, "Zur Einsteinschen Gastheorie," recorded as being received by *Physikalische Zeitschrift* on 15 December 1925. In an important and still unpublished letter to Einstein dated 28 April 1926, Schrödinger gave the following evaluation of his results: "I can . . . assert categorically that I have really achieved the liberation I mentioned above. . . . I stress the determination of the frequency spectrum in § 3. This whole conception falls entirely within the framework of 'wave mechanics'; it is simply the mechanics of waves applied to the gas instead of to the atom or the oscillator."

Schrödinger, who generally expressed his judgments in an intensely emotional way, termed the earlier Bohr-Sommerfeld quantum theory unsatisfactory, sometimes even disagreeable. Seeking to apply the new ideas to the problem of atomic structure, he "took seriously the de Broglie-Einstein wave theory of moving particles, according to which the particles are nothing more than a kind of 'wave crest' on a background of waves." As is evident in a letter of 16 November 1925, from Schrödinger to Alfred Landé, Schrödinger's conjectures on this topic date from the beginning of November 1925 and therefore from before the conclusion of his paper on Einstein's gas theory.

The intensity of Schrödinger's work on the problem increased as he saw that he was on the track of a "new atomic theory," and it reached a peak during his winter vacation in Arosa. On 27 December 1925 he wrote to Wilhelm Wien, editor of the *Annalen der Physik* in Munich that he was very optimistic: "I believe that I can give a vibrating system . . . that yields the hydrogen frequency *levels* as

its eigenfrequencies." The frequencies of the emitted light rays are then obtained, as Schrödinger observed, by establishing the differences of the two eigenfrequencies respectively.

> Consequently the way is opened toward a real understanding of Bohr's frequency calculation—it is really a vibration (or, as the case may be, interference) process, which occurs with the same frequency as the one we observe in the spectroscope.
>
> I hope that I will soon be able to report on this subject in a little more detail and in a more comprehensible fashion. In the meantime I must learn more mathematics, in order to fully master the vibration problem—a linear differential equation, similar to Bessel's, but less well known, and with remarkable boundary conditions that the equation 'carries within itself' and that are not externally predetermined.

The letter confirms what is already known from Schrödinger's publications and from other statements: that, as must have seemed logically consistent from the physics of the problem, he originally developed a relativistic theory. It must be emphasized, therefore, that Schrödinger worked out the relativistic version only at the end of 1925 and not, as historians of science had believed, in the middle of that year. The equation now known as the "Klein-Gordon equation" does yield the correct nonrelativistic Balmer term, but it gives an incorrect description of the fine structure. Schrödinger was deeply disappointed by this failure and must have thought at first that his whole method was basically wrong. Today it is known that the reason for the failure lay not in his bold initial approach but in the application of the theory of relativity, which, however, has itself been abundantly confirmed. The relativistic Schrödinger equation is obviously correct, but it describes particles without spin, whereas a description of electrons requires the Dirac equation. At the time, however, only the first steps had been taken toward an understanding of electron spin.

After a brief interruption Schrödinger took up his method again, but this time he treated the electron nonrelativistically. It soon became apparent that he had arrived at a theory that correctly represented the behavior of the electron to a very good approximation. The result was the emergence of wave mechanics in January 1926.

Schrödinger published the results of his research in a series of four papers in the *Annalen der Physik* bearing the overall title "Quantisierung als Eigenwertproblem." The first installment, sent on 26 January and received by Wien the next day, contains the first appearance in the literature of his famous wave equation, written out for the hydrogen atom. The solution of this equation follows, as Schrödinger put it, from the "well-known" method of the separation of variables. The radial dependency gives rise to the differential equation

$$\frac{d^2\chi}{dr^2} + \frac{2}{r}\frac{d\chi}{dr} + \left(\frac{2mE}{K^2} + \frac{2me^2}{K^2 r} - \frac{n(n+1)}{r^2}\right)\chi = 0.$$

In fulfilling the boundary conditions one obtains solutions only for certain values of the energy parameters, the stationary values. This seemed to Schrödinger to be the "salient point," but in Bohr's original theory—as its creator stressed from the beginning—it was one of the two fundamental postulates that had remained unexplained. Schrödinger emphasized that, in his theory,

> the ordinary quantization rule can be replaced by another condition in which the term "integral number" no longer appears. Rather, the integrality occurs in the same natural way as, say, the integrality in the modal numbers of a vibrating string. The new conception can be generalized and, I believe, penetrates very deeply into the true nature of the quantum rules.

In solving the differential equation for the radial function, Schrödinger received expert assistance from Hermann Weyl. A crucial element in their rapid success was the fact that the mathematical theory had already been completely worked out by Richard Courant and David Hilbert in their *Methoden der mathematischen Physik* (1924).

In his second paper (23 February 1926) Schrödinger gave a sort of "derivation" of his *undulatorischer Mechanik* in which he drew on the almost century-old work of William Rowan Hamilton. Hamilton was aware that geometrical optics was only a special case of wave optics valid for infinitely small wavelengths, and he showed how to make the transition from the characteristic (iconal) equation of geometrical optics to the differential equation of wave optics. Hamilton introduced the methods of geometrical optics into mechanics and obtained an equation similar to the iconal equation and now known as the Hamilton-Jacobi differential equation. In it the index of refraction is replaced, essentially, by the potential energy and the mass of the mechanical particle.

In Hamilton's work Schrödinger thus found an analogy between mechanics and geometrical optics. And, since geometrical optics "is only a gross approximation for light," he conjectured that the same cause was responsible for the failure of classical mechanics "in the case of very small orbital dimensions and very strong orbital curvature." Both would be only approximations for small wavelengths. Therefore, he said:

> Perhaps this failure is a complete analogy to the failure of geometrical optics, that is, the optics with infinitely small wavelengths; [a failure] that occurs, as is known, as soon as the "obstacles" or "openings" are no longer large relative to the real, finite wavelength. Perhaps our classical mechanics is the *complete* analogue of geometrical optics and, as such, false. . . . Therefore, we have to seek an "undulatory mechanics"—and the way to it that lies closest at hand is the wave-theoretical elaboration of Hamilton's model.

Consequently, Schrödinger introduced into his development of wave mechanics conceptions that differed completely from those underlying the quantum mechanics formulated by the Göttingen school. He himself stated: "It is hardly necessary to emphasize how much more agreeable it would be to represent a quantum transition as the passage of energy from one vibrational form into another, rather than to represent it as the jumping of electrons." In many passages Schrödinger (like Heisenberg) expressed his views in an almost polemical tone: "I . . . feel intimidated, not to say repelled, by what seem to me the very difficult methods [of matrix mechanics] and by the lack of clarity."

Despite his distaste for matrix mechanics, Schrödinger was "convinced of [its] inner connection" with wave mechanics. Hermann Weyl, to whom he had presented his purely mathematical problem, was unable to "provide the connecting link." Thereupon Schrödinger temporarily put aside his conjectures on the matter; but by the beginning of March 1926, much earlier than he had thought possible, he was able to show the formal, mathematical identity of the two theories.

The starting point for this analysis was the following observation:

> Given the extraordinary disparity, it is . . . odd that these two new quantum theories agree with each other even where they deviate from the old quantum theory. I note above all the peculiar "half-integrality" in the case of the oscillator and the rotator. This is truly remarkable, for the starting point, conception, method, and . . . entire mathematical apparatus appear to be fundamentally different for each theory.

Schrödinger remarked that Heisenberg's peculiar computational rules for functions of the $2n$

variables — $q_1, q_2, \cdots, q_n, p_1, p_2, \cdots, p_n$ space and impulse coordinates — agree exactly with the computational rules that are valid in ordinary analysis for linear differential operators of n variables $q_1, \cdots, q_n$. The correspondence is of such a nature that each p_i in the function is replaced by the operator $\delta/\delta q_i$. As a result Schrödinger rewrote the equation $pq - qp = h/2\pi i$ (first formulated by Born) simply as $\frac{\delta}{\delta q} q - q \frac{\delta}{\delta q} = 1$, because the operator on the left side, applied to an arbitrary function of q, reproduces this function. On this basis Schrödinger proceeded to show the complete mathematical equivalence of the two theories. The matrices can be constructed from Schrödinger's eigenfunctions and vice versa.

With the demonstration of the mathematical identity of wave mechanics and matrix mechanics, physicists at last came into possession of the "new quantum theory" that had been sought for so long. In working with it they could use either of two mathematical tools: matrix computation or the method of setting up and solving a partial differential equation. Schrödinger's wave equation proved to be easier to handle. Moreover, physicists were more familiar with partial differential equations than with the new matrices. Therefore, Schrödinger's methods were more widely adopted for the mathematical treatment of the new theory. He contributed substantially to the elaboration of that treatment in his next two papers, especially through the development of his perturbation theory.

In his first publications Schrödinger had spoken of the wave function ψ as something that could be directly visualized — a vibration amplitude in three-dimensional space. He sought to interpret $\psi\bar{\psi}$ as electric charge density and hoped to establish physics on a thoroughgoing wave conception. Since, however, experiments clearly indicated the existence of strongly localized particles, he attempted to introduce the concept of the wave group: "One can try to construct a wave group of relatively small dimensions in all directions. Such a wave group presumably will obey the same laws of motion as an individual image point of the mechanical system."

Schrödinger attempted to develop this conception in "Der stetige Übergang von der Mikro- zur Makromechanik." It soon became apparent, however, that in almost all cases such a wave group disappears in infinitely short time and therefore cannot possibly represent a real particle. Schrödinger also observed that in the many-electron problem, the interpretation he originally had in mind is necessarily invalid in ordinary space: "$\psi\bar{\psi}$ is a sort of weight function in the configuration space of the system."

Shortly afterward Max Born interpreted $\psi\bar{\psi}$ as a probability, a view that Schrödinger considered a complete misinterpretation of his theory. From this time on, quantum theory developed in a way wholly different from the one Schrödinger had foreseen. In 1927 Heisenberg and Bohr succeeded in establishing, on a statistical foundation, an independent and consistent interpretation of quantum theory, the "Copenhagen interpretation." Schrödinger was "concerned and disappointed" that this "transcendental, almost psychical interpretation of the wave phenomena" had become "the almost universally accepted dogma." Schrödinger never changed his attitude on this subject, repeatedly defending the notion of "the electron as wave" and seeking to elaborate it without having recourse to the idea of "the electron as particle."

In 1927 Schrödinger accepted the prestigious offer, which had been declined by Arnold Sommerfeld, to succeed Max Planck in the chair of theoretical physics at the University of Berlin. At the same time he became a member of the Prussian Academy of Sciences. The University of Zurich vainly sought to persuade him to stay, offering him, among other inducements, a double professorship jointly with the Eidgenössische Technische Hochschule. Schrödinger was content in Zurich, despite occasional complaints; and his stay there had been very fruitful for the development of his scientific thought. Clearly, however, the city could not compete with Berlin, where, in the truest sense of the phrase, "physics was done." Berlin, with its two universities, the Kaiser Wilhelm Institute, the Physikalisch-Technische Reichsanstalt, and numerous industrial laboratories, offered the possibility of contact with a large number of first-rate physicists and chemists. Still, Schrödinger did not find it easy to make the decision. It was Max Planck who finally brought the vacillating Schrödinger to Berlin with the words: "It would make me happy" — as Schrödinger himself recorded in the Planck family guest book.

Although Schrödinger was extremely fond of nature, especially the Alps, and dreaded the prospect of living in a big city, he very much enjoyed his years in Berlin. He developed a close friendship with Planck, whose scientific and philosophical views were similar to his own. After the "wandering years from 1920 to 1927," this time of his life was "the very beautiful teaching and learning period."

In 1933 Schrödinger was deeply outraged at the new regime and its dismissal of outstandingly qualified scientists. Frederick A. Lindemann (later Viscount Cherwell) offered him the support of Imperial Chemical Industries; and after a summer vacation in Wolkenstein in the Grödnertal (Val Gardena), where he had a depressing meeting with Born and Weyl, Schrödinger moved to Oxford at the beginning of November. The fifth day after his arrival, he was accepted as a fellow of Magdalen College. At the same time the *Times* of London called his hotel to tell him that he had been awarded the Nobel Prize in physics for 1933, jointly with P. A. M. Dirac.

At Oxford, Schrödinger gradually became so homesick for Austria that he allowed himself to be persuaded to accept a post at Graz in the winter semester of 1936–1937. After the *Anschluss* he was subjected to strong pressure from the National Socialists, who had not forgotten his emigration from Germany in 1933. His friends at Oxford observed his difficulties with great concern.

As early as May 1938 Eamon de Valera, who had once been professor of mathematics at the University of Dublin, attempted to find a way of bringing Schrödinger to Ireland. By the time Schrödinger was dismissed, without notice, from his position at Graz on 1 September 1938, the first steps had already been taken. Fortunately, Schrödinger had been left his passport and was able to depart unhindered, although with only a small amount of baggage and no money. Passing through Rome and Geneva, he first returned to Oxford. De Valera had a law passed in the Irish Parliament establishing the Dublin Institute for Advanced Studies; but in order to keep busy until it opened, Schrödinger accepted a guest professorship at the Francqui Foundation in Ghent.

At the beginning of September 1939, Schrödinger, as a German émigré, suddenly found himself an enemy alien; but once more de Valera came to his assistance. Through the Irish high commissioner in Great Britain, he arranged for a letter of safe conduct to be issued for Schrödinger, who on 5 October 1939 passed through England on his way to Dublin with a transit visa valid for twenty-four hours. Schrödinger spent the next seventeen years in the Irish capital, where he was able to work in his new position undisturbed by external events. He later called these years of exile "a very, very beautiful time. Otherwise I would have never gotten to know and learned to love this beautiful island of Ireland. It is impossible to imagine what would have happened if, instead, I had been in Graz for these seventeen years."

The new Institute for Advanced Studies consisted of two sections, theoretical physics and Celtic languages, both located in a former townhouse on Merrion Square in Dublin. Young physicists from all over the world were given stipends enabling them to spend one or two years there. On the average there were ten to fifteen scholars in residence. Among them were Walter Thirring, Friedrich Mautner, Bruno Berdotti, and H. W. Peng. Like many of the others, Peng had previously worked with Max Born at Edinburgh. The yearly "summer school" in Dublin became famous as an informal gathering for the discussion of current problems of physics. Born and Dirac were frequent participants, and de Valera often came too.

In the years after his departure from Germany, Schrödinger published many works on the application and statistical interpretation of wave mechanics, on the mathematical character of the new statistics, and on its relationship to the statistical theory of heat. He also dealt with questions concerning general relativity, notably the relativistic treatment of wave fields, in contradistinction to the initial, nonrelativistic formulation of wave mechanics. In addition he wrote on a number of cosmological problems. Schrödinger, however, devoted an especially fervent effort, as did Einstein in his later years, to expanding the latter's theory of gravitation into a "unified field theory," the metric determination of which was to be established from a consideration of all the known forces between particles.

In his last creative period Schrödinger turned to a thorough study of the foundations of physics and their implications for philosophy and for the development of a world view. He wrote a number of studies on this subject in book form, most of them appearing first in English and then in German translation. It becomes particularly evident from the posthumously published *Meine Weltansicht* that Schrödinger was greatly concerned with the ancient Indian philosophy of life (Vedanta), which had led him to concepts that closely approximate Albert Schweitzer's "reverence for life." In "What Is Life?" Schrödinger points out why physics had amassed so little empirical evidence that might be applicable to the study of cell development: aperiodic crystals, in terms of which a gene should be considered, had not been investigated. But according to Delbrück's model, quantum physics made it possible to understand general persistence as well as the case of spontaneous mutation. Schrödinger was convinced that the biological process of growth could also be conceived on the basis of quantum theory according to the schema "order out of order." His analysis is outdated today; but during his lifetime it exerted enormous appeal among physicists (as Francis Crick corroborated) and induced many young people to study biology. Thus the great advances of molecular biology are indirectly linked to Schrödinger. He was a master of exposition, and Arnold Sommerfeld even spoke of a special "Schrödinger style." Schrödinger wrote and spoke four modern languages (as well as Greek and Latin), translated various items, and published a volume of poetry—while continuing to bestow great care on the preparation of his lectures, as is evident from their exceptional accuracy. To keep up this pace he required a marked alternation of intensely productive periods with creative pauses.

Soon after the end of the war, Austria tried to convince Schrödinger to return home. Even the president, Karl Renner, personally intervened in 1946; but Schrödinger was not willing to return while Vienna was under Soviet occupation. In the succeeding years he often visited the Tirol with his wife, but he did not return definitively until 1956, when he was given his own chair at the University of Vienna. A year later he turned seventy, the customary retirement age in Austria, but lectured for a further year (Ehrenjahr).

In his last years Austria honored Schrödinger with a lavish display of gratitude and recognition. Immediately after his return he received the prize of the city of Vienna. The national government endowed a prize bearing Schrödinger's name, to be awarded by the Austrian Academy of Sciences, and Schrödinger was its first recipient. In 1957 he was awarded the Austrian Medal for Arts and Science. He wrote that "Austria had treated me generously in every respect, and thus my academic career ended happily at the same Physics Institute where it had begun."

On 27 May 1957 Schrödinger was accepted into the German order Pour le mérite. He was also granted honorary doctorates from a number of universities and was a member of many scientific associations, including the Pontifical Academy of Sciences, the Royal Society of London, the Prussian (later German) Academy of Sciences in Berlin, and the Austrian Academy of Sciences. In 1957 Schrödinger survived an illness that threatened his life, and he never fully recovered his health. He died on 4 January 1961 and is buried in the small village of Alpbach, in his beloved Tirolean mountains.

BIBLIOGRAPHY

I. ORIGINAL WORKS. Schrödinger's important papers on wave mechanics are reprinted in *Abhandlungen zur Wellenmechanik* (Leipzig, 1927; 2nd ed., 1928); and *Die Wellenmechanik*, vol. 3 of Dokumente der Naturwissenschaft (Stuttgart, 1963), which contains an extensive bibliography compiled by E. E. Koch of Schrödinger's writings (pp. 193–199).

Some important correspondence is in Karl Przibram, ed., *Schrödinger. Einstein. Lorentz, Briefe zur Wellenmechanik* (Vienna, 1963), also translated into English by Martin J. Klein as *Letters on Wave Mechanics* (New York, 1967), which does not, however, contain Schrödinger's letter to Einstein (28 Apr. 1926). Unpublished letters to Arnold Sommerfeld are at the Sommerfeld estate in the library at the Deutsches Museum, Munich. Two letters to Hermann Weyl were published by Johannes Gerber in *Archive for History of Exact Sciences*, **5** (1969), 412–416. The sources of other letters to and from Schrödinger are in T. S. Kuhn *et al.*, *Sources for History of Quantum Physics. An Inventory and Report* (Philadelphia, 1967), 83–86.

II. SECONDARY LITERATURE. See Johannes Gerber, "Geschichte der Wellenmechanik," in *Archive for History of Exact Sciences*, **5** (1969), 349–416; Armin Hermann, "Erwin Schrödinger—eine Biographie," in *Die Wellenmechanik* (see above), 173–192; Max Jammer, *The Conceptual Development of Quantum Mechanics* (New York, 1966), 236–280; Martin J. Klein, "Einstein and the Wave-Particle Duality," in *Natural Philosopher*, **3** (1964), 1–49; V. V. Raman and Paul Forman, "Why Was It Schrödinger Who Developed de Broglie's Ideas?" in *Historical Studies in the Physical Sciences*, **1** (1969), 291–314; William T. Scott, *Erwin Schrödinger, an Introduction to His Writings* (Amherst, Mass., 1967); Robert Olby, "Schrödinger's Problem: What Is Life?" in *Journal of the History of Biology*, **4** (1971), 119–148.

ARMIN HERMANN

SCHROEDER VAN DER KOLK, JACOBUS LUDOVICUS CONRADUS (*b.* Leeuwarden, Netherlands, 14 March 1797; *d.* Utrecht, Netherlands, 1 May 1862), *medicine.*

Schroeder van der Kolk began the study of medicine in 1812 at the University of Groningen. As a student, he wrote two prize essays: one on the benefits accruing to the animal economy from the latent or combined caloric of air and water (1816) and the other on blood and its circulation (1819). In 1820 he received the M.D. for his dissertation on the coagulation of blood. He then established a medical practice in Hoorn but the following year was appointed resident physician at the Buitengasthuis in Amsterdam, where he treated about 400 patients daily. He also performed many postmortem examinations and did much on behalf of the 150 mental patients in the hospital. Thus he had abundant opportunity to acquire an extensive practical knowledge of various diseases. He prepared anatomical specimens and also formed a collection of pathological specimens. In 1826 he published his anatomical researches, *Observationes anatomico-pathologici et practici argumenti;* and in the same year he established a medical practice in Amsterdam. In 1827 he was appointed professor of anatomy and physiology at the University of Utrecht; he held this post until his death.

Schroeder van der Kolk's many articles on anatomy reveal both his skill in fine anatomical examination and his wide reading. At Utrecht he compared the anatomy of man with that of other vertebrates and often used the microscope to examine organs and tissues, a practice that was still uncommon. He also lectured on morbid anatomy and emphasized the value of anatomical investigations. In 1845 he discovered that tuberculous pulmonary tissue is easily recognized by the presence of elastic threads in the sputum. But he mistakenly concluded that these threads originate only from a tuberculous cavity.

To gain a better insight into brain disorders Schroeder van der Kolk closely examined the structure of the central nervous system. He conducted anatomical-physiological, pathological-anatomical, and clinical researches on the structure of the human brain and on that of higher animals. From 1855 he studied microscopically the spinal cord and the medulla oblongata. His most important discovery was the connection between the nervous fibers of the anterior roots of the medulla oblongata and the large branched cells of the anterior gray horns of the spinal cord.

Schroeder van der Kolk's studies are characterized by his accurate descriptions and fine illustrations. He published works on the anatomy of the tarsier *Stenops kukang* of the East Indies (1841); on the anatomy and physiology of the larva of the horse botfly *Gasterophilus intestinalis* (1845); on the structure of the lungs of birds (1858); on the liver of the elephant (1861); and, with Willem Vrolik, professor of anatomy at Amsterdam, on the comparative anatomy of the half-apes (1848). He also wrote on the brain of the chimpanzee (1849) and the orangutan (1861), the vascular plexuses of the three-toed sloth *Bradypus tridactylus,* and on the limbs of birds (1848).

Schroeder van der Kolk was deeply influenced by vitalism, and he often proposed extreme teleological points of view, especially in his lectures on physiology (*ca.* 1840); he was resolute against the rising materialism of his time. Besides the primitive forces in nature (attraction and repulsion) and the imponderables (light, heat, electricity, galvanism, and magnetism), he saw in the vegetable and animal kingdoms various life-forces. In man, he believed that the nervous-force informs the sensibility with its impression of the outer world and that this force communicates the commands of the will to the muscles. Although he sought an empirical foundation for this philosophy, he was unable to escape from the concepts of *vis vitalis* and teleology. He was convinced that all events in the universe are focused on a good and just aim.

Besides his work in physiology and anatomy, Schroeder van der Kolk always strove for better care for the insane; his *Oratio de debita cura infaustam maniacorum sortem emendandi eosque sanandi in nostra patria neglecta* (1837) dealt with this subject. In 1827 he became a governor of the Utrechtsche Dolhuis and sought to improve both the treatment and housing of the insane. His reforms prompted legislation for general reform in the care of the mad; and after passage of the Lunacy Act in 1841, he was appointed inspector of lunatic asylums (1842–1862).

Schroeder van der Kolk's textbook on psychiatry was published posthumously by his pupil F. A. Hartsen. His clinical psychiatric concepts were also influenced by vitalism. He thought that body and soul interact in the life-force (or "brain-force"): in the insane the brain-force, rather than the soul (the "higher principle" in man), is ill. Thus the soul receives wrong data from the nervous-force and consequently reaches a wrong judgment.

BIBLIOGRAPHY

I. ORIGINAL WORKS. Schroeder van der Kolk's works include "Responsio ad quaestionem: quae sunt emolumenta praecipua, quae ex calorico latente, seu ligato, aëris et aquae ad oeconomiam animalem redundant," in *Annales Academiae Groninganae* (1815–1816); "Commentatio ad quaestionem, ab ordine medico anno 1818 propositam, de sanguinis vase effluentes coagulatione," *ibid.* (1818–1819); *Dissertatio physiologica-medica inauguralis, sistens sanguinis coagulantis historiam, cum experimentis ad eam illustrandam institutis* (Groningen, 1820); *Observationes anatomico-pathologici et practici argumenti* (Amsterdam, 1826); *Oratio de anatomiae pathologicae praecipue subtilioris studio utilissimo et ad morborum naturam investigandam maxime commendando* (Utrecht, 1827); and *Eene Voorlezing over het verschil tusschen doode natuurkrachten, levenskrachten en ziel* (Utrecht, 1835), with German trans. reprinted in *Opuscula selecta Neerlandicorum de arte medica*, **11** (1932), 283–359.

Later writings are *Oratio de debita cura infaustam maniacorum sortem emendandi eosque sanandi in nostra patria neglecta* (Utrecht, 1837), with English trans. reprinted in *Opuscula selecta Neerlandicorum de arte medica*, 7 (1927), 294–352; "Anatomisch-physiologisch onderzoek over het fijnere zamenstel en de werking van het ruggemerg," in *Verhandelingen der Koninklijke akademie van wetenschappen*, 2 (1855); and "Over het fijnere zamenstel en de werking van het verlengde ruggemerg en over de naaste oorzaak van epilepsie en hare rationele behandeling," *ibid.*, 6 (1858). The last two were translated by W. D. Moore as *On the Minute Structure and Functions of the Spinal Cord and Medulla Oblongata and On the Proximate Cause and Rational Treatment of Epilepsy* (London, 1859). See also *Handboek van de Pathologie en Therapie der Krankzinnigheid* (Utrecht, 1863), with trans. by J. T. Rudall as *The Pathology and Therapeutics of Mental Diseases* (London, 1870). Schroeder van der Kolk's lectures on physiology, "Physiologia corporis humani" (1840), are in G. ten Doesschate, *J. L. C. Schroeder van der Kolk als physioloog* (Utrecht, 1961).

II. SECONDARY LITERATURE. On Schroeder van der Kolk and his work, see C. A. Pekelharing, in *Nieuw Nederlandsch Biografisch Woordenboek*, II (Leiden, 1912), col. 700–705; W. Vrolik, in *Jaarboek van de Koninklijke Akademie van wetenschappen gevestigd te Amsterdam* (1862), 161–191; and P. van der Esch, *Jacobus Ludovicus Conradus Schroeder van der Kolk. 1797–1862. Leven en werken* (Amsterdam, 1954), with an extensive bibliography, pp. 95–119.

H. A. M. SNELDERS

SCHROETER, HEINRICH EDUARD (*b.* Königsberg, Germany [now Kaliningrad, R.S.F.S.R.], 8 January 1829; *d.* Breslau, Germany [now Wrocław, Poland], 3 January 1892), *mathematics*.

The son of a merchant, Schroeter attended the Altstädtische Gymnasium of his native city. In the summer of 1848 he began to study mathematics and physics at the University of Königsberg, and after his military service he continued his studies at Berlin for two years. He earned the doctorate at Königsberg in 1854 and qualified as lecturer in the fall of 1855 at the University of Breslau, where he

became extraordinary professor in 1858 and full professor in 1861. He taught at Breslau until his death but was severely handicapped by paralysis during the final years of his life.

As a student at Königsberg, Schroeter attended the mathematics lectures of Friedrich Richelot, a follower of Jacobi. At Berlin his most important teachers were Dirichlet and Jakob Steiner. The influence of Steiner's ideas, on synthetic geometry in particular, was so strong that Schroeter later devoted almost all his research to this branch of mathematics. For his doctoral dissertation (under Richelot) and *Habilitationsschrift*, however, he chose topics from the theory of elliptic functions. Schroeter became more widely known through his association with Steiner—specifically, by editing the second part of Steiner's lectures on synthetic geometry.

The publication of Steiner's lectures ended with this second part, but Schroeter's extensive book of 1880 on the theory of second-order surfaces and third-order space curves can be considered a continuation of Steiner's work. Among the topics Schroeter treated were many metric properties of quadrics and cubic space curves; for unlike Staudt, for example, he did not confine himself to pure projective geometry. Schroeter pursued Steiner's fundamental aim of generating more complicated geometric elements from simpler ones (for instance, generating conic sections from the intersections of corresponding straight lines of projectively related pencils). Schroeter's name has been given to the generation of a third-degree plane curve c starting from six points of the plane, given that c should pass through six points of the plane and that further points are to be obtained using only a ruler; and to two generations of a third-degree surface when only one point and four straight lines in P_3 are given.

In 1888 Schroeter published a book in which he applied his approach to third-order plane curves. His last separately printed publication (1890) was devoted to fourth-order space curves of the first species, that is, to total intersections of two quadrics. Examining this topic from the viewpoint of synthetic geometry, Schroeter obtained many results on these curves, which are closely related to plane cubics. In his last years he studied various plane and spatial configurations, employing—as in all his writings—a purely elementary approach. In his view, all multidimensional considerations were not elementary, as were all those that were later designated by Felix Klein as belonging to higher geometry.

Schroeter's most important student in synthetic geometry was Rudolf Sturm.

BIBLIOGRAPHY

Schroeter's ed. of Steiner's work is . . . *Vorlesungen über synthetische Geometrie. Zweiter Teil: Die Theorie der Kegelschnitte, gestützt auf projectivische Eigenschaften* (Leipzig, 1867; 2nd ed., 1876). His own writings include *Die Theorie der Oberflächen 2. Ordnung und der Raumkurven 3. Ordnung als Erzeugnisse projectivischer Gebilde* (Leipzig, 1880); *Die Theorie der ebenen Kurven 3. Ordnung, auf synthetischem Wege abgeleitet* (Leipzig, 1888); and *Grundzüge einer reingeometrischen Theorie der Raumkurven 4. Ordnung, I. Spezies* (Leipzig, 1890).

A biography is R. Sturm, "Heinrich Schroeter," in *Jahresberichte der Deutschen Mathematikervereinigung,* **2** (1893), 32–41.

WERNER BURAU

SCHRÖTER, JOHANN HIERONYMUS (*b.* Erfurt, Germany, 30 August 1745; *d.* Erfurt, 29 August 1816), *astronomy.*

Schröter studied law at Göttingen but also attended lectures in mathematics, physics, and astronomy, the last under Kästner. Upon completing his law studies he was appointed junior barrister in Hannover. Through his appreciation of music he met the Herschel family, who revived his interest in astronomy. In 1781 he became chief magistrate at Lilienthal, a post that left him free time to devote to astronomy. With the aid of the optician J. G. Schrader he built and equipped an observatory that subsequently became world-famous for the excellence of the instruments. Some were made in his own workshop; others he bought from Herschel, the latter including a reflector with a twenty-seven-foot focal length, the largest on the Continent. George III of England enabled Schröter to continue his astronomical work by buying all of his instruments, with the stipulation that they remain in Schröter's possession until his death, when they would become the property of the University of Göttingen. Schröter was also awarded a grant to hire an assistant. K. L. Harding and, later, F. W. Bessel were among those who held the post.

For thirty years the observatory at Lilienthal was a center of astronomical research and was visited by foreign astronomers. On 21 September 1800 it was the site of the congress organized to search the space between Mars and Jupiter for a planetary body.

Lilienthal was occupied during the Napoleonic Wars by the French, who looted and partly destroyed the observatory, although most of the instruments were saved. In the ensuing fire Schröter lost all copies of his own works, which he had published himself. He returned to Erfurt and built a new observatory, but his health failed and he did little observing. He died soon afterward.

Schröter was the first to observe the surface of the moon and the planets systematically over a long period. He made hundreds of drawings of lunar mountains and other features, and discovered and named the lunar rills. Unfortunately, his drawings were rough; and the standard of the images obtainable with the large reflectors was soon greatly improved by the refractors from the Munich workshops. *Selenotopographische Fragmente zur genauern Kenntniss der Mondfläche* was published at Lilienthal in 1791–1802. His observations of Venus appeared in *Aphroditographische Fragmente* . . . (Helmstedt, 1796), in which he estimated a rotation period of twenty-three hours and twenty-one minutes. He also thought that he observed mountains on the surface of Venus. In other works he noted lines on Mars (but did not call them canals), and he thought that the ring of Saturn was a solid body.

Schröter's reputation has been damaged by the many extravagant conclusions he drew from his observations. It may well be that his lasting influence on astronomy lies in the fact that he enabled Bessel and Harding to work in astronomy and that the selenographer J. F. J. Schmidt acquired his lifelong interest in the moon after he had read a copy of Schröter's work.

BIBLIOGRAPHY

A list of Schröter's publications can be found in Poggendorff, II, 846–847.

Secondary literature includes H.-B. Brenske, "Johann Hieronymus Schröter, der Amateurastronom von Lilienthal," in Walter Stein, ed., *Von Bremer Astronomen und Sternfreunden* (Bremen, 1958), 64–74; Gunther's article on Schröter in *Allgemeine deutsche Biographie,* XXXII, 570–572; and Dieter B. Herrmann, "Johann Hieronymus Schröter im Urtel seiner Zeit," in *Sterne,* **41** (1965), 136–143.

LETTIE S. MULTHAUF

SCHRÖTTER, ANTON VON (*b.* Olmütz, Austria [now Olomouc, Czechoslovakia], 26 November 1802; *d.* Vienna, Austria, 15 April 1875), *chemistry.*

Schrötter's father was an apothecary, and his mother was daughter of the mayor of Olmütz. In 1822, at his father's request, he entered the University of Vienna to study medicine but two years later turned to his true interest, mathematics and the natural sciences. On the advice of the mineralogist Friedrich Mohs, he devoted his attention to chemistry, learning applied analytical chemistry at the artillery school. Schrötter became assistant in physics and mathematics at the Technische Hochschule of Graz in 1827 and was promoted to professor of physics and chemistry three years later. Shortly thereafter he took a leave of absence and visited the important chemical laboratories in Germany and Paris. Using the experience gained on his trip, especially during his stay with Liebig at Giessen, he set up an impressive laboratory at Graz. In 1843 he was named professor of chemical technology at the Technische Hochschule in Vienna, and in 1845 he became professor of general chemistry. Appointed chief director of the mint in 1868, he held that position until his retirement in 1874.

Although he published over sixty papers on pure and applied chemistry, chiefly on the behavior of metals at very high and low temperatures, Schrötter is best known for his conclusive demonstration that red phosphorus (believed to be an oxide of white phosphorus) is truly an allotropic form of the element. In 1847 he demonstrated before the Vienna Academy that white phosphorus in a hermetically sealed bulb tube would turn red upon exposure to light although no oxygen or moisture was present. His suggestion of using amorphous phosphorus in the manufacture of matches led to the development of the safety match. This achievement brought him the Montyon Prize of the French Academy in 1856 and the Legion of Honor at the Paris Exhibition of 1855 for his great contribution to public safety. One of the active promoters of the Vienna Royal Academy of Sciences, Schrötter was a founding member and served as general secretary from 1850 until his death.

BIBLIOGRAPHY

I. Original Works. Schrötter's important paper on red phosphorus appeared in several journals under several different titles. One is "Über einen neuen allotro-

pischen Zustand des Phosphors," in *Annalen der Physik und Chemie* (Poggendorff), **81** (1850), 276–298. An English abstract was published as "On the Allotropic Condition of Phosphorus," in *Report of the British Association for the Advancement of Science,* **19**, pt. 2 (1849), 42. His work on the safety match is described in his chapter on phosphorus and matches in August W. Hofmann, ed., *Bericht über die Entwickelung der chemischen Industrie während des letzten Jahrzehnts,* 2 vols. (Brunswick, 1875–1877). A bibliography of Schrötter's publications is in an unsigned obituary, "Anton Schrötter," in *Berichte der Deutschen chemischen Gesellschaft,* **9** (1876), 90–108.

II. Secondary Literature. The obituary notice cited above is the most detailed of several short sketches of Schrötter's life. The most complete English obituary is an unsigned, untitled article in *Journal of the Chemical Society,* **29** (1876), 622–625. On his work with phosphorus, see Moritz Kohn, "The Discovery of Red Phosphorus (1847) by Anton von Schrötter (1802–1875)," in *Journal of Chemical Education,* **21** (1944), 522–554.

Sheldon J. Kopperl

SCHUBERT, HERMANN CÄSAR HANNIBAL (*b.* Potsdam, Germany, 22 May 1848; *d.* Hamburg, Germany, 20 July 1911), *mathematics.*

Schubert, the son of an innkeeper, attended secondary schools in Potsdam and Spandau. He first studied mathematics and physics in 1867 at the University of Berlin and then went to Halle, where he received the doctorate in 1870. Soon afterward he became a secondary school teacher; his first post was at the Andreanum Gymnasium in Hildesheim (1872–1876). In 1876 he accepted the same post at the Johanneum in Hamburg. He remained there until 1908, having been promoted in 1887 to the rank of professor. Besides this school activity he was engaged by the Hamburg authorities to teach adult courses in which he dealt with various fields of mathematics for teachers already in the profession. In 1905 Schubert began to suffer from circulatory disorders that forced him to retire three years later. He died after a long illness that, toward the end, left him paralyzed. Schubert married Anna Hamel in 1873; they had four daughters.

Schubert published sixty-three works, including several books. His place in the history of mathematics is due chiefly to his work in enumerative geometry. He quickly established a reputation in that field on the basis of his doctoral dissertation, "Zur Theorie der Charakteristiken" (1870), and two earlier papers on the system of sixteen spheres that touch four given spheres. When he was only twenty-six, Schubert won the Gold Medal of the Royal Danish Academy of Sciences for the solution of a prize problem posed by H. G. Zeuthen on the extension of the theory of characteristics in cubic space curves (1874). A member of the Société Mathématique de France and honorary member of the Royal Netherlands Academy of Sciences, Schubert knew and corresponded with such famous geometers as Klein, Loria, and Hurwitz.

Schubert was content to remain in Hamburg, which had no university until 1919. Like Hermann Grassmann, he never became a university teacher and, in fact, declined offers that would have enabled him to do so. Mathematics in Hamburg centered in this period on the Mathematische Gesellschaft (founded in 1690 and still in existence), in the *Mitteilungen* of which Schubert published a number of papers.

In 1879 Schubert was able to present the methods and many individual results of his research in *Kalkül der abzählenden Geometrie.* Many further results were in papers he published until 1903.

Enumerative geometry is concerned with all those problems and theorems of algebraic geometry that involve a finite number of solutions. For example:

1. Bézout's theorem of the plane: two algebraic curves of orders a and b with no common elements have no more than ab points of intersection in common; this number can be reached.

2. Apollonius' theorem, according to which there are eight circles that simultaneously touch three given circles in the plane. Schubert's earliest works dealt with a spatial generalization of this theorem.

3. A somewhat more difficult result of enumerative geometry, Halphen's theorem: two algebraic linear congruences of P_3, one of order a and class $b,$ and the other of order a' and class $b',$ have in general $aa' + bb'$ straight lines in common.

Algebraically, the solution of the problems of enumerative geometry amounts to finding the number of solutions for certain systems of algebraic equations with finitely many solutions. Since the direct algebraic solution of the problems is possible only in the simplest cases, mathematicians sought to transform the system of equations, by continuous variation of the constants involved, into a system for which the number of solutions could be determined more easily. Poncelet devised this process, which he called the principle of continuity; in

his day, of course, the method could not be elucidated in exact terms. Schubert's achievement was to combine this procedure, which he called "the principle of the conservation of the number," with the Chasles correspondence principle, thus establishing the foundation of a calculus. With the aid of this calculus, which he modeled on Ernst Schröder's logical calculus, Schubert was able to solve many problems systematically.

In *Kalkül der abzählenden Geometrie* Schubert formulated his fundamental problem as follows: Let C_k be a given set of geometric objects that depend on k parameters. Then, on the model of Bézout's theorem, formulate theorems on the number of common objects of two subsets C_a and C'_{k-a} of $C_k.$ Here C_a (and analogously C'_{k-a} are designated by certain characteristics, that is numbers $\rho_1, \cdots, \rho_s$ of objects that C_a has in common with certain previously designated elementary sets $E^1_{k-a}, \cdots, E^s_{k-a}$ of C_k of dimension $k - a.$ The best known of Schubert's investigations are those for the case where C_k is the totality of all subspaces P_d of the projective $P_n,$ where $k = (n - d)(d + 1).$ The appropiate elementary sets have since been known as Schubert sets, defined as follows: Let P_{a_i} ($i = 0, 1, \cdots, d$) be subspaces of $P_n,$ each of them of dimension a_i with $0 \leqslant a_0 < a_1 < \cdots < a_d \leqslant n$ and $P'_{a_0} \subset P'_{a_1} \subset \cdots \subset P'_{a_d}.$ Then Schubert designated as $[a_0, a_1, \cdots, a_d]$ the set of those P_d that intersect P'_{a_i} in at least i dimensions ($i = 0, 1, \cdots, d$). If the totality of all P_d in P_n is mapped into the points of the Grassmann-manifold $G_{n,d},$ there corresponds to $[a_0, a_1, \cdots, a_d]$ a subset of dimension $a_0 + a_1 + \cdots + a_d - \binom{d+1}{2}$ on $G_{n,d}.$ Later investigations have shown that the Schubert sets are precisely the basic sets of $G_{n,d}$ in Severi's sense.

Another set that Schubert studied is the totality C_6 of all plane triangles. His results on this set were rederived and confirmed from the modern standpoint by J. G. Semple.

Schubert could not rigorously demonstrate the principle of the conservation of number with the means available in his time, and E. Study and G. Kohn showed through counterexamples that it could lead to false conclusions. Schubert avoided such errors through his sure instinct. In 1900, in his famous Paris lecture David Hilbert called for an exact proof of Schubert's principle (problem no. 15). In 1912 Severi published a rigorous proof, but it was little known outside Italy. B. L. van der Waerden independently established the principle in 1930 on the basis of the recently created concepts of modern algebra and topology.

Schubert was known to a broader public as the

editor of Sammlung Schubert, a series of textbooks in wide use before World War I. He wrote the first volume of the series, on arithmetic and algebra, and a subsequent volume on lower analysis. He also edited tables of logarithms and collections of problems for schools and published a simple method for computing logarithms.

Schubert was very interested in recreational mathematics and games of all kinds, including chess and skat, and in the mathematical questions that arise in connection with them. In 1897 he published the first edition of his book on recreational mathematics, *Mathematische Mussestunden;* the second edition, expanded to three volumes, appeared in 1900; and a thirteenth edition, revised by J. Erlebach, appeared in 1967. Schubert also was the author of the first article to appear in the *Encyklopädie der mathematischen Wissenschaften:* "Grundlagen der Arithmetik." His article, however, was subjected to severe criticism by the great pioneer in this area, Gottlob Frege.

BIBLIOGRAPHY

I. ORIGINAL WORKS. Schubert's writings include "Zur Theorie der Charakteristiken," in *Journal für die reine und angewandte Mathematik,* **71** (1870), 366–386; *Kalkül der abzählenden Geometrie* (Leipzig, 1879); "Abzählende Geometrie der Dreiecke," in *Mathematische Annalen,* **17** (1880), 153–212; *Mathematische Mussestunden* (Leipzig, 1897; 2nd ed., 3 vols., 1900; 13th ed., enl. by J. Erlebach, 1967); "Grundlagen der Arithmetik," in *Encyklopädie der mathematische Wissenschaften,* I, pt. 1 (1898), 1–29; *Arithmetik und Algebra* (Leipzig, 1898–1904); and *Niedere Analysis* (Leipzig, 1902).

II. SECONDARY LITERATURE. See W. Burau, "Der Hamburger Mathematiker Hermann Schubert," in *Mitteilungen der Mathematischen Gesellschaft in Hamburg,* 9th ser., **3** (1966), 10–20; G. Kohn, "Über das Prinzip von der Erhaltung der Anzahl," in *Archiv der Mathematik und Physik,* 3rd ser., **4** (1902), 312–316; J. G. Semple, "The Triangle as a Geometric Variable," in *Mathematica,* **1** (1954), 80–88; F. Severi, "Sul principio della conservazione del numero," in *Rendiconti del Circolo mathematico di Palermo,* **33** (1912), 313–327; "I fondamenti della geometria numerative," in *Annali di matematica pura ed applicata,* 4th ser., **19** (1940), 153–242; and *Grundlagen der abzählenden Geometrie* (Wolfenbüttel, 1948); and B. L. van der Waerden, "Topologische Begründung des Kalküls der abzählenden Geometrie," in *Mathematische Annalen,* **102** (1930), 337–362.

WERNER BURAU

SCHUCHERT, CHARLES (*b.* Cincinnati, Ohio, 3 July 1858; *d.* New Haven, Connecticut, 20 November 1942), *paleontology.*

Schuchert began his career as an untrained amateur collector of fossils and completed it as perhaps the most influential synthesizer of historical geology in North America. The oldest of six children of an impoverished immigrant Bavarian cabinetmaker, he received formal schooling only between the ages of six and twelve in a Catholic parochial school, which he was forced to leave to work in the family business. By the time he reached twenty, his father's health had failed and Schuchert was forced to support the entire household. In the meanwhile, fortunately, he had developed an intense interest in fossils and had amassed a significant collection.

Cincinnati, Ohio, lies in an area of Late Ordovician shales and limestone. These rocks are so crowded with fossils that before widespread urban paving specimens could even be collected from the street gutters after every rain. The city may well be built on the most fossiliferous spot on earth. For much of the nineteenth century, the "Cincinnati school" of enthusiastic amateurs was a vital part of the American study of paleontology.

In 1878 Schuchert joined forces with E. O. Ulrich, another local worker who rose to worldwide prominence as a paleontologist. Subsequently, Schuchert's business was destroyed by fire, but in the interim he had learned the art of lithographic illustration. Between 1884 and 1887 he was employed by Ulrich, and they drew more than 100 plates of illustrations of bryozoans—complex colonial organisms—for the geological surveys of Minnesota and Illinois. Concurrently he built up a magnificent collection of fossil brachiopods.

Both Schuchert's skill as an illustrator and the value of his collection induced James Hall, state geologist of New York, to employ him. Beginning in November 1888 he spent thirty months in Albany assisting in both the illustration and the writing of a classic text on brachiopods, but he received scant credit for his work. Schuchert worked for the Minnesota Geological Survey from 1891 to 1892, when available funds were exhausted. He then assisted C. E. Beecher at Yale in the preparation of fossils on large slabs that were exhibited at the Columbian Exposition in Chicago (1893).

C. D. Walcott, who had also worked under Hall's supervision, which bordered on the tyrannical, arranged in 1893 for Schuchert to join the U.S. Geological Survey in Washington. When Walcott became director of the Survey in 1894, most fossil collections were transferred to the U.S. National Museum, where Schuchert remained as curator for a decade. His summers were spent in fieldwork, including one season with R. E. Peary in western Greenland. During the winter he reorganized museum exhibits, curated collections, and studied fossils. He published about thirty papers during this decade, of which *Synopsis of American Fossil Brachiopoda* (1897) is the most enduring. He also prepared the section on Brachiopoda for the Zittel-Eastman *Text-Book of Paleontology* (1900).

Following Beecher's death in 1904, Schuchert was invited to join the Yale University faculty. At the age of forty-six he began a second career as a professor; the transition from museum to classroom apparently was painful but eventually highly successful. For the next twenty-one years he trained and influenced dozens of graduate students. His portion of *A Text-Book of Geology* (1915), written with L. V. Pirsson, went through several revisions and for at least three decades was the definitive American text of historical geology. For ten years Schuchert was chairman of the geology department of the Sheffield Scientific School and then served two additional years as head of a university-wide department.

A direct outgrowth of Schuchert's teaching efforts was the summarization of numerous stratigraphic details on maps to give a better picture of the changing distribution of land and seas during 600 million years. Although there is some doubt as to whether Schuchert or Ulrich was the first in North America to utilize this method of synthesizing data, there is no question as to the volume of work accomplished and the worldwide preeminence of Schuchert in this field. His 1910 "Paleogeography of North America" was a pioneer work and remains a classic. More than seventy-five other papers were written during this twenty-year interval. His work on older fossil starfish and a revision of the brachiopod section in the second edition (1913) of the Zittel-Eastman treatise are particularly noteworthy. He also directed substantial amounts of fieldwork with students in eastern Canada, a region in which he had special interest.

Schuchert completed his formal teaching career in 1923 but continued to advise and assist graduate students for almost two decades. His later research accomplishments were formidable, even for a bachelor "wedded to his science." With the aid of Clara Mae LeVene, he prepared another summary of published data on brachiopods, as well as a popular geology book and the definitive biography of the vertebrate paleontologist O. C. Marsh (1940).

Schuchert and Cooper (1932) is a standard reference for the study of two orders of brachiopods, but only one of many papers produced. In keeping his textbook on historical geology current, he became increasingly concerned with worldwide problems of correlation and methodology in the science, and this breadth of interest is reflected in the titles of his papers

The capstone of Schuchert's career was the publication of volume I of *Historical Geology of North America* (1935), on the Antillean-Caribbean region. A second volume, on the stratigraphy of the eastern and central United States, was published the year following his death; and a third was left partially completed. Without question Schuchert was the leader in synthesizing the geologic history of North America and was the last to grasp the entire literature encompassing details of 600 million years of change.

BIBLIOGRAPHY

Adolf Knopf, "Biographical Memoir of Charles Schuchert 1858–1942," in *Biographical Memoirs. National Academy of Sciences,* **27** (1952), 363–389, is the principal source that lists other memorials. In particular the memorial by C. O. Dunbar in *Proceedings of the Geological Society of America for 1942* (1943), 217–240, should be consulted. The esteem in which the Schuchert and Dunbar text on historical geology was held may be gathered from a review of the fourth edition (1941) by Cary Croneis in *Journal of Geology,* **49** (1941), 776–779.

ELLIS L. YOCHELSON

SCHULTZE, MAX JOHANN SIGISMUND (*b.* Freiburg im Breisgau, Germany, 25 March 1825; *d.* Bonn, Germany, 16 January 1874), *anatomy, microscopy.*

Schultze played a leading role in the movement to reform the cell theory as originally set forth by Schleiden and Schwann. Above all, Schultze and the other reformers disputed Schleiden and Schwann's emphasis on the cell wall and directed attention instead to the living substance (protoplasm) found within all cells, whether plant or animal.

Schultze was born to Frederike Bellermann and Karl August Sigismund Schultze, then professor of anatomy and physiology at the University of Freiburg. In 1830, when Schultze was five, his father became professor of anatomy at the University of Greifswald. After early education at home, where his interests in natural history, music, and drawing were nurtured and encouraged, Schultze attended the Gymnasium at Greifswald, and studied there from 1835 to 1845. In the summer of 1845 he entered the University of Greifswald as a medical student. He received all of his formal training there, except for the winter semester of 1846–1847, when he went to the University of Berlin. There he heard Johannes Müller lecture on anatomy and physiology and Ernst Brücke on the theory and use of the microscope. With a dissertation on the structure, function, and chemical composition of the arteries, Schultze graduated M.D. from Greifswald on 16 August 1849.

After another winter in Berlin, where he passed the state medical examination, Schultze returned to Greifswald as prosector in anatomy to his father. Later in 1850 he was also named *Privatdozent* in the faculty of medicine at Greifswald. He moved to Halle as assistant professor of anatomy in October 1854. In 1859 he became professor of anatomy and director of the anatomical institute at Bonn, where he remained despite offers from the universities of Strasbourg and Leipzig. At Bonn he planned and supervised the construction of a new anatomical institute, completed in 1872. Schultze was twice married; in 1854, to his cousin Christine Bellermann, who died of typhoid fever in 1865; and in 1868, to Sophie Sievers of Bonn. His death in 1874 was attributed to a perforated duodenal ulcer.

In 1851 Schultze found chlorophyll in the flatworm Turbellaria, thereby contributing to the recognition that animals as well as plants can contain that substance. His achievement won him an honorary Ph.D. from the University of Rostock in 1852 and the Blumenbach Traveling Scholarship from the University of Berlin in 1853. Schultze used this scholarship to go to Italy, where he studied marine zoology on the shores of the Adriatic Sea. Like Dujardin before him, he focused on the semifluid substance within the calcareous shells of the foraminifera. In a monograph of 1854 he described the results of this work and proposed the creation of a new class of shelled rhizopods, the Monothalamia, which lacked the internal partitions of Ehrenberg's Polythalamia. The monograph earned him Ehrenberg's lasting enmity.

In 1858 Schultze drew attention to the remarkable similarity between cyclosis in lower plants (notably the marine diatoms) and the streaming of granules in the pseudopodia of foraminifera and other lower animals. He also found that physical and chemical agents produced strikingly uniform effects on the contractile contents of plant and animal cells. By 1860 his studies of protozoa had led him to a generalization that implied a redefinition of the cell: "The less perfectly the surface of the protoplasm is hardened to a membrane, the nearer to the primitive membraneless condition does the cell find itself, a condition in which it exhibits only a small lump of protoplasm with nucleus."[1]

This definition of the cell as "ein nacktes Protoplasmaklümpchen mit Kern" became famous chiefly through Schultze's paper "Ueber Muskelkörperchen und das was man eine zelle zu nennen habe" (1861). At the time, controversy surrounded these "muscle corpuscles"—small, granular, spindlelike, nucleated masses of protoplasm found among the contractile fibers of striated muscle. Some histologists took these bodies to be complete cells while others supposed they were merely isolated nuclei. Schultze claimed that the argument stemmed mainly from disagreement over the definition of a cell. If histologists would only abandon the old "botanical" conception of the cell as a "bladderlike structure with membrane, contents, and nucleus," if they would recognize instead that a cell need not have a chemically distinct membrane, then they might agree with Schultze that the muscle corpuscles were wall-less cells that had fused to form a colonial muscle fiber. This particular conclusion eventually lost favor among histologists, who came to regard the muscle fiber as a single, multinucleated cell rather than as fused colony of many independent cells. But Schultze's redefinition of the cell and his emphasis on the cell substance won widespread support, despite the opposition of Remak and Reichert.

Even before Schultze entered the arena, Alexander Braun, Ferdinand Cohn, and Franz Leydig, among others, had sought to establish an identity between plant and animal cell substances and to insist that a cell need not have a distinct membrane. Schultze himself admitted that he intended only "to dress in words that which many have long perceived, though perhaps less definitely."[2] That his work nonetheless attracted so much attention can be ascribed to two factors: (1) unlike his predecessors, Schultze gave prominent attention to a tissue (muscle) characteristic of higher, differentiated animals; (2) he also campaigned for the adoption of a single word—protoplasm—to refer to the cell substance of both plants and animals. Following Dujardin, zoologists had generally used the name "sarcode" for the contractile contents of animal cells. Schultze urged them to adopt instead the name used by botanists for the plant cell substance and thereby to acknowledge "the complete correspondence that exists between plant and animal cells in all essential respects."[3]

This seemingly trivial suggestion helped to crystallize thinking about the substance of life, and the 1860's became "a heyday for speculation upon the nature of protoplasm and for the celebration of its amazing properties."[4] Gradually, as it became clear that protoplasm was not a unitary chemical substance but a dynamic emulsion of several substances, and as the quest for a substance of life focused increasingly on the nucleus, protoplasm lost much of its allure. Moreover, the detection of the plasma membrane—notably through Overton's plasmolytic studies of the 1890's—qualified Schultze's claim that a cell required no limiting boundary. Nonetheless, Schultze's critique of the original cell theory—and especially of the place of the cell wall in that theory—retained much of its cogency.

Apart from his role in the reform of the cell theory, Schultze did his most important work on the sense organs, particularly the retina, which was the subject of his inaugural lecture at Bonn in 1859. In a monograph of 1867 Schultze sought especially to elucidate the physiological role of the rods and cones. Emphasizing that the rods predominated in nocturnal animals (including the bat, the cat, and the owl), he suggested that these structures were better adapted than the cones for the simple perception of light. Partly because the sense of color in humans was proportional to the number of cones in a given region of the retina, he argued that the cones probably acted as the terminal nerve organs of the color sense, although they obviously served other visual functions as well.

Schultze also did valuable descriptive and taxonomic work, especially on rhizopods and sponges, although he shared the common skepticism of German naturalists toward Darwinian evolutionary theory. In 1864 he described prickles in the stratified squamous epithelium of mammalian tongue and skin, but without recognizing them as plasmodesmata. In 1865 he gave a clear description of the blood platelets. His studies of bioluminescence and of the electric organs of fishes also attracted considerable attention.

Schultze founded in 1865 and edited until his death the *Archiv für mikroskopische Anatomie und Entwicklungsmechanik*. This esteemed journal, in which he published most of his later papers, won the support of many of the leading German histologists and microscopists of the day. A consummate master of microscopic technique, Schultze introduced osmic acid as a fixative and iodized serum as a preservative "physiological fluid." He also designed a "hot stage" for the microscope, allowing the investigator to heat his preparations within reasonably precise temperatures. In the judgment of N. E. Nordenskiöld, Schultze "brought cytology to the farthest point possible" before the introduction of the microtome.[5]

NOTES

1. Max Schultze, "Die Gattung Cornuspira unter den Monothalamien und Bemerkungen über die Organisation und Fortpflanzung der Polythalamien," in *Archiv für Naturgeschichte*, **26** (1860), 299. Cf. *ibid.*, 305. See also Baker, "The Cell Theory," pt. 3, pp. 164–165.
2. Schultze, "Ueber Muskelkörperchen," 8.
3. *Ibid.*, 2, n. 2.
4. Coleman, "Cell, Nucleus, and Inheritance," 128.
5. Nils Erik Nordenskiöld, *The History of Biology: A Survey*, trans. from the Swedish by Leonard Bucknall Eyre (New York, 1949), 533–534.

BIBLIOGRAPHY

I. Original Works. Schultze's published monographs include *Beiträge zur Naturgeschichte der Turbellarien. Erste Abtheilung* (Greifswald, 1851); *Ueber den Organismus der Polythalamien (Foraminiferen) nebst Bemerkungen über die Rhizopoden im Allgemeinen* (Leipzig, 1854); *Das Protoplasma der Rhizopoden und der Pflanzenzelle* (Leipzig, 1863); and *Zur Anatomie und Physiologie der Retina* (Bonn, 1867). For his famous paper on "muscle corpuscles," see "Ueber Muskelkörperchen und das was man eine Zelle zu nennen habe," in *Archiv für Anatomie, Physiologie und wissenschaftliche Medizin* (1861), 1–27.

In his obituary notice Schwalbe (see below) gives a chronological bibliography of eighty-two items by Schultze. The Royal Society *Catalogue of Scientific Papers*, V. 571–573; VIII, 894–895; XII, 66, lists eighty-eight papers by Schultze alone and one written with M. Rudneff. Nonetheless, Schwalbe's bibliography is probably complete, for the Royal Society *Catalogue* sometimes gives a separate listing to trans. or to multiple items that Schwalbe includes under one entry.

II. Secondary Literature. G. Schwalbe's obituary notice, in *Archiv für mikroskopische Anatomie und Entwicklungsmechanik*, **10** (1874), i–xxiii, provides the basis for the article by Theodor H. Bast, in *Annals of Medical History*, n.s. **3** (1931), 166–178. Brief sketches, also derivative from Schwalbe, appear in *Allgemeine deutsche Biographie*, LIV (1908), 256–257; and in *Biographisches Lexicon der hervorragenden Ärzte aller Zeiten und Völker*, 2nd ed., V (1934), 162–163.

More generally, see William Coleman, "Cell, Nucleus, and Inheritance: An Historical Study," in *Proceedings* of the American Philosophical Society, **109** (1965), 124–158; G. L. Geison, "The Protoplasmic Theory of Life and the Vitalist-Mechanist Debate," in *Isis*, **60** (1969), 273–292; and "Towards a Substance of Life: Concepts of Protoplasm, 1835–1870" (M.A. thesis, Yale Univ., 1967), esp. ch. 4; and John R. Baker, "The Cell Theory: A Restatement, History, and Critique," in *Quarterly Journal of Microscopical Science*, in five parts: **89** (1948), 103–125; **90** (1949), 87–108; **93** (1952), 157–190; **94** (1953), 407–440; and **96** (1955), 449–481. References to Schultze will be found in pt. 2, pp. 95–96, and in pt. 3, pp. 164–165, 172, 176, 180, 189.

Gerald L. Geison

SCHULZE, FRANZ FERDINAND (b. Naumburg, Germany, 17 January 1815; d. Rostock, Germany, 15 April 1873), *chemistry, microbiology.*

Schulze's career was centered principally around teaching agricultural chemistry at Eldena and chemistry and pharmacy at Rostock. Although his particular interests were wide-ranging, the core of much of his work was his expertise in analytical chemistry. He was not a great innovator but made a number of useful modifications to existing analytical techniques and equipment, such as in gas analysis and in the use of the blowpipe in the production of laboratory glassware (1).

Many of Schulze's activities were in the field of applied science, for example his long paper (1868) on the examination of well water for "those particles which are most relevant in hygiene"(2). In this study, prompted by an outbreak of cholera in Rostock in 1866, Schulze included a judicious summary of the difficulties of interpreting the nature and significance of airborne organic matter. He thus contributed to the current, far-reaching debate on whether microorganisms could be spontaneously generated from, for example, the floating organic matter that was widely believed also to cause fermentation and putrefaction. Schulze indicated that much organic matter was harmless, but the difficulty lay in identifying that which was undoubtedly poisonous. He felt, too, that the latter might be synonymous with the "mysterious domain" of microorganisms, as was being suggested by Pasteur. Schulze's interest in the subject of spontaneous generation of microorganisms extended back to 1836. At that time he demonstrated that after air was bubbled slowly through sulfuric acid, no growth of organisms occurred in a sterile culture medium through which the air was next passed (3). This carefully conducted experiment had consider-

able influence, for it was repeated frequently (sometimes with contradictory results) during the peak of controversy (from the late 1850's to the 1870's) over the question of spontaneous generation of microorganisms. It thus contributed significantly to the developing awareness of the experimental difficulties involved in handling microorganisms.

Although the title of Schulze's paper suggested that it was a preliminary communication, he published nothing more on spontaneous generation and immersed himself in agricultural and chemical topics. Much of his chemistry involved natural products, including the difficult areas of lignins and carbohydrates (4). Although current chemical techniques limited what he could accomplish, some of his results on the chemical similarities of lignins from various sources, and on the properties of starch, were sound. Apart from his laboratory achievements, Schulze also contributed to education, including his translation into German (5) of J. F. W. Johnston's *Elements of Agricultural Chemistry and Geology* (Edinburgh, 1841). Johnston was notably successful in stimulating interest in the application of science to agriculture, and Schulze wrote in his preface to the translation that "the more we [Germans] have reason to turn our attention to the practical sense and high level of development of [English] agriculture, the greater must be our trust in their judgment" (6). This comment—although apparently forgetting Liebig's agricultural studies—was just, and it also illustrates Schulze's own practical outlook.

BIBLIOGRAPHY

Schulze's writings include (1) "Die gasvolumetrische Analyse, als Hülfsmittel für wissenschaftliche agriculturchemische und technische Untersuchungen," in *Zeitschrift für analytische Chemie*, **2** (1863), 289–300; and "Beschreiben eines für chemische Laboratorien anwendbaren gebläse Apparates," in *Journal für praktische Chemie*, **43** (1848), 368–372; (2) "Ueber die Untersuchung der Brunnenwässer auf diejenigen Bestandtheile, welche für die Gesundheitspflege am meisten in betracht kommen," in *Dinglers polytechnisches Journal*, **188** (1868), 197–219; (3) "Vorläusige Mittheilung resultate einer experimentallen Beobachtung über generatio aequivoca," in *Annalen der Physik*, **39** (1836), 487–489; (4) "Beitrag zur Kenntniss des Lignins," in *Chemisches Zentralblatt*, n.s. 2 (1857), 321–325; and "Ueber die Metamorphose des Amylums," in *Annalen der Physik*, **39** (1836), 489–493; (5) *Anfangsgründe der praktischen Agricultur-Chemie und Geologie* (Neubrandenburg, 1845); and (6) *ibid.*, p. 4.

Schulze's many publications are in a variety of journals. No comprehensive list has been compiled, but most of his works are referred to in F. Ferchl, *Chemisch-pharmazeutisches Bio- und Bibliographikon* (Mittenwald, 1938), 490. Some background to his teaching career, particularly at Rostock, is in R. Schmitz, *Die Deutschen pharmaceutische chemischen Hochschulinstitute* (Stuttgart, 1969).

J. K. CRELLIN

SCHUMACHER, HEINRICH CHRISTIAN (*b*. Bad Bramstedt, Holstein, Germany, 3 September 1780; d. Altona, Germany, 28 December 1850), *astronomy, geodesy.*

Schumacher was the son of Andreas Schumacher, a magistrate, who died when the boy was nine. Schumacher was then placed under the care of a minister named Dörfer at the Lutheran church of Altona. He attended the Gymnasium at Altona, where he was introduced to mathematics, astronomy, and the use of astronomical instruments; studied jurisprudence at the universities of Kiel and Göttingen; and was awarded the LL.D. at Göttingen in 1806. In 1805–1806 he was a *Dozent* at the Faculty of Law of Dorpat and wrote two legal treatises. It was at Dorpat that Schumacher's interest in astronomy was revived by J. Pfaff.

In 1807 Schumacher obtained a salaried position at the University of Göttingen and studied astronomy under the direction of Gauss. His firm friendship with Gauss, begun at this time, was lifelong. From 1808 to 1810 Schumacher studied mathematics in Hamburg and translated Lazare Carnot's *La géométrie de position.* J. G. Repsold gave Schumacher access to the observatory at Hamburg, where he made a series of observations that served as the basis of a new star catalog.

In 1810 Schumacher was named extraordinary professor of astronomy at the University of Copenhagen; but he did not assume the duties connected with this post until after Thomas Bugge's death in 1815, serving in the meantime as director of the observatory at Mannheim (1813–1815). In 1817 the Danish government released Schumacher from his duties so that he could take part in the geodetic survey of Schleswig and Holstein.

During the years 1800–1825, the mapping of territory was in progress in many European states including Holland, Prussia, Hesse, and Bavaria. The work simultaneously in progress in many centers had to be coordinated. Schumacher was involved in the measurement of a degree between Skagen and Lauenburg, and also in the determination of the longitude along the arc between Copenhagen and the west coast of Jutland.

In 1821 Schumacher was appointed to direct the survey by the Royal Danish Academy of Copenhagen. In the same year the king, Frederick VI, arranged for the building and equipping of the observatory at Altona, where Schumacher worked for many years. His determination of the base line for the measurement of a degree between Skagen and Lauenburg was a masterpiece of accuracy and was in almost perfect agreement with the Hannoverian measurement by Gauss and the Hessian and Bavarian triangulations. Bessel used Schumacher's results in his calculations of the figure of the earth.

Schumacher rendered considerable service to astronomers of his day by the institution of various publications. Between 1820 and 1829 he published astronomical ephemerides and auxiliary tables in a form that did not necessitate reduction calculations. From 1829 the *Berliner astronomisches Jahrbuch,* edited by Bessel, continued to publish similar tables. In 1823 Schumacher edited the first volume of *Astronomische Nachrichten,* a journal to which astronomers of all nations could contribute. The founding of this journal, which is still published, is perhaps his greatest contribution to astronomy. He was at the center of a lively correspondence with the leading astronomers of his day, including Gauss, Olbers, and Bessel.

In conjunction with the English Board of Longitude, Schumacher in 1824 determined the difference in longitude between the observatories of Greenwich and Altona, using English and Danish chronometers. In 1830 he determined the length of a seconds pendulum at the castle of Güldenstein in Holstein, and between 1837 and 1839 he carried out experimental work for the Danish government on a comparison of the most important legal units of weight. Schumacher continued his topographical work until 1837, when the preparation of maps was taken over by the army.

Schumacher was elected to the Royal Society of London in 1821, and his portrait by H. Wolf was presented to the Society by the artist in 1847. Schumacher was honored by the Danish kings Frederick VI and Christian VIII.

BIBLIOGRAPHY

I. ORIGINAL WORKS. Sixty-four titles of papers and scientific writings by Schumacher are listed in the Royal Society *Catalogue of Scientific Papers*, V, 576–577. See also Poggendorff, II, cols. 866–867.

II. SECONDARY LITERATURE. A biographical account

of Schumacher is given in a lengthy obituary by C. F. R. Olufsen in *Astronomische Nachrichten,* **36**, supp. 864 (1853), cols. 393–404. Further biographical information appears in *English Cyclopaedia,* Biography Div., V (London, 1867), 343; *Allgemeine deutsche Biographie,* XXXIII, 32–33; and *Dansk biografisk Leksikon,* XXI, 429–432.

SISTER MAUREEN FARRELL, F.C.J.

SCHUMANN, VICTOR (*b.* Markranstädt, near Leipzig, Germany, 21 December 1841; *d.* Leipzig, 1 September 1913), *photography.*

Schumann is known among physicists as UV Schumann because of his development of photographic plates capable of registering ultraviolet light. The son of Karl Ferdinand Schumann, a physician, he attended the local elementary school and was then sent to a *Realschule* in Leipzig. Following a year of practical training in an engineering works, he studied mechanical engineering from 1861 to 1864 at the Royal Technical College at Chemnitz (now Karl-Marx-Stadt). In 1865 he was cofounder of an engineering works in Leipzig of which he served as technical director. Schumann was obliged to retire in 1893 because of overwork and damage to his eyes that appeared to be leading to blindness. His first wife, Auguste Baumgarten, daughter of a factory owner in Chemnitz, whom he married in 1871 after a youthful romance, died only seven years later. He remained a widower until 1909, when he married Elise Börner.

Schumann was an extremely successful engineer and designer, especially of machines for book production. It was, however, in photography that he won international recognition. Schumann took up photography as a hobby in 1872 and, after the death of his wife, spent all his limited leisure time on it. He became a member of the Berlin Photographic Society in 1882 (and later an honorary member), and in 1894 the University of Halle awarded him an honorary doctorate. During the last three years of his life he was also a full member of the Royal Saxon Academy of Sciences in Leipzig.

Schumann took up photography while it was still in its infancy. The necessity for long exposures was further complicated by the impossibility of representing various tints by different degrees of photographic density: a red or yellow object, for example, appeared as dark as a black one. Schumann found, however, that adding a small amount of silver iodide to the customary silver bromide emulsion not only permitted significantly shorter exposures, but also yielded markedly improved contrasts for red and yellow objects. This finding contradicted the publications of experts in England and on the Continent, who claimed that the addition of silver iodide produced still weaker contrasts. Accepting the challenge implicit in this disagreement, Schumann demonstrated that both sides were justified in their claims. The experts had prepared silver bromide and silver iodide emulsions separately and then mixed them, a technique that resulted in inferior plates. By reversing the procedure—dissolving the light-sensitive salts together in water and then adding the gelatin—Schumann produced plates that were far superior. Earlier, in 1873, he had increased sensitivity to red by allowing solutions of certain organic dyes to act on prepared plates. The announcement of this technique stimulated a wealth of further research by both amateurs and industry.

Schumann held that the most informative way of investigating the sensitivity of photographic plates to color was to expose them through a spectroscope. He was particularly interested in the ultraviolet region. As George Stokes had shown, this region could be made strikingly visible through a device in which the collector is formed by placing quartz lenses and calcite prisms on plates of fluorescent uranium glass. A problem remained, however: Why did shorter wavelengths of light darken the plates less than longer wavelengths? Schumann discovered two reasons for this. First, because the gelatin absorbed the light before it reached the silver bromide, he prepared plates in which these particles were not dispersed throughout the layer of gelatin but, rather, adhered to the top of it. Second, he established that the air in the spectrograph was highly disruptive, creating problems of both dispersion and, especially, absorption. Schumann discovered that a layer of air even 0.10 millimeter thick could completely absorb a spectral line.

Since no firm could furnish or build him a vacuum spectrograph, Schumann constructed one himself. The prisms and plates had to be adjusted precisely from outside the apparatus, and it took him a full year to devise an aperture that fulfilled his requirements. When finished, the device produced sharper spectra than any previously seen; with his plates it became possible to photograph spectra as low as 1,270 Å, whereas the limit had been 4,000 Å. (Theodore Lyman subsequently recorded spectra at 1,030 Å.) This further advance made it possible to demonstrate the Lyman series of hydrogen (predicted by J. J. Balmer), the first member of which lies at 1,215 Å. Since the majority of spectral lines of the elements lie in the ultraviolet region, the amateur photographer Schumann also became a pioneer of spectroscopy and of atomic physics.

BIBLIOGRAPHY

I. ORIGINAL WORKS. Schumann's writings include "Wirkung d. AgJ auf die Lichtempfindlichkeit d. AgBr-Gelatine," in *Photographisches Archiv* (1882); "Über die Photographie der Lichtstrahlen kleinster Wellenlänge," in *Sitzungsberichte der Akademie der Wissenschaften in Wien*, **102**, sec. 2a (1893), 415–475, 625–694; "Über ein neues Verfahren zur Herstellung ultraviolettempfindlicher Platten," *ibid.*, 994–1024; "New Method of Preparing Plates Sensitive to Ultraviolet Rays," in *Astrophysical Journal*, **3** (1896), 220–226, 387–395; and **4** (1896), 144–154; and "Verbessertes Verfahren zur Herstellung ultraviolettempfindlicher Platten," in *Annalen der Physik*, 4th ser., **5** (1901), 349–374. He also made many contributions to *Jahrbuch für Photographie und Reproductionstechnik* between 1887 and 1903.

II. SECONDARY LITERATURE. Obituaries are T. Lyman, in *Astrophysical Journal*, **39** (1914), 1–4, with portrait; and O. Wiener, "Victor Schumann," in *Berichte über die Verhandlungen der Sächsischen Gesellschaft der Wissenschaften*, **65** (1913), 409–413.

F. FRAUNBERGER

SCHUNCK, HENRY EDWARD (*b.* Manchester, England, 16 August 1820; *d.* Kersal, near Manchester, 13 January 1903), *organic chemistry.*

Schunck was of German descent, his father having settled in Manchester as the founder of the firm Schunck, Mylius and Co., textile merchants and calico-printers; his mother was a daughter of Johann Mylius. He was educated privately and received his first instruction in practical chemistry in the laboratory of William Henry, a family friend. He then studied under Heinrich Rose and H. G. Magnus at Berlin, and with Liebig at Giessen, before returning about 1842 to enter his father's printing works at Rochdale. After a few years, however, his increasing wealth enabled him to detach himself from the day-to-day management of the firm and to devote himself to research, mainly on the chemistry of the natural coloring matters.

Soon after returning to England, Schunck published the results of his work on the isolation and analysis of a pure crystalline compound (lecanorin) from the lichens that furnished the old dyestuffs archil and cudbear and the indicator litmus. Later (1847) he isolated the glycoside rubian, the precursor of alizarin in madder root, and studied other colored substances that accompany it. In 1853 he isolated the colorless precursor of indigo; this was indican, later shown to be a glycoside of indoxyl, which forms indigo as a result of oxidative hydrolysis in the dyebath.

Although a skillful and painstaking practical chemist and analyst, Schunck had little interest in theory. It was only while Hermann Roemer was serving as his assistant (1875–1879) that he began to relate his analyses to structural formulas. He and Roemer made important contributions to the study of the polyhydroxy anthraquinones, which were then becoming available synthetically; and they were among the first to use absorption spectroscopy as a tool for the identification of colored compounds. Later, assisted by Leon Marchlewski, Schunck made extensive studies of chlorophyll and its congeners, again using absorption spectroscopy. This problem was so difficult, however, that they achieved little, except to demonstrate a chemical relationship between chlorophyll and hemoglobin. Schunck's son Charles also participated in this work.

Although Schunck never held an academic post, he was the leading figure in the scientific life of Manchester for fifty years. He was four times president of the Manchester Literary and Philosophical Society, one of the earliest members of the Chemical Society, and a founder-member (later president) of the Society of Chemical Industry. He was elected fellow of the Royal Society in 1850. Shortly before his death he gave Manchester University the then huge sum of £20,000 for the endowment of research. His laboratory—reputedly the best private laboratory in the world—and his extensive library were bequeathed to the University, to which they were moved. He married in 1850 and had seven children, of whom only four survived him.

BIBLIOGRAPHY

I. ORIGINAL WORKS. Schunck and his assistants wrote nearly 100 papers. Of special interest is his address to the British Association, in *Report of the British Association for the Advancement of Science*, **57** (1887), 624–635, expressing the opinion that the future of organic chemistry lay in the elucidation of biological processes; and his presidential address to the Society of Chemical Industry, in *Journal of the Society of Chemical Industry*, **17** (1897), 586–594, in which he recalls the scientific personalities of Manchester in his younger days.

II. SECONDARY LITERATURE. There are notices on Schunck in *Manchester Faces and Places*, IX (1898), 1–6, with portrait; and in *Dictionary of National Biography, 1901–1911*, 274–275. The main obituaries are in *Memoirs and Proceedings of the Manchester Literary and Philosophical Society*, **47** (1902–1903), xlix–liii; *Berichte der Deutschen chemischen Gesellschaft*, **36** (1903), 305; *Journal of the Society of Chemical Industry*, **22** (1903), 84; *Journal of the Society of Dyers and Colourists*, **19** (1903), 35–36, with portrait; *Nature*, **67** (1903), 274; and *Proceedings of the Royal Society*, **75** (1904–1905), 261–264. A short account of his scientific work is W. H. Perkin, Jr., "The Chemical Researches of Edward Schunck. . . .," in *Memoirs and Proceedings of the Manchester Literary and Philosophical Society*, **47**, no. 6 (1902–1903), 1–8.

For an obituary, see *Berichte der Deutschen chemischen Gesellschaft*, **18** (1885), 285–289.

W. V. FARRAR

SCHUR, ISSAI (*b.* Mogilev, Russia, 10 January 1875; *d.* Tel Aviv, Palestine [now Israel], 10 January 1941), *mathematics*.

Schur was one of the most brilliant Jewish mathematicians active in Germany during the first third of the twentieth century. He attended the Gymnasium in Libau (now Liepaja, Latvian S.S.R.) and then the University of Berlin, where he spent most of his scientific career. From 1911 until 1916, when he returned to Berlin, he was an assistant professor at Bonn. He became full professor at Berlin in 1919. Schur was forced to retire by the Nazi authorities in 1935 but was able to emigrate to Palestine in 1939. He died there of a heart ailment two years later. Schur had been a member of the Prussian Academy of Sciences before the Nazi purges. He married and had a son and daughter.

Schur's principal field was the representation theory of groups, founded a little before 1900 by his teacher Frobenius. Schur seems to have completed it shortly before World War I; but he returned to the subject after 1925, when it became important for physics. Further developed by his student Richard Brauer, it is in our time experiencing an extraordinary growth through the opening of new questions. Schur's dissertation (1901) became fundamental to the representation theory of the general linear group; in fact English mathematicians have named certain of the functions appearing in the work "S-functions" in Schur's honor. In 1905 Schur reestablished the theory of group characters—the keystone of representation theory. The most important tool involved is "Schur's lemma." Along with the representation of groups by integral linear substitutions, Schur was also the first to study representation by linear fractional substitutions, treating this more difficult problem almost completely in two works (1904, 1907). In 1906 Schur considered the fundamental problems that appear when an algebraic number field is taken as the domain; a number appearing in this connection is now called the Schur index. His works written after 1925 include a complete description of the rational and of the continuous representations of the general linear group; the foundations of this work were in his dissertation.

A lively interchange with many colleagues led Schur to contribute important memoirs to other areas of mathematics. Some of these were published as collaborations with other authors, although publications with dual authorship were almost unheard of at that time. Here we can only indicate the areas. First there was pure group theory, in which Schur adopted the surprising approach of proving without the aid of characters theorems that had previously been demonstrated only by that means. Second, he worked in the field of matrices. Third, he handled algebraic equations, sometimes proceeding to the evaluation of roots, and sometimes treating the so-called equations without affect, that is, with symmetric Galois groups. He was also the first to give examples of equations with alternating Galois groups. Fourth, he worked in number theory, notably in additive number theory; fifth in divergent series; sixth in integral equations; and lastly in function theory.

BIBLIOGRAPHY

Schur's writings are collected in *Gesammelte Abhandlungen*, A. Brauer and H. Rohrbach, ed., 3 vols. (Berlin, 1973). Moreover, two lectures have been published as *Die algebraischen Grundlagen der Darstellungstheorie der Gruppen: Zürcher Vorlesungen 1936*, E. Stiefel, ed.; and *Vorlesungen über Invariantentheorie*, H. Grunsky, ed. (Berlin, 1968).

On Schur and his work, see *Mathematische Zeitschrift*, **63** (1955–1956), a special issue published to commemorate Schur's eightieth birthday, with forty articles dedicated to his memory by leading mathematicians. See also Alfred Brauer, "Gedenkrede auf Issai Schur, gehalten 1960 bei der Schur-Gedenkfeier an der Humboldt-Universität Berlin," in *Gesammelte Abhandlungen*, I, which contains a detailed report of Schur's life and work.

H. BOERNER

SCHUSTER, ARTHUR (*b.* Frankfurt, Germany, 12 September 1851; *d.* Yeldall, near Twyford,

Berkshire, England, 14 October 1934), *physics, applied mathematics.*

Schuster was the son of Francis Joseph Schuster, a well-to-do Jewish textile merchant with business connections in Great Britain. After the Seven Weeks' War the family firm moved to Manchester, England, when Frankfurt was annexed by Prussia. Schuster, baptized as a young boy, was educated privately and at the Frankfurt Gymnasium. He attended the Geneva Academy from 1868 until he joined his parents at Manchester in the summer of 1870.

By the age of sixteen Schuster had developed an interest in physical science, mainly through Henry Roscoe's elementary textbook on spectrum analysis. His parents saw at once that he lacked enthusiasm for business; and they consulted Roscoe, then professor of chemistry at Owens College, Manchester, who arranged for Schuster to enroll as a day student in October 1871. He studied physics under Balfour Stewart and was directed in research in spectrum analysis by Roscoe. Within a year he produced his first research paper, "On the Spectrum of Nitrogen." Again at Roscoe's suggestion, Schuster enrolled at Heidelberg under Kirchhoff and received his Ph.D. after a less-than-brilliant examination in 1873.

Schuster served at Owens in 1873 as unpaid demonstrator in the new physics laboratory and later, at the request of Lockyer, joined an eclipse expedition to the coast of Siam. Upon his return to England in 1875, Schuster remained at Owens for a semester and then joined Maxwell as a researcher at the Cavendish Laboratory, where he remained for five years, ultimately joining Lord Rayleigh in an absolute determination of the ohm.

In 1879 Schuster applied for a post at Mason Science College, Birmingham, but was rejected in favor of his friend J. H. Poynting. Two years later, when a professorship of applied mathematics was founded at Owens, Schuster was selected for the chair over his former student J. J. Thomson and Oliver Lodge. Subsequently he was rejected as Rayleigh's successor at the Cavendish in 1884; but after Balfour Stewart's death in 1887 he succeeded in the following year to the chair of physics at Manchester.

At the beginning of his Owens College career, Schuster resumed his interest in what was by then termed "spectroscopy." In an important paper, "On Harmonic Ratios in the Spectra of Gases" (*Proceedings of the Royal Society,* **31** [1881], 337–347), he refuted G. J. Stoney's explanation of spectral lines that used simple harmonic series

by demonstrating statistically that the spectra of five chosen elements conform more closely to a random distribution than to Stoney's "law." He concluded, however, that "Most probably some law hitherto undiscovered exists which in special cases resolves itself into the law of harmonic ratios." In 1897 Schuster independently discovered and published the relationship known as the Rydberg-Schuster law, which relates the convergence frequencies of different spectral series of the same substance.

Schuster's interests led him to investigate the spectra produced by the discharge of electricity through gases in otherwise evacuated tubes. Such electrical discharges were imperfectly understood, and he began a series of detailed investigations that led to his Bakerian lectures before the Royal Society in 1884 and 1890. Schuster's findings were of major importance: he showed that an electrical current was conducted through gases by ions and that once a gas was "dissociated" (ionized), a small potential would suffice to maintain a current.

Schuster was also the first to indicate the path toward determining the ratio e/m for cathode rays by using a magnetic field, a method that ultimately led to the discovery of the electron. In 1896, shortly after the appearance of Roentgen's researches, he offered the first suggestion that X rays were small-wavelength transverse vibrations of the ether.

Schuster's interests were too wide-ranging to give even a brief account here. His work on terrestrial magnetism, however, deserves special notice. In 1889 he showed that daily magnetic variations are of two kinds, internal and atmospheric. He attributed the latter to electric currents in the upper atmosphere, and the former to induction currents in the earth. In a later estimate of the ionization of the upper atmosphere he helped lay the groundwork for the studies of Heaviside and Kennelly.

In 1907 Schuster resigned his chair at Manchester and secured Ernest Rutherford as his successor, thus reinforcing Manchester's prominence in physical research.

Elected a fellow of the Royal Society in 1879, Schuster served twice on its Council and was secretary from 1912 to 1919. He was founder and first secretary of the International Research Council and served as president of the British Association in 1915. He was knighted in 1920.

A man of remarkable originality and ingenuity, Schuster often pointed the way toward novel areas but left the task of reaching research summits to others, a pattern perhaps inevitable in a period of exploding possibilities for one of such wide interests and perception.

BIBLIOGRAPHY

I. ORIGINAL WORKS. A record of Schuster's scientific papers from 1881 to 1906 is in *The Physical Laboratories of the University of Manchester* (Manchester, 1906), 45–60; papers published to 1901 are listed in the Royal Society *Catalogue of Scientific Papers*, VIII, 899; XI, 359–360; XVIII, 623–625. Schuster's major books include *Spectrum Analysis*, 4th ed. (London, 1885), written with H. E. Roscoe; *Introduction to the Theory of Optics* (London, 1904; 3rd ed., 1924); *The Progress of Physics During 33 Years (1875–1908)* (Cambridge, 1911); and *Biographical Fragments* (London, 1932). With Arthur Shipley he wrote *Britain's Heritage of Science* (London, 1917), a fascinating Victorian view of the history of science.

II. SECONDARY LITERATURE. On Schuster's life and work the following are of special value: G. C. Simpson, "Sir Arthur Schuster, 1851–1934," in *Obituary Notices of Fellows of the Royal Society of London*, 1 (1932–1935), 409–423; "Sir Arthur Schuster, FRS," in *Nature*, **134** (1934), 595–597; and his article in *Dictionary of National Biography*; G. E. Hale, "Sir Arthur Schuster," in *Astrophysical Journal*, **81** (1935), 97–106; R. S. Hutton, *Recollections of a Technologist* (London, 1964), pp. 103–106; and J. G. Crowther, *Scientific Types* (London, 1968), 333–358. See also *Manchester Faces and Places*, IV (1892–1893), 158–159; and *Commemoration of the 25th Anniversary of the Election of Arthur Schuster, F.R.S., to a Professorship in the Owens College* (Manchester, 1906).

On Schuster's work see Edmund Whittaker, *History of the Theories of Aether and Electricity*, I (New York, 1960), pp. 355–360; Norah Schuster, "Early Days of Roentgen Photography in Britain," in *British Medical Journal* (1962), **2**, 1164–1166; D. L. Anderson, *The Discovery of the Electron* (Princeton, 1964), pp. 30, 42, 74; and William McGucken, *Nineteenth-Century Spectroscopy* (Baltimore, 1969), *passim*.

On Schuster at Owens, see P. J. Hartog, *The Owens College Manchester* (Manchester, 1900), pp. 54–59; and H. B. Charlton, *Portrait of a University* (Manchester, 1951), pp. 78–84.

ROBERT H. KARGON

SCHWABE, SAMUEL HEINRICH (*b.* Dessau, Germany, 25 October 1789; *d.* Dessau, 11 April 1875), *astronomy*.

Schwabe's father was a physician, and the family apothecary business was derived from his mother's family. After working from 1806 to 1809 as an as-

sistant in the business, Schwabe continued his pharmaceutical studies at the University of Berlin in 1810–1812, under Klaproth and Hermbstädt. While at Berlin he became interested in astronomy and botany. Schwabe worked as an apothecary from 1812 until 1829, when he sold the business in order to give his time fully to his scientific interests.

On 17 December 1827 Schwabe rediscovered the eccentricity of Saturn's rings. In 1843 he made his first definite statement regarding the periodicity of sunspots, giving statistics for 1826–1843. He tabulated his results under four headings: the year, the number of groups of sunspots in the year, the number of days free from sunspots, and the number of days when observations were made. Schwabe realized that with the modest apparatus in his private observatory, numerical determination was difficult; for instance, on days when there was a large number of spots, he had probably underestimated them. His carefully compiled results demonstrated the existence of periodicity, although he wrongly estimated the period to be about ten years. His discovery remained unnoticed until Humboldt drew attention to it in 1851. Because Schwabe was an amateur astronomer, his discovery was all the more noteworthy, for the investigation of the occurrence of sunspots had been judged unprofitable by Lalande and Delambre.

After Schwabe's discovery, Rudolf Wolf collated all existing sunspot data and recalculated the period as just over eleven years. In 1857 the Royal Astronomical Society awarded Schwabe its gold medal. He was elected a member of the Royal Society of London in 1868.

BIBLIOGRAPHY

I. ORIGINAL WORKS. The Royal Society *Catalogue of Scientific Papers*, V, 582–585; and VIII, 901, lists 109 of Schwabe's printed papers and scientific works, including papers on the phenomena of frost patterns, haze, and mock suns. In 1865 he published a flora of Anhalt. Thirty-one volumes of Schwabe's astronomical observations were transferred after his death into the keeping of the Royal Astronomical Society. They cover his work from 1825 to 1867 and are held in the Society archives at Burlington House, London. See also Poggendorff, II, 871; III, 1223; VI, 2391.

II. SECONDARY LITERATURE. Biographical information is in *Allgemeine deutsche Biographie*, XXXIII, 159–161; T. Arendt, *Schwabe: Leben und Wirken* (Dessau, 1925), which I have not been able to see; and Gustav Partheil, "Samuel Heinrich Schwabe der dessauer Astronom und Botaniker," in *Jahrbuch, Heimat-*

liches, für Anhalt 1926. Accounts of his work appear in Alexander von Humboldt, *Kosmos: Entwurfeiner physischen weltbeschreibung*, III (Stuttgart–Augsburg, 1851), 379–405; and H. H. Turner, *Astronomical Discovery* (London, 1904), 155–176.

SISTER MAUREEN FARRELL, F.C.J.

SCHWANN, THEODOR AMBROSE HUBERT (*b.* Neuss, Germany, 7 December 1810; *d.* Cologne, Germany, 11 January 1882), *physiology.*

An account of Schwann's early life has some of the qualities of an edifying tale of saintly childhood. To his teachers and fellow pupils in primary school and at the progymnasium, Schwann was a cooperative child, diligent and modest. Little tempted by the delights of society, lacking self-confidence, and excessively shy, he withdrew into study, family life, and piety. Equally brilliant in all branches of learning, he showed a particular inclination for mathematics and physics. Given his lack of interest in the outside world, it was accepted that his vocation should be directed toward the Church when he left his native town in 1826 to enter the Jesuit College of the Three Crowns in Cologne.

Here Schwann came under the influence of an exceptional religious teacher, Wilhelm Smets. To Schwann, until then acquainted only with the strict aspects of piety, but also endowed with a brilliant intelligence and a lively sensibility, Smets's teaching of religion was the revelation of an entirely new aspect of God and especially of the singular fact of the liberty of man with regard to the whole of nature. It was from him that Schwann learned the lesson of the elevation of man by personal perfection.

Increasingly enamored with reason, Schwann renounced theology to take up medical studies. His philosophical position became that of a Christian rationalist whose personal philosophy was in the tradition of Descartes and Leibniz.

In October 1829 Schwann entered the University of Bonn, where he enrolled in the premedical curriculum and obtained his bachelor's degree in 1831. During this time, he attended Johannes Müller's lectures on physiology and began to assist him in the laboratory. In the autumn of 1831 he moved to Würzburg, where he studied for three semesters, attending clinical lectures. In April 1833 he left Würzburg for Berlin, where Müller had been appointed to teach anatomy and physiology. In Berlin, Schwann attended clinical demonstrations and, under Müller's guidance, prepared a dissertation on the necessity of air for the development of chicken eggs. He obtained the M.D. on 31 May 1834 and passed the state examination on 26 July. Schwann immediately became one of Müller's assistants and devoted all his time and efforts to research.

Although he remained a practicing Catholic, Schwann abandoned himself, especially after the death of his mother in 1835, to an extreme mechanistic tendency, which guided him in the impressive work he accomplished at Müller's laboratory in Berlin between 1834 and 1839. Schwann's conception of God at this time was the philosophical and impersonal God of Descartes.

During this period, Müller was working on the *Handbuch der Physiologie*, which introduced into Germany Magendie's experimental method in medical studies. Until his death Müller remained a convinced vitalist. Recourse to experimentation was for him (as it had been for Bichat) a means of studying the effects of the vital force peculiar to each organ. Restricted in his chemical and physical background, he progressively detached himself from physiology and devoted himself entirely to comparative morphology, in which field he acquired fame. On the other hand, from the beginning of his career as a researcher Schwann took a completely different position, which inaugurated the quantitative period of physiology.

Müller's *Handbuch* was not merely a compilation; he critically examined all the notions that he printed. Repeating the experiments of others, suggesting new ones, opening avenues not yet explored, this treatise is a work as unique in its conception as in its realization. In the section entrusted to him, Schwann enriched Müller's *Handbuch* with the results of extensive work and contributed numerous new notions. This book also contains an account of a study clearly showing Schwann's innovating tendency; his first experiments can be dated, on the basis of his laboratory notebooks, at 16 April 1835. In these Schwann envisaged experiments in which it would be possible to subject the physiological properties of an organ or of a tissue to physical measurement. One such method involved measuring the secretion of a gland. But it was the muscle that seemed to him likely to furnish the most rewarding results. He planned to measure the length of a muscle contracted by the action of the same stimulus for different loads or, further, to compare the intensity of the contraction with that of the stimulus. He accomplished this experiment by means of the "muscular balance" and in a sense established the first tension-length diagram.

The influence in physiological circles of this simple experiment is difficult for us to appreciate. "It was the first time," as du Bois-Reymond emphasized, "that someone examined an eminently vital force as a physical phenomenon and that the laws of its action were quantitatively expressed." In a milieu where the idealistic philosophy and the theories of Fichte and Hegel were still dominant, the *fundamental Versuch* came as a revelation and constituted the point of departure for a new physiology. Dissociating itself from the teaching of Müller and resolutely abandoning the notion of vital force for the study of molecular mechanisms, the school stemming from Schwann's experiment was distinguished particularly by the work of his successors at the Berlin laboratory, Emil du Bois-Reymond and Hermann von Helmholtz.

Parallel with his experiments on muscle, Schwann pursued the researches that led to his discovery of pepsin. About 1835, however, Gay-Lussac's observations, prompted by Nicolas Appert's experiments, made acceptable the notion that oxygen was the agent of both fermentation and putrefaction. This observation stimulated a recrudescence of the theories of spontaneous generation and a tendency to return to the ideas of Needham, for whom the effect of heat was to deprive the air of the oxygen necessary for the birth of "animalcules."

Having observed that neither infusorians nor the smell of putrefaction appeared in a maceration of meat that had been boiled, Schwann noted the appearance of both these phenomena when he used an unboiled maceration or unheated air. Convinced that it was the destruction of germs that prevented the development of infusorians and molds, and that prevented putrefaction, Schwann wished to make a counterproof by showing that the heating of air did not prevent the operation of a chemical process to which it contributed oxygen, and not germs. He demonstrated that a frog breathes normally in previously heated air; and he investigated alcoholic fermentation, which also depended, in the current opinion, on the presence of oxygen. To his great astonishment, Schwann observed that heating the air he bubbled through a boiled suspension of yeast in a sugary solution prevented fermentation in certain experiments. In January 1836 he noted in his laboratory notebook the conclusion that alcoholic fermentation is the work of a live organism.

The description of the multiplication of yeast cells appears in Schwann's laboratory notebook under the date 16 February 1836. The first public announcement of the relationship between alcoholic fermentation and the life cycle of yeast was by Cagniard de La Tour, who described the multiplication of yeast in the issue of *L'Institut* for 25 November 1836. Schwann's paper (1837), however, independently demonstrated the living nature of the agent of fermentation and presented arguments of a new sort.

Schwann was led to the idea that alcoholic fermentation was related to the metabolism of yeast by his conception that putrefaction was related to the metabolism of live organisms. The prevailing doctrine in Müller's laboratory was the vitalism derived from Paracelsus, and his principles were hostile to the Cartesian unity of natural forces. Schwann's mechanistic and unitarian antagonism toward this intellectual attitude had already been clearly manifested in his studies of muscle, of the mechanism of digestion, and of fermentation. His tendency to introduce a more exact mode of explanation than the current one in terms of the "vital force" culminated in the formulation of the cell theory.

The cell theory prolonged, on the biological terrain, the old debate over continuity and discontinuity in nature. The search for a common structural principle of live organisms, excluding such imaginary entities as Buffon's "molecules," has preoccupied many scientists. In his biography of Virchow, E. H. Ackerknecht distinguished several searches for a common principle. In the eighteenth century the principle was the "fiber." According to this view, which Ackerknecht designated as the first cell theory, the development of fibers began in little globules, like those recognized by Prochaska (1797). After these views were abandoned, a new theory appeared that John R. Baker termed "globulist," Ackerknecht's second cell theory. Its adherents included Lorenz Oken, Meckel, Mirbel, Dutrochet, Purkyně, Valentin, and Raspail. The notion of "globule" embraced a great variety of elementary units: particles and nuclei, as well as optical illusions. The globulists often included some form of cell among their "globules"; but none of them can be regarded as having conceived of the organism as composed *solely* of cells, of modified cells, or of products of cells. It was not until 1830 that the perfecting of the microscope permitted Robert Brown to recognize the presence of the nucleus as the essential characteristic of the plant cell.

In 1839, in his *Mikroskopische Untersuchungen,* Schwann formulated what Ackerknecht called the third cell theory, which insists on the common cellular origin of every living thing. By "cell" Schwann meant "a layer around a nucleus" that could differentiate itself: covered by a membrane, as the site of deposit of a more consistent substance; growing hollow, as a vacuole; or fusing itself with the "layer" of other cells. He also thought (incorrectly) that cells form around a nucleus within a "blastema," an amorphous substance that can be intracellular or extracellular. Ackerknecht's fourth cell theory, which remains current, is that of Remak and Virchow, the first part of which follows Schwann in acknowledging the cellular composition of organisms, with the cell as the vital element, the bearer of all the characteristics of life. The second part of this theory, expressed in the dictum "omnis cellula e cellula," contradicts Schwann's erroneous belief in the formation of cells within a "blastema."

The *Mikroskopische Untersuchungen* is composed of three parts. The first is devoted to a microscopic study of the *chorda dorsalis* in frog larvae. Studying that structure, Schwann found that it consists of polyhedral cells that have in or on the internal surface of their wall a structure corresponding to the nucleus of plant cells. New cells are formed within parent cells. He also found the structure of cartilage to be in accordance with the tissues of plants, and he believed that he had observed that the cartilage cells contain a nucleus and that they originate by formation of the nucleus, around which the cell develops. Schwann therefore was convinced that the cells of the *chorda dorsalis* and of cartilage were derived from structures of the same kind as the plant cells, with nucleus, membrane, and vacuole.

In the second part Schwann presented a demonstration of the same notion with regard to much more specialized elementary parts. He found that the varied forms of the "elementary parts" of tissues—be they epithelium, hoof, feather, crystalline lens, cartilage, bone, tooth, muscle tissue, fatty tissue, elastic tissue, nerve tissue—are products of cellular differentiation. The conclusion he drew from this observation was that "elementary parts," although quite distinct in a physiological sense, may be developed according to the same laws. The elementary parts of most tissues, when traced back from their state of complete development to their primary conditions, are only developments of cells.

In the third part, of a philosophical nature, Schwann, on the basis of his cell theory expounded in the first two parts, developed a theory of the

cells that he presented as purely hypothetical. He stated that according to the cell theory, one may suppose that an organized body is not produced, as was accepted by theological theories, by a fundamental power guided in its operation by a definite idea, but is developed, according to blind laws of necessity, by powers that, like those of inorganic nature, are established by the very existence of matter. He believed that the source of life phenomena resided in another combination of the materials of the inorganic world, whether it be in a peculiar mode of union of the atoms to form molecules, or in the arrangement of these conglomerate molecules to form the parts of organisms.

Schwann stated that two groups of phenomena attend the formation of cells: those relating to the combination of molecules to form a cell (plastic phenomena) and those resulting from chemical changes in the component particles of the cells (metabolic phenomena). The cell attracts particles from its medium, which is not a mere solution of cell material but contains this material in other combinations, and it produces chemical changes in these particles. In addition, all the parts of the cell itself may be chemically modified during the process of its growth by a "metabolic power" that is an attribute of the cell itself; this is demonstrated by alcoholic fermentation, which provides a representation of the process that is repeated in all the cells of an organism. Metabolic changes occur not only in the cell contents but also in the solid parts, for example, the nucleus and the membrane. The metabolic processes, in which heat is evolved, are produced only at certain temperatures. All cells demonstrate respiration, a fundamental condition of metabolism; and each cell produces chemical changes in particular organic substances.

Schwann discerned a relation between the phenomena of cell formation, as he conceived it, and the phenomena of crystallization, a comparison developed at length, but only as a hypothesis.

Schwann defined his attitude toward the vital force, as it was accepted by Müller, who proposed the notion of the proper energy of tissues, thus:

> A simple force different from matter, as it is supposed, the vital force would form the organism in the same way as an architect constructs a building according to a plan, but a plan of which he is not conscious. Furthermore, it would give to all our tissues that which is called their proper energy, that is, the properties that distinguish living tissues from dead tissues: muscles would owe it their contractility, nerves their irritability, glands their secretory func-

tion. Here, in a word, is the doctrine of the vitalist school. Never was I able to conceive the existence of a simple force that would itself change its mode of action in order to realize an idea, without, however, possessing the characteristic attributes of intelligent beings. I have always preferred to seek in the Creator rather than in the created the cause of the finality to which the whole of nature evidently bears witness; and I have also always rejected as illusory the explanation of vital phenomena as conceived by the Vitalist school. I laid down as a principle that these phenomena must be explained in the same way as those of inert nature [*Manifestation en l'honneur de M. le professeur Th. Schwann . . .*].

Schwann sought to replace theological explanation with physical explanation. For him the phenomena of life were not produced by a force acting according to an idea, but by forces acting blindly and with necessity, as in physics. Individual finality, as it was observed in each organism, was determined in the same manner as in inert nature: its explanation depended entirely upon the characteristics of matter and upon the blind forces with which it had been created by an infinitely intelligent being.

Schwann found the confirmation of this view in the notion of the uniformity of the texture and the growth of animals and plants, as he developed it in his cell theory. "The uniformity of this development demonstrated that it is the same force that everywhere unites molecules into cells, and that this force could be nothing but that of molecules or atoms: the fundamental phenomenon of life therefore had to have its *raison d'être* in the properties of atoms." The error suggested to Schwann by Schleiden—the formation of cells within a blastema, which Schwann tentatively compared to the phenomenon of crystallization—satisfied his chemical and physical preferences to such a high degree that one can understand a little more easily why he accepted it on the strength of arguments as weak as those he presented to demonstrate it: those concerning an alleged preexistence of the nucleus in the cartilages, for example.

The solution to the philosophical problem of finality proposed by Schwann transferred it from biology to the universe and its constituent particles, and from the vital force to the Creator. It continued to be influential philosophically, and Lotze was notably inspired by it in his celebrated article on the nature of life, "Leben, Lebenskraft" (1842). Schwann's cell theory can be regarded as marking the origin in biology of the school of mech-

anistic materialism that Brücke, du Bois-Reymond, Helmholtz, and Carl Ludwig made famous. According to Schwann, the theory that led from the molecule (the molecule of the chemist) to the organism by way of the universal stage of the cell, was inspired by an intellectual, mechanistic reaction to Müller's vitalism. Erroneous as it appears now in certain of its aspects, this theory led him to the inestimably significant discovery of the development of organisms through cellular differentiation.

Schwann's short and brilliant scientific career extended from 1834 to 1839, after which he abandoned rationalism and became a mystic. The scientist gave way to the professor, the inventor, and the theologian. The beginning of this transformation dates from the attacks directed at Schwann by the chemists. Having shown an exceptional insensitivity to epistemological obstacles during his years of fruitful work, he nevertheless succumbed to a particularly violent attack dictated by one of these obstacles. At the beginning of 1839, there appeared in the *Annalen der Pharmacie,* following a translation of a general paper by Turpin on the mechanism of alcoholic fermentation considered as a result of the activity of yeast, an article entitled "Das enträthselte Geheimnis der geistigen Gährung." The work of Wöhler, embellished by Liebig with some particularly ferocious touches, this satirical text presented a caricature of the views of Cagniard, Schwann, and Kützing on the role of yeast in alcoholic fermentation.

According to this facetious article, yeast suspended in water assumes the form of animal eggs that hatch with an unbelievable rapidity in a sugary solution. These animals, in the shape of an alembic, have neither teeth nor eyes but do have a stomach, an intestine, an anus (in the form of a pink dot), and urinary organs. Immediately upon leaving the eggs, they throw themselves on the sugar and devour it; it penetrates their stomachs, is digested, and produces excrements. In a word, they eat sugar, expelling alcohol through the anus and carbonic acid through the urinary organs. Moreover, their bladder has the shape of a champagne bottle.

Shortly afterward, a lengthy memoir by Liebig appeared in the same periodical. In it he formulated the theory of alcoholic fermentation as the result of instability produced in sugar by the instability of a substance formed through the access of air to the nitrogenous substances of plant juices. This theory enjoyed a long popularity among chemists, and it was not until Pasteur that justice was done to Cagniard, Schwann, and Kützing. The cruel treatment of Schwann by the scientific leaders of his time made it impossible for him to pursue a scientific career in Germany.

At the same time Schwann's ardent rationalism grew lukewarm; he became preoccupied with religious meditations, doubtless fostered by the influence of his brother Peter, a theologian. The brother was the author (under the pseudonym Dr. J. F. Müller) of an edition of *The Imitation of Christ*. His failure in his candidature for a chair at the University of Bonn, added to his other disappointments, sent Schwann into exile in 1839, when he became professor of anatomy at Louvain. But the mainspring of enthusiasm and discovery was broken. Like Pascal before him, he abandoned rationalism to return to the God of his childhood, the "God of the heart, not of reason." A conscientious professor at Louvain and at Liège (from 1848), Schwann spent the rest of his life in a solitary existence darkened by episodes of depression and anxiety.

Before he went to Liège in 1848, Schwann had been approached by his friend J. A. Spring, who presented the proposals of the Belgian government, including a substantial increase of salary and the promise, never fulfilled, of the construction of an institute of anatomy. When Schwann was appointed, he first received the chair of anatomy, which previously had been held by Spring, who also taught physiology. In 1858 Spring became professor of general pathology and clinical medicine, and Schwann of physiology as well as of general anatomy and embryology. In 1872 he abandoned general anatomy and in 1877 embryology, teaching only physiology until he retired in 1879.

During his stay at Louvain (1839–1848), Schwann developed a method of utilizing the biliary fistula for the study of the role of bile in digestion, and concluded that a lack of bile secretion in the digestive tract is incompatible with survival. He received the Sömmering Medal (1841); and in 1847 the Sydenham Society published an English version of his *Mikroskopische Untersuchungen*, translated by Henry Smith, who in his introduction presented the following judgment: "The treatise has now been seven years before the public, has been most acutely investigated by those best competent to test its value, and the first physiologists of our day have judged the discoveries which it unfolds as worthy to be ranked among the most

important steps by which the science of physiology has ever been advanced."

The papers of 1844 and 1845 that record Schwann's work on the biliary fistula were his last physiological works. After that time, although he never ceased to work in the laboratory, his scientific inquiry lost its impact. Following his arrival in the prosperous industrial region of Liège, he became more of an inventor, developing a number of instruments used in mining technology, including pumps for the aspiration of water in coal mines and a respiratory apparatus for rescue operations. This instrument is the ancestor of the apparatus for measuring metabolism in man and of the devices used by divers.

Schwann's religious meditations occupied most of his time after his arrival at Liège. He composed what he intended to be a complement to the three parts of the *Mikroskopische Untersuchungen*, starting from the definition of the atom and extending the cell theory to a general system of organisms, including psychology and religion. His *Theoria* consisted of the three parts of the *Mikroskopische Untersuchungen* and of still unpublished chapters; a fourth part was two chapters on irritability and on brain function, and a fifth part concerned the theory of creation. The fourth and fifth parts are purely theological and philosophical. After his retirement Schwann remained in Liège, where he had formed many friendships. His life was troubled by very few incidents, the main one being the case of the "stigmatized" Louise Lateau. High Church authorities having wrongly interpreted what they considered to be a testimonial by him in favor of the miraculous nature of the phenomena, Schwann was forced to publish a statement of rectification.

During a Christmas visit to a brother and sister living in Cologne, he suffered a stroke and died on 11 January 1882, after two weeks of agony, during which he several times expressed the regret that he had not been able to publish the whole of his *Theoria*.

BIBLIOGRAPHY

I. ORIGINAL WORKS. Schwann's earlier writings include *De necessitate aëris atmospherici ad evolutionem pulli in ovo incubito* (Berlin, 1834); "Uber die Nothwendigkeit der atmosphärischen Luft zur Entwicklung des Hühnchens in dem bebrüteten Ei," in *Notizen aus dem Gebiete der Natur- und Heilkunde*, **41** (1834), 241–245; Johannes Müller, *Handbuch der Physiologie des Menschen*, 2 vols. (Koblenz, 1834–1838), *passim*: reports by Schwann on his research on muscle structure, ends of motor nerves, laws of muscle contraction, walls of capillary vessels, contractility of arteries, division of primitive nerve fibers, regeneration of cut nerves, nerve conduction, movements of lymph in the mesentery, ciliary movements, erectile tissues; "Gefässe," "Hämatosis," "Harnsekretion," "Hautsekretion," in *Encyclopädisches Wörterbuch der medizinischen Wissenschaft,* XIV (Berlin, 1836); "Versuche über die künstliche Verdauung des geronnenen Eiweisses," in *Archiv für Anatomie und Physiologie* (1836), 66–90, written with Müller; "Über das Wesen des Verdauungsprocesses," *ibid.,* 90–119; "Über die feinere Nervenausbreitung im Schwanze von Froschlarven," in *Medizinische Zeitung,* **6** (1837), 169; "Verdauung," "Muskelkraft," "Generatio equivoca," in Oken's *Isis* (1837), no. 5, 509–510; no. 6, 523–524; and no. 7, 524, respectively; "Vorläufige Mittheilung betreffend Versuche über Weingährung und Fäulniss," in *Annalen der Physik und Chemie,* **41** (1837), 184–193; preliminary notes on the cell theory in *Neue Notizen aus dem Gebiete der Natur-und Heilkunde,* no. 91 (1838), 34–36; no. 103 (1838), 225–229; no. 112 (1838), 21–23; *Mikroskopische Untersuchungen über die Übereinstimmung in der Struktur und dem Wachstum der Thiere und Pflanzen* (Berlin, 1839), also in English (London, 1847) and Russian (Moscow, 1939), and repr. as no. 176 of Ostwald's Klassiker der Exakten Wissenschaften (Leipzig, 1910); and "Übersicht über die Entwicklung der Gewebe," in R. Wagner, *Lehrbuch der Physiologie,* I (Leipzig, 1839), 139–142.

During the 1840's and 1850's Schwann published "Instructions pour l'observation des phénomènes périodiques chez l'homme," in *Bulletin de l'Académie royale de Belgique,* **9** (1842), 120–137; "Recherches microscopiques sur la conformité de structure et d'accroissement des animaux et des plantes," in *Annales des sciences naturelles,* Zoologie, 2nd ser., **17** (1842), 5–19; "Mensuration d'organes," in *Nouveaux mémoires de l'Académie royale de Belgique,* **16** (1843), 51–52, and **18** (1845), 145; "Versuche um auszumitteln, ob die Galle im Organismus eine für das Leben wesentliche Rolle spielt," in *Archiv für Anatomie, Physiologie und wissenschaftliche Medicin* (1844), 127–159; "Expériences pour constater si la bile joue dans l'économie animale un rôle essentiel pour la vie," in *Nouveaux mémoires de l'Académie royale de Belgique,* **18** (1845), 3–29; a letter to Wagner concerning his last experiments on the biliary fistula, in R. Wagner, *Handwörterbuch der Physiologie,* III (Brunswick, 1846), 837; "Sur des graines tombées de l'air dans la Prusse rhénane," in *Bulletin de l'Académie royale de Belgique,* **19** (1852), 5–6; *Anatomie du corps humain,* 2 vols. (Brussels, 1852); *Rapport sur la situation exceptionnelle dans laquelle s'est trouvée la province de Liège à l'époque de l'épidémie cholérique de 1854 et 1855* (Liège, 1857); and *Erklärung der stöchiometrischen Tafel* (Cologne, 1858).

Schwann's latest works include "Réponse à l'interpre-

tation de M. d'Omalius relative à la force vitale," in *Bulletin de l'Académie royale des sciences de Belgique,* **24** (1870), 683; "Notice sur Frédéric-Antoine Spring," in *Annuaire de l'Académie royale de Belgique* (1874); *Mein Gutachten über die Versuche die an der stigmatisirten Louise Lateau am 26. März 1869 angestellt wurden* (Cologne–Neuss, 1875); "Appareil permettant de pénétrer et de vivre dans un milieu irrespirable," in *Bulletin du musée de l'industrie de Belgique,* **21** (1877), 5–9; and *Description de deux appareils permettant de vivre dans un milieu irrespirable* (Liège, 1878), repr. in *Revue universelle des mines, de la métallurgie, des travaux publics, des sciences et des arts appliqués à l'industrie,* **7** (1880), 601–609. See also *Manifestation en l'honneur de M. le professeur Th. Schwann, Liège, 23 juin 1878. Liber memorialis publié par la Commission organisatrice* (Düsseldorf, 1879), which contains Schwann's reply to speeches of congratulation.

II. SECONDARY LITERATURE. See M. Florkin, *Théodore Schwann et les débuts de la médecine scientifique* (Paris, 1956), Conférences du Palais de la Découverte, ser. D, no. 43; *Naissance et déviation de la théorie cellulaire dans l'oeuvre de Théodore Schwann* (Paris, 1960); *Lettres de Théodore Schwann* (Liège, 1961); and "Théodore Schwann. 1810–1882," in *Florilège des sciences en Belgique* (Brussels, 1968); L. Fredericq, *Théodore Schwann, sa vie et ses travaux* (Liège, 1884); A. Le Roy, "Schwann, Théodore," in *L'Université de Liège depuis sa fondation* (Liège, 1869), 919–938; and R. Watermann, *Theodor Schwann. Leben und Werk* (Düsseldorf, 1960).

MARCEL FLORKIN

SCHWARZ, HERMANN AMANDUS (*b.* Hermsdorf, Silesia [now Sobiecin, Poland], 25 January 1843; *d.* Berlin, Germany, 30 November 1921), *mathematics.*

Schwarz, the son of an architect, was the leading mathematician in Berlin in the period following Kronecker, Kummer, and Weierstrass. He may be said to represent the link between these great mathematicians and the generation active in Germany in the first third of the twentieth century, a group that he greatly influenced. After attending the Gymnasium in Dortmund, he studied chemistry in Berlin at the Gewerbeinstitut (now the Technische Universität) but, under the influence of Kummer and Weierstrass, soon changed to mathematics. Schwarz received the doctorate in 1864 and then completed his training as a *Mittelschule* teacher. Immediately thereafter, in 1867, he was appointed assistant professor at Halle. In 1869 he became a full professor at the Eidgenössische

Technische Hochschule in Zurich and in 1875 assumed the same rank at the University of Göttingen. Schwarz succeeded Weierstrass at the University of Berlin in 1892 and lectured there until 1917. During this long period, teaching duties and concern for his many students took so much of his time that he published very little more. A contributing element may have been his propensity for handling both the important and the trivial with the same thoroughness, a trait also evident in his mathematical papers. Schwarz was a member of the Prussian and Bavarian academies of sciences. He was married to a daughter of Kummer.

Schwarz's greatest strength lay in his geometric intuition, which was brought to bear in his first publication, an elementary proof of the chief theorem of axonometry, which had been posed by Karl Pohlke, his teacher at the Gewerbeinstitut. The influence of Weierstrass, however, soon led Schwarz to place his geometric ability in the service of analysis; and this synthesis was the basis of his contribution to mathematics. Schwarz tended to work on narrowly defined, concrete, individual problems, but in solving them he developed methods the significance of which far transcended the problem under discussion.

Schwarz's most important contribution to the history of mathematics was the "rescue" of some of Riemann's achievements. The demonstrations had been justly challenged by Weierstrass. The question centered on the "main theorem" of conformal (similar in the least parts) mapping, which stated that every simply connected region of the plane can be conformally mapped onto a circular area. In order to prove it, Riemann had employed the relation of the problem to the first boundary-value problem of potential theory (Dirichlet's problem), which requires a solution of the partial differential equation $\Delta u = 0$ with prescribed values at the boundary of the region. Dirichlet believed he had disposed of this problem with the observation (Dirichlet's principle) that such a function yields an extreme value for a certain double integral; Weierstrass had objected that the existence of a function which can do that is not at all self-evident but must be demonstrated.

Schwarz first solved the mapping problem explicitly for various simple geometric figures—the square and the triangle—and then in general for polygons. He also treated the conformal mapping of polyhedral surfaces onto the spherical surface. These results enabled him to solve the two problems mentioned, that is, to present the first com-

pletely valid proofs for extended classes of regions by approximating the given region by means of polygons. These works contained the first statement of principles that are now familiar to all: the principle of reflection; the "alternating method," which provides a further method for the approximation of solution functions, and "Schwarz's lemma."

Schwarz also worked in the field of minimal surfaces (surfaces of least area), a characteristic problem of the calculus of variation. Such a surface must everywhere have zero mean curvature, and in general all surfaces with this property are termed minimal surfaces. The boundary-value problem requires in this case that a minimal surface be passed through a given closed space curve, a procedure that can be carried out experimentally by dipping a wire loop into a soap solution. Following his preference for concrete geometrical problems, Schwarz first solved the problem explicitly for special space curves, mostly consisting of straight sections, of which the curve composed of four out of six edges of a tetrahedron has become the best known.

In his most important work, a *Festschrift* for Weierstrass' seventieth birthday, Schwarz set himself the task of completely answering the question of whether a given minimal surface really yields a minimal area. Aside from the achievement itself, which contains the first complete treatment of the second variation in a multiple integral, this work introduced methods that immediately became extremely fruitful. For example, a function was constructed through successive approximations that Picard was able to employ in obtaining his existence proof for differential equations. Furthermore, Schwarz demonstrated the existence of a certain number, which could be viewed as the (least) eigenvalue for the eigenvalue problem of a certain differential equation (these concepts did not exist then). This was done through a method that Schwarz's student Erhard Schmidt later applied to the proof of the existence of an eigenvalue of an integral equation—a procedure that is one of the most important tools of modern analysis. In this connection Schwarz also employed the inequality for integrals that is today known as "Schwarz's inequality."

Algebra played the least role in Schwarz's work; his dissertation, however, was devoted to those surfaces developable into the plane that are given by algebraic equations of the first seven degrees. Much later he answered the question: In which cases does the Gaussian hypergeometric series represent an algebraic function? In approaching this matter, moreover, he developed trains of thought that led directly to the theory of automorphic functions, which was developed shortly afterward by Klein and Poincaré.

Of a series of minor works, executed with the same devotion and care as the major ones, two that involve criticism of predecessors and contemporaries remain to be mentioned. Schwarz presented the first rigorous proof that the sphere possesses a smaller surface area than any other body of the same volume. Earlier mathematicians, particularly Steiner, had implicitly supposed in their demonstrations the existence of a body with least surface area. Schwarz also pointed out that in the definition of the area of a curved surface appearing in many textbooks of his time, the method employed for determining the length of a curve was applied carelessly and that it therefore, for example, led to an infinitely great area resulting for so simple a surface as a cylindrical section.

BIBLIOGRAPHY

I. ORIGINAL WORKS. Schwarz's writings were collected in his *Gesammelte mathematische Abhandlungen*, 2 vols. (Berlin, 1890). He also compiled and edited *Nach Vorlesungen und Aufzeichnungen des Hrn. K. Weierstrass*, 12 pts. (Göttingen, 1881–1885), brought together in the 2nd ed. (Berlin, 1893), and also in French (Paris, 1894).

II. SECONDARY LITERATURE. See *Mathematische Abhandlungen Hermann Amandus Schwarz zu seinem fünfzigjährigen Doktorjubiläum gewidmet von Freunden und Schülern*, C. Carathéodory, G. Hessenberg, E. Landau, and L. Lichtenstein, eds. (Berlin, 1914), with portrait; L. Bieberbach, "H. A. Schwarz," in *Sitzungsberichte der Berliner mathematischen Gesellschaft*, **21** (1922), 47–51, with portrait and list of works not included in *Gesammelte Abhandlungen;* C. Carathéodory, "Hermann Amandus Schwarz," in *Deutsches biographisches Jahrbuch*, III (1921), 236–238; G. Hamel, "Zum Gedächtnis an Hermann Amandus Schwarz," in *Jahresberichte der Deutschen Mathematikervereinigung*, **32** (1923), 6–13, with portrait and complete bibliography; F. Lindemann, obituary in *Jahrbuch der bayerischen Akademie der Wissenschaften* (1922–1923), 75–77; R. von Mises, "H. A. Schwarz," in *Zeitschrift für angewandte Mathematik und Mechanik*, **1** (1921); and E. Schmidt, "Gedächtnisrede auf Hermann Amandus Schwarz," in *Sitzungsberichte der Preussischen Akademie der Wissenschaften zu Berlin* (1922), 85–87.

H. BOERNER

SCHWARZSCHILD, KARL (*b*. Frankfurt am Main, Germany, 9 October 1873; *d*. Potsdam, Germany, 11 May 1916), *astronomy.*

Schwarzschild was the eldest of five sons and one daughter born to Moses Martin Schwarzschild and his wife Henrietta Sabel. His father was a prosperous member of the business community in Frankfurt, with Jewish forebears in that city who can be traced back to Liebmann "of the Black Shield" (died 1594), and possibly even further, to one Elieser, also known as Liebmann, who came to Frankfurt from Cologne in 1450.

From his mother, a vivacious, warm person, Schwarzschild undoubtedly inherited his happy, outgoing personality; from his father, a capacity for sustained hard work. His childhood was spent in comfortable circumstances among a large circle of relatives, whose interests included art and music; he was the first to become a scientist.

After attending a Jewish primary school, Schwarzschild entered the municipal Gymnasium in Frankfurt at the age of eleven. His curiosity about the heavens was first manifested then; he saved his allowance and bought lenses to make a telescope. Indulging this interest, his father introduced him to a friend, J. Epstein, a mathematician who had a private observatory. With Epstein's son (later professor of mathematics in the University of Strasbourg), Schwarzschild learned to use a telescope and studied mathematics of a more advanced type than he was getting in school. His precocious mastery of celestial mechanics resulted in two papers on double star orbits, written when he was barely sixteen. They appeared in the *Astronomische Nachrichten* (1890).

In 1891 Schwarzschild began two years of study at the University of Strasbourg, where Ernst Becker, director of the observatory, guided the development of his skills in practical astronomy—skills that later were to form a solid underpinning for his masterful mathematical abilities.

At age twenty Schwarzschild went to the University of Munich. Three years later, in 1896, he obtained his Ph.D., *summa cum laude.* His dissertation, written under the direction of Hugo von Seeliger, was an application of Poincaré's theory of stable configurations in rotating bodies to several astronomical problems, including tidal deformation in satellites and the validity of Laplace's suggestion as to how the solar system had originated. Before graduating, Schwarzschild also found time to do some practical work: having read about Michelson's interferometer with two slits variably spaced, he devised a multislit instrument for himself. This instrument consisted of a coarse wire grating at a variable angle above the objective lens of a ten-inch telescope. He used it to measure the separation of close double stars; with a micrometer he found the distance between the tiny first-order spectra that resulted, and was able to detect separations as small as 0.88″ of arc. Later workers, notably Comstock and Hertzsprung, used this device to find the "effective wavelengths" of individual stars and so a clue to stellar surface temperatures.

After graduating, Schwarzschild became assistant at the Kuffner observatory in Ottakring (a western suburb of Vienna), where Leo de Ball was then director. Here Schwarzschild remained from October 1896 until June 1899, and here he began what became a lifetime avocation—giving lectures that conveyed to nonastronomers his own feelings about the excitement and significance astronomy holds for everyone.

During this period Schwarzschild published several papers on celestial mechanics, dealing with special cases of the three-body problem. But the main thrust of his work now became a coordinated attack on one of astronomy's most fundamental problems: stellar photometry. Measurement of the radiant energy reaching us from the stars was then still being done by eye, in principle just as Hipparchus had done two millennia earlier. Schwarzschild decided to try substituting a photographic plate for the human eye at the telescope. The many advantages of photography had been recognized (permanent record; coverage of a whole field of stars at once, and of invisible stars merely by increasing the time of exposure), but much work remained to be done before photography could even equal the eye of a trained observer. This work, both theoretical and practical, Schwarzschild now began. It culminated with the publication of his "Aktinometrie," so called because light producing a photochemical effect was then referred to as "actinic." Part A of "Aktinometrie," published in 1910, contains the earliest catalog of photographic magnitudes; it preceded Parkhurst's "Yerkes Actinometry" by several years.

Of the two likely ways of converting from black dots on a photographic plate to actual stellar magnitudes, Schwarzschild rejected measuring diameters of the images as inaccurate. He had investigated the theory of diffraction patterns as produced at various angular distances from the optic axis and found that the distribution of intensity in the concentric rings was not constant over an extended field. He therefore decided to smear out the images by putting his plate inside the focal plane, and then to measure the density of the resulting blurs with a photometer. This technique had been suggested by Janssen in 1895, but Schwarzschild was actually the first to use it.

Next Schwarzschild investigated the response of the photographic emulsion in order to determine whether photographs taken at different exposure times could be directly compared. According to the photochemical law enunciated by Bunsen and Roscoe in 1862, the image of a given star should be identical with that produced for a star half as bright when exposed for twice the time. But other workers, such as Abney, noted deviations from such strict reciprocity. Schwarzschild was the first to quantify the particular "failure of reciprocity" that occurs under low levels of illumination such as from faint stars. He performed a series of laboratory experiments and concluded that the law must be modified by raising the exposure time to the power p, with p less than unity but a constant for any given combination of emulsion and development process. This relation is still known as Schwarzschild's law, and p as Schwarzschild's exponent, although subsequent work has shown that p is not as unvarying as Schwarzschild had thought.

Now Schwarzschild was ready to try out his techniques on the sky over Vienna. He photographed an aggregate of 367 stars, which included two that were known to vary in brightness. In following one of the variables, eta Aquilae, through several of its cycles, Schwarzschild found that its changes covered a considerably larger range of magnitude photographically than visually. He correctly attributed this difference to a rhythmic change in surface temperature and was therefore the first both to observe and to explain this phenomenon. It is one that occurs in all similar stars—the Cepheids.

These photometric results were presented to the University of Munich as Schwarzschild's monograph qualifying him to teach. He returned to Munich and served as *Privatdozent* for two years.

At a meeting of the German Astronomical Society held in Heidelberg in August 1900, Schwarzschild—once more under Seeliger's influence—discussed quite a different aspect of astronomy, namely the possibility that the geometry of space was non-Euclidean. He suggested two kinds of curvature: elliptic (positively curved and finite, like the surface of a sphere but with antipodal points considered identical) and hyperbolic (negatively curved and infinite). After considering the astronomical evidence then available, he concluded that, if space were curved, the radius of curvature of the universe must exceed the earth-sun distance by at least four million times for a hyperbolic universe, and by a hundred million times for an elliptic universe. The latter case carried the proviso that space absorption of about forty stellar magnitudes must occur, otherwise the returning light emitted from the far side of our sun would refocus into a visible countersun in the sky. These estimates of size, even as lower limits, are decidedly small; yet if the paper shows how small a universe Schwarzschild thought he lived in, it also demonstrates the unlimited boldness of his thought.

In another publication dating from this period, Schwarzschild considered the suggestion, published by Arrhenius a few months previously, that the tails of comets point away from the sun because the repulsive pressure of solar radiation outweighs gravity. Assuming that the tails were made up of completely reflecting spherical particles of a reasonable density, he found that the pressure of radiation could just barely exceed the gravitational attraction by the necessary twenty times, if the particles had diameters between 0.07 and 1.5 microns; below that size scattering would occur, and above it gravitation would predominate. He remarked that the occasional tail in which even greater repulsion seemed to be present could not be shaped by radiation pressure alone. Such is still believed to be the case.

In the fall of 1901 Schwarzschild was named associate professor at the University of Göttingen and also director of its observatory. The observatory, with the director's living quarters in one wing, had been built and equipped eighty years earlier by Gauss.

Less than a year later, at the age of twenty-eight, Schwarzschild was promoted to full professor. He remained eight years in Göttingen, the most productive and probably the happiest time in his life. He sharpened his ideas in discussions with a brilliant circle of colleagues; for example, during the summer semester of 1904 he was one of four men in charge of the mathematical-physical seminar, the other three being Klein, Hilbert, and Minkowski. He carried a heavy teaching load but each year managed to include a course entitled "Popular Astronomy." The observatory soon became a center for young intellectuals of all disciplines. But it did not at first offer Schwarzschild the instruments he needed to pursue his observational work.

Gauss's original meridian circle was obsolete, while the other main piece of equipment, a Repsold heliometer, was unsuitable. In 1904, however, A. Schobloch donated a seven-inch refractor. Schwarzschild and his collaborators used this telescope to photograph 3,522 stars, data on which appeared in the "Aktinometrie."

For this enterprise Schwarzschild had a new idea. Instead of using extrafocal images as before, he decided to use a special plateholder—his "Schraffierkassette"—held in the focal plane but moved mechanically during a three-minute exposure so that all the images came out as squares 0.25 mm. on a side. This plateholder, revised several times, was effective but cumbersome and was not used by subsequent investigators. The methods of reducing the plates were also refined. The final publication, *Aktinometrie, Teil B* (1912), contains for each star its fully corrected photographic magnitude and an indication of its surface temperature in the form of its color index (photographic minus visual magnitude). Schwarzschild used the Potsdam visual magnitudes and also those obtained at Harvard, for comparison.

To the tradition of geodetic measurements at Göttingen, initiated by Gauss, Schwarzschild contributed in 1903 a suspended zenith camera of his own design, to be used for photographic latitude determination. He also became interested in ballooning—in balloons filled with gas from the city plant, making it as hazardous a sport as Schwarzschild's other favorites, mountain climbing and skiing. To simplify the problem of navigating while in the swinging basket of a balloon, Schwarzschild developed a form of bubble sextant, with ancillary tables and nomograms.

While in Göttingen, Schwarzschild also became interested in the sun. He obtained a small grant and went by freighter from Hamburg to Algeria for the total solar eclipse of 30 August 1905. His companions were Carl Runge, an applied mathematician at the University of Göttingen, and Robert Emden, a physicist, then teaching in Munich, and Schwarzschild's brother-in-law. Their modest equipment, pictured in the published report (and including a rare photograph of Schwarzschild himself), was set up on the ruined stage of an old Roman amphitheater in Guelma, with a makeshift darkroom nearby. The ambient temperature was 108° F., but the planned program was carried out to the last detail. Of greatest interest were Schwarzschild's flash spectra: using a camera fitted with an objective prism (all the glass being transparent to near ultraviolet light) and roll film pulled through by hand, he got sixteen photographs of the solar spectrum in a period of thirty seconds, beginning ten seconds before second contact. Since the speed with which the moon passed across the solar disc was known, these spectrograms could be analyzed to give the chemical composition, both qualitative and quantitative, of regions at various heights on the sun. This ingenious method was later revived by Menzel in his jumping film spectrograph.

Returning to Germany, Schwarzschild enlisted the aid of his old friend Villiger (who had helped him to measure double star separations in 1896) to investigate how the intensity of ultraviolet light varied across the disc of the sun. The observations were made at Jena, in the Zeiss factory, using a thin film of silver on the objective of the telescope, to screen out all radiation longer than 3,200 Å. They found that the drop-off between center and limb was even more pronounced at these short wavelengths than in either the visible or the infrared.

In 1906 Schwarzschild published a theoretical work on the transfer of energy at and near the surface of the sun. In discussing the results of the 1905 eclipse he had assumed that equilibria in the different modes of energy transfer could occur simultaneously and therefore be treated separately. He had also remarked that the rapid decrease in density necessary to explain the observed sharpness of the solar disc favored the predominance of radiative over convective (adiabatic) transfer near the photosphere. He now developed a theory of radiative exchange and equilibrium that was quantitative, and therefore susceptible to experimental verification. He assumed that near its surface the sun was horizontally layered into regions, each of which received radiation from below and reemitted it outward. His first approximation to a solution of the integral equations involved was similar to one proposed by Schuster in 1905. It is therefore usually referred to as the Schuster-Schwarzschild model for a gray atmosphere, although they arrived at it independently. It represented a major step toward understanding stellar structure, but as it did not predict the correct flux it was superseded by Eddington's model, which did.

Other theoretical work that Schwarzschild did at Göttingen includes three papers on electrodynamics, written in 1903. In them he attempted to formulate the fundamental equations in terms of direct action at a distance, using Hamilton's principle of least action. This approach has been used again at least once, by Wheeler and Feynmann in 1945.

In 1905 Schwarzschild published three papers on geometrical optics, dealing exhaustively with the aberrations encountered in optical systems. Here he used Hamilton's "characteristic function" (called the "eikonal" by Bruns). In the first paper he showed how spherical aberrations originate, including those of higher order. In the second paper he demonstrated how, by combining two mirrors with aspherical surfaces, a telescope free of aberrations would result. In the third paper he provided formulas for computing a variety of compound optical systems. Max Born, writing in 1955, acknowledged that these papers formed the backbone of his own "Optik," first published in 1932.

Schwarzschild also made contributions to stellar statistics, at a time when the structure of our galaxy and the way it rotates were still mysterious. He considered, in two articles published in 1907 and 1908, the motions of nearby stars through space as related to estimates of their distances. The sparse observational material then available, including proper motions as tabulated in the Groombridge-Greenwich catalog, had already been analyzed by Kapteyn, who was surprised to find that peculiar motions (obtained from proper motions of the stars by correcting for the motion of the sun) were not random but seemed to favor two preferential directions. Kapteyn derived from this his "two stream hypothesis," which had stars moving past each other from opposite directions. Such a picture was intellectually unacceptable to Schwarzschild, who developed instead what he called a unitary picture, namely his hypothesis of an ellipsoidal velocity distribution, which he showed would fit the observed facts equally well. A third article, published in 1911 after he had left Göttingen, gave details of his methods and compared his results to those of Seeliger, Kapteyn, and Hertzsprung.

Schwarzschild's cosmological thoughts are available in a collection of four popular lectures, entitled "On the System of Fixed Stars." Perhaps of the greatest interest is the lecture read before the Scientific Society of Göttingen on 9 November 1907, dealing with Lambert's cosmological letters. Schwarzschild discussed the type of teleological arguments used (successfully) by Lambert to reach many of the same conclusions about the universe—including the plurality of inhabited worlds—that are adhered to even by those physical scientists to whom teleological arguments are anathema. Schwarzschild includes a wry comment that teleology is still fruitful in biological sciences, in the theory of evolution.

In 1909 Schwarzschild's life changed. He was appointed successor to Vogel as director of the Astrophysical Observatory in Potsdam. This was the most prestigious post available to an astronomer in Germany, but accepting it meant increased administrative burdens, and also giving up the academic surroundings so congenial to him. Potsdam had been an army town since the time of Frederick the Great, and the University of Berlin would be fully fifteen miles away. Nevertheless, he decided to go, and took up his duties on Telegraph Hill (where the observatory was located) late in 1909. With him he brought Else Rosenbach, the daughter of a professor of surgery at Göttingen, whom he had married on 22 October 1909. Their marriage was successful despite initial family misgivings (she was not Jewish) and was blessed with three children: Agathe, Martin (professor of astronomy in Princeton University), and Alfred.

Also making the move to Potsdam at this time was Ejnar Hertzsprung, who had come to Göttingen at Schwarzschild's invitation in April 1909.

In August 1910 Schwarzschild went to California to attend the Fourth Meeting of the International Union for Cooperative Solar Research, stopping off along the way to visit the major observatories in the United States. The published account of this trip sheds an interesting light on the differences between American and European astronomy just before World War I. Notwithstanding the better skies and the larger instruments, Schwarzschild's envy was directed mainly toward the installations both Harvard and Lick had in the Southern hemisphere. He came home ready to push for a German observatory south of the equator, and suggested Windhoek, then in German Southwest Africa, as a possible site.

The year 1910 also brought a return of Halley's comet. Schwarzschild, with E. Kron, measured photographs of this comet, taken by a Potsdam expedition to Tenerife. In their discussion of how the brightness diminished outward, there appeared for the first time the suggestion that fluorescent radiation occurs in comet tails (later amply verified).

At Potsdam, Schwarzschild's interests turned more toward spectroscopy. He designed a spectrographic objective, which was built by Zeiss. Appreciating the need for a quick and reliable way to determine the radial velocities of stars (to supplement proper motions for work in stellar statistics), he expanded, in 1913, upon the way E. C. Pickering had used an objective prism for this purpose. In 1914, anticipating his own later work in general

relativity, Schwarzschild attempted — unsuccessfully, as it turned out — to observe a gravitational red shift in the spectrum of the sun.

When World War I began in August 1914, Schwarzschild carried over into political life the unitary concepts that guided his scientific life. He volunteered for military service, feeling that loyalty to Germany should come ahead of professional ties and his personal background as a Jew. After an initial delay, because of his high government position, he was accepted and placed in charge of a weather station in Namur, Belgium. Subsequently he was commissioned as a lieutenant and attached to the headquarters staff of an artillery unit, serving first in France and later on the Eastern front. His assignment was to calculate trajectories for long-range missiles; a communication to the Berlin Academy in 1915 (not published until 1920 for security reasons) dealt with the effect of wind and air density on projectiles.

While serving in Russia, Schwarzschild wrote two papers on general relativity, presented to the Berlin Academy for him by Einstein, and published in 1916. The first paper, dealing with the gravitational field of a point mass in empty space, was the first exact solution of Einstein's field equations; Schwarzschild's comment is that this work of his "permits Mr. Einstein's result to shine with increased purity."

The well-known "Schwarzschild radius" appears in the second of these papers, which treated the gravitational field of a fluid sphere with constant density throughout. Such a simplification cannot, of course, represent any real star, but it does permit of an exact solution. This solution has a singularity at $R = 2MG/c^2$, where R is the (Schwarzschild) radius for an object of mass M, G the universal constant of gravitation, and c the velocity of light. Should a star, undergoing gravitational collapse, shrink down inside this radius, it becomes a "black hole" that emits no radiation and can be detected only by its gravitational effects. (As an example of how far a star has to shrink, R for our sun is less than two miles.) The black holes resulting from Schwarzschild's solution differ from those of Kerr's 1963 solution in that they have no angular momentum.

For some time — dating back to his studies of the solar atmosphere — Schwarzschild had been interested in the problem of relating spectral lines to the underlying structure of the atoms producing them. His last paper was an attempt to enlarge upon several recent papers on the quantum theory written by Planck and by Sommerfeld. This subject,

Schwarzschild said, awaits a Kepler — but he did not live to see who it would be.

While serving at the front in Russia, Schwarzschild developed symptoms of a rare, painful, and at the time incurable, malady called pemphigus. This is a metabolic disease of the skin, tentatively believed today to have an "auto-immune" mechanism. Schwarzschild was invalided home in March 1916 and spent the last two months of his life in a hospital. He was buried, according to his own wish, in the central cemetery in Göttingen.

The honors Schwarzschild received before he died at age forty-two were few, considering his accomplishments. He was elected to the Scientific Society of Göttingen in 1905, became a foreign associate of the Royal Astronomical Society of London in 1909, and a member of the German Academy of Science in Berlin in 1913. For his war work he was awarded an Iron Cross. In 1960 the Berlin Academy dedicated to him, as "the greatest German astronomer of the last hundred years," the Karl Schwarzschild telescope, a seventy-nine-inch reflector located at Tautenburg, a few miles from Jena, where the optical parts were made. In 1959 the German Astronomical Society established the Karl Schwarzschild lectureship in his honor, with invited lectures to be given by distinguished astronomers.

BIBLIOGRAPHY

I. ORIGINAL WORKS. Schwarzschild's schoolboy publications on celestial mechanics are "Zur Bahnbestimmung nach Bruns," in *Astronomische Nachrichten*, **124** (1890), cols. 211–216; and "Methode zur Bahnbestimmung der Doppelsterne," *ibid.*, cols. 215–218. His coarse wire objective grating is described in "Über Messung von Doppelsternen durch Interferenzen," *ibid.*, **139** (1896), cols. 353–360. His dissertation is "Die Poincaré'sche Theorie des Gleichgewichts einer homogenen rotierenden Flüssigkeitsmasse," in *Neue Annalen der K. Sternwarte in München*, **3** (1898), 231–299.

Schwarzschild's publications on the photographic determination of stellar magnitudes and color indices include "Die Beugungsfigur im Fernrohr weit asserhalb des Focus," in *Sitzungsberichte der Bayerischen Akademie der Wissenschaften zu München*, Math.-Phys. Kl., **28** (1898), 271–294, with figure following p. 362; "Über Abweichungen vom Reciprocitätgesetz für Bromsilbergelatine," in *Photographische Korrespondenz*, **36** (1899), 109–112, trans. as "On the Deviations from the Law of Reciprocity for Bromide of Silver Gelatine," in *Astrophysical Journal*, **11** (1900), 89–91; "Die Bestimmung von Sternhelligkeiten aus extrafokalen photographischen Aufnahmen," in *Publikationen der von Kuffnerschen Sternwarte*, **5** (1900), B1–B23; his Habilitationsschrift, "Beiträge zur photographischen Photometrie der Gestirne," *ibid.*, **5** (1900), C1–C135; "Über die photographische Vergleichung der Helligkeit verschiedenfarbiger Sterne," in *Sitzungsberichte der Akademie der Wissenschaften in Wien*, Math.-Natur. Kl., **109**, sec. 2a (1900), 1127–1134; "Über eine Schraffierkassette zur Aktinometrie der Sterne," in *Astronomische Nachrichten*, **170** (1906), cols. 277–282, written with Br. Meyermann; "Über eine neue Schraffierkassette," *ibid.*, **174** (1907), cols. 297–300, written with Br. Meyermann; "Aktinometrie der Sterne der BD bis zur Grösse 7,5 in der Zone 0° bis +20° Deklination": Teil A in *Abhandlungen der K. Gesellschaft der Wissenschaften zu Göttingen*, Math.-Phys. Kl., n.s. **6**, no. 6 (1910), written with Br. Meyermann, A. Kohlschütter, and O. Birck; Teil B, *ibid.*, n.s. **8**, no. 3 (1912), written with Br. Meyermann, A. Kohlschütter, O. Birck, and W. Dziewulski; and "Über die Schlierkorrektion bei der Halbgittermethode zur Bestimmung photographischer Sterngrössen," in *Astronomische Nachrichten*, **193** (1912), cols. 81–84.

Publications by Schwarzschild dealing with comets include "Der Druck des Lichts auf kleine Kugeln und die Arrheniussche Theorie der Cometenschweife," in *Sitzungsberichte der Bayerischen Akademie der Wissenschaften zu München*, Math.-Phys. Kl., **31** (1901), 293–338; and "Über die Helligkeitsverteilung im Schweife des Halleyschen Kometen," in *Nachrichten von der Gesellschaft der Wissenschaften zu Göttingen*, Math.-Phys. Kl., **1911** (1911), 197–208, written with E. Kron, trans. as "On the Distribution of Brightness in the Tail of Halley's Comet," in *Astrophysical Journal*, **34** (1911), 342–352.

The suspended zenith camera devised by Schwarzschild is described in "Über Breitenbestimmung mit Hilfe eines hängenden Zenithkamera," in *Astronomische Nachrichten*, **164** (1903), cols. 177–182.

Schwarzschild discussed the sun and its atmosphere, including the formation of Fraunhofer lines, in papers among which are "Über die totale Sonnenfinsternis vom 30. August 1905," *Abhandlungen der Gesellschaft der Wissenschaften zu Göttingen*, Math.-Phys. Kl., n.s. **5**, no. 2 (1907), with three halftone plates; "Über die Helligkeitsverteilung des ultravioletten Lichtes auf der Sonnenscheibe," in *Physikalische Zeitschrift*, **6** (1905), 737–744, written with W. Villiger, trans. as "On the Distribution of Brightness of the Ultra-Violet Light on the Sun's Disc," in *Astrophysical Journal*, **23** (1906), 284–305, which includes additional material; "Über das Gleichgewicht der Sonnenatmosphäre," in *Nachrichten von der Gesellschaft der Wissenschaften zu Göttingen*, Math.-Phys. Kl., **1906** (1906), 41–53; and "Über Diffusion und Absorption in der Sonnenatmosphäre," in *Sitzungsberichte der Preussischen Akademie der Wissenschaften zu Berlin*, **1914** (1914), 1183–1200.

Schwarzschild's three articles on electrodynamics, "Zur Elektrodynamik," appeared in *Nachrichten von der Gesellschaft der Wissenschaften zu Göttingen*,

Math.-Phys. Kl. (1903), I, 126–131; II, 132–141; III, 245–278. His three articles on optical aberrations appeared as "Untersuchung zur geometrischen Optik," in *Abhandlungen der K. Gesellschaft der Wissenschaften zu Göttingen*, Math.-Phys. Kl., n.s. **4** (1905): I as no. 1, II as no. 2, III as no. 3.

Schwarzschild's papers on stellar motions and stellar statistics include "Über die Eigenbewegung der Fixsterne," in *Nachrichten von der Gesellschaft der Wissenschaften zu Göttingen*, Math.-Phys. Kl., **1907** (1907), 614–631; "Über die Bestimmung von Vertex und Apex nach der Ellipsoidhypothese aus einer geringeren Anzahl beobachteter Eigenbewegung," *ibid.*, **1908** (1908), 191–200; "Zur Stellarstatistik," in *Astronomische Nachrichten*, **190** (1911), cols. 361–376; and "Beitrag zur Bestimmung von Radialgeschwindigkeiten mit dem Objektivprisma," in *Publicationen des Astrophysikalischen Observatoriums zu Potsdam*, **23**, pt. 1 (1913), no. 69.

Schwarzschild's publications dealing with space curvature and general relativity are "Über das zulässige Krummungsmass des Raumes," in *Vierteljahrsschrift der Astronomischen Gesellschaft*, **35** (1900), 337–347, with a summary of the discussion that followed his talk on 311–312; "Über die Verschiebung der Bande bei 3883 Å in Sonnenspektrum," in *Sitzungsberichte der Preussischen Akademie der Wissenschaften zu Berlin*, **1914** (1914), 1201–1213; "Über das Gravitationsfeld eines Massenpunktes nach der Einsteinschen Theorie," *ibid.*, **1916** (1916), 189–196; and "Über das Gravitationsfeld einer Kugel aus inkompressibler Flüssigkeit nach der Einsteinschen Theorie," *ibid.*, **1916** (1916), 424–434.

Schwarzschild's last paper was "Zur Quantenhypothese," *ibid.*, **1916** (1916), 548–568; his classified work on ballistics appeared as "Über den Einfluss von Wind und Luftdichte auf die Geschossbahn," *ibid.*, **1920** (1920), 37–63.

For Schwarzschild's general attitude toward astronomy, including its relation to other disciplines, see "Über Himmelsmechanik," in *Physikalische Zeitschrift*, **4** (1903), 765–773. See also the collection of his popular lectures, reprinted in pamphlet form in honor of Seeliger's sixtieth birthday, *Uber das System der Fixsterne* (Leipzig, 1909; 2nd ed., Leipzig, 1916) (the talk "Über Lamberts kosmologische Briefe," found in this pamphlet, first appeared in *Nachrichten von der Gesellschaft der Wissenschaften zu Göttingen*, *Geschäftliche Mitteilungen*, **1907**, 88–102); "Die grossen Sternwarten der Vereinigen Staaten," in *Internationale Wochenschrift für Wissenschaft, Kunst und Technik*, **49** (1910), cols. 1531–1544; and his inaugural address to the Berlin Academy, in *Sitzungsberichte der Preussischen Akademie der Wissenschaften zu Berlin*, **1913** (1913), 596–600, followed by Planck's reply, 600–602.

A list of 116 publications by Schwarzschild is appended to the obituary written by O. Blumenthal. Apart from official director's reports from Göttingen and Potsdam, which appeared yearly in *Vierteljahrsschrift der Astrono-* *mischen Gesellschaft*, and similar special reports in *Astronomische Nachrichten*, it seems to be complete, with the exception of a contribution, "Stationare Geschwindigkeitsverteilung in Sternsystem," printed posthumously (and marked "fragment") in *Probleme der Astronomie, Festschrift für Hugo v. Seeliger* (Berlin, 1924), 94–105.

II. SECONDARY LITERATURE. Obituary notices on Schwarzschild include O. Blumenthal, in *Jahresbericht der Deutschen Mathematikervereinigung*, **26** (1918), 56–75, with photograph, facs. signature, and list of publications starting on p. 70; A. S. Eddington, in *Monthly Notices of the Royal Astronomical Society*, **77** (1917), 314–319; A. Einstein, in *Sitzungsberichte der Preussischen Akademie der Wissenschaften zu Berlin*, **1916** (1916), 768–770; and E. Hertzsprung, in *Astrophysical Journal*, **45** (1917), 285–292, with portrait facing p. 285. S. Oppenheim wrote an essay commemorating the fiftieth anniversary of Schwarzschild's birth, which appeared in *Vierteljahrsschrift der Astronomischen Gesellschaft*, **58** (1923), 191–209. Max Born's reminiscences of Schwarzschild as a professor at Göttingen are included in his "Astronomical Recollections," in *Vistas in Astronomy*, **1** (1955), 41–44.

Author's Note: I am indebted to Professor Martin Schwarzschild for a number of facts about his parents that are not available in print.

SALLY H. DIEKE

SCHWEIGGER, JOHANN SALOMO CHRISTOPH (*b.* Erlangen, Bavaria, 8 April 1779; *d.* Halle, Prussia, 6 September 1857), *physics, chemistry.*

Schweigger was the son of Friedrich Schweigger, extraordinary professor of theology at the Protestant University of Erlangen and archdeacon of a parish in that city. In addition to attending the Gymnasium in Erlangen, he received a thorough education in classical and Semitic languages and in philosophy from his father and several of his father's learned friends. On 7 April 1800 he received the Ph.D. at Erlangen; his dissertation, "De Diomede Homeri," dealt with the unifying characteristics of Homer's heroes. Having also studied mathematics and physics, he lectured on mathematics and natural science as a *Privatdozent* at Erlangen until 1803, when he was called to Bayreuth as professor of mathematics and physics at the Gymnasium. He then was professor of chemistry and physics at the Physikotechnisches Institut (called also the Höhere Realschule) in Nuremberg from 1811 until its dissolution in 1816. A corresponding member of the Bavarian Academy of Sciences since 1813, Schweigger went to Munich in 1817 as an ordinary member but left that year probably to become ordinary professor of physics and chemistry at the University of Erlangen. His status at the Academy thereby reverted to corresponding member, although he later became a foreign member (probably in 1847). In 1819 he was called to the University of Halle as ordinary professor of physics and chemistry, and remained there until his death. In 1816 he had become a corresponding member of the Göttingen Gesellschaft der Wissenschaften and a member of the Kaiserliche Leopoldino-Carolinische Deutsche Akademie der Naturforscher, of which he was an *Adjunkt des Direktoriums* by 1817. Schweigger, who married late in life, had three sons and one daughter.

Schweigger is perhaps best known as founder of the *Journal für Chemie und Physik*, of which he edited fifty-four volumes between 1811 and 1828.[1] This important journal published both original articles and translations and, being somewhat less prestigious than the *Annalen der Physik*, served as the organ of publication of the first papers of a number of scientists, including Wilhelm Weber and Gustav Theodor Fechner. Schweigger's literary output consisted largely of review articles and commentaries on the papers of others.

At the start of his scientific career Schweigger published several papers (1806, 1808) that questioned the validity of Volta's contact theory of electricity by describing an active pile that, according to that theory, should not have been capable of producing any electricity. At first content to conclude merely that the liquid conductor must play a more important role in the pile than simply preventing metallic contact, he subsequently offered an explanation in terms of a polarization of the water by the metal plates. This work was extended in 1817 by the discovery that in certain piles chemical action caused a reversal in polarity of the normally positive zinc and negative copper. Schweigger did not, however, refine or extend his experiments and thus cannot be counted among the major protagonists of the chemical theory of the pile.

Schweigger shared with Poggendorff the honor of constructing the first simple galvanometer, his *Multiplicator*, or multiplier, which he demonstrated before the Naturforschende Gesellschaft of Halle on 16 September and 4 November 1820. Schweigger's device consisted of a figure-eight-shaped coil of wire, a construction he preferred to a simple loop because he wished to demonstrate the equal and opposite electromagnetic effects on a magnetic needle placed in either side. Indeed, his use of the device never went much beyond such simple demonstrations, nor did he show any inclination to refine it into a measuring instrument or to discover its laws of operation. Schweigger thought the operation of the multiplier provided vivid proof of the existence of a "double magnetic polarity" perpendicular to the current in a connecting wire (that is, a wire connecting the poles of a pile). He envisioned this polarity as a succession of magnetic axes oppositely directed along the top and bottom of the wire, so that a compass would point in opposite directions when held above or below it. That he regarded this hypothesis on the nature of electromagnetism as a direct expression of the simple facts was characteristic of Schweigger's concretely pictorial approach to physical theory.

NOTES

1. The journal was continued until 1833 (vol. **69**) by his adopted son, Franz Wilhelm Schweigger-Seidel, who had been coeditor since 1825 (vol. **45**). Johann Ludwig Georg Meinecke also had been a coeditor, from 1819 (vol. **26**) until 1823 (vol. **38**). From the beginning of 1821 (vol. **31**) to 1830 the journal also bore the title *Jahrbuch der Chemie und Physik*, with its own volume numbers. Finally, from 1825 (vol. **45**) to 1827 (vol. **51**) it was subtitled *als eine Zeitschrift des wissenschaftlichen Vereins zur Verbreitung von Naturkenntniss und höherer Wahrheit.*

BIBLIOGRAPHY

I. ORIGINAL WORKS. Extensive bibliographies are found in the Royal Society *Catalogue of Scientific Papers*, V, 589–592; and in Poggendorff, II, cols. 873–875. Many more of his commentaries on others' papers are listed in G. C. Wittstein, ed., *Autoren- und Sach-Register zu sämmtlichen neunundsechzig Bänden des Schweigger'schen Journals für Chemie und Physik. (Jahrgänge 1811–1833)* (Munich, 1848), 88–91. See also Snelders' article (below).

II. SECONDARY LITERATURE. On Schweigger's life and work, see Carl Friedrich Philipp von Martius, "Denkrede auf Joh. Salomo Christoph Schweigger," in *Gelehrte Anzeigen der k. Bayerischen Akademie der Wissenschaften*, **46**, Jan.–June 1858, cols. 81–99, repr. in Martius' *Akademische Denkreden* (Leipzig, 1866), 345–364. Also useful is the article by "K" in *Allgemeine deutsche Biographie*, XXXIII (1891), 335–339. For his contribution to the founding of the Gesellschaft Deutscher Naturforscher und Ärzte, see Heinz Degen, "Die Gründungsgeschichte der Gesellschaft deutscher Naturforscher und Ärzte," in *Naturwissenschaftliche Rundschau*, **8** (1955), 421–427, 472–480.

An informative account of an important aspect of his work is H. A. M. Snelders, "J. S. C. Schweigger: His Romanticism and His Crystal Electrical Theory of Matter," in *Isis*, **62** (1971), 328–338, which should be read to supplement the information given here. Some of his work on the pile and the multiplier is discussed in Wilhelm Ostwald, *Elektrochemie, ihre Geschichte und Lehre* (Leipzig, 1896), 301–304, 371–373.

KENNETH L. CANEVA

SCHWEIKART, FERDINAND KARL (*b.* Erbach, Germany, 28 February 1780; *d.* Königsberg, Germany [now Kaliningrad, R.S.F.S.R.], 17 August 1859), *mathematics.*

Schweikart studied law at the University of Marburg from 1796 to 1798 and received his doctorate in law from Jena in the latter year. After practicing at Erbach from 1800 to 1803, he worked as a private tutor until 1809; his pupils included the prince of Hohenlohe-Ingelfingen. In 1809 Schweikart became extraordinary professor of law at the University of Giessen; from 1812 to 1816 he was full professor at the University of Kharkov; and from 1816 to 1820 he taught at Marburg. From 1821 until his death he was professor of law at Königsberg, where he also earned a doctorate in philosophy.

Schweikart published extensively in his principal field of endeavor, including a work on the relationship of natural and positive law (1801). Early in his life he also became interested in mathematics, and he holds an important place in the prehistory of non-Euclidean geometry. While a student at Marburg, the lectures of J. K. F. Hauff had stimulated him to consider the problem of parallel lines, which provided the subject of his only publication in mathematics (1807). His approach was still completely Euclidean; but later he arrived at the beginnings of a hyperbolic geometry, which he called astral geometry. He made this advance independently of Gauss, Bolyai, and Lobachevsky, as is proved by the correspondence cited by Engel and Stäckel in *Die Theorie der Parallellinien von Euklid bis Gauss.* The astronomer Christian Gerling, a student of Gauss, wrote in a letter to Wolfgang Bolyai, the father of János Bolyai, that in 1819 Schweikart had reported on the basic elements of his "astral geometry" to colleagues at Marburg. Schweikart also wrote on this topic to his nephew Taurinus in Cologne. Stimulated by his uncle's work, Taurinus had virtually discovered hyperbolic trigonometry; but unlike his uncle, he still believed in the sole validity of Euclidean geometry.

The three chief founders of hyperbolic geometry surpassed Schweikart only because of the thoroughness with which they examined specific topics of this subject. The demands of his legal career undoubtedly prevented him from finding sufficient time to undertake similarly extensive research.

BIBLIOGRAPHY

Schweikart's only mathematical work is *Die Theorie der Parallellinien, nebst einem Vorschlag ihrer Verbannung aus der Geometrie* (Jena–Leipzig, 1807).

A secondary source is Friedrich Engel and Paul Stäckel, *Die Theorie der Parallellinien von Euklid bis Gauss* (Leipzig, 1895), 243–252.

WERNER BURAU

SCHWENDENER, SIMON (*b.* Buchs, St. Gallen, Switzerland, 10 February 1829; *d.* Berlin, Germany, 27 May 1919), *plant anatomy.*

Schwendener was the son of a farmer; he himself worked on his grandfather's farm during summer vacations from school. His father wished him to become a teacher, so in 1847 Schwendener began to prepare himself for this career, although he had little inclination for it. From 1849 to 1850 he studied science at the Academy of Geneva. His father could not afford to allow him to attend the University of Zurich for further study, as he had planned, and Schwendener then accepted a teaching position in Wädenswil. In 1853 his grandfather died and left him a small legacy, which he employed to support himself at the university. He graduated from the University of Zurich in 1854 and was awarded the Ph.D., *summa cum laude,* in 1856.

Schwendener's Ph.D. thesis, *Ueber die periodische Erscheinungen der Natur, insbesondere der Pflanzenwelt,* was inspired by Candolle and finished under the direction of Oswald Heer. Another early—and lasting—influence on Schwendener's work was that of Carl Naegeli, whose Zurich lectures Schwendener had attended. Both Naegeli and Schwendener were interested in plant morphology and ontogeny, and Schwendener attracted Naegeli's attention while attending his courses at the Zurich Eidgenössische Technische Hochschule. As a result, when Naegeli was later, in 1857, appointed professor at the University of Munich, he invited Schwendener to be his assistant, and thus initiated a close collaboration. Their two-volume work *Das Mikroskop* (published in 1865–1867) represented three years' mutual effort; in it Naegeli and Schwendener not only demonstrated a number of details of plant anatomy but also set out the principles that Abbe used in his optical work. Schwendener also did independent research on lichens, and published the first of his several works on that subject in 1860, the same year in which he became *Privatdozent*.

In 1867 Schwendener returned to Switzerland to take up an appointment as *professor ordinarius* and director of the botanic garden at the University of Basel. He here continued the work on lichens that culminated in his *Die Algentypen der Flechtengonidien. Programm für die Rektoratsfeier der Universität*, published in 1869. In this book Schwendener first stated that lichens are a composite of algae and fungi (later termed "symbiosis" by De Bary and confirmed by the work of Bornet and Stahl). In support of his thesis, Schwendener offered a considerable amount of histological evidence.

Schwendener then began to examine the mechanical properties of plants, seeking an analogue in plants to the animal skeleton or to the materials used in constructing a bridge. He found that the principles of mechanics govern the structure of the stems of plants, with maximum rigidity resulting from minimum materials; he presented his findings in *Das mechanische Prinzip im anatomischen Bau der Monocotylen*, in which, however, he gave no account of the causal development of the structures that he described. The book, published in 1874, was received unenthusiastically by his fellow botanists.

At Basel Schwendener worked in comparative isolation and taught only a few students; he was therefore happy to accept an appointment in 1877 to succeed Wilhelm Hofmeister at Tübingen. Here he studied phyllotaxy, again applying mechanical principles. Hofmeister had been the first to refute the spiral theory of leaf development, stating that each point on the growing region of a stem is a potential leaf and adding that new leaves occur within the largest gaps between existing ones. Schwendener went on to demonstrate, using mechanical models, that leaf arrangement was the result of displacement by contact between leaf primordia; his theory was at first fully accepted, then attacked. It remains an important one in the development of the theory of phyllotaxy, and was stated in *Mechanische Theorie der Blattstellungen*, published in 1878, the same year that Schwendener went to Berlin to succeed Alexander Braun.

Schwendener stayed in Berlin for thirty-one years, during which time he taught a great number of students and wrote articles in defense of his theory of phyllotaxy and on the movement of fluids in plants, the structure and mechanics of stomata, the theory of descent in botany, and torsion in plants. He was elected to the Berlin Academy of Sciences in 1880 and in 1882 was one of the founders of the Deutsche Botanische Gesellschaft. He served as rector of the university from 1887 and retired in 1909. He was, in addition, an honorary member of a number of foreign scientific societies.

Schwendener never married. He was interested in the arts and in literature, and composed several poems. Music, however, he found "a rather disagreeable noise."

BIBLIOGRAPHY

I. ORIGINAL WORKS. Schwendener's most important writings are his dissertation, *Ueber die periodische Erscheinungen der Natur, insbesondere der Pflanzenwelt* (Zurich, 1856); *Das Mikroskop*, 2 vols. (Leipzig, 1865–1867), written with Carl Naegeli; *Die Algentypen der Flechtengonidien. Programm für die Rektoratsfeier der Universität* (Basel, 1869); *Das mechanische Prinzip im anatomischen Bau der Monocotylen* (Leipzig, 1874); and *Mechanische Theorie der Blattstellungen* (Leipzig, 1878). A number of the results of his work at Berlin are collected in *Gesammelte botanische Abhandlungen* (Berlin, 1898).

II. SECONDARY LITERATURE. A short autobiography, written in 1900, and a bibliography are included in A. Zimmermann, "Simon Schwendener," in *Berichte der Deutschen botanischen Gesellschaft*, **40** (1922), 53–76. A detailed biography is G. Haberlandt, *ibid*., **47** (1929), 1–20.

A. P. M. SANDERS

SCILLA, AGOSTINO (*b*. Messina, Sicily, 10 August 1629; *d*. Rome, Italy, 31 May 1700), *geology*.

Having shown an aptitude for painting since childhood, Scilla was sent to Rome to study art. After his return to Messina, he soon became well known and is still considered one of the best painters of the seventeenth-century Sicilian school. The failure of the Messina revolt against the Spanish (1674–1678), in which Scilla had taken part, forced him into exile, first at Turin and then at Rome. He is famous not only as a painter but also as a scholar, a man of culture well versed in science and the humanities; the latter field is illustrated by his knowledge of ancient Sicilian coins. In the domain of science he was a good mathematician, but he is particularly remembered as the author of *La vana speculazione disingannata dal* senso (1670), today considered one of the classics of geology.

In the seventeenth century most scientists still considered fossils to be *lusus naturae,* sports of nature, born within rocks through the influence of the stars or by other strange means. At the Accademia dei Lincei, in which the supporters of the new science gathered around Galileo, one of its first members, Francesco Stelluti, persisted in this view. It seems highly likely that Stelluti was the academician who moved Scilla to claim the right, in his book, of denouncing *vana speculazione* ("vain speculation"). Fabio Colonna, Scilla, and Niels Stensen put the study of geology in the seventeenth century on the right path, even if they still placed the universal deluge as the origin of those phenomena they were so carefully and objectively observing in Italy.

Convinced that "to doubt things is the best and only way to begin to know them, even approximately," Scilla described with admirable clarity and critical sense the observations he had made on the fossiliferous sedimentary terrains of both shores of the Strait of Messina, dealing with the succession of strata, the genesis of the rocks, and particularly the nature of the fossils. He anticipated the principle that the present is the key to the past when he explained the repetition of coarse, medium, and fine-grained materials in terms of what he could see actually happening in the same places under the action of rapid torrents. He considered fossils to be animal remains imprisoned in rocks that are now hard but were originally muddy or sandy soil.

Extending his researches to other parts of Sicily and to Malta, Scilla studied the zoological features of each fossil, comparing them with those of analogous living species. He did not limit himself to the study of mollusks, the origins of which seemed obvious to him, but tackled more difficult problems, recognizing the presence of fossil corals and echinoderms and showing that the much-discussed *glossopetrae* are the teeth of sharks. To deny the organic origin of fossils, he concluded, was to "commit the sin of disputing a known truth."

BIBLIOGRAPHY

La vana speculazione disingannata dal senso (Naples, 1670) includes 28 beautifully executed engravings of fossil and living marine animals that reveal the keen spirit of observation of the painter and the naturalist. The volume was later published in Latin as *De corporibus marinis quae defossa reperiuntur* (Rome, 1747).

The main secondary source is G. Seguenza, *Discorso intorno Agostino Scilla* (Messina, 1868). Other studies deal exclusively with Scilla as a painter.

FRANCESCO RODOLICO

SCLATER, PHILIP LUTLEY (*b.* Tangier Park, Hampshire, England, 4 November 1829; *d.* Odiham, Hampshire, England, 27 June 1913), *ornithology.*

Sclater was the second son of William Lutley Sclater and Anne Maria Bowyer. His family were landed gentry, and his elder brother became a member of Parliament and later the first Lord Basing. Educated at Oxford, Sclater took the B.A. degree in 1849 and remained at Corpus Christi College for another two years, studying natural history. In 1851 he entered Lincoln's Inn and was later admitted to the bar. He practiced law for a number of years, but he constantly maintained his interest in natural history. Sclater often traveled abroad during this decade, both on the Continent, where he was a frequent visitor to the home of Charles Lucien Bonaparte, and to America, where he met Cassin, Leidy, and John LeConte.

Elected a fellow of the Zoological Society of London in 1850, Sclater became a member of its Council in 1857 and its secretary in 1860, a post he held for forty-three years. In 1858 he took a prominent part in founding *Ibis,* the journal of the British Ornithologists' Union. He became the first editor and continued to be for fifty-four years, except during the period 1865–1877.

This was the great age of zoological travel and exploration, of classification and anatomy. Among Sclater's first major contributions to zoology, and perhaps one of his greatest, was the 1858 paper "On the General Geographic Distribution of the Members of the Class Aves" (*Journal of the Linnean Society,* Zoology, **2**, 130–145), in which he classified the zoogeographical regions of the world on the basis of their bird life. The division into six distinct regions that he proposed was later adopted for all other animals, and is still used by students of zoogeography.

In 1862 Sclater married Jane Anne Eliza Hunter Blair, daughter of a baronet, by whom he had six children. His eldest son, William Lutley, also became an outstanding ornithologist and succeeded his father as editor of *Ibis* just before the latter's death in 1913; he continued as editor until 1930.

In 1861 Sclater was elected a fellow of the Royal Society and served two terms on its Council. He was a member of the British Association for the Advancement of Science (1847) and served as one of its two general secretaries for five years. He was also a life fellow of the Linnean and the Royal Geographical societies and the Geological Society of London, and a corresponding or honorary member of more than forty other scientific societies in Great Britain and abroad.

Sclater's most engrossing duties were with the Zoological Society of London. He spent a number of years reorganizing its affairs, increasing its membership and income, rebuilding the main buildings in the Zoological Gardens, repaying its debts, and keeping the society solvent. He also saw to it that the various publications of the society—the *Proceedings* (now titled *Journal of Zoology*), *Transactions, Zoological Record,* and sundry lists of animals and garden guides—were issued regularly and on schedule.

When his elder brother accepted (1874) a position as president of the Local Government Board in Disraeli's second administration, Sclater acted as his private secretary for two years and subsequently was offered a permanent position in the civil service. He declined this offer because it would take him from his work in natural history.

In connection with his work on zoogeography, Sclater wrote monographs on the tanager genus *Calliste* (1857) and on the jaçanas and puffbirds (1882). With Osbert Salvin, he published *Exotic Ornithology* (1869), which described many new and rare Central and South American birds, and *Nomenclator avium neotropicalum* (1873). A series of papers in the *Proceedings of the Zoological Society of London* in 1877 and 1878 reported on the birds collected by the *Challenger* expedition. In 1888 and 1889 Sclater issued his *Argentine Ornithology,* with notes by W. H. Hudson on the habits of the birds. He also wrote four volumes of the monumental *Catalogue of the Birds in the British Museum*—he prepared volume XI in 1886, XIV in 1888, XV in 1890, and half of XIX in 1891.

Sclater's close friends were the great zoologists of the time—Alfred Newton, who succeeded him as editor of *Ibis* (1865–1871); Salvin, who succeeded Newton until 1877; Canon Tristram; and Alfred Henry Garrod, the anatomist. One of his closest friends was T. H. Huxley, who was also one of his staunchest supporters on the Council of the Zoological Society. Charles Darwin often visited him in his office, bringing long lists of memoranda to discuss.

Sclater was a man of strong personality. Proba-

bly this quality is reflected best in his association with the British Ornithologists' Club, which he helped R. Bowdler Sharpe establish in 1892, and of which he was elected chairman. He chaired the monthly meetings and delivered an inaugural address at the beginning of each session.

After resigning as secretary of the Zoological Society in 1903, Sclater retired to his home in Odiham, where he was widely known as an active justice of the peace and a frequent rider with the Hampshire Hunt, of which he was by far the oldest member. He continued to visit the library of the Zoological Society and the collection of his birds at the British Museum (Natural History) until his death, at the age of eighty-three, following a carriage accident.

BIBLIOGRAPHY

I. ORIGINAL WORKS. Sclater was one of the most prolific writers of scientific papers, books, articles, and notes of his time. His publications, listed in the several bibliographies below, total almost 1,400 titles. Many of these were short notes of a few pages or less in periodical literature, some only a few lines announcing new acquisitions by the Zoological Society or exhibits at the British Ornithologists' Club, describing new taxa, or making corrections in the systematic literature. On the other hand, the several volumes he contributed to the *Catalogue of the Birds in the British Museum* are weighty tomes of substance and importance.

II. SECONDARY LITERATURE. A detailed biography is included in G. Brown Goode, "Bibliography of the Published Writings of Philip Lutley Sclater, F.R.S., Secretary of the Zoological Society of London," *Bulletin. United States National Museum,* no. 49 (1896). This lists 1,289 titles to that year, contains a portrait, and names the new families, genera, and species he described. This biography was abridged (with slight corrections) for *Ibis,* 9th ser., **11,** jubilee supp. (1908), 129–137, commemorating the "original members" of the British Ornithologists' Union. His longest obituary, by A. H. Evans, in *Ibis,* 10th ser., **1** (1913), 672–686, lists 582 titles on birds alone.

OLIVER L. AUSTIN, JR.

SCOT. See **Michael Scot.**

SCOTT, DUKINFIELD HENRY (*b.* London, England, 28 November 1854; *d.* Basingstoke, England, 29 January 1934), *botany, paleobotany.*

Scott was the youngest son of George Gilbert Scott, an eminent architect, and Caroline Oldrid.

An unusually well-informed botanist, he was among those who laid the foundations of scientific botany and paleobotany.

He was educated privately at home, where he became an avid collector of the local flora. From an early age he used a standard work on systematic botany, and his interests and reading were surprisingly profound. At the age of fourteen he read Joseph Hooker's presidential address to the British Association for the Advancement of Science (1868) in support of Darwinism, and soon thereafter (using English translations), the books of the Continental botanists Alexander Braun, Hugo von Mohl, Carl Wilhelm von Naegeli, and Wilhelm Hofmeister. In addition, he studied Henfrey and Griffith's *Micrographic Dictionary*, with its many German citations. (German literature was ahead of the field in those days.)

Upon entering Christ Church, Oxford, Scott's botanical interests and scholarship, which had sustained his boyhood, slackened or failed, probably through lack of encouragement. In 1876 he received his B.A. and from 1876 to 1879 studied engineering. Upon the death of his father in 1878, Scott came into independent means. His old enthusiasm for botany reasserted itself, and in 1880 he went to Würzburg to study botany with Sachs.

In August 1882 Scott graduated as doctor of philosophy, *summa cum laude*, with a thesis on plant structure: "The Development of the Milk Vessels in Plants." Upon returning to England he succeeded Bower in 1883 as assistant to Daniel Oliver at University College and in 1885 as lecturer in the Royal College of Science under T. H. Huxley. During this period Bower and Scott, great friends, labored on their individual anatomical projects in the small Jodrell Laboratory in Kew Gardens, where Scott produced further evidence for his interpretation of the nature of milk vessels. Later he became honorary keeper of the laboratory and wrote (sometimes in collaboration) several excellent anatomical papers on the fleshy roots of *Sesbania;* on the stems of species (*Strychnos, Ipomoea, Yucca, Dracaena*) with peculiar or anomalous stem vascular tissues; and on the pitchers of *Dischidia*. Scott's associations with the many distinguished visiting botanists and his sojourn in Germany—his "spiritual home"—made him something of an internationalist.

In 1889–1890 the aging W. C. Williamson of the University of Manchester invited Scott and Bower to see his collection of fossil plants and sections thereof—in the hope that they might continue his novel investigations. As Scott himself said, he became an instant convert to the study of fossil plants. While he never ceased to emphasize the importance of comparative anatomical studies of fossil and living plants, he also kept in close touch with virtually the whole field of botany, including plant physiology and genetics. For example, although he did not work in physiology or genetics, both active fields of research, he was alert to their importance. Scott wrote two admirable textbooks, which together make up *An Introduction to Structural Botany:* pt. I, *Flowering Plants;* pt. II, *Flowerless Plants* (1896). Essentially based on the detailed study of selected "types," the textbooks contain many drawings by Scott's wife.

Williamson's pioneering work on Carboniferous fossils had been published in a series of memoirs in *Philosophical Transactions of the Royal Society* (1871–1893). Unfortunately many of his contemporaries had but little understanding of his remarkable achievements. In Scott, Williamson recruited as a co-worker a first-class scholar and plant anatomist, who had an eye for detail and possessed an enviable objectivity. In a joint memoir to the Royal Society on "Further Observations on the Organization of Fossil Plants of the Coal Measures," Williamson and Scott in 1894 gave an important general review of the morphological characters of *Calamites, Calamostachys,* and *Sphenophyllum,* including comparisons with recent plants. The complex strobili (cones) of some of these plants must have taxed their techniques and powers of interpretation. Scott pointed out, with convincing vigor, that studies of the diverse anatomy of extinct and of living species were essentially reciprocal in character and quite essential to any basic consideration of the evolution of plants. In 1895 (the year of Williamson's death) two further memoirs, which dealt with the roots of *Calamites, Lyginodendron,* and *Heterangium,* were published, again under joint authorship. In the memoirs the anatomy of fossil species, with relevant comparisons with recent ferns and cycads, was impeccably portrayed for the first time.

In a notable memoir, contributed to the Royal Society in 1897, Scott described *Cheirostrobus,* a new and exceptional type of cone from the Lower Carboniferous beds at Pettycur on the Firth of Forth. This paper affords a good example of Scott's skill in investigation and interpretation.

In 1900 Scott gave a course of lectures at University College, London, published in *Studies in Fossil Botany*. Because of the beautiful illustrations and engaging clarity of the book, it became, and has remained, a classic. In 1908 the original volume was so enlarged that it was necessary to issue the work in two volumes, and a third edition appeared in 1920–1923. These volumes and Scott's various public lectures did much to bring a proper awareness of the importance of the study of fossils to the botanical world.

During this period Scott also continued to work on selected living plants, for example, cycads and *Isoetes hystrix*. In 1901 he described the seedlike fructifications of *Lepidocarpon*, which were of special interest because they afforded an indication of how early seeds—"in a nascent stage of evolution"—might have originated. In 1902 he published an account of *Dadoxylon* and of its curious vascular structure. In the same year there appeared *The Old Wood and the New*, in which the common anatomical features of Paleozoic stems were closely and critically examined. Later he elucidated the structure and probable affinity of *Stauropteris, Botryopteris, Trigonocarpus, Mesoxylon*, and *Ankyropteris*.

Numerous investigations of ancient Pteridophyta, Cycadofilicales, and other groups, with discoveries by contemporaries, provided Scott with a wide range of information on ancient plants and enabled him to write *The Evolution of Plants* (1911). At the time, the book was of rather special interest, for Scott gave an unusually concise and clear account of the possible affinity of the Jurassic-Cretaceous Bennettitales, that is, of plants that vegetatively seem close to recent cycads but which, on the evidence of their reproductive structures, must be far apart. Scott raised the question: Could plants with these remarkable reproductive organs perhaps have prepared the way for the evolution of the flowering plants? In 1922 he included a wider range of materials in *Extinct Plants and Problems of Evolution*.

In 1887 Scott married Henderina Victoria Klaassen, who had written several botanical papers. In addition to illustrating some of Scott's books and papers, she also provided secretarial help. They had two sons who survived infancy: the younger died suddenly at school in 1914; the elder was killed in the British Ypres salient in 1917. Four daughters survived.

Scott received many academic honors. In 1894 he was elected a member of the Royal Society and in 1906 received the Royal Medal. From 1908 to 1912 he was president of the Linnean Society. In 1926 he was awarded the Darwin Medal and two years later, the Wollaston Medal of the Geological Society.

BIBLIOGRAPHY

Besides the works listed in the text, Scott wrote "The Present Position of Morphological Botany," in *Reports of the British Association for the Advancement of Science* (1896), 922–1010; and "The Present Position of the Theory of Descent, in Relation to the Early History of Plants," *ibid.* (1922), 170–186, his presidential addresses to the botany section of the Association. See also "Reminiscences of a Victorian Botanist," A. B. Rendle, ed., in *Journal of Botany, British and Foreign* (1934). A bibliography is given in *Annals of Botany*, **72** (1935), with portrait.

On Scott and his work, see F. O. Bower, *Sixty Years of Botany (1875–1935): Impressions of an Eyewitness* (London, 1938); and A. C. S., "Dukinfield Henry Scott," in *Obituary Notices of Fellows of the Royal Society of London,* **1** (1932), 205–227.

C. W. WARDLAW

SCOTT, WILLIAM BERRYMAN (*b.* Cincinnati, Ohio, 12 February 1858; *d.* Princeton, New Jersey, 29 March 1947), *vertebrate paleontology, geology.*

The son of William McKendree Scott and Mary Elizabeth Hodge, and a great-great-great-grandson of Benjamin Franklin, Scott lived virtually his entire life in Princeton, New Jersey, where his family moved when he was three years old. He attended the College of New Jersey (now Princeton University) and began his scientific career with field trips to Bridger Basin, Wyoming, in 1877 and 1878, accompanied by his lifelong friend, Henry Fairfield Osborn.

After completion of graduate studies in England and Germany (where he obtained the doctorate at the University of Heidelberg), Scott returned to Princeton in order to join the faculty, where he served for fifty years and then for seventeen years more, after his formal retirement. In 1883 he married Alice Adeline Post; they had seven children. In 1884, at the age of twenty-six, he became a full professor, and in 1904, first chairman of the department of geology, a post he held until his retirement in 1930.

Scott devoted a large part of his life to quiet teaching and research on fossil mammals. After a few expeditions at the beginning of his career, he abandoned the search for fossils in the field, although he was an inveterate traveler throughout most of his life. His research, almost entirely devoted to fossil mammals, produced some 177 published contributions. His viewpoint was pragmatic, and little of his attention was devoted to the more theoretical aspects of his subject. Perhaps his two greatest efforts were the editing and writing in part of the impressive *Reports of the Princeton University Expeditions to Patagonia* (1905–1912) and the writing of several large volumes on the Oligocene mammals of the beds of the White River, South Dakota (1936–1941). He also wrote a standard geology textbook and the widely used *History of Land Mammals in the Western Hemisphere* (1913).

BIBLIOGRAPHY

Scott wrote an autobiography, *Memoirs of a Palaeontologist* (Princeton, N.J., 1939). The full bibliography of W. B. Scott is G. G. Simpson, "Biographical Memoir of William Berryman Scott," in *Biographical Memoirs. National Academy of Sciences,* **25** (1948), 175–203.

EDWIN H. COLBERT

SCOTUS. See **Duns Scotus, John.**

SCROPE, GEORGE JULIUS POULETT (*b.* London, England, 10 March 1797; *d.* Fairlawn [near Cobham], Surrey, England, 19 January 1876), *geology.*

Scrope was the son of John Poulett Thomson, head of a firm engaged in trade with Russia, and Charlotte Jacob. Scrope's younger brother was Charles Edward Poulett Thomson, Lord Sydenham. Scrope was educated at Harrow; at Pembroke College, Oxford (1815–1816); and at St. John's College, Cambridge (1816–1821). Upon his marriage (22 March 1821) to Emma Phipps Scrope, heiress of William Scrope, of Castle Combe, Wiltshire, he assumed her name (which is pronounced Scroop).

Scrope was elected to the Geological Society in 1824 and served as secretary in 1825; he was later awarded the Society's Wollaston Medal (1867). He was elected also to the Royal Society (1826) and was founder and first president of the Wiltshire Archaeological and Natural History Society (1853–1855). From 1833 to 1868 he was a Liberal member of Parliament for Stroud, Gloucestershire. He was an advocate of free trade and various social and economic reforms, especially the poor law, but he took no part in parliamentary debate. He instead wrote extensively on a variety of political

and economic subjects. He was said to have written nearly seventy anonymous pamphlets, earning him the nickname "Pamphlet Scrope." About 1867, after the death of his wife, who had been an invalid as the result of a riding accident soon after their marriage, he sold Castle Combe and moved to Fairlawn, near Cobham, Surrey. On 14 November 1867 he married Margaret Elizabeth Savage, who survived him. There were no children from either marriage.

Scrope's interest in geology was first aroused in Italy by the sight of Vesuvius in continual eruption during the winters of 1817–1818 and 1818–1819. In 1819–1820 he visited Sicily and the Lipari Islands, studying Mount Etna and Stromboli. On the advice of Edward Clarke and Adam Sedgwick at Cambridge, he studied the extinct volcanic region of Auvergne in central France in the summer and fall of 1821. He then went to northern Italy and eventually to Naples, where he arrived in time to observe the violent eruption of Vesuvius in October 1822. During his return to England in the summer of 1823, he visited the volcanic regions of the Eifel in Germany.

On the basis of his geological fieldwork, Scrope wrote two books. The first book, *Considerations on Volcanos* (1825), has been called "the earliest systematic treatise on vulcanology."[1] It was poorly received by geologists, since it put forth in a dogmatic fashion hypotheses about every phase of volcanic activity and concluded with a "new theory of the earth." At this time Scrope was an ardent advocate of the theory of a cooling earth, which implied that the frequency and intensity of earthquakes and volcanic eruptions had declined over geological time. He believed that the forces of heat within the earth were still capable of producing, on rare occasions, cataclysmic upheavals (perhaps of whole mountain ranges or continents), causing destructive diluvial waves. At the same time he argued that

> The laws or processes of nature we have every reason to believe invariable. Their *results* from time to time vary, according to the combinations of influential circumstances [p. 242]. . . . Until, after a long investigation, and with the most liberal allowances for all possible variations, and an unlimited series of ages, [present-day processes] have been found wholly inadequate to the purpose, it would be the height of absurdity to have recourse to any gratuitous and unexampled hypothesis [pp. v–vi].

These ideas were indebted in part to the writings

of James Hutton, John Playfair, and James Hall, but Scrope's restatement in combination with the theory of a cooling earth was to provide the basis for a catastrophist opposition to the uniformitarianism of Lyell.

Scrope's second book, *Memoir on the Geology of Central France* (1827, but written in 1822), was more uniformitarian in approach, being devoted to a small region during geologically recent times. Improving upon the work of French geologists in Auvergne, he showed that currents of lava, which had flowed into valleys at various times, appeared at different heights above the river beds, marking successive steps in the progress of erosion of the valleys by the rivers. Scrope refuted the arguments for a recent deluge in the region and showed the untenability of attempts to classify the volcanic cones into antediluvian and postdiluvian on the basis of the amount of erosion they had undergone. As additional evidence that rivers are capable of producing impressive valleys unaided by a deluge, he cited in 1830 the presence of entrenched meanders in the valleys of the Meuse and Moselle.[2] These arguments were effective in undermining the Cuvier-Buckland theory of a recent universal deluge, identical with the Biblical flood, that had deposited debris and had carved the major valleys. The theory was eventually abandoned by its remaining supporters in the Geological Society.

Scrope always believed that his two books had greatly influenced the development of Lyell's uniformitarian views; and Lyell's dependence is traceable in two articles that he wrote in 1826 and 1827 for the *Quarterly Review*. The latter was a very favorable review of Scrope's second book. Lyell soon after verified Scrope's observations in central France and Italy (1828–1829). Therefore, Scrope can, paradoxically, be regarded as a parent of both uniformitarianism and its catastrophist opposition in Great Britain. He never committed himself to either side and always occupied a middle ground.

As one of a number of younger geologists who wished, as he expressed it, to free geology "from the clutches of Moses," Scrope assisted Lyell in the completion of the first volume of his *Principles of Geology* (1830), which had as a principal objective the extermination of theological influence on geology. A favorable review was ensured, since the publisher also owned the *Quarterly Review*; and its editor, after consulting Lyell, chose Scrope as the reviewer. Scrope wrote the review with Lyell's advice, and he also reviewed Lyell's third volume for the same journal (1835). In these and later reviews, Scrope argued strongly against religious influence in geology, yet he asserted that there was no conflict between the Bible and geology and wrote enthusiastically about the great contributions of geology to natural theology. He put forth, in opposition to Lyell, the evidence for progressive change in the histories of the earth and of life; and he was unimpressed by Lyell's hypothesis of a chemical source of heat within the earth.

Scrope rejected Lyell's metamorphic theory, which asserted that the "stratified primary rocks," such as gneiss and schist, were normal sedimentary rocks altered by internal heat. He contended instead that the stratified primary rocks had originally been disintegrated granite deposited in hot agitated water when the primitive earth was hot and barren.[3] He later gave up this explanation but continued to believe that the foliation of these rocks was caused by differential movement. Scrope regarded the earth as essentially solid in its interior, kept in this state by intense pressure brought about by the expansive forces of heat and steam. The subterranean matter was thus in a state of tension so that any slight reduction of external pressure, caused perhaps by a change in atmospheric pressure or by the tidal action of the sun and moon, or an increase in internal temperature brought about by a local influx of heat would be sufficient to cause local melting accompanied by fracturing of the surrounding rock and the penetration of the fractures by the molten rock.

Scrope saw no essential difference between the causes of volcanoes and of earthquakes; a volcano was the result of fracturing at shallow depths, which allowed the fluid material to reach the surface. In 1856 he argued that this same cause could also produce a violent fracture and elevation of the overlying crust and the extrusion through a fissure of a ridge of crystalline matter. As the central axis of this protruded ridge or mountain range rose, the hot and partially fluid matter on the sides would be subject to friction, causing differential movement and the formation of parallel striations. In support of this theory he argued that mountain ranges typically show granite in the center, passing on the sides into gneiss (or "squeezed granite") and, further on, into schist.[4]

To the end of his life, Scrope continued to believe in the possibility of rare cataclysmic earth movements far in excess of anything that Lyell would allow, although Scrope's early catastrophism was soon modified to the extent that he believed that a mountain range had been formed by a succession of upheavals rather than by one grand upheaval, as advocated by Élie de Beaumont.

Scrope adopted a mean position between the two extremes following the analogy with volcanic eruptions, which vary greatly in violence. By 1872 he had also sufficiently changed his views so that he could regard the theory of a cooling earth as only a conjecture, belonging rather to astronomy than to geology. He therefore rejected T. H. Huxley's attempt to replace the uniformitarian interpretation of earth history by an evolutionary one, asserting that there was no evidence to show that the overall rate of earth movement had varied perceptibly during geological time. He did not, however, contest the evidence for biological evolution.[5]

Scrope's original scientific work virtually ceased for many years after he entered Parliament. He returned to geology in the mid-1850's, prompted by his desire to assist Lyell in combating a revival of the theory of "craters of elevation" of Humboldt, Buch, and Élie de Beaumont—a theory that he had first attacked in 1825. This theory regarded some volcanic cones as produced by a single explosive upheaval of strata rather than being built slowly by successive deposits of volcanic materials erupted from a vent, as Scrope and Lyell had always maintained. In two articles (1856, 1859) Scrope helped to refute the theory, pointing out its inconsistencies and the lack of agreement among its supporters as to the criteria for distinguishing these cones from cones formed by ordinary eruptions.[6]

After revisiting Auvergne in the summer of 1857, Scrope published a revised edition of his work on central France (1858); he dedicated the work to Lyell. This was followed by a greatly altered edition of his work on volcanoes (1862). During the last fifteen years of his life, he wrote many letters and short articles, which appeared mostly in the *Geological Magazine*. These writings served to correct the errors of others, to reaffirm or revive theories that Scrope had published in his first books, and to remind the world of his priority. He gave a general summary of his views in a new preface that accompanied the reissue of his work on volcanoes in 1872.

Among the "errors" attacked by Scrope in his last years were (1) the theory of a hot liquid earth with a thin crust, the contractions of which cause the earth to crumple, forming mountain ranges; (2) the tendency of German geologists to postulate a rigid law of succession of different types of lava from a volcanic vent; (3) the theory, held by Lyell, that the influx of seawater into the interior of the earth is the triggering cause of earthquakes and volcanic activity; and (4) any theory that ignored the primary importance of subterranean forces in the history of the earth. Thus, in a controversy with Jukes over the origin of valleys (1866), Scrope felt it necessary to remind the extreme fluvialists of the primacy of internal forces in creating the topography of the earth. Scrope believed that stream erosion was insignificant in comparison, yet he had long been among the leading advocates of "rain and rivers" as agencies of denudation in opposition to the tendency of Lyell and others to stress marine denudation.[7] Later (1872) he warned the fluvialists of the probability of vast denudational effects produced in the past by gigantic waves accompanying cataclysmic earth movements.

One of Scrope's favorite theories was that most lavas at the time of their appearance on the surface are not in a state of fusion but consist of solid crystals sliding over one another because of the expansive force of the steam mixed with them. In support of this theory he pointed to the rarity of glassy textures in most lavas. Despite the criticism his theory incurred from Lyell, after he first proposed it in 1825, Scrope continued to advance it, although without much success.

Like Lyell, Scrope was virtually blind during his last years. He generously encouraged young geologists to continue his investigations of volcanic phenomena, and his financial support enabled Archibald Geikie (1870) and John W. Judd (1876) to study Vesuvius and the Lipari Islands.

Scrope remained an amateur in geology in the sense that his knowledge never extended far beyond his principal fields of interest. He had little knowledge of paleontology, and his theories on tectonic mechanisms and on the origin of metamorphic rocks exhibit a deficient knowledge of chemistry and physics. His books of the 1820's showed considerable originality, and, principally by means of their influence on Lyell, helped steer geology into a more uniformitarian path. His later writings may have helped to keep geology on a middle course by combating extreme views from whatever side.

NOTES

1. See John W. Judd, *Volcanoes: What They Are and What They Teach*, 6th ed. (London, 1903), p. 5. Judd credits Scrope with a number of contributions to vulcanology.
2. *Philosophical Magazine*, **7** (1830), 210–211 (Geological Society Proceedings).
3. *Quarterly Review*, **43** (1830), 411–469, and **53** (1835), 406–448.
4. *Geological Society Quarterly Journal*, **12** (1856), 326–350; cf. *Volcanos* (1862), pp. 265ff.
5. *Volcanos* (London, 1872), Preface.

6. *Geological Society Quarterly Journal,* **12** (1856), 326–350, and **15** (1859), 505–549.

7. *Geological Magazine,* **3** (1866). Cf. *Geology and Extinct Volcanos of Central France* (1858), 208.

BIBLIOGRAPHY

I. ORIGINAL WORKS. Scrope's major geological works are *Considerations on Volcanos* (London, 1825), 2nd ed., *Volcanos* (London, 1862; reissued with new preface, 1872), and *Memoir on the Geology of Central France* (London, 1827), 2nd ed., *Geology and Extinct Volcanos of Central France* (London, 1858). The Royal Society *Catalogue of Scientific Papers* lists some 36 scientific articles by Scrope, omitting at least four articles in the *Geological Magazine,* two letters in *Nature* (1875), and four reviews of geological works in the *Quarterly Review* (listed in the *Wellesley Index to Victorian Periodicals,* vol. I). Besides many pamphlets, Scrope wrote a number of reviews on nonscientific subjects, a biography of his brother, a history of Castle Combe, and works on economics and other subjects. Some 32 of Scrope's letters to Lyell (1828–1874) are at the American Philosophical Society.

II. SECONDARY WORKS. There is no biography of Scrope. T. G. Bonney's article in the *Dictionary of National Biography,* XVII (1897), 1073–1074, is rather uninformative about Scrope's personal life, as are the various obituaries. Scrope's contributions to geology are listed in *Geological Magazine,* **13** (1876), 96. His geological work is discussed in Karl Alfred von Zittel, *History of Geology and Palaeontology* (London, 1901), 259–263, and in R. J. Chorley, A. J. Dunn, and R. P. Beckinsale, *History of the Study of Landforms,* I (London, 1964), 125–130, 146–147, 357, 390–391, 400.

L. E. PAGE

SCUDDER, SAMUEL HUBBARD (*b.* Boston, Massachusetts, 13 April 1837; *d.* Cambridge, Massachusetts, 17 May 1911), *systematic entomology.*

Scudder was the son of Charles Scudder and Sarah Lathrop Coit, both of whom were Congregationalists. He attended Williams College (1853–1857) and studied with Louis Agassiz at Harvard (1857–1864).

Scudder held various positions in Cambridge and Boston and was instrumental in founding the Cambridge Entomological Club and *Psyche* in 1874. Between 1858 and 1902 he published 791 papers. His noteworthy works include *Catalogue of Scientific Serials of All Countries . . . 1633–1876* (1879); *Nomenclator zoologicus,* 2 pts. (1882–1884), a list of the generic names proposed in zoology; and the three-volume *Butterflies of the Eastern United States and Canada* (1888–1889).

Scudder's main contributions were in the study of Orthoptera—of which he described 630 species—and fossil insects. He named about 1,144 species of fossil insects, mostly while employed as paleontologist in the United States Geological Survey between 1886 and 1892.

Scudder was one of the most learned and productive American systematic entomologists of his day. As recently as 1920 Willis Stanley Blatchley said that "to him more than to all his predecessors and contemporaries combined is due our present knowledge of the Orthoptera." Scudder drew whatever taxonomic and evolutionary conclusions his data indicated, although new methods, especially studies of genitalia, and more extensive series of specimens, have required the modification of some of his conclusions. It is also doubtful whether fossils like the Coleoptera, which he studied, can always be named with as much taxonomic precision and be integrated as precisely with living species as Scudder held that they could. The beetles, for instance, do not exhibit the characters on which contemporary classification depends. To date no one has attempted either to continue or to revise Scudder's work on fossil beetles, at least in anything like Scudder's detail.

Scudder's personal life was unfortunate. In 1867 he married Ethelinda Jane Blatchford, who died in 1872. Their son died at the age of twenty-seven in 1896, the same year that Scudder began to show signs of Parkinson's disease. Realistic about his prospects, Scudder ended his work in 1902. He transferred his personal collection to the Museum of Comparative Zoology at Harvard College and his library to the Boston Society of Natural History and to Williams College. He died in 1911 after years of seclusion and invalidism.

BIBLIOGRAPHY

On Scudder and his work, see J. S. Kingsley, William L. W. Field, T. D. A. Cockerell, and Albert P. Morse, "Appraisals of Scudder as a Naturalist," in *Psyche,* **18** (1911), 174–192, with portrait; and Alfred Goldsborough Mayor, "Samuel Hubbard Scudder 1837–1911," in *Biographical Memoirs. National Academy of Sciences,* **17** (1919), 79–104, with portrait and bibliography of 791 titles.

MELVILLE H. HATCH

SEARES, FREDERICK HANLEY (*b.* near Cassopolis, Michigan, 17 May 1873; *d.* Honolulu, Hawaii, 20 July 1964), *astronomy.*

Seares was associated with the Mount Wilson Observatory for thirty-six years, fifteen of them as assistant director. His principal contribution lay in the field of photographic photometry: he standardized the stellar magnitude system and extended it to include stars fainter than the eighteenth magnitude.

The son of Isaac Newton Seares and his wife, the former Ella Ardelia Swartwout, Seares was born on a farm in the southwest corner of Michigan. By the time he was fourteen, the family was living in California, where he attended the Pasadena high school. He received a B.S. degree (with honors) from the University of California in Berkeley in 1895. This was his highest earned degree, although he remained at Berkeley four more years, two with the title of fellow and two more as instructor in astronomy.

In 1896 Seares married Mabel Urmy. Their only child, Richard, was born in Paris in 1900, while Seares was studying at the Sorbonne; the previous year Seares attended the University of Berlin.

Returning to the United States in 1901, Seares served for eight years as professor of astronomy and director of the Laws Observatory at the University of Missouri in Columbia. Then, at the invitation of G. E. Hale, he returned to Pasadena as superintendent of the computing division of the Mount Wilson Solar Observatory, but also to do research with the then brand-new sixty-inch telescope.

In this latter connection Seares was soon photographing stars in "selected areas" of the sky that had been chosen by Kapteyn. This collaboration culminated, more than twenty years later, in a catalog listing 67,941 stars, located in 139 areas (none of which were larger than 23′ of arc in diameter) systematically scattered over the sky north of declination −15°. Seares's problem was to intercompare, in a reliable way, light signals from widely separated stars that differed by as much as ten million times in brightness. His method was to photograph each area several times on the same plate, using absorbing wire gauze screens and reduced apertures to introduce known reductions in light, up to eleven magnitudes, between successive images of each star. Relative magnitudes could then be read off, and a common zero point applied to give absolute values.

The preliminary results of Seares's photometric program were so impressive that in 1922 he was elected president of the committee on stellar photometry of the International Astronomical Union. In 1932 the IAU adopted international magnitude standards based on his work, but Seares himself was not yet satisfied: he then began work on a catalog that appeared in 1941, providing data on 2,271 stars within 10° of the North celestial pole, to be used for both visual and photographic magnitude standards.

Seares also wrote a number of papers on galactic structure. His conclusion as to the relative brightness of our Milky Way compared to other "spiral nebulae" was influential in the stand taken by Shapley (his student at Missouri and his co-worker at Mount Wilson) in the Curtis-Shapley debate of 1920. Seares also investigated the way interstellar material obscures and reddens the light from distant stars.

Seares was elected to the American Philosophical Society in 1917, an associate of the Royal Astronomical Society in 1918, and to the National Academy of Sciences in 1919. He received an LL.D. degree from the University of California in 1930 and another from the University of Missouri in 1934. In 1940 he was awarded the Bruce Gold Medal of the Astronomical Society of the Pacific. That same year his wife died; two years later he married his longtime assistant Mary Cross Joyner, and with her eventually retired to Honolulu, where he died at age ninety-one.

BIBLIOGRAPHY

I. ORIGINAL WORKS. For a description of the Laws Observatory, see "Report of the Director of the Laws Observatory of the University of Missouri," in *Publications of the Astronomical Society of the Pacific,* **15** (1903), 167–168.

Seares's photometric techniques are described in "Photographic Photometry with the 60-inch Reflector of the Mount Wilson Solar Observatory," in *Astrophysical Journal,* **39** (1914), 307–340; his so-called exposure ratio method for direct determination of the color index (a number to be subtracted from the photographic magnitude of a star to get its visual magnitude) is outlined in "A Simple Method of Determining the Colors of the Stars," in *Proceedings of the National Academy of Sciences of the United States of America,* **2** (1916), 521–525. His paper entitled "The Surface Brightness of the Galactic System as Seen From a Distant External Point and a Comparison With Spiral Nebulae," appeared in *Astrophysical Journal,* **52** (1920), 162–182.

The *Mount Wilson Catalogue of Photographic Magnitudes in Selected Areas 1–139* is vol. IV of the Papers of the Mount Wilson Observatory and appeared in 1930 as Carnegie Institution of Washington Publication no. 402; the authors are given as F. H. Seares, J. C. Kapteyn, and P. J. van Rhijn (although Kapteyn had been dead almost eight years), assisted by Mary C. Joyner and Myrtle L. Richmond. *Magnitudes and Colors of Stars North of +80°*, written with Frank E. Ross and Mary C. Joyner, appeared as vol. VI of the same series and as Carnegie Publication no. 532 (1941); this work is Seares's final attempt to provide a set of absolute standard magnitudes in the North Polar region, replacing those printed in *Transactions of the International Astronomical Union*, **4** (1932), 140–152, that had been adopted as international standards.

Seares's ideas on interstellar obscuration are summarized in "The Dust of Space," based on his Bruce Gold Medal lecture, in *Publications of the Astronomical Society of the Pacific*, **52** (1940), 80–115.

A list of 161 publications by Seares follows Joy's 1967 biographical memoir (see below).

II. SECONDARY LITERATURE. For a contemporary discussion of Seares's work, see Alfred H. Joy, "The Award of the Bruce Gold Medal to F. H. Seares," in *Publications of the Astronomical Society of the Pacific*, **52** (1940), 69–79, with photograph facing p. 69. Joy also wrote the entry on Seares in *Biographical Memoirs, National Academy of Sciences*, **39** (1967), 417–431 with bibliography 432–444. An obituary by R. O. Redman appeared in *Quarterly Journal of the Royal Astronomical Society*, **7** (1966), 75–79.

SALLY H. DIEKE

SECCHI, (PIETRO) ANGELO (*b*. Reggio nell' Emilia, Italy, 18 June 1818; *d*. Rome, Italy, 26 February 1878), *astronomy, astrophysics*.

Secchi's father was a cabinetmaker, and the family was of modest circumstances. Secchi himself attended the Jesuit school in Reggio nell'Emilia, then, toward the end of 1833, when he was fifteen, entered the Jesuit novitiate in Rome. Two years later he entered the Collegio Romano, where he distinguished himself in a course that included physics and mathematics. In 1841 he was appointed instructor in these subjects at the Jesuit college in Loreto and soon became known for the originality of his lectures. Between 1844 and 1848 Secchi was obliged to return to his theological studies, but was able simultaneously to continue his astronomical work under Francesco de Vico, director of the observatory of the Collegio Romano and professor of astronomy at the Gregorian University in Rome.

When the Jesuits were expelled from Rome in 1848, Secchi went first to the flourishing Jesuit college at Stonyhurst, Lancashire, England. He then established himself at Georgetown University in Washington, D.C., where he acted as assistant to the director of the observatory, Father P. Curley, and made further studies in both theoretical and practical astronomy. He met the hydrographer M. F. Maury, and became acquainted with Maury's important meteorological works. In 1849 the ban against the Jesuits was lifted, and Secchi was able to return to Rome, where he took up an appointment as director of the observatory of the Collegio Romano.

Secchi recognized immediately that the observatory and its equipment were inadequate. He determined both to build a new observatory and to reshape the course of the research to be performed there, placing a new emphasis on astrophysics. His predecessor de Vico had already conducted important observations on comets, the rotation of Venus, and the satellites of Saturn, and Secchi, using the outmoded instruments of the old installation, began to examine the physical aspect of the ring of Saturn. In 1851 he began to study the sun, measuring the intensity of solar radiation with a thermoelectric pile, a technique previously employed by Joseph Henry to determine the temperature of a sunspot. Secchi first measured the radiation of the sun during the eclipse of 1851, then applied this method to the full solar disk in an attempt to establish the relationship between the temperature of the disk at its center and that at its edges. In the course of his work during the eclipse he made several daguerreotypes that must be reckoned among the earliest applications of photography in the study of the celestial bodies. His results indicated that the center of the solar disk emits almost twice as much radiation as does its borders.

The following year Secchi collated the two fragments into which Biela's comet had split during its appearance in 1846. He was able to observe a weak star through one of the segments, and was thereby able to demonstrate the thinness of the matter of which the comet was constituted. In 1853 Secchi discovered a comet with a multiple nucleus. He was, during this period in which astronomers were first beginning to understand the true nature of comets, more interested in determining their physical composition than in observing their position, and his interest extended to falling stars, which he introduced as a subject for study by his students at the Collegio Romano. His own observations led him to the conclusion that falling stars were of cosmic origin and thus paved the way for the work of Schiaparelli. At about the same time he made his first investigations of nebulae, by which he sought to confirm the results obtained by William Herschel, James Clark Ross, William Huggins, and Hermann Vogel.

Secchi was further engaged in preparing the new observatory that was being constructed over the church of St. Ignatius, part of the Collegio Romano. He installed a Merz equatorial telescope with an aperture of 24.5 centimeters and a focal distance of 4.3 meters, and with it resumed his observations of Saturn. With the new instrument, Secchi was able to determine the physical characteristics of the planet, including its polar flattening and the eccentricity of its ring. Having made further observations of Mars, during its opposition of 1859, Secchi announced that he had seen two permanent "canals" between the two reddish equatorial continents of that planet; he thus introduced a term which was widely taken up by his successors. In the same year he made studies of the moon, during which he measured and and made a detailed drawing of the crater of Copernicus for the purpose of noting seasonal variations, should such occur. He attempted to apply photography to the study of that body, but determined that his refractor was not suitable for photographic use, since its visual objective was corrected for the human eye, rather than for the special qualities of photographic emulsions.

About 1860 Secchi began to make observations and drawings of Jupiter. He noted that disturbances similar to terrestrial storms occurred in its atmosphere and, with the Merz objective, studied its satellites in some detail. In particular, he observed the spots on the Jovian moons, their periods of rotation about their axes, and the characteristics of their reflected light. He made spectroscopic studies of both Jupiter and Saturn and discovered the presence of special absorption bands in their spectra, which led him to conclude that the atmospheres of these planets contained elements different from terrestrial ones. He also made note of the almost permanent transparency of the atmosphere of Mars and proved that Uranus and Neptune do not have discontinuous spectra, but rather demonstrate bands that have the same qualities (although of much greater intensity) as those that he had found in the spectra of Jupiter and Saturn.

Secchi soon turned his attention to the sun. From the beginning he was convinced of the applicability of his research to a wide variety of celestial and terrestrial phenomena, a belief that he later summed up (in the introduction to his *Le soleil*), when he wrote that

Whatever our researches and [whatever] the knowledge that we acquire from them, it will not be in our power to regulate the influence of the sun. Nevertheless, the action of this star is too intimately related to the phenomena of life, heat, and light to render useless the studies that may enable us to investigate its nature. And, on the other hand, who knows whether or not an intimate relationship may exist between certain solar phenomena and some terrestrial ones that it would be important for us to predict with some degree of certainty?

Secchi made use of a good helioscopic eyepiece and projections to observe, on the photosphere, a great number of small luminous granules. These granules were of a variety of sizes and shapes, although the commonest were oval; they stood out upon a darker (although not entirely black) ground. This granulation was broken, most notably at the edges of the disk, by luminous tongues, which Secchi named "facole," and by the small black holes (which he called "pori") that are the points from which sunspots originate. Secchi noted that the luminous granules represented the extremities of columns of the warmer gases that arise from the cooler and less luminous solar surfaces. Having observed that the formation of sunspots, which generally appeared after a period of surface agitation, was usually accompanied by the appearance of less brilliant luminous tongues (now called "flares"), Secchi determined to investigate them. He concluded that these flares were, in fact, complex groups of gases with several nuclei (or dark central shadows), surrounded by half-shadows.

Secchi also observed the chromospheric eruptions that cross the nuclei of sunspots and split them into segments. It was clear to him that such wide, rapid, and complex surface movements could not occur in a solid substance, and he therefore suggested that the entire photosphere must be composed of an elastic fluid, similar to a gas, through which the sunspots move in a manner similar to terrestrial cyclones. He noticed that these vortices are more frequent during a period in which sunspots are being formed, when the surface movements that create the spots create currents that converge toward the nuclei. This represented further evidence of the gaseous nature of the sunspots and of the photosphere. Secchi lastly applied the law of diminution of angular velocity to the movement of sunspots from the equator to the poles of the solar surface to ascertain that the sun, or at least the photosphere, moves in accordance with the laws that govern a fluid mass.

Secchi wished to study the sun spectroscopically, and to that end commissioned Hofmann and

Merz to construct spectroscopes incorporating a series of prisms, while G. B. Amici constructed instruments for direct viewing. Taking up Kirchhoff's researches, Secchi demonstrated that the absorbing stratum of the sun, later identified as an inversion layer, must be very thin. With a large dispersion spectroscope, which he attached to the Merz equatorial, Secchi was able to observe the inversion of the hydrogen line on the chromosphere, which occurred an instant before the appearance of the dark D lines of Fraunhofer. Since the continuous spectra, with the exception of a few lines of sodium and magnesia, were also inverted, Secchi concluded that the stratum that in that instant partially inverts the dark lines of certain metals (such as the rose stratum of the chromosphere) also inverts the dark lines of hydrogen. This spectral analysis provided further confirmation of a solar atmosphere similar to the terrestrial one, although containing many lines of unknown origin, possibly those of elements that did not exist on earth. Secchi's spectroscopic examination of sunspots led him to recognize that the lines they exhibit are those of the solar atmosphere, although more or less widened, intensified, or weakened.

Secchi also realized the importance of observing the chromosphere and the corona during total eclipses of the sun. His first opportunity to do so occurred in 1860, when the totality of a solar eclipse was visible in Spain. Secchi traveled to Desierto de las Palmas, near Castellón de la Plana, where he made observations with a Cauchoix refractor; he then compared his results with those De la Rue had made with a Kew photoheliograph at Rivabellosa. Secchi thus concluded that the prominences seen during the eclipse were real, rather than a play of light as some had suggested; that they were solar in origin; and that the corona was also real and thicker at the equator than at the poles, and thickest at forty-five degrees. After the 1868 eclipse Secchi used the technique, simultaneously developed by Janssen and Lockyer, of enlarging the aperture of the spectroscope directed toward the solar border to observe the prominences and chromosphere in full sunlight. He applied this method further in 1869, when he began, with Respighi, the series of observations of the "spectroscopic images of the solar border" that he published in *Memorie della Società degli spettroscopisti italiani* in the following year.

Secchi also published a number of observations on solar prominences in his treatise *Le soleil*, issued in French in 1875–1877. This work was illustrated with magnificent color plates of the chromosphere and of the various types of prominences. Among those shown were the small flames (now called "spiculae") that he observed in the region of sunspots, converging toward the center of the eruption. These, he noted, became higher, more slender, and extremely luminous at the solar poles, where considerable activity manifested itself even during periods of relative calm on the solar surface. He classified the prominences as "quiescent" and "eruptive" — terminology that is still current.

Secchi made an especially careful study of the forces to which solar prominences are subjected, measuring the velocity of the masses expelled by the sun and their movement in the solar atmosphere. He used the spectroscope to observe the shifts, caused by the Doppler effect, of the lines present in the spectra of the prominences and observed that the expelled matter is not only launched upward but also frequently animated by vortical movements that give a spiral appearance to the luminous spouts. He speculated that the variations in velocity now attributed to the presence of magnetic fields must be caused by an as yet unrecognized periodic force. He observed that secular variations, of very short duration, also occurred at the diameter of the sun, and pointed out that irregularities in the shape of the sun were most apparent during periods of (and in the regions of) maximum photospheric agitation.

While conducting his solar studies, Secchi was further concerned with the study of the physical constitution of comets. During the appearance of the comet of 1861 he observed that the head of the comet emitted jets of discontinuous gases, which formed parabolic envelopes about it and, by a backward movement, produced the tail. In observing the comet in 1862, he was able to see that the jets of gases altered from night to night in correspondence to the comet's distance from the sun. He established the presence of carbon in the spectrum of the comet of 1866 and noted, in addition to the lines of emission, the continuous spectrum that indicated the existence of direct or reflected light. He found carbon associated with hydrogen or oxygen in the bands exhibited by comets of later years.

In 1862 Secchi, in furtherance of the early work on falling stars that had been performed at the Collegio Romano, carried out simultaneous observations at Rome and at Civitavecchia in order to determine the altitude of falling stars, which he calculated as being between seventy-five and 250 kilometers, with a falling velocity of ninety kilometers per second. From these and later observations he also established the similarity of falling stars, asteroids, and aerolites. Using the spectrosope he demonstrated that all these phenomena contained such metals as iron, magnesium, and sodium; he was particularly active during the rain of fire of 27 November 1872, "in which," he wrote, "the layers of distant light resemble the surge of snowflakes."

Secchi's spectroscopic research on luminous stars began in 1863, when he was visited in Rome by Janssen, who had a small spectroscope with him. Together they attached the spectroscope to a Merz equatorial and observed the stars, communicating their joint findings to the Paris Academy. Secchi and Janssen found Fraunhofer lines in the stellar spectra they examined, and identified some of these with terrestrial elements; Secchi then began to work with more sophisticated equipment to define the differences in solar spectra already noted by Donati and Huggins. He determined to investigate the spectra of a large number of stars, and set out his plan in a communication to the Pontificia Accademia Tiberina on 27 January 1868. He prefaced his report with the statement that: "In substance I wanted to see whether, just as the stars are countless, their composition is also proportionately varied. This was my query, and having been fortunate enough to perfect the observation instrument, the harvest was abundant, even more than I had hoped." The instrument to which he referred was a spectroscope equipped with a luminous aperture with which he could analyze even the weakest stars; with it Secchi was able to recognize a specific spectral type in a number of principal stars.

Secchi then determined to examine other stars by means of simple differential methods. Toward the end of 1869 he decided to adopt the apparatus that Fraunhofer had used, which consisted of a flint prism, fifteen centimeters in diameter, with a refracting angle of twelve degrees. He mounted this prism directly in front of the twenty-three-centimeter objective of the Merz equatorial telescope; he thus obtained greater luminosity and a larger dispersion than had been possible with the direct-vision prism, inserted between the objective and the ocular piece, that he had used previously. He next experimented with a circular prism, constructed by Merz, which he attached to the Cauchoix equatorial, the objective having an aperture equal to that of the prism. With this new combination he discovered that "whereas the stars are very numerous, their spectra are reduced to a few well-defined and distinct forms, which for the sake of brevity we may call types." He went on to note

that he had examined at least 4,000 stars, and was able to divide them into five types, with the high-temperature white stars at one end of the scale and the low-temperature red stars at the other. This classification still bears Secchi's name; it was soon adopted almost universally.

Secchi also classified nebulae according to his spectroscopic examination, into planetary, elliptical, and irregular forms. He examined examples of each type and found spectral lines of emission produced both by hydrogen and by elements then unknown on earth. The presence of these unknown elements led him to deduce that some nebulae are masses of pure gas—that is, that not all of them are resolvable into stars—a confirmation of a theory put forth by Herschel and accepted by Secchi himself. Of the elliptical nebulae of the external galaxies he was particularly interested in Andromeda, of which he studied the continuous spectrum.

In his observations of Andromeda Secchi noticed two black canals transversing the nebula. It seemed to him that these must be zones of non-luminous matter, projected on the nebula proper and intercepting the light of the stars, a phenomenon that he discovered in other parts of the Milky Way. He noted that it was improbable that these canals should, in fact, represent apertures, particularly given the gaseous nature of nebulae; many years later observations confirmed the presence of dark masses dispersed in space, which are seen projected on the background of a sky made luminous by light-emitting cosmic matter.

Secchi had almost ceased to make observations by 1873, when the Jesuits were again expelled from the Collegio Romano. He was nonetheless allowed to remain at his observatory through the intervention of the government, and he spent his last years preparing his scholarly writings for their final editions. He also continued to publish notes in the *Memorie della Società degli spettroscopisti italiani*, of which he had been, with Tacchini, a founder in 1870.

BIBLIOGRAPHY

I. ORIGINAL WORKS. Secchi's works include *Le soleil* (Paris, 1875–1877); *Le stelle* (Milan, 1877); and *L'astronomia in Roma nel pontificato di Pio IX* (Rome, 1877). A complete list of his writings is given by Bricarelli, cited below.

II. SECONDARY LITERATURE. On Secchi and his works, see G. Abetti, *Padre Angelo Secchi* (Milan, 1928); and *Storia dell'astronomia* (Florence, 1963), 159, 187–203, 205–206, 228–229, 255, 259, 266, 270, 278,

299, 301, 304, 352, 364, 377, 383, 389–391, 395, 401; and Bricarelli, "Della vita e delle opere del P. Angelo Secchi," in *Memorie dell'Accademia pontificia dei Nuovi Lincei*, **4** (1888).

GIORGIO ABETTI

SECHENOV, IVAN MIKHAYLOVICH (*b.* Teply Stan [now Sechenovo], Simbirsk guberniya [now Arzamas oblast], Russia, 1 August 1829; *d.* Moscow, Russia, 2 November 1905), *physiology, physical chemistry, psychology.*

Sechenov's father was a landowner, and his mother was of peasant stock. He was educated at home and then attended the Military Engineering School in St. Petersburg (1843–1848). From 1848 to 1850 he was a military engineer at Kiev, and for the following six years he studied medicine at Moscow University. Upon graduation he went to Germany, where, until 1860, he studied and worked in the laboratories of Johannes Müller, E. du Bois-Reymond, Helmholtz, and Ludwig.

In 1860 Sechenov presented his dissertation *Materialy dlya budushchey fiziologii alkogolnogo opyanenia* ("Data for the Future Physiology of Alcoholic Intoxication") to the St. Petersburg Medico-Surgical Academy, at which he was appointed professor (1860–1870) and founded the first Russian school of physiology. After resigning to protest the rejection of Elie Metchnikoff, his candidate for the chair of zoology, Sechenov conducted chemical research in Mendeleev's laboratory in St. Petersburg. The following year he accepted the chair at the Novorossysk University at Odessa (1871–1876) and subsequently became professor at St. Petersburg (1876–1888) and Moscow (1891–1901). Sechenov was elected an honorary fellow of the Russian Academy of Sciences in 1904.

His first investigations were devoted to gaseous exchange (his dissertation) and electrophysiology *O zhivotnom elektrichestve* ("On Animal Electricity," 1862). In November 1862, while working in the Paris laboratory of Claude Bernard (who did not, however, collaborate on this work), Sechenov reported on "central inhibition"— the repressive effects of thalamic nerve centers on spinal reflexes. He thus inaugurated research on inhibition phenomena in the central nervous system.

His discovery led Sechenov to suggest the theory of cerebral behavior mechanisms, according to which all conscious and unconscious acts are reflexes in terms of their structure ("means of origin"). This theory provided the basis for the development of neurophysiology and objective psychology in Russia, including the investigations of Pavlov and Bekhterev. Although accepted by the intelligentsia as an aspect of a scientific view of the nature of man, the theory was interpreted in more conservative circles as a threat to moral principles and social order. In elaborating the theory of the functions of higher nerve centers, Sechenov established a principle of self-regulation that was set forth in works published in 1866, 1891, and 1898. The main role was attributed to the coordination between nerve centers. Sechenov emphasized not only "form but activity, not only topographical isolation of organs but the combination of central processes into natural groups"—an interpretation that contradicted conceptions based on "anatomical principle."

In 1881 Sechenov established the existence of periodic spontaneous fluctuations of bioelectric potentials in the brain. Proceeding from the conception of muscle as a "receptor" of sensory information, and having analyzed disorders of nerve and muscle activities (ataxia), he concluded that signals reflecting the muscle effects are involved in the regulation of motor activity in animals and man. This was a precursor of the conception of feedback as an essential factor in the organization of behavior. He introduced an essentially new interpretation of reflex by declaring that it consisted of sensation (a signal) and movement. Sensation, he believed, was determined not by information at the level of consciousness but on the basis of objective functions of vital activity and served to distinguish among conditions and to regulate actions.

Maintaining that the reality of sensation is rooted in the reality of the motor act, Sechenov developed a new approach to the functions of the sensory organs in *Fiziologia organov chuvstv* ("Physiology of the Sensory Organs," 1867). A receptor was responsible merely for a signal and thus constituted only half of the complete physiological mechanism, the other half being muscle activity. (This represented "the principle of coordinating movement and sensation, a unity between reception by and action of a muscle.") The signals of muscle sensation were the main source of information on the space-time characteristics of the environment.

On the basis of the new "reflective" scheme, Sechenov suggested a plan for reorganizing psychology into an objective natural science based on physiology (1873). Instead of being an adjunct of physiology, psychology should become a study of the psychic regulation of behavior using the methods and conceptions of natural sciences.

Sechenov also investigated the chemistry of respiration; the physiology of respiration, particularly at reduced atmospheric pressure; and the physics and chemistry of solutions. He designed a new type of absorptiometer and used it to establish the law of solution of gases in salt solutions with which they did not react. He also constructed a device for studying respiration when a man was moving or at rest. His *Ocherk rabochikh dvizheny u cheloveka* ("A Survey of the Working Movements of Man," 1901) laid the foundation for later investigations into the physiology of work in Russia.

Sechenov was active in the struggle for equal rights for women and for self-government of the universities. His students and followers included many outstanding Russian physiologists: Vvedensky, Pavlov, Ukhtomsky, I. P. Tarkhanov, Samoylov.

BIBLIOGRAPHY

I. ORIGINAL WORKS. Sechenov's main writings are *Materialy dlya budushchey fiziologii alkogolnogo opyanenia* ("Data for the Future Physiology of Alcoholic Intoxication"; St. Petersburg, 1860); *O zhivatnom elektrichestve* ("On Animal Electricity"; St. Petersburg, 1862); "Refleksy golovnogo mozga" ("Reflexes of the Brain"), in *Meditsinsky vestnik*, nos. 47–48 (1863); *Fiziologia nervnoy sistemy* ("Physiology of the Nervous System"; St. Petersburg, 1866); "Komu i kak razrabatyvat psikhologiyu" ("Who Must Investigate Psychology and How"), in *Vestnik Evropy* (1873), no. 4; "Elementi mysli" ("The Elements of Thought"), *ibid.*, (1878), nos. 3–4; *O pogloshchenii ugolnoy kisloty solyanymi rastvorami i krovyu* ("On Absorption of Carbon Acid by Salt Solutions and Blood"; St. Petersburg, 1879); *Fiziologia nervnykh tsentrov* ("Physiology of Nerve Centers"; St. Petersburg, 1891); and *Ocherk rabochikh dvizheny u cheloveka* ("A Survey of the Working Movements of Man"; Moscow, 1901).

Collections of his writings are available in French as *Études psychologiques* (Paris, 1889) and in English as *Selected Works*, A. A. Subkov, ed. (Moscow–Leningrad, 1935).

II. SECONDARY LITERATURE. See K. S. Koshtoyants, *I. M. Sechenov* (Moscow, 1950); A. F. Samoylov, "I. M. Sechenov i ego mysli o roli myshtsy v nashem poznanii prirody" ("Sechenov and His Ideas on the Role of Muscle in Our Knowledge of Nature"), in *Nauchnoe slovo* (1930), no. 5; N. E. Vvedensky, "I. M. Sechenov," in his *Polnoe sobranie sochineny* ("Complete Works"), VII (Leningrad, 1963); and M. G. Laroshevsky, *I. M. Sechenov* (Leningrad, 1968).

M. G. LAROSHEVSKY

SEDERHOLM, JOHANNES JAKOB (*b.* Helsinki, Finland, 20 July 1863; *d.* Helsinki, 26 June 1934), *geology, petrology.*

Sederholm was the third of eight children of Claes Theodor Sederholm and Maria Sofia Christina Blomquist. His father, owner of a printing plant, founded and published the major daily newspaper of Helsinki and also published books. In 1882 Sederholm entered the University of Helsinki to study philosophy. His health was weak, however, and his doctor, doubtful of his recovery, recommended that he abandon formal academic pursuits for a branch of the natural sciences that would get him outdoors. He chose geology. Sederholm had to fight against illness throughout his life.

In the department of natural history at Helsinki, Sederholm met Axel Palmén, later a renowned ornithologist, and Wilhelm Ramsay, who became a leading geologist of Fennoscandia; they became lifelong friends. After receiving his B.A. in 1885, Sederholm continued his studies from 1886 to 1888 at the University of Stockholm, where he met Brøgger, who was teaching mineralogy and geology there. His imposing, multifaceted personality inspired several generations of Fennoscandian geologists, and Sederholm always spoke of him as "my dear teacher and master"; they remained lifelong friends.

During the summers Sederholm served as assistant geologist (1883–1887), and in 1888 was appointed a member, of the Geological Commission (Geological Survey). To become more familiar with modern trends in petrology, he studied with Rosenbusch at Heidelberg, where he met American geologists and thus began a lifelong link with America. Sederholm completed two important papers while at Heidelberg, on the eruptive rocks of southern Finland and on the rapakivi granites. In the first he showed that many of these rocks are metamorphosed and that two degrees of metamorphism can be distinguished, an idea that was developed (metamorphic depth zones) more than ten years later by Becke and Grubenmann. The paper on the rapakivi granites marked the starting point of research that remained a lifelong concern. The former was also presented as a dissertation on 30 May 1891 with F. J. Wiik, a declared antiactualist, as critic.

After having passed his examination in 1892, Sederholm received the doctorate at the age of twenty-nine, became director of the Geological Commission, and married Anna Ingeborg Mathilde von Christierson. They had two daughters and one son. As director of the Geological Commission for over forty years, he not only created a modern research institution for basic and economic geology but also established new standards for the study of the world's crystalline basements, the Precambrian continental shields. He retired during the summer of 1933 and died the following June.

Established in 1877 under the directorship of Karl Adolf Moberg, the Geological Commission was the first geological survey of Finland with geological mapping. The first sheet appeared in 1879 on a scale of 1:200,000; bedrock and superficial deposits were represented on the same sheet. Thirty-seven quadrangles of this atlas were subsequently published, but only a few principal petrological groups were distinguished within the basement. Under Sederholm's enthusiastic leadership, however, another type of map was adopted, with bedrock and superficial deposits published on separate sheets on a scale of 1:400,000. Whereas the earlier maps had been based on petrological distinctions, the new series employed principles proposed in Sederholm's paper of 1893. Age relationships were of primary importance, but the methods of classical stratigraphy were scarcely applicable; and new principles for determining the succession of geological events were needed. During the course of this long and exacting work, methods and classifications were constantly adjusted to conform with the growth of knowledge and were influenced by critics and exchanges with other geologists. The continuing feedback from field observations modified and improved the manner of mapping over the years. The dominant thread was always actualism.

One of the methods chiefly responsible for the final success of the survey was Sederholm's idea of mapping crucially important areas or outcrops on a finer scale, and the geology of Finland was thus represented at different enlargements. Some outcrops were mapped at 1:10, others at 1:50, 1:200, or 1:10,000. In the limit, photographs of ice-smoothed hillocks, of hand specimens, and of thin sections under the microscope completed the spectrum of scales.

With Sederholm's method of multiple levels of research, Finland became the classic example of a Precambrian basement; for in addition to various mapping scales, the Commission was also administered at various levels of organization. In this way the project, rather than becoming merely the sum of its parts, acquired new properties and the individual parts assumed new functions at different levels. Studies conducted at each level had their own methodology and governing principles. Because of qualitative differences, the same methods of study are best applied to closely related levels. This distinction between different levels was not understood by those who sought a unity of methods to study the entire spectrum: for instance, those who advocated mapping only petrographic differences without paying attention to formations having the same or a different geological history.

The large units of sedimentary and volcanic formations are separated by unconformities, breaks in geological history that are most evident if they are marked by conglomerates representing specimens of a former erosional surface. Sederholm's eagerness to find conglomerates was rewarded by his important discovery of such formations in the sedimentary series of Lake Näsijärvi, near Tampere, in 1899. Many other sedimentary structures are well preserved, such as the varves containing some of the very ancient fossils *Corycium enigmaticum*. This was a triumph for uniformitarian principles, and the area became a classic that was often visited by foreign geologists. Another important member of these series consists of basic volcanic rocks transformed into uralite-porphyrites.

In order to obtain a uniformitarian picture of the events that occurred in the Svecofennian area of the Precambrian basement, it was necessary to find the basement supporting the sedimentary series and the piles of volcanic effusions, as well as the source areas for the clastic rocks. But again, new obstacles appeared that could not be eliminated until the possibility of the reactivation of old basements was recognized. Observations of relevant exposures were described, and interpretive principles proposed, in 1897, when an official excursion of the Seventh International Geological Congress visited the shores of Näsijärvi; these views spread rapidly and soon appeared in textbooks.

Dikes of volcanic and granitic intrusions with their ramifications provided, by their intersections, still another means of establishing a chronological sequence; but continuing in this way, geologists soon became ensnared in riddles that at first sight appeared insoluble. Before further progress was possible, such problems had to be pursued on several levels. During the summer of 1906 Sederholm, then a member of the Diet, was obliged to remain near Helsinki and was unable to travel to the wilderness. He decided to study the *roches moutonnées* of southern Finland with his assistant Hans Hausen. The multitude of phenomena of these southern rocks, varying from one step to the next although the number of mineral components and their combinations were sharply limited, was initially extremely confusing. These phenomena were only partly intelligible through methods of classical petrology, for which reason they had not been observed earlier, even though they occupy vast areas in crystalline basements of any age. A new set of ideas and methods was needed to describe and interpret the observations and to enable others to see these phenomena. Thus a new level of research was intercalated between the petrographic level, based mainly on microscopic study, and large-scale mapping. After the variegated patterns visible on the flat rock surfaces of southern Finland were mapped on scales from 1:10 to 1:200, an unsuspected wealth of new phenomena was revealed and time sequences were established. The apparatus of descriptive and interpretive terms that was created gave petrologists of the old school cause to shudder. Nevertheless, a new domain, existing from unknown ages and hitherto invisible, was revealed; and a new model for mass circulation within the sialic crust was proposed.

The mixed rocks, previously considered impure, were named migmatites and became the center of petrologic interest. Different patterns of such mixed rocks were distinguished, from "agmatites" (with angular fragments) to "nebulites" (with cloudy appearance), and from ptygmatic veins to palingenetic and anatectic granites (older granites, gneisses, or schists grading into rocks that resembled granite). Sederholm considered these areas to be former "granite factories" or "granite works" (1907), arrested during their activity by cooling and rendered accessible by deep erosion, smoothed by glacial polishing, and washed bare by wave action. A new cyclic model was proposed, similar in some points to Hutton's hypothesis; but in this sequence every phase was represented by visible outcrops, so that the whole of the events could be observed in the field. It was a new victory for uniformitarianism. The granites in this model came not from "unknown depths," as a result of differentiation from a basic magma, but from reactivation *in situ* of older materials (anatexis and palingenesis). These mobilized granites could then rise in the crust.

The case of the "paradoxical inclusions" illustrates the sort of problem that confronted Sederholm and his method of solution. These inclusions are both older and younger than the enclosing rocks. The explanation was that basic dikes were intruded into former gneisses or schists, which were later reactivated and transformed into palingenetic granite enclosing the fragments of the for-

mer dikes. These phenomena made it possible to distinguish the chronological sequence of events in areas characterized as ultrametamorphic and to coordinate these sequences over more extended areas.

On another level, belts characterized by distinct historical evolution could be distinguished and mapped, some with definite limits (such as the Karelian belt, well discernible from the much older basement in eastern Karelia) or more indistinct (such as the Svecofennian belt in southern Finland, characterized by the Bottnian formation). Sederholm published a series of maps of the basement of Finland, perfected after the progressive mapping. Most of them were included in the *Atlas of Finland*, a work in which he was deeply interested.

The study of fracture patterns cutting the old basement was conducted on the scale of the old shield (1911, 1913, 1932). After the deep erosion that removed the upper zones and exposed the metamorphic and ultrametamorphic levels, the brittle crust was broken into a mosaiclike pattern, undergoing weathering, erosion, and glacial scouring, and thus producing some of the most characteristic features of the Fennoscandian landscape.

In "The Average Composition of the Earth's Crust in Finland" (1925), another study of old crystalline basements, Sederholm attempted to characterize the average geochemical composition of deeply eroded crustal areas. The investigation differed from the usual means of rock analyses (for example, Frank Wigglesworth Clarke's) because the analyses entering into the calculation were weighted according to the areas actually underlain by the corresponding rocks. By establishing the weighted average composition, the result offered a valuable example—the only one thus far—of an extended crystalline basement cut at this deep level and represented an important contribution to the geochemical knowledge of the sialic crust.

Sederholm was a keen observer for whom a granite was not an abstract concept but the embodiment of a distinct "personality." Appearance and behavior, related to composition and variability, formed the characteristic profile. Thus he was often able to predict other qualities invisible to the naked eye, such as a percentage of fluorine or other mineral components. These granite individuals were grouped into four families, which also were groups of different relative age that occupy special places in the evolution of the crustal sector.

To learn more about these individual characteristics, Sederholm studied special textures: orbicular, spotted, and nodular granites and the rapakivi

(1928). His paper on "synantectic" minerals (1916) was representative of work on the component material of the rocks. Here his main aim was to establish the sequence of events, and the phenomena of synantectic minerals are a good example. The interfaces of two adjacent minerals, formed in stable association, can begin to produce new minerals by interaction of the primary minerals; in this way two, and sometimes more, stages are marked in the evolution of the rock, characterized by different physicochemical conditions. More interested in transformations than in phase equilibriums, Sederholm noted the results of laboratory experiments but could hardly consider them final criteria. For him, they were useful only insofar as they could be integrated within the organic interdependence of different levels of apprehension.

In this way a spectrum of new methods of observation and interpretations, each set adapted to its own level, was created; it produced a hitherto unsuspected picture of crustal evolution in a historical perspective. Those accustomed to a taxonomic approach found it difficult to accept this manner of reasoning, which was unusual at the beginning of the twentieth century; and it became necessary to reply to the vigorous opposition.

Most of the old crystalline basements are more or less peneplained with low relief, and it was considered impossible to distinguish three-dimensional structures of higher orders of magnitude. Fortunately for Sederholm, a young Swiss geologist, C. E. Wegmann, appeared and showed how to obtain a three-dimensional interpretation, how to reconstruct ancient mountain chains with their different axial culminations and depressions, and how to discover the movements that they had undergone. The former belts became orogens with visible cross sections that were many kilometers in depth. Although in his sixties, Sederholm was still so open-minded and eager to complete his work that he became an ardent student of structural methods, even though their results contradicted some of his former hypotheses. On the other hand, they offered further evidence against the theory of the ubiquity of folding and furnished new conceptual tools for uniformitarian reconstruction.

Sederholm's outstanding scientific achievements brought him many honors and medals, and the respect accorded him was turned to the welfare of his native land. In 1906 he became a member of the Diet, representing the third estate. An active member of the Workers Institution, he lectured on scientific and other topics and was the author of semipopular and popular articles, papers, and books, on social questions as well as earth sciences. He was a founder of the Geographical Society of Finland and served five times as president, and was one of the most active members of the editorial staff of the *Atlas of Finland* (1899–1925). With the establishment of the Republic of Finland in July 1919, Sederholm was entrusted with several important missions to the League of Nations, including that concerning the issue of whether the Åland Islands should be Swedish or Finnish. The League also appointed him a member of the Commission for the Independence of Albania. He made two journeys to that country to inspect its frontiers. Unarmed and without military escort, he met the Serbian guerrillas and arranged for their peaceful withdrawal.

Sederholm directed much attention to economic questions, not only economic geology but also general problems. As a member, and twice chairman, of the Economic Society of Finland, he delivered several lectures, one of them on the reasons for North American industrial supremacy (1905). F. W. Taylor's system of scientific management interested him deeply, probably because of its multileveled reasoning, and in 1915 Sederholm published a noted monograph entitled *Arbetets vetenskap* ("The Science of Work").

Sederholm was greatly interested in America, first in the Precambrian shield and its chronology, but also in the politics, economics, industry, social conditions, hospitals, and many other facets of the nation's life. He traveled several times in Canada and the United States on lecture tours, accepting honors (including the Penrose Medal, in 1928), visiting important outcrops, collecting documents, and observing general conditions. He particularly enjoyed recalling his discussions with N. L. Bowen, the foremost leader of the diametrically opposed magmatist school of petrology. This great scientist admitted that many of the phenomena described by Sederholm were inexplicable by his own theory—in sharp contrast with other petrologists, who simply denied the possibility that they had occurred. One of Sederholm's favorite projects was a book on America for Europeans, to have been entitled *The Country of Brobdingnag*. But after retiring, so many matters awaited completion that the time left him was too limited to reap the entire harvest on the land he had tilled.

BIBLIOGRAPHY

I. Original Works. There is a bibliography of all Sederholm's main geological publications and a selection of his more important nongeological work in Sederholm's *Selected Works* (New York, 1967), 589–594.

His earlier writings include "Über die finnländischen Rapakiwigesteine," in *Tschermaks mineralogische und petrographische Mitteilungen*, **12** (1891), 1–31; "Studien über archäische Eruptivgesteine aus dem südwestlichen Finnland," *ibid.*, 97–142; "Om bärggrunden i södra Finland. Deutsches Referat," in *Fennia*, **8**, no. 3 (1893), 1–137; "Les excursions en Finlande," in *Guide du VII Congrès géologique international*, XIII (St. Petersburg, 1897), 1–22, written with W. Ramsay; "Über eine archäische Sedimentformation im südwestlichen Finnland und ihre Bedeutung für die Erklärung der Entstehungsweise des Grundgebirges," in *Bulletin de la Commission géologique de la Finlande*, **6** (1899); "Über die Entstehung des Urgebirges," in *Förhandlingar vid Nordiska Naturforskare och läkaremötet* (Helsinki) (7 July 1902), 88–109; "Über den gegenwärtigen Stand unserer Kenntnis der kristallinischen Schiefer von Finnland," in *Comptes rendus du IX Congrès géologique international* (Vienna, 1903), 609–630; "Om granit och gneis, deras uppkomst, uppträdande och utbredning inom urberget i Fennoskandia," in *Bulletin de la Commission géologique de la Finlande*, **23** (1907); and "Einige Probleme der präkambrischen Geologie von Fennoskandia," in *Geologische Rundschau*, **1** (1910), 126–135.

Subsequent works include "Om palingenesen i den sydfinska skärgården samt den finska urbergsindelningen," in *Geologiska föreningens i Stockholm förhandlingar*, **34** (1912), 285–316; "Sur les vestiges de la vie dans les formations proterozoiques," in *Comptes rendus du XI Congrès géologique international* (1912), 515–523; "Die regionale Umschmelzung (Anatexis) erläutert an typischen Beispielen," *ibid.*, 573–586; "Subdivision of the Pre-Cambrian of Fennoscandia," *ibid.*, 683–698; "Hutton och Werner," in *Festskrift tillägnad Edvard Westermarck* (Helsinki, 1912), 279–291; "Über ptygmatische Faltungen," in *Neues Jahrbuch für Mineralogie, Geologie und Paläontologie*, supp. **35** (1913), 491–512; "Über die Entstehung der migmatitischen Gesteine," in *Geologische Rundschau*, **4** (1913), 174–185; "On Regional Granitization or Anatexis," in *Comptes rendus du XII Congrès géologique international* (Toronto, 1913), 319–324; *Arbetets vetenskap* ("The Science of Work"; 1915); "Different Types of Pre-Cambrian Unconformities," *ibid.*, 313–318; "On Synantectic Minerals and Related Phenomena," in *Bulletin de la Commission géologique de la Finlande*, **48** (1916); "On Migmatites and Associated Pre-Cambrian Rocks of Southwestern Finland. I: The Pellinge Region," *ibid.*, **58** (1923); "The Average Composition of the Earth's Crust in Finland," *ibid.*, **70** (1925), also in *Fennia*, **45**, no. 18 (1925), 1–20; "On Migmatites and Associated Pre-Cambrian Rocks of Southwestern Finland. II: The Region Around the Barösundsfjärd West of Helsingfors and Neighbouring Areas," *ibid.*, **77** (1926); "On Orbicular Granites, Spotted and Nodular Granites and the Rapakivi Texture," *ibid.*, **83** (1928);

"On Migmatites and Associated Pre-Cambrian Rocks of Southwestern Finland. III: The Åland Islands," *ibid.*, **107** (1934); and "Ultrametamorphism and Anatexis," in *Pan-American Geologist*, **61** (1934), 241–250.

II. SECONDARY LITERATURE. See Pentti Eskola, "Outline of Sederholm's Life and Work," in Sederholm's *Selected Works* (New York, 1967), 577–594, with portrait and bibliography; Victor Hackman, "Jakob Johannes Sederholm," *Bulletin de la Commission géologique de la Finlande*, no. 117 (1935), with portrait and bibliography; Hans Hausen, "J. J. Sederholm," in *Svenska folkskolans vänners kalender* (1934), 151–159, with two portraits; and Hans Hausen, *The History of Geology and Mineralogy in Finland, 1828–1918* (Helsinki, 1968), with bibliography; Aarne Laitakari, "Geologische Bibliographie Finnlands 1555–1933," *Bulletin de la Commission géologique de la Finlande*, no. 108 (1934); and Väinö Tanner, *Jakob Johannes Sederholm* (Helsinki, 1937), read to the Swedish Academy of Technical Sciences in Finland on 22 Mar. 1935.

EUGENE WEGMANN

SEDGWICK, ADAM (*b*. Dent, Yorkshire, England, 22 March 1785; *d*. Cambridge, England, 27 January 1873), *geology*.

Sedgwick was the second son of Richard Sedgwick, vicar of the rural parish of Dent. From a local grammar school he went to Trinity College, Cambridge, where he graduated in 1808 with distinction in mathematics. He was elected a fellow of Trinity in 1810 and was ordained in 1817. He never married, and Trinity College remained his home for the rest of his life.

In 1818 Sedgwick was elected Woodwardian professor of geology at Cambridge and immediately took to his new work with boundless energy and enthusiasm (his later assertion of his complete ignorance of geology at this time probably was exaggerated). He made his first geological expedition that summer, and became a fellow of the Geological Society of London later in the year. In 1819 he played a leading part in the founding of the Cambridge Philosophical Society, which was designed to promote the study of the natural sciences at Cambridge; and the same year he gave the first of his annual courses of lectures on geology (a series that he continued without interruption until 1870). Although Sedgwick's lectures were, until the latter part of his life, optional and extracurricular, they were immensely popular; and their influence on successive generations of Cambridge students, and hence on the shaping of English educated opinion on geology, is hard to overestimate.

Sedgwick's lecturing style was clear and vivid,

and he had a direct and informal manner that made him accessible to and popular with students. But he found the formal composition of scientific papers irksome, and their completion repeatedly was delayed by recurrent ill health (dating from a serious breakdown in 1813) and by his political activities and administrative responsibilities within the college and the university. His published works, therefore, hardly reflect the full extent of his achievement.

Sedgwick inherited a geological collection somewhat enlarged from Woodward's original bequest; but he himself expanded it during his long tenure of the chair into one of the finest geological museums in the world, partly through his own and his students' collecting activities, and partly through purchasing fine specimens and collections with his own resources or with funds raised from public appeals. In 1841 a new museum building was opened to accommodate this rapidly growing collection; by the end of his life this in turn was inadequate, and the present Sedgwick Museum was erected as a memorial to him.

Sedgwick was president of the Geological Society of London from 1829 to 1831, and of the British Association at its first visit to Cambridge in 1833. In 1834 his appointment as a prebendary of Norwich gave him greater financial independence (the stipend of his chair was very small), but at the cost of requiring his residence at Norwich for part of every year for the rest of his life.

In politics Sedgwick was one of the most prominent Liberals at Cambridge, and was in the forefront of the movement for university reform; Prince Albert, on becoming chancellor of the university in 1847, chose him to act as his "secretary" at Cambridge, and Sedgwick was later (1850–1852) a member of the royal commission on the reform of the university.

Sedgwick began his geological work under the influence of William Conybeare, and his earliest major studies were on the stratigraphy of the problematical and poorly fossiliferous deposits of the New Red Sandstone. In a monograph published in 1829 he successfully used the distinctive Magnesian Limestone of northeastern England as a key to these strata, and was able to correlate them with the classic successions in Germany. This work showed Sedgwick to be a field geologist with an exceptional flair for grasping the regional significance of local details. The wider relevance of its conclusions lay in his interpretation of the strata as the products of long-continued processes, and in his emphasis on the strata as conformable "con-

necting links" from the Coal Measures below to the Lias (Jurassic) above. The same emphasis on stratigraphical continuity is evident in his joint work with Roderick Murchison on the eastern Alps at about the same period, in which he clearly was concerned to bridge the apparent faunal break between "Secondary" and Tertiary strata.

Sedgwick therefore naturally welcomed some aspects of Charles Lyell's work: in his presidential addresses to the Geological Society in 1830 and 1831 he agreed with Lyell that incalculably vast periods of time must be inferred for many geological events, and he retracted his earlier view (derived from William Buckland) that a single paroxysmal episode could account for all the "diluvial" deposits. But in reviewing the first volume of Lyell's *Principles of Geology* he sharply criticized Lyell's confusion of different meanings of "uniformity." He agreed that the "primary laws of matter" were "immutable," but he felt it was "a merely gratuitous hypothesis" to assume that the geological processes based on those laws must have been rigidly uniform in their intensity throughout earth-history: uniformity in the latter sense had to be tested by empirical observation, not assumed a priori.

In conformity with this empiricist program, Sedgwick approved Élie de Beaumont's theory of occasional paroxysmal elevation of mountain ranges, because it made explicable many common phenomena (local folding of strata and local unconformities) in terms of events that, although abrupt and uncommon in occurrence, were perfectly natural in their mechanism. Similarly, he rejected Lyell's assertion of steady-state uniformity in the organic realm, because the facts of the fossil record seemed to indicate unequivocally a gradual approach to the "present system of things." Above all, Sedgwick felt that the geologically recent appearance of man was "absolutely subversive" of Lyell's Huttonian conclusion.

Sedgwick's most important geological work, which led to the foundation of the Cambrian system, seems to have been motivated by a desire to penetrate the fossil record back to its farthest limits, and to demonstrate that life had indeed had a beginning in time. Some of his earliest fieldwork was an attempt to unravel the complex structure of the old rocks of Devon and Cornwall, and later he studied in detail those of the Lake District (where for many years he enjoyed the friendship of William Wordsworth). In the classic paper "Remarks on the Structure of Large Mineral Masses" (1835) he combined his mathematical training with his skill as a field geologist in the first clear analysis of the effects of diagenesis and low-grade metamorphism. In particular, his exposition of the distinction between stratification, jointing, and slaty cleavage provided the crucial technical key for the interpretation of the structure of regions with complex folding.

This had already enabled him, as early as 1832, to discover the essential structure and succession of the ancient rocks of North Wales (on his first expedition there, in 1831, he gave Charles Darwin his first training as a field geologist). In the same years Murchison was studying apparently younger "Transition" strata in the Welsh Borderland. During their first and only joint study (1834) of the relation between their two areas, Murchison assured Sedgwick that his strata (later termed "Silurian") lay wholly above Sedgwick's "Cambrian" (so named in 1835), although there was clear—and not unexpected—faunal similarity between Murchison's Lower Silurian strata and Sedgwick's Upper Cambrian Bala series.

Their collaboration continued fruitfully in their solution of the anomalous problem of the slaty rocks of Devonshire, where De La Beche's discovery of Carboniferous plants in rocks of ancient appearance had seemed for a time to threaten the validity of both Murchison's and Sedgwick's stratigraphy. They worked closely in discovering first that the anomalous fossils had come from a syncline of slaty rocks of Carboniferous age, and then that the older rocks in the region were not Silurian or Cambrian but the lateral equivalents of the Old Red Sandstone, which they termed "Devonian." This interpretation was confirmed by a joint expedition to the Continent in 1839.

Sedgwick then turned his attention back to the problem of the Cambrian strata in Wales, as part of a larger program for a synoptic work (never completed) on all the Paleozoic strata of Britain. Although he could not point to a Cambrian fauna as distinctive as Murchison's Silurian fauna, he rightly emphasized that the vast thickness of the Cambrian strata and the apparent beginning of the fossil record within them justified their status as a "system" of comparable importance. Indeed, he underlined their theoretical significance by including them with the Silurian in a broader category of "Protozoic." He was therefore disconcerted and eventually exasperated when Murchison claimed that the upper (and fossiliferous) part of his Cambrian was nothing other than Murchison's Lower Silurian. Murchison gradually extended this claim until he had annexed virtually the whole of the Cambrian and reduced it to a synonym of Lower Silurian.

Sedgwick later was angered by what he regarded as editorial tampering with a crucial paper on the subject submitted to the Geological Society. His stratigraphical nomenclature was altered, apparently in the interests of editorial uniformity, and possibly in innocence of the massive theoretical and personal implications. Reacting with characteristic vehemence, he later broke off all dealings with the Society.

Only gradually did Sedgwick detect the root cause of the controversy. Murchison earlier had misinterpreted the order of succession of his Lower Silurian strata in their type area, so that they were not in fact younger than Sedgwick's Upper Cambrian Bala series, but of the same age. Even more seriously, Sedgwick found in 1854 that Murchison had confused some Upper Silurian strata (May Hill sandstone) with these much earlier Lower Silurian strata (Caradoc series), thus giving the Silurian faunas a spurious uniformity down into Sedgwick's Upper Cambrian.

But Murchison naturally was reluctant to admit these errors, and his position as head of the Geological Survey (from 1855) allowed him to retain his interpretation in all the Survey's official publications. What had begun as a controversy with important implications for the understanding of the earliest part of the fossil record gradually degenerated into a priority dispute between two equally obstinate old men. The conflict was not settled until much later, when the discovery of earlier faunas in Wales rehabilitated the term Cambrian for what had been Sedgwick's Lower Cambrian; and an "Ordovician" system was proposed irenically for the disputed strata (that is, Sedgwick's "Upper Cambrian" and Murchison's "Lower Silurian") between the newly restricted Cambrian and Silurian systems.

The Geological Society acknowledged the outstanding value of Sedgwick's work in 1850 (before he was estranged from it) by awarding him their highest honor, the Wollaston Medal; and in 1863 the Royal Society, to which he had been elected in 1830, awarded him the Copley Medal.

Sedgwick was seventy-four when Darwin's *Origin of Species* was published, but his rejection of his pupil's evolutionary theory was not simply a consequence of old age. Thirty years earlier, while welcoming naturalistic explanations for geological events (including those responsible for "diluvial" deposits), he had felt that no purely natural mechanism could ever account for the origin of new organic species. This belief was grounded in his strong sense of the "designful" beauty of organisms: although he was not primarily a paleontologist, his favorite lecture subject was the adaptive significance of fossil mammals. But his concept of teleology was philosophically unsophisticated, and like Paley (whose work had influenced him deeply) he simply wished the contemplation of organic design to nourish the sense of wonder that would lead the mind toward God.

Any theory of the transmutation of species by natural means therefore seemed to Sedgwick to threaten this preparatory function of natural theology and to lead to a "train of monstrous consequences." Above all, since he saw clearly that whatever applied to other species ultimately must apply to man, the consequences of any evolutionary theory seemed to him to include the denial of the reality of the "moral" realm. Although a devout Christian, Sedgwick was no fundamentalist in religious matters: he was a prominent member of the Broad Church party within the Anglican Church, and was greatly concerned to see progressive science and enlightened theology working independently toward an ultimate synthesis of truth. But this meant that he was as much concerned to expose the pretensions of a naïve materialism that undermined man's moral responsibility as he was to attack simplistic "reconciliations" between geology and Scripture. Thus in his presidential addresses of 1830 and 1831 he criticized the popular "Scriptural geologists" even more vehemently than the proponents of transmutation. His influential *Discourse on the Studies of the University* (1833) linked a reassertion of the place of geology within the tradition of natural theology with a trenchant criticism of utilitarian moral philosophy; and the same concerns later were expressed vehemently in a major anonymous review (1845) of Robert Chambers' *Vestiges of the Natural History of Creation*.

Sedgwick was angered not only by the inaccuracies and pseudoscientific pretensions of Chambers' unsigned book: more fundamentally he feared that the specious plausibility of its all-embracing principle of naturalistic "development" would undermine the sense of personal responsibility that he believed was basic to the nature of man in society. He reiterated his views even more vehemently in a vastly enlarged fifth edition of the *Discourse* in 1850; by the time Darwin sent him a copy of the *Origin of Species,* Sedgwick's antipathy to the "materialistic" tendencies of evolutionary theories

had become so obsessive that his reaction was predictable.

By the end of his long life Sedgwick had in effect survived into a new period in the history of science; and although he was widely admired and even loved as a warmhearted and noble character, many of his scientific views seemed remote and antiquated. But in his prime he had been one of the most distinguished geologists within an exceptionally talented generation; and his concern for the broader implications of science had left an enduring mark on the place of science in university education.

BIBLIOGRAPHY

I. ORIGINAL WORKS. Sedgwick's more important earlier works include *A Syllabus of a Course of Lectures on Geology* (Cambridge, 1821); "On the Origin of Alluvial and Diluvial Formations," in *Annals of Philosophy,* n.s. **9** (1825), 241–247, and **10** (1825), 18–37; "On the Geological Relations and Internal Structure of the Magnesian Limestone, and on the Lower Portions of the New Red Sandstone Series . . .," in *Transactions of the Geological Society of London,* 2nd ser., **3**, pt. 1 (1829), 37–124; "Address[es] to the Geological Society, Delivered on the Evening of the Anniversary . . .," in *Proceedings of the Geological Society of London,* **1** (1830), 187–212, and (1831), 281–316; "A Sketch of the Structure of the Eastern Alps . . .," in *Transactions of the Geological Society of London,* 2nd ser., **3**, pt. 2 (1832), 301–420, written with Murchison; *A Discourse on the Studies of the University* (Cambridge, 1833; 5th ed., 1850; repr. Leicester, 1969); "Remarks on the Structure of Large Mineral Masses, and Especially on the Chemical Changes Produced in the Aggregation of Stratified Rocks During Different Periods After Their Deposition," in *Transactions of the Geological Society of London,* 2nd ser., **3**, pt. 3 (1835), 461–486; "Introduction to the General Structure of the Cumbrian Mountains . . .," *ibid.,* **4**, pt. 1 (1835), 47–68; and "A Synopsis of the English Series of Stratified Rocks Inferior to the Old Red Sandstone," in *Proceedings of the Geological Society of London,* **2** (1838), 675–685, and "Supplement [to the same]," *ibid.,* **3** (1841), 541–554.

In the 1840's he published "On the Physical Structure of Devonshire, and on the Subdivisions and Geological Relations of Its Older Stratified Deposits, &c.," in *Transactions of the Geological Society of London,* 2nd ser., **5**, pt. 3 (1840), 633–704, written with Murchison; "On the Distribution and Classification of the Older or Palaeozoic Deposits of the North of Germany and Belgium, and Their Comparison With Formations of the Same Age in the British Isles," *ibid.,* **6**, pt. 2 (1842), 221–301, written with Murchison; "Three Letters

Upon the Geology of the Lake District Addressed to W. Wordsworth, Esq.," in John Hudson, ed., *A Complete Guide to the Lakes* . . . (Kendal, 1842)—two further letters were published in later eds. (1846, 1853); "On the Older Palaeozoic *(Protozoic)* Rocks of North Wales," in *Quarterly Journal of the Geological Society of London,* **1** (1845), 5–22; and [Anonymous review of] "Vestiges of the Natural History of Creation," in *Edinburgh Review,* **82** (1845), 1–85.

His last works include *A Synopsis of the Classification of the British Palaeozoic Rocks With a Systematic Description of the British Palaeozoic Fossils in the Geological Museum of the University of Cambridge* (Cambridge, 1851–1855), the description of fossils by Frederick McCoy; "On the Classification and Nomenclature of the Lower Palaeozoic Rocks of England and Wales," in *Quarterly Journal of the Geological Society of London,* **8** (1852), 136–168; and "On the May Hill Sandstone, and the Palaeozoic System of England," in *Philosophical Magazine,* 4th ser., **8** (1854), 301–317, 359–370.

University Library, Cambridge, has a large collection of scientific letters to Sedgwick; his geological collections and field notebooks are in the Sedgwick Museum, Cambridge.

II. SECONDARY LITERATURE. The principal biographical source is John Willis Clark and Thomas McKenny Hughes, *The Life and Letters of Adam Sedgwick . . .,* 2 vols. (Cambridge, 1890), which contains balanced assessments of Sedgwick's geological work from a late nineteenth-century viewpoint but relatively little of his more strictly scientific correspondence.

For an important modern essay on the cultural milieu of Sedgwick's work, see Walter F. Cannon, "Scientists and Broad Churchmen: An Early Victorian Intellectual Network," in *Journal of British Studies,* **4** (1964), 65–88. The biography by Clark and Hughes contains a fairly full list of Sedgwick's work, excluding items published anonymously but including most of his political pamphlets and other writings as well as his scientific papers.

M. J. S. RUDWICK

SEDOV, GEORGY YAKOVLEVICH (*b.* Krivaya Kosa, on the Sea of Azov, Russia, 1877; *d.* during an expedition to the North Pole, 5 March 1914), *hydrography, polar exploration.*

The son of a fisherman, Sedov attended the local church school. In 1894 he served as a sailor on a trading ship, and the following year he entered the naval school at Rostov-on-Don. After qualifying as a long-distance navigator in 1898, he sailed on the Sea of Azov and the Black Sea as navigator and captain. In 1900 Sedov entered naval service; he passed the examinations for the naval corps the next year and, with the rank of ensign, was assigned to the Main Hydrographical Administration of the Naval Ministry in St. Petersburg. In 1902 he joined an expedition to Novaya Zemlya. His work included a survey of the island of Vaygach and soundings of Yugorsky Shar.

In 1909 Sedov headed an expedition to explore the mouth of the Kolyma River and to investigate the possibility of approaching it from the sea. The group made a plane-table survey and sounding of the river, conducted meteorological and hydrological observations, surveyed the seacoast, and, before beginning navigation, gave a complete description of the mouth of the Kolyma. At the same time Sedov gathered ethnographical and geological material and made astronomical observations. In 1910 he explored and mapped Krestovaya Gulf on the western shore of Novaya Zemlya.

In 1912 Sedov proposed a sled expedition to the North Pole. His project was not supported by the government, so he organized an expedition with voluntary contributions, collecting 108,000 rubles and chartering a ship. On 10 September 1912 the *St. Fok* sailed from Arkhangelsk with twenty-two crew members and scientists. At Novaya Zemlya she encountered a severe storm, began to leak, and shipped water. On the way to Franz Josef Land the route was blocked by heavy ice, and the expedition was forced to winter at Novaya Zemlya. During the winter Sedov organized expeditions by sleigh into the interior and along the shores; reached Cape Zhelania, on foot; and mapped the shore of the unexplored portion of Novaya Zemlya. The expedition reached Franz Josef Land on 13 September 1913 and began its second wintering at Bukhta Tikhaya on Hooker Island.

On 15 February 1914 Sedov, suffering from scurvy, headed for the North Pole with three dog teams and two sailors, G. Linnik and A. Pustoshny. He died en route and was buried at Cape Auk on Rudolf Island.

Sedov and the members of his expedition to the North Pole made meteorological and magnetic observations, investigated and mapped the northwestern and Karskiye Vorota shores of Novaya Zemlya, crossed the northern island of Novaya Zemlya, corrected maps of Novaya Zemlya, gave geological descriptions of Hooker Island and Franz Josef Land, made observations on the condition of the ice, and determined astronomical points. Energetic and, as his friends wrote, "bold to the point of madness," Sedov passionately strove to reach the North Pole.

BIBLIOGRAPHY

I. ORIGINAL WORKS. Sedov's writings include "Puteshestvie v Kolymu v 1909 g." ("Journey to the Kolyma in 1909"), in *Zapiski po gidrografii*, **41**, no. 2–3 (1917), 263–326; "Ekspeditsia po issledovaniyu guby Krestovoy na Novoy Zemle v 1910 g." ("Expedition to Investigate Krestovaya Bay on Novaya Zemlya in 1910"), *ibid.*, **43**, no. 1 (1919), 119–136; "Tsarskoe pravitelstvo i polyarnaya ekspeditsia G. Y. Sedova, 1912–1916 gg. Dokumenty" ("The Tsarist Government and the Polar Expedition of G. Y. Sedov. Documents"), in *Krasny arkhiv*, **88** (1938), 16–76, with intro. by S. Nagornow; and "Materialy rabot G. Y. Sedova za vremya pervoy zimovki polyarnoy ekspeditsii 1912–1913 gg." ("Materials From the Works of G. Y. Sedov on the First Wintering of the Polar Expedition of 1912–1913"), K. A. Bogdanov, ed., in *Izvestiya Akademii nauk SSSR*, geographical ser. (1957), no. 3, 85–90.

II. SECONDARY LITERATURE. See A. F. Laktionov, *Severny polyus* ("The North Pole"; Moscow, 1955); B. G. Ostrovsky, *Bezvremenno ushedshie (G. Y. Sedov, V. A. Rusanov, G. L. Brusilov i E. V. Tol)* ("Those Who Died Prematurely [G. Y. Sedov, V. A. Rusanov, G. L. Brusilov and E. V. Tol]"; Leningrad, 1934), 3–31; N. V. Pinegin, "Georgy Sedov," foreword to V. Y. Vize, *Glavny sevmorput* ("The Main Northern Sea Routes"), 2nd ed. (Moscow–Leningrad, 1953), 345; A. I. Soloviev and G. V. Karpov, "Georgy Yakovlevich Sedov," in *Otechestvennye fiziko-geografy* ("Native Physical Geographers"; Moscow, 1959), 434–439; and V. Y. Vize, "Posledny put Sedova" ("Sedov's Last Trip"), in *Sovetskaya arktika* (1939), no. 3, 86–93; and "Georgy Yakovlevich Sedov," in *Russkie moreplavateli* ("Russian Seafarers"; Moscow, 1953), 317–327.

VERA N. FEDCHINA

SEE, THOMAS JEFFERSON JACKSON (*b.* near Montgomery City, Missouri, 19 February 1866; *d.* Oakland, California, 4 July 1962), *astronomy.*

See graduated from the University of Missouri in 1889 and received his doctorate from Berlin in 1892. After three years at the University of Chicago, he spent two years directing the Lowell survey of southern double stars. In 1899 See was appointed U.S. Navy professor of mathematics. He spent three years at the Naval Observatory and one year at the Naval Academy before becoming director of the observatory at Mare Island, California, where he remained until his retirement in 1930.

See's early investigations of double stars led him to study stellar evolution and the evolution of the earth and of the solar system. He was the first to postulate that matter was expelled from stars by repulsive forces, the material condensing into multiple stars or, frequently, solar systems, and that the orbits of the planets become circular because of a resisting medium. Satellites, including the moon, were small planets captured by their primaries. He also believed that planets without dense atmospheres preserved evidence of their formation in their cratered surfaces. See was the first to perform an experimental study of craters formed by high-velocity projectiles. He noted the evidence for lunar erosion by impact and melting, blanketing by dust, and subsidence.

See did not accept the prevalent belief that mountains and ocean trenches resulted from cooling and shrinkage of the earth, postulating instead a dynamic relationship between these features that involved an exchange of material from beneath the continents.

He also formulated the wave theory of gravitation and suggested that the red shift of galaxies was due not to an expanding universe but to the interaction of light and gravity waves.

See's numerous publications were considered unorthodox and were dismissed by scientists of his time. Many of his ideas, however, are in striking agreement with current theories.

BIBLIOGRAPHY

I. ORIGINAL WORKS. See's voluminous publications may best be sampled in *Researches on the Evolution of Stellar Systems*, 2 vols. (Lynn, Mass., 1896–1910), esp. vol. II, *The Capture Theory of Cosmical Evolution*. A number of his earlier papers are reprinted by William Larkin Webb in his *Brief Biography and Popular Account of the Unparalleled Discoveries of T. J. J. See* (Lynn, Mass., 1913). See's "New Theory of the Aether" is presented in *Astronomische Nachrichten*, **211** (1920), 49–86, 137–190; **212** (1920), 233–302, 385–454; **214** (1921), 281–359; **215** (1922), 49–138; **217** (1922), 193–284; and **226** (1926), 401–497 (special ed.). See also *Wave Theory!*, 3 vols. (Lynn, Mass., 1941–1950).

II. SECONDARY LITERATURE. Obituary notices are by J. Ashbrook, in *Sky and Telescope*, **24** (1962), 193, 202; and New York *Times* (5 July 1962). The only biography of See is that by W. L. Webb (above), which, however, deals only with See's life before 1913. A classic demolition of See's "capture theory" is F. R. Moulton, "Capture Theory and Capture Practice," in *Popular Astronomy*, **20** (1912), 67–82. Moulton had previously shown that See's "discovery" of an invisible body in the system of 70 Ophiuchi was impossible in "The Limits of Temporary Stability of Satellite Motion, With an Application to the Question of the Existence of an Unseen Body in the Binary System F. 70 Ophiuchi," in *Astronomical Journal,* **20** (1899), 33–37. See's reply, and his dismissal from that journal, are *ibid.,* 56.

R. A. J. SCHORN
L. D. G. YOUNG

SEEBECK, THOMAS (*b.* Tallinn, Estonia, 9 April 1770; *d.* Berlin, Germany, 10 December 1831), *electricity, magnetism, optics.*

Thomas Seebeck, the discoverer of thermoelectricity and one of the most distinguished experimental physicists of the early nineteenth century, was born in Estonia, to a well-to-do merchant family. After graduating from a Gymnasium he studied medicine at Berlin and at the University of Göttingen, receiving an M.D. from the latter in 1802. As a student Seebeck developed a strong interest in the natural sciences and decided to devote himself to scientific research rather than to medical practice. He married in 1795 and shortly thereafter began the career of a rich scientific enthusiast.

As a natural philosopher Seebeck was attracted to Jena, where an important intellectual circle was developing in the early 1800's around the philosophers Schelling and Hegel, the scientists Ritter and Oken, and the poet-philosopher Goethe. Here, partly inspired by Goethe's anti-Newtonian theory of colors (the *Farbenlehre*), Seebeck undertook his first research in optics in 1806. Its goal was to investigate the heating and chemical effects of the different colors of the solar spectrum.

Several scientists before Seebeck—Marsiglio Landriani, A. M. de Rochon, William Herschel, and John Leslie—had examined the heating effects of rays of different colors, and Herschel had shown in 1800 that heating could be detected in the region beyond the red end of the visible spectrum. Seebeck confirmed Herschel's finding and added to it the discovery of a slight rise in temperature beyond the violet region. He also found that the position of the point of greatest heat in the spectrum varied with the nature of the prism producing the colors. Seebeck also repeated and expanded upon Ritter's experiments on the coloration effects of different rays on silver salts.

Malus's discovery of polarization in 1808 led Seebeck to his next research in optics. In 1812 and 1813 he observed the "entoptic" patterns in pieces of glass under stress or subject to uneven heating and viewed through a polarizer. He also discovered optical rotatory polarization in certain oils,

the power of tourmaline to produce a single polarized ray of light, and the system of colored rings produced in polarized light by Iceland spar cut orthogonal to its axis. All these discoveries, unfortunately, were partially anticipated by Brewster or Biot. Nonetheless, Seebeck shared the Paris Academy of Science's annual prize in 1816 for his work on polarization in stressed glass, and was elected to the Berlin Academy in 1814.

In the 1820's Seebeck, having moved to Berlin, became interested in the phenomena of magnetism. He repeated the discovery made independently by Arago and Davy, that an electric current can induce magnetism in iron and steel, and that a steel needle is strongly magnetized when drawn around a conductor. Next, he expanded upon Arago's discovery that the oscillations of a magnetized iron needle about the magnetic meridian can be damped by placing a slab of almost any material in the immediate vicinity. He performed a large number of experiments on the magnetizability of different metals and first noticed the anomalous behavior of magnetized red-hot iron, an early indication of the phenomenon known as hysteresis.

By far Seebeck's most significant discovery, however, was that of thermoelectricity—or thermomagnetism, as he called it—in 1822. While he was studying the influence of heat on galvanic arrangements, it occurred to him that heat might create magnetism in two different metals joined to form a closed circuit. He joined a semicircular piece of bismuth with a similar piece of copper and fastened the ends together to form a circle. When heat was applied to either of the bismuth-copper junctions, a magnetic needle placed nearby behaved as if the circle were a closed, current-carrying circuit. By repeating this experiment many times with different pairs of metals and other conductors, Seebeck was able to order the various conducting materials in a thermoelectric series with bismuth at the extreme negative end and tellurium at the extreme positive end. He did not, however, believe that an electric current was actually set up in the bimetallic rings and preferred to describe his effect as "thermomagnetism."

BIBLIOGRAPHY

I. ORIGINAL WORKS. Seebeck's studies on the heating effects of the solar spectrum are presented in "Über die ungleiche Erregung der Wärme in prismatischen Sonnenbilde," in *Abhandlungen der Preussischen Akademie der*

Wissenschaften (1818–1819), 305–350. His work on the chemical effects of different colored rays appears in *Journal für Chemie und Physik,* **2** (1811), 263–264. The two memoirs on polarized light are "Einige neue Versuche und Beobachtungen über Spiegelung und Brechung des Lichtes," *ibid.,* **7** (1812), 259–298, 382–384; and "Von den entoptischen Farbenfiguren und den Bedingungen ihrer Bildung in Gläsern," *ibid.,* **12** (1814), 1–16. His discovery of thermoelectricity is described in "Magnetische Polarisation der Metalle und Erze durch Temperatur-Differenz," in *Abhandlungen der Preussischen Akademie der Wissenschaften* (1822–1823), 265–373. Other works are listed in the Royal Society *Catalogue of Scientific Papers,* V, 620–621; and at the end of Poggendorff's "Gedachtnissrede auf T. J. Seebeck" (see below).

II. SECONDARY LITERATURE. The only substantial biography of Seebeck is J. C. Poggendorff, "Gedachtnissrede auf Thomas Johann Seebeck, gehalten in den öffentlichen Sitzung vom 7 Juli 1839," in *Abhandlungen der Preussischen Akademie der Wissenschaften* (1841), xix–xxvii. *Encyclopaedia Britannica,* 7th ed. (1842), contains brief discussions of Seebeck's principal discoveries in electromagnetism, VIII, 574, and XXI, 684; thermoelectricity, VIII, 574, and XXI, 695; the prismatic spectrum, XIII, 332; magnetism, XIII, 694, 709, 712; and optics, XIII, 370, 420, 464.

EUGENE FRANKEL

SEELIGER, HUGO VON (*b.* Biala, near Bielitz, Austrian Silesia [now Bielsko Biala, Poland], 23 September 1849; *d.* Munich, Germany, 2 December 1924), *astronomy.*

Seeliger's father was mayor of Biala. After graduating from the Gymnasium at Teschen, he studied astronomy at Heidelberg and Leipzig, where he took his doctorate under Bruhns in 1871. From 1871 to 1873 he was assistant at the Leipzig observatory and, from 1873 to 1878, observer at the Bonn observatory. He served as *Privatdozent* at Leipzig until 1881, when he became director of the Gotha observatory. The following year he succeeded Lamont as professor of astronomy and as director of the Munich observatory, retaining both posts until his death.

One of the most famous astronomers of his time, Seeliger was interested mainly in theoretical astronomy. His activities, however, also included observations, and in 1874 he led an expedition to the Pacific to observe the transit of Venus. His papers on stellar statistics were his most important contribution to theoretical astronomy. He was the first astronomer to develop the fundamental equations of the relations between various statistical

functions of the stars. The immense number of stars in the Milky Way precludes a determination of its constitution by studying each star separately. Seeliger found that there are integral equations relating the function of stellar density in space with the distribution of stars of apparent magnitude; the first of these functions can be calculated after the distribution has been determined by observation. Although later improved and simplified in certain points, Seeliger's theory established the fundamental principles of stellar statistics.

Seeliger's important papers on the illumination of cosmic objects deal especially with Saturn and the zodiacal light. His speculations on the occurrence of novae were later abandoned by astronomers. His research on the law of gravitation provided a strong impetus to astronomical cosmology. He found that the Euclidean structure of space, nonvanishing mean density of matter, and overall validity of Newton's law of gravitation were incompatible, because a universe constructed on these principles would be unstable. In an attempt to resolve this difficulty, Seeliger assumed that Newton's law required small corrections. Later cosmological research, partly stimulated by his results, made it clear that no instability occurs if all matter in the universe moves—for instance, if the universe expands, as has been believed since about 1930.

In 1885 Seeliger married Sophie Stoeltzel, daughter of a professor at the Munich Technische Hochschule; they had two sons. Seeliger was president of the Astronomische Gesellschaft from 1896 to 1921 and of the Munich Academy of Sciences from 1918 to 1923. Many students took their doctorates under his supervision, the best known being Karl Schwarzschild. Seeliger's influence on the development of astronomy was thus much greater than many astronomers believe.

BIBLIOGRAPHY

I. ORIGINAL WORKS. Seeliger's papers on stellar statistics are in the *Abhandlungen* and *Sitzungsberichte der Bayerischen Akademie der Wissenschaften,* Math.-phys. Kl. (1884–1920). Some papers also appeared in *Astronomische Nachrichten;* three articles in the latter— **137** (1895), 129–136; and **138** (1895), 51–54, 255–258— deal with Newton's law of gravitation. See also "Zur Theorie der Beleuchtung der grossen Planeten, insbesondere des Saturn," in *Abhandlungen der Bayerischen Akademie der Wissenschaften,* Math.-phys. Kl., **16** (1887), 403–516; and "Theorie der Beleuchtung staubförmiger Massen, insbesondere des Saturnringes," *ibid.,* **18** (1893), 1–72.

A complete bibliography of Seeliger's publications and of all doctoral theses supervised by him is given by H. Kienle, in *Vierteljahrsschrift der Astronomischen Gesellschaft*, **60** (1925), 18–23.

II. SECONDARY LITERATURE. See G. Deutschland, "Die Untersuchungen H. V. Seeliger's über das Fixsternsystem," in *Vierteljahrsschrift der Astronomischen Gesellschaft*, **54** (1919), 25–131; and E. von der Pahlen, *Lehrbuch der Stellarstatistik* (Leipzig, 1937), 370–409.

F. SCHMEIDLER

SEGNER, JÁNOS-ANDRÁS (JOHANN ANDREAS VON) (*b.* Pressburg, Hungary [now Bratislava, Czechoslovakia], 9 October 1704; *d.* Halle, Germany, 5 October 1777), *mathematics, physics.*

Segner was the son of Miklós Segner, a merchant. He was educated in the Gymnasiums of Pressburg and Debrecen and then at the University of Jena (1725–1730), from which he received the M.D. Simultaneously he also studied physics and mathematics and in 1728 he published a work containing a demonstration of Descartes's rule of signs for the determination of the number of positive and negative roots of an algebraic equation when all roots are real; later he devoted another article to the derivation of this rule (1758). Segner practiced medicine in Pressburg and Debrecen for a short time. He went to Jena in 1732 as assistant professor and in 1733 became extraordinary professor of mathematics. In 1735 he was named ordinary professor of mathematics and physics at Göttingen; and from 1755 until his death he held the same chair at the University of Halle. He was a foreign member of the Berlin (1746) and St. Petersburg (1754) academies of science.

Segner's invention of one of the first reaction hydraulic turbines, named for him, was of outstanding importance. It consists of a wheel rotating under the action of water streaming from parallel and oppositely directed tubes. He wrote of this invention in a letter to Euler dated 11 January 1750, and in the same year he described in detail the construction and action of his machine, which he later improved; further improvements in construction were added by Euler. Segner's letters to Euler give detailed evidence of the progress of early work in the theory and construction of reaction hydraulic turbines (Euler's letters to Segner are lost). Segner's wheel is now used for horticultural irrigation and serves as a demonstration device in schools. Segner generally spent much time constructing and perfecting scientific devices, from a slide rule to clocks and telescopes.

While studying the theory of tubes, Segner introduced the three principal axes of rotation (axes of inertia) of a solid body and offered first considerations on this problem. Euler made considerable use of this discovery and, referring motion to principal axes of inertia, deduced his important equations of the motion of a solid body (1765).

Segner also wrote on various problems of physics and mathematics. He defended Newton's theory of the emanation of light (1740), developed an original graphic device for the construction of roots of algebraic equations (1761), and presented a recurrent solution of Euler's famous problem of the number of possible dissections of an n-gon into triangles by means of noncrossing diagonals (1761). In mathematical logic Segner developed Leibniz' ideas and was one of the first to make extensive use of an entire system of symbolic designations to formalize logical conclusions; he did not, however, confine himself to classical syllogistics.

Segner wrote a number of mathematical manuals, proceeding, to a certain extent, from Euler's works and using his advice, which were popular in their time.

BIBLIOGRAPHY

I. ORIGINAL WORKS. Bibliographies of Segner's works are in Poggendorff, II, cols. 892–894; and C. von Wurzbach, ed., *Biographisches Lexikon des Kaiserthums Oesterreich*, XXXIII (1877), 318–320. His writings include *Dissertatio epistolica . . . qua regulam Harriotti, de modo ex aequationum signis numerum radicum eas componentium cognoscendi demonstrare conatur* (Jena, 1728); *Specimen logicae universaliter demonstratae* (Jena, 1740); *Programma in quo computatio formae atque virium machinae nuper descriptae* (Göttingen, 1750); *Programma in quo theoriam machinae cujusdam hydraulicae praemittit* (Göttingen, 1750); *Specimen theoriae turbinum* (Halle, 1755); *Cursus mathematicus*, 5 vols. (Halle, 1758–1767); and *Elementa analyseos infinitorum*, 2 vols. (Halle, 1761–1763).

II. SECONDARY LITERATURE. See *Allgemeine deutsche Biographie*, XXXIII (1891), 609–610; M. Cantor, *Vorlesungen über Geschichte der Mathematik*, III–IV (Leipzig, 1900–1908), see index; *Leonhardi Euleri Opera omnia*, fourth series, *Commercium epistolicum*, I, A. Juškerič, V. Smirnov, and W. Habicht, eds. (Basel, 1975), 403–426; Jakusc István, "Segner András," in *Fizikai szemle*, **5** (1955), 56–65; N. M. Raskin, "Voprosy tekhniki u Eylera" ("Technical Problems of Euler"), in M. A. Lavrentiev, A. P. Youschkevitch, and A. T. Grigorian, eds., *Leonard Eyler. Sbornik statey . . .* (Moscow, 1958), 509–536; and F. Rosenberger, *Die*

Geschichte der Physik in Grundzügen, II (Brunswick, 1884), 345.

A. P. YOUSCHKEVITCH
A. T. GRIGORIAN

SEGRE, CORRADO (*b*. Saluzzo, Italy, 20 August 1863; *d*. Turin, Italy, 18 May 1924), *mathematics*.

Segre studied under Enrico D'Ovidio at the University of Turin, where he formed a long friendship with his fellow student Gino Loria. Segre submitted his doctoral dissertation in 1883, when he was only twenty; and in the same year he was named assistant to the professor of algebra and to the professor of analytic geometry. Two years later he became an assistant in descriptive geometry, and from 1885 to 1888 he replaced Giuseppe Bruno in the courses on projective geometry. In 1888 he succeeded D'Ovidio in the chair of higher geometry, a post he held without interruption until his death.

Segre was much influenced by D'Ovidio's course on the geometry of ruled spaces (1881–1882). D'Ovidio started from the ideas of Plücker, which had been taken up and developed by Felix Klein. According to these ideas, the geometry of ruled space is equivalent to the study of a quadratic variety of four dimensions imbedded in a linear space of five dimensions. In his lectures D'Ovidio examined the works of Veronese on the projective geometry of hyperspaces and those of Weierstrass on bilinear and quadratic forms. These topics inspired much of Segre's research, beginning with his thesis. The latter consists of two parts: a study of the quadrics in a linear space of arbitrary dimension and an examination of the geometry of the right line and of its quadratic series. Before completing his thesis, Segre collaborated with Loria on a twenty-two-page article in French that they sent to Klein, who published it in *Mathematische Annalen* (1883). A long and active correspondence between Segre and Klein then ensued.

Segre's mathematical work can be divided into four distinct areas, all of which are linked by a common concern with the problem of space. The first of these areas comprises Segre's articles on the geometric properties that are invariant under linear transformations of space. In this connection Segre showed the value of investigating hyperspaces in the study of three-dimensional space S_3. For example, a ruled surface of S_3, which is composed of right lines, can be represented by a curve in S_5; it thus becomes possible to reduce the classification of surfaces to that of curves. The insufficiencies of the earlier theories proposed by A. Möbius, Grassmann, Cayley, and Cremona were thus soon revealed.

According to Segre, a ruled surface in a space S_n can also be considered a variety of ∞^2 points distributed on ∞^1 right lines. Further, Segre generalized the theory of the loci formed by ∞^1 right lines of S_n to the theory of the loci formed by ∞^1 planes. He took as his point of departure certain problems on bundles of quadrics that Weierstrass and L. Kronecker had treated in a purely algebraic manner.

At this time it was known that the intersection of two quadrics of S_3 is a quartic the projection of which from a point exterior to it onto a plane is a quartic with two double points. John Casey and Gaston Darboux had shown that its study is useful for that of fourth-order surfaces, called cyclides. Segre reexamined and generalized the problem by placing the two quadrics in a space S_4. He also investigated the locus resulting from the intersection of two quadrics of S_5 and discovered that it is no longer a surface but rather a three-dimensional variety that can be interpreted as a complex quadratic of S_3. From this result he confirmed in an elegant manner the famous fourth-order surface with sixteen double points, which had been found by Kummer in 1864 and bear his name. Before Segre's findings, the study of this surface required the use of extremely complicated algebraic procedures.

Segre next began a series of works on the properties of algebraic curves and ruled surfaces subjected to birational transformations. Alfred Clebsch, Paul Gordan, Alexander Brill, and Max Noether had already studied these transformations with a view toward giving a geometric interpretation to the theory of Abelian functions. Segre showed the advantage gained by operating in a hyperspace. His article of 1896 on the birational transformations of a surface contains the invariant that Zeuthen had encountered under another form in 1871, now called the Zeuthen-Segre invariant.

Segre's interest in 1890 in the properties of the Riemann sphere led him to a third area of research: the role of imaginary elements in geometry. He laid the basis of a new theory of hyperalgebraic entities by representing complex points of S_n by means of the ∞^{2n} real points of one of the varieties V_{2n}. (This variety has since been named for Segre.) Certain of Segre's hyperalgebraic transformations possess invariant properties, and he was led to enlarge the concept of a point. To this end, he introduced points that he called bicomplex, which correspond to the ordinary complex points of the real image. Their coordinates are bicomplex numbers constructed with the aid of the two unities i and j, such that:

$$i \cdot j = j \cdot i$$

and

$$i^2 = j^2 = -1.$$

Later, in 1912, Segre returned to this subject, when, utilizing the works of Von Staudt, he studied another type of complex geometry.

Darboux's *Leçons sur la théorie générale des surfaces*, which Segre often used in his courses, inspired him to investigate (from 1907) infinitesimal geometry. Extending the work of Darboux, Segre studied a certain class of surfaces in S_n defined by second-order linear partial differential equations. These surfaces are described by a moving point of which the homogeneous coordinates—functions of two independent parameters u and v—are the solutions of a second-order partial differential equation. Among the surfaces of a hyperspace, Segre was particularly interested in those that lead to a Laplace equation. In an article of 1908 on the conjugate tangents of a surface, he established a relationship between the points of the tangent plane and those of the planes passing through the origin. To establish this relationship he employed infinitesimals of higher order in a problem concerning the neighborhood of a point. This procedure led him to introduce a new system of lines, analogous to those studied by Darboux, traced on the surface; they were named Segre lines, and their differential equation was established by Fubini. It may be noted that Segre's last publication dealt with differential geometry. Segre wrote a long article on hyperspaces for the *Encyklopädie der mathematischen Wissenschaften*, containing all that was then known about such spaces. A model article, it is notable for its clarity and elegance.

Segre became a member of the Academy of Turin in 1889. He long served on the editorial board of the *Annali di matematica pura ed applicata*, on which he was succeeded by his former student Severi of the University of Rome.

Through his teaching and his publications, Segre played an important role in reviving an interest in geometry in Italy. His reputation and the new ideas he presented in his courses attracted many Italian and foreign students to Turin. Segre's contribution to the knowledge of space assures him a place after Cremona in the ranks of the most illustrious members of the new Italian school of geometry.

BIBLIOGRAPHY

I. ORIGINAL WORKS. The complete works of Segre have been published as *Opere*, 4 vols. (1957–1963), but it does not contain the paper "Mehrdimensionale Räume" (see below). A complete list of Segre's publications, 128 titles, is given in G. Loria (see below). A. Terracini lists ninety-eight titles. See also Poggendorff, V, 1151–1152.

Segre's most important works include "Sur les différentes espèces de complexes du 2e degré des droites qui coupent harmoniquement deux surfaces du 2e ordre." in *Mathematische Annalen*, **23** (1883), 213–234, written with G. Loria; "Studio sulle quadriche in uno spazio lineare ad un numero qualunque di dimensioni," in *Memorie dell'Accademia delle scienze di Torino*, **36** (1883), 3–86; "Sulla geometria della retta e delle sue serie quadratiche," *ibid.*, 87–157; "Note sur les complexes quadratiques dont la surface singulière est une surface du 2e degré double," in *Mathematische Annalen*, **23** (1883), 235–243; "Sulle geometrie metriche dei complessi lineari e delle sfere e sulle loro mutue analogie," in *Atti dell'Accademia delle scienze*, **19** (1883), 159–186; "Sulla teoria e sulla classificazione delle omografie in uno spazio lineare ad un numero qualunque di dimensioni," in *Memorie della R. Accademia dei Lincei*, 3rd ser., **19** (1884), 127–148; and "Étude des différentes surfaces du quatrième ordre à conique double ou cuspidale (générale ou décomposée) considérées comme des projections de l'intersection de deux variétés quadratiques de l'espace à quatre dimensions," in *Mathematische Annalen*, **24** (1884), 313–444.

Later writings are "Le coppie di elementi imaginari nella geometria proiettiva sintetica," in *Memorie dell' Accademia delle scienze di Torino*, **38** (1886), 3–24; "Recherches générales sur les courbes et les surfaces réglées algébriques," in *Mathematische Annalen*, **30** (1887), 203–226, and **34** (1889), 1–25; "Un nuovo campo di ricerche geometriche," in *Atti dell'Academia delle scienze*, **25** (1889), 276–301, 430–457, 592–612, and **26** (1890), 35–71; "Su alcuni indirizzi nelle investigazioni geometriche," in *Rivista di matematica*, **1** (1891), 42–66, with English trans. by J. W. Young as "On Some Tendencies in Geometric Investigations," in *Bulletin of the American Mathematical Society*, 2nd ser., **10** (1904), 442–468; "Le rappresentazioni reali delle forme complesse e gli enti iperalgebrici," in *Mathematische Annalen*, **40** (1891), 413–467; "Intorno ad un carattere delle superficie e delle varietà superiori algebriche," in *Atti dell'Accademia delle scienze*, **31** (1896), 485–501; and "Su un problema relativo alle intersezioni di curve e superficie," *ibid.*, **33** (1898), 19–23.

See also "Intorno ai punti di Weierstrass di una curva algebrica," in *Atti dell'Accademia nazionale dei Lincei. Rendiconti*, 5th ser., **8** (1889), 89–91; "Gli ordini delle varietà che annullano i determinanti dei diversi gradi estratti da una data matrice," *ibid.*, **9** (1900), 253–260; "Su una classe di superficie degli iperspazi, legata con le equazioni lineari alle derivate parziali di 2° ordine," in *Atti dell'Accademia delle scienze*, **42** (1907), 1047–1079; "Complementi alla teoria delle tangenti coniugate di una superficie," in *Atti dell'Accademia nazionale dei Lincei. Rendiconti*, 5th ser., **17** (1908), 405–412; "Mehrdimensionale Räume," in *Encyklopädie der mathematischen Wissenschaften*, III, pt. 3, fasc. 7 (1918), 769–972; "Sulle corrispondenze quadrilineari tra forme di prima specie e su alcune loro rappresentazioni spaziali," in *Annali di matematica pura ed applicata*, 3rd ser., **29** (1920), 105–140; "Sui fochi di 2° ordine dei sistemi infiniti di piani e sulle curve iperspaziali con una doppia infinità di piani plurisecanti," in *Atti dell'Accademia nazionale dei Lincei. Rendiconti*, 5th ser., **30** (1921), 67–71; "Le superficie degli iperspazi con una doppia infinità di curve piane o spaziali," in *Atti dell'Accademia delle scienze*, **56** (1921), 143–157; "Sugli elementi lineari che hanno comuni la tangente e il piano osculatore," in *Atti dell'Accademia nazionale dei Lincei. Rendiconti*, 5th ser., **33** (1924), 325–329; "Le curve piane d'ordine n circoscritte ad un $(n + 1) = latero$ completo di tangenti ed una classe particolare di superficie con doppio sistema coniugato di coni circoscritti," in *Atti dell'Accademia delle scienze*, **59** (1924), 303–320.

II. Secondary Literature. Obituary notices are L. Berzolari, in *Rendiconti dell'Istituto lombardo di scienze e lettere*, **57** (1924), 528–532; G. Castelnuovo, in *Atti dell'Accademia nazionale dei Lincei. Rendiconti*, 5th ser., **33** (1924), 353–359; E. Pascal, in *Rendiconti dell'Accademia delle scienze fisiche e matematiche*, **30** (1924), 114–116; and V. Volterra, in *Atti dell'Accademia nazionale dei Lincei. Rendiconti*, 5th ser., **33** (1924), 459–461. See also Poggendorff, VI, 2407, for a list of notices.

On Segre and his work, see H. F. Baker's article in *Journal of the London Mathematical Society*, **1** (1926), 263–271, with trans. by G. Loria in *Bollettino dell'Unione matematica italiana*, **6** (1927), 276–284; J. L. Coolidge, in *Bulletin of the American Mathematical Society*, **33** (1927), 352–357; G. Loria, in *Annali di matematica pura ed applicata*, 4th ser., **2** (1924), 1–21; and A. Terracini, in *Jahresbericht der Deutschen Mathematikervereinigung*, **35** (1926), 209–250, with portrait. The articles by Loria, Terracini, and Baker are especially helpful.

Pierre Speziali

SÉGUIN, ARMAND (*b.* Paris, France, March 1767; *d.* Paris, 24 January 1835), *chemistry, chemical technology, physiology.*

Séguin's father was the treasurer (apparently corrupt) of the duke of Orléans. Although little is known of his education, it is evident that he had some training in the sciences, for by the mid-1780's he had become part of Lavoisier's circle. Séguin was Lavoisier's assistant from 1789 until the latter's death in 1794. During this time, Séguin produced those memoirs (some written with Lavoisier) on heat and respiration for which he is best known. In 1796 he assisted Mme Lavoisier in preparing her husband's memoirs for publication. But they soon ended this collaboration because Séguin was unwilling to denounce in print Lavoisier's executioners and because, in a preface prepared by Séguin, he took more credit for Lavoisier's later work than Mme Lavoisier rightly thought he deserved.

Meanwhile, Séguin had become director of a tanning works at Sèvres, an enterprise that was based on processes of his own devising and that won the contract to supply the revolutionary armies with boot leather. Although Séguin made no fundamental innovations in tanning, he found several ways to rationalize and accelerate the operation, being unhampered by craft mysteries. He shortened the time for tanning hides from more than a year to a few weeks. Understandably, he received support, encouragement, and subsidies from the Comité de Salut Public.

Séguin made money out of the wars, but Napoleon, who had no love for profiteers, later reduced his fortune by taxes and fines (even to the point of imprisoning him), but did not succeed in impoverishing him. Séguin survived the Empire and Restoration and lived thereafter the life of an eccentric, Balzacian *rentier*, devoting most of his intellectual energies after 1815 to the composition of pamphlets on government finances. He was also devoted to horseracing and wrote a number of works on that subject.

Séguin's scientific contributions were made chiefly in collaboration with others. In the work he published with Fourcroy and Vauquelin on the synthesis of water, and in the papers he wrote with, or under the tutelage of, Lavoisier, he wrote crisply and authoritatively. Thereafter he lost his grip, and, with the exception of his research on tannin, his independent investigations were trivial. Although he contributed a number of "first memoirs" on several subjects, mostly pharmaceutical, to the *Annales de chimie* in 1814, these papers had been written years before and were never followed up.

In May 1790 Séguin read to the Académie des

Sciences the report on the large-scale synthesis of water carried out in Fourcroy's laboratory by himself, Fourcroy, and Vauquelin. The purpose of this experiment was to establish finally that water is composed only of hydrogen and oxygen and that the weight of water is fully accounted for by the weights of the two gases. They also sought to determine accurately the combining ratio of the components of water, an especially important constant in oxygen chemistry. They found that the ratio hydrogen:oxygen is 2.052:1 by volume and 14.338:85.662 by weight. (The discrepancies from the true figures probably arose from the difficulties of weighing the gases.)

Séguin's papers on respiration, animal heat, and caloric are all derivative from Lavoisier's work and ideas, although the evidence suggests that Séguin was an enthusiastic collaborator and one who made the master's ideas his own. Séguin's series of papers on caloric competently summarized and systematized Lavoisier's later thinking on the subject and also, as Robert Fox has recently shown, thoroughly refuted the Irvinist theory of caloric. This work helped to consolidate the Lavoisier-Laplace version of caloric theory and thus paved the way for the developments of that theory in the following three decades.

BIBLIOGRAPHY

I. Original Works. Séguin's works are listed in the Royal Society *Catalogue of Printed Papers,* V, 628–629; those which he contributed to Lavoisier's *Mémoires de chimie,* 2 vols. (Paris, 1805), are listed in Denis I. Duveen and Herbert S. Klickstein, *A Bibliography of the Works of Antoine Laurent Lavoisier 1743–1794* (London, 1954), 204–214. His papers written with Lavoisier are "Premier mémoire sur la respiration," in *Mémoires de l'Académie royale des sciences* (1789), 566–584; "Premier mémoire sur la transpiration des animaux," *ibid.* (1790), 601–612; "Second mémoire sur la transpiration," in *Annales de chimie,* 90 (1814), 5–28; "Second mémoire sur la respiration," *ibid.,* 91 (1814), 318–334; and "Sur la respiration des animaux," in Lavoisier, *Mémoires de chimie,* II, 52–64 (in the separately paginated last section). See also "Observations générales sur la respiration et sur la chaleur animale," in *Observations sur la physique, sur l'histoire naturelle et sur les arts,* 37 (1790), 467–472. Séguin's paper with Fourcroy and Vauquelin is "Mémoire sur la combustion du gaz hydrogène dans des vaisseaux clos," in *Annales de chimie,* 8 (1791), 230–307; reprinted in Lavoisier, *op. cit.,* II, 313–413.

The Bibliothèque Nationale *Catalogue des livres imprimés* lists Séguin's financial and miscellaneous writings.

II. Secondary Literature. On Séguin and his work, see Michaud, ed., *Biographie universelle;* and J. R. Partington, *History of Chemistry,* III (London, 1962), 106–107. For his contribution to the theory of heat, see Robert Fox, *Caloric Theory of Gases* (Oxford, 1971), chap. 2, especially pp. 38–39; for his relations with Mme Lavoisier, see Édouard Grimaux, *Lavoisier* (Paris, 1888), 330–336, and Duveen and Klickstein, *op. cit.,* 199–204; and for his work on tanning, see C. H. Lelièvre and Pelletier, "Rapport au Comité de Salut Public, sur les nouveaux moyens de tanner les cuirs, proposés par le cit. Armand Séguin," in *Annales de chimie,* 20 (1797), 15–77.

Stuart Pierson

SEGUIN, MARC, also known as **SEGUIN AÎNÉ** (*b.* Annonay, France, 20 April 1786; *d.* Annonay, 24 February 1875), *engineering, physics.*

The eldest son of a small but prosperous manufacturer in the Ardèche, Seguin completed his formal education at an undistinguished Parisian boarding school. From his arrival in Paris in 1799 his interest in science and engineering was stimulated and decisively shaped through his informal contact with his granduncle Joseph Montgolfier, the famous balloonist. Closely related by birth and later by marriage to the Montgolfier family, Seguin always regarded himself as Montgolfier's leading disciple. From Montgolfier Seguin acquired several scientific perspectives seldom expressed by the contemporary scientific community, notably an emphasis on *vis viva* (mv^2) as the quantity that is conserved not only in heat engines and machines but also in the universe. Seguin also credited Montgolfier with rejecting the caloric theory of heat and suggesting, instead, that heat and motion, both manifestations of an unknown but common cause, were interconvertible. Montgolfier died in 1810, and shortly thereafter Seguin returned to Annonay.

Over the next two decades Seguin, aided by his younger brothers, executed a series of successful and innovative engineering projects. In 1825, at Tournon on the Rhone, he erected the first successful suspension bridge in France to use cables of iron wire. After a brief attempt to establish regular steamboat service on the Rhone, the Seguin brothers organized the company that built France's first modern railroad, a line between Saint-Étienne and Lyons completed in 1832. Finding the Stephenson locomotive unable to generate enough steam for high-speed operation, in 1827 Seguin invented the multitubular, or fire tube, boiler. After working briefly on the Left Bank railroad between

Paris and Versailles, Seguin retired from active engineering and moved to Fontenay in 1838. Marked both by numerous technical innovations and by shrewd economic planning, his engineering projects provide one of the earliest examples in France of large-scale civil engineering undertaken and financed by private companies. For these engineering achievements Seguin was elected a correspondent of the Académie des Sciences in 1845.

Except for some contact with J. B. Biot, who had invested heavily in the engineering enterprises, Seguin always remained on the periphery of professional French science. Through numerous visits to England, however, he became acquainted with several prominent British scientists, notably John Herschel, Michael Faraday, and Humphry Davy. Two letters from Seguin to Herschel and to Brewster were published in Edinburgh journals in 1824 and 1825. These contain his first statements, perhaps derived from Montgolfier, of an extreme form of Newtonianism in which all physical forces are to be explained as the result of the inverse-square law of attraction between molecules. Matter, Seguin argued, consists of small, dense molecules in constant motion in miniature solar systems. Magnetic, electrical, and thermal phenomena are the result of particular velocities and orbits. Faster molecules escape from orbit along tangential paths, producing light and radiant heat. Explicitly identifying heat as molecular velocity, Seguin added that when molecules transmit their velocity to external objects, a conversion of heat into mechanical effect occurs. The qualitative, synthetic style of Seguin's papers and his conceptions of heat and light were in sharp contrast with the mathematical caloric and wave theories then dominant in France. In spite of a close similarity to contemporary British science, the papers apparently had no influence.

In 1839 Seguin returned to the problem of heat in his most important publication, *De l'influence des chemins de fer,* a handbook for the design and construction of railroads. In the chapter on steam locomotive performance, he first rejected the caloric theory because its major premise, the existence of heat as a fluid conserved in all processes, would allow the reuse of heat in an engine and thus would imply perpetual motion. "It appears more natural to me to suppose that a certain quantity of heat disappears in the very act of the production of force or mechanical power, and conversely; and that the two phenomena are linked together by conditions that assign to them invariable relationships" (p. 382). This assumption was the basis for

his later claim to priority over Joule and Mayer for the statement of the convertibility and conservation of heat and work.

To determine the numerical relationship, Seguin imagined a unit weight of steam generated under pressure in a cylinder and allowed to expand adiabatically until its temperature fell twenty degrees Centigrade. Assuming that steam is a perfect gas that remains saturated during expansion, he used standard engineering formulas and steam tables to calculate the work performed against the piston. The results, given in a table for different twenty-degree intervals, showed a steady decrease in the amount of work produced as the intervals were located higher on the temperature scale, a result indicating either that the conversion of heat into work did not follow an invariable law or, as Seguin chose to conclude, that the heat loss of twenty degrees as measured on a thermometer was not a true measure of the heat lost by the steam. Unable to specify the relation between temperature loss and total loss of heat content, he made no attempt to define a unit of heat or to state its mechanical equivalent.

Joule's determination of the mechanical equivalent was published in France in 1847, and one month later Seguin responded with a note to the Academy supporting Joule's conclusions. Seguin called attention to his 1839 work as an earlier attempt to find the numerical equivalent and demonstrated that the average of his tabular results, converted to Joule's units, gave a value very close to the figure Joule had obtained by completely different methods. Conversely, Seguin regarded Joule's experiments as a confirmation of his own more general theory outlined in 1824, and his paper concluded with an announcement of his intention to explain the identity of heat and work through an extension of the law of universal attraction.

In the later priority controversy surrounding the principle of energy conservation, it became clear that Mayer, Joule, and Helmholtz had worked independently of Seguin and that, despite Seguin's repeated claims, only in retrospect could his 1839 suggestions be clearly interpreted as a mechanical equivalent of heat. Although Seguin's theory of forces implied a conservation of energy, he focused his attention on the motion of molecules and made no attempt to define a concept of energy or to state its conservation.

From 1848 until his death Seguin conducted a broad campaign to win acceptance for his program of reducing all physical forces to the single Newtonian law of molecular attraction. In 1853 he bought a bankrupt journal and began publishing a weekly scientific magazine, *Cosmos*. Under the editorship of the abbé François Moigno the journal served as an important vehicle for the popularization of science and as a forum for Seguin's theories. In 1856 Seguin commissioned a French translation of William Grove's *Correlation of Physical Forces* and added notes and commentary. Throughout Seguin's prolific publications the earlier themes of 1824 were repeated and elaborated. The only major addition was a strong emphasis, adopted from Biot, on crystal structure and polarized light. Seguin developed gravitational models for the structure of matter and presented particle theories for heat, light, electricity, and magnetism. These theories, together with his attacks on the ether hypothesis and on the reduction of physics to analytical mathematics, were completely contrary to contemporary scientific opinion and had no apparent subsequent influence.

BIBLIOGRAPHY

I. ORIGINAL WORKS. Seguin's thirty-six journal articles are listed in the Royal Society *Catalogue of Scientific Papers*, V and VIII. The most important are "Letter to Sir. J. Herschel: Observations on the Effects of Heat and of Motion," in *Edinburgh Philosophical Journal*, **10** (1824), 280–283; "Letter to Dr. Brewster on the Effects of Heat and Motion," in *Edinburgh Journal of Science*, **3** (1825), 276–281; and "Note à l'appui de l'opinion émise par M. Joule, sur l'identité du mouvement et du calorique," in *Comptes rendus . . . de l'Académie des sciences*, **25** (1847), 420–422. Seguin published nearly thirty books, many of them reprints of earlier journal articles. Of special interest are *Des ponts en fil de fer* (Paris, 1824; 2nd ed., 1826); *De l'influence des chemins de fer et de l'art de les tracer et de les construire* (Paris, 1839; repr. 1887); and *Mémoire sur les causes et sur les effets de la chaleur, de la lumière et de l'électricité* (Paris, 1865).

II. SECONDARY LITERATURE. The only biography, P. E. Marchal and Laurent Seguin, *Marc Seguin 1786–1875: La naissance du premier chemin de fer français* (Lyons, 1957), is useful, but uncritical. Seguin is discussed in the context of the several men who approached energy conservation by various routes in T. S. Kuhn, "Energy Conservation as an Example of Simultaneous Discovery," in Marshall Clagett, ed., *Critical Problems in the History of Science* (Madison, Wis., 1959), 321–356.

JAMES F. CHALLEY

SEIDEL, PHILIPP LUDWIG VON (*b.* Zweibrücken, Germany, 24 October 1821; *d.* Munich, Germany, 13 August 1896), *astronomy, mathematics.*

Seidel was the son of Justus Christian Felix Seidel, a post office official, and Julie Reinhold. Because of his father's work he began school in Nördlingen, continued in Nuremberg, and finished in Hof. After passing the graduation examination in the fall of 1839 he took private lessons from L. C. Schnürlein, a teacher of mathematics at the Hof Gymnasium who had studied under Gauss. In the spring of 1840, Seidel entered Berlin University, where he attended the lectures of Dirichlet and Encke, for whom he subsequently carried out calculations at the astronomical observatory. In the fall of 1842 he moved to Königsberg, where he studied with Bessel, Jacobi, and F. E. Neumann. When Jacobi left Königsberg because of his health in the fall of 1843, Seidel, on Bessel's recommendation, moved to Munich and obtained the doctorate with the dissertation "Über die beste Form der Spiegel in Teleskopen" in January 1846. Six months later he qualified as a *Privatdozent* on the basis of his "Untersuchungen über die Konvergenz und Divergenz der Kettenbrüche."

These two works treat two fields investigated by Seidel throughout his life, dioptrics and mathematical analysis. He also produced works in probability theory and photometry, the latter stimulated by his collaboration with Steinheil. In his mathematical investigations he depended on Dirichlet but filled important gaps left by his teacher—for instance, introducing the concept of nonuniform convergence.

Seidel's photometric measurements of fixed stars and planets were the first true measurements of this kind. The precise evaluation of his observations by methods of probability theory, considering atmospheric extinction, are worthy of special mention. At Steinheil's suggestion Seidel derived trigonometric formulas for points lateral to the axis of an optical system; they soon became important for astronomical photography and led to the production of improved telescopes.

Besides the application of probability theory to astronomy, Seidel investigated the relation between the frequency of certain diseases and climatic conditions at Munich. His pioneer work in several fields was acknowledged by Bavaria. In 1847 he became assistant professor, in 1855 full professor, and later royal privy councillor; he also received a number of medals, one of them connected with nobility. Seidel was a member of the Bavarian Academy of Sciences (1851) and corresponding member of the Berlin and Göttingen academies, as well as a member of the Commission for the European Measurement of a Degree and of a group observing a transit of Venus.

Seidel suffered from eye problems and was obliged to retire early. A bachelor, he was cared for by his unmarried sister Lucie until 1889, and later by the widow of a clergyman named Langhans.

Seidel's lectures covered mathematics, including probability theory and the method of least squares, astronomy, and dioptrics. He never accepted Riemannian geometry.

BIBLIOGRAPHY

I. ORIGINAL WORKS. Seidel's earlier works include "Über die Bestimmung der Brechungs- und Zerstreuungs-Verhältnisses verschiedener Medien," in *Abhandlungen der Bayerischen Akademie der Wissenschaften,* Math.-phys. Kl., **5** (1848), 253–268, written with K. A. Steinheil; "Note über eine Eigenschaft der Reihen, welche discontinuierliche Functionen darstellen," *ibid.,* 381–393; "Untersuchungen über die gegenseitigen Helligkeiten der Fixsterne erster Grösse, und über die Extinction des Lichtes in der Atmosphäre," *ibid.,* **6,** no. 3 (1852), 539–660; "Zur Theorie der Fernrohr-Objective," in *Astronomische Nachrichten,* **35** (1852), 301–316; "Zur Dioptrik," *ibid.,* **37** (1853), 105–120; "Bemerkungen über den Zusammenhang zwischen dem Bildungsgesetze eines Kettenbruches und der Art des Fortgangs seiner Näherungsbrüche," in *Abhandlungen der Bayerischen Akademie der Wissenschaften,* Math.-phys. Kl., **7** (1855), 559–602; "Entwicklung der Glieder 3.ter Ordnung, welche den Weg eines ausserhalb der Ebene der Axe gelegenen Lichtstrahles durch ein System brechender Medien bestimmen," in *Astronomische Nachrichten,* **43** (1856), 289–332; "Über den Einfluss der Theorie der Fehler, mit welchen die durch optische Instrumente gesehenen Bilder behaftet sind, und über die mathematischen Bedingungen ihrer Aufhebung," in *Abhandlungen der naturwissenschaftlich-technischen Commission der Bayerischen Akademie der Wissenschaften,* **1** (1857), 227–267; and "Untersuchungen über die Lichtstärke der Planeten vergleichen mit den Sternen, und über die relative Weisse ihrer Oberfläche," in *Monumenta saecularum der Bayerischen Akademie der Wissenschaften* (1859), 1–102.

Among his later writings are Resultate photometrischer Messungen an 208 der vorzüglichsten Fixsterne," in *Abhandlungen der Bayerischen Akademie der Wissenschaften,* Math.-phys. Kl., **9** (1863), 419–607; "Über eine Anwendung der Wahrscheinlichkeitsrechnung, bezüglich auf die Schwankungen in den Durchsichtigkeitsverhältnissen der Luft," in *Sitzungs-*berichte der Bayerischen Akademie der Wissenschaften zu München* (1863), pt. 2, 320–350; "Trigonometrische Formeln für den allgemeinsten Fall der Brechung des Lichtes an centrirten sphärischen Flächen," *ibid.* (1866), pt. 2, 263–284; "Über ein Verfahren, die Gleichungen, auf welche die Methode der kleinsten Quadrate führt, sowie lineäre Gleichungen überhaupt," in *Abhandlungen der Bayerischen Akademie der Wissenschaften,* Math.-phys. Kl., **11,** no. 3 (1874), 81–108; and "Über eine einfache Entstehungsweise der Bernoulli'schen Zahlen," in *Sitzungsberichte der Bayerischen Akademie der Wissenschaften,* Math.-phys. Kl., n.s. **7** (1877), 157–187.

II. SECONDARY LITERATURE. See F. Lindemann, *Gedächtnisrede auf L. Ph. von Seidel* (Munich, 1898).

H.-CHRIST. FREIESLEBEN

SEKI, TAKAKAZU (*b.* Huzioka[?], Japan, 1642[?]; *d.* Edo [now Tokyo], Japan, 24 October 1708), *mathematics.*

Knowledge of Seki's life is meager and indirect. His place of birth is variously given as Huzioka or Edo, and the year as 1642 or 1644. He was the second son of Nagaakira Utiyama, a samurai; his mother's name is unknown. He was adopted by the patriarch of the Seki family, an accountant, whom he accompanied to Edo as chief of the Bureau of Supply. In 1706, having grown too old to fulfill the duties of this office, he was transferred to a sinecure and died two years later.

Seki is reported to have begun the study of mathematics under Yositane Takahara, a brilliant disciple of Sigeyosi Mōri. Mōri is the author of *Warizansyo* ("A Book on Division," 1622), believed to be the first book on mathematics written by a Japanese, but little is known about Takahara. Of particular influence on Seki's mathematics was *Suan-hsüeh ch'i-mêng* ("Introduction to Mathematical Studies," 1299), compiled by Chu Shih-chieh, a collection of problems solved by a method known in Chinese as *t'ien-yuan shu* ("method of the celestial element"); this method makes it possible to solve a problem by transforming it into an algebraic equation with one variable. Kazuyuki Sawaguchi, allegedly the first Japanese mathematician to master this method, used it to solve 150 problems proposed by Masaoki Satō in his *Sanpô Kongenki* ("Fundamentals of Mathematics," 1667). He then organized these problems, together with their solutions, into the seven-volume collection *Kokon sanpōki* ("Ancient and Modern Mathematics," 1670). At the end of the last volume Sawaguchi presented fifteen problems that he believed to be unsolvable by means of *t'ien-yuan shu.*

Seki's solutions to these problems were published in 1674 as *Hatubi sanpō*. Because mathematicians of those days were unable to grasp how the solutions had been accomplished, Katahiro Takebe (1664–1739), a distinguished disciple of Seki, published *Hatubi sanpō endan genkai* ("An Easy Guide to the *Hatubi sanpō*," 1685), the work that made Seki's method known.

In Chinese mathematics operations were performed by means of instruments called *suan-ch'ou* ("calculating rods") and therefore could not treat any algebraic expressions except those with one variable and numerical coefficients. Seki introduced Chinese ideographs and wrote them to the right of a vertical—such as |a—where a is used, for typographical reasons, instead of a Chinese ideograph. Seki called this notation *bōsyohō* ("method of writing by the side") and used it as the basis of his *endan zyutu* ("*endan* method"). *Endan zyutu* enabled him to represent known and unknown quantities by Chinese ideographs and led him to form equations with literal coefficients of any degree and with several variables. The technique was later renamed *tenzan zyutu* by Yosisuke Matunaga (1693–1744), the third licensee of the secret mathematical methods of Seki's school.

The *Hatubi sanpō* did not include Seki's principal theorems, which were kept secret; but in order to initiate students he arranged the theorems systematically. Parts of these works and some more extended theorems were collected and published posthumously by his disciples as *Katuyō sanpō*—which, with *Sekiryū sanpō sitibusyo* ("Seven Books on the Mathematics of Seki's School," 1907), is sufficient to grasp his mathematics.

Seki first treated general theories of algebraic equations. Since his method of side writing was inconvenient for writing general equations of degree n, he worked with equations of the second through fifth degrees. But his treatment was so general that his method could be applied to equations of any degree. Seki attempted to find a means of solving second-degree algebraic equations with numerical coefficients but, having no concept of algebraic solution, directed his efforts at finding an approximate solution. He discovered a procedure, used long before in China, that was substantially the same as Horner's. The notion of a discriminant of an algebraic equation also was introduced by Seki. Although he had no notion of the derivative, he derived from an algebraic expression $f(x)$ another expression that was the equivalent of $f'(x)$ in modern notation. Eliminating x from the pair of equations $f(x) = 0$ and $f'(x) = 0$, he obtained what is now called a discriminant. With the help of this expression Seki found double roots of the equation $f(x) = 0$. He also developed a method similar to Newton's by which an approximate value of the root of a numerical equation can be computed. Seki's *tenzan zyutu* was important in the treatment of problems that can be transformed into the solution of a system of simultaneous equations. In order to solve the problem of elimination, he introduced determinants and gave a rule for expressing them diagrammatically. For third-order equations his formula was basically similar to Sarrus'.

The method that Seki named *syōsahō* was intended to determine the coefficients of the expression $y = a_1 x + a_2 x^2 + \cdots + a_n x^n$, when n values of $x_1, x_2, \cdots, x_n$ of x and the corresponding n values of $y_1, y_2, \cdots, y_n$ of y are given. Since his notation was not suitable for the general case corresponding to an arbitrary n, Seki treated the case that corresponds to the special value of n. His solution was similar to the method of finite difference.

Another method, *daseki zyutu*, also is important in Seki's mathematics. Its purpose is to find values of $s_p = 1^p + 2^p + \cdots + n^p$ for $p = 1, 2, 3, \cdots$. Using the *syōsahō*, Seki calculated $s_1, s_2, \cdots, s_6$ for a particular value of n:

$$s_1 = \frac{n^2}{2} + \frac{n}{2}$$

$$s_2 = \frac{n^3}{3} + \frac{n^2}{2} + \frac{1}{6} \cdot \frac{2n}{2}$$

$$s_3 = \frac{n^4}{4} + \frac{n^3}{2} + \frac{1}{6} \cdot \frac{3n^2}{2}$$

$$s_4 = \frac{n^5}{5} + \frac{n^4}{2} + \frac{1}{6} \cdot \frac{4n^3}{2} - \frac{1}{30} \cdot \frac{4 \cdot 3 \cdot 2n}{2 \cdot 3 \cdot 4}$$

$$s_5 = \frac{n^6}{6} + \frac{n^5}{2} + \frac{1}{6} \cdot \frac{5n^4}{2} - \frac{1}{30} \cdot \frac{5 \cdot 4 \cdot 3n^2}{2 \cdot 3 \cdot 4}$$

$$s_6 = \frac{n^7}{7} + \frac{n^6}{2} + \frac{1}{6} \cdot \frac{6n^5}{2} - \frac{1}{30} \cdot \frac{6 \cdot 5 \cdot 4n^3}{2 \cdot 3 \cdot 4} +$$

$$\frac{1}{42} \cdot \frac{6 \cdot 5 \cdot 4 \cdot 3 \cdot 2n}{2 \cdot 3 \cdot 4 \cdot 5 \cdot 6}.$$

The numbers 1/6, 1/30, 1/42 are Bernoulli numbers, which were introduced in his *Ars conjectandi* (1713).

Enri ("principle of the circle"), one of Seki's important contributions, consists of rectification of the circumference of a circle, rectification of a circular arc, and cubature of a sphere. In the rectification of a circumference, Seki considered a circle of diameter 1 and an inscribed regular polygon of 2^n sides. He believed that the inscribed polygon gradually loses its angularities and finally becomes a circumference of the circle when the number of sides is increased without limit. He therefore calculated the perimeter c_i of the regular polygon of 2^i sides, where i represents any integer not greater than 17, and devised a method by which he was able to obtain a better result from c_{15}, c_{16}, c_{17}. The formula was

$$s = c_{16} + \frac{(c_{16} - c_{15})(c_{17} - c_{16})}{(c_{16} - c_{15}) - (c_{17} - c_{16})},$$

where

$$c_{15} = 3.1415926487769856708,$$
$$c_{16} = 3.1415926523565913571,$$

and

$$c_{17} = 3.1415926532889027755.$$

Therefore, $s = 3.14159265359$, where s is the circumference of the circle; this value is accurate except for the last figure. Also in connection with this problem Seki created a method of approximation called *reiyaku zyutu*, by which he theoretically obtained 355/113 as an approximate value of π, a value found much earlier in China.

In the rectification of a circular arc, Seki considered an arc of which the chord is 8 and the corresponding sagitta is 2. He considered an inscribed open polygon of 2^{15} sides and, using the above formula, calculated the approximate value of the arc as 9.272953. In the cubature of a sphere, Seki calculated the volume of a sphere of diameter 10 and obtained $523\frac{203}{339}$ as an approximate value. Using the approximate value of π as 355/113, Seki observed that if d is the diameter of this sphere,

$$\frac{\pi}{6} d^3 = \frac{355}{678} \times (10)^3 = 523\frac{203}{339}.$$

Certain other geometrical problems, which do not belong among the *enri*, concern ellipses. Seki believed that any ellipse can be obtained through cutting a suitable circular cylinder by a plane. In order to obtain the area of an ellipse, he cut off from a circular cylinder two segments with generatrices of equal length such that one has elliptical bases and the other has circular bases. These two cylinders have the same volume. By equating the volumes of these two pieces of the cylinder, Seki obtained the result that the area of an ellipse is $\pi/4 \times AA' \times BB'$, where AA' and BB' denote, respec-

tively, the major and minor axis of an ellipse. Among the problems of cubature, that of a solid generated by revolving a segment of circle about a straight line that lies on the same plane as the segment is noteworthy. His result in this area had generality, and the theorem that he established was substantially the same as that now called the theorem of Pappus and Guldin.

BIBLIOGRAPHY

I. ORIGINAL WORKS. Seki's published writings are *Hatubi sanpō* (Edo, 1674) and *Katuyō sanpō* (Tokyo–Kyoto, 1709), copies of which are owned by the Mathematical Institute, Faculty of Science, Kyoto University. *Sekiryū sanpō sitibusyo* ("Seven Books on the Mathematics of Seki's School"; Tokyo, 1907), is a collection of Seki's papers (1683–1685) that were transmitted from master to pupils, who were permitted to copy them. An important collection of MS papers, "Sanbusyō" ("Three Selected Papers"), is discussed by Fujiwara (see below). See also *Collected Papers of Takakazu Seki* (Osaka, 1974).

II. SECONDARY LITERATURE. See the following, listed chronologically: Katahiro Takebe, *Hatubi sanpō endan genkai* ("An Easy Guide to the Hatubi sanpō"; n.p., 1685), a copy of which is owned by the Mathematical Institute, Faculty of Science, Kyoto University, with a facs. of the text of *Hatubi sanpō* and an explanation of Seki's method of solution; Dairoku Kikuchi, "Seki's Method of Finding the Length of an Arc of a Circle," in *Proceedings of the Physico-Mathematical Society of Japan*, **8**, no. 5 (1899), 179–198; and Matsusaburo Fujiwara, *Mathematics of Japan Before the Meiji Era*, II (Tokyo, 1956), 133–265, in Japanese. There are many other works that treat Seki's mathematics, such as Yoshio Mikami, *The Development of Mathematics in China and Japan* (Leipzig–New York, 1913; repr. New York, n.d.), but only those of scientific importance are cited here.

AKIRA KOBORI

SELWYN, ALFRED RICHARD CECIL (*b.* Kilmington, Somerset, England, 28 July 1824; *d.* Vancouver, British Columbia, 19 October 1902), *geology.*

Selwyn was born into an English upper-class family. His father was a canon in the church and his mother was the daughter of a nobleman. His education began at home under private tutors and was completed in Switzerland, although to what level is not known. He was interested in the natural sciences and especially in geology; at the age of twenty-one he was engaged by the Geological Survey of Great Britain. His mapping assignments were in the lower Paleozoic graptolitic sediments and black volcanics of western Shropshire and North Wales. Selwyn is credited with sixteen map sheets, which were described by his superior, and sometime field associate, Sir A. C. Ramsay, as "the perfection of beauty."

At the end of 1852 Selwyn accepted the post of director of the Geological Survey of Victoria, Australia, which he held for seventeen years. About the same time he married Matilda Charlotte Selwyn, daughter of the Rev. Edward Selwyn of Hemmingford Abbotts, and they had nine children. The area of Victoria is ten times that of Wales, but the rocks are generally similar in type and age. Although he had only a small staff of geologists, sixty-one geological maps (with accompanying sections at a scale of two inches to a mile) were produced. Since Victoria was the scene of intensive gold prospecting, particular attention was given to the distribution of auriferous veins and the extension of gold-bearing placer deposits beneath younger Tertiary lava flows. He administered the survey, actively participated in field mapping, and served as a commissioner to international exhibitions in London (1862), Dublin (1865), and Paris (1866). The survey was abruptly terminated in 1869, when the colonial legislature refused to vote a budget.

In December 1869 Selwyn became the second director of the Geological Survey of Canada, succeeding Sir William Logan, who had established a small but effective organization. The following year Selwyn investigated the gold fields of Nova Scotia. With the confederation of Canada in 1867 the jurisdiction of the survey over Ontario and Quebec had been expanded to include the Maritime Provinces. Moreover, negotiations for union were in progress with the western provinces, and such a unification would require the construction of a railroad to the Pacific coast. Thus, in 1871, at the request of the government, Selwyn went via San Francisco to British Columbia to traverse on horseback possible rail routes in the southern part of the province. The dense forest and raging streams made progress so difficult that a distance of only five miles a day was normal. At one point, a hungry horse seems to have eaten the records of two days' observations. Selwyn strengthened the assumption by feeding the horse blank pages from the same notebook.

In 1873 Selwyn made a geological reconnaissance of the western provinces, traveling by horse cart from Winnipeg to the Rocky Mountains, and in 1875 he examined a proposed northern railroad route via the Peace River. On this latter trip he was accompanied by a botanist because the survey had been expanded to include all aspects of natural history. Thus within five years Selwyn had a broad knowledge of Canadian geology and the hardships of fieldwork in Canada. Later his responsibilities as director of the survey prevented him from conducting prolonged fieldwork; but he still visited in the field on a regular basis, usually to inspect mineral finds of economic importance.

During his directorship, the staff of the Geological Survey was increased to over thirty employees, including some of the most highly qualified geologists graduating from Canadian universities. Sections within the survey were set up for chemistry, mineralogy, paleontology, natural history, topographic mapping, and administration. The survey library was greatly expanded and was described as one of the great scientific libraries in North America. Selwyn initiated new sections for mines, borings, water supply, and statistics of mineral production. The survey was represented at international exhibits in Philadelphia (1876), Paris (1878), London (1886), and Chicago (1893), all of which drew attention to the mineral industry of Canada and credit to Selwyn's organization. The Survey Act of 1890 required that the geologists had to be graduates of recognized universities.

Selwyn's term as director, however, was marked by much internal dissension, possibly because of his authoritarian attitude, and agitation by malcontents both inside and outside the survey. A government inquiry in 1884 into the operations of the survey has been described as breaking open a hornet's nest. Some of the problems arose from the expansion of Canada, devoting too much time to one provincial area rather than another, low pay and different salaries for individuals with the same qualifications, slow promotions, the delay or suppression of publications, poor accounting, lack of public relations, pursuing a purely scientific (rather than practical) goal, and following in the footsteps of Logan. Although the final report was critical of the discord, the level of activity, and the delay and seeming suppression of publications, Selwyn remained as director and none of the employees resigned. Selwyn's superannuation at age seventy in 1894 proved embarrassing when the government, during his absence in England, issued an order for his immediate retirement and the appointment of G. M. Dawson as director, about which Selwyn learned upon his return.

BIBLIOGRAPHY

I. ORIGINAL WORKS. A complete list of Selwyn's publications is given in the biographical sketch by H. M. Ami (see below). His most notable contributions are the sixty-one geological maps of Victoria, which, according to the present director of the Geological Survey of Victoria, are still held in the highest regard. His thirty-seven publications for Canada, listed by J. M. Nickles in "Geologic Literature of North America 1785–1918," in *Bulletin of the United States Geological Survey*, **746** (1923), 931–932, are mainly the annual summary reports of the Geological Survey of Canada. Selwyn admitted after retirement that he had "an antipathy to the mechanical labour of writing," but he was described as a master of clear English expression. His broad interests are evident in "Notes and Observations on the Gold Fields of Quebec and Nova Scotia," in *Canadian Geological Survey, Report of Progress 1870–71* (1872), 252–282; "The Stratigraphy of the Quebec Group," in *Canadian Naturalist and Geologist*, n.s. **9** (1879), 17–31; and "Tracks of Organic Origin in the Animikie Group," in *American Journal of Science*, 3rd ser. (1890), 145–147.

II. SECONDARY LITERATURE. See H. M. Ami, "Memorial or Sketch of the Life of the Late Dr. A. R. C. Selwyn, C.M.G., LL.D., F.R.S., F.G.S., etc., etc., Director of the Geological Survey of Canada from 1869 to 1894," in *Transactions of the Royal Society of Canada*, Section IV, Geological Sciences and Mineralogy (1904), 173–205. An interpretative account of Selwyn as director of the Geological Survey can be found in M. Zaslow, *Reading the Rocks: The Story of the Geological Survey of Canada, 1842–1972* (Toronto, 1975), *passim*.

C. GORDON WINDER

SEMMELWEIS, IGNAZ PHILIPP (*b*. Buda, Hungary, 1 July 1818; *d*. Vienna, Austria, 13 August 1865), *medicine*.

Semmelweis was one of the most prominent medical figures of his time. His discovery concerning the etiology and prevention of puerperal fever was a brilliant example of fact-finding, meaningful statistical analysis, and keen inductive reasoning. The highly successful prophylactic hand washings made him a pioneer in antisepsis during the prebacteriological era in spite of deliberate opposition and uninformed resistance.

Semmelweis was born in Tabán, an old commercial sector of Buda. The fifth child of a prosperous shopkeeper of German origin, he received his elementary education at the Catholic Gymnasium of Buda, then completed his schooling at the University of Pest between 1835 and 1837.

In the fall of 1837, Semmelweis traveled to Vienna, ostensibly to enroll in its law school. His father wanted him to become a military advocate in the service of the Austrian bureaucracy. Soon after his arrival, however, he was attracted to medicine; and seemingly without parental opposition he matriculated in the medical school.

After completing his first year of studies at Vienna, Semmelweis returned to Pest and continued at the local university during the academic years 1839–1841. The backward conditions in the school, however, caused his return to Vienna in 1841 for further studies at the Second Vienna Medical School, which became one of the leading world centers for almost a century with its amalgamation of laboratory and bedside medicine. During the last two years of study, Semmelweis came in close contact with three of the most promising figures of the new school: Karl von Rokitansky, Josef Skoda, and Ferdinand von Hebra.

After voluntarily attending seminars led by these teachers, Semmelweis completed his botanically oriented dissertation early in 1844. He remained in Vienna after graduation, repeating a two-month course in practical midwifery and receiving a master's degree in the subject. He also completed some surgical training and spent almost fifteen months (October 1844–February 1846) with Skoda learning diagnostic and statistical methods. Finally Semmelweis applied for the position of assistant in the First Obstetrical Clinic of the university's teaching institution, the Vienna General Hospital.

In July of 1846 Semmelweis became the titular house officer of the First Clinic, which was then under the direction of Johann Klein. Among his numerous duties were the instruction of medical students, assistance at surgical procedures, and the regular performance of all clinical examinations. One of the most pressing problems facing him was the high maternal and neonatal mortality due to puerperal fever, 13.10 percent. Curiously, however, the Second Obstetrical Clinic in the same hospital exhibited a much lower mortality rate, 2.03 percent. The only difference between them lay in their function. The First was the teaching service for medical students, while the Second had been selected in 1839 for the instruction of midwives. Although everyone was baffled by the contrasting mortality figures, no clear explanation for the differences was forthcoming. The disease was considered to be an inevitable aspect of contemporary hospital-based obstetrics, a product of unknown agents operating in conjunction with elusive atmospheric conditions.

After a temporary demotion to allow the reinstatement of his predecessor, who soon left Vienna for a professorship at Tübingen, Semmelweis resumed his post in March 1847. During his short vacation in Venice, the tragic death of his friend Jakob Kolletschka, professor of forensic medicine, occurred after his finger was accidentally punctured with a knife during a postmortem examination. Interestingly, Kolletschka's own autopsy revealed a pathological situation akin to that of the women who were dying from puerperal fever.

Prepared through his intensive pathological training with Rokitansky, who had placed all cadavers from the gynecology ward at his disposal for dissection, Semmelweis made a crucial association. He promptly connected the idea of cadaveric contamination with puerperal fever, and made a detailed study of the mortality statistics of both obstetrical clinics. He concluded that he and the students carried the infecting particles on their hands from the autopsy room to the patients they examined during labor. This startling hypothesis led Semmelweis to devise a novel system of prophylaxis in May 1847. Realizing that the cadaveric smell emanating from the hands of the dissectors reflected the presence of the incriminated poisonous matter, he instituted the use of a solution of chlorinated lime for washing hands between autopsy work and examination of patients. Despite early protests, especially from the medical students and hospital staff, Semmelweis was able to enforce the new procedure vigorously; and in barely one month the mortality from puerperal fever declined in his clinic from 12.24 percent to 2.38 percent. A subsequent temporary resurgence of the dreaded ailment was traced to contamination with putrid material from a patient suffering from uterine cancer and another with a knee infection.

In spite of the dramatic practical results of his washings, Semmelweis refused to communicate his method officially to the learned circles of Vienna, nor was he eager to explain it on paper. Hence, Hebra finally wrote two articles in his behalf, explaining the etiology of puerperal fever and strongly recommending use of chlorinated lime as a preventive. Although foreign physicians and the leading members of the Viennese school were impressed by Semmelweis' apparent discovery, the papers failed to generate widespread support.

During 1848 Semmelweis gradually widened his prophylaxis to include all instruments coming in contact with patients in labor. His statistically documented success in virtually eliminating puerperal fever from the hospital ward led to efforts by Skoda to create an official commission to investigate the results. The proposal was ultimately rejected by the Ministry of Education, however, a casualty of the political struggle between the defeated liberals of the 1848 movement and the newly empowered conservatives in both the university and the government bureaucracy.

Angered by favorable reports concerning the new methods that indirectly represented an indictment of his own beliefs and actions, Klein refused to reappoint Semmelweis in March 1849. Undaunted, he applied for an unpaid instructorship in midwifery. In the meantime he began to carry out animal experiments to prove his clinical conclusions with the aid of the physiologist Ernst Brücke and a grant from the Vienna Academy of Sciences.

Semmelweis was at last persuaded to present his findings personally to the local medical community. On 15 May 1850 he delivered a lecture to the Association of Physicians in Vienna, meeting under the presidency of Rokitansky. The following October he received the long-awaited appointment as a *Privatdozent* in midwifery, but the routine governmental decree stipulated that he could only teach obstetrics on a mannequin. Faced with financial difficulties in supporting his family, and perhaps discouraged, Semmelweis abruptly left the Austrian capital, returning to Pest without notifying even his closest friends. Such a hasty decision jeopardized forever his chances to overcome the Viennese skeptics gradually with the dedicated help of Rokitansky, Skoda, Hebra, and other colleagues.

In Hungary, Semmelweis found a backward and depressed political and scientific atmosphere following the crushing defeat of the liberals in the revolution of 1848. Despite the unfavorable circumstances, he managed to receive an honorary appointment and took charge of the maternity ward of Pest's St. Rochus Hospital in May 1851, remaining there until 1857. He soon was able to implement his new prophylaxis against puerperal fever, with great success, while building an extensive private practice.

Following the death of the incumbent, Semmelweis was appointed by the Austrian Ministry of Education to the chair of theoretical and practical midwifery at the University of Pest in July 1855, although he had been only the second choice of the local medical faculty. He subsequently devoted his efforts to improving the appalling conditions of the university's lying-in hospital, a difficult task in the face of severe economic restrictions. In 1855 Semmelweis instituted his chlorine hand washings in the clinic, and he gradually achieved good results despite initial carelessness by the hospital staff. His lectures, delivered in Hungarian by decree of the Austrian authorities, attracted large student audiences. Semmelweis also became active in university affairs, serving on committees dealing with medical education, clinical services, and library organization.

In 1861 Semmelweis finally published his momentous discovery in book form. The work was written in German and discussed, at length, the historical circumstances surrounding his discovery of the cause and prevention of puerperal fever. A number of unfavorable foreign reviews of the book prompted Semmelweis to lash out against his critics in a series of open letters written in 1861–1862, which did little to advance his ideas.

After 1863 Semmelweis' increasing bitterness and frustration at the lack of acceptance of his method finally broke his hitherto indomitable spirit. He became alternately apathetic and pathologically enraged about his mission as a savior of mothers. In July 1865 Semmelweis suffered what appeared to be a form of mental illness; and after a journey to Vienna imposed by friends and relatives, he was committed to an asylum, the Niederösterreichische Heil- und Pflegeanstalt. He died there only two weeks later, the victim of a generalized sepsis ironically similar to that of puerperal fever, which had ensued from a surgically infected finger.

Semmelweis' achievement must be considered against the medical milieu of his time. The ontological concept of disease insisted on specific disease entities that could be distinctly correlated both clinically and pathologically. Puerperal fever, however, exhibited multiple and varying anatomical localizations and a baffling symptomatology closely related to the evolution of generalized sepsis. The apparent connection between this fever and erysipelas further clouded the issue. Moreover, the idea of a specific contagion causing the disease was not borne out by the clinical experience.

In the face of such theoretical uncertainties and the profusion of causes attributable to the disease, Semmelweis displayed a brilliant methodology borrowed from his teachers at the Second Vienna Medical School. He partially solved the puzzle through extensive and meticulous dissections of those who had succumbed to the disease, eventu-

ally recognizing the crucial similarities of all septic states. The methodical exclusion of possible etiological factors—one variable at a time—followed Skoda's diagnostic procedure, while the employment of statistical data was transferred from therapeutic analysis to the elucidation of the decisive factor responsible for the disease. In finally arriving at his discovery, Semmelweis successfully seized upon his built-in control group of women at the Second Clinic, a fortunate situation unparalleled elsewhere.

The subsequent lack of recognition for Semmelweis' prophylaxis can be attributed to several factors. An initial lack of proper publicity among Viennese and foreign visiting physicians led to misunderstandings and an incomplete assessment of the intended procedure. Further, political feuds led to an identification of Semmelweis with the liberal and reform-oriented faction of the Viennese medical faculty, a group temporarily thwarted in their objectives by the crushing defeat of 1848. Finally, Semmelweis' abrupt departure from the arena robbed him of the possibility of eventually persuading his Viennese colleagues of the soundness of the chlorine washings. Operating from a politically suppressed and scientifically backward country with a second-rate university, Semmelweis was effectively hampered in the promulgation of his ideas. His later, rather violent and passionate polemics added little further credence to a somewhat cumbersome method that was difficult to implement among hospital staff members content with the status quo. Most important, however, was the lack of a good explanation for Semmelweis' empirically derived procedure, a development made possible only through the ensuing work of Pasteur.

BIBLIOGRAPHY

I. Original Works. Semmelweis' meager writings are listed in *Medical Classics*, **5** (1941), 340–341; and in *Bulletin of the History of Medicine*, **20** (1946), 653–707. His most important work was *Die Aetiologie, der Begriff und die Prophylaxis des Kindbettfiebers* (Pest-Vienna–Leipzig, 1861), reprinted with a new introduction by A. F. Guttmacher (New York–London, 1966). This work was translated into English by F. R. Murphy and appeared as "The Etiology, the Concept and Prophylaxis of Childbed Fever," in *Medical Classics*, **5** (1941), 350–773. However, Semmelweis first published his ideas in 1858 under the title "A gyermekagyi láz koroktana" ("The Etiology of Childbed Fevers") in *Orvosi hétilap* (1858): no. 1, 1–5; no. 2, 17–21; no. 5,

65–69; no. 6, 81–84; no. 21, 321–326; no. 22, 337–342; no. 23, 353–359.

In 1903 the Hungarian Society for the Publication of Medical Works collected and published Semmelweis' works in Hungarian while the Hungarian Academy simultaneously arranged for an edition of the collected writings in German: *Semmelweis gesammelte Werke,* edited and partially translated from the Hungarian by T. von Győry (Jena, 1905). This book contains articles dealing with gynecological subjects originally published in *Orvosi hétilap.* A short letter written by Semmelweis in English and dated at Pest, 21 April 1862, is "On the Origin and Prevention of Puerperal Fever," in *Medical Times and Gazette* (London), **1** (1862), 601–602.

II. Secondary Literature. Bibliographies of works on Semmelweis are Emerson C. Kelly, in *Medical Classics,* **5** (1941), 341–347, and Frank P. Murphy, in *Bulletin of the History of Medicine,* **20** (1946), 653–707.

Among the numerous biographies, the following standard ones are mentioned in chronological order: Alfred Hegar, *Ignaz Philipp Semmelweis. Sein Leben und seine Lehre, zugleich ein Beitrag zur Lehre der fieberhaften Wundkrankheiten* (Freiburg–Tübingen, 1882); Fritz Schürer von Waldheim, *Ignaz Philipp Semmelweis, sein Leben und Wirken* (Vienna–Leipzig, 1905); William J. Sinclair, *Semmelweis, His Life and Doctrines* (Manchester, 1909); and, more recently, the English version of a Hungarian work initially published in 1965; György Gortvay and Imre Zoltán, *Semmelweis—His Life and Work,* translated by E. Róna (Budapest, 1968). Shorter biographical accounts are E. Podach, *Ignaz Philipp Semmelweis* (Berlin–Leipzig, 1947); and Henry E. Sigerist, in *The Great Doctors,* translated by Eden and Cedar Paul (Baltimore, 1933), ch. 41, 338–343.

A great number of articles and monographs concerning aspects of Semmelweis' life (especially the question of his terminal illness) and discovery have been published in Europe, especially in Hungary and Austria. Many of these papers were delivered during the celebrations commemorating the 150th anniversary of Semmelweis' birth in 1968 and appeared in two special numbers of the journal *Communicationes de historia artis medicinae Orvostörténeti közlemények,* nos. 46–47 (1968) and 55–56 (1970). Other articles appeared previously in *Orvosi hétilap,* **106** (1965); *Orszagos orvostörténeti* (Communicationes ex Bibliotheca historiae medicae hungarica), no. 42–43 (1967); and *Zentralblatt für Gynäkologie,* **87** (1965).

Among the main essays printed in both Hungarian and English in *Orvostörténeti közlemények,* no. 55–56 (1970), are I. Zoltán, "Semmelweis," 19–29; G. Regöly-Mérei, "The Pathological Reconstruction of Semmelweis' Disease on the Basis of the Catamnestic Analysis and Paleopathological Examination," 65–92; I. Benedek, "The Illness and Death of Semmelweis," 103–113; and L. Madai, "Semmelweis and Statistical Science," 157–174.

Other valuable contributions concerning Semmelweis' Viennese period are Erna Lesky, "Ignaz Philipp Semmelweis und die Wiener medizinische Schule," in *Sitzungsberichte der Österreichischen Akademie der Wissenschaften,* phil.-hist. Kl., **245** (1964), 3. Abh., 1–93, summarized in "Ignaz Philipp Semmelweis, Legende und Historie," in *Deutsche medizinische Wochenschrift,* **97** (1972), 627–632. The same author also published additional background material in "Wiener Aktenmaterial zur Berufung Semmelweis' im Jahre 1855," in *Orvostörténeti közlemények,* no. 46–47 (1968), 35–54; and *Die Wiener medizinische Schule im 19. Jahrhundert* (Graz–Vienna–Cologne, 1964), 209–220.

Selected recent articles on the subject are S. Fekete, "Die Geburtshilfe zur Zeit Semmelweis," in *Clio Medica,* **5** (1970), 35–44; H. Böttger, "Förderer der Semmelweisschen Lehre," in *Sudhoffs Archiv für Geschichte der Medizin und der Naturwissenschaften,* **39** (1955), 341–362; D. Tutzke, "Die Auswirkungen der Lehre von Semmelweis auf die öffentliche Gesundheitspflege," in *Medizinische Monatsschrift,* **20** (1966), 459–462; and S. D. Elek, "Semmelweis and the Oath of Hippocrates," in *Proceedings of the Royal Society of Medicine,* **59** (1969), 346–352.

Guenter B. Risse

SEMON, RICHARD WOLFGANG (*b.* Berlin, Germany, 22 August 1859; *d.* Munich, Germany, 27 December 1918), *zoology, anatomy.*

Semon's father, Simon Joseph Semon, a banker and stockbroker, and his mother, Henrietta Aschenheim, came from well-to-do Jewish families. His older brother Felix was a leading laryngologist in England, becoming physician in ordinary to King Edward VII and receiving a knighthood.

After reading the works of Charles Darwin and Ernst Haeckel, Semon became interested in biology while still at the Gymnasium. In 1879 he began to study zoology at Jena under Haeckel, whose views on natural philosophy had a lasting influence on Semon. He later stated that Haeckel's school was characterized by "the feeling for the connection of all branches of human knowledge [and] monism as a method of thinking and research." Beginning in 1881, Semon studied medicine at Heidelberg and at the same time prepared under Otto Bütschli's supervision a dissertation on "Das Nervensystem der Holothurien." He obtained the Ph.D. with this work at Jena in 1883, and a year later he passed the state medical examination at Heidelberg.

In 1885 Semon served as physician on an expedition to Africa led by Robert Flegel, but he had to withdraw from the expedition because of malaria. He then worked at the zoology station in Naples (1885–1886) before becoming an assistant at the

Jena anatomical institute in 1886. After receiving his medical degree that same year, Semon qualified as a university lecturer at Jena in 1887 with a work "Die indifferente Anlage der Keimdrüsen beim Hünchen und ihre Differenzierung zum Hoden" ("The Undifferentiated Rudiments of the Genital Glands of the Chick and Their Differentiation Into Testicles"). In 1891 Semon was named extraordinary professor at Jena.

From 1891 to 1893 Semon supervised an expedition to Australia. He published the results with the assistance of a number of co-workers.

In 1897 Semon gave up his teaching activities at Jena for personal reasons and began working as a private scholar in Munich. Two years later he married Maria Krehl (born Geibel), who became widely known for her translations of the works of Auguste-Henri Forel, L. Morgan, and the young Charles Darwin.

Semon based his zoological works on comparative anatomical and embryological studies of echinoderms, snails, fish, and birds. In Australia he was concerned mainly with the habitats, sexual reproduction, and development of the lungfish *Ceratodus forsteri*, as well as with the monotremata. His travel accounts contain remarks on animal geography, paleontology, and geology, as well as ethnographic and anthropological observations, and vivid descriptions of landscapes.

After 1900 Semon devoted himself primarily to an attempt to bring together into a unified concept "all those phenomena in the organic world that involve reproduction of any kind." Out of this attempt emerged his hypothesis of "the mneme as the enduring principle in changes occurring in organic life." Semon used the concept of the mneme (cell memory) to designate a particular property of organic substance, pursuing ideas first put forth in 1870 by Ewald Hering, who saw in memory "a universal function of organic matter." According to Semon, not only can a stimulus influence irritable organic substance temporarily, but it can also effect a persisting, latent change. In this case, the stimulus inscribes itself by means of an engram. These engrams can, he thought, be eliminated by certain influences, or ecphoria. The mneme consists of the sum of the engrams that an organism has individually acquired in the course of its life or that have been produced within it by heredity. In Semon's view, under favorable circumstances the individually acquired adaptations can be passed on to offspring (somatogenic inheritance).

Semon's Lamarckian concepts were rejected by,

among others, August Weismann and Wilhelm Ludwig Johannsen, but were welcomed by Forel and his student Eugen Bleuler (the founder of Mnemismus). According to Jürgen Schatzmann, modern research on memory and on heredity provides partial justification for Semon's ideas, since "in both processes entirely similar chemical structures are involved." Nevertheless, the idea of an identity of the two processes is no more acceptable today than it was when Semon proposed it.

BIBLIOGRAPHY

I. ORIGINAL WORKS. A complete list of Semon's publications can be found in Otto Lubarsch, ed., *Bewustseinsvorgang im Gehirnprozess. Eine Studie von R. Semon* (Wiesbaden, 1920), xlv–xlviii.

Semon's principal works are *Zoologische Forschungsreisen in Australien und dem Malayischen Archipel-Denkschriften der medizinisch naturwissenschaftlichen Gesellschaft Jena*, **4–8** (Jena, 1893–1913)—this contains all Semon's works on the Ceratodus as well as on the monotremata and Marsupialia; *Im australischen Busch und an den Küsten des Korallenmeeres* (Leipzig, 1896); *Die Mneme als erhaltendes Prinzip im Wechsel des organischen Geschehens* (Leipzig, 1904; 3rd ed. 1911); *Das Problem der Vererbung 'erworbener Eigenschaften'* (Leipzig, 1912); and "Aus Haeckels Schule," in H. Schmidt, ed., *Was wir Ernst Haeckel verdanken* (Leipzig, 1914).

Semon's letters for Forel can be found in the archives of the Medizinhistorische Institut of the University of Zurich. Semon's letters to Haeckel are held at the Ernst-Haeckel-Haus of the Friedrich-Schiller-Universität in Jena; Haeckel's letters to Semon are held at the Bavarian State Library in Munich.

II. SECONDARY LITERATURE. See the article by Lubarsch in the book he edited under the title *Bewustseinsvorgang und Gehirnprozess von Richard Semon* (Wiesbaden, 1920). See also Auguste-Henri Forel, "Richard Semons Mneme als erhaltendes Prinzip im Wechsel des organischen Geschehens," in *Archiv für Rassen- und Gesellschaftsbiologie*, **2**, no. 2 (1905), and "Richard Semon," in *Journal für Psychologie und Neurologie*, **25** (1919); O. Lubarsch, "Richard Wolfgang Semon," in *Münchener medizinische Wochenschrift*, **66**, no. 11 (1919); August Weismann, "Semons 'Mneme' und die Vererbung erworbener Eigenschaften," in *Archiv für Rassen- und Gesellschaftsbiologie*, **3**, no. 1 (1906); Georg Uschmann, in *Geschichte der Zoologie und der zoologischen Anstalten in Jena* (Jena, 1959); and Jürgen Schatzmann, "Richard Semon (1859–1918) und seine Mnemetheorie," in *Zürcher medizingeschichtliche Abhandlungen*, n.s. no. 58 (1968).

GEORG USCHMANN

SEMPER, CARL GOTTFRIED (*b*. Altona, Germany, 6 July 1832; *d*. Würzburg, Germany, 29 May 1893), *zoology, ecology*.

Semper's father was a manufacturer; his uncle was the famous architect Gottfried Semper. Carl first studied engineering at Hannover (1851–1854) but eventually chose to become a naturalist and explorer. Thus he studied zoology, histology, and comparative anatomy (particularly of the invertebrates) at the University of Würzburg under Koelliker, Leydig, and Gegenbaur. His thesis (1856) dealt with the anatomy and physiology of the pulmonate snails. From 1857 to 1865 he traveled in Europe and then in the eastern tropics.

Except for a year (1862) on the Palau Islands of Babelthaup and Peleliu, Semper devoted the period from December 1858 to May 1865 to the exploration of the Philippines. During this time, he endured extreme hardship, frequent serious illness (malaria and dysentery), and great danger (hostile natives and travel in unseaworthy boats). Nevertheless, it was a period of outstanding achievement, chiefly because of Semper's dogged determination. He acquired magnificent zoological and ethnographic collections on the islands of Luzon, Bohol, Cebu, Leyte, and Mindanao, thus laying a permanent foundation for future research in the Philippines.

After his return to Germany, Semper was appointed *Privatdozent* (1866) at the University of Würzburg and later full professor of zoology and director of the zoological institute (1869). He was an active teacher with numerous students, but in 1887 a stroke left him a semi-invalid and forced him, in 1893, to retire.

Semper's bibliography of ninety titles reveals his broad interests. In addition to his journal articles, in which he reported his Philippine travels, he published two books on geography and ethnology—one dealing with the Philippines, the other with the Palau Islands. Mollusks were his favored group of animals and more than half of his publications are devoted to this group; but he also published on corals, holothurians, pycnogonids, ascidians, annelids, crustaceans, and sharks. His interests included taxonomy, anatomy, histology, and phylogeny. He was especially interested in evolution, and contributed his share to the construction of phylogenetic trees, basing his investigation in part on the (erroneous) belief that the urogenital system of the sharks could be homologized with that of the annelids. This assumption involved him in a heated controversy with Max Fürbringer and others.

The ten-quarto-volume *Reisen im Archipel der Philippinen*, which contains Semper's scientific reports on his collections, is a monument to his industry and determination. It remains, to this day, an important source book, particularly for the Philippine mollusks.

Probably Semper is best known for his two-volume *Die natürlichen Existenzbedingungen der Thiere*, the first textbook on animal ecology. The work was based on a series of twelve lectures given in 1877 at the Lowell Technological Institute in Boston. In this volume on physiological ecology he discussed the influence of the physical and biotic environment on the structure, distribution, and habits of organisms. Food, light and darkness, temperature, water, water currents, and various aspects of symbiosis, parasitism, and predator-prey relations are treated. Semper's emphasis on the living animal was of decisive importance in an age that placed an exaggerated value on the study of morphology.

BIBLIOGRAPHY

I. ORIGINAL WORKS. Semper's works include vols. I (Holothuria), III (Terrestrial Mollusks), V, and VI (Lepidoptera) of *Reisen im Archipel der Philippinen*, 10 vols. (Wiesbaden, 1868–1905) (for a complete collation of the 100 parts in which this work was issued, see R. I. Johnson, in *Journal of the Society for the Bibliography of Natural History*, **5** [1969], 144–147); and *Die natürlichen Existenzbedingungen der Thiere*, 2 vols. (Leipzig, 1880), with English trans., *Animal Life as Affected by the Natural Conditions of Existence* (London, 1880).

II. SECONDARY LITERATURE. On Semper's life and work, see A. Schuberg, "Carl Semper," in *Reisen . . .* , X (1895), vi–xxi, with complete bibliography.

ERNST MAYR

SEMYONOV-TYAN-SHANSKY, PETR PETROVICH (*b*. near Urusov, Ryazan guberniya, Russia, 14 January 1827; *d*. St. Petersburg, Russia, 11 March 1914), *geography, statistics*.

Semyonov's father, Petr Nikolaevich Semyonov, was a landowner and well-known playwright; his mother, Aleksandra Petrovna Blank, came from a French family that had immigrated to Russia at the end of the seventeenth century. Semyonov was interested in botany and history as a child and was educated at home by private tutors. In 1842 he entered the school for guard cadets at St. Petersburg, from which he graduated with distinction. Three years later he enrolled in the natural sciences section of St. Petersburg University. After graduating in 1848 he was elected a member of the Russian Geographical Society, and by the end of his life he had held honorary memberships in seventy-three Russian and foreign scientific societies and institutions.

In addition to his scientific activity, Semyonov was an expert on Dutch painting and collected 700 pictures and 3,500 prints by Dutch and Flemish masters of the sixteenth and seventeenth centuries; the collection was presented to the Hermitage Museum in 1910. He also published works on seventeenth-century Dutch painting and in 1874 was elected an honorary member of the Academy of Arts in St. Petersburg. His abiding interest in entomology was reflected in his collection of 700,000 specimens, given to the Zoological Museum of the Academy of Sciences.

Semyonov began his geographical research in 1849, when, at the request of the Free Economic Society, he and Nikolai Danilevsky investigated the chernozem zone of European Russia. The botanical material that they collected provided the basis for his master's thesis, defended in 1851, on the flora of the Don basin in relation to the geographical distribution of plants in European Russia. In the same year, at the request of the Russian Geographical Society, he began work on a translation of Karl Ritter's *Die Erdkunde von Asien*, taking into consideration material obtained after 1830. This project stimulated his interest in the then almost unknown Tien Shan. From 1853 to 1855 he lived in Berlin and became acquainted with Ritter.

In preparation for an expedition to Tien Shan, Semyonov attended lectures at Berlin University, studied geography and geology, traveled on foot through the mountainous regions of western Europe and Switzerland, studied volcanic phenomena, and made seventeen ascents of Vesuvius. His acquaintance with Humboldt and study of his scientific work especially influenced his scientific outlook; Humboldt, in turn, enthusiastically encouraged Semyonov to explore Tien Shan.

In 1855 Semyonov returned to Russia, and the following year he published the first volume of his translation of Ritter's *Die Erdkunde von Asien*, devoted to Mongolia, Manchuria, and northern China. Semyonov's extensive additions constituted half the volume, and his edition subsequently acquired the significance of an independent work. In the introduction he emphasized the need for geography to deal with the particulars of nature as they related

to agriculture and discussed the importance of developing a Russian orthography—especially for Chinese place names—and geographical terminology; he himself introduced "upland" (*nagore*), "plateau" (*ploskogore*), "hollow" (*kotlovina*), and "foothills" (*predgore*). In his annotations he corrected Ritter's text and also disputed the author's assertion that the junctions of the Caspian with the Aral and Black seas could have occurred only in prehistoric times. This problem is still unresolved. He also corrected Humboldt and accounted for the Caspian depression "by the gradual drying up of the seas and not by a volcanic collapse, as in the Dead Sea."

In 1856 Semyonov reached Tien Shan. He had traveled through the cities of Ekaterinburg (now Sverdlovsk), Omsk, Barnaul, Semipalatinsk, and the fortress of Verny (now Alma-Ata); and en route he had met the geographers G. N. Potanin and C. C. Valikhanov, and the exiled F. Dostoevsky. From Verny he made two excursions to Lake Issyk Kul and one to Kuldja. In 1857 Semyonov wrote to the Russian Geographical Society: "My second long trip to the Chu River exceeded my expectations. I not only succeeded in crossing the Chu but even in reaching Issyk Kul by this route, that is, by its western extremity, on which no European had yet set foot and which no scientific research of any kind had touched."

In 1857 Semyonov crossed the northern chain of the Terskey Ala-Tau range; discovered the upper reaches of the Naryn River—the main source of the Syr Darya; and climbed along the canyon of the Dzhuuk, having observed the hill and valley topography of the elevated watersheds. He then crossed the Tien Shan to the basin of the Tarim, climbed the Khan Tengri group, and discovered broad glaciers in the upper reaches of the Sazydzhas River. On his return he studied the Trans-Ili Ala-Tau range, Dzungarian Ala-Tau, Lake Alakol, and the Tarbagatai range.

Semyonov's route enabled him to trace the overall configuration of the country and to discover the actual structure of the interior of Asia. He refuted Humboldt's assertion of the volcanic origin of the mountains of central Asia and of the presence of the north-south Bolor (Muztagh Ata) range. His observations provided a basis for refuting Ritter's and Humboldt's assertion that the Chu River arises from Lake Issyk Kul. The river, he discovered, only approaches the lake, which has no outlet and only provisional connections with the Chu along the channel of the Kutemalda. He pointed out the great altitude of the snow line in the mountains of central Asia (from 11,000 to 15,000 feet), convincing Humboldt that "the dryness of the climate elevates the snowline to an unusual extent." He established the existence of extensive glaciation in the Tien Shan, first suggested by Humboldt, and compiled the first orographical scheme of the area. He discussed the tectonics and geological structure, noting the line of east-west elevations and intermontane depressions, in which young sedimentary rock had developed. Semyonov also described the vertical division of the landscape in the mountains of the Trans-Ili Ala-Tau into five zones of vegetation and evaluated their agricultural potential. The vast collection of geological and botanical specimens that he amassed included insects, mollusks, and ethnographical material.

After his return to Russia in 1857 Semyonov became active as a scientific encyclopedist. His thirty-year study of Russian economics and statistics was reflected in publication of the five-volume *Geografichesko-statistichesky slovar* ("Geographical-Statistical Dictionary," 1863–1885), a basic reference work. As head of the Central Statistical Committee from 1864 Semyonov organized important studies and introduced the geographical method into the study of landed property, sowing area, and yields; the material was grouped by districts classified according to their natural and economic features. In 1870 he organized the First All-Russian Statistical Congress. He conducted a classic investigation of the peasant economy in 1880, and the first general census of Russia (1897) was carried out on his initiative. In 1882 Semyonov became a senator, and from 1897 he was a member of the State Council.

In 1860 Semyonov was elected president of the Section of Physical Geography of the Russian Geographical Society, and from 1873 he was vice-president of the Society. He organized many expeditions to central Asia, including those of N. M. Przhevalsky, M. V. Pevtsov, G. N. Potanin, P. K. Kozlov, and V. A. Obruchev, the results of which substantially altered existing ideas about Asia. He actively assisted the expedition of N. N. Miklukho-Maklai and G. Sedov; organized, with Shokalsky, the Kamchatka expedition of the Russian Geographical Society; and assisted scientists in political exile, including Potanin, A. L. Chekanovsky, and I. D. Chersky.

In 1888 Semyonov visited central Asia for the second time, passing through Ashkhabad and Bukhara to Samarkand and Tashkent. He traveled up the valley of the Zeravshan River and climbed the mountains of Turkestan and the Gissar range. His descriptions of the natural history and economy of the area are still of scientific value.

As a popularizer of geographical knowledge, Semyonov wrote and edited many works. He translated and supplemented Ritter's *Die Erdkunde von Asien* with sections on the Altai, Sayan, Baikal, and regions around Lake Baikal. He edited the multivolume *Zhivopisnaya Rossia* ("Scenic Russia") and wrote a three-volume history of the Russian Geographical Society. In 1906, on the fiftieth anniversary of his expedition to Tien Shan, the epithet "Tyan-Shansky" was officially added to the family name.

BIBLIOGRAPHY

I. ORIGINAL WORKS. Semyonov's earlier writings include "Neskolko zametok o granitsakh geologicheskikh formatsy v sredney i yuzhnoy Rossii" ("Some Notes on the Boundaries of Geological Formations in Central and Southern Russia"), in *Geograficheskie izvestiya* (1850), 513–518; *Pridonskaya flora v ee otnosheniakh s geograficheskim raspredeleniem rasteny v Evropeyskoy Rossii* ("Flora of the Don in Relation to the Geographical Distribution of Plants in European Russia"; St. Petersburg, 1851), his master's diss.; "Obozrenie Amura v fiziko-geograficheskom otnoshenii" ("Review of the Amur in Its Physical-Geographical Aspects"), in *Vestnik Russkogo geograficheskogo obshchestva*, no. 15 (1855), 227–255; *Zemlevedenie Azii K. Rittera* (Ritter's *Die Erdkunde von Asien*), translated and supplemented by Semyonov, 5 vols. (St. Petersburg, 1856–1879); "Pervaya poezdka na Tyan-Shan ili Nebesny khrebet do verkhoviev r. Yaksarta ili Syr-Dari v 1857 g." ("First Trip to the Tien Shan or Heavenly Range as Far as the Upper Reaches of the Jaxartes or Syr Darya River in 1857"), in *Vestnik Russkogo geograficheskogo obshchestva*, no. 23 (1858), 7–25; "Zapiska po voprosu ob obmelenii Azovskogo morya" ("Note on . . . the Shallowness of the Sea of Azov"), *ibid.*, no. 30 (1860); and *Geografichesko-statistichesky slovar Rossyskoy imperii* ("Geographical-Statistical Dictionary of the Russian Empire"), 5 vols. (St. Petersburg, 1863–1885).

Subsequent works are "Naselennost Evropeyskoy Rossii v zavisimosti ot prichin, obuslovlivayushchikh raspredelenie naselenia imperii" ("Population of European Russia in Relation to the Conditions That Determine the Distribution of the Population of the Empire"), in *Statistichesky vremennik Rossyskoy imperii*, **2**, no. 1 (1871), 125–156; articles in *Statistika pozemelnoy sobstvennosti i naselennykh mest Evropeyskoy Rossii* ("Statistics on Landed Property and Settled Localities of European Russia"), pts. 1–2, 4–5 (St. Petersburg, 1880–1884); "O vozvrashchenii Amu-Dari v Kaspyskom more" ("On the Return of the Amu Darya Into the

Caspian Sea"), in *Moskovskie vedomosti*, nos. 45–46 (1881); "Oblast kraynego severa Evropeyskoy Rossii v eyo sovremennom ekonomicheskom sostoyanii" (". . . the Extreme North of European Russia in Its Present Economic Condition"), in Semyonov, ed., *Zhivopisnaya Rossia* ("Scenic Russia"), I (St. Petersburg–Moscow, 1881), 313–336; "Ozernaya oblast v eyo sovremennon ekonomicheskom sostoyanii" ("The Lake Region in Its Present Economic Condition"), *ibid.*, 817–834; "Ermitazh i kartinnye gallerei Peterburga" ("The Hermitage and Picture Galleries of St. Petersburg"), *ibid.*, 687–720; "Obshchy obzor ekonomicheskogo sostoyania Finlyandii" ("A General Survey of the Economic Conditions of Finland"), *ibid.*, II (St. Petersburg–Moscow, 1882), 119–128; "Belorusskaya oblast v eyo sovremennom ekonomicheskom sostoyanii" ("The Belorussian Region in Its Present Economic Condition"), *ibid.*, III (St. Petersburg–Moscow, 1882), 473–490; "Zapadnaya Sibir v eyo sovremennom ekonomicheskom sostoyanii" ("Western Siberia in Its Present Economic Condition"), *ibid.*, IX (St. Petersburg–Moscow, 1884), 349–370; and "Nebesny khrebet i Zailysky kray" ("The Heavenly Range and the Trans-Ili Region"), *ibid.*, X (St. Petersburg–Moscow, 1885), 333–376.

Among his later works are *Kratkoe rukovodstvo dlya sobirania zhukov ili zhestkokrylykh (Coleoptera) i babochek ili cheshuekrylykh (Lepidoptera)* ("A Short Guide to Collecting Beetles . . . and Butterflies . . ."; St. Petersburg, 1882; 2nd ed., 1893); "Turkestan i Zakaspysky kray v 1888 godu" ("Turkestan and the Transcaspian Region in 1888"), in *Izvestiya Russkogo geograficheskogo obshchestva*, **24**, no. 4 (1888), 289–347; *Istoria poluvekovoy deyatelnosti Russkogo geograficheskogo obshchestva 1845–1895* ("History of a Half-Century . . . of the Russian Geographical Society . . ."), 3 vols. (St. Petersburg, 1896); "Kharakternye vyvody iz pervoy vseobshchey perepisi" ("Characteristic Conclusions From the First General Census"), in *Izvestiya Russkogo geograficheskogo obshchestva*, **33** (1897), 249–270; "Sibir" ("Siberia"), in Semyonov, ed., *Okrainy Rossii. Sibir, Turkestan, Kavkaz, i polyarnaya chast Evropeyskoy Rossii* ("Outlying Districts of Russia. Siberia, Turkestan, the Caucasus, and the Polar Part of European Russia"; St. Petersburg, 1900); "Rastitelny i zhivotny mir" ("The Plant and Animal World"), II, ch. 3; and "Istoricheskie sudby srednerusskoy chernozemnoy oblasti i kulturnye eyo uspekhi" ("The Historical Fate of the Central Russian Chernozem Regions and Their Cultural Progress"), II, ch. 4, written with V. I. Lamansky, in *Rossia* (St. Petersburg, 1899–1914); and *Memuary* ("Memoirs"), 4 vols. (I, III, IV, Petrograd, 1916–1917; II, Leningrad, 1946–1947).

II. SECONDARY LITERATURE. See L. S. Berg, "Petr Petrovich Semyonov-Tyan-Shansky," in his *Ocherki po istorii russkikh geograficheskikh otkryty* ("Sketches in the History of Russian Geographical Discoveries"; Moscow–Leningrad, 1946), 232–272; and *Vsesoyuznoe geograficheskoe obshchestvo za sto let* ("The All-

Union Geographical Society for the Last Hundred Years"; Moscow–Leningrad, 1946), 57–77; V. I. Chernyavsky, *P. P. Semyonov-Tyan-Shansky i ego trudy po geografii* ("Semyonov . . . and His Work in Geography"; Moscow, 1955), 296; A. A. Dostoevsky, "P. P. Semyonov-Tyan-Shansky kak issledovatel, geograf i statistik" (". . . Semyonov . . . as Researcher, Geographer, and Statistician"), in *Pamyati P. P. Semyonov-Tyan-Shansky* ("Recollections of Semyonov . . ."; Petrograd, 1914), 9–22; G. Y. Grumm-Grzhimaylo, "P. P. Semyonov-Tyan-Shansky kak geograf" (". . . Semyonov . . . as Geographer"), in A. A. Dostoevsky, ed., *Petr Petrovich Semyonov-Tyan-Shansky, ego zhizn i deyatelnost* (". . . Semyonov . . ., His Life and Work"; Leningrad, 1928), 161–165; V. I. Lavrov, "Petr Petrovich Semyonov-Tyan-Shansky," in *Lyudi russkoy nauki* ("People of Russian Science"; Moscow, 1962), 460–468; S. I. Ognev, "P. P. Semyonov-Tyan-Shansky," in *Byulleten Moskovskogo obshchestva ispytateley prirody*, Biol. ser., **51**, no. 3 (1946), 122–137; and Y. K. Efremov, "Petr Petrovich Semyonov-Tyan-Shansky kak fiziko-geograf" (". . . Semyonov . . . as Physical Geographer"), in *Otechestvennye fiziko-geografy* ("Native Physical Geographers"; Moscow, 1959), 284–293.

VERA N. FEDCHINA

SENAC, JEAN-BAPTISTE (*b.* near Lombez, Gascony, France, *ca.* 1693; *d.* Paris, France, 20 December 1770), *anatomy, physiology, medicine, chemistry* (?).

Nothing definite is known either of Senac's family or of his early life; nor is it certain where he received the M.D.—although Montpellier and Reims are possibilities. He was elected to the Académie des Sciences in 1723 as an anatomist and in 1741 was made *associé vétéran*, a sign that he was no longer an active member. He served as a doctor with the army and became personal physician to the Maréchal de Saxe. In 1752 he succeeded François Chicoyneau as chief physician to Louis XV and was appointed a councillor of state.

In 1724 Senac published anonymously *L'anatomie d'Heister*, a detailed account of human anatomy and physiology in which he advocated mechanical rather than chemical explanations of bodily functions. Between 1724 and 1729 he wrote several anatomical memoirs, principally on the respiratory organs; and he established that, contrary to popular belief, little water enters the lungs and stomach of the drowned. After twenty years of research on the structure, action, and diseases of the heart, he published in 1749 his most important work, *Traité de la structure du coeur.* . . . He made important new observations on both healthy and diseased hearts, and the book remained authoritative for many years.

Two anonymous medical books have been attributed to Senac. *Traité . . . de la peste* (1744) includes observations made by Chicoyneau and others during the Marseilles plague of 1720; but a treatise on fevers, *De recondita febrium* (1759), is clearly based on the author's personal experience as a physician.

Senac has also been suspected of writing *Nouveau cours de chymie, suivant les principes de Newton et de Sthall* [sic] (1723), a book consisting partly of extracts from the writings of John Freind. It introduced early Newtonian chemical ideas to French readers—although with little immediate impact—and helped to spread knowledge of the phlogiston theory.

BIBLIOGRAPHY

I. ORIGINAL WORKS. There are four publications by Senac in *Histoire et Mémoires de l'Académie Royale des Sciences*; "Sur les organes de la respiration," in *Mémoires* for 1724 (1726), 159–175; "Sur les noyés," in *Histoire* for 1725 (1727), 12–15; "Sur les mouvements des levres," in *Histoire* for 1727 (1729), 13–15; and "Sur le diaphragme," in *Mémoires* for 1729 (1731), 118–134.

The only book with Senac's name on the title page is *Traité de la structure du coeur, de son action, et de ses maladies*, 2 vols. (Paris, 1749; 2nd ed., corrected and enlarged by Senac, with additions by Antoine Portal, 2 vols., Paris, 1774). Eds. dated 1777 and 1783 have also been recorded.

It is certain that Senac wrote *L'anatomie d'Heister, avec des essais de physique sur l'usage de parties du corps humain, & sur le méchanisme de leurs mouvemens* (Paris, 1724; 2nd ed., 1735; 3rd ed., 1753). When discussing drowning (2nd ed., p. 618), the author cites his own publication in the memoirs of the Académie for 1725, and this can refer only to Senac's "Sur les noyés" (see above). In the preface (2nd ed., pp. xii–xiii) Senac stated that the book was based on lessons that he had given to foreign students recommended to him by Freind; he had used Heister's *Compendium anatomicum* (Altdorf, 1717) as a text, but had added much new material, some of which contradicted Heister.

The *Nouveau cours de chymie suivant les principes de Newton et de Sthall* [sic] was attributed to Senac in the sale catalog of E. F. Geoffroy's library (*Catalogus librorum . . . Stephani-Francisci Geoffroy* [Paris, 1731], 94, item 1363). P. J. Macquer described it as "a work of Senac's youth which he has never acknowledged" (Macquer to T. O. Bergman, 22 February 1768, in G. Carlid and J. Nordström, eds., *Torbern Bergman's Foreign Correspondence*, I [Stockholm, 1965], p. 230). It

may be significant that *Nouveau cours* and *L'anatomie d'Heister* had the same publisher, Jacques Vincent, and appeared about the same time, and also that Senac was evidently in touch with Freind (see above), whose writings were utilized by the author of *Nouveau cours*. But in 1778 Eloy (see below) denied that Senac was the author, as did de la Porte and Renauldin (see below), and the attribution cannot be regarded as certain. There is an Italian trans., *Nuovo corso di chimica secondo i principe di Newton e di Sthall*, only the 2nd ed. of which (Venice, 1750) has been located (Wellcome Institute of the History of Medicine Library, London); the censorship license is dated 29 September 1737 and the date of registration is 9 April 1738 (p. 483), so the 1st ed. probably appeared in 1738.

According to Eloy, Senac wrote the anonymous *Traité des causes, des accidens, et de la cure de la peste . . .* (Paris, 1744). He also attributed to Senac *De recondita febrium intermittentium, tum remittentium natura, et de earum curatione . . .* (Amsterdam, 1759; enl. ed., Geneva, 1769); the Amsterdam ed. was translated into English, with a few notes, by Charles Caldwell: *A Treatise on the Hidden Nature, and the Treatment of Intermitting and Remitting Fevers . . . by Jean Senac* (Philadelphia, 1805).

II. SECONDARY LITERATURE. A short account of Senac is in N. F. J. Eloy, *Dictionnaire historique de la médecine, ancienne et moderne*, IV (Mons, 1778), 245–247; further information is given by H. de la Porte and L. J. Renauldin in Michaud's *Biographie universelle*, XLII (Paris, 1825), 1–2, and by G. Degris, *Étude sur Senac, premier médecin de Louis XV* (Paris, 1901).

Senac's work on the heart and its diseases is placed in its historical context by D. Guthrie, "The Evolution of Cardiology," in E. A. Underwood, ed., *Science, Medicine and History, Essays in Honour of Charles Singer*, II (London, 1953), 508–517, esp. 511; and by J. O. Leibowitz, *The History of Coronary Heart Disease* (London, 1970), 75–76. The contents of the *Nouveau cours de chymie . . .* are discussed by J. R. Partington, *History of Chemistry*, III (London, 1962), 58–59; and its importance in the development of Newtonian chemistry is assessed by A. Thackray, *Atoms and Powers* (Cambridge, Mass., 1970), 94–95.

W. A. SMEATON

SÉNARMONT, HENRI HUREAU DE (*b.* Broué, Eure-et-Loire, France, 6 September 1808; *d.* Paris, France, 30 June 1862), *crystallography, mineralogy.*

At Sénarmont's request, no obituaries appeared after his death; thus little is known of his private life. He was the son of Amédée Hureau Sénarmont, a landowner in Badonville in the commune of Broué, and Amélie Rey. After attending the Collège Rollin and the Collège Charlemagne in Paris, he entered the École Polytechnique in 1826.

Three years later he joined the state mining administration as *élève-ingénieur*. In this capacity he visited (1831) the arsenal in Toulouse and was assigned to the steel mills in Rive-de-Gier and Le Creusot. In 1833 he worked temporarily with the engineer Conte, who was carrying out special assignments in the Autun basin. In 1835 he became a mining engineer, second class.

Sénarmont's work brought him to Nantes and Angers in 1835–1836. In the summer of the latter year he was assigned to prepare geological maps of Aube and Seine-et-Oise. (Seine-et-Marne was added in 1837, and the map of Aube was canceled in 1839.) In 1843 he published *Sur la géologie des départements de Seine-et-Oise et Seine-et-Marne*, which appeared in two sections the following year.

From 1840 to 1847 Sénarmont was engaged in inspecting steam engines in the Seine department. He was promoted to mining engineer, first class, in 1841 and then, in 1848, to assistant chief engineer. In 1847 he was made an examiner at the École Polytechnique; but in the same year he was transferred to the École des Mines, where he received the chair of mineralogy. In 1849 Sénarmont joined the editorial staff of the *Annales des mines*. Later he was named dean of students, librarian, and secretary of the council at the École des Mines. In 1852, following the death of Beudant, Sénarmont became a member of the mineralogy section of the Académie des Sciences; he served as vice-president in 1858 and as president in 1859. In 1854 he became an editor of the *Annales de chimie et de physique* and held this post until his death. He also received the chair of physics at the École Polytechnique (1856–1862).

Sénarmont's enthusiasm for crystallography was first awakened by Fresnel. His importance is based on his demonstration of the directional dependency of the physical properties of crystals and on his experiments on the synthesis of minerals under conditions corresponding to those in nature. In his first paper, "Mémoire sur les modifications que la réflexion spéculaire à la surface des corps métalliques imprime à un rayon de lumière polarisée" (1840), Sénarmont introduced, for the purpose of measuring phase differences, a thin layer of mica known as the 1/4 λ plate. In "Mémoire sur la réflexion et la double réfraction de la lumière par les cristaux doués de l'opacité métallique" (1847), he discussed perpendicular incidence on calcite and stated (1) that a rotation of the plane of polarization can be observed and (2) that an analogous rotation of the plane of polarization occurs for re-

flected light on stibnite (antimony sulfide) and is evidence of double refraction. The difficulty of the problems that Sénarmont investigated is evident when one considers that it was only in 1887 that Drude attempted to determine quantitatively the optical properties of stibnite, and not until 1931 that problems of quantitative ore microscopy were clarified by Max Berek.

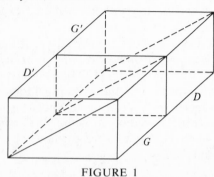

FIGURE 1

In 1850 Sénarmont described his polariscope (Figure 1), a plate composed of four quartz prisms with its upper and lower faces normal to the optic axis (*D* and *D'* are optically rotatory clockwise and *G* and *G'* counterclockwise):

> If this parallel-sided plate is set at right angles to a beam of polarized, parallel light—that is to say, in such a way that the light is traveling along the optic axis—the plate will be seen to be covered with straight fringes parallel to the refracting edges of the prisms. If the principal section of the analyzer is the same as the initial plane of polarization, the dark central fringe will be situated in the middle of the plate, where the thickness of each of the crossed prisms is the same; hence it will form a straight line along the front and back halves of the plate.[1]

Sénarmont made important contributions to isomorphism in "Recherches sur les propriétés optiques biréfringentes des corps isomorphes" (1851). Besides an exact description of his procedures, he furnished a considerable amount of crystallographic data and described many isomorphic compounds. To determine the character of the axes of optical elasticity, he utilized quartz plates and wedges: "The thickness is always that which is required to produce colors by compensation if the slightly prismatic laminae recommended by M. Biot are employed; and the axis of the plate parallel to the optical axis of the quartz will always be the one of greatest optical elasticity."[2]

In his "Recherches" Sénarmont also provided a method for measuring the binormal angle (optic

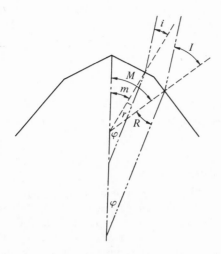

FIGURE 2

axial angle) in convergently polarized light (Figure 2). If $m = r + \varphi = i + \theta$ and $M = R + \varphi = I + \Theta$, it follows that

$$\sin(m - \theta) = l \sin(m - \varphi), \sin(M - \Theta) = l \sin(M - \varphi);$$

$$\tan\left(\frac{M+m}{2} - \varphi\right) = \tan\left(\frac{M-m}{2}\right) \frac{\left[\frac{M+m}{2} - (\theta + \Theta)\right]}{\left[\frac{M-m}{2} + (\theta - \Theta)\right]}.$$

Here, i and I are the corresponding angles of emergence, θ and Θ the apparent half-angles of the optic axes after this emergence, and l the index of refraction. Thus Sénarmont was able to determine the binormal angle of K_2SO_4 without knowing the index of refraction. In this work he also described the dispersion of the optic axes and the shift of the plane of these axes toward red in crystalline solid solutions of potassium Rochelle salt and ammonium Rochelle salt.

In "Recherches sur la double réfraction" (1856), Sénarmont provided a thorough account of all of the phenomena related to parallel and convergent polarized light beams. He also observed carefully the boundary cones of rays in total reflection. In "Sur la réflexion totale de la lumière extérieurement à la surface des cristaux biréfringents" (1856), he developed the formulas for conic sections in optically uniaxial crystals and in certain optically biaxial crystals. Virtually the only fluid refractive medium available to him was carbon disulfide. In "Note sur quelques formules propres à la détermination des trois indices principaux dans les cri-

staux biréfringents" (1857), he applied the method of minimal diffraction to prisms of doubly refractive crystals in order to determine the principal indexes of refraction.

In "Mémoires sur la conductibilité des substances cristallisées pour la chaleur" (1847), Sénarmont demonstrated that thermal conductivity is dependent on crystal symmetry. He bored through the middle of thin crystal plates, waxed them, and through the hole placed a silver tube, which he heated. The swelling of the wax indicated an isothermal corresponding to the melting temperature of the wax. On all the slices of isometric crystals and on all the basal slices of tetragonal and hexagonal crystals, the isotherms were circular; in all other cases they were elliptical. From these patterns of swelling in the wax he recognized the optically positive nature of quartz. In 1848 he showed that, when subjected to unilateral pressure, melting isotropic bodies (like glass) yield isotherms that resemble those that are characteristic of anisotropic materials.

Analogously, Sénarmont established the directional dependence of surface conductivity in crystals in "Mémoire sur la conductibilité superficielle des corps cristallisées pour l'électricité de tension" (1850). He discovered this dependence by wrapping a crystal in tinfoil (which had been grounded) and by placing a metal point on the crystal surface at a point where a circular piece of the tinfoil had been cut out; the point was then connected to the positive conductor of an electrostatic machine, and the whole apparatus was placed under the glass bell of an air pump. At reduced pressure he was able to observe, in the dark, circular or elliptical figures of light, depending on the nature of the crystal. He stated that: "The continuous and silent flux of the electricity of the rarefied air does not, it is true, leave permanent traces; but it does manifest itself in the darkness by a faint light that persists throughout the whole experiment and that makes all its details visible. . . ."[3]

In "Expériences sur la production artificielle de polychromisme dans les substances cristallisées" (1851), Sénarmont was the first to describe the production of artificial pleochromism in strontium nitrate pentahydrate, which had been prepared by saturating the substance with ammoniacal logwood extract and other organic dyestuffs. He also reported on less successful experiments involving rock candy (sugar), Rochelle salt, potassium nitrate, and sodium nitrate.

The syntheses that Sénarmont carried out in the

years 1849–1851 are recounted in "Expériences sur la formation des minéraux par la voie humide dans les gîtes métallifères concrétionnées" (1851) and are an essential contribution to the understanding of mineral formation. Since CO_2, H_2S, alkali salts, sulfides, and carbonates predominate in thermal springs, he assumed that the formation of ore veins from these components would necessarily occur at elevated temperatures and pressures. Thus he placed those components that he wished to have interact in sealed glass tubes, which were inserted into a sealed pipe filled with water. The apparatus was then embedded in coal dust and heated in the gas ovens of the steel mills at Ivry-sur-Seine. Through either double decomposition of a soluble salt with Na_2CO_3 or $CaCO_3$, or precipitation of a soluble salt using alkali carbonate in a supersaturated CO_2 solution, Sénarmont produced magnesite, siderite, rhodochrosite, cobalt carbonate, nickel carbonate, smithsonite, and malachite, as well as barite, fluorite, and quartz in crystalline form.

Sénarmont also synthesized pure silver, copper, arsenic, and hematite. From metallic salts and alkali sulfides he obtained mostly amorphous sulfides—including marcasite, pyrite, manganese sulfide, hauerite, NiS, CO_3S_4, sphalerite, galena, and chalcopyrite; and he obtained realgar, orpiment, stibnite, bismuthinite, arsenopyrite, proustite, and pyrargyrite in crystalline form. He was similarly successful in crystallizing PbS and ZnS in a supersaturated H_2S solution and in obtaining pyrite and chalcopyrite in the form of a granulated powder with metallic luster. If he wished to avoid an immediate reaction, he inserted into the glass tube a thin ampul containing a salt and a gas bubble. When heat was applied the gas bubble burst the ampul. Altogether Sénarmont succeeded in synthesizing twenty-nine vein minerals from the alkali sulfides and carbonates commonly found in thermal springs with metallic salts. In these syntheses the temperature rarely exceeded 350° C. He gave an exact crystallographic description of all the compounds he was able to crystallize. In addition, he described the effect of the solutions employed on the glass tubes, the flaking off of pieces of glass from the tubes, and the danger of explosion involved in the use of sealed tubes (bombs).

In 1851 Sénarmont described for the first time both rhombic antimony bloom (valentinite) from Sensa in Algeria and natural isometric antimony oxide from Minina (near Sensa), thus confirming the dimorphism of Sb_2O_3. Dana gave the name senarmontite to the isometric form of Sb_2O_3.

Sénarmont also demonstrated that common silicon carbide belongs to the isometric system (1856).

NOTES

1. *Annales de chimie et de physique*, 3rd ser., **28** (1850), 281.
2. *Ibid.*, **33** (1851), 401.
3. *Ibid.*, **28** (1850), 261.

BIBLIOGRAPHY

I. ORIGINAL WORKS. For many of Sénarmont's important papers written between 1840 and 1851, see *Annales de chimie et de physique*, 2nd and 3rd ser. The Royal Society *Catalogue of Scientific Papers*, V (1871), 641–643, lists thirty-eight titles by Sénarmont. Poggendorff, curiously, omits most of the papers that appeared in German journals, as well as "Extraits de minéralogie," which appeared in *Annales des mines*, 5th ser., **6–19** (1854–1861). Sénarmont's personal instructions from and reports to the French mining administration are recorded in *Annales des mines*, 3rd ser. (1833–1841) and 4th ser. (1842–1851).

II. SECONDARY LITERATURE. See J. L. F. Bertrand, "Éloge de Sénarmont, lu à la Société des amis des sciences, 16 avril 1863," in *Société de secours des amis des sciences* (1863), 27–56; Walter Fischer, *Gesteins- und Lagersstättenbildung im Wandel der wissenschaftlichen Anachauung* (Stuttgart, 1961); E. Hoppe, *Geschichte der Physik* (Brunswick, 1926); F. von Kobell, *Geschichte der Mineralogie 1650–1860* (Munich, 1864); T. Liebisch, *Physikalische Kristallographie* (Leipzig, 1891); Joseph Michaud, ed., *Biographie universelle ancienne et moderne*, XXXIX (1969), 56; F. Pockels, *Lehrbuch der Kristalloptik* (Leipzig–Berlin, 1906); and *Nouvelle biographie générale*, XLIII (Paris, 1864).

WALTER FISCHER

SENDIVOGIUS (SĘDZIMIR or SĘDZIWÓJ), MICHAEL (*b.* Skorsko or Łukawica, Poland, 2 February 1566; *d.* Cravar, Silesia, June [?] 1636), *alchemy.*

Sendivogius' parents, Jacob Sędzimir and Catherine Pielsz Rogowska, were both of noble families and had a small estate near Nowy Sącz, in the Cracow district. After studying in Italy, Sendivogius entered the University of Leipzig in 1590, moving a year later to the University of Vienna. In 1593 he entered the service of Emperor Rudolf II in Prague as a courier, and in 1594 he also became courier and later secretary to the Polish king Sigismund III; this dual service was made possible by the close friendship of the two rulers and their common enmity to Turkey. Also in 1594 Sendivogius married Veronica Stieber, a wealthy widow. He soon came to Rudolf's attention and participated in his alchemical experiments, becoming his favorite and trusted friend. In Cracow and Prague, and on his many official missions, Sendivogius met prominent political figures and scientists; his friends included the alchemists Joachim Tancke, Oswald Croll, J. Orthel, J. Kapr von Kaprstein, V. Lavinius, R. Egli, Martin Ruland, and Michael Maier.

Sendivogius' name appears in the rolls of the University of Altdorf for 1595 — probably as an imperial official, rather than as a student. As mentioned by his biographer Carolides a Carlsperga (1598), he may also have visited the universities of Rostock, Ingolstadt, and Cambridge. In 1597 Sendivogius bought the Fumberg estate, near Prague, from the widow of the English alchemist Edward Kelley. Around this time, and under the influence of the Polish master of heraldry Bartłomiej Paprocki, he changed his family name to the nobler-sounding Sędziwój (latinized as Sendivogius) and began to sign his name Michael Sendivogius Liberbaro de Skorsko et Łukawica. In 1599 he was accused before the municipal court of Prague of being responsible for the death of a friend and fellow alchemist, a rich Bohemian merchant named Louis Koralek, and was sentenced to prison. He was released as a result of the diplomatic intervention of Sigismund III.

At this time Sendivogius' wife and two of their four children died. Offended by the noninterference of Rudolf in the Koralek affair and by his failure to defend him before the arrest, Sendivogius sold his estate at Fumberg and, with his surviving children, Veronica and Christopher, returned to Poland. In 1602 he was recalled to Prague and was appointed imperial privy councillor. In 1605, while on a diplomatic mission to France, Sendivogius was lured to the court of Duke Frederick of Württemberg at Stuttgart. Having claimed in *De lapide philosophorum* (1604) to be the "true possessor" of the "mystery of the philosophical stone," he was soon imprisoned. Sigismund III, Rudolf II, and several German princes intervened on his behalf; alarmed by this, Frederick arranged for Sendivogius to escape and laid the blame on his court alchemist, Heinrich Mühlenfells. Put to torture, Mühlenfells pleaded guilty and was condemned to the gallows.

In 1607 Sendivogius visited Cologne, where he published *Dialogus mercurii . . .*, a kind of satire on alchemy. On his return to Poland he became courtier to Queen Constantia, the second wife of Sigismund III. With crown marshall Mikołaj Wolski he established many smithies and iron and brass foundries in Krzepice, which later became a leading industrial center. His collaboration with Wolski was undoubtedly lucrative, for Sendivogius soon became the owner of several houses in Cracow. In 1615–1616 he visited Johannes Hartmann's laboratory in Marburg. Around 1619 Sendivogius transferred his allegiance to Emperor Ferdinand II, for whom he established lead foundries in Silesia. In 1626 he was appointed privy councillor and in 1631, as compensation for long-unpaid salaries, he received the estates of Cravar and Kounty in Crnow county, Moravia. In ruinous condition following the Thirty Years War, the estates proved to be the source of great expense.

Mysterious and intriguing, Sendivogius was undoubtedly a political double agent. His adventures with the Scottish alchemist Alexander Seton in Saxony seem to be a literary fiction, created years after his death; there is no mention of them in the materials of the Landesarchiv in Dresden. Sendivogius was considered by contemporary and succeeding generations of alchemists to be the true possessor of the "great mystery" and a member of the Rosicrucians. He was greatly admired and was frequently cited in seventeenth- and eighteenth-century alchemical treatises.

His alchemical writings had no influence on the development of chemistry, but his treatise *De lapide philosophorum* is of great value for the history of science. Besides recipes for the philosophers' stone, it contains interesting notes concerning the components of air. Sendivogius believed that the air contained a hidden life-giving and fire-supporting agent, the "invisible niter" or "philosophical saltpeter" — the food of life without which nothing could live or grow. This "invisible niter" was born in the rays of the sun and moon, from which it flowed down to the earth in rain or dew. During rainstorms the "niter" passed from the air into the earth, combining with its constituents to form "saltpeter." This process, Sendivogius maintained, occurred continuously and in plain view, although no one noticed or understood it. This argument contains the first idea of the existence of oxygen.

An exponent of the then fashionable Hermetic philosophy, Sendivogius was greatly influenced by Paracelsus and Alexander von Suchten. The *ignis naturae* or *balsamum vitae* of Paracelsus and the *spiritus vitae* of Suchten were redefined by Sendivogius as "philosophical niter" — with the important added explanation of its role in nature. His views on the fire-supporting and life-giving "saltpeter" apparently were derived from the current belief that fires in the salt mines at Wieliczka, near Cracow, were caused by the abundance of saltpeter in the air.

Several seventeenth-century alchemists, including Bathurst and Mayow, investigated Sendivogius' recipes for the philosophers' stone and as a first step searched for the "philosophical niter" in the air.

BIBLIOGRAPHY

I. ORIGINAL WORKS. Sendivogius' main writings are *De lapide philosophorum tractatus duodecim e naturae fonte et manuali experientia depromti* (n.p., 1604), since Jean Beguin's ed. (Paris, 1608) also known as *Cosmopolitani novum lumen chymicum; Dialogus mercurii, alchimistae et naturae* (Cologne, 1607); and *Tractatus de sulphure altero naturae principio* (Cologne, 1616). All three treatises are known in over eighty eds. and have been translated into German, English, French, Russian, and Polish. Sendivogius' *Processus super centrum universi seu sal centrale* was edited by Johann Becher in his *Chymischer Glückshafen* (Frankfurt, 1682), 231–240.

The fifty-five letters allegedly by Sendivogius, first published by J. Manget in *Bibliotheca chemica curiosa,* II (Geneva, 1702), 493 ff. and also published in German, were written in the second half of the seventeenth century, long after his death.

Bibliographies of Sendivogius' works are in the following (listed chronologically); John Ferguson, *Bibliotheca chemica,* II (Glasgow, 1906), 364–370; C. Zibrt, *Bibliographie česke historia,* III (Prague, 1906), 523–526; K. Estreicher, *Bibliografia polska,* XXVII (Cracow, 1929), 332–342; and R. Bugaj, *Michał Sędziwój* (Wrocław–Warsaw–Cracow, 1968), 280–304.

II. SECONDARY LITERATURE. Early biographies of Sendivogius include Georgius Carolides a Carlsperga, *Praecepta institutionis* (Prague, 1598); Bartłomiej Paprocki, *Jina czastka, nove kratochwile* (Prague, 1598); and J. Chorinus, *Illustris foeminae D. Dn. Veronicae Stiberiae* (Prague, 1604). Later biographies (listed chronologically) are P. N. Lenglet Dufresnoy, *Histoire de la philosophie hermétique,* I (The Hague, 1742), 332–333; A. Batowski, "List Poliarka Micigna," in *Rozmaitości–Gazeta Lwowska,* 19 (1858), 153–156; W. Szymanowski, "Michał Sędziwój," in *Tygodnik ilustrowany,* 5 (1862), 181–218; M. Wiszniewski, *Bakona metoda tłumaczenia natury* (Warsaw, 1876), 130–136; J. Brincken, "O życiu i pismach Michała Sędziwoja," in *Biblioteka Warszawska,* 2 (1846), 479–506; J. Svatek, *Culturhistorische Bilder aus Böhmen* (Vienna, 1879), 78–84; J. Read, *Humour and Humanism in Chemistry* (London, 1947), 52–65; and R. Bugaj, *W poszukiwaniu kamienia filozoficznego* (Warsaw, 1957). These works,

however, have little value in terms of history or the history of science.

Archival materials concerning the life of Sendivogius are presented in the following (cited chronologically): B. Peška, "Praski meštan a polsky alchymista," in *Svêtozor,* VI (1872), 471–495; C. R. Elvert, "Der Alchemist Sendivogius," in *Notizenblatt der k. und k. Mährisch-schlesischen Gesellschaft zur Beförderung des Ackerbaues,* Hist.-stat. Kl., 12 (1883), 20–22; J. Zukal, "Alchymista Michael Sendivoj," *Vestnik matice opavske,* 3 (1909), no. 17; O. Zachar, *Z dejin alchymie v zemich ceskych* (Kladno, 1910); W. Hubicki, "Michael Sendivogius's Theory, Its Origin and Significance in the History of Chemistry," in *Proceedings of the Tenth International Congress on the History of Science, Ithaca, 1962* (Paris, 1964), II, 829–833; "The True Life of Michael Sendivogius," in *Actes du XI Congrès international d'histoire des sciences,* IV (Warsaw, 1965), 31–35; and "Zapomniana teoria," in *Problemy,* 22 (1966), 98–103; and *Ossolineum PAN,* IV (Wrocław–Warsaw–Cracow, 1968), 41–45.

WŁODZIMIERZ HUBICKI

SENEBIER, JEAN (*b.* Geneva, Switzerland, 6 May 1742; *d.* Geneva, 22 July 1809), *physiology.*

Although Senebier, the son of Jean-Antoine Senebier, a merchant, and Marie Tessier, was interested in natural history, his family intended him to be a minister. After having presented a distinguished thesis on polygamy, he was ordained pastor of the Protestant church of Geneva in 1765. He then spent a year in Paris, where he became acquainted with more people in the scientific and theatrical worlds than in the church. In 1770 he published *Contes moraux* and became friends with Abraham Trembley, who influenced the young Protestant minister profoundly.

Charles Bonnet encouraged Senebier to work in the natural sciences and enabled him to perform his first experiments in plant physiology. Following Bonnet's advice, in 1768 Senebier answered a question on the art of observing posed by the Netherlands Society of Sciences at Haarlem. It received an honorable mention and was published in 1772. He became pastor of Chancy, near Geneva, in 1769 but four years later resigned his post to become librarian for the Republic of Geneva. In 1777 Senebier published the first volume of Spallanzani's *Opuscules de physique animale et végétale,* thereby introducing French readers to his work. He later translated most of the works of Spallanzani, with whom he maintained close contact. In 1779 Senebier began to publish his *Action de la lumière sur la végétation,* the study of photosynthesis that established his reputation as a physiologist. The first edition of this voluminous *Traité de physiologie végétale* appeared in 1800.

Senebier became the center of a group of young life scientists, and he taught them all: Pierre Huber (1777–1840); A.-P. de Candolle; Jean-Antoine Colladon (1758–1830), the pharmacist whom many consider to be one of Mendel's precursors; and N. T. de Saussure, who started photochemistry. He was particularly close to François Huber (1750–1831), with whom he conducted experiments on bees and published *Influence de l'air . . . dans la germination* (1801).

Two of Senebier's publications can still repay attention today: his research on photosynthesis and his works on the experimental method, which he defined with precision fifty years before Claude Bernard.

In several works, but especially in *Expériences sur l'action de la lumière solaire dans la végétation* (1788), Senebier paid particular attention to the gas exchanges of green plants exposed to light. He was the first to observe that in sunlight such plants absorb carbonic acid gas and emit oxygen while manufacturing a substance with a carbon base.

As an extension of his communication on the "art of observing" of 1769, Senebier published the two-volume *Art d'observer* in 1775. The three-volume *Essai sur l'art d'observer et de faire des expériences* (1802) sums up the fundamental theses of the experimental method. This work is impressive for the closeness of Senebier's thought to that of Claude Bernard and for the degree to which the ideas expressed in Bernard's *Introduction à l'étude de la médecine expérimentale* were formulated in the work of Senebier.

BIBLIOGRAPHY

I. ORIGINAL WORKS. Senebier's works include *Art d'observer* (Geneva, 1775); *Expériences sur l'action de la lumière solaire dans la végétation* (Geneva, 1788); *Physiologie végétale*, 5 vols. (Geneva, 1800); and *Essai sur l'art d'observer et de faire des expériences* (Geneva, 1802).

II. SECONDARY LITERATURE. See J. Briquet, "Bibliographie des botanistes à Genève," in *Bulletin de la Société botanique suisse,* **50** (1940), 433; J. P. Maunoir, *Éloge historique de M. Jean Senebier* (Geneva, 1810); P. E. Pilet, "Jean Senebier, un des précurseurs de Claude Bernard," in *Archives internationales d'histoire des sciences,* **15** (1962), 303–313; P. Revilliod, *Physiciens et naturalistes genevois* (Geneva, 1942), 48.

P. E. PILET

SENECA, LUCIUS ANNAEUS (*b.* Córdoba, Spain, *ca.* 4 B.C.–A.D. 1; *d.* near Rome, April A.D. 65), *physical science.*

Seneca came from a distinguished provincial family of Italian origin; his father, for whom he was named, wrote on history and rhetoric. The younger Seneca was educated at Rome and then for a time devoted himself to philosophy, particularly to the teaching of the eclectic Sextians and the Stoics. Ethics was his main concern; but his interests extended to physics, for in his youth he produced a book, now lost, on earthquakes. In accordance with his father's wishes he entered politics, beginning his senatorial career soon after A.D. 31 with the post of quaestor. During the next ten years he became established as one of Rome's leading orators and writers and won influential friends within the imperial family. In A.D. 41 he was implicated in a court intrigue and banished to Corsica, a grave setback to his career; but eight years later his fortunes were restored when Agrippina, wife of the Emperor Claudius, recalled him and appointed him tutor to her son Nero. In A.D. 54 Nero, then aged sixteen, became emperor; and for the next eight years he governed with the assistance of Seneca and Sextus Afranius Burrus, the commander of the Praetorian Guard. Toward the end of this period of generally sound government Nero turned to different, less scrupulous advisers, so that when Burrus died in A.D. 62, Seneca withdrew from the court, his influence with Nero at an end. Three years later he was accused of involvement in the abortive Pisonian conspiracy against Nero. The evidence against him was weak, but Nero ordered him to commit suicide.

Writing and philosophy occupied Seneca's leisure throughout his life. The tragedies and ethical works have always been his best-known writings, but also extant is one of his scientific books, *Naturales quaestiones,* written around A.D. 62. It is typical of Roman scientific writing, a popularizing work largely derived from Greek sources. Seneca shows the eclectic's independence in choosing between rival theories, but he has no original ideas to contribute. He writes of the need for further careful investigation of natural phenomena but did not conduct any fresh research, although casual observation did provide him with some valuable new information.

The extant part of the *Naturales quaestiones,* which has survived incomplete, deals with meteorological phenomena, rivers, earthquakes, meteors, and comets, topics that all belonged to "meteorology" in the ancient sense. Apart from Aristotle's

Meteorologica it is the longest extant ancient work on the subject; hence it is the main source for the history of Greek meteorology after Aristotle, since it draws heavily on Greek sources and mentions the theories of many individuals whose works are lost. Admittedly Seneca had little interest in the historical development of the subject; knowing few of his predecessors' works at first hand, he sometimes misunderstood or oversimplified their ideas and did not always sharply distinguish his own interpretations and comments. Furthermore, his characteristically terse and brilliant prose lacked the clarity and precision of expression needed for scientific writing. Yet despite these limitations the work greatly enlarges our knowledge of Greek meteorology after Aristotle.

The *Naturales quaestiones* owes more to the meteorological works of Posidonius than to any other single source, although the loss of these works prevents the extent of the debt from being known in detail. Posidonius had followed Aristotle closely, although he placed Aristotelian theories in the context of his own world system, a modification of the Stoic one. The main features of Seneca's world view were probably Posidonian. He thought that the stars and planets are nourished by vapors given off from the earth. An innate energy possessed by air, and the Aristotelian exhalations, account for most events in the atmosphere. (Aristotle had attributed most meteorological phenomena to the activity of moist and dry "exhalations" emitted from the earth's surface, roughly equivalent to water vapor and radiated heat.) To explain earthquakes and rivers, Seneca assumed that the earth is like a living creature, permeated by channels for water and air analogous to veins and arteries. But he disagreed with Posidonius and Aristotle about the nature of comets, effectively criticizing their theory that these are a variety of meteor and using his own observations of the comets that appeared in A.D. 54 and 60 to support the view that they are heavenly bodies like planets, with regular orbits. Based on good evidence and well argued, this part of the *Naturales quaestiones* is in sharp contrast with the rest, which, like most Greek meteorology, abounds in untested speculation and analogy.

Certain broader issues also interested Seneca. As a Stoic he rejected Epicurean physics, particularly the atomic theory of matter, and the denial that the world was created and ordered by a rational God. Like most Stoics he accepted the principles of astrology and divination, and attempted to answer some of the skeptical arguments against

them. The problem of relating science to moral life was of especial importance to him, for almost a third of the *Naturales quaestiones* is about ethical and theological subjects: Seneca thought that through the rational investigation of the universe, men may learn what their attitude toward the material world should be and may reach a true awareness of God's nature, free from all superstition.

After the immediate popularity enjoyed by all Seneca's writings, the scientific works were little read in the ancient world and never became established textbooks. The *Naturales quaestiones* survived the Middle Ages, contributing to the rediscovery of ancient science in Western Europe during the twelfth century, and was still read as a scientific work during the Renaissance. Today it gives an instructive picture of the state of Roman science in the first century A.D., and of the history of Greek meteorology, has considerable literary interest, and illuminates our knowledge of Seneca himself.

BIBLIOGRAPHY

I. Original Works. Modern eds. of the *Naturales quaestiones* are by A. Gercke (Leipzig 1907; repr. Stuttgart, 1970); P. Oltramare, with French trans. and notes (Paris, 1929; repr. 1961); and T. H. Corcoran, with English trans., 2 vols. (London–Cambridge, Mass., 1971–1972). For recent eds. of other works, see Motto's bibliography (cited below).

II. Secondary Literature. Bibliographies are by W. Schaub, of works since 1900 relating to the *Naturales quaestiones*, in the 1970 repr. of Gercke's ed., pp. xlvii–lxi; and by A. L. Motto, of works on all of Seneca's prose since 1940, in *Classical World*, **54** (1960–1961), 13–18, 37–48, 70–71, 111–112; **64** (1970–1971), 141–158, 177–186, 191. A few of the works are O. Gilbert, *Die meteorologischen Theorien des griechischen Altertums* (Leipzig, 1907; repr. Hildesheim, 1967); R. Waltz, *Vie de Sénèque* (Paris, 1909); and G. Stahl, "Die *Naturales Quaestiones* Senecas. Ein Beitrag zum Spiritualisierungsprozess der römischen Stoa," in *Hermes*, **92** (1964), 425–454. The following articles in Pauly-Wissowa, *Real-Encyclopädie der classischen Altertumswissenschaft* refer to Seneca: W. Gundel, "Kometen," XI, 1143–1193; W. Capelle, "Erdbebenforschung," supp. IV, 344–374; and "Meteorologie," supp. VI, 315–358; A. Rehm, "Nilschwelle," XVII, pt. 1, 571–590; and R. Böker and H. Gundel, "Winde," 2nd ser., VIIIa, pt. 2, 2211–2387.

H. M. Hine

SENNERT, DANIEL (*b.* Breslau, Germany [now Wrocław, Poland], 25 November 1572; *d.* Wittenberg, Germany, 21 July 1637), *medicine, chemistry*.

Sennert was the son of a shoemaker, Nicolaus Sennert, and Catharina Helmania, both of whom came from Silesia (from Lähn and Zopten, respectively). After attending the schools in his native Breslau, Sennert enrolled at the University of Wittenberg on 6 June 1593. He followed the basic course of study in the philosophy faculty and was awarded the master's degree on 5 April 1598. He originally intended to become a teacher, but studied medicine instead for three years at the universities of Leipzig, Jena, and Frankfurt an der Oder. In 1601 he entered medical practice in Berlin under the supervision of the physician Johann Georg Magnus. After a short stay at the University of Basel, he obtained the doctor of medicine degree from Wittenberg on 10 September 1601. Altering his plans immediately to open a medical practice, he successfully sought the professorship of medicine at Wittenberg, which he was named to on 15 September 1602 and held until his death.

In 1603 Sennert married Margarethe Schatt of Wittenberg, by whom he had seven children. One of them, Andreas, became a famous Orientalist. Margarethe died in 1622, and in 1624 Sennert married Helene Burenius of Dresden. Following her death, Sennert married, in 1633, Margarethe Kramer of the principality of Sachsen-Altenburg. The last two marriages were childless. Sennert died from what was diagnosed as "plague," after he himself had survived six epidemics of the disease while serving as physician in Wittenberg.

Sennert was a well-known teacher, physician, and scientific writer. His medical ideas have never received a thorough treatment, although his publishing activity began[1] in 1611 with the lengthy *Institutionum medicinae libri V* and continued with other large works on medicine, such as *De febribus libri IV* of 1619 and *Practicae medicinae*, which appeared successively in six books between 1628 and 1636. Closely related to these works were others in which he dealt in detail with *chymia*, a subject that had been placed in the service of medicine by Paracelsus. This group began with the revealingly titled *De chymicorum cum Aristotelicis et Galenicis consensu ac dissensu liber I* (Wittenberg, 1619). Sennert's views are generally difficult to judge, because he attempted to reconcile the theories of Aristotle, Galen, Paracelsus, and the supporters of the traditional atomic hypotheses. For this reason Lasswitz judged Sennert too one-sidedly from the point of view of atomism, while Thorndike and Partington gave equally distorted assessments, but from the standpoints, respectively, of magic and modern chemistry. Even Ramsauer's attempt to describe Sennert's amalgamation of the various doctrines remained incomplete, in part because he lacked sufficient knowledge of the requisite languages.[2]

In medicine, Sennert defended Galen's humoral pathology. From the three Paracelsian principles, sulfur, salt, and mercury, he derived, like Jean Béguin, properties suitable for the chemical treatment of disease. Sennert thought that sulfur, which he considered to be the principle of burning, "phlogiston" (1619), was responsible for the heat of the heart. Salt supposedly served as the radical of the liver, and mercury as the spiritual principle of the brain. Sennert assumed that these three principles cannot be isolated; otherwise, their medicinal properties would be destroyed—an opinion still held in 1662 by Robert Boyle with respect to chemical action.[3] Sennert broke with Paracelsus, however, in rejecting the macroscopic influence of the celestial bodies. He also rejected Paracelsus' view that diseases are caused by the *ens deale*, *ens astrale*, *ens naturale*, *ens spirituale*, and *ens veneni*.[4] Further, unlike Paracelsus, Sennert thought that the *tria prima* are actually *prima mista* (first combinations), specifically, that they are composed of the four Peripatetic elements. He agreed with Paracelsus, however, that all natural bodies contain a *vis seminalis* that bestows life on them (and that, for example, causes the growth of metals). He joined this seminal force in a Neoplatonic fashion with the logos to produce a *principium plasticum* (formative principle).

From the above, it is obvious how strongly rooted the academic physician Sennert was in the ancient tradition. Even where he conceived from a corpuscular point of view the constituents joined together under the form, he retained the Peripatetic notion of form (which is independent of celestial influence).

In the theory proper of change in natural processes—which includes what we call "chemistry"—Sennert followed to some extent the views of the physicians Jean Fernel and Ibn Sīnā, according to whom the forms of the constituents persist under the new *forma superior* of the *mixtum* (for example, of the chemical compound) (1629). In 1619 Sennert, still following Ibn Rushd in this respect, held that the parts of the form persist and therefore that the form persists as such individually: *eadem numero*. Notwithstanding, in order to allow the new natural body (*mixtum*) to come into being, Sennert posited the existence of an *impetus* (*natura*, ὁρμή), which functions as a causal force. This is in addition to the *spiritus architectonicus*, which first creates the new forms, but then also the occult forms (or properties, as stated in the writings of Fernel). Sennert also retained until at least 1636 the notion he took from Albertus Magnus and Jacopo Zabarella of a multiplication of the forms responsible for the properties.

The fact that Sennert, like Ibn Sīnā, assumed the persistence of the forms of the constituents was made easy for him by notions dominant in the medical tradition since the time of Galen (for example, in the interpretation of the analysis of milk). To be sure, Sennert did not think it necessary to prove this theory through an actual separation of the constituents. This is evident from his theory of the elements. On the basis of J. C. Scaliger's principle, as *in essendo*, so *in causando*, Sennert inferred, in a direct, *a posteriori* manner, the existence of the four Peripatetic elements and the three Paracelsian principles from the perceptible properties of substances. For Sennert, as for Aristotle, this reasoning sufficed as a demonstration of the existence of the elementary constituents. The constituents must, of course, already be present in the body *potentia*, that is to say, with respect to their possible effect. Otherwise the formations of the new body (*mixtum*) would not be a qualitative change (*alteratio*) but a destruction or new creation. Combustibility, for example, demonstrates that the principle "sulfur" does have an effect. Sennert held that it was the concern of the wise, not of the common people, to discover these basic conceptions (the elements and the *tria prima*).

Sennert's fundamental principle of analysis was: *ex iis corpora naturalia constant, in quae resolvuntur* ("natural bodies consist of that into which they are decomposed"). He also correctly inverted this proposition, which, incidentally, he attributed to Hippocrates. He felt that he was faithful to the medical tradition not only in adopting this proposition, but also in accepting Galen's definition of the elements as very small particles (*minima*). In order to arrive at the elements, he added—true to the Aristotelian tradition—the necessity of the *ultima resolutio* (1635). In his view, the *prima mista* combined from the elements are the direct causes of the perceptible properties (*prima qualitates*: color, taste, smell). Thus, sulfur gives rise to the ability to burn and to smell, and salt to crystallization and to taste. Sennert was not sure what properties to assign to mercury.

Sennert held that the mechanism of reaction consisted of two stages: (1) the bodies split up into *minimae particulae*; (2) they then move about and reform as a new body. Although Sennert referred to a corresponding definition of Scaliger's, Galen had already put forth the idea of the comminution and reciprocal action of the fragments. The end product is no mere assemblage of the particles; rather, its properties are determined by the *natura quinta* associated with the form. In 1619 Sennert named this comminution and recombination *diacrisis* and *syncrisis*, respectively. (For Jungius' different terminology, see the article on him in this Dictionary.) A novel element in this account is that Sennert, an Aristotelian, went beyond the concepts of *actio* (influence) and *passio* (being influenced by) and raised the question of a *re-actio* and *re-passio*, perhaps on grounds of symmetry.

Sennert made use of an atomic theory properly so-called only in certain cases where he wished to show the persistence of the nature of a substance (1629). Specifically, he adopted this point of view in discussing distillation, sublimation, coagulation, the melting of the gold-silver alloy, and the solution of silver in nitric acid and of common salt in water. It was not until 1636, however, that he spoke of the unalterable persistence of the particles themselves.

Between 1611 and 1636 Sennert developed a compromise atomic hypothesis starting from the assumptions of the Averroistic school of Padua.

At first sight it appears surprising that in 1624 Sennert argued (falsely) for a *transmutatio* (that is, genuine transformation) of iron into copper during precipitation. He held that since many authors had confirmed it, it was a waste of time to continue the dispute.

For Sennert (as for A. G. Billich) chemistry is not an auxiliary art, but has its own inner goal (*finis internus*, 1629): to decompose natural substances and to prepare them for use. It thus possesses an independent character. Its external goals are healing and the metamorphosis of metals. An academic physician, Sennert incorporated the craft *chymia* into scientific medicine. First one conducts chemical experiments; the reasons that account for them will not fail to be discovered. In 1629 he stated that both medicine and chemistry must, because they are parts of a single knowledge of nature, seek to discover natural laws in such a way that the doctrine of nature (*Physica*) supplies *chymia* with the theory of natural principles, whereas *chymia* furnishes *Physica* with the experience acquired from chemical operations.

NOTES

1. Robert Multhauf, *The Origins of Chemistry* (London, 1966), 265, n. 27; and H. Kangro, *Joachim Jungius' Experiment und Gedanken zur Begründung der Chemie als Wissenschaft* (Wiesbaden, 1968). R. Hooykaas devotes a chapter to Sennert's chemical procedures in *Het begrip element in zijn historisch-wijsgeerige ontwikkeling* (Utrecht, 1933), 160–167.
2. R. Boyle, *The Sceptical Chymist*, conclusion.
3. Multhauf, *op. cit.*, 265, notes that these *entia* are five in number, as are the eternal substances of al-Rāzī. It may be added that the notion of the *natura quinta* appeared in the third century B.C. and that Étienne de Clave (1624) employed five principles: *tria prima, phlegma, caput mortuum.*
4. Kangro, *op. cit.*, 144.

BIBLIOGRAPHY

I. ORIGINAL WORKS. There does not exist a complete bibliography of Sennert's works; some are listed in the catalogs of the Bibliothèque Nationale, Paris, and of the Library of the British Museum. See also J. R. Partington, *A History of Chemistry,* II (London–New York, 1961), 271–272; H. Kangro, *Joachim Jungius' Experimente und Gedanken zur Begründung der Chemie als Wissenschaft* (Wiesbaden, 1968), 407; the titles given in *Biographisches Lexikon der hervorragenden Ärzte aller Zeiten und Völker,* A. Hirsch, E. Gurlt, and A. Wernich eds., 2nd ed., V (Berlin–Vienna, 1934), 230, are not very exact.

The main works are *Epitome naturalis scientiae, comprehensa disputationibus viginti sex, in . . . Academia Witebergensi . . . propositis a M. Daniele Sennerto* (Wittenberg, 1600) (I have not seen this); *Institutionum medicinae libri V.* (Wittenberg, 1611); *Disputatio medicina, qua suam de occultis, seu totius substantiae quas vocant morbis sententiam defendit D. Sennertus* ([Wittenberg], 1616); *Epitome naturalis scientiae* (Wittenberg, 1618), including atomism, most probably for the first time and so different from the disputations in 1600; *De chymicorum cum Aristotelicis et Galenicis consensu ac dissensu liber I* (Wittenberg, 1619); *De febribus libri IV* (Wittenberg, 1619); *De scorbuto tractatus* (Wittenberg, 1624); *De dysenteria tractatus* (Wittenberg, 1626); *Disputatio physica de gustu et tactu* (Wittenberg, 1626); *Disputatio physica de auditu et olefactu* (Wittenberg, 1626); *Practicae medicinae, liber I, II, III, IV, V, VI* (appeared at different places from 1628 till 1636); *De chymicorum cum Aristotelicis et Galenicis consensu ac dissensu liber: cui accessit appendix de constitutione chymiae* (Wittenberg, 1629), very different from the work ed. in 1619; *De arthritide tractatus* (Wittenberg, 1631); *Epitome institutionum medicinae* (Wittenberg, 1631); *Epitome librorum de febribus* (Wittenberg, 1634); *Hypomnemata Physica* (Frankfurt am Main, 1636); *Paralipomena cum praemissâ methodo discendi medicinam, tractatus posthumus* (Wittenberg, 1642); Sennertus (Daniel), Culpeper (Nicholas), Cole (Abdiah), *Thirteen Books on Natural Philosophy* (London, 1660).

A work of unknown authorship (see Kangro [1968], pp. 126–127, note 178) is *Auctarium epitomes physicae . . . Danielis Sennerti* (edited simultaneously at Wittenberg and Hamburg, 1635).

Moreover Sennert has written many *Disputationes,* which still wait to be revealed among the occasional writings of various authors bound together in volumes of the seventeenth century.

II. SECONDARY LITERATURE. No full presentation of Sennert's life and work is known. Biographical details are included in the works of August Buchner, *Dissertationum Academicarum volumen II* (Wittenberg, 1651); J. Graetzer, *Lebensbilder hervorragender schlesischer Ärzte* (Breslau, 1889); and *Allgemeine Deutsche Biographie,* R. V. Liliencron and F. X. von Wegele, eds., published by the Historische Commission bei der Königlichen Akademie der Wissenschaften (at Munich), XXXIV (Munich–Leipzig, 1892), 34–35.

On chemical views of Sennert, consult Reijer Hooykaas (1933: see note 1), 160–167; J. F. Partington, *A History of Chemistry,* XXIII (London, 1961), 271–276; Robert P. Multhauf (1966: see note 1), *passim*; Hans Kangro (1968: see note 1), *passim*; Allen G. Debus, "Guintherius, Libavius and Sennert: The Chemical Compromise in Early Modern Medicine," in *Science, Medicine and Society in the Renaissance,* A. G. Debus, ed. (New York, 1972), 157–165, and "The Paracelsians and the Chemists: the Chemical Dilemma in Renaissance Medicine," in *Clio medica,* 7 (1972), 195. Sennert's atomism is particularly treated by Kurd Lasswitz, "Die Erneuerung der Atomistik in Deutschland durch Daniel Sennert und sein Zusammenhang mit Asklepiades von Bithynien," in *Vierteljahrsschrift für wissenschaftliche Philosophie,* 3 (1879), 408–434; idem, in *Geschichte der Atomistik vom Mittelalter bis Newton,* 2 vols. (Hamburg–Leipzig, 1890), vol. I, 436–454 and *passim* in vols. I and II; and Rembert Ramsauer, *Die Atomistik des Daniel Sennert* (Kiel, 1935), the last not always reliable.

A few thoughts extracted from Sennert's large medical work are briefly dealt with by Walter Pagel, "Daniel Sennert's Critical Defence of Paracelsus," in *Paracelsus, An Introduction to Philosophical Medicine in the Era of Renaissance* (Basel–New York, 1958), 333–343; "William Harvey Revisited," in *History of Science,* 8 (1969), 10, and 9 (1970), 7, 11–20; and Peter H. Niebyl, "Sennert, van Helmont, and Medical Ontology," in *Bulletin of the History of Medicine,* 45 (1971), 115–137.

On older sources dealing with views of Sennert, see Ferguson.

HANS KANGRO

SERENUS (*b.* Antinoupolis, Egypt, *fl.* fourth century A.D. [?]), *mathematics.*

Serenus was the author of two treatises on conic sections, *On the Section of a Cylinder* and *On the Section of a Cone,* which have survived, and a commentary on the *Conics* of Apollonius, which has not. From a subscription in a later hand to the Vatican archetype of the first-named work and from the title of the second as given in a Paris manuscript from Mount Athos, Serenus' birth can be placed at Antinoupolis, a city founded by Hadrian in A.D. 122. This birthplace gives an upper limit for his date. As Serenus reckoned Apollonius among the "ancient" writers on conics, and used two lemmas proved by Pappus to transform certain unequal proportions,[1] he is generally thought to have flourished in the fourth century. Certainly his surviving works belonged to an age when Greek geometry had passed its creative phase.[2]

On the Section of a Cylinder, dedicated to an otherwise unknown Cyrus, consists of an introduction, eight definitions, and thirty-three propositions. It counters what is said to have been a prevalent belief—that the curve formed by the oblique section of a cylinder differs from the curve formed by the oblique section of a cone known as the ellipse. In the final five propositions Serenus defended a friend Peithon, who, not satisfied with Euclid's treatment, had defined parallels to be such lines as are cast on a wall or a roof by a pillar with a light behind it. Even in the decline of Greek mathematics this description had been a source of amusement to Peithon's contemporaries.[3]

On the Section of a Cone, also dedicated to Cyrus, consists of an introduction and sixty-nine propositions. It deals mainly with the areas of triangular sections of right or scalene cones made by planes passing through the vertex. Serenus specified the conditions for which the area of a triangle in a certain class is a maximum, those for which two triangles in a particular class may be equal, and so on. In some instances he also evaluated areas.

Serenus himself bore witness to his lost commentary on Apollonius.[4] Certain manuscripts of Theon of Smyrna preserve a fragment that may have come from that work or from a separate collection of lemmas. It is introduced with the words, "From Serenus the philosopher out of the lemmas," and it lays down that if a number of rectilineal angles be subtended at a point on the diameter of a circle (not being its center) by equal arcs of the circle, an angle nearer the center is always less than an angle farther away; this is applied to angles subtended at the center of the ecliptic by equal arcs of the eccentric circle of the sun.

NOTES

1. *De sectione coni,* Prop. XIX, in J. L. Heiberg, *Sereni Antinoensis opuscula,* pp. 160.15–162.11; Pappus, *Collectio* VII. 45 and 47, in F. Hultsch, *Pappi Alexandrini Collectionis quae supersunt,* II (Berlin, 1877), pp. 684.20–686.4, 686.15–27.
2. Halley's beliefs (*Apollonii Pergaei Conicorum libri octo,* Praefatio *ad finem*) that Serenus was born at Antissa in Lesbos and that a lower date for his life is given by an apparent reference to him in the commentary of Marinus (*fl.* A.D. 425) on Euclid's *Data* (David Gregory, *Euclidis quae supersunt omnia* [Oxford, 1703], p. 457.3) have been shown philologically by Heiberg in his review of M. Cantor, *Vorlesungen über Geschichte der Mathematik* in *Revue critique d'histoire et de Littérature,* **11** (1881), 381, and by Menge (*Euclidis opera omnia,* J. L. Heiberg and H. Menge, eds., VI [Leipzig, 1896], p. 248.3–4, where there is no mention of Serenus) to be erroneous.
3. J. L. Heiberg, *Sereni Antinoensis opuscula,* p. 96.14–25.
4. *Ibid.,* pp. 26–27.

BIBLIOGRAPHY

I. ORIGINAL WORKS. It seems likely that from the seventh century the two surviving works of Serenus and the commentary of Eutocius were bound with the *Conics* of Apollonius—Theodorus Metochita certainly read them together early in the fourteenth century—and their survival is probably due to these circumstances. A Latin trans. of Serenus' *De sectione cylindri* and *De sectione coni* was published by F. Commandinus at the end of his *Apollonii conicorum libri quatri* (Bologna, 1566). The Greek text was first published by E. Halley in *Apollonii Pergaei Conicorum libri octo et Sereni Antissensis De sectione cylindri et coni libri duo* (Oxford, 1710). A definitive critical ed. with Latin trans. was published by J. L. Heiberg, *Sereni Antinoensis opuscula* (Leipzig, 1896). A German trans. was made by E. Nizze, *Serenus von Antissa: Ueber den Schnitt des Cylinders* (Stralsund, 1860) and *Ueber den Schnitt des Kegels* (Stralsund, 1861); and there is an excellent French trans. with intro. and notes by Paul Ver Eecke, *Serenus d'Antinoë: Le livre De la section du cylindre e le livre De la section du cône* (Paris–Bruges, 1929).

The fragment from the lemmas has been published by T. H. Martin, *Theonis Platonici Liber De astronomia* (Paris, 1849; repr. Groningen, 1971), 340–343, with a Latin trans. and by J. L. Heiberg, *Sereni Antinoensis opuscula,* XVIII–XIX.

II. SECONDARY LITERATURE. See Thomas Heath, *History of Greek Mathematics,* II (Oxford, 1921), 519–526; J. L. Heiberg, "Über der Geburtsort des Serenos," in *Bibliotheca mathematica,* n.s. **8** (1894), 97–98; Gino Loria, *Le scienze esatte nell' antica Grecia,* 2nd ed. (Milan, 1914), 727–735; T. H. Martin, *Theonis Platoni-*

ci *Liber De astronomia* (Paris, 1849; repr. Groningen, 1971), 79–81; and Paul Tannery, "Serenus d'Antissa," in *Bulletin des sciences mathématiques et astronomiques,* 2nd ser., **7** (1883), 237–244, repr. in *Mémoires scientifiques,* I (Paris–Toulouse, 1912), 290–299.

IVOR BULMER-THOMAS

SERGENT, EDMOND (*b.* Philippeville [now Skikda], Algeria, 23 March 1876; *d.* Andilly-en-Bassigny, France, 20 August 1969), *epidemiology, immunology.*

The son of a French career soldier stationed in North Africa, Sergent studied medicine at Algiers. In 1900 he began to study under Émile Roux, assistant director of the Institut Pasteur in Paris. Shortly before, Grassi had demonstrated the role of mosquitoes in the propagation of malaria, and at Roux's suggestion Sergent went to Algeria to investigate the implications of this discovery. From 1900 to 1910 Sergent spent the malaria season in Algeria and the rest of the year in Paris. In 1912 he became director of the Institut Pasteur at Algiers, a post he held until 12 April 1963, when he was suddenly removed from office for political reasons. He left his native country and spent the rest of his life in France.

Sergent produced an extensive body of scientific work. He often collaborated with other researchers, notably his brother Étienne. A large portion of this research dealt with malaria. For more than forty-five years, both in the laboratory and in the field, the Sergent brothers tirelessly studied the factors involved in the spread of the disease: the protozoan (pathogenic agent), the *Anopheles* (vector), and man (reservoir of the parasite). This work culminated in 1926 in the creation, near Algiers, of an experimental station known as Marais des Ouled Mendil. Henceforth men were able to live where previously the presence of malaria had precluded settlement.

Sergent demonstrated that malaria is not the only disease in which an insect acts as the vector of the pathogenic agent. He was able to show this by studying the mode of transmission of various diseases including relapsing fever (spread by lice), bouton d'Orient (sandflies of the genus *Phlebotomus*), and various types of babesioses (ticks). Sergent also devised the concept of "premunition," according to which an organism's immunity to certain infections (including malaria and tuberculosis) can be assured only if it permanently carries the pathogenic agent in an attenuated state.

Sergent had great administrative ability and was placed in charge of many missions. He was known for his warmth and kindness, qualities most memorably displayed in his filial relationship with Roux. Sergent belonged to many scientific societies and received a number of honors, including the coveted Manson Medal (1962).

BIBLIOGRAPHY

I. ORIGINAL WORKS. With his brother Étienne, Sergent wrote *Vingt-cinq années d'étude et de prophylaxie du paludisme en Algérie* (Algiers, 1928) and *Histoire d'un marais algérien* (Algiers, 1947). Alone he wrote *Les travaux scientifiques de l'Institut Pasteur en Algérie de 1900 à 1962* (Paris, 1964). Many of his works can be found in *Archives de l'Institut Pasteur d'Algérie.*

II. SECONDARY LITERATURE. See Albert Delaunay, *L'Institut Pasteur des origines à aujourd'hui* (Paris, 1962); and "Edmond Sergent (1876–1969)," in *Annales de l'Institut Pasteur,* **118** (May 1970), 593.

ALBERT DELAUNAY

SERRES, ANTOINE ÉTIENNE REYNAUD AUGUSTIN (*b.* Clairac, France, 12 September 1786; *d.* Paris, France, 22 January 1868), *comparative anatomy, embryology.*

Serres was trained in Paris and received his medical degree in 1810. From 1808 to 1822 he worked at the Hôtel Dieu. In 1820 he was awarded the prize for physiological research by the Académie des Sciences and the following year gained a special prize for his two-volume work on the comparative anatomy of the brains of vertebrate animals. In 1822 Serres was appointed chief medical officer at the Hôpital de la Pitié. He was elected to the Académie de Medecine in 1822 and to the Académie des Sciences in 1828. In 1839 he preceded Flourens as professor of comparative anatomy at the Jardin des Plantes and two years later became president of the Académie des Sciences. He was created an officer (1841) and a commander (1848) of the Légion d'Honneur.

Serres did research into the development of the bones and teeth in normal and abnormal fetuses and studied the comparative anatomy of a number of vertebrate organs. He noted that many organs start from a number of isolated centers, which eventually unite to form a single adult organ—an observation that he regarded as a complete confirmation of epigenesis. In his general approach to the nature of life and the harmony between the organs he was clearly influenced by Cuvier, who mentioned Serres's work with admiration.

Serres's theoretical position was more closely akin to that of Geoffroy Saint-Hilaire, who regarded Serres as his collaborator. Serres believed that there was only one underlying animal type and that in the course of their development, the organs of the higher animals repeated the form of the equivalent organs in lower organisms. These ideas were not new; the nature philosophers in Germany had suggested similar ideas, and Meckel claimed that the higher animals pass through developmental stages analogous to the adult forms of lower animals. The distinction between a repetition of the organs of lower forms and the repetition of the actual organisms is often blurred; the latter view is sometimes called the Serres-Meckel Law.

After 1828 belief in either version of the Serres-Meckel law was gradually abandoned as the result of Baer's criticism, but throughout the 1840's and 1850's Serres continued to write papers in which he maintained his original views. These publications brought him into conflict with his younger colleagues and especially with Milne-Edwards; nevertheless, in 1859 Serres produced a final memoir in which he still maintained his original views.

A careful and precise observer of anatomical detail, Serres's work was neglected by the next generation, who were converts to an evolutionary outlook and scorned Serres's type of speculation. Haeckel's biogenetic law (1866)—each animal in its development recapitulates its evolutionary history—has much in common with the Serres-Meckel law.

Historians tend to treat Serres as a mere disciple of Geoffroy Saint-Hilaire, which again is to do him less than justice.

BIBLIOGRAPHY

I. ORIGINAL WORKS. Serres's chief writings are *Anatomie comparée du cerveau dans les quatre classes des animaux vertébrés*, 2 vols. plus atlas (Paris, 1824–1826); and *Anatomie comparée, transcendante. Principes d'embryogénie de zoogénie et de teratogénie* (Paris, 1859). His early works appeared in *Annales des sciences naturelles*, **11**, **12** (1827); **16** (1829); **21** (1830). Other publications are listed in *Catalogue de la Bibliothèque Nationale*.

II. SECONDARY LITERATURE. On Serres and his work, see Ch. Coury, "L'identification de la fièvre 'entéro-mésentérique' (ou typhoide) par Petit et Serres (1813)," in *Semaine des hôpitaux de Paris*, **40** (1964), 3056–3064; Ch. Coury and R. Rullière, "Deux grands iniciateurs de la recherche clinique moderne—Petit et Serres—leur étude de la fièvre entéro-mésentérique (1811–1813)," in *Presse médicale*, **72** (1964), 2487–2490, and in *Aktuelle Probleme aus der Geschichte der Medizin* (Basel–New York, 1966), 596–603; P. Huard, "A propos du centenaire de la mort d'Étienne Serres (1786–1868)," in *Pagine di storia delle medicina*, **14**, no. 5 (1970), 11–15; E. J. Russell, *Form and Function* (London, 1916); and an inaugural diss. by M. M. Kraegel von der Heyden, *Étienne-Renaud-Augustin-Serres (1787–1868) Entdecker des Abdominaltyphus* (Zurich, 1972), which lists also most of the earlier literature.

ELIZABETH B. GASKING

SERRES, OLIVIER DE (or **DES**) (*b.* Villeneuve-de-Berg, Ardèche, France, 1539; *d.* Villeneuve-de-Berg, 2 July 1619), *agronomy.*

Serres's father, Jacques de Serres, and his mother, Louise de Leyris, came from families long established as small landowners and lawyers in Vivarais; it is uncertain at what point the estate of Pradel, which was to be Serres's home, passed into their hands. Since his father died while Olivier was still a boy, it is uncertain what his education was; he may have studied for a while at the University of Valence, but presumably he did not graduate. In 1559 he married Marguerite d'Arcons; they had seven children. Although he had to travel from time to time, possibly to Germany and Italy, Pradel and its improvement were his life's work. As a young man he was converted to Protestantism; as early as 1561 he seems to have been regarded as a leader of the local Huguenots, obtaining a preacher for them from Geneva.

Much of the little that is known of Serres's life relates to his position in the Reformed community in time of civil war. In 1562 the parish church vessels were entrusted to him for sale. He also commanded forces in local campaigns of the various wars of the 1560's and 1570's and played a leading role in the capture of Villeneuve by the Huguenots in 1573, although he should almost certainly be exonerated of all blame for the massacre that followed. In fact, he was driven from Pradel more than once during these years and participated at least three times in conferences to arrange a local peace. At the end of the century he spent some time at Paris, where he presented his plans for the expansion of sericulture and diffusion of the mulberry to Henry IV.

At the same time Serres saw to the publication of his book *Théâtre d'agriculture* (1600). Since he was by then over sixty, the work can be regarded as the fruit of his life's experience. His aim was to present a complete survey of all aspects of agriculture, starting with advice on the proper way to run a household and proceeding, by way of discussions of various types of soil, to describe all the domesticated animals and plants known to him and to give useful hints on their cultivation. He also was an enthusiastic advocate of the use of irrigation to improve meadows, of careful drainage, and of the conservation of water.

Unlike most books of that period on farming and estate management, which tended to limit themselves to the codification and dissemination of the best current practice, Serres's was among the first, at least north of the Alps, to argue for widespread innovation and experiment. By the time his book appeared, he had acquired a national reputation as an authority on the silkworm, so much so that the relevant portion of his book appeared as a kind of preprint, *La cueillette de la soye,* the year before the main body, and was translated into German and English. In it he gave one of the first detailed accounts of the life cycle of the silkworm, although he did not eliminate the possibility of spontaneous generation (but acknowledged that he had never observed it). He believed that the silkworm could be reared much farther north than was then accepted. Serres also devised, or promoted, a method of manufacturing coarse cloth from the bark of the mulberry trees, the leaves of which fed the worms. His work on this, *La seconde richesse du meurier-blanc,* also was printed independently and was translated. With this new motive added to the needs of the silk industry, Serres bore a large part of the responsibility for the mulberry craze of the next decades and, in particular, inspired the king to make extensive plantings at Paris.

Serres was also keen on introducing crops previously unknown to France. An advocate of the sowing of artificial grasses, he devoted a chapter of his *Théâtre* to sainfoin, the use of which was then spreading north from Italy and Spain. Serres introduced hops to France and was the first French agricultural writer to describe and encourage the cultivation of maize and potatoes. Among exotic barnyard fowl—which gave him some difficulty in distinguishing one species from another—he appears to have known the turkey.

But the proportion of novelty in the whole should not be exaggerated. Although it is a treatise of agricultural improvement, his *Théâtre* is also a depiction of the old ideal of the self-sufficient and patriarchal small estate, whose master, while trying to increase his patrimony, seeks above all to be content with his lot and holds fast to the simplicity of rural life.

BIBLIOGRAPHY

I. ORIGINAL WORKS. Serres's main work is *Théâtre d'agriculture et mesnage des champs* (Paris, 1600), of which at least nineteen eds. had appeared by 1675; there is also an annotated ed., 2 vols. (Paris, 1804–1805). Sections of it that were published separately are *La cueillette de la soye* (Paris, 1599) and *La seconde richesse du meurier-blanc* (Paris, 1603).

II. SECONDARY LITERATURE. See M. de Fels, *Olivier de Serres* (Paris, 1963); G. Lizerand, *Le régime rural de l'ancienne France* (Paris, 1942), 79–80; and H. Vaschalde, *Olivier de Serres, seigneur du Pradel, sa vie et ses travaux* (Paris, 1886).

A. G. KELLER

SERRES DE MESPLÈS, MARCEL PIERRE TOUSSAINT DE (*b.* Montpellier, France, 3 November 1780; *d.* Montpellier, 22 July 1862), *zoology, geology.*

Serres (or de Serres) came from a rich family of drapers that belonged to the nobility of the robe. His mother died when he was very young, and he became a rebellious and lazy student, indifferent to punishment. Following his adolescence, however, Serres became a tireless scientific author whose 300 writings are noteworthy both in number and in diversity and encompass the natural and physical sciences, technology, jurisprudence, social and economic statistics, and travel accounts.

Serres studied law and in 1805 became deputy public prosecutor at the court of Montpellier; he was nevertheless more attracted by scientific research. Although his family suffered sudden financial ruin, Serres was able to go to Paris to study in 1807 through the generosity of Count Pierre Daru, a close collaborator of Napoleon. In Paris he attended the lectures of Haüy, Cuvier, Lamarck, and Geoffroy Saint-Hilaire. He also had the support of Berthollet and became friendly with Alexandre Brongniart and Constant Prévost. At the request of Daru, Serres spent 1809–1811 in Austria and Bavaria, studying technical processes of possible value to French industry. His account of this mission filled sixteen volumes (1813–1823), three of which were devoted specifically to technology. In 1813 Serres translated into French a partially unpublished work by the physicist H. C. Oersted:

Recherches sur l'identité des forces chimiques et électriques.

In 1809 Daru arranged for Serres to receive the chair of mineralogy and geology at the reorganized University of Montpellier. Serres assumed the post in 1811 but continued to spend much time in Paris. After the fall of the Empire and Daru's disgrace (1814), he settled permanently in Montpellier and reentered the magistracy, remaining in office until 1852. This responsibility accounts for his authorship, in 1823, of a large *Manuel des cours d'assises.*

Among Serres's earliest works were some dealing with the anatomy of insects, particularly the Orthoptera. The most detailed and original of these studies concerned the organs of vision. In an extensive work published in 1842 Serres presented the first synthesis of knowledge of animal migrations. In geology he accepted the theory that present causes have always been sufficient, as proposed by Lamarck and Prévost; this view was under attack from Cuvier and had not yet been developed by Lyell into uniformitarianism. Serres applied his knowledge of chemistry to the study of rocks, particularly flints of the chalk formations (1850). Serres was apparently the first, in 1817, to consider dating fossil bones by their fluorine concentration.

Serres, who was friendly with William Buckland, stimulated interest on the Continent in cave excavations and discovered human bones that he believed to be contemporary with the semifossilized bones of extinct animal species. He was unaware, however, of the existence of chipped flint tools. In 1836 Serres published an excellent synthetic work on caves, and three years later he wrote a monumental monograph on the cave of Lunel-Viel. In 1829 Jules Desnoyers had proposed the word *Quaternaire* to designate the most recent geological period; Serres redefined it soon afterward in a more valid fashion and spread its use.

Influenced by Lamarck and Étienne Geoffroy Saint-Hilaire, Serres stated in his *Géognosie* (1829) that "extinct species [*générations*] appear to be linked by an uninterrupted chain to present species." An English summary of this book, published the following year, emphasized the increasing complexity of organisms during the course of geological time. Serres subsequently adopted a new approach to the problem, however, as did Brongniart, Deshayes, and E. R. A. Serres. They rejected the idea of the variability of species. At the same time they relaxed the notion of fixity of species by accepting the evidence for successive creations—an idea that seemed to be confirmed by stratigraphic geology.

Serres sought to reconcile science and the Bible in *Cosmogonie de Moïse comparée aux faits géologiques*, which went through three editions (1838–1859) and appeared in at least two translations (German and Spanish). In this work he asserted that only cultivated or domestic species are variable. In 1851, however, he again stressed the "gradual perfecting of organized beings," in effect adopting an unacknowledged evolutionary view.

BIBLIOGRAPHY

I. ORIGINAL WORKS. The works listed in the bibliography given by Rouville (see below) and in Royal Society *Catalogue of Scientific Papers,* V, 651–659; and VIII, 937, total about 300. The major ones are *Mémoire sur les yeux composés et les yeux lisses des Orthoptères . . .* (Montpellier, 1813), also in German (Berlin, 1826); *Géognosie des terrains tertiaires* (Montpellier–Paris, 1829), summarized in *Edinburgh Journal of Natural and Geographical Science,* **2** (1830), 294–295; *Essai sur les cavernes à ossements et sur les causes qui les y ont accumulés* (Montpellier, 1836; 3rd ed., Paris, 1838); *Cosmogonie de Moïse comparée aux faits géologiques* (Paris, 1838; 3rd ed., 1859); *Des causes des migrations des animaux* (Haarlem, 1842; 2nd ed., enl., Paris, 1845); and "Du perfectionnement graduel des êtres organisés," in *Actes de la Société linnéenne de Bordeaux,* **17** (1851), 5–32, 85–117, 181–213, 389–421; **18** (1852), 5–37, 97–129, 193–257, 427–459; and **19** (1853), 1–37, 77–113.

II. SECONDARY LITERATURE. See P. G. de Rouville, *Éloge historique de Marcel de Serres* (Montpellier, 1863); and Rumelin, "Marcel de Serres," in Michaud, *Biographie générale,* 2nd ed., XXXIX, 128–131.

FRANCK BOURDIER

SERRET, JOSEPH ALFRED (*b.* Paris, France, 30 August 1819; *d.* Versailles, France, 2 March 1885), *mathematics.*

Serret is sometimes confused with Paul Joseph Serret (1827–1898), a mathematician at the Université Catholique in Paris. After graduating from the École Polytechnique in 1840, Serret decided on a life of science and in 1848 became an entrance examiner at the École. After several other academic appointments he was named professor of celestial mechanics (1861) at the Collège de France and then, in 1863, professor of differential and integral calculus at the Sorbonne. In 1873 he joined the Bureau des Longitudes.

With his contemporaries P.-O. Bonnet and J. Bertrand, Serret belonged to that group of mathematicians in Paris who greatly advanced differential calculus during the period 1840–1865, and the fundamental formulas in the theory of space curves bear his name and that of J. F. Frenet. Serret also worked in number theory, calculus, mechanics, and astronomy and wrote several popular textbooks, including *Cours d'algèbre supérieure* (1849) and *Cours de calcul différentiel et intégral* (1867–1868).

In 1860 Serret succeeded Poinsot in the Académie des Sciences. After 1871 Serret's health declined; and he retired to Versailles, where he lived quietly with his family until his death.

BIBLIOGRAPHY

I. Original Works. The *Journal des mathématiques pures et appliquées* contains several of Serret's papers, including "Mémoire sur les surfaces orthogonales," **12** (1847), 241–254; "Sur quelques formules relatives à la théorie des courbes à double courbure," **16** (1851), 193–207; and "Mémoire sur les surfaces dont toutes les lignes de courbure sont planes ou sphériques," **18** (1853), 113–162. See also "Sur la moindre surface comprise entre des lignes droites données, non situées dans le même plan," in *Comptes rendus hebdomadaire des séances de l'Académie des sciences*, **40** (1855), 1078–1082.

Serret edited the *Oeuvres de Lagrange*, 14 vols. (Paris, 1867–1892), and the fifth ed. of Monge's *Application de l'analyse à la géométrie* (Paris, 1850), with annotations.

II. Secondary Literature. An obituary notice is given in *Bulletin des sciences mathématiques*, 2nd ser., **9** (1885), 123–132.

D. J. Struik

SERTOLI, ENRICO (*b.* Sondrio, Italy, 6 June 1842; *d.* Sondrio, 28 January 1910), *physiology, histology.*

Sertoli studied medicine at the University of Pavia, where, with Giulio Bizzozero and Camillo Golgi, he was a pupil of the physiologist Eusebio Oehl, who systematically developed studies in microscopic anatomy and histology at Pavia. After graduating in 1865, Sertoli moved to Vienna to study physiology under Brücke; but he returned to Italy the following year to take part in the campaign against Austria. After the war, he went to Tübingen in 1867 to work in Hoppe-Seyler's laboratory there.

From 1870 to 1907 Sertoli was professor of anatomy and physiology, and after 1907 of physiology only, at the Advanced Royal School of Veterinary Medicine in Milan, which, at that time, enjoyed university status. There he founded the Laboratory of Experimental Physiology.

Sertoli was an outstanding exponent of microscopic anatomy. In his first scientific work (1865) he identified and described the branched cells in the seminiferous tubules of the human testicle, which are still known as Sertoli cells. This research, carried out under Oehl's direction at the Pavia Institute of Physiology, was the starting point for further investigations; Sertoli later studied the structure of the testicle and spermatogenesis.

With Hoppe-Seyler, Sertoli reported (1867) on the importance of the blood proteins, and especially of the globulins, as mediators of alkalies in the alternating process of fixation and clearance of carbon dioxide; they discovered that this process is carried out in the capillary beds of the greater and lesser circulation, respectively. Sertoli's findings in this field were subsequently confirmed by Zuntz and Otto Loewi.

In Milan, Sertoli studied (1882–1883) the persistent excitability and extreme sensitivity to thermal stimuli of the smooth muscles. He is also credited with the first leiomyogram, which he obtained by using the retractor muscle of the penis, which was particularly suitable for the purpose because of its length, uniformity, and parallel fibrocells.

BIBLIOGRAPHY

I. Original Works. A list of Sertoli's publications is given in Pugliese (see below). His major works include "Dell'esistenza di particolari cellule ramificate nei canalicoli seminiferi del testicolo umano," in *Morgagni*, **7** (1865), 31–40, with one plate; "Ueber die Bindung der Kohlensäure im Blute und ihre Ausscheidung in der Lunge," in *Medicinisch-chemische Untersuchungen*, **2** (1867), 350–365; and in *Zentralblatt für die medizinischen Wissenschaften*, **6** (1868), 145–147; "Osservazioni sulla struttura dei canalicoli seminiferi del testicolo," in *Gazzetta medica lombarda*, 4 d.s. **6** (1871), 413–415; "Sulla struttura dei canalicoli seminiferi del testicolo studiata in rapporto allo sviluppo dei nemaspermi," *ibid.*, 2 d.s. **7** (1875), 401–403; "Di un pseudo-ermafrodismo in una capra," in *Archivio di medicina veterinaria*, **1** (1876), 22–33, written with G. Generali; "Sulla struttura dei canalicoli seminiferi dei testicoli studiata in rapporto allo sviluppo dei nemaspermi," in *Archivio per le scienze mediche*, **2** (1878), 107–146, 267–295, and plates 3–4; "Contribuzioni alla fisiologia generale dei muscoli lisci," in *Rendiconti dell'Istituto lombardo di scienze e lettere*, **15** (1882), 567–582; "Contribution à la physiologie général des muscles lisses," in *Archives italiennes de biologie*, **3** (1883), 78–94; "Della cariocinesi nella spermatogenesi," in *Rendiconti dell'Istituto lombardo di scienze e lettere*, **18** (1885), 833–839; and "Sur la caryokinèse dans la spermatogénèse," in *Archives italiennes de biologie*, **7** (1886), 369–375.

II. SECONDARY LITERATURE. On Sertoli and his work, see L. Belloni, "Enrico Sertoli in la medicina a Milano dal settecento al 1915," in *Storia di Milano*. Fondazione Treccani degli Alfieri, **16** (1962), 1028; A. Pugliese, "Henri Sertoli," in *Archives italiennes de biologie*, **53** (1910), 161–164; and F. Usuelli, "Enrico Sertoli (1842–1910)," in *Annuario veterinario italiano* (1934–1935), 455–461.

BRUNO ZANOBIO

SERTÜRNER, FRIEDRICH WILHELM ADAM FERDINAND (*b.* Neuhaus, near Paderborn, Germany, 19 June 1783; *d.* Hameln, Germany, 20 February 1841), *pharmacology.*

Sertürner's parents were Austrian. His father, Joseph Simon Serdinner (the spelling varies), married Marie Therese Brockmann and entered the service of Friedrich Wilhelm, prince-bishop of Paderborn, his son's godfather, as engineer and state building inspector. In 1798 Sertürner's father and his princely patron both died. The youth, then fifteen, was apprenticed to Cramer, the court apothecary, and in 1803 passed his assistant's test with excellent marks. In 1806 Sertürner became assistant to Hink, the town apothecary of Einbeck. In 1809 the French government of Westphalia licensed him to open his own pharmacy. Upon the return of the Hanoverian government, the license was revoked as an act of the French occupation forces. After a long, unsuccessful litigation, Sertürner took over the town pharmacy of Hameln in 1820. The following year he married Leonore von Rettberg. A capable assistant relieved him of the routine work in the prosperous pharmacy and thus, financially secure, he was able to devote himself to his scientific interests.

In later years Sertürner apparently suffered increasingly from mental disturbances, and his hypochondria became quite evident during his last years.

Aside from his chemical-pharmaceutical work, his passion was the construction of firearms. He designed a breechloader and tested new alloys for bullets. An arms manufacturer named Stürmer undertook the manufacture of these novelties and demonstrated them to the war ministries of Hannover and Prussia.

In his first scientific work Sertürner endeavored to isolate the "sleep-inducing factor" in opium and discovered a process whereby he could use ammonia to separate practically pure morphine from aqueous clarified opium extract. Until then Scheele's work had led to the assumption that all active substances in plants were acids. Sertürner called the newly discovered "sleep-inducing factor" a "vegetable alkali." He stated that this was most certainly the first representative of a new class of plant matter and called for the further search for other vegetable alkalies. Thus the foundation was laid for alkaloid chemistry. The introduction of morphine into pharmaceutics was later compared to the introduction of iron into metallurgy.

Sertürner's first publications on morphine in 1805 and 1806 failed to attract attention. In 1817, when Sertürner republished the results of his research in enlarged and more detailed form, the importance of his work was recognized.

Considering the obstacles confronting Sertürner's work on morphine, it is surprising that he succeeded at all. An autodidact with only sparse knowledge of the relevant literature, he conducted his research with the simplest equipment while performing the strenuous duties of an apothecary's assistant. Sometimes years elapsed between his research projects. Sertürner played an important part in that period of organic chemistry—between Scheele and F. F. Runge—when fundamental research was carried out by gifted investigators (mostly pharmacists) with only limited equipment.

Before Davy, Sertürner established in 1806 that caustic alkalies are not elements, but compounds of oxygen plus another combustible element similar to hydrogen. He failed, however, to interest a scientific journal in publishing his paper.

Sertürner's tendency toward speculation became so pronounced that even his most advanced colleagues often failed to comprehend him. His views on the life element "zoon," on the "cold nature of sunlight," on "atmospheric heat," and on "fire oxide" were unfounded and failed to stimulate productive thinking. Consequently, Sertürner acquired a dubious reputation, which partly explains why his two further important discoveries were ignored.

He developed a theory on the formation of ether from alcohol and sulfuric acid and established the formulas for three different "sulphovinic acids" (ethyl sulfuric acids). Although he came close to being correct, he met with universal rejection.

No attention was paid to his paper dealing with the cholera epidemics prevalent at the time. In this work he was the first to point out the real cause of the disease. On the basis of the known fact that objects exposed to severe cold or heat no longer transmitted the disease, he ascribed its cause to a toxic, self-reproducing living agent.

Only his work on morphine brought Sertürner numerous honors.

BIBLIOGRAPHY

I. ORIGINAL WORKS. Sertürner's writings include *System der chemischen Physik*, 2 vols. (Göttingen, 1820–1822); *Annalen für das Universalsystem der Elemente*, 3 vols. (Göttingen, 1826–1829); *Dringende Aufforderung an das deutsche Vaterland, in Beziehung der orientalischen Brechruhr* (Göttingen, 1831); *Einige Belehrungen für das gebildete und gelehrte Publikum über den gegenwärtigen Zustand der Heilkunde und der Naturwissenschaften im allgemeinen, mit besonderer Rücksicht auf das gemeine Leben . . .* (Göttingen, 1838); and Franz Krömeke, ed., *Friedrich Wilhelm Sertürner, der Entdecker der Morphiums. Lebensbild und Neudruck der Original-Morphiumarbeiten* (Jena, 1925).

II. SECONDARY LITERATURE. See Hermann Coenen, "Über das Jahr der Morphiumentdeckung Sertürners in Paderborn," in *Archiv der Pharmazie*, **287** (1954), 166–180; F. von Gizyki, "Die Aufnahme des Morphins in den Arzneischatz," in *Deutsche Apotheker-Zeitung*, **96** (1956), 583–584; P. J. Hanzlik, "125th Anniversary of the Discovery of Morphine by Sertürner," in *Journal of the American Pharmaceutical Association*, **18** (1929), 375–384; Georg Lockemann, "Friedrich Wilhelm Sertürner," in *Zeitschrift für angewandte Chemie*, **37**, no. 30 (1924), 526–532; Hermann Trommsdorff, "Trommsdorff und Sertürner; Johann Bartholomä Trommsdorff und seine Zeitgenossen. Teil 2," in *Jahrbücher der Akademie gemeinnütziger Wissenschaften in Erfurt*, **55** (1941), 133–243; and J. Valentin, "Der erkenntnistheoretische Wandel Sertürners im Jahre 1804," in *Deutsche Apotheker-Zeitung*, **97** (1957), 573–574.

EBERHARD SCHMAUDERER

SERULLAS, GEORGES-SIMON (*b.* Poncin, Ain, France, 21 November 1774; *d.* Paris, France, 25 May 1832), *chemistry, pharmacy.*

Serullas was the son of a notary and seemed destined to follow his father's profession. After doing well in his early studies, however, he enrolled in a pharmacy course in 1793 and became a military pharmacist. During a campaign in the Alps he learned botany, physics, and chemistry. He spent several years in Italy, where, following the European blockade, he was put in charge of preparing a huge amount of grape syrup as a sugar substitute for consumption in the military hospitals. He was chief pharmacist under the command of Ney throughout the Italian, German, and Russian campaigns.

After the siege of Torgau, where he lived for a time, Serullas became chief pharmacist as well as the first professor of pharmacy at the military hospital in Metz. From then on, he devoted himself to intellectual pursuits; for example, at the age of forty-two he began to study Greek and mathematics. In 1825 Serullas became chief pharmacist and professor at the Val de Grâce and was named professor of chemistry at the Jardin des Plantes. In 1829 he was elected a member of the Paris Academy, succeeding Vauquelin. He died of cholera, which he contracted at the funeral of Georges Cuvier.

Serullas's earliest research, which involved sugar and sugar substitutes, was followed by investigations of alloys of sodium and potassium. He probably is best known, however, for his studies of iodine and bromine and their compounds. In 1823 he discovered iodoform (CHI_3), which he called *hydriodure de carbone*. Serullas's confusion, which reflects the state of organic chemistry of the period, is indicated by the fact that he called presumably the same compound *protoiodure de carbone* in 1823 and *periodure de carbone* in 1828. In 1824 he prepared cyanogen iodide (discovered by Humphry Davy in 1816) by a more efficient method.

His studies with bromine led to the preparation of ethyl bromide; cyanogen bromide; a selenium bromide; several compounds of bromine with arsenic, bismuth, and antimony; and an *éther hydrobromique*. Serullas found that the *hydrocarbure de brome* (bromoform) remains solid up to 7°C., a fact ignored during previous work. He also experimented with chlorine and in 1828 discovered cyanuric chloride. This work on halogen compounds led to the publication of the well-received book *Sur quelques composés d'iode, tels que le chlorure d'iode, sur l'action mutuelle de l'acide iodique et de la morphine ou de ses sels, sur l'acide iodique cristallisé* (1830), which became an important reference work in legal medicine. In 1827 he discovered cyanamide and cyanuric acid. His other investigations involved perchloric acid, phosphonium iodide (PH_4I), and ether.

BIBLIOGRAPHY

I. ORIGINAL WORKS. J. R. Partington, *A History of Chemistry*, IV (London, 1964), 83–84, 89, 254, 325,

342, 349–350, 358, gives references to the papers describing most of Serullas's studies that were published in the *Annales de chimie* or the *Mémoires* of the Paris Academy. In addition, the following early books and memoirs are significant: *Mémoires pour le perfectionnement des moyens d'obtenir la matière sucrée des végétaux indigènes*, 2 vols. (Paris, 1810–1813); *Mémoire sur la conversion de la matière sucrée en alcool* (Paris, 1817); *Sur les fumigations chloriques* (Paris, 1817); *Observations physico-chimiques sur les alliages du potassium et du sodium avec d'autres métaux* (Metz, 1821); *Moyen d'enflammer la poudre sous l'eau* (Metz, 1822); and *Sur quelques composés d'iode . . .* (Paris, 1830).

II. Secondary Literature. A short, relatively accessible sketch of Serullas is in F. Hoefer, ed., *Nouvelle biographie générale*, XLIII (1867), 802–803. Longer obituary notices are Jean Antoine Lodibert, *Éloge historique de Serullas* (Paris, 1837); and Julien Joseph Virey, *Notice sur Serullas* (Paris, 1832). Partington (see above) makes several references to Serullas's investigations of organic halides in relation to the work of other French chemists.

Sheldon J. Kopperl

SERVETUS, MICHAEL (*b*. Villanueva de Sixena [?], Spain, 29 September 1511 [?]; *d*. Geneva, Switzerland, 27 October 1553), *biology, philosophy*.

There is controversy as to the date and place of birth of Michael Servetus. The conflicting data were supplied by Servetus himself during his trials at Lyons and Geneva, when he was anxious to mislead his inquisitors. The more likely date, 29 September 1511 as against the traditional 1509, is corroborated by two separate statements made by Servetus: that he was forty-two at the time of his trial in Lyons and that he was twenty when he published his first book. Villanueva de Sixena, in the province of Huesca, has been authenticated as the place where his family resided; hence Servetus' choice of Villanovanus as a pseudonym. He also had stated, however, that he was born at Tudela, Navarre, thus leading some historians to suppose that his family lived there at the time of his birth and later moved to Villanueva. Evidence is lacking to support this inference.

Servetus' parents were Antonio Serveto, alias Reves (a pseudonym Servetus also used), a notary, and Catalina Conesa. They were "Old Christian" nobles; and one of his brothers was a priest. Not much is known of his early education. Possibly, after completing church school, he attended the University of Zaragoza, which was not far from his home. There he learned Latin.

A combination of intellectual precocity and family connections led Servetus, at the age of fifteen, to enter the service of the learned Franciscan friar Juan de Quintana, who held a doctorate from the Sorbonne and was a member of the Cortes of Aragon. The influence of Erasmianism in Spain was well manifested in Quintana, who at the Diet of Augsburg told Melanchthon that he was unable to understand why Luther's doctrine of justification by faith should have aroused so much controversy.

Servetus temporarily left Quintana's employ to pursue legal studies at the University of Toulouse in 1528. This institution was considered preeminent in the field of law, and Servetus described it as "the mother of those skilled in law." (All quotations are from the O'Malley translation.) It was here that Servetus became interested in scriptural studies, and he may have studied Greek and Hebrew as linguistic aids. His stay in Toulouse was brief; for Quintana, having been named confessor to Emperor Charles V, recalled him to his service in 1529. In Quintana's train Servetus witnessed Charles V's coronation as Holy Roman Emperor at Bologna and later traveled to Germany, where the emperor hoped to settle the Protestant problem.

Servetus' earlier studies of the Bible had raised grave doubts in his mind. Nowhere in the Bible did he find the word "Trinity." He must have realized that he could no longer stay in Quintana's employ, for he left his patron in 1530. By July of that year he was in Basel. He hoped to meet Erasmus, but the latter had left Basel more than a year earlier. Johannes Oecolampadius was now the chief reformer of that city; and Servetus stayed in his house as a guest, probably for the ten months that he remained in Basel.

Oecolampadius, who was forty-eight, showed great forbearance toward the nineteen-year-old Servetus, who, aside from voicing anti-Trinitarian doctrines, was a contentious, vain, and stubborn young man. Oecolampadius made every effort to convert Servetus, but to no avail. At the conference of reformers in Zurich, he was driven to complain about this Spaniard who was spreading the Arian heresy in his city. On his return to Basel, Oecolampadius heeded Zwingli's admonition that every possible means be taken to prevent Servetus' heresy from spreading, and Servetus left Basel.

He chose to go to Strasbourg, for he had befriended Martin Bucer and the city was well-known for its tolerant attitude toward sectarian movements. At Hagenau, near Strasbourg, Servetus found a printer, Johannes Setzer, who had published some 150 titles, and convinced him to print his first work. In July 1531, *De trinitatis erroribus* went on sale.

In this work, published when he was only twenty, Servetus displayed a very wide range of reading. He cited many authors and pitted their views against the Bible in its original Greek and Hebrew texts. Thus he was able to show the discrepancy between later Scholastic theories and the original Biblical statements on the Trinity. Servetus denied the doctrine of three equal persons in Godhead and brought on himself the condemnation of both Catholics and Protestants.

Bucer refuted *De trinitatis* publicly, and the city magistrates banned its sale in Strasbourg. Servetus returned to Basel; but the reception of his work there was, if anything, harsher than in Strasbourg. Partly in order to allay criticism, he published *De trinitate* (1532). Although the tone of this second work was not as unrestrained, Servetus fundamentally stuck to his doctrines. It therefore was advisable for him to leave Switzerland.

Assuming the name of Michel de Villeneuve, Servetus moved to France. In 1533 he was studying in Paris at the Collège Calvi. At this time Paris was beginning to crack down on heretics, however; and a meeting between Servetus and Calvin did not take place, probably because of the former's fear of being apprehended. Servetus decided to go to Lyons, where he may have stopped briefly before going to Paris. Being a trade center, Lyons was a relatively more tolerant city; moreover, there were many great printing houses there where he could find work.

Servetus became a corrector and editor for the most famous publishers in Lyons, the brothers Trechsel. For them he prepared two editions of Ptolemy's *Geography* (1535, 1541) and three editions of the Bible (an octavo Bible and the Santis Pagnini Bible, both in 1542, and a seven-volume edition that appeared in 1542). His edition of the Santis Pagnini Bible is the best-known and is remarkable for its theory of prophecy.

Ptolemy's *Geography* had been the standard work on the subject since the second century and had often appeared in Greek and Latin editions. Servetus used Bilibald Pirckheimer's edition of 1524 and compared it with the Greek text and other editions. With great relish he pointed out the many errors that had crept into the Pirckheimer edition. Subsequent geographers have acknowledged the validity of these corrections.

In the preparation of the text that accompanied the fifty maps, Servetus stated that he had consulted eighty works. In reference to the New World,

he wrote that "those err to high heaven . . . who contend that this continent should be called America, since Amerigo approached that land long after Columbus. . . ." Some historians have gone so far as to claim that he was the founder of comparative geography because of his comments on national characteristics and his interest in national psychology, which were new for the time. The success of this work was attested to by the fact that Servetus was commissioned to do another edition, with minor alterations, in 1541.

Servetus' interest in medicine was aroused in connection with his proofreading duties. Many medical works were published in Lyons, and the Trechsel firm published the writings of the distinguished medical humanist Symphorien Champier, with whom Servetus struck up a close friendship. Significantly, Servetus' first medical work, *In Leonardum Fuchsium apologia* (1536), was a defense of Champier, who had become involved in a controversy with Leonhard Fuchs. In the *Apologia* Servetus expounded his belief in the healing powers of certain herbs.

It was probably Champier who advised Servetus to return to Paris and study medicine. The preface of the *Apologia* was dated 12 November 1536, from Paris. There Servetus became part of a distinguished medical circle, and his teachers included Sylvius (Jacques Dubois), Fernel, and Johannes Guinter. The last singled him out, together with Vesalius, as his most able assistant in dissection. (Servetus and Vesalius may not have known each other personally; evidence suggests that the latter had returned to Louvain by the time Servetus reached Paris.)

In 1537 Servetus published what was essentially a continuation of the *Apologia*, the *Syruporum universa ratio*, which was so successful that it went through six editions and helped finance his stay in Paris. This fundamentally Galenic work centered on the use of syrups for curative purposes and contained a significant passage on the use of "correct" foods, especially citrus fruits, as an aid in the assimilative process of digestion. Servetus also maintained that sickness was the perversion of the natural functions of body organs and was not caused by the introduction of new elements into the body. The *Apologia* and the *Syruporum* were noteworthy contributions to modern pharmacology.

Contrary to university regulations, which at any rate were only laxly enforced, Servetus supplemented his dwindling funds by giving lectures, although he did not have a Master of Arts degree. His original subject was geography, in which his edition of Ptolemy had given him enough reputation. He then moved on to astronomy and became involved in judicial astrology or forecasting and its relation to medicine. He was charged before the Faculty of Medicine with lecturing on astrology. In his defense Servetus wrote the *Apologetica disceptatio pro astrologia* (1538), which he hastened to publish despite indications that the Parlement of Paris had been asked to issue an injunction against its publication. Too late to prevent its appearance, the Parlement confiscated all copies of the *Astrologia* and reprimanded its author. Because of the absence of any record that he received a degree in medicine, many authors have surmised that this incident prevented Servetus from completing his studies. Nevertheless, his 1541 contract to edit the Bible referred to him as a *docteur en médecine;* and, although this document was drafted in Lyons, there certainly were persons in that city who had known him well in Paris.

In 1538 Servetus returned to Lyons; then moved to Charlieu, where he practiced medicine for three years; then returned to Lyons. During most of the latter time Servetus lived at Vienne in the palace of Archbishop Pierre Palmier, the outstanding churchman of the region, who had attended his lectures in Paris and whom he now served as personal physician. He also practiced medicine at large for the next twelve years; and his colleagues elected him prior of the Confraternity of St. Luke, with responsibility to supervise the apothecaries and tend to the indigent hospital patients.

Although outwardly living as a Catholic, Servetus did not abandon his theological studies and his original doctrines. He had been at work on his *magnum opus,* the *Christianismi restitutio,* which was published on 3 January 1553. This theological treatise contained Servetus' imperishable contribution to science as the first man in the West to discover the lesser circulation of the blood. His primary concern, however, was theological: the problem of the introduction of the divine spirit into the blood and its dissemination throughout the body. He stated that the blood was not transmitted from the right ventricle of the heart to the left by way of the septum, for "that middle wall, since it is lacking in vessels and mechanisms, is not suitable for that communication and elaboration, although something may possibly sweat through." Rather, noting the size of the pulmonary artery, Servetus concluded that it was too large for simply transporting a small portion of the blood for the nutriment of the lungs, the function that Galen had as-

cribed to it. Servetus asserted that blood passed through the lungs for oxygenation. A further statement that the "vital spirit is then transfused from the left ventricle of the heart into the arteries of the whole body" showed that Servetus had arrived at the threshold of the complete circulation. Since his interest was primarily theological, however, he did not pursue this; and we have no way of knowing whether he could have done so.

Servetus' claim to the discovery of the lesser circulation has been questioned. Reference has been made to Realdo Colombo's *De re anatomica,* which, although published in 1559, was written earlier. Nonetheless, a manuscript of *Christianismi restitutio* in the Bibliothèque Nationale bears evidence of having been written before 1546. Ibn al-Nafis described the lesser circulation in a work that dates from the mid-thirteenth century, but Servetus' finding was made independently.

The publication of *Christianismi restitutio* and his earlier letters to Calvin, including drafts of some chapters of the book, led to Servetus' undoing, for Calvin allowed these letters to be used to inform the authorities in Lyons as to the true identity of Michel de Villeneuve. On 4 April 1553, Servetus was arrested and imprisoned but managed to escape three days later. In the meantime most of the thousand copies of his work were confiscated and burned; it was not until 1694 that Servetus' discovery of the lesser circulation became known. When Harvey announced the discovery of the general circulation in 1628, he did not know of Servetus' contribution.

Servetus remained out of sight for four months in France and then decided to go to Italy. He chose the route that passed through Geneva, where on 13 August he was recognized and denounced by Calvin to the magistrates. He was sentenced to be burned at the stake; his last cry was a reaffirmation of his views on the Trinity.

BIBLIOGRAPHY

I. ORIGINAL WORKS. A complete listing of Servetus' works is in John F. Fulton, *Michael Servetus: Humanist and Martyr* (New York, 1953), which also shows where copies may be found. An able translation of the scientific writings of Servetus is C. D. O'Malley, *Michael Servetus: A Translation of His Geographical, Medical and Astrological Writings* (Philadelphia, 1953).

II. SECONDARY LITERATURE. The most readable biography is Roland H. Bainton, *Hunted Heretic: The Life and Death of Michael Servetus, 1511–1553* (Boston, 1953; repr., 1960), which also contains a good list of periodical literature, including the sixty-eight articles and six books of the assiduous nineteenth-century Servetus scholar Henri Tollin. The following emphasize various aspects of Servetus' life: B. Becker, ed., *Autour de Michel Servet et de Sebastien Castellion* (Haarlem, 1953); Eloy Bullón y Fernández, *Miguel Servet y la geografía del Renacimiento,* 3rd ed. (Madrid, 1945); Pierre Cavard, *Le procès de Michel Servet de Vienne* (Vienne, 1953); and Juan-Manuel Palacios Sánchez, *El ilustre aragonés Miguel Servet* (Huesca, 1956).

Two works that place the doctrines of Servetus in their wider theological context are Earl Morse Wilbur, *A History of Unitarianism,* I (Cambridge, Mass., 1947), 3–4 and *passim*; and George Huntston Williams, *The Radical Reformation* (Philadelphia, 1962).

VICENTE R. PILAPIL

SERVOIS, FRANÇOIS-JOSEPH (*b.* Mont-de-Laval, Doubs, France, 19 July 1767; *d.* Mont-de-Laval, 17 April 1847), *mathematics.*

Servois was the son of Jacques-Ignace Servois, a merchant, and Jeanne-Marie Jolliet. He was ordained a priest at Besançon at the beginning of the Revolution, but in 1793 he gave up his ecclesiastical duties in order to join the army. In 1794, after a brief stay at the artillery school of Châlons-sur-Marne, he was made a lieutenant. While serving in several campaigns as staff officer, he devoted his leisure time to the study of mathematics. With the support of Legendre, he was appointed professor of mathematics at the artillery school of Besançon in July 1801. A few months later he transferred to the school at Châlons-sur-Marne; in 1802, to the artillery school at Metz; and in 1808, to the school at La Fère. After a brief return to Metz as professor at the artillery and engineering school, he was appointed curator of the artillery museum at Paris in 1816. He held the post until 1827, when he retired to his native village.

Like a number of his colleagues who taught at military schools, Servois closely followed developments in mathematics and sought, at times successfully, to make an original contribution. His first publication was a short work on pure and applied geometry: *Solutions peu connues de différents problèmes de géométrie pratique . . .* (1805). Drawing upon Mascheroni's *Geometria del compasso* and upon Lazare Carnot's *Géométrie de position* (1803), Servois formulated some notions of modern geometry and applied them to practical problems. The book was well received, and Poncelet considered it a "truly original work, notable for presenting the first applications of the

theory of transversals to the geometry of the ruler or surveyor's staff, thus revealing the fruitfulness and utility of this theory" (*Traité des propriétés projectives* [Paris, 1822], xliv).

Servois presented three memoirs before the Académie des Sciences. The first was on the principles of differential calculus and the development of functions in series (1805; new version, 1810); the second, which was never published, was devoted to the elements of dynamics (1809; additions in 1811); the third, also never published, dealt with the "determination of cometary and planetary orbits." In 1810 Servois published a study on the principle of virtual velocities in the *Mémoires* of the Turin Academy, but most of his subsequent papers appeared in Gergonne's *Annales de mathématiques pures et appliquées.* In his first contribution to the latter, he solved two construction problems by projective methods and introduced the term *pôle*. His ability in geometry was recognized by Poncelet, who consulted him on several occasions while writing his *Traité des propriétés projectives.*

In a letter to Gergonne of November 1813, Servois criticized, in the name of the primacy of algebraic language, the geometric representation of imaginary numbers that had recently been proposed by J. R. Argand and J. F. Français: "I confess that I do not yet see in this notation anything but a geometric mask applied to analytic forms the direct use of which seems to me simple and more expeditious" (*Annales de mathématiques . . . ,* **4**, no. 7 [January 1814], 230). This formalist conception of algebra made Servois one of the chief precursors of the English school of symbolic algebra. It can be seen still more clearly in his "Essai sur un nouveau mode d'exposition des principes du calcul différentiel," which contains the most important aspects of the memoir presented to the Academy in 1805 and 1810. Familiar with the work of Hindenburg's combinatorial school and with L. F. A. Arbogast's *Calcul des dérivations,* Servois sought in the "Essai" to provide differential calculus with a rigorous foundation. In the course of this effort he developed the first elements of what became the calculus of operations. Observing that this calculus is based on the conservation of certain properties of the operations to which it is applied, he introduced the fundamental notions of "commutative property" and "distributive property" (*Annales,* **5**, no. 5 [November 1814], 98). He did not, however, always distinguish between "function" and "operation." Servois's memoir, which more or less directly inspired the work of

Robert Murphy and of George Boole, was followed by an interesting critique of the various presentations of the principles of differential calculus, particularly the theory of the infinitely small and the method of Wronski.

Although Servois did not produce a major body of work, he made a number of original contributions to various branches of mathematics and prepared the way for important later developments.

BIBLIOGRAPHY

I. ORIGINAL WORKS. Servois's book on geometry, *Solutions peu connues de différents problèmes de géométrie pratique pour servir de supplément aux traités de cette science* (Metz–Paris, 1805), was followed by *Lettre de S . . . à F . . . professeur de mathématiques sur le Traité analytique des courbes et surfaces du second ordre* (Paris, 1802). He also published "De principio velocitatum virtualium," in *Mémoires de l'Académie impériale des sciences de Turin,* **18** (1809–1810), pt. 2, 177–244.

The following articles appeared in Gergonne's *Annales de mathématiques pures et appliquées:* "Solutions de deux problèmes de construction," **1,** no. 11 (May 1811), 332–335, 337–341; "Démonstrations de quelques formules de trigonométrie sphérique," **2,** no. 3 (Sept. 1811), 84–88; "Remarques relatives à la formule logarithmique" (dated 2 Oct. 1811), **2,** no. 7 (Jan. 1812), 178–179; "Calendrier perpétuel," **4,** no. 3 (Sept. 1813), 84–90; "Sur la théorie des quantités imaginaires. Lettre de M. Servois" (dated 23 Nov. 1813), **4,** no. 7 (Jan. 1814), 228–235, also in J. R. Argand, *Essai sur une manière de représenter les quantités imaginaires . . .,* 2nd ed. (Paris, 1874), 101–109; "Essai sur un nouveau mode d'exposition des principes du calcul différentiel," **5,** no. 4 (Oct. 1814), 93–140; "Réflexions sur les divers systèmes d'exposition des principes du calcul différentiel, et, en particulier, sur la doctrine des infiniment petits" (La Fère, 10 Aug. 1814), **5,** no. 5 (Nov. 1814), 141–170. The last two articles were printed together in a pamphlet (Nîmes, 1814).

See also "Note de M. Servois (Sur la trigonométrie des Indiens)," in *Correspondance sur l'École polytechnique,* **3,** no. 3 (Jan. 1816), 265–266; "Mémoire sur les quadratures," in *Annales de mathématiques . . .,* **8,** no. 3 (Sept. 1817), 73–115; "Lambert (Henri-Jean)," in Michaud, ed., *Biographie universelle,* XXIII (1819), 46–51; "Trajectoire," in *Dictionnaire de l'artillerie,* G.-H. Cotty, ed. (Paris, 1822), 464–471; "Lettre sur la théorie des parallèles" (dated 15 Nov. 1825), in *Annales de mathématiques . . .,* **16,** no. 7 (Feb. 1826), 233–238. Royal Society *Catalogue of Scientific Papers,* V, 665, gives only a portion of this bibliography.

II. SECONDARY LITERATURE. The principal account of Servois's career and writings is J. Boyer, "Le mathématicien franc-comtois François-Joseph Servois, an-

cien conservateur du Musée d'artillerie d'après des documents inédits," in *Mémoires de la Société d'émulation du Doubs,* 6th. ser., **9** (1894), 5–37, also separately printed as a 26-page pamphlet (Besançon, 1895).

Comments on Servois's work are given by S. F. Lacroix, in *Procès-verbaux des séances de l'Académie des sciences,* V (Hendaye, 1914), 99–101; and in *Traité du calcul différentiel et du calcul intégral,* 2nd ed., III (Paris, 1819), see index; by J. V. Poncelet, in *Traité des propriétés projectives . . .* (Paris, 1822), v–vi, xliv; and in *Applications d'analyse et de géométrie,* II (Paris, 1864), 530–552; by M. Chasles, in *Aperçu historique . . .* (Paris, 1875), see index; by O. Terquem, in *Bulletin de bibliographie, d'histoire et biographie mathématique,* **1,** 84, 93, 110, 185, supp. to *Nouvelles annales de mathématiques,* **14** (1855); and by S. Pincherle, "Équations et opérations fonctionnelles," in *Encyclopédie des sciences mathématiques,* II, pt. 5, fasc. 1 (Paris–Leipzig, 1912), 4–5; and in *Intermédiaire des mathématiciens,* **2** (1895), 58, 220, and **23** (1916), 195. The most recent study, N. Nielsen, *Géomètres français sous la Révolution* (Copenhagen–Paris, 1929), 221–224, analyzes certain aspects of Servois's work in greater detail but contains a number of errors.

RENÉ TATON

SESSÉ Y LACASTA, MARTÍN DE (*b.* Baraguas, Aragón, Spain, 11 December 1751 [?]; *d.* Madrid, Spain, 4 October 1808), *botany.*

Sessé studied medicine, practiced in Madrid (1775–1776), then served as an army doctor in Spain and in Cuba. He moved to Mexico City in 1785. On 13 March 1787 he was named director of the Royal Botanical Expedition to New Spain and director of the Royal Botanical Garden in Mexico City. Early in 1789 Sessé gave up his medical work to devote full time to botany. He continued to hold his two directorships until he returned to Spain. In spite of the pressure of administrative detail involving the expedition and the garden, he took part in long field excursions to western Mexico (1789–1792), to the Atlantic slope of Mexico (1793), and to Cuba and Puerto Rico (1795–1798). Sessé left Mexico for the last time about April 1803 and reached Spain in November, having stopped in Cuba to arrange for the shipment of his West Indian collection, the bulk of which reached Madrid in June 1804. He seems to have accomplished little in his remaining years.

Sessé was a competent botanist, as is shown by his existing manuscript notes and botanical descriptions. He apparently enjoyed collecting and analyzing plants in the field and understood thoroughly the standard practices and concepts of his day. Sessé's contribution to botany is linked with that of José Mariano Mociño and can hardly be considered apart from it. The posthumous works *Plantae Novae Hispaniae* and *Flora Mexicana* were attributed to Sessé and Mociño as joint authors, but it is probable that a major part of the botanical study and writing was done by Mociño under the nominal direction of Sessé, whose principal contribution to science seems to have been related to his administrative and executive functions.

It was Sessé who originally conceived and proposed the Botanical Expedition to New Spain, and with Vicente Cervantes he helped plan and maintain the Botanical Garden in Mexico. He dealt with several viceroys in turn, keeping them informed of progress and trying to convince them of the continuing value of the botanical work. Under his direction the members of the expedition conducted or took part in major excursions to all parts of Mexico except the extreme north, to Central America as far as Costa Rica, to the Greater Antilles, and to the northern Pacific. For about fifteen years he kept a group of temperamental naturalists and artists occupied and relatively contented (with the conspicuous exception of Longinos Martínez), sometimes under very trying circumstances. Finally, he managed to return to Spain with all the expedition's collections, manuscripts, and paintings intact.

BIBLIOGRAPHY

I. ORIGINAL WORKS. Two volumes, attributed to Sessé and Mociño jointly, were published in Mexico between 1887 and 1897. These appeared first in parts, as supplements to the periodical *La Naturaleza*. *Plantae Novae Hispaniae* (1887–1891) was based on a MS written by Mociño, completed at Guadalajara, Jalisco, forwarded from there to the viceroy, the Conde de Revilla-Gigedo, in July 1791, and now in the archives of the Instituto Botánico "A. J. Cavanilles," Madrid. It is a complete flora, including the species of flowering plants studied by the Botanical Expedition up to about the beginning of 1791. A 2nd ed. was published in book form at Mexico City in 1893.

Flora Mexicana (1891–1897) was based on a very heterogeneous series of notes on individual plant-species, from many parts of Spanish America. These comprised a part, but by no means all, of the notes prepared by the members of the Botanical Expedition. Discovered, in no particular order, in the archives at Madrid, the notes were organized by the editor into the Linnaean classes and were published without careful study or collation. A 2nd ed. was published in book form at Mexico City in 1894, before the later parts of the first edition appeared in *Naturaleza*.

Original letters, memoranda, and other documents relative to the Botanical Expedition to New Spain are to be found in the Mexican National Archives, sec. "Historia," vols. 460–466, 527. A few documents apparently of similar origin are in the William L. Clements Library, University of Michigan, Ann Arbor. Sessé's official correspondence as director of the Expedition and of the Royal Botanical Garden is voluminous. The papers of Revilla-Gigedo, acquired in 1954 by a private collector in the United States, contain some information not accessible elsewhere but have been little studied in this connection.

The richest source of MS material in Spain is the archive of the Instituto Botánico "A. J. Cavanilles," Madrid. It contains most of the existing MSS dealing with strictly botanical matters of the expedition to New Spain: the MS of *Plantae Novae Hispaniae*, various botanical descriptions, fragments of unpublished floras (including a "Flora guatemalensis" by Mociño), inventories of paintings, and collections from the various excursions carried out in Mexico. Descriptions or copies of most of these inventories have been published by Arias Divito (see below) or in the papers cited by him. Arias Divito also lists (p. 307) the other major sources of MS material in Madrid and Seville.

II. SECONDARY LITERATURE. An extensively documented account of Sessé, Mociño, and their co-workers, based primarily upon materials in the Archivo General de la Nación, Mexico City, is H. W. Rickett, "The Royal Botanical Expedition to New Spain," in *Chronica botanica*, **11** (1947), 1–86. Juan Carlos Arias Divito, *Las expediciones científicas españolas durante el siglo XVIII* (Madrid, 1968), is based primarily on Spanish archival sources. It includes copies of many previously unpublished inventories of plants, animals, and paintings, and a considerable bibliography that supplements the references cited by Rickett. Additional information, especially relative to the members of the Malaspina Expedition who were in Mexico at the same time as the Royal Botanical Expedition, is in Iris Higbie Wilson, "Scientific Aspects of Spanish Exploration in New Spain During the Late Eighteenth Century" (Ph.D. diss., Univ. of Southern California, 1962).

The story of the disaffected naturalist Longinos Martínez, who left the Botanical Expedition after a long and bitter quarrel with Sessé, is told in Lesley Bird Simpson, *Journal of José Longinos Martínez* (San Francisco, 1961).

The botanical specimens collected in New Spain from about 1787 to 1799 number more than 10,000; perhaps 8,000 compose the "Sessé and Mociño" herbarium at the Instituto Botánico "A. J. Cavanilles," Madrid; and several thousand duplicates are scattered through the larger European herbaria, especially those in London, Paris, Geneva, Florence, and Oxford. After the death of Sessé and the flight of Mociño with the retreating French in 1812, the Spanish botanist José Antonio Pavón sold to collectors at least 15,000 duplicate specimens, including many of those collected by the expedition of Sessé and Mociño. As these found their way gradually into large public and private herbaria, they were much studied and cited by botanists, and thus ironically became of more scientific value than the original herbarium, which remained unstudied in Madrid. Much effort has been expended in recent years, as more has become known of the work of the Botanical Expedition, in documenting these specimens that constitute perhaps the most valuable part of the legacy of Sessé and Mociño. A part of the story of their sale and the dispersal of duplicate specimens from New Spain is told by Arthur Robert Steele in *Flowers for the King* (Durham, N.C., 1964), 291–315, which describes in detail Pavón's dealings with Aylmer Bourke Lambert and Philip Barker Webb. An uncataloged MS in the department of botany, British Museum (Natural History), lists the plants sold by Pavón to Lambert and later bought for the Museum.

ROGERS McVAUGH

SETCHELL, WILLIAM ALBERT (*b.* Norwich, Connecticut, 15 April 1864; *d.* Berkeley, California, 5 April 1943), *botany, geography.*

Setchell was the acknowledged authority on marine algae of the northern Pacific, and on the role of crustaceous algae in coral reef formation. He also advanced knowledge of the role of temperature in delimiting plant distributions, and initiated studies on the genus *Nicotiana.*

Setchell was the son of George Case Setchell and Ann Davis Setchell. With George R. Case, Setchell published a catalog of local wild plants before he was twenty; and the botanist Daniel Cady Eaton encouraged his interest in botany while he was an undergraduate at Yale. His lifetime predilection for algae dated from his Harvard years, when, as a Morgan fellow, he came under the tutelage of William Gilson Farlow. For twenty-five years Setchell, with his associates F. S. Collins and Isaac Holden, issued *Phycotheca Boreali-Americana* (1895–1919), numbering 200,000 specimens of algae. In 1920 Setchell went to Samoa under the aegis of the Carnegie Institution of Washington, the first of many journeys to the South Pacific to study coral reef formation, ethnobotanical subjects, and patterns of plant distribution. From these and other trips he collected and donated hundreds of objects, including a notable pipe collection now at the Robert H. Lowie Museum of Anthropology. Meanwhile Setchell amassed a collection of living tobaccos and began an investigation of their morphology and hybridization. His colleague Thomas Harper Goodspeed took up this study and published a comprehensive monograph entitled *The Genus Nicotiana* (1954).

The history of botany was one of Setchell's pleasures, and his course in that subject attracted students and colleagues alike. He enjoined students to compare various topics among the herbals which he presented to the Biology Library of the University of California at Berkeley.

Setchell emphasized the critical role of temperature in the delimitation of algal and flowering plant ranges; this led to his "waves of anthesis" principle: species succeed one another in flowering with every rise of 5°F. in the vernal temperature. He also predicated the critical role of establishment in the distribution of organisms, as a biologic corollary of Liebig's law of the minimum.

Setchell's wife, Clara Ball Pearson Caldwell, whom he married in 1920, shared his enthusiasms for fourteen years. His foil in the laboratory preparation of algae was Nathaniel L. Gardner (1864–1937), with whom he wrote several revisions of Pacific marine algae. Setchell's close associates described him as "of commanding presence, magnetic personality, catholic taste, and congenial disposition" (Clausen, Bonar, and Evans, p. 39).

BIBLIOGRAPHY

I. ORIGINAL WORKS. Setchell's chief works are "Marine Algae of the Pacific Coast of North America," in *University of California Publications in Botany,* **8**, pts. 1–3 (1919–1925); "American Samoa," in *Publications. Carnegie Institution of Washington,* no. 341 (1924), 1–275; "Temperature and Anthesis," in *American Journal of Botany,* **12** (1925), 178–188; and "Geographic Elements of the Marine Flora of the North Pacific Ocean," in *American Naturalist,* **69** (1935), 560–577. Prophetic of his later phenological interests was *A Catalogue of Wild Plants Growing in Norwich and Vicinity, Arranged in Order of Flowering for the Year 1882* (Norwich, Conn., 1883), written with George R. Case. A bibliography of his publications, prepared by T. H. Goodspeed and Lee Bonar, was appended to D. H. Campbell's sketch (see below). Copies of 210 papers (1890–1935) are bound in 35 vols. in the Biology Library, University of California, Berkeley. His correspondence is preserved in the department of botany. His unpublished outline for his history of botany course was extensively utilized by Howard S. Reed in his *Short History of the Plant Sciences* (Waltham, Mass., 1942).

II. SECONDARY LITERATURE. The best obituary of Setchell, with interpretive background comment, was written by his Stanford colleague D. H. Campbell, in *Biographical Memoirs. National Academy of Sciences,* **23** (1945), 127–147, with portrait by Peter van Valkenburgh. *Essays in Geobotany in Honor of William Albert Setchell* (Berkeley, 1936) includes a biographical intro. by the editor, T. H. Goodspeed. Other sketches were published by Roy E. Clausen, Lee Bonar, and Herbert M. Evans, in *University of California In Memoriam* (Berkeley, 1943) 37–39; by A. D. Cotton, in *Proceedings of the Linnean Society of London*, **156** (1943–1944), 232–233; by Francis Drouet, in *American Midland Naturalist*, **30** (1943), 529–532; and by Herbert L. Mason, in *Madroño*, **7** (1943), 91–93, with portrait. A disparate estimate will be read in the private journals of his colleague Willis Linn Jepson when they are made available to the public.

JOSEPH EWAN

SEVERGIN, VASILY MIKHAYLOVICH (*b.* St. Petersburg, Russia, 19 September 1765; *d.* St. Petersburg, 29 November 1826), *mineralogy, chemistry, technology.*

The son of a court musician, Severgin was accepted, on his father's petition, in 1776 at the private Gymnasium of the St. Petersburg Academy of Sciences. In 1784 he enrolled at the Academy's university, choosing mineralogy as his specialty. The following year he was sent to the University of Göttingen, where he studied the outcrops of basalt near Göttingen and became involved in the controversy between the neptunists and the plutonists.

In 1789 Severgin returned to St. Petersburg and presented two scientific papers to the Academy, on the properties and formation of basalt and on alkaline salts. In the first paper, directed against the neptunists, he argued that basalt originated in a fiery liquid fusion. On 25 June 1789 Severgin was elected adjunct to the chair of mineralogy. His chief orientation was toward mineral chemistry, in which he applied the ideas of Lavoisier.

In his enlarged and supplemented Russian translation of Kirwan's *Elements of Mineralogy* (1791) Severgin classified and described minerals on the basis of their chemical composition. Two years later he was elected professor of mineralogy, a post that carried with it the title of academician. Much of his subsequent work was devoted to the study of Russian minerals, their regional distribution, and methods of extracting and processing them. Severgin disseminated chemical and mineralogical knowledge through his many textbooks and lectures at the Institute of Mines and at the Medical and Surgical Academy.

His *Pervye osnovania mineralogii* ("Foundations of Mineralogy," 1798) was the first textbook in Russian on the subject. Besides describing minerals and rocks, Severgin classified petrifactions as "simple" or "complex." Among the former

were marble, jasper, and flint (quartz), which lack foreign particles. He gave detailed descriptions of the physical and chemical properties of minerals, developing "wet" methods of analysis as well as methods using the blowpipe; his techniques of determining the external characteristics of minerals are still used, substantially unchanged. In 1804 Severgin founded *Tekhnologichesky zhurnal*. A frequent contributor to the journal, he was also its editor until 1824. His mineralogical dictionary (1807) contained detailed explanations and was an important contribution to the literature.

Concentrating on mineral chemistry rather than on crystallography, Severgin reported in 1798 on the significance of mineral associations—galena and sphalerite, for example—on the basis of which he developed a theory of the contiguity of minerals: "What I call the contiguity of minerals is the joint occurrence of two or more minerals in one place . . . for example, the association of quartz with mica, virgin gold, and others" (*Pervye osnovania mineralogii*, p. 85–86).

The mineral collections of the Institute of Mines, the Free Economic Society, and the many St. Petersburg amateur collectors, as well as his personal collection, served Severgin as the material for *Opyt mineralogicheskogo zemleopisania Rossyskogo gosudarstva* ("An Attempt at the Mineralogical Description of the Territory of the Russian State"). The first volume, a physical-geographical survey, describes structures and lithology as well as the hydrographic network; the second volume deals with the geographical distribution of minerals.

In 1819 Severgin published his translation of the book on minerals of Pliny's *Natural History*. He also contributed to the development of scientific terminology, introducing Russian terms still used for oxide, silicon dioxide, alkali, and splintery and conchoidal fracture of minerals. His chemical works had a practical orientation and dealt with the extraction of mineral salts, the testing of medicinal chemical substances, assaying, and the production of saltpeter.

BIBLIOGRAPHY

I. ORIGINAL WORKS. Severgin's writings include *Nachalnye osnovania estestvennoy istorii* . . . ("The Foundations of Natural History"), a trans. of Kirwan's *Elements of Mineralogy*, enl. and supp., 2 vols. (St. Petersburg, 1791); *Mineralogicheskie, geograficheskie i drugie smeshannye izvestia o Altayskikh gorakh, prinadlezhashchikh k Rossyskomu vladeniyu* ("Mineralogical,

Geographical, and Other . . . Information on the Altai Mountains, Which Belong to the Russian Domain"), trans. from the German of H. M. Renovanz (St. Petersburg, 1792); "Opisanie Dalgrenevoy payalnoy trubki, deystvuyushchey pomoshchyu mekha s pokazaniem upotreblenia onoy" ("Description of the Dahlgren Blowpipe, Which Works With the Aid of a Bellows, With Instructions for Its Use"), in *Trudy Volnogo ekonomicheskogo obshchestva* (1792), nos. 14 and 15; *Pervye osnovania mineralogii . . .* ("Foundations of Mineralogy"), 2 vols. (St. Petersburg, 1798); "O estestve i obrazovanii bazalta, ili stolbchatogo kamnya" ("On the Nature and Formation of Basalt or of Basaltiform Rock"), in *Akademicheskie sochinenia* (1801), no. 1, 332–359; *Probirnoe iskusstvo* ("Assaying"; St. Petersburg, 1801); *Zapiski puteshestvia po zapadnym provintsiam Rossyskogo gosudarstva . . . 1802 i 1803* ("Notes of a Journey Through the Western Provinces of the Russian State . . . in 1802 and 1803"; St. Petersburg, 1803).

They also include *Prodolzhenie zapisok puteshestvia po zapadnym provintsiam Rossyskogo gosudarstva* ("Continuation of the Notes of a Journey Through the Western Provinces of the Russian State"; St. Petersburg, 1804); *Obozrenie Rossyskoy Finlyandii* ("A Survey of Russian Finland"; St. Petersburg, 1804); *Podrobny slovar mineralogichesky . . .* ("A Detailed Mineralogical Dictionary . . ."), 2 vols. (St. Petersburg, 1807); *Opyt mineralogicheskogo zemleopisania Rossyskogo gosudarstva* ("An Attempt to Describe Mineralogically the Territory of the Russian State"), 2 vols. (St. Petersburg, 1809); *Slovar khimichesky* ("Chemical Dictionary"), trans. of the work of Charles-Louis Cadet de Gassicourt, 4 vols. (St. Petersburg, 1810–1813); "Obozrenie mineralnogo kabineta imperatorskoy Akademii nauk" ("A Survey of the Mineral Cabinet of the Imperial Academy of Sciences"), in *Tekhnologichesky zhurnal*, **11**, no. 1 (1814); *Novaya sistema mineralov, osnovannaya na naruzhnykh otlichitelnykh priznakakh* ("A New System of Minerals, Based on External Distinctive Characteristics"; St. Petersburg, 1816); and *Kaya Plinia sekunda—Estestvennaya istoria iskopaemykh tel*, trans. of the mineralogical section from Pliny the Elder's *Natural History* (St. Petersburg, 1819).

II. SECONDARY LITERATURE. See G. P. Barsanov, "V. M. Severgin i mineralogia ego vremeni v Rossii" ("Severgin and the Mineralogy of His Time in Russia"), in *Izvestiya Akademii nauk SSSR*, geol. ser. (1949), no. 5; *Bolshaya sovetskaya entsiklopedia* ("Great Soviet Encyclopedia"), 2nd ed., XXXVIII, 303; A. E. Fersman, "Mineralogia v Akademii nauk za 220 let" ("220 Years of Mineralogy in the Academy of Sciences"), in *Ocherki po istorii Akademii nauk* ("Essays on the History of the Academy of Sciences"; Moscow–Leningrad, 1945); D. P. Grigorev and I. I. Shafranovsky, "V. M. Severgin," in *Vydayushchiesya russkie mineralogi* ("Outstanding Russian Mineralogists"; Moscow–Leningrad, 1949); A. N. Ivanov, "Vasily Mikhaylovich Severgin," in *Lyudi russkoy nauki* ("People of Russian Science"; Moscow, 1962), 7–15; A. V. Nemilova, and

I. I. Shafranovsky, "Akademik Severgin V. M. i ego rol v istorii russkoy mineralogii (k 120 letiyu so dnya smerti, 1765–1826)" ("Academician Severgin and His Role in the History of Russian Mineralogy [on the 120th Anniversary of His Death]"), in *Priroda*, **36** (1947), no. 3, 72–75; D. P. Rezvoy, "Akademik Vasily Severgin — Russky mineralog i geognost (1765–1826)" ("Academician Severgin — Russian Mineralogist and Geognost"), in *Mineralogicheskii sbornik* (1953), no. 7; and M. I. Sukhomlinov, "Ocherk zhizni i deyatelnosti akademika Severgina" ("An Essay on the Life and Career of Academician Severgin"), in *Istoria Rossyskoy Akademii* ("History of the Russian Academy"), appendix to *Zapiski Imperatorskoi akademii nauk*, **32**, no. 1 (1878).

G. D. KUROCHKIN

SEVERI, FRANCESCO (*b.* Arezzo, Italy, 13 April 1879; *d.* Rome, Italy, 8 December 1961), *mathematics*.

From 1898 until his death, Severi published more than 400 books and papers on mathematics, history of science, education, and philosophy. His most outstanding contributions, however, were in the field of algebraic geometry. Severi acquired the taste for elegant synthetic arguments while studying with Segre at the University of Turin, from which he graduated in 1900 under Segre's guidance. At Turin he became interested in algebraic and enumerative problems and developed a broad geometric eclecticism and a formidable dexterity in the projective geometry of higher spaces.

In the latter field Segre published (1894) an interesting reworking of geometry on an algebraic curve. In Italy, Bertini and Castelnuovo also contributed to this field, while in Germany, Brill and Max Noether, in the footsteps of Riemann, made more studies using different methods. A more invariant view, derived from the transformations introduced by Cremona thirty years earlier, led Castelnuovo and Enriques to lay the foundations of a similar theory for algebraic surfaces. This theory anticipated the work of Picard in France on the same subject.

Having served as *assistente* to Enriques at Bologna in 1902 and to Bertini at Pisa in 1903, Severi was drawn to these new developments. He attempted, with great success, to explain important and still unsolved problems along with work in new areas. He perfected the theory of birational invariants of algebraic surfaces and created an analogous (but more complex) theory for algebraic varieties of arbitrary dimension. The completion of this work was to take him another fifty years. Severi's work on algebraic geometry can best be described by dividing it into five sections, rather than maintaining a chronological order.

1. Enumerative and Projective Geometry, Intersections, and Questions on the Foundations of Algebraic Geometry. The proof of the principle of the "conservation of number," established heuristically by Schubert in the nineteenth century, was listed by Hilbert at the Paris Congress of 1900 as one of the fundamental unsolved problems of mathematics. Severi subsequently found and proved the conditions under which this principle is true. Thus he refined Schubert's work and also advanced it through the theory of the base and the theory of characteristics.

Twenty years later this research by Severi inspired several mathematicians, including William V. D. Hodge, Wei L. Chow, and Bartel van der Waerden. Severi also introduced the important notion of the invariant order of an algebraic variety, which led to the theory of minimal models; and he studied improper double points of algebraic surfaces, characters of embedding of one variety in another, and generalizations of Bezout's theorem from intersections of plane curves to those of arbitrary varieties in higher projective spaces.

2. Series and Systems of Equivalence. This theory, created almost wholly by Severi, added to algebraic geometry many important entities, for example, the canonical varieties of arbitrary dimension—a theory (completed later by Beniamino Segre and J. A. Todd) that has had considerable connections and implications in both algebra and topology. He generalized the theory of linear equivalence to arbitrary subvarieties of a given variety and also made lengthy fundamental studies of rational equivalence, algebraic equivalence, and algebraic correspondences between varieties.

3. Geometry on Algebraic Surfaces. At the beginning of the twentieth century, the geometry of algebraic surfaces had reached a dead end. Although Castelnuovo and Enriques had defined the genera, irregularity, and plurigenera of surfaces and had characterized those surfaces that are birationally equivalent to a plane or to a ruled surface, there were still several unsolved problems; and Picard's introduction of three types of integrals on a surface suggested many additional questions, a large number of which were successfully explained by Severi. Also, Severi reduced Picard's three types of integrals to normal form and found conditions of integrability for certain linear differential equations on a surface.

Severi introduced the notion of semiexact differentials of the first type and, using Hodge's findings,

surprisingly showed that they are always exact. An important property utilized in these investigations was the completeness of the characteristic series of a continuous complete system. Much effort was later required to establish this result in its correct generality.

4. Geometry on Algebraic Varieties. The extension from surfaces to varieties of three or more dimensions is no less difficult than that from curves to surfaces. In an early memoir (1909), Severi established the basis for the extended theory with his study of linear systems of hypersurfaces. He gave various definitions of the arithmetic genus of a variety and proved their equivalence, thus partially extending the Riemannn-Roch theorem and also Picard's theorem on the regularity of the adjoint.

Besides his work on the foundations of the general theory of algebraic varieties, Severi established the theory of irregularity and made important studies of continuous systems of curves in the plane and in higher projective spaces.

5. Abelian and Quasi-Abelian Varieties. The theory of Abelian varieties V_p, of dimension p, originated in 1889 with Picard, who investigated algebraic V_p possessing a continuous, transitive, Abelian group of ∞^p birational automorphisms. The infinitesimal transformations of the group led to p independent integrals. Picard maintained that these integrals were all of the first type, but Severi showed that this is not true for $p = 2$ if the group is not absolutely transitive.

The study of these V_p is connected with that of a particular type of functions of several complex variables—a generalization of elliptic functions. These functions are related to particular varieties, called Picard and Albanese varieties, to which Severi devoted several works. When the group of the V_p is transitive, but not necessarily absolutely transitive, V_p is called quasi-Abelian. Severi discussed these V_p in a lengthy paper written during the turbulent period October 1944–May 1945.

Algebraic geometry has undergone several revolutionary changes in the twentieth century that have led to many schools and to several widely differing methods of approach. Severi's work remains not merely a monument to him but also a valuable source from which all algebraic geometers continue to draw ideas. He himself characterized his approach to mathematical research with the following admonition:

> Let us not pride ourselves too much on perfect rigour, which we today believe to be capable of reducing so large a part of mathematics to nothing, and let us not discard what does not appear quite as rigorous,

for tomorrow we will certainly find imperfections in our perfection and from some brilliant, intuitive thought which had not yet the blessing of rigour will be drawn unthinkable results [Severi, "Intuizionismo e astrattismo nella matematica contemporanea," in *Atti del congresso. Unione matematica italiana* (Sept. 1948), p. 30].

BIBLIOGRAPHY

I. ORIGINAL WORKS. Severi's works include *Vorlesungen über algebraische Geometrie*, L. Löffler, ed. and trans. (Leipzig, 1921; repr., New York–London, 1968); "Geometria delle serie lineari," in *Trattato di geometria algebrica*, **1**, pt. 1 (1926), 145–169; *Serie, sistemi d'equivalenza e corrispondenze algebriche sulle varietà algebriche*, F. Conforto and E. Martinelli, eds. (Rome, 1942); *Funzioni quasi abeliane* (Vatican City, 1947); *Memorie scelte*, B. Segre, ed. (Bologna, 1950); *Geometria dei sistemi algebrici sopra una superficie e sopra una varietà algebrica*, II (Rome, 1957), III (Rome, 1959); and *Il teorema di Rimann-Roch per curve, superficie e varietà* (Berlin, 1958). Severi's mathematical papers, collected in seven volumes, will soon be published by the Lincei Academy (vols. I and II have already appeared in 1971 and 1974).

II. SECONDARY LITERATURE. On Severi and his work, see B. Segre, *L'opera scientifica di Francesco Severi* (Rome, 1962), with complete bibliography.

BENIAMINO SEGRE

SEVERIN, CHRISTIAN, also known as **Longomontanus** (*b*. Longberg, Jutland, Denmark, 4 October 1562; *d*. Copenhagen, Denmark, 8 October 1647), *astronomy*.

Severin was the son of Søren Poulsen and Maren Christensdatter, both of whom were humble peasants. Finding education an uncertain and intermittent luxury, especially after the early death of his father, Severin did not complete his basic education until 1588. At that time he entered the service of Tycho Brahe and stayed with him until 1597, when Tycho left Denmark. After his *Wanderjahre* in Germany, Severin received the M.A. at the University of Rostock and then returned home to begin his career. By 1607 he was professor of mathematics and astronomy at the University of Copenhagen, where he remained until his death.

When Tycho died in 1601, his program for the restoration of astronomy was unfinished. The observational aspects were complete, but two important tasks remained: the selection and integration of the data into accounts of the motions of the planets, and the presentation of the results of the entire program in the form of a systematic treatise. Severin, Tycho's sole disciple, assumed the re-

sponsibility and fulfilled both tasks in his voluminous *Astronomia danica* (1622). Regarded as the testament of Tycho, the work was eagerly received and quickly won a place in seventeenth-century astronomical literature. Even after the appearance of Kepler's *Tabulae Rudolphinae* (1627), a rival work that bore the imprimatur of Tycho, Severin's *Astronomia danica* retained sufficient prestige (despite its staidness) to warrant reprinting in 1640 and 1663.

Unfortunately Severin found himself looking backward to Tycho, instead of forward into the seventeenth century. Although Severin worked and wrote in the era of Kepler and Galileo, he denounced ellipses, denied heliocentrism, denigrated the telescope, and ignored logarithms. Severin departed from Tycho in only one significant respect—he assumed diurnal rotation of the earth.

Because Severin's career was virtually determined by his unique status as the literary heir of Tycho, it is impossible to form an independent estimate of his contemporary reputation. He was highly esteemed by Tycho for his skill at manipulating observational data, and he may have played an important role in Tycho's remarkable research on the lunar theory. Regardless of his competence as a planetary theorist, Severin's reputation will always suffer in comparison with Kepler's achievements in the same task. In addition to his astronomical interests, Severin also displayed considerable enthusiasm for pure mathematics, but with notably less success. Concerned principally with the quadrature of the circle, he believed that he had solved the problem with a precise evaluation of π as equal to $78/43 \sqrt{3}$.

BIBLIOGRAPHY

A complete bibliography of Severin's works is in H. Ehreneron-Müller, *Forfatterlexicon*, V (Copenhagen, 1929), 181–185. His major works are *Cyclometria ex lunulis reciproce demonstrata* (Copenhagen, 1612); *Astronomia danica* (Amsterdam; 1622, 1640, 1663); *Inventio quadraturae circuli* (Copenhagen, 1634); and *Introductio in theatrum astronomicum* (Copenhagen, 1639).

On Severin and his work, see J.-B.-J. Delambre, *Histoire de l'astronomie moderne*, I (Paris, 1821), 262–287.

VICTOR E. THOREN

SEVERINO, MARCO AURELIO (*b*. Tarsia, Calabria, Italy, 2 November 1580; *d*. Naples, Italy, 12 July 1656), *biomedical sciences*.

Severino was the son of Beatrice Orangia and Jacopo Severino, a successful lawyer who died when his son was seven. Marco Aurelio's mother directed his early education, in Latin, Greek, rhetoric, poetry, and law, at various schools in Calabria. He then continued his studies at Naples, soon moving from law to medicine as his chosen field. At Naples he met Tommaso Campanella, who, although not officially one of Severino's teachers, was nevertheless an important influence in the formation of his thought. From Campanella, he learned the rudiments of Telesio's philosophical system, which formed the basis of the critical anti-Aristotelianism that marked Severino's later work. After taking a medical degree at Salerno in 1606 (although his studies had largely been at Naples), Severino returned to Tarsia to begin medical practice. Three years later he returned to Naples to study surgery with Giulio Iasolino. From 1610 Severino taught surgery and anatomy privately at Naples. When the university chair in these subjects fell vacant in 1615, Severino was named to fill it and shortly afterward was also named first surgeon at the Ospedale Degli Incurabili.

Severino's fame as a surgeon spread rapidly, and students came from all parts of Europe to study with him. Ultimately his published works were better known and more frequently published north of the Alps than in Italy. He corresponded with many of the important physicians and scientists of his time, including William Harvey and John Houghton in England; Thomas Bartholin and Ole Worm in Denmark; J. G. Volkamer and Joannes Vesling in Germany; and Campanella, Iasolino, and Tommaso Cornelio in Italy. Severino was called before the Inquisition for allegedly unorthodox religious and philosophical views but was eventually acquitted. He died of the plague in Naples and was buried without a marker in the church of S. Biagio de' Librai.

Severino's writings are marked by a general emphasis on observation and experience, which he traced back to a medical tradition stemming from Democritus. But he remained deeply influenced by metaphysical ideas and accepted teleology in nature, neo-Platonic hierarchical schemes, and the Paracelsian version of the microcosm-macrocosm relationship. His strongly anti-Aristotelian sentiments (which are especially evident in *Zootomia Democritea* and in *Antiperipatias*) derived in part from the native southern Italian intellectual heritage of Telesio, della Porta, and Campanella.

The bulk of Severino's printed works dealt with surgery and anatomy. He published both comprehensive treatises and specific detailed monographs on these subjects. His fame as a surgeon is illustrated by the broad distribution of works like *De efficaci medicina,* in which he championed surgery as a legitimate medical technique in opposition to the iatrochemical approach of some contemporaries.

Severino's permanent contributions, however, seem to lie in his anatomical works, especially *Zootomia Democritea.* This work might with some justification be called "the earliest comprehensive treatise on comparative anatomy" (Cole) and, indeed, it emphasized throughout an approach in which human anatomy is related to that of other animals. Severino viewed the study of anatomy as one way to uncover a clearer knowledge of divine creation. Since man, animals, and plants form a continuous hierarchical structure, the anatomy of all three must be studied in conjunction. Severino recognized a close similarity between the anatomy of man and of animals and considered important the detailed study of nonhuman anatomy. He himself dissected and studied a wide range of specimens, both vertebrate and invertebrate. He contended that even tiny animals and insects must be studied by the anatomist, if necessary with the aid of a microscope, although he does not seem to have made much use of that instrument himself.

The *Antiperipatias* illustrates Severino's critical attitude toward the Aristotelians. He argued against the Peripatetic view—that fish do not breathe air—by trying to demonstrate, following the atomistic philosophy of Democritus, that fish actually utilize the air that is dissolved in water.

Severino's full significance in the flourishing scientific culture of Naples during his time and also his importance as a figure of international renown in the seventeenth century have not been studied in detail. Particularly important are his relations to Harvey and his place in the discussions arising from the publication in 1628 of Harvey's *De motu cordis.* Most of the key documents touching on this aspect of his activities remain in manuscript and have never been properly evaluated, nor is there an adequate survey of his other unpublished writings. Thus his place in the development of seventeenth-century biomedicine is not firmly fixed.

BIBLIOGRAPHY

I. ORIGINAL WORKS. A more complete bibliography is in Schmitt and Webster (below). See also *Therapeuta Neapolitanus* (Naples, 1653), fols. §§2r–§§4r and Severino's trans. of Antonio Colmenero de Ledesma, *Chocolata Inda* (Nuremberg, 1644), 69–73.

Severino's major works include *De recondita abscessuum natura* (Naples, 1632); *Zootomia Democritea* (Nuremberg, 1645); *De efficaci medicina* (Frankfurt, 1646); *Vipera Pythia* (Padua, 1650); *Trimembris chirurgia* (Frankfurt, 1653); *Therapeuta Neapolitanus* (Naples, 1653); *Seilo-phlebotome castigata* (Hanau, 1654); *Quaestiones anatomicae quatuor* (Frankfurt, 1654); *Antiperipatias. Hoc est adversus Aristoteleos de respiratione piscium diatribe . . . De piscibus in sicco viventibus . . . Phoca illustratus*, 2 pts. (Naples, 1655, 1659); *Synopseos chirurgiae* (Amsterdam, 1644).

At his death Severino left numerous unpublished works, some of which appeared in print posthumously. Most of his MSS went first to Antonio Bulifon, then to Giammaria Lancisi; they remain in the Biblioteca Lancisiana in Rome. For some information see V. Ducceschi, "L'epistolario di Marco Aurelio Severino (1580–1656)," in *Rivista di storia delle scienze mediche e naturali,* **5** (1923), 213–223, and the article by Schmitt and Webster, which summarizes the extant MS sources thus far uncovered. For a list of the seventy-seven vols. of MSS in the Biblioteca Lancisiana, which contain Severino materials, see P. De Angelis, *Giovanni Maria Lancisi, La Biblioteca Lancisiana, L'Accademia Lancisiana* (Rome, 1965), 151–163.

II. SECONDARY LITERATURE. The anonymous *Vita,* prefaced by Severino's *Antiperipatias* (1659), fols. 3v–4v, remains the most important contemporary source for his life. Of the more recent works, see esp. L. Amabile, "Marco Aurelio Severino," in *Rivista critica di cultura calabrese,* **2** (1922); "Due artisti ed uno scienziato . . . Marco Aurelio Severino nel Santo Officio Napoletano," in *Atti della Reale Accademia di scienze morali e politiche* (Società reale di Napoli), **24** (1891), 433–503: N. Badaloni, *Introduzione a G. B. Vico* (Milan, 1961), 25–37; L. Belloni, "Severino als Vorläufer Malpighis," in *Nova acta Leopoldina,* n.s. **27** (1963), 213–224, and "La dottrina della circulazione del sangue e la Scuola Galileiana, 1636–61," in *Gesnerus,* **28** (1971), 7–33; and *Biographisches Lexikon der hervorragenden Ärzte,* V (Munich–Basel, 1962), 242–243.

See also P. Capparoni, *Profili biobibliografici di medici e naturalisti celebri italiani dal secolo XV al secolo XVIII,* II (Rome, 1925–1928), 75–78; F. J. Cole, *History of Comparative Anatomy* (London, 1949), 132–149; Pietro Magliari, *Elogio istorico di M. A. Severino* (Naples, 1815); A. Portal, *Histoire de l'anatomie et de la chirurgie,* II (Paris, 1770), 493–505; C. B. Schmitt and C. Webster, "Harvey and M. A. Severino: A Neglected Medical Relationship," in *Bulletin of the History of Medicine,* **45** (1971), 49–75; and "Marco Aurelio Severino and His Relationship to William Harvey: Some Preliminary Considerations," in A. G. Debus, ed., *Science, Medicine and Society in the Renaissance,* II (New York, 1972), 63–72; and J. C. Trent, "Five Letters of Marcus Aurelius Severinus . . . ," in *Bulletin of the History of Medicine,* **15** (1944), 306–323.

An immense amount of material concerning Severino was collected by Luigi Amabile, who was prevented by his death from publishing a major work on him. His notes, including transcriptions from manuscripts in various libraries, are preserved in Naples, Biblioteca nazionale, MSS XI.AA.35–37.

CHARLES B. SCHMITT

SEVERINUS, PETRUS (or **PEDER SØRENSON**) (*b.* Ribe, Jutland, Denmark, 1542 [or 1540]; *d.* Copenhagen, Denmark, July 1602), *chemistry, medicine.*

Severinus attended the University of Copenhagen, where he lectured on Latin poetry at the age of twenty. After studying medicine briefly in France, he returned to Copenhagen to take his Master of Arts degree. He was officially appointed Professor Paedagogicus, and, with the offer of financial support from the University of Copenhagen, he set out with Johannes Pratensis (also a noted sixteenth-century Paracelsist) to study abroad. From 1565 to 1571 Severinus traveled throughout Germany, France, and Italy, attending various universities. Although he first matriculated at the University of Padua, he took his M.D. degree in France. Later, in Florence, he completed his major work, *Idea medicinae philosophicae* (1571), which he dedicated to the Danish king, Frederick II, a monarch genuinely interested in the sciences. On his return home Severinus was appointed canon of Roskild and became a physician to the court, a post he held for the next three decades. In 1602 he was offered the chair of medicine at the University of Copenhagen, but he died of the plague before the appointment officially began.

Severinus was widely known in the iatrochemical circles of his time. In Denmark he was closely associated at court with Tycho Brahe, who was claimed by sixteenth- and seventeenth-century chemists as a leading authority in this field. The writings of Severinus attest to his close relationship with the Paracelsians Livinius Battus and Theodor Zwinger the elder. The English iatrochemist Thomas Moffett, who visited Denmark in 1582, dedicated his important *De jure et praestantia chemicorum medicamentorum* (1585) to Severinus.

Only two of Severinus' many papers were published: *Idea medicinae philosophicae* (1571) and *Epistola scripta Theophrasto Paracelso* (1572). The latter, a short panegyric, was written thirty years after the death of Paracelsus and it reached its greatest audience when it was included in the

Latin edition of Paracelsus' works (1658). Far more important is the *Idea medicinae philosophicae,* which purported to contain the "entire doctrine of Paracelsus, Hippocrates, and Galen." Although earlier syntheses of the Paracelsian corpus had been written by Leo Suavius (1568) and Albert Wimpenaeus (1569), the work of Severinus was immediately accepted as one of the most authoritative documents of the Paracelsian school.

The *Idea* was a defense of the Paracelsian doctrines in opposition to the traditional medicine. In his attack Severinus labeled Galen as little more than a compiler who had been forced to arrange the work of his predecessors into some sort of order; seeking a unifying principle for this task, Galen had chosen the methods of the geometricians. His attempt to make medicine a part of geometry, with its own principles, axioms, and mathematical explanations, had been finally disproved, Severinus argued, only in recent years, when a number of new diseases had ravaged the Continent. Because they could not be controlled by physicians trained only in the traditional methods, it was therefore proper to seek something new and more effective. The answer was to be found in the medicine that was the glory of Paracelsus, a scholar whose method was devoid of the "mathematical" approach of the Galenists. In contrast, the truths to be found in his work were based on the fresh observations of the chemists. In one of the most frequently quoted passages of the sixteenth-century scientific literature, Severinus tells his readers to discard their books and to seek a knowledge of nature through personal experience.

The *Epistola* indicates in a few pages those Paracelsian texts known to Severinus, while the *Idea* shows just how deeply steeped in those sources he was. He fully accepted Paracelsus' endorsement of the macrocosm-microcosm universe; and he wrote that man has within him rivers, seas, mountains, and valleys in a fashion analogous to the greater world. Severinus accepted the doctrine of signatures and firmly condemned the humoral pathology of the ancients. Again, like Paracelsus, he broke with traditional medicine in affirming that the harmony of nature requires that like must cure like. In contrast, the Galenists insisted that contraries cured.

Much of the *Idea medicinae philosophicae* is devoted to the elements and the principles. The influence of traditional alchemy may be seen in the acceptance of both material and insensible elements, while the inconsistencies of Paracelsus regarding the relationship of the Aristotelian elements and the Paracelsian principles also is mirrored. Severinus' view of the universe was vitalistic and he believed that naturalists should seek out the vital principle in all substances. He stated that the elements contained certain forces, or *astra,* that, in connection with the chemical principles, formed *semina.* These *semina* were to be found in all parts of a given body—in man, however, they were perfected in the generative organs. The seed was properly called "astral" in nature because it had the magisterial power of life, which could not be destroyed even through the processes of putrefaction and dissolution.

As Pagel has shown, Severinus was the most eloquent exponent of epigenesis in the period between Aristotle and Harvey. He believed that the *semen* could give rise to a complex organism, not by virtue of the matter present but through its internal endowment, an intrinsic "knowledge" within it. While his views were significant, they were not based on embryological observations. In his role as defender of Paracelsus, Severinus placed strong emphasis on the supremacy of the heart because of its relationship to the vital spirit. Nevertheless, to him the role of the heart was somewhat less important than that of the blood, since the essential life force reached all parts of the body through this vehicle. Thus, although Severinus adopted the hard line of the Paracelsians against the ancients, his views on the primacy of the heart and the blood—as well as his espousal of epigenesis—show an Aristotelian influence and also mark him as a significant precursor of Harvey.

As the first major synthesis of the Paracelsian corpus, the *Idea medicinae philosophicae* was highly influential. Printed three times between 1571 and 1660, it was widely quoted not only by adherents of the new Paracelsian medicine but also by its opponents. Thomas Erastus wrote against Severinus in his attack on Paracelsus (1572–1573), and Daniel Sennert similarly discussed the views of Severinus in his *De chymicorum cum Aristotelicis et Galenicis consensu ac dissensu liber* (1619). Francis Bacon thought highly of the ability of Severinus, and he regretted only that he had devoted his time and talent to supporting the "useless" opinions of Paracelsus. Perhaps the greatest impact of the *Idea medicinae philosophicae* is to be found in the work of William Davison, who was appointed the first lecturer in chemistry at the Jardin des Plantes in Paris. In 1660 Davison's *Commentariorum in . . . Petri Severini Dani Ideam medicinae philosophicae . . . prodromus* was published along with the much shorter original text of the *Idea*. A condensed commentary, also by Davison, appeared in 1663.

BIBLIOGRAPHY

I. ORIGINAL WORKS. *Epistola scripta Theophrasto Paracelso: In qua ratio ordinis et nominum, adeoque totius philosophiae adeptae methodus compendiose et erudite ostenditur a Petro Severino Dano, philosophiae et medicinae doctore* (Basel, 1572) is most conveniently found in the Latin *Opera omnia* of Paracelsus, Fridericus Bitiskius, ed., I (Geneva, 1658), 4v–2r. The *Idea medicinae philosophicae. Continens fundamenta totius doctrinae Paracelsicae Hippocraticae & Galenicae* (Basel, 1571; 2nd ed., Erfurt, 1616) was reprinted (The Hague, 1660) with a long commentary by William Davison, the *Commentariorum in . . . Petri Severini Dani Ideam medicinae philosophicae . . . prodromus.* Davison's brief commentary entitled *Commentaria in Ideam medicinae philosophicae Petri Severini Dani, medici incomparabilis & philosophi sublimis* (The Hague, 1663) is an entirely different work. A contemporary English trans., probably made by A. Bartlet *ca.* 1600, of the *Idea medicinae philosophicae* exists in MS at the British Museum (Sloane MS 11).

II. SECONDARY LITERATURE. The secondary literature on Severinus is scanty, and Kurt Sprengel, *Versuch einer pragmatischen Geschichte der Arzneikunde*, 2nd ed., 5 vols. (Halle, 1800–1803), III (1801), 408–413, remains of interest. Important material on the Scandinavian Paracelsians is in Sten Lindroth, *Paracelsismen i Sverige till 1600-talets mitt* (Uppsala, 1943), 21–25, and *passim*; more recent are Eyvind Bastholm, "Petrus Severinus (1542–1602). A Danish Paracelsist," in *Proceedings of the XXI International Congress of the History of Medicine* (Siena, 1968), 1080–1085; and "Petrus Severinus (1542–1602). En dansk paracelsist," in *Särtryck ur Sydsvenska medicinhistoriska sällskapets årsskrift* (1970), 53–72.

On the relationship of the work of Severinus to the Paracelsian corpus, see Walter Pagel, *Paracelsus. An Introduction to Philosophical Medicine in the Era of the Renaissance* (Basel–New York, 1958), *passim*. More specifically, Pagel has investigated Severinus as a precursor of William Harvey in *William Harvey's Biological Ideas. Selected Aspects and Historical Background* (Basel–New York, 1967), 239–347.

The relationship of Severinus' views on mathematics to those of other Paracelsians is discussed in Allen G. Debus, "Mathematics and Nature in the Chemical Texts of the Renaissance," in *Ambix*, **15** (1968), 1–28, 211; and a summary of his thought from the standpoint of the chemist is included in J. R. Partington, *A History of Chemistry*, II (London, 1961), 163–164.

The impact of the work of Severinus on the contemporary English medical literature is treated in Allen G. Debus, *The English Paracelsians* (London, 1965; New York, 1966), 20 and *passim*. The extent of his influence throughout European medical circles is reflected in the many references in John Ferguson, *Bibliotheca chemica* (Glasgow, 1906; repr. London, 1954), II, 378–379.

ALLEN G. DEBUS

SEVERTSOV, ALEKSEY NIKOLAEVICH (*b.* Moscow, Russia, 11 September 1866; *d.* Moscow, 16 December 1936), *comparative anatomy, evolutionary morphology.*

Severtsov spent his early childhood in the village of Petrov, Voronezh gubernia, with his father, N. A. Severtsov, a zoologist and explorer, and his mother, S. A. Severtsova. He received his secondary education in a private gymnasium. After his graduation in 1885, Severtsov entered the department of physics and mathematics at Moscow University. Severtsov's teachers were M. A. Menzbir, I. M. Sechenov, K. A. Timiryazev, and V. V. Markovnikov.

While a student Severtsov, with P. P. Sushkin, entered a department competition on the organization and taxonomy of the Apoda and was awarded a gold medal. In 1895 Severtsov defended his master's dissertation, "O razvitii zatylochnoy oblasti nizshikh pozvonochnykh v svyaz; s voprosom o metamerii golovy" ("On the Development of the Occipital Area of the Lower Vertebrates in Connection With Metameres of the Head"). For the next three years he worked in the marine biological stations at Banyuls-sur-Mer, Villefranche, and Naples, and in the zoological laboratories at Munich and Kiel. The research done abroad was included in his doctoral dissertation, "Metameria golov elektricheskogo skata" ("Metameres of the Head of the Torpedo Ray"), which he defended in 1898. Severtsov did scientific and administrative work at Dorpat (now Tartu, Estonian S.S.R.), where from 1898 to 1902 he occupied the chair of zoology, then at Kiev (1902–1911), and at Moscow (1911–1930).

In 1930 Severtsov founded at Moscow University a laboratory of evolutionary morphology that later became the Institute of Evolutionary Morphology (now the A. N. Severtsov Institute of Evolutionary Morphology and Animal Ecology). In recognition of his scientific contributions he was elected an academician of the Soviet Academy of Sciences and of the Academy of Sciences of the Ukrainian S.S.R.

Severtsov chose comparative anatomy as his specialty, for he early recognized the necessity of extending morphology and evolutionary theory. Rather than study morphological regularities of evolution however, for a long time he limited himself to problems of comparative anatomy and phylogeny. His classic research on metameres of the vertebrate head (1895) revealed the evolution of the head. Severtsov devoted a number of works to explaining the origin and evolution of the extremities of vertebrates; he believed that the pentadactylic limbs of terrestrial vertebrates arose from the many-rayed fins of fish. In 1926 and 1934 he supplemented this conclusion with the idea that the fins had originated from the lateral folds. Clarifying the course of vertebrate phylogenetic development also was facilitated by Severtsov's research on the origin of the osseous scales and the evolution of the osseous skulls of fish. He believed that the covering parts of the skull arose from the osseous rhombic scales of the cutaneous cover. Severtsov also investigated the origin of the maxillary apparatus, the branchial skeleton, and breathing organs in fish.

Using material obtained through his own work and that of his pupils, Severtsov attempted to restate the evolution of the lower vertebrates in three articles (1916, 1917, 1925). He considered the lower cartilaginous fish, the basic groups of osseous fish, and the ancestors of land vertebrates. Severtsov proposed uniting Ostracodermi with the Cyclostomata in one group of ancient agnathous vertebrates. He tried to re-create the structure of the ancestors of the vertebrates—the primary Acrania and Gnathostomata, ancestors of agnathous and gnathostomatous vertebrates—and to draw a family tree of the lower vertebrates. The first two parts of "Issledovania ob evolyutsii nizshikh pozvonochnykh" ("Research on the Evolution of the Lower Vertebrates") were awarded the K. E. Baer Prize in 1919.

In 1910 Severtsov presented a report at the Twelfth Congress of Russian Natural Scientists and Physicians that defined the purposes and methodology of the evolutionary morphology of animals. In it he pointed to the scarcely touched area of research opened after the discovery of the biogenetic law by Haeckel, the principle of change of function by A. Dohrn, the law of substitution by N. Kleinenberg, and the phyletic correlation and certain other regularities of evolution.

Supporting the materialistic view of the evolution of the organic world, Severtsov denied the concepts of vitalism and autogenesis. Without

knowledge of the laws of evolution, he held, it is impossible to understand either the laws of individual development or the laws of life in general. Opposing a dogmatic interpretation of Darwin's theory, he favored a bold posing of new problems and the introduction of new ideas. Severtsov devoted twenty-five years to the realization of this program. The result was the strict theory of the morphological regularities of evolution, the nucleus of which was the theory of phyloembryogeny and the morphobiological theory of evolution. Having rehabilitated the Darwinist principle of the variability of all ontogenetic stages in the process of evolution, Severtsov investigated modes of phylogenetic transformation of ontogenesis and their influence on the character and tempo of evolution. The theory of phyloembryogeny helped to overcome the limitations of the two opposing points of view: that ontogeny is a function of phylogeny, and vice versa. Severtsov saw the evolution of form and the evolution of ontogeny as mutually interacting processes.

Severtsov first studied the relations of ontogeny and phylogeny. The lively polemic concerning the theory of the gastraea, the theory of embryonic layers, problems of homology, and other phylogenetic questions indicated that the biogenetic law and theory of recapitulation in the form given by Haeckel was unsatisfactory for explaining the correlation of the individual and historical development of organisms. Turning from isolated consideration of the biogenetic law, Severtsov tried to free it from the traditional Haeckelian treatment and to give a new basis to the phenomenon of recapitulation in terms of his own theory of phyloembryogeny.

According to the latter, evolutionary changes arise through changes in the first stages of ontogeny (archallaxis), changes in the intermediate stages (deviation), and the addition of new final stages (anabolism). Thus this theory rehabilitated and supplemented the Darwinian principle of variations in all stages of ontogeny during evolution with concrete morphological data.

According to the theory of phyloembryogeny, the biogenetic law is the consequence of evolution by means of anabolism. Archallaxis and deviation limit the completeness of recapitulation. Severtsov showed that Baer's law, which asserted that the characteristics of small systematic groups appear late in ontogeny while the signs of larger systematic groups appear early, was not a general rule. He related the development of characteristics of animals in a determinate order to anabolic evolution, and viewed Baer's statement that characteristics of large systematic groups appear in the early stages of ontogeny as the consequence of the anabolic divergent monophyletic evolution.

The theory of phyloembryogeny also can be viewed as a morphological theory of ontogenetic evolution. Severtsov proposed an addition to it in 1934: the hypothesis of ontogenetic evolution of many-celled animals was invoked as an aid in determining the origin and regularity of development of modes of phyloembryogeny. Severtsov considered anabolism the primary method of ontogenetic evolution and the reason for the origin of primary recapitulation. His hypothesis assumed that ontogenetic evolution was completed in the early stages, not only through "piecing" of stages but also by means of archallaxis, deviation, and heterochronism. These secondary modes changed the linear order of stages of ontogeny and caused a reduction in recapitulation. Severtsov also included cenogenesis in the regular processes of ontogenetic evolution, showing the irregularity of its opposite, polygenesis.

The study of the relationship of ontogeny and phylogeny on the level of the whole organism, of separate organs, and of tissues showed the universality of the theory of phyloembryogeny. First formulated on the basis of the study of vertebrates, this theory was later recognized in the morphology of vertebrates, the morphology of plants, histology, physiology, and anthropology.

Darwin's theory presented evolution as a gradual progressive increase in organization, a replacement of lower forms by higher. Darwin gave a basically correct but also highly general solution to the problem of the development of species. His followers—T. H. Huxley, M. Neumayr, Mechnikov, V. O. Kovalevsky—continued the analysis of this problem. Ideas on progress that were alien to Darwinism were widespread, however: the mechanical-Lamarckian theory of ontogeny and autogenetic views. There was no coherent theory showing the basic trends of progress in the organic world from a Darwinian point of view. Severtsov's morphological theory of evolution filled that lack.

According to Severtsov (1925, 1931), biological progress occurs by means of a general increase in the life activity of the organism (aromorphosis), individual adaptation (idioadaptation or adaptation in the narrow sense), embryonic adjustment, and morphophysiological regression (for example, the transition to parasitism). In all but the first case the level of organization does not rise (and in the case of morphophysiological regression it is lowered); but, because it is better adapted to the conditions of existence, the group of organisms that is retarded in development gains the opportunity to compete successfully with more highly organized forms. Thus the existence of both highly organized and primitive forms among contemporary fauna is explained.

Using the theory of phyloembryogeny and the studies of the main directions of the evolutionary process, Severtsov closely associated the methods of the phylogenetic transformation of organs ("methods of transition," according to Darwin) with his hypothesis of correlation. According to this theory, in evolution a few characteristics change at first through heredity; the remaining characteristics and the organism as a whole then change in correlation with these primary changes. His hypothesis served as the basis for the solution of the problem of mutual adaptation (coadaptation) of organs in phylogenesis.

With the appearance of evolutionary morphology, work proceeded on the problem of reduction. Severtsov provided a detailed concept of the courses of reduction, distinguishing the sequential shedding of the final stages of development during the decrease in original formation of the organ (rudimentation) and the reduction of a normally formed organ until it disappears completely (aphanisia).

Severtsov limited his investigations to morphological regularities of evolution and to the routes by which the evolution of form and structure was achieved. Nevertheless, he clearly saw and upheld the tendency to synthesize the data and generalizations achieved by descriptive and experimental biology. Thus he understood and stated that a complete theory of the relation of individual development and evolution cannot be constructed exclusively from morphological material. In his opinion such a theory could be created only by synthesizing the data of evolutionary morphology, genetics, mechanics of development, and ecology. His prognosis was justified: in the 1930's and 1940's Severtsov's student I. I. Shmalgauzen achieved such a synthesis, creating the theory of the organism as a whole in its individual and historical development and the theory of the course and regularities of the evolutionary process.

BIBLIOGRAPHY

I. ORIGINAL WORKS. Severtsov's works have been collected in *Sobranie Sochinenii*, I. I. Shmalgauzen and

E. N. Pavlovsky, eds., 5 vols. (Moscow–Leningrad, 1945–1951). His basic writings are "O razvitii zatylochnoy oblasti nizshikh pozvonochnykh v svyazi s voprosom o metamerii golovy" ("On the Development of the Occipital Area of the Lower Vertebrates in Connection With Metameres of the Head"), in *Uchenye zapiski Moskovskogo universiteta,* Nat.-hist. cl. (1895), no. 2, 1–95; *Ocherki po istorii razvitia golovy pozvonochnykh* ("Sketches in the History of the Development of the Vertebrate Head"; Moscow, 1898); "Evolyutsia i embriologia" ("Evolution and Embryology"), in *Dnevnik XII Sezda russkikh estestvoispytateley i vrachey* ("Daily Journal of the XII Congress of Russian Natural Scientists and Physicians"; Moscow, 1910), 262–275; *Etyudy po teorii evolyutsii* ("Studies in the Theory of Evolution"; Kiev, 1912); *Sovremennye zadachi evolyutsionnoy teorii* ("Contemporary Problems in Evolutionary Theory"; Moscow, 1914); "Issledovania ob evolyutsii nizshikh pozvonochnykh" ("Research on the Evolution of the Lower Vertebrates"), in *Russkii arkhiv anatomii, gistologii i embriologii,* **1,** no. 1 (1916), 1–114; no. 3 (1917), 503–656; and **3,** no. 2 (1924), 279–360—the first two parts are available in French as "Études sur l'évolution des vertébrés inférieures. I. Morphologie du squelette et de la musculature de la tête des Cyclostomes" and "II. Organisation des ancêtres des vertébrés actuels," in *Archives russes d'anatomie, d'histologie et d'embryologie,* **1,** no. 1 (1916) and no. 3 (1917); *Glavnye napravlenia evolyutsionnogo protsessa* ("Main Trends in the Evolutionary Process"; Moscow, 1925); *Morphologische Gesetzmässigkeiten der Evolution* (Jena, 1931); and *Morfologicheskie zakonomernosti evolyutsii* ("Morphological Regularities in Evolution"; Moscow–Leningrad, 1939).

II. Secondary Literature. See B. S. Matveev and A. N. Druzhinin, "Zhizn i tvorchestvo A. N. Severtsova" ("Life and Work of Severtsov"), in *Pamyati akademika A. N. Severtsova* ("Memories of Academician Severtsov"), I (Moscow–Leningrad, 1939); L. B. Severtsova, *Aleksey Nikolaevich Severtsov* (Moscow–Leningrad, 1946; 1951); and I. I. Shmalgauzen, *Nauchnaya deyatelnost akademika A. N. Severtsova kak teoretika-evolyutsionista* ("Scientific Activity of Severtsov as Evolutionary Theorist"), in *Pamyati akademika A. N. Severtsova,* I.

E. Mirzoyan

SEWARD, ALBERT CHARLES (*b.* Lancaster, England, 9 October 1863; *d.* London, England, 11 April 1941), *paleobotany.*

Seward's interest in geology was first inspired by John Marr's lectures. At Cambridge he took his degree in geology and botany, and on the advice of Thomas McKenny Hughes, decided to work on fossil plants. Botany at Cambridge was then emerging from a period of neglect, and Seward stated that it was quite late in his career when he first heard of living cells and protoplasm—"a revelation." To further his training as a paleobotanist he spent a year at Manchester with W. C. Williamson and then traveled to European countries where work was being done in that field.

Seward worked on the whole range of fossil plants, but about half his papers dealt with the Mesozoic. He was appointed a lecturer at St. John's College, Cambridge, in 1890 and later was made a fellow of the college; he became professor of botany in 1906. His steady stream of papers began in 1888, but it was his great revision of the English Weald flora (1895) that brought him fame and election at the age of thirty-five to the Royal Society. Collections of fossil plants from all over the world poured into Seward's laboratory. He collected very little until late in his life, when he spent a summer on the western Greenland Cretaceous.

Seward's synthetic papers dealt with the history of floras, especially with past climates as deduced from fossil plants and with the ways in which changing climates altered the geographical distribution of vegetation. His anatomical descriptions were careful, but he preferred the gross specimen on a large slab to the minute detail. Seward was not interested in the subtleties of comparative and evolutionary morphology and would, if possible, lump species rather than divide them. Impatient with the intricacies of nomenclature that had arisen during his working life, he often proceeded on the basis of what he considered good sense.

Seward became professor of the large and growing department of botany in 1906 and master of Downing College in 1915, both posts that many treated as full-time. In addition he gave generous help to the British Museum and British Association. Although he undertook nearly all of the elementary teaching in botany in addition to giving advanced lectures, he was able to set aside time almost every day for research. Not until he took on yet another full-time post, that of vice-chancellor of the university, was his paleobotanical research suspended.

Seward's retirement years were as well organized as his working life. At seventy-three he retired voluntarily from his chair and the mastership, and settled down to work near the British Museum. He made it a rule to finish all work before Easter and before Christmas; and so on Good Friday eve of 1941 he left on his desk the finished manuscript of his final paper and answers to all his letters, and went to bed. He died in his sleep.

BIBLIOGRAPHY

Seward's major works include *The Wealden Flora,* 2 pts. (London, 1894–1895); *The Jurassic Flora,* 2 vols. (London, 1900–1904); *Fossil Plants,* 4 vols. (Cambridge, 1898–1919); and *Plant Life Through the Ages* (Cambridge, 1931). See also "A Petrified Williamsonia From Scotland," in *Philosophical Transactions of the Royal Society,* **B204** (1912), 201; and "The Cretaceous Plant Bearing Rocks of Western Greenland," *ibid.,* **218** (1926), 215.

A bibliography of Seward's works is in his obituary in *Obituary Notices of Fellows of the Royal Society of London* (1941).

Tom M. Harris

SEXTUS EMPIRICUS (*fl. ca.* A.D. 200), *medicine, skeptical philosophy.*

The rediscovery of Sextus' writings in the sixteenth century and the publication of his *Pyrrhonian Hypotyposes* (or *Outlines of Pyrrhonism*) in a Latin translation in 1562 led to an epistemological crisis at the time of the Reformation. About the man himself, almost nothing is known. The name Sextus is Latin, but he wrote in Greek; and in *Against the Grammarians* he used the first person plural: "We say . . . whereas the Athenians and Coans say. . . ."[1] The name Empiricus signifies that he was a member of the Empirical school of medicine, which claimed to understand and treat diseases without postulating theoretical causes like "humors" or "spirits." Presumably Sextus was a practicing physician of this school, although he observed that of the medical schools it was the Methodists rather than the Empiricists who were closest to skepticism.[2] He also mentioned a work of his called *Medical Notes* (Ιατρικὰ ὑπομνήματα),[3] but this does not survive. His historical importance is in the field of philosophy, not medicine.

Sextus' surviving works include *Pyrrhonian Hypotyposes,* in three books, of which the first outlines the skeptical position and the second and third criticize other philosophical schools, subject by subject. The criticisms contained in these latter books are expanded in the rest of his work, which is usually grouped under the single title Πρὸς μαθηματικούς (*Adversus mathematicos,* or *Against the Professors*). There are eleven books, referred to by individual titles in the English edition by R. G. Bury (and in this article), as follows: I, *Against the Grammarians*; II, *Against the Rhetoricians*; III, *Against the Geometers*; IV, *Against the Arithmeticians*; V, *Against the Astrologers*; VI, *Against*

the *Musicians*; VII–VIII, *Against the Logicians,* I–II; IX–X, *Against the Physicists,* I–II; and XI, *Against the Ethicists.*

Sextus probably derived most of his knowledge of earlier philosophers from handbooks and compendia, rather than from original sources; but he is a valuable source of information nonetheless. Occasionally he transcribed verbatim; for example, the prologue of Parmenides' great philosophical poem,[4] some fragments of Empedocles,[5] and Critias' poem on the invention of the gods[6] are known to us only from the text of Sextus. More often he gave summaries, some of which are very important: his critique of Pythagoreanism[7] gives details of that theory that are otherwise unknown. (P. Wilpert, *Zwei aristotelische Frühschriften über die Ideenlehre* [Regensburg, 1949], has claimed that much of this was derived from Plato's lectures, but the claim has not found much agreement.) Sextus gives the only surviving account of Diodorus Cronus' "arguments against motion."[8]

The Stoic school, however, founded by Zeno of Citium in Athens about 300 B.C. and by Sextus' time the most firmly established of all the philosophical schools, was his chief target. The division of philosophy into logic, physics, and ethics was Stoic, and he organized his own books according to this scheme. Logic, for him and also for the Stoics, included epistemology, and consequently was the most important division. *Against the Logicians* and the summary in book II of *Pyrrhonian Hypotyposes* constitute the fullest source of information on Stoic logic and have been used extensively in the recent reconstruction of the logical theory of the Stoics.[9]

Sextus' own professed philosophy of skepticism is derived ultimately from Pyrrho of Elis, but more directly from Aenesidemus. In *Pyrrhonian Hypotyposes*[10] Sextus enumerated the ten "tropes" for bringing about suspension of judgment, which elsewhere[11] he attributed to Aenesidemus. These tropes constitute a systematic exposition of arguments that throw doubt on the ability of the senses to give knowledge of the external world. They are followed by a critique of the notions of cause and sign, also derived from Aenesidemus.

Sextus' own position, which has to be collected from statements scattered over his works, amounts to an extreme form of skepticism. He distinguished between the external object and the phenomenon, and asserted that our sense perceptions are of phenomena only, that the external object is unknowable, and that nothing is true.[12] To count as true a statement must be verifiable and be about a real object: the first condition eliminates statements about the external world, and the second those about sense impressions. It follows that not even the statements of the skeptical philosopher are true. Sextus used the famous image of the ladder: just as a man can climb up to a high place and then kick the ladder down, so the skeptical philosopher can use argument to reach his position and ultimately demolish his own argument.[13] The result, according to Sextus, should be *ataraxia*, or peace.[14]

NOTES

1. *Against the Grammarians*, 246.
2. *Pyrrhonian Hypotyposes*, bk. I, 237–241.
3. *Against the Logicians*, bk. I, 202.
4. *Ibid.*, 111.
5. *Ibid.*, 122–124; *Against the Physicists*, bk. I, 127–129.
6. *Against the Physicists*, bk. I, 54.
7. *Ibid.*, bk. II, 248–309.
8. *Against the Physicists*, bk. I, 85–120.
9. See esp. B. Mates, "Stoic Logic"; and William and Martha Kneale, *Development of Logic* (Oxford, 1962), chap. 3.
10. Bk. I, 36–163.
11. *Against the Logicians*, bk. I, 345.
12. *Pyrrhonian Hypotyposes*, bk. II, 88 ff.
13. *Against the Logicians*, bk. II, 481; cf. L. Wittgenstein, *Tractatus Logico-philosophicus* (London, 1922), prop. 6.54.
14. *Pyrrhonian Hypotyposes*, bk. I, 8.

BIBLIOGRAPHY

I. ORIGINAL WORKS. The main source is Sextus Empiricus, *Opera*, 4 vols. (Leipzig, 1912–1962), volš. I–II, H. Mutschmann, ed.; vol. III, J. Mau, ed.; vol. IV, K. Janáček, ed., is an index. See also *Sextus Empiricus*, R. G. Bury, ed. and trans., 4 vols. (London–Cambridge, 1933–1949); and *Scepticism, Man and God: Selections From the Major Writings of Sextus Empiricus*, P. Halle, ed., Sanford Etheridge, trans. (Middletown, Conn., 1964).

II. SECONDARY LITERATURE. The most recent and best source is Charlotte Stough, *Greek Scepticism: A Study in Epistemology* (Berkeley–Los Angeles, 1969). See also V. Brochard, *Les Sceptiques Grecs*, 2nd ed. (Paris, 1955); Roderick Chisholm, "Sextus Empiricus and Modern Empiricism," in *Philosophy of Science*, **8** (1941), 371–384; A. Goedeckemeyer, *Die Geschichte des griechischen Skeptizismus* (Leipzig, 1905); K. Janáček, "Prolegomena to Sextus Empiricus," in *Acta Universitatis Palackianae Olomucensis*, **4** (1948), "Sextus Empiricus en der Arbeit," in *Philologus*, **100** (1956), 100–107, and *Sextus Empiricus' Sceptical Methods*, Acta Universitatis Carolinae Philologica, Monographia XXXVIII (Prague, 1972); Benson Mates, "Stoic Logic and the Text of Sextus Empiricus," in *American Journal of Philology*, **70** (1949), 290–298, and *Stoic Logic*

(Berkeley–Los Angeles, 1961); A. Philip McMahon, "Sextus Empiricus and the Arts," in *Harvard Studies in Classical Philology*, **42** (1931), 79–137; and Richard Popkin, *History of Scepticism From Erasmus to Descartes* (Assen, 1960).

DAVID J. FURLEY

SEZAWA, KATSUTADA (*b.* Yamaguchi, Japan, 21 August 1895; *d.* Tokyo, Japan, 23 April 1944), *applied mathematics, theoretical seismology.*

The son of a judge, Sezawa entered the Imperial University of Tokyo in 1918 and graduated as a shipbuilding engineer in 1921. He was then appointed assistant professor of engineering at the university and became a full professor in 1928. He first worked on problems of shipbuilding engineering and of vibration, in which he acquired a considerable reputation. In 1925 he started a lifelong association with the Earthquake Research Institute of the university, becoming its director in 1943. In 1932 he visited Britain, Germany, and the United States to further his studies in theoretical seismology, the field in which he is now best known. Sezawa was associated with many Japanese research organizations, including the Seismological Society of Japan, the Aeronautical Research Institute, and the Aviation Council. During World War II his responsibilities were greatly extended: he was supervisor of research projects at the Admiralty and a member of the Air Force Weapons Research Committee and was closely connected with army research.

When Sezawa began his research career, the new science of seismology presented challenging problems requiring sophisticated mathematical analysis. Sezawa's pioneering work on many of these problems provided the basis for important later developments both in Japan and elsewhere, and his mathematical ability was a significant factor in raising the world standard of seismological research. Much of this work was carried out in collaboration with his brilliant former pupil Kiyoshi Kanai.

Sezawa is particularly noted for his contributions to the theory of seismic surface waves, one of the main wave types generated by earthquakes. These waves tend to become increasingly regular in form as they move away from an earthquake source. Mathematical analysis of this property throws light on the structure of the outer part of the earth. By this means Sezawa derived useful estimates of layering in the earth's crust and produced evidence indicating that the Pacific crust is thinner than the Eurasian. More profoundly, his work pointed the way to important developments of the existing mathematical theory of seismic surface waves.

Sezawa produced a body of theory important to such seismological problems as seiches in lakes and tsunami (seismic sea waves) generated by large earthquakes, and the mechanism of earthquake generation. He applied his earlier studies of vibration theory to the problems of vibrations excited in buildings and bridges by strong earthquakes, contributed to the theory of designing structures to withstand earthquakes, and participated in related experimental work.

Although he was often unwell, Sezawa drove himself hard and lived very austerely. His health deteriorated seriously during the war, and he died at the age of forty-eight. The Imperial Academy of Sciences of Japan awarded him its highest honor, the Imperial Order of Merit, in 1931 and elected him a member in 1943.

BIBLIOGRAPHY

Most of Sezawa's 140 research papers on seismology and earthquake engineering were published as *Bulletins* of the Earthquake Research Institute of Tokyo Imperial University. Forty-six of his more important papers are listed in W. M. Ewing, W. S. Jardetzky, and F. Press, *Elastic Waves in Layered Media* (New York, 1957). He also wrote 50 papers on aeronautics, published in *Reports of the Aeronautical Research Institute, Tokyo University*; and 20 papers on ship construction, published as Reports of the Society of Naval Architecture of Japan.

An obituary was published in Japanese in *Jishin*, **16**, no. 5 (May 1944), 1–2.

K. E. BULLEN

SHAKERLEY, JEREMY (*b*. Halifax, Yorkshire, England, November 1626; *d*. India, *ca.* 1655), *astronomy.*

Shakerley was the son of William Shakerley of North Owram, Halifax. After a childhood in Yorkshire and a visit to Ireland, he settled in Pendle Forest, Lancashire, the address on his first surviving astronomical letter, sent to the London astrologer William Lilly in January 1648. The correspondence with Lilly, spanning 1648–1650, comprises nine letters and is concerned largely with patronage and astrology. It also shows that Shakerley

first became interested in mathematics around 1646. Over the years Lilly supplied him with books, stationery, and other aids, although he never extended to him the complete patronage he craved.

In 1649 Shakerley was taken into the Towneley household at Carré Hall, Burnley, Lancashire, where he was encouraged in his scientific pursuits. The Towneleys were prominent patrons of learning in the north of England and assisted the astronomers Crabtree and Gascoigne as well as Shakerley. While in the household of the Towneleys, who were Royalist Catholics, Shakerley continued to correspond with Lilly, a Parliamentarian and a Protestant—seemingly with the full knowledge of Towneley. Nothing is known of Shakerley's own religious allegiance, although he appears to have been a latitudinarian Protestant.

Like other practitioners of astronomy in the region, Shakerley was self-educated, having acquired his knowledge from the works of Kepler and Boulliau, whose achievements he greatly admired, as well as other authors. He was remarkably well versed in the literature of the "new philosophy"; and in his printed works he took great delight in ridiculing more conservative astronomers.

Many of the early letters to Lilly deal with a mixture of astronomical and astrological matters. They show that although Shakerley had a completely physical explanation for celestial mechanics, he nonetheless accepted that the natural motions of the planets also contained a supernatural element that vindicated his astrological beliefs. A letter describing the appearance of two mock suns in 1648 clearly illustrates this harmony of physical and astrological beliefs, for after giving a purely optical explanation for the mock suns, he invited Lilly to pronounce "astrological judgment" upon them. But as the correspondence progressed, Shakerley became increasingly skeptical about the validity of astrology, despite his enthusiasm for Lilly's intention to reform the science.

Shakerley was the first mathematician to recognize the significance of the work of the Liverpool astronomer Jeremiah Horrocks, whose papers had been acquired by Christopher Towneley and had been taken to Carré Hall after Horrocks' death. In each of his three published works, Shakerley spoke of Horrocks' researches with the highest praise, especially his discoveries concerning the lunar theory. When attacking Vincent Wing's *Urania practica* (1649), he used material from Horrocks' surviving papers to frame his own critique of

Wing's faulty lunar theory. The debt to Horrocks was again recognized by Shakerley in his *Tabulae Britannicae* (1653).

As a supplement to his almanac for 1651, Shakerley predicted a transit of Mercury on 24 October 1651. He described how best to observe it, using the projection method, and enumerates the new astronomical data that could be gained by doing so. Horrocks, who first observed a transit of Venus in 1639, was again cited; and it is clear that Shakerley had access to his unpublished papers on the transit, then at Carré Hall. He also referred to Gassendi, who in 1631 had been the first astronomer to observe a transit of Mercury. As the 1651 transit would occur during the night in European latitudes, he stated that it would be observed most advantageously in eastern lands.

Probably as a result of his attack on Vincent Wing, Lilly withdrew his support from Shakerley in 1650. No doubt because of the bleakness of his prospects at home, Shakerley emigrated to India. It was from Surat that he observed the Mercury transit predicted in his almanac. The observation began at 6:40 A.M.; but the proximity of adjacent buildings along with other demands on his time prevented him from making more than one sighting, and even this was impeded by his lack of adequate instruments. Mercury appeared to be "brownish black" and was less than half a minute in diameter. This information, and a drawing of the solar disk with Mercury delineated, was sent to Henry Osborne in London. The letter gives no indication as to Shakerley's occupation in Surat; but it is certain that he did not make the voyage merely to see the transit, as Vincent Wing suggested in 1669. He was probably an employee of the East India Company, although no mention of his name occurs in the company's records for the early 1650's.

Apart from reporting the Mercury transit, the Osborne letter relates other astronomical observations, such as that of a comet in 1652. Scarcely any references to astrology occur in this letter, and Shakerley confined himself to reporting purely physical data. While in India he became deeply interested in Brahmin astronomy. By the time of his letter to Osborne in January 1653, he had already learned a considerable amount, especially about the Indian calendar, and promised to devote more time to its study.

Shakerley was the second man ever to witness a Mercury transit, was probably the first Englishman to undertake systematic astronomical observations in India, and was one of the earliest men of science to seriously interest himself in the astronomy of the Brahmins.

After his letter to Osborne in 1653, nothing more was heard of Shakerley, although his *Tabulae Britannicae* was published at London in the same year. John Booker wrote to him in India in 1655, but he does not record having received a reply. In 1675 Edward Sherburne laconically remarked that Shakerley had "dyed in the East Indies."

BIBLIOGRAPHY

I. ORIGINAL WORKS. Twelve of Shakerley's letters are extant. Eleven are in the Bodleian Library, Ashmole 242 and 423, including his correspondence with Lilly and Osborne. Shakerley's letter on astrology and the doubts that he entertained therein, sent to John Matteson on 5 Mar. 1649, is published in the *Historical Manuscripts Commission Report, Various Collections,* **8** (1913), p. 61. Shakerley's three published works are *Anatomy of "Urania Practica"* (London, 1649); *Synopsis compendiana* (London, 1651), his almanac for 1651, which includes a supplement predicting the impending Mercury transit; and *Tabulae Britannicae* (London, 1653).

II. SECONDARY LITERATURE. Shakerley obtained posthumous recognition in Vincent Wing's *Astronomia Britannica,* 2nd ed. (London, 1669); and in the appendix to Edward Sherburne's *The Sphere of Marcus Manilius* (London, 1675).

ALLAN CHAPMAN

SHALER, NATHANIEL SOUTHGATE (*b.* Newport, Kentucky, 20 February 1841; *d.* Cambridge, Massachusetts, 10 April 1906), *geology.*

Shaler was the son of Nathaniel Burger Shaler, a physician, and Anne Hinde Southgate, daughter of a prosperous lawyer. He entered Lawrence Scientific School of Harvard University; studied under Louis Agassiz, although he came to reject Agassiz's anti-Darwinism, and earned the S.B. *summa cum laude* in 1862. His Civil War service in Kentucky curtailed by illness, Shaler returned to Harvard in 1864 as a university lecturer and remained there until his death, at which time he had become professor of geology and dean of the Lawrence Scientific School. Shaler worked intermittently for the U.S. Coast Survey and was director of the Kentucky Geological Survey (1873–1880), undertaking the first systematic survey of that state. In

1880 he joined the U.S. Geological Survey on a part-time basis and was head of its Atlantic Coast division from 1884 to 1900.

Shaler made a notable contribution to reclamation geology. His reports on inundated lands of the eastern United States and their reclamation value appeared within a decade after John Wesley Powell's *Report on the Lands of the Arid Region of the United States* (1878). Shaler said that an interesting reclamation alternative to irrigation of arid western lands would be the drainage of swamps and marshes. His concern with inundated lands reflected his broader interest in relating geology to the effects of man's activity upon the earth's surface. Shaler's *Aspects of the Earth* (1889), similar in mood to George Perkins Marsh's *Nature and Man* (1864), was intended to show the necessity for human understanding of the environment. This theme was later applied in his *Nature and Man in America* (1891), an important work on the environmental interpretation of history.

Shaler attained recognition through his popularization of geology, the sheer volume of his writing, and his national prominence within the profession (he was elected president of the Geological Society of America in 1895). Optimistic, enthusiastic, and sometimes prone to exaggeration, he contributed to the dissemination of geological knowledge and linked geology to human progress.

BIBLIOGRAPHY

I. ORIGINAL WORKS. The following scientific writings provide some indication of the range of Shaler's geological interests: "On the Formation of Mountain Chains," in *Geological Magazine*, **5** (1868), 511–517; "Sea Coast Swamps of the Eastern United States," in United States Geological Survey, *Sixth Annual Report* (Washington, D.C., 1886), 359–398; "The Geology of the Island of Mount Desert, Maine," *ibid.*, *Eighth Annual Report* (Washington, D.C., 1889), 987–1061; "General Account of the Fresh-Water Morasses of the United States, With a Description of the Dismal Swamp District of Virginia and North Carolina," *ibid.*, *Tenth Annual Report* (Washington, D.C., 1890), 255–339; "The Origin and Nature of Soils," *ibid.*, *Twelfth Annual Report* (Washington, D.C., 1892), 213–345; "Preliminary Report on the Geology of the Common Roads of the United States," *ibid.*, *Fifteenth Annual Report* (Washington, D.C., 1895), 255–306.

Representative of Shaler's effort to popularize geological knowledge are *Illustrations of the Earth's Surface: Glaciers* (Boston, 1881); *The First Book of Geology* (Boston, 1884); *Aspects of the Earth* (New York, 1889); *Sea and Land: Features of Coasts and Oceans* (New

York, 1892); and *Outlines of the Earth's History* (New York, 1898). The last work was castigated by the geologist Israel C. Russell, who termed it a "nature-novel" in his review in *Science*, n.s. **8** (1898), 712–715.

Shaler's application of geology and geography to history is revealed in *Kentucky: A Pioneer Commonwealth* (Boston, 1884) and in *Nature and Man in America* (New York, 1891).

Shaler's memoirs were published as *The Autobiography of Nathaniel Southgate Shaler With a Supplementary Memoir by His Wife* (Boston, 1909).

II. SECONDARY LITERATURE. Brief assessments of Shaler are "Professors N. S. Shaler and I. C. Russell," in *Nature*, **74** (1906), 226–227; and "Nathaniel Southgate Shaler," in *Science*, n.s. **23** (1906), 869–872. A lengthy account is Walter L. Berg, "Nathaniel Southgate Shaler: A Critical Study of an Earth Scientist," unpub. diss., University Microfilms (Ann Arbor, Mich., 1957). A full bibliography of Shaler's writings is in John E. Wolff, "Memoir of Nathaniel Southgate Shaler," in *Bulletin of the Geological Society of America*, **18** (1908), 592–608.

WALTER L. BERG

SHANKS, WILLIAM (*b.* Corsenside, Northumberland, England, 25 January 1812; *d.* Houghton-le-Spring, Durham, England, 1882), *mathematics.*

Shanks's contributions to mathematics lie entirely in the field of computation, in which he was influenced by William Rutherford of Edinburgh. From 1847 his life was spent in Houghton-le-Spring, a small town in the coal-mining area of County Durham. There he kept a boarding school, and carried out his laborious and generally reliable calculations, most of which concerned the constant π, the ratio of the circumference of a circle to its diameter.

Modern methods for the calculation of π rely mainly on the formula

$$\text{arc tan } x = x - \frac{x^3}{3} + \frac{x^5}{5} - \cdots,$$

discovered independently by James Gregory (1670) and Leibniz (1673). With $x = 1$ it yields

$$\frac{1}{4}\pi = 1 - \frac{1}{3} + \frac{1}{5} - \cdots;$$

but the series converges too slowly to be of use, and more rapid processes may be obtained by using the Gregory series in formulas derived from the addition theorem

$$\text{arc tan } x + \text{arc tan } y = \text{arc tan } \{(x+y)/(1-xy)\}.$$

By repeated application of this theorem, John Machin (1706) found the convenient formula

$$\frac{1}{4}\pi = 4 \text{ arc tan} \left(\frac{1}{5}\right) - \text{arc tan} \left(\frac{1}{239}\right),$$

and calculated π to 100 decimal places.

This and similar formulas encouraged more extended calculations: here it is enough to note that in 1853 Rutherford gave 440 decimal places; and in the same year Shanks, in conjunction with Rutherford, gave 530 places, which proved to be his most accurate value. Also in 1853 Shanks gave 607 places, and the value to 500 places was independently checked. Some errors were corrected in 1873; and by that year Shanks, using Machin's formula, carried his calculations to 707 decimal places. There the matter rested for a considerable period. Subsidiary calculations provided the natural logarithms of 2, 3, 5, 10 to 137 decimal places and the values of 2^n, with $n = 12m + 1$ for $m = 1, 2, \cdots, 60$. Shanks also computed the value of e and of Euler's constant γ to a great many decimal places, and prepared a table of the prime numbers less than 60,000.

In 1944 D. F. Ferguson of the Royal Naval College, Dartmouth, attracted by the formula

$$\frac{1}{4}\pi = 3 \text{ arc tan} \left(\frac{1}{4}\right) + \text{arc tan} \left(\frac{1}{20}\right) + \text{arc tan} \left(\frac{1}{1985}\right),$$

proceeded to calculate π and compare his value with that given by Shanks. At the 528th decimal place there was a disagreement that was not reduced when Ferguson rechecked his own work, which he eventually carried to 710 decimal places. This discrepancy was communicated to R. C. Archibald, editor of *Mathematical Tables and Aids to Computation*, who suggested to J. W. Wrench, Jr., and L. B. Smith that they might recalculate π by Machin's formula; their value, to 808 decimal places, confirmed Ferguson's result and his identification of two terms omitted by Shanks, which had caused the latter's errors. Modern computing machinery has carried the calculation of π to great lengths: in 1949 the first such determination, by ENIAC, went to 2,000 decimal places; by 1960 at least 100,000 places were known.

BIBLIOGRAPHY

I. Original Works. Shanks's book was *Contributions to Mathematics, Comprising Chiefly the Rectification of the Circle* . . . (London–Cambridge–Durham, 1853). His papers are listed in Royal Society *Catalogue of Scientific Papers,* V, 672; VIII, 941; and XI, 401; and include nine memoirs published in *Proceedings of the Royal Society,* **6–22** (1854–1874).

II. Secondary Literature. Poggendorff mentions Shanks briefly, in III, 1241; but his reference in IV, 1390, to an obituary by J. C. Hoffmann in *Zeitschrift für mathematischen und naturwissenschaftlichen Unterricht,* **26** (1895), is misleading; this item merely reproduces Shanks's 1873 figures, with a little comment. Local sources could supply only the information that Shanks kept a school. A. Fletcher, J. C. P. Miller, and L. Rosenhead, *An Index of Mathematical Tables,* 2nd ed. (London, 1962), gives full bibliographical details and critical notes. A concise history of the evaluation of π is given by E. W. Hobson, *Squaring the Circle* (London, 1913; repr. 1953).

Ferguson's two notes on his evaluation of π are in *Mathematical Gazette,* no. 289 (May 1946), 89–90; and no. 298 (Feb. 1948), 37. A note by R. C. Archibald, J. W. Wrench, Jr., L. B. Smith, and D. F. Ferguson, in *Mathematical Tables and Other Aids to Computation,* **2** (Apr. 1947), gives agreed figures (as in Ferguson's second note) and adds some details.

T. A. A. Broadbent

SHAPLEY, HARLOW (*b.* Nashville, Missouri, 2 November 1885; *d.* Boulder, Colorado, 20 October 1972), *astronomy.*

Shapley was born in a farmhouse near Carthage, Missouri, the son of Willis Shapley, a farmer and schoolteacher, and Sarah Stowell. He received the equivalent of a fifth-grade education in a nearby rural school, and later took a short business course in Pittsburg, Kansas. At age sixteen he was a reporter on the Chanute, Kansas, *Daily Sun,* and a year later worked briefly as a police reporter in Joplin, Missouri. Determined to qualify for college, he and his younger brother John applied to the high school in Carthage, but they were turned down as unprepared. Instead, they attended the Presbyterian Carthage Collegiate Institute, from which Harlow graduated after two semesters. (Although Harlow's intellectual ambition was not shared by his twin brother, Horace, his younger brother John became an eminent art historian.)

In 1907 Shapley enrolled at the University of Missouri, intending to enter the projected School of Journalism, only to find that the school would not open for another year. Consequently, he took up astronomy almost by accident. Shapley's choice of astronomy was reinforced in his third year when Frederick H. Seares, director of the Laws Observatory, offered him a teaching assistantship. After three years at the university, Shapley received a B.A. with high honors in mathematics and physics in 1910 and an M.A. in 1911. When recommending him for the Thaw fellowship in astronomy at Princeton, Seares mentioned Shapley's "phenomenal industry," his "independence of thought and a certain originality," and his "diversity of interest."

Upon receiving the fellowship in 1911, Shapley began working on eclipsing binaries with Henry Norris Russell, who became one of his closest friends and confidants. Their joint work, based on the use of new computing methods, for the first time yielded extensive knowledge of the sizes of stars. Besides the new methods of computing, Shapley used the polarizing photometer with the 23-inch refractor at Princeton, obtaining nearly 10,000 measurements. Within two years he had completed his doctoral dissertation. In an expanded version of his thesis, eventually published as a 176-page quarto volume in the *Princeton University Observatory Contributions*, Shapley analyzed ninety eclipsing binaries; scarcely ten orbits had previously been computed. Otto Struve later called this "the most significant single contribution toward our understanding of the physical characteristics of very close double stars."

As an important by-product of his research, Shapley disproved the commonly accepted opinion that Cepheid variables were binary stars. He showed that if the Cepheids were indeed double stars, the two components of their prototype, Delta Cephei, would have to fall inside each other. He therefore concluded that the Cepheid variables are not double but single stars that pulsate, thus changing their brightness as they change in size. Arthur Eddington carried out the theoretical analysis that made the pulsation hypothesis creditable but, as the extant correspondence reveals, there was always a close interaction between Shapley, the observer, and Eddington, the theoretician.

In 1913, as Shapley was finishing his thesis, he inquired about job prospects with Seares, who had left Missouri for the Mount Wilson Observatory. Seares arranged for Shapley to have an interview with George Ellery Hale, and shortly thereafter Shapley obtained a post at the California observatory. He did not go west immediately, but first took a five-month European tour with his brother John, and then stayed several months longer in Princeton to complete his monograph on eclipsing binaries. En route to Pasadena, on 15 April 1914, he married Martha Betz, whom he had met in a mathematics class at Missouri. Later she collaborated with Shapley on several papers and eventually became an expert in her own right on eclipsing binaries. The Shapley family grew to include a daughter and four sons.

The nature and direction of Shapley's research at Mount Wilson was foreshadowed by a visit he made to the Harvard College Observatory shortly before completing his graduate work at Princeton. There he discussed his future plans with Solon I. Bailey, who suggested that Shapley use the Mount Wilson sixty-inch telescope to study variable stars in globular clusters. It was precisely this suggestion that led to Shapley's most remarkable discoveries.

The globular clusters that became the focal point of Shapley's work are extremely remote and highly concentrated stellar systems, arranged in a spherical form and consisting of tens of thousands of stars. Before Shapley began his research at Mount Wilson, Bailey had already detected a number of Cepheid variables in the globular clusters. In addition, Henrietta Leavitt of Harvard had identified many variable stars in the two Magellanic Clouds. Her investigations indicated that the longer the periodic cycle of light variation, the brighter the star.

Shapley enlarged on Bailey's and Leavitt's work first by discovering many new Cepheid variables in globular clusters and second by devising a method of measuring distances to these clusters based on the relationship between Cepheid brightness and period. Before he could exploit this so-called period-luminosity relationship, Shapley had to calibrate the absolute brightness or luminosity of at least one Cepheid. Because no Cepheids are close enough to be measured by direct trigonometric methods, he relied on an ingenious statistical procedure to establish the distance and hence the luminosity of a typical Cepheid variable.

With his newly calibrated standard candle for the measurement of stellar distances, Shapley established a radically altered conception of the size of the Milky Way system. It is difficult to convey a sense of the intensive amount of work required to set up the magnitude sequences and to obtain the multiple plates needed to determine the periods of the variable stars. The fact that Shapley produced a series of eleven papers on star clusters before reaching his remarkable conclusions on galactic structure is indicative of the extraordinary number of hours devoted exclusively to data gathering. On 6 February 1917, Shapley wrote to the Dutch astronomer Kapteyn, who had been a regular visitor at Mount Wilson, that "the work on clusters goes on monotonously—monotonous so far as labor is concerned, but the results are continual pleasure. Give me time enough and I shall get something out of the problem yet."

A year later, on 8 January 1918, Shapley wrote to Eddington about a new breakthrough:

I have had in mind from the first that results more important to the problem of the galactic system than to any other question might be contributed by the cluster studies. Now, with startling suddenness and definiteness, they seem to have elucidated the whole sidereal structure. . . .

The luminosity-period law of Cepheid variation—a fundamental feature in this work—is now very prettily defined. It is based upon 230 stars with periods ranging from about 100 days to five hours. The measurement of the magnitudes necessary for the determination of the distances and space distribution of the clusters took a painful amount of stupid labor, but I am forgetting that for now we have the parallaxes of every one of them. . . .

To be brief, the globular clusters outline the sidereal system, but they avoid the plane of the Milky Way. . . . All of our naked-eye stars, the irregular nebulae, eclipsing binaries—everything we know about, in fact, and call remote, [belong to this system] except those compactly formed globular clusters, a few outlying cluster-type variables, the Magellanic clouds, and perhaps, the spiral nebulae. The globular clusters apparently can form and exist only in the parts of the universe where the star material is less dense and the gravitational forces less powerful than along the galactic plane. This view of the general system, I am afraid, will necessitate alterations in our ideas of star distribution and density in the galactic system.

The widely accepted view of the Milky Way in 1918 had resulted largely from the statistical work of Kapteyn. According to those laborious studies, the sun lay near the center of a flat lens-shaped stellar aggregation with the great majority of stars encompassed within a disk about 10,000 light-years in diameter. In contrast, Shapley maintained that Kapteyn's system, containing most of the stars and clusters that we can see, constituted only a small part of a much larger galactic system that was centered within the remote congregation of globular clusters in the direction of Sagittarius. In writing to Eddington, Shapley indicated that the equatorial diameter of the system was about 300,000 light-years, with a center some 60,000 light-years distant.

Walter Baade later described Shapley's achievement in his own picturesque way:

I have always admired the way in which Shapley finished this whole problem in a very short time, ending up with a picture of the Galaxy that just about smashed up all the old school's ideas about galactic dimensions.

It was a very exciting time, for these distances seemed to be fantastically large, and the "old boys" did not take them sitting down. But Shapley's determination of the distances of the globular clusters simply demanded these larger dimensions [*Stars and Galaxies*, p. 9].

Among the other very exciting things then going on at Mount Wilson was the discovery of novae in the spiral nebulae. At that time it was uncertain whether the spiral nebulae were satellites of our own Galaxy or "island universes," that is, stellar systems comparable in form and structure to the Milky Way but located far beyond our galactic system. Shapley realized that if the luminosities of the novae were known, these stars could then provide a key to the distances of the spirals. In 1917 he suggested that the Andromeda nebula had a distance of some one million light-years, a measure close to the result now accepted. Yet, almost immediately, Shapley withdrew his statement. The reason for his action was twofold. First, Adriaan van Maanen at Mount Wilson had studied the proper motions of stars in spiral nebulae and had found that the spirals were rotating. His investigation of the spiral M 101 led to the conclusion that if this object were actually located at the distance indicated by its nova, it would be an enormous galaxy and hence its linear motions would be just incredibly large—an appreciable fraction of the speed of light. (Those who argued that the spirals lay outside the galactic system were obliged to consider van Maanen's measures spurious, and subsequent research proved their view correct.)

By 1918 Shapley had a second reason for questioning the validity of the island universe theory. The Milky Way, as he had begun to envision it, was an enormous and lumpy structure that seemed to bear little resemblance to the spirals. He was loath to believe that the spirals could be comparable to the immense galactic system.

Shapley's indefatigable researching, speculating, and publicizing of his own views eventually led to the now famous debate on the scale of the universe presented before the National Academy of Sciences in Washington in April 1920. Throughout the encounter, Shapley maintained a cordial relationship with his opponent, Heber D. Curtis of the Lick Observatory, even though Curtis had written that the two speakers should go after each other "hammer and tongs." Shapley outlined his findings on the large dimensions of the Galaxy, presenting his points mainly in a nontechnical fashion. Curtis, on the other hand, spoke rather technically, trying his best to demolish Shapley's hypotheses about the luminosity of stars in globular clusters and to deflate the concept of a large distance scale for the galactic system. At the same time, Curtis argued quite correctly about the great distances of the spiral nebulae, a topic that Shapley tried to ignore. Before the debate there had been little direct communication between Shapley and Curtis, but for the joint publication, they freely exchanged working drafts. Hence Shapley's published version differs greatly from his comparatively popular oral presentation.

Shapley's alert and inquisitive nature led him to still other investigations on Mount Wilson. For example, he discovered a quantitative linear relation between temperature and the running speed of ants on the mountain, and he was always particularly proud of his five technical papers on ants in *Proceedings of the National Academy of Sciences*, *Psyche*, and *Bulletin of the Ecological Society of America*. Altogether, during his seven years at Mount Wilson he published over 100 papers.

Shapley's enthusiastic researching and his penchant for speculation sometimes led him astray. In the spring of 1918 he became excited about an explanation for the phenomenon of star streaming that completely missed the correct reasons. Ironically enough, it was the analysis of star streaming in terms of the rotation of our Galaxy, set forth by Bertil Lindblad in the 1920's, that provided one of the convincing finishing touches to Shapley's picture of the Milky Way.

While at Mount Wilson, Shapley had recognized that his own interests in variable stars and clusters were closely akin to the main concerns of the research programs carried out at Harvard under Edward C. Pickering's directorship, and he sometimes contemplated the possibility of becoming Pickering's successor. In his reminiscences Shapley wrote:

> The day I heard that Pickering had died, on my way home for lunch, I stopped at the corner of two streets—I could name them now—and pondered on whether I should give up a research career. Should I, or should I not? Should I curb my ambition? Finally I said to myself, "All right. I'll take a shot at it" [*Through Rugged Ways to the Stars*, p. 82].

In fact, the directorship was first offered to Henry Norris Russell, who on 13 June 1920 wrote frankly to Hale at Mount Wilson Observatory:

> If they accept this plan, I will then propose Shapley for second in command . . . consider what Shapley and I could do at Harvard!

> Between us, we cover the field of sidereal astrophysics rather fully. We can both do some theory,— and I might keep Shapley from too riotous an imagination,—in print. Moreover, Shapley knows the field of modern photographic photometry and is familiar with big reflectors. He would have good ideas for the use of the 60-inch mirror which is at Harvard, but has never been utilized. . . .
>
> Shapley couldn't swing the thing alone, I am convinced of this after trying to measure myself with the job. . . . But he would make a bully second, and would be sure to grow—I mean in knowledge of the world and of affairs; if he grew intellectually he would be a prodigy!

In the end, Russell turned down the position, President Lowell of Harvard then offered Shapley a staff appointment, but not the directorship. When Shapley promptly declined the job, Hale informed Lowell that the Mount Wilson Observatory would grant Shapley a year's leave of absence if Harvard wished to make a trial arrangement. Lowell agreed, and in April 1921 Shapley took up residence in Cambridge; on 31 October he was awarded the appointment as full director.

At Harvard Observatory, Shapley immediately offered his encouragement for the completion and extension of the *Henry Draper Catalogue* of stellar spectral classifications, and with various collaborators, including Annie Jump Cannon and Lindblad, he began extensive researches into the distribution and distances of stars of various spectral types. Even while at Mount Wilson, Shapley had hoped to use the Harvard objective prism plates to determine spectrographically the distances of bright southern stars, but Walter S. Adams, the acting director, had made him return the plates on the grounds that it was inappropriate for a Mount Wilson staff member to use observational material from elsewhere.

At Harvard, Shapley seized the opportunity to study the Magellanic Clouds, the objects in the southern hemisphere in which the period-luminosity relation for Cepheids had first been established. Because Harvard Observatory had maintained a southern station for many years, photographic plates were already available, and Shapley in 1924 revised his earlier distance estimate for the Small Magellanic Cloud upward to 100,000 light-years, at that time the largest published distance for any object. Throughout his tenure as director, Shapley was always proud of the existence of a southern station, and with it he established a virtual monopoly on the study of the Magellanic Clouds. In 1927 the station was moved from Arequipa, Peru, to Bloemfontein, South Africa, and simultaneously Shapley persuaded the Rockefeller Foundation to provide a sixty-inch reflector for the new site. The giant emission nebula, 30 Doradus, in the Large Magellanic Cloud received special study, and in 1937 he and John S. Paraskevopoulos published photographs from the Rockefeller reflector that showed for the first time the obscured nuclear cluster of blue-white supergiants. They also identified the red (M-type) supergiants in the association.

In February 1924 Edwin Hubble wrote to Shapley about his discovery of two Cepheid variables in the Andromeda nebula, M 31. Shapley responded that the letter was "the most entertaining literature I have seen for a long time," and promised to send a revised period-luminosity curve. Shapley must have realized at once that the spirals were, after all, extremely distant objects. His research interests turned increasingly toward these nebulae, which he called galaxies. By the end of the decade a considerable rivalry developed with Hubble, who called the spirals "extragalactic nebulae," and these terms became shibboleths in an even broader competition between east coast and west coast American astronomy. The rivalry was exacerbated by the Rockefeller Foundation decision to sponsor a 200-inch telescope for the Mount Wilson Observatory; Shapley naturally had hoped for greater development of his southern station.

Shapley's principal work on galaxies took the form of vast surveys that recorded tens of thousands of these objects in both hemispheres of the sky. His work showed not only the enormous numbers of galaxies, but also their irregular distribution, a point he emphasized in contrast to Hubble, who tended to stress the homogeneity necessary for simple cosmological modeling. An early result of these surveys was the "Shapley-Ames Catalogue" of 1,249 galaxies, including 1,025 brighter than the thirteenth magnitude.

Shapley's major discovery of the 1930's, a consequence of the galaxy surveys, was the identification of the first two dwarf systems, in the southern constellations Sculptor and Fornax, both now firmly established as members of our local family of galaxies.

After leaving Mount Wilson, Shapley's greatest contribution was not so much any particular astronomical discovery, but rather the extraordinarily stimulating environment he created at the Harvard College Observatory. Cambridge, Massachusetts, in the 1920's became the crossroad through which nearly every major astronomer passed, a status that culminated in the congress of the International Astronomical Union there in 1932. Cecilia Payne and Donald Menzel came to Harvard to pursue pioneering astrophysical problems, and Payne's doctoral thesis on stellar atmospheres, published as the first of the *Harvard Observatory Monographs*, was pronounced by Henry Norris Russell as the best he had ever read with the possible exception of Shapley's. Previously there had been no graduate program in astronomy at Harvard. Shapley quickly set about building a distinguished department whose alumni in turn became the leaders in other graduate programs throughout the country. Among the staff members Shapley brought to Harvard in the late 1920's to assist in building a graduate program were H. H. Plaskett and Bart J. Bok. The first Radcliffe and Harvard astronomy Ph.D.'s after Miss Payne, were Frank Hogg, Emma Williams, and Helen Sawyer. Graduates in the 1930's included Peter Millman, Carl Seyfert, Frank Edmondson, Jesse Greenstein, and Leo Goldberg.

Under Shapley the Harvard Observatory became a mecca for young astronomers throughout the world. In his early days there he became a confirmed internationalist, and during the late 1930's he helped rescue European refugee scientists and bring them to the United States. Bok reports, "One of these who came to Harvard [Richard Prager of Berlin] told me quietly and seriously that every night at least a thousand Jewish scientists were saying a prayer of thanks for Harlow Shapley's humanitarian efforts to help save them and their families."

A brilliant and witty speaker, Shapley accepted numerous lecture assignments, including the Halley lecture in Oxford (1928), the Darwin lecture of the Royal Astronomical Society (London, 1934), and the Henry Norris Russell lecture of the American Astronomical Society (Haverford, 1950), as well as popular lectures in churches and small colleges. His original insights dramatized the vastness of the universe and the peripheralness of man. A confirmed agnostic, he nevertheless frequently participated in conferences on science and religion and edited the book *Science Ponders Religion* (New York, 1960).

Shapley was the recipient of many honors, beginning with his election to the National Academy of Sciences in 1924 and the Draper Medal awarded him by the Academy in 1926. His other numerous awards included the Rumford Medal of the American Academy of Arts and Sciences in 1933, the Gold Medal of the Royal Astronomical Society in 1934, and the Pope Pius XI Prize in 1941. He became an honorary national academician in a dozen foreign countries, and won even more honorary doctorates. Shapley served as president of the American Astronomical Society (1943–1946), of the Society of the Sigma Xi (1943–1947), and of the American Academy of Arts and Sciences (1939–1944), which he was particularly instrumental in revitalizing.

After World War II, Shapley gave increasing priority to national and international affairs. Consequently, his effectiveness as an astronomer began to decline, and Harvard began to lose the leading position it had reached in astronomy during the 1930's, according to Bok, in his "Biographical Memoir of Harlow Shapley," in *Biographical Memoirs. National Academy of Sciences.* Bok adds that in retrospect it seems a pity that Shapley did not resign his directorship to assume some important administrative post in science commensurate with his role as citizen of the world.

One of Shapley's proudest achievements during the late 1940's was his role in the formation of the United Nations Educational, Scientific, and Cultural Organization. Kirtley Mather has written, "Shapley almost singlehandedly prevented the deletion of the 'S' from UNESCO." In 1945 Shapley was one of the Americans sent to London by the State Department to write the UNESCO Charter, and he firmly believed the opening lines: "Since wars begin in the minds of men, it is in the minds of men that the defenses of peace must be constructed."

In 1945 Shapley was Harvard's representative at the celebration of the 220th anniversary of the Academy of Sciences in Moscow. One of the few Americans permitted to visit the Soviet Union in that era, he became an outspoken champion of cooperation with Soviet intellectuals when such a view was becoming increasingly unpopular. For several years Shapley served as chairman of the Independent Citizens Committee of the Arts, Sciences, and Professions, an organization that helped raise money to support liberal candidates for Congress. In November 1946 he was subpoenaed by the House Committee on Un-American Activities. Congressman John Rankin, who had been sitting behind closed doors as a one-man subcommittee, emerged to state, "I have never seen a witness treat a committee with more contempt." A month later Shapley was elected president of the American Association for the Advancement of Science, a move interpreted as a rebuke to the committee and a vote of confidence in the Harvard astronomer. In the late 1940's Shapley made headlines when he chaired several meetings of left-wing organizations to which Russian delegates were invited. In March 1950 he was named by Senator Joseph McCarthy as one of five alleged Communists connected with the State Department, but later in the year Shapley was completely exonerated by the Senate Foreign Relations Committee.

Shapley continued as director of the Harvard College Observatory until the fall of 1952. In his seventies, he was still very active, giving much time to the grants committees of the American Philosophical Society and the Society of the Sigma Xi, and thoroughly enjoying himself as he traveled far and wide on lecture tours. Following his eighty-fifth birthday, his strength began to fail rapidly. He moved to Boulder, Colorado, where his son Alan resided, and there he died in 1972.

A versatile and imaginative thinker with a vivid personality, Shapley made devoted allies and bitter enemies. His friends called him a Renaissance man and forgave his vanity, while even his detractors conceded that he was one of the most stimulating figures in twentieth-century science.

BIBLIOGRAPHY

I. ORIGINAL WORKS. A. *Books and Articles.* An extensive bibliography of Shapley's writings (about 600 items), prepared by Mildred Shapley Matthews and based on an earlier version by Thomasine Brooks, will appear in *Biographical Memoirs. National Academy of Sciences.* Only his most noteworthy publications are listed here.

Shapley's doctoral dissertation was published as "A Study of the Orbits of Eclipsing Binaries," in *Princeton University Observatory Contributions*, no. 3 (1915). A related and pioneering paper was "On the Nature and Cause of Cepheid Variation," in *Astrophysical Journal*, **40** (1914), 448–465. Two dozen additional articles on binaries and variable stars appeared in *Astrophysical Journal* and *Publications of the Astronomical Society of the Pacific* during the years 1913–1916.

Shapley's Mount Wilson studies of clusters and galactic structure appeared between 1916 and 1921 primarily in two long series, "Studies of the Magnitudes in Star Clusters" (13 parts in *Proceedings of the National Academy of Sciences*) and "Studies Based on the Colors and Magnitudes in Stellar Clusters" (19 parts mostly in the *Astrophysical Journal*, but the first three only in *Contributions from the Mount Wilson Solar Observatory*); the most important of these studies are "Sixth Paper: On the Determination of the Distances of Globular Clusters," in *Astrophysical Journal*, **48** (1918), 89–124; "Seventh Paper: The Distances, Distribution in Space, and Dimensions of 69 Globular Clusters," *ibid.*, **48** (1918), 154–181; and "Twelfth Paper: Remarks on the

Arrangement of the Sidereal Universe," *ibid.*, **49** (1919), 311–336. An excellent review of his early ideas on the arrangement of the Milky Way is "Star Clusters and the Structure of the Universe," in *Scientia*, **26** (1919), 269–276, 353–361, and **27** (1920), 93–101, 185–193.

His changing views on the nature of the spiral nebulae are revealed in "Note on the Magnitudes of Novae in Spiral Nebulae," in *Proceedings of the National Academy of Sciences*, **29** (1917), 213–217, and "On the Existence of External Galaxies," *ibid.*, **31** (1919), 261–268. The famous Shapley-Curtis debate, in a much revised form, appears as "The Scale of the Universe," in *National Research Council Bulletin*, **2**, no 11; Shapley's argument is found on pages 171–193 and H. D. Curtis' on pages 194–217. Shapley's work on clusters culminated in his monograph *Star Clusters* (New York, 1930), and in the extended summary "Stellar Clusters," in *Handbuch der Astrophysik*, **5**, part 2 (1933), 698–773. A later review of this work is "A Half Century of Globular Clusters," in *Popular Astronomy*, **57** (1949), 203–229.

While at Harvard, Shapley produced a series of eight articles on "The Magellanic Clouds," in *Harvard College Observatory Circulars* (1924–1925), and, with Adelaide Ames, another series of five parts on "The Coma-Virgo Galaxies," in *Harvard College Observatory Bulletin* (1929). He also prepared, with Miss Ames, "A Survey of the External Galaxies Brighter than the Thirteenth Magnitude," in *Annals of Harvard College Observatory*, **88**, no. 2 (1932), commonly called the "Shapley-Ames catalogue." For descriptions of Shapley's vast galaxy surveys recorded in *Annals of Harvard College Observatory*, **88**, no. 5 (1935), and **105**, no. 8 (1938), see "A Study of 7900 External Galaxies," in *Proceedings of the National Academy of Sciences*, **21** (1935), 587–592, and "A Survey of Thirty-six Thousand Southern Galaxies," *ibid.*, **23** (1937), 449–453. The discovery of the Sculptor and Fornax dwarf galaxies is announced in "Two Stellar Systems of a New Kind," in *Nature*, **142** (1938), 715–716. From 1939 to 1942 Shapley published the first sixteen pages of a series entitled "Galactic and Extragalactic Studies," in *Proceedings of the National Academy of Sciences*; he completed the series finally with paper 23 in 1955.

At least as early as 1935 Shapley had outlined a proposed book on the structure of the Milky Way and the Magellanic Clouds, and had by 1948 planned a monograph solely on the Magellanic Clouds. Although the work was never completed in this form, its development strongly influenced the scope of his *Galaxies* (Philadelphia, 1943; rev. ed., Cambridge, Mass., 1961), in the semipopular Harvard Books on Astronomy series, as well as his Henry Norris Russell lecture to the American Astronomical Society in 1950 (summarized in "A Survey of the Inner Metagalaxy," in *American Scientist*, **39** (1951), 609–628. The Russell lecture and a Sigma Xi lecture, "The Clouds of Magellan, a Gateway to the Sidereal Universe," *ibid.*, **44** (1956), 73–97, were later expanded into *The Inner Metagalaxy* (New Haven,

1957). Among the research works synthesized in this volume was a series of seventeen papers, mostly by Shapley, entitled "Magellanic Clouds," appearing in the *Proceedings of the National Academy of Sciences* between 1951 and 1955. See also "Comparison of the Magellanic Clouds with the Galactic System," in *Publications of the Observatory of the University of Michigan*, **10** (1951), 79–84.

Shapley wrote several distinguished popular books of essays on astronomy: *Starlight* (New York, 1926), *Flights from Chaos: A Survey of Material Systems from Atoms to Galaxies* (New York, 1930), *Of Stars and Men* (Boston, 1958), *Beyond the Observatory* (New York, 1967), and *The View from a Distant Star* (New York, 1963). The last of these volumes incorporates one of his most influential and widely reprinted essays, "A Design for Fighting," originally in *American Scholar*, **14** (1945), 19–32. Another essay that Shapley held as one of his most significant was "Cosmography: an Approach to Orientation," in *American Scientist*, **42** (1954), 471–486.

Shapley prepared several anthologies including *A Source Book in Astronomy*, with H. E. Howarth (New York, 1929), and *Source Book in Astronomy 1900–1950* (Cambridge, Mass., 1960).

B. *Manuscripts.* The Harvard University Archives contains 216 archival boxes of Shapley's correspondence, manuscripts, and memorabilia. Under shelf mark HUG 4773.10 are filed the so-called personal papers deposited by Shapley and his family, with access and literary rights under the discretion of the Archives. Boxes 1a to 5d contain manuscripts including scientific papers and associated research, book typescripts, and radio scripts; found here also is the original manuscript of the 1920 debate with Curtis, as well as numerous other lectures. Boxes 23b and 23c contain early correspondence from about 1910 to 1921. Later personal correspondence, mostly after Shapley's retirement from the Harvard Observatory directorship in 1952, is found in boxes 18a–23a. Other large blocks of correspondence and memoranda relating mostly to non-observatory committees and assignments (including political affairs) are found in boxes 10a–17d. Travel diaries and biographical materials are found in 25a–26c. The second group of boxes, ninety in all, shelf mark UA V 630.22, contain the observatory director's correspondence for 1921–1954, with access by permission of Harvard College Observatory. In this category can be found Shapley's voluminous correspondence with Henry Norris Russell, for example, plus letters to and from George Ellery Hale, Edwin Hubble, Adriaan van Maanen, and many others.

II. SECONDARY LITERATURE. Shapley's book of autobiographical reminiscences, *Through Rugged Ways to the Stars* (New York, 1969), was produced from an oral interview, although with reliance on memories of an earlier anecdotal book that he researched but never wrote. (The original tapes are in the Niels Bohr Library, American Institute of Physics, in New York.) "It is not the very best of autobiographies, but it does show the true

Harlow Shapley with all his wonderful ideals, his vanity, his compassion and his greatness," writes Bart J. Bok in "Biographical Memoir of Harlow Shapley," in *Biographical Memoirs. National Academy of Sciences*, **48** (1976). An unpublished book-length biography has been written by Shapley's daughter Mildred Shapley Matthews. See also Bart J. Bok, "Harlow Shapley, Cosmographer," in *American Scholar*, **40** (1971), 470–474, and "Harlow Shapely—Cosmographer and Humanitarian," in *Sky and Telescope*, **44** (1972). 354–357. An extensive obituary appeared in *The New York Times*, 21 October 1972; see also Hudson Hoagland, "Harlow Shapley—Some Recollections," in *Publications of the Astronomical Society of the Pacific*, **77** (1965), 422–430.

Earlier accounts include Frank Robbins, "The Royal Astronomical Society's Gold Medallist," in *Journal of the British Astronomical Association*, **44** (1934), 177–179, and the entry in Anna Rothe and Evelyn Lohr, eds., *Current Biography 1952* (New York, 1953), 533–535. For other aspects of Shapley's career, see Kirtley Mather, "Harlow Shapley, Man of the World," in *American Scholar*, **40** (1971), 475–481, and Don K. Price, "The Scientist as Politican," in *American Academy of Arts and Sciences Bulletin*, **26** (1973), 25–34.

Shapley's earlier work is reviewed by Owen Gingerich, "Harlow Shapley and Mount Wilson," *ibid.*, 10–24; Otto Struve, "A Historic Debate About the Universe," in *Sky and Telescope*, **19** (1960), 398–401; Bart J. Bok, "Harlow Shapley and the Discovery of the Center of Our Galaxy," in J. Neyman, ed., *The Heritage of Copernicus—Theories "Pleasing to the Mind"* (Cambridge, 1975); Helen Sawyer Hogg, "Harlow Shapley and Globular Clusters," in *Publications of the Astronomical Society of the Pacific*, **77** (1965), 336–346; and Bart J. Bok, "Shapley's Researches on the Magellanic Clouds," *ibid.*, 416–421. See also Richard Berendzen, Richard Hart, and Daniel Seeley, *Man Discovers the Galaxies: Case Studies on the Development of Modern Astronomy, 1900–1940* (in press), especially sections I and II and the Reader.

OWEN GINGERICH

Al-SHARĪF AL-IDRĪSĪ. See Al-Idrīsī, Abū ʿAbd Allāh Muḥammad ibn Muḥammad ibn ʿAbd Allāh ibn Idrīs, al-Sharīf al-Idrīsī.

SHARONOV, VSEVOLOD VASILIEVICH (*b.* St. Petersburg, Russia, 10 March 1901; *d.* Leningrad, U.S.S.R., 26 November 1964), *astronomy, geophysics*.

Sharonov was the son of an Imperial opera singer. After graduating from the Gymnasium in 1918, he entered the Faculty of Physics and Mathematics of Petrograd University, from which he graduated only in 1926 after having served in the Red Army (1919–1924). From his youth Sharonov systematically conducted various astronomical observations, particularly of sunspots. While still a student he headed the section of solar research of the Russian Society of Amateurs of Astronomy and published instructions for conducting observations throughout the country; the results were then sent to Sharonov. He later recounted his experiences in *Solntse i ego nablyudenia* ("The Sun and Observations of It"; 1948, 1953).

As a graduate student (1926–1929) at the Leningrad Astronomical Institute (now the Institute of Theoretical Astronomy of the Soviet Academy of Sciences) Sharonov conducted a substantial part of his experimental work at the State Optical Institute in Leningrad and at the Pulkovo, Simeiz, Tashkent, and Leningrad University observatories. He defended his dissertation, on the theory and application of the photometric wedge, in October 1929. After working at the Tashkent observatory, he returned to Leningrad in 1930 as senior scientific worker. In 1932 Sharonov organized a photometric laboratory at the University of Leningrad (later the Laboratory of Planetary Astronomy) and carried out important projects on absolute photometry, on the colorimetry of the moon and planets, and on atmospheric optics. He devised and tested a number of photometric instruments for solving the problem of "visibility of distant objects and sources of light." In December 1940 Sharonov defended his doctoral dissertation, on "indexes of visibility."

From 1938 to 1941 Sharonov was a docent at Leningrad University, and from 1941 to 1944 he directed the astrophysics laboratory of the part of Leningrad University evacuated to Yelabuga, Tatar A.S.S.R. From 1944 he was professor at Leningrad University and, from 1951, director of its astronomical observatory.

Having studied the photometric wedge as the most convenient instrument for astronomical and geophysical observations, Sharonov worked from 1930 to 1936 at the Institute of Air Surveys on problems of aerophotometry applied to the aerial photographic survey of landscapes under various conditions of illumination and visibility. The original instruments that he developed for this purpose included an aeroexponometer, a sensitoscope, a haze measurer, an epsilometer, a diaphanometer, a universal wedge photometer, and a visual colorimeter. He used them in his photometrical laboratory and on expeditions to measure the transparency of the atmosphere and the visibility of distant objects. One group of his works was devoted to methods of spectrophotometry applied to the measurement of the color of the clear sky and to the determination of the solar light constant, which he found to be 135,000 lux.

Sharonov applied the absolute methods of photometry and colorimetry to study the lunar surface and the solar corona, which he observed successfully during seven total solar eclipses (1936–1963). He published tables and graphs of the variation in several photometric properties of more than 100 objects on the lunar surface. Comparing them with analogous investigations of rock and mineral specimens, he found confirming evidence of the "meteor-slag theory" advanced by his wife, N. N. Sytinskaya. According to this theory, almost all lunar rocks are covered with porous, spongy layers formed by the caking of particles that result from the fall of meteoric bodies, the latter being accompanied by explosions and sharp local rises in temperature.

Sharonov observed the oppositions of Mars at Tashkent in 1939, 1956, and 1958. His photometric and colorimetric research on the planets was summarized in *Fotometricheskie issledovania prirody planet i sputnikov* ("Photometric Research on the Nature of the Planets and Satellites"; 1954), *Priroda planet* ("The Nature of the Planets"; 1958), and *Planeta Venera* ("The Planet Venus"; 1965). He also developed the hypothesis that the surface of Mars is covered with limonite dust.

Sharonov was in charge of the Soviet study of noctilucent clouds for the International Geophysical Year in 1957–1959.

BIBLIOGRAPHY

I. ORIGINAL WORKS. Sharonov's more than 200 basic writings include "Issledovanie fotometricheskogo klina" ("Research on the Photometric Wedge"), in *Trudy Tashkentskoi astronomicheskoi observatorii*, **3** (1930), 84–100; "O sisteme i nomenklature astronomicheskikh svetovykh velichin" ("On the System and Nomenclature of Astronomical Light Quantities"), in *Astronomicheskii zhurnal*, **9**, nos. 1–2 (1932), 82–101; "O kharakteristikakh otrazhatelnoy sposobnosti nebesnykh tel" ("On the Properties of the Reflecting Capacity of Heavenly Bodies"), *ibid.*, **11**, no. 5 (1934), 473–483; "On the Determination of the Absolute Reflectivity of the Moon and Planetary Surfaces," in *Trudy Astronomicheskoi observatorii Leningradskogo gosudarstvennogo universiteta*, **6** (1936), 26–33; "A Simple Method of Checking the Purkinje Effect in Variable Star Observations," in *Variable Stars*, **5**, no. 3 (1936), 68–70; "Absolute Photographic Photometry of Saturn's Disk," in *Poulkovo Observatory Circular*, nos. 26–27 (1939), 37–51;

"Opyt izmerenia absolyutnykh znacheny koeffitsientov yarkosti razlichnykh uchastkov lunnoy poverkhnosti" ("Experiment in Measuring the Absolute Values of the Coefficients of Brightness of Various Parts of the Lunar Surface"), in *Trudy Astronomicheskoi observatorii Leningradskogo gosudarstvennogo universiteta*, **10** (1939), 28–60; and "Universalny klinovoy fotometr" ("Universal Wedge Photometer"), *ibid.*, 72–81, repr. in *Uchenye zapiski Leningradskogo universiteta*, no. 31, Math. Ser., no. 3.

Later works are "Absolute Photographic Photometry and Colorimetry of Jupiter's Disk at the Opposition of 1928," in *Poulkovo Observatory Circular*, no. 30 (1940), 48–64; "Problemy absolyutnoy fotometrii tel solnechnoy sistemy" ("Problems of Absolute Photometry of Bodies in the Solar System"), in *Uchenye zapiski Leningradskogo Universiteta*, no. 53 (1940), 5–36; "Osveshchennost v lunnye nochi" ("Illumination on Moonlit Nights"), in *Astronomicheskie zhurnal*, **20**, no. 1 (1943), 21–33; *Vidimost dalekikh predmetov i ogney* ("The Visibility of Distant Objects and Sources of Light"; Moscow–Leningrad, 1944); *Izmerenie i raschet vidimosti dalekikh predmetov* ("Measurement and Calculation of Visibilities of Distant Objects"; Moscow–Leningrad, 1947); *Mars* (Moscow–Leningrad, 1947); "Diafanoskop, ego teoria, issledovanie i primenenie" ("The Diaphanometer, Its Theory, Research, and Use"), in *Trudy Glavnoi geofizicheskoi observatorii imeni A. I. Voeikova* (1948), no. 11, 73–110; and "Opyt absolyutnoy fotometrii serebristykh oblakov" ("Experiment on the Absolute Photometry of Noctilucent Clouds"), in *Nauchny byulleten Leningradskogo universiteta*, no. 22 (1948), 5–16.

See also "Issledovanie otrazhatelnoy sposobnosti lunnoy poverkhnosti" ("Research on the Reflecting Capacities of the Lunar Surface"), in *Trudy Astronomicheskoi observatorii Leningradskogo gosudarstvennogo universiteta*, **16** (1952), 114–154, written with N. N. Sytinskaya; "'Yavlenie Lomonosova' i ego znachenie dlya astronomii" ("'Lomonosov's Phenomenon' and Its Importance for Astronomy"), in *Astronomicheskii zhurnal*, **29**, no. 6 (1952), 728–737; "Problema fotometricheskikh nablyudeny lunnykh zatmeny" ("The Problem of Photometric Observations During Lunar Eclipses"), in *Vestnik Leningradskogo Universiteta*, no. 2 (1953), 47–61; "Fotometricheskie issledovania prirody planet i sputnikov" ("Photometric Researchs on the Nature of Planets and Satellites"), in *Uspekhi astronomicheskikh nauk*, **6** (1954), 181–249, which has a bibliography of 256 titles; and "Fotometricheskie i kolorimetricheskie sravnenia poverkhnosti Marsa s obraztsami limonita i gornykh porod krasnotsvetnykh tolshch" ("Photometric and Colorimetric Comparisons of the Surface of Mars With Specimens of Limonite and of Rock From the Red Layers"), in *Izvestiya Komissii po fizike planet Astrosoveta Akademii nauk SSSR*, no. 2 (1960), 30.

II. SECONDARY LITERATURE. See the obituary in *Astronomicheskii tsirkulyar. Byuro astronomicheskikh soobshchenii, Akademiya nauk SSSR*, no. 311 (1964); V. A. Bronshten, "Leningradsky issledovatel planet"

("Leningrad Investigator of the Planets"), in *Zemlya i vselennaya*, no. 5 (1969), 70–71; *Izvestiya Komissii po fizike planet Astrosoveta Akademii nauk SSSR*, no. 5 (1965), 105–111; L. N. Radlova, in *Astronomicheskii Kalendar na 1966* (Moscow, 1965), 242–245, with portrait; and *Uchenye zapiski Leningradskogo universiteta*, no. 328 (1965), 175–177.

P. G. KULIKOVSKY

SHARPEY, WILLIAM (*b*. Arbroath, Scotland, 1 April 1802; *d*. London, England, 11 April 1880), *anatomy, physiology.*

Sharpey was the posthumous son and fifth child of Henry Sharpey, a shipowner of Folkestone who had settled in Arbroath, Scotland, and his wife Mary Balfour. He was educated at Arbroath and at the University of Edinburgh, where he graduated M.D. in 1823. He became a fellow of the Royal College of Surgeons of Edinburgh in 1830. From 1831 to 1836 he taught anatomy extramurally in Edinburgh and in the latter year was appointed to the chair of anatomy and physiology at University College, London, in which post he spent the remainder of his professional life, retiring in 1874. He never married.

Sharpey became a fellow of the Royal Society of Edinburgh in 1834 and five years later was elected a fellow of the Royal Society, of which he was secretary from 1853 to 1872. At various times he was a member of many other official and learned bodies. He appears, after his London appointment, largely to have given up original work in favor of teaching and administration.

Although many who knew Sharpey considered him the real founder of the British school of physiology, comparing him in this respect with Johannes Müller in Germany, he made no great impact as a young man, and his appointment to the London chair evoked much surprise. He was of course a product of the famous Edinburgh medical school, still deeply influenced by the tradition of Cullen, John Gregory, and the first two Monros. Little is known of his early life, other than that he traveled extensively in Europe, studying under Panizza, Rudolphi, and Tiedemann and became familiar with French and German science and medicine. He published little original work—a few papers on cilia and ciliary motion, a long note on decidual structure in the English translation of Müller's *Handbuch der Physiologie des Menschen*, and a description in Quain's *Elements of Anatomy* of what are still referred to as Sharpey's bone fibers.

Sharpey's considerable authority stemmed from his membership of what would now be called the scientific "establishment," and from the fact that he was a great and inspiring teacher, who from his chair and by virtue of his position in the Royal Society did all that he could to further the development of physiology. His pupils included Joseph Lister; Michael Foster, who founded the Cambridge school of physiology; and E. A. Schäfer, who many years later added Sharpey's name to his own. He also collaborated with Burdon-Sanderson, who succeeded him and later became first holder of the chair of physiology at Oxford. These men, writing in the atmosphere of the late nineteenth century, were inclined to attribute much of Sharpey's influence to his firm opposition to vitalism in biology; but he was not averse to using vitalistic concepts in certain contexts, and the philosophy underlying his physiology must be interpreted with some care.

In the last years of his life Sharpey was much disturbed by the increasing agitation in Britain against experiments on living animals, and he kept in close touch with the negotiations that culminated in the act of 1876 "to amend the Law relating to Cruelty to Animals." In 1876 he was elected, along with Darwin, to honorary membership of the newly founded Physiological Society, an expression of the widely held opinion that for many years he had been the mainstay of physiology in Britain.

BIBLIOGRAPHY

The outlines of Sharpey's career are given in the obituary notice in *Proceedings of the Royal Society,* **31** (1880), xi–xix; in the *Dictionary of National Biography;* and in E. A. Sharpey-Schäfer, *History of the Physiological Society* (London, 1927), esp. 17–19, 31. The only modern and the only full-length study, by D. W. Taylor in *Medical History,* **15** (1971), 126–153, 241–259, includes a bibliography of his published work and draws to a considerable extent on unpublished MSS: sets of lecture notes including those taken by Lister, miscellaneous papers, referees' reports to the Royal Society, and letters written toward the end of his life to E. A. Schäfer and others. Sharpey's presidential address to the Physiological Section of the British Medical Association, in *British Medical Journal* (1862), ii, 162–171, is of considerable interest because it sets out his views about the state of his science after a lifetime of teaching and from a position of eminence among his contemporaries.

DOUGLASS W. TAYLOR

SHARPEY-SCHÄFER, EDWARD ALBERT (*b.* London, England, 2 June 1850; *d.* North Berwick, Scotland, 29 March 1935), *histology, physiology.*

Schäfer was the third son of J. W. H. Schäfer, who was born in Hamburg but had become a naturalized Englishman and a merchant in the City of London, and Jessie Browne. He was educated at University College, London, where he came under the lasting influence of William Sharpey and where he qualified in medicine in 1874. When Sharpey retired from his chair in that year and Burdon-Sanderson was appointed his successor and first Jodrell professor of physiology, Schäfer became assistant professor, succeeding Burdon-Sanderson in 1883. He was appointed to the chair of physiology at the University of Edinburgh in 1899 and retired in 1933. In 1878 he married Maud Dixey, who died in 1896; they had two sons and two daughters. In 1900 he married Ethel Roberts. One daughter died young in tragic circumstances, and both sons were killed in World War I. In 1918 he took the name of Sharpey-Schäfer "partly on Jack's account [his elder son, John Sharpey Schäfer], partly because it was the name of my old teacher and master in Physiology—the best friend I ever had."

Schäfer received many distinctions. He was elected a fellow of the Royal Society in 1878, and was awarded a Royal Medal in 1902 and the Copley Medal in 1924. He was president of the British Association in 1912, of the Eleventh International Physiological Congress, which met at Edinburgh in 1923, and of the Royal Society of Edinburgh in 1933. He also received many honorary degrees and was knighted in 1913.

In the laboratory Schäfer's catholicity of interest was impressive. He edited and contributed six chapters on topics as diverse as the biochemistry of blood, the ductless glands, the neuron, and cerebral localization to the *Textbook of Physiology*, a work for advanced students, in which each chapter was written by a leading authority.

Schäfer's early work was histological and embryological. His *Essentials of Histology* (1885) was one of the most widely used books on the subject in English; the sixteenth edition was published in 1954. One paper from those years in particular deserves to rank as a classic although its importance was not appreciated at the time. Whether nerve cells were separate and individual units, or whether their processes anastomosed to form a nerve net, was an eagerly debated question in the latter part of the nineteenth century. The main protagonists were Golgi and Ramón y Cajal. As a re-

sult of the interest of his friend G. J. Romanes in the problem of locomotion in Medusae, Schäfer was led to study the structure of the subumbrellar nervous plexus in *Aurelia aurita.* He found that each nerve fiber was distinct from and nowhere structurally continuous with any other; he thought it reasonable to assume fiber-to-fiber transmission from "inductive action," possibly electric, the result being the same as if there were a real network.

With E. Klein and J. N. Langley, Schäfer was appointed in 1881 to adjudicate on the conflicting claims of Goltz, on the one hand, and of Ferrier and Yeo, on the other, about the effects of ablation of defined areas of the mammalian cerebral cortex. This aroused his interest in cerebral localization and led him to seek the collaboration of Victor Horsley in a series of experiments that appreciably added to the results of Ferrier. This interest was later extended to include the spinal cord, and until the end of his career he worked intermittently on neurophysiological problems.

Schäfer made his most notable contributions in the field of endocrinology, and his papers with George Oliver on the effects of suprarenal and of pituitary extracts are landmarks in the history of physiology. Oliver, a practicing physician, sought Schäfer's advice on the supposed effects of orally administered suprarenal and other extracts. The two men showed that while most were inactive, intravenous injections of suprarenal extract produced a dramatic rise in arterial blood pressure, arterial constriction, vagal stimulation (reflex, as we now know), and an increase in the rate and force of cardiac contraction in vagotomized animals. They also pointed out that these effects derived from the medulla, not from the cortex of the gland. They then demonstrated the pressor effect of pituitary extract given intravenously. After Howell's discovery that this depended only on the posterior lobe of the gland, Schäfer continued to investigate the problem, which was the subject of his Croonian lecture to the Royal Society in 1909. He found, however, that posterior lobe extract apparently caused an increase in renal volume and a diuresis, independent of its pressor effect. These observations on the kidney led to considerable confusion among workers in the field, which was dissipated only by E. B. Verney's unequivocal demonstration of the antidiuretic effect in 1926.

The importance of the pancreas in carbohydrate metabolism had been obvious since the experiments of Joseph von Mering and Minkowski in 1889. As early as 1894 Schäfer pointed out on morphological grounds that the islet tissue might act collectively as an organ of internal secretion by means of which the pancreas produced its effect on the blood sugar level, an illustration of his prescience and of his oft-stated belief in the value of histology to physiology. In 1913, in his Lane lectures, he suggested the name "insuline" for the still hypothetical substance and also introduced the terms "autacoid" and "chalone" into endocrinology. (He later pointed out [*The Endocrine Organs*, 2nd ed., II, 343] that he was not the first to use the word "insuline.")

Schäfer's practical turn of mind showed itself in the invention of new laboratory methods and useful modifications of existing procedures. His name became familiar to many who could have had only the haziest idea of his eminence as a physiologist following the publication in 1903 of his method of artificial respiration—now superseded by mouth-to-mouth inflation of the lungs—for which he was awarded the Distinguished Service Medal of the Royal Life Saving Society in 1909.

An uncompromising opponent of the antivivisection movement, Schäfer did not mince words in public about what he regarded as the hypocrisy of those opposed to experiments on living animals. His presidential address to the British Association in 1912 offended many lay people, who considered it a dogmatically materialistic explanation of the origins of life in terms of physics and chemistry. During World War I, when anti-German hysteria was at its height, his forthright but unavailing defense of his colleague W. Cramer did not increase his popularity, even in academic circles.

Schäfer was an original member of the Physiological Society; and in 1926 he was appointed to write its history for its jubilee, a task for which he was uniquely qualified—knowing personally almost all the members since its inception. In 1908 he founded the *Quarterly Journal of Experimental Physiology*, which he continued to edit until 1933; in that year a special number was dedicated to him, written entirely by his pupils, the number and worldwide distribution of whom testified to his influence as a teacher. He remained an active experimentalist almost until his retirement, and one of his last papers reported his observations on the results of nerve section and regeneration. He himself, at the age of seventy-seven, had been the experimental subject.

BIBLIOGRAPHY

I. ORIGINAL WORKS. Schäfer's output of published work was very large. It includes numerous short contri-

butions to the *Proceedings* of the Physiological and Royal societies, about sixty full-length scientific papers, an impressive number of textbooks, and lectures and addresses.

His contributions to science, apart from his textbooks, are to be found mainly in the *Philosophical Transactions* and the *Proceedings of the Royal Society*, in *Brain*, in *Journal of Physiology*, and in *Quarterly Journal of Experimental Physiology*. Of those on the nervous system, the most important are "Observations on the Nervous System of *Aurelia aurita*," in *Philosophical Transactions of the Royal Society*, **169** (1878), 563–575; "A Record of Experiments Upon the Functions of the Cerebral Cortex," ibid., **B179** (1888), 1–45, written with Victor Horsley; "An Investigation Into the Functions of the Occipital and Temporal Lobes of the Monkey's Brain," ibid., 303–328, written with S. M. Brown; and "The Nerve Cell Considered as the Basis of Neurology," in *Brain*, **16** (1893), 134–169.

His fundamental work with G. Oliver on the suprarenal gland was reported in preliminary form in *Journal of Physiology*, **16** (1894), i–iv, and **17** (1895), ix–xiv, and, in full, as "The Physiological Effects of Extracts of the Suprarenal Capsules," **18** (1895), 230–276. The results of his research with Oliver on the pituitary are to be found briefly in *Journal of Physiology*, **18** (1895), 277–279; more fully, with S. Vincent, in "The Physiological Effects of Extracts of the Pituitary Body," ibid., **25** (1899), 87–97; and, with P. T. Herring, in "On the Action of Pituitary Extracts on the Kidney," in *Philosophical Transactions of the Royal Society*, **199** (1908), 1–29. His Oliver-Sharpey lectures, "The Present Condition of Our Knowledge Regarding the Suprarenal Capsules," in *British Medical Journal* (1908), **1**, 1277–1281, 1346–1351; and his Croonian lecture, "The Functions of the Pituitary Body," in *Proceedings of the Royal Society*, **B81** (1909), 442–468, also should be consulted.

Schäfer's early statements about the possible function of the islets of Langerhans are given in his address to the Physiological Section of the British Association, in *Report of the British Association for the Advancement of Science*, **64** (1894), 795–814; that to the British Medical Association, in *British Medical Journal* (1895), ii, 341–348; and in his *Textbook of Physiology*, I (Edinburgh–London, 1898), 930; this book is a well-documented and valuable historical guide to the physiological knowledge of the time.

Schäfer's Lane lectures, given at Stanford University in 1913, were published as *An Introduction to the Study of the Endocrine Glands and Internal Secretions* (Stanford, 1914) and include a lengthy discussion on the terminology of the subject. They were published in a revised form as *The Endocrine Organs: An Introduction to the Study of Internal Secretion* (London–New York, 1916; 2nd ed., enl., 2 vols., 1924–1926).

His work on artificial respiration was reported as "Description of a Simple and Efficient Method of Performing Artificial Respiration in the Human Subject Especially in Cases of Drowning. To Which Is Appended Instructions for the Treatment of the Apparently Drowned," in *Medico-Chirurgical Transactions*, **87** (1904), 609–623.

Schäfer's presidential address to the British Association, in *Report of the British Association for the Advancement of Science*, **82** (1912), 3–36, is an interesting exposition of his views on physiology in general; as is his Horsley memorial lecture, "The Relations of Surgery and Physiology," in *British Medical Journal* (1923), **2**, 739–745. In addition to his *History of the Physiological Society During Its First Fifty Years 1876–1926* (London, 1927), an invaluable source of material is the collection of Sharpey-Schäfer papers in the Library of the Wellcome Institute of the History of Medicine, London. These include his private diaries, from which the quoted explanation of his change of name was taken, letters from physiologists all over the world covering a period of sixty years, and many other documents and newspaper clippings.

II. SECONDARY LITERATURE. The only secondary sources appear to be the obituary notices in *Quarterly Journal of Experimental Physiology* . . ., **25** (1935), 99–104; *Nature*, **135** (1935), 608–610; *Lancet* (1935), **1**, 843–845; *British Medical Journal* (1935), i, 741–742; *Obituary Notices of Fellows of the Royal Society*, no. 4 (1935); *Dictionary of National Biography, 1931–1940*; and Sherrington's Sharpey-Schäfer lecture, in *Edinburgh Medical Journal*, n.s. **42** (1935), 393–406.

DOUGLASS W. TAYLOR

SHARROCK, ROBERT (*b.* Adstock, England, June [?] 1630; *d.* Bishop's Waltham, England, 11 July 1684), *botany.*

Sharrock, the son of a clergyman, was educated at Winchester College and became a perpetual fellow of New College, Oxford, on 5 March 1649. After taking the B.C.L. in 1654 and the D.C.L. in 1661, he was ordained and held several church benefices, becoming a canon in 1669 and archdeacon of Winchester in 1684.

Sharrock took a scientific interest in the cultivation of plants. He was well acquainted with the classical work on plants and with the prevalent myths and superstitions concerning agriculture and horticulture, and he tested these against his own observations. His *History of the Propagation and Improvement of Vegetables* (1660) was dedicated to Robert Boyle and shows Sharrock's experimental approach to botany as well as a profound knowledge of methods of propagating plants by seeds, vegetative reproduction, budding, and grafting, and of the improvement of soil by cultivation and by leguminous crops. He was skeptical about the transmutation of species at a time when some professors of botany believed in it, and he

showed Boyle how the belief arose from insufficient investigation. He demonstrated that shreds and ashes of plants could not grow into new plants, and that grafting a red rose onto a white did not produce the striped *Rosa mundi*. He also conducted experiments on phototropism and made observations on the morphology of seeds and on phyllotaxy.

Had he devoted his life to the study of plants, Sharrock's experimental approach might have made him one of the most important botanists. But he also wrote other books on law, religion, and political philosophy, in which he attacked Hobbes's views on ethics. He also contributed prefaces to three of Boyle's treatises on physics.

BIBLIOGRAPHY

Sharrock's book on botany is *The History of the Propagation and Improvement of Vegetables by the Concurrence of Art and Nature* (Oxford, 1660, 1666, 1672; London, 1694), the last under the title *An Improvement to the Art of Gardening*.

Secondary literature includes *Athenae Oxoniensis*, II (London, 1692), 580–581; J. Britten and G. S. Boulger, *A Biographical Index of Deceased British and Irish Botanists* (London, 1931), 152; J. Foster, *Alumni Oxonienses* (Oxford, 1892), 1340; J. R. Green, *A History of Botany* (London, 1914), 56, 125; and B. Porter, "Robert Sharrock," in *Dictionary of National Biography*, XVII, 1368–1369.

F. A. L. CLOWES

IBN AL-SHĀṬIR, ᶜĀLĀᵓ AL-DĪN ABUᵓL-ḤASAN ᶜALĪ IBN IBRĀHĪM (*b.* Damascus, Syria, *ca.* 1305; *d.* Damascus, *ca.* 1375), *astronomy.*

Ibn al-Shāṭir (Suter, no. 416) was perhaps the most distinguished Muslim astronomer of the fourteenth century. Although he was head *muwaqqit* at the Umayyad mosque in Damascus, responsible for the regulation of the astronomically defined times of prayer, his works on astronomical timekeeping are considerably less significant than those of his colleague al-Khalīlī. On the other hand, Ibn al-Shāṭir shared the interest of his earlier contemporaries Ibn al-Sarrāj, Ibn al-Ghazūlī, and al-Mizzī (Suter, nos. 508, 412, and 406) in astrolabes and quadrants; and he constructed sundials. Nevertheless, Ibn al-Shāṭir's most significant contribution to astronomy was his planetary theory. In his planetary models he incorporated various ingenious modifications of those of Ptolemy. Also, with the reservation that they are geocentric, his models are the same as those of Copernicus. Ibn al-Shāṭir's planetary theory was investigated for the first time in the 1950's, and the discovery that his models were mathematically identical to those of Copernicus raised the very interesting question of a possible transmission of his planetary theory to Europe. This question has since been the subject of a number of investigations, but research on the astronomy of Ibn al-Shāṭir and his sources, let alone on the later influence of his planetary theory in the Islamic world or Europe, is still at a preliminary stage.

Only a few details of the life of Ibn al-Shāṭir are known. His father died when the boy was six years old; and he was brought up by his grandfather, who taught him the art of inlaying ivory. At the age of about ten he traveled to Cairo and Alexandria to study astronomy, and, presumably, his interest in spherical astronomy was fired by the extensive compendium on spherical astronomy and instruments compiled in Cairo about 1280 by Abū ᶜAlī al-Marrākushī (Suter, no. 363). In his early work Ibn al-Shāṭir revealed something of his debt to al-Mizzī, who also had worked in Egypt. In his treatise on the "perfect" quadrant, he depended on a pair of distinctive parameters also used, but not derived, by al-Mizzī: 33;27° for the latitude of Damascus and 23;33° for the obliquity of the ecliptic. In A.H. 765 (1363/1364) he derived the new pair of values 33;30° and 23;31°, which he employed in his later works.

Planetary Astronomy. Ibn al-Shāṭir appears to have begun his work on planetary astronomy by preparing a *zīj*, an astronomical handbook with tables. Some two hundred *zījes* were compiled by the astronomers of medieval Islam, and several had been prepared in Damascus prior to the time of Ibn al-Shāṭir (for example, Kennedy, nos. 15/16, 89, 41, and 42). Ibn al-Shāṭir's first *zīj*, which has not survived, was inappropriately called *Nihāyat al-ghāyāt fī 'l-aᶜmāl al-falakiyyāt* ("The Final Work on Astronomical Operations") and was based on strictly Ptolemaic planetary theory. In a later treatise entitled *Taᶜlīq al-arṣād* ("Comments on Observations"), he described the observations and procedures with which he had constructed his new planetary models and derived new parameters. No copy of this treatise is known to exist in the manuscript sources. Later, in *Nihāyat al-sūl fī taṣḥīḥ al-uṣūl* ("A Final Inquiry Concerning the Rectification of Planetary Theory"), Ibn al-Shāṭir presented the reasoning behind his new planetary models. This work has survived.[1] Finally, Ibn al-Shāṭir's *al-Zīj al-jadīd* ("The New Astronomical Handbook"), which survives in a number of manuscript copies, contains a new set of planetary tables based on his new theory and parameters.[2]

Ibn al-Shāṭir introduced this later *zīj* in the following way:

God granted me success in working on this science [astronomy] and made it easy for me after I had mastered arithmetic, surveying, geometry, instrument making, and had actually invented many kinds of astronomical instruments. I came across the books of certain of my predecessors among the noted scholars in this branch of science, and I found that the most distinguished of the later astronomers, such as al-Majrīṭī Abu'l-Walīd al-Maghribī [Ibn Rushd?], Ibn al-Haytham, Naṣīr al-Ṭūsī, Muᵓayyad al-ᶜUrdī [assistant to al-Ṭūsī, *fl.* Damascus and Persia *ca.* 1250], Quṭb al-Shīrāzī, and Ibn Shukr al-Maghribī [Suter, no. 376], and others, had adduced doubts concerning the well-known astronomy of the spheres according to Ptolemy. These doubts were indisputable and [concerned matters] incompatible with the geometrical and physical models that had been established [by Ptolemy]. These scholars took pains to make models that would adequately represent the longitudinal and latitudinal motions of the planets, and not introduce inconsistencies. They were not granted success, however, and they admitted this in their writings.

I therefore asked Almighty God to give me inspiration and help me to invent models that would achieve what was required, and God—may He be praised and exalted, all praise and gratitude to Him—did enable me to devise universal models for the planetary motions in longitude and latitude and all other observable features of their motions, models that were free—thank God—from the doubts surrounding previous models. I described these new models and gave the necessary proof of their viability in my book called *Taᶜlīq al-arṣād*, "Comments on Observations," and I gave a short description of the models themselves in my book called *Nihāyat al-sūl fī taṣḥīḥ al-uṣūl*, "A Final Enquiry Concerning the Rectification of Planetary Theory." Then I asked God—may He be exalted—for guidance in compiling a book that would contain [rules for] the precise determination of planetary positions and motions and the secrets of the planetary attributes, according to the mean motions that I found by observation, the distances that I computed, and the tables that I compiled on the basis of the new corrected astronomy. This book should be a fundamental work for people to rely on, in which astronomical operations and problems are precisely formulated. . . .

Of the surviving works by the scholars mentioned by Ibn al-Shāṭir, only the *Tadhkira* of al-Ṭūsī and the *Nihāyat al-idrāk* and the *Tuḥfa shāhīya* of Quṭb al-Dīn al-Shīrāzī describe non-Ptolemaic planetary models.[3] Quṭb al-Dīn remarked several times in his treatises that most contemporary astronomers preferred such-and-such a non-Ptolemaic model, suggesting that he was one of several scholars who tried to modify the Ptolemaic models.

The essence of Ibn al-Shāṭir's planetary theory is the apparent removal of the eccentric deferent and equant of the Ptolemaic models, with secondary epicycles used instead. The motivation for this was aesthetic rather than scientific; the ultimate object was to produce a planetary theory composed of uniform motions in circular orbits rather than to improve the bases of practical astronomy. In the case of the sun, no apparent advantage was gained by the additional epicycle. In the case of the moon, the new configuration to some extent corrected the major defect of the Ptolemaic lunar theory, since it considerably reduced the variation of the lunar distance. In the case of the planets, the relative sizes of the primary and secondary epicycles were chosen so that the models were mathematically equivalent to those of Ptolemy.[4]

Below is a brief outline of Ibn al-Shāṭir's new planetary theory. All numbers are expressed sexagesimally (see Kennedy, p. 139).

The Solar Theory. The mean sun, $\bar{S}$, is situated on the deferent circle, radius $r = 60$, which rotates from west to east about the center of the universe O. The apogee moves from west to east about O at a rate of one degree in sixty Persian years of 365 days each. (Ibn al-Shāṭir accepted the rate of precession as one degree in seventy Persian years.)

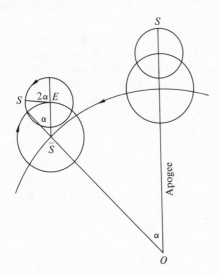

FIGURE 1. Ibn al-Shāṭir's solar model (α: apogee distance).

The primary epicycle has center $\bar{S}$ and radius $r_1 = 4;37$ and rotates with the motion of $\bar{S}$ relative to

the apogee and in the opposite sense. The radius $\bar{S}E$ thus remains parallel to the apsidal line. The true sun, S, is situated on the secondary epicycle, center E and radius $r_2 = 2;30$, which rotates with double the motion of $\bar{S}$ relative to the apogee and in the same sense.

The resultant maximum equation in this model is $2;2,6°$ and occurs when $\bar{S}$ is about 97° from the apogee, the position of which is given as Gemini $29;12°$ in December 1331. Ibn al-Shāṭir retained the Ptolemaic eccentricity 2;30 in his value of r_2; and his maximum equation corresponds to a resultant eccentricity of about 2;8, which is close to his value for $r_1 - r_2$. The solar distances at apogee and perigee are now 52;53 and 1,7;7, as against Ptolemy's 57;30 and 1,2;30. Ibn al-Shāṭir's new solar model appears to be the result of an attempt to make the variation of the solar distance correspond closely to the variation of the lunar distance in his new lunar model.

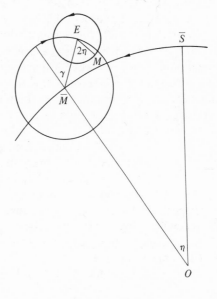

FIGURE 2. Ibn al-Shāṭir's lunar model (γ: mean anomaly; 2η: double elongation).

The Lunar Theory. The orbit of the moon is inclined at an angle of 5° to the plane of the ecliptic, and the nodes move from east to west with a constant motion. The mean moon, $\overline{M}$, is situated on the deferent, radius $r = 60$, which rotates about O from west to east in such a way that the resultant motion of $\overline{M}$ is the mean sidereal motion. The primary epicycle, center $\overline{M}$ and radius $r_1 = 6;35$, rotates with the mean anomaly in the opposite direction. The true moon, M, is situated on a secondary epicycle, centered at E on the first epicycle and having radius $r_2 = 1;25$, which rotates from west to east at twice the difference between the lunar and solar mean motions.

As a consequence of the resultant motion, the moon will always be at the perigee of the second-ary epicycle at mean syzygies and at its apogee at quadrature. The apparent epicycle of radius $r_1 - r_2 = 5;10$ at syzygies accounts for the equation of center, and the gradual increase in its apparent ra-dius to $r_1 + r_2 = 8;0$ as it approaches quadrature accounts for the evection. The maximum equa-tion of the resultant epicycle is $7;40°$, which is Ptolemy's value. Also the lunar distance now varies between $r - (r_1 - r_2) = 54;50$ and $r + (r_1 - r_2) = 1,5;10$ at the syzygies and between $r - (r_1 + r_2) = 52;0$ and $r + (r_1 + r_2) = 1,8;0$ at the quadratures. Thus the major objection to the Ptolemaic model—in which the moon could come as close as $34;7$ to the earth at quadrature, so that its apparent diameter should be almost twice its mean value—was eliminated.

Planetary Theory. The mean planet, $\bar{P}$, here con-sidered in the plane of the ecliptic, is situated on the deferent, radius $r = 60$, which rotates about the center of the universe from west to east with the mean longitudinal motion. The primary epicycle, radius r_1, rotates in the opposite direction at the same rate corrected for the motion of the apogees, again one degree in sixty Persian years. Thus the radius $\bar{P}E$ remains parallel to the apsidal line. The secondary epicycle, radius r_2, rotates about E from west to east at twice this rate. The true planet, P, is situated on the tertiary epicycle, radius r_3, which rotates with the mean anomaly about point F on the secondary epicycle. The anomaly is reckoned from the true epicyclic apogee, which is point G such that FG is parallel to $O\bar{P}$. In the case of the outer planets, FP remains parallel to the line joining O to $\bar{S}$. In the case of the inner planets, the direction $O\bar{P}$ defines $\bar{S}$.

In order to preserve the Ptolemaic distances in the apsidal line and at quadrature, the geometry of the models requires that

$$r_1 - r_2 = e \quad \text{and} \quad r_1 + r_2 = 2e,$$

where e is the Ptolemaic eccentricity, so that $r_1 = 3e/2$ and $r_2 = e/2$. At least in the case of the three outer planets, Ibn al-Shāṭir's values of r_1 and r_2 are precisely these. For Venus he takes

$$r_1 - r_2 = e \quad \text{and} \quad r_1 + r_2 = 2e',$$

where $e = 1;15$ is Ptolemy's eccentricity for Venus and $2e' = 2;7$ is the resultant double eccentricity of Ibn al-Shāṭir's own solar model.

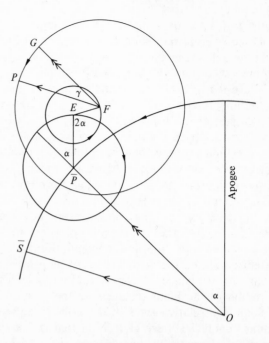

FIGURE 3. Ibn al-Shāṭir's model for the outer planets (α: apogee distance; γ: mean anomaly).

Because of the large eccentricity of the orbit of Mercury, Ibn al-Shāṭir's model was more elaborate than those for the other planets. Two additional epi-cycles placed at the end of r_3 have the effect of ex-panding and contracting its length in simple har-monic motion, with a period twice that of the mean longitudinal motion corrected for the motion of the apogee. Also, the sense of rotation of the epicycle with radius r_2 is the reverse of that for the other planets.

The solar, lunar, and planetary equation tables in *al-Zīj al-jadīd* were based on these new models. The accompanying mean motion tables, however, were based on parameters different from those stat-ed in the *Nihāyat al-sūl*. Also, although in this treatise Ibn al-Shāṭir presented a new theory of planetary latitudes to accompany his new longitude theory, the latitude tables in *al-Zīj al-jadīd* were, with the exception of those for Venus, ultimately derived from Ptolemy's *Almagest*.[5]

Astronomical Timekeeping. Ibn al-Shāṭir com-piled prayer tables, that is, a set of tables displaying the values of certain spherical astronomical functions relating to the times of prayer. The lati-tude used for these tables was $34°$, correspond-ing to an unspecified locality just north of Damas-cus. These tables, not discovered until 1974, dis-play such functions as the duration of morning and evening twilight and the time of the afternoon prayer, as well as such standard spherical astronomical functions as the solar meridian altitude, the lengths of daytime and nighttime, and right and oblique ascensions. Values are given in degrees and minutes for each degree of solar longitude, corresponding roughly to each day of the year.

A more extensive set of tables for timekeeping at Damascus was compiled by al-Mizzī; but it was replaced by the corpus of tables compiled by al-Khalīlī, which were based on slightly different parameters.

Sundials. In A.H. 773 (1371/1372) Ibn al-Shāṭir designed and constructed a magnificent horizontal sundial that was erected on the northern minaret of the Umayyad mosque. The instrument now on the minaret is an exact copy made in the late nineteenth century by the astronomer al-Ṭanṭāwī, the last of a long line of Syrian *muwaqqits* working in the medieval astronomical tradition. Fragments of the original instrument are preserved in the garden of the National Museum, Damascus. Ibn al-Shāṭir's sundial, described for the first time in 1971 by L. Janin, consisted of a slab of marble measuring approximately one meter by two meters. A complex system of curves engraved on the marble enabled the *muwaqqit* to read the time of day in equinoctial hours since sunrise or before sunset and to reckon time with respect to daybreak and nightfall and with respect to the beginning of the interval during which the afternoon prayer should be performed, this being defined in terms of shadow lengths. The curves on this sundial probably were drawn according to a set of tables, compiled especially for the purpose, that displayed the coordinates of the points corresponding to the hours on the solstitial and equinoctial shadow traces. Tables of such coordinates for horizontal sundials to be used in Mecca, Medina, Cairo, Baghdad, and Damascus had been compiled early in the ninth century by al-Khwārizmī; and less than a century before Ibn al-Shāṭir's time, new sets of sundial tables for various latitudes had been compiled in Cairo by al-Marrākushī (Suter, no. 363) and al-Maqsī (Suter, no. 383). None of the several later sets of Islamic sundial tables that are still extant is attributed to Ibn al-Shāṭir. One such set based on his parameters survives, however, in MS Damascus Ẓāhirīya 9353, where it is attributed to al-Ṭanṭāwī.

A considerably less sophisticated sundial made by Ibn al-Shāṭir in A.H. 767 (1365/1366) is preserved in the Aḥmadiyya *madrasa* in Aleppo. It is contained in a box called *ṣandūq al-yawāqīt* ("jewel box"), measuring twelve centimeters by twelve centimeters by three centimeters. It could be used to find the times (*al-mawāqīt*) of the midday and afternoon prayers, as well as to establish the local meridian and, hence, the direction of Mecca.[6]

Astrolabes and Quadrants. Among the astronomers of Damascus and Cairo in the thirteenth, fourteenth, and fifteenth centuries, many varieties of quadrants rivaled the astrolabe as a handy analog computer. Certain instruments devised for solving the standard problems of spherical astronomy for any latitude were more of theoretical interest than of practical value. It should also be remembered that tables were available to Ibn al-Shāṭir for solving all such problems with greater accuracy than was possible using any of the several available varieties of quadrant.

Ibn al-Shāṭir wrote on the ordinary planispheric astrolabe and designed an astrolabe that he called *al-āla al-jāmiᶜa* ("the universal instrument").[7] Ibn al-Shāṭir also wrote on the two most commonly used quadrants, *al-rubᶜ al-muqanṭarāt* (the almucantar quadrant) and *al-rubᶜ al-mujayyab* (the sine quadrant). The first bore a stereographic projection of the celestial sphere for a particular latitude, and the second a trigonometric grid for solving the standard problems of spherical astronomy. A given instrument might have markings of each kind on either side.

Two special quadrants designed by Ibn al-Shāṭir were called *al-rubᶜ al-ᶜAlāʾī* (the ᶜAlāʾī quadrant, the appellation being derived from ᶜAlāʾ al-Dīn, part of his name) and *al-rubᶜ al-tāmm* (the "perfect" quadrant). Both quadrants were modifications of the simpler and ultimately more useful sine quadrant. No examples of either are known to survive. The ᶜAlāʾī quadrant bore a grid, like the sine quadrant, of orthogonal coordinate lines dividing each axis into sixty (or ninety) equal parts and also a family of parallel lines joining corresponding points on both axes. (In modern notation, if we denote the axes by $x = 0$ and $y = 0$, and the radius of the quadrant by $R = 60$, the grid consists of the lines $x = n$, $y = n$, $x + y = n$, for $n = 1, 2, \cdots, R$.) Ibn al-Shāṭir described how to use the instrument for finding products, quotients, and standard trigonometric functions, and for solving such problems as the determination of the first and second declination and right ascension for given ecliptic longitude, the length of daylight and twilight for a given terrestrial latitude and solar longitude, and the time of day for a given terrestrial latitude, solar longitude, and solar altitude. The "perfect" quadrant bore a grid of two sets of equispaced lines drawn parallel to the sides of an equilateral triangle inscribed in the quadrant with one axis as base. (In algebraic notation, the grid consisted of lines $y = \pm x \tan 60° + n$, for $n = 1, 2, \cdots, 60$.) The instrument could be used for solving the same problems as the ᶜAlāʾī quadrant. Ibn al-Shāṭir's treatise on the perfect quadrant concludes with a hundred questions and answers on topics relating to spherical astronomy.

Mechanical Devices. The Arab historian al-Ṣafadī reported that he visited Ibn al-Shāṭir in A.H. 743 (1343) and inspected an "astrolabe" that the latter had constructed. His account is difficult to understand, but it appears that the instrument was shaped like an arch, measured three-quarters of a cubit in length, and was fixed perpendicular to a wall. Part of the instrument rotated once in twenty-four hours and somehow displayed both the equinoctial and the seasonal hours. The driving mechanism was not visible and probably was built into the wall. Apart from this obscure reference we have no contemporary record of any continuation of the sophisticated tradition of mechanical devices that flourished in Syria some two hundred years before the time of Ibn al-Shāṭir.

Later Influence. There is no indication in the known sources that any Muslim astronomers after Ibn al-Shāṭir concerned themselves with non-Ptolemaic astronomy. The *zījes* of al-Kāshī and of Ulugh Beg (Kennedy, nos. 20 and 11), compiled in Samarkand in the first half of the fifteenth century, were the only astronomical works of major consequence prepared by Muslim astronomers after Ibn al-Shāṭir; and they are based on strictly Ptolemaic planetary theory following the tradition of the thirteenth century *Īlkhānī zīj* of al-Ṭūsī (Kennedy, no. 6). Nevertheless, later astronomers in Damascus and Cairo prepared commentaries on, and new versions of, Ibn al-Shāṭir's *Zīj al-jadīd*. His *zīj* was used in Damascus for several centuries, but it had to compete with adaptations of other works in which the planetary mean motion tables were modified for Damascus: a recension of al-Ṭūsī's *Īlkhānī zīj* prepared by al-Ḥalabī (*fl. ca.* 1425, Suter, no. 434); a recension of the *zīj* of Ulugh Beg prepared by al-Ṣāliḥī (*fl. ca.* 1500, Suter no. 454); and a recension of al-Kāshī's *Khāqānī zīj* prepared by Ibn al-Kayyāl (*fl. ca.* 1550, Suter, no. 474).

Another Damascus astronomer, Ibn Zurayq (*fl. ca.* 1400, Suter, no. 426), prepared an abridgment of Ibn al-Shāṭir's *zīj*, called *al-Rawḍ al-ᶜāṭir*, that was very popular. Al-Ḥalabī, in one source (see Kennedy, no. 34) reported to have been a *muwaqqit* at the Hagia Sofia mosque in Istanbul but more probably to be identified with the Damascus astronomer mentioned above, compiled a *zīj* called *Nuzhat al-nāẓir*, based on that of Ibn al-Shāṭir. An astronomer named al-Nabulusī (*fl. ca.* 1590), who may have worked in Damascus or Cairo, compiled a *zīj* called *al-Misk al-ᶜāṭir* based on *al-Zīj al-jadīd*.

In Cairo, al-Kawm al-Rīshī (*fl. ca.* 1400, Suter, no. 428) adapted Ibn al-Shāṭir's planetary tables to the longitude of Cairo in his *zīj* entitled *al-Lumᶜa*. The contemporary Egyptian astronomer Ibn al-Majdī (Suter, no. 432; Kennedy, no. 36) compiled another set of planetary tables entitled *al-Durr al-yatīm*, from which planetary positions could be found with relative facility from a given date in the Muslim lunar calendar; he stated that the parameters underlying his tables were those of Ibn al-Shāṭir. Another Egyptian astronomer, Jamāl al-Dīn Yūsuf al-Khiṭāʾī, prepared an extensive set of double-argument planetary equation tables based on those of Ibn al-Shāṭir.

Each of these works was used in Cairo for several centuries, alongside solar and lunar tables extracted from the *Ḥākimī zīj* of the tenth-century astronomer Ibn Yūnus (Kennedy, no. 14) and recensions of the *zīj* of Ulugh Beg prepared by Ibn Abi l-Fatḥ al-Ṣūfī (*fl. ca.* 1460; Suter, no. 447; Kennedy, no. 37) and Riḍwān ibn al-Razzāz (*fl. ca.* 1680; Kennedy, no. X209). The popularity of Ibn al-Shāṭir in Egypt is illustrated by the fact that a commentary on al-Kawm al-Rīshī's *zīj al-lumᶜa* was written in the mid-nineteenth century by Muḥammad al-Khuḍrī. There is evidence that Ibn al-Shāṭir's *zīj* was known in Tunis in the late fourteenth century but was replaced by a Tunisian version of Ulugh Beg's *zīj*. None of the numerous works purporting to be based on Ibn al-Shāṭir's *zīj* has been studied in modern times.

Ibn al-Shāṭir's principal treatises on instruments remained popular for several centuries in Syria, Egypt, and Turkey, the three centers of astronomical timekeeping in the Islamic world. Thus his influence in later Islamic astronomy was widespread but, as far as we can tell, unfruitful. On the other hand, the reappearance of his planetary models in the writings of Copernicus strongly suggests the possibility of the transmission of some details of these models beyond the frontiers of Islam.

NOTES

1. A critical edition of the Arabic text and an English translation have been prepared by V. Roberts but both are unpublished.
2. A brief summary of the contents of this *zīj* has been published by E. S. Kennedy.
3. These have been discussed in the secondary literature by E. S. Kennedy and W. Hartner, but more research is necessary before the extent of Ibn al-Shāṭir's debt to them and to other sources can be ascertained.

4. Ibn al-Shāṭir's planetary theory has been described in a series of four articles by E. S. Kennedy, V. Roberts, and F. Abbud. Before the theory may be more fully understood, however, the complete text of the *Nihāyat al-sūl* must be published with a translation and commentary, and also the relevant parts of the *Zīj al-jadīd*, including the planetary tables. It is also necessary to continue the search for his other works amidst the vast numbers of Arabic astronomical manuscripts which survive in libraries around the world untouched by modern scholarship. The manuscript (no. 66/5) in the Khālidiyya Library, Jerusalem, of a work attributed to Ibn al-Shāṭir that is entitled *Risāla fi 'l-hayʾa al-jadīda* ("Treatise on the New Astronomy"), is unfortunately only a copy of his *Nihāyat al-suʾl*.

5. For the other contents of *al-Zīj al-jadīd*, see the summary by E. S. Kennedy. The topics treated are the standard subject matter of *zījes*, although some of Ibn al-Shāṭir's tables for parallax and lunar visibility are of a kind not attested in earlier works.

6. A treatise on the use of Ibn al-Shāṭir's "jewel box" was written by the Egyptian astronomer Ibn Abi 'l-Fatḥ al-Ṣūfī (*fl. ca.* 1475; Suter, no. 447/7).

7. Two examples of this instrument, both made by Ibn al-Shāṭir in A.H. 738 (1337/1338) are preserved at the Museum of Islamic Art, Cairo, and the Bibliothèque Nationale, Paris, but have not been properly studied. Another astrolabe made by him in 1326 is preserved at the Observatoire National, Paris.

BIBLIOGRAPHY

I. ORIGINAL WORKS. For lists of Ibn al-Shāṭir's works and MSS thereof, consult H. Suter, no. 416; C. Brockelmann, *Geschichte der arabischen Literatur*, 2nd ed., II (Leiden, 1943–1949), 156, and supp., II (Leiden, 1937–1942), 157; and the much less reliable A. Azzawi, *History of Astronomy in Iraq* (Baghdad, 1958), 162–171, in Arabic.

The following titles are attributed to Ibn al-Shāṭir:

On planetary astronomy, *Nihāyat al-ghāyāt fi 'l-aʿmāl al-falakiyyāt*, an astronomical handbook with tables (not extant but mentioned in *Zīj Ibn al-Shāṭir*); *Nihāyat al-sūl f ʿī taṣḥīḥ al-usūl*, on planetary theory (extant); *Taʿlīq al-arṣād*, on observations (not extant but mentioned in *Zīj Ibn al-Shāṭir*); and *Zīj Ibn al-Shāṭir* or *al-Zīj al-jadīd*, astronomical handbook with tables (extant).

His sole work on astronomical timekeeping is a set of prayer tables for latitude 34° (extant in MS Cairo Dār al-Kutub *mīqāt* 1170, fols. 11r–22v; intro. in MS Leiden Universitetsbibliothek Or. 1001, fols. 108r–113r).

Works on instruments are *al-Nafʿ al-ʿāmm fi 'l-ʿamal bi-l-rubʿ al-tāmm li-mawāqīt al-Islām*, on the "perfect" quadrant (extant); *Iḍāḥ al-mughayyab fi 'l-ʿamal bi-l-rubʿ al-mujayyab*, on the sine quadrant (extant); *Tuḥfat al-sāmiʿ fi 'l-ʿamal bi-l-rubʿ al-jāmiʿ*, on the "universal" quadrant (not extant, but see *Nuzhat al-sāmiʿ fi 'l-ʿamal bi-l-rubʿ al-jāmiʿ*); *Nuzhat al-sāmiʿ fi 'l-ʿamal bi-l-rubʿ al-jāmiʿ*, a shorter version of *Tuḥfat al-sāmiʿ* (extant); *al-Ashiʿʿa al-lāmiʿa fi 'l-ʿamal bi-l-āla al-jāmiʿa*, on the "universal instrument" (extant); *al-Rawḍāt al-muzhirāt fi 'l-ʿamal bi-rubʿ al-muqanṭarāt*, on the use of the almucantar quadrant (extant); *Risāla fi 'l-rubʿ al-ʿAlāʾī*, on the *ʿAlāʾī* quadrant (extant); *Risāla fi 'l-asṭurlāb*, on the astrolabe (extant); *Risāla fi uṣūl ʿilm al-asṭurlāb*, on the principles of the astrolabe (extant); and *Mukhtaṣar fi 'l-ʿamal bi-l-asṭurlāb wa-rubʿ al-muqanṭarāt wa-l-rubʿ al-mujayyab*, on the use of the astrolabe, almucantar quadrant, and sine quadrant (extant).

Miscellaneous writings are *Fi 'l-nisba al-sittīniya*, probably on sexagesimal arithmetic (extant); *Urjūza fi 'l-kawākib*, a poem on the stars (extant); *Risāla fi istikhrāj al-taʾrīkh*, on calendrical calculations (extant); and *Kitāb al-jabr wa-l-muqābala*, on algebra (Azzawi, p. 165, states that there is a work with this title by Ibn al-Shāṭir preserved in Cairo).

II. SECONDARY LITERATURE. References to Suter and Kennedy are to the basic bibliographical sources: H. Suter, *Die Mathematiker und Astronomen der Araber und ihre Werke* (Leipzig, 1900), and E. S. Kennedy, "A Survey of Islamic Astronomical Tables," in *Transactions of the American Philosophical Society*, n.s. **46**, no. 2 (1956), 121–177.

The only biographical study thus far is E. Wiedemann, "Ibn al Schâtir, ein arabischer Astronom aus dem 14. Jahrhundert," in *Sitzungsberichte der physikalisch-medizinischen Sozietät in Erlangen*, **60** (1928), 317–326, repr. in his *Aufsätze zur arabischen Wissenschaftsgeschichte*, II (Hildesheim, 1970), 729–738.

On the *Zīj* of Ibn al-Shāṭir, consult E. S. Kennedy, "A Survey of Islamic Astronomical Tables," in *Transactions of the American Philosophical Society*, n.s. **46**, no. 2 (1956), no. 11. See also A. Sayili, *The Observatory in Islam* (Ankara, 1960), 245.

On Ibn al-Shāṭir's planetary theory, see the following, listed chronologically: V. Roberts, "The Solar and Lunar Theory of Ibn al-Shāṭir: A Pre-Copernican Copernican Model," in *Isis*, **48** (1957), 428–432; E. S. Kennedy and V. Roberts, "The Planetary Theory of Ibn al-Shāṭir," *ibid.*, **50** (1959), 227–235; F. Abbud, "The Planetary Theory of Ibn al-Shāṭir: Reduction of the Geometric Models to Numerical Tables," *ibid.*, **53** (1962), 492–499; V. Roberts, "The Planetary Theory of Ibn al-Shāṭir: Latitudes of the Planets," *ibid.*, **57** (1966), 208–219; E. S. Kennedy, "Late Medieval Planetary Theory," *ibid.*, **57** (1966), 365–378; and W. Hartner, "Ptolemy, Azarquiel, Ibn al-Shāṭir, and Copernicus on Mercury: A Study of Parameters," in *Archives internationales d'histoire des sciences*, **24** (1974), 5–25.

The possible transmission of late Islamic planetary theory to Europe is discussed in W. Hartner, "Naṣir al-Dīn's Lunar Theory," in *Physis: Rivista internazionale di storia della scienza*, **11** (1969), 287–304; E. S. Kennedy, "Planetary Theory in the Medieval Near East and Its Transmission to Europe," and W. Hartner, "Trepidation and Planetary Theories: Common Features in Late Islamic and Early Renaissance Astronomy," in *Accademia Nazionale dei Lincei*, *13° Convegno Volta*, (1971), 595–604 and 609–629, respectively; I. N. Veselovsky, "Copernicus and Naṣīr al-Dīn al-Ṭūsī," in *Journal for the History of Astronomy*, **4** (1973), 128–130; G. Rosinska, "Naṣīr al-Dīn al-Ṭūsī and Ibn al-

Shāṭir in Cracow?" in *Isis*, **65** (1974), 239–243; and W. Hartner, "The Astronomical Background of Nicolaus Copernicus," in *Studia Copernicana* (1975).

On the quadrants designed by Ibn al-Shāṭir, see P. Schmalzl, *Zur Geschichte des Quadranten bei den Arabern* (Munich, 1929). On his sundial, see L. Janin, "Le cadran solaire de la mosquée Umayyade à Damas," in *Centaurus*, **16** (1971), 285–298. Ibn al-Shāṭir's "jewel box" is described and illustrated in S. Reich and G. Wiet, "Un astrolabe syrien du XIVᵉ siècle," in *Bulletin de l'Institut français d'archéologie orientale du Caire*, **38** (1939), 195–202. See also L. A. Mayer, *Islamic Astrolabists and Their Works* (Geneva, 1956), 40–41.

DAVID A. KING

SHATUNOVSKY, SAMUIL OSIPOVICH (*b.* Znamenka, Melitopol district, Tavricheskaya guberniya, Russia, 25 March 1859; *d.* Odessa, U.S.S.R., 27 March 1929), *mathematics.*

Shatunovsky was the ninth child in the family of an impoverished artisan. In 1877 he graduated from a technological high school in Kherson and the following year completed a specialized supplementary course at Rostov. He then studied for a short time at the Technological College and the College of Transport in St. Petersburg. Shatunovsky, however, was interested in mathematics rather than technology; instead of following the curriculum at the college, he attended the lectures of Chebyshev and his disciples at St. Petersburg University. Unable to enroll at the university (he did not have the prerequisite diploma from a classical high school), Shatunovsky attempted to acquire a higher mathematical education in Switzerland. In 1887 lack of money forced him to return to Russia, where he was a private teacher in small towns in the south. One of his works that was sent to Odessa was well received by local mathematicians, who invited him to move there. He was elected a member (1897) and secretary (1898) of the mathematical department of the Novorossysky (Odessa) Society of Natural Scientists, and for some time taught school. In 1905 Shatunovsky passed the examinations for the master's degree and became assistant professor at Novorossysky (Odessa) University, where he worked until his death, becoming professor in 1920. In 1906–1920 he also taught at the Women's School for Higher Education.

Shatunovsky's principal works concern the foundations of mathematics. Independently of Hilbert he elaborated an axiomatic theory of the measurement of areas of rectilinear figures and reported on the subject to the Society of Natural Scientists in Odessa (1897) and at the Tenth Congress of the All-Russian Society of Natural Scientists and Physicians (1898). Publication of Hilbert's *Die Grundlagen der Geometrie* (1899) probably kept Shatunovsky from stating his theory, which was almost identical with Hilbert's, in print. From 1898 to 1902 Shatunovsky developed his theory for measuring the volumes of polyhedrons. In his theory of areas the principal concept is that of the invariant of one triangle (the product of base times corresponding height), and in the theory of volumes the principal notion is the invariant of the tetrahedron (the product of the area of some face times corresponding height). These studies led Shatunovsky to an axiomatic general theory of scalar quantities.

From 1906 Shatunovsky taught introduction to analysis; his lectures contain an original description of the theory of sets and functions, particularly of the definition of irrational and real numbers. The generalization of the concept of limit suggested in them is close to that introduced by E. H. Moore in 1915 ("Definition of Limit in General Integral Analysis," in *Proceedings of the National Academy of Sciences* [1915], no. 12). For a long time Shatunovsky's *Vvedenie v analiz* could be obtained only as a lithograph (Odessa, 1906–1907), however, and was not printed until 1923.

In a report to the Society of Natural Scientists in Odessa (1901), Shatunovsky critically approached the problem of applying the logical law of the excluded third to the elements of infinite sets. He discussed the subject in print in the introduction to his master's thesis, published in 1917. Pointing out the logical inadmissibility of the purely formal use of the logical law of the excluded third, the applicability of which needs special verification every time, Shatunovsky did not reach conclusions as radical as those presented by L. E. J. Brouwer in his works on intuitionism. Shatunovsky's thesis contains a new construction of Galois's theory that does not presuppose the existence of the roots of algebraic equations, which is demonstrated only in the final part of this work.

Shatunovsky also wrote articles and books on elementary mathematics. In them, for example, he stated a general principle for solving trigonometrical problems and a classification of problems connected with this principle.

BIBLIOGRAPHY

I. ORIGINAL WORKS. Shatunovsky's writings include "Ob izmerenii obemov mnogogrannikov" ("On the

Measurement of Volumes of Polyhedrons"), in *Vestnik opytnoi fiziki i elementarnoi matematiki* (1902), 82–87, 104–108, 127–132, 149–155; "Über den Rauminhalt der Polyeder," in *Mathematische Annalen*, **57** (1903), 496–508; "O postulatakh lezhashchikh v osnovanii ponyatia o velichine" ("On the Basic Postulates of the Concept of Quantity"), in *Zapiski Matematicheskago otdeleniya Novorossiiskago obshchestva estestvoispytatelei*, **26** (1904); *Algebra kak uchenie o sravnenyakh po funktsionalnym modulyam* ("Algebra as the Theory of Congruences With Respect to the Functional Modulus"; Odessa, 1917); *Vvedenie v analiz* ("Introduction to Analysis"; Odessa, 1923); and *Metody reshenia zadach pryamolineynoy trigonometrii* ("Methods of Solving Problems in Rectilinear Trigonometry"; Moscow, 1929).

II. Secondary Literature. See E. Y. Bakhmutskaya, "O rannikh rabotakh Shatunovskogo po osnovaniam matematiki" ("On Shatunovsky's First Research on the Foundations of Mathematics"), in *Istoriko–matematicheskie issledovaniya*, **16** (1965), 207–216; N. G. Chebotarev, "Samuil Osipovich Shatunovsky," in *Uspekhi matematicheskikh nauk*, **7** (1940), 316–321; V. F. Kagan, "S. O. Shatunovsky," in Shatunovsky's *Metody . . . trigonometrii* (above); and "Etudy po osnovaniam geometrii" ("Essays on the Foundations of Geometry"), in *Vestnik opytnoi fiziki i elementarnoi matematiki*, (1901), 286–292, also in Kagan's book *Ocherki po geometrii* ("Geometrical Essays"; Moscow, 1963), 147–154; *Matematika v SSSR za tridtsat let* ("Mathematics in the U.S.S.R. for Thirty Years"; Moscow–Leningrad, 1948), see index; F. A. Medvedev, "O formirovanii ponyatia obobshchennogo predela" ("On the Development of the Concept of the Generalized Limit"), in *Trudy Instituta istorii estestvoznaniya i tekhniki. Akademiya nauk SSSR*, **34** (1960), 299–322; *Nauka v SSSR za pyatnadtsat let. Matematika* ("Science in the U.S.S.R. During Fifteen Years. Mathematics"; Moscow–Leningrad, 1932), see index; J. Z. Shtokalo, ed., *Istoria otechestvennoy matematiki*, 4 vols. ("A History of [Russian] Mathematics"; Kiev, 1966–1970), see index; and A. P. Youschkevitch, *Istoria matematiki v Rossii do 1917 goda* ("History of Mathematics in Russia Until 1917"; Moscow, 1968), see index.

A. P. Youschkevitch
A. T. Grigorian

SHAW, PETER (*b.* Lichfield, Staffordshire, England, March or April 1694; *d.* London, England, 15 March 1764), *chemistry.*

Shaw's father was master of the Lichfield Grammar School, so it is probable that the boy received a good education, although nothing is recorded of his life between 1704, when his father died, and 1723, when his first publication appeared. Since he translated from Latin easily and well, he evidently had a good grounding in the classics. He

also learned medicine and chemistry, and made his living by translating, writing, and editing books on these two subjects and by practicing medicine. His edition of Boyle's works, and his translations of Boerhaave and Stahl, were popular and influential. The most important of his own early writings was *A New Practice of Physic*, based on the teachings of Sydenham and Boerhaave.

Shaw's interest in chemistry evidently was deepened by his study of Boerhaave and Stahl. He welcomed Stahl's search for a "universal chemistry" but rejected his mysticism and his doctrine of phlogiston; indeed, he never translated any part of Stahl's writings on those subjects. His rational, experimental, and eclectic approach is revealed in the title he gave to his chemical lectures, the text of which he later published. From 1733 to 1737 he practiced at Scarborough and was active in promoting its spa. He became involved with the notorious Joanna Stephens' remedies, which, as she claimed, dissolved urinary calculi *in situ*. They were a complex mixture that included calcined snail shells and soap, and Shaw believed in their efficacy.

In 1740 Shaw was admitted licentiate of the College of Physicians and soon established an extensive and fashionable practice. He was made M.D. of Cambridge by mandamus in 1751, fellow of the Royal Society in 1752, candidate of the College of Physicians in 1753, and physician in ordinary to George III in 1760. Shaw was active in promoting the aims of the newly founded Society for the Encouragement of Arts, Manufactures and Commerce, and was highly influential in chemical and medical circles.

BIBLIOGRAPHY

I. Original Works. Shaw's own writings are *A Treatise of Incurable Diseases* (London, 1723); *The Juice of the Grape, or Wine Preferable to Water* (London, 1724), published anonymously but traditionally ascribed to Shaw; *A New Practice of Physic* (London, 1726; 1728; 5th ed., 1753); *Three Essays in Artificial Philosophy, or Universal Chemistry* (London, 1731); *Chemical Lectures Publickly Read in London in . . . 1731 and 1732; and Since at Scarborough, in 1733, for the Improvement of Arts, Trades, and Natural Philosophy* (London, 1734; 1755; Paris, 1759); *An Enquiry Into the Contents, Virtues and Uses of the Scarborough Spaw-Waters* (London, 1734); *Examination of the Reasons for and Against the Subscription for a Medicament for the Stone* (London, 1738); *Inquiries on the Nature of Miss Stephens's Medicaments* (London, 1738); and

Essays for the Improvement of Arts, Manufactures and Commerce by Means of Chemistry (London, 1761).

With Francis Hauksbee the younger he wrote *An Essay for Introducing a Portable Laboratory, by Means Whereof All the Chemical Operations Are Commodiously Performed for the Purposes of Philosophy, Medicine, Metallurgy, and Family. With Sculptures* (London, 1731) and *Proposals for a Course of Chemical Experiments: With a View to Practical Philosophy, Arts, Trade and Business* (London, 1731).

His translations include *The Dispensatory of the Royal College of Physicians of Edinburgh* (London, 1727), 5th ed. (London, 1753); *A New Method of Chemistry*, 2 vols. (London, 1727), trans. of Hermann Boerhaave's *Institutiones chemiae* (Paris, 1724), incorporating student notes in collaboration with Ephraim Chambers; also new, rev. ed. (London, 1741, 1753); *Philosophical Principles of Universal Chemistry* (London, 1730), trans. of all but the last part of G. E. Stahl's *Collegium Jenense: The Philosophical Works of Francis Bacon*, 3 vols. (London, 1733; French ed. Paris, 1765); and B. Varenius, *A Compleat System of . . . Geography*, rev. and corrected by Shaw (London, 1733; 1734; 1736; 1765).

Shaw edited John Quincy, *Praelectiones pharmaceuticae; or a Course of Lectures in Pharmacy, Chymical and Galenical, Published From His Original Manuscript, With a Preface, . . .* (London, 1723); and *Philosophical Works of the Honourable Robert Boyle, Abridged, Methodised and Disposed Under the General Heads of Physics, Statics, Pneumatics, Natural History, Chemistry, and Medicine*, 3 vols. (London, 1725).

II. SECONDARY LITERATURE. The definitive account is F. W. Gibbs, "Peter Shaw and the Revival of Chemistry," in *Annals of Science*, 7 (1951), 211–237, which corrects the accounts in *Dictionary of National Biography* and in W. Munk, *The Roll of the Royal College of Physicians of London*, 2nd ed. (London, 1878), upon which all earlier accounts were based.

MARIE BOAS HALL

SHAW, WILLIAM NAPIER (*b.* Birmingham, England, 4 March 1854; *d.* London, England, 23 March 1945), *meteorology, physics.*

Shaw received his education at King Edward's School in Birmingham and Emmanuel College, Cambridge, where he studied mathematics and natural sciences. After his graduation in 1876 he was elected a fellow of his college. In 1879, after a semester of study under Helmholtz at Berlin, he was appointed demonstrator at the Cavendish Laboratory, jointly with his lifelong friend R. T. Glazebrook. He became lecturer in experimental physics in 1887 and assistant director of the laboratory in 1898. His publications during this time

dealt with experimental physics. He also began work on problems of ventilating buildings.

Partly on the basis of his work on hygrometric methods and instruments, begun in 1879, Shaw was appointed a member of the Meteorological Council in 1897. With his appointment as secretary in 1900, he forsook the opportunity of a university career at Cambridge. He became director of the Meteorological Office in 1905 and held this post until his retirement in 1920. In 1907 he became reader in meteorology at the University of London, and he was first professor of meteorology at Imperial College from 1920 to 1924. He was president of the International Meteorological Committee from 1906 to 1923.

Shaw's contributions to meteorology were more far-reaching than his writings would indicate. Under his administration the Meteorological Office was transformed through the introduction of a trained scientific staff and the consequent emphasis on studies of the physics of the atmosphere. This activity complemented the customary statistical treatment of observations.

One of Shaw's most important publications, *The Life History of Surface Air-Currents*, pointed the way toward air-mass analysis and the concept of fronts (later developed by the Norwegian school of meteorologists) by showing that trajectories of air converging toward various parts of mid-latitude storms originated in widely different regions. Shaw did not pursue these results, however, and his work had little influence on meteorological practice and theory. In association with W. H. Dines, he subsequently turned to the study of the upper atmosphere by means of kites and balloons. Shaw introduced the principle of isentropic analysis, later developed by C.-G. Rossby and his collaborators, and devised a thermodynamic diagram (the tephigram) that is widely used in meteorology. His enthusiasm for the observational and diagrammatic approach was based on the conviction, dating from his student years under Maxwell, that atmospheric problems should be handled by determining the dynamics from the observations of motion.

Shaw took a particular interest in educating the public on meteorology and related subjects, and served on a number of advisory committees. After his retirement he completed his four-volume *Manual of Meteorology*, a unique account of the historical roots and the physical and mathematical basis of the subject. His writings in general reflect a deep interest and insight into the historical development of meteorology.

Shaw was knighted in 1915 and was a fellow of the Royal Society and honorary or foreign member of many academies and societies. He received the Symons Medal (1910), the Buys Ballot Medal (1923), and the Royal Medal (1923).

BIBLIOGRAPHY

I. ORIGINAL WORKS. A complete bibliography of Shaw's works is in *Selected Meteorological Papers of Sir Napier Shaw* (London, 1955). His publications included *Practical Physics* (London, 1885), written with R. T. Glazebrook; "Report on Hygrometric Methods," in *Philosophical Transactions of the Royal Society,* **A179** (1888), 73–149; "Ventilation and Warming," in T. Stevenson and S. Murphy, eds., *A Treatise on Hygiene and Public Health,* I (London, 1890), 31–148; *The Life History of Surface Air-Currents* (London, 1906), written with R. G. K. Lempfert; *Weather Forecasting* (London, 1911); *The Air and Its Ways* (Cambridge, 1923); and *Manual of Meteorology,* 4 vols. (Cambridge, 1926–1931). Shaw's MSS and correspondence are in the archives of the Meteorological Office, Bracknell, England.

II. SECONDARY LITERATURE. Obituaries are in *Obituary Notices of Fellows of the Royal Society of London,* **5** (1945), 202–230, with selected bibliography; and *Quarterly Journal of the Royal Meteorological Society,* **71** (1945), 187–194. See also D. Brunt, "A Hundred Years of Meteorology (1851–1951)," in *Advancement of Science,* **8** (1951), 114–124.

GISELA KUTZBACH

SHAYN, GRIGORY ABRAMOVICH (*b.* Odessa, Russia, 19 April 1892; *d.* Abramtsevo, near Moscow, U.S.S.R., 4 August 1956), *astrophysicist.*

The son of a joiner, Shayn completed only elementary school; but in 1911 he passed with distinction the examinations for the graduation certificate as an extramural student. He became interested in astronomy at the age of ten, and at fourteen or fifteen he seriously observed meteors with binoculars; in 1910 his first scientific work, "Vychislenie radianta Perseid" ("A Calculation of the Radiant of the Perseids"), was published in *Izvestiya Russkogo astronomicheskogo obshchestva* (**16**, no. 5, 194–197).

In 1912 Shayn entered the Faculty of Physics and Mathematics at Yurev (Dorpat) University. After serving in the army from 1914 to 1917, he completed his university education in 1919 at Perm, to which the university had been evacuated, and began his teaching career. The following year he passed the examinations for the master's degree

and became an assistant in the department of astronomy at Tomsk University. In 1921 he transferred to Pulkovo and devoted himself completely to scientific work.

In 1925 Shayn and his wife, Pelageya Fedorovna Sannikova, moved to the Simeiz section of the Pulkovo observatory, where Shayn supervised the installation of a 102-centimeter reflector, which had been ordered before the war from the British firm of Grubb. In January 1926 the first spectrogram was obtained with it. Shayn worked with this instrument until World War II. In 1935 he was awarded the doctorate in physical and mathematical sciences. Two years later he was elected foreign member of the Royal Astronomical Society, and in 1939 he became an academician of the Soviet Academy of Sciences.

During World War II part of the staff of the Simeiz observatory was evacuated to the Abastumani astrophysical observatory in Georgia, and there Shayn continued to study spectrograms evacuated from Simeiz. After the war Shayn participated in restoring the destroyed Simeiz observatory and in building a large modern astrophysical observatory in the mountains of the central Crimea. In 1945 he was named director of the Crimean Astrophysical Observatory of the Soviet Academy of Sciences. Seven years later, having asked, for reasons of health, to be relieved of his responsibilities as director, Shayn was named head of the section on the physics of nebulae and interstellar mediums. During the following four years he carried out important investigations of nebulae and galactic magnetic fields.

In the 1920's Shayn became interested in the evolution of stars and turned to double stars, correctly asserting that their components must be of the same age. He compared the most reliable data obtained from the literature on the components of double stars, in order to construct a "spectrum-luminosity" (Hertzsprung-Russell) diagram. Shayn studied the evolution of doubles, the changes in the proportions of the masses of the components, and the mass-luminosity and spectrum-luminosity relationships. He drew the important conclusion, later fully confirmed, that the evolution of the larger component must be more rapid than that of the smaller.

At the same time as O. Struve, and in partial collaboration with him by means of correspondence, Shayn discovered the rapid rotation of a number of stars of early spectral classes by analyzing the form of the spectral lines. Theoretically considering the forms of spectral lines of rotating and non-rotating stars, he provided a method of determining the velocity of rotation. With V. A. Albitsky, Shayn obtained precise determinations of the radial velocity of about 800 stars, discovered several dozen spectroscopic binaries, and computed the elements of the orbits of many of them.

Spectrophotometry was a natural continuation of Shayn's study of spectroscopic binaries. His aim was to investigate the behavior of the absorption lines and bands and their influence on the color of the stars, their apparent bolometric magnitudes and other properties, and the relation of the normal color to luminosity. Research on the spectra of the long-period variables was associated with the elucidation of all the peculiarities of the spectrum-luminosity and period-luminosity relationships. A number of Shayn's spectrophotometric investigations dealt with planetary nebulae, the integral spectrum of the Milky Way clouds, and the spectrum of the rings of Saturn. His observations of the total solar eclipse of 1936 provided material for the study of the physics of the solar corona.

At Abastumani, Shayn used spectrograms from Simeiz to offer an original interpretation of the coexistence of emission lines and lines of absorption (high- and low-temperature spectra) in the spectra of long-period variables such as Mira Ceti. A paradox was removed by the hypothesis that the physical obscuration of the source of high-temperature radiation was provided by the extended atmosphere of such a star. Shayn indicated the possible similarity of the turbulent phenomena of solar activity (chromospheric flares and similar processes) to phenomena that cause the outward motion of hot matter from a star and the appearance of emission lines in its spectrum.

Shayn conducted important research on isotopes in the atmospheres of stars. In 1940 he discovered that the isotope C^{13} content in several stars was very great: for the earth the proportion of C^{13} to C^{12} is approximately $1:70 - 1:90$, for the sun it is less than $1:10$, while on certain red so-called carbon stars it reaches $1:2$. Besides the two known bands of the heavy molecule of cyanogen $C^{13}N^{14}$, Shayn also demonstrated the presence of many bands in the red and violet range of the spectra of these stars. American physicists were thus led to make a new experimental determination of the cross section of the capture of protons by the nuclei of C^{12} and C^{13}. As a result it was unexpectedly shown that the amount of isotope C^{13} on earth and on the sun is abnormally small. For his work on isotopes in the atmospheres of carbon stars Shayn was awarded the State Prize in 1950.

By 1948 Shayn and his collaborator of many years, Vera F. Gaze, had developed a special method of photography based on the fact that gas nebulae radiate all their energy in certain bright emission lines. Using two meniscus cameras with objectives of 450 millimeters of high optical efficiency (1 : 1.4) and a field of about 4°, they discovered more than 150 new emission nebulae and published several catalogs of diffuse nebulae, as well as the photographic *Atlas diffuznykh gazovykh tumannostey* ("Atlas of Diffuse Gas Nebulae"; 1952). Using the same method, Shayn also found emission objects in other galaxies. All these nebulae appeared to be distributed along the branches of spirals. From 1950 Shayn used a more powerful 640-millimeter camera.

In the galactic emission nebulae he noted peculiarities in the distribution of the matter in the so-called peripheral nebulae, and he concluded that the nebulae expanded over the course of time. From this he formulated the important cosmogonic statement of the common formation of the association of hot stars and nebulae. Studying the continuous spectra of certain diffuse nebulae, he showed that in accord with the hypothesis of A. Y. Kipper (Tartu), the continuous spectrum of nebulae is related not to the scattering of light by interstellar dust but to the "two-quantum jump" in hydrogen atoms. Shayn concluded that the role of the dust had been exaggerated, for its density proved to be much less than that of the gaseous medium (for example, 1/100 in the Orion nebula).

Studying the filamentary nebulae, Shayn found that in most cases the filaments were oriented parallel to the galactic equator; to explain their elongation and orientation he posited the existence in the galaxy of powerful magnetic fields. He discovered that the direction of the elongated nebulae was similar to the direction of the plane of polarization of light. This made it possible to define the borders of the branches of our galaxy more precisely and to assert the presence of an "arm" in the direction of the constellation Sagittarius. The magnetic theory explained why the gas does not disperse beyond the branches and does not fill the space between the "arms" of the spirals.

BIBLIOGRAPHY

I. ORIGINAL WORKS. A complete bibliography of 249 titles, compiled by N. B. Lavrova, is *Istoriko-astronomicheskie issledovaniya*, **3** (1957), 596–607. Among them are "On the Rotation of Stars," in *Monthly No-*

tices of the Royal Astronomical Society, **89** (1929), 222–239, written with O. Struve; "The Absorption Continuum in the Violet Region of the Spectra of Carbon Stars," in *Astrophysical Journal*, **106** (1947), 86–91, written with O. Struve; "Otnoshenie kontsentratsii isotopov C¹³ i C¹⁴ v atmosferakh zvezd" ("The Relative Concentration of the Isotopes C¹³ and C¹⁴ in the Atmosphere of Stars"), in *Uspekhi fizicheskikh nauk*, **43** (1951), 3–10, written with V. F. Gaze; "Certain Peculiar Structures in Interstellar Clouds," in *Gas Dynamics of Cosmic Clouds* (Amsterdam, 1955), 37–38; and "On the Groups of Diffuse Emission Nebulae," in *Vistas in Astronomy*, II (London, 1955), 1066–1069.

II. SECONDARY LITERATURE. See "Akademik Grigory Abramovich Shayn. 1892–1956," in *Vestnik Akademii nauk SSSR* (1956), no. 10, 84; "Akademik Grigory Abramovich Shayn," in *Voprosy kosmogonii*, **5** (1957), 3–5; P. P. Dobronravin, "Grigory Abramovich i Pelageya Fedorovna Shayn," in *Peremennye zvezdy*, **11**, no. 4 (1958), 321–324; "G. A. Shayn (1892–1956)," in *Astronomicheskii zhurnal*, **33**, no. 4 (1956), 465–468, with portrait; "Grigory Abramovich Shayn," in *Izvestiya Krymskoi astrofizicheskii observatorii*, **17** (1957), 3–10; "Grigory Abramovich Shayn (1892–1956)," in *Materialy k biobibliografii uchenykh SSSR*, Astron. ser. (1960), no. 2, intro. by P. P. Dobronravin and bibliography by O. V. Isakova; S. B. Pikel'ner, "G. A. Shayn," in *Astronomicheskii tsirkulyar. Byuro astronomicheskikh soobshchenii, Akademiya nauk SSSR*, no. 172 (1956), 1–2; and "G. A. Shayn (1892–1956)," in *Istoriko-astronomicheskie issledovaniya*, **3** (1957), 551–607, with complete bibliography of 249 titles compiled by N. B. Lavrova, 596–607; the article "Shayn" in *Bolshaya sovetskaya entsiklopedia* ("Great Soviet Encyclopedia"), 2nd ed., XLVII, 499; and O. Struve, "G. A. Shain and Russian Astronomy," in *Sky and Telescope*, **17**, no. 6 (1958), 272–274.

P. G. KULIKOVSKY

SHEN KUA[1] (*b.* 1031, registered at Ch'ien-t'ang[2] [now Hangchow, Chekiang province], China; *d.* Ching-k'ou, Jun prefecture[3] [now Chinkiang, Kiangsu province], China, 1095), *polymathy, astronomy.*

Shen was the son of Shen Chou[4] (*ca.* 978–1052) and his wife, whose maiden name was Hsu.[5] Shen Chou came of a gentry family with neither large landholdings nor an unbroken tradition of civil service. He spent his life in minor provincial posts, with several years in the capital judiciary. Shen Kua apparently received his early education from his mother. A native of Soochow (the region of which was known for its flourishing manufactures, commerce, and agriculture), she was forty-four or forty-five years old when he was born. Shen's background made possible his entry into the imperial bureaucracy, the only conventional road to advancement for educated people of his time. Unlike colleagues who came from the ancient great clans, he could count on few advantages save those earned by his striving and the full use of his intellectual talents. Shortly after he was assigned to the court, he became a confidant of the emperor and played a brilliant part in resolving the crises of the time. But within slightly over a decade his career in the capital was ended by impeachment. After a provincial appointment and five years of meritorious military accomplishment, he was doubly disgraced and politically burned out. The extremes of Shen's career and the shaping of his experience and achievement in science and technology become comprehensible only if the pivotal circumstances of his time are first considered.

Historical Background. Shen's time was in many senses the climax of a major transition in the Chinese polity, society, and economy.

Three centuries earlier the center of gravity in all these respects still lay in the north, the old center of civilization of the Han people. Wealth and power rested in the hands of the old aristocratic landowning families. Governmental institutions incorporated the tension between their private interests and the inevitable desire of their foremost peer, the emperor, to concentrate authority. The civil service examination system was beginning to give the central government a means to shape a uniform education for its future officials; but since birth or local recommendation determined who was tested, the mass of commoners remained uninvolved. The social ideals prevalent among the elite were static; the ideal past was cited to discourage innovation; and the moral example of those who ruled, rather than responsive institutions or prescriptive law, was held to be the key to the healthy state. The classicist's paradigm of a two-class society—self-sufficient agriculturalists ruled and civilized by humane generalists, with land as the only true wealth—did not encourage commerce, industry, or the exploitation of natural resources. The wants of the great families, whose civil servant members were becoming city dwellers by the middle of the eighth century, nonetheless gave momentum to all of these activities; but the majority of the population still took no part in the rudimentary money economy.

The T'ang order began a long, slow collapse about 750, until in the first half of the tenth century the empire of "All Under Heaven" was reduced to a succession of ephemeral and competing kingdoms. When the universal state was reconstructed in the Northern Sung (960–1126), its foundations were in many important respects different from those of the early T'ang. A new dynasty was not only, as classical monarchic theory had it, a fresh dispensation of the cosmos; it was also the occasion for institutionalizing a new distribution of power in society. The cumulative result of changes in taxation had been to make the old families accountable for their estates as they had not been earlier, and to encourage smaller landholdings—and, thus, a wider diffusion of wealth.

The center of vitality had moved southeast to the lower Yangtze valley, which had long before emerged as the major rice-yielding region. By this time its fertility, combined with its relative freedom from restrictive social arrangements, had bred a new subculture that was more productive in industry than elsewhere and hospitable to the growth of commerce and stable markets, the beginnings of a uniform money economy, and the great broadening of education that printing had just made possible. The new southern elite was, on the whole, small gentry, and lacked the military traditions of the ancient northern clans and of power holders in the period of disunion. Their families were often too involved in trade for them to despise it. Although conservative, as all Chinese elites have been, they were prepared to think of change as a useful tool. The novelties of attitude and value were often slighter or subtler than such a brief account can convey, but within the established limits of Chinese social ideals their consequences were very considerable.

In Shen Kua's time the old families still provided many of the very highest officials and thus wielded great influence, positive or obstructive, in discussions about the future of China. But they had become merely influential members of a new political constellation that brought a variety of convictions and interests to that perennial debate. An especially obvious new element was that many southern small gentry families like Shen's established traditions of civil service, either as a main means of support or to protect and further their other concerns. Once a family's social standing was achieved, one or more members could enter the bureaucracy freely because of experience as subordinates in local administration or because they were amply prepared by education for the examinations. Their sons could enter still more freely because special access to both direct appointment and examination was provided to offspring of officials.

Not sharing the old vision of a virtue-dominated social order fixed by precedent, men of the new elite were willing to sponsor institutional renovation in order to cope directly with contemporary problems. Dependent on their own talents and often needing their salaries, they were dedicated to building a rational, systematic, and in most respects more centrally oriented administration. They were willing to make law an instrument of policy, and insisted that local officials be rated not only on the moral example they set but also quantitatively—on how effectively they made land arable and collected taxes. In the name of efficiency they devoted themselves to removing customary curbs on imperial authority and (with only partial success in the Sung) to dismantling the structures of privilege that underlay regional autonomy. Only later would it become clear that they were completing the metamorphosis of the emperor from paramount aristocrat to autocrat. At the same time they were successfully demanding more policy-making authority as the emperor's surrogates, although at the cost to themselves of greater conformity than officials of the old type had willingly accepted.

This irreversible transition did not lead to a modern state, but only to a new and ultimately stagnant pattern. The most accelerated phase of change was the activity of what is called the New Policies[6] group (actually a shifting coalition) between 1069 and 1085. Its leader, Wang An-shih[7] (1021–1086), was brought to the capital in 1068 by the young emperor Shen-tsung, who had just taken the throne. Within two years Wang had become first privy councillor. He resigned for nine months in 1074, when pressure from his antagonists persuaded the emperor to be less permissive, and returned permanently to private life in 1076. The New Policies continued to be applied and extended, but with less and less attention to their founding principles, until Shen-tsung's death in 1085. Under the regency of the empress dowager, enemies of the reform attempted for eight years to extirpate Wang's influence and take revenge upon his adherents. When Emperor Che-tsung came of age in 1093, the New Policies were revived, but were so bent toward selfish ends and administered so disastrously that the word "reform" is hardly applicable.

Wang An-shih's opponents were many: the old aristocrats, career bureaucrats of the sort who would oppose any change as disruptive, officials whose individual or group interests ran in other directions —and men of high ideals who found his proposals ill-advised and his personal style too intolerant.*

No institution had evolved through Chinese history to work out and resolve conflicts of political viewpoint. This lack was filled by cliques, intrigues, and appeals to imperial intervention. Division and corruption among active supporters of the New Policies also had been a problem from the start. The scope of Wang's program was so large that he had to take competent support where he found it. The new access to power that he offered attracted ambitious men, many of whom had little real sympathy for his convictions and dedicated themselves primarily to manipulation and graft. Once Wang was gone, the leadership of his group tended to become a battleground for aspirations of this kind. The internal and external enemies of the New Policies left the program a shambles by the time the Chin Tartars drove the Sung south in 1127.

A primary aim of the reforms was financial security of the state, which prompted initiatives in water control and land reclamation, encouragement of extractive industries and agriculture, intervention in commerce, and rationalization of taxes. Another goal, particularly at the emperor's insistence, was military strength. There had been a long confrontation between the Chinese and the powerful Khitan empire, pastoral masters of mounted combat to the north (renamed Liao in 1066). Seventy years of fitful peace were punctuated by humiliating Chinese failures to recapture territory south of the Great Wall and maintained by large annual bribes. For three decades the Tangut people of the northwest had posed an almost equally unpalatable demand for appeasement. Victory or détente through strength, the emperor hoped, could be bought on both fronts with the wealth that the New Policies generated from man's exploitation of nature. Here too expertise was needed in cartography, strategic theory and tactical doctrine (both of which contained cosmological elements), design and manufacture of war matériel, fortification, troop organization and training, and development of a stable economy in border regions.

*In the successive reform movements of the Northern Sung there were considerable differences in the alignment of men with different beliefs and backgrounds. See the discussion in James T. C. Liu, "An Early Sung Reformer: Fan Chung-yen," in John K. Fairbank, ed., *Chinese Thought and Institutions* (Chicago, 1957), 105–131, esp. 107–109. The generalizations of the present article and of current scholarship as a whole are crude and tentative, pending the "comparative analysis of the interrelationships between ideology and family, class, status-group, and regional interests" that Robert M. Hartwell has called for in "Historical Analogism, Public Policy, and Social Science in Eleventh- and Twelfth-Century China," in *American Historical Review*, **76** (1971), 690–727.

Shen Kua contributed to nearly every field of New Policies activity, both civil and military. His social background and political commitments cannot be considered responsible for his scientific talent or curiosity; the antecedents and loyalties of other major contemporary scientific figures were very different from his. But a review of his career and of his work will show how regularly his involvement with particular technical themes and problems grew out of his activities in government.

Life. From about 1040 Shen traveled with his father to successive official posts from Szechwan in the west to the international port of Amoy. He was exposed not only to the geographical diversity of China but also to the broad range of technical and managerial problems—public works, finance, improvement of agriculture, maintenance of waterways—that were among the universal responsibilities of local administrators. Because his physical constitution was weak, he became interested in medicine at an early age.

Late in 1051, when Shen was twenty, his father died. As soon as the customary inactivity of the mourning period ended in 1054, Shen received the first of a series of minor local posts; his father's service exempted him from the prefectural examination. His planning ability became almost immediately apparent when he designed and superintended a drainage and embankment system that reclaimed some hundred thousand acres of swampland for agriculture. This was the first of a series of projects that established his reputation for skill in water control. In 1061, as a subprefect in Ning-kuo[8] (now Fu-hu,[9] Anhwei province), after a cartographic survey and a historical study of previous earthworks in the region, he applied the labor of fourteen thousand people to another massive land reclamation scheme that won the recognition of the emperor. In a series of floods four years later, Shen noted, it was the only such project not overwhelmed. He wrote characteristically that in the first year it returned the cost of the grain used, and that there was more than a tenfold profit on cash expended. In 1063 he passed the national examinations. Posted to Yangchow, he impressed the fiscal intendant (a post then equivalent to governor), Chang Ch'u[10] (1015–1080), who recommended him for a court appointment leading to a career in the professional financial administration.*

*The succession of fiscal posts that often led to a seat on the Council of State in the eleventh century has been documented by Robert M. Hartwell in "Financial Expertise, Examinations, and the Formulation of Economic Policy in Northern Sung China," in *Journal of Asian Studies*, **30**, 281–314.

Shen apparently used the time not occupied by his early metropolitan appointments, which were conventional and undemanding, to study astronomy. In reply to the informal questions of a superior he set down clear explanations, still extant, of the sphericity of the sun and moon as proved by lunar phases, of eclipse limits, and of the retrogradation of the lunar nodes. They demonstrate an exceptional ability to visualize motions in space, which were at best implicit in the numerical procedures of traditional astronomy and seldom were discussed in technical writing. In 1072 Shen was given an additional appointment as director of the Astronomical Bureau. With the collaboration of his remarkable commoner protégé Wei P'u[11] and the aid of other scholarly amateurs, using books gathered from all over the country, he undertook a major calendar reform. He planned an ambitious series of daily observations to extend over five years, using renovated and redesigned instruments. When he took office, the bureau was staffed with incompetents. He forced the dismissal of six whom he caught falsifying records of phenomena, but the obstruction of those who remained doomed his program of observations and kept his new system of ephemerides computation from being among the two or three most securely founded before modern times. Shen's personal involvement in later stages of the reform undoubtedly was limited by his gradual movement into the vortex of factional politics.

Shen was early known to Wang An-shih, who composed his father's epitaph while a young provincial official; Shen eventually came to be publicly identified by enemies of the New Policies as among the eighteen members of Wang's intimate clique. In late 1072, in support of Wang's program, Shen surveyed the silting of the Pien Canal near the capital by an original technique, dredged it, and demonstrated the value of the silt as fertilizer. Until mid-1075 he spent much time traveling as a troubleshooter of sorts, inspecting and reporting on water control projects, military preparations, and local administrations—and, it has been conjectured, providing encouragement to Wang's provincial supporters. Shen was put in charge of arsenal activities and, in 1075, was sponsored by Wang (then head of government) to revise defensive military tactics, a task the throne had proposed for Wang himself.

In 1074 the Khitan were pressing negotiations to move their borders further south. Incompetent and timorous Chinese negotiators were conceding unfounded Liao assertions about the language and substance of previous agreements. Shen built a sol-id Chinese case by going to the archives, as no one had bothered to do before. His embassy in mid-1075 to the camp of the Khitan monarch on Mt. Yung-an[12] (near modern P'ing-ch'üan,[13] Hopei) was triumphant. He described himself surrounded by a thousand hostile onlookers, calling on his staff, who had memorized the old documents of the Khitan themselves, to cite without pause or flurry the exact reference to refute one historical claim after another.

Shen returned to China—with biological specimens and maps of the territories he had passed through—to become a Han-lin academician, to be given charge of a large-scale water control survey in the Yangtze region, and then to become head of the Finance Commission. While in this very powerful position he untangled a variety of contradictory policies, producing in the process some of the most penetrating writings before modern times on the operation and regulation of supply and demand, on methods of forecasting prices in order to intervene effectively in the market, and on factors that affect the supply of currency (varying through hoarding, counterfeiting, and melting) as the value of the metal in it fluctuates about its controlled monetary value. In the autumn of 1077, just as his revision of critical fiscal measures was well launched, he was impeached by the corrupt and vindictive censor Ts'ai Ch'ueh[14] (1036–1093). The charge was that Shen had opposed a New Policies taxation measure in an underhanded, inconsistent, and improper way. It was credited by historians for centuries, but its truth has been refuted in every detail by recent Chinese research. His protector Wang An-shih had just left government; it is believed, given the mood of the time, that by threatening an established budget item in order to ease the burdens of the poor, Shen became an easy victim of factional maneuvering.

The emperor was not only the ritual synapse between the political and natural orders; he was a human being whose likes and dislikes were indulged within broad limits that could be further widened by force of his personal charisma and will. The closer to him an official penetrated, the more achievement and even survival became subject to imperial whim and the intrigue of colleagues. Although the record is fragmentary, it gives the impression that Shen Kua was maneuvered by Wang An-shih into the proximity of the throne because of his brilliance, judgment, and effectiveness at complicated tasks. Nothing indicates that he was adept at protecting himself. He attracted the most damaging animosity not from opponents of the

New Policies but from designing members of his coalition. Once the emperor qualified his support of the New Policies in 1074, the risk of debacle remained great and imminent. Many officials who had risen with Wang fought furiously for the power that would keep them afloat even though the program sank. They did not wish to be deterred by a colleague who judged issues on their own merits. They probably also felt, as others did, that a man of Shen's age and rank did not deserve the emperor's confidence.

Ts'ai Ch'ueh was rising into the vacuum that Wang's retirement had left. The emperor depended increasingly on Ts'ai's monetary counsel and could not easily disregard what he insisted upon. For three years it was impossible to overcome his objections and those of another censor, and to rehabilitate Shen. Finally Shen was sent to Yen-chou[15] (now Yenan, Shensi province), on the necessary route for military operations by or against the Tanguts, as commissioner for prefectural civil and military affairs.[16] The Tanguts were then divided and weakened, minor Chinese conquests around 1070 had set the stage for a war, and the treasury had ample funds. Shen played an important part in organizing and fortifying for the victorious offensive of the autumn of 1081. In extending Sung control he showed a practical as well as a theoretical mastery of the art of warfare. He was cited for merit and given several honorary appointments. It was probably at the same time that he was ennobled as state foundation viscount.[17] In his sixteen months at Yen-chou, Shen received 273 personal letters from the emperor. His standing at the court was in principle reestablished. Whether he had become shrewd enough to survive there was never tested.

Shen and a colleague followed up the victory by proposing fortifications to close another important region to the Tanguts. The emperor referred the matter to an ambitious and arrogant official who, ignoring the proposal, changed the plan to provide defenses for what Shen argued was an indefensible and strategically useless location. Shen was commanded to leave the vicinity of the new citadel so as not to share in the credit for the anticipated victory. When the Tangut attack came, the emissary's force was decimated while Shen, with imperial permission, was successfully defending a key town on the enemy invasion route to Yen-chou. The campaign thus provided the Tanguts with no opening for advance—but Ts'ai Ch'ueh was now a privy councillor. As titular military commander Shen was held responsible for the defeat and considerable loss of life. At the age of fifty-one his career was over. The towns he saved were later abandoned by the anti–New Policies regime to no advantage, just as the lands he had saved from the Khitan through diplomacy had since been lost by another negotiator.

Shen spent six years in fixed probationary residence, forbidden to engage in official matters. He used at least two of these years to complete a great imperially commissioned atlas of all territory then under Chinese control. He had been working on this atlas intermittently since, as finance commissioner a decade earlier, he had had access to court documents. His reward included the privilege of living where he chose.

Ten years earlier Shen had bought, sight unseen, a garden estate on the outskirts of Ching-k'ou. In 1086, visiting it for the first time, he recognized it as a landscape of poignant beauty that he had seen repeatedly in dreams, and named it Dream Brook (*Meng ch'i*,[18] alternately read *Meng hsi*). He moved there in 1088. Despite a pardon and the award of sinecures to support him in his old age, he spent seven years of leisure, isolation, and illness until his death there.*

Shen's writings, of which only a few are extant even in part, include commentaries on Confucian classics, two atlases, reports on his diplomatic missions, a collection of literary works, and monographs on rituals, music, mathematical harmonics, administration, mathematical astronomy, astronomical instruments, defensive tactics and fortification, painting, tea, medicine, and poetry. Of three books compiled during his last years at Dream Brook, one, "Good Prescriptions" (*Liang fang*[19]), was devoted to medical therapy, theory, and philology; the other two belong to particularly Chinese genres. "Record of Longings Forgotten" (*Wang huai lu*[20]), a collection of notes on the life of the gentleman farmer in the mountains, contains useful information on implements and agricultural technique and, unlike more conventional agricultural treatises up to that time, on the culture of medicinal plants.

"Brush Talks From Dream Brook" (*Meng ch'i pi t'an*[21]) and its sequels, extant and well-edited in modern times, is by any reckoning one of the most remarkable documents of early science and technology. It is a collection of about six hundred recollections and observations, ranging from one or two sentences to about a page of modern print—"because I had only my writing brush and ink slab

_____

*For a translation that conveys the flavor of Shen's autobiography, see Donald Holzman, "Shen Kua," 275–276.

to converse with, I call it Brush Talks." They are loosely grouped under topics (seventeen in all current versions), of which seven contain considerable matter of interest in the study of nature and man's use of it: "Regularities Underlying the Phenomena"[22] (mostly astronomy, astrology, cosmology, divination), "Technical Skills"[23] (mathematics and its applications, technology, medicine), "Philology"[24] (including etymology and meanings of technical terms), "Strange Occurrences"[25] (incorporating various natural observations), "Artifacts and Implements"[26] (techniques reflected in ancient objects), "Miscellaneous Notes"[27] (greatly overlapping other sections), and "Deliberations on Materia Medica"[28] (most of it on untangling historic and regional confusions in identities of medical substances).

Notices of the highest originality stand cheek by jowl with trivial didacticisms, court anecdotes, and ephemeral curiosities under all these rubrics; other sections were given to topics conventional in collections of jottings—memorable people, wisdom in emergencies, and so on. Shen's theoretical discussions of scientific topics employed the abstract concepts of his time—yin-yang, the Five Phases (wu-hsing[29]), ch'i,[30] and so on. A large fraction of the book's contents is devoted to fate, divination, and portents, his belief in which has been ignored by historians seeking to identify in him the prototype of the modern scientist. The author of "Brush Talks" has been compared with Leibniz; and in an era of happier relations with the Soviet Union, Hu Tao-ching, the foremost authority on Shen, referred to him as the Lomonosov of his day. But Shen was writing for gentlemen of universal curiosity and humanistic temperament; custom, wisdom, language, and oddity were as important themes as nature and artifice.

Because Shen's interests were multifarious, the record unsystematic, and its form too confining for anything but fragmentary insight, only accumulation can provide a fair impression of what constitutes his importance. What follows is the mere sample that space allows of his attempts to deepen the contemporary understanding of nature, his observations that directed the attention of his educated contemporaries to important phenomena or processes, and his own technical accomplishments. They are grouped to bring out contiguity of subject matter without interposing the radically different disciplinary divisions of modern science. These samples will become the basis of discussion—which, given the state of research, must be highly

tentative—of the epistemological underpinnings of Shen's work, and of the unity of his scientific thought with elements that today would be considered unscientific, primitive, or superstitious. Finally, it will be possible to evaluate Shen's life as a case study in the reconcilability of Confucianism and science, which the conventional wisdom among sinologists for over a generation has tended to place in opposition.

Quantity and Measure. Mathematics was not the queen of sciences in traditional China. It did not exist except as embodied in specific problems about the physical world. Abstract thought about numbers was always concerned with their qualities rather than their properties, and thus remained numerology. This art, although it blended into arithmetic, was only partly distinct from other symbolic means (in the anthropologist's sense: magical, ritual, religious, divinatory) for exploring the inherent patterns of nature and man's relation to it. Computation, on the other hand, was applied to a great variety of mensurational, accounting, and other everyday tasks of the administrator in a coherent tradition of textbooks. Occasionally curiosity and skill pushed beyond these pragmatic limits, but never very far. Some of the problems that Shen presented in "Brush Talks" had no application, but his enthusiasm for them was in no way qualified.

In addition to this accumulation of individual problems there were two exact sciences, in which mathematics served theory to advance knowledge of the patterns underlying the phenomena. One was mathematical harmonics (lü lü[31]), which explored the relations between musical intervals and the dimensions of instruments that produced them, in ways analogous to the Pythagorean art. Its appeal was much the same in both China and Greece: it demonstrated how deeply the power of number was grounded in nature. For this reason in China mathematical harmonics was often put into the same category as mathematical astronomy, which also had foundations in metaphysics. Astronomy, by far the more technically sophisticated of the two exact sciences, was normally employed on behalf of the monarch. Unpredictable phenomena and failures of prediction were either good or bad omens. Bad omens were interpreted as warnings that the emperor's mediating virtue, which maintained concord between the cosmic and political orders, was deficient. Successful prediction of celestial events was symbolic preservation or enhancement of the charisma of the ruling dynasty.

The annual calendar (or almanac) issued by authority of the throne was thus of great ceremonial importance. It encompassed all predictable phenomena, including planetary phenomena and eclipses. The utilitarian calendrical aspects—lunar months and solar years—had long since been refined past any practical demand for accuracy, but astronomical reinforcement of the Mandate of Heaven called forth endless attempts at greater precision of constants. As it became conventional to institute a complete new system for computing these ephemerides when a new emperor was enthroned, technical novelty was at a premium. When new ideas were unavailable, trivial recasting of old techniques was usually substituted. Repeated failures of prediction were another motive for reform of the astronomical system. In such cases too the system was in principle replaced as a unit rather than repaired. Most systems survived or fell on their ability to predict eclipses, particularly solar eclipses. These were the least amenable of all celestial phenomena to the algebraic, nongeometric style of mathematics. Prior to Shen's time little effort had gone into predicting the apparent motions of the planets, which lacked the immediacy of solar and lunar phenomena. This was, in fact, an omission that Shen seems to have been the first to confront.

General Mathematics. As wood-block printing became widespread, the government used it to propagate carefully edited collections of important ancient textbooks for use in education. This was being done in medicine at the time Shen entered the capital bureaucracy. In 1084 a collection of ten mathematical manuals, made four centuries earlier and reconstituted as well as extant texts allowed, was printed. The authority of these projects served both to fix textual traditions, preserving selected treatises from further attrition, and passively to encourage the fading into oblivion of books left out. Shen thus lived at a pivotal period in the development of mathematics, and his judgments on lost techniques and disused technical terms (such as 300, 306) have played an important part in later attempts to interpret them.*

*Numbers in parentheses are item numbers in the Hu Taoching edition of *Meng ch'i pi t'an* (the latter is referred to hereafter as "Brush Talks"). Roman volume numbers followed by page numbers refer to translations in Joseph Needham *et al.,* *Science and Civilisation in China.* Where my own understanding differs considerably from Needham's, an asterisk follows the page reference. All quotations below are from Shen, and all translations are my own. Full bibliographical data are given in the notes only for sources of too limited pertinence to be included in the bibliography. Chinese and Japanese family names precede personal names throughout this article.

"Brush Talks" is also an essential source for the study of pre-Sung metrology, currency, and other subjects related to computation.

Shen used mathematics in the formulation of policy arguments more consistently than most of his colleagues; examples are his critique of military tactics in terms of space required for formations (579) and his computation that a campaign of thirty-one days is the longest that can feasibly be provisioned by human carriers (205). But of the computational methods discussed in his "Technical Skills" chapter, those not related to astronomy are almost all abstractly oriented.

This original bent emerges most clearly in two problems. One departs from earlier formulas for computing the frustum of a solid rectangular pyramid. Shen worked out the volume of the same figure if composed of stacked articles (he mentioned *go* pieces, bricks, wine vats) that leave interstices (301). Since Shen intended this "volume with interstices" (*ch'i chi*[32]) method to be applicable regardless of the shape of the objects stacked, what he gave is a correct formula for the number of objects, which are thus to be considered of unit volume. His presentation has several interesting features. Needham has suggested that the concern with interstices (and, one would add, unit volumes) may have been a step in the direction of geometric exhaustion methods (III, 142–143)—although it was tentative and bore fruit only in seventeenth-century Japan. Second, instead of the worked-out problem with actual dimensions that is conventional in early textbooks, Shen simply gave a generalized formula: "double the lower length, add to the upper length, multiply by the lower width," and so on. Third, this was the earliest known case in China of a problem involving higher series. Built on earlier numerical approaches to arithmetical progressions, it provided a basis for more elaborate treatment by Yang Hui[33] (1261) and Chu Shih-chieh[34] (1303).

The second problem of interest was said "in a story" to have been solved by one of China's greatest astronomers, the Tantric Buddhist patriarch I-hsing[35] (682–727): the number of possible situations on a *go* board, with nineteen by nineteen intersections on which any number of black or white pieces may be placed. Whether I-hsing actually solved this problem we do not know; Shen's single paragraph was the first and last known discussion of permutations in traditional mathematics. It stated the order of magnitude of the answer— "approximately speaking one must write the character *wan*[36] (10,000) fifty-two times in succession"—adding exact answers for smaller arrays, three methods of solution, and a note on the limited traditional notation for very large numbers (304).*

Mathematical Harmonics. The Pythagoreans were fascinated by the relations of concordant intervals to the plucked strings that produced them, since the lengths between stops were proportionate to simple ratios of integers. The Chinese built up a similar science on a gamut of standard pipes. Beginning with a pipe eight inches long and 0.9 inch in diameter, they generated the lengths of subsequent pipes by multiplying the previous length alternately by 2/3 and 4/3, making twelve pipes within an approximate octave. The dozen were then related to such categories as the twelve divisions of the tropical year, in order to provide a cosmic basis for the system of modes that the pipes determined. A pentatonic scale, which could be used in any of the twelve modes, provided similar associations with the Five Phases. This basis was extended to metrology by defining the lengths and capacities of the pipes in terms of millet grains of standard dimensions. Shen provided a lucid and concise explanation of these fundamentals of mathematical harmonics, and corrected grotesque complications that had crept into a canonic source through miscopying of numbers (143, 549). He also experimentally studied stringed instruments. By straddling strings with paper figures, he showed that strings tuned to the same notes on different instruments resonate, as do those tuned an octave apart on the same instrument (537; cf. IV.1, 130). His two chapters on music and harmonics[37] are also a trove of information on composition and performance.

Astronomy. Shen's major contributions in astronomy were his attempts to visualize celestial motions spatially, his arc-sagitta methods that for the first time moved algebraic techniques toward trigonometry, and his insistence on daily observational records as a basis for his calendar reform. The first had no direct application in computation of the ephemerides, although it may well have inspired (and at the same time have been inspired by) the second, which grew out of traditional mensurational arithmetic. It has been suggested that the clarity of Shen's cosmological explanations led to his appointment to the Astronomical Bureau, which provided opportunity for his contributions in the second and third areas. But circumstances that arose from the bureaucratic character of mathematical astronomy made these contributions futile in his lifetime.

Shen's discussions of solar, lunar, and eclipse phenomena (130–131; excerpts, III, 415–416) have been mentioned. By far the most remarkable of his cosmological hypotheses attempted to account for variations in the apparent planetary motions, including retrogradation. This concern is not to be taken for granted, since traditional astronomers preferred purely numerical approaches to prediction, unlike the spatial geometric models of Greek antiquity, and showed little interest in planetary problems. Noting that the greatest planetary anomaly occurred near the stationary points, Shen proposed a model in which the planet traced out a figure like a willow leaf attached at one side to the periphery of a circle (see Figure 1). The change in direction of the planet's motion with respect to the stars was explained by its travel along the pointed ends of the leaf (148).* The willow leaf, in other words, served one of the same functions that the epicycle served in Europe. It is characteristic that, having taken a tack that in the West was prompted entirely by geometric reasoning, Shen's first resort should have been a familiar physical object. Use of a pointed figure doubtless would not have survived a mathematical analysis of observational data, but this remained an offhand suggestion.

Another early outcome of Shen's service at the court was a series of proposals for the redesign of major astronomical instruments: the gnomon, which was still employed to measure the noon shadow and fix the solstices; the armillary sphere, with which angular measurements were made; and the clepsydra, used to determine the time of observations (and to regulate court activities). Shen's improved versions of the latter two apparently were not built until late 1073, after he had taken charge of the Astronomical Bureau. The armillary at least was discarded for a new one in 1082, a casualty of his personal disgrace.

Shen's clepsydra proposals represent a new design of the overflow-tank type (Needham's Type B; III, 315–319, 325), but the most significant outcome of his work on this instrument was a jotting on problems of calibration. Day and night were by custom separately divided into hours, the

---

*This was translated in part by Needham (III, 139). The extant text, even in Hu's edition, is very corrupt. It has been edited and considerably emended by Ch'ien Pao-tsung in *Sung Yuan shu-hsueh-shih lun-wen-chi*, 266–269.

*Translated by N. Sivin, *Cosmos and Computation in Early Chinese Mathematical Astronomy* (Leiden, 1969), also published in *T'oung Pao*, **55** (1969), 1–73 (see 71–73), from which the figure is reproduced with permission of E. J. Brill.

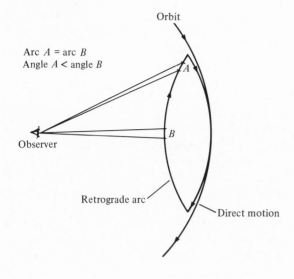

Arc *A* = arc *B*
Angle *A* < angle *B*

Observer

Orbit

A

B

Retrograde arc

Direct motion

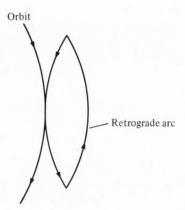

Orbit

Retrograde arc

FIGURE 1. Shen Kua's explanation of planetary anomaly. He suggested that the "willow leaf" could be either inside or outside the orbit. No drawings appear with the text in "Brush Talks."

length of which varied with the season. The time was read off graduated float rods, day and night sets of which were changed twenty-four times a year. Shen pointed out that this crude and inadequate scheme amounted to linear interpolation, "treating the ecliptic as a polygon rather than a circle," and argued for the use of higher-order interpolation (128).

The best armillary sphere available in the central administration when Shen first worked there was based on a three-hundred-year-old design "and lacked ease of operation" (150). The most interesting of Shen's improvements was in the diameter of the naked-eye sighting tube. At least from the first millennium B.C. a succession of stars had been taken up and abandoned as the pole star. In the late fifth century of the current era Tsu Keng[38] discovered that the current polestar, 4339 Camelopardi, rotated about a point slightly more than a

degree away. This determination of the true pole was incorporated in subsequent instruments by making the radius of their sighting tubes 1.5 Chinese degrees (each 360/365.25°). The excursion of the pole star just inside the field of view thus provided a nightly check on orientation. Six hundred years later Shen found that the polestar could no longer be kept in view throughout the night. He gradually widened the tube, using plots of the polestar's position made three times each night for three months to adjust aim, until his new calibration revealed that the distance of the star from "the unmoving place at the celestial pole" was now slightly over three degrees (127; III, 262). Shen's successors followed him in treating the distance as variable, although the relation of this secular change to the equinoctial precession was not explored. Aware of the periodic retrogradation of the lunar nodes, Shen also discarded the armillary ring representing the moon's path, which could not reflect this motion; it was never used again.

Calendar Reform. On the accession of Shen-tsung in 1068, a new computational system was expected. The inability of the incumbent specialists to produce one left Shen with a clear mandate when he took over the Astronomical Bureau in 1072. The situation became even more awkward when he was forced to bring in Wei P'u and others from outside the civil service, although few of the incompetents already in the bureau could be dislodged, in order to begin work on the calendar reform. It is not yet possible to tell what part of the work was done by Shen and what part by his assistants, although it is clear that Wei took responsibility for compiling the system as Shen became increasingly occupied elsewhere in government. Wei, a commoner whose connection with Shen was first reported in 1068, bore the brunt of fervent opposition within the bureau. He was even formally accused of malfeasance.

Shen knew that previous Sung astronomical systems had suffered greatly from reliance on old observations, and had a clear conception of what new data were needed for the first major advance in centuries. Unabating opposition within the bureau and his own demanding involvements outside it limited the number of innovations of lasting importance in his Oblatory Epoch (*Feng-yuan*[39]) system. It was the official basis of calendar computation from 1075, the year of its completion, to 1094, a period very close to the average for systems of the Northern Sung. That the system was not used longer has little to do with its merits, since except in cases of spectacular failure, Sung astronomical systems changed as rulers changed. Shen's was replaced when a new era was marked by the coming of age of Che-tsung. The immediate vicissitudes and long-term influence of three special features will give a general idea of the limits that historical actuality set upon Shen's astronomical ambitions.

The boldest aspect of Shen's program was the attempt to master the apparent motions of the planets—not merely their mean speeds and prominent phenomena—for the first time. This could not be done with a few observations of stationary points, occultations, and maximum elongations. Shen and Wei therefore planned a series of observations of a kind not proposed in Europe until the time of Tycho Brahe, five centuries later: exact coordinates read three times a night for five years. Similar records were to be kept for the moon's positions, since previous Sung systems had still used the lunar theory of I-hsing, which after 350 years had accumulated considerable error. These records were the most unfortunate casualty of the antagonism within the Bureau. Shen and Wei had no recourse but to produce a conventional planetary theory based mainly on old observations. They were able to correct the lunar error, but even this proposal provoked such an outcry that it could be vindicated only by a public demonstration using a gnomon (116).

A second issue was the central one of eclipse prediction. Previous attempts to add or subtract correction factors showed the futility of this approach. It was Wei P'u who "realized that, because the old eclipse technique used the mean sun, [the apparent sun] was ahead of it in the accelerated phase of its motion and behind it in the retarded phase." He therefore incorporated apparent solar motion into the eclipse theory (139). This had been done centuries earlier but abandoned.

A major obstacle in eclipse prediction, as well as in such workaday problems as the projection of observations in equatorial coordinates onto the ecliptic, was the absence of spherical geometry. Shen's evolution of arc-chord-sagitta relations out of some inferior approximations for segment areas given in the arithmetical classics was a first step toward trigonometry, making it possible in effect to apply sine relations and a fair approximation of cosine relations (301; III, 39, with diagram). The great remaining lack, as in planetary theory, was a mass of fresh observations on which to base new parameters. That this weakness could threaten the continuance of the system became clear the year after it was adopted (1076), when the failure of a predicted lunar eclipse to occur left Shen and his associates open to attack. Shen parried with a successful request that astronomical students at the Han-lin Academy observatory be ordered to carry out his observational program "for three or five years" and to communicate the results to the original compilers. Whether this attempt to bypass the stalemate at the Astronomical Bureau's observatory was well-conceived remains unknown, for in the next year Shen's impeachment aborted it.

In sum, the immediate outcome of the Oblatory Epoch calendar reform was undistinguished, and within half a century the official documents embodying it had been lost. It is impossible to be sure, for instance, to what extent arc-sagitta relations had been incorporated after Shen invented them. But enough information survived in proposals, reports, Shen's writings, and compendiums of various sorts for his astronomical system to play a considerable part in the highest achievement of traditional Chinese mathematical astronomy, the Season-Granting (*Shou shih*[40]) system of Kuo Shouching[41] (1280). Kuo carried out a sustained program of observation using instruments that incorporated Shen's improvements. He took up Shen's arc-sagitta formula, greatly improving the cosine approximation, and applied it to the equator-ecliptic transform. Aware of Shen's emphasis on the continuous variation of quantities in nature, and of his criticism of linear interpolation in clepsydra design, Kuo used higher-order interpolation to an unprecedented extent in his calendar reform.

Shen recorded another scheme for reform of the civil calendar that was most remarkable for his time and place. It almost certainly occurred to him in the last decade of his life. The traditional lunisolar calendar was a series of compromises in reconciling two incommensurable quantities. The modern value for the tropical year is 365.2422 days, and that for the synodic month 29.53059 days, so that there are roughly 12.37 lunar months per solar year. The practical problem was to design a civil calendar with an integral number of days each month, and an integral number of months each year, in such a way that the long-term averages approach the astronomical constants. Hardly two of the roughly one hundred computational systems recorded in early China solved this problem in exactly the same way, just as there was endless tactical variety in other traditional societies, but strategy was generally the same. Months of twenty-nine and thirty days alternated, with occasional pairs of long months to raise the average slightly. Intercalary thirteenth months were inserted roughly seven times every nineteen years, which comes to 0.37 additional months per year.

By a millennium before Shen's time the calendar was more than adequate in these respects for every civil need, although attempts to further refine the approximation led to endless retouching. The rhythms of administration, and to some extent of commerce, were of course paramount in the design of the lunisolar calendar, despite pieties about imperial concern for agriculture. It is most unlikely that Chinese peasants ever needed a printed almanac by which to regulate their activity; what they consulted, if anything, was its notations of lucky and unlucky days. Division of the year by lunar months is, in fact, useless for agriculture, since the seasons that pace the farmer's work vary with the sun alone. The Chinese calendar also incorporated twelve equal divisions of the tropical year (ch'i[30], like the Babylonian tithis), further subdivided into twenty-four periods with such names as Spring Begins, Grain Rains, and Insects Awaken. These provided a reliable notation for seasonal change in the part of northern China in which the series originated.

Shen's suggestion was a purely solar calendar, based on the twelve divisions of the tropical year (average 30.43697 days in his system) instead of on the lunation. The civil calendar would thus alternate months of thirty and thirty-one days, with pairs of short months as necessary to approach the average. This would provide truly seasonal months and at the same time do away with "that goitrous excrescence" the intercalary month. "As for the waxing and waning of the moon, although some phenomena such as pregnancy and the tides are tied to them, they have nothing to do with seasons or changes of climate; let them simply be noted in the almanac" (545). Shen was aware that because the lunisolar calendar went back to hoary antiquity "it is by no means appropriate to criticize it." He predicted that his discussion "will call forth offense and derision, but in another time there will be those who use my arguments." This proposal was in fact considered by later scholars the greatest blemish on Shen's astronomical talent. His posterity appeared in the mid-nineteenth century, with the even more radical solar calendar enacted for a few years by the T'ai-p'ing rebels.* His work was

*Kuo T'ing-i,[42] T'ai-p'ing t'ien kuo li-fa k'ao-ting[43] ("Review of the Calendrical Methods of the T'ai-p'ing Heavenly Kingdom," 1937; reprinted Taipei, 1963); Lo Erh-kang,[44] T'ien li k'ao chi t'ien li yü yin yang li jih tui-chao-piao[45] ("On the T'ai-p'ing Calendar, With a Concordance Table for the Lunar and Gregorian Calendars"; Peking, 1955).

cited to justify historically more respectable proposals between that time and the adoption of the Gregorian calendar in 1912.

Configuration and Change. Chinese natural philosophers, unlike the majority in the postclassical West, did not dismiss the possibility that terrestrial phenomena could conform to mathematical regularities. But given the strength of Chinese quantitative sciences in numerical rather than geometric approaches, the very late and partial development of mathematical generalization, and the complete absence of notions of rigor, it is only consistent that much of the effort to discover such regularities produced numerology. Thus the most obvious of Shen's contributions to understanding of the earth and its phenomena are qualitative.

Magnetism. For more than a millennium before Shen's time, south-pointing objects carved from magnetite had been used from time to time in ceremonial and magic, and in 1044 objects cut from sheet iron and magnetized by thermoremanence were recommended for pathfinding in a book on military arts. Shen took up the matter of needles rubbed against lodestone by contemporary magi, discussed floating and other mountings, recommended suspension, noted that some needles point north and some south, and asserted that "they are always displaced slightly east rather than pointing due south"—all in about a hundred characters (437; IV.1, 249–250). This recognition of magnetic declination depended not only on consideration of a suspended needle but also on the improved meridian determined by Shen's measurement of the distance between the polestar and true north; declination in his part of China at the time has been estimated as between five and ten degrees (Needham and Peter J. Smith, "Magnetic Declination in Mediaeval China," in *Nature* [17 June 1967], 1213–1214. See the historical table in *Science and Civilisation in China*, IV.1, 310).

Shen may have been anticipated by geomancers, who practiced a sophisticated protoscience of land configuration and siting, but the dates of texts on which such claims have been based are questionable. The use of compass needles in navigation is recorded shortly after Shen's death, and later descriptions provide enough detail to show that the twenty-four-point rose that Shen substituted for the old eight compass points (perhaps also under the stimulus of the better meridian, if not of geomantic practice) had become widely used. He apparently was unaware of the polarity of magnetite itself, since in another article he explained the difference between north-pointing and south-pointing needles as "perhaps because the character of the stone also varies" (588; IV.1, 250).

Cartography. It has been conjectured that Shen was the first to use a compass in mapmaking, although traditional methods would have sufficed. Neither his early maps of Khitan territory nor the atlas of China completed in 1087 have survived to answer this question. But in an enclosure to the latter he did separately record bearings between points using his twenty-four-point compass rose, as well as rectilinear distances rather than, as customary, distances along established routes (he calls the use of distances "as the bird flies" ancient, but we have no earlier record). "Thus although in later generations the maps may be lost, given my book the territorial divisions may be laid out according to the twenty-four directions, and the maps speedily reconstructed without the least discrepancy" (575; III, 576). His great atlas included twenty-three maps drawn to a uniform scale of 1:900,000; the general map was ten by twelve Chinese feet. There is no evidence that the handbook outlasted the maps.

Three-dimensional topographic maps go back at least to Hsieh Chuang[46] (421–466), who had a demountable wooden model carved, apparently on the basis of an ancient map. In 1075, while inspecting the Khitan border, Shen embodied information gathered from the commander and the results of his own travels in a series of relief maps modeled, for the sake of portability, in plastic media—wheat paste and sawdust until the weather turned freezing, then beeswax—on wooden bases. These were carried to the capital and duplicated in wood; similar models were thenceforth required from other frontier regions (472; III, 580).

Shen's regular use of both historical research and special on-the-ground surveys to solve such cartographic problems as tracing changes in watercourses also is noteworthy (431). Typical of his ingenious topographic survey methods were those used in 1072 to measure the slope of the Pien Canal near the capital. There he built a series of dikes in temporary, narrow parallel channels to measure incremental changes in water level (457; III, 577*).

Formation of the Earth. In 1074, in the T'ai-hang mountain range (Hopei), Shen noticed strata of "bivalve shells and ovoid rocks running horizontally through a cliff like a belt. This was once a seashore, although the sea is now hundreds of miles east. What we call our continent is an inundation of silt. . . . This mud year by year flows eastward, forming continental land." A similar stratum

had been observed long before by Yen Chen-ch'ing[47] (708–784), who vaguely suggested its origin in the sea; but Shen—whose duties had made him intimately familiar with the process of silting—opened a new line of investigation by proposing a mechanism (430; III, 604).

Probably on his southward drought survey earlier in the same year, Shen saw the Yen-tang range (Chekiang), a series of fantastic rock formations "invisible from beyond the ridgeline [opposite], but towering to the sky when seen from the valleys. If we trace the underlying pattern, it must be that great waters in the valleys have attacked and washed away all the sand and earth, leaving only the great rocks erect and looming up." His explanation proceeded to generalize the shaping role of erosion, and then to apply it to the hills that divide streams in the loess country of northwest China—"miniatures of the Yen-tang mountains, but in earth rather than stone" (433; III, 603–604).

Shen reported a variety of contemporary finds of petrified plants and animals (373–374; III, 614–618). He remarked particularly on a stony formation he identified as originally a grove of interconnected bamboo roots and shoots, found dozens of feet below ground level at Yenan (Shensi). He knew from his military service there that the climate was too dry to grow bamboo: "Can it be that in earliest times [literally, 'before antiquity'] the land was lower and the climate moister, suitable for bamboo?" (373). About a century later the great philosopher and polymath Chu Hsi[48] (1130–1200), who knew Shen's jottings well and often extended ideas from them in his teaching, suggested that the stone of certain mountains was itself petrified silt deposits. But Shen's notion of prehistoric climatic change, like that of the reshaping of land by erosion, was not pushed further soon after his lifetime.

Atmospheric Phenomena. Although Shen did not report important original discoveries of his own, he preserved a number of interesting observations not recorded elsewhere. Perhaps the most important is a vivid description of a tornado (385; translated in Holzman, "Shen Kua," 286), the veracity of which was questioned by modern meteorologists until, in the first decade of the twentieth century, the Sikawei Observatory in Shantung reported phenomena of the same kind, previously thought restricted to the western hemisphere. Shen was also responsible for transmitting an explanation of the rainbow by Sun Ssu-kung,[49] an elder contemporary in the court who was also considered one of the best mathematical astronomers of his era. "The rainbow is the image [literally, 'shadow'] of the sun in rain, and occurs when the sun shines upon it." This sentence does not, as often claimed, adduce refraction (pinhole or mirror images were regularly called "shadows"; see 44). Shen was prompted to determine by experiment that the rainbow is visible only opposite the sun (357). Later Chu Hsi, aware of Shen's account, added that by the time the rainbow appears "the rain ch'i[30] has already thinned out; this in turn is because sunlight has shone on and attenuated the rain ch'i."[30] Ch'i must mean vapor here; the notion of reflections off individual drops is, as in Sun's explanation, implicit at best. Shen also recorded the fall of a fist-sized meteorite in more detail and with less mystification than previous reports. The particulars of its fall came from a careful account by another of Wang An-shih's associates. The object was recovered and exhibited, but Shen did not claim that he himself had observed that "its color is like that of iron, which it also resembles in weight" (340; III, 433–434).

Products of the Earth. Responsibilities with respect to fiscal policy gave Shen a detailed knowledge of important commodities, their varieties, and the circumstances of their production, as may be seen from his descriptions of tea (208) and salt (221). Inflammable seepages from rock had been known a millennium before Shen's time, and for centuries had been used locally as lamp fuel and lubricant. While civil and military commissioner near Yen-chou, he noted the blackness of soot from petroleum and began an industry to manufacture the solid cakes of carbon ink used for writing and painting throughout China. Good ink was then made by burning pine resin, but Shen knew that North China was being rapidly deforested. He remarked that, in contrast with the growing scarcity of trees, "petroleum is produced inexhaustibly within the earth." The name Shen coined for petroleum[50a] is the one used today, and the source in Shensi province that he developed is still exploited. In the same article he quoted a poem of his that is among the earliest records of the economic importance of coal, then beginning to replace charcoal as a fuel (421; III, 609, partial).

Optical Phenomena. Shen's interest in image formation was not directly connected with his worldly concerns. His motivation is more plausibly traced to the play of his curiosity over old artifacts than to the improvement of naked-eye astronomical instruments.

In the canons of the Mohist school (ca. 300 B.C.) is a set of propositions explaining the formation of shadows and of optical images (considered a kind of shadow) in plane, convex, and concave mirrors. One proposition is widely believed to concern pinhole images, although textual corruption and ambiguity make this uncertain. These propositions are in many respects correct, although very schematic, and rays of light are not presupposed. Shen concerned himself with the single question of why a concave mirror forms an inverted image. He posited an "obstruction" (ai[50]), analogous to an oarlock, that constricts the "shadow" to a shape like that of a narrow-waisted drum—or, as we would put it, to form two cones apex to apex, the second constituting the inverted image. Like the Mohists, Shen clearly believed that inversion takes place before the image is reflected. He expressly likened the inverted image to that of a moving object formed on the wall of a room through a small opening in a paper window. Aware for the first time that there is a range of distances from a concave mirror within which no image is formed (that is, between the center of curvature and the focal point), he explained that this blank region, corresponding to the pinhole, is the locus of "obstruction" (44; translated in A. C. Graham and N. Sivin, "A Systematic Approach to the Mohist Optics," in S. Nakayama and N. Sivin, eds., *Chinese Science: Explorations of an Ancient Tradition* [Cambridge, Mass., 1973], 145–147). His pinhole observation was adventitious, but his approach to the burning-mirror was experimental in its details.

Two other observations of optical interest are found under the rubric "Artifacts and Implements." The first, in the "Sequel to Brush Talks," noted that when the ancients cast bronze mirrors, they made the faces just convex enough that, regardless of size, every mirror would reflect a whole face. By Shen's time this refinement had been abandoned and the reasoning behind the curvature forgotten, so that collectors were having the faces of old mirrors scraped flat (327; IV.1, 93).

The second jotting is the oldest record of a Far Eastern curiosity still being investigated: "magic mirrors," or, as Shen called them, "transparent mirrors." Shen described a bronze mirror with a smooth face and an integrally cast inscription in relief on its back (both conventional features). When the mirror was used to reflect the sun onto a wall, the inscription was duplicated within the image. Shen cited with approval an anonymous explanation: "When the mirror is cast, the thinner parts cool first; the raised design on the back, being thicker, cools later and the shrinkage of the bronze is greater. Although the inscription is on the obverse, there are imperceptible traces of it on the face, so that it becomes visible within the light." He then qualified this explanation as incomplete, because he had tried mirrors in his own and other collections that were physically indistinguishable from the "transparent" ones and found that they did not cast images (330; IV.1, 94*). His doubt was justified, although the approach taken by his informant was at least as good as those of some modern metallurgists. Although cooling rate plays no discernible part, the variation in thickness is indeed responsible for the image in this sort of mirror, the most common among several types extant. Filing considerable bronze off the face of the mirror after casting is the key. This releases tensions in the metal and gives rise to slight deformations that produce the image.

Productive Techniques and Materials. The technologies of Shen's time were not cumulative and linked to science, but independent artisanal traditions transmitted from master to pupil. Shen left so many unique and informative accounts of ancient and contemporary processes among his jottings that "Brush Talks" has become a major source for early technology. Shen's interests in contemporary techniques can in most cases be linked to broad concerns of his official career; but the exceptional richness of his record bespeaks a rare curiosity, and the trenchancy of his descriptions a seriousness about mechanical detail unusual among scholar-officials. His notes on techniques lost by his time reflect the application of this technical curiosity and seriousness to archaeology, which was just becoming a distinct branch of investigation in the eleventh century.

Most of Shen's cultured contemporaries had a keen appreciation for good workmanship but considered the artisans responsible for it beneath notice except for occasional condescension. Shen wrote about resourceful craftsmen and ingenious laborers with much the same admiration he gave to judicious statesmen. He did not lose sight of the social distance between himself and members of the lower orders, but in his writing there is no snobbishness about the concert of hand, eye, and mind.

Contemporary Techniques. The most famous example is Shen's account of the invention of movable-type printing by the artisan Pi Sheng[51] (*fl.* 1041–1048). Shen described the carving and firing of ceramic type and the method of imbedding and leveling them in a layer of resin, wax, and paper ash in an iron form, one form being set as a second is printed. As in xylography, water-base ink was used. Since the porous, thin paper took it up with little pressure, no press was needed. Shen also remarked, with his usual acumen, that the process could become faster than carving wood blocks only with very large editions[52] (the average then has been estimated at between fifty and a hundred copies). Unevenness of the surface and absorption of ink by the fired clay must have posed serious problems. Abandonment of the process after Pi died was probably due to the lack of economic incentive that Shen noted. The long series of royally subsidized Korean experiments in the fifteenth century that perfected cast-metal typesetting still began with Pi Sheng's imbedding technique as described by Shen. Whether he knew Pi is unclear, but Shen's cousins preserved Pi's original font (307; translated in full, but not entirely accurately, in T. F. Carter, *The Invention of Printing in China and Its Spread Westward*, L. C. Goodrich, ed., 2nd ed. [New York, 1955], 212).

Shen left a number of descriptions of metallurgical interest—for instance, an account of the recovery of copper from a mineral creek by replacement of iron, a process then being carried out on an industrial scale to provide metal for currency (455; II, 267); observations of two of the three steelmaking processes used in early China (56; translated in Needham, *The Development of Iron and Steel Technology in China* [London, 1958], 33–34; the book was reprinted at Cambridge, England, in 1964); and remarks on a little-known cold-working method used by smiths of the Ch'iang[53] people of western China to make extremely tough steel armor (333). Water control techniques of which he records details include pound-locks with double slipways (213; IV.3, 351–352), piles for strengthening embankments (210; IV.3, 322–323), and sectional gabions for closing gaps after embankment repairs (207; IV.3, 342–343).

Ancient Techniques. The concern for understanding ancient techniques began with the commentators on the Confucian and other classics more than a millennium earlier. Exegesis remained an important activity in China, and the productive methods of golden antiquity were investigated with the same assiduity as anything else mentioned in its literary remains. For various reasons—among them the recovery of ancient artifacts in large numbers for the first time, the growth of collecting, and the elaboration of a conscious aesthetics—archaeology began to emerge from the footnotes less than a century before Shen's time, especially in monographs on ancient implements and ritual institutions. He was familiar with this literature and responded to it critically. Much of his writing in the "Artifacts and Implements" chapter falls squarely in this tradition, drawing on the testimony of both objects and books.

Shen's vision of the past as a repertory of lost processes introduced an influential new theme. A constant concern in his writing was not only that the workmanship of the past be esteemed for its excellence, but also that the present be enriched through understanding what the practical arts had been capable of. Although the belief was still current that the inventions that first made civilization possible were all due to semidivine monarchs of archaic times, in a letter Shen saw the technological past as successful for just the opposite reason: "How could all of this have come from the Sages? Every sort of workman and administrator, the people of the towns and those of the countryside—none failed to take part" (*Ch'ang-hsing chi* [1718 ed.], 19:53b).

Shen's remarks on magic mirrors are typical of his effort to understand lost processes. Another example is his reconstruction (and personal trial) of ancient crossbow marksmanship, interpreting a gnomic aiming formula in an ancient footnote with the aid of a graduated sight and trigger assembly that he examined after it was unearthed (331; III, 574–575*). The most famous instance of Shen's use of literary sources for the study of techniques has to do with the remarkable modular system of architecture used in public buildings. The set of standard proportions is well-known from an official compilation printed about a decade after Shen's death. Shen, by describing the proportion system of the Timberwork Canon (*Mu ching*[54]), attributed to a great builder of about 1000 and already falling out of use, demonstrates the antiquity of this art (299; IV.3, 82–83).

Medicine. By Shen's time medicine, which from the start drew heavily upon natural philosophy for its conceptual underpinnings, had accumulated a classical tradition. Not only was each new treatise consciously built upon its predecessors, but a major goal of new work was restoring an understanding that medical scholars believed was deepest in the oldest writings. The revealed truth of the archaic canons was too concentrated for ordinary latter-day minds, who could hope to recapture it only as the culmination of a lifetime of study. Writers in the intervening centuries referred to the early classics as the ultimate source of significance even while aware that empirical and practical knowledge had considerably advanced since antiquity. The major contribution of the continuous tradition of medical writing was to fit new experiences into the old framework and, when necessary, to construct new frameworks in the spirit of the old. As woodblock printing became feasible, standard editions of the chief classics were compiled and disseminated by government committees. This increased the respectability of the curing arts as a field of study. Large numbers of men from the scholar-official class began to take up medicine, not in competition with those who made a living by it but as a means of self-cultivation allied to cosmology and occasionally useful. The initial motivations commonly were personal ill health and the desire to serve one's sick parents.

Shen, as noted earlier, began the study of medicine early, for the former reason. One of his two therapeutic compilations survives in somewhat altered form. Its preface is a long disquisition on the difficulty of adequate diagnosis and therapy, as well as on the proper selection, preparation, and administration of drugs. His criticisms of contemporary trends toward simplification remind us that the development of urban culture and education in Sung China had led to increased medical practice among ordinary people as well as study by the literati. As protoscientific medicine began to displace magico-ritual folk remedies (at least in the cities), there were more half-educated physicians to be criticized by learned amateurs such as Shen. Shen's most characteristic contribution was undoubtedly his emphasis on his own experience, unusual in a tradition whose literature in the Sung still tended to depend heavily on copying wholesale from earlier treatises. Shen not only omitted any prescription the efficacy of which he had not witnessed, but appended to most a description of the circumstances in which it had succeeded. He provided many precise descriptions of medicinal substances of animal, vegetable, and mineral origin. Although he had no more interest in general taxonomic schemes than other pharmacognostic scholars of his time, his concern for exact identification and for philological accuracy gave his critical remarks enduring value. Many were incorporated into later compilations on materia medica, and Shen's writing also served as a stimulus to the work a few decades later of the great pharmacognostic critic K'ou Tsung-shih[55] in his "Dilatations Upon the Pharmacopoeias" (*Pen-ts'ao yen i,*[56] 1116).

A recent discovery of considerable interest is that certain medical preparations from human urine collectively called "autumn mineral" (*ch'iu shih*[57]), which have a long history in China, contain high concentrations of steroid hormones and some protein hormones as well. In "Good Prescriptions" Shen gives one of the earliest accounts, in the form of detailed instructions for two such preparations that he performed in 1061 (other accounts by contemporaries are harder to date).*

Perhaps Shen's most famous writing on general medical matters is one in which he refutes the common belief that there are three passages in the throat—as shown, for instance, in the first book of drawings of the internal organs based directly on dissection (1045).† His supporting argument is not from independent dissection but from sufficient reason—"When liquid and solid are imbibed together, how can it be that in one's mouth they sort themselves into two throat channels?" He thus saw the larynx as the beginning of a network for distributing throughout the body the vital energy carried in atmospheric air, and the esophagus as carrying nutriment directly to the stomach cavity, where its assimilation begins. This was a significant increase in clarity as well as accuracy (480).

A passage that has been praised for its simple but beautiful language takes issue with the ancient principle that medicinal plants should be gathered in the second and eighth lunar months (when they were thought easiest to identify). In a few hundred words it epitomizes the variation of ripening time with the identity and variety of the plant; the part used in therapy; the physiological effect needed for the application; altitude; climate; and, for domesticated medicinal plants, variation with planting time, fertilization, and other details of horticulture. The sophistication of this passage reflects not only increasing domestication (exceptional in earlier eras) but also the integration of drugs from every corner of China into the expanding commercial network.

Conclusion. The expansiveness of Northern Sung society and its relative openness to talent, not to mention increasing government sponsorship

---

*See Lu Gwei-djen and Joseph Needham, "Medieval Preparations of Urinary Steroid Hormones," in *Medical History,* **8** (1964), 101–121; Miyashita Saburō,[58] *Kanyaku shūseki no yakushigakuteki kenkyū*[59] ("A Historical Pharmaceutical Study of the Chinese Drug 'Autumn Mineral' the *Ch'iu-shih*"; Osaka, 1969), esp. 9–12.

†Persons untrained in medicine performed the dissection upon executed bandits in 1045 and recorded what was found under the direction of an enthusiastic amateur. Another episode of the same kind, undertaken explicitly to correct the earlier drawings, took place at the beginning of the twelfth century. There is no reliable account of either in any European language, but see Watanabe Kōzō,[60] "Genson suru Chūgoku kinsei made no gozō rokufu zu no gaisetsu"[61] ("A Survey of Extant Chinese Anatomical Drawings Before Modern Times"), in *Nihon ishigaku zasshi,* **7** (1956), 88.

of learning, made this an important period in the history of every branch of science and technology. Shen was not the first polymath it produced. There was also Yen Su[62] (*fl.* 1016), who designed an odometer and south-pointing chariot (in which a differential gear assembly kept figures pointing in a constant direction as the chariot turned), improved the design of the water clock and other astronomical instruments, and wrote on mathematical harmonics and the tides. In Shen's lifetime there was Su Sung[63] (1020–1101), who was first privy councillor during the last part of the reaction against the New Policies (1092–1093). Through the 1060's he played a major part in a large imperially sponsored compilation of materia medica, and in the editing and printing of ancient medical classics. In 1088 a group that he headed completed a great water-driven astronomical clock incorporating an escapement device. Their detailed description of the mechanism included the oldest star map extant in printed form, based on a new stellar survey. (The book has been studied and translated in Wang Ling, Joseph Needham, Derek J. de Solla Price, *et al., Heavenly Clockwork* [Cambridge, England, 1960].) That Yen, Su, and Shen were all in the central administration is not surprising. The projects on which they were trained and those in which they worked out many of their ideas were of a scale that only the imperial treasury could (or at least would) support.

Breadth of interest alone does not account for Shen's importance for the study of the Chinese scientific intellect. Another aspect is his profound technical curiosity. A number of the phenomena he recorded were mentioned by others; but even when others' descriptions happen to be fuller, they usually are of considerably less interest because their subject matter is treated as a mere curiosity or as an occasion for anecdote rather than as a challenge to comprehension. Above all, one is aware in Shen, as in other great scientific figures, of a special directness. A member of a society in which the weight of the past always lay heavily on work of the mind, he nevertheless often cut past deeply ingrained structures and assumptions. This was as true in his program of astronomical observations and his audacious solar calendar as in his work on government policies. People in the Sung were aware that man's world had greatly expanded since antiquity, and questioning of precedent (in the name of a return to classical principles) was inherent in the New Policies. Shen's commitment to this political point of view can only have reinforced the sense of cumulative improvement of techniques and increasing accuracy over time that one finds in major Chinese astronomers. But given these predispositions and opportunities, Shen remains in many senses an atypical figure, even in his time and among his associates.

There certainly is much that a modern scientist or engineer finds familiar, not only in the way Shen went about making sense of the physical world but also in the temper of his discourse, despite the profoundly antique nature of the concepts he used. One comes away from his writings confident that he would see much of modern science as a culmination (not the only possible culmination) of his own investigations—more confident than after reading Plato, Aristotle, or St. Thomas Aquinas. But does Shen's special configuration of abilities and motivations suggest that a genetic accident produced, out of time, a scientific rationalist-empiricist of essentially modern type? To answer this question it is necessary to look at Shen's larger conception of reality, of which his scientific notions compose only a part but from which they are inseparable.

The Relation of Scientific Thought to Reality. The sense of cumulative enterprise in mathematical astronomy did not imply the positivistic conviction that eventually the whole pattern could be mastered. Instead, from the earliest discussions there was a prevalent attitude that scientific explanation—whether in terms of number or of abstract qualitative concepts, such as yin-yang—merely expresses, for human purposes, limited aspects of a pattern of constant relations too subtle to be understood directly. No one expressed this attitude more clearly than Shen. In instance after instance he emphasized the inability of secular knowledge to encompass phenomena: the reason for magnetic declination (437), why lightning striking a house can melt metal objects without burning the wooden structure (347), and so on.

Shen made this point most clearly in connection with astronomy. In one passage he discussed the fine variations that astronomers must, in the nature of their work, ignore. Every constant, every mean value obscures continuous variation of every parameter (123). In his official proposals on the armillary sphere,[64] he argued that measure is an artifact, that it allows particular phenomena to be "caught" (po[65]) in observational instruments, where they are no longer part of the continuum of nature. That Shen saw as the condition of their comprehensibility. This and similar evidence amount not merely to an appreciation of the role of abstraction in science, but also to the steady conviction that abstraction is a limited process incapable of producing universal and fundamental knowledge of the concrete phenomenal world. Nature is too rich, too multivariant, too subtle (wei[66]). This limitation did not detract from the interest or worth of theoretical inquiry, and did not lead intellectuals to question whether learning could contribute to the satisfaction of social needs; but the ambit of rationalism in traditional scientific thought was definitely circumscribed.

In this light Shen's explanatory metaphors become more comprehensible. In his remarkable suggestion that variations in planetary speed may be represented by a compounded figure, he chose to fasten to the periphery of his circle a willow leaf, whereas in Europe no figure but another circle was thinkable (148). When explaining optical image inversion in terms of converging and diverging rays, the images of the oarlock and waisted drum occurred to him (44). The variation in polarity of different magnetized needles was likened to the shedding of antlers by two species of deer in opposite seasons (588; IV.1, 250), and so on. Geometric figures, numbers, and quantities were useful for computation but had very limited value, not so great as cogent metaphors from the world of experience, in understanding the pattern inherent in physical reality.

Many Chinese thinkers, even in the Sung, did believe in number as a key to the pattern of physical reality; but their search was concentrated in numerology (especially as founded on the "Great Commentary" to the *Book of Changes*) rather than in mathematics. This is not to imply that numerology was a distraction from mathematics. The two were not considered alternate means to the same goal.

Other Kinds of Knowledge. Did Shen believe that other ways of knowing complemented and completed empirical and theoretical investigation? Aside from its scientific aspects, Shen's thought has been so little studied that only some tentative suggestions can be offered. Contemplation and disciplined self-examination were ancient themes in Confucianism, and by Shen's time illumination was widely considered among the learned as a source of knowledge complementary to that given by experience of the external world. The domestication and secularization of Buddhist and Taoist meditation were gradually leading to a more introspective and less ritualistic approach to self-realization. This tendency was later elaborated with great variety of emphasis and weight in the schools of neo-Confucianism.

To understand what part contemplation and meditation played in the thought of Shen Kua requires a clearer view than we now have of their currency and coloring in his time, of the considerable role of Wang An-shih's thought in his intellectual development, and of Shen's own attitudes as indirectly expressed in his literary remains. There is as yet no sound basis for evaluating his interest in Taoist arcana that seems to have peaked in his thirties, his public remarks that express sympathetic interest in illuminationist (Ch'an, Japanese "Zen") Buddhism, and his statement in an autobiographical fragment that Ch'an meditation was one of the things to which he turned his attention after retirement. In any case these involvements refract aspects of his epistemology that cannot be overlooked without badly distorting our recognition of the whole.

Teraji Jun has recently demonstrated this point in examining how strong a factor in Shen's motivation and individuality was his belief in destiny and prognostication. There are crucial passages, especially in his commentary on Mencius, where Shen spoke of the necessity for choosing what is true and holding to it, and called the rule of the heart and mind by sensory experience "the way of the small man." The basis of moral choice was an autonomous inner authority defined in an original way but largely in Mencian terms, a centeredness "filling the space between sky and earth," unquestionably linked with the self-reliance that marked his unhappy career.

It is not immediately obvious why someone who so valued individual responsibility should have been fascinated by fate and divination, which in fact are the themes of whole chapters of "Brush Talks." Shen does not seem to have viewed these enthusiasms as in conflict with his scientific knowledge. His delight in strange occurrences and his tendency to place matters of scientific interest under that rubric begin to make sense under the hypothesis that he accepted the odd, the exceptional, and the affront to common sense as a challenge for explanation at another time, or by someone else—without assuming that explanation was inevitable. In his hundreds of jottings on people, the person he chose to praise is most often the one who did not do the obvious thing, even when it seemed the sound thing to do.

At one point Shen provided a thoroughly rational explanation of the relations between fate and prognostication. The future can of course be foreknown by certain people, he said, but it is a mistake to conclude that all matters are preordained. The vision of the future is always experienced in present time; the years in the interim also become simultaneous. One can do nothing to avoid an undesirable future so glimpsed. Authentic foreknowledge would have witnessed the evasive measures; a vision that failed to see them could not be authentic foreknowledge (350).

In addition to the visionary ability of certain minds, Shen pondered universally accessible methods of divination, which (he seems to have believed) do not describe the future or the spatially distant so much as provide counsel about them or aid thought about them. In one of his chapters, "Regularities Underlying the Phenomena," he explained why the same divinatory technique gives different outcomes when used by different people, and thus has no inherent verifiability. He quoted the "Great Commentary" to the *Book of Changes* to the effect that understanding is a matter of the clarity and divinity (in a very abstract sense) within one's mind. But because the mind is never without burdens that hinder access to its divinity, Shen reasoned, one's communion with it may take place through a passive mediating object or procedure (144, 145). This divinity is, for Shen's sources, the moral center of the individual. Prognostication, however ritualized (as we would put it), thus draws indirectly upon the power of self-examination. Access to the future, whether by vision or by divination, is a perfectly natural phenomenon that is imperfectly distinct, on the one hand, from the moral faculties, the choices of which condition the future, and, on the other, from science, the rational comprehension of the natural order as reflected in all authentic experience.

Thus it appears that introspection supplemented by divinatory procedures was a legitimate means to knowledge in Shen Kua's eyes, just as painstaking observation and measurement of natural phenomena were another. He neither confused the two approaches nor attempted to draw a clear line between them. Nor was he inclined to assess the comparative importance of these ways of knowing.

The complementarity in Shen's attitudes toward knowledge is echoed by another in the external world of his work. Computational astronomy and divination of various kinds (including judicial astrology) were equally weighty functions carried out by the central government on the emperor's behalf, for both kinds of activity were established supports of his charisma. The need to combine science with ritual in this sphere is implied in an important memorial of Wang An-shih: because the monarch acts on behalf of the natural order, he can safeguard the empire and command the assent of the governed only through knowledge of nature. Ritually expressed awe of that order, without knowledge, is not enough (*Hsu tzu chih t'ung chien ch'ang pien*[67] ["Materials for the Sequel to the Comprehensive Mirror for Aid in Government"], presented to the throne 1168 [1881 ed.], 236:16b). Teraji has acutely pointed out that this is precisely the political justification for Shen's research, and the reason that traditional bureaucrat-scientists who were concerned mainly with maintaining ancient practices were not what Wang wanted.

Confucianism and Science. Recent attempts in both East and West to construct a historical sociology of Chinese science have in large part been built around a contrast between Confucianist and Taoist ideology. The values of the Confucian elite are often described as oriented toward stasis, hierarchy, bureaucracy, and bookishness. These characteristics are seen as perennially in tension with the appetite of socially marginal Taoists for novelty and change, their tendency to contemplate nature and the individual in it as a system, and their fascination with techniques, which kept them in touch with craftsmen and made them willing to engage in manual work themselves. It will no doubt be possible eventually to excavate a falsifiable, and thus historically testable, hypothesis from the mound of observations and speculations in this vein that have accumulated over the last half-century. For the moment, all one can do is point out how relentlessly unsociological this discussion has been.

Sociology is about groups of people. Doctrines are germane to sociology to the extent that their effect on what groups of people do, or on how they form, can be demonstrated. Generalizations about people who accept a certain doctrine have no sociological significance unless such people can be shown to act as a group, or at least to identify themselves as a group. The term "Confucian" is commonly used indifferently even by specialists to refer to a master of ceremonial, a professional teacher of Confucian doctrines, a philosopher who contributes to their elaboration, someone who attempts to live by Confucius' teachings, any member of the civil service, any member of the gentry regardless of ambition toward officialdom, or any conventional person (since it was conventional to quote Confucian doctrines in support of conventional behavior). A "Taoist" can be anyone from a hereditary priest ordained by the Heavenly Master to a retired bureaucrat of mildly unconventional tastes living on a city estate. Either group, by crite-

ria in common use, includes people who would make opposite choices on practically any issue. This being so, the proposition "Taoists were more friendly toward science and technology than Confucians" reduces to "Educated individuals who hold unconventional sentiments are more inclined to value activities unconventional for the educated than are educated people who hold conventional sentiments." That is probably not quite a tautologous statement, but it is sociologically vacuous and historically uninteresting.

Unease of this sort is probably the most obvious outcome of reflection on Shen Kua's career. By sentimental criteria he can be assigned to Confucianism, Taoism, or Buddhism, to suit the historian's proclivities.* He was a member of the elite, a responsible official, a writer of commentaries on several of the Confucian classics, and a user of the concepts of Confucius' successor Mencius to explore the depths of his own identity. He spoke well and knowledgeably of Buddhism. He practiced arcane disciplines, such as breath control, that he called Taoist.

As for his allegiances, Shen was prominently associated with a powerful but shifting group of background very generally similar to his own. Social stasis and institutional fixity were impediments to their aims in reshaping government. At the same time, the new balance of power toward which they strove was more authoritarian than the old. Underlying their common effort was an enormous disparity of motivation, from the well-intentioned (Shen) to the simultaneously manipulative and corrupt (Ts'ai Ch'ueh).

Were these Confucians more or less Confucian than their Confucian opponents? Wang An-shih earned enduring stature for his commentaries on the classics and his thought on canonic themes. His followers seem to have found inspiration in the

---

*A new element was introduced in 1974 in a book issued as part of the "anti-Confucius anti-Lin Piao" campaign against current ideological trends. Two of its essays (pp. 118–140) portray Shen as a legalist and a relentless opponent of Confucianism. "Legalist" is a term applied to writers on government and administration concentrated in the last centuries before the Christian era, especially those who argued that polity must be built on law and regulation, in contrast with the traditionalist faith of Confucius in rites and moral example. Although the arguments in this book are too distorted and too selective in their use of sources to be of interest as history, they become intelligible when "legalism" and "Confucianism" are understood as code words for the political convictions of two contending power groups in China today, as portrayed by spokesmen for one of the two. The book is *Ju-Fa tou-cheng yü wo kuo ku-tai k'o-hsueh chi-shu ti fa-chan*[68] ("The Struggle Between Confucianism and Legalism and the Development of Science and Technology in Our Country in Ancient Times"; Peking, 1974). The first printing was 31,000 copies.

classics as often as their enemies and as those who avoided taking a political position. This is not to say that everyone understood the Confucian teachings in the same way. The latter were not, from the viewpoint of intellectual history, a set of tightly linked ideas that set fixed limits on change; rather, they were a diverse and fragmentary collection of texts reinterpreted in every age. They were understood differently by every individual and group who looked to them for guidance when coping with problems of the moment.

The major commentaries, which attempted to define the meanings of Confucian teachings philologically, carried enormous authority; and governments (that of Wang An-shih, for instance) repeatedly attempted to make one interpretation orthodox. But the urge to pin down meanings was always in conflict with precisely what made these books classic. Their unlimited depth of significance depended more on what could be read into them than on precisely what their authors had meant them to say. That depth made them applicable to an infinity of human predicaments and social issues, unprecedented as well as perennial. Late neo-Confucian philosophers striking out in new directions demonstrated again and again how little the bounded intellectual horizons and social prejudices of the classics' authors objectively limited what may be drawn from them.

In other words, the Confucian canon had the influence it did because it provided a conceptual language that over the centuries educated people used and redefined in thinking out decisions and justifying action and inaction. The classics were often cited as a pattern for static social harmony and willing subordination in arguments against the New Policies. Shen, on the other hand, used them to argue for flexibility in social relations and for greater receptivity toward new possibilities than was usual in his time. Either as a social institution or as an ideology, Confucianism is too protean and thus too elusive a base for generalizations about the social foundations of science and techniques in China.

Institutions also changed constantly, but at least they were tangible entities. It is essential to consider them when tracing the social connections of science. Very little is known about how scientists were educated in the Northern Sung period; the obvious next step is a collective study of a great many biographies. In Shen's case we can see a pattern that certainly was not unique. He was, so far as we know, self-educated in astronomy, but with many learned associates to draw upon. In medicine

and breath control he probably received teaching in the traditional master-disciple relationship. Defined in the ages before printing made possible access to large collections of books, this relationship involved the student's memorizing the classics (more often one than several) that the teacher had mastered. This verbatim transmission of a text was supplemented by the teacher's oral explanations. The relation was deepened by ceremonial formality; the master took on the obligation to monitor the disciple's moral as well as intellectual growth, and the disciple accepted the responsibility of becoming a link in an endless chain of transmission. Schools were largely communities of masters and disciples. The scale of government-sponsored elementary schools in the provinces was small in Shen's youth, and began to compete with private academies only in the New Policies period. The two sorts together did not serve more than a small minority of youth.

By the eighth century there were small schools in the central government to train technical specialists. The masters, usually several in number, were functionaries, representing the departments of the bureau that the disciples were being trained to staff. The schools for medicine and astronomy could not lead to the top of government, but guaranteed steady advancement between minor sinecures. Very few of the great physicians or astronomers of traditional China began in these schools.

In the absence of evidence to the contrary, there is no reason to believe that Shen Kua ever attended a school of any sort, nor does that make him untypical. His early education by his mother, his training in medicine by an obscure physician and others who remain unknown, and his catch-as-catch-can studies of most other matters do not set him apart from his contemporaries. With no knowledge of particulars one cannot even guess how his personal style in technical work was formed. But to say that we are ignorant is not to say everything. The intimate relations of master and teacher and the isolation of the autodidact were themselves important institutions in the Northern Sung, institutions of a sort that did not discourage the emergence of unforeseen abilities in the small number of people who had the opportunity to be educated. Shen did not have to cope with a standard curriculum, for better or worse. If we are searching for the decisive curriculum of science and technology, it is necessary to look outside the realm of education.

The Civil Service and Science. One institution above all others influenced the mature ideas and attitudes of the ruling stratum: the bureaucracy. What can be said about its influence on science and technology in the life of Shen Kua? First, like every bureaucracy, it depended upon science and technology. It supported both sorts of activity on a scale otherwise unattainable, and unheard of in Europe at the time. Shen's curiosity, experience, and skills were so largely shaped by the civil service that it is absurd to ask what he would have become had he lived as a country gentleman or a Taoist priest. On the other hand, as elsewhere, technicians were certainly less important to the priorities of the state than administrators. The responsibility of the former was to provide the emperor and his administrators with wealth and other tools for the realization of policy. Specialist positions in science and engineering did not often serve as the beginnings of great careers.

By the New Policies period a career stream for economic experts had been established. It could assimilate people who combined technological acumen with fiscal skills, and carry them to the central councils of the empire. Shen's early technical feats were performed in general administrative posts, but his talents came to be valued and he rose quickly through formal and informal structures. It is not irrelevant that his directorship of the Astronomical Bureau was never more than a concurrent position. His attempt to combine an effective voice in the shaping of change with scientific contributions ended in personal disaster. He was ruined by men of his own faction, apparently for his political seriousness and naïveté. His astronomical work was rendered futile by subordinates because of his professional demands upon them. The bureaucracy was not neutral; it was a two-edged sword.

The civil service provided a form for great projects in science and technology, and practically monopolized certain disciplines, such as mathematical astronomy and observational astrology. Printing gave it the wherewithal to determine much of the content of elementary technical education (as in medicine and mathematics). A man of Wei P'u's genius, who had not had the opportunity to enter the bureaucracy by a regular route, was looked down upon and deliberately frustrated. Had Shen himself chosen to be a mere technician, his standing in the civil service would have been sufficient to protect him from personal attack. He would have had more time but less power. It would be rash indeed to speculate that his calendar reform would not have failed. But there is a larger issue.

Shen's mind was shaped for the civil service, as were those of his ancestors and peers, by an early education centered in moral philosophy and letters. He was a generalist. The development of depth in thought and work was left to his own proclivities. Only a superficial knowledge of technical matters was expected of him as a youth—a situation not very different from that of the British civil service generalist of some decades ago. Shen's growing responsibilities in fiscal affairs were the one aspect of his career that we can be sure encouraged him to draw coherence out of his varied experiences and studies. For this reason and others of which we are still ignorant, the great breadth of his knowledge was accompanied by enough depth to let him write monographs of some importance and, even through his brief jottings, to reshape Chinese knowledge of certain phenomena. But distraction is a theme that runs through his writings: promising studies laid aside; endless skirmishes to defend administratively measures that spoke for themselves technically and strategically; proposals negated by political setbacks. Regardless of his capacity for scientific depth and his willingness to find his way to it, the sheer busyness of his career drastically limited him. The works of his final leisure, however valuable, were all superficial in form. Was this the result of habit, of distance necessitated by disillusion, or of an aesthetic choice of the style appropriate for conversing with one's brush and ink slab in a silent garden? That remains for deeper study to decide.

What, then, was responsible for Shen Kua's scientific personality? We do not know the answers to all sorts of prior questions. The greatest difficulty comes in learning what these questions should be—in isolating the important issues, in coming to terms with the paucity and partiality of the sources, and in doing justice to a rich mind that, despite its absorption in a quest that transcends people and eras, partook fully of its time and place. It is not a matter of mechanically juxtaposing the usual factors: intelligence, subjectivity, philosophical convictions, social background, career, and other experiences. We have already seen how problematic the last three are. The most conspicuous traits of Shen's consciousness were open curiosity, mental independence (without the intolerance for intellectual disagreement that was a major limitation of Wang An-shih), sympathy for the unconventional, ambition, loyalty, and lack of snobbishness. The first four are considered marks of promise among technical people today, although one often meets great scientists who lack one or more of them. Were these characteristics in Shen due to heredity, to early experiences and education, or to influences encountered in adult life? This is an example of the sort of question that bars understanding; surely Shen was the sum of all three. The secret of his uniqueness will not yield itself to historical method, however powerful, unless it is applied with imagination, artifice, and awareness of the springs of human complexity.

Attitudes Toward Nature. When examined closely, attitudes toward nature in the late eleventh century become as elusive as attitudes toward Confucian humanism. The richly articulated philosophic vision of man in harmony with his physical surroundings was proving quite incapable of preventing the deforestation of northern China, which was virtually complete a generation after Shen's death. One cannot even speak of the defeat of that vision in an encounter of ideas, for no intellectual confrontation is recorded. What happened? The most obvious part of the answer is that the people who were chopping down the trees for charcoal were not the people who were seeking union with the ineffable cosmic Tao. Since that social difference was of very long standing, however, it does not explain the crescendo of exploitation in the Northern Sung. The coincidence of that fateful shift with the rise of large-scale industry and market networks is again obvious enough.* What needs to be explained, in fact, is the survival of the naturalist ideal until modern times.

The dilemma emerges clearly in the attitudes of Shen Kua and Wang An-shih toward nature. The orientations that pervade "Brush Talks" are in most respects the same as those of literati thinking about nature a millennium earlier. Philosophical pigeonholes are largely beside the point. Some "Confucians" thought about nature a great deal, and some, convinced that human society is the sole proper object of reflection and action, as little as possible; but their perspectives were, on the whole, the ones common to all Chinese who could read and write. Nature was an organismic system, its rhythms cyclic and governed by the inherent and concordant pattern uniting all phenomena.

---

*It was made obvious in a brilliant series of papers by Robert M. Hartwell: "A Revolution in the Chinese Iron and Coal Industries During the Northern Sung, 960–1126 A.D.," in *Journal of Asian Studies,* **21** (1962), 153–162; "Markets, Technology, and the Structure of Enterprise in the Development of the Eleventh-Century Chinese Iron and Steel Industry," in *Journal of Economic History,* **26** (1966), 29–58; "A Cycle of Economic Change in Imperial China: Coal and Iron in Northeast China, 750–1350," in *Journal of the Economic and Social History of the Orient,* **10** (1967), 102–159.

It comes as a shock to see Shen's definition of salt in a memorial: "Salt is a means to wealth, profit without end emerging from the sea" (*Hsu tzu chih t'ung chien ch'ang pien,* 280:17b–21b). This was not a slip, nor is it difficult to find philosophical precedents. Shen saw the fiscal function of the state (for which he briefly had supreme responsibility) as the provision of wealth from nature. His recommendations encouraged extractive industries and manufactures, and mobilization of the popular strength for land reclamation, in order to increase national wealth. In that respect he was faithful to the priorities of Wang An-shih. This is a far cry from the senior civil servant in China in the 1960's designing a campaign to convince farmers that nature is an enemy to be conquered, tamed, and remolded to social ends. But neither is it the pastoral ideal.

Why this discrepancy between nature as the ideal pattern to which man adjusts and nature as a (still beneficent) means of enrichment? Why does Shen seem not to be conscious of it as contradictory? These are questions on which the research has yet to be done. But Shen Kua's career, considered in the round, suggests a working hypothesis. Such notions as yin-yang, the Five Phases, and certain related ideas associated with the *Book of Changes* are often considered to have been hindrances to an autochthonous scientific revolution in traditional China. This is, of course, an elementary fallacy, comparable to considering the railroad, because it filled a need satisfactorily for so long, an impediment to the invention of the airplane. The old Chinese world view had much in common with cosmological ideas practically universal in Europe until the consummation of the Scientific Revolution—the four elements and so on—but that gave way soon enough. Historically speaking, Chinese organismic naturalism was not a rigid framework of ideas that barred change; rather, it was the only conceptual language available for thinking about nature and communicating one's thoughts, new or old, to others. Like any language, it imposed form and was itself malleable. Its historical possibilities were less a matter of original etymology or definition than of the ambiguity and extensibility that let people in later ages read new and often drastically changed import into old words. There is no true paradox in appeals to the harmony of man and nature by Shen and others before and after him who favored the exploitation of nature in the interests of the state. Although such activist thinkers stretched the old pattern of understanding, its fabric remained seamless. Their definition of what they wanted could not transcend it. Only the more desperate urgencies of another time could finally stretch it until it tore.

BIBLIOGRAPHY

I. ORIGINAL WORKS. The best attempt at a complete list of Shen's writings is in an appendix to Hu Tao-ching's standard ed. of "Brush Talks," *Meng ch'i pi t'an chiao cheng*[69] ("Brush Talks From Dream Brook, a Variorum Edition"), rev. ed., 2 vols. (Peking, 1960 [1st ed., Shanghai, 1956]), 1151–1156. There are forty titles, including some only mentioned in early writings about Shen. A portion of the list belongs to parts or earlier versions of larger writings. It has been suggested that the high rate of attrition was due to the campaign of Ts'ai Ching[70] (1046–1126), virtual dictator during the revival of the New Policies in the first quarter of the twelfth century, to obliterate the literary remains of his predecessors as well as their enemies. (See Ch'en Teng-yuan,[71] *Ku-chin tien-chi chü-san k'ao*[72] ["A Study of the Collection and Dispersion of Classical Writings in Ancient and Modern Times"; Shanghai, 1936], 54.) Six works are extant, although only two appear to be substantially unaltered, and considerable fragments of four others exist. Those of scientific interest are described below:

1. *Meng ch'i pi t'an*[21] ("Brush Talks From Dream Brook"), written over the greater part of Shen's retirement and possibly printed during his lifetime. It was first quoted in a book dated 1095. Originally it consisted of thirty *chüan* (a chapterlike division); but all extant versions, descended from a xylograph of 1166, follow an unknown prior editor's rearrangement into twenty-six *chüan*. The editor of the 1166 reprint noted a number of errors already in the text that he could not correct for want of variants. There are 587 jottings.

The practically definitive ed. of this book and its sequels (items 2 and 3 below), and in many other respects the foundation of future studies, is the Hu Tao-ching recension mentioned two paragraphs above. It includes a carefully collated and corrected text with variorum notes and modern (but occasionally faulty) punctuation, based on all important printed versions and on five previous sets of notes on variants. It also provides exegetic and explanatory notes and generous quotations from documents concerning Shen, from his other books, from the reflections of other early writers on his subject matter, and from modern Chinese (and to some extent Japanese and Western) scholarship. Appendixes include thirty-six additional jottings or fragments that have survived only in the writings or compilations of others; all known prefaces and colophons; notes on eds. by early bibliographers and collators; a chronological biography; a list of Shen's writings; and an index to names and variant

names of all persons mentioned in "Brush Talks" (a tool still very rare in Chinese publications). A 1-vol. version of the text with minimal apparatus was published by Hu as *Hsin chiao cheng Meng ch'i pi t'an*[73] ("Brush Talks From Dream Brook, Newly Edited"; Peking, 1957).

2. *Pu pi t'an*[74] ("Supplement to Brush Talks"), listed in most early bibliographies as two *chüan* but rearranged into three *chüan* with some alteration of order in the 1631 ed. Ninety-one jottings. Hu suggests that this and the next item were edited posthumously from Shen's notes. There is even stronger evidence for this hypothesis than he adduces, for some articles appear to be rejected drafts of jottings in "Brush Talks" (compare 588 with 437, 601 with 274).

3. *Hsu pi t'an*[75] ("Sequel to Brush Talks"), eleven jottings in one *chüan*, mostly on literature.

4. *Hsi-ning Feng-yuan li*[76] ("The Oblatory Epoch Astronomical System of the Splendid Peace Reign Period," 1075), lost, but listed in a Sung bibliography as seven *chüan*. This was the official report embodying Shen's calendar reform. It would have followed the usual arrangement, providing lists of constants and step-by-step instructions for computation, with tables as needed, so that the complete ephemerides could be calculated by someone with no knowledge of astronomy. Since a *Hsi-ning Feng-yuan li ching*[77] ("Canon of the Oblatory Epoch Astronomical System . . .") in three *chüan* is separately recorded, the remaining four *chüan* may have been, as in other instances, an official critique (*li i*[78]) outlining the observational basis of the system and reporting on tests of its accuracy. The Sung standard history also records a ready reckoner (*li ch'eng*[79]) in fourteen *chüan*, used to simplify calculations, and a detailed explanation of the mathematics with worked-out examples (*pei ts'ao*[80]) in six *chüan*. Surviving fragments of the basic document have been gathered by the great student of ancient astronomy Li Jui[81] (1765–1814) under the title *Pu hsiu Sung Feng-yuan shu*[82] ("Restoration of the Sung Oblatory Epoch Techniques"), printed in his *Li shih i shu*[83] ("Posthumous works of Mr. Li," 1823).

5. *Liang fang*[19] ("Good Prescriptions"), a work of ten or fifteen *chüan* compiled during Shen's retirement. In the Sung it was combined with a smaller medical miscellany by the greatest literary figure of Shen's time, Su Shih[84] (1036–1101), a moderate but influential opponent of the New Policies. The conflation is called *Su Shen nei-han liang fang*[85] ("Good Prescriptions by the Han-lin Academicians Su and Shen"), often referred to as *Su Shen liang fang*. The most broadly based text is that in the *Chih pu-tsu chai ts'ung-shu*[86] collection and modern reprints descended from it. One copy of an illustrated Ming ed. still exists. Shen's original compilation was lost sometime after 1500. There is some overlap between *chüan* 1 of *Su Shen liang fang* and jottings in *chüan* 26 of *Meng ch'i pi t'an*; see the comparison in Hu's *Chiao cheng*, pp. 880–882. A lost collection of prescriptions in twenty *chüan*, *Ling yuan fang*[87] ("Prescriptions From the Holy Garden"), is quoted in Sung treatises on mate-

ria medica. Hu has shown that it was written before *Liang fang* (*Meng ch'i pi t'an chiao cheng*, pp. 830–831).

6. *Wang huai lu*[20] ("Record of Longings Forgotten"), three *chüan*, compiled during Shen's retirement. It incorporates a lost book of observations on mountain living written (or at least begun) in Shen's youth and entitled *Huai shan lu*[88] ("Record of Longings for the Mountains"). His retirement to Dream Brook satisfied his early longings, hence the title of the later collection. It was lost soon after his death. The only well-known excerpts, in the *Shuo fu*[89] collection, are on implements useful to the well-born mountain dweller, but Hu Tao-ching in a recent study has shown that the book was correctly classified by early bibliographers as agricultural. See "Shen Kua ti nung-hsueh chu-tso *Meng ch'i Wang huai lu*"[90] ("Shen Kua's Agricultural Work . . ."), in *Wen shih*,[91] **3** (1963), 221–225. Hu's collection of all known fragments has not yet appeared.

7. *Ch'ang-hsing chi*[92] ("Collected Literary Works of [the Viscount of] Ch'ang-hsing"), originally forty-one *chüan*, almost certainly a posthumous compilation. Includes prose, poetry, and administrative documents prized for their language. By the time this work was reprinted in the Ming (*ca.* fifteenth century), only nineteen *chüan* of the Sung version remained. An additional three *chüan* were collected from other works and printed at the head of the recension in *Shen shih san hsien-sheng wen chi*[93] (1718). This is now the best ed. available. The collection includes important astronomical documents and a great deal of information on Shen's intellectual formation, in particular his commentary on Mencius (*Meng-tzu chieh*[94]) in *chüan* 23.

The only book in any Western language that translates more than a few examples of Shen's writings is Joseph Needham *et al.*, *Science and Civilisation in China*, 7 vols. projected (Cambridge, 1954–   ), particularly from vol. III on. The translations always occur in context, usually with fuller historical background than given in Chinese publications. Occasionally the English version is extremely free, as when "Meng ch'i" is translated "Dream Pool." Translations into modern Chinese are sprinkled through Chang Chia-chü,[95] *Shen Kua* (Shanghai, 1962). A complete Japanese trans. of "Brush Talks" and its sequels is an ongoing project of the History of Science Seminar, Research Institute for Humanistic Studies (Jimbun Kagaku Kenkyūsho[96]), Kyoto University. A representative selection of English translations will be included in a sourcebook of Chinese science being compiled by N. Sivin.

II. SECONDARY LITERATURE. There is no bibliography devoted to studies of Shen's life or work, but most primary and secondary sources in Chinese have been cited in Hu's ed. or in the footnotes to the biography of Shen by Chang Chia-chü (see above). The latter is the fullest and most accurate account of Shen's life, and pays attention to the whole range of his work. It is generally critical in method, but sometimes careless. Like

other recent Chinese accounts, it is extremely positivistic, patronizing toward "feudal" aspects of Shen's mentality, and inclined to exaggerate his sympathies toward the common people. A concise survey of Shen's life and positive contributions by a great historian of mathematics is Ch'ien Pao-tsung,[97] "Shen Kua," in Seminar in the History of the Natural Sciences, ed., *Chung-kuo ku-tai k'o-hsueh-chia*[98] ("Ancient Chinese Scientists"; Peking, 1959), 111–121. Another work of interest by Hu Tao-ching, overlapping to some extent the preface to his ed. of "Brush Talks," is "Shen Kua ti cheng-chih ch'ing-hsiang ho t'a tsai k'o-hsueh ch'eng-chiu-shang ti li-shih t'iao-chien"[99] ("Shen Kua's Political Tendencies and the Historical Conditions Bearing on His Scientific Accomplishments"), in Li Kuang-pi and Ch'ien Chün-yeh,[100] eds., *Chung-kuo li-shih jen-wu lun-chi*[101] ("Essays on Chinese Historical Figures"; Peking, 1957), 330–347. Its summary of scientific and technical accomplishments in the Northern Sung period from 960 to *ca.* 1100 is especially useful.

In addition to discursive biographical studies, Shen's life has been the subject of four chronologies (*nien-p'u*[102]), an old form in which individual events are simply listed year by year along with related data. The fullest in print (although obsolete in a number of respects) is Chang Yin-lin,[103] "Shen Kua pien nien shih chi"[104] ("A Chronicle of Shen Kua"), in *Ch'ing-hua hsueh-pao*,[105] **11** (1936), 323–358. That appended to the 2-vol. Hu Tao-ching ed. of "Brush Talks," 1141–1156, is especially handy because of its references to jottings and to sources cited in the book's notes. The most up-to-date and accurate chronology is the one at the end of Chang Chia-chü, *Shen Kua*, 235–259. Hu Tao-ching, in his colophon to the 1960 ed. of "Brush Talks," remarked that his own book-length chronology was in the press, but it has not yet appeared.

Yabuuchi Kiyoshi,[106] Japan's leading historian of science, has provided a characteristically reflective discussion of the historic circumstances of Shen's career in "Shin Katsu to sono gyōseki,"[107] ("Shen Kua and His Achievements"), in *Kagakushi kenkyū*,[108] **48** (1958), 1–6. The most stimulating contribution to the study of Shen in the past decade is Teraji Jun,[109] "Shin Katsu no shizen kenkyū to sono haikei"[110] ("The Natural Investigations of Shen Kua and Their Background"), in *Hiroshima daigaku bungakubu kiyō*,[111] **27**, no. 1 (1967), 99–121. Rejecting the prevalent tendency to prove Shen's greatness by citing anticipations of European science and technology, the author has made a fruitful and original effort to grasp the inner coherence of his thought and work. This article provided a point of departure for the first two sections of the "Conclusion" of the present article.

The first, and so far the only, European introduction to Shen's life is Donald Holzman, "Shen Kua and his *Meng-ch'i pi-t'an*," in *T'oung Pao* (Leiden), **46** (1958), 260–292, occasioned by the first publication of Hu's ed. of "Brush Talks." In addition to providing a critical and well-proportioned biographical sketch, Holzman has paid more attention to Shen's humanistic scholarship than has any other author discussed in this section. He also considers some of the evidence for Shen's position in the history of science, but reaches no conclusion. He tends to ask whether Shen's ideas are correct from today's point of view rather than what they contributed to better understanding of nature in the Sung. The most reliable and compendious introduction to the New Policies is James T. C. Liu, *Reform in Sung China. Wang An-shih (1021–1086) and His New Policies* (Cambridge, Mass., 1959). A full-length intellectual biography of Shen is under way by N. Sivin.

The first modern study of any aspect of Shen's interests, largely responsible for the attention paid him by Chinese educated in modern science, is Chu K'o-chen,[112] "Pei Sung Shen Kua tui-yü ti-hsüeh chih kung-hsien yü chi-shu"[113] ("Contributions to and Records Concerning the Earth Sciences by Shen Kua of the Northern Sung Period"), in *K'o-hsüeh*,[114] **11** (1926), 792–807. Chu's erudite and broadly conceived article has influenced much of the later writing on the subject. A great number of observations on Shen's scientific and technical ideas are distributed through Needham *et al.*, *Science and Civilisation in China*, as well as through the topical studies by leading Japanese specialists in Yabuuchi Kiyoshi, ed., *Sō Gen jidai no kagaku gijutsu shi*[115] ("History of Science and Technology in the Sung and Yuan Periods"; Kyoto, 1967).

There is no recent investigation in depth of Shen's astronomical activities, but a good technical description of what were traditionally considered his most important contributions is found in Juan Yuan,[116] *Ch'ou jen chuan*[117] ("Biographies of Mathematical Astronomers" [1799]; Shanghai, 1935), 20:238–243. Shen's most noteworthy mathematical problems have been studied in the various articles in Ch'ien Pao-tsung, ed., *Sung Yuan shu-hsüeh-shih lun-wen-chi*[118] ("Essays in the History of Mathematics in the Sung and Yuan Periods"; Peking, 1966). The considerable portion of "Brush Talks" devoted to music is evaluated and used in Rulan C. Pian, *Sonq [sic] Dynasty Musical Sources and Their Interpretation* (Cambridge, Mass., 1967), esp. 30–32. Shen's ideas concerning economic theory, the circulation of money, and similar topics have been related to traditions of thought on these subjects in an unpublished study by Robert M. Hartwell. A number of interesting ideas are found in Sakade Yoshinobu's[119] positivistic discussion of Shen's use of theory, "Shin Katsu no shizenkan ni tsuite"[120] ("On Shen Kua's Conception of Nature"), in *Tōhōgaku*,[121] **39** (1970), 74–87. Shen's remarks on ancient techniques are elucidated in Hsia Nai,[122] "Shen Kua ho k'ao-ku-hsüeh"[123] ("Shen Kua and Archaeology"), in *K'ao-ku*,[124] no. 5 (1974), 277–289, also in *K'ao-ku hsüeh-pao*,[125] no. 2 (1974), 1–14, with English summary, 15–17.

N. SIVIN

NOTES

1. 沈括	29. 五行	53. 羌	筆談
2. 錢塘	30. 氣	54. 木經	74. 補筆談
3. 潤州京口	31. 律呂	55. 寇宗奭	75. 續筆談
4. 沈周	32. 隙積	56. 本草衍義	76. 熙寧奉元曆
5. 許	33. 楊輝	57. 秋石	77. 曆經
6. 新法	34. 朱世傑	58. 宮下三郎	78. 曆議
7. 王安石	35. 一行	59. 漢薬秋石の薬	79. 立成
8. 寧國	36. 萬	史学的研究	80. 備草
9. 蕪湖	37. 樂律	60. 渡辺幸三	81. 李銳
10. 張蒭	38. 祖暅	61. 現存する中国	82. 補修宋奉元術
11. 衛朴	39. 奉元	近世までの五	83. 李氏遺書
12. 永安	40. 授時	藏六府図の概	84. 蘇軾
13. 平泉	41. 郭守敬	説	85. 蘇沈內翰良方
14. 蔡確	42. 郭廷以	62. 燕肅	86. 知不足齋叢書
15. 延州	43. 太平天国曆法	63. 蘇頌	87. 靈苑方
16. 經略安撫使	考訂	64. 渾儀議	88. 懷山錄
17. 開國子	44. 羅爾綱	65. 搏	89. 說郛
18. 夢溪	45. 天曆考及天曆	66. 微	90. 沈括的農學著
19. 良方	與陰陽曆日對	67. 續資治通鑑長編	作《夢溪忘懷錄》
20. 忘懷錄	照表	68. 儒法斗爭与我	91. 文史
21. 夢溪筆談	46. 謝莊	国古代科学技	92. 長興集
22. 象數	47. 顏眞卿	术的发展	93. 沈氏三先生文集
23. 技藝	48. 朱熹	69. 胡道靜, 校證	94. 孟子解
24. 辯證	49. 孫思恭	70. 蔡京	95. 張家駒
25. 異事	50. 礙	71. 陳登原	96. 人文科學研究所
26. 器用	50a. 石油	72. 古今典籍聚	97. 錢寶琮
27. 雜識	51. 畢昇	散考	98. 中國古代科學家
28. 藥議	52. 十百千	73. 新校證夢溪	99. 沈括的政治傾向

和他在科學成就	119. 坂出祥伸
上的歷史条件	120. 沈括の自然觀に
100. 李光璧, 錢君曄	ついて
101. 中國歷史人物	121. 東方學
論集	122. 夏鼐
102. 年譜	123. 沈括和考古学
103. 張蔭麟	124. 考古
104. 編年事輯	125. 学報
105. 清華學報	
106. 藪內清	
107. 沈括とその業績	
108. 科学史研究	
109. 寺地遵	
110. 沈括の自然研	
究とその背景	
111. 広島大学文学	
部紀要	
112. 竺可楨	
113. 北宋沈括對於	
地學之貢獻與	
紀述	
114. 科學	
115. 宋元時代の科	
学技術史	
116. 阮元	
117. 疇人傳	
118. 宋元数学史論	
文集	

SHERARD, WILLIAM (*b*. Bushby, Leicestershire, England, 27 February 1659; *d*. London, England, 11 August 1728), *botany*.

William Sherard was the eldest son of George and Mary Sheerwood, or Sherwood. He received his secondary education at Merchant Taylors' School and in 1677 was elected to St. John's College, Oxford, where he developed a lasting interest in botany and established a close friendship with Jacob Bobart. In December 1683 Sherard took the bachelor's degree in common law and was elected law fellow of St. John's College. Granted leave for foreign travel, he studied three years with Tournefort in Paris and spent the summer of 1688 studying with Paul Hermann in Leiden. He collected plants in the Swiss Alps, Geneva, Rome, Naples, Cornwall, and Jersey, supplying lists of plants that were published by John Ray in his *Synopsis methodica stirpium Britannicarum* (1690) and *Stirpium Europaearum . . . sylloge* (1694).

Between 1690 and 1702, Sherard, as tutor to various young noblemen, made two more tours of the Continent and received the degree of doctor of common law from St. John's College on 23 June 1694. During this period, Sherard began a revision of Gaspard Bauhin's *Pinax*. This work, which occupied the remainder of his life, was never finished; the manuscript is with his library at Oxford.

After a brief appointment as "Commissioner for the Sick and Wounded, and for the Exchange of Prisoners" in 1702, Sherard received an appointment by the Levant Company as consul at Smyrna in 1703. While there he collected plants in Greece and Anatolia, copied antiquarian artifacts, and collected coins. He returned to England in 1717 with a considerable fortune. In 1718 he was elected a fellow of the Royal Society. His brother, James Sherard (1666–1937), a physician and apothecary, who had amassed a fortune in business, retired in 1720 and bought a country house at Eltham in Kent, where he established one of the finest botanical gardens in England. Sherard himself made three trips to the Continent between 1721 and 1727, bringing Dillenius from Giessen in August 1721 to assist with the *Pinax*. He was particularly impressed with Dillenius' knowledge of cryptogams and thought that bringing him to Oxford would enhance the department and the progress of the science.

On his death in 1728, Sherard left to Oxford his herbarium of 12,000 to 14,000 specimens, still preserved intact, and his library of more than 600 volumes. In addition, he bequeathed £3,000 to establish the Sherardian chair of botany, naming Dillenius the first Sherardian professor. Unfortunately, his brother James Sherard, who acted as executor, delayed settlement of his estate until 1734.

Sherard's contemporaries considered him an excellent and knowledgeable botanist. Nevertheless, he wrote and published little during his lifetime. He became the friend and correspondent of nearly every major botanist of his day, and his letters, which occupy four volumes, reveal his generosity in gifts of specimens, seeds, living plants, books, and subscriptions. In 1695 he edited Paul Hermann's manuscript of *Paradisus Batavus* for his widow's benefit. He assisted Pier Antonio Micheli and Paolo Boccone with subscriptions for publications and contributions of plants. In 1721 Sherard prevailed upon Boerhaave to edit the lifework of the ailing Sébastien Vaillant and assisted in cataloguing specimens for it. Sherard's assistance is acknowledged by Bobart in his *Historia oxoniensis* and by Ray in his *Historia plantarum*. Specimens with his notations are found in the herbaria of Tournefort, Ray, Dillenius, Vaillant, and Sloane. Concerning Sherard's problem in completing the *Pinax*, Clokie stated, "His difficulty seems to have been to concentrate on his work instead of helping his friends. His generosity to his friends seems to have known no limit."

BIBLIOGRAPHY

I. ORIGINAL WORKS. Sherard's most important work is *Schola botanica, sive catalogus plantarum quas ab aliquot annis in Horto Regio Parisiensi studiosis indigitavit vir clarissimus Joseph Pitton Tournefort, D.M., ut et Pauli Hermanni P.P. Paradisi Batavi prodromus, in quo plantae rariores omnes, in Batavorum Hortis hactenus cultae, et plurimam partem à nemine antea descriptae, recensentur* (Amsterdam, 1689). This publication is a list of the plants found in the Royal Garden in Paris, arranged according to the Tournefort system with the prodromus for Paul Hermann's *Paradisus Batavus* that Sherard subsequently edited. It was published under the initials S. W. A., which have been interpreted by various authors to stand for Simone Wartono Anglo or some variation thereof. Gorham (p. 12) gives the name as Sherardus Wilhelmus Anglus. Regardless of the name for which the initials stand, all authorities agree that it is the work of William Sherard. (See also Jackson, pp. 136–137 and Clokie, pl 18.)

Other writings are "The Way of Making Several China Varnishes Sent From the Jesuits in China to the Great Duke of Tuscany, Communicated by Dr. William Sherard," in *Philosophical Transactions of the Royal*

Society, **22** (1700), 525 (Sherard probably gained the information while in Rome with his pupil, the Duke of Beaufort): "An Account of the Strange Effects of the Indian Varnish, Wrote by Dr. Joseph del Papa, Physician to the Cardinal de Medices, at the Desire of the Great Duke of Tuscany. Communicated by Dr. William Sherard," *ibid*. (1701), 947; "An Account of a New Island Raised Near Sant-Erini in the Archipelago; Being Part of a Letter to Mr. James Petiver, F.R.S. From Dr. W. Sherard, Consul at Smyrna . . .," *ibid*., **26** (1708), 67 (date of writing was 24 July 1707; the news came to Smyrna from the English consul at Milo); "An Account of the Poyson Wood Tree in New England. By the Honourable Paul Dudley, Esq., F.R.S. Communicated by John Chamberlain, Esq.," *ibid*., **31** (1721), 145: "A Farther Account of the Same Tree. By William Sherard, LL.D., R.S.S.," *ibid*., p. 147.

II. SECONDARY LITERATURE. A complete list of literature on Sherard and his work is in J. Britten and G. S. Boulger, *A Biographical Index of Deceased British and Irish Botanists,* 2nd ed. (London, 1931). See especially *Dictionary of National Biography,* XVIII, p. 67; G. Druce and S. Vines, *The Dillenian Herbaria* (Oxford, 1907); M. Epstein, *The Early History of the Levant Company* (New York, 1968); J. Green, *History of Botany* (New York, 1914); R. T. Günther, *Oxford Gardens* (Oxford, 1912); D. P. Micheli, *Targioni-Tozzetti* (Florence, 1858); R. Pulteney, *Pulteney's Sketches* (London, 1790); D. Richardson, ed., *Richardson Correspondence* (Yarmouth, 1835); and A. C. Wood, *A History of the Levant Company* (New York, 1964).

Sources to which specific reference has been made are H. N. Clokie, *An Account of the Herbaria of the Department of Botany in the University of Oxford* (Oxford, 1964); G. C. Gorham, *Memoirs of John and Thomas Martyn* (London, 1830); and B. D. Jackson, "A Sketch of the Life of William Sherard," in *Journal of Botany,* **12** (1874), 129–138.

CAROLYN D. TOROSIAN

SHERRINGTON, CHARLES SCOTT (*b*. London, England, 27 November 1857; *d*. Eastbourne, England, 4 March 1952), *neurophysiology.*

Sherrington was the son of Anne Brookes and James Norton Sherrington. After his father's death, in Sherrington's early childhood, his mother married Dr. Caleb Rose, Jr., of Ipswich. The Rose home, a gathering place for artists and scholars, helped to shape Sherrington's broad interests in science, philosophy, history, and poetry. After attending the Ipswich Grammar School from 1870 to 1875, Sherrington, encouraged by his stepfather, began medical training at St. Thomas's Hospital in London. In 1879 improved family finances enabled

him to enter Caius College, Cambridge, where he studied physiology in Sir Michael Foster's laboratory. He worked chiefly under John Newport Langley and Walter Gaskell, who imparted to him their dominant interest in how anatomical structure reflects, or is expressed in, physiological function. From 1884 to 1887 Sherrington completed his medical courses and did graduate study and research in Europe under Friedrich Goltz, Rudolph Virchow, and Robert Koch, gaining a superb grounding in physiology, morphology, histology, and pathology. In 1887 he was appointed a lecturer in systematic physiology at St. Thomas's, and from 1891 to 1895 he served as physician-superintendent of the Brown Institution, a London animal hospital. From 1895 to 1912 Sherrington held the Holt professorship of physiology at Liverpool and from 1913 to 1935 the Wayneflete chair of physiology at Oxford.

Sherrington married Ethel Wright of Suffolk, England, on 27 August 1891; their only child, Carr E. R. Sherrington, was born in 1897. He himself was a man of diverse interests. Outside of the laboratory his activities included sports (a feature event during his years in London was Sunday morning parachute jumping from the tower of St. Thomas's), work in many scientific organizations, academic affairs at Liverpool and Oxford, and studies for the government on such problems as industrial fatigue. After his retirement from Oxford, his pursuits included lecturing and writing, trusteeship of the British Museum, and service as governor of the Ipswich School and Ipswich town adviser on museums and health services. In a career that spanned sixty-nine years, Sherrington is remembered mainly for his scientific contributions but he was also the teacher who prepared *Mammalian Physiology. A Course of Practical Exercises* (1919), the poet who wrote *The Assaying of Brabantius* (1925), and the philosopher and historian whose writings included *Man on His Nature* (1941) and *The Endeavour of Jean Fernel* (1946). His numerous honors included the presidency of the Royal Society of London (1920–1925), Knight Grand Cross of the British Empire (1922), Order of Merit (1924), and the Nobel Prize for physiology or medicine (1932); at his death he was an honorary fellow, member, or associate of more than forty academies and had received honorary degrees from twenty-two universities.

Sherrington's classic investigations dealt primarily with reflex motor behavior in vertebrates, detailing the nature of muscle management at the spinal level. The data, terms, and concepts that he introduced have become such a fundamental part of the neurosciences that it is perhaps not surprising their authorship is often forgotten: such terms as proprioceptive, nociceptive, recruitment, fractionation, occlusion, myotatic, neuron pool, motoneuron, and synapse, and such concepts as the final common path, the motor unit, the neuron threshold, central excitatory and inhibitory states, proprioception, reciprocal innervation, and the integrative action of the nervous system.

Sherrington's scientific work may be broadly divided into two phases: from the 1880's to the publication of *The Integrative Action of the Nervous System* in 1906, and from 1906 to his receipt of the Nobel Prize in 1932. When he began his work, in the 1880's, the data and theories about the structure and function of the nervous system that had developed over the centuries were at best piecemeal. Controversy was rampant in almost every area and, apart from some textbook presentations, few attempts had been made to correlate structural and functional data within a given field of study, much less to interrelate the various separate channels of work on the nervous system.

The study of reflex actions, for example, went on almost independently of work on such problems as the structure and interconnection of nerve cells, the differentiation of the sensory and motor functions of the spinal cord, and the determination of brain structure and function. A fairly extensive fund of techniques, data, and theories about reflexes was available, but the field of reflex physiology was greatly in need of reorganization. Techniques were generally imprecise; sounder anatomical knowledge was needed; above all, experimentally based concepts—with which to interpret the known facts of reflex action and evaluate their role in the animal economy—were singularly lacking.

Sherrington decided to concentrate on neurophysiology rather than on pathology, his initial interest, when he returned to England in 1887 from Koch's laboratory in Berlin. He credited Gaskell with directing his attention from his first neurophysiological investigations into brain–spinal cord connections to the physiology of the spinal cord. Sherrington began by studying the little-understood phenomenon of the knee jerk, reporting the results of his first analyses (1891, 1892) of the muscles and nerves upon which the jerk depends. In these studies, however, he found that he could not deal satisfactorily with functional problems in the face of a major gap in neuroanatomical knowledge—the distribution of the sensory and motor fibers of the spinal cord. For a decade of what

seemed to him often "boring" and "pedestrian" research, Sherrington therefore surveyed the field of distribution of each spinal root, creating the anatomical foundation necessary for physiological work. His three major contributions to neuroanatomy were mapping motor pathways, chiefly those in the lumbosacral plexus (1892), establishing the existence of sensory nerves in muscles (1894), and tracing the cutaneous distribution of the posterior spinal roots (1894, 1898).

Concomitant with his anatomical work, and often deriving from it, was a profusion of ideas and observations on the reflex functions of the spinal cord. The two major, intertwined lines of these researches were the analyses of antagonistic muscle action and of larger pieces of reflex "machinery" such as the extension, flexion, and scratch reflexes of the hind limb. Out of these studies emerged Sherrington's conviction that the "main secret of nervous co-ordination . . . lies in the compounding of reflexes," a compounding built up by the play of reflex arcs about their "common paths." Behind this play lie the key processes of inhibitory and excitatory actions at the junctional regions between nerve cells—the synapses.

Like other investigators of the nervous system, Sherrington faced the task of devising techniques for reducing and controlling the complexity of the nervous system to the point where meaningful data could be obtained. His first steps were to concentrate upon the reflex functions of the cord rather than on the more complex field of the brain; to choose an appropriate experimental animal, the monkey; and to make parallel control and comparison experiments on lower forms to establish the necessary points of anatomical knowledge.

Sherrington's basic method was to study simple motor acts which could be made to occur in isolation, correlating his exacting analyses of input-output relations of reflex responses with anatomical and histological data. He used two types of experimental preparations: the classic spinal animal and the decerebrate animal. The effects of decerebration had been partially described by many earlier workers, such as Magendie, Bernard, and Flourens, but it was Sherrington who named decerebrate rigidity and, in a fundamental paper of 1898 and later publications, established it as a phenomenon in its own right and as a major tool for examining the reflex functions of the spinal cord, particularly the nature of inhibition.

The last decades of the nineteenth century saw the rise and fall of numerous theories about the nature of central inhibition, such as the controversial and influential center theory advanced by Johann Setchenov in 1863. It was against the background of these theories and the emergence of the neuron theory that Sherrington began to work out his ideas on the roles of inhibition and excitation in motor behavior and on the reflex nature of inhibition itself. The most important theme in Sherrington's functional researches up to 1900, for both his understanding of the operation of spinal reflexes per se and his comprehension of the mechanisms of nervous coordination, was his analysis of the reciprocal innervation of antagonistic muscles. It was the principle of reciprocal innervation, as Lord Adrian commented, "which opened the way to the further advance from the simple to the complex. It was the clue to the whole system of traffic control in the spinal cord and throughout the central pathways."[1]

The results of Sherrington's exhaustive study of reciprocal innervation, which stemmed from his observations on the knee jerk, are found chiefly in his fourteen classic "Notes" in the *Proceedings of the Royal Society* from 1893 to 1909. He first used the term "reciprocal innervation" in the title of the third "Note," read before the Royal Society on 21 January 1897; the term, he explained, denoted the "particular form of correlation" in which one muscle of an antagonistic couple is relaxed as its mechanical opponent actively contracts. Four months later, as the Royal Society's Croonian lecturer, he proposed his classic definition of reciprocal innervation as that form of coordination in which "inhibito-motor spinal reflexes occur quite habitually and concurrently with many of the excito-motor."

Another critical event of 1897 was Sherrington's introduction of the term and concept of synapse in Michael Foster's *Textbook of Physiology*. "So far as our present knowledge goes we are led to think that the tip of a twig of the [axon's] arborescence is not continuous with but merely in contact with the substance of the dendrite or cell body on which it impinges. Such a connection of one nerve-cell with another might be called a synapsis."

Sherrington's statement reflects the impact upon ideas of the structural and functional interrelations of the nervous system created by the neuron theory, introduced in 1889 by Ramón y Cajal. Prior to Ramón y Cajal's researches the dominant neurohistological view was the reticular theory, which held that nerve impulses are transmitted throughout the body over a continuous network or reticulum of anastomosing nerve processes. Ramón y Cajal's preparations showed that definitely limited conduction paths exist in the gray matter and that

nerve impulses are somehow transmitted by contact or contiguity, not by continuity. The significance of Sherrington's choice of the neuron theory and his coining of synapse has been well stated by Ragnar Granit: "When Sherrington decided in favor of nerve-cell contacts he refashioned thinking in this field along lines that determined its future course for all time and also tied it to the newly born science of electrophysiology. . . . Only a contact theory could bridge the gap between reflex transmission and electrophysiology; such is the power of a fundamental concept like the synapse."[2]

Between 1897 and 1900 Sherrington formulated a comprehensive picture of the motor functions of the spinal cord. His conception of these functions, of the rules that govern them, their mechanisms of control, and their role in the unitary functioning of the nervous system, were set forth in his Croonian and Marshall Hall lectures and in E. A. Schäfer's *Text Book of Physiology*. By 1900 Sherrington had assembled the major ingredients of the integrative action concept. From a study of the seemingly simple anatomy and physiology of the knee jerk he had become engaged in a series of broader problems, such as the nature and mechanisms of antagonistic muscle action, the production and maintenance of decerebrate rigidity, and the nature and significance of spinal shock. From these and other researches he developed a number of basic functional principles: reciprocal innervation; interaction between higher and lower level centers of motor control; and muscular sense, inhibition, and facilitation as the three key mechanisms of muscle management at the spinal level. Recognizing the import of the neuron theory, he had perceived that many of the characteristic properties of reflex pathways might be explicable by the events at the synapse.

The next phase of his work was to determine how reflex arcs combine to form successively larger and more complex reflex patterns. Sherrington's analysis of the scratch and other hind limb reflexes confirmed his earlier findings: the same functional principles obtain in both the simplest and most complex reflex actions. And, because of their very complexity, the hind limb reflexes further illuminated a wide range of phenomena underlying motor coordination, such as inhibition, facilitation, spinal induction, and the events at the synapse. In his definitive paper on the scratch reflex ("Observations on the Scratch Reflex in the Spinal Dog," *Journal of Physiology*, **34** [1906], 1–50), the properties of reflexes as found in the isolated spinal cord were described more minutely and fully than ever before in the annals of neurophysiology.

In 1904 Sherrington enunciated the essentials of the integrative action concept to the Physiological Section of the British Association for the Advancement of Science in a presidential address entitled "The Correlation of Reflexes and the Principle of the Common Path." It was his most important published conceptual statement before *The Integrative Action of the Nervous System* (1906). The main theme was the reflex chain of the synaptic system: the receptive neuron forms a private path into the brain or cord; within the "great central organ" many private paths converge at an internuncial neuron to form a public or common path which runs to the motor neuron; from the motor neuron, impulses travel over a final common path to converge upon the effector organ. "The singleness of action from moment to moment," assured by the principle of the common path, Sherrington declared, "is a keystone in the construction of the individual whose unity it is the specific office of the nervous system to perfect."

The immediate fruitfulness of the common path principle can be seen in Sherrington's papers of 1905 and 1906, in which he extended his analysis of the mechanisms controlling reflex actions. Working with the hind limb reflexes, he now focused on spinal induction, inhibition, and his fundamental concept of the proprioceptive system.

Sherrington journeyed to the United States to deliver ten lectures on "Integrative Action by the Nervous System" as the second Silliman Memorial Lecturer at Yale University in April 1904. His oral delivery, complex and difficult to follow even for those familiar with his work, left the majority of his steadily dwindling audience less than enthusiastic; but publication of the lectures in 1906 was recognized as an epochal event in the development of neurophysiology. The lasting value of *The Integrative Action of the Nervous System* for students of neurophysiology is reflected in the numerous reviews of its fifth reprinting, in 1947. F. M. R. Walshe, writing in the *British Medical Journal,* asserted:

> I have called it "an imperishable work," for it is one of those works, rare in science, the permanent value of which is unquestionable, and I believe that future generations of physiologists will so acclaim it. In physiology, it holds a position similar to that of Newton's *Principia* in physics. . . . For it is more than an orderly record of precise observations: it is a product of sustained thought upon what is essential-

ly—though only his genius revealed it as such—a single problem—namely, the mode of nervous action.[3]

The Integrative Action consists, in essence, of a synthesis of Sherrington's own researches and concepts and a chronicle of relevant work by other investigators. The structure and major concepts of the book may be divided into six parts: (1) Sherrington's definition of his topic in the first seven and one-half pages of lecture I; (2) lectures I–III, treating of coordination in the simple reflex; (3) lectures IV–VI, concerned with coordination between reflexes—their interaction and compounding by simultaneous and successive combination; (4) lecture VII, reflexes as adapted reactions; (5) lectures VIII–IX, the brain's role in integrative motor action; and (6) lecture X, sensual fusion. Sherrington's written analysis of the integrative action of the nervous system followed basically the same pattern as his research work. He began by delineating the characteristics of the simple reflex, the smallest functional unit of integrative action as seen in the spinal animal, and then built toward the complex patterns of reflex muscle management, guided by the brain, in the intact animal.

For a person unfamiliar with Sherrington's work, the first pages of lecture I provide a succinct statement of the meaning and scope of the concept of integrative action. In them he laid down three central propositions: (1) the nervous system is one, if not the only, major integrating agent in complex multicellular organisms; (2) the reflex is the unit reaction in nervous integration; (3) there are two grades of reflex coordination, that effected by the simple reflex and that effected by the simultaneous and successive combination of reflexes. Working from these premises he proceeded to demonstrate in meticulous detail the basic theme of the integrative action concept: "The nervous synthesis of an individual from what without it were a mere aggregation of commensal organs resolves itself into coordination by reflex action."

Sherrington continued his active life as researcher, teacher, writer, and prominent member of the international scientific community in the years after 1906, moving from Liverpool to Oxford in 1913. When his research was curtailed by World War I, Sherrington devoted himself to government war work with his customary drive and efficiency. Few episodes better illustrate his character than his activities during the summer of 1915, when he disappeared from home on a bicycle, presumably for a holiday, leaving no address. His whereabouts were finally revealed when he needed to replace a lost collar stud—having decided to study industrial fatigue *in situ*, he was working incognito as an unskilled workman at the Vickers-Maxim shell factory in Birmingham.

At the end of the war Sherrington resumed his extensive research program, and until he was almost seventy-five he performed at least one long experiment every week and spent many hours analyzing data. When he retired in 1935, the "Sherrington school" at Oxford had issued a series of influential papers on such topics as afterdischarge, summation, recruitment, postural contraction, and the motor unit, to illuminate the finer details of the reflex activity of the spinal cord. Two of Sherrington's last comprehensive reviews of muscle management at the spinal level, summarizing and synthesizing the work of the Oxford years, are his 1931 Hughlings Jackson lecture, "Quantitative Management of Contraction in Lowest Level Coordination," and chapter seven of *Reflex Activity of the Spinal Cord* (1932). His coauthors for the later work exemplify the continuing prominence of the Sherrington school in modern neurophysiology: R. S. Creed, D. Denny-Brown, J. C. Eccles, and E. G. T. Liddell.

Sherrington's tenure at Oxford may be characterized as a period of quantitation, testing and refining the concepts set forth in *The Integrative Action*. New techniques, in particular the development of isometric myography, made possible the accurate measurement of muscle tensions in various preparations. Sherrington could now measure and balance excitatory and inhibitory processes against each other, learning virtually everything about reflexes that was possible without the aid of the more sophisticated electronic methods that were developed as his career drew to a close.

Three fundamental publications of the Oxford period were Sherrington's papers on the stretch reflex (1924), central excitatory and inhibitory states (1925), and the motor unit (1930). These papers presented both the culmination of issues raised by his earlier work and the basis for many subsequent major advances in unraveling the operations of the nervous system. Sherrington and Liddell's analysis of the stretch reflex, the basic reflex used in standing, grew out of Sherrington's studies in the 1890's on the response of the "muscular sense organs" to stretching and contraction. By 1905 he had observed and described the stretch reflex, although its naming and definition awaited his and Liddell's later work. In their 1924 and 1925 papers, they reported the results of using individual isolated knee extensor muscles in a decerebrate preparation, with the free ends of the muscle attached to an isometric myograph. These researches, in turn, led to the definition of the nature of autogenetic excitation and inhibition and to our present understanding of muscle tonus, attitude, and posture.

Sherrington's work on central excitatory and inhibitory states and the motor unit were the culmination, for him, of the research he had begun forty years earlier on the functional anatomy of sensory and motor pathways, and led to the studies of the finer details of synaptic conduction, which now fill volumes.

After 1906 one of the chief problems occupying Sherrington's attention was inhibition. By 1925, in "Remarks on Some Aspects of Reflex Inhibition," he was ready to state his concept of central excitatory and inhibitory states and, as he had first suggested in 1908, of excitation and inhibition interacting algebraically at the synapse. In the 1925 paper, Sherrington marshaled the evidence developed in over twenty-five years of experiments, reasoning back from the phenomena of muscle contraction, as seen principally in the crossed extensor and ipsilateral flexor reflexes, to the events at the synapse. Inhibition, he demonstrated, is a distinct phenomenon although it is almost identical in its properties to excitation and obeys the same laws. The further testing and development of his ideas on central excitation and inhibition occupied much of Sherrington's time during his last decade of research. His concept of central excitatory and inhibitory states has been confirmed, expanded, and reformulated in terms of postsynaptic excitatory and inhibitory potentials by Sir John Eccles and others, using such techniques as intracellular recordings from motoneurons.

The concept of the motor unit, Sherrington's last major contribution to neurophysiology, can be seen as a more sophisticated, experimentally based development of the principle of the common path. The motor unit, in simple terms, is a spinal motoneuron (or motor cell in the ventral horn of the spinal cord) which, by the branching of its axon, controls and coordinates the actions of more than 100 muscle fibers. Years of exacting study by Sherrington and his colleagues went into the paper on the motor unit which he published with Eccles in 1930: the writing of the paper itself occupied Sherrington for over two years. A glimpse of Sherrington the scientist, at seventy-two, working on his last major paper, is offered by John Fulton's diary entry for 2 April 1930:[4]

> It is remarkable to see how at this time of his life he is beginning to correlate all the various aspects of his own work; structure of fibers, reflexes, series of central excitations, etc., etc., into a beautifully synthesized body of knowledge. For him the days simply weren't long enough, and there are all manner of things that need investigation. The rest of the world in his eyes is a little slow because it does not see all these things staring it in the face.

Sherrington received the Nobel Prize in 1932 specifically for his isolation and functional analysis of the motor unit. Somewhat ironically, the man who developed the single-unit concept never used the then newly available electrical recording techniques, but Sherrington can scarcely be held at fault for not making such studies when he was in his seventies. Sherrington shared the Nobel award with Edgar Douglas Adrian, Foulerton professor of physiology at Cambridge, for his analysis of the frequency discharge of single units. Both men had long sought to define the properties of the nerve cell as the functional unit of the central nervous system—Adrian through investigating the afferent input from sense organs, Sherrington the nature of motor input—and Adrian's work during the 1920's probably had the most immediate influence on the direction and development of Sherrington's ideas. To many, particularly those who had worked with him over the years, Sherrington's award was long overdue—a circumstance perhaps partly explained by the Nobel Committee's difficulties in citing a specific discovery on which to base the prize.

The work noted above is a small, but highly important, portion of the experiments and ideas generated by Sherrington and his pupils and colleagues during his twenty-three years at Oxford. It would be a difficult task indeed to select the most important single achievement from among the vast program of researches in which Sherrington was engaged from the 1880's to his retirement in 1935: brain-cord connections and spinal degenerations; the distribution of motor and sensory roots; the proprioceptive system; the characteristics of synaptic reflex arc conduction; reciprocal innervation and the nature of central inhibition; the reflex patterns of the spinal, decerebrate, and intact animal; and the nature of supraspinal control as seen in the functional organization of the motor cortex. Perhaps most significant are his inseparable analysis of reciprocal innervation and inhibition, his studies

of muscle tonus (posture), and his conceptual definition of the nature of synaptic action in effecting the unitary or integrated behavior of nerve cells.

In more general terms, by examining the antecedents to, and tracing the course and content of, Sherrington's researches, one sees how strikingly the new outweighed the old in his work: in instance after instance Sherrington himself "made the time ripe" for answering a given problem. He pioneered new techniques and apparatus, such as the method of successive degenerations, surgical procedures for mammalian decerebration, and the use of the myograph for reflex recordings, and established new methodological canons with his meticulously designed and executed experiments. Second, he marshaled extant facts and theories and added a host of new ones about each topic he studied, emphasizing particularly the correlation of structural and functional data.

The scope of his specific contribution clearly marks Sherrington as a major figure in the history of the neurosciences. The greater significance of his work, however, lies in his "synthetic attitude," his perception of the interrelatedness of his varied researches. One of his goals was to explain the functional unity of motor behavior, primarily by interpreting central nervous system function in histological terms. From the content of his 1897 Croonian lecture on the mammalian spinal cord as an organ of reflex action, it appears that he was moving toward the concept of integrative action by that date.

Sherrington's work is resolvable into a threefold study of reflex actions, using the nerve cell and its interconnections as his basic analytical unit: their gross and histological architecture, the spinal and higher level mechanisms controlling them, and their functions in vertebrate motor behavior. Although his most fundamental experiments were performed around the turn of the century, it was the work during the 1920's at Oxford which has shaped many facets of neurophysiological research up to the present.

Sherrington's name remains linked most closely, however, with his integrative action concept, although the idea of nervous integration did not originate with him. The fact of motor coordination and the participation of the nervous system in its operation had been recognized since antiquity, and prototypes of the integrative action concept may be found from the ancient idea of "sympathy" to Flourens's studies of how specific brain regions affect an animal's functional unity. The uniqueness and significance of Sherrington's work, epitomized by the integrative action concept, lies in the fact that it provided the first comprehensive, experimentally documented explanation of how the nervous system, through the unit mechanism of reflex action, produces an integrated or coordinated motor organism. It was this watershed achievement, synthesizing the work of one era and opening a new one, that led Sherrington's peers to designate him as "the main architect of the nervous system," "the supreme philosopher of the nervous system," "the author of the *Principia* of physiology," and the "man who almost singlehandedly crystallized the special field of neurophysiology."

Sherrington's work was motivated, in large measure, by a desire to explain organized, purposeful behavior, and he looked upon reflexes as very simple items of such behavior. Thus, in the Silliman lectures and in subsequent writings he voiced distinct reservations about the ability of his analysis of reflex action to account for the functional solidarity of vertebrates, especially among primate forms. These reservations stemmed, in part, from the realization that his work left unanswered many questions about the nature of reflex motor control that would be resolved by others using more sophisticated techniques and types of experiments.

His other reservations about his work stemmed from his belief that reflex action was only a small part of the integration of higher vertebrates. Sherrington himself might have written the words of the sixteenth-century physician Jean Fernel, quoted in *Man on His Nature*: " . . . our task, now that we have dealt with the excellent structure of the body, cannot stop there, because man is a body and a mind together." As the quotation suggests, this aspect of Sherrington's self-appraisal is intimately related to his position on the question of the relation of mind and body. In this realm Sherrington was a dualist. For Sherrington man is the product of natural forces, yet he encompasses a territory which neurophysiology cannot reach—the realm of mind and thought. One senses, however, that Sherrington was not a dualist by philosophical choice but, rather, felt constrained to adopt the position because the sciences of his day offered no evidence or means of bridging the gap between mind and brain.

In the foreword to the 1947 reissue of *The Integrative Action*, Sherrington summarized his years of study and thought about the roles and relations of body and mind in animal integration, distinguishing three systems or levels of integrative action. At the first level, physicochemical processes weld the body's organs into a "unified machine." This welding is exemplified by the integrative action of the nervous system, of which the unit mechanism, as Sherrington had shown, is reflex action.

Reflex action vanished completely as a mechanism in Sherrington's second system of integrative action, "the field of the psyche." At this level, he held, "the physical creates from psychical data a percipient, thinking, and endeavouring individual." For Sherrington "the physical is never anything but physical, or the psychical anything but psychical," yet the two systems "are largely complemental and life brings them co-operatively together at innumerable points." This mind-body liaison was, to Sherrington, the third and highest level of integrative action. "In all of those types of organisms in which the physical and psychical coexist, each of the two achieves its aim only by reason of a *contact utile* between them. And this liaison can rank as the final and supreme integration completing the individual."

To Sherrington, called the "supreme philosopher of the nervous system," the most baffling and challenging problem for both scientists and philosophers was how the mind-body liaison is effected. In 1947, he commented succinctly that the issue "remains where Aristotle left it 2,000 years ago." While Sherrington could not explain a dualistic interaction, neither could he find any valid basis for reducing mind to a manifestation of physical energy. Thus, as he explained in the closing sentence of the foreword, dualism seemed to be as reasonable an assumption as monism. "That our being should consist of *two* fundamental entities offers I suppose no greater inherent probability than that it should rest on one only."

Near the end of his life Sherrington made one of his final and most positive statements about the levels of integrative action that produce the totality of an animal such as man. During a conversation with Sir Russell Brain, he said "the reflex was a very useful idea, but it has served its purpose. What the reflex does is so banal. You don't think that what we are doing now is reflex, do you? No, no, no."[5]

Although Sherrington's dualistic philosophy was disturbing to many of his scientific colleagues, it did not diminish their estimate of his contributions to neurophysiology. Of the scores of tributes which marked his death on 4 March 1952, none more simply expressed the sentiments of those who knew him than the words of Henry Viets: "A great and good man has died. . . . We stand on mighty shoulders."[6]

NOTES

1. E. D. Adrian, "The Analysis of the Nervous System: Sherrington Memorial Lecture," in *Proceedings of the Royal Society of Medicine,* **50** (1957), 993.
2. Ragnar Granit, *Charles Scott Sherrington,* p. 43.
3. F. M. R. Walshe, "A Foundation of Neurology. *The Integrative Action of the Nervous System,*" in *British Medical Journal* (1947), 2, 823.
4. John F. Fulton Papers, Historical Library, Yale University School of Medicine.
5. Quoted in G. E. W. Wolstenholme and C. M. O'Connor, eds., *Ciba Foundation Symposium on the Neurological Bases of Behaviour, in Commemoration of Sir Charles Scott Sherrington* (Boston, 1948), p. 24.
6. Henry Viets, "Charles Scott Sherrington, 1857–1952," in *New England Journal of Medicine,* **246** (1952), 981.

BIBLIOGRAPHY

I. ORIGINAL WORKS. A complete Sherrington bibliography is in Fulton (1952); an extensive although not complete listing is in Swazey (1969). Both are cited below. For those wishing to explore the development of Sherrington's scientific ideas and his nonscientific works, the following are suggested: *The Central Nervous System,* vol. III of Michael Foster, *A Textbook of Physiology,* 7th ed. (London, 1897); "The Mammalian Spinal Cord as an Organ of Reflex Action. Croonian Lecture," in *Proceedings of the Royal Society,* **61** (1897) 220–221, an abstract that was printed in full as sec. 4 of Sherrington's "Experiments in Examination of the Peripheral Distribution of the Fibres of the Posterior Roots of Some Spinal Nerves (II)," in *Philosophical Transactions of the Royal Society,* **190B** (1898), 45–186; "Decerebrate Rigidity, and Reflex Co-ordination of Movements," in *Journal of Physiology,* **22** (1898), 319–332; "On the Spinal Animal (The Marshall Hall Lecture)," in *Medico-Chirurgical Transactions,* **82** (1899), 449–477; "The Spinal Cord," "The Parts of the Brain Below the Cerebral Cortex," "Cutaneous Sensations," and "The Muscular Sense," in E. A. Schäfer, ed., *Text Book of Physiology,* II (Edinburgh, 1900), 783–1025; "The Correlation of Reflexes and the Principle of the Common Path," in *Report of the British Association for the Advancement of Science,* **74** (1904), 1–14; *The Integrative Action of the Nervous System* (New Haven, 1906); "Reflex Inhibition as a Factor in the Co-ordination of Movements and Postures," in *Quarterly Journal of Experimental Physiology,* **6** (1913), 251–310; "Some Aspects of Animal Mechanism. Presidential Address, British Association for the Advancement of Science," in *Report of the British Association for the Advancement of Science* (1922), 1–15; "Reflexes in Response to Stretch (Myotatic Reflexes)," in *Proceedings of the Royal Society,* **86B** (1924), 212–242, written with E. G. T. Liddell; *The Assaying of Brabantius and Other Verses* (Oxford, 1925); "Remarks on Some Aspects of Reflex Inhibition," in *Proceedings of the Royal Society,* **97B** (1925), 519–545; "Numbers and Contraction-values of Individual Motor-units Examined in Some Muscles of the Limb," *ibid.,* **106B** (1930), 326–357, written with J. C. Eccles; *Reflex Activity of the Spinal Cord* (Oxford, 1932), written with R. S. Creed *et al.; Inhibition as a Co-ordinative Factor* (Stockholm, 1932), the Nobel lecture delivered at Stockholm, 12 Dec. 1932; *The Brain and Its Mechanism* (Cambridge, 1933); *Man on His Nature* (Cambridge, 1941), the Gifford lectures, Edinburgh, 1937–1938; *The Endeavour of Jean Fernel* (Cambridge, 1946); and "Marginalia," in E. A. Underwood, ed., *Science, Medicine and History,* II (Oxford, 1954), 545–553.

II. SECONDARY LITERATURE. See Edgar D. Adrian, "The Analysis of the Nervous System: Sherrington Memorial Lecture," in *Proceedings of the Royal Society of Medicine,* **50** (1957), 991–998; Mary Brazier, "The Historical Development of Neurophysiology," in John Field, H. W. Magoun, and V. E. Hall, eds., *Handbook of Physiology. Section I: Neurophysiology* (Washington, D.C., 1959): Georges Canguilhem, *La formation du concept de réflexe au XVIIᵉ et XVIIIᵉ siècles* (Paris, 1955); Lord Cohen of Birkenhead, *Sherrington: Physiologist, Philosopher, Poet* (Liverpool, 1958), vol. IV of the University of Liverpool Sherrington Lectures; Derek Denny-Brown, "The Sherrington School of Physiology," in *Journal of Neurophysiology,* **20** (1957), 543–548; Franklin Fearing, *Reflex Action: A Study in the History of Physiological Psychology* (Baltimore, 1930; repr. New York, 1964); John F. Fulton, "Sir Charles Scott Sherrington, O. M.," in *Journal of Neurophysiology,* **15** (1952), 167–190; and "Historical Reflections on the Backgrounds of Neurophysiology: Inhibition, Excitation, and Integration of Activity," in Chandler M. Brooks and P. F. Cranefield, eds., *The Historical Development of Physiological Thought* (New York, 1959); Ragnar Granit, *Charles Scott Sherrington: An Appraisal* (London, 1966); E. G. T. Liddell, "Charles Scott Sherrington, 1857–1952," in *Obituary Notices of Fellows of the Royal Society of London,* **8** (1952), 241–259; and *The Discovery of Reflexes* (Oxford, 1960); Wilder Penfield, "Sir Charles Sherrington, Poet and Philosopher," in *Brain,* **80** (1957), 402–410; Carr E. R. Sherrington, *Memories* (privately printed, 1957), the Beaumont lecture, Yale University, 15 Nov. 1957; Judith P. Swazey, "Sherrington's Concept of Integrative Action," in *Journal of the History of Biology,* **1** (1968), 57–89; and *Reflexes and Motor Integration: Sherrington's Concept of Integrative Action* (Cambridge, Mass., 1969).

A major source of information about Sherrington and his life and work is contained in the papers of the late Dr. John F. Fulton, who had a long and close personal and professional association with him. Fulton first studied under Sherrington in 1921, when he went to Oxford as a Rhodes Scholar. The Fulton papers are housed at the Historical Library, Yale University School of Medicine, New Haven, Connecticut.

JUDITH P. SWAZEY

SHIBUKAWA, HARUMI (*b.* Kyoto, Japan, 27 December 1639; *d.* Edo [now Tokyo], Japan, 11 November 1715), *astronomy*.

Harumi was the son of Yasui Santetsu, a professional *go* player in the service of the Tokugawa shogunate. After his father's death he assumed his name and profession, becoming known as Yasui Santetsu II. Trained in *go*, Harumi studied Chinese and Japanese classics, Shintoism, and calendrical astronomy with various teachers. His distinguished service in calendar reform led to his appointment in 1685 as official astronomer. He later returned to his original name, Shibukawa.

The Chinese lunisolar Hsuan-ming calendar, adopted in Japan in 862, had not been reformed for more than eight hundred years. Over the centuries the discrepancy in the length of a solar year had increased so that by Harumi's time there was a two-day delay in the winter solstice. Moreover, it had become of little use for its traditional purpose, the precise prediction of solar and lunar eclipses. Although the error caused little inconvenience or confusion in daily life, reformation of the official calendar became an event of major political importance—to strengthen the prestige and authority of the imperial court vis-à-vis the shogunate by providing the people with an accurate calendar.

An able mathematician and skilled diplomat, Harumi urged calendar reform by pointing out faults in the Hsuan-ming calendar, seeking to prove the discrepancy by actual observation of winter and summer solstices and by demonstrating the possibility of establishing a calendar that would be more accurate—as confirmed by observation—in predicting eclipses.

In 1669 Harumi began conducting astronomical observations, probably the first systematic observations made in Japan. Following the procedures of traditional astronomy, he set up a gnomon and measured the lengths of shadows at various points before and after the winter solstice, in order to calculate the time of occurrence. He was especially interested in the Shou-shih calendar of the Yüan dynasty (1279–1368), a crowning achieve-

ment of calendrical astronomy adopted in China in 1282; and his observations were based upon its methods.

In 1673 Harumi proposed to the emperor the adoption of the Shou-shih calendar. In a report entitled "On the Eclipses" he compared the differing calculations, derived from both calendars, of solar and lunar eclipses, for the period 1673–1675. Of the six subsequently observed eclipses, however, the solar eclipse of 1675 was found in better agreement with the calculations based on the Hsuan-ming calendar.

Stunned and disheartened by this experience, Harumi improved his calculations and subsequently devised a calendar that agreed with the incorrectly predicted eclipse. In 1683 he again proposed a calendar revision to the emperor, the first calendar devised by a Japanese that was completely independent of the Chinese calendars.

However, the tendency of Japanese astronomers to follow Chinese practice was not easily overcome. In 1684 the fifteen-member Board of Astronomy decided to adopt a newer Chinese calendar, the Ta-t'ung. Appalled by this decision, Harumi engaged in some quiet behind-the-scenes maneuvering and finally succeeded in reversing the decision. Later that year his own calendar revision (the Jokyo calendar) was implemented.

Like the Shou-shih calendar, the Jokyo incorporated the secular variation term of the length of the tropical year. Such correctional terms were used to explain the records of winter solstices in the remote past. The Ta-t'ung, although following the substance of the Shou-shih, had abandoned secular variation terms in the belief that such minimal revisions could not be proved by observation; Harumi's own adoption of them was based on his conviction that it would render his calendar more profound.

The Jokyo and Shou-shih calendars can be considered the culmination of traditional Chinese calendrical astronomy, distinguished—like Babylonian astronomy—in their concentration on numerical and algebraic matters. Neither used the geometrical approach or the schematic model of Western astronomy, and thus, taken together, neither surpassed Ptolemy's *Almagest*.

During his career, the Shih-hsien calendar, compiled by Jesuits, had been introduced in 1644 in China, and Harumi frequently referred to it. There was, unfortunately, no way for him to learn about the system adopted in compiling it. The Japanese government's closed-door policy, begun in the 1630's, included a ban directed mainly against

403

Jesuit writings and prevented him from obtaining an important work on Sino-Jesuit astronomy, *Hsi-yang hsin-fa li-shu* ("Treatises on Calendrical Science According to New Western Methods," 1645).

In his references to Western theory, Harumi based his information exclusively on *T'ien-ching huo-wen* ("Queries on the Classics of Heaven," 1675), by Yu I. Rather than a scientific treatment of observational values or of the methods of calculation derived from them, the work was merely a popular explanation of various astronomical and cosmological theories. Harumi was especially impressed by its clear explanation, using a geometrical model, of eclipses, which he had never found in Chinese calendrical writings. Yet, as an astronomer focusing on useful parameters or numerical values that could be borrowed to improve the precision of a calendar, he found the work disappointing and came to regard Western astronomers as "barbarians who may have theories but cannot prove methods." It is regrettable that sufficient material for evaluating Western theories was not available to him.

During the eighteenth century Japanese astronomy altered its orientation from China to the West. Harumi belonged to the first generation of astronomers who, with only limited knowledge of Western astronomy, began evaluating the merits of both systems. He was a leader of those Japanese astronomers who, through their science, initiated the acknowledgment of Western superiority and the modernization of Japan.

BIBLIOGRAPHY

In English, see Shigeru Nakayama, *A History of Japanese Astronomy, Chinese Background and Western Impact* (Cambridge, Mass., 1969).

In Japanese, works on Harumi and his work are Endo Toshisada, "Shibukawa Harumi," MS preserved at the Japan Academy, begun in 1904; Shigeru Nakayama, "Shibukawa Harumi's Solstitial Observation and the Hsiao-chang Method," in *Tenmon Geppo*, no. 58 (1965); and *A History of Japanese Astronomy, Chinese Background and Western Impact* (Cambridge, Mass., 1969); Nishiuchi Masaru, *Study of Shibukawa Harumi* (Tokyo, 1940); Shibukawa Takaya, "Biography of Master Harumi," in *Nihon Kyoiku Shiryo*, **9** (1889); Tani Jinzan, "Shinro Menmei," in *Nihon Bunko*, **4** (1890); and *Jinzan Shu* (Tokyo, 1909); and Watanabe Toshio, *Shibukawa Harumi, the Pioneer of Japanese Calendrical Astronomy, and the History of Astronomy in the Edo Period* (Tokyo, 1965).

SHIGERU NAKAYAMA

SHILOV, NIKOLAY ALEKSANDROVICH (*b.* Moscow, Russia, 10 July 1872; *d.* Gagry, U.S.S.R., 17 August 1930), *chemistry.*

Shilov graduated from Moscow University in 1895. In 1896–1897 and 1901–1904 he worked in Ostwald's physics and chemistry laboratory at Leipzig, where he began research on chemical kinetics. From 1910 he was professor in the department of inorganic chemistry at the Moscow Technical College and from 1911, professor at the Moscow Commercial Institute. From 1915 to 1918 he headed the technical section on gas, attached to the headquarters on the Western Front. In 1919–1921 Shilov helped organize the Institute of Chemical Research in Moscow.

Shilov's master's thesis (1905) systematized a large amount of experimental material on conjugate oxidation reactions. He there offered several theoretical generalizations and developed terminology for all the processes and active components, namely chemical induction, induction factor, actor, inductor, and acceptor (terms used in the field of catalysis). Subsequently these terms became generally accepted in chemical literature. Shilov gave special attention to the study of self-induction and to transitional phenomena between induction and catalysis.

Shilov's research demonstrated the central role of intermediary products in the kinetics of conjugate oxidation reactions. Using the conjugate oxidation reactions as a model, he developed a theory of the action of photographic developers.

Shilov began his study of gas adsorption during World War I. Introducing Zelinsky's charcoal filter gas mask into the Russian army, Shilov established a laboratory at the front, where he conducted a broad investigation of the adsorption of gases in an air flow containing poisonous substances. He established the relationship between the length of the layer of adsorbent and the duration of its effectiveness.

In 1919 Shilov began to study the adsorption of substances from solutions and the distribution of substances between two liquid phases. He also constructed a formula for the distribution of a substance between two solvents.

Investigating hydrolytic adsorption, Shilov demonstrated that, according to the surface oxides of carbon, the latter element manifests the characteristics of either a positive or a negative adsorbent. Shilov's representation of active carbon, as an adsorbent having various surface functional groups that enter into exchange reactions with adsorbing substances, must be considered the first explanation of the principle of the action of ion exchangers (cation and anion exchange resins).

BIBLIOGRAPHY

I. ORIGINAL WORKS. Shilov's writings include "Zur Systematik und Theorie gekoppelter Oxydations-Reduktionsvorgänge," in *Zeitschrift für physikalische Chemie*, **46** (1903), 777–817, written with R. Lüther; *O sopryazhennykh reaktsiakh okislenia* ("On Conjugate Oxidation Reactions"; Moscow, 1905); "K teorii fotograficheskogo proyavitelya" ("Toward a Theory of Photographic Developers"), in *Sbornik posvyashchenny K. A. Timiryazevu ego uchenikami* ("A Collection Dedicated to Timiryazev by His Students"; Moscow, 1916), 111–129; "Adsorbtsia elektrolitov i molekulyarnye sily" ("Molecular Forces and the Adsorption of Electrolytes"), in *Vestnik Lomonosovskogo fiziko-khimicheskogo obshchestva v Moskve*, **1**, no. 1 (1919), 1–137, written with L. K. Lepin; "Raspredelenie veshchestva mezhdu dvumya rastvoritelyami i silovoe pole rastvora" ("The Distribution of a Substance Between Two Solvents and the Strength Field of a Solution"), *ibid.*, no. 2 (1920), 1–103, written with L. K. Lepin; "K voprosu ob adsorbtsii postoronnego gaza iz toka vozdukha" ("Toward the Question of the Adsorption of Foreign Gases From an Air Flow"), in *Zhurnal Russkogo fiziko-khimicheskogo obshchestva*, chem. sec., **61** (1929), 1107; written with L. K. Lepin and A. S. Voznesensky; and "Studien über Kohleoberflächenoxyde," in *Zeitschrift für physikalische Chemie*, **150** (1930), 31–36, written with E. G. Shatunovskaya and K. V. Chmutov.

II. SECONDARY LITERATURE. See "Krupny russky ucheny Nikolay Aleksandrovich Shilov" ("The Outstanding Russian Scientist Shilov"), in *Uspekhi khimii*, **15**, no. 2 (1946), 233–264; and N. N. Ushakova, *Nikolay Aleksandrovich Shilov* (Moscow, 1966).

Y. I. SOLOVIEV

SHIRAKATSÍ, ANANIA (also known as **Ananias of Shirak**) (*b.* Shirakavan [now Ani], Armenia, *ca.* 620; *d.* shortly after 685), *mathematics, geography, philosophy, astronomy.*

A representative of the progressive Armenian scholars of the seventh century and a follower of the best traditions of Hellenistic science and culture, Shirakatsí lived during the period when Armenia had lost her political independence; the western part being ruled by Byzantium and the eastern by Persia. He received his basic education at a local monastery school. After several journeys in search of a teacher of mathematics, which he considered the "mother of all sciences," Shirakatsí reached Trebizond and entered the school of the Greek scientist Tychicus, who taught the children of many Byzantine nobles. During the next eight years he studied mathematics, cosmography, philosophy, and several other sciences, before returning to his native region of Shirak, where he opened a school. In addition to teaching, he conducted scientific research and wrote works on astronomy, mathematics, geography, history, and other sciences. He possessed truly encyclopedic knowledge and the ability to reach the essence of matters.

Shirakatsí produced his most important scientific work from the 650's through the 670's. In 667–669 he was concerned with the reform of the Armenian calendar, anticipating the modern desire for an "immovable" calendar.

Shirakatsí's scientific works are known through manuscripts of the eleventh through seventeenth centuries that are scattered in the Soviet Union, Italy, Great Britain, Austria, Israel, and perhaps other countries. His advanced philosophical and cosmological views brought him to the attention of official circles, and he was persecuted by both lay and ecclesiastical authorities.

Like the scientists of antiquity, Shirakatsí believed that the world consists of four elements: earth, water, air, and fire. The world, in which he included plants, animals, and man, is a "definite composition of intermixed elements."

All things in nature move and are subject to change. Old substances decompose in due course, and new forms arise in their place. Creation, wrote Shirakatsí, is the basis of destruction; and destruction in its turn is the basis of creation; "as a consequence of this harmless contradiction, the world acquires its eternal existence."

On the form of the earth, Shirakatsí wrote: "The earth seems to me to have an egg-shaped form: as the yolk in spherical form is in the middle, the white around it, and a shell surrounds it all, so the earth is in the center like the yolk, the air around it like the white, and the sky surrounds it all like the shell." In the early Middle Ages such ideas were very daring.

In connection with the spherical form of the earth, Shirakatsí spoke of the mountains and canyons "on the other side" of the earth. He wrote about the antipodes, of animals and people "like a fly, moving on an apple equally well on all sides. When it is night on one side of the earth, the sun lights the other half of the earth's sphere."

Shirakatsí believed that the earth is in equilibrium in space because the force of gravity, which pulls it down, is opposed by the force of the wind, which tries to raise it.

Criticizing numerous legends that explained the Milky Way, Shirakatsí gave an explanation that was correct and bold for the time: "The Milky Way is a mass of thickly clustered and weakly shining stars."

The moon, in Shirakatsí's opinion, does not emit its own light but reflects that of the sun. He associated the phases of the moon, which proceed from changes in the mutual positions of the sun and moon, with this reflection of the sun's light.

Shirakatsí gave a correct explanation for solar and lunar eclipses and composed a special table for calculating their occurrence, using the nineteen-year "lunar cycle."

In his *Geometry of Astronomy* Shirakatsí tried to determine the distance from the earth to the sun, the moon, and the planets, and to estimate the true dimensions of the sun. Such a problem was of course beyond the observational techniques of his time.

Shirakatsí's works on the calendar were of great importance. He studied and compared the calendar systems of fourteen nations, among them the Agvancians (ancient inhabitants of Azerbaidjan), who did not leave any written records, and the Cappadocians.

Of special interest is his *Tables of the Lunar Cycle*, the authorship of which was established in the mid-twentieth century. The Yerevan Matenadaran, a repository of ancient manuscripts and books, possesses ten records that contain this work, which was based on his own observations. He wrote in his foreword:

I, Anania Shirakatsí, have faithfully studied the course and changes in the appearance of the moon through all the days of its passage and, noting them, have fixed this information in tables, wishing to lighten the work of those who are interested. And I have drawn first the newborn moon, and then the full moon, on what day it takes place, at what time—in the night or in the day, at what hour and what minute.

Shirakatsí considered not only the days of the various phases of the moon but also the hours, which had not been done in any previous calendar. A comparison of his lunar tables with modern data shows the former's great precision.

Shirakatsí's textbook of arithmetic is one of the oldest known Armenian textbooks. Its mathematical tables—of multiplication and of arithmetical and geometrical progression—also are the oldest.

BIBLIOGRAPHY

I. ORIGINAL WORKS. Shirakatsí's writings include *Ananiayi Širakunwoy mnatsordk' panic'* ("Collected Works of Anania Shirakatsí"), K. P. Patkanian, ed. (St. Petersburg, 1877), in classical Armenian; his autobiography in English, in F. C. Conybeare, "Ananias of Širak," in *Byzantinische Zeitschrift*, 11 (1897), 572–584, also translated into French by H. Berberian in *Revue des Études Arméniennes*, n.s. 1 (1964), 189; *T'uabanut'iwn* ("Arithmetic"), A. G. Abrahamean, ed. (Erevan, 1939); *Tiezeragitut'iwn ew Tomar* ("Cosmography and Chronology"), A. G. Abrahamean, ed. (Erevan, 1940), also in Armenian; *Tablitsy lunnogo kruga* ("Tables of the Motions of the Moon"), A. G. Abrahamean, ed. (Erevan, 1962), in Russian and Armenian; and a collection of Shirakatsí's other works, *Anania Širakac'u matenadrut'iwn* ("The Works of Anania Shirakatsí"), A. G. Abrahamean, ed. (Erevan, 1944), in Armenian.

II. SECONDARY LITERATURE. See A. G. Abrahamean and G. B. Petrosian, *Ananias Shirakatsy* (Erevan, 1970), in Russian; F. C. Conybeare, "Ananias of Shirak, 'On Christmas,'" in *Expositor* (London), 5th ser., 4 (1896), 321–337; R. H. Hewsen, "Science in VIIth Century Armenia: Ananias of Širak," in *Isis*, 59 (1968), 32–45; I. A. Orbely, *"Voprosy i reshenia" Ananii Shirakatsi* ("The Problems and Solutions of Anania Shirakatsi") (Petrograd, 1918); W. Petri, "Anania Shirakazi—ein armenischer Kosmograph des 7. Jahrhunderts," in *Zeitschrift der Deutschen morgenländischen Gesellschaft*, 114, no. 2 (1964), 269–288, also in *Mitteilungen der Sternwarte München*, 1, no. 14 (1964), 269–288; G. Ter-Mkrtchian, "Anania Shirakatsy," in *Ararat* (1896), 96–104, 143–152, 199–208, 292–296, 336–344; and B. E. Tumanian and R. A. Abramian, "Ob astronomicheskikh rabotakh Ananii Shirakatsi" ("On the Astronomical Works of Anania Shirakatsi"), in *Istoriko-astronomicheskie issledovaniya*, no. 2 (1956), 239–246.

P. G. KULIKOVSKY

AL-SHĪRĀZĪ. See **Quṭb al-Dīn al-Shīrāzī.**

SHIZUKI, TADAO (*b.* Nagasaki, Japan, 1760; *d.* Nagasaki, 22 August 1806), *natural philosophy.*

Tadao's surname by birth was Nakano, but he was adopted by the Shizuki family, whose head was a government interpreter from the Dutch. His nickname was Tadajiro, and professionally he was known as Ryuho. In 1776 he became an assistant interpreter, succeeding his adoptive father, but he retired from that post the following year because of ill health. After leaving public service, he spent the rest of his life in the private study of Dutch books and in contemplation. Although his health was delicate and he had a reputation for unsociability, he attracted brilliant followers. He wrote books about the Dutch language and partially translated the Dutch translation of Engelbert Kaempher's *Geschichte und Beschreibung von Japan*. But Tadao's major work was *Rekisho shinsho*, a compilation of his own theories on natural philosophy, inspired by his translation of the Dutch version of John Keill's *Introductio ad veram physicam* and the *Introductio ad veram astronomiam*.

Tadao's natural philosophy was unusual within the Japanese intellectual tradition. His approach to problems was close to that of modern Western natural philosophers: he attempted to find fundamental explanations for all natural phenomena rather than merely describe them as moral, aesthetic, or practical problems.

Western mechanistic philosophy must have seemed remote and uninteresting in an intellectual climate dominated by Confucius' moral supreme doctrine, but Tadao nonetheless absorbed himself for twenty years in translating Keill's book and constructing his own natural philosophy. Perhaps he was able to do so because he was removed from the intellectual tradition centered around the Japanese Confucians and because he was able to pursue his study in Nagasaki, which was then the only opening to the outside world. Japanese knowledge of western science was at that time very limited. While Chinese translations of Western books on science had just been released from governmental ban, these were the work of Jesuits stationed in China and covered only Tychonic astronomy. The only sources for Copernicanism and Newtonianism were books brought in by the Dutch, who were the only Westerners permitted to trade with Japan and who were permitted to land only at Nagasaki. Tadao was thus ideally situated.

Other interpreters and physicians had contributed to introducing modern Western science into Japan, but Tadao had a far better understanding of the Dutch language and a superior insight into philosophical concepts. It is therefore curious that he chose to spend so much of his life translating Keill's book. If he meant simply to introduce Western natural science, why did he not choose other popular, up-to-date books and well-arranged texts, such as, for example, Benjamin Martin's *Philosophical Grammar*, the Dutch translation of which must have been easy to obtain despite the limited availability of Dutch books?

Although he translated other works on request, Tadao probably concentrated on Keill's book because it was difficult, under the import restrictions, to find an equally sophisticated work and because

the other textbooks and popular books available to him did not give him the same intellectual satisfaction. In advocating Newtonianism, Keill's work had a polemical tone, and more importantly and quite unlike the readjusted interpretations of later authors, it dealt in abstractions and included a great many elements of natural philosophy. The book especially suited Tadao's inclination toward natural philosophy and Tadao thus became the first Newtonian in the East.

The earliest extant manuscript of Tadao's translation of Keill's work is "On Attractive Force" (1784). Considering the level of knowledge of Western science in the Orient at that time, it would seem that Tadao struggled excellently with a very difficult subject. Since Copernican theory can be grasped as problems of angular variations, it presented no conceptional difficulty to the Oriental mind; but Newtonianism was being introduced into the Orient for the first time, and there was no Japanese vocabulary to embrace the concepts of corpuscle, vacuum, gravity, or force. Tadao therefore had to invent such words, and some of his inventions became standard in countries in which Chinese characters are used. The concept of atomism was also unknown in the Orient, and Tadao attempted to adopt the neo-Confucian idea of *ch'i* as a corresponding notion; but since the concept of *ch'i* is based on the model of a continuously changing fluid, he found it difficult to combine the idea of discrete atoms with the monistic *ch'i* concept of condensation and rarefaction.

Atomism requires a clear distinction between atom and vacuum, but for Tadao vacuum was a rarefied state of *ch'i*; and atom and vacuum were continuously caught in the spectrum of rarefaction of *ch'i*. Keill, however, explained electrical phenomena by means of effluvia, and Tadao found the concept of effluvia much more congenial to interpretation by *ch'i* than that of the atom. Tadao also claimed that effluvia offered an explanation for not only electrical force but also gravity. Since he considered weight to be the accumulation of *ch'i*, both electromagnetic force and gravity could be explained thereby.

Tadao's commentary contains many original ideas. He applied Western principles of attractive force and the traditional idea of Yin-Yang to the explanation of the phenomenal world. His adaptation of Yin-Yang incorporated two different — positive and negative — forces, and he used the variation in the balance of these two forces to explain what Western scientists considered to be a variation in the magnitude of only one force. Had

Tadao developed this idea further he might have constructed his own system, which would probably have been significantly different from its Western counterpart. His method seems particularly suitable to the explanation of electromagnetic force.

Although Tadao and Keill were from completely different academic environments, Tadao's native aptitude seems superior to Keill's, and he himself even experimented with a barometer, at a time when a Japanese experimental science barely existed. The subjects that Tadao tried to explain by attractive force—other than the data he obtained from Dutch books—were, however, limited to spontaneously occurring phenomena—as, for example, atmospheric events and plant life. (He even tried to construct a primitive vegetable physiology based upon attractive force.).

In his work on attractive force Keill developed the ideas of Newton's *Opticks* and tried to explain chemical and other phenomena by means of homogeneous particles and their intermolecular force, using the inverse third or fourth powers of their distances. But he could neither measure nor test what he wanted to prove and thus failed to achieve his objective. Unlike Keill and other Newtonians who sought to prove quantitative change in chemical phenomena, Tadao lacked the social background that might have fostered an interest in chemistry; and no such academic discipline had yet developed in Japan. Thus his interest in attractive force remained purely that of a natural philosopher.

The theory of cosmic dual forces in Tadao's commentary "On Attractive Force" is compatible with modern science, and there is the possibility that one subsumes the other: it is an acceptable and permissible concept for modern scientists. But in his later studies Tadao's ideas conformed more closely to traditional natural philosophy, and they became more speculative. During this time he completed his *Rekisho shinsho*, in which he commented systematically on Newtonian dynamics—although he was concerned primarily with their metaphysical basis: "All things have the property of gravity. Although gravity originally emerged from the inexplicable process of creation, it can be comprehended by the intelligence and hence is not absolutely inexplicable. Yet the cause of gravity is quite inscrutable. Even with advanced Western instruments and mathematics, the fundamental cause is indeterminable."

Although the second volume of *Rekisho shinsho* was entitled *Immeasurable*, Tadao sought in Oriental thinking a solution for matters that in the West would have been explained as acts of God. He established unitary *ch'i* and its dual function (rarefaction and condensation) as the basis for his natural philosophy and thus wrote that

> The space of the universe contains only one substance, *ch'i*, but it can also be either empty or full. Thus in one there is two, and in two, one. If there were only the one, there could be no difference between the rarefied and the condensed. Is there not then a difference between the rarefied and the condensed? By the existence of these two contrary principles the phenomena are caused in endless succession. Because of the oneness of the substance, the universe is monistic. The cause of these principles is beyond my comprehension, but the best way to comprehend the subtlety of these principles is to study the teaching of the *Book of Changes* [*I-Ching*].
>
> If there were only the two, the *ch'i* of heaven and earth could not be transmitted from one to the other. The shining *ch'i* of the sun and heavenly bodies is reflected from one to the other, and goes to and from the extremities of heaven. Permeating space without a single gap, it rises and falls, undergoing countless transformations. We must, then, admit that there is only a single *ch'i* . . . , which differs in respect to condensation and rarefaction. Condensation and rarefaction are the same in causal origin as emptiness and plenitude. The extreme of rarefaction is emptiness. Perfect plenitude and perfect emptiness, combining with each other, make a single state. This is why Laotzu said, "Nonexistence occupies nonspace." Nevertheless, even in the extremities of heaven, there is not the slightest space of pure plenitude or nonemptiness.
>
> We must acknowledge that the light of the stars can permeate the broad heavens, and that the *ch'i* of fire can penetrate rock and metal. For example although winter is cold, and summer hot, even in winter there is still some warm *ch'i* and even in summer there is some cold *ch'i*. Or take the case of soil, placed in water. As the soil is condensed and heavy, the water, being light and rarefied, is like heaven. The soil, mixing with the water, discolors it; and the water, permeating the soil, moistens it. Therefore in the water there is nowhere where the soil *ch'i* is absent, and in the soil, nowhere where the water *ch'i* is absent.

Accordingly, Tadao arranged the subjects of Newtonian dynamics, including gravity, into a series of chapters on divination, theory of monistic *ch'i*, and Newtonian dynamics. He was not as successful, however, in relating the natural philosophy that he derived from the theory of monistic *ch'i* to Newtonian dynamics.

Tadao was one of the first to introduce Copernican theory into the Orient, although his interest was not in heliocentric theory. The locational relationship between the sun and the universe was for him simply a problem of changing the coordinate system; and, from the natural-philosophical point of view, it was not a substantial problem. In traditional neo-Confucian cosmology the problem involved the dynamics of motion and inactivity. Tadao did not refer to Copernicanism as a heliocentric theory but, rather, as an earth-moving theory, in which heaven and earth are composed of the cosmic dual forces of *ch'i*. The fast and light *ch'i* ascend and become heaven while the heavy and slow *ch'i* gather together and become earth. This system represents Chu Hsi's dynamic cosmogony and, unlike Aristotelian celestial-terrestrial dichotomy, makes no sharp distinction between heaven and earth, motion and inactivity. Another neo-Confucian philosopher also thought that the earth did not have absolute fixation in the middle of the universe but was situated at one end of a continuous spectrum binding Yin-Yang polar concepts (for example, shade and light, inactivity and motion, slow and fast) and that it rotated in relation to its surroundings.

Tadao viewed Copernicanism as absolute relativism but could not decide whether earthly or heavenly motion was more correct. He also pointed out that he had found the word "earth moving" in an ancient Chinese book and went on to suggest that the Chinese first conceived the earth-moving theory. (The word "earth moving" as it appears in this ancient text can also be translated as "earthquake," however.) The term "earth moving," as Tadao used it, has been retained as a scientific, technical word, even though it does not distinguish rotation from revolution.

Tadao also raised the question of why the planets rotate and revolve in the same direction in planes not greatly inclined to the ecliptic. In a section entitled "Kenkon bunpan zusetsu" ("The Formulation of the Cosmos, Illustrated") he proposed a hypothesis concerning the formation of the planetary system. His hypothesis recalls immediately the celebrated hypotheses of Kant and Laplace. Because of the relative inaccessibility of Western treatises, however, it is unlikely that Tadao derived his idea from anyone else. In view of his background in neo-Confucian ideas, his hypothesis was not a titanic leap—many aspects of it were already present in neo-Confucian vortex cosmogony. Hence, an infusion of ideas concerning attraction and centrifugal force provided Tadao with a more elaborate mechanical hypothesis, which he formulated in accordance with the heliocentric system.

BIBLIOGRAPHY

Tadao's major works are *Rekisho Shinsho* ("New Treatise on Calendrical Phenomena"; Heibon-sha, 1956), 2 vols., Japanese Philosophical Thoughts no. 9; and *Kyurikiron* ("On Attractive Force"; Iwanami, 1972).

On Tadao and his work in Western languages, see Yoshio Mikami, "On Shizuki Tadao's Translation of Keill's Astronomical Treatise," in *Nieuw archief voor wiskunde*, **11** (1913), 1–11; Shigeru Nakayama, *History of Japanese Astronomy* (Cambridge, Mass., 1969); Ohmori Minoru, "A Study of the *Rekisho Shinsho*," in *Japanese Studies in the History of Science*, no. 2 (1963), 146–153, and no. 3 (1964), 81–88; S. Yajima, "Théorie nébulaire de Shizuki (1760–1806)," in *Archives internationales d'histoire des sciences*, **12** (1956), 169–173; and Tadashi Yoshida, "The Rangako of Shizuki Tadao: the Introduction of Western Science in Tokugawa Japan," Ph.D. thesis at Princeton University (1974).

In Japanese are Kanda Shigeru, "Translations by Shizuki Tadao," in *Rangaku shiryo Kenkyukai Hokoka*, no. 107 (1961); Hiroto Saigusa, "On Newton, Who Existed in Japan the Past Two Centuries," in *Yokohama Daigaku Ronso*, Social Science, no. 1 (1958); Watanabe Kurasuke, "Summary on Work of Dutch Translator, Shizuki," in *Nagasaki Gakkai Sosho*, 4th ed. (1957).

S<small>HIGERU</small> N<small>AKAYAMA</small>

SHMALHAUZEN, IVAN IVANOVICH (*b.* Kiev, Russia, 23 April 1884; *d.* Moscow, U.S.S.R., 7 October 1963), *biology.*

The son of a professor of botany at Kiev University, Shmalhauzen graduated from the natural sciences section of the Physics and Mathematics Faculty of Kiev University in 1909. He remained there as assistant to A. N. Severtsov until 1911, passed his master's degree examination in 1912, and in 1914 presented his thesis, "Neparnye plavniki ryb; ikh filogeniticheskoe razvitie" ("Unpaired Fins of Fish; Their Phylogenetic Development"), at Moscow University. In 1916 Shmalhauzen defended his doctoral dissertation, "Razvitie konechmostey amfiby i ikh znachenie v voprose proiskhozhdenia nazemnykh pozvonochnykh" ("The Development of Extremities in Amphibians and Their Significance in the Origin of Land Vertebrates"). He was professor at Yuriev (Tartu) University, from 1916 to 1920 and headed the department of embryology and dynamics of development at Kiev from 1920 to 1937. At Kiev he organized the Biological Institute (later the Institute of Zoology) at the Ukrainian Academy of Sciences and was its director from 1941. From 1936 to 1948 Shmalhauzen was director of the A. N. Severtsov

Institute of Evolutionary Morphology and of the Academy of Sciences of the U.S.S.R., and was head of the department of Darwinism at Moscow University from 1939 to 1948. During his last years he worked at the Zoological Institute of the Academy of Sciences. He was elected academician of the Ukrainian Academy of Sciences (1922) and of the Academy of Sciences of the U.S.S.R. (1935).

Beginning his scientific career as a comparative anatomist, Shmalhauzen later expanded his research to the study of individual development and directed research in experimental embryology. Studying the growth of animals, he formulated a theory of growth according to which that process has an exponential character exhibiting an inverse relationship between growth and differentiation: attenuation of growth is described by a parabolic curve, since the specific rate of growth decreases in inverse proportion to age. During various distinct periods of individual life the energy of growth can be expressed by the constant of growth C_v, for the computation of which Shmalhauzen proposed

the formula $C_v = \dfrac{\log v_1 - \log v_0}{0.4343\,(t_1 - t_0)} = \text{constant}$, where

v_0 and v_1 are the mass of the body at the moments t_0 and t_1. He later studied the correlations of growth in individual and historic development that are the basis of the integrity of the organism and arise through the effect of natural selection.

In specialized monographs (1938, 1939, 1946) Shmalhauzen examined the course and regularities of the evolutionary process. In particular he provided a basis for classifying the types of natural selection. He established, in addition to an "active" natural selection that stabilizes mutational changes favoring survival under changed conditions, the existence of "stabilizing" natural selection. The latter preserves "normal" characteristics and eliminates deviations as long as the environment remains relatively unchanged. In the process of stabilizing selection "under the cover of the normal phenotype," recessive or balancing genes accumulate; with environmental changes they can serve as material for "active" natural selection.

In 1938, while studying the relations that exist in ontogeny and in phylogeny, Shmalhauzen suggested the idea, later (1968) substantiated in detail, that methods of cybernetics might be applied to the study of ontogenetic and phylogenetic development. His many years of teaching resulted in textbooks on comparative anatomy and on Darwinism. During the last years of his life Shmalhauzen re-

sumed the study of the origin of land vertebrates and published a monograph on that subject (1964).

BIBLIOGRAPHY

I. ORIGINAL WORKS. Shmalhauzen wrote more than 200 works, including the following monographs: *Rost organizmov* ("The Growth of Organisms"; Kiev, 1932), in Ukrainian; *Organizm kak tseloe v individualnom i istoricheskom razvitii* ("The Organism as a Whole in Individual and Historical Development"; Moscow–Leningrad, 1938; 2nd ed., 1942); *Puti i zakonomernosti evolyutsionnogo protsessa* ("The Ways and Regularities of the Evolutionary Process"; Moscow–Leningrad, 1939); *Faktory evolyutsii. Teoria stabiliziruyushchego otbora* ("Factors of Evolution. Theory of Stabilizing Selection"; Moscow–Leningrad, 1946; 2nd ed., 1968); also in English trans. (Philadelphia, 1949); *Proiskhozhdenie nazemnykh pozvonochnykh* ("The Origin of Terrestrial Vertebrates"; Moscow, 1964), also in English trans. (New York, 1968); and *Kiberneticheskie voprosy biologii* ("Cybernetic Questions of Biology"; Novosibirsk, 1968).

II. SECONDARY LITERATURE. See A. A. Makhotin, "Ivan Ivanovich Shmalhauzen (1884–1963)," in *Zoologicheskii zhurnal*, **43**, pt. 2 (1964), 297–302; and L. P. Tatarinov and B. A. Trofimov, "Akademik Ivan Ivanovich Shmalhauzen (1884–1963)," in *Paleontologicheskii zhurnal* (1964), no. 2, 169–173.

L. J. BLACHER

SHNIRELMAN, LEV GENRIKHOVICH (*b*. Gomel, Russia, 2 January 1905; *d*. Moscow, U.S.S.R., 24 September 1938), *mathematics*.

The son of a teacher, Shnirelman displayed remarkable mathematical abilities even as a child. In his twelfth year he studied an entire course of elementary mathematics at home; and in 1921 he entered Moscow University, where he attended courses taught by N. N. Lusin, P. S. Uryson, and A. Y. Khinchin. While still a student he obtained several interesting results in algebra, geometry, and topology that he did not wish to publish, considering them of insufficient importance. After two and a half years Shnirelman graduated from the university, then remained for further study. Having completed his graduate work, he became professor and head of the department of mathematics at the Don Polytechnical Institute in Novocherkassk (1929). In the following year Shnirelman returned to Moscow and taught at the university. He was elected a corresponding member of the Soviet Academy of Sciences in 1933, and from 1934 he worked in the Mathematical Institute of the Academy.

In 1927–1929 Shnirelman, with his friend L. A. Lyusternik, made important contributions to the qualitative (topological) methods of the calculus of variations. Their starting point was Poincaré's problem of the three geodesics, which they first solved completely and generally by showing the existence of three closed geodesics on every simply connected surface (every surface homeomorphic to a sphere). For the proof of this theorem the authors used a method, which they broadly generalized, that had been devised by G. Birkhoff, who in 1919 showed the existence of one closed geodesic. Shnirelman and Lyusternik also applied their "principle of the stationary point" to other problems of geometry "im Grossen." They also presented a new topological invariant, the category of point sets.

In 1930 Shnirelman introduced an original and profound idea into number theory, using the concept of the compactness α of the sequence of natural numbers, $n_1, n_2, n_3, \ldots$ so that $\alpha = \inf \dfrac{N(x)}{x}$ $(x \geq 1)$ where $N(x)$ is a number of the members of the sequence not exceeding x, and proving that every natural number n is representable as the sum of a finite (and independent of n) number of members of the sequences with a positive compactness. This allowed Shnirelman to prove, in particular, that any natural number is the sum of a certain finite number k of prime numbers—the Goldbach hypothesis in a less rigid form. According to the Goldbach hypothesis $k = 3$; by Shnirelman's method it is now possible to show that k is not greater than 20. Shnirelman also stated several arithmetical propositions, among them a generalization of Waring's theorem.

BIBLIOGRAPHY

I. Original Works. Shnirelman's writings include "Sur un principe topologique en analyse," in Comptes rendus . . . de l'Académie des sciences, **188** (1929), 295–297, written with L. A. Lyusternik; "Existence de trois géodésiques fermées sur toute surface de genre 0," ibid., 534–536, written with Lyusternik; "Sur le problème de trois géodésiques fermées sur les surfaces de genre 0," ibid., **189** (1929), 269–271, written with Lyusternik; "Ob additivnykh svoystavakh chisel" ("On the Additive Properties of Numbers"), in Izvestiya Donskogo politekhnicheskogo instituta v Novocherkasske, **14**, nos. 2–3 (1930), 3–28, also in Uspekhi matematicheskikh nauk, **6** (1939), 9–25; "Über eine neue kombinator-ische Invariante," in Monatshefte für Mathematik und Physik, **37** (1930), 131–134; Topologicheskie metody v variatsionnykh zadachakh ("Topological Methods in Variational Problems"; Moscow, 1930), written with Lyusternik; "Über additive Eigenschaften von Zahlen," in Mathematische Annalen, **107** (1933), 649–690; "Ob additivnykh svoystvakh chisel" ("On the Additive Properties of Numbers"), in Uspekhi matematicheskikh nauk, **7** (1940), 7–46; and "O slozhenii posledovatelnostey" ("On Addition of Sequences"), ibid., 62–63.

II. Secondary Literature. See "L. G. Shnirelman (1905–1938)," in Uspekhi matematicheskikh nauk, **6** (1939), 3–8; Matematika v SSSR za pyatnadtsat let ("Mathematics in the U.S.S.R. for Fifteen Years"; Moscow–Leningrad, 1932); Matematika v SSSR za tridtsat let ("Mathematics in the U.S.S.R. for Thirty Years"; Moscow–Leningrad, 1948); and Matematika v SSSR za sorok let ("Mathematics in the U.S.S.R. for Forty Years"), 2 vols. (Moscow, 1959), esp. II, 781–782.

A. P. Youschkevitch

SHOKALSKY, YULY MIKHAYLOVICH (b. St. Petersburg, Russia, 17 October 1856; d. Leningrad, U.S.S.R., 26 March 1940), *oceanography, geography.*

Fascinated by geography as a child, Shokalsky enrolled at the Naval College in St. Petersburg in 1873. Although it became apparent on his first student voyages that he was strongly inclined to seasickness, he did not abandon his chosen career. After graduating in 1877, he began service with the Baltic fleet; but realizing that his command responsibilities did not leave him time to pursue his scientific interests, he completed his education at the Naval Academy from 1878 to 1880.

In 1881 Shokalsky became head of the marine meteorology division at the Central Physics Observatory (now the A. I. Voeykov Central Geophysical Observatory in Leningrad). A year later his first scientific paper, on weather forecasting, was published. From 1883 to 1908 he taught geography and marine description at the Naval College; and, from 1908, physical geography, meteorology and, later, oceanography at the Naval Academy, where he was the first professor of this subject in Russia. Shokalsky was a member of the fleet's department of hydrography, directing its central naval library from 1890 and the hydrometeorological section from 1907.

From 1900 to 1915 Shokalsky developed a large-scale project for oceanographic research and participated in the preparations for the expedition of the icebreakers *Taymyr* and *Vaygach* to the

Arctic Ocean—the expedition that discovered Severnaya Zemlya. He was also one of the organizers of the Eleventh International Congress on Navigation, held in St. Petersburg in 1908. Shokalsky's plan, formulated in 1902, for the creation of a marine science center was realized in 1921 with the establishment in Monaco of the International Hydrographic Organization.

Elected president of the Russian Geographic Society in 1914, Shokalsky made a major contribution to cartography, geomorphology, terrestrial hydrology, glaciology, and geodesy. In *Okeanografia* (1917), his most important work, he postulated the mutual dependence of all marine phenomena; this concept was subsequently elaborated to include the idea of a "worldwide ocean," an unbroken totality of all interconnected bodies of salt water. In addition to discussing physical phenomena, Shokalsky gave a full description of the methodology and techniques of shipboard observation. The work, which became extremely popular both in the Soviet Union and elsewhere, was awarded prizes by the Russian Academy of Sciences (1919) and by the Paris Academy of Sciences (1923). It is still of value.

In 1909 the Hydrographic Administration had commissioned Shokalsky to plan and determine the methodology of a comprehensive oceanographic expedition to the Black Sea. The project was to include all branches of marine science and would extend to adjacent basins: the Kerchenskiy Proliv, Bosporus, and Dardanelles straits, and the seas of Azov and Marmara. Although Shokalsky completed plans for the expedition in 1914, it was delayed for nine years by the outbreak of World War I and the Soviet Revolution.

During the first year the study comprised only two hydrological sections taken from the narrowest part of the Black Sea—from Cape Sarych, in the southern Crimea, to Inebolu, on the Anatolian coast of Turkey. By 1925 Shokalsky had extended the survey to the entire Black Sea, and its work was completed in 1935 with a long winter cruise. During the twelve-year expedition fifty-three voyages were made, and over 1,600 hydrological samples and approximately 2,000 soil and biological samples were taken. Data obtained on the density of seawater in relation to depth discredited the concept of an upper layer, containing atmospheric oxygen in solution, distinct from a lower, hydrosulfidic layer. Instead, the information indicated a high mobility of both layers and a constant interexchange. Extremely long cores of earth were also

taken from the seabed; one, 380 centimeters in length, was a record at the time.

Despite his advanced age, Shokalsky remained active during the 1930's. He served on the commission to develop the programs of the Second International Polar Year (1932–1933) and, with V. V. Shuleykin and N. N. Zubov, strove for the inclusion of oceanographic studies. He also was responsible for compiling a new physical map of the North Polar region. In 1933 he was a member of the organizational committee of the Fourth Hydrologic Conference of Baltic Nations, held at Leningrad; was a member of the presidium of the marine section; and the chairman of the Commission on the [Aquatic] Balance of the Baltic Sea. The following year, at the age of almost eighty, he was the Soviet delegate to the Fourteenth International Geographical Congress, in Warsaw.

From 1929 until his death Shokalsky taught oceanography at Leningrad University; his lectures in general oceanography were supplemented by a course in regional oceanography that was entirely of his own devising.

Shokalsky was a member of fifteen foreign geographic societies and received an honorary doctorate in geography from the University of Bordeaux. He was an honorary member of the Soviet Academy of Sciences, honorary president of the Russian Geographic Society, and received the title "honored scientist."

BIBLIOGRAPHY

I. ORIGINAL WORKS. The most important of Shokalsky's more than 1,300 publications are "O predskazanii veroyatnoy pogody i shtormov" ("On Forecasting Weather and Storms"), in *Morskoi sbornik*, **192**, no. 10 (1882), 87–125, his first scientific paper; "Ocherk razvitia fiziki okeanov" ("Essay on the Development of the Physics of Oceans"), in *Fiziko-matematichesky ezhegodnik*, **1** (1900), 158–207; "Vzglyad na sovremennoe sostoyanie okeanografii" ("View of the Contemporary State of Oceanography"), in *Izvestiya Russkogo geograficheskogo obshchestva*, **43** (1911), 503–520; *Okeanografia* (Petrograd, 1917; 2nd ed., 1959), his major work; *Geografichesky atlas v 32 tablitsakh* ("Geographic Atlas in 32 Tables"; Leningrad, 1930); *Fizicheskaya okeanografia* (Moscow, 1933); "Okeanografia Chernogo morya" ("Oceanography of the Black Sea"), in *Doklady sovetskoy delegatsii na Mezhdunarodnom geograficheskom kongresse v Varshave*, no. 14 (1934); "O rabotakh po okeanografii v Mirovom okeane" ("On Papers About Oceanography in the World Ocean"), in *Doklady prochitannye na Tretem* *plenume gruppy geografii i geofiziki Akademii nauk SSSR* ("Reports Read at the Third Plenum of the Geography and Geophysics Group of the Soviet Academy of Sciences"; Moscow, 1937), 5–18; "Okeanograficheskie issledovania Soyuza SSR za 20 let" ("Twenty Years of Oceanographic Investigation in the U.S.S.R."), in *Matematika i estestvoznanie v SSSR* ("Mathematics and Natural Science in the U.S.S.R."; Moscow, 1938), 901–917; and "Kartografirovanie morey Sovetskogo Soyuza," in *Dvadtsat let sovetskoy kartografii i geodezii, 1919–1939* (Moscow, 1939), pt. 2, 162–190.

II. SECONDARY LITERATURE. See E. Andreeva, *Y. M. Shokalsky* (Leningrad, 1956); *Pamyati Yulia Mikhaylovicha Shokalskogo. Sbornik statey i materialov,* I (Moscow–Leningrad, 1946); and Z. Y. Shokalskaya, *Zhiznenny puty Y. M. Shokalskogo* ("The Life of . . . Shokalsky"; Moscow, 1960).

A. F. PLAKHOTNIK

SHORT, JAMES (*b.* Edinburgh, Scotland, 10 June 1710; *d.* Stoke Newington, Essex, England, 15 June 1768), *optics.*

Short, whose father was an Edinburgh joiner and burgess, was orphaned at the age of ten. He was educated at Heriot's Hospital, a school for the sons of poor burgesses, and at the Edinburgh High School. In 1726 he entered the University of Edinburgh. His M.A., however, was awarded by the University of St. Andrews in 1753. Because of his excellent academic record, his grandmother hoped that Short would enter the ministry, but he became instead a protégé of Colin Maclaurin, professor of mathematics at Edinburgh. Encouraged by Maclaurin, Short started making mirrors for reflecting telescopes, first of glass, then of speculum metal. His skill in this work received immediate recognition and was the source of his subsequent success. Indeed, the perfecting of these metal mirrors was his lifework, for, unlike other instrument makers of his time, he was a specialist.

Short settled permanently in London in 1738, having been elected a fellow of the Royal Society the previous year. A bachelor, Short's devotion to his chosen profession, "Optician, solely for reflecting telescopes," brought him an international reputation and a fortune that was estimated at £20,000 at the time of his death. Short was one of forty-five founder members of the Philosophical Society of Edinburgh; was a founder member, in 1754, of the Society for the Encouragement of Arts, Manufactures and Commerce; and, in 1757, became a foreign member of the Royal Swedish Academy of Sciences.

From 1738 to the end of his life, Short's home and workshop were in Surrey Street, off the Strand. There he made astronomical observations that were frequently reported in the *Philosophical Transactions.* Short's portrait, painted by Benjamin Wilson, shows him in his observatory at Surrey Street, overlooking the Thames; behind him is the five-foot-focal-length reflecting telescope that he habitually used.

Short generously encouraged the work of his fellow telescope maker, and potential rival, John Dollond, by communicating to the Royal Society, in 1758, Dollond's experimental work on the correction of chromatic aberration in the refracting telescope. Because of Dollond's achievement, the refractor was, by the end of Short's life, beginning to supersede the reflector. Another friend to whom Short gave active support was John Harrison, the chronometer maker. Had Short not championed the notoriously difficult and unpopular Harrison in his disputes with the Board of Longitude, Short might well have become Astronomer Royal. According to Alexander Small, writing to Benjamin Franklin, who was a friend of Short, the help that Short gave to Harrison annoyed the Earl of Morton, who consequently opposed Short's appointment to the Royal Observatory.

The most reliable source of information about Short's method of work is the Plymouth physician John Mudge, who visited Short's workshop and who read two papers to the Royal Society on the founding and figuring of metal mirrors for reflecting telescopes. This art was partly in the composition and founding of the metal and partly in the polishing (or figuring) of the mirror. Apparently it was in the latter skill that Short particularly excelled; Mudge wrote of his mirrors, "they are all exquisitely figured." Recent studies show that Short made a total of 1,370 reflecting telescopes, of which 110 still exist.

The two most important astronomical events of the mid-eighteenth century were the transits of Venus in 1761 and 1769. The purpose of making worldwide observations of the transits was to calculate the solar parallax, and hence to discover the dimensions of the solar system. Astronomers throughout Europe were eager to acquire the best possible instruments for the task. They turned naturally to London, the reputation of whose instrument makers was unrivaled, and, for telescopes, to Short. A week before his death he was still concerned with the despatch of instruments to the Russian Imperial Academy. Short was also, as a mathematician, involved in the calculations of the parallax, and he published two long papers on this problem in the *Philosophical Transactions of the Royal Society* (1762, 1763). Short became a member of the council of the Royal Society in 1760 and was appointed to its special committee set up to study the 1769 transit. He died before he could take an active part in the plans he had helped to formulate, but his instruments were used to observe the second transit from stations throughout the world. Two of his instruments traveled with Cook on the *Endeavour* to Tahiti.

BIBLIOGRAPHY

I. ORIGINAL WORKS. Short's works include "Description and Uses of the Equatorial Telescope, or Portable Observatory," in *Philosophical Transactions of the Royal Society*, **46** (1749–1750), 241–246; "The Observations of the Internal Contact of Venus With the Sun's Limb, in the Late Transit, Made in Different Places of Europe, Compared With the Time of the Same Contact Observed at the Cape of Good Hope, and the Parallax of the Sun From Thence Determined," *ibid.*, **52** (1762), 611–628; "The Difference of Longitude Between the Royal Observatories of Greenwich and Paris, Determined by the Observations of the Transits of Mercury Over the Sun in the Years 1723, 1736, 1743, and 1753," *ibid.*, **53** (1763), 158–169; and "Second Paper Concerning the Parallax of the Sun Determined From the Observations of the Late Transit of Venus; in Which This Subject is Treated of More at Length, and the Quantity of the Parallax More Fully Ascertained," *ibid.*, 300–345. Short published twenty-eight additional papers in the *Philosophical Transactions of the Royal Society*, volumes **41** to **59**, most of these being brief accounts of astronomical observations. MS material is in the British Museum Add. MS 4434. Short's telescopes are housed in museums throughout the world; the Museum of the History of Science, Oxford, holds the longest (twelve-foot focal length) and also seven others.

II. SECONDARY LITERATURE. See D. J. Bryden, *James Short and His Telescopes. Royal Scottish Museum, Edinburgh, July 26th–September 7th, 1968* (Edinburgh, 1968); "Note on a Further Portrait of James Short, FRS," in *Notes and Records. Royal Society of London*, **24** (1969), 109–112; and "A Portrait Sketch of James Short by the 11th Earl of Buchan," in *Journal of the Royal Society of Arts*, **118** (1970), 792; V. L. Chenakal, "James Short and Russian Astronomy," in *Istoriko-astronomicheskie issledovaniya*, **5** (1959), 11–82; and G. L'E. Turner, "A Portrait of James Short, FRS, Attributed to Benjamin Wilson, FRS," in *Notes and Records. Royal Society of London*, **22** (1967), 105–112; "James Short, FRS, and His Contribution to the Construction of Reflecting Telescopes," *ibid.*, **24** (1969), 91–108; and "Mr James Short, Optician, Founding Member of the Society," in *Journal of the Royal Society of Arts*, **118** (1970), 788–792.

G. L'E. TURNER

SHTOKMAN, VLADIMIR BORISOVICH (*b.* Moscow, Russia, 10 March 1909; *d.* Moscow, 14 June 1968), *earth science, oceanography.*

In 1928 Shtokman entered the Faculty of Physics and Mathematics of Moscow University and chose to specialize in the geophysics of the earth's hydrosphere. The death of his parents in 1930 and his own illness in 1931 obliged him to interrupt his studies, and he began work as a laboratory assistant at the Institute of Oceanography in Moscow. By 1932 he had become a junior staff member as a result of his first independent scientific work, an investigation of the form of the curved underwater section of a cable carrying oceanographic instruments. He was promoted to senior staff member the following year, after having planned and led an oceanographic expedition in Motovskiy Gulf of the Barents Sea that yielded important results.

In 1934 Shtokman was sent to the Azerbaydzhan branch of the All-Union Scientific Research Institute of Ocean Fisheries and Oceanography (VNIRO) at Baku, where he organized and directed a laboratory of physical oceanography.

By applying probability theory and random functions to the study of ocean turbulence, Shtokman was a pioneer in introducing new statistical ideas and methods of studying this phenomenon into the U.S.S.R. He also developed direct techniques of measuring turbulent pulsation and current velocity at a series of points. These investigations were carried out in the central and southern Caspian Sea during a series of oceanographic expeditions, the majority of which Shtokman led personally. As a result he derived completely new results for turbulent pulsations in the horizontal velocity of marine currents. He also was the first to obtain the coefficients of horizontal turbulent exchange by direct methods.

In 1938 Shtokman was awarded the candidate's degree in physical-mathematical sciences, without defending a dissertation. In the late 1930's and early 1940's he worked in Moscow as director of the hydrology section of VNIRO and as senior staff member at the Institute of Theoretical Geophysics of the U.S.S.R. Academy of Sciences, and during the first years of World War II he was at Krasnoyarsk as senior staff member of the Arctic Institute, which had been evacuated there. During these years Shtokman conducted and published investigations on the theoretical bases of the computation of geostrophic currents from oceanographic measurements; on indirect methods for computing geostrophic currents in the Greenland Sea; on the analysis of water masses of the central part of the northern Arctic Ocean; and on the peculiarities of distribution of Atlantic waters in the Arctic Ocean. Shtokman employed temperature-salt curves in his critical examination of the widely used Jacobsen method of determining the intensity of intermixing of masses of water, and showed that the geometrical part of the method contained serious error. This work led him to research on the application of temperature-salt curves in the analysis of marine water masses, as a result of which a strict theory of these curves (geometry of temperature-salt curves) was developed.

In 1943 Shtokman returned to Moscow, defended his dissertation for the doctorate in physical-mathematical sciences, and began work at the newly created laboratory of oceanography of the Soviet Academy of Sciences, where he remained for the last twenty-five years of his life. During this time the laboratory of oceanography grew into the Institute of Oceanography of the Soviet Academy of Sciences; and Shtokman was director of the section of physical oceanography, the laboratory of ocean dynamics, and the theoretical section.

By the mid-1940's Shtokman had become widely known as an eminent Soviet specialist in the theory of ocean currents. He made an important step forward from the relations, proposed by Ekman, between currents and wind at a given point of the ocean and discovered the connections between currents and wind over the area of the ocean. Shtokman was the first to show clearly the important role in the dynamics of ocean currents of the transverse irregularities of tangential stress exerted by wind on water. In research published in 1945 he showed that the transverse irregularity of tangential stress of a following wind is an important reason for the horizontal circulation in the ocean. In 1941 Shtokman had shown that the presence of transverse irregularities of tangential stress of a wind over a closed sea inevitably results in countercurrents. The countercurrents exist not only in closed seas, however, but also in the open ocean, particularly in the equatorial zone.

In 1947 Shtokman published a special investigation, *Vozmozhny li protivotechenia v bezbrezhnom more, obuslovlennye lokalnoy neravnomernostyu vetra?* ("Are Countercurrents Caused by Local Ir-

regularity of the Wind Possible in an Open Sea?"). The answer was affirmative. In a work published in 1948 Shtokman showed that the main peculiarities of equatorial countercurrents are explained by the dynamic effect of a stable zone irregularity (trade winds) in the lower latitudes.

In 1946 research on the influence of the wind field on currents led Shtokman to develop a theoretical method of computing mean velocities of wind currents as a function of depth – the method of full streams. The closed system of hydrodynamic equations used in this method proved easy to solve and stimulated significant progress in the development of theoretical models of ocean currents for many years. Soon after Shtokman's work appeared, a method of full streams was developed in the United States by Sverdrup (1947). Unlike Shtokman's work, which dealt with the basin of a limited area and thus did not consider extensive change in the Coriolis parameter (β effect), Sverdrup, by developing the same method for the open sea, did consider the β effect.

In subsequent research Shtokman sought an easier method of mapping the full streams of the seas of the U.S.S.R., and the theoretical model of density that he introduced made it possible to compute approximately the velocity of currents at various depths.

In the last years of his life, Shtokman did mathematical work on the circulation of water, especially around islands in a direction opposite to the circulation in the surrounding ocean. Such a situation occurs in the area around Taiwan in winter and around Iceland and the Kurile Islands throughout the year. In 1966 Shtokman showed that the reason for this phenomenon is the disturbance effect (violation of water exchange), introduced by the island into the horizontal circulation stimulated by the transverse irregularity of wind within the limits of a closed area.

BIBLIOGRAPHY

I. ORIGINAL WORKS. Shtokman's major published writings are "Turbulentny obmen v rayone Agrakhanskogo poluostrova v Kaspyskom more" ("Turbulent Exchange in the Region of the Agrakhansky Peninsula in the Caspian Sea"), in *Zhurnal geofiziki*, 6, no. 4 (1936), 340–388; "O turbulentnom obmene v sredney i yuzhnoy chasti Kaspyskogo morya" ("On Turbulent Exchange in the Middle and Southern Parts of the Caspian Sea"), in *Izvestiya Akademii nauk SSSR*, geog.-geophys. sec. (1940), no. 4, 569–592; "O pulsatsiakh gorizontalnykh komponent skorosti morskikh techeny, obuslovlennykh turbulentnostyu bolshogo masshtaba" ("On the Pulsations of the Horizontal Components of Velocity of the Ocean Currents Caused by Large-Scale Turbulence"), *ibid.* (1941), nos. 4–5, 475–486; "Osnovy teorii temperaturno-solenostnykh krivykh, kak metoda izuchenia peremeshivania i transformatsii vodnykh mass morya" ("Bases of the Theory of Temperature-Salt Curves as a Method of Studying the Mixing and Transformation of Masses of Seawater"), in *Problemy arktiki* (1943), no. 1, 32–71; "Geometricheskie svoystva temperaturno-solenostnykh krivykh pri smeshenii trekh vodnykh mass v neogranichennom more" ("Geometrical Properties of Temperature-Salt Curves in the Mixing of Three Water Masses in the Open Ocean"), in *Doklady Akademii nauk SSSR,* **43,** no. 8 (1944), 351–355; "Poperechnaya neravnomernost nagonnogo vetra kak odna iz vazhnykh prichin gorizontalnoy tsirkulyatsii v more" ("Transverse Irregularity of a Following Wind as One of the Important Reasons for Horizontal Circulation in the Ocean"), *ibid.,* **49,** no. 2 (1945), 102–106; and "Teoria ekvatorialnykh protivotecheny v okeanakh" ("Theory of Equatorial Countercurrent in the Oceans"), *ibid.,* **52,** no. 4 (1946), 311–314.

Subsequent works are "Uravnenia polya polnykh potokov, vozbuzhdaemykh vetrom v neodnorodnom okeane" ("Equations of the Fields of Full Streams Generated by Wind in the Nonuniform Ocean"), in *Doklady Akademii nauk SSSR,* **54,** no. 5 (1946), 407–410; "Ispolzovanie analogii mezhdu polnym potokom v more i izgibom zakreplennoy plastiny . . ." ("Use of the Analogy Between a Full Stream in the Ocean and the Curve of a Strengthened Plate . . ."), *ibid.,* **54,** no. 8 (1946), 689–692; "Novye dokazatelstva znachenia neravnomernosti vetra kak odnoy iz prichin tsirkulyatsii v more" ("New Proof of the Significance of the Irregularity of Wind as One of the Reasons for Circulation in the Ocean"), *ibid.,* **58,** no. 1 (1947), 53–56; *Ekvatorialnye protivotechenia v okeanakh* ("Equatorial Countercurrents in the Oceans"; Leningrad, 1948); "Issledovanie vlania vetra i relefa dna na rezultiruyushchuyu tsirkulyatsiyu i raspredelenie mass v neodnorodnom okeane ili more" ("Research on the Influence of Wind and the Surface of the Bottom on the Resulting Circulation and Distribution of Masses in a Nonuniform Ocean or Sea"), in *Trudy Instituta okeanologii Akademii nauk SSSR,* **3** (1949), 3–65; "Vlianie vetra na techenia v Beringovom prolive . . ." ("Influence of the Wind on the Currents in the Bering Strait . . ."), *ibid.,* **25** (1957), 17–24; "Ob odnoy probleme dinamiki okeanicheskoy tsirkulyatsii" ("On One Problem of the Dynamics of Ocean Circulation"), in *Simpozium po matematicheskim i gidrodinamicheskim metodam izuchenia fizicheskikh protsessov v okeane, Moskva, 25–28 maya 1966, tezisy dokladov* ("Symposium on Mathematical and Hydrodynamical Methods of Studying the Physical Processes in the Ocean . . . Abstracts of Reports"; Moscow, 1966), 60–61; and "Razvitie teorii morskoy i okeanicheskoy tsirku-

lyatsii v SSSR za 50 let" ("Development of the Theory of Sea and Ocean Circulation in the U.S.S.R. for Fifty Years"), in *Okeanologia,* **7,** no. 5 (1967), 761–773.

II. Secondary Literature. See the obituaries by his editorial colleagues, "Vladimir Borisovich Shtokman," in *Izvestiya Akademii nauk SSSR,* Fiz. atmos. i okeana ser., **4,** no. 9 (1968), 1012–1013; "Vladimir Borisovich Shtokman," in *Okeanologia,* **8,** no. 4 (1968), 771, by a group of his colleagues.

A. F. Plakhotnik

SHUJĀᶜ IBN ASLAM, AL-MIṢRI. See Abū Kāmil Shujāᶜ ibn Aslam ibn Muḥammad ibn Shujāᶜ

SHULL, AARON FRANKLIN (*b.* Miami County, Ohio, 1 August 1881; *d.* Ann Arbor, Michigan, 7 November 1961), *genetics, evolution.*

Shull was one of eight children born to Harrison and Catherine Ryman Shull. Although they had relatively little formal education, both parents encouraged intellectual activity among their children. The father was a farmer and lay minister; the mother had strong interests in serious reading, especially topics relating to natural history, and in her later years became an accomplished horticulturist with a firsthand knowledge of plants. Because the family moved from farm to farm in south-central Ohio, Shull's early schooling was largely informal. In 1904 he enrolled as an undergraduate at the University of Michigan, completing his A.B. degree in 1908. In the summer following his graduation he worked with the Michigan Biological Survey, and in the fall of that year he entered Columbia University for graduate work in zoology. Stimulated by the work of T. H. Morgan and E. B. Wilson, both at Columbia, Shull became interested in problems of heredity, particularly sex determination, on which he wrote his thesis. After obtaining his Ph.D. in 1911, he returned to the University of Michigan as an instructor in zoology (1911–1912), assistant professor (1912–1914), associate professor (1914–1921), and professor (1921–1951). His only break with this university occurred in the summer of 1938, when he was a visiting professor at the University of California, Berkeley. Although a researcher of considerable merit, Shull perhaps is best remembered in American biology for his teaching and writing. A stimulating lecturer, he was also a prolific writer of monographs and textbooks that introduced countless students to modern, experimental biology and to rigorous concepts in general biology, heredity, and evolution.

Shull studied in considerable depth the life cycle of and sex determination problem in rotifers, a subject that had been variously interpreted by workers in the last part of the nineteenth and first part of the twentieth centuries. A study of developmental physiology and sex determination in aphids, expanded the earlier work to the problem of sex determination in general. In the 1920's and 1930's he experimented with induction of crossing-over in *Drosophila* by physical factors, most notably heat. In all these studies, Shull's focus was on the relationship between heredity and environment in determining the phenotype of an organism. His interests centered on some of the highly controversial questions, which received so much prominence at the time, concerning the influence of environment on heredity. A Mendelian from his earliest days, Shull was interested not only in working out specific problems of heredity—was food a factor in determining sex, or does heat induce crossing-over in *Drosophila?*—but also in the relationships between these phenomena and the process of organic evolution. Recognizing earlier than many biologists that one side of the evolutionary coin was the problem of the origin of hereditary variation (the other side was the effect of selection on these variations), he concentrated much of his research on determining the relationship between genetic and environmental factors in producing the phenotypes on which selection acted.

In his studies and writings on evolution, Shull was incisive and penetrating in his analyses of such subsidiary problems as the nature and origin of mimicry. A fervent advocate of drawing conclusions only from the data at hand, he severely criticized the concept of mimicry advanced by G. D. Hale Carpenter. To Shull, phenotypic properties such as mimicry (in which one species comes to resemble another as a means of protection against predators) could not always be judged as being of survival value simply because, to man, the two species appeared to resemble each other. He pointed out that two forms resembling each other in human vision might appear quite distinct to some predator (such as a bird). Shull cited the work of W. L. McAtee, who, in 1912, had shown from analysis of the contents of birds' stomachs that mimics were eaten, like nonmimics, roughly in proportion to their availability. Thus, whatever resemblance the mimics may or may not have borne to the model appeared to be of little value in helping the

prey escape its predators. Shull's opposition to the theory of warning coloration and mimicry was based largely on what he considered the tendency to misuse evidence, to interject anthropomorphism and subjective speculation into an area where the collection of solid facts would be more beneficial. A strong empiricist and experimentalist, Shull was one of a group of younger biologists who rejected the nonrigorous and speculative tradition in biology represented by the older morphologists and neo-Darwinians. Although a strong proponent of Darwin's theory of natural selection, Shull felt that among evolutionists there was a preponderance of purely descriptive, nonrigorous, and nonanalytical thinking that did not take into consideration the recent findings in such experimental areas as physiology, development, and genetics.

Shull carried his concern for new methods in biology into his teaching and educational writings. A strong advocate of the "principles" approach to biology, he organized his courses and teaching monographs in terms of generally applicable biological concepts; cell structure and function, transport, unity and control, embryonic development, genetics, systematics, and geographic distribution. To the modern reader this may appear to be a customary and routine type of organization; it was in fact quite novel in Shull's day. During the first three decades of the twentieth century, most biology courses were organized along phylogenetic and "type specimen" lines. Students were given a detailed, descriptive, and anatomically oriented survey of animal or plant types (poriferans, annelids, crustaceans, echinoderms, vertebrates, tracheophytes, angiosperms, and so on). To Shull, this method of organization not only was uninteresting for most students but also offered a limited view of biology. Why not, he asked, study the characteristics of cells by using examples of many cell types from many different species of animals and plants? Biological principles are what the student is going to remember most; the anatomical detail will be important if—and only if—the student decides to pursue some area of biology in depth. Besides, he argued, the old "type specimen" course did not even do what it claimed to do: give the student a picture of evolutionary development. Shull pointed out, for example, that most such courses involved detailed consideration of a modern echinoderm (starfish, sand dollar, sea urchin); yet echinoderms as a group represent an evolutionary offshoot that was by no means to be found in the mainstream of animal phylogeny. In *Principles of Animal Biology* (1934), *Evolution* (1936), and *Heredity* (1938), Shull gave this approach a concrete form that he hoped would aid others in developing a "principles" approach to biology at the undergraduate and graduate levels.

During his academic career Shull received numerous honors and was a member of many professional societies. He was a fellow of the American Association for the Advancement of Science and was appointed Russel lecturer for 1951. He was a member of the American Society of Naturalists, serving as secretary (1920–1926), vice-president (1929), and president (1934). He also belonged to the American Society of Zoologists, the Genetics Society of America, the Society for the Study of Evolution, the Eugenics Society (London), and the National Association of Biology Teachers; was a fellow of the Entomological Society of America; and served as president of the Michigan Academy of Sciences (1921–1922). In 1911 Shull married Margaret Jeffrey Buckley; they had four children.

BIBLIOGRAPHY

I. ORIGINAL WORKS. Shull wrote a large number and variety of scholarly papers on sex determination, heredity, evolution, and education. A few of the most notable are "Color Sport Among Locustidae," in *Science,* **26** (1907), 218–219; "Nutrition and Sex Determination in Rotifers," *ibid.,* **38** (1913), 786–788; "Biological Principles in the Zoology Course," *ibid.,* **48** (1918), 648–649; "Crossovers in Male *Drosophila melanogaster* Induced by Heat," *ibid.,* **80** (1934), 103–104, written with Maurice Whittingill; "Weismann and Haeckel: One Hundred Years," *ibid.,* **81** (1935), 443–452; and "Needs of the Mimicry Theory," *ibid.,* **85** (1937), 496–498.

II. SECONDARY LITERATURE. There is no detailed biographical sketch of Shull's life or work. He is listed in *American Men of Science*, 9th ed. (Lancaster, Pa., 1955), 1030. Letters to and from Shull can be found at the American Philosophical Society, in the Jennings, Blakeslee, Demerec, Dunn, and Davenport papers.

GARLAND ALLEN

SIDGWICK, NEVIL VINCENT (*b.* Oxford, England, 8 May 1873; *d.* Oxford, 15 March 1952), *chemistry.*

Sidgwick was born into a family of unusual distinction. His father, William Carr Sidgwick, was a fellow of Merton College, Oxford. His uncles included Henry Sidgwick, professor of moral philosophy at Cambridge; Arthur Sidgwick, reader in Greek at Oxford; and (by marriage) Edward White Benson, archbishop of Canterbury. From them he may well have inherited or absorbed his power of mental organization and his command of language. Until he was twelve years old Sidgwick was educated at home, mainly by his mother, Sarah Isabella Thompson. Her uncle was General Thomas Perronet Thompson, F.R.S., and it was to her that he owed his introduction to botany and natural history and his general love of science.

Sidgwick went to Rugby School when he was thirteen and, unusually for that time, studied both the classics and science. In 1892 he returned to Oxford as a scholar of Christ Church. His tutor was Vernon Harcourt, a pioneer in reaction kinetics. Sidgwick earned a first-class degree in chemistry in 1895. Then, reputedly because of a disparaging remark by a relative about science, he studied *literae humaniores* and gained a brilliant first in 1897, largely by his performance in philosophy. Next he went to Germany, where he studied physical chemistry under Georg Bredig in Ostwald's laboratory at Leipzig and then organic chemistry with Hans von Pechmann at Tübingen.

In 1900 Sidgwick was elected a fellow of Lincoln College, Oxford, and there spent the rest of his working life. Until 1920 he had published only eighteen papers. Most of these were concerned with the kinetics of organic reactions, the others mainly with the relation of solubility and chemical structure. These papers described good, careful work; but none was of great importance. He would have been unknown outside Oxford had he not written *Organic Chemistry of Nitrogen* (1910). This was his first essay in applying the ideas and quantitative methods of physical chemistry to the facts and systematics of descriptive chemistry, a task that gradually became his major interest. The book was a great success, not only because of his shrewd selection of topics and his clarity of thought but also because of the intellectual excitement conveyed by his style.

From 1920 Sidgwick's rate of publication increased rapidly, probably because the introduction of a year of research as a part of the chemistry course provided him with more research pupils. His major accomplishment was establishing that there can be a definite bond between a group containing a fairly acidic hydrogen atom (for example, hydroxyl group) and an oxygen-rich group (for example, nitro group). Such a bond via a hydrogen atom had already been postulated by various people; but the clear, systematic attack by Sidgwick and his pupils played a major part in gaining general acceptance of the idea. He was elected a fellow of the Royal Society in 1922.

In 1914, while traveling to Australia for a meeting of the British Association, Sidgwick met Ernest Rutherford and immediately came under his spell. This friendship was of crucial importance, for it inspired Sidgwick to try to explain chemical behavior in terms of atomic structure, as G. N. Lewis and Langmuir were also doing. The first major fruit of this new interest was the publication in 1927 of *Electronic Theory of Valency*, which was intended as an exposition of principles to be followed by a second volume applying them systematically. One of the most novel and important parts of this book was that concerned with the coordination compounds or complexes so extensively studied by A. Werner. Sidgwick showed that, by using the concept of the dative bond (wherein both bonding electrons are provided initially by one of the two atoms involved, instead of one by each), it is possible to rationalize these compounds more successfully than had been done previously. Lewis had already put forward the concept of this bond, but it was Sidgwick's systematic application of the idea that made chemists realize its value and wide importance. Sidgwick also emphasized that both ionic and covalent bonds exist, that generally they are sharply distinguished, and that a given bond might exist in either form, for example, when an acid ionizes. The book presented a brilliant discussion of a wide range of topics on a simple basis, and it had a profound effect.

Even as the book was written, however, the theoretical basis that Sidgwick had used, namely, the quantum mechanics of Bohr, Sommerfeld, and W. Wilson, was being discarded by physicists in favor of a much more general mechanics formulated in matrix form by W. Heisenberg and as a wave equation by Schrödinger. In 1927 W. Heitler and F. London produced an explanation of the covalent bond that was far more fundamental than anything previously advanced. A year later F. Hund produced an alternative treatment. Both theories were quickly taken up and developed. From the former, J. C. Slater and L. Pauling derived, in the early 1930's, a basis for stereochemistry; and they also introduced the concept of "resonance" in molecules; electrons holding a set of atoms together may not be localized as pairs between pairs of atoms but may be more generally distributed or "delocalized," so that each electron can be considered to play a part in holding several atoms together. From Hund's explanation R. S. Mulliken and E. Hückel developed an alternative treatment for many-atom molecules, the "molecular orbital" method.

Sidgwick went to the United States for the first time in 1931, as George Fisher Baker nonresident lecturer in chemistry at Cornell University, and in his travels met Pauling. They immediately became fast friends. Thereafter one of Sidgwick's main preoccupations was to expound the concept of resonance to British chemists. He did so in various articles and in his presidential addresses to the Chemical Society (1936, 1937). He had a flair for extracting the essence of a mathematical argument and expressing it verbally.

Sidgwick had become embarrassed by the success of his books. There had long been a demand for a new edition of his book on nitrogen compounds. Twenty-five years after publication secondhand copies were selling for four times the original price. But realizing that he could not prepare a new edition, he had his colleagues T. W. J. Taylor and W. Baker take over the task and prepare a reworked edition in 1937. Another edition was produced in 1966 by I. T. Millar and H. D. Springall. To meet the requirements of his Cornell appointment Sidgwick published *Some Physical Properties of the Covalent Link in Chemistry* (1933), which dealt mainly with the new experimental methods for investigating structure, such as heats of formation, lengths, and electric dipole moments of bonds. Because of its relatively limited scope, it did not have the importance of the book on valence theory.

Sidgwick then began writing volume II of his *Electronic Theory of Valency*. Curiously, the hardships created by World War II may have helped Sidgwick to complete this task, the size of which became clearer and more daunting as he proceeded. The limitations on travel meant fewer outside demands on his time; and still more important was the diminution in the world output of primary publications. He consulted 10,000 papers, mostly on his own but also with help from H. M. Powell and R. V. G. Ewens. Eventually, in 1950 when he was seventy-seven, the work appeared as *Chemical Elements and Their Compounds,* two large volumes of about 750,000 words. While it did not have the impact of volume I, it was still a landmark in the development of chemistry. Once again he had brought unification, this time to an even vaster body of fact. His clear critical mind and easy style illuminate every word. Although the book has become dated it still is a prime source of earlier references. The emphasis by chemists on the molecular orbital method began just as his writing finished. In the 1950's the ligand field treatment of complexes was developed at Oxford by L. E. Orgel, a pupil of a pupil. Accurate determinations of geometric structures of molecules began to pour forth after 1945. Completely unforeseen developments occurred, notably in the discovery of new organometallic compounds and of compounds of the once inert gases.

Today it is impossible for a large book about descriptive chemistry to remain in date for more than a few years after it is started; and no satisfactory technique for dealing with this situation has yet been devised. What is certain is that no one man can ever again attempt such a task with any hope of being effective; thus Sidgwick may be regarded as the last of a line. He showed shrewdness, or had luck, in applying his talents when they were particularly useful in the development of chemistry.

Sidgwick did not live long enough to enjoy his final success. His health had been slowly failing for more than ten years, and he had completed his writing only because of his indomitable will. But he was able to achieve again his dearest ambition, to revisit the United States, to meet his old friends, and to see the beauty of New England in the fall. On the return voyage he collapsed aboard ship. He was brought back to Oxford, where he died in his sleep.

Sidgwick's influence on those who knew him was as much due to his personality as to his writings. He never married, although he enjoyed the company of women—provided that they were intelligent. He lived in college—very simply save when he entertained. He was a generous and genial host, delighting in lively discussions and pungent repartee.

BIBLIOGRAPHY

I. ORIGINAL WORKS. A complete bibliography is given by Tizard (see below). Sidgwick's books are *Organic Chemistry of Nitrogen* (Oxford, 1910); *Electronic Theory of Valency* (Oxford, 1927); *Some Physical Properties of the Covalent Link in Chemistry* (Ithaca, N. Y., 1933); and *Chemical Elements and Their Compounds,* 2 vols. (Oxford, 1950).

II. SECONDARY LITERATURE. The most helpful source is Sir Henry Tizard's article in *Obituary Notices of Fellows of the Royal Society of London,* **9** (1954), 237–258, with bibliography. See also L. E. Sutton's obituary in *Proceedings of the Chemical Society* (1958), 310–319.

L. E. SUTTON

SIEBOLD, CARL THEODOR ERNST VON (*b.* Würzburg, Germany, 16 February 1804; *d.* Munich, Germany, 7 April 1885), *medicine, zoology.*

Siebold was the third child of Elias von Siebold, professor of medicine and midwifery at Würzburg, and Sophie von Schäffer. His happy childhood was punctuated by fondly remembered vacations in Regensburg at the home of his grandfather Jakob Christian Gottlieb von Schäffer, whose extensive natural history collection first stimulated Siebold's interest in the subject. Siebold accompanied his older brother Eduard (who later became professor of medicine and midwifery at Marburg and then at Göttingen) and their friend Ignaz Döllinger on entomological and botanical excursions in the woods near Würzburg. In a short autobiography Siebold wrote of his friendship with Döllinger:

This relationship gave me the opportunity one day to enter the study of Döllinger's father, the famous founder of embryology. And it was there that I glimpsed a saucer filled with black wax placed on a desk near the window; a flea was affixed to the saucer with needles so that the arrangement of its intestines could easily be examined. This anatomical preparation made a deep and lasting impression on me.

Siebold began his schooling in Würzburg and continued it at the Gymnasium zum Grauen Kloster in 1816, when his father assumed a post at the University of Berlin. During these years Siebold collected and identified butterflies and dug up newts, snails, and mussels. He passed the final secondary school examination in the fall of 1823 and, acceding to his father's wishes, began to study medicine, although even at this early date he would have preferred to devote himself exclusively to zoology. He spent the first two semesters of his medical studies at Berlin, attending the lectures of Karl Martin Lichtenstein, Link, and Rudolphi, among others. In the fall of 1824 he went to Göttingen, where his interest in natural history was encouraged by Blumenbach and Johann Hausmann. Three years later he returned to Berlin, and on 28 April 1828 received the M.D. The sudden death of his father on 12 July 1828 obliged Siebold to find some means of support. Accordingly, he prepared to practice medicine, passing the two official qualifying examinations in 1829 and 1830. In the spring of 1831 he was named district physician in Heilsberg (now Lidzmark). On 10 April 1831, shortly before assuming his duties, he married the twenty-six-year-old Fanny Nöldechen.

In Königsberg, en route to Heilsberg, Siebold met Karl Ernst von Baer, who offered him guidance and assistance in his scientific studies during the next three years by sending him technical literature and information. Siebold's wish to be near a university again was fulfilled by his transfer in 1834 to the post of municipal physician in Königsberg. He still hoped for the opportunity to qualify as a university lecturer, and within a few months it seemed that he would have his chance. Both Baer, who had received a post in St. Petersburg, and Lichtenstein supported Siebold's candidacy at Albertus University, but their efforts were futile — a ruling dating to 1544 prohibited Catholics from teaching there.

Following this disappointment Siebold accepted a post in the same year (1834) in Danzig as municipal physician and director of a school of midwifery. His investigations during this period on the phenomena of generation in jellyfish, intestinal worms, and insects can be viewed as preliminary studies for Steenstrup's fundamental work on the alternation of generations (1842). Siebold also published extensively on invertebrates of Prussia.

Siebold's many publications soon attracted the attention of zoologists. No less a figure than Alexander von Humboldt — who was a guest at Siebold's house in Danzig on 12 and 13 September 1840 — intervened successfully with King Ludwig I of Bavaria in favor of Siebold's appointment to the chair of zoology and comparative anatomy at the Friedrich Alexander University in Erlangen, left vacant by the departure of Rudolph Wagner. On 1 March 1841 Siebold returned with his family to his native Franconia. In addition to his regular lectures, Siebold also taught veterinary medicine, physiology, and histology, requiring his students to use the microscope. At the beginning of 1845 Siebold accepted an offer from the University of Freiburg, and on 28 October 1845 he was formally welcomed by the university senate.

Siebold developed a close friendship at Freiburg im Breisgau with the botanist Alexander Braun, who accompanied him in 1847 to the congress of Swiss scientists at Schaffhausen. On this occasion Siebold realized a long-cherished plan: he and Braun agreed to join with Naegeli and Koelliker in editing a new journal of botany and zoology. Various circumstances, including Braun's election to the office of vice-chancellor of the University of Berlin and Naegeli's departure for Freiburg, prevented the journal from appearing in the form originally envisioned. Instead, Siebold and Koelliker created the *Zeitschrift für wissenschaftliche Zoologie*, first published in 1848. In the same year Siebold completed his *Lehrbuch der vergleichenden*

Anatomie der wirbellosen Thiere, begun in 1845 and one of the most important systematic reforms since the work of Cuvier. In it Siebold divided the Radiata into groups and characterized the Protozoa as single-celled organisms.

The political disturbances of 1848 led Siebold, in the spring of 1850, to Breslau, where he succeeded Purkyně as professor of physiology. At Breslau, Siebold continued his research on the development of the Cestoda and discovered the parthenogenesis of the honeybee. Wagner considered the discovery of parthenogenesis to be "one of the most disconcerting obstacles impeding the formulation of so-called general laws of animal life processes." Siebold remained at Breslau for only two years. Disappointed with the university, he was delighted when the Bavarian ministry of education in June 1852 began negotiations concerning his assuming the professorship of physiology and comparative anatomy at Munich. The discussions lasted until the late fall, but on 26 November Siebold informed the dean of the Breslau medical faculty that he had accepted the post.

Siebold became a member of the medical faculty of the Ludwig Maximilian University in Munich on 13 April 1853; and on 18 January 1854 he was accepted as a member of the Bavarian Academy of Sciences, of which he had been a corresponding member since 1848. According to the terms of Siebold's contract, he was required to establish an institute of physiology in Munich. Thus he lectured on both zoology and physiology only until he was able to relinquish the chair of physiology, along with the post of curator of the anatomical institute, to Theodor Bischoff. Siebold's lectures encompassed zoology, comparative anatomy, the reproductive biology of man and animals, and parasitology. He also was curator of the Bavarian state collections of comparative anatomy, physiology, and zoology.

While in Munich, Siebold completed *Über die Band- und Blasenwürmer nebst einer Einleitung über die Enstehung der Eingeweidewürmer* and actively participated in the research of his student Bilharz. Siebold's most important topic of research, however, was parthenogenesis; and in 1856 he published *Wahre Parthenogenesis bei Schmetterlingen und Bienen*. In addition, he obtained a royal contract (dated 3 May 1854) to produce a monograph on the fishes of Central Europe, a task that required extended travel and an intensive study of the specialized literature. The result of nine years' work, *Die Süsswasserfische von Mitteleuropa*, illustrated with sixty-four woodcuts and two colorplates, finally appeared in 1863.

Siebold's wife died on 26 December 1854, one of the last victims of the cholera epidemic. A year later, in Göttingen, Siebold married her younger sister, Antoynie Nöldechen. Siebold was acquainted with artists and scholars, and she made their home a center of stimulating social gatherings. He also belonged to the Munich poets' circle, whose members were regularly guests of the king.

At a congress of German scientists and physicians in Königsberg in 1860, Siebold met the young Ernst Haeckel, with whom he felt closely united in discussions of the Darwinian theory of evolution. Their common enthusiasm provided the basis of a lifelong correspondence and friendship. In a letter to Haeckel on his fortieth birthday, the seventy-year-old Siebold wrote:

> Oh, how I wish I could see this reform carried through! For I must tell you that brilliant though it is, it is not easy for a zoologist trained in the old school. Instead of being able to relax in my later years, I have to learn just as much—no, even more—than I did during all my younger days. If you reflect that in old age it is much harder to learn than to forget, you will bear with me.

At the end of the winter semester of 1882–1883, during which he gave a two-hour lecture course, Siebold submitted his request for retirement. In a birthday letter to Haeckel dated 18 February 1883, he confessed: "I have been much upset recently by the fact that in my lectures, which I was accustomed to give without the aid of notes, I cannot always remember the scientific names of animals with their genus and species designations—this causes me the greatest embarrassment." Ludwig II granted him permission to retire on 11 March 1883, two years before his death.

BIBLIOGRAPHY

I. ORIGINAL WORKS. Siebold's works include *Observationes quaedam de Salamandris et Tritonibus* (Berlin, 1828), his M.D. thesis; "Über die Spermatozoen der Crustaceen, Insecten, Gastropoden und einiger anderer wirbelloser Thiere," in *Archiv für Anatomie, Physiologie und wissenschaftliche Medicin*, **3** (1836), 13–53; "Fernere Beobachtungen über die Spermatozoen der wirbellosen Thiere," *ibid.*, 232–255; "Fernere Beobachtungen über die Spermatozoen der wirbellosen Thiere. 3. Die Spermatozoen der Bivalven. 4. Die Spermatozoen in den befruchteten Insecten-Weibchen," *ibid.*, **4** (1837), 381–439; "Zur Entwicklungsgeschichte der Helminthen," in K. F. Burdach, ed., *Die Physiologie als Erfah-*

rungswissenschaft, II (Leipzig, 1837), 183–213; "Beiträge zur Naturgeschichte der wirbellosen Thiere. Über Medusa, Cyclops, Loligo, Gregarina und Xenos," in *Neueste Schriften der Naturforschenden Gesellschaft in Danzig*, **3** (1839), 1–94; *Observationes quaedam entomologicae de oxybelo uniglume atque miltogramma conica* (Erlangen, 1841); and *Viro summe reverendo collegae . . .* (Erlangen, 1844).

Later writings are "Parasiten," in R. Wagner, ed., *Handwörterbuch der Physiologie mit Rücksicht auf physiologische Pathologie*, II (Brunswick, 1844), 641–692; *Lehrbuch der vergleichenden Anatomie der wirbellosen Thiere* (Berlin, 1848); "Über den Generationswechsel der Cestoden nebst einer Revision der Gattung Tetrarhynchus," in *Zeitschrift für wissenschaftliche Zoologie*, **2** (1850), 198–253; *Über die Band- und Blasenwürmer nebst einer Einleitung über die Entstehung der Eingeweidewürmer* (Leipzig, 1854); *Wahre Parthenogenesis bei Schmetterlingen und Bienen. Ein Beitrag zur Fortpflanzungsgeschichte der Thiere* (Leipzig, 1856); *Über Parthenogenesis* (Munich, 1862); *Die Süsswasserfische von Mitteleuropa* (Leipzig, 1863); and *Beiträge zur Parthenogenesis der Arthropoden* (Leipzig, 1871).

A short autobiography, used by A. Koelliker for his biographical sketch, is still extant in MS in a private collection in Freiburg im Breisgau.

II. SECONDARY LITERATURE. On Siebold and his work, see E. Ehlers, "Carl Theodor Ernst von Siebold. Eine biographische Skizze," in *Zeitschrift für wissenschaftliche Zoologie*, **42** (1885), i–xxiii; R. Hertwig, *Gedächtnisrede auf Carl Theodor von Siebold gehalten in der öffentlichen Sitzung der k. Bayerischen Akademie der Wissenschaften . . .* (Munich, 1886); A. Koelliker, "Carl Theodor von Siebold, eine biographische Skizze," in *Zeitschrift für wissenschaftliche Zoologie*, supp. **30** (1878), v–xxix; H. Körner, "Die Würzburger Siebold. Eine Gelehrtenfamilie des 18. und 19. Jahrhunderts," in *Deutsches Familienarchiv*, nos. 34–35 (1967), 451–1080; G. Olpp, *Hervorragende Tropenärzte in Wort und Bild* (Munich, 1932), 378–379; and F. Winckel, "Carl Theodor Ernst von Siebold," in *Allgemeine deutsche Biographie*, XXXIV (1892), 186–188.

ARMIN GEUS

SIEDENTOPF, HENRY FRIEDRICH WILHELM (*b.* Bremen, Germany, 22 September 1872; *d.* Jena, Germany, 8 May 1940), *physics.*

Siedentopf was a distinguished practitioner of scientific microscopy and a pioneer in ultramicroscopy and microphotography. After graduating from the Gymnasium in Bremen, he studied at Leipzig and Göttingen and became assistant to the mineralogist and crystallographer Theodor Liebisch. In 1896 Siedentopf received the doctorate at Göttingen under Woldemar Voigt for the dissertation

"Über die Capillaritätsconstanten geschmolzener Metalle." He became assistant to Franz Richarz at Greifswald in 1898 but the following year accepted an offer from Ernst Abbe to join the Zeiss optical works in Jena. Siedentopf first worked in Abbe's laboratory, and from 1907 to 1938 he was director of the company's microscopy division. In 1918 he was named both titular and ordinary professor at the University of Jena, where he lectured on scientific microscopy. With Hermann Ambronn and August Köhler he gave courses at Jena every summer.

Siedentopf's most important achievement was the development of the "slit ultramicroscope," which he perfected in 1902–1903 in collaboration with Richard Zsigmondy. They constructed the instrument in order to make visible the gold particles in ruby glass, which Zsigmondy had unsuccessfully attempted to do alone. The device was based on the principle that under intense illumination with an electric arc lamp, the ultramicroscopic particles can be made to act as origins of small diffraction cones, which are visible in the objective. In the instrument the smallest particles were no longer illuminated from below, as in the ordinary microscope, but from the side; and the light that they refracted appeared in the ultramicroscope's field of view. Zsigmondy later developed this instrument into the immersion microscope, and Siedentopf created the cardioid ultramicroscope. From 1907 Siedentopf devoted his attention to microcinematography and in 1911 devised a stationary apparatus with a time-lapse camera and a slow-motion camera. Between 1919 and 1923 he constructed skin and capillary microscopes, and in 1922 he developed the photomicroscope with "Phoku" eyepiece and attached miniature camera. The latter device was a milestone in the development of microphotography.

BIBLIOGRAPHY

I. ORIGINAL WORKS. Siedentopf wrote about 50 scientific papers and obtained a number of patents for optical and microscopical devices. See Poggendorff, IV, 1394; V, 1162; VI, 2442; VIIa, 4, 405. His works include "Über die Sichtbarmachung und Grössenbestimmung ultramikroskopischer Teilchen mit besonderer Anwendung von Goldrubingläsern," in *Annalen der Physik*, 4th ser., **10** (1903), 1–39, written with R. Zsigmondy; "Bisphärische Spiegelkondensatoren für Ultramikroskopie," ibid., **39** (1912), 1177–1186; *Übungen zur wissenschaftlichen Mikroskopie* (Leipzig, 1913); "Über den Nachweis der Form von Ultramikronen," in *Kolloid-Zeitschrift*, supp. to **36** (1925), "Zsigmondy-Festschrift," 1–14; "Über die optische Abbildung von Nicht-Selbstleuchtern," in *Zeitschrift für Physik*, **50** (1928), 297–309; and "Mikroskopische Beobachtungen an Strichgittern mit periodischen Teilungsfehlern," ibid., **107** (1937), 251–257; **108** (1938), 279–287; **109** (1938), 260–272; and (with similar title) **112** (1939), 704–726.

II. SECONDARY LITERATURE. Obituary notices are in *Deutsche optische Wochenschrift*, **61** (1940), 110; and *Kolloid-Zeitschrift*, **91** (1940), B218; a biography is being prepared by F. Stier for *Neue deutsche Biographie*. See also the following, listed chronologically: F. Hauser, "Die Entwicklung mikroskopischer Apparate bei der Firma Zeiss in dem ersten Jahrhundert ihres Bestehens," in *Jenaer Jahrbuch* (1952), 1–64, see 47–48, 55; R. Jobst, "120 Jahre wissenschaftlicher Gerätebau in Jena," in *Jenaer Rundschau* (1966), no. 4, supp., "Carl Zeiss 150. Geburtstag," 25; and H. Gause, "Das Spaltultramikroskop nach Siedentopf und Zsigmondy—eine historische und optische Betrachtung," ibid., no. 6, 327–333.

HANS-GÜNTHER KÖRBER

SIEDLECKI, MICHAŁ (*b.* Cracow, Poland, 1873; *d.* Sachsenhausen, Germany, January 1940), *zoology, cytology.*

Siedlecki was born into a middle-class family. He studied at Jagiellonian Cracow University at Cracow and received the M.D. in 1895. The following year he went to Berlin to work with Schulze, whose assistant at that time was Schaudinn. From 1897 to 1899 Siedlecki worked at the Pasteur Institute under Metchnikoff and also at the Zoological Station in Naples under Anton Dohrn.

Siedlecki's first paper dealt with leukocytes of Urodela (1895). He later studied the phagocytes of Annelida (1903) and, with Caullery, Echinodermata (1903). With Kostanecki, he published an interesting paper on the cytology of *Ascaris*. In 1908–1909, Siedlecki went to Java, where he became interested in frogs of the genus *Rhacophorus* and in fishes and birds.

Siedlecki's outstanding scientific contributions, however, were in protozoology, which he first studied at Schulze's laboratory. When Siedlecki went there he intended to work under Schaudinn on Foraminifera. But Schaudinn was also interested in the life histories of Sporozoa and suggested to Siedlecki that they work together in this area, studying the Coccidia of *Lithobius forficatus*. In a joint, preliminary paper (1897), they described the life histories of *Coccidium schneideri* and *Adelea ovata*. This paper, a classic in protozoology, was the first to describe correctly the life cycle of Coccidia. Siedlecki's trip to Naples and Schaudinn's military obligations prevented them from publishing the full results of their researches.

Siedlecki was the first (1898) to describe the sexual cycle of *Klossia octospina* (or *Aggregata eberthi*) in *Sepia*, the only known host until 1908, when Léger and Duboscq found an asexual cycle in *Portunus*. The following year he published the first complete life cycle of a gregarine *(Adelea ovata)* living in *Lithobius forficatus.*

In 1900 Siedlecki was appointed lecturer of zoology at Cracow and in 1912 professor and also director of the Zoological Laboratory and Museum. From 1919 to 1921 he was rector at the University of Vilna, helping to plan its reconstruction after World War I. Later he returned to Cracow. He also served as the Polish representative to the Permanent Council for Marine Exploration and to the International Committee for Bird Preservation.

After the Nazi invasion of Poland, Siedlecki and many of his colleagues were arrested on charges of promoting Polish nationalism. He was jailed first at Cracow but was later transferred to a prison in Breslau, and finally to a concentration camp at Sachsenhausen-Oranienburg, where reportedly he died of heart failure and "ill treatment."

BIBLIOGRAPHY

I. ORIGINAL WORKS. Siedlecki's works include "Beiträge zur Kenntnis der Coccidien," in *Verhandlungen der Deutschen zoologischen Gesellschaft,* **7** (1897), 192–203, written with F. Schaudinn; "Étude cytologique et cycle évolutif de la coccidie de la seiche," in *Annales de l'Institut Pasteur,* **12** (1898), 799–836; and "Étude cytologique et cycle évolutif de *Adelea ovata* Schneider," *ibid.,* **13** (1898), 169–192.

II. SECONDARY LITERATURE. On Siedlecki and his work, see "Michael Siedlecki," in *Nature,* **145** (22 June 1940), 963; "Michał Siedlecki," in *Zoologica poloniae,* **4** (1948), 51; and Clifford Dobell, "Michał Siedlecki (1873–1940)," in *Parasitology,* **33** (1949), 1–7.

ENRIQUE BELTRÁN

SIEMENS, CHARLES WILLIAM (CARL WILHELM) (*b.* Lenthe, near Hannover, Germany, 4 April 1823; *d.* London, England, 19 November 1883), *engineering.*

The seventh son of Christian Ferdinand Siemens, a prosperous farmer, and Eleonore Deichmann, Siemens was naturalized as a British subject on 19 March 1859. He married Anne Gordon on 23 July of that year. Siemens was a member of the Institution of Civil Engineers, the Institution of Mechanical Engineers (president, 1872), the Iron and Steel Institute (president, 1877), the Society of Telegraph Engineers (first president, 1872), the British Association (president, 1882), and the Royal Society of Arts (chairman, 1882) and a fellow of the Royal Society.

Having received a sound German technical education, Siemens went at age twenty to England and profitably promoted an electroplating invention of his older brother Werner (who in 1847 founded the German company of Siemens and Halske). After several years of indifferent success with other inventions, including regenerative steam engines, an engine governor, and a printing technique, he became agent in Britain for his brother's telegraph equipment and later a partner in his subsidiary British company. During the same period (1850–1858) Siemens developed a highly successful meter for measuring water consumption. These activities, combined with his important invention (1861) of the regenerative gas furnace and its application to open-hearth steelmaking and other industrial processes, made him independently wealthy before 1870.

In 1874 Siemens designed the cable ship *Faraday* and assisted in the laying of the first of several transatlantic cables that it completed. During the last fifteen years of his life he actively supported the development of the engineering profession and its societies and stimulated public interest in the conservation of fuel, the reduction of air pollution, and the potential value of electric power in a wide variety of engineering applications.

BIBLIOGRAPHY

Siemens' writings are collected in *The Scientific Works of C. William Siemens, Kt.,* E. F. Bamber, ed., 3 vols. (London, 1889).

A biography is William Pole, *The Life of Sir William Siemens* (London, 1888). See also H. T. Wood in *Dictionary of National Biography,* XVIII (Oxford, 1922). Many incidental references are in Georg Siemens, *History of the House of Siemens,* 2 vols. (Freiburg, 1957), and in a collection of his brother's memoirs, *Werner von Siemens, Inventor and Entrepreneur* (Clifton, N.J., 1966).

ROBERT A. CHIPMAN

SIEMENS, ERNST WERNER VON (*b.* Lenthe, near Hannover, Germany, 13 December 1816;

d. Berlin-Charlottenburg, Germany, 6 December 1892), *electrical science, technology.*

Siemens' father, Christian Ferdinand, was a farmer and estate manager descended from a middle-class family long prominent in the affairs of Goslar. His mother, Eleonore Deichmann, bore fourteen children and, of the ten surviving, he was the oldest. In 1832 he entered a Gymnasium in Lübeck, where he gave early indication of an abiding interest in science. Although economic difficulties at home thwarted his plan to study at the *Bauakademie* in Berlin, Siemens won an appointment as an officer candidate at the Prussian artillery and engineering school in Berlin. From 1835 to 1838 he studied mathematics, physics, and chemistry under instructors who also lectured at the university.

Stationed as an officer at a provincial garrison, Siemens used his free time to apply science to practical inventions. After the death of his mother and of his father months later in 1840, he was spurred on by the financial need of his brothers and sisters. His first successful invention was an improved process for gold- and silverplating. Rights to the process were sold in England in 1843 by his brother Wilhelm (later Sir William) to Elkington of Birmingham. Transferred to the staff of the Berlin artillery works, he soon joined the circle of Gustav Magnus, professor of physics at the University of Berlin. The group, which included du Bois-Reymond, Clausius, and Helmholtz, heard Siemens lecture on his indicator telegraph in 1845.

After improving upon the indicator telegraph of Charles Wheatstone, Siemens developed an entire telegraph system, including a method of providing the wire with a seamless insulation of gutta-percha. In 1847, together with Johann Georg Halske, the university's scientific instrument maker, he founded the Telegraphenbauanstalt von Siemens & Halske to manufacture and construct telegraph systems.

The firm obtained government contracts to build a telegraph network in northern Germany, including the line that in 1849 carried the dramatic news from the revolutionary Frankfurt Parliament to the Prussian king, Frederick William IV, in Berlin, that he had been elected German emperor (a dubious honor he declined). Although disagreements cut off Prussian government contracts after 1850, Siemens, having left the army, visited Russia and planned an extensive telegraph network, including a line from St. Petersburg to the Crimea, used during the Crimean War. The Russian business was so extensive that Siemens' brother Carl was made resident Russian representative, and so profitable that Siemens could conduct research that resulted not only in telegraph improvements but also in advances in underwater cable telegraphy.

Siemens became scientific consultant to the British government on underwater telegraphy; and Siemens Brothers in London, headed by William, manufactured and laid cable. For that company Siemens helped design the first special cable-laying ship, the *Faraday,* which, after 1875, laid five Atlantic cables in ten years. An even more dramatic achievement was Siemens' organization and construction of the Indo-European telegraph from London via Berlin, Odessa, and Teheran to Calcutta, completed in 1870.

Siemens' outstanding contribution to scientific technology was his discovery of the dynamo principle, announced to the Berlin Academy of Sciences in January 1867. Having already introduced the double-T armature, he found it possible to connect the armature, the electromagnetic field, and the external load of an electrical generator in a single circuit, thereby avoiding the costly permanent magnets previously used in the field. Other inventors and scientists—Sóren Hjorth, Anyos Jedlik, Alfred Varley, Charles Wheatstone, and Moses Farmer—discovered the dynamo principle at about the same time; but Siemens foresaw the consequences of his "dynamo" for heavy-current, or power, uses and developed practical applications. His company pioneered in using electricity for streetcars and mine locomotives, in electrolysis, and in central generating stations. In 1889 Siemens retired from active management of the family firm, which, including the daughter firms in London, St. Petersburg, and Vienna, employed about five thousand workers.

Unlike many major inventor-engineers of the nineteenth century, Siemens valued science highly, steadfastly advocating that technology not only should be based upon scientific theory but also should be analyzed to derive theory. His own efforts provided an excellent example, for he often published his analyses of telegraph and cable technology in *Dinglers polytechnisches Journal,* Poggendorff's *Annalen der Physik,* and in the reports of the Berlin Academy of Sciences. Siemens helped to establish scientific standards of measurement, designing among other things a universal galvanometer. In a period of sharp international competition, he advised the Prussian government that a nation would never gain and maintain international status if it did not excel in research and base its technology and science upon it. His determination and financial assistance resulted in the establishment of the Physikalische-Technische Reichsanstalt in Berlin (1887), a government-supported research institution first headed by Helmholtz.

Siemens received an honorary doctorate from the University of Berlin (1860), was a member of the Berlin Academy of Sciences (1873), and was ennobled in 1888. He died a few days after publication of the first edition of his *Lebenserinnerungen,* a memoir still in print.

BIBLIOGRAPHY

I. ORIGINAL WORKS. Siemens' autobiography was *Lebenserinnerungen* (Berlin, 1892; 17th ed. Munich, 1966), also available in English as . . . *Recollections* (London, 1893; 2nd ed., London–Munich, 1966). His papers were collected as *Wissenschaftliche und technische Arbeiten,* 2 vols. (Berlin, 1889–1891); a selection of his letters and a 190-page biography are in *Werner Siemens: Ein kurzgefasstes Lebensbild nebst einer Auswahl seiner Briefe,* Conrad Matschoss, ed., 2 vols. (Berlin, 1916). Six thousand letters of the Siemens brothers from 1842 to 1892 are in the Werner von Siemens Institut, Munich.

II. SECONDARY LITERATURE. A concise, well-informed biography by the head of the Siemens archives in Munich is Sigfrid von Weiher, *Werner von Siemens: Ein Leben für Wissenschaft, Technik und Wirtschaft* (Göttingen, 1970); the same author also contributed to the series of pamphlets published by the Deutsches Museum: *Werner von Siemens, ein Wegbereiter der deutschen Industrie* (Munich, 1966). Also useful are Karl Burhenne, *Werner Siemens als Sozialpolitiker* (Munich, 1932); Richard Ehrenberg, *Die Unternehmungen der Brüder Siemens* (Jena, 1906); Friedrich Heintzenberg, *Werner von Siemens in Briefen an seine Familie und an Freunde* (Stuttgart, 1953); and Conrad Wandrey, *Werner Siemens—Geschichte seines Lebens und Wirkens* (Munich, 1942).

THOMAS PARKE HUGHES

SIERPIŃSKI, WACŁAW (*b.* Warsaw, Poland, 14 March 1882; *d.* Warsaw, 21 October 1969), *mathematics.*

Sierpiński was the son of Constantine Sierpiński, a prominent physician, and Louise Łapińska. He entered the University of Warsaw in 1900 and studied under G. Voronoi, an outstanding expert on number theory who influenced his scientific career for the next decade or more. Sierpiński's important contributions to number theory (for instance, in the theory of equipartitions) were continued and developed in G. H. Hardy, Edmund Landau, and H. Weyl. In 1903 the university awarded

Sierpiński a gold medal for mathematics; his abilities in this area were evident from childhood. He received his degree the following year.

Sierpiński's most important work, however, was in set theory, and in 1908 he was the first to teach a systematic course on that subject. He investigated set theory and related domains (point-set topology, theory of functions of a real variable) for fifty years; he devoted the last fifteen to number theory. He also served as editor in chief of *Acta arithmetica.*

Sierpiński published some six hundred papers on set theory and a hundred on number theory. The most important of his books and monographs on set theory are *Hypothèse du continu* (1934) and *Cardinal and Ordinal Numbers* (1958). His chief work on number theory was *Elementary Theory of Numbers* (1964). His papers contained new and important theorems (some of which bear his name), geometrical constructions (Sierpiński curves), concepts, and original and improved proofs of earlier theorems. His findings stimulated further research by his students and by mathematicians throughout the world.

Sierpiński was a foreign member of twelve academies of science (among them the French, the Lincei, and Pontifical), and he received honorary doctorates from ten universities (including Paris, Moscow, and Amsterdam). He was also elected vice-president of the Polish Academy of Sciences and was awarded the scientific prize of the first degree (1949) and the Grand Cross of the Order of Polonia Restituta (1958).

Sierpiński's career spanned more than sixty years; he lectured at the University of Lvov until 1914 and then, after World War I, at the University of Warsaw. He was considered an excellent and stimulating teacher. About 1920 Sierpiński, Janiszewski, and Mazurkiewicz created a Polish school of mathematics centered on foundations, set theory, and applications, and also founded in 1919 a periodical to specialize in these areas, *Fundamenta mathematicae.* The first editor in chief was Janiszewski, and after his death in 1920 Sierpiński and Mazurkiewicz carried on the work for decades.

BIBLIOGRAPHY

I. ORIGINAL WORKS. Sierpiński's most important works are *Hypothèse du continu* (Warsaw, 1934); *Cardinal and Ordinal Numbers* (Warsaw, 1958); and *Elementary Theory of Numbers* (Warsaw, 1964).

II. SECONDARY LITERATURE. Works on Sierpiński

and his work are M. Fryde, "Wacław Sierpiński-Mathematician," in *Scripta mathematica*, **27** (1964), 105–111; S. Hartman, "Les travaux de W. Sierpiński sur l'analyse," in *Oeuvres choisies*, I (1974), 217–221; S. Hartman, K. Kuratowski, E. Marczewski, A. Mostowski, "Travaux de W. Sierpiński sur la théorie des ensembles et ses applications," *ibid.*, II (1975), 9–36; K. Kuratowski, "Wacław Sierpiński (1882–1969)," in *Acta arithmetica*, **21** (1972), 1–5; A. Schinzel, "Wacław Sierpiński's Papers on the Theory of Numbers," *ibid.*, 7–13.

KAZIMIERZ KURATOWSKI

SIGAUD DE LAFOND, JOSEPH-AIGNAN (*b*. Bourges, France, 5 January 1730; *d*. Bourges, 26 January 1810), *experimental physics, chemistry, medicine.*

Sigaud de Lafond was the son of a clockmaker who was an artisan and man of letters. He began his education by studying for the priesthood with the Jesuits in Bourges, but later he decided to become a physician instead. He went to Paris and enrolled as a medical student at the school of Saint-Côme.

While preparing for his medical degree, Sigaud attended the famous course of public lectures given by the Abbé Nollet, who aroused in him such a lively interest in experimental science that Sigaud became first a tutor in philosophy and mathematics and then a demonstrator in experimental science at the Collège Louis-le-Grand. In 1760 he succeeded the Abbé Nollet in his chair at Louis-le-Grand, where he taught courses in anatomy, physiology, and also those courses in experimental physics that had been taught by his famous predecessor.

In 1770 Sigaud became a professor of surgery at the school of Saint-Côme. In 1782 he returned to Bourges, where, after four years, he obtained a chair in physics at the local *collège*. The Revolution closed the *collèges*, making his position temporarily difficult; but with the reorganization of public instruction under the National Convention and Directory, he became in 1795 professor of physics and chemistry at Bourges at the École Centrale, which replaced the old *collège*. With the creation of the *lycées*, Fourcroy, a former student of Sigaud's and a member of the Council of State, appointed him *proviseur* (headmaster) of the school at Bourges. He resigned this position in 1808, two years before his death.

On 28 February 1796 Sigaud was elected a nonresident associate of the section of experimental physics of the National Institute. He belonged also to the academies of Montpellier, Florence, and St. Petersburg. In 1795 the Convention included him on a list of savants who were to receive a subsidy of 3,000 francs in gratitude for their services.

Sigaud was a prolific writer in the fields of experimental physics, chemistry, medicine, and (apparently as a consequence of his early Jesuit training) theology. Experimental science was a fashionable pursuit among the leisured classes in eighteenth-century France, and Sigaud was one of several illustrious popularizers who satisfied the intellectual appetites and curiosities of an ever-increasing number of amateurs of science. Popular interest tended toward the more spectacular examples of natural phenomena; and lectures accompanied by demonstrations, especially on electricity and on the newly discovered gases, always attracted large and enthusiastic crowds. As a follower of the Abbé Nollet, Sigaud was apparently quite successful in appealing to this group of virtuosi, and most of his publications were written for the enlightened layman rather than the professional researcher. As a result, his work was generally not profound, creative, or original. He avoided theoretical explanations and instead emphasized phenomenological aspects. There is something, too, in his writing of the vulgar catering to the "goût des merveilles"—the popular fascination with the strange, the unusual, the bizarre. He devoted an entire two-volume work to the "marvels of nature," which went through at least two French editions and was translated into German. His positive contributions to science were in the area of experimental technique. He is sometimes attributed with the invention of the glass insulator and the circular glass plate (to replace the glass globe) in electrical machines. (A. Wolf [see Bibliography] attributes the latter invention to Ingenhousz and Ramsden, and perhaps also to Planta.)

In the 1770's Sigaud collaborated with Macquer in investigating the aeriform fluids or "airs," newly discovered by Priestley. In 1776 they burned a quantity of the so-called "inflammable air" (hydrogen), and by holding a porcelain saucer over the flame they managed to collect a few drops of a colorless liquid that both researchers agreed was water. The experiment is often cited as an anticipation of some of the work later done by Cavendish, Lavoisier, and Monge on the synthesis of water, but neither Macquer nor Sigaud de Lafond fully recognized the significance of their observation.

In medicine, Sigaud achieved a certain notoriety for proposing, in a communication to the Royal Academy of Surgery, that section of the pubic symphysis could, in certain cases, be substituted for cesarean section. The Academy rejected the idea, but Sigaud was resolved to try it anyway. Specializing in midwifery, he established his medical practice in Paris, and finally in October 1777, he found an opportunity to put his new operation into practice. A pregnant woman, about forty years of age and deformed from rickets, came to him for help. She had already lost four babies, and the consensus of medical opinion was that she had no chance of bearing live children without a cesarean section. Sigaud, assisted by Alphonse Le Roy, performed instead a section of the pubic symphysis, and mother and child both survived the operation. Before the faculty of medicine in Paris, Sigaud read a memoir describing his procedure. The faculty ordered that the memoir be published in Latin and French and had a silver medal struck in honor of Sigaud and his assistant.

BIBLIOGRAPHY

I. ORIGINAL WORKS. Sigaud's works include *Leçons de physique expérimentale*, 2 vols. (Paris, 1767); *Traité de l'électricité . . .* (Paris, 1771); *Description et usage d'un cabinet de physique expérimentale*, 2 vols. (Paris, 1775); *Élémens de physique théorique et expérimentale . . .*, 4 vols. (Paris, 1777); *Essai sur différentes espèces d'air, qu'on désigne sous le nom d'air fixe . . .* (Paris, 1779); *Dictionnaire des merveilles de la nature*, 2 vols. (Paris, 1781); *Dictionnaire de physique*, 5 vols. (1781–1782); *Précis historique et expérimental des phénomènes électriques . . .* (Paris, 1781); *Physique générale*, 5 vols. (Paris, 1788–1792); *Examen de quelques principes erronés en électricité* (Paris, 1796); and *De l'électricité médicale* (Paris, 1803).

II. SECONDARY LITERATURE. On Sigaud and his work, see *Biographie universelle*, XLII (Paris, 1825), 316–318; H. Boyer, in *Nouvelle biographie générale*, XLIII (Paris, 1864), 966–967; Mechin-Desquins, *Notice historique sur Sigaud de Lafond* (Bourges, 1841); and A. Wolf, *History of Science, Technology, and Philosophy in the Eighteenth Century*, I (New York, 1961), 220. For details concerning Sigaud's course of public demonstrations, see Jean Torlais, "La physique expérimentale," in R. Taton, ed., *Enseignement et diffusion des sciences en France au XVIIIè siècle* (Paris, 1964), 619–645.

J. B. GOUGH

SIGER OF BRABANT (*b.* Brabant, *ca.* 1240; *d.* Orvieto, Italy, 1281/1284), *philosophy.*

Nothing is known of Siger's birthplace, his family, or his early education. He arrived in Paris probably between 1255 and 1260, was admitted to the Picard *nation* of the University of Paris, and became master of arts between 1260 and 1265. His name is first cited in a document dated 27 August 1266, in which he appears as a boisterous and pugnacious young teacher at the Faculty of Arts. He received a special rebuke in Thomas Aquinas' *De unitate intellectus* (1270); and on 10 December 1270 the bishop of Paris, Étienne Tempier, condemned thirteen heterodox propositions taken from the writings of Siger and his partisans. After 1270 Siger tempered his doctrinal positions, but remained the leader of the dissident minority party in the Faculty of Arts. Later he was summoned by the inquisitor of France but fled in late 1276 with two other teachers and took refuge at the papal court, the tribunal of which was reputedly more lenient than that of the inquisitors. (On 7 March 1277 Tempier, with Siger's teaching particularly in mind, condemned 219 propositions.) At the papal court, Siger was placed under house surveillance in the company of a cleric. Sometime during the pontificate of Martin IV (1281–1285), the cleric, in a fit of madness, stabbed Siger to death. John Peckham attests his death in a letter dated 10 November 1284.

Dante esteemed Siger and in his *Divine Comedy* consigned him to Paradise (canto X) beside Thomas Aquinas, in the crown of twelve sages, where he represented autonomous philosophy. A firm believer in the separation of the two powers in Christianity, Dante viewed Siger as the victim of attacks by conservative theologians. Although Siger's career ended prematurely, his historical role was nevertheless fundamental because of the reactions he provoked in university circles—and on such men as Bonaventure, Thomas Aquinas, Albert the Great, and John Peckham.

On the basis of his writings discovered to date, it is known that Siger was concerned primarily with metaphysics and psychology, and secondarily with logic and natural philosophy; several questions on ethics also have been discovered. His contributions to science can be found in his writings on psychology and natural philosophy, in which areas connections can be made between philosophy and science.

Siger's writings on psychology are devoted to problems of the intellective soul, and these are treated in an exclusively philosophical manner: the works contain only those few elements of descriptive psychology that are indispensable for formulating the philosophical problems.

Siger wrote several works on natural philosophy. Of the three *Quaestiones naturales* found in Paris, the first is purely philosophical and deals with the uniqueness of the substantial form; the second defends the Aristotelian principle "Everything that moves is moved by something else"; and the third discusses the problem of gravity, which is resolved in the spirit of Ibn Rushd.

Six other *Quaestiones naturales* have been found in Lisbon. The third and sixth are purely philosophical, and two others are patterned on Aristotle's pseudophilosophical hypotheses on the "natural place" of simple bodies (the first question) and on the influence of the heavens (*orbis*) in human generation (the fourth question), which are of no interest for experimental science. Only the second and fifth questions have some scientific taste. The second interprets an experiment in physics: "If a lighted candle is placed in a vessel put on water, why does the water then rise in the vessel?" Siger's answer is inspired by Aristotle. The candle warms the air, which then rises to the top of the vessel. Because a vacuum is impossible and water is fluid, the water rises (remaining in contact with the air), compresses the air, and thus increases its own ascending motion. But the vessel would shatter if placed mouth down on the earth, since the latter cannot rise because of its cohesion and weight. The fifth question is a brief, abstract discussion of the paradox of Achilles and the tortoise.

In *Impossibilia* the problem of gravity is again examined in chapter 4. After a long discussion, in which he rejects the opinions of Albertus Magnus and of Thomas Aquinas, Siger again adopts (but modifies) Ibn Rushd's thesis. The entire discussion is developed according to Aristotelian physics (with all its prejudices).

De aeternitate mundi treats the eternity of mankind in a purely philosophical context. *Compendium de generatione et corruptione*, a fragment of which has been discovered in a manuscript in Lilienfeld, Austria, is a brief, unoriginal analysis of Aristotle's treatise. Almost all of the twenty-four *Quaestiones super libros I et II Physicorum*, discovered at the Vatican, deal with purely philosophical problems. The only questions of possible interest from a scientific viewpoint are II, 1 and 2, on the natural movement of light and heavy bodies (which is explained in the same way as in the other writings), and II, 5, in which Siger explains that *musica*, *perspectiva*, and *astrologia* are intermediary between the purely natural and mathematical sciences.

Siger's contribution to experimental science seems insignificant. Even those problems that could have been treated scientifically were given a philosophical explanation and were solved without originality by relying on the principles of Aristotle and Ibn Rushd. If the commentaries of Munich MS 9559, which have been attributed to him by Martin Grabmann, were truly by Siger, this assessment would be different, for then Siger would be the author of an important series of commentaries on natural philosophy in which many scientific questions are discussed. Formerly the author accepted Grabmann's attribution; but serious difficulties have since been raised concerning the authenticity of several commentaries, and it seems preferable not to take them into account here.

BIBLIOGRAPHY

I. Original Works. All the works of Siger quoted in the article are in B. Bazán, ed., *Siger de Brabant. Quaestiones in tertium de anima. De anima intellectiva. De aeternitate mundi* (Louvain, 1972), and B. Bazán, ed., *Siger de Brabant. Écrits de logique, de morale et de physique* (Louvain, 1974).

II. Secondary Literature. See P. Mandonnet, *Siger de Brabant et l'averroïsme latin au XIIIe siècle*, 2nd ed., 2 vols. (Louvain, 1908–1911); F. Van Steenberghen, *Siger de Brabant d'après ses oeuvres inédites*, 2 vols. (Louvain, 1931–1942); *La philosophie au XIIIe siècle* (Louvain, 1966), 357–402; and *Introduction à l'étude de la philosophie médiévale* (Louvain, 1974), *passim* (see *Table onomastique*, p. 603).

F. Van Steenberghen

SIGORGNE, PIERRE (*b.* Rembercourt-aux-Pots, France, 24 October 1719; *d.* Mâcon, France, 10 November 1809), *physics, science popularization.*

The son of Pierre Sigorgne, a minor judicial official, and Marguerite du Moulin, Sigorgne received his theological degrees at the Sorbonne and assumed the chair of philosophy at the Collège Duplessis (Paris) in 1740. He quickly established himself as a gifted educator and popularizer of science, and was prominent in introducing Newtonian theories into the French university curriculum. His promising Paris career ended, however, when he was arrested in 1749 as the alleged author of satirical verses concerning Louis XV and Madame de Pompadour. He spent the remainder of his life in exile at Mâcon, where he continued his scientific work while proving himself a distinguished ecclesiastical administrator. Sigorgne maintained an active correspondence with many of the important scientists and *philosophes* of the period, winning a reputation as a genial and enlightened reconciler of science and theology. He was named *correspondant* of the Académie des Sciences in 1778 and *correspondant* of the Institut de France in 1803, and was one of the founders of the Mâcon Academy.

Sigorgne's *Institutions léibnitiennes* (1767), an accurate but critical account of Leibniz's cosmological theories, contributed to the more informed discussion of German philosophy in France; but his main importance for the history of science lies in his vigorous and effective popularization of Newtonian ideas. Although the introduction of Newton's theories into France was well advanced by 1740, Cartesian ideas still exerted a powerful influence. Sigorgne's courses of lectures at the Collège Duplessis provided a detailed and sophisticated treatment of recent physical theories, notably the Newtonian concept of universal gravitation; and his courses in philosophy included systematic instruction in mathematics and contributed to the spread of ideas on the calculus.

His cautious advocacy of Newtonian science was broadened with the publication of Sigorgne's *Examen et refutation des leçons de physique expliquées par M. de Molières* (1741). Primarily an attack on Privat de Molières's influential attempt to reconcile Cartesian and Newtonian theories, the *Examen* demolished the vortex theory as emended by Privat de Molières to obviate the major objections to Cartesian physics. Sigorgne forcefully demonstrated the Newtonian arguments for the physical instability of the hypothetical vortices and the mathematical incompatibility between vortex motion and Kepler's laws. His *Institutions newtoniennes* (1747), a clear introduction to Newtonian mathematical and physical principles, contributed to the acceptance of the attraction theory by the French scientific community. A Latin résumé of the *Institutions newtoniennes* (1748) was rapidly recognized as a standard Newtonian textbook in Western Europe.

The most successful of Sigorgne's efforts to apply the concept of universal gravitation is his explanation of capillary phenomena by the laws of attraction, which was awarded a prize by the Rouen Academy in 1748. His chemical theories, in contrast, were of little significance. Sigorgne shared the misguided vision of those eighteenth-century Newtonians who sought to explain observed chemical behavior on the basis of interparticulate forces, the operation of which would be subject to exact mathematical treatment. Thus, ironically, those ideas that had been skillfully exploited by Sigorgne in defense of the new physics at mid-century reappeared at the end of his long career

in a series of ill-tempered attacks on modern chemistry.

A minor but respected *savant* of Enlightenment France, Sigorgne used his gifts of exposition to bring developing scientific ideas before a broad public.

BIBLIOGRAPHY

I. ORIGINAL WORKS. Sigorgne's first important writings, his polemics against Privat de Molières and his Cartesian supporters, include *Examen et refutation des leçons de physique expliquées par M. de Molières au Collège royal de France* (Paris, 1741); *Réplique à M. de Molières ou démonstration physico-mathématique de l'insuffisance et de l'impossibilité des tourbillons* (Paris, 1741); and "A Physico-Mathematical Demonstration of the Impossibility and Insufficiency of Vortices," in *Philosophical Transactions of the Royal Society*, **41**, no. 457 (1740), 409–435.

His major work is *Institutions newtoniennes, ou introduction à la philosophie de Newton* (Paris, 1747; 2nd ed., 1769). A Latin résumé of *Institutions newtoniennes, Astronomiae physicae juxta Newtoni principia breviarium, methodo scolastica ad usum studiosae juventutis* (Paris, 1748), was widely used in France and Germany as a standard Newtonian textbook and was translated into Italian by Giulio Carbonara as *Istituzioni neutoniane* (Lucca, 1757).

Sigorgne published a summary of his prize essay on the effects of attraction in capillary tube phenomena as an appendix to the 2nd ed. of *Institutions newtoniennes*; the essay had been submitted to the Rouen Academy in 1748 as "Dissertatio physico-mecanica de ascensu et suspensione liquorum intra tubos capillares." Sigorgne's critical exposition of Leibnizian cosmology is *Institutions léibnitiennes, ou précis de la monadologie* (Lyons, 1767). An example of Sigorgne's enduring fascination with Newtonian explanations is the merely curious *Examen nouveau de la chimie moderne, avec une dissertation sur la force* (Mâcon, 1807).

II. SECONDARY LITERATURE. The fullest recent account of Sigorgne's life and work is Martial Griveaud, "Un physicien oublié du XVIIIe siècle: L'Abbé Pierre Sigorgne de Rembercourt-aux-Pots," in *Annales de l'est*, 4th ser., **3** (1935), 77–107. J.-M. Guerrier, "Étude critique sur les oeuvres de l'Abbé Sigorgne," in *Annales de l'Académie de Mâcon*, 3rd ser., **14** (1909), 432–458, is concerned mainly with an analysis of Sigorgne's literary output but has some brief comments on his scientific writings. A short account of Sigorgne's life and work appears in F. Hoefer, ed., *Nouvelle biographie générale*, XLIII (1864), 988–989. Useful comments on the significance of Sigorgne's university courses appear in René Taton, *Enseignement et diffusion des sciences en France au XVIIIe siècle* (Paris, 1964), 142, 627.

MARTIN FICHMAN

SIGÜENZA Y GÓNGORA, CARLOS DE (*b*. Mexico City, 20 August 1645; *d*. Mexico City, 22 August 1700), *mathematics, astronomy, natural history.*

Sigüenza's father was tutor to Prince Baltazar before going to New Spain. After receiving his first education at home, Sigüenza entered the Jesuit Colegio de Tepozotlán and took his first vows in 1662. He continued his studies at the Colegio del Espíritu Santo at Puebla until 1667, when he was expelled for disciplinary reasons; he remained a secular priest. During the following years Sigüenza was a student at the University of Mexico and chaplain at Amor de Dios Hospital. In 1672 he was awarded the chair of astrology and mathematics at the university and occupied it for more than twenty years.

In 1680, to calm the fears aroused by a comet, Sigüenza wrote *Manifiesto filosófico contra los cometas* (1681), which drew a reply from Martín de la Torre the same year. To answer it Sigüenza wrote *El Belerofonte matemático* (now lost), which aroused the antagonism of Father Eusebio Kino, a Jesuit missionary who was a renowned mathematician and astronomer, leading him to publish a strong response to Sigüenza's arguments: *Exposición astronómica del cometa* (1681). Kino's book gave Sigüenza the opportunity to publish in 1690 *Libra astronómica y philosóphica*, a short book of great significance for its sound mathematical background, anti-Aristotelian outlook, and familiarity with modern authors: Copernicus, Galileo, Descartes, Kepler, and Tycho Brahe.

As royal cosmographer, Sigüenza made valuable observations and drew good charts. These included a general map of New Spain, probably the first by a Mexican, best known through a reproduction by Beaumont in 1873–1874; a map of the lakes of the Valley of Mexico, probably made in 1691, but not published until 1748, and reprinted in 1768, 1783, and 1786; and a map of the bay of Santa María de Galve (Pensacola), 1693. In 1692 the viceroy's palace was set on fire during a riot and Sigüenza risked his life to save valuable papers in the archives.

Sigüenza projected writing a history of ancient Mexico and collected much material, but little was published. His manuscripts, now lost, were considered by contemporaries of great value. He assembled a large library, said to be the best in the realm. In 1693 Sigüenza was sent with Admiral Andrés de Pez to reconnoiter Pensacola Bay; he kept an interesting diary and made valuable charts.

BIBLIOGRAPHY

I. ORIGINAL WORKS. Besides those works cited in text, Sigüenza wrote *Piedad heróica de don Fernando Cortes* (Mexico City, 1689); *Trofeo de la justicia española* (Mexico City, 1691); *Mercurio volante* (Mexico City, 1693), and several unpublished MSS.

II. SECONDARY LITERATURE. See F. Pérez Salazar, *Obras de Carlos de Sigüenza y Góngora con una biografía* (Mexico City, 1928); J. Rojas Garcidueñas, *Don Carlos de Sigüenza y Góngora. Erudito barroco* (Mexico City, 1945); I. A. Leonard, *Don Carlos de Sigüenza y Góngora. A Mexican Savant of the Seventeenth Century* (Berkeley, 1929).

ENRIQUE BELTRÁN

AL-SIJZĪ, ABŪ SAʿĪD AḤMAD IBN MUḤAMMAD IBN ʿABD AL-JALĪL (*b*. Sijistān, Persia, *ca*. 945; *d. ca*. 1020), *geometry, astronomy, astrology.*

Al-Sijzī is also known as al-Sijazī, al-Sijizī, or al-Sijarī. The following evidence indicates that he was an older contemporary of al-Bīrūnī (973–*ca*. 1050): he is not mentioned in Ibn al-Nadīm's *Fihrist* (987), but al-Bīrūnī quoted him in his *Chronology*. Al-Bīrūnī wrote to al-Sijzī on the determination of the *qibla* (direction of Mecca, for prayer) and on a proof by his teacher Manṣūr ibn ʿIrāq for the theory of the transversal figure. Conversely, al-Sijzī quoted three propositions by al-Bīrūnī in his treatise on trisecting an angle, which he ended with five problems of al-Bīrūnī. Around 969 al-Sijzī had written and copied mathematical works at Shīrāz, a later version of which is in Paris (Bib. Nat. arabe 2457). Presumably around the same time (*ca*. 967) he composed his *Kitāb al-qirānāt* ("Book of the Conjunctions"), which contains references to an even earlier work of his, *Muntakhab Kitāb al-ulūf* ("Summary of the Thousands of Abū Maʿshar"). In 969–970 al-Sijzī assisted at the observations of the meridian transits in Shīrāz conducted by ʿAbd al-Raḥmān al-Ṣūfī.

Al-Sijzī may have spent some time in Khurāsān, since he answered questions by mathematicians of that region. He dedicated works to the Sayyid Amīr Abū Jaʿfar Aḥmad ibn Muḥammad, a prince of Balkh (*d*. 1019) (L. Massignon, *Opera omnia*, I [Beirut, 1963], 650–666), and to the Buwayhid Caliph ʿAḍud al-Dawla (Shīrāz–Baghdad, 949–983).

Al-Sijzī's main scientific activity was in astrology, and he had a vast knowledge of the older literature. He usually compiled and tabulated, adding his own critical commentary. Al-Sijzī summarized three works by Abū Maʿshar and wrote on the second of the five books ascribed to Zoroaster in his *Kitāb Zarādusht ṣuwar darajāt al-falak* ("The Book of Zoroaster on the Pictures of the Degrees of the Zodiac"). In his *Kitāb al-qirānāt*, which treats general astrology and its history, he used Sassanid material and sources from the time of Hārūn al-Rashīd and from the late Umayyad period. In *Zāʾirjāt*, a book on horoscopes, he gave tables based on Hermes, Ptolemy, Dorotheus, and "the moderns." Al-Sijzā's tables, together with those of Ptolemy, are quoted by Iḥtiyāzuʿ l'Dīn Muḥammad in his *Judicial Astrology* (Trinity College, Cambridge). Al-Bīrūnī described in his *Kitāb fī istīʿāb* three degenerate astrolabes constructed by al-Sijzī: one fish-shaped, one anemone-shaped, and one skiff-shaped.

Al-Sijzī's mathematical papers are less numerous but more significant than his astrological ones, and he is therefore better known as a geometer. He wrote original treatises on spheres and conic sections, the construction of a conic compass, and the trisection of an angle by intersecting a circle with an equilateral hyperbola. This method became widely accepted: Abū'l-Jūd, for example, describes it in the Leiden manuscript Or 168(13). Al-Sijzī mentioned several other methods for solving this problem, including one by "mobile geometry," which he ascribed to the ancients; but he omitted any reference to Pappus. His treatise on proportions in the transversal figure is especially useful for astronomy, and his emphasis on the position of the lines was new and important. Al-Sijzī constructed the regular heptagon according to the same principle as that used by al-Qūhī. He also wrote articles on subdividing segments and several letters on problems related to the work of Euclid and Archimedes.

BIBLIOGRAPHY

I. ORIGINAL WORKS. Al-Sijzī's available mathematical MSS are listed in F. Sezgin, *Geschichte des arabischen Schrifttums*, V (Leiden, 1974), 331–334. On the astrological MSS see M. Krause, "Stambuler Handschriften islamischer Mathematiker," in *Quellen und Studien zur Geschichte der Mathematik, Astronomie und Physik*, B.3 (1934), 468–472; and W. Thomson and G. Junge, *The Commentary of Pappus on Book X of Euclid's Elements* (Cambridge, 1930), 48–51. C. Brockelmann, *Geschichte der arabischen Literatur*, I (Leiden, 1943), 246–247; and supp. I (Leiden, 1937), 388–389, lists a few more MSS and additional copies. Neither mentions *Kitāb al-qirānāt wa tahāwīl sinī al-ʿālam*, a MS that David Pingree dealt with in *The Thousands of Abū Maʿshar* (London, 1968). In this work Pingree also discusses the *Muntakhab Kitāb al-ulūf*, which was partly translated by E. S. Kennedy in "The World-Year of the Persians," in *Journal of the American Oriental Society*, **83**, no. 3 (1963), 315–327. Translations or discussions of mathematical treatises are found in: F. Woepcke, *L'Algèbre d'Omar Alkhayāmī* (Paris, 1851), 117–127; and "Trois traités arabes sur le compas parfait," in *Notices et extraits de la Bibliothèque nationale*, **22**, part 1 (1874), 112–115; C. Schoy, "Graecoarabische Studien," in *Isis*, **8** (1926), 21–40; H. Bürger and K. Kohl, "Thabits Werk über den Transversalensatz," in *Abhandlungen zur Geschichte der Naturwissenschaften und der Medizin*, **7** (1924), 49–53; and L. A. Sédillot, "Notice de plusieurs opuscules mathématiques," in *Notices et extraits de la Bibliothèque nationale*, **13** (1838), 136–145. Edited by the Osmania Oriental Publications Bureau is *Risāla fī 'l-shakl al-gaṭṭāʿ* ("On the Transversal-Theorem"; Hyderabad, 1948).

II. SECONDARY LITERATURE. There are few biographical references to al-Sijzī. On the observations in Shīrāz see al-Bīrūnī, *Taḥdīd nihāyāt al-amākin li-taṣḥīḥ masāfāt al-masākin* (Cairo, 1962), 99; and E. S. Kennedy, *A Commentary Upon Bīrūnī's Kitāb Taḥdīd al-Amākin* (Beirut, 1973), 42. On al-Sijzī as an astrologer see Pingree (see above), 21–26, 55, 63–67, 70–127. On his mathematics consult Sezgin (see above), 46–47, 329–334; Thomson and Junge (see above), 43–51; and the notes of G. Bergsträsser in "Pappos Kommentar zum Xten Buch von Euklid's Elementen," in *Islam*, **21** (1938), 195–198. On his astrolabes see Josef Frank, "Zur Geschichte des Astrolabs," in *Sitzungsberichte der Physikalisch-medizinischen Sozietät in Erlangen*, **50–51** (1918–1919), 290–293; and al-Bīrūnī, *Al-Qānūn al Masʿūdī*, I (Hyderabad, 1954), introduction, 17–18.

YVONNE DOLD-SAMPLONIUS

SILLIMAN, BENJAMIN (*b.* North Stratford [now Trumbull], Connecticut, 8 August 1779; *d.* New Haven, Connecticut, 24 November 1864), *chemistry, mineralogy, geology.*

Graduated from Yale College in 1796, Silliman was diverted from following his father and grandfather in the law when he was offered the newly established (1802) professorship of chemistry and natural history at Yale. Untrained in these subjects, Silliman went to Philadelphia to study, profiting greatly not only from formal course work in the medical school there but also from occasional visits with John Maclean at Princeton and from informal chemical experiments with his classmate and fellow boarder Robert Hare. In the spring of 1805 Silliman sailed for Britain to continue his scientific education and to purchase books and apparatus for Yale College. After visiting Liverpool, Manchester, London, Holland, and the mining districts of Cornwall, he settled in Edinburgh, where he spent the winter studying chemistry, geology, and medicine.

In the years following his return to the United States, Silliman established himself as a leading figure in American science less through his original research than through his teaching and educational statesmanship at Yale, his editorship of the *American Journal of Science,* his public lectures on chemistry and geology, his textbooks, and his role in founding and strengthening scientific organizations.

As an original investigator, Silliman made his chief contributions during the early part of his career, the best-known being his description and chemical analysis of the Weston meteor of 14 December 1807 and his experiments with the oxy-hydrogen blowpipe and the deflagrator, both invented by his friend Robert Hare. Silliman's analysis of fragments of the Weston meteor was widely reprinted in Europe and won him election to the American Philosophical Society. His experiments on the fusion of refractory substances also attracted considerable attention abroad. Using his own improved version of Hare's blowpipe, Silliman added substantially to the list of substances proved capable of fusion by heat, including zircon, lime, magnesia, chalcedony, beryl, and corundum (1813). In his experiments with the deflagrator on the fusion of carbon (1822), Silliman noted the transfer of volatilized carbon from the positive electrode to the negative, an observation subsequently confirmed by César Despretz. Silliman's geological papers were mostly descriptive essays on New England localities, but George P. Merrill credits him with anticipating the aqueo-igneous theory of eruptive rocks in his views on rock crystallization.

By 1820 Silliman had made Yale College the leading center in the United States for training in chemistry, geology, and mineralogy. Through his friendship and collaboration with George Gibbs of Newport, Rhode Island, he secured for Yale the splendid collection of minerals that Gibbs had purchased in Europe during his travels there. Arranged according to Haüy's system, these specimens served as an invaluable teaching aid for Silliman's lectures. Meanwhile, Silliman published four American editions of William Henry's *Epitome of Chemistry* with notes and additions. In 1830–1831 he brought out his own *Elements of Chemistry*, a solid, up-to-date work that compared favorably with European textbooks of that day. Silliman also prepared three American editions of Robert Bakewell's *Introduction to Geology*, accompanied

by an appendix in which he outlined his own geological lectures and endeavored to demonstrate the harmony of geology and Genesis.

An excellent teacher, Silliman trained a generation of American chemists, geologists, and mineralogists, including Denison Olmsted, Amos Eaton, Edward Hitchcock, Chester Dewey, Oliver P. Hubbard, George T. Bowen, Charles U. Shepard, James Dwight Dana, and Benjamin Silliman, Jr. He also took the lead in establishing graduate and professional training in the sciences at Yale. He helped to found a medical school at Yale (1813) and served as professor of chemistry and pharmacy in that institution for nearly forty years. In 1846 Silliman joined with his son to establish a professorship of agricultural chemistry and plant and animal physiology at Yale, for the express purpose of providing graduate training in chemistry and its applications to agriculture. The eventual result was the Department of Philosophy and the Arts, from which grew the Graduate School of Yale University and the Sheffield Scientific School.

In 1818 Silliman launched the *American Journal of Science,* which quickly became the leading American scientific journal and gave Silliman an international reputation. By 1830 the *Journal* was self-sustaining and was drawing important contributions from all fields of American science, including applied science. Deeply interested in the applications of science, Silliman kept his readers posted on the progress of the industrial arts. As a consulting chemist and geologist, he inspected mining properties in New England, Pennsylvania, Maryland, and Virginia, and published excerpts of his reports in the *Journal.* In 1838 Silliman's son joined him in editing the journal, and nine years later his son-in-law James Dwight Dana began assisting in the work.

Meanwhile, Silliman had begun to carry the cause of science to the American public as a lecturer on chemistry and geology. Beginning in 1834, at Hartford, Connecticut, Silliman extended his lecturing activities to Boston and thence to New York, Baltimore, Washington, Pittsburgh, St. Louis, Mobile, and New Orleans. These lectures did much to generate interest in science throughout the country, as Charles Lyell noted during his American travels. They also served to allay religious opposition to science, since Silliman went out of his way to harmonize Genesis and geology.

As his reputation increased, Silliman became a member of a great many scientific societies both at home and abroad. Elected early to the Connecticut Academy of Arts and Sciences, the American Philosophical Society, and the American Academy of Arts and Sciences, he joined with George Gibbs in founding the short-lived American Geological Society in 1819. More successful was the Association of American Geologists, formed in 1840 by Edward Hitchcock and several geologists from the New York and Pennsylvania surveys. Silliman served as president of this organization in 1841–1842 and remained active in it as it evolved into the American Association for the Advancement of Science.

On his second trip abroad in 1851 Silliman, now well-known in the world of science, was warmly received by his European colleagues. He was a charter member of the National Academy of Sciences, established in 1863. His scientific work is commemorated in the name of the mineral sillimanite.

BIBLIOGRAPHY

I. ORIGINAL WORKS. Extensive Silliman MSS, including much correspondence, his student diary for 1795–1796, account books, daybook for 1840–1864, and a 9-vol. MS, "Origin and Progress in Chemistry, Mineralogy, and Geology in Yale College and in Other Places, With Personal Reminiscences," are at the Yale University Library. Numerous other letters may be found at the Historical Society of Pennsylvania, the Library of the American Philosophical Society, the Library Company of Philadelphia, and the New-York Historical Society. Silliman's scientific papers are listed in the Royal Society *Catalogue of Scientific Papers*, V, 694–697. Other writings are listed in F. B. Dexter, *Biographical Sketches of the Graduates of Yale College, With Annals of the College History*, V (New York, 1911), 220–227. Silliman's European travels are narrated in his *A Journal of Travels in England, Holland and Scotland . . . in the Years 1805 and 1806*, 2 vols. (New York, 1810) and *A Visit to Europe in 1851*, 2 vols. (New York, 1853).

II. SECONDARY LITERATURE. For a nineteenth-century view of Silliman's life and work, see George P. Fisher, *Life of Benjamin Silliman, M.D., LL.D.*, 2 vols. (New York, 1866), which contains extensive quotations from the MS sources. A more recent and very well balanced account of Silliman's career is John F. Fulton and Elizabeth H. Thomson, *Benjamin Silliman 1779–1864, Pathfinder in American Science* (New York, 1947), containing a useful section, "Bibliography and Sources." See also Alexis Caswell's article in *Biographical Memoirs. National Academy of Sciences*, **1** (1877), 99–112; R. H. Chittenden, *History of the Sheffield Scientific School of Yale University 1846–1922*, I (New Haven, 1928), chs. 1–2; E. S. Dana, Charles Schuchert, *et al.*, *A Century of Science in America, With Special Reference to the American Journal of Science, 1818–1918* (New Haven,

1918), ch. 1; *Memorial of the Centennial of the Yale Medical School* (New Haven, 1915), ch. 1; George P. Merrill, *The First 100 Years of American Geology* (New Haven, 1924), 157; and Margaret Rossiter, "Benjamin Silliman and the Lowell Institute: The Popularization of Science in Nineteenth-Century America," in *New England Quarterly*, **44** (1971), 602–626.

JOHN C. GREENE

SILLIMAN, BENJAMIN, JR. (*b*. New Haven, Connecticut, 4 December 1816; *d*. New Haven, 14 January 1885), *chemistry, geology.*

Silliman was the fourth child and second son of Benjamin Silliman, professor of chemistry at Yale College, and Harriet Trumbull. After graduation from Yale College in 1837, he studied and did research in his father's laboratory, earning an M.A. in 1840. He also worked briefly in the private laboratory of the well-known Boston chemist Charles T. Jackson.

In 1838 Silliman began to assist his father on the internationally known *American Journal of Science and Arts*. His name appeared on the masthead in 1841, and he continued in various editorial capacities until his death. This work brought him into contact with many foreign scientists, a number of whom visited his father's house and later his own, and gave him a broad knowledge of the progress of scientific research.

In the late 1830's Silliman also began to assist his father on lecture tours and mining surveys. These trips widened his acquaintance with American scientists, gave him experience in the effective presentation of science, of which his father was a master, and offered training in practical geology.

On 14 May 1840 Silliman married Susan Huldah Forbes. They had seven children, of whom a son (Benjamin) and four daughters lived to maturity. A man of great personal charm, tremendous energy, and enthusiasm, Silliman was warmhearted and trusting to a fault. He dispensed hospitality generously, sent his daughters to Europe to study, and in general lived on a scale beyond his professional salary.

Silliman was one of the fifty original members of the National Academy of Sciences, incorporated by act of Congress in 1863. He was an associate fellow of the American Academy of Arts and Sciences and a member of many other societies in the United States and abroad. He received an honorary M.D. from the Medical College of South Carolina in 1849 and an LL.D. from Jefferson Medical College in 1884.

Silliman's professional career may be divided into four areas: contributions as an editor of the *American Journal of Science*, as a teacher and author of textbooks, as an analytical chemist doing experimental work, and as a consultant in chemistry and geology.

Silliman's long and effective career as a teacher started in 1842, when he began providing laboratory experience for his father's students interested in advanced training. Many were only slightly his junior; and together they turned out creditable work in the small laboratory, several studies appearing in the *American Journal of Science and Arts*. One of these students, John Pitkin Norton, who later studied in Europe, succeeded on his return, with the help of the Sillimans, in persuading the Corporation of Yale College to establish two professorships in 1846: agricultural chemistry (to which Norton was appointed) and applied chemistry (to 'which Silliman was appointed). The need to provide a degree for graduates of the School of Applied Chemistry (later the Yale Scientific School and finally the Sheffield Scientific School) led to the establishment in 1847 of the Department of Philosophy and the Arts (subsequently the Graduate School) and of the degree of Doctor of Philosophy, the first to be awarded in the United States (1863).

Since he and Norton received no salary from Yale, Silliman had to leave Norton to carry on alone in 1849 and accepted the professorship of medical chemistry and toxicology in the medical department at the University of Louisville, Kentucky. He returned to Yale in 1854 as professor of general and applied chemistry when his father retired.

In 1847 Silliman published the first of two textbooks that were clearly written, well arranged, and justifiably popular for many years in American colleges. Some fifty thousand copies of the *First Principles of Chemistry*, to which T. Sterry Hunt contributed the section on organic chemistry, were sold in the first twenty-five years. His *First Principles of Physics or Natural Philosophy* (1859) was, according to J. D. Dana, long the best-known textbook in physics in the country. Both volumes showed broad knowledge and Silliman's remarkable ability to synthesize, explain, and extract from the work of others with great clarity and effectiveness, which made his books especially useful to students.

As a laboratory investigator Silliman never had a well-defined program. His choice of research projects reflected his own wide-ranging interests and

the practical problems addressed to him by men who were concerned with economic development of the country's resources but had no scientific knowledge. Certain interests persisted, however—mineralogy, petroleum, coal, precious metals, and combustion of gases for illumination (he was a director of the New Haven Gas Works for many years).

Silliman's selected bibliography, which includes thirteen books and pamphlets and nearly a hundred papers, does not list many of the often extensive reports written for private clients. One of these was probably his most important publication, for it launched the world's petroleum industry. In a report dated 16 April 1855, he set forth his methods and results in a chemical analysis of rock oil from Venango County, Pennsylvania, and recommended uses of the several products discovered. Silliman used fractional distillation to break down the components—a method utilized in Europe but little employed in America for that purpose. He identified kerosene, an inexpensive and safe illuminant; paraffin, better than tallow for candles; lubricants, to replace animal grease; and, by passing crude petroleum through heated coke, an illuminating gas of high quality. For a low-boiling fraction (gasoline) he could propose no use. That had to await the development of the internal combustion engine, but for the next half century the petroleum industry utilized the other components and the methods (including steam distillation) that Silliman suggested for preparing and purifying them. This report showed his potential as an original, imaginative investigator—a potential not realized in subsequent work.

Another important publication, not supplanted to this day, was *American Contributions to Chemistry*, a biographical dictionary of American chemists including bibliographies of their work prepared for the "centennial of chemistry," a celebration of the hundredth anniversary of the discovery of oxygen, and presented in part on 1 August 1874 at Northumberland, Pennsylvania, Priestley's place of residence in America. It involved a tremendous amount of work and, on the whole, was remarkably complete and accurate.

Silliman had of necessity been augmenting his meager professorial salary for some time, as did his father[1] and most other members of the academic community, by outside commissions of various sorts; and in 1864 he made a year-long trip to California to seek new opportunities. It was a time of great excitement about the resources of the country, and Silliman shared the general curiosity about undeveloped lands in the West. On this and several subsequent trips he examined many properties for clients eager to capitalize on his reputation as a geologist—both potential oil-yielding sites and gold and silver mines. Enthusiasm excited by the promise of great oil and mineral wealth, coupled with his natural optimism, resulted in generally favorable reports, useful to promoters in the formation of companies with authorized capital in the millions. Never quoted were more guarded statements or conditions that Silliman specified must be met if results were to justify promise. Although they were based on sometimes brief and insufficient study, the majority of his predictions ultimately were realized, partly because of his sound knowledge of geology and an intuitive ability to sense unseen potentials.

Silliman's enthusiastic lectures on California's rich resources, with special mention of oil in the southern part of the state, brought him into conflict with the head of the California Geological Survey, Josiah D. Whitney, and his former assistant, Silliman's friend and student William H. Brewer, professor of agriculture in the Scientific School (1864–1903); both were on record as saying that there was no oil in southern California. Fearing that Silliman's opinion would jeopardize the Survey, Whitney mounted a vicious attack, one of the most acrimonious and bitter in the annals of science, that continued intermittently, with Brewer's help, until Silliman's death. He accused Silliman of deliberately swindling the public for large fees and thus of degrading all scientists. Whitney was aided by the failure of the oil company formed on the basis of Silliman's report and by the fact that the oil sample on which Silliman had based part of his judgment proved to be "salted."[2] Damaging, too, to Silliman was the subsequent failure of silver and gold mining companies the formation of which had also been assisted by his enthusiastic reports.

Silliman's enemies were unable to have him ousted from the National Academy of Sciences, the American Academy of Arts and Sciences, or Yale; but they did hurt his scientific reputation and they forced him to resign (1870) from Yale College (but not from the medical faculty) and to sever connections with the Sheffield Scientific School. They also turned friends against him and brought disgrace and anguish to him and his family.

Silliman amassed an enormous file of evidence to support his opinions in response to Whitney's charges before the National Academy of Sciences, printed the "salted" oil report in the *American Journal of Science and Arts,* and promised an investigation; but thereafter he maintained a dignified silence and outwardly cheerful mien. He did not gloat, publicly or privately, when improved methods and machinery yielded rich oil strikes in the late 1870's in southern California, or when the Bodie mine (California) produced gold beyond even his great expectations and a report of a Congressional investigation of the Emma mine (Utah) contained no criticism of his judgment.[3]

Silliman's excellent reputation as an editor, teacher, and author of useful books remains undiminished. As a laboratory investigator he was careful and methodical but showed originality only on rare occasions, as in the investigation of rock oil in 1855 and in the use of certain techniques—such as the production of daguerreotype pictures by the light of the carbon arc and the use of an improved goniometer, based on a modification of a European model, in his examination of American micas. Had his energies not been diverted into so many channels, Silliman might have made more notable contributions to chemistry. His geological work showed excellent training, extensive knowledge, and sound judgment. It was when he ventured from academic surroundings into the commercial world that his optimism and guilelessness helped to create circumstances that led to his undoing. The ultimate vindication of his judgment on the important issues could not erase his personal tragedy, but it did restore for the record his reputation as a scientist.

NOTES

1. See, for example, Margaret W. Rossiter, "Benjamin Silliman and the Lowell Institute: The Popularization of Science in Nineteenth-Century America," in *New England Quarterly,* **44** (1971), 602–626.
2. It was later thought that Silliman never explained what he discovered in his investigation of the salted sample because John B. Church, the husband of his eldest sister, might have been implicated.
3. Silliman's testimony before the Committee on Foreign Affairs of the House of Representatives (the investigation ran from February to May 1876) gave him the opportunity to state under oath that his fee for two trips to the mine in Utah was $25,000, less than half the amount that his adversaries had claimed.

BIBLIOGRAPHY

I. ORIGINAL WORKS. Silliman's most important books include *First Principles of Chemistry* (Philadelphia–Boston, 1847; rev. 1850, 1853); *First Principles of Physics, or Natural Philosophy* (Philadelphia, 1859; 2nd ed., 1861); *A Century of Medicine and Chemistry* (New Haven, 1871); and *American Contributions to Chemis-*

try (Philadelphia, 1874). Pamphlets are *Fuel for Locomotive Steam Use* (New York, 1855) and *Report on the Rock Oil, or Petroleum, From Venango Co., Pennsylvania* (New Haven, 1855).

His papers include "A Daguerreotype Experiment by Galvanic Light," in *American Journal of Science*, **43** (1842), 185–186, written with W. H. Goode; "On the Use of Carbon in Grove's Battery," *ibid.*, 393; "Report on the Intrusive Trap of the New Red Sandstone of Connecticut," *ibid.*, **47** (1844), 107–108; "On the Chemical Composition of the Calcareous Corals," *ibid.*, 2nd ser., **1** (1846), 189–199; "Optical Examination of Several American Micas," *ibid.*, **10** (1850), 372–383; "On the Existence of the Mastodon in the Deep-Lying Gold Placers of California," *ibid.*, **45** (1868), 378–381; "On Flame Temperatures in Their Relations to Composition and Luminosity," *ibid.*, **49** (1870), 339–347, written with Henry Wurtz (repr. in *Chemical News, Journal of the Franklin Institute, Philosophical Magazine*, and *Journal of Gas-lighting, Water-supply and Sanitary Improvement* [London]); "Researches on Water-Gas," in *Journal of Gas-lighting, Water-supply, and Sanitary Improvement*, **24** (1874), 544–545, 574–576, 608–610, 640–641, 675–677, written with Henry Wurtz—this paper appeared first as a book in 1869 and in the *American Gas-Light Journal and Chemical Repertory*, beginning with the issue of 16 Jan. 1874, p. 21.

There are important collections of letters, diaries, reports, and memorabilia pertaining to Silliman and his work at the Yale University Library, in the archives of the National Academy of Sciences, at the Bancroft Library (University of California), the Stanford University Library, the Huntington Library (San Marino, California), and the DeGolyer Foundation Library (Dallas, Texas). For details concerning these materials and further sources, see Gerald T. White (below).

II. SECONDARY LITERATURE. There is no full-length biography of Silliman. The best source for the period 1865–1885 is Gerald T. White, *Scientists in Conflict. The Beginnings of the Oil Industry in California* (San Marino, Calif., 1968), which contains the substance of a number of earlier papers by White and, through its bibliographical note and extensive footnotes, is an excellent guide to the sources by and about Silliman. Other sources are Russell H. Chittenden, *History of the Sheffield Scientific School of Yale University 1846–1922*, I (New Haven, 1928), esp. 38, 42, 45–51, 64, 66, 69, 110, 116, 122, 287; [James Dwight Dana], "Benjamin Silliman," in *American Journal of Science*, **29** (1885), 85–92; W. L. Kingsley, *Yale College: A Sketch of Its History*, II (New York, 1879), 81–83, 105–107; Louis I. Kuslan, "The Founding of the Yale School of Applied Chemistry," in *Journal of the History of Medicine and Allied Sciences*, **24** (1969), 430–451; and Arthur W. Wright, "Biographical Memoir of Benjamin Silliman 1816–1885," in *Biographical Memoirs. National Academy of Sciences*, **7** (1913), 115–141.

ELIZABETH H. THOMSON

SIMON, FRANZ EUGEN (FRANCIS) (*b.* Berlin, Germany, 2 July 1893; *d.* Oxford, England, 31 October 1956), *physics*.

The son of a wealthy estate dealer, Simon, and his two sisters, grew up in comparative affluence. Although he received a classical education, he developed a strong interest in science; and in 1912 he went to Munich to read physics. A year later he was called up for military service; and from 1914 to 1918 he served as lieutenant in the field artillery. He resumed his studies at the University of Berlin in 1919, and the following year he started work for his Ph.D. under the supervision of Nernst. His dissertation concerned the measurement of specific heats at low temperatures, a line of research that was closely connected with Nernst's heat theorem, now generally known as the third law of thermodynamics. The subject remained the basis of Simon's scientific interest throughout his life. After obtaining his doctorate in 1921, Simon remained at Berlin, where in 1924 he became *Privatdozent* and, three years later, associate professor. It was during this period that his school of low-temperature physics was founded and that he did his outstanding work combining low-temperature and high-pressure techniques.

In 1931 Simon was appointed to the chair of physical chemistry at the Technical University of Breslau, succeeding Eucken. With some of the former members of his Berlin school he began to assemble and to set up low-temperature equipment, but the economic depression and political uncertainty severely hampered these efforts. Simon spent part of 1932 as visiting professor at Berkeley. When, a few months after his return from America, Hitler assumed power, Simon realized that despite his war service, his days in Germany were numbered. He tendered his resignation in June 1933 and accepted the invitation of F. A. Lindemann (later Lord Cherwell) to work at the Clarendon Laboratory, Oxford, where a small helium liquefaction plant had been set up by one of Simon's former co-workers, K. Mendelssohn. Another member of his Berlin School, Nicholas Kurti, accompanied Simon to Oxford and worked with him until Simon's death.

At first Simon occupied no regular position in Oxford but received a grant from Imperial Chemical Industries, which, through Lindemann's efforts, was helping many scientific refugees to establish themselves. In 1935 Simon was appointed to the readership in thermodynamics, and in 1945 he became professor of thermodynamics. He held this post until 1956, when Lindemann retired as Lee professor of experimental philosophy and Simon became his successor. Simon died while making plans for the further development of the Clarendon Laboratory, only a few weeks after taking up his new appointment.

Except for the interruption by the war years, Simon devoted all his time at Oxford to building up a new research school in low-temperature physics. At his suggestion Kurti, while still at Berlin, had begun work on the low-temperature properties of paramagnetic salts; and after settling at Oxford, much of Simon's work was taken up with developing the method of cooling by adiabatic demagnetization and with investigating the properties of matter at temperatures below 1° K. During the last years of his life his interest shifted from the ordering of electron spins to that of nuclear spins, and in 1951 the first nuclear alignment was achieved by members of his research group. Although Simon was greatly interested in this combination of low temperatures and nuclear physics, it took second place to the aim that he and Kurti had pursued for many years, the cooling by adiabatic demagnetization of nuclear spins. After long preparations and often disappointing pilot experiments, the final goal was reached a few months before Simon's death. The nuclear spin system of copper had been cooled to a temperature of less than 20 microdegrees absolute.

In addition to his magnetic work, Simon continued his interest in the general properties of matter at liquid helium temperatures, such as specific heats and thermal conductivities. He also resumed the research at high pressures, but perhaps not quite with the vigor it deserved. During the war Simon took part in the work on the atomic bomb and was particularly concerned with isotope separation by gaseous diffusion. In his later years he was much concerned with the problems of utilizing scientific advances technologically; and in his writings on these subjects politicians, as well as industry, came in for a good deal of criticism.

In 1941 Simon was elected a fellow of the Royal Society, and in 1948 he received its Rumford Medal. Two years later he was the first recipient of the Kamerlingh Onnes Medal of the Dutch Institute of Refrigeration, and in 1952 he was awarded the Linde Medal; in the same year he was elected an honorary foreign member of the American Academy of Arts and Sciences. For his war work on atomic energy he was given the C.B.E. in 1946, and in 1955 he was knighted.

When assessing Simon's scientific achievement, it is tempting to rate the spectacular success of nuclear cooling highest, but this would not do justice to the large body of outstanding work directed toward the proof and elucidation of the third law of thermodynamics. When Simon came to Nernst in 1920, the latter had just written the famous monograph in which he had proved to his own satisfaction that the heat theorem was correct and that it should be regarded as a basic law of physics. There were many who did not share this conviction, however, and it was left to Simon to prove the validity of the law in which Nernst was now beginning to lose interest. The law requires that, as absolute zero is approached, any system must tend to a state of zero entropy (that is, to maximum statistical orderliness). It was pointed out that many systems, such as glasses, retained an obvious degree of disorder, even when cooled to the lowest possible temperatures. Simon noticed that these systems were not in thermodynamic equilibrium and that, if by magic or by waiting for immensely long times they could be guided into equilibrium, the process would be accompanied by the liberation of heat. In other words, none of these systems could be used to reach absolute zero and thereby infringe upon the third law.

Simon and his school also investigated systems, such as ortho-hydrogen, the chemical constant of which seemed to suggest the existence of a zero-point entropy. Their experiments proved that some ordering always occurs, sometimes at less than 1° K., which brings the system into agreement with the third law. Simon also provided the explanation for the very strange fact that under its own vapor pressure helium remains a liquid, even at absolute zero. He showed that this is due to the vibration of the atoms under the quantum-mechanical zero-point energy that again is a consequence of Nernst's theorem.

Simon's work on high pressure was an investigation of the melting curves of solidified gases, especially that of helium. It was known that up to the highest pressures, the equilibrium between the solid and the fluid phase of any pure substance follows a smooth curve with no indication of a critical point or of a change in the temperature function. He had the brilliant idea of extending investigations to the substance with the lowest critical data: helium. Thus, using it as a model system, Simon eventually was able to explore the melting curve up to ten times the liquid-gas critical temperature. Even under these extreme conditions, however, no solid-fluid critical point was found. In fact, parallel experiments on the thermodynamic properties showed that with rising pressure and temperature, the two phases become increasingly dissimilar.

Curiously, Simon was at first less known through his scientific results than through the methods of obtaining them. When he began his work, only three laboratories in the world commanded the expensive means of liquefying helium. It was Simon's great achievement to develop small-scale apparatus of novel and ingenious design that eventually permitted not only his but many other laboratories to experiment in this otherwise closed domain.

BIBLIOGRAPHY

Simon and his co-workers published more than 150 papers, only a few of which can be cited here: "Zur Frage der Nullpunktsenergie," in *Zeitschrift für Physik*, **16** (1923), 183–199, written with K. Bennewitz; "Die Bestimmung der freien Energie," in H. Geiger and K. Scheel, eds., *Handbuch der Physik*, X, pt. 7 (Berlin, 1926), 350; "Fünfundzwanzig Jahre Nernstscher Wärmesatz," in *Ergebnisse der exakten Naturwissenschaften*, **9** (1930), 222–274; "The Approach to the Absolute Zero of Temperature," in *Proceedings of the Royal Institution*, **28** (1935), 515–541; "On the Range of Stability of the Fluid State," in *Transactions of the Faraday Society*, **33** (1936), 65–73; "The Determination of Temperature Below 1° K.," in *Science Progress*, **34** (July 1939), 31–46; *The Neglect of Science* (Oxford, 1951); "Low Temperature Problems, A General Survey," in F. E. Simon *et al.*, *Low Temperature Physics* (London, 1952), 1–29; and "The Third Law of Thermodynamics—a Historical Survey (40th Guthrie Lecture)," in *Yearbook of the Physical Society* (1956), 1.

For Simon's life see N. Kurti's obituary in *Biographical Memoirs of Fellows of the Royal Society*; and Nancy Arms, *A Prophet in Two Countries: The Life of F. E. Simon* (London, 1966).

KURT MENDELSSOHN

SIMON BREDON. See **Bredon, Simon.**

SIMON DE PHARES (*b*. Meung-sur-Loire [?], France, *ca*. 1450; *d*. Paris, France, after 1499), *astrology.*

All that is known about Simon is what he wrote in his *Recueil des plus célèbres astrologues*.[1] Born perhaps in Meung-sur-Loire, he studied law in Orléans and then entered the Faculty of Arts in Paris, where he studied Sacrobosco's *De sphaera* and al-Qabīṣī's *Introductorium*. He then joined the service of Mathieu de Nanterre,[2] no doubt as astrologer, and later that of Duke John II of Bourbon. While serving the latter, Simon completed his training with the German astrologer Conrad Heingarter, whom he subsequently considered his master. After studying for two years at Oxford, he traveled in Scotland and Ireland; returned to France to take courses at the Faculty of Medicine in Montpellier; journeyed in Italy (Rome, Venice) and Egypt (Cairo, Alexandria); then traveled through the Alps of Savoy and Switzerland for four years, botanizing and examining rocks.

After the death in 1488 of John II, to whose service he had returned, Simon moved to Lyons, married, and raised a family. His house, near the cathedral, was furnished with a library of two hundred books and was his astrological office. He was so famous that King Charles VIII, while passing through Lyons on All Saints' Day of 1490, was anxious to consult him. Such glory and success were bound to arouse jealousy. Accused of sorcery before the episcopal court of Lyons, Simon was ordered to cease his activities and his library was confiscated. His appeal to the Parlement of Paris failed, and the books in his library were censured by the Faculty of Theology. He subsequently moved to Paris, where he was still living in 1499, apparently having failed to obtain royal intervention, although he had composed a work justifying his activities for Charles VIII.

This justification is known today by the title *Recueil des plus célèbres astrologues et quelques hommes doctes*, which was added at the end of the sixteenth century to the only existing manuscript, which appears to be the original. It is the first part of a work in which Simon had also planned to present the principles of astrology and of the divinatory arts, in order that the scientific contributions of the former could easily be separated from the charlatanism of the latter. That the planned parts probably were never written is unfortunate, for Simon's experience in a trade that he practiced rather like a liberal profession, his curiosity in the most varied areas of science, and his training in at least four universities and through extensive travels would have imparted considerable value to the work.

Composed in French, Simon's justification of astrology was conceived as a panegyric of astrologers who had honored their profession by the success of their predictions, and he should therefore be considered the first historiographer of astronomy. The *Recueil* is a series of accounts, arranged in theoretically chronological order, devoted to famous astrologers and their works. It is thus a priceless source of information, since Simon went so far as to give the incipits of some works of his colleagues.

The quality of the information obviously is highly variable, and the reports on Simon's contemporaries are of greater interest than the mythical biographies of the founders of astrology. Even for the fourteenth century the chronology is often defective: John of Murs and Firmin de Belleval are assigned dates that are too recent, as are Roger Bacon and "Barthelemy de Morbecha" (William of Moerbeke), who are placed in the middle of the fourteenth century. Because erroneous information is presented side by side with precise data, the *Recueil* must be read very critically.[3] Nevertheless, it is a tool of very great importance for historians of medieval astronomy and medicine.

NOTES

1. The information provided by the *Recueil* on the circumstances of Simon's trial before the Parlement has been completed by E. Wickersheimer with the aid of archival documents, and by the material published by Charles Du Plessis d'Argentré in his *Collectio judiciorum de novis erroribus*, I (Paris, 1728).
2. Mathieu de Nanterre was the premier president of the Parlement of Paris. The minutes of *étude* VIII in the *minutier central* of the Archives Nationales preserve several documents on Mathieu de Nanterre for 1480–1485.
3. Among the errors is Simon's dating of his work from the sixteenth year of the reign of Charles VIII, who actually died in April 1498, before having completed the fifteenth year of his reign.

BIBLIOGRAPHY

An excellent ed. of the only known work by Simon de Phares is *Recueil des plus célèbres astrologues et quelques hommes doctes faict par Symon de Phares du temps de Charles VIIIᵉ, publié d'après le manuscrit unique de la Bibliothèque nationale par Ernest Wickersheimer* (Paris, 1929). The biography included in this ed. (pp. vi–xii) was reprinted in E. Wickersheimer, *Dictionnaire biographique des médecins en France au moyen âge* (Paris, 1936), 743–744. It also is the basis of the account by L. Thorndike in *A History of Magic and Experimental Science*, IV (New York, 1934), 545–557, which contains interesting speculations concerning the reasons for Simon's travels in the Alps and the relations of Simon and of Charles VIII to the Parlement of Paris.

EMMANUEL POULLE

SIMPLICIUS (*b.* Cilicia, *ca.* 500; *d.* after 533), *philosophy.*

Simplicius was one of the most famous representatives of Neoplatonism in the sixth century. An outstanding scholar, he was the author of extensive commentaries on Aristotle that contain much valuable information on previous Greek philosophy, including the pre-Socratics.

Very little is known of his life. According to Agathias (*History*, II,30,3), he was born in Cilicia. He received his first philosophical education in Alexandria at the school of Ammonius Hermiae,[1] the author of a large commentary on the *Peri Hermeneias* and on some other logical, physical, and metaphysical treatises of Aristotle. These works strongly influenced not only the commentaries of Simplicius but also those written by the philosophers of the Alexandrian School: Asclepius, Philoponus, and Olympiodorus.[2] Simplicius also studied philosophy at Athens in the school of Damascius,[3] the author of *Problems and Solutions About the First Principles*, known for his doctrine of the Ineffable First Principle. According to Damascius no name is capable of expressing adequately the nature of that Principle, not even the Plotinian name of "the One." Damascius was the last pagan Neoplatonist in the unbroken succession of the Athenian school, where he was teaching when Justinian closed it in 529. Simplicius, who at that time was a member of Damascius' circle, left Athens with him and five other philosophers and moved to Persia (531–532). Their exile was only temporary, for they returned to the empire after the treaty of peace between the Byzantines and the Persians (533). According to Agathias (*History*, II,31,4), the terms of the treaty would have guaranteed to the philosophers full security in their own environment: they were not to be compelled to accept anything against their personal conviction, and they were never to be prevented from living according to their own philosophical doctrine.[4]

There are grounds for supposing that Simplicius settled in Athens after returning from Persia.[5] Presumably he was not allowed to deliver public lectures and thus could devote all his time to research and writing. Hence his commentaries are not related to any teaching activity; rather, they show the character of written expositions that carefully analyze the Aristotelian text and interpret it in the light of the whole history of Greek philosophy. Simplicius always endeavored to harmonize and reconcile Plato and Aristotle by reducing the differences between them to a question of vocabulary, point of view, or even misunderstanding of some Platonic theories by the Stagirite.

Simplicius was not the first to take this approach. According to W. Jaeger, this trend can be traced to Posidonius and to Neoplatonic philosophy in general. The same method was certainly used by Ammonius, who always attempted to reduce the opposition between Plato and Aristotle to different viewpoints. For example, in dealing with Aristotle's criticism of the theory of ideas, Ammonius believed this criticism to concern not the authentic doctrine of Plato, but rather the opinion of some philosophers who attributed to the Ideas an independent subsistence, separate from the Intellect of the Demiurge (Asclepius, *In Metaphysicorum*, 69,24–27; 73,27).

Apparently Simplicius was persuaded that this approach was in agreement with the attitude of the φιλομαθεῖς and that it uncovered the true meaning of philosophical doctrines. At first glance, he said, some theories seem to be quite contradictory, but a more accurate inquiry shows them to be reconcilable (*In de Caelo*, 159,3–9). Moreover, in explaining a philosophical text, one should not be biased for or against its author. Hence Simplicius opposed the method of Alexander, who from the beginning is suspicious of Plato in the same way that others are inspired with prejudice against Aristotle (*In de Caelo*, 297,1–4). Since agreement on an opinion, even a prephilosophical one, has often been considered a criterion of truth, Aristotle and the Stoics frequently used the argument of universal agreement. Therefore, having to cope with the increasing influence of Christianity, late Neoplatonic philosophers wanted to argue against the presumed disaccord between the main representatives of Greek philosophy, Plato and Aristotle, in order to enhance their own doctrine. As a Christian, Philoponus did not have the same motives for harmonizing Plato and Aristotle; he firmly opposed attempts to reconcile them and called this interpretation a kind of mythology. Aristotle, he held, did not argue against those who misunderstood Plato but against the authentic Platonic doctrine.

As a commentator Simplicius did not overestimate his own contributions but was quite aware of his debt to other philosophers, especially to Alexander, Iamblichus, and Porphyry (*In Categorias*, 3, 10–13). He did not hesitate to call his own commentaries a mere introduction to the writings of these famous masters (*In Categorias*, 3,13–17), nor did he cling fanatically to his own interpretations; he was happy to exchange them for better explanations (*In Categorias*, 350,8–9). On the other hand, the work of a commentator is far from being a neutral undertaking or a question of mere erudition; it is chiefly an opportunity to become more familiar with the text under consideration and

to elucidate some intricate passages (*In Enchiridion*, Praefatio, 2,24–29; *In de Caelo*, 102,15; 166,14–16; *In Categorias*, 3,4–6); hence Simplicius' constant concern to obtain reliable documents and to check the historical value of this information, as when he verified the information provided by Alexander about the squaring of the circle according to Hippocrates of Chios (*In Physicorum*, 60, 22–68, 32).

Simplicius adhered to the Aristotelian doctrine of the eternity of the world, as a theory that fits perfectly into the Neoplatonic ontology insofar as the eternal movement of the heavens is a necessary link between the pure eternity of the intelligible reality and the temporal character of material beings. With respect to this question, Simplicius strongly opposed Philoponus, who asserted the beginning of the world through divine creation. Philoponus, however, did not argue as a Christian, nor did he base his refutation of the Aristotelian doctrine on arguments drawn from his Christian faith. According to him, God is the principle of whatever exists: if time is infinite, nothing may ever come to be, because an infinite number of conditions of possibility are to be fulfilled before anything could begin to exist—which is clearly impossible. Simplicius' notion of "infinite" is different; it does not mean an infinity existing at once, but a possibility of transcending any boundary. Consequently the conception of time exposed by both authors is not the same. Simplicius professed a cyclical conception; Philoponus adhered to a linear view without regular return of the same events. Philoponus also substantiated divine creation in time, without preexisting matter; whereas Simplicius maintained that although heaven, the first and highest corporeal reality, is totally dependent upon God, it has never come to exist; it must be eternal, because it springs immediately from God.

In his *Corollarium de tempore* (*In Physicorum*, 773,8–800,25) Simplicius drew a general survey of the different theories about time, dealing with older as well as with more recent philosophers. According to his view, time is closely related to the life of the soul; but the activity of the soul does not merely coincide with time, because it occurs in time. Previous to all things existing in time, there is a time that makes them temporal and arranges the extension of their existence in an orderly fashion. The nature of that time, like the nature of the soul, is intermediary between being and becoming. Consequently the soul does not exist in time but is the principle of the temporal character of its own activity, as it is the origin of the time of the cosmos.

To a certain extent, soul and time may be identified, although the conceptual distinction must be maintained. Simplicius wondered whether this logical distinction may entail an ontological one; his reply was rather hesitant. In stressing the connection between time and soul, Simplicius approached Plotinus; on the other hand, he was also influenced by Iamblichus and Proclus insofar as he dealt not only with the numbered time, but also with the numbering time, that is, the regulating principle of movement.

The earliest preserved work of Simplicius seems to be his commentary on Epictetus' *Enchiridion*. K. Praechter was the first to believe that this work predates the Aristotelian commentaries or even that it was written during Simplicius' stay at Alexandria. Praechter argued mainly from the text that has been chosen for explication; from the absence of references to Iamblichus, Proclus, or Damascius; from the less intricate doctrine of the first principles; and finally from its kinship with the commentary of Hierocles on the *Carmen aureum*.[6] Praechter's thesis is certainly questionable. In two contributions I. Hadot has shown that the influence of Proclus and even of Damascius is undeniable.[7] In his discussion of the Manichaean cosmogony Simplicius also seemingly relied on information drawn from conversations with Manichaean sages; this is probably related to his stay in Persia with King Chosroes, who always showed a keen interest in philosophical problems.[8] The allusion to the "tyrannic circumstances" that afforded him an opportunity for dealing with Epictetus' *Enchiridion* (138,17–19) may suggest that Simplicius wrote his commentary after the Edict of Justinian (529). From these and other similar anti-Christian statements that occur in the commentary, and also from the way in which the duty of a philosopher in corrupt states is presented, A. Cameron argued that this work may have been written precisely during the years 529–531.[9]

Among the commentaries on Aristotle, the first to be mentioned according to chronological order seems to be the *In de Caelo*; some passages in the first book of this work, where the criticisms of Philoponus against Aristotle are refuted, are referred to in the commentary on the *Physics* (1118,3; 1146,27; 1169,7; 1175,32; 1178,36; 1330,2; 1335,1). In 529 Philoponus published his *De aeternitate mundi contra Proclum*. Between this work and his *De aeternitate mundi contra Aristotelem*, he completed two other works, one of

which is the commentary on the *Meteorologica*.[10] Hence the *In de Caelo* could hardly be dated before 535; presumably the work was written shortly after Simplicius' stay in Persia.

The commentary on the *Physics* is certainly later than the *In de Caelo* because of its references to this work already noted. On the other hand, it is prior to the commentary on the *Categoriae*, because it is referred to in this last work (*In Categorias*, 435,23–24). The commentary was written after the death of Damascius, but we do not know this date. According to A. Cameron,[11] Damascius was alive as late as 538; consequently the commentary could hardly have been written before 540.

Both the commentaries on the *Categoriae* and the *De anima* are to be dated after the *In Physicorum*. To date, the authenticity of the commentary on the *De Anima* has hardly been questioned; nevertheless, certain features may suggest that this work has been erroneously attributed to Simplicius. The solution of this problem is of some importance, because our information about some lost works of Simplicius depends on it. The author of the *In de Anima* six times refers to earlier writings: to an *Epitome Physicorum Theophrasti* (136,29), to a work on the *Metaphysics* (28,20; 217,26), and to a commentary on the *Physics* (35,14; 120,4; 198,5). If Simplicius is to be considered the author of the *In de Anima*, then perhaps only two not unimportant works, namely the *Epitome Physicorum Theophrasti* and a commentary on the *Metaphysics*, have been lost.

Only fragments have been preserved of the commentary on the *Premises* of the first book of the *Elementa Euclidis* (see *Anaritii in decem libros priores Elementorum Euclidis commentarii*). On the other hand, some scholia on Proclus' *In Platonis Timaeum commentaria* may have been composed by Simplicius.[12] As to the *Scholia in Hermogenis artem oratoriam* (see Fabricius-Harles, V,770, referring to Lambeck-Kollar, VII, 549–553), there is no reference to Simplicius in the description of the codex Vindob. Phil. gr. 15 by H. Hunger.[13] Fabricius-Harles (IX,567) also mentions a commentary on Iamblichus' *De Pythagorica secta libri tres* and a *Commentarius brevis de Syllogismis*; no trace of either work has ever been found.

Simplicius' work was very influential, especially his commentary on the *Categoriae*, translated into Latin by William of Moerbeke in 1266. Part of the commentary on the *De Caelo* was first translated by Robert Grosseteste;[14] and a complete Latin version was executed by William of Moerbeke in 1271.

NOTES

1. In his commentaries Simplicius frequently mentions Ammonius as his master: *In de Caelo*, 271,19; 462,20–21; *In Physicorum*, 59,23–24; 59,30–31; 183,18; 192,14; 198,17; 1363,8.
2. Cf. *Anonymous Prolegomena to Platonic Philosophy*, L. G. Westerink, ed. (Amsterdam, 1962), xi.
3. For references to Damascius as the master of Simplicius see *In Physicorum*, 462,17; 601,19; 630,35; 644,10; 774,28; 778,27; 795,14.
4. Some serious criticisms against the reliability of the information given by Agathias were recently raised by A. Cameron; see "The Last Days of the Academy at Athens," 18.
5. *Ibid.*, 22–26.
6. See K. Praechter, *Simplikios*, cols. 206–210.
7. See I. Hadot, *Le Système théologique de Simplicius dans son commentaire sur le manuel d'Epictète*, 270, 272–273, and 278–279.
8. See I. Hadot, *Die Widerlegung des Manichäismus im Epiktetkommentar des Simplikios*, 46, 56–57.
9. See A. Cameron, *op. cit.*, 13–17.
10. See É. Evrard, "Les convictions religieuses de Jean Philopon et la date de son commentaire aux 'Météorologiques,'" in *Bulletin de l'Académie royale de Belgique. Classe des lettres et des sciences morales et politiques*, 5th ser., **39** (1953), 345.
11. A. Cameron, *op. cit.*, 22.
12. Proclus, *Théologie Platonicienne*, H. D. Saffrey and L. G. Westerink, ed. and trans., Bk. 1 (Paris, 1968), clii–cliii.
13. H. Hunger, *Katalog der griechischen Handschriften der oesterreichischen Nationalbibliothek*, I (Vienna, 1961), 147–148.
14. See D. Allan, "Mediaeval Versions of Aristotle's 'De Caelo' and of the Commentary of Simplicius," in *Mediaeval and Renaissance Studies*, **2** (1950), 82–120.

BIBLIOGRAPHY

I. ORIGINAL WORKS. Simplicius' works are *Commentarius in Enchiridion Epicteti*, Jo. Schweighäuser, ed., in *Theophrasti Characteres*, . . . Fr. Dübner, ed. (Paris, 1840); *In Aristotelis physicorum libros quattuor priores commentaria*, H. Diels, ed., Commentaria in Aristotelem Graeca, vol. IX (Berlin, 1882); *In libros Aristotelis de Anima commentaria*, M. Hayduck, ed., *ibid.*, XI (Berlin, 1882); *In Aristotelis de Caelo commentaria*, J. L. Heiberg, ed., *ibid.*, VII (Berlin, 1894); *In Aristotelis physicorum libros quattuor posteriores commentaria*, H. Diels, ed., *ibid.*, X (Berlin, 1895); *In Aristotelis Categorias commentarium*, C. Kalbfleisch, ed., *ibid.*, VIII (Berlin, 1907); and *Commentaire sur les Catégories d'Aristote*, in *Corpus Latinum commentariorum in Aristotelem graecorum*, I (Louvain–Paris, 1971), II (Leiden, 1975), a critical ed. by A. Pattin of William of Moerbeke's translation.

II. SECONDARY LITERATURE. On Simplicius and his work, see *Anaritii in decem libros priores Elementorum Euclidis commentarii, ex interpretatione Gherardi Cre-monensis in codice Cracoviensi 569 servata*, M. Curtze, ed. (Leipzig, 1899); A. Cameron, "The Last Days of the Academy at Athens," in *Proceedings of the Cambridge Philological Society*, n.s. **15** (1969), 7–29; E. Ducci, "In τὸ ἐὸν parmenideo nella interpretazione di Simplicio," in *Angelicum*, **40** (1963), 173–194, 313–327; I. Hadot, "Die Widerlegung des Manichäismus im Epiktetkommentar des Simplikios," in *Archiv für Geschichte der Philosophie*, **51** (1969), 31–57; and "Le système théologique de Simplicius dans son commentaire sur le manuel d'Épictète," in *Le néoplatonisme. Colloques internationaux du C.N.R.S.* (Royaumont, 1969), 265–279.

See also H. Meyer, *Das Corollarium de Tempore des Simplikios und die Aporien des Aristoteles zur Zeit* (Meisenheim am Glan, 1969); B. Nardi, "Il commento di Simplicio al De anima nelle controversie della fine del secolo XV e del secolo XVI," in *Saggi sull' Aristotelismo padovano dal secolo XIV al XVI* (Florence, 1958), 365–442; K. Praechter, "Simplikios," in Pauly-Wissowa, *Real-Encyclopädie der classischen Altertumswissenschaft*, 2nd ser., III, 204–213; A. I. Sabra, "Simplicius's Proof of Euclid's Parallels Postulate," in *Journal of the Warburg and Courtauld Institutes*, **32** (1969), 1–24; and W. Wieland, "Die Ewigkeit der Welt (Der Streit zwischen Joannes Philoponus und Simplicius)," in *Die Gegenwart der Griechen im neuerem Denken. Festschrift für H.-G. Gadamer zum 60. Geburstag* (Tübingen, 1960), 291–316.

G. VERBEKE

SIMPSON, THOMAS (*b.* Market Bosworth, Leicestershire, England, 20 August 1710; *d.* Market Bosworth, 14 May 1761), *mathematics*.

Simpson's father, a weaver, wanted him to take up the same trade. After limited education the son moved to Nuneaton, where he was influenced by the 1724 eclipse and by a visiting peddler, who lent him a copy of Cocker's *Arithmetic* and a work by Partridge on astrology. Young Simpson made such progress with his studies that he acquired a local reputation as a fortune-teller. He was able to leave his weaving and marry his landlady, a widow Swinfield, whose son was a little older than her new husband. About 1733 an unfortunate incident obliged him to move to Derby, where he taught at an evening school and resumed his trade as a weaver during the day.

By the beginning of 1736 Simpson had moved to London and settled in Spitalfields, where the Mathematical Society had flourished for two decades. In 1736 his first mathematical contributions were published in the well-known *Ladies' Diary*. One of these showed that he was already versed in the subject of fluxions, which had elicited a growing interest, as illustrated by the famous controversy sparked by Bishop George Berkeley in 1734.[1] In December 1735 Simpson had issued proposals[2] for publishing his first book, *A New Treatise of Fluxions*, which appeared in 1737. Although publication may have been delayed by the author's teaching duties, it indicated his success, which enabled him to bring his family from Derby, and his future career as a mathematics teacher, editor, and textbook writer.

Robert Heath's accusation of plagiarism probably brought Simpson useful publicity, which was supplemented by the publication in 1740 of *The Laws of Chance* and *Essays on Several Subjects*. They were rapidly followed by *Annuities and Reversions* (1742) and *Mathematical Dissertations* (1743), the latter being dedicated to Martin Folkes, then president of the Royal Society, with whom he had been in correspondence for some months. Apart from Francis Blake, Simpson's other correspondents were relatively humble philomaths. Largely through Folkes's support, Simpson was appointed second mathematical master at the Royal Military Academy, Woolwich, in August 1743 and was elected fellow of the Royal Society two years later.

Simpson seems to have been quite successful as a teacher, and his duties left him time for other activities. Three subsequent textbooks were best-sellers, partly because of his position and partly because of their scope: *Algebra*, with ten English editions in 1745–1826, besides American and German versions; *Geometry*, six London editions between 1747 and 1821, five at Paris, and one at Amsterdam; and *Trigonometry*, five London editions in 1748–1799, besides French and American versions. *Geometry*, which led to an argument with Robert Simson (whose editions of Euclid became very popular), represented a significant revision of the original Greek treatment along the lines of Clairaut and other Continental mathematicians.

Simpson's influence on English mathematics was extended by his editorship of the annual *Ladies' Diary* from 1754.[3] This post demanded an extensive correspondence with contributors throughout the country, in addition to the normal responsibility of seeing the work through the press; and Simpson seems to have worn himself out with his many activities and aged prematurely. In 1760 he became involved as a consultant on the best form for a new bridge across the Thames at Blackfriars.[4] The intense work on this project accelerated his death.

Simpson obtained a reputation as "the ablest Analyst (if we regard the useful purposes of Analytical Science) that this country [Britain] can boast of" and as author of one of the two best treatises "on the Fluxionary Calculus."[5] He was aware of the importance of Continental mathematicians, for the first book on the subject he read was a translation from the French of L'Hospital's *Analyse des infiniment petits*; and the final paragraph of the preface to his last work, *Miscellaneous Tracts* (1757), was by nature of a testament. Having mentioned in the latter that he had "chiefly adhered to the analytic method of Investigation," he warned that "by a diligent cultivation of the Modern Analysis, . . . Foreign Mathematicians have, of late, been able to push their Researches farther, in many particulars, than Sir Isaac Newton and his Followers here, have done. . . ."

Although Simpson clearly was more interested in the applications to problems in series and mechanics[6] than in the foundations of analysis, he avoided the difficulties of infinitesimals by his definition: "The Fluxions of variable Quantities are always measured by their Relation to each other; and are ever expressed by the finite spaces that would be uniformly described in equal Times, with the Velocities by which those Quantities are generated." F. M. Clarke has detailed the correspondence with Francis Blake, author of an anonymous but influential pamphlet, *Explanation of Fluxions* (1741), which clarified his and Simpson's ideas on the subject before the appearance, in an enlarged and revised form, of Simpson's *Doctrine and Applications of Fluxions* (1750); this work inspired another polemic.

Until his death in 1754, one of the leading mathematicians in England was Abraham De Moivre, whose well-known *Doctrine of Chances* (1718) included work on annuities. In *Laws of Chance* (1740) Simpson wrote approvingly of De Moivre but claimed to have investigated two problems in probability for which the latter had given only the results; two years later he issued *Annuities and Reversions*. The latter was criticized by De Moivre, and Simpson replied immediately with an appendix that seems to have effectively terminated the dispute. In 1752 Simpson issued a supplementary essay that included his much-quoted tables on the valuation of lives according to London bills of mortality. Paradoxically he is now best remembered for Simpson's rule, discovered long before him, for determining the area under a curve,

$$\frac{Aa + 4Bb + Cc}{3} \times AB,$$

obtained by replacing the curve by a parabola with vertical axis going through the points *a*, *b*, and *c*.[7] Fifty years after Simpson's death Robert Woodhouse and his disciples achieved Simpson's aim with the reform of mathematical analysis at Cambridge, which brought English mathematics once more into the front rank of European developments.

NOTES

1. Details are in F. Cajori, *A History of the Conceptions of Limits and Fluxions in Great Britain From Newton to Woodhouse* (Chicago, 1919), chs. 3, 4.
2. D. F. McKenzie and J. C. Ross, *A Ledger of Charles Ackers* (Oxford, 1968), no. 398, quotes 750 copies costing £1 each. The only known copy is that in the Simpson papers, IV.
3. Simpson also contributed to other periodicals. See R. C. Archibald, "Notes on Some Minor English Mathematical Serials," in *Mathematical Gazette*, **14**, no. 200 (Apr. 1929), 379–400.
4. A brief account in F. M. Clarke, *Simpson and His Times*, can be supplemented by J. Nichols, *The History and the Antiquities of the County of Leicester*, IV (London, 1811), 510–514.
5. The assessments by R. Woodhouse and J. Playfair are quoted in Simpson's *Fluxions* (1823), iv.
6. See I. Todhunter, *A History of the Mathematical Theories of Attraction* (London, 1873), ch. 10, for an estimate of Simpson's contributions to this subject and (sec. 294) his estimate that Simpson was "at the head of the non-academical body of English mathematicians" and second only to Newton.
7. Given in *Mathematical Dissertations* (1743), p. 110, for the equidistant ordinates *Aa*, *Bb*, and *Cc*.

BIBLIOGRAPHY

I. ORIGINAL WORKS. Clarke (see below) gives the full titles, but not details of the eds., of Simpson's works except the last: *Miscellaneous Tracts on Some Curious and Very Interesting Subjects in Mechanics, Physical-Astronomy and Speculative Mathematics; Wherein the Precessions of the Equinox, the Nutation of the Earth's Axis, and the Motion of the Moon in Her Orbit, Are Determined* (London, 1757). Simpson's books reprinted many of his *Philosophical Transactions* articles, listed in Poggendorff, II, 937.

II. SECONDARY LITERATURE. The main source for this article is Frances M. Clarke, *Thomas Simpson and His Times* (New York, 1929), based on her 1929 Columbia University thesis but incompletely documented and unindexed. This often quotes from the 8 vols. of Simpson papers in Columbia University Library, which kindly sent a microfilm to the writer. Most other biographies depend on Charles Hutton, "Memoirs of the Life and Writings of the Author," prefixed to Simpson's *Select Exercises* (London, 1792), itself an extended version of an account in the *Annual Register* (1764), 29–38.

P. J. WALLIS

SIMSON, ROBERT (*b.* West Kilbride, Ayrshire, Scotland, 14 October 1687; *d.* Glasgow, Scotland, 1 October 1768), *geometry.*

Simson's father, Robert, was a prosperous merchant in Glasgow who had acquired the small estate of Kirktonhall in West Kilbride; his mother, Agnes, whose maiden name was also Simson, came from a family that had provided parish ministers for the Church of Scotland from the time of the Reformation. It was with the intention of training for the Church that Simson matriculated at the University of Glasgow in 1701. He followed the standard course in the faculty of arts (Latin, Greek, logic, natural philosophy) and then devoted himself to the study of theology and Semitic languages. During these years, one of his teachers was his maternal uncle, John Simson, professor of divinity. He also acquired a knowledge of natural history that was a source of pleasure to him throughout his life; it is interesting to note that until his death he was held by his contemporaries to be one of the best botanists of his time.

At this time no instruction in mathematics was given at the University of Glasgow. The chair of mathematics had been revived in 1691 and during the years 1691–1696 it was occupied by George Sinclair, a mathematician and engineer of some repute. On his death Sinclair was succeeded by his son, Robert, who flagrantly neglected the duties of his chair. Thus Simson had no formal tuition in mathematics. It would appear to have been through reading George Sinclair's *Tyrocinia Mathematica in Novem Tractatus* (Glasgow, 1661) that Simson's interest in the subject was first aroused and it was this work that encouraged him to read Euclid's *Elements* (in the edition of Commandinus). He soon became absorbed in the study of geometry and acquired such a reputation as an "amateur" mathematician that in 1710 the senate of the university, having relieved Sinclair of his office, offered Simson the chair of mathematics. Simson declined the invitation on the grounds that he had received no formal training in mathematics; when the senate reaffirmed its confidence in his ability to discharge the duties of the chair, Simson suggested that the appointment be left open for a year, during which he would devote himself entirely to the study of mathematics.

Simson chose to spend the academic year 1710–1711 in London. He had originally intended to study in Oxford, but his efforts to make contact with mathematicians there were unsuccessful; so he spent the year at Christ's Hospital (the Blue Coat school), where, under the aegis of Samuel

Pepys, a mathematical school had been founded for the purpose of training navigation officers for the Royal Navy. More important than the formal instruction that Simson received there were the personal relationships he established with several prominent mathematicians: John Caswell, James Jurin (secretary of the Royal Society), and Humphrey Ditton. He was most profoundly influenced by Halley, who had recently been appointed Savilian professor of geometry at Oxford while still a captain in the Royal Navy; not only was Halley regarded as second only to Newton in the field of scientific research, he was also a distinguished scholar (and editor) of the works of the Greek mathematicians.

While Simson was still in London the senate of the University of Glasgow elected him (on 11 March 1711) to the chair of mathematics on the condition that "he give satisfactory proof of his skill in mathematics previous to his admission." On his return to Glasgow he submitted to a simple test and was duly admitted professor of mathematics on 20 November 1711.

At Glasgow, Simson's first task was to design a proper course in mathematics. The course extended over two complete academic years, each of seven months' duration; to each class he lectured for five hours a week. Although his own interest was entirely in geometry, he lectured on Newton's theory of fluxions; on Cartesian geometry, algebra, and the theory of logarithms; and on mechanics and geometrical optics. Among his students were Maclaurin, Matthew Stewart, and William Trail, all of whom subsequently occupied chairs of mathematics in Scottish universities.

Simson lived the rest of his life in rooms within the College of Glasgow; outwardly his life gave every appearance of being uneventful—so much so that it was highlighted only by the conferment upon him in 1746 of the M.D. (*honoris causa*) by the University of St. Andrews. In 1761 John Williamson was appointed his assistant and successor.

Simson's lifework was devoted to the restoration of "lost" works of the Greek geometers and to the preparation of definitive editions of those works that had survived. Halley had encouraged this predilection for the works of the Greek geometers. (Simson's classical education and his knowledge of oriental languages were especially useful to him.) He first turned his attention to the restoration of Euclid's porisms, which are known only from the scant account in Pappus' *Mathematical Collections*. Although Fermat claimed to have restored Euclid's work, and Halley had edited the Greek

text of the preface to Pappus' seventh book, Simson is usually regarded as the first to have thrown real light on the matter. In a paper, "Two General Propositions of Pappus, in Which Many of Euclid's Porisms Are Included" (*Philosophical Transactions of the Royal Society*, **32** [1723], 330), Simson elucidated two general propositions of Pappus and showed that they contained several of the porisms as special cases. He continued to work on this topic throughout his life, but nothing further was published until *De porismatibus tractatus* appeared posthumously in 1776. Simson's only other genuine research paper, "An Explanation of an Obscure Passage in Albert Girard's Commentary on Simon Stevin's Works, p. 169, 170," appeared in 1753 (*Philosophical Transactions of the Royal Society*, **48**, 368).

Simson's book on conic sections (1735) used only geometrical methods. Although he was familiar with the methods of coordinate geometry—and lectured upon them—he developed the subject in the style of the classical Greek authors. His authoritative account of the *loci plani* of Apollonius appeared in 1749. But his most influential work was his definitive edition (1756) of Euclid's *Elements*. This edition was the basis of every subsequent edition of the *Elements* until the beginning of the twentieth century. Simson adopted the perhaps naïve view that Euclid's treatise in its original form had been free from logical faults—any blemishes were regarded by him as being due to the bungling of editors such as Theon. Simson's restoration of Euclid's *Data* was added to his second edition of the *Elements* (1762).

A posthumous edition of Simson's unpublished mathematical works was published as *Opera Quaedam Reliqua R. Simson* (1776) at the expense of Philip Stanhope, second earl of Stanhope. It consists of four books: *De porismatibus tractatus*; *De sectione determinata*; *De logarithmis liber*; and *De limitibus quantitatum et rationum, fragmentum*. The last two books are based on his lectures to students; *De logarithmis* is a purely geometrical theory of logarithms. *De limitibus* is of great interest because it shows that Simson perceived that the fluxionary calculus of Newton rested on insecure foundations; accordingly, he attempted to place the theory of limits on a rigorous foundation. His failure lies probably in the fact that he tried to formulate the theory entirely in terms that would have been intelligible to a Greek geometer of the Alexandrian School.

Simson's manuscripts contain a great variety of miscellaneous geometrical propositions and many interesting reflections on various aspects of mathematical teaching and research, but none of it in a state for publication. He also prepared a draft of an edition of the complete works of Pappus that was based on material he had received from Halley many years earlier, and it is perhaps for this reason that a transcript was obtained by the Clarendon Press at Oxford.

On his death Simson bequeathed to the University of Glasgow his collection of mathematical books—at that time recognized as the most complete in the British Isles. They are preserved as the Simson Collection of the university library.

BIBLIOGRAPHY

I. ORIGINAL WORKS. Simson's works include *Sectionum Conicarum Libri V* (Edinburgh, 1735; 2nd ed., enlarged, 1750); *Apollonii Pergaei Locorum Planorum Libri II, restituti a R. Simson* (Glasgow, 1749); *Elements of Euclid* (Glasgow, 1756), of which the 2nd ed. (1762) contained Euclid's *Data*; and *Opera Quaedam Reliqua R. Simson*, James Clow, ed. (Glasgow, 1776).

II. SECONDARY LITERATURE. The best source is William Trail, *Life and Writings of Robert Simson* (Bath, 1812).

IAN N. SNEDDON

IBN SĪNĀ (or **Avicenna**), **ABU ALI AL-HUSSEIN IBN ABDALLAH** (*b.* Kharmaithen, near Bukhara, Persia [now Uzbekistan, U.S.S.R.], 980; *d.* Hamadān, Persia [now Iran], 1037), *philosophy, medicine, biology, astronomy.*

For a detailed study of his life and work, see Supplement.

SINĀN IBN THĀBIT IBN QURRA, ABŪ SAʿĪD (*b. ca.* 880; *d.* Baghdad, 943), *medicine, astronomy, mathematics.*

The son of Thābit ibn Qurra al-Ḥarrānī (*ca.* 830–901), and the father of Ibrāhīm ibn Sinān ibn Thābit (908–946), Sinān belonged to the sect of the Sabians originating in Ḥarrān. One of the most famous physicians of his time, Sinān worked mainly in Baghdad. He was born probably around 880: al-Masʿūdī mentions a description by Sinān of the life at the court of Caliph al-Muʿtadid (892–902), his father's protector. Apparently, Sinān held no position before 908. He was then physician to the caliphs al-Muqtadir (908–932), al-Qāhir (932–934), and al-Rāḍī (934–940).

Under al-Muqtadir, Sinān brilliantly directed the hospitals and medical administration of Baghdad. He was not a Muslim, and he cared for the faithful and unfaithful without discrimination. In 931, after a fatal malpractice, every Baghdad doctor, except a few famous ones, had to pass a test before Sinān.

Under al-Qāhir, Sabians were persecuted, and Sinān had to become Muslim and later fled to Khurāsān, returning under al-Rāḍī. After the latter's death he served Amīr Abu 'L-Ḥusayn Baḥkam in Wāsiṭ, looking after his character and physical health.

None of Sinān's work is extant. As listed by Ibn al-Qifṭī, it can be divided into three categories: historical-political, mathematical, and astronomical; no medical texts are mentioned. A treatise of the first kind contained the already mentioned description of life at the court of al-Muʿtadid, and, among other things, a sketch for a government according to Plato's *Republic*. Al-Maʿsūdī criticizes it, adding that Sinān should rather have occupied himself with topics within his competence, such as the science of Euclid, the *Almagest*, astronomy, the theories of meteorological phenomena, logic, metaphysics, and the philosophical systems of Socrates, Plato, and Aristotle.

Four mathematical treatises are listed: one addressed to ʿAḍud al-Dawla; a correction of a commentary on his entire work by Abū Sahl al-Qūhī, made on the latter's request; one connected with Archimedes' *On Triangles*; and a correction, with additions, of Aqāṭun's *On Elements of Geometry* (Is this the Aya Sofya MS 4830, 5, *Kitāb al-Mafrūḍāt* by Aqāṭun?). The first two treatises cannot be Sinān's, since the addressees were active in the second half of the tenth century.

As to the third category, only the content of the *Kitāb al-Anwāʾ* (dedicated to al-Muʿtadid) is somewhat known through excerpts by al-Bīrūnī; it is probably identical with *Kitāb al-Istiwāʾ* listed in the *Fihrist* and Ibn al-Qifṭī. The anwaʾ are the meteorological qualities of the individual days. Scholars disagree on their cause. Some scholars deduce them from the rising and setting of the fixed stars, others by comparing the weather in the past. Sinān maintains the latter opinion and disapproves of Galen, who wants to decide between the two only after prolonged experimental examination. Sinān agrees on the difficulty of testing them in a short period. He advises to verify whether the Arabs and Persians agree on a *nawʾ* (singular form of *anwāʾ*); if they do, it is most probable. According to al-Bīrūnī, Sinān also relates an Egyptian theory and one by Hipparchus, on where to fix the beginnings of the seasons.

One of the other astronomical treatises, directed to the Sabian Abū Isḥāq Ibrāhīm ibn Hilāl (*ca.* 924–994), is on the assignment of the planets to the days of the week. The seven planets were important in Sabian religion; each one had its own temple. Ibn al-Qifṭī lists several works on Sabian rites and religion.

BIBLIOGRAPHY

I. ORIGINAL WORKS. Fuat Sezgin, *Geschichte des arabischen Schrifttums*, V (Leiden, 1974), 291; Ibn al-Qifṭī, *Ta'rīkh-al-ḥukamā'*, J. Lippert, ed. (Leipzig, 1903), 195 and the Ibn Abī Uṣaybiʿa, *Ṭabaqāt al-aṭibbā'*, I. A. Müller, ed. (Cairo, 1882), 224, list Sinān's work, of which nothing is extant. Al-Bīrūnī gives excerpts from the *Kitāb al-anwā'* in his *Chronology of Ancient Nations*, C. E. Sachau, ed. (London, 1879), 232, 233, 262, 322; see on this subject also O. Neugebauer, "An Arabic Version of Ptolemy's Parapegma From the 'Phaseis,'" in *Journal of the American Oriental Society*, **91**, no. 4 (1971), 506. A translation of the Aya Sofya MS 4830, 5, of which Sinān might be the author, is in preparation by the writer of this article.

II. SECONDARY LITERATURE. Biographical references can be found in Ibn al-Qifṭī, *Ta'rīkh al-ḥukamā'*, J. Lippert, ed. (Leipzig, 1903), 190–195; Ibn Abī Uṣaybiʿa, *Ṭabaqāt al-aṭibbā'*, I. A. Müller, ed. (Cairo, 1882), 220–224; and C. Brockelmann, *Geschichte der arabischen Literatur*, I (Leiden, 1943), 244–245 and supp. I (Leiden, 1937), 386. Yaʿqub al-Nadīm, *Kitāb al-Fihrist*, G. Flügel, ed. (Leipzig, 1871–1872), 272, 302, mentions Sinān, without giving much information. D. Chwolson, *Die Ssabier und der Ssabismus*, I (St. Petersburg, 1856; repr., Amsterdam, 1965), 569–577, elucidates Sinān's biography and Sabian religion. L. Leclerc, *Histoire de la médecine arabe* (Paris, 1876), 365–368, emphasizes Sinān the physician. Al-Masʿūdī's description and criticism is to be found in al-Masʿūdī, *Murūj al-dhahab wa maʿādin al-jawhar, Les prairies d'or*, I, Arabic text and French translation by C. Barbier de Meynard and Pavet de Courteille (Paris, 1861), 19–20.

YVONNE DOLD-SAMPLONIUS

SITTER, WILLEM DE (*b.* Sneek, Netherlands, 6 May 1872; *d.* Leiden, Netherlands, 20 November 1934), *astronomy.*

De Sitter was the son of L. U. De Sitter, a judge, who became president of the court at Arnhem, and T. W. S. Bertling. After preparatory education at Arnhem he entered the University of Groningen, where he studied mathematics and physics. Later he became interested in astronomy while participating (under Kapteyn's guidance) in the work of the astronomical laboratory. From 1897 to 1899 he worked under David Gill at the Royal Observatory in Cape Town, South Africa, and next served as an assistant to Kapteyn at Groningen until 1908, when he was appointed professor of astronomy at the University of Leiden. From 1919 until his death he also was director of the Leiden observatory.

De Sitter's main contributions to astronomy lie in the fields of celestial mechanics (particularly his research into the intricate problem of the dynamics of the satellites of Jupiter), the determination of the fundamental astronomical constants, and the theory of relativity applied to cosmology. He also contributed significantly, during his early years, to stellar photometry and to the measurement of stellar parallaxes in the context of Kapteyn's general program of researches on the structure of the Milky Way. Throughout his career De Sitter often acknowledged that his scientific approach was strongly influenced by Kapteyn and Gill.

Of the twelve satellites of Jupiter, four (Io, Europa, Ganymede, and Callisto) are of the fifth and sixth stellar magnitude, whereas the remaining ones are of thirteenth magnitude and fainter. These four, discovered by Galileo in 1610, were used by Römer in 1675 to determine the velocity of light. Their brightness enabled accurate determinations to be made of their projected positions on the sky with respect to Jupiter and to each other, first by heliometer observations and then photographically. De Sitter first participated at the Cape Observatory in the heliometer observations started by Gill and W. H. Finlay and then undertook their reduction and discussion, which led to his doctoral thesis at Groningen, "Discussion of Heliometer Observations of Jupiter's Satellites" (1901).

Satellites of a planet slightly disturb the motions of each other by their mutual attractions, and a study of these perturbations enables the mass of a satellite to be determined with its orbital elements. This problem was one of high mathematical complexity, requiring critical appreciation of both the value and limitations of the observations. De Sitter was particularly well prepared for the task. The satellites of Jupiter continued to interest him for the next thirty years. At his instigation a series of photographic observations were obtained at observatories in Cape Town, Greenwich, Johannesburg, Leiden, and Pulkovo. Their analysis, and a discussion of old observations of the eclipses of these satellites (by Jupiter) dating from 1668, led to an extensive series of publications by De Sitter in various journals and observatory publications, culminating in his "New Mathematical Theory of Jupiter's Satellites" (1925).

Shortly after Einstein's first publication on the restricted principle of relativity, De Sitter discussed its consequences for the small deviations in the motions of the moon and the planets; and after Einstein's paper on the generalized theory of relativity, De Sitter published (1916–1917) a series of three papers on "Einstein's Theory of Gravitation and Its Astronomical Consequences" in *Monthly Notices of the Royal Astronomical Society*. In the third of these papers he introduced what soon became known as the "De Sitter universe" as an alternative to the "Einstein universe." Because of his broad knowledge of dynamical astronomy, De Sitter was able to discuss fully the astronomical consequences of the theory of relativity, and he was among the first to appreciate its significance for astronomy. Apparently De Sitter's papers contributed uniquely to the introduction into the English-speaking countries of Einstein's theory during and shortly after World War I, and, for instance, led to Eddington's solar eclipse expeditions of 1919 to measure the gravitational deflection of light rays passing near the sun. De Sitter showed that in addition to the solution given by Einstein himself for the Einstein field equation (representing a static universe) a second model was possible with systematic motions—particularly the "expanding universe"—provided the density of matter could be considered negligible. Subsequent work by Georges Lemaître, Eddington, and De Sitter led to solutions satisfying more accurately both theory and observations, from which modern cosmology has emerged.

Closely related to De Sitter's work on the satellites of Jupiter were his investigations of the rotation of the earth and of the fundamental astronomical constants. Starting in 1915 with a discussion of the figure and composition of the earth, he tried to combine in a coherent system results from geodetic and gravity measurements with those from astronomical observations. In his paper "Secular Accelerations and Fluctuations of the Longitude of the Moon, the Sun, Mercury and Venus" (1927), De Sitter showed that these phenomena can be understood by assuming that varying tidal friction influences the rotation of the earth as well as the motion of the moon and by assuming internal changes in the moment of inertia of the earth. A comprehensive discussion of the fundamental, but observationally interrelated, astronomical constants—for example, the parallax of the sun, the constant of aberration, and the constant of nuta-

tion—appeared in "The Most Probable Values of Some Astronomical Constants; 1st Paper: Constants Connected With the Earth" (1927). An unfinished manuscript extending this work was edited and commented upon by D. Brouwer and was published posthumously in 1938 as "On the System of Astronomical Constants."

As director of the Leiden observatory, De Sitter successfully reorganized the institute, adding an astrophysical department and modern observing facilities. The latter included an arrangement with the Union Observatory in Johannesburg for the use of the telescopes there. This arrangement later led to the establishment of a Leiden station in Johannesburg that was equipped with a twin astrograph donated by the Rockefeller Foundation. These organizational efforts and nearly uninterrupted research were carried out by De Sitter despite repeated periods of illness. In 1933 he published a *Short History of the Observatory of the University at Leiden, 1633–1933* to commemorate its third centennial. In 1921 he created the *Bulletin of the Astronomical Institutes of the Netherlands*.

De Sitter was president of the International Astronomical Union from 1925 to 1928 and in that capacity did much to reestablish relations between scientists of formerly hostile countries. He received many honors, including the Gold Medal of the Royal Astronomical Society of London (1931), the Bruce Medal of the Astronomical Society of the Pacific, and honorary degrees from Cambridge, Cape Town, Oxford, and Wesleyan universities.

BIBLIOGRAPHY

I. ORIGINAL WORKS. A list of principal publications is given in C. H. Hins's obituary (see below). De Sitter's works include "Secular Accelerations and Fluctuations of the Longitude of the Moon, the Sun, Mercury and Venus," in *Bulletin of the Astronomical Institutes of the Netherlands*, **4**, no. 124 (1927), 21–38; "The Most Probable Values of Some Astronomical Constants; 1st Paper: Constants Connected With the Earth," *ibid.*, 57–61; "New Mathematical Theory of Jupiter's Satellites," in *Annalen van de Sterrewacht te Leiden*, **12**, pt. 3 (1925), 1–83, and in his George Darwin lecture "Jupiter's Galilean Satellites," which appeared in *Monthly Notices of the Royal Astronomical Society*, **91** (1931), 706–738; *Kosmos, a Course of Six Lectures on the Development of Our Insight Into the Structure of the Universe* (Cambridge, Mass., 1932); *The Astronomical Aspect of the Theory of Relativity* (Berkeley, Calif., 1933); and "On the System of Astronomical Constants," D. Brouwer, ed., in *Bulletin of the Astronomical Institutes of the Netherlands*, **8** (1938), 213–231.

II. SECONDARY LITERATURE. Extensive obituaries are given by C. H. Hins, in *Hemel en Dampkring*, **33** (1935), 3–18, with bibliography; H. Spencer Jones, in *Monthly Notices of the Royal Astronomical Society*, **95** (1935), 343–347; and J. H. Oort, in *Observatory*, **58** (1935), 22–27. De Sitter's wife, Eleonora De Sitter-Suermondt, wrote *Willem de Sitter, een Mensenleven* (Haarlem, 1948), a memoir.

A. BLAAUW

ŠKODA, JOSEF (*b.* Pilsen, Bohemia [now Czechoslovakia], 10 December 1805; *d.* Vienna, Austria, 13 June 1881), *internal medicine.*

Since Škoda was frequently ill during childhood, he entered high school in Pilsen only at the age of twelve. He graduated near the top of his class in 1825 and entered the Faculty of Medicine at Vienna. His dissertation, on the "De morborum divisione," may be considered the first evidence of his critical turn of mind.

After graduation on 18 July 1831, Škoda returned to Pilsen and established a medical practice. At this time the first pandemic of Asiatic cholera was approaching Czechoslovakia; and he became the district cholera specialist, first in the Chrudim region, then in Kouřim, and finally in Pilsen (1831–1832). He realized how little his formal training in medicine had prepared him for medical practice, and further that in the fight against cholera, more could be achieved through preventive hygienic measures than by means of many officially recommended medicines. Škoda therefore returned to Vienna for further study. Before obtaining an unsalaried post as a doctor in the internal department of the General Hospital (autumn of 1833), he worked in Karl Rokitansky's Pathology-Anatomy Institute and developed a close relationship with him. The collaboration did not cease when Škoda moved to clinical work; indeed, it was only when Škoda confirmed his clinical diagnoses on the dissection table and was able to perform experiments in the dissection room that his collaboration with Rokitansky achieved its real purpose.

Around 1836 Škoda began investigating the fundamentals of percussion and auscultation, two of the modern examination methods in clinical medicine. Both had been propagated in France (Corvisart, Laënnec, Gaspard Bayle) and in Great Britain (Charles Williams, Robert Graves, William Stokes) within clinics but had not penetrated into general medical practice because they were difficult to master. Škoda used his knowledge of physics, which he had learned at the high school in Pilsen and had studied further at the University of Vienna under Julius Baumgärtner.

Škoda based his research into percussion and auscultation on physical acoustics. He simplified and unified the terminology, defined concepts, and supplemented them with his own observations and experience. After his first publications in 1836 and 1837, he elaborated his doctrine and in 1839 published it formally as *Abhandlung über Perkussion und Auskultation*. Škoda improved each of the five new editions, responding to criticism and to new ideas. The book was also translated into English and French.

Škoda critically evaluated the doctrines of the French school of medicine, which distinguished percussion sounds according to the organ—the thigh, the liver, the intestine, the lung, or whatever—and substituted a physical classification of percussion sound in four categories: from full to empty, from clear to muffled, from tympanous to nontympanous, from high to deep. A part of modern diagnostics is Škoda's discovery of tympanous percussion in the presence of serous pleurisy.

In the theory of auscultation Škoda first distinguished reverberations (heart sounds) from cardiac murmurs. On the basis of comparative observations of healthy people and those known to have heart disease he learned to diagnose various heart illnesses from the presence of murmurs in individual valves. He also evaluated pulsations of the neck veins and accentuation of further reverberations in the pulmonary artery. Through his lucid account of functional changes and symptoms attendant upon various changes in valves of the heart or the pericardium, he established the principles of the clinical physiology of heart diseases.

By comparing manifestations of sickness in the body, and its physical and chemical signs, with pathological findings at autopsies, Škoda was able to make accurate diagnoses. His critical approach to therapy led him to replace obsolete, inefficient methods (venesection) with rational new methods (puncture of empyema of the pericardium and pleura); he also introduced effective medicines, such as chloral hydrate and salicylic acid. His principles formed the basis of diagnoses and a simpler and more humane therapy. He also evaluated the results of medical treatment by means of statistical methods. Because of this, he was unjustly regarded as a therapeutic nihilist.

Škoda was a born teacher. In high school he taught his classmates, and while studying medicine he earned money by giving private lessons. About 1836, while on a hospital staff, he began courses in percussion and auscultation for doctors, which were his sole source of income; he continued them until his appointment as professor of internal diseases at the Vienna Faculty of Medicine on 26 September 1846. These courses carried his doctrines to foreign universities.

Škoda almost entirely eliminated typhoid fever in Vienna by securing the construction of a water main from mountain springs at a time when the true cause of the disease was unknown. (He had already demonstrated preventive measures during the cholera epidemic in Czechoslovakia.) Thus he enlarged the sphere of his activities into public health and epidemiology.

BIBLIOGRAPHY

I. ORIGINAL WORKS. Škoda's most important works are "Ueber die Perkussion," in *Medizinischer Jahrbücher des K. K. osterreichischen Staates*, **20** (1836), 453–473, 514–566; "Ueber den Herzstoss und die durch Herzbewegungeñ verursachten Töne," *ibid.*, **22** (1837), 227–266; "Anwendung der Perkussion bei Untersuchung der Organe des Unterleibes," *ibid.*, **23** (1837), 236–262, 410–439; "Ueber Abdominaltyphus und desse Behandlung mit Alumen crudum," *ibid.*, **24** (1838), 5–46, written with A. Dobler; "Untersuchungsmethode zur Bestimmung des Zustandes des Herzens," *ibid.*, **27** (1839), 528–559; "Ueber Pericarditis in pathologischer und diagnostischer Beziehung," *ibid.*, **28** (1839), 55–74, 227–272, 397–433, written with J. Kolletschka; *Abhandlung über Perkussion und Auskultation* (Vienna, 1839; 6th ed., 1864); "Äuszug aus der Eintrittsrede," in *Zeitschrift der Gesellschaft der Aerzte in Wien*, **3** (1847), 258–265; "Fälle von Lungenbrand behandelt und geheilt durch Einathmen von Terpentinöldampfen," *ibid.*, **9** (1853), 445–447; and "Ueber die Funktion der Vorkammern des Herzens und über den Einfluss der Kontraktionskraft der Lunge und der Respirationsbewegungen auf die Blutzirkulation," *ibid.*, 193–213.

II. SECONDARY LITERATURE. See the following, listed chronologically: Constantin Wurzbach, *Biographisches Lexikon des Kaiserthums Oesterreich*, XXXV (Vienna, 1877), 66–72; Maximillian Sternberg, *Josef Skoda* (Vienna, 1924); Erna Lesky, *Die Wiener medizinische Schule im 19 Jahrhundert* (Graz–Cologne, 1965), 142–149; and Zdeněk Hornof, "Josef Škoda als Choleraarzt in Böhmen," in *Clio Medica*, **2** (1967), 55–62; and "The Study of Josef Škoda at the Medical Faculty in Vienna in the Period 1825–1831," in *Plzeňský lékařský sborník*, **31** (1968), 131–148, in Czech with English summary.

ZDENĚK HORNOF

SKOLEM, ALBERT THORALF (*b.* Sandsvaer, Norway, 23 May 1887; *d.* Oslo, Norway, 23 March 1963), *mathematics.*

Skolem was the son of Even Skolem, a teacher, and Helene Olette Vaal. He took his *examen artium* in Oslo in 1905 and then studied mathematics (his preferred subject), physics, chemistry, zoology, and botany. In 1913 he passed the state examination with distinction.

In 1909 Skolem became an assistant to Olaf Birkeland and in 1913–1914 traveled with him in the Sudan to observe the zodiacal light. Then, in 1915–1916, he studied in Göttingen. In the latter year he returned to Oslo, where he was made *Dozent* in 1918. He received his doctorate in 1926.

Skolem conducted independent research at the Christian Michelsens Institute in Bergen from 1930 to 1938, when he returned as full professor to the University of Oslo. He retired in 1950. On several occasions after 1938 he was a visiting professor in America. Skolem served as editor of various mathematical periodicals and was a member of several learned societies. In 1962 he received the Gunnerus Medal in Trondheim.

Skolem published more than 175 works. His main field of research was the foundations of mathematics; but he also worked on algebra, number theory, set theory, algebraic topology, group theory, lattice theory, and Dirichlet series. Half of his works are concerned with Diophantine equations, and in this connection he developed a p-adic method. In 1920 he stated the Skolem-Löwenheim theorem: If a finite or denumerably infinite sentential set is formulable in the ordinary predicate calculus, then it is satisfiable in a denumerable field of individuals.

Skolem freed set theory from Cantor's definitions. In 1923 he presented the Skolem-Noether theorem on the characterization of the automorphism of simple algebras. According to this theorem, it is impossible to establish within a predicate calculus a categorical axiom system for the natural numbers by means of a finite or denumerably infinite set of propositions (1929).

Most of Skolem's works appeared in Norway, although his monograph *Diophantische Gleichungen* (1938) was published in Berlin. With Viggo Brun, he brought out a new edition (1927) of Netto's textbook on combinatorial analysis, for which he wrote all the notes and an important addendum.

Skolem also investigated the formal feasibility of various theories and concerned himself with the discovery of simpler, more constructive demonstrations of known theorems. He was especially influenced by the mathematicians Sylow and Thue.

BIBLIOGRAPHY

For a bibliography of Skolem, see T. Nagell, "Thoralf Skolem in Memoriam," in *Acta mathematica*, **110** (1963), which lists 171 titles. On his life, see also Erik Fenstadt, "Thoralf Albert Skolem in Memoriam," in *Nordisk Mathematisk Tidsskrift*, **45** (1963), 145–153, with portrait; and Ingebrigt Johansson, "Minnetale over Professor Thoralf Skolem," in *Norske Videnskåps-Akademi i Oslo Arbok 1964* (1964), 37–41.

H. OETTEL

SKRAUP, ZDENKO HANS (*b.* Prague, Czechoslovakia, 3 March 1850; *d.* Vienna, Austria, 10 September 1910), *chemistry*.

Skraup came from a Czech family of musicians; his father composed church music and popular songs, and his uncle is remembered to this day for his composition of the Czech national anthem. Although musically gifted as well, Skraup turned to chemistry, which he studied at the German Technische Hochschule in Prague. He became a fervent German-Austrian patriot, abandoning the national allegiance of his Czech forebears. After completing his studies and briefly working in a porcelain factory near Karlovy Vary (Karlsbad) and in the mint in Vienna, Skraup became assistant under Friedrich Rochleder and then Adolf Lieben, who held professorships at the University of Vienna. In 1886 Skraup moved to Graz, where he was appointed professor of chemistry first at the Technische Hochschule and then a year later at the University of Graz. In 1906 he accepted the invitation to succeed Lieben at Vienna.

The development of science in Austria and Bohemia was closely linked during the years before 1918, as is clearly evident from an examination of the activities of the group of eminent chemists including Adolph Martin Pleischl, Jacob Redtenbacher, Rochleder, Heinrich Hlasiwetz, Lieben, and Skraup, in Prague and Vienna (and other Austrian university towns). It was because of the influence of Rochleder, one of the founders of modern phytochemistry, that Skraup became interested in quinine alkaloids, an area of study important to medical and structural chemistry. In turn it was Skraup who guided young co-workers, among them Fritz Pregl, in the field of physiological chemistry.

Skraup's most renowned scientific contribution was his synthesis of quinoline. The published account of his work resulted in the development of heterocyclid chemistry of the quinoline series. Although the relation of quinoline to various alkaloids was recognized at the time, there was no easy way to prepare the substance. From the investigations of Karl Graebe on alizarin blue and of Wilhelm Königs on quinoline, it became evident to Skraup that heating nitrobenzene and glycerol in the presence of sulfuric acid could produce the compound

$$C_6H_5NO_2 + C_3H_8O_3 = C_9H_7N + 3H_2O + O_2.$$

Skraup tried out the reaction and confirmed this conjecture but found that the yield of quinoline was rather low. He believed that this drawback was mainly the result of the evolution of oxygen, and in order to avoid it he proceeded to combine aniline with glycerol under the same conditions:

$$C_6H_7N + C_3H_8O_3 = C_9H_7N + 3H_2O + H_2,$$

only finding that the amount of quinoline was again small. After combining the two methods, thus effectively oxidizing oxygen to water, Skraup obtained a satisfactory yield of quinoline:

$$2C_6H_5NH_2 + C_6H_5NO_2 + C_3H_8O_3 = 3C_9H_7N + 11H_2O.$$

Skraup's synthesis became a general method for the preparation of quinolines, in which an aromatic primary amine is heated with glycerol and sulfuric acid in the presence of nitrobenzene or some other oxidizing agent.

BIBLIOGRAPHY

The fundamental paper "Eine Synthese des Chinolins" appeared in the *Sitzungsberichte der mathematischnaturwissenschaftlichen Classe der Kaiserlichen Akademie der Wissenschaften*, **81** (1880), pt. II,I–V. Skraup's works are listed in succeeding volumes of Poggendorff, III (1898), 1254; IV, pt. II (1904), 1402, and V, pt. II (1926), 1173. The obituary by H. Schrötter in *Berichte der Deutschen chemischen Gesellschaft*, **43** (1910), 3683–3702, is informative. See also the article by M. Kohn, "A Chapter of the History of Chemistry in Vienna," in *Journal of Chemical Education*, **20** (1943), 471–473.

M. TEICH

SKRYABIN, KONSTANTIN IVANOVICH (*b.* St. Petersburg, Russia [now Leningrad, U.S.S.R.], 7 December 1878; *d.* Moscow, U.S.S.R., 17 October 1972), *helminthology, public health*.

The son of a communications engineer, Skryabin attended the Dorpat (now Tartu) Veterinary Institute while auditing classes at the Faculty of Biology of Dorpat University. From 1905 he was a veterinarian in Kazakhstan. Sent abroad to continue his research on helminthology, he worked in the laboratories of Max Braun, Lue, Alcide Railliet, and Furman.

In 1917 Skryabin became professor in the first chair of parasitology in Russia, at Novocherkassk, and from 1920 he headed the chair of parasitology of the Moscow Veterinary Institute (now the K. I. Skryabin Moscow Veterinary Academy). Three important helminthological research institutes were organized in Moscow under his direction: the helminthological section of the State Institute of Experimental Veterinary Medicine, reorganized in 1931 as the All-Union Institute of Helminthology and named for Skryabin in 1939; the helminthological section of the Central Tropical Institute (now the I. E. Martsinovsky Institute of Medical Parasitology and Tropical Medicine), which Skryabin directed from 1921 to 1949; and a small parasitological laboratory of the Faculty of Physics and Mathematics of Moscow University that he headed for several years. In 1942 the Laboratory of Helminthology of the U.S.S.R. Academy of Sciences was established, and it was headed by Skryabin until his death.

Skryabin's more than 700 works are devoted to morphology, biology, phylogeny, taxonomy, the geography of helminths, epidemiology (epizootiology), helminthiasis, clinical pathogenesis, preventive and therapeutic measures, and the development of principles and radical methods for eliminating helminths in man and animals. The more than 340 expeditions organized under his general direction—and frequently with his participation—played a major role in disseminating knowledge of helminths of man and animals. Material gathered on these expeditions was amassed through the method of complete helminthological dissection, which Skryabin elaborated. In addition to his revisions of many taxonomic groups, Skryabin described more than 200 new species and 100 new genera of helminths.

Skryabin's methods of prophylaxis against helminthiases were widely used in the Soviet Union and in other countries, and his principles of the complete elimination of various species of pathogenic helminths led, in certain areas, to the total liquidation of a number of helminthiases, including ascariasis, ancylostomiasis, and taeniarhynchosis. Through his work such helminthiases of animals as echinococcosis, cysticercosis of cattle, dictyocaulosis of large horned animals, fascioliasis of cattle, and *Moniezia* infections have been virtually eliminated in many districts in the Soviet Union.

Skryabin's special interest in the trematode and the diseases it causes resulted in the important monograph *Trematody zhivotnykh i cheloveka* ("Trematodes of Animals and Man"), of which twenty-five of twenty-seven projected volumes were published. Each volume included a description of a given taxonomic group and presented a new system and tables for diagnostic determinations of trematodosis in animals. His concern to further the progress of helminthology led him to create and head a commission, established in 1922 at the zoological museum of the U.S.S.R. Academy of Sciences, to coordinate biological, medical, veterinary, and agronomical research. The commission was reorganized in 1940 as the All-Union Society of Helminthologists of the U.S.S.R. Academy of Sciences.

His emphasis on the maintenance of relations with foreign scientists led Skryabin to travel frequently after World War II and to present many reports to the International Epizootic Bureau in Paris (1930–1937) and to the Eleventh International Veterinary Congress in London in 1930. His proposal for the international coordination of research on measures against trichinosis, echinococcosis, and fascioliasis was accepted at a meeting of parasitologists in Hungary in 1959. The international journal *Helminthologia* was founded that year at his request, and he served as president of its editorial board.

Skryabin was an honorary or active member of many foreign academies and scientific societies. He was twice awarded the State Prize of the U.S.S.R. (1941, 1950), received the Lenin Prize in 1957, and in 1958 was awarded the honorary title Hero of Socialist Labor.

N. P. SHIKHOBALOVA

SLIPHER, EARL C. (*b.* Mulberry, Indiana, 25 March 1883; *d.* Flagstaff, Arizona, 7 August 1964), *planetary astronomy.*

After receiving his B.S. degree at Indiana University, Slipher joined the staff of the Lowell Observatory at Flagstaff, Arizona, in 1905; he worked there until the day before his death. Slipher was a pioneer in planetary photography, and the quality of his photographs has seldom been surpassed. He regularly observed the brighter planets during their favorable oppositions over a period of more than fifty-five years, and his photographic sequences that show long-term changes on Mars and Jupiter and the various aspects of Saturn are unique.

Slipher's special interest, like that of Percival Lowell, was the study of Mars. He obtained almost 200,000 images of the planet, nearly half of them through telescopes during expeditions to Chile in 1907 and to South Africa in 1939, 1954, and 1956. At these sites he obtained sharper photographs because Mars crossed the meridian close to the observer's zenith, where the turbulent effects of the atmosphere were minimal.

Slipher was one of the first to recognize that multiple-image printing could improve the quality of information extracted from a series of photographs taken within a sufficiently brief interval to avoid blurring because of planetary rotation. He would make a single print by accurately superimposing a number of unusually sharp individual images. He also was one of the first to standardize his plates for photometric measures; this practice, which he initiated in 1918, is now generally followed.

Slipher found that features on Mars's surface, which normally are invisible when photographed in the violet, sometimes stand out as clearly as they do in yellow light. He referred to this phenomenon as "blue clearing." His other discoveries about Mars include the "W" clouds, the appearance of a very large dust cloud in 1956, and many secular and transient changes.

The culmination of Slipher's work on Mars was *Mars, the Photographic Story* (1962), a compilation of 512 photographs that graphically illustrated many facts known about the planet. *The Brighter Planets* was published two years later. Only two weeks before his death he saw a preliminary copy of the deluxe edition, which contained photographic reproductions instead of halftones.

Photographs and scientific discoveries made from space vehicles have, since Slipher's death, drastically changed the thinking of many on the idea that canals, oases, and valleys of vegetation have been seen and sometimes photographed on Mars. Slipher shared this older point of view, which had been widely publicized many years before by Percival Lowell. These classical interpretations do not importantly detract, however, from the value of the unique and extensive series of photographs that is his legacy to planetary science. His photographic sequence of Venus, one image of which shows a complete halo around the planet,

has been frequently reprinted; and his photograph taken on 4 December 1911, showing Mars about to be occulted by the moon, is a striking illustration of the relative apparent size and surface brightness of these two objects.

Slipher's many honors included an honorary D.Sc. from the University of Arizona, Tucson, and an honorary LL.D. from Arizona State College (now Northern Arizona University in Flagstaff).

BIBLIOGRAPHY

Slipher published a number of short papers usually based on photographs. The best of these were reproduced in the two books mentioned above. An interim summary of his work is "The Planets From Observations at the Lowell Observatory," in *Proceedings of the American Philosophical Society*, **79** (1938), 441–470.

An obituary by A. P. Fitzgerald is in *Irish Astronomical Journal*, **6** (1964), 297.

JOHN S. HALL

SLIPHER, VESTO MELVIN (*b*. Mulberry, Indiana, 11 November 1875; *d*. Flagstaff, Arizona, 8 November 1969), *astronomy*.

Slipher, a son of David Clarke and Hannah App Slipher, perfected techniques in spectroscopy and achieved great advances in galactic astronomy. He earned his B.A. (1901), his M.A. (1903), and his Ph.D. (1909) degrees at Indiana University, and received honorary degrees from the University of Arizona (1923), Indiana University (1929), the University of Toronto (1935), and Northern Arizona University (1965).

Soon after receiving his B.A., Slipher was asked by Percival Lowell to join the staff of the Lowell Observatory at Flagstaff, Arizona. Lowell had selected the site because its high altitude was conducive to good visibility. He had obtained a twenty-four-inch Alvan Clark refractor and a John Brashear spectrograph. Slipher installed the spectrographic equipment in 1902 and began work under Lowell's enthusiastic, driving direction.

Slipher's main contributions were to spectroscopy, in which he both pioneered instrumental techniques and made major discoveries. His research can be divided into three areas: planetary atmospheres and rotations, diffuse nebulae and the interstellar medium, and rotations and radial velocities of spiral nebulae.

Shortly after arriving at Lowell Observatory, Slipher began studying the rotations of the planets.

Since Venus shows no surface markings, optical determinations of its rotation period proved difficult. Slipher oriented the slit of his spectrograph perpendicular to the terminator of Venus and measured the inclination of the spectral lines. In 1903, after taking twenty-six plates, he determined that the period was surprisingly long—certainly much greater than the twenty-four hours that it was commonly believed to be. And in the next issue of the *Lowell Observatory Bulletin*, Slipher announced his measurements for the rotation of Mars. These results, obtained in the same manner as for Venus, are close to presently accepted values. He continued spectrographic observations of planetary rotation periods, and by 1912 he had measured them for Jupiter, Saturn, and Uranus.

Slipher's spectrograms also clearly showed, for the first time, bands in the spectra of the Jovian planets. In 1934 Rupert Wildt identified some of the spectral features as being caused by ammonia and methane, and Slipher and Arthur Adel identified many of the remaining bands. For his work on planetary spectroscopy, Slipher was awarded the gold medal of the Royal Astronomical Society in 1933.

In the area of diffuse nebulae and interstellar material, in 1912 Slipher noticed that the diffuse nebulosity in the Pleiades shows a dark-line spectrum similar to that of the stars surrounding the Pleiades; he therefore concluded that the nebula shines by reflected light. This discovery, one of the first to give incontrovertible evidence of particulate matter in interstellar space, paved the way for the work of Hertzsprung and Hubble on emission and absorption nebulae.

In 1908, while studying the spectrum of a binary star, Slipher discovered a sharp calcium line that did not exhibit the oscillatory motion of its companions. Recalling that J. F. Hartmann had found a similar line in 1904, he studied more spectra and found several other such lines. To explain the phenomenon, he correctly reasoned that there must be gas between the stars and the earth.

Thus Slipher's research on interstellar space was extremely important, for he demonstrated the existence of both dust and gas. During the late 1920's and early 1930's, the studies of the interstellar medium by Eddington, Plaskett, Trumpler, and others were directly influenced by his work.

Probably the most significant aspect of Slipher's research, however, dealt with spiral nebulae. During the fall and winter of 1912, he obtained a series of spectrograms indicating that the Andromeda Nebula is approaching the sun at a mean velocity of 300 kilometers per second, the greatest radial velocity that had been observed.

Slipher continued such observations; and by 1914, when he released his results, he had obtained Doppler shifts for fourteen spirals. Despite the initially enthusiastic response of the astronomical community, many questioned Slipher's findings. For over a decade—until others began to believe and understand the implications of his findings—he was virtually the only observer investigating the velocities of extragalactic nebulae.

By 1925 Slipher had measured thirty-nine of the forty-four known radial velocities of spirals, the majority of which showed large velocities of recession, as much as 1,125 kilometers per second. Although the nature of spirals was not definitely known until Hubble proved in 1924 that they are external galaxies similar to the Milky Way, Slipher's early results suggested to a few perceptive astronomers that spirals are exterior to our system. Since the radial velocities of the spirals are so extraordinarily great, they probably could not be contained within the Milky Way. On 14 March 1914, just weeks after Slipher's original announcement, Hertzsprung wrote to him:

> My harty [sic] congratulations to your beautiful discovery of the great radial velocity of some spiral nebulae.
>
> It seems to me, that with this discovery the great question, if the spirals belong to the system of the Milky Way or not, is answered with great certainty to the end, that they do not. . . .

Moreover, H. D. Curtis, the chief proponent of the revival of the "island universe" theory (before Hubble's discovery of Cepheids in spirals), appears to have been influenced by Slipher's findings.

Hubble's velocity-distance relationship, first presented in 1929, was made possible by Slipher's velocity measurements. To construct the relationship, Hubble used these velocities and the distance measurements available for eighteen isolated nebulae and four objects in the Virgo cluster. The relationship also was used to compute distances for the nebulae on Slipher's list in which no stars could be detected.

The possibility of a relationship between distances and velocities of galaxies had been considered for years; C. Wirtz, K. Lundmark, and others had attempted unsuccessfully to construct such a relationship. Reliable distances were needed, but they were unobtainable without large instruments (like Mount Wilson's Hooker telescope) and ingenious techniques (like Shapley's period-luminosity law). Credit deservedly belongs to Hubble for his work on measuring these distances and in recognizing their relationship to the velocities; nevertheless, Slipher's findings were crucial to the discovery. His work prepared the way for investigations of the motions of galaxies and for cosmological theories based on an expanding universe.

Slipher also measured rotations of spirals, using the technique he had developed in his studies of planetary rotation. He found rotational velocities on the order of a few hundred kilometers per second and the direction of motion to be such as to "wind up" the spirals. These results contradicted the controversial proper motion measurements of Adriaan van Maanen. This discrepancy was not entirely resolved until the 1930's, when it was demonstrated conclusively that van Maanen's measurements had been subject to systematic errors.

Other areas of Slipher's research included the determination of radial velocities of globular clusters, spectroscopic studies of comets and aurorae, and observations of bright lines and bands in night sky spectra.

Slipher was also an unusually competent administrator; indeed, in recognition of that ability, as well as for his research, the Astronomical Society of the Pacific awarded him the Bruce Medal in 1935. He received his first experience in administration in 1915, when Lowell made him assistant director of the observatory. He became acting director upon Lowell's death in 1916 and continued in that capacity until he was made director in 1926, a post he held until 1952. During his directorship he supervised the trans-Neptunian planet search, which culminated in 1930 in the discovery of Pluto by Clyde Tombaugh, a staff member at Lowell.

Slipher's other administrative experience included serving as president of the Commission on Nebulae (no. 28) of the International Astronomical Union (1925 and 1928), vice-president of the American Astronomical Society (1931), and vice-president of the American Association for the Advancement of Science (1933).

In his work with the I.A.U. commission, Slipher made another important contribution to astronomy. As its president he became the center for all information concerning nebulae, serving as coordinator and organizer during the mid- and late 1920's, when the nature of galaxies and their relationship to the universe as a whole were being discovered by Hubble, Lundmark, and others.

Slipher was a member of the American Academy of Arts and Sciences, the American Philosoph-

ical Society, the Astronomical Society of France, Phi Beta Kappa, and Sigma Xi. He received the Lalande Prize of the Paris Academy of Sciences in 1919 and the Draper Gold Medal of the National Academy of Sciences in 1922.

BIBLIOGRAPHY

I. ORIGINAL WORKS. Slipher's most important publications include "A Spectrographic Investigation on the Rotational Velocity of Venus," in *Lowell Observatory Bulletin*, no. 3 (1903), 9–18; "On the Efficiency of the Spectrograph for Investigating Planetary Rotations and on the Accuracy of the Inclination Method of Measurement: Tests on the Rotation of the Planet Mars," *ibid.*, no. 4 (1903), 19–33; "The Lowell Spectrograph," in *Astrophysical Journal*, **28** (1908), 397–404; "Peculiar Star Spectra Suggestive of Selective Absorption of Light in Space," in *Lowell Observatory Bulletin*, no. 51 (1909), 1–2; "The Radial Velocity of the Andromeda Nebula," *ibid.*, no. 58 (1913), 56–57; "Spectrographic Observations of Nebulae," in *Popular Astronomy*, **23** (1915), 21–24; and "Spectroscopic Studies of the Planets," in *Monthly Notices of the Royal Astronomical Society*, **93** (1933), 657–668.

II. SECONDARY LITERATURE. Obituaries are in *Publications of the Astronomical Society of the Pacific*, **81** (1969), 922–923; and *New York Times* (10 Nov. 1969), 47. Two excellent biographies of Slipher have been prepared by John S. Hall: "V. M. Slipher's Trailblazing Career," in *Sky and Telescope*, **39** (1970), 84–86; and "Vesto Melvin Slipher," in *Yearbook. American Philosophical Society* (1970), 161–166. Comments on Slipher's research were published on the occasion of several of his awards: S. Einarsson, "The Award of the Bruce Gold Medal to Dr. Vesto Melvin Slipher," in *Publications of the Astronomical Society of the Pacific*, **47** (1935), 5–10; and "Gold Medal Award, President's Speech," in *Monthly Notices of the Royal Astronomical Society*, **93** (1933), 476–477. For additional, related information, see Otto Struve and Velta Zebergs, *Astronomy of the 20th Century* (New York, 1962); A. Pannekoek, *A History of Astronomy* (London, 1961); and J. D. Fernie, "The Historical Quest for the Nature of the Spiral Nebulae," in *Publications of the Astronomical Society of the Pacific*, **82** (1970), 1189–1230. Slipher's private papers and correspondence (including the Hertzsprung letter cited above) are cataloged and are on microfilm at Lowell Observatory, Flagstaff, Arizona.

RICHARD HART
RICHARD BERENDZEN

SLOANE, SIR HANS (*b.* Killyleagh, County Down, Northern Ireland, 16 April 1660; *d.* Chelsea, London, England, 11 January 1753), *medicine, natural history.*

Sloane was the youngest of seven sons born to Alexander Sloane and Sarah Hickes, daughter of the chaplain to Archbishop Laud. The Sloane family emigrated to Ireland from Scotland during the reign of James I (VI), and the name was originally written Slowman or Slowan. Hans Sloane's first name was a compliment to the Hamiltons, earls of Clanbrassill, a family in which it was common.

After the Restoration, Sloane's father, receiver-general of taxes from County Down for the earl of Clanbrassill, became one of the commissioners of array. In a census of the previous year he is shown as having twenty-two people on his land, so he must have been a man of standing and property. He died in 1666.

In his youth Sloane turned his interest toward natural history: "I had from my youth been very much pleas'd with the Study of Plants, and other Parts of Nature, and had seen most of those Kinds of Curiosities, which are to be found either in the Fields, or in the Gardens or Cabinets of the Curious in these Parts." Killyleagh was a center of learning and had a school of philosophy, founded by the Hamilton family; and County Down, with Strangford Lough, presented many opportunities for the study of natural history. Sloane visited Copeland Island and saw "how the sea-mews laid their eggs on the ground, so thick that he had difficulty in passing along without treading on them"; and he was much intrigued with the seaweed on the shore, which the Irish were accustomed to chew in order to cure scurvy. These experiences, involving natural history and medicine, were the basis of his career.

At the age of sixteen, Sloane was taken with spasms of spitting blood and probably suffered from an attack of tuberculosis; but "by temperance, and abstaining from wine, and other fermented liquors, and the prudent management of himself in all other respects, he avoided the consequences of a disorder which must otherwise have proved fatal to him." Three years later, in 1679, he was well enough to go to London to study medicine. He lodged in Water Lane, next to the laboratory of the Worshipful Society of Apothecaries, where he studied chemistry under Nicolaus Staphorst and botany at the Apothecaries' Physick Garden at Chelsea. He attended lectures on anatomy and medicine, but most important at this period of his life were his friendships with two of the greatest English men of science of the day, John Ray and Robert Boyle.

In 1683 Sloane started on his grand tour of Europe. On his way to Paris he met Nicolas Lemery;

in Paris he frequented the Charité hospital and heard botany lectures by Tournefort and anatomy lectures by Duverney. It was impossible for a Protestant to take a degree in France, but at that time the town of Orange in Provence was still under the House of Orange. Its university gave examinations and conferred degrees but provided no instruction in medicine. Sloane graduated Doctor of Physick there on 28 July 1683, then went to Montpellier to complete his studies, working under the physicians Charles Barbeyrac, Pierre Chirac, and Pierre Magnol.

The persecution of Protestants in France was starting in 1684, when Sloane returned to London with the intention of practicing medicine. For the contributions that he had already made to botany, he was elected Fellow of the Royal Society on 21 January 1685. Robert Boyle recommended Sloane as a skillful anatomist and good botanist to the surgeon Thomas Sydenham. The latter exclaimed "That is all moghty [sic] fine, but it won't do; . . . no, young man, all this is Stuff: you must go to the bedside, it is there alone that you can learn disease." The secret of Sydenham's fame lay in his systematic approach to the symptoms observed in his patients, and this method fitted perfectly into Sloane's systematic study of botany; diagnosis of disease became a part of natural history. Sloane was admitted a fellow of the Royal College of Physicians of London on 12 April 1687.

Christopher Monck, second duke of Albemarle, was at that time appointed governor of Jamaica; and Sloane accompanied him as physician, sailing on 12 September 1687. The expedition was of great value to Sloane, not only giving him firsthand experience of the flora and fauna of a relatively little-known island but also enabling him to search for new drugs; it was not long since the bark of *Cinchona vera* had been brought to Europe and used as a febrifuge. The description of the voyage and the observations on the inhabitants, diseases, plants, animals (some of which he brought back alive), and meteorology of the West Indies make Sloane's book on the natural history of Jamaica indispensable even today. On his return to England in 1689, Sloane found James II fled and William III on the throne.

On 11 May 1695, Sloane married Elizabeth, daughter of John Langley and widow of Fulk Rose, formerly of Jamaica; they lived in a house that is now 4 Bloomsbury Place. Sloane was now launched not only in the highest and scientifically the most distinguished society — his friends included Ray, Boyle, John Locke, Samuel Pepys, Edmond Halley, and Sir Isaac Newton—but also in his profession of medicine, which became very lucrative. One guinea an hour was the value of his time, although he treated the poor for nothing. His fees, his investments in quinine bark and in sugar, and his wife's fortune—derived from her first husband's estates in Jamaica—made Sloane a rich man.

Sloane had four children, of whom two daughters survived infancy. The elder, Sarah, married George Stanley of Paultons, from whom the family of Sloane Stanley is descended; the younger, Elizabeth, married Colonel Charles Cadogan of Oakley, afterwards second Lord Cadogan, and ancestor of the Earls Cadogan.

Appointed physician to Queen Anne in 1712, Sloane played a small but vital (although unrecognized) part in the history of England. On 27 July 1714, a political battle was fought in the Privy Council between Henry St. John, Viscount Bolingbroke, and Robert Harley, earl of Oxford. The latter lost and was dismissed; and nothing seemed to stand in the way of the succession of the Jacobites upon the queen's death, which appeared imminent because she had fainted at the Privy Council meeting. Rumors circulated constantly that the queen was dead (on which government stocks rose 3 percent) or that she was still alive. Sloane urged that she be bled, which was done; and she recovered sufficiently to preside over another meeting of the Privy Council, at which she had just strength enough to hand the treasurer's staff of office to Charles Talbot, duke of Shrewsbury. The Protestant succession of George, elector of Hanover, in accordance with the Act of Settlement, was then assured. It was her certified death, after so much uncertainty, that gave rise to the expression "as dead as Queen Anne."

On 3 April 1716, George I conferred a baronetcy on Sloane, and on 30 September 1719 he was elected president of the Royal College of Physicians of London. In that post he inspired the petition to Parliament drawing attention to the evils of alcoholism that resulted in the Gin Acts, at a time when dissolute crowds thronged the streets of London shouting "No gin, no King." Another event of his presidency was the publication of the fourth *London Pharmacopoeia,* which reflected Sloane's efforts to rationalize medical prescriptions, get rid of the disgusting ingredients that had hitherto disgraced them, discard the fetishes of superstition, and include a catalog of medicinal herbs with clear definitions of their properties and the methods by which they could be identified. When

he bought his property in Chelsea, including the Physick Garden, he conveyed it to the Society of Apothecaries for £5 a year, on condition that every year for forty years, fifty specimens of plants of different species, grown in the garden, be supplied to the Royal Society.

It may be claimed that Sloane introduced the scientific method into medicine. In a volume of the *Philosophical Transactions of the Royal Society* edited by him, he was at pains to emphasize the difference between "Matters of Fact, Experiment, or Observation, and what is called Hypothesis," in which latter category he included the old notion of "humours." The humoral theory could not explain the fact, made evident by experiment, that quinine reduced fever. "A poor Indian who first taught the cure of an Ague, of which the Lady of the Count of Cinchon was sick, overthrew with one simple medicine, without any Preparation, all the *Hypotheses* and Theories of Agues, which were supported by some Scores not to say Hundreds of Volumes."

A great believer in the importance of diet, Sloane, who became familiar with chocolate in Jamaica, found it to be more digestible when mixed with milk. The resulting product was known as "Sir Hans Sloane's Milk Chocolate," a recipe used by Messrs. Cadbury until 1885. He was consulted by the British government on the preservation of the health of ships' crews in the Royal Navy and on the precautions to be taken against the threat of the plague of Marseilles of 1720. He also played an important part in establishing the practice of inoculation for smallpox, brought to England by Lady Mary Wortley Montagu in 1718.

In 1739 Sloane was associated with Thomas Coram in the foundation of the Foundling Hospital, and in the same year his godson, Sir Richard Manningham, founded the first Lying-in Ward in the parochial hospital of St James's, Westminster. Sloane's secretary, Cromwell Mortimer, started a health insurance scheme, offering to treat patients "for a certain salary, by the year." Since he followed the principle that "Sobriety, temperance and moderation, are the best and most powerful preservatives that Nature has granted to Mankind," it is not surprising that at a time when most remedies were useless if not injurious, Sloane's reputation as a physician was so deservedly high.

Sloane was elected one of the two secretaries of the Royal Society in 1693. In 1727 the president, Sir Isaac Newton, died; Sloane was elected to succeed him, a post he occupied until 1741.

In 1712 Sloane felt it desirable to acquire a country house and bought the manor house at

Chelsea from Lord Cheyne; but he did not move into it until 1742. Throughout his life he amassed collections. The first were botanical specimens collected in France and the West Indies; and they formed the material for his catalog of plants. His herbarium fills 337 folio volumes in the British Museum (Natural History). Sloane soon bought and added other collections of plants, animals, insects, fossils, minerals, precious stones, and ethnographical specimens; he also branched out into Egyptian, Assyrian, Etruscan, Roman, Oriental, American Indian, and Peruvian antiquities. To these were added works of art by Albrecht Dürer, Hans Holbein, and Wenzel Hollar, and a rich collection of coins and medals. Sloane's library contained over 50,000 books and 3,500 bound volumes of manuscripts.

Such treasures demanded careful provisions in a will. Sloane might have left them to his family, but there would then have been no guarantee of their preservation intact. Eventually, in a will made in 1739, to which codicils were added in 1749 and 1751, "desiring very much that these things, tending many ways to the Glory of God, the confutation of Atheism and its consequences, the use and improvement of Physic, and other Arts and Sciences, and Benefit of Mankind, may remain together, and not be separated, and that chiefly in and about the City of London . . . where they may by the great confluence of people be of most use," he offered them to the British nation, provided the sum of £20,000 was paid to his daughters.

After Sloane's death in 1753, the trustees whom he had appointed met; the matter was brought before Parliament, which on 7 June 1753 received the royal assent for the act enabling purchase of the museum or collection of Sir Hans Sloane. To this were added the Harleian collection of manuscripts and the Cotton Library, and the British Museum was founded. It was installed in Montague House, Great Russell Street, and was opened to the public in 1759. The natural history departments, which had been the original kernel of Sloane's collections, were moved to the British Museum (Natural History) in South Kensington, which was opened to the public in 1881.

The names of Sloane and of his sons-in-law are dotted all over his former property in Chelsea: Sloane Street, Hans Crescent, Paultons Square, Cadogan Gardens, Oakley Street; and the Physick Garden, where Sloane worked and its curator Philip Miller established the part played by insects in pollination, still continues to serve botany.

Sloane was a fellow of the Royal Society for all but twenty-one days in sixty-eight years, the longest fellowship. When he was young, Thomas Hobbes, born at the time of the Armada, was alive; when he was old, he knew Thomas Martyn, a botanist who died after the birth of Queen Victoria.

BIBLIOGRAPHY

I. ORIGINAL WORKS. Sloane's writings include *Catalogus plantarum quae in Jamaica sponte proveniunt* (London, 1696); and *Voyage to Madeira, Barbadoes, and Jamaica; With the Natural History of Jamaica*, 2 vols. (London, 1707–1725).

II. SECONDARY LITERATURE. See Gavin de Beer, *Sir Hans Sloane and the British Museum* (London, 1953), which contains bibliographical references to all the chief MSS and printed sources of information on the life and work of Sloane; William Eric St. John Brooks, *Sir Hans Sloane. The Great Collector and His Circle* (London, 1954); and *The Sloane Herbarium. An Annotated List of the Horti Sicci Composing It; With Biographical Accounts of the Principal Contributors,* based on records compiled by James Britten and with an intro. by Spencer Savage, revised and edited by J. E. Dandy (London, 1954).

GAVIN DE BEER

SLUSE, RENÉ-FRANÇOIS DE (*b.* Visé, Principality of Liège [now Belgium], 2 July 1622; *d.* Liège, 19 March 1685), *mathematics.*

Although the family name is variously spelled in the archives and documents, its correct form is de Sluse in French and Slusius in Latin. Sluse was a nephew of Gualthère Waltheri, secretary of papal briefs to Innocent X. Destined by his well-to-do family for an ecclesiastical career, Sluse went to Louvain in the fall of 1638 and remained through the summer of 1642. In 1643 he obtained a doctorate in law from the University of Rome. He lived in Rome for ten years more, becoming proficient in Greek, Hebrew, Arabic, Syriac, and astronomy. But his natural gifts led him to mathematics and a thorough study of the teachings of Cavalieri and Torricelli on the geometry of indivisibles.

On 8 October 1650, Innocent X appointed Sluse canon of the cathedral of Liège. His understanding of law and his great knowledge brought him many high positions. But his success in the administration of a small state severed him from the life he had known in Rome and thrust him into an intellectual vacuum; and his administrative duties left him little leisure for scientific work, particularly after 1659, when he became a member of the Privy Council of Prince-Bishop Maximilian Henry, who was also elector of Cologne. The only way that Sluse could survive as a scientist was, according to the practice of the time, to conduct an extensive correspondence with the leaders of mathematical studies: Blaise Pascal, Huygens, Oldenburg, Wallis, and M. A. Ricci.

In June 1658, Pascal, under the name of A. Dettonville, challenged mathematicians to solve a number of problems related to the cycloid. The evaluation of the area between a cycloid and a line parallel to its base, and the calculation of the volume generated by a rotation of this area around the base or around a line parallel to the base, were among the problems proposed, and already solved, by Pascal. In his work on the cycloid (1658) Pascal paid homage to the elegance of the solutions Sluse had sent to him, and the two remained regular correspondents. In his correspondence with Pascal, Sluse discussed the areas limited by curves corresponding to the equation

$$Y^m = Kx^p (a-x)^n$$

and the cubature of various solids; and as an example he found the volume generated by the rotation of a cissoid around its asymptote. These questions were discussed in his *Miscellanea,* published in 1668 as a section of the second edition of his *Mesolabum.*

One of the questions widely studied by the geometers of Greek antiquity was the duplication of the cube, that is, the construction of a cube of a volume double that of a given cube. This led to the solution of a cubic. More generally, Sluse discussed the solutions of third- and fourth-degree equations. Descartes had shown that their solution corresponds to the intersection of a parabola and a circle, and Sluse demonstrated that any conic section can be substituted for the parabola. He developed his method in *Mesolabum* (1659), particularly in the second edition.

In his *Géométrie,* Descartes had demonstrated the application of geometrical loci to the solution of equations of higher degrees. Sluse was among those who perfected the methods of Descartes and Fermat to draw tangents and determine the maxima and minima. By completing Descartes's construction for the solution of third- and fourth-degree equations and using a circle and any conic section, Sluse generalized the method for the solution of equations through the construction of roots by means of curves. In 1673 he published a digest of the results of his work in the *Philosophical*

Transactions and became a member of the Royal Society in the following year.

The discovery of a general method for the construction of tangents to algebraic curves places Sluse among the pioneers in the discovery of the calculus. At Huygens' suggestion, Leibniz learned analytical geometry through the writings of Sluse and Descartes. Sluse deserved the judgment formulated by Huygens in a letter to Oldenburg: "(Slusius) est geometrarum, quos novi, omnium doctissimus candidissimusque."

Sluse was also a historian and wrote a book on the death of St. Lambert, the bishop of Tongres, who was killed on the spot to which St. Hubert, his successor, transferred the seat of his bishopric (which became Liège). Another historical study concerns the famous bishop of Maastricht, St. Servatius. Among his unpublished manuscripts is a history of Cologne.

The breadth of Sluse's interests is attested by the variety of subjects covered in the hundreds of pages of his unpublished manuscripts now preserved at the Bibliothèque Nationale, Paris. Although concerned mainly with mathematics, they also treat astronomy, physics, and natural history.

BIBLIOGRAPHY

Sluse's writings include *Mesolabum seu duae mediae proportionales inter extremas datas per circulum et ellipsim vel hyperbolam infinitis modis exhibitae* (Liège, 1659; 2nd ed., enl., 1668); "An Extract of a Letter From the Excellent Renatus Franciscus Slusius, Canon of Liège and Counsellor of His Electoral Highness of Collen [Cologne], Written to the Publisher in Order to Be Communicated to the R. Society, Concerning His Short and Easier Method of Drawing Tangents to All Geometrical Curves Without Any Labour of Calculation," in *Philosophical Transactions of the Royal Society,* **7** (1672), 5143–5147; "Illustrissimi Slusii modus, quo demonstrat methodum suam ducendi tangentes ad quaslibet curvas . . .," *ibid.,* **8** (1673), 6059; *De tempore et causa martyrii B. Lamberti, Tungrensis episcopi, diatriba chronologica et historica* (Liège, 1679); and *De S. Servatio episcopo Tungrensi, ejus nominis unico: Adversus nuperum de sancto Arvatio vel duobus Servatiis commentum* (Liège, 1684).

M. C. Le Paige published more than 100 letters from Sluse to Pascal, Huygens, Oldenburg, Lambeck, Sorbière, and Pacichelli in "Correspondance de René-François de Sluse publiée pour la première fois," in *Bullettino di bibliografia e di storia delle scienze matematiche e fisiche,* **17** (1884), 494–726, and his introduction is the best available biography of Sluse. Secondary literature also includes C. Le Paige, "Notes pour servir à l'histoire des mathématiques dans l'ancien Pays de

Liège," in *Bulletin de l'Institut archéologique liègeois*, **21** (1890), 457–565; P. Gilbert, *René de Sluse* (Brussels, 1886); F. Van Hulst, *René Sluse* (Liège, 1842); and L. Godeaux, *Esquisse d'une histoire des sciences mathématiques en Belgique* (Brussels, 1943).

MARCEL FLORKIN

SLUTSKY, EVGENY EVGENIEVICH (*b.* Novoe, Yaroslavskaya guberniya, Russia, 19 April 1880; *d.* Moscow, U.S.S.R., 10 March 1948), *mathematics, statistics.*

Slutsky's father was an instructor at a teachers' seminary and, from 1886, director of a school in Zhitomir. After graduating from a classical Gymnasium, Slutsky enrolled in the mathematics department of Kiev University in 1899. He participated in student disturbances there and consequently was inducted into the army in 1901; readmitted to the university shortly thereafter, he was again expelled in 1902. He then studied for three years at the Munich Polytechnikum.

In 1905 Slutsky received permission to continue his studies in Kiev. His interest in political economy led him to enroll at the Faculty of Law, from which he graduated in 1911 with a gold medal. From 1913 he taught at the Kiev Institute of Commerce, and from 1926 he worked in Moscow in the government statistical offices. He began teaching at Moscow University in 1934 and, in 1938, at the Institute of Mathematics of the Academy of Sciences of the U.S.S.R.

Slutsky belonged to the generation of Russian statisticians that developed under the influence of Pearson and his school. His interest in both practical statistical problems (economics and later the natural sciences) and their theoretical background led Slutsky into purely mathematical studies, which although sometimes not fully extended in their generality, nevertheless contained fundamental new ideas.

A pioneer of the theory of random functions, Slutsky generalized or introduced stochastic concepts of limits, derivative, and integral (1925–1928), and obtained the conditions of measurability of random functions (1937). In 1927 he demonstrated that the subjection of a sequence of independent random variables to a succession of moving averages generated a series that is almost periodic; this finding stimulated the creation of the theory of stationary stochastic processes and constituted an important contribution to business cycle theory. An important group of Slutsky's papers is devoted to the classical theory of correlations of

related series for a limited number of trials. In 1915 he contributed to economics what is now known as the fundamental equation of value theory, which partitions the effect of a change in the price of a commodity into the income and substitution effects.

Slutsky's applied work included studies of the pricing of grain, the mean density of population, the periodicity of solar activity (using information on aurorae boreales from 500 B.C.), and statistical studies of chromosomes.

BIBLIOGRAPHY

Slutsky's basic writings were collected in *Izbrannye trudy. Teoria veroyatnostey i matematicheskaya statistika* ("Selected Works. Probability Theory and Mathematical Statistics"; Moscow, 1960). Separately published works include *Teoria korrelyatsii i elementy uchenia o krivykh raspredelenia* ("Correlation Theory and Elements of the Theory of Distribution Curves"; Kiev, 1912); *Ser Viliam Petty. Kratky ocherk ego ekonomicheskikh vozzreny* ("Sir William Petty. A Short Essay on His Economic Views"; Kiev, 1914); *Tablitsy dlya vychislenia nepolnoy Γ-funktsii i funktsii veroyatnosti ψ^2* ("Tables for the Calculation of an Incomplete Γ-Function and the Probability Function ψ^2"; Moscow–Leningrad, 1950); and "Sulla teoria del bilancio del consumatore," in *Giornale degli economisti*, **51** (1915), 1–26, trans. by American Economic Association, as "On the Theory of the Budget of the Consumer," in *Readings in Price Theory* (Chicago, 1952), 27–56.

On Slutsky and his work, see A. N. Kolmogorov, in *Uspekhi matematicheskikh nauk,* **3**, no. 4 (July–Aug. 1948), 143–151, with bibliography of 47 works by Slutsky (1912–1946); and N. V. Smirnov's obituary in *Izvestiya Akademii nauk SSSR*, Seria mat., **12** (1948), 417–420.

A. A. YOUSCHKEVITCH

SLYKE, DONALD DEXTER VAN. See **Van Slyke, Donald Dexter.**

SMEATON, JOHN (*b.* Austhorpe, England, 8 June 1724; *d.* Austhorpe, 28 October 1792), *civil engineering, applied mechanics.*

One of the foremost British engineers of the eighteenth century, Smeaton also gained a reputation as a man of science and distinguished himself through experimental research on applied hydraulics. He was descended from a family of Scots, one of whom, Thomas Smeton, turned to Protestantism late in the sixteenth century and held important positions in the church and in the University of

Glasgow. By the time of Smeaton's birth, the family resided near Leeds, where his father, William, practiced law. Smeaton was encouraged to follow a legal career, and after a sound elementary education he served in his father's office and was later sent to London for further employment and training in the courts. An early inclination toward the mechanical arts soon prevailed, however; and, with his father's consent, he became a maker of scientific instruments, a pursuit that allowed ample scope for both his scientific interests and his mechanical ingenuity.

Early in the 1750's Smeaton began the experiments that constituted his chief contribution to science; and during this period he also busied himself with several technical innovations, including a novel pyrometer with which he studied the expansive characteristics of various materials. The pace of industrial and commercial progress was quickening in Britain, however, and the attention of technical men was being directed increasingly toward large-scale engineering works. From 1756 to 1759 Smeaton was occupied with his best-known achievement, the rebuilding of the Eddystone lighthouse. By the end of the decade it had become evident that structural engineering and river and harbor works were more profitable than making scientific instruments. Accordingly, Smeaton established himself as a consultant in these fields; indeed, it was he who adopted the term "civil engineer" to distinguish civilian consultants and designers from the increasing number of military engineers who were being graduated from the Royal Military Academy at Woolwich. During the last thirty-five years of his life he was responsible for many engineering projects, including bridges, steam engine facilities, power stations run by wind or water, mill structures and machinery, and river and harbor improvements.

Smeaton became a fellow of the Royal Society, a member of the Royal Society Club, and an occasional guest at meetings of the Lunar Society. He also was a charter member of the first professional engineering society, the Society of Civil Engineers (not to be confused with the later Institution of Civil Engineers), founded in 1771; after his death it became known as the Smeatonian Society. Its founding reflected the growing sense of professionalization among British civilian engineers during the eighteenth century.

In 1759 Smeaton's engineering and scientific careers were crowned with outstanding success. In that year he completed the Eddystone lighthouse, which confirmed his reputation as an engineer, and

published a paper on waterwheels and windmills, for which he received the Copley Medal of the Royal Society.

In his research on waterwheels Smeaton reopened the question of the relative efficiency of undershot wheels (which operate through the impulse of the water against the blades) and overshot wheels (where the water flows from above and moves the wheel by the force of its weight). Through experiments on a model wheel he showed that, contrary to common opinion, overshot wheels are twice as efficient as undershot. Beyond this empirical generalization Smeaton displayed his scientific bent by speculating on the cause of the greater loss of energy ("mechanic power," as he termed it) in the undershot wheel and by concluding that it was consumed in turbulence—"nonelastic bodies [water], when acting by their impulse or collision, communicate only a part of their original power; the other part being spent in changing their figure in consequence of the stroke."

Following this initial success in research on applied mechanics, Smeaton's interests drifted toward natural philosophy and he devoted two further experimental investigations to the *vis viva* dispute and the laws of collision. He maintained that these seemingly abstract studies were of importance in practice, inasmuch as the conclusions of natural philosophers might, if incorrect, mislead practical men to adopt unsound procedures. The results he obtained, however, were more consequential in theory than in practice, for they confirmed not only the belief that mechanical effort could indeed be "lost" but also that mv^2 (*vis viva*) was a measure of "mechanic power." Smeaton recognized that his conclusions were in opposition to those favored by the disciples of Newton, and he diplomatically specified that both mv and mv^2 were useful values when properly interpreted.

Smeaton's career provides an early example of the interaction of engineering and applied science. His technical interests influenced the direction of his scientific research; and he used the results of his research in his own waterwheel designs, consistently favoring breast wheels and overshot wheels and almost never using the undershot system. There is reason to believe that Smeaton's work led other designers to foresake the long-preferred undershot wheel. Moreover, the continued economic importance of waterwheels contributed a sense of urgency to the recurrent controversy over the measure of "force"; and in these discussions Smeaton's research and his support of the *vis viva* school of thought played a prominent role.

Smeaton also performed extensive tests on an experimental Newcomen engine, optimizing its design and significantly increasing its efficiency. These studies, however, never rose above the level of systematic empiricism and, moreover, were soon overshadowed by James Watt's invention of the separate condenser. A few minor contributions to observational astronomy rounded out Smeaton's scientific work.

BIBLIOGRAPHY

I. ORIGINAL WORKS. Many of Smeaton's papers were collected and published posthumously: *Reports of the Late John Smeaton*, 4 vols. (London, 1812–1814). Vol. IV, *The Miscellaneous Papers of John Smeaton* (1814), contains the papers he contributed to the *Philosophical Transactions of the Royal Society*, of which the most important are his Copley Medal paper, "An Experimental Enquiry Concerning the Natural Powers of Water and Wind to Turn Mills and Other Machines Depending on a Circular Motion," **51** (1759–1760), 100–174; "An Experimental Examination of the Quantity and Proportion of Mechanic Power Necessary to Be Employed in Giving Different Degrees of Velocity to Heavy Bodies From a State of Rest," **66** (1776), 450–475; and "New Fundamental Experiments Upon the Collision of Bodies," **72** (1782), 337–354. These three papers were reprinted together as *Experimental Enquiry Concerning the Natural Powers of Wind and Water* (London, 1794) and are also conveniently collected in Thomas Tredgold, ed., *Tracts on Hydraulics* (London, 1826). P. S. Girard translated them into French as *Recherches expérimentales sur l'eau et le vent* (Paris, 1810). For the results of his experiments on the steam engine, see John Farey, *A Treatise on the Steam Engine* (London, 1827), 158 ff.

John Smeaton's Diary of His Journey to the Low Countries 1755, Newcomen Society for the Study of the History of Engineering and Technology, Extra Publication no. 4 (London, 1938); and "Description of the Statical Hydraulic Engine, Invented and Made by the Late Mr. William Westgarth, of Colecleugh in the County of Northumberland," in *Transactions of the Royal Society of Arts*, **5** (1787), 185–210, throw some additional light on the engineering sources of Smeaton's scientific interests.

II. SECONDARY LITERATURE. The fullest biography of Smeaton is still Samuel Smiles, "Life of John Smeaton," in *Lives of the Engineers*, 3 vols. (London, 1861–1862), II, 1–89. John Holmes, who knew Smeaton well, published *A Short Narrative of the Genius, Life and Works of the Late Mr. J. Smeaton, Civil Engineer* (London, 1793). For a recent biographical article, see Gerald Bowman, "John Smeaton—Consulting Engineer," in *Engineering Heritage*, 2 vols. (New York, 1966), II, 8–12. None of these treats Smeaton's scientific work adequately.

D. S. L. Cardwell has interpreted Smeaton's research in the context of the developing relationship between power technology and thermodynamics; see "Some Factors in the Early Development of the Concepts of Power, Work and Energy," in *British Journal for the History of Science*, **3** (1966–1967), 209–224; and *From Watt to Clausius* (Ithaca, N.Y., 1971), see index. The influence of Smeaton's research on the controversy over the measurement of "force" may be seen in Peter Ewart, "On the Measure of Moving Force," in *Memoirs of the Literary and Philosophical Society of Manchester*, 2nd ser., **2** (1813), 105–258. On his water power engineering, see Paul N. Wilson, "The Waterwheels of John Smeaton," in *Transactions. Newcomen Society for the Study of the History of Engineering and Technology*, **30** (1955–1957), 25–48.

The little that is known of the Society of Civil Engineers in the eighteenth century is presented fully in T. E. Allibone, "The Club of the Royal College of Physicians, the Smeatonian Society of Civil Engineers and Their Relationship to the Royal Society Club," in *Notes and Records of the Royal Society of London*, **22** (1967), 186–192; S. B. Donkin, "The Society of Civil Engineers (Smeatonians)," in *Transactions. Newcomen Society for the Study of the History of Engineering and Technology*, **17** (1936–1937), 51–71; and Esther Clark Wright, "The Early Smeatonians," *ibid.*, **18** (1937–1938), 101–110.

HAROLD DORN

SMEKAL, ADOLF GUSTAV STEPHAN (*b*. Vienna, Austria, 12 September 1895; *d*. Graz, Austria, 7 March 1959), *physics*.

Adolf Smekal was the elder child and only son of Gustav Smekal, an artillery officer. Because of repeated shifts of residence, he gained admission to university study by the "back door" of a Realschule diploma (1912) and a year at the Technische Hochschule in Vienna (1912–1913). He then attended the University of Graz for four years, receiving his doctorate (14 June 1917) under Michael Radakovič, to whose family the Smekals were closely related. Extreme nearsightedness had rendered Smekal unfit for military service. Yet neither that handicap nor his short stature prevented the young man from becoming a skilled and tireless alpinist, who however in middle age succumbed to corpulence and heart disease.

From the autumn of 1917 to the spring of 1919 Smekal continued his study of mathematics and physics at the University of Berlin. In June 1919 he took up an assistantship in the physical institutes of Heinrich Mache and Ludwig Flamm at the Technische Hochschule in Vienna, where he immediately joined the circle of young theorists around Hans Thirring at the university. In the autumn of 1920 Smekal accepted an assistantship to Gustav Jaeger at the university, where he qualified simultaneously as *Privatdozent* in both theoretical and experimental physics. The following year this *venia legendi* was extended to the Technische Hochschule, where in 1923 Smekal was appointed *Honorardozent* in the newly established Abteilung für Technische Physik.

In the autumn of 1928 Smekal was appointed professor of theoretical physics at the University of Halle. He was especially pleased by the experimental facilities of the institute attached to that post, in which he continued until deported by the Americans to West Germany in June 1945. After some years of professional and financial uncertainty, Smekal obtained a chair and institute of his own in 1949 at the University of Graz, as professor of experimental physics. Smekal married twice, in 1924 and 1942, and had one child of the latter marriage.

Like virtually all Austrian theoretical physicists of his generation, Smekal was thoroughly trained in statistical mechanics; and his first publications were on the foundations of quantum statistics. (His doctoral dissertation aimed to show "that such radical assumptions as those of the quantum theory are by no means necessary in order to avoid the equipartition of energy.") Smekal also assimilated, and soon exemplified, the Austrian critical-encyclopedic style. In the 1920's he was the principal abstractor of publications on quantum theory for the *Physikalische Berichte* and wrote several extraordinarily learned handbook articles and a veritable fountain of research papers that, although distinguished for their recherché bibliographic citations, generally were conceptually derivative and often lacking in physical as well as personal "tact."

The year and a half in Berlin (1917–1919) was extremely important for Smekal's scientific development and subsequent research. There he took up the quantum, the Bohr theory, and the problem of X-ray spectra. After delivering a crushing blow to the faltering Sommerfeld-Debye theory, which deduced X-ray spectra from hypothetical intra-atomic mechanisms, Smekal, in competition with Dirk Coster and Gregor Wentzel, induced from the experimental data the number, arrangement, and allowed transitions between the atomic energy levels resulting in X-ray spectral lines.

Although these papers of 1920–1921 are probably his most original achievement as a theorist, Smekal's name is better known through the effect predicted by him in September 1923 and discovered experimentally by C. V. Raman in 1928. This is the alteration of the frequency of light upon being scattered by an atomic-molecular system—a decrease, or increase, by an amount equal to the frequency of the light that would be absorbed or emitted in transitions between the stationary states of that system. It was the radical light quantum viewpoint that enabled Smekal to foresee this effect; but its necessity was immediately accepted also by theorists who rejected that viewpoint, particularly those around Niels Bohr. Smekal implied that his considerations were independent of A. H. Compton's; he did not, however, preclude influence from William Duane, with whose particulate theory of X-ray diffraction Smekal's considerations appear to bear considerable affinity.

Smekal's interest in the great discrepancy between the mechanical strength of ideal and of real crystals, apparently aroused by contact with the Austro-Hungarians staffing the Kaiser-Wilhelm-Institut für Faserstoffchemie in Berlin, was first expressed in a paper extending A. A. Griffith's theory of fracture (1922). There Smekal first advanced his conception of irregularities in the structure of real crystals arising as a "frozen Brownian molecular motion."[1] After 1925 he advocated it as a kind of "universal remedy"[2] in solid-state physics. In 1925–1927 Smekal turned from fundamental questions in quantum theory and atomic physics to the technical physics of structure-dependent properties of solids. By 1933 he had become, and at his death he remained, a world authority on brittleness and the technology of pulverization.

NOTES

1. A. Smekal, "Kristalleigenschaften und Kristallisationsbedingungen," in *Forschungen und Fortschritte*, 5 (1929), 385–387.
2. A. Joffé, letter to the editor, *Naturwissenschaften*, 16 (1928), 744–745. Cf. Joffé, *Begegnungen mit Physikern* (Leipzig, 1967), 83–84.

BIBLIOGRAPHY

I. Original Works. The only bibliography of Smekal's publications is in Poggendorff, V, 1176; VI, 2473–2474; and VII, 427–429. Smekal's most important monograph is "Allgemeine Grundlagen der Quantenstatistik und Quantentheorie," in *Encyklopädie der mathematischen Wissenschaften*, V, pt. 3 (Leipzig, 1926), 816–1214. His papers on the X-ray term scheme, "Zur Feinstruktur der Röntgenspektren," in *Zeitschrift für Physik*, 4 (1920), 26–45, and 5 (1921), 91–106, are based upon "le système de Smekal" (adopted by the marginal French but not by better-informed theorists), according to which every degree of freedom of every electron in an atom is entitled to its own quantum number. Smekal's prediction of the Raman effect is "Zur Quantentheorie der Dispersion," in *Naturwissenschaften*, **11** (1923), 873–875; and his initial publication on fracture theory is "Technische Festigkeit und molekulare Festigkeit," *ibid.*, **10** (1922), 799–804.

II. SECONDARY LITERATURE. The informative obituaries are by Ludwig Flamm: *Almanach. Österreichische Akademie der Wissenschaften*, **109** (1959), 421–427; *Acta physica austriaca*, **13** (1960), 140–143; Technische Hochschule, Vienna, *150 Jahre Technische Hochschule in Wien, 1815–1965* (Vienna, 1965), I, 359–361, and II, 166. See also H. Rumpf, "Zur Entwicklungsgeschichte der Physik der Brucherscheinungen; A. Smekal zum Gedächtnis," in *Chemie-Ingenieur-Technik*, **31** (1959), 697–705; and A. Faessler, "Adolf Smekal," in *Glastechnische Berichte*, **32** (1959), 180. For Smekal's criticism of the Debye-Vegard theory of X-ray spectra, see John L. Heilbron, "The Kossel-Sommerfeld Theory and the Ring Atom," in *Isis*, **58** (1967), 451–485.

PAUL FORMAN

SMITH, EDGAR FAHS (*b.* York, Pennsylvania, 23 May 1854; *d.* Philadelphia, Pennsylvania, 3 May 1928), *chemistry.*

After graduating from Gettysburg College, Smith studied under Friedrich Wöhler at the University of Göttingen, where he received the Ph.D. in 1876. He taught chemistry at the University of Pennsylvania (1876–1881), Muhlenberg College (1881–1883), Wittenberg College (1883–1888), and the University of Pennsylvania again (1888–1920). At Pennsylvania he also held the important executive offices of vice-provost (1898–1911) and provost (1911–1920) of the university. Smith was three times president of the American Chemical Society and served as scientific adviser to the federal government.

Smith's most important research was in electrochemistry. In 1901 he developed the rotating anode, which permitted the application of higher cathode current densities and greatly decreased the time required for electroanalysis. In turn this led to broader application of electroanalysis in research and industry.

In studies on atomic weights Smith and his students endeavored to determine more precisely the atomic weights of eighteen elements, using electrolytic and chemical methods. Other research was on complex inorganic acids. He and his collaborators prepared many salts of complex acids (for example, ammonium vanadico-phospho-tungstate) and elucidated their relationships.

A prominent historian of chemistry in the United States, Smith wrote mainly from a biographical viewpoint. He collected and endowed a notable library of books, manuscripts, prints, and other memorabilia, now known as the Edgar Fahs Smith Memorial Collection in the History of Chemistry, at the University of Pennsylvania.

BIBLIOGRAPHY

A complete list of Smith's books, translations, and brochures, and of doctoral theses by his students, is in the biography by Meeker (below) and in *Memorial Service for Edgar Fahs Smith . . . December 4, 1928* (n.p., 1928[?]). His books include *Electrochemical Analysis* (Philadelphia, 1890; 6th ed., 1918); *Elements of Electrochemistry* (Philadelphia, 1913); and *Chemistry in America: Chapters From the History of the Science in the United States* (New York, 1914).

George H. Meeker, "Biographical Memoir of Edgar Fahs Smith, 1854–1928," in *Biographical Memoirs. National Academy of Sciences*, **17** (1936), 103–149, has a portrait and references to seven other biographical accounts of Smith.

WYNDHAM D. MILES

SMITH, EDWARD (*b.* Heanor, Derbyshire, England, 1818[?]; *d.* London, England, 16 November 1874), *physiology, nutrition, public health.*

Strikingly little is known about Edward Smith, a competent and highly influential nineteenth-century British physiologist and public health worker. His birth was not recorded in the parish register at Heanor, and the exact date is unknown. His father was Joseph Smith, apparently a successful businessman in Derbyshire; the surname of his mother, whose Christian name was Martha, is not recorded. Smith obtained his initial medical degree (M.B.) at the Royal Birmingham Medical School in 1841, and the M.D. degree followed in 1843. The medical school shortly afterward became Queen's College, and its certificates were recognized by the University of London. In 1848 Smith received the London B.A. and LL.B. from Queen's College. He is known to have practiced medicine in Birmingham from 1841 to about 1848.

Smith's religion seems to have been Wesleyan, a matter of some significance at the time and for much of the nineteenth century. Candidates for admission to Oxford or Cambridge (although not to the University of London system) were required to subscribe to the tenets of the Church of England and could not be Dissenters. To adhere to doctrines not sanctioned by the official church was a handicap in other ways as well; it made easy access to Britain's highest intellectual and political strata considerably more than a matter of course. Smith's religious convictions, at least as a young man, would seem to have been intense, judging from a prize essay written while he was in medical school. The essay was basically a theological tract that employed the aortic system to support various fundamentalist religious theses. Smith married Matilda Frearson Clarke (an American citizen, according to the census of 1861) at Nottingham on 4 May 1843. Two daughters were born between 1847 and 1850. Smith made a rapid survey of living conditions in Texas in 1849, possibly requested by relatives of his wife, and published the results within a few weeks of his return to Britain.

Sometime in 1851 Smith established practice in London, having become fellow of the Royal College of Surgeons by examination in that year. Late in 1851 he was appointed lecturer in botany at the Charing Cross Medical School, and within a short time he became demonstrator in anatomy there. He also held an appointment as physician-accoucheur at the West London Lying-in Institution. All went well for a short time; but within a year he was involved in acrimonious dispute with the medical committee of Charing Cross Hospital. The incident was the first in a series of controversies with authorities and colleagues that characterized much of his professional career. It resulted in his dismissal from Charing Cross Medical School in 1853.

For several years Smith occupied himself with practice and writing on medical topics for the layman as well as for the professional. On 29 March 1855 he was appointed assistant physician at the Brompton Hospital for Consumption, a post he held for ten years. No later than 1862 Smith became known to public health officials in Britain, and in 1866 he was appointed inspector and medical officer to the Poor Law Board. For a time he was very influential in medical aspects of Britain's welfare system. But he ultimately came into conflict with Sir John Simon, head of the Local Government Board's medical department, and the remaining years of his life were spent somewhat in limbo.

Smith was elected fellow of the Royal Society in 1860. He was also a fellow of the Royal College of Physicians (1863), president of the Physiological Subsection of the British Association, and member of the National Association for the Promotion of Social Science.

Smith's claim to scientific distinction rests on his pioneering work in respiratory physiology, metabolism, and nutrition. It is also clear that scientific curiosity was not his primary motivating force; he was at heart a social reformer and was unique among scientific investigators of his time in that he mobilized his research to support reform movements.

While on the staff at Brompton Hospital, Smith devised ingenious and original methods for measurement of respiratory function and related metabolic phenomena. His interest in measuring the effects of physical exertion on respiration seems to have directed his attention to the punitive treadmill, a device then used in Britain's prisons. Prisoners sentenced to hard labor were required to spend many hours each day on the treadmill; and Smith, perceiving an opportunity, asked prison authorities for permission to use prisoners as experimental subjects. This experience seems to have led him to consider the diet and living conditions of prisoners. His published work dealt with both subjects and ultimately brought him election to the Royal Society.

The work also allied Smith with groups and individuals seeking to reform Britain's prisons and may have been a factor in arousing a more general interest in the plight of Britain's lower classes. In 1863 he testified before a parliamentary commission investigating prison conditions and presented physiological evidence to show that the treadmill, as it was used, was a cruel and inhumane device.

The work on respiration at rest and during exercise led naturally to a consideration of metabolism of foodstuffs and energy sources under the same conditions. Once again Smith's emphasis was on measurement, this time of foods ingested and metabolic products excreted. He made short work, in the process, of Liebig's dogmatic assertion that the energy for muscle exercise comes entirely from protein.

The cotton famine of 1862 (in Lancashire) brought Smith formally into what is now known as public health. In December of that year Sir John Simon, then medical officer of health, asked him to visit six stricken towns in order to determine the general state of nutrition of the unemployed and "the least outlay of money which [will] procure food enough for life." A second and larger survey was carried out in the summer of 1863. The results, although in many respects imperfect, provided very valuable quantitative information concerning diet and economic conditions. Probably more important is that Smith's surveys pointed the way to, and the necessity for, health research on entire populations. They were, in fact, the forerunners of larger and more elaborate field studies done before and after both world wars.

Smith subsequently did additional studies of nutrition and working conditions of specific types of workers, reporting the results in the language of the reformer. Tailors in the London area, he found, had mortality rates that were higher, at all ages, than the rates for farmers. In London's printshops the condition of young boys, working twelve hours a day, six days a week, demanded "instant amelioration." As a Poor Law official, Smith had a great deal of influence on workhouse dietary practice, the provision of medical care, and the design of the workhouses themselves.

The last ten years of Smith's life undoubtedly were anticlimactic. He was involved in almost continuous controversy and, in some instances, did not acquit himself well. One such case was the bitter quarrel with Sir John Simon. An obituary in the *British Medical Journal* said: ". . . medically, Dr. Edward Smith met with little success in practice nor did he contrive to conciliate the affections of his colleagues." This was probably a fair assessment. But neither the *Journal* nor other publications at the time credited him with his great innovations in the quantitative study of respiration and metabolism, and in the nutrition of populations. Smith was the first to devise quantitative methods suitable for studies on the human being during exercise. His monumental data on inspiratory volume, respiratory and pulse rates, and carbon dioxide production at rest and at various levels of exercise served as the basis for much of the work on muscular exercise in the latter part of the nineteenth century. But most British physiologists, in sharp contrast to those on the Continent, seem to have known little of Smith and his work, although both groups built on his concepts and results. His work on nutrition, although innovative and fundamental, fared little better until quite recently.

Smith's reputation may well have suffered during his life and after his death owing to the numerous quarrels in which he was involved. But he was also very much ahead of his time: he was not only scientifically gifted and innovative; he also believed in seeing that his results were applied *pro bono publico*. Partly for this reason and partly because of belated recognition of the excellence of his scientific work, Smith's life and work have recently been rescued from obscurity.

BIBLIOGRAPHY

I. ORIGINAL WORKS. Smith's writings include "The Spirometer: Its Construction, Indications and Fallacies," in *Medical Circular*, 9 (1856), 294, 305, 313–314; 10 (1857), 5, 40, 64–65; "The Influence of the Labour of the Treadwheel Over Respiration and Pulsation, and Its Relation to the Waste of the System, and the Dietary of the Prisoners," in *Medical Times and Gazette*, n.s. 14 (1857), 601–603; "Inquiries Into the Quantity of Air Inspired Throughout the Day and Night and Under the Influence of Exercise, Food, Medicine, Temperature, etc.," in *Proceedings of the Royal Society*, 8 (1857), 451–454; "Inquiries Into the Phenomena of Respiration," *ibid.*, 9 (1858), 611–614; "Experimental Inquiries Into the Chemical and Other Phenomena of Respiration, and Their Modifications by Various Physical Agencies," in *Philosophical Transactions of the Royal Society*, 149 (1859), 681–714; "On the Immediate Source of the Carbon Exhaled by the Lungs," in *Philosophical Magazine*, 4th ser., 18 (1859), 429–436; "Report on the Action of Prison Diet and Discipline on the Bodily Functions of Prisoners. Part I," in *Report of the British Association for the Advancement of Science*, 31 (1861), 44–81, written with W. R. Milner; "Report on the Food of the Poorer Labouring Classes in England," in *Sixth Report of the Medical Officer Privy Council* (London, 1864), 216–329 (app. 5); "Report on the Sanitary Circumstances of Printers in London," *ibid.*, 383–415; "Report on the Sanitary Circumstances of Tailors in London," *ibid.*, 416–430; "Dietaries for the Inmates of Work Houses," in House of Commons, *Parliamentary Papers* (Reports From Commissioners for 1866), XXXV, 321–629; "Metropolitan Workhouse Infirmaries and Sick Wards," *ibid.* (Accounts and Papers) (1866), LXI, 171–388; and "Report on the Sufficiency of the Existing Arrangements for the Care and Treatment of the Sick in Forty-Eight Provincial Workhouses Situated in Various Parts of England and Wales," *ibid.* (1867–1868), LX, 325–483.

II. SECONDARY LITERATURE. See T. C. Barker, D. J. Oddy, and John Yudkin, *The Dietary Surveys of Dr. Edward Smith, 1862–3*, Occasional paper no. 1, Dept. of Nutrition, Queen Elizabeth College (London, 1970); and Carleton B. Chapman, "Edward Smith (?1818–1874). Physiologist, Human Ecologist, Reformer," in *Journal of the History of Medicine and Allied Sciences*, 22 (Jan. 1967), 1–26.

CARLETON B. CHAPMAN

SMITH, ERWIN FRINK (*b.* Gilbert's Mills, New York, 21 January 1854; *d.* Washington, D.C., 6 April 1927), *plant pathology, bacteriology*.

Smith was the son of Rancellor King Smith and Louisa Frink Smith, who left New York to farm near Hubbardston, Michigan. Smith graduated from high school in Ionia, Michigan, then attended the University of Michigan, from which he received the B.Sc. in 1886 and the doctorate in 1889. From his youth, Smith was profoundly interested in botany; he served in the United States Department of Agriculture from 1899 and later was director of the plant pathology laboratory of the Bureau of Plant Industry. His researches made him the most distinguished of the early American plant pathologists. His work fully established that bacteria cause plant disease—a view that was vigorously contested by his European counterparts.

One of Smith's earliest investigations concerned yellows, a perplexing disease of the peach of which the etiology is not yet fully understood. Smith established the infectious nature of the disease and attempted its control by eradication. Although he was personally disappointed by his inability to discover the causative agent, he nevertheless disproved a number of earlier misconceptions about the malady.

Smith was more successful in demonstrating that bacterial pathogens invade plants through wounds and natural openings. He also showed insect transmission in certain diseases and provided a workable classification of genera of bacterial plant pathogens. He demonstrated that certain soil fungi (Fusaria) cause widespread and devastating vascular wilts. Smith's later years were taken up with the study of crown gall disease, which he compared to animal cancer. His studies on tumor formation in plants in its relation to cancer in man and animals won him the certificate of honor of the American Medical Association in 1913. His researches are summarized in a number of papers and, especially, in his three-volume *Bacteria in Relation to Plant Diseases*.

Smith was a member of a number of scholarly societies and received many honors. He had broad interests in biology and was a lover and patron of music, art, and literature (a collection of his sonnets was brought out privately in 1915). He was twice married, first to Charlotte May Buffett, who died in 1906, then to Ruth Warren, who survived him. His home life was simple to the point of austerity, and, although not an active churchman, he was deeply religious.

BIBLIOGRAPHY

I. ORIGINAL WORKS. Smith's most important works are *Bacteria in Relation to Plant Diseases*, 3 vols. (Washington, D.C., 1905–1914); and *An Introduction to Bacterial Diseases of Plants* (Philadelphia–London, 1920). He published widely in journals, and bibliographies of his works may be found in notices by L. R. Jones and R. H. True, cited below.

II. SECONDARY LITERATURE. On Smith and his work, see Florence Hedges, "Dr. Erwin F. Smith, Scientist, is Dead," in *United States Department of Agriculture Official Record*, 6 (1927), 1, 5, 8; L. R. Jones, "Biographical Memoir of Erwin Frink Smith," in *Biographical Memoirs. National Academy of Sciences*, 21 (1939), 1–71, with portrait, synopsis of researches, and bibliography; L. R. Jones, W. H. Welch, and F. V. Rand, "To Erwin Frink Smith," in *Phytopathology*, 18 (1928), 1–5, testimonials to Smith given at a dinner in Philadelphia in December 1926; F. V. Rand, "Erwin F. Smith," in *Mycologia*, 20 (1928), 181–186, with portrait; A. D. Rodgers, III, "Erwin Frink Smith, a Story of North American Plant Pathology," *Memoirs of the American Philosophical Society*, 31 (1952); and R. H. True, "Erwin F. Smith (1854–1927)," in *Phytopathology*, 17 (1927), 675–688, with portrait and bibliography.

ROBERT AYCOCK

SMITH, GRAFTON ELLIOT. See **Elliot Smith, Grafton.**

SMITH, HENRY JOHN STANLEY (*b.* Dublin, Ireland, 2 November 1826; *d.* Oxford, England, 9 February 1883), *mathematics.*

Smith's contributions to mathematics, although relatively few, were not slight in importance. His best work was done in number theory, but he also wrote on elliptic functions and geometry.

Smith was the youngest of four children of John Smith, an Irish barrister, and the former Mary Murphy. His mother's family were country gentry from near Bantry Bay. After his father's death in 1828, Smith's mother took the family to the Isle of Man in 1829 and to the Isle of Wight in 1831. Smith was taught entirely by his mother until 1838, when he was given instruction by a Mr. R. Wheler. In 1840 the family moved to Oxford, and Henry Highton was engaged as tutor. When Highton went to teach at Rugby School in 1841, Smith accompanied him as a pupil but was soon removed, following his brother's death, and spent some time in France and Switzerland. He won a scholarship to Balliol College, Oxford, in 1844. Benjamin Jowett later described his natural abilities as greater than those of anyone he had ever known at Oxford, and T. H. Huxley made a similar comment. While on a visit to Rome, Smith was obliged by illness to interrupt his studies at Oxford between 1845 and

1847; but during his convalescence in Paris he attended the lectures of Arago and Milne-Edwards. After returning to Oxford he won the Dean Ireland scholarship in classical learning in 1848, and took a first class in the schools of both mathematics and *literae humaniores* in 1849. He was elected a fellow of Balliol and in 1851 was senior mathematical scholar in the university. Smith was long undecided between a career in classics and one in mathematics. He was elected Savilian professor of geometry in 1860, fellow of the Royal Society in 1861, and president of the Mathematical Section of the British Association and fellow of Corpus Christi College, Oxford, in 1873; from 1874 he was keeper of the University Museum, and in 1877 he became first chairman of the Meteorological Council in London. Smith devoted considerable effort to educational administration and reform, and was appointed an Oxford University commissioner in 1877. Smith was an unsuccessful Liberal candidate for Parliament. He died unmarried. The many eulogies to his powers and character are tempered with hints that he was lacking in ambition; and this was, no doubt, the secret of his undoubted popularity.

After graduating, Smith published a few short papers on number theory and geometry but soon turned to an intensive study of Gauss, Dirichlet, Eisenstein, and other writers on number theory. His reports to the British Association between 1859 and 1865, which contain much original work, were the outcome of this study. He presented important papers to the Royal Society on systems of linear indeterminate equations and congruences, and established a general theory of n-ary quadratics permitting the derivation of theorems on expressing any positive integer as the sum of five and seven squares. (Eisenstein had proved the theorem for three squares, and Jacobi for two, four, and six.) Smith's general theory with n indeterminates has been described by J. W. L. Glaisher as possibly the greatest advance made between the publication of Gauss's *Disquisitiones arithmeticae* (1801) and Smith's time.

Smith gave only an abstract of his results in 1864, and in 1868 he provided the general formulas without proofs. In 1882 the French Academy, not knowing of his work, set the problem of five squares for its Grand Prix des Sciences Mathématiques; the last of his published memoirs contains his entry, with proofs of the general theorems so far as they were needed. The prize of 3,000 francs was awarded to Smith posthumously in March 1883. An apology was subsequently made for awarding the prize jointly to a competitor (Minkowski), who seems to have followed Smith's published work.

Smith extended many of Gauss's theorems for real quadratic forms to complex quadratic forms. During the last twenty years of his life he wrote chiefly on elliptic functions; in a field marred by an excessive number of alternative methods and notations, his work is especially elegant. At the time of his death Smith had almost completed his "Memoir on the Theta and Omega Functions," which was written to accompany Glaisher's tables of theta functions. The memoir is a very substantial work running to 208 large quarto pages in the second volume of Smith's collected papers. As an appendix to the same volume there is an introduction written by Smith for the collected papers of W. K. Clifford, and papers written for the South Kensington Science Museum on arithmetical and geometrical instruments and models. Smith was one of the last mathematicians to write an original and significant memoir in Latin, "De fractionibus quibusdam continuis" (1879).

BIBLIOGRAPHY

Smith's mathematical works are assembled in *The Collected Mathematical Papers of Henry John Stephen Smith*, J. W. L. Glaisher, ed., 2 vols. (Oxford, 1894). This collection includes a comprehensive mathematical introduction by the editor (I, lxi–xcv), a portrait, and biographical sketches containing references to nonmathematical writings and to forty mathematical notebooks, more than a dozen of which include unpublished works.

Apart from the introduction to the collected papers, the best biographical notice is the obituary by J. W. L. Glaisher, in *Monthly Notices of the Royal Astronomical Society*, **44** (1884), 138–149. For references to similar notices by P. Mansion, L. Cremona, W. Spottiswoode, and others, see G. Eneström, "Biobibliographie der 1881–1900 verstorbenen Mathematiker," in *Bibliotheca mathematica*, 3rd ser., **2** (1901), 345. For a different collection of references, see A. M. Clerke's article on Smith in *Dictionary of National Biography*. See also A. Macfarlane, *Lectures on Ten British Mathematicians of the Nineteenth Century* (New York, 1916), 92–106.

The introductory material for *Collected Mathematical Papers*, by C. H. Pearson, Benjamin Jowett, Lord Bowen, J. L. Strachan-Davidson, Alfred Robinson, and J. W. L. Glaisher, is reprinted without change in *Biographical Sketches and Recollections (With Early Letters) of Henry John Stephen Smith* (Oxford, 1894). It includes new material in the form of fifteen early letters, one to Smith's mother and the rest to his sister Eleanor.

J. D. NORTH

SMITH, HOMER WILLIAM (*b.* Denver, Colorado, 2 January 1895; *d.* New York, N.Y., 25 March 1962), *physiology, evolutionary biology.*

The youngest of six children, Smith grew up in Cripple Creek, Colorado, where his family encouraged his early fascination with science. He attended high school in Cripple Creek and in Denver, and received his A.B. degree from the University of Denver in 1917. After graduation Smith served in the armed forces, first in a battalion of engineers and ultimately as chemist in the Chemical Warfare Station of the American University in Washington, D.C. Shortly after the end of World War I, he began studies with the physiologist William H. Howell at Johns Hopkins University, where he earned a D.Sc. in 1921. He was a research fellow in the Harvard laboratory of Walter B. Cannon from 1923 to 1925 and subsequently became chairman of the department of physiology at the University of Virginia School of Medicine. In 1928 Smith was appointed professor of physiology and director of the physiological laboratories at the New York University College of Medicine. He retired in 1961 and died of a cerebral hemorrhage a few months later.

Smith's research interests gradually shifted from physical chemistry through chemotherapy to the chemical physiology of the body fluids. By the late 1920's he had focused his energies on problems of renal physiology. Toward the end of his life, however, he wrote: "Superficially, it might be said that the function of the kidneys is to make urine; but in a more considered view one can say that the kidneys make the stuff of philosophy itself." He took the position, originating with Claude Bernard, that an animal's true ambience is its own *milieu intérieur,* not the external environment. The kidneys are the chief regulators of this milieu, upon the constancy of which all other physiological processes depend. Smith thus used questions arising from functional considerations of the kidney to probe phenomena as diverse as paleontology, the biology of consciousness, and the history of religion.

In 1928 Smith began his investigations on the African lungfish *(Protopterus aethiopicus),* summarizing its biological significance in his philosophical novel *Kamongo: The Lungfish and the Padre* (1932, revised 1949) and in his book on the evolutionary history of kidney function, *From Fish to Philosopher* (1953). He also published a number of papers on the comparative renal physiology of the seal, the goosefish *(Lophius piscatorius),* and both fresh- and salt-water elasmobranchs. Smith spent many summers in Maine at the Mount Desert Island Biological Laboratory, and he brought his comparative studies to bear on the problems that became central to his later research: the functions of the mammalian (and especially human) kidney.

Smith played a major part in the development of contemporary understanding of the kidney. In the 1930's he and A. N. Richards independently discovered that inulin, a kind of sugar, is filtered by the human and canine renal glomeruli and is then neither excreted nor absorbed by the tubules and collecting ducts. Inulin thus made possible the accurate measurement of glomerular filtration rate (GFR), a concept introduced in the nineteenth century by Carl Ludwig. Smith did much to make van Slyke's felicitous notion of "renal clearance" fundamental to the study of kidney function; and he and his collaborators elucidated the manner in which the kidney "clears" creatinine, urea, mannitol, sodium, and inulin. He also performed classic experiments on differential blood flow in both normal and diseased kidneys, and investigated the role of the kidneys in the pathogenesis of hypertension.

Smith's New York University laboratory became an international center of renal physiology where he trained and collaborated with more than one hundred clinicians and physiologists. Despite his lack of formal medical training, Smith's work possessed immediate clinical significance; and the ties between his laboratory and clinical departments were close and mutually fruitful.

Smith's preeminence in his specialty was demonstrated by two monographs. *The Physiology of the Kidney* (1937) was the first comprehensive study of renal physiology in English since Cushny's *The Secretion of the Urine* (1917). In his *magnum opus, The Kidney: Structure and Function in Health and Disease* (1951), a massive yet readable tome, Smith judiciously surveyed the entire field of renal physiology and pathology. Its depth and scope made the book definitive.

Smith's last book, *Principles of Renal Physiology* (1956), was an engaging summary written primarily for medical students. He was in the process of revising it when he died.

BIBLIOGRAPHY

In addition to the works mentioned in the text, Smith wrote two historical and philosophical studies in which he spelled out his own naturalistic humanism: *The End of Illusion* (New York, 1935) and *Man and His Gods* (Boston, 1952). which includes an autobiographical account of his Colorado boyhood.

A complete bibliography of his published writings through 1962 is in Herbert Chasis and William Goldring, eds., *Homer William Smith: His Scientific and Literary Achievements* (New York, 1965), 259–268. This volume, edited by two of his colleagues, contains selections from Smith's writings; a list of his awards, honors, and appointments; a partial list of the scientists associated with him at New York University; and a short memoir by Robert F. Pitts that was reprinted (with bibliography) in *Biographical Memoirs. National Academy of Sciences*, **39** (1967), 445–470.

WILLIAM F. BYNUM

SMITH, JAMES EDWARD (*b.* Norwich, England, 2 December 1759; *d.* Norwich, 17 March 1828), *botany*.

Smith was the eldest of the seven children of James Smith, a textile merchant, and Frances Kinderley. During his childhood he showed an interest in botany. Encouraged by several competent botanists who lived in Norwich, Smith wanted to study botany formally, but his father insisted that he should also read medicine. Consequently, in 1781 he went to the University of Edinburgh to study under John Hope, an exponent of the Linnaean method; and in 1783 he moved to London to read anatomy under John Hunter. He came with an introduction from Hope to Joseph Banks, who entertained freely and encouraged young scientists. Smith was with Banks when a letter arrived from Linnaeus' executors offering to sell his library, manuscripts, herbarium, and specimens. Having tried and failed to purchase the collection earlier, Banks was disinclined to take it, but he urged Smith to acquire the collection for himself. Smith negotiated the sale for about £1,000 and deposited the collection in rooms in Chelsea. He later moved to other houses in London, and upon his marriage to Pleasance Reeve in 1796, he took his whole establishment back to Norwich.

The Linnaean collections gave Smith both a purpose to his work and standing in scientific society in London. He studied the material, some of which he rearranged and relabeled, and in 1796 he auctioned off the minerals. His first published works were translations of Linnaeus' *Reflections on the Study of Nature* (1785) and *Dissertation on the Sexes of Plants* (1786). He later published a translation of Linnaeus' *Flora Lapponica* and, in 1821, *Correspondence of Linnaeus and Other Naturalists*, which was based on the manuscripts in his possession. Although a devoted admirer and follower of Linnaeus, Smith—once attacked as

"bigotedly attached to the Linnean system"— was aware of the need for change and latterly acknowledged the importance of Jussieu's system. Probably the most important effect of the purchase was the founding in 1788 of the Linnean Society, with a high proportion of foreign members. Smith was elected the first president and held the office until his death. His inaugural address was a "Discourse on the Rise and Progress of Natural History," and he published many papers in the *Transactions* of the society. After Smith's death there was some resentment that he had not left the Linnaean collection to the Society, but the collection was eventually purchased by the Society for £3,000.

The remainder of Smith's life was shaped and influenced by the collection. He was elected fellow of the Royal Society in 1785; and from 1786 to 1787 he traveled in Europe, where he visited famous sites, libraries, and botanical gardens, and met botanists, including Antoine-Laurent de Jussieu. At Leiden in 1786 he took his M.D. with a thesis "De generatione." He published a very personal account of his tour, including an assessment of the state of science in the countries he visited. Upon his return he did some work on the irritability of vegetables and read a paper on the subject to the Royal Society in 1888, but most of his work was on taxonomy. He instructed the queen and princesses in botany, and was knighted in 1814. A popular teacher, Smith lectured regularly at the Royal Institution and for a time at the University of Cambridge; but he was mortified by the refusal to appoint him professor of botany on the grounds that he was a Dissenter, and wrote two pamphlets protesting against the system. His textbooks *Introduction to Physiological and Systematic Botany* (1807) and *Grammar of Botany* (1821) went through several editions, including some published in the United States.

At his home in Norwich, Smith grew many of the plants that he studied and he was in contact with gardeners who grew specimens from overseas, described in his *Exotic Botany* (1804–1805). He prided himself that whenever possible, he personally checked all descriptions that he issued. It was characteristic of his work that before writing on the genus *Salix*, he spent five years collecting and growing all available kinds of willow. Smith's importance in the history of botany rests on his ability to popularize the subject and on his meticulous accuracy and comprehensiveness in describing the flora of Great Britain and of other countries previously little known.

BIBLIOGRAPHY

I. ORIGINAL WORKS. The most enduring memorial of Smith's work in botany is the series of taxonomic books, which often include fine illustrations. The works are *English Botany*, 36 vols. (London, 1790–1814; 2nd ed., 12 vols., 1832–1846; 3rd ed., 1863), with colored plates (highly regarded for their accuracy) by James Sowerby; *Flora Britannica*, 3 vols. (London, 1800–1804), also condensed into a *Compendium* (1800), both of which were issued in German. The *English Flora*, 4 vols. (London, 1824–1828), which was not merely a translation, but was revised, was the most complete treatise of its kind; it was followed by the *Compendium* (1829). He wrote the botanical part of *Zoology and Botany of New Holland and the Isles Adjacent. . . .* (London, [1793]), the first substantial work on the flora of Australia, and edited vols. I–VII of J. Sibthorp's *Flora Graeca* (London, 1806–1840). Smith wrote most of the articles on botany in Rees's *Cyclopaedia*.

A bibliography of Smith's publications never has been fully worked out. The most accessible comprehensive list is appended to G. S. Boulger's article on Smith, in the *Dictionary of National Biography*, XVIII, 469–472. F. A. Stafleu, *Taxonomic Literature* (Utrecht, 1967), 449–451, gives more bibliographical details and several references, including one to the *Catalogue of Herbarium and Types*, which is available on microfilm (IDC 5074). The Royal Society *Catalogue of Scientific Papers*, V, 725–727, lists 57 papers by Smith; and Stafleu, in an article, "Taxonomic Literature," in *Journal and Proceedings of the Royal Society of New South Wales*, **42** (1928), 80–81, lists all his papers on Australian plants and gives a complete list of the one genus and several species named after Smith. The MS sources are well documented. Lady Smith gave her late husband's library and over 3,000 of his letters to the Linnean Society; the letters have been recorded by W. R. Dawson, in *Catalogue of the Manuscripts in the Library of the Linnean Society of London, Part I: the Smith Papers* (London, 1934).

II. SECONDARY LITERATURE. The official biography of Smith is *Memoir and Correspondence of the Late Sir James Edward Smith . . . Edited by Lady Smith*, 2 vols. (London, 1832). Other accounts shortly after Smith's death are John Nichols, *Illustrations of the Literary History of the Eighteenth Century*, VI (London, 1831), 830–850; and E. B. Ramsay, "Biographical Notice of the Late Sir J. E. Smith . . . With an Estimate of His Character and Influence of His Botanical Labours," in *Edinburgh Journal of Science*, n.s. 1 (1829), 1–16. See also G. S. Boulger, in the *Dictionary of National Biography*, LIII (1898), 61–64. Many more articles are listed in J. Britten and G. S. Boulger, *A Bibliographical Index of Deceased British and Irish Botanists, 2nd ed., Revised and Completed by A. B. Rendle* (London, 1831). For a careful analysis of Smith's taxonomic decisions see W. J. Hooker's review of *English Flora*, vols. I–II, in *Edinburgh Journal of Science*, 3 (1825), 159–169;

later vols. also were reviewed extensively. Smith's work in editing Sibthorp was described by W. T. Stearn, "Sibthorp's Smith, The 'Flora Graeca' and the 'Florae Graecae Prodromus,'" in *Taxon*, **16** (1967), 168–178. A comprehensive account of Smith's life, mainly from sources in Norwich, is A. M. Geldart, "Sir James Edward Smith and Some of His Friends," in *Transactions of the Norfolk and Norwich Naturalists' Society*, **9** (1914), 645–692, with bibliography. Smith's relationship to the Linnean Society is covered in A. T. Gage, *A History of the Linnean Society of London* (London, 1938), and in B. D. Jackson, "History of the Linnean Collections, Prepared for the Centenary Anniversary," in *Proceedings of the Linnean Society of London* (1890), 18–34. For probable dates of publication for most of Smith's 3,045 articles in Rees's *Cyclopaedia*, see B. D. Jackson, "Dates of Rees's *Cyclopaedia*," in *Journal of Botany*, **34** (1896), 307–311.

DIANA M. SIMPKINS

SMITH, PHILIP EDWARD (*b.* DeSmet, South Dakota, 1 January 1884; *d.* Florence, Massachusetts, 8 December 1970), *anatomy, endocrinology.*

Prior to Smith many investigators had attempted to study the effects of the removal of the hypophysis (pituitary gland). Since this gland lies at the base of the brain, most workers used an intracranial approach, which involved some possibility of damage to the brain. For many years there was an intensive controversy as to which of the symptoms of hypophyseal removal (hypophysectomy) were due to brain damage and which to actual removal of the gland. Smith developed a surgical approach through the neck to the base of the skull, where he drilled a small hole that exposed the hypophysis directly without any contact being made with the brain. The results of removal of the gland by this route resulted in a number of symptoms, which were completely reversible by daily implants of the anterior lobe of the hypophysis from donor animals into the operated animal. He further placed lesions in the base of the brain close to the hypophyseal region and demonstrated that these were the cause of the remarkable adiposity that many previous investigators had attributed to hypophyseal insufficiency. He showed that uncomplicated hypophysectomy in mammals resulted in cessation of growth; loss of weight; atrophy of the reproductive system, the thyroid gland, and the cortex of the adrenal gland; and a number of other symptoms.

Philip E. Smith was the youngest of the three children of John E. Smith, a congregationalist minister, and his wife, Lydia Elmina Stratton. Not long after Philip's birth, the family moved to Niobrara, Nebraska, where his father was both a government agent and a schoolteacher at a Ponca Indian mission.

The Smith family remained in Niobrara until Philip was about six years old, at which time they acquired an eighty-acre farm in Moorpark, California (Ventura County).

Smith attended the local elementary school and spent much of his time helping with the farm work. There was no high school near the farm and all three children had to leave home to attend the Pomona Preparatory School. They subsequently went to Pomona College. Philip and his older brother did plumbing work for the college and helped to run the college heating plant. When he graduated with a B.S. degree in 1908, Philip was president of his class.

After his graduation from Pomona, he worked for a year as an entomologist engaged in the control of certain insect infestations on citrus fruit trees in southern California. During this year his sister Hope died of appendicitis.

Probably influenced by one of his instructors at Pomona, William Atwood Hilton, who had obtained his degree in histology at Cornell, Smith applied for admission to the Cornell Graduate School. He requested a first major in advanced systematic entomology and a first minor in advanced economic entomology. He entered Cornell in the fall of 1909. Shortly afterward, Smith asked to change his minor subject (for his M.S. degree) to histology under Kingsbury in the anatomy department, but it seems that the M.S. (1910) was in entomology. In October 1910 Smith applied for candidacy for a Ph.D. with a major in histology and embryology, a minor in vertebrate zoology, and a minor in systematic entomology. Sometime later he requested a change of his minor in vertebrate zoology to a minor in human anatomy. It appears that this request was granted; Smith obtained his Ph.D. in anatomy under Kingsbury in 1912.

In his doctoral thesis, "Some Features in the Development of the Central Nervous System of *Desmognathus fusca*," Smith discussed in depth the development of the hypophysis cerebri (pituitary gland), but he also devoted an almost equal amount of attention to the pineal body. It is clear from his thesis that even before he left Cornell, Smith faced the scientific crossroads of his career. He was intensely interested in the embryology, morphology, and function of the pituitary gland, but he also appeared to have an equally intense interest in the pineal body. It is also clear

which road he decided to follow. All of his many subsequent published papers were directly or indirectly concerned with the pituitary gland. It is probable that Smith selected this path because he had already foreseen possible approaches to experimental ablation of the hypophysis in the amphibian embryo.

In the summer of 1912 Smith accepted a position as an instructor in the Department of Anatomy at the University of California (Berkeley). Here he shared an office with Irene A. Patchett, an assistant in anatomy. It is significant that she shortly obtained her master's degree with a thesis on the development of the hypophysis of the frog.

Irene Patchett and Philip Smith were married in December 1913.

During this time, Smith was preparing to start his experimental operations aimed at the ablation of the pituitary anlage in the amphibian embryo. Research funds were scarce, and Smith and his wife spent much of their time on field trips collecting frogs, tadpoles, and frog eggs. He set up facilities in the laboratory to raise amphibia and at the same time he devoted many hours to the meticulous task of hand-grinding sewing needles into the microscalpels which he needed for his work. He launched his first classic experiments on the pituitary gland. He surgically removed the anlage of the pars distalis of the hypophysis at a very early stage in the developing frog embryo (early tail bud stage). Although this work progressed rapidly and successfully, it was not published until 1916.

During the same period, B. M. Allen, an investigator at the University of Kansas, was conducting almost identical research. He and Smith chanced to meet socially and thus discovered their common interest and discussed their experiments fully and frankly. It is said that there was an understanding between them in regard to the initial publication of this very important work. Allen's work was published in the same journal as Smith's and in the same year, but several issues later. Throughout his life Smith retained the highest admiration for Allen as a scientist.

Meanwhile an event occurred which significantly influenced Smith's subsequent scientific career. In 1915 Herbert M. Evans came from Johns Hopkins to Berkeley as professor of anatomy (he was only a few years older than Smith). He brought with him from Hopkins another brilliant young anatomist, George W. Corner. During the first few years of this new departmental regime Smith and Evans were the best of friends. But with the passage of time Smith developed rather negative feelings toward Evans. Smith and Corner remained lifelong friends.

This change in Smith's attitude may have been due to Evans' rather close observation of Smith's work. In his memorial biography of Evans (*Anatomical Record*, 1971), Corner stated: "Daily observations of Philip Smith's pioneering study of the effects of ablation of the hypophysis of frog larvae (begun at Berkeley before Evans took over the department of anatomy) turned Evans' attention to the hypophyseal hormones." It seemed that Smith felt that this "daily observation" of his work overstepped the bounds of scientific propriety. Smith remained at Berkeley until 1926, and it appears that he continued to feel that Evans might be taking advantage of his work.

Smith continued his work on hypophysectomy in amphibia, which ultimately led to his classic monograph "The Pigmentary, Growth and Endocrine Disturbances Induced in the Anuran Tadpole by the Early Ablation of the Pars Buccalis of the Hypophysis" (1920).

In 1919 Smith took a six-month sabbatical leave from the University of California. He moved his family to Boston, where he worked with W. B. Cannon. Smith was greatly stimulated to repeat in mammals what he had done in amphibia and he had been considering approaches to this problem. Probably the greatest obstacle blocking the progress of endocrinology was the confusion and controversy about the function of the hypophysis.

Many investigators in Europe had already published reports on hypophysectomy in various mammals. The results were as varied as the investigators. In 1912, in the United States, Harvey Cushing "hypophysectomized" dogs and came to the conclusion that survival for more than a few days was impossible without the hypophysis.

Most of the investigators in this field had used an intracranial approach to the pituitary gland. This procedure led to considerable difference of opinion as to whether the results obtained in various experiments were the consequence of ablation of the pituitary gland or the result of damage done to the brain along the course of the surgical approach employed.

After his return to Berkeley from Cannon's laboratory, Smith continued his work on amphibia, but he now started to concentrate on an approach to the mammalian hypophysis. It is interesting that his first efforts (in the rat) utilized the intracranial approach. But the method Smith used was novel. He designed and constructed a microsyringe which was capable of accurately injecting quantities of

less than .002 milliliters. He used this instrument to inject .010 to .013 milliliters of a chromic acid solution into the anterior lobe of the hypophysis. In 1923, in a little-known paper ("The Production of the Adiposogenital Syndrome in the Rat, With Preliminary Notes Upon the Effects of a Replacement Therapy"), Smith described one single rat in which he had obtained adequate histological evidence of the complete destruction of the anterior lobe and at the same time he could find no evidence of any damage to neural components of the hypophysis or of brain damage. In this single rat, Smith was able to demonstrate that there was ovarian and uterine atrophy with no adiposity. He also showed that the genital atrophy was reversible by replacement therapy with a material derived from anterior pituitary extracts. It may seem strange that Smith should have published a paper which included his findings on a single rat. However, it is typical of the man that his extreme intellectual honesty and his intelligence never permitted any of his intuitive feelings or theories to interfere with the objective realities of an experiment. When one single experimental animal did not fit in with his previous ideas on hypophyseal function, he thought that this was worthy of public comment. Smith later published extensive accounts of this chromic acid injection technique and its results.

Nevertheless, he realized that this intracranial approach was unsatisfactory. He proceeded to develop a parapharyngeal approach to the hypophysis in the rat. This involved a surgical route through the neck to reach the sphenoid bone at the base of the skull; by drilling through the sphenoid at the proper site he exposed the gland. By means of suction applied through a glass cannula he attained a complete hypophysectomy without touching the brain. The very vital hypothalamic region in the floor of the brain is separated from the pituitary body by the very tough double reflection of dura mater (the diaphragma sella) which is pierced by the pituitary stalk. This adequately protected the floor of the brain from any possible damage during the course of the operation, and made it possible to clearly distinguish the effects of hypophysectomy from the symptoms which followed damage to the hypothalamic region. Furthermore he was able to reverse the symptoms which followed this hypophysectomy by daily implants of anterior pituitary tissue into his operated animals.

In 1921 Smith had been promoted to associate professor of anatomy at the University of California. In 1926 he refused an offer of a full professorship in physiology. He felt that he was primarily an anatomist. In the same year he was offered an associate professorship in anatomy at Stanford and he accepted. Both he and his family were quite happy in this new location and he quickly set up his laboratory to continue his work on hypophysectomy in rats. Smith probably did not realize that as a result of his work on amphibia, he was already internationally known in scientific circles. Although at this date he had published little on his mammalian work, the news of his great breakthrough in this field had spread.

He had barely become settled at Stanford when he was offered a position as a full professor of anatomy at the College of Physicians and Surgeons at Columbia. He accepted this position as of July 1927 but proceeded with a planned leave. He visited various laboratories in Europe, spending three months in one laboratory in Vienna. Smith returned to New York in December 1927 to assume his new position.

Smith's years at Columbia were his most productive. His classic paper "Hypophysectomy and a Replacement Therapy in the Rat" (1930) was published there. This work gave a complete account of his great breakthrough in hypophyseal physiology.

Smith continued his studies of the mammalian hypophysis and finally extended this work to the monkey (rhesus). This later work made possible the study of the role of the hypophysis in a primate whose reproductive cycle was very similar to that of the human species.

During this period many young postdoctoral students from the United States and Europe came to spend a year or more in his laboratory. Also a number of graduate students obtained their Ph.D. degrees under Smith's direction.

Smith was also instrumental in bringing two of his former co-workers from the West Coast to Columbia; Earl Theron Engle, an anatomist from Stanford, and Goodwin Lebaron Foster, a biochemist from the University of California. Both these men remained at Columbia for the balance of their careers.

In the late fall and winter of 1939–1940 Smith and his wife spent three months at the School of Tropical Medicine in Puerto Rico. The U.S. Public Health Service maintained a large colony of rhesus monkeys on a small island off the coast of Puerto Rico. Smith thus had access to a supply of monkeys that was far superior to his own colony at Columbia and this gave great stimulus to his work on the rhesus monkey, which he continued at Columbia until his retirement.

Smith's work was interrupted for some months in 1951 when he was run over by a small cultivator tractor while working on a hillside on his property in Westwood, New Jersey. He returned to active work in his laboratory. Smith became professor emeritus of anatomy in 1952; but he continued at Columbia with an appointment as a lecturer in anatomy until 1954, at which time he decided to retire. He and his wife settled in Sunderland, Massachusetts, near their daughter Fredrika, a pediatrician in Northhampton.

Smith was obviously restless without a laboratory, and in 1956 he returned to Stanford as a research associate. His wife received an appointment as his research assistant. Their work at Stanford was supported by the National Science Foundation. The Smiths intended to spend a year at Stanford, but remained in active work there for seven years. Shortly before his final retirement in 1963, the endocrinologists A. S. Parkes and E. C. Amoroso journeyed from London to Stanford to present to Smith the Sir Henry Dale Medal of the Society of Endocrinology of Great Britain.

After the Smiths left Stanford they returned to Florence, Massachusetts. They also had a cabin in Maine, where they spent the summer months. All his life, from the five-year-old boy riding his pony with the Ponca Indians to the eighty-five-year-old man fly-fishing for salmon in Maine, he loved the outdoors. He remained active until a few weeks before his death.

BIBLIOGRAPHY

I. ORIGINAL WORKS. Smith's writings include "A Study of Some Specific Characters of the Genus *Pseudococcus*," in *Journal of Entomology and Zoology*, **5** (1913), 69–84; "Some Features in the Development of the Central Nervous System of *Desmognathus fusca*," in *Journal of Morphology*, **25** (1914), 511–557; "The Development of the Hypophysis of *Amia calva*," in *Anatomical Record*, **8** (1914), 490–508; "Experimental Ablation of the Hypophysis in the Frog Embryo," in *Science*, **44** (1916), 280–282; "On the Effects of the Ablation of the Epithelial Hypophysis on the Other Endocrine Glands," in *Proceedings of the Society for Experimental Biology and Medicine*, **16** (1919), 81; "Studies on the Conditions of Activity in the Endocrine Glands," in *American Journal of Physiology*, **60** (1922), 476–494, written with W. B. Cannon; "The Pigmentary, Growth and Endocrine Disturbances Induced in the Anuran Tadpole by the Early Ablation of the Pars Buccalis of the Hypophysis," in *American Anatomical Memoirs*, **11** (1920), 1–151; "The Production of the Adiposogenital Syndrome in the Rat With Preliminary Notes on the Effects of a Replacement Therapy," in

Proceedings of the Society for Experimental Biology and Medicine, **21** (1923), 204–206, written with A. T. Walker and J. B. Graeser; "The Function of the Lobes of the Hypophysis as Indicated by Replacement Therapy With Different Portions of the Ox Gland," in *Endocrinology,* **7** (1923), 579–591; "The First Occurrence of Secretory Products and of a Specified Structural Differentiation in the Thyroid and Anterior Pituitary During the Development of the Pig Foetus," in *Anatomical Record,* **33** (1926), 289–298; "Hastening Development of the Female Genital System by Daily Homoplastic Pituitary Transplants," in *Proceedings of the Society for Experimental Biology and Medicine,* **24** (1926), 131–132; "The Genital System Responses to Daily Pituitary Transplants," *ibid.,* **24** (1927), 337–338; "Induction of Precocious Sexual Maturity in the Mouse by Daily Pituitary Homeo and Heterotransplants," *ibid.,* **24** (1927), 561–562, written with E. T. Engle; "The Induction of Precocious Sexual Maturity by Pituitary Homotransplants," in *American Journal of Physiology,* **80** (1927), 114–125; "Hypophysectomy and Replacement Therapy," in *Journal of the American Medical Association,* **87** (1926), 2151–2153, written with G. L. Foster; "A Comparison in Normal, Thyroidectomized and Hypophysectomized Rats of the Effects Upon Metabolism and Growth Resulting From Daily Injections of Small Amounts of Thyroid Extract," in *American Journal of Pathology,* **3** (1927), 669–687, written with C. L. Greenwood and G. L. Foster; "Experimental Evidence Regarding the Role of the Anterior Pituitary in the Development and Regulation of the Genital System," in *American Journal of Anatomy,* **40** (1927), 159–217, written with E. T. Engle; "The Disabilities Caused by Hypophysectomy and Their Repair," in *Journal of the American Medical Association,* **88** (1927), 158–161; "The First Appearance in the Anterior Pituitary of the Developing Pig Foetus of Detectible Amounts of the Hormones Stimulating Ovarian Maturity and General Body Growth," in *Anatomical Record,* **43** (1929), 277–297, written with C. Dortzbach; "Hypophysectomy and a Replacement Therapy in the Rat," in *American Journal of Anatomy,* **45** (1930), 205–273; "Disorders Induced by Injury to the Pituitary and the Hypothalamus," in *Journal of Nervous and Mental Diseases,* **74** (1931), 56–61; "The Effect of Hypophysectomy on Ovulation and Corpus Luteum Formation in the Rabbit," in *Journal of the American Medical Association,* **97** (1931), 1861–1863; "The Non-essentiality of the Posterior Hypophysis in Parturition," in *American Journal of Physiology,* **99** (1932), 345–348; "Prevention of Uterine Bleeding in the Macacus Monkey by Corpus Luteum Extract (Progestin)," in *Proceedings of the Society for Experimental Biology and Medicine,* **29** (1932), 12–25, written with E. T. Engle; "Effect of Injecting Pregnancy Urine Extracts in Hypophysectomized Rats. I. The Male," in *Proceedings of the Society for Experimental Biology and Medicine,* **30** (1933), 1246–1250, written with S. L. Leonard; "Effect of Injecting Pregnancy Urine Extracts in Hypophysectomized Rats. II, The

Female," *ibid.,* **30** (1933), 1248, written with S. L. Leonard; "Increased Skeletal Effects in Anterior Pituitary Growth Hormone Injections by Administration of Thyroid in Hypophysectomized, Thyroparathyroidectomized Rats," *ibid.,* **30** (1933), 1252–1254; "The Effect of Castration Upon the Sex Stimulating Potency and the Structure of the Anterior Pituitary in Rabbits," in *Anatomical Record,* **57** (1933), 177–195, written with A. E. Severinghaus and S. L. Leonard; "Responses of the Reproductive System of Hypophysectomized and Normal Rats to Injections of Pregnancy Urine Extracts, I. The Male," *ibid.,* **58** (1934), 145–173, written with S. L. Leonard; "Responses of the Reproductive System of Hypophysectomized and Normal Rats to Injections of Pregnancy Urine Extracts, II. The Female," *ibid.,* **58** (1934), 175–203, written with S. L. Leonard; "Differential Ovarian Responses After Injections of Follicle Stimulating and Pregnancy Urine in Very Young Female Rats," in *Proceedings of the Society for Experimental Biology and Medicine,* **31** (1934), 744–746, written with E. T. Engle and H. H. Tyndal; "The Role of Estrin and Progestin in Experimental Menstruation," in *American Journal of Obstetrics and Gynecology,* **29** (1935), 787–798; "Effect of Hypophysectomy on Blood Sugar of Rhesus Monkeys," in *Proceedings of the Society for Experimental Biology and Medicine,* **34** (1936), 247–749, written with L. Dotti, H. H. Tyndal, and E. T. Engle; "The Reproductive System and Its Responses to Ovarian Hormones in Hypophysectomized Rhesus Monkeys," *ibid.,* **34** (1936), 245–247; "Response of Normal and Hypophysectomized Rhesus Monkeys to Insulin," in *Proceedings of the Society for Experimental Biology and Medicine,* **34** (1936), 250–251, written with H. H. Tyndal, L. Dotti, and E. T. Engle; "Is the Blood Calcium Level of Mammals Influenced by Estrogenic Hormones?," in *Endocrinology,* **22** (1938), 315–321, written with L. Levin; "The Endometrium of the Monkey and Estrone-Progesterone Balance," in *American Journal of Anatomy,* **63** (1938), 349–365, written with E. T. Engle; "Responses of Normal and Hypophysectomized Immature Rats to Menopause Urine Injections," in *American Journal of Physiology,* **124** (1938), 174–184, written with L. Levin and H. H. Tyndal; "Certain Actions of Testosterone on the Endometrium of the Monkey and on Uterine Bleeding," in *Endocrinology,* **25** (1939), 1–6, written with E. T. Engle; "Effect of Equine Gonadotropin on Testes of Hypophysectomized Monkeys," in *Endocrinology,* **31** (1942), 1–12; "Continuation of Pregnancy in Rhesus Monkeys (*Macaca mulatta*) Following Hypophysectomy," in *Endocrinology,* **55** (1954), 655–664; "The Endocrine Glands in Hypophysectomized Pregnant Rhesus Monkeys (*Macaca mulatta*) With Special Reference to the Adrenal Glands," in *Endocrinology,* **56** (1955), 271–284; "Postponed Homotransplants of the Hypophysis Into the Region of the Median Eminence in Hypophysectomized Male Rats," in *Endocrinology,* **68** (1961), 130–143; "Postponed Pituitary Homotransplants Into the Region of the Hypophysial Portal Circulation in Hypophysectomized Female Rats," in *Endocrinology*, **73** (1963), 793–806, written with Irene P. Smith; and *Baileys Textbook of Histology*, 7th–13th eds. (1932–1958), coauthor.

II. SECONDARY LITERATURE. On Smith and his work, see Frederic J. Agate, Jr., "Philip Edward Smith," in *Anatomical Record*, **4**, no. 1 (1971), 135–138; Nicholas P. Christy, "Philip Edward Smith," in *Endocrinology*, **90**, no. 6 (1972), 1415–1416; and Aura E. Severinghaus, "Philip Edward Smith," in *American Journal of Anatomy*, **135**, no. 2 (1972), 161–163.

FREDERIC J. AGATE, JR.

SMITH, ROBERT (*b.* Lea, near Gainsborough, England, 1689; *d.* Cambridge, England, 2 February 1768), *physics*.

Smith's father, John Smith, was rector of the parish of Lea; his mother, Hannah Smith, was the aunt of Roger Cotes, Plumian professor of astronomy at Cambridge. Smith was educated at the Leicester Grammar School and from 1708 at Trinity College, Cambridge, where he lived with and assisted his cousin Cotes. Smith graduated B.A. in 1711 and M.A. in 1715. He was elected a fellow of his college in 1714, Plumian professor in 1716, and fellow of the Royal Society in 1718. He received the LL.D. in 1723 and the D.D. in 1739. Appointed master of Trinity College in 1742, Smith was vice-chancellor of the University in 1742–1743, and he held the Plumian professorship until 1760. Among his many bequests to the university and to his college, he founded the two Smith's prizes for undergraduate attainment in mathematics and natural philosophy.

Smith wrote on optics and harmonics. In 1738 he published *A Compleat System of Opticks in Four Books, viz. A Popular, a Mathematical, a Mechanical, and a Philosophical Treatise*. Both comprehensive and reliable, the work became probably the most influential optical textbook of the eighteenth century. It was also published in Dutch in 1753, in German in 1755, and in two different French translations in 1767. In 1778 an abridged version was published in English. In turn, its popularity helped to establish the eighteenth-century conviction that light is particulate.

Although Newton had expressed some uncertainty about the nature of light, Smith asserted in the "Popular Treatise" that there was no reason to doubt that light consisted of material particles. He then gave a plausible explanation of most known optical phenomena in terms of particles of light that were acted upon by attractive and repulsive forces. In these explanations Smith never even

suggested that any vibrating medium might exist to produce light or "Newton's rings," nor did he even mention Newton's theory of "fits." Rather he repeated Newton's assertion that the rings were caused by the disposition of varying thicknesses of air or films that reflect or refract different colors of light.

In the "Mathematical Treatise," Smith developed a very comprehensive set of geometric propositions for the computation of the focus, location, magnification, brightness, and aberrations of systems of lenses and mirrors. Apparently he was the first person to construct images by means of an unrefracted central ray and a ray parallel to the axis that is refracted through the focus.[1] He also derived a particular case of the relationship now known as the Smith-Helmholtz formula or the theorem of Lagrange. Using a relationship between the magnification and location of object and image for one lens, Smith showed that the same relationship was invariant within a system of any combination of lenses.[2]

In the "Mechanical Treatise," Smith gave methods for making optical instruments, and in the "Philosophical Treatise," he gave an account of astronomical discoveries.

In 1749 Smith published *Harmonics, or the Philosophy of Musical Sounds*, which had a second edition in 1759 and a postscript in 1762. Although it was partly a textbook, Smith's principal objective was to describe his system of tempering a musical scale by making "all the consonances . . . as equally harmonious as possible. . . ."[3] He derived the "equally harmonic" intervals by a mathematical theory and confirmed his results on an organ and a harpsichord. Smith's temperament was an improvement on existing systems, but its use required impractical mechanical changes in the instruments.

NOTES

1. Ernst Mach, *The Principles of Physical Optics* (New York, 1953), 57.
2. Smith credits Roger Cotes with the discovery of the relationship for one lens. See Smith, *A Compleat System*, bk. II, ch. 5, esp. arts. 247–249, 261–263, 267, 465–474. See also Lord Rayleigh, "Notes, Chiefly Historical. . . ," in *Philosophical Magazine*, 5th ser., **21** (1886), 466–469.
3. Smith, *Harmonics* (1749), p. vi.

BIBLIOGRAPHY

I. ORIGINAL WORKS. Smith's works are *A Compleat System of Opticks in Four Books, viz. A Popular, a Mathematical, a Mechanical, and a Philosophical Trea-*

tise (Cambridge, 1738) and *Harmonics, or the Philosophy of Musical Sounds* (Cambridge, 1749; repr., New York, 1966).

II. Secondary Literature. There is no full biography of Smith. Biographical information in this article is from the *Dictionary of National Biography*, XVIII, 517–519. Smith is mentioned in Ernst Mach, *The Principles of Physical Optics* (New York, 1953), 57, 62. The most useful article on the Smith-Helmholtz formula is Lord Rayleigh, "Notes, Chiefly Historical, on Some Fundamental Propositions in Optics," in *Philosophical Magazine*, 5th ser., **21** (1886), 466–476. The best discussion of Smith's historical importance is in an unpublished master's thesis by Henry John Steffens, "The Development of Newtonian Optics in England, 1738–1831" (Ithaca, New York: Cornell University, 1965). On Smith's *Harmonics*, see Lloyd S. Lloyd, "Robert Smith," in *Grove's Dictionary of Music and Musicians*, 5th ed., VII (London, 1954), 857–858; and "Temperaments," *ibid.*, VIII, 377.

Edgar W. Morse

SMITH, ROBERT ANGUS (*b.* Glasgow, Scotland, 15 February 1817; *d.* Colwyn Bay, North Wales, 12 May 1884), *chemistry*.

Smith was the son of a manufacturer. Having demonstrated some talent for classics, he prepared at the Glasgow grammar school and at the University of Glasgow for a career in the church. His interest in chemistry, however, was kindled by the public lectures of Thomas Graham at Anderson's College. After leaving the University of Glasgow, Smith spent a few years as tutor to the children of several families, eventually traveling to Germany with the Reverend H. E. Bridgeman.

During his German sojourn, Smith's interests in chemistry were reawakened, and in 1839 he made his way to Giessen, where he worked in Liebig's laboratory. His fellow students at that time included Lyon Playfair and Henry Edward Schunck, both of whom were later his colleagues in Manchester. He took the Ph.D. and returned to Great Britain in 1841. Soon afterward he published a translation of Liebig's paper "On the Azotised Nutritive Principles of Plants." Smith's chemical prospects were dim, and in 1843, when Playfair offered him the post of assistant at the Royal Manchester Institution, he eagerly accepted, ultimately joining Playfair in the "health of towns" investigation. Thus Smith commenced a long and distinguished career as a sanitary chemist.

As early as 1845 Smith began to publish a series of analyses of the air and water of large towns. In 1864 he served as consultant to the Condition of Mines Inquiry and published a report on the analysis of the atmosphere in mines and the methods of analysis that were used. Smith's studies on atmospheric and water pollution are collected in his *Air and Rain* (1872).

Smith pioneered also in the chemistry of disinfection. He joined with Frederick Crace-Calvert and Alexander McDougall in experimenting with sewage deodorants in the River Medlock. With McDougall, Smith took out a patent (1854) on a disinfectant powder (largely carbolic acid), which was later manufactured by McDougall and widely used. At Carlisle, McDougall's powder caught the attention of Lister. By 1869 the *Chemical News* reported that "By common consent Dr. Smith has become the first authority in Europe on the subject of disinfection" (*Chemical News*, **9** [1869], 105). Many of Smith's papers on the subject were integrated into his *Disinfectants and Disinfection* (1869). His national reputation as a sanitary chemist made Smith the logical choice for the position of first inspector under the Alkali Act of 1863. He was popular with the manufacturers, providing both constructive regulation and much-needed technical advice. He served also as an inspector under the Rivers Pollution Act of 1876.

In 1845 Smith was elected a member of the Manchester Literary and Philosophical Society and after 1859 served regularly as its president and vice-president. His honors included election as a fellow of the Royal Society (1857) and honorary degrees from Glasgow (1881) and Edinburgh (1882). His concern with the local scientific community is reflected in his historical works, for example, his sketch of the life of Dalton and the atomic theory (1856) and his history of the Manchester scientific community (1883).

BIBLIOGRAPHY

I. Original Works. More than 45 of Smith's articles are listed in the Royal Society *Catalogue of Scientific Papers*, V, 731–732; VIII, 974; XI, 440; XVIII, 812. His major works are "Memoir of John Dalton . . . and History of the Atomic Theory Up to His Time," in *Memoirs and Proceedings of the Manchester Literary and Philosophical Society*, 2nd ser., **13** (1856), 1–29; *Disinfectants and Disinfection* (Edinburgh, 1869); *Air and Rain, the Beginnings of Chemical Climatology* (London, 1872); and "A Centenary of Science in Manchester," in *Memoirs and Proceedings of the Manchester Literary and Philosophical Society*, 3rd ser., **9** (1883), 1–475.

II. Secondary Literature. The best accounts of Smith's life are P. J. Hartog, in the *Dictionary of Na-*

tional Biography, XVIII, 520–522; H. E. Schunck, "Memoir of Robert Angus Smith," in *Memoirs and Proceedings of the Manchester Literary and Philosophical Society*, 3rd ser., **10** (1887), 90–102; and T. E. Thorpe, in *Nature*, **30** (1884), 104–105. On Smith's career as Alkali Acts inspector, see R. MacLeod, "Alkali Acts Administration, 1863–1884," in *Victorian Studies*, **9** (1965), 85–112. An excellent article, A. Gibson and W. V. Farrar, "Robert Angus Smith, F.R.S. and 'Sanitary Science,'" in *Notes and Records of the Royal Society of London*, **28** (1974), 241–262, appeared too late for inclusion in the preparation of this article.

ROBERT H. KARGON

SMITH, SIDNEY IRVING (*b.* Norway, Maine, 18 February 1843; *d.* New Haven, Connecticut, 6 May 1926), *zoology.*

Smith's parents, Elliot Smith and Lavinia Barton, were of old New England families, and he spent his life studying the fauna of New England. His first work in natural history, a collection of the insects of Maine, was so comprehensive that Agassiz purchased it for Harvard. In 1864 Smith went to the Sheffield Scientific School at Yale to work with Addison E. Verrill. He graduated in 1867 and was then appointed assistant in zoology. As an undergraduate he started his life's work on the little-known subject of marine invertebrates. Spending all his summers on dredging expeditions and afterward identifying the collected specimens, he soon specialized in Crustacea. In 1875 he was appointed first professor of comparative anatomy in the same department of zoology, where he remained until his retirement in 1906. He married Eugenia P. Barber in 1882.

Expeditions in which Smith was involved were first those in which he was working with Verrill between 1864 and 1870 to Long Island Sound and the Bay of Fundy. He was zoologist to the U.S. Lake Survey in 1871, studying the deeper parts of Lake Superior. The following year he joined the U.S. Coast Survey, went to St. George's Bank (Newfoundland), and became a member of the U.S. Fish Commission. He was at Kerguelen Island in 1876, and he dredged off the New England coast with the *Fish Hawk* in 1880 and the *Albatross* (mainly in deep water) in 1883. He did little scientific work thereafter.

The value of Smith's work was the large volume of careful identification and description, with accurate drawings, and some observations of behavior, of many species of aquatic Crustacea, hitherto little studied. He discovered many new species and

genera, and worked out their relationships. He also collected extensive data on distribution, including bathymetric distribution, and found that deep-sea samples often contained known species not previously found at great depths, as well as new species.

The large number of available specimens, carefully ordered, allowed Smith to trace the developmental stages of many crustacean larvae formerly thought to be different species from their adult forms. His early papers on the North American lobster are models, and later work on other species threw new light on their relationships. Implications of the details found and generalizations about the group did not come easily to Smith. He never wrote a monograph on the Crustacea, and comments on the size, structure, color, form of eye, and breeding habits of the deep-sea Crustacea collected by the *Albatross* were made by Verrill.

Smith's excellent collections of preserved specimens were given to the Peabody Museum of Natural History at Yale and to the National Museum of Natural History (Washington, D.C.). He was active in the foundation of the Woods Hole Oceanographic Institution.

Smith had a number of minor professional interests. His first published work in 1864 was on the fertilization of orchids, but he did not continue this work. In 1868 he was awarded the Berzelius Prize at Yale for an essay on the geographical distribution of animals, which was concerned largely with fossil forms. He never lost his early interest in entomology. He wrote an occasional paper in the field and was for a time state entomologist of Maine and Connecticut. Smith was also an enthusiastic teacher and started one of the first courses in biology for premedical students.

BIBLIOGRAPHY

I. ORIGINAL WORKS. Smith's most important work, "The Metamorphosis of the Lobster, and Other Crustacea," is in A. E. Verrill, "Report of the Invertebrate Animals of Vineyard Sound and the Adjacent Waters," in *Report of the United States Commission of Fish and Fisheries, 1871/72, Supplementary paper 18*, **2** (1873), 522–537. A fuller account of the development of the lobster is "The Early Stages of the American Lobster (Homarus Americanus Edwards)," in *Transactions of the Connecticut Academy of Arts and Sciences*, **2** (1873), 351–381.

Other papers describing new species, and lists of Crustacea from the various expeditions were published in later *Reports of the Commission of Fish and Fisheries*, the *Bulletin* and the *Proceedings of the United States*

National Museum, Transactions of the Connecticut Academy of Arts and Sciences, and American Journal of Science. They can be traced through the Royal Society Catalogue of Scientific Papers, VIII, 974–975; XI, 440–441; XII, 690; XVIII, 814; or the bibliography of Coe (see below).

II. SECONDARY LITERATURE. The best account of Smith is Wesley R. Coe, in Biographical Memoirs. National Academy of Sciences, 14 (1932), 3–16, with a portrait. There is also an obituary by Smith's colleague A. E. Verrill, in Science, 64 (1926), 57–58. For the background to Smith's work at Yale, see R. H. Chittenden, History of the Sheffield Scientific School, Yale, 2 vols. (New Haven, 1928).

DIANA M. SIMPKINS

SMITH, THEOBALD (b. Albany, New York, 31 July 1859; d. New York, N.Y., 10 December 1934), microbiology, comparative pathology.

The scope and thoroughness of Smith's researches in bacteriology, immunology, and parasitology produced many discoveries of theoretical import and immediate utility to public health and veterinary medicine. He was the most distinguished early American microbiologist and probably the leading comparative pathologist in the world. His greatest accomplishment—elucidation of the causal agent and mode of transmission of Texas cattle fever—first conclusively proved that an infectious disease could be arthropod-borne. Unlike many contemporary bacteriologists in the United States, he received no training in France or Germany.

Smith's parents were Philipp Schmitt, a tailor and the son of a farmer, and Theresia Kexel, whose recent forebears were village schoolmasters. Both born in Nassau, Germany, they married in 1854 and emigrated to America, settling in Albany, N.Y., where Philipp followed his trade for more than forty years. They took in boarders, worked hard, and were very thrifty. Their second child and only son was baptized in his mother's Roman Catholic faith (the father being Lutheran) and given the surname of his godparent, Jacob Theobald, a friendly immigrant neighbor. He appears in the parish register as Theobald Schmitt but in high school lists as Theobald J. Smith, for he temporarily adopted his godfather's first name. Before entering Cornell University, he discarded the second initial and rejected the Roman church.

At home, German was spoken, and Smith's education began at a German-speaking private academy. As a youth he quoted Goethe, enjoyed Schil-

ler, and subsequently mastered the original reports of Robert Koch and Paul Ehrlich. In 1872, after two years of parish schooling, he entered the recently founded Albany Free Academy, where he excelled in all subjects, became president of the debating society, and was valedictorian in 1876. With a state scholarship supplementing his earnings from piano lessons, organ-playing, and bookkeeping, he entered Cornell in 1877. His industry, versatility, and inclination for scientific studies brought durable friendships with the physiologist and comparative anatomist Burt G. Wilder and with the microscopist Simon H. Gage. In 1881 he received the Ph.B. degree with honors and enrolled at the Albany Medical College, where he headed the 1883 M.D. class. His thesis was entitled "Relations Between Cell-activity in Health and Disease."

Smith felt unready for private practice. With Gage's help he obtained an assistantship with Daniel E. Salmon, chief of the veterinary division of the U.S. Department of Agriculture, commencing December 1883. Six months later he became inspector in the new Bureau of Animal Industry, established by Congress under Salmon's charge to combat bovine pleuropneumonia, glanders, infectious diseases of swine, and Texas cattle fever. Smith taught himself Koch's culture-plate methods and improved on them. Through careful field and laboratory studies of swine epizootics, he differentiated hog cholera from the multiplex swine plague (Schweineseuche), implicating distinctive bacillary species for each disease. These findings appeared in the annual reports of the Bureau from 1885 to 1895 and in two monographs, Hog Cholera: Its History, Nature and Treatment (1889) and Special Report on the Cause and Prevention of Swine Plague (1891). In 1886 pioneer observations involving hog cholera bacilli were made by Smith on bacterial variation—a phenomenon that excited his continuing speculative interest—and on the immunity developed by pigeons inoculated with heat-killed cultures, thus heralding a new approach to bacterial vaccine production. Salmon's assumption of sole or senior authorship of several reports on this bacillus led to the selection of the species in 1900 as the prototype of an eponymous Salmonella genus. Some twenty years after Smith discovered Salmonella cholerae-suis, however, the actual etiological agent of hog cholera proved to be viral, and the bacillus was accepted thereafter as a secondary invader.

These projects overlapped with another major assignment, Texas cattle fever, on which Smith worked intermittently, restricted by its summer incidence. In November 1892, more than six years after first observing "small round bodies" in red blood corpuscles from stricken cattle, he completed his classic monograph *Investigations Into the Nature, Causation, and Prevention of Texas or Southern Cattle Fever* (1893). He found that the disease resulted from erythrocyte destruction by a protozoan microparasite, *Pyrosoma bigeminum,* carried in the blood of apparently healthy southern cattle and transmitted to susceptible northern cattle by the progeny of blood-sucking ticks *(Boophilus bovis).* The complex, meticulously verified tick-borne mechanism was viewed incredulously by many, but never refuted—a situation that facilitated acceptance within a decade of the mosquito-borne nature of malaria and yellow fever.

Smith's international recognition was hastened by his publications in German journals. In Washington he was promoted in 1891 to chief of the division of animal pathology of the Bureau of Animal Industry, but Salmon sought unduly to divert credit for Smith's work to himself and to other veterinarians. For example, F. L. Kilborne, superintendent of the experimental farm, was overgenerously made coauthor of the Texas fever monograph. Smith chafed under the repeated injustices but delayed resigning because of fresh research opportunities, including a novel protozoal disease of turkeys, and observations on two varieties of tubercle bacilli from mammals, which presaged a lifelong involvement with human and animal tuberculosis. Moreover, he had developed other interests, including the bacteriology of water supplies. Beginning in 1885–1886 with unofficial observations on the total bacterial count of samples from the Potomac River, he systematically examined (1892) microflora in the Hudson River for fecal bacteria. In a report to the New York Department of Health (1893), he advocated quantitative assays of *Bacillus coli communis* as an index of intestinal pollution and introduced the fermentation tube to demonstrate the presence of gas-producing coliforms. His techniques and detailed studies of *B. coli* and related microorganisms were incorporated in recommendations of the committee of American bacteriologists appointed in 1895 (on which Smith served under W. H. Welch's chairmanship) that culminated in the first edition of the *Standard Methods of Water Analysis* (1905) of the American Public Health Association.

Smith recognized that improved sanitation of sewage, milk, and water supplies required an aroused public interest. He disliked the limelight but nevertheless addressed farmers and sanitarians and regularly participated in meetings of the Biological Society of Washington. In 1886 he became lecturer and professor of bacteriology at the National Medical College (the medical department of Columbian University, now known as George Washington University). This appointment, one of the first chairs of bacteriology at an American medical school, was held until 1895. His industry was leavened and his dissatisfactions eased by a happy marriage in 1888 to Lilian Hillyer Egleston, a clergyman's daughter. Her intelligence, high principles, and social graces furthered her husband's work and life aims. They had two daughters (born in Washington) and a son.

In 1895 Smith resigned from the Bureau, becoming director of an antitoxin laboratory for the Massachusetts State Board of Health and professor of zoology at Harvard University. In six months, in improvised quarters at the Bussey Institution in Jamaica Plain, near Boston, he produced potent diphtheria antitoxin. Through a cooperative arrangement devised by H. P. Walcott, chairman of the State Board of Health, and President Charles Eliot of Harvard, both of whom admired Smith, he was appointed in 1896 to the new George F. Fabyan chair of comparative pathology, endowed by a wealthy Bostonian. Smith retained his directorship of the antitoxin laboratory and was privileged to reside in a mansion nearby, commuting daily to Harvard Medical School. Although he took teaching and committee duties seriously, his class lectures were more thorough than inspiring. The dual position intensified his resolute pursuit of new knowledge on the etiology, pathology, and prevention of communicable disease.

During a European trip in 1896, Smith met many leading microbiologists, including Ehrlich and Koch. To the latter he imparted preliminary observations on two varieties of mammalian tubercle bacilli, which he expanded in another classic report, "A Comparative Study of Bovine Tubercle Bacilli and of Human Bacilli From Sputum" (1898). Three years later Koch confirmed these distinctions but failed to acknowledge Smith's priority until 1908. Koch's extreme views on the negligible role of bovine bacilli in human tuberculosis were not endorsed by Smith.

In 1903 Smith inspected several European vaccine lymph manufacturing facilities, prior to designing an enlarged antitoxin and vaccine laboratory, erected in 1904. Smith was the first scientist in North America to adopt Ehrlich's standardized antitoxic unit; and he introduced many improvements in titration methods, which Ehrlich praised on visiting his laboratory in 1904. Irregularities in guinea pig susceptibility to toxin could be reduced through careful breeding and selection of animals (1905), especially by eliminating passively immune progeny of females previously used for titrations (1907). In studying the antigenic properties of toxin-antitoxin mixtures, Smith foresaw their application to the active immunization of humans (1909, 1910). Incidentally, he mentioned to Ehrlich his observation of the sudden death of guinea pigs following second injections of antitoxin. Ehrlich's colleague R. Otto verified this serum-hypersensitivity, designating it the "Theobald Smith phenomenon" (1906).

In 1903 Smith and A. L. Reagh reported agglutination relationships between certain members of the typhoid-paratyphoid-coliform group of bacilli. A second paper, again involving the hog-cholera bacillus, revealed the nonidentity of its flagellar and somatic agglutinogens. These immunologic contributions were fundamental to subsequent development of the Kauffmann-White schema for identifying *Salmonella* organisms serologically.

Research opportunities in parasitology were plentiful. Malaria was endemic in parts of Massachusetts, and as early as 1896 Smith conjectured that the disease was mosquito-borne. The reluctance of the State Board of Health to support his hypothesis, and difficulties in studying malaria in an unfavorable latitude, discouraged him from this field and the palm soon went to Ronald Ross. Other parasitic diseases studied by Smith were murine sarcosporidiosis (1901), coccidiosis of mouse kidney (1902) and rabbit intestine (1910), and amebiasis in the pig (1910). In 1913 he revived investigations into turkey blackhead begun twenty years earlier in Washington.

The output and functions of the pioneer state laboratory multiplied, and administrative duties mounted. Smith was consulted by bacteriologists, veterinarians, and sanitarians; and Eliot encouraged his defense of animal experimentation during an antivivisectionist campaign (1902), his membership on the Charles River Dam committee (1903), and his inquiry into possible damage to animals by smelter smoke from the Anaconda Copper Mining Company in Montana (1906). Before retiring from the presidency of Harvard University in 1909, Eliot persuaded Smith to give eight Lowell lectures (never published) to popularize comparative pathology. In 1912, as Harvard exchange professor at the University of Berlin, Smith took his family to Germany for six months. His inaugural address,

"Parasitismus und Krankheit," abstractly developed the theme of his Harvey lecture (1906) on the parasitism of the tubercle bacillus. His convictions about the importance of comparative pathology were permeated increasingly by the concept of host-parasite interrelationships.

Smith's acknowledged leadership in this field and his unmatched reputation for productive research led early in 1914 to an invitation from Simon Flexner, director of the Rockefeller Institute for Medical Research, to head the newly endowed department of animal pathology to be established at Princeton, N. J. (In 1901, at the inception of the Institute, he had rejected an offer to become its director but had agreed to join the board of scientific directors under Welch's chairmanship.) Although fifty-five years old and not in robust health, Smith resigned from the State Board of Health that summer, but remained at Harvard for a year until preliminaries for the new department had been fulfilled. At a testimonial dinner in June 1915 extraordinary tributes were paid to Smith by distinguished colleagues from all over the world.

For more than two years after this move, Smith was largely responsible, in consultation with Rockefeller Institute representatives, for the general plans of the new division, design of laboratories and animal quarters, and selection of equipment. By the end of 1917 antipneumococcus and antimeningococcus sera were being manufactured in horses, researches into cattle diseases had begun, and a commodious director's house was under construction. In 1920 Smith and H. W. Graybill showed that the protozoon causing turkey blackhead was transmitted in novel fashion, involving ingestion by the healthy host of the embryonated eggs of a small nematode, *Heterakis papillosa*, which was parasitic in the ceca of infected birds. (The infective agent, erroneously designated *Amoeba meleagridis* by Smith many years before, was recognized by E. E. Tyzzer, his successor at Harvard, as a unique flagellate, which he renamed *Histomonas meleagridis*.) Proximity to a large dairy herd infected with Bang's disease reawakened Smith's early interest in *Bacillus abortus* and bovine contagious abortion; and he published, sometimes with R. B. Little, twelve papers and a monograph in this field. In 1926 they described the protection induced by vaccinating heifers with living *B. abortus* culture of low virulence. Other investigations concerned *Vibrio fetus*, a spirillar cause of cattle abortion, hitherto unrecognized in America; a possible new species, *Bacillus actinoides*, producing bronchopneumonia in calves;

the vitally protective antibodies in colostrum for newborn calves; and the pathogenicity of certain bovine strains of *B. coli* in calves deprived of colostrum.

In 1929, at age seventy, Smith relinquished his directorship of the division of animal pathology and was succeeded by Carl Ten Broeck, a long-time associate. He continued working at Princeton as member emeritus of the Rockefeller Institute. Smith had become vice-president of the board of scientific directors in 1924 and succeeded Welch as president in 1933. In November 1934 increasing weakness forced his hospitalization in New York, where he died just before an exploratory operation for intestinal cancer. His ashes and, six years later, those of his wife were buried in the woods at their summer home at Silver Lake, New Hampshire. In 1967 they were reinterred in the nearby Chocorua cemetery.

Honors came to Smith rather late in life. Between 1917 and 1933 he delivered the Herter, Mellon, Pasteur, Gross, De Lamar, Milbank Memorial, Welch, and Thayer lectures. A climactic series of five Vanuxem lectures, given at Princeton in 1933, and published in book form as *Parasitism and Disease* (1934), philosophically embodied his scientific credo. He received a dozen honorary doctorates from renowned American and European universities. He held membership in numerous scientific and medical societies, and was president of the Society of American Bacteriologists (1903), the National Tuberculosis Association (1926), and the Triennial Congress of Physicians and Surgeons (1928). He was elected a trustee of the Carnegie Institution in 1917. Smith was a foreign member of the Royal Society of London and eleven other ancient societies. Further honor awards were the Mary Kingsley, Flattery, Kober, Trudeau, Holland, Sedgwick, Manson, and Copley medals. Recommended several times for the Nobel prize, this ultimate distinction eluded him, although he surely deserved it. His portrait in oils is at the entrance to the Theobald Smith Building of the Rockefeller Institute, now known as the Rockefeller University, which he served so faithfully in various capacities for thirty-three years.

Smith unpretentiously summarized his own life work as "a study of the causes of infectious diseases and a search for their control." His outstanding success in this quest derived from a farsighted, dispassionately critical intelligence, linked to capacities for unsparing industry, punctilious concern for detail, technical inventiveness, and indomitable persistence. These qualities were applied to realis-

tically chosen problems. Between 1883 and 1934 he published at least one scientific research report annually, and in several of these years the annual output was ten or more such publications—a record demanding rare degrees of self-discipline and dedication to the work ethic. As a director he was fair in judgment but sparing of praise, painstakingly conscientious, and abhorrent of waste or extravagance. All who knew Smith and his work respected him. Individuals as diverse as Osler, Welch, Simon Flexner, Prudden, Rous, Richard Shope, and Ten Broeck held him in profound admiration. Smith was too reticent to be popular, and he displayed an element of restraint even with Gage, despite their half-century of close friendship. Hans Zinsser observes, "there was about him an unobtrusive pride, a reserve tinged with austerity which did not invite easy intimacy."

Smith's relaxations were modest and quiet, befitting his nature. When tired, he sought solace in reading, piano-playing, or calculus. During the hot summer months, he found refreshment at his lakeside home, where besides preparing manuscripts, he enjoyed boating, making household repairs, and landscaping. His pattern of life was consistently rational, yet he did not lack emotion. He hated war and wastefulness, for example, but knew that great ideas must be both launched and defended, often at high cost in a hostile environment. That a scientist of such unswerving probity and fine accomplishments should carry so little fame among his countrymen testifies partly to his self-effacing character. Many of his discriminating contemporaries thought him comparable to Pasteur and Koch, and the passage of time has not dimmed the luster of his contributions to the conquest of disease.

BIBLIOGRAPHY

I. ORIGINAL WORKS. Mimeographed bibliographies were prepared by Earl B. McKinley and Ellen G. Acree, and also by the library of the Rockefeller Institute for Medical Research (now Rockefeller University), New York. Published versions accompany the sketch of Smith's life in *Medical Classics*, **1** (1936–1937), 347–371, and the biographical memoir by Hans Zinsser (see below), which respectively cite 224 and 247 items. These are all incomplete and contain inaccuracies. The actual total, excluding unverifiable editorials and multiple publications of the same article, is almost 300 titles.

His more important monographs include *Hog Cholera: Its History, Nature and Treatment* (Washington, 1889), written with D. E. Salmon and F. L. Kilborne; *Special Report on the Cause and Prevention of Swine Plague* (Washington, 1891); *Investigations Into the*

Nature, Causation, and Prevention of Texas or Southern Cattle Fever (Washington, 1893), written with F. L. Kilborne, repr. in *Medical Classics,* **1** (1936–1937), 372–597; *Studies in Vaccinal Immunity Towards Disease of the Bovine Placenta Due to Bacillus Abortus (Infectious Abortion)* (New York, 1923), written with R. B. Little; and *Parasitism and Disease* (Princeton, N.J., 1934), the Vanuxem lectures.

Smith's lasting interest in the bacteriology and immunology of tuberculosis is expressed in "The Diagnostic and Prognostic Value of the Bacillus Tuberculosis in the Sputum of Pulmonary Diseases," in *Albany Medical Annals,* **5** (1884), 193–198; "Some Practical Suggestions for the Suppression and Prevention of Bovine Tuberculosis," in *Yearbook of the United States Department of Agriculture* (1895), 317–330; "Two Varieties of the Tubercle Bacillus From Mammals," in *Transactions of the Association of American Physicians,* **11** (1896), 75–93; "A Comparative Study of Bovine Tubercle Bacilli and of Human Bacilli From Sputum," in *Journal of Experimental Medicine,* **3** (1898), 451–511, repr. in *Medical Classics,* **1** (1936–1937), 599–669; "The Thermal Death-point of Tubercle Bacilli in Milk and Some Other Fluids," in *Journal of Experimental Medicine,* **4** (1899), 217–233; "The Relation Between Bovine and Human Tuberculosis," in *Medical News,* **80** (1902), 343–346; "Studies in Mammalian Tubercle Bacilli. III. Description of a Bovine Bacillus From the Human Body. A Culture Test for Distinguishing the Human From the Bovine Type of Baccilli," in *Transactions of the Association of American Physicians,* **18** (1903), 109–151; "The Parasitism of the Tubercle Bacillus and Its Bearing on Infection and Immunity," in *Journal of the American Medical Association,* **46** (1906), 1247–1254, 1345–1348, the Harvey lecture; "Certain Aspects of Natural and Acquired Resistance to Tuberculosis and Their Bearing on Preventive Measures," *ibid.,* **68** (1917), 669–674, 764–769, the Mellon lecture; and "Focal Cell Reactions in Tuberculosis and Allied Diseases," in *Bulletin of the Johns Hopkins Hospital,* **53** (1933), 197–225, the Thayer lectures.

His main contributions to the bacteriology and immunology of diphtheria are "Antitoxic and Microbicide Powers of the Blood Serum After Immunization, With Special Reference to Diphtheria," in *Albany Medical Annals,* **16** (1895), 175–189; "The Production of Diphtheria Antitoxin," in *Journal of the Association of Engineering Societies,* **16** (1896), 83–92; "The Conditions Which Influence the Appearance of Toxin in Cultures of the Diphtheria Bacillus," in *Transactions of the Association of American Physicians,* **11** (1896), 37–61; "The Relation of Dextrose to the Production of Toxin in Bouillon Cultures of the Diphtheria Bacillus," in *Journal of Experimental Medicine,* **4** (1899), 373–397; "The Antitoxin Unit in Diphtheria," in *Journal of the Boston Society of Medical Sciences,* **5** (1900), 1–11; "The Degree and Duration of Passive Immunity to Diphtheria Toxin Transmitted by Immunized Female Guinea-pigs to Their Immediate Offspring," in *Journal of Medical Research,* n.s. **11** (1907), 359–379; and "Active Immunity Produced by So-called Balanced or Neutral Mixtures of Diphtheria Toxin and Antitoxin," in *Journal of Experimental Medicine,* **11** (1909), 241–256.

Other fundamental contributions to immunology are "On a New Method of Producing Immunity From Contagious Diseases," in *Proceedings of the Biological Society of Washington,* **3** (1886), 29–33, and "Experiments on the Production of Immunity by the Hypodermic Injection of Sterilized Cultures," in *Transactions of the IX International Medical Congress, Washington,* **3** (1887), 403–407, both written with D. E. Salmon; "The Agglutination Affinities of Related Bacteria Parasitic in Different Hosts," in *Journal of Medical Research,* n.s. **4** (1903), 270–300, and "The Non-identity of Agglutinins Acting Upon the Flagella and Upon the Body of Bacteria,"*ibid.,* n.s. **5** (1903), 89–100, both written with A. L. Reagh; "Agglutination Affinities of a Pathogenic Bacillus From Fowls (Fowl Typhoid) Bacterium sanguinarium, Moore) With the Typhoid Bacillus of Man," *ibid.,* n.s. **26** (1915), 503–521, written with C. Ten Broeck; "The Significance of Colostrum to the New-born Calf," in *Journal of Experimental Medicine,* **36** (1922), 181–198, written with R. B. Little; and "The Relation of the Capsular Substance of B. coli to Antibody Production," *ibid.,* **48** (1928), 351–361.

His studies on the properties and differentiation of new or unusual bacterial species include "A New Chromogenous Bacillus," in *Proceedings of the American Association for the Advancement of Science,* **34** (1885), 303–309, written with D. E. Salmon; "The Bacterium of Swine Plague," in *American Monthly Microscopical Journal,* **7** (1886), 204–205; "A Contribution to the Study of the Microbe of Rabbit Septicaemia," in *Journal of Comparative Medicine and Surgery,* **8** (1887), 24–37; "Zur Unterscheidung zwischen Typhus- und Kolonbacillen," in *Centralblatt für Bakteriologie und Parasitenkunde* (Original-Mittheilung), **11** (1892), 367–370; "On a Pathogenic Bacillus From the Vagina of a Mare After Abortion," in *Bulletin. Bureau of Animal Industry. United States Department of Agriculture,* no. 3 (Washington, 1893), 53–59; "Spontaneous Pseudo-tuberculosis in a Guinea-pig, and the Bacillus Causing It," in *Journal of the Boston Society of Medical Sciences,* **1** (1897), 5–8; "Ueber die pathogene Wirkung des Bacillus abortus Bang," in *Centralblatt für Bakteriologie, Parasitenkunde und Infektionskrankheiten,* I. Abteilung (Originale), **61** (1912), 549–555; "A Pleomorphic Bacillus From Pneumonic Lungs of Calves Simulating Actinomyces," in *Journal of Experimental Medicine,* **28** (1918), 333–344; "Spirilla Associated With Disease of the Fetal Membranes in Cattle (Infectious Abortion)," *ibid.,* 701–719; "Some Cultural Characters of Bacillus abortus (Bang) With Special Reference to CO_2 Requirements," *ibid.,* **40** (1924), 219–232; "Studies on a Paratyphoid Infection in Guinea Pigs," *ibid.,* **45** (1927), 353–363, 365–377, written with J. B. Nelson; and "Studies on Pathogenic B. coli From Bovine Sources," *ibid.,* **46** (1927), 123–131, written with R. B. Little.

Smith's persistent concern with bacterial variation is apparent from "On the Variability of Pathogenic Organisms, as Illustrated by the Bacterium of Swine-plague," in *American Monthly Microscopical Journal,* **7** (1886), 201–203; "Observations on the Variability of Disease Germs," in *New York Medical Journal,* **52** (1890), 485–487; "Modification, Temporary and Permanent, of the Physiological Characters of Bacteria in Mixed Cultures," in *Transactions of the Association of American Physicians,* **9** (1894), 85–106; "Variations Among Pathogenic Bacteria," in *Journal of the Boston Society of Medical Sciences,* **4** (1900), 95–109; "Animal Reservoirs of Human Disease With Special Reference to Microbic Variability," in *Bulletin of the New York Academy of Medicine,* 2nd ser., **4** (1928), 476–496; and "Koch's Views on the Stability of Species Among Bacteria," in *Annals of Medical History,* n.s. **4** (1932), 524–530.

His pioneering work on the bacteriological analysis of water is expressed in "Some Recent Investigations Concerning Bacteria in Drinking Water," in *Medical News,* **49** (1886), 399–401; "Quantitative Variations in the Germ Life of Potomac Water During the Year 1886," *ibid.,* **50** (1887), 404–405; "The Relation of Drinking Water to Some Infectious Diseases," in *Albany Medical Annals,* **9** (1888), 297–302; "On Pathogenic Bacteria in Drinking Water and the Means Employed for Their Removal," *ibid.,* **13** (1892), 129–150; "A New Method for Determining Quantitatively the Pollution of Water by Fecal Bacteria," in *New York State Board of Health. Thirteenth Annual Report for the Year 1892* (1893), 712–722; "Notes on Bacillus coli communis and Related Forms, Together With Some Suggestions Concerning the Bacteriological Examination of Drinking-water," in *American Journal of the Medical Sciences,* **110** (1895), 283–302; and "Water-borne Diseases," in *Journal of the New England Water Works Association,* **10** (1896), 203–225.

On other aspects of sanitation he wrote "Recent Advances in the Disinfection of Dwellings as Illustrated by the Berlin Rules," in *New York Medical Journal,* **48** (1888), 117–120; "The Sanitary Aspects of Dairying," in *Maine Farmer* (15 Dec. 1898), 1, 4; "The House-fly as an Agent in the Dissemination of Infectious Diseases," in *American Journal of Public Hygiene,* n.s. **4** (1908), 312–317; "What Is Diseased Meat and What Is Its Relation to Meat Inspection?," *ibid.,* n.s. **5** (1909), 397–411; and "Insects as Carriers of Disease," in *Monthly Bulletin of the State Board of Health of Massachusetts,* **5** (1910), 112–119.

The scope and duration of Smith's work in parasitology is exemplified by "Some Observations on Coccidia in the Renal Epithelium of the Mouse," in *Journal of Comparative Medicine and Surgery,* **10** (1889), 211–217; "Preliminary Observations on the Microorganism of Texas Fever," in *Medical News,* **55** (1889), 689–693; "Some Problems in the Etiology and Pathology of Texas Cattle Fever, and Their Bearing on the Comparative Study of Protozoan Diseases," in *Transactions of*

the Association of American Physicians, **8** (1893), 117–134; "An Infectious Disease Among Turkeys Caused by Protozoa (Infectious Entero-hepatitis)," in *Bulletin. Bureau of Animal Industry. United States Department of Agriculture,* no. 8 (1895), 7–38; "The Etiology of Texas Cattle Fever, With Special Reference to Recent Hypotheses Concerning the Transmission of Malaria," in *New York Medical Journal,* **70** (1899), 47–51; "The Etiology of Malaria With Special Reference to the Mosquito as an Intermediate Host," in *Journal of the Massachusetts Association of Boards of Health,* **11** (1901), 99–113; "The Production of Sarcosporidiosis in the Mouse by Feeding Infected Muscular Tissue," in *Journal of Experimental Medicine,* **6** (1901), 1–21; "On a Coccidium (Klossiella muris, gen. et spec. nov.) Parasitic in the Renal Epithelium of the Mouse," *ibid.,* **6** (1902), 303–316, written with H. P. Johnson; "The Sources, Favoring Conditions and Prophylaxis of Malaria in Temperate Climates, With Special Reference to Massachusetts," in *Boston Medical and Surgical Journal,* **149** (1903), 57–64, 87–92, 115–118, 139–144, the Shattuck lecture; "Some Field Experiments Bearing on the Transmission of Blackhead in Turkeys," in *Journal of Experimental Medicine,* **25** (1917), 405–414; "Coccidiosis in Young Calves," *ibid.,* **28** (1918), 89–108; and "Encephalitozoon cuniculi as a Kidney Parasite in the Rabbit," *ibid.,* **41** (1925), 25–35.

Technological innovations and elucidations are reported in "A Few Simple Methods of Obtaining Pure Cultures of Bacteria for Microscopical Examination," in *American Monthly Microscopical Journal,* **7** (1886), 124–125; "The Fermentation Tube With Special Reference to Anaërobiosis and Gas Production Among Bacteria," in *Wilder Quarter-Century Book 1868–1893* (Ithaca, 1893), 187–233; "Ueber die Bedeutung des Zuckers in Kulturmedien für Bakterien," in *Centralblatt für Bakteriologie und Parasitenkunde,* I. Abteilung (Originale), **18** (1895), 1–9; "A Modification of the Method for Determining the Production of Indol by Bacteria," in *Journal of Experimental Medicine,* **2** (1897), 543–547; and "One of the Conditions Under Which Discontinuous Sterilization May be Ineffective," *ibid.,* **3** (1898), 647–650.

Smith's advocacy of research in comparative pathology and his emphasis on the host-parasite relationship are expressed in "Comparative Pathology in Its Relation to Human Medicine," in *Bulletin of the Harvard Medical Alumni Association,* **9** (1896), 50–69; "Adaptation of Pathogenic Bacteria to Different Species of Animals," in *Boston Medical and Surgical Journal,* **142** (1900), 473–476; "Some Problems in the Life History of Pathogenic Microorganisms," in *Science,* n.s. **20** (1904), 817–832; "The Relation of Animal Life to Human Diseases," in *Boston Medical and Surgical Journal,* **153** (1905), 485–489; "Animal Diseases Transmissible to Man," in *Monthly Bulletin of the State Board of Health of Massachusetts,* **4** (1909), 264–276; "Parasitismus und Krankheit," in *Deutsche medizinische Wochenschrift,* **38** (1912), 276–279, inaugural address as visiting professor, University of Berlin; "Parasitism as a Factor in Disease," in *Science*, **54** (1921), 99–108; "Some Biological and Economic Aspects of Comparative Pathology," in *Edinburgh Medical Journal*, **31** (1924), 221–240; and "Disease a Biological Problem," in *Bulletin of the Harvard Medical Alumni Association*, **5** (1931), 2–6.

Correspondence and other data relating to Smith are among the Simon Henry Gage Papers at the Olin Research Library, Cornell University, Ithaca, N. Y., and the Simon Flexner Papers in the American Philosophical Society Library, Philadelphia. The Countway Library of Medicine, Harvard University, Boston, Mass., and the Archives of the Rockefeller University, New York, also contain material bearing on his work at Boston and at Princeton. Bronze bas-reliefs of him hang in the School of Public Health at Harvard University and in the library of the Rockefeller University. Small medallions of another such portrait were distributed to all members attending the third International Congress of Microbiology, held in New York in 1939.

II. SECONDARY LITERATURE. Obituaries include J. H. Brown, "Theobald Smith, 1859–1934," in *Journal of Bacteriology*, **30** (1935), 1–3, with photograph of bronze plaque; W. Bulloch, "*In Memoriam* Theobald Smith, 1859–1934," in *Journal of Pathology and Bacteriology*, **40** (1935), 621–635, with portrait; A. E. Cohn, "Obituary: Theobald Smith, 1859–1934," in *Bulletin of the New York Academy of Medicine*, 2nd ser., **11** (1935), 107–116, with portrait; E. G. Conklin, "Theobald Smith," in *Proceedings of the American Philosophical Society*, **75** (1935), 333–335; S. Flexner's minute on Smith, read at the meeting of the board of scientific directors of the Rockefeller Institute for Medical Research, on 20 April 1935; S. H. Gage, "Theobald Smith, 1859–1934," in *Cornell Veterinarian*, **25** (1935), 207–228, with portrait; and "Theobald Smith, Investigator and Man, 1859–1934," in *Science*, **84** (1936), 365–371, with portrait; Preston Kyes, "Theobald Smith, M.D., 1859–1934," in *Archives of Pathology*, **19** (1935), 234–238; E. B. McKinley, "Theobald Smith," in *Science*, **82** (1935), 575–586; C. R. Stockard, "Theobald Smith," *ibid.*, **80** (1934), 579–580; S. B. Wolbach, "Dr. Theobald Smith," in *Bulletin of the Harvard Medical Alumni Association*, **9** (1935), 35–38; and H. Zinsser, "Biographical Memoir of Theobald Smith, 1859–1934," in *Biographical Memoirs. National Academy of Sciences*, **17**, no. 12 (1936), 261–303, with portrait and bibliography. Obituaries in foreign languages include O. Seifried, "Theobald Smith †. 1859–1934," in *Tierärztliche Rundschau*, **41** (1935), 46–48; and V. L. Yakimoff, "Theobald Smith," in *Priroda*, no. 5 (1935), 81–86.

Other references to Smith's life and work are P. F. Clark, "Theobald Smith, Student of Disease (1859–1934)," in *Journal of the History of Medicine and Allied Sciences*, **14** (1959), 490–514, with photograph of bronze medallion; I. S. Cutter, "Theobald Smith and His Contributions to Science," in *Journal of the American Veterinary Medical Association*, **90** (1937), 245–

255; C. E. Dolman, "Texas Cattle Fever. A Commemorative Tribute to Theobald Smith," in *Clio Medica*, **4** (1969), 1–31; and "Theobald Smith, 1859–1934: Life and Work," in *New York State Journal of Medicine*, **69** (1969), 2801–2816; D. Fairchild, *The World Was My Garden. Travels of a Plant Explorer* (New York, 1938), 24–25; M. C. Hall, "Theobald Smith as a Parasitologist," in *Journal of Parasitology*, **21** (1935), 231–243, and "Theobald Smith on Disease," in *Journal of Heredity*, **26** (1935), 419–422, a review of Smith's *Parasitism and Disease;* Paul de Kruif, "Theobald Smith: Ticks and Texas Fever," in *Microbe Hunters* (New York, 1926), 234–251; J. Middleton, "A Great American Scientist," in *World's Work* (July 1914), 299–302; T. M. Prudden, "Professor Theobald Smith and a New Outlook in Animal Pathology," in *Science*, n.s. **39** (1914), 751–754; Anna M. Sexton, "Theobald Smith: First Chairman of the Laboratory Section, 1900," in *American Journal of Public Health*, **41** (1951), 125–131; and P. H. Smith, "Theobald Smith," in *Land*, **8** (1949), 363–368.

CLAUDE E. DOLMAN

SMITH, WILLIAM (*b.* Churchill, Oxfordshire, England, 23 March 1769; *d.* Northampton, England, 28 August 1839), *geology.*

Smith's father, John, was a village blacksmith; but his grandparents and great-grandparents were small farmers in Oxfordshire and Gloucestershire. His mother, Ann, daughter of an unrelated William Smith, was also descended from a farming family. William was the eldest of five children and was only seven when his father died. His first eighteen years were spent in the village of Churchill, with the exception of two years spent in London. He attended the village school until he was eleven; there he learned simple arithmetic and how to write in a good, clear hand. Later, with some older friends and neighbors, he pursued further studies, including mathematics.

The year 1787, when he was eighteen, was a turning point in Smith's life. A local surveyor, Edward Webb of Stow-on-the-Wold, came to Churchill to make a detailed survey of the parish preparatory to the enclosure of the common lands. He needed the assistance of an intelligent lad to hold the chain and to take notes, and Smith got the job. Evidently Webb realized that he had made a good choice, for he took Smith into his business, carried on in the large house (now known as Manor House) on the corner of the market square in Stow. Here Smith lived with Webb and his family for nearly five years. There is no evidence that he was articled to Webb, but he learned all the duties of a land surveyor and valuer and must have become well qualified.

In the autumn of 1791 Webb sent Smith to survey and value an estate in north Somerset. He went there on foot and lodged at Rugborne Farm, near High Littleton, about eight miles southwest of Bath. Smith later designated this farmhouse "the birth-place of English geology," for it was there that he began to think about the succession of the strata. The house is still standing, almost unaltered since Smith lodged there. At that time the district had many active coal mines, and Smith went underground to examine some of them and draw plans. He also prepared a map of High Littleton that still exists.

In 1793 Smith was engaged by a group of local landowners to make a survey for a proposed canal, on which the coal from their mines could be carried to a wider market at a lower cost. In March 1794 he gave evidence before Parliament in connection with the act authorizing the canal construction; and in August he went with two members of the canal committee on a carriage tour to the north of England to see other canals and collieries. The tour provided him with valuable additions to his knowledge of the strata, a subject in which he was increasingly interested. While in London he had visited booksellers in order to find books on geology, but with little success.

Work on the canal, which became known as the Somerset Coal Canal, began in July 1795. Two branches, each extending from the coal-mining areas along nearly parallel valleys and each about six miles long, were to be constructed. From their meeting point a canal two miles long would connect with the Kennet and Avon Canal, also under construction; the latter was intended to link Bath with the towns of Newbury and Reading in the Thames Valley.

Smith was employed by the Canal Company from 1794 to 1799; and during this period, he became familiar with the strata through which the canal passed, from Triassic marls to the Lias and Oolites of the Jurassic. He collected fossils, and his notes show that by January 1796 he had made the great discovery that lithologically similar beds can be distinguished by the assemblage of fossils found in them, a concept virtually unrecognized by the geologists of that period. He also began to color maps to show how the different beds outcropped around the neighboring hills. In June 1799 his engagement with the Canal Company was terminat-

ed; and about this time he dictated to two local clergymen, Joseph Townsend and Benjamin Richardson, both collectors of fossils, a list of the strata found around Bath and the fossils characteristic of each. This list is deservedly famous. A contemporary copy, and also a map by Smith of the country five miles around Bath "colored geologically in 1799," is held by the Geological Society of London.

Smith had already drained some land for local landowners, and this type of work offered him prospects of traveling about the country and seeing more of its geology. In 1800 he was employed by a famous landowner and agriculturist Thomas Coke of Holkham in Norfolk; and in 1801 Coke introduced him to Francis, Duke of Bedford, who then employed Smith on his Woburn estate. Both Coke and the duke held large annual meetings on their estates to coincide with the June sheepshearings, and these were attended by many prominent landowners, including distinguished foreigners. From 1801 Smith went to these meetings, exhibited his maps, and talked about geology and its economic value. Several small maps of England and Wales colored geologically by Smith around 1801–1803 are still extant.

In 1802 Smith first met Sir Joseph Banks, president of the Royal Society, and explained his ideas to him. Banks greeted Smith's proposal for a geological map of England and Wales with enthusiasm and encouraged him to complete it. Smith had already issued a printed prospectus, dated 1 June 1801, of his projected work; and a list of subscribers had been opened. The book was to be called "Accurate Delineations and Descriptions of the Natural Order of the Various Strata That Are Found in Different Parts of England and Wales"; it was to be accompanied by a "correct map of the strata."

Nevertheless, during the next ten years, Smith's only publication was a nongeological book on irrigation and water meadows (1806). From this venture he learned that books are not necessarily profitable to their authors. He continued to make numerous notes and write portions of his proposed work on geology but was constantly employed on different projects and had little spare time for concentrated writing, even though he employed an amanuensis to copy his notes. His work varied from the construction of sea defenses on the east coast of England and in South Wales, to supervising sinkings for coal in Yorkshire and Lancashire, and to reporting on the value of estates. In 1804 he leased a large house in London. There he set up his collection of fossils on sloping shelves to represent the different strata. This collection was inspected in 1808 by members of the newly formed Geological Society of London.

In 1812 a London map engraver and publisher, John Cary, offered to publish Smith's geological map of England and Wales on a scale of five miles to the inch. Plates were specially engraved, and Smith himself decided what place names were to be inserted. During 1813 and 1814 he added the geological lines; and when the coloring was carried out he insisted on the use of a novel feature—each formation was colored a darker shade at its base to make clear how the beds were superimposed. In May 1815 the completed map, *A Delineation of the Strata of England and Wales, With part of Scotland*, was exhibited in London to the Board of Agriculture, to the Royal Institution, and to the Society for the Encouragement of Arts, Manufactures and Commerce. This society had offered annually since 1802 a premium of fifty guineas for a mineralogical map of England and Wales. Smith received this award. By March 1816, 250 copies of the geological map had been colored and issued to subscribers; most of the maps were numbered and signed by Smith and duly noted in his diary. Probably 400 copies in all were issued, of which fewer than a hundred are known to be extant.

The map was sold at five guineas (£5.25) a copy, but the costs of production and coloring must have absorbed most of the proceeds. About this time he found himself in severe financial difficulties. In 1812 he had leased a quarry near the Coal Canal and had set up a sawmill and stoneworks under the management of his brother John; but the stone proved to be of poor quality because the quarry was intersected by unsuspected faults. Smith's debts had rapidly increased. For this reason he decided to sell his vast collection of fossils, arranged stratigraphically, to the British Museum; and he began negotiations with the government in 1815. Unfortunately the sum he eventually received was well below his expectations—£500 in installments with a further £100 in 1818 for some additional fossils. About 2,000 of these fossils, mostly bearing Smith's original reference marks, are still in the collections of the British Museum (Natural History). Also, museum officials demanded a catalog; and Smith had to give much time to its compilation, although he was aided by his nephew John Phillips, then aged fifteen.

Despite his difficulties, during the next few years Smith published several works. *Strata Identified*

by Organized Fossils, in four parts (London, 1816–1819), in which fossils from the London Clay (Tertiary) down to the Fuller's Earth Rock (Middle Jurassic) were shown on nineteen colored plates. *Stratigraphical System of Organized Fossils Part I* (London, 1817) described fossils from the London Clay down to the Marlstone of the Lias, with particular reference to those purchased by the British Museum, and contained a "Geological Table of British Organized Fossils Which Identify the Course and Continuity of the Strata in Their Order of Superposition, as Originally Discovered by W. Smith Civil Engineer; With Reference to His Geological Map of England and Wales." This table was also issued separately and later was included in a volume of geological sections (1819), five large folding sheets of hand-colored panoramic horizontal sections, across different parts of southern England. A geological section from London to Snowdon, the highest mountain in Wales, usually included in this work, had also been issued separately in 1817.

Cary, who published these geological sections, now provided Smith with maps of the English counties to color geologically; and in May 1819 geological maps of Kent, Sussex, Norfolk, and Wiltshire were published. This work continued up to 1824. In all, twenty-four maps of twenty-one counties were issued; Yorkshire, the largest English county, required four sheets. Other county maps were in an advanced state of preparation, but never appeared with geological coloring.

From 1820 Smith lived in the north of England. For many years he had no settled home—but lived in lodgings wherever his work or inclination led him. During 1824 and 1825 he and his nephew John Phillips (who later became professor of geology at Oxford) lectured on geology in several Yorkshire towns, but rheumatism and increasing deafness made it difficult for Smith to continue this occupation. In 1828 he was offered a post as land steward to Sir John Johnstone of Hackness (a village near Scarborough in Yorkshire), a great admirer of Smith's work. Smith lived at Hackness for about five years and while there mapped, on a scale of six-and-a-half inches to the mile, the Jurassic rocks of the Hackness Hills. This beautiful and accurate map was published in 1832.

In 1831 Adam Sedgwick, president of the Geological Society of London, announced that the first Wollaston Medal had been awarded to Smith "in consideration of his being a great original discoverer in English Geology; and especially for his having been the first, in this country, to discover and teach the identification of strata, and to determine their succession by means of their imbedded fossils" (*Proceedings of the Geological Society*, **1** [1834], 271). The gold medal (not then ready) was presented to Smith the following year at the British Association meeting in Oxford. This recognition of Smith's fundamental contribution to geology was followed by an award by the government of an annuity of £100. In 1835 whilst at a British Association meeting the LL.D. was bestowed on him at Trinity College, Dublin. In 1834 he left Hackness to live at Scarborough, and in 1835 moved into Newborough Cottage, Bar Street. He regularly attended the annual meetings of the British Association, to which he twice contributed papers; and at Scarborough he spent many hours writing reminiscences, fragments of geology, and notes on many topics.

Smith's last geological task was performed in 1838, when he accompanied Henry de la Beche, director of the newly established Geological Survey, Charles Barry, the architect, and C. H. Smith, a sculptor and mason, on a horse-and-carriage tour of the principal quarries of England and Scotland in order to choose a suitable stone for the new Houses of Parliament. On this tour particular attention was paid to the condition of the stone in old abbeys and churches. In 1839 the official report recommended the use of a magnesian limestone from certain quarries at Bolsover Moor, Derbyshire. As building proceeded, the supply of stone proved inadequate; and further supplies of magnesian limestone were obtained from the Anston quarries eight miles to the north in Yorkshire. Although this stone proved excellent when used for the Museum of Practical Geology, opened in 1851, it failed badly in parts of the Parliament buildings; and as early as 1861 an inquiry was held about its decay. The present view is that the stone was unsuitable for the highly decorated Parliament buildings, although satisfactory for the classic style of the museum. Smith's notes made at the time of the tour indicate that he was well aware of the many factors that can affect the condition of stone buildings. Had he not died suddenly from a chill on his way to a British Association meeting in Birmingham, his specialized knowledge and supervision might have made a marked difference in the selection of stone for the more deeply sculptured portions of the Houses of Parliament.

Smith's contributions to the advancement of geology were chiefly practical and were based on field geology; and to seek in his works, published or unpublished, theoretical considerations of a pro-found nature is a waste of time. Smith was a surveyor, a working man, not an academic; and he saw his discoveries as tools that could be used to promote the economic development of his country, in agriculture and in industry. Many of his unpublished notes confirm this viewpoint.

It is perhaps not widely realized how the geological succession in England itself contributed to William Smith's rapid progress in interpreting its order. In England it is possible to find sedimentary rocks of every age from Precambrian through Paleozoic to Mesozoic and Tertiary, and only the older Paleozoic rocks are so folded and compressed that interpretation of their succession is difficult. In only a few places in England does the intrusion of granites or other igneous rocks cause some disorder and irregularity; local folding and faulting also occur, but the intense folding and faulting that gave rise to the complicated Alpine structures of Europe reached only the very south of England, as minor ripples. Nor are there vast gaps in the succession, such as occur, for example, in the eastern United States, where the Jurassic beds are entirely absent and Cretaceous sediments directly overlie Triassic ones. In the former kingdom of Saxony, where Werner sought to distinguish "formations," the Jurassic rocks are also absent and the Cretaceous ones rest directly on Paleozoic or even older rocks.

This view is confirmed by T. H. Huxley, in his address to the British Association in 1881, "The Rise and Progress of Palaeontology." He stated that "this modest land-surveyor, whose business took him into many parts of England, profited by the peculiarly favourable conditions offered by the arrangement of our secondary strata . . ." (*Collected Essays*, IV [London, 1895], 37).

Unlike certain naturalists, Smith did not concern himself with the extinction of species or the living analogues of fossils. His knowledge of biology was minimal and he regarded fossils solely as a means of identifying a particular stratum, such as the Cornbrash or the Coral Rag. He did not recognize any age difference in these beds. Hence his approach was quite different from that of the naturalists Buffon and Soulavie, who earlier had concluded that rocks containing fossils of which there were no known living representatives must be older than those containing fossils part or all of which resembled creatures living in modern oceans. Smith did, however, recognize before 1800 that fossils worn by attrition found in alluvial beds indicated that the beds were deposited later than those containing the unworn fossils.

Smith's major achievements were (1) the recognition of a regular succession in the strata of England, first confirmed in the southwest and then established across most of the country; (2) the discovery that many individual beds have a characteristic fossil content that can be used to distinguish them from other beds that are lithologically similar; and (3) the utilization of these two discoveries in the preparation of a large-scale geological map of the whole country. Since this map was Smith's first geological publication, it is necessary to make clear how his discoveries became known long before its publication in 1815.

The earliest extant list of English strata prepared by Smith was written in 1797; more than twenty different strata from Chalk (Cretaceous) down to the Coal Measures and the limestone (Carboniferous) beneath them are briefly described, but no reference is made to fossils. His next list, dictated to Richardson and Townsend in June 1799, enumerated the strata around Bath, their particular characteristics, and the fossils found in certain beds. Twenty-three different beds are named, from Chalk to Coal; and in most cases the thickness of each, as then known to Smith, is given. Under the heading "Fossils, petrifactions, &c., &c." are listed the fossils found in ten of the named beds. Their names were provided mostly by the two clergymen. Besides the general terms ammonite, belemnite, and gryphite, more specific ones—high-waved cockle, prickly cockle, and large Scollop—are also given. These details were written down in tabular form by Richardson, and copies were made. Although the table was not printed until 1815, when it was inserted in a memoir accompanying the map, it is certain that manuscript copies were in circulation within a year or so, at first apparently unknown to Smith himself. To whom copies were distributed is not known, although in 1831 Richardson stated that he "without reserve gave a card of the English strata to Baron Rosencrantz, Dr Muller of Christiana, and many others, in the year 1801" (*Proceedings of the Geological Society*, **1** [1834], 276).

The first printed account of Smith's order of strata and of the fossils contained in different beds was published in the Reverend Richard Warner's *History of Bath* (Bath, 1801). Although brief and incomplete—and clearly not fully understood by Warner himself—on account of the date of publication it is of considerable significance. Warner, a Bath curate and also a well-known author, lived at Widcombe Cottage, situated between Bath and the Coal Canal. He was acquainted with Smith, who examined Warner's collection of fossils and arranged them stratigraphically. In the *History of Bath*, a short chapter (pp. 394–399) is entitled "Mineralogy and Fossilogy of Bath"; in this Warner stated that he would give a general view of the strata and their "fossilogical contents" and that a "more scientific and particular account" would soon be given in a work written by "the very ingenious Mr. Smith, of Midford, near Bath. . . ." Warner then briefly described the principal strata found near Bath, the "Forest Marble," the Bath freestone (Upper Oolite), the fuller's-earth beds, the lower freestone (Inferior Oolite), the sands and marls beneath it, and the Lias. Each description included the names (in a far more detailed form than in Smith's 1799 list) of the fossils associated with the particular bed. This account seems to be the first printed description of a succession of different strata accompanied by details of their fossil content, and it was certainly derived from Smith. The account could have been read by many visitors to Bath, where there were several subscription libraries.

After 1800 Smith's knowledge of the English strata and its fossils was made known to others by Richardson (whose rectory near Bath was frequented by many persons interested in geology); by Farey, who from 1806 published references to Smith and his discoveries; and by Townsend, who published *The Character of Moses Established for Veracity as an Historian* (Bath, 1813). Although this title appears to have little connection with geology, the book contains a detailed account of the English strata from Chalk to Carboniferous Limestone, with plates illustrating the fossils from different formations. Townsend readily acknowledged his debt to Smith and used a number of Smith's names for different strata, names designated "uncouth" by geologists of the Wernerian school but still familiar to every English geologist.

In 1822, W. D. Conybeare and W. Phillips wrote that Smith "had freely communicated the information he possessed in many quarters, till in fact it became by oral diffusion the common property of a large body of English geologists, and thus contributed to the progress of the science in many quarters where the author was little known" (*Outlines of the Geology of England and Wales* [London, 1822], xlv).

Smith's great work, *Delineation of the Strata of England and Wales With Part of Scotland*, was undoubtedly a major cartographic and scientific achievement. It represented about 65,000 square miles, was the first large-scale geological map of any country, and was based on the scientific principles discovered by Smith himself. Moreover, the coloring was designed to indicate not only the surface area of any one geological formation, but, by using a deeper shade along the base of a formation, an attempt was also made to show how the beds were superimposed; thus a structural factor was introduced.

This map owed remarkably little to the work of others. Smith's manuscript maps of 1801 and 1802 show his early grasp of the general succession across England; and a comparison of his 1815 map with a modern geological map of England, on the same scale, shows the extent of his knowledge. Errors, of course, were made, and the more important were pointed out in 1818 by Fitton (*Edinburgh Review*, **29**, 310–337). But the amount of correct detail that Smith recorded is amazing and still impresses modern geologists. A stratigraphical succession of twenty-one sedimentary beds or groups of beds was shown in different colors, and one more color was used for large masses of granite or other crystalline rocks. Different signs were used to indicate mines of tin, lead, and copper; for collieries; and for salt and alum works. Not content with the map as issued in 1815, during the next few years Smith continued to make small alterations and additions, marked by changes of coloring and engraving. A noteworthy addition, made soon after April 1816, was the insertion of another limestone distinguished by its fossils, the Coral Rag, colored in orange. This outcrop was added first in Berkshire, Oxfordshire, Somerset, and Wiltshire and later, perhaps in 1817, in Yorkshire.

Smith's other cartographic publications—his geological sections across parts of England and his county maps—demonstrate his continued interest in field geology and its economic importance. This interest is particularly well shown by his four-sheet map of Yorkshire (1821), which has many details concerning the coal seams and their accompanying grits and sandstones.

Although Smith's map was superseded in 1820 by the geological map compiled by Greenough (published by the Geological Society), his county maps were used by geologists for many years; and their value was acknowledged by Sedgwick in 1831 (*Proceedings of the Geological Society*, **1**, 278).

Smith's two publications on fossils, *Strata Iden-*tified and *Stratigraphical System*, were complementary to his cartographic work. They appeared at a time when some prominent geologists were still unwilling to admit the value of fossils in determining the stratigraphical succession, but within a few years this opposition was overcome. Smith's publications no doubt contributed to the changed outlook. Certainly no one could deny Smith's right to the title "Founder of Stratigraphical Geology."

BIBLIOGRAPHY

I. ORIGINAL WORKS. All known publications by Smith are listed in Joan M. Eyles, "William Smith (1769–1839): A Bibliography of His Published Writings, Maps and Geological Sections, Printed and Lithographed," in *Journal of the Society for the Bibliography of Natural History*, **5** (1969), 87–109. A large collection of his MSS is in the possession of the Department of Mineralogy and Geology, University of Oxford. His portrait in oils by Fourau (1837) is owned by the Geological Society of London.

II. SECONDARY LITERATURE. John Phillips published a biography soon after his uncle's death: *Memoirs of William Smith, LL.D.* (London, 1844). This work was the principal source of information about Smith until the discovery of his papers at Oxford in 1938. These were examined and arranged by L. R. Cox, who gave an account of them in "New Light on William Smith and His Work," in *Proceedings of the Yorkshire Geological Society*, **25** (1942), 1–99. A detailed and well-illustrated, although uncritical, account of Smith's principal publications is in T. Sheppard, "William Smith: His Maps and Memoirs," *ibid*, **19** (1917), 75–253; repr. (Hull, 1920). Both Sheppard and Cox provide extensive bibliographies, that by Cox being supplemental to Sheppard's. An account of Smith's 1797 MS list is given by J. A. Douglas and L. R. Cox, "An Early List of Strata by William Smith," in *Geological Magazine*, **86** (1849), 180–188.

The principal sources of information about Smith available to 1967 are described by J. M. Eyles in "William Smith: Some Aspects of His Life and Work," in C. J. Schneer, ed., *Toward a History of Geology*, (Cambridge, Mass., 1969), 142–158; details of Smith's work as related to the construction of the Somerset Coal Canal are also in this paper. Smith's work in Somerset is also described by John G. C. M. Fuller, "The Industrial Basis of Stratigraphy: John Strachey, 1671–1743 and William Smith, 1769–1839," in *American Association of Petroleum Geologists Bulletin*, **53** (1969), 2256–2273.

A useful collection of quotations by and about Smith is in D. A. Bassett, "William Smith, the Father of English Geology and Stratigraphy: An Anthology," in *Geology: Journal of the Association of Teachers of Geolo-*

gy, **1** (1969), 38–51. One aspect of Smith's economic work is described by J. M. Eyles, "William Smith (1769–1839) and the Search for Coal in Great Britain," in *Geologie*, **20** (1971), 710–714; his interest in technological developments is described in "William Smith, Richard Trevithick and Samuel Homfray: Their Correspondence on Steam Engines, 1804–06," in *Transactions of the Newcomen Society*, **43** (1974), 137–161; and the correct identification of Smith's property near Bath is made in "William Smith's Home Near Bath: the Real Tucking Mill," in *Journal of the Society for the Bibliography of Natural History*, **7** (1974), 29–34. A detailed account of the progressive changes in Smith's 1815 map is in V. A. Eyles and J. M. Eyles, "On the Different Issues of the First Geological Map of England and Wales," in *Annals of Science*, **3** (1938), 190–212.

A journey by Smith in 1813 is described by J. E. Hemingway and J. S. Owen, "William Smith and the Jurassic Coals of Yorkshire," in *Proceedings of the Yorkshire Geological Society*, **40** (1975), 297–308, and an account of his lectures in Yorkshire is given by J. M. Edmonds, "The Geological Lecture-Courses Given in Yorkshire by William Smith and John Phillips, 1824–1825," *ibid.*, **40** (1975), 373–412.

JOAN M. EYLES

SMITH, WILSON (*b.* Great Harwood, Lancashire, England, 21 June 1897; *d.* Newbury, Berkshire, England, 10 July 1965), *microbiology.*

Smith, whose father, John Howard Smith, kept a small retail drapery shop, grew up in a modest and serious-minded environment. This upbringing had a lasting influence on him, and he remained throughout his life a most earnest person with an intense devotion to his work. He served as a private in the Royal Army Medical Corps in World War I, an experience that determined his career in medicine. He qualified at Manchester University in 1923 and afterward practiced medicine for three years. From 1926 to 1927 he took his diploma in bacteriology at Manchester under W. W. C. Topley, who was mainly responsible for Smith's interest in medical research.

In 1927 Smith married Muriel Nutt, one of Topley's demonstrators, and moved to the National Institute for Medical Research in London. Here he associated with many notable scientists, including H. H. Dale, S. R. Douglas, Percival Hartley, Clifford Dobell, P. P. Laidlaw, and C. H. Andrewes, and entered what was then a comparatively new field, the study of viruses. In 1939 he became professor of bacteriology at Sheffield University and in 1946 returned to London as professor of bacteriology at University College Hospital Medical School.

In 1960 he retired but continued his researches at the Microbiological Research Establishment, Porton, and gave up working only a few months before his death.

At the National Institute for Medical Research, Smith first worked with vaccinia and herpes viruses, directing his researches toward elucidating the mechanisms of protection that immunized animals acquire against viral infections (1, 2, 3, 4). But his most important contribution to virology concerned influenza. Intensive efforts were being made at the National Institute to isolate the influenza virus, and many different species of animals were being inoculated with the throat garglings from suspected cases and also with lung material from fatal cases. No success was achieved until Smith decided to inoculate ferrets intranasally. The first isolation of influenza virus was made in February 1933, when two ferrets were inoculated with throat washings from Andrewes, who had suffered a serious attack of influenza. Unfortunately this strain of influenza virus was lost, because of an outbreak of distemper in the ferrets, but a month later Smith himself had influenza. It was suspected he had caught it from a ferret, and the virus was isolated from his throat garglings by inoculating them into ferrets. The WS strain still remains one of the classic strains (5).

The isolation of the influenza virus opened up a wide field of work at the institute, most of it being shared by Laidlaw, Smith, and Andrewes. It was shown that the virus can be serially transmitted in ferrets and that virus material from infected ferrets can infect mice on intranasal inoculation. This finding led to the development of methods of determining the degree of infectivity of viral material and of estimating the neutralizing antibody present in human sera. Further, it was shown that the virus can grow in fertile eggs and in tissue culture and that there are antigenic differences between strains of virus (6–16).

Smith's work in virology was interrupted by his move to Sheffield in 1939 and by the administrative responsibilities he took on because of the war, and also by a heavy load of teaching. On returning to London in 1946, he again worked in virology and led a team of young workers, many of whom now hold important positions in microbiology.

Smith became one of the leading virologists in the United Kingdom; and his advice was sought by many institutions, including the Medical Research Council, the Ministry of Health, the Agricultural Research Council, and the Microbiological Research Establishment. The value of his work was widely recognized, and he was elected a fellow of the Royal Society of London (1949) and of the Royal College of Physicians of London (1959).

BIBLIOGRAPHY

A complete bibliography of Smith's works is given by D. G. Evans in *Biographical Memoirs of Fellows of the Royal Society*, **12** (1966), 479–487. Among those mentioned above are:

(1) "The Distribution of Virus and Neutralizing Antibodies in the Blood and Pathological Exudates of Rabbits Infected With Vaccinia," in *British Journal of Experimental Pathology*, **10** (1929), 93–95.

(2) "Generalized Vaccinia in Rabbits With Especial Reference to Lesions in the Internal Organs," in *Journal of Pathology and Bacteriology*, **32** (1929), 99–100, written with Douglas and Price.

(3) "A Study of Vaccinal Immunity in Rabbits by Means of *in vitro* Methods," in *British Journal of Experimental Pathology*, **11** (1930), 96–99, written with Douglas.

(4) "Specific Antibody Absorption by Viruses of Vaccinia and Herpes," in *Journal of Pathology and Bacteriology*, **33** (1930), 273–276.

(5) "A Virus Obtained from Influenza Patients," in *Lancet* (1933), **2**, 66–68, written with Andrewes and Laidlaw.

(6) "The Susceptibility of Mice to the Viruses of Human and Swine Influenza," *ibid.* (1934), 859–864, written with Andrewes and Laidlaw.

(7) "Cultivation of the Virus of Influenza," in *British Journal of Experimental Pathology*, **16** (1935), 508–511.

(8) "Influenza: The Preparation of Immune Sera in Horses," *ibid.*, 275–282, written with Laidlaw *et al.*

(9) "Influenza: Experiments on the Immunization of Ferrets and Mice," *ibid.*, 291–301, written with Andrewes and Laidlaw.

(10) "Influenza: Observations on the Recovery of Virus From Man and on the Antibody Content of Human Sera," *ibid.*, 566–568, written with Andrewes and Laidlaw.

(11) "Influenza Infection of Man from the Ferret," in *Lancet* (1936), **2**, 121–125, written with Stuart-Harris.

(12) "The Complement Fixation Reaction in Influenza," *ibid.*, 1256–1258.

(13) "Influenza: Further Experiments on the Active Immunization of Mice," in *British Journal of Experimental Pathology*, **18** (1937), 43–46, written with Andrewes.

(14) "Immunological Observation on Experimental Influenza," in *Proceedings of the International Congress of Microbiology* (1937), 107–110.

(15) "A Study of Epidemic Influenza: With Special Reference to the 1936–1937 Epidemic," *Report of the Medical Research Council*, no. 228 (1938), written with Stuart-Harris and Andrewes.

(16) "Serological Races of Influenza Virus," in *British Journal of Experimental Pathology*, **19** (1938), 293–297.

D. G. EVANS

SMITHELLS, ARTHUR (*b.* Bury, Lancashire, England, 24 May 1860; *d.* Highgate, London, England, 8 February 1939), *chemistry*.

Smithells was an articulate spokesman for chemistry, chemical education, and the larger cultural dimensions of chemistry. His research contributed to the understanding of combustion and the structure of flames.

Smithells was the third son of James Smithells, a railway manager, and Martha Livesey. From 1875 to 1877 he studied physics and chemistry under Kelvin and Ferguson at the University of Glasgow, where he developed an abiding interest in the latter. Then, for the next five years, he studied chemistry under Roscoe and Schorlemmer at Owens College in Manchester. He received the B.Sc. in 1881 from the University of London and then became an "Associate" of Owens College until 1882, when he went to Munich to pursue his studies in chemistry with Baeyer and then to Heidelberg to study with Bunsen. The following year he returned to Manchester as assistant lecturer in chemistry. In 1885, at the age of only twenty-five, he succeeded T. E. Thorpe as professor of chemistry at the University of Leeds.

Smithells discovered a method for separating the two cones of the flame of a Bunsen burner and found that the inner cone contains residual hydrogen. Since it had been thought previously that hydrogen was burned preferentially, Smithells' discovery led to further investigations in combustion. He also conducted extensive research into the structure of flames and the luminosity of gases, but this work was inhibited by his administrative duties.

In 1901 Smithells was elected a fellow of the Royal Society, and in 1918 he was made a companion of the Order of St. Michael and St. George for his skilled organization of antigas training. He was also involved in educational reform: he strongly opposed specialized universities and advocated the integration of pure and applied science in the university curriculum. He also wished to extend science to the practical problems of daily life.

In 1907 Smithells was elected president of the chemistry section of the British Association for the Advancement of Science. In his presidential address he stressed the importance of atomic research and of the new investigations prompted by the discovery of radioactivity. Because of these scientific developments, the chemist, whose work had previously been "confined to comparatively gross quantities of matter," was called upon to examine and reinterpret earlier theories concerning the ultimate constituents of matter.

In 1923 Smithells resigned his chair at Leeds and moved to London, where, as director of Salters' Institute of Industrial Chemistry, he was influential in admitting students of chemistry. He retired in 1937, two years before his death.

BIBLIOGRAPHY

I. ORIGINAL WORKS. Many of Smithells' scientific works are listed in the Royal Society *Catalogue of Scientific Papers*, **18**, p. 820. His major works are "The Structure and Chemistry of Flames," in *Journal of the Chemical Society*, **61** (1892), 204–216, written with H. Ingle; and "The Electrical Conductivity and Luminosity of Flames Containing Vaporised Salts," in *Philosophical Transactions of the Royal Society*, **193A** (1900), 89–128, written with H. M. Dawson and H. A. Wilson. His address to the British Association appeared in *Report of the British Association for the Advancement of Science* (1907), 469–479; he also published a collection of his addresses in *From a Modern University* (Oxford, 1921). Smithells edited Schorlemmer's *The Rise and Development of Organic Chemistry*, 2nd ed. (London, 1894).

An autobiographical letter dated 2 May 1893 exists in the Krause *Album*, IV, MSS 7766, Sondersammlungen, Bibliothek, Deutsches Museum, Munich. MacLeod, *Archives*, indicates that many of his papers are held by Professor Phillip Smithells, 2 Pollock St., Maori Hill, Dunedin, New Zealand. There are several items in the Royal Institution, Imperial College, and at the University of Leeds.

II. SECONDARY LITERATURE. Smithells' former student J. W. Cobb wrote "Professor A. Smithells, C.M.G., F.R.S.," in *Nature*, **143** (1939), 321–322. He also wrote the article in the *Dictionary of National Biography 1931–1940*, 820–821, and one in *Journal of the Chemical Society* (July 1939), 1234–1236. H. S. Raper, another student, wrote the article in *Obituary Notices of Fellows of the Royal Society*, **8** (1940), 97–107. An anonymous note appeared in *The Annual Register* (1939), 428.

THADDEUS J. TRENN

SMITHSON, JAMES LOUIS MACIE (*b.* Paris, France, 1765; *d.* Genoa, Italy, 27 June 1829), *chemistry.*

Smithson was the illegitimate son of Hugh Smithson Percy, first duke of Northumberland, and Elizabeth Hungerford Keate Macie, who was the widow of James Macie, a country gentleman of Bath, England. While pregnant, his mother had gone to Paris, where Smithson was born in 1765; but no record has been found of the exact date of birth. Until the age of thirty-six he was known as James Louis Macie. He took the surname Smithson on 16 February 1801. Upon the death of his mother in 1800, James acquired a small fortune, which enabled him to support his researches and extensive travels.

At the age of ten, Smithson returned to England with his mother, where he was naturalized a British subject; but a provision was made at the time that he could not hold public office (civil or military) or have any grant of land from the crown. On 7 May 1782 he entered Pembroke College, Oxford, and subsequently took his master of arts on 26 May 1786. He was attracted to the study of chemistry and mineralogy, and having been sponsored by Kirwan and Cavendish, he became a fellow of the Royal Society on 26 April 1787. He also may have worked in the private laboratory of Cavendish at that time.

Smithson read his first paper before the Royal Society on 7 July 1791. The paper concerned a study of the chemical properties of tabasheer, a substance found in bamboo. He also was listed as a charter member of the Royal Institution. His most important work, "A Chemical Analysis of Some Calamines," was read before the Royal Society on 18 November 1802 and published in the *Philosophical Transactions*. He analyzed zinc ores from various European deposits and showed them to be primarily zinc carbonate. Since his analytical techniques were creditable, and as a result of his study, the mineral zinc carbonate was named smithsonite in his honor. Smithson published twenty-seven papers on chemical subjects in the *Philosophical Transactions* and the *Annals of Philosophy*, but his importance as a chemist is minimal.

Smithson is remembered chiefly because he left money for founding the Smithsonian Institution in Washington, D.C. On 23 October 1826 Smithson prepared his will, according to which he left his estate to Henry James Hungerford, his nephew. There was the following stipulation:

In the case of the death of my said Nephew without leaving a child or children, or the death of the child or children he may have had under the age of twenty-one years or intestate, I then bequeath the whole of my property subject to the Annuity of One Hundred pounds to John Fitall, & for the security & payment of which I mean Stock to remain in this Country, to the United States of America, to found at Washington, under the name of the Smithsonian Institution, an Establishment for the increase & diffusion of knowledge among men.

On 27 June 1829 James Smithson died in Genoa, Italy, at the age of sixty-four; his estate passed to his nephew. On 5 June 1835 the nephew died without heirs, and the United States Government was notified of its claim to the estate. The claim was prosecuted, and within three years the estate, which amounted to $508,318.46, was shipped to the United States Mint at Philadelphia. It was not until 10 August 1846 that Congress agreed to the disposition of the money and the founding of the Smithsonian Institution. This delay was due to disagreement among Congressional leaders as to the nature of the proposed institution. Among the schemes suggested were an observatory, a library, a university, and a museum. On 3 December 1846 Joseph Henry was elected the first secretary of the Smithsonian Institution, and he guided its development as primarily a scientific institution.

In 1904 the remains of James Smithson were brought to Washington from Genoa and interred in the original Smithsonian building.

BIBLIOGRAPHY

I. ORIGINAL WORKS. Much of the papers, personal library, and mineral collections of James Smithson, which were brought to the United States and housed in the Smithsonian Institution, were destroyed in a fire of 1865. His twenty-seven published scientific papers were edited by William J. Rhees and published in 1879 by the Smithsonian Institution; see *Smithsonian Miscellaneous Collections*, **21** (1881).

II. SECONDARY LITERATURE. Many of the details of Smithson's life have been documented by biographers, but much of his life remains unrecorded. Some of the notable biographical sketches include Leonard Carmichael and J. C. Long, *James Smithson and the Smithsonian Story* (New York, 1965); Samuel P. Langley, "Biographical Sketch of James Smithson," in George Brown Goode, ed., *The Smithsonian Institution 1846–1896, the History of Its First Half-Century* (Washington, D.C., 1897), 1–24; Paul H. Oehser, *Sons of Science* (New York, 1949), 1–25; and W. J. Rhees, *James Smithson and His Bequest* (Washington, D.C., 1880), also in *Smithsonian Miscellaneous Collections*, **21** (1881).

DANIEL P. JONES

SMITS, ANDREAS (*b.* Woerden, Netherlands, 14 June 1870; *d.* Doorn, Netherlands, 13 November 1948), *physical chemistry.*

Smits first studied chemistry at the University of Utrecht and then entered the University of Giessen, from which he received the Ph.D. *magna cum laude* (1896) for his dissertation "Untersuchungen mit dem Mikromanometer." Two years later he was appointed chemist at the Municipal Gasworks in Amsterdam, and in 1901 he became a privatdocent in chemistry at the University of Amsterdam. He subsequently was named professor of general chemistry at the University of Technology at Delft (1906), and in 1907 succeeded Roozeboom as professor of chemistry at Amsterdam. He held this latter post until his retirement in 1940.

During these years, Smits's scientific research covered three fields. Prior to 1905 he studied the relationship in dilute solutions between the decrease in vapor pressure and the elevation of the boiling point. Also, he determined the so-called van't Hoff factor i (or ionic coefficient) for different aqueous concentrations of various salts. After 1924 he investigated the possibility of metal interconvertibility — especially of lead into mercury — by various means, using a quartz-lead lamp; sparks or electric arc between lead electrodes; and solar, X, and ultraviolet radiation.

Smits's major research, however, was in phase theory, especially in three-component systems with critical endpoints where two phases are identical; and in so-called pseudobinary systems. Smits thought that every component of a pseudobinary system actually contains two types of molecules. A pseudobinary system is a one-component system the molecules of which are chemically the same, but nevertheless may be divided into two types differing from one another in respect of "physical" properties, and there exists an equilibrium between the two types. He defended this theory throughout his career and tried to apply it to allotropic forms; the phenomena of passivity, polarization, and overvoltage in metals; electromotive equilibriums; ortho- and para-hydrogen systems; intensively dried substances; and continuous transitions.

Many of Smits's investigations (both independent and with his students) are summarized in two books: *Die Theorie der Allotropie* (1921) and *Die Theorie der Komplexität und der Allotropie* (1938).

BIBLIOGRAPHY

I. ORIGINAL WORKS. A complete bibliography of Smits's writing is in *Chemisch weekblad*, **3** (1906), 582–

583; **28** (1931), 561–566; **37** (1940), 435–436; and **45** (1949), 151. His major works include "Untersuchungen mit dem Mikromanometer" (Ph.D. diss., Univ. of Giessen, 1896), which appeared in part in *Verslagen en mededeelingen der Koninklijke Akademie van Wetenschappen*, **5** (1897), 292–295; *Die Theorie der Allotropie* (Leipzig, 1921), with trans. by J. S. Thomas as *The Theory of Allotropy* (London, 1922); and *Die Theorie der Komplexität und der Allotropie* (Berlin, 1938).

II. Secondary Literature. On Smits and his work, see J. M. Bijvoet, "Prof. Dr. A. Smits. 4 October 1906–4 October 1931," in *Chemisch weekblad*, **28** (1931), 555–559; F. E. C. Scheffer, "Het 25-jarig hoogleeraarschap van Prof. Dr. A. Smits. Enkele persoonlijke herinneringen," *ibid.*, **28** (1931), 560–561; the unsigned "Professor Dr. A. Smits. 14 Juni 1870–14 Juni 1940," *ibid.*, **37** (1940), 430–435; and E. H. Buchner, "Andreas Smits 1870–1948," *ibid.*, **45** (1949), 149–151.

H. A. M. Snelders

SMOLUCHOWSKI, MARIAN (*b.* Vorderbrühl, near Vienna, Austria, 28 May 1872; *d.* Cracow, Poland, 5 September 1917), *physics*.

Born to a Polish family, Smoluchowski spent his youth in Vienna. His father, Wilhelm, was a senior official in the chancellery of Emperor Franz Josef; his mother was the former Teofila Szczepanowska. Smoluchowski attended the Collegium Theresianum from 1880 to 1885 and was an outstanding student. From 1890 to 1895 he studied at the University of Vienna under the direction of Josef Stefan and F. Exner; his doctoral dissertation was entitled "Akustische Untersuchungen über die Elastizität weicher Körper."

From November 1895 to August 1897 Smoluchowski worked under Lippmann in Paris, with Lord Kelvin in Glasgow, and with Warburg in Berlin. Two papers published during his stay in Paris dealt with thermal radiation (the Kirchhoff-Clausius law). At Glasgow he investigated the influence of Röntgen and Becquerel rays on the conductance of gases. In 1901 Smoluchowski received the LL.D. from Glasgow, where he had been a research fellow. In Berlin he worked on the discontinuity of temperature in gases, a problem suggested to him by Warburg. In 1875 Warburg and A. Kundt, on the basis of the kinetic theory of gases, had predicted that if the temperature of a gas differed from that of the container wall, the former temperature would not pass continuously to the latter: there would be a discontinuity of temperature between the gas and the wall. Their experiments, successful in the case of the analogous phenom-enon of the slipping of gases, had not been decisive for temperature discontinuity. Smoluchowski, observing the cooling time of a thermometer in a gas-filled container, demonstrated that such an effect exists and reached significant values with rarefied gas in "Uber Wärmeleitung in verdünnten Gasen" (1898).

This work was of special importance, for by publishing it Smoluchowski joined the dispute on the validity of atomic conceptions. These, represented in physics mainly by the kinetic theory of gases developed by Boltzmann, were far from accepted at the end of the nineteenth century; and their recognition was partly due to Smoluchowski. At that time only a few phenomena were predicted by the kinetic theory or required it for intelligibility. Among them was discontinuity of temperature, for its existence was wholly unexplained from a classical point of view. Moreover, in 1897, after his return to Vienna, Smoluchowski pointed out the quantitative agreement of his experimental results with the kinetic theory. In 1898 the University of Vienna admitted him *veniam legendi*.

From 1899 Smoluchowski worked at the University of Lvov. Appointed professor in 1900, he held the chair of mathematical physics there until 1913. His first works at Lvov concerned atmospheric physics, aerodynamics and hydrodynamics, electrophoresis, and the theory of mountain folding. Recognition for these specialized works was shown by his being asked to write the chapter on endosmosis phenomena in *Handbuch der Elektrizität und des Magnetismus,* edited by J. A. Barth (Leipzig, 1914).

From about 1900 Smoluchowski worked on Brownian movement. He wished to use experimental data to verify the theory he had obtained, a desire complicated by the confused situation of experimental research. In the meantime Einstein, in papers of 1905 and 1906, had presented a solution to the problem. Smoluchowski then decided to publish his results in "Zarys kinetycznej teorii ruchów Browna" ("An Outline of the Kinetic Theory of Brownian Movement," 1906), which presented his different method. Einstein started from general relations of statistical physics, an approach that was universal but did not lend itself to visualization. For example, Einstein said nothing of the collisions between a Brownian particle and the surrounding molecules. Smoluchowski started by examining the effects of successive collisions and obtained a final formula that differed little from Einstein's. Smoluchowski's further works in this field extend through an examination of the Brownian movement of a particle undergoing the influence of a quasi-elastic force to the Brownian movements of macroscopic bodies. At the Conference of Natural Scientists at Münster in 1912, Smoluchowski proposed the observation of the Brownian rotative movement of a small mirror suspended on a thin quartz fiber and the observation of a free end of a similar fiber. The first experiment was performed by W. Gerlach and E. Lehrer in 1927, and later by Eugen Kappler; the second, by A. Houjdik and P. Zeeman, and by E. Einthoven, in 1925. Both experiments confirmed Smoluchowski's calculations.

Another of Smoluchowski's interests concerned fluctuations and was related to the second law of thermodynamics. The kinetic approach to the second law proposed by Boltzmann implied the occurrence of spontaneous deviations from a state of maximum entropy. Because the occurrence of such deviations had not been experimentally confirmed, however, the kinetic theory lay open to attack. Boltzmann, in defense, calculated the time of return for given micro states and showed how rare and difficult to observe these phenomena are. Smoluchowski, on the other hand, laid the foundations of the theory of fluctuations, calculated the times of return for macro states, linked the theory to measurable parameters, and proved the actual existence of fluctuations.

In his first paper dealing with this problem, "Über Unregelmässigkeiten in der Verteilung von Gasmolekülen" (1904), Smoluchowski gave a theoretical approach to the fluctuations of density in a gas. At the same time he indicated the experimental possibility of detecting these fluctuations either by optical methods or when the number of particles is not too great, as in the case of colloidal suspensions. In 1910 Theodor Svedberg based his experiments on Smoluchowski's calculations, observing how many particles of a suspension can be seen in the field of vision of a microscope at a given time and experimentally confirming Smoluchowski's predictions to an astonishingly high degree. Smoluchowski himself had previously proved the existence of fluctuations of density in a pure gas by demonstrating that they are responsible for the known but unexplained phenomenon of the opalescence of a gas at a critical state. His paper "Teoria kinetyczna opalescencji gazów w stanie krytycznym" ("Kinetic Theory of Gas Opalescence at the Critical State," 1907) shows why the critical point plays such an important role and

states that the opalescence of a pure gas also should be observable under normal conditions: "Each of us has observed it innumerable times when admiring the blue of the sky or the glow of the rising sun." Smoluchowski combined the theory of fluctuations with the results of Lord Rayleigh's researches on the blue of the sky; his finding (Einstein also took part in the discussion) was that the blueness of the sky was caused by fluctuations in the density of the air. Smoluchowski's laboratory production of sky blue closed the investigation to a certain extent. In "Experimentelle Bestätigung der Rayleighschen Theorie des Himmelsblaus" (1916) Smoluchowski demonstrated that pure air can opalesce in the laboratory under normal conditions.

Experimental proofs of the existence of fluctuations and the revelation of the causes of Brownian movement have limited the validity of the classical formulation of the second law of thermodynamics. A new, statistical formulation of this principle that had been initiated by Boltzmann was developed by Smoluchowski. He concluded that the deeper one goes into microscopic processes, the more visible the reversibility becomes. Macroscopic processes, although theoretically reversible, are practically irreversible because of the unimaginably long times of return. Statistical interpretation of the second law gave ground, at that time, for hopes of constructing the *perpetuum mobile* of the second kind. Smoluchowski resolved this question in his lectures at Münster (1912) and Göttingen (1914): If we expect great deviations from the state of maximum entropy, the efficiency of the machine will be infinitesimal, since great deviations are extremely rare; and if we hope for microscopic deviations, the valves and other parts needed to eliminate deviations occurring in an adverse direction will have to be so fine that they themselves will undergo Brownian movement and will not be able to perform their task. Thus it is not possible to construct a *perpetuum mobile* of the second kind if we mean a machine with any finite efficiency.

Smoluchowski obtained important results in the physics of colloids. His interest in the methodology of teaching physics can be seen in the chapters he wrote for *Poradnik dla samouków* ("Primer for Home Studies"), edited by A. Heflich and S. Michalski (Warsaw, 1917). The title of the book is a bit misleading, for it is really a report on physical research and aims.

In 1913 Smoluchowski became professor of experimental physics at the Jagiellonian University in Cracow. In 1917 he was elected rector of the university. Later that year he died of dysentery, at the age of forty-five.

BIBLIOGRAPHY

I. ORIGINAL WORKS. Smoluchowski's writings were collected as *Pisma Mariana Smoluchowskiego* ("The Works of Marian Smoluchowski"), W. Natanson, ed., 3 vols. (Cracow, 1924–1928). Besides texts in Polish, this collection includes versions published in other languages.

His most important works are "Über Wärmeleitung in verdünnten Gasen," in *Annalen der Physik und Chemie*, **64** (1898), 101–130; "Uber Unregelmässigkeiten in der Verteilung von Gasmolekülen und deren Einfluss auf Entropie und Zustandsgleichung," in *Boltzmann-Festschrift* (Leipzig, 1904), 626–641; "Zur kinetischen Theorie der Brownschen Molekularbewegung und der Suspensionen," in *Annalen der Physik*, 4th ser., **21** (1906), 756–780; "Molekular-kinetische Theorie der Opaleszenz von Gasen im kritischen Zustande, sowie einiger verwandter Erscheinungen," *ibid.*, **25** (1908), 205–226; "Beitrag zur Theorie der Opaleszenz von Gasen im kritischen Zustande," in *Bulletin international de l'Académie des sciences et des lettres de Cracovie*, ser. A (1911), 493–502; "Experimentell nachweisbare, der üblichen Thermodynamik widersprechende Molekularphänomene," in *Physikalische Zeitschrift*, **13** (1912), 1069–1079; "Gültigkeitsgrenzen des zweiten Hauptsatzes der Wärmetheorie," in *Vorträge über die kinetische Theorie der Materie und der Elektrizität* (Leipzig–Berlin, 1914), 89; "Studien über Molekularstatistik von Emulsionen und deren Zusammenhang mit der Brownschen Bewegung," in *Sitzungsberichte der Akademie der Wissenschaften in Wien*, Math.-nat. Kl., Abt. IIa, **123** (1914), 2381–2405; "Molekular-theoretische Studien über umkehr thermodynamisch irreversibler Vorgänge und über Wiederkehr abnormaler Zustände," *ibid.*, **124** (1915), 339–368; "Über Brownsche Molekularbewegung unter Einwirkung äusserer Kräfte und deren Zusammenhang mit der verallgemeinerten Diffusionsgleichung," in *Annalen der Physik*, **48** (1915), 1103–1112; "Experimentelle Bestätigung der Rayleighschen Theorie des Himmelsblaus," in *Bulletin international de l'Académie des sciences et des lettres de Cracovie*, ser. A (1916), 218–222; "Drei Vorträge über Diffusion, Brownsche Molekularbewegung und Koagulation von Kolloidteilchen," in *Physikalische Zeitschrift*, **17** (1916), 557–571, 585–599; and "Über den Begriff des Zufalls und den Ursprung der Wahrscheinlichkeitsgesetze in der Physik," in *Naturwissenschaften*, **6** (1918), 253–263.

II. SECONDARY LITERATURE. Polish sources are W. Kapuściński, "Poglądy filozoficzne Mariana Smoluchowskiego" ("Marian Smoluchowski's Philosophical Views"), in *Fizyka i chemia*, **6** (1953), 200; W. Krajewski, *Swiatopogląd Mariana Smoluchowskiego* ("Marian Smoluchowski's *Weltanschauung*"; Warsaw, 1956); S. Loria, "Marian Smoluchowski i jego dzieło" ("Marian Smoluchowski and His Work"), in *Postępy fizyki*, **4** (1953), 5; and A. Teske, *Marian Smoluchowski—życie i twórczość* ("Marian Smoluchowski—Life and Work"; Warsaw, 1955).

Other sources are A. Einstein, "Marian von Smoluchowski," in *Naturwissenschaften*, **5** (1917), 737–738; A. Sommerfeld, "Zum Andenken an Marian von Smoluchowski," in *Physikalische Zeitschrift*, **18** (1917), 533–539, with bibliography; A. Teske, "An Outline Account of the Work of Marian Smoluchowski," in *Études consacrées à Maria Skłodowska-Curie et à Marian Smoluchowski* (Wrocław–Warsaw–Cracow, 1970); and S. Ulam, "Marian Smoluchowski and the Theory of Probabilities in Physics," in *American Journal of Physics*, **25** (1957), 475–481.

ANDRZEJ A. TESKE

SMYTH, CHARLES PIAZZI (*b*. Naples, Italy, 3 January 1819; *d*. Clova, near Ripon, Scotland, 21 February 1900), *astronomy, meteorology*.

Smyth was named after Giuseppe Piazzi, the astronomer-friend of Smyth's father, William Henry Smyth (1788–1865), who was stationed in Italy with the Royal Navy when Smyth was born. In 1825 the Smyth family returned to England and settled at Bedford, where Smyth's father established the Bedford observatory, the best-equipped private observatory in England.

Smyth was educated at the Bedford grammar school. From 1835 to 1845 he served as assistant to Maclear at the royal observatory, Cape of Good Hope. There Smyth observed and drew the great comets of 1836 and 1843, and participated in the verification and extension of Lacaille's arc of meridian. In 1845 Smyth was appointed successor to Thomas Henderson as director of the Edinburgh observatory, a position that included the additional titles astronomer royal for Scotland and professor of practical astronomy in the University of Edinburgh. Although under his direction the Edinburgh observatory produced observations of the positions of the sun, moon, planets, and stars, Smyth was primarily interested in more experimental and speculative matters.

In 1856 Smyth led an expedition to the Peak of Tenerife, primarily "to ascertain how much astronomical observation can be benefited, by eliminating the lower third or fourth part of the atmosphere" (C. P. Smyth, *Report on the Teneriffe Astronomical Experiment* [London, 1858]). Financial support for this experiment was given by the British Admiralty, and moral support by the entire British scientific community. In addition to telescopic observations of planets and stars, Smyth measured the radiant heat of the moon; observed the solar spectrum and noted which lines of absorption were of terrestrial origin; and made various other observations of the meteorology, geology, and botany of the island.

With his wife Smyth spent four months in 1865 in Egypt, where he measured the orientation, sizes, and angles of the various parts of the Great Pyramid at Giza, and correlated the results with astronomical phenomena. Smyth's measurements earned him the Keith Prize of the Royal Society of Edinburgh. His speculations on the mysteries hidden within the pyramid sparked an acrimonious debate, which led to his resignation from the Royal Society of London.

Smyth also charted the spectra of the sun, aurora, zodiacal light, the atmosphere under different meteorological conditions, and—in the laboratory—of various luminous gases. In order to resolve difficult solar lines, he obtained Rutherfurd and then Rowland diffraction gratings; and, in search of clearer atmosphere than Edinburgh afforded, Smyth traveled to Palermo, Portugal, Madeira, and Winchester. For his spectroscopic studies Smyth won the Makdougall-Brisbane Prize of the Royal Society of Edinburgh.

Like his father, Smyth was a member of numerous societies. Toward the end of his life he signed his name "C. Piazzi Smyth, F.R.S.E., F.R.A.S., F.R.S.S.A., Corresponding Member of the Academies of Science in Munich and Palermo; honorary member of the Royal Society of Modena, of the Institute of Engineers in Scotland, and of the Edinburgh Photographic Society; Regius Professor of Practical Astronomy in the University of Edinburgh, and Astronomer-Royal for Scotland; also Ex-Member of the Royal Society, London" (*Astronomical Observations Made at the Royal Observatory, Edinburgh*, **15** [1886]).

BIBLIOGRAPHY

I. ORIGINAL WORKS. Smyth's works include *Astronomical Observations Made at the Royal Observatory, Edinburgh*: vols. VI–X (1847–1852) contain observations made by T. Henderson, reduced and edited by C. P. Smyth; vols. XI–XV (1852–1880) contain observations made under Smyth's directorship; *Paris Universal Exposition of 1855 . . . Description of New or Improved Instruments for Navigation and Astronomy* (Edinburgh, 1855); *Teneriffe: An Astronomer's Experiment; or Specialities of a Residence Above the Clouds . . . Illustrated With Photo-Stereographs* (London, 1858); *Report on the Teneriffe Astronomical Experiment of 1856, Addressed to the Lords Commissioners of the Admiralty* (London, 1858), repr. from *Philosophical Transactions of the Royal Society*; and *Three Cities in Russia*, 2 vols. (London, 1862).

See also *Our Inheritance in the Great Pyramid . . .* (London, 1864; 5th enl. ed., 1890); *Life and Work at the Great Pyramid During the Months of January, February, March, and April, A.D. 1865; With a Discussion of the Facts Ascertained*, 3 vols. (Edinburgh, 1867); *On the Antiquity of Intellectual Man, From a Practical and Astronomical Point of View* (Edinburgh, 1868); *A Poor Man's Photography at the Great Pyramid in . . . 1865, Compared With That of the Ordnance Survey Establishment . . .* (London, 1870); *On an Equal-Surface Projection for Maps of the World, and Its Application to Certain Anthropological Questions* (Edinburgh, 1870); *The Great Pyramid and the Royal Society (London)* (London, 1874); *Madeira Spectroscopic, Being a Revision of 21 Places in the Red Half of the Solar Visible Spectrum, With a Rutherfurd Diffraction Grating, at Madeira . . . During the Summer of 1881* (Edinburgh, 1882); and *Madeira Meteorologic* (Edinburgh 1882). In addition to the above, the catalog of the British Museum Library lists several responses to Smyth's ideas about the Great Pyramid. The Royal Society *Catalogue of Scientific Papers*, V, 735–737; VIII, 976; XI, 443–444; XVIII, 823; and Poggendorff, III, 1261–1262, list over 130 articles by Smyth.

II. SECONDARY LITERATURE. On Smyth and his work, see the obituaries by Ralph Copeland, in *Monthly Notices of the Royal Astronomical Society*, **61** (1901), 189–196; in *Popular Astronomy*, **8** (1900), 384–387 (also in *Astronomische Nachrichten*, **152** [1900], 189); and in *Observatory*, **23** (1900), 145–147. See also the article by Agnes Clerk, in *Dictionary of National Biography*, XXII, 1222–1223.

DEBORAH JEAN WARNER

SNEL (Snellius or **Snel van Royen), WILLEBRORD** (*b.* Leiden, Netherlands, 1580; *d.* Leiden, 30 October 1626), *mathematics, optics, astronomy.*

Snel was the son of Rudolph Snellius, or Snel van Royen, professor of mathematics at the new University of Leiden, and of Machteld Cornelisdochter. He studied law at the university but became interested in mathematics at an early age. Through the influence of Van Ceulen, Stevin, and his father, he received permission in 1600 to teach mathematics at the university. Soon afterward he left for Würzburg, where he met Van Roomen. He then went to Prague to conduct observations under Tycho. He also met Kepler, and traveled to Altdorf and Tübingen, where he saw Mästlin, Kepler's teacher. In 1602 Snel studied law in Paris. He returned home in 1604, after having traveled to Switzerland with his father, who was then in Kassel at the court of the learned Prince Maurice of Hesse.

At Leiden, Snel prepared a Latin translation of Stevin's *Wisconstighe Ghedachtenissen*, which was then being published; Snel's translation appeared as *Hypomnemata mathematica* (1608). He also busied himself with the restoration of the two books of Apollonius on plane loci, preserved only in abstract by Pappus. Related tasks on other books of Apollonius also occupied Viète (*Apollonius gallus* [1600]) and Ghetaldi (*Apollonius redivivus* [1607–1613]). Snel's work was in three parts: the first remained in manuscript and is preserved at the library of the University of Leiden; the second appeared under the title Περὶ λόγου ἀποτομῆς καὶ περὶ χωρίου ἀποτομῆς *resuscita geometria* (1607); and the third was published as *Apollonius batavus* (1608).

In 1608 Snel received the M.A. and married Maria De Lange, daughter of a burgomaster of Schoonhoven; only three of their eighteen children survived. After his father's death in March 1613, Snel succeeded him at the university, and two years later he became professor. He taught mathematics, astronomy, and optics, using some instruments in his instruction.

Sharing the admiration of his father and of Maurice of Hesse for Ramus, Snel published Ramus' *Arithmetica*, with commentary, in 1613. He later published *P. Rami Meetkonst* (1622), an annotated Dutch translation by Dirck Houtman of Ramus' *Geometria*. It was the only one of Snel's works to be published in Amsterdam; all the others appeared at Leiden. Snel's *De re numeraria* (dedicated to Grotius), a short work on money in Israel, Greece, and Rome, also dates from 1613.

During this period Snel prepared the Latin translation of two books by Van Ceulen, probably at the request of his widow, Adriana Symons. His rather careless translation of *Van den Circkel* includes some notes by Snel, among them the expression $\sqrt{(s-a)(s-b)(s-c)(s-d)}$ for the area of a cyclic quadrilateral. Although this expression had already appeared in the work of Brahmagupta, it seems to be the first time that it was used in Europe.

Snel's lack of attention to this translation may have been due to preoccupation with geodetic work. In 1615 he became deeply involved in the determination of the length of the meridian, selecting for this work the method of triangulation, first proposed by Gemma Frisius in 1533 and also used

by Tycho. Snel developed it to such an extent that he may rightfully be called the father of triangulation. Starting with his house (marked by a memorial plaque in 1960), he used the spires of town churches as points of reference. Thus, through a net of triangles, he computed the distance from Alkmaar to Bergen-op-Zoom (around 130 kilometers). The two towns lie on approximately the same meridian. Snel used the distance from Leiden to Zoeterwoude (about 5 kilometers) as a baseline. His instruments were made by Blaeu; and the huge, 210-centimeter quadrant used for his triangulations is suspended in the hall of the Leiden astronomical observatory. The unit of measure was the Rhineland rod (1 rod = 3.767 meters), recommended by Stevin to the States General in 1604 (Stevin, *Principal Works*, IV [1964], 24); and, following Stevin, the rod was divided into tenths and hundredths. The results were presented in *Eratosthenes batavus* (1617).

In order to locate his house with respect to three towers in Leiden, Snel solved the so-called recession problem for three points. The problem is often named after Snel, as well as after L. Pothenot (1692); and claims have been made for Ptolemy.

Dissatisfied with his geodetic work, Snel began to correct it, aided by his pupils, and extended his measurements to include the distance from Bergen-op-Zoom to Mechelen. Unaided by logarithms, he continued this work throughout his life. His early death in 1626 prevented him from publishing his computations, which are preserved in his own copy of *Eratosthenes batavus* at the Royal Library in Brussels. They were recently checked by N. D. Haasbroek and were found to be conscientious and remarkably accurate. Haasbroek could not say as much for the way in which Musschenbroek handled these notes in his "De magnitudine terrae," in *Physicae experimentales* . . . (1729).

Snel published some observations by Bürgi and Tycho in 1618, and his descriptions of the comets of 1585 and 1618, published in 1619, show Snel to be a follower of the Ptolemaic system. Although he demonstrated from the parallax that the comet was beyond the moon and therefore could not consist of terrestrial vapors, he still believed in the character of comets as omina.

In the *Cyclometricus* (1621) π was found, by Van Ceulen's methods, to thirty-four decimals; and the thirty-fifth decimal, found in Van Ceulen's papers, was added. Snel also explained his own shorter method, following and improving on Van Lansberge's *Cyclometria nova* (1616), establishing the inequality

$$\frac{3\sin\varphi}{2+\cos\varphi} < \varphi < \tan\frac{\varphi}{3} + 2\sin\frac{\varphi}{3},$$

of which the inequality to the left agrees with Cusa's result in *Perfectio mathematica* (1458).

In 1624 Snel published his lessons on navigation in *Tiphys batavus* (Tiphys was the pilot of the *Argo*). The work is mainly a study and tabulation of Pedro Nuñez' so-called rhumb lines (1537), which Snel named "loxodromes." His consideration of a small spherical triangle bounded by a loxodrome, a parallel, and a meridian circle as a plane right triangle foreshadows the differential triangle of Pascal and later mathematicians.

The last works published by Snel himself were *Canon triangulorum* (1626) and *Doctrina triangulorum* (1627), the latter completed by his pupil Hortensius. The *Doctrina*, which comprise a plane and spherical trigonometry, includes the recession problem for two points, often named after P. A. Hansen (1841). It uses the polar triangle for the computation of the sides of a spherical triangle.

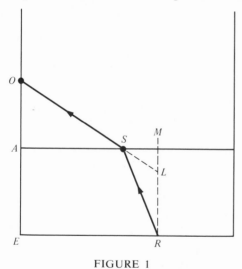

FIGURE 1

Snel's best-known discovery, the law of refraction of light rays, which was named after him, was formulated probably in or after 1621, and was the result of many years of experimentation and of the study of such books as Kepler's *Ad Vitellionem paralipomena* (1604) and Risner's *Optica* (1606), both of which quote Ibn al-Haytham and Witelo. Snel's manuscript, which contained his results, has disappeared, but it was examined by Isaac Vossius (1662) and by Huygens, who commented on it in his *Dioptrica* (1703, 1728). Snel's wording of his law has been preserved in what C. De Waard considered to be an index of the manuscript preserved in Amsterdam, and it checks with the account of

Snel's law given by Vossius: If the eye O (in the air) receives a light ray coming from a point R in a medium (for example, water) and refracted at S on the surface A of the medium, then O observes the point R as if it were at L on the line $RM \perp$ surface A. Then $SL:SR$ is constant for all rays. This agrees with the present formulation of the law, which states that $\sin r : \sin i$ is constant, where i and r are the angles that OS and SR make with the normal to A at S.

The priority of the publication of the law remains with Descartes in his *Dioptrique* (1637), stated without experimental verification. Descartes has been accused of plagiarism (for example, by Huygens), a fact made plausible by his visits to Leiden during and after Snel's days, but there seems to be no evidence for it.

Snel was buried in the Pieterskerk in Leiden. The monument erected to him and his wife, who died in 1627, is still there.

BIBLIOGRAPHY

Snel's works are cited in the text. On his life and work see C. De Waard, in *Nieuw nederlandsch biographisch woordenboek*, **7** (1927), 1155–1163; and P. van Geer, "Notice sur la vie et les travaux de Willebrord Snellius," in *Archives néerlandaises des sciences exactes et naturelles*, **18** (1883), 453–468. On his trigonometric work, see A. von Braunmühl, *Geschichte der Trigonometrie*, I (Leipzig, 1900), 239–246. On his geodetic work, see H. Bosmans, "Le degré du méridien terrestre mesuré par la distance de Berg-op-Zoom et de Malines," in *Annales de la Société scientifique de Bruxelles*, **24**, pt. 2, 113–134; N. D. Haasbroek, *Gemma Frisius, Tycho Brahe and Snellius, and Their Triangulations* (Delft, 1968), with references to three previous papers by Haasbroek, in *Tydschrift voor kadaster en landmeetkunde* (1965–1967); and J. J. Delambre, *Histoire de l'astronomie moderne*, II (Paris, 1821), 92–110.

On the recession problem, see J. Tropfke, *Geschichte der Elementarmathematik*, 2nd ed., V (Berlin 1923), 97; and J. A. Oudemans, "Het problema van Snellius, opgelost door Ptolemaeus," in *Verslagen en mededeelingen der K. Akademie van wetenschappen*, 2nd ser., **19** (1884), 436–440.

For Snel's formulation of the law of refraction, see E. J. Dyksterhuis, *The Mechanization of the World Picture*, pt. 4, sec. 170 (Oxford, 1961), also in Dutch and German; this follows the text of Isaac Vossius, *De lucis natura et proprietate* (Amsterdam, 1662), 36 (see J. A. Vollgraff's ed. of *Risneri optica cum annotationibus W. Snellii pars I liber I* [Ghent, 1918], 216). Other works are D. J. Korteweg, "Descartes et les manuscrits de Snellius," in *Revue de métaphysique et de morale*, **4** (1896), 489–501; C. de Waard, "Le manuscrit perdu de

Snellius sur la réfraction," in *Janus*, **39** (1935), 51–75); J. A. Vollgraff, "Snellius' Notes on the Reflection and Refraction of Rays," in *Osiris*, **1** (1936), 718–725; and Huygens' remarks in *Oeuvres complètes de Christiaan Huygens, publiées par la Société Hollandaise des Sciences,* XIII, and esp. X (1903), 405–406.

DIRK J. STRUIK

SNOW, JOHN (*b.* York, England, 15 March 1813; *d.* London, England, 16 June 1858), *medicine, anesthesiology, epidemiology.*

Snow was the eldest son of a farmer. Little is known of his early life, but at the age of fourteen he was apprenticed to William Hardcastle, surgeon, of Newcastle upon Tyne. He is said to have been industrious and studious, and at the age of seventeen became imbued with vegetarianism and temperance, beliefs which he held—almost to the extent of obsession—to the end of his life, and which he carried into his medical practice. (Although it is reported that later in life he occasionally and of necessity took a little wine.)

In 1831 the first cholera epidemic struck England, entering through Sunderland, a seaport near Newcastle, which suffered a disastrous visitation. Snow was sent to the nearby Killingworth colliery, where in appalling conditions he worked indefatigably and laid the foundations of his interest in, and knowledge of, cholera, for which no cure was known, and which was frequently fatal.

Moving to London in 1836, Snow studied at Westminster Hospital and became a member of the Royal College of Surgeons and a licentiate of the Society of Apothecaries. In 1843 he graduated M.B. from the University of London and in the following year proceeded M.D. The only course then open to him was to enter general practice, and to use his own words, Snow "nailed up his colours" at 54 Frith Street, Soho. He never married, and his life in practice consisted in assiduous attention to his patients (mostly of the working classes), to posts such as that of visitor to outpatients in Charing Cross Hospital, and to his two great contributions to medicine. Snow's friend and biographer, Benjamin Ward Richardson, described him as reserved and lonely with a dry sense of humor.

In 1841 Snow read to the Westminster Medical Society "Asphyxia and the Resuscitation of Newborn Children." In this paper he described a double air pump and gave some of his ideas on lack of oxygen. Since he had made other similar studies on the physiology of respiration, his knowledge placed him in a favorable position when ether was introduced as an anesthetic in 1846. The first major operation in England in which the new drug was used was an amputation of a leg performed by Robert Liston at University College Hospital, London, on 21 December 1846, with William Squire administering the ether. Snow at once began experimenting with the substance and invented an apparatus for its administration, based on physiological principles. He demonstrated its use at St. George's Hospital with so much smoothness and success that he was invited to work with Liston, and later with most of the well-known surgeons of London. Rapidly Snow became the premier anesthetist of the country. In September 1847 he published his masterly little book *On Ether*, which included a description of his apparatus and of the properties of the drug, together with physiological and practical information regarding its administration. His division of the stages of anesthesia into five degrees was not improved upon until the work of Arthur Guedel in 1917.

When chloroform was introduced into anesthesia by James Young Simpson in November 1847, Snow was quick to appreciate the advantages and disadvantages of the new drug. Snow's expertise in apparatus led him to construct new pieces for the administration of chloroform. He laid emphasis on the use of such apparatus as a means of delivering low and exact percentages of chloroform in air; this was in direct contrast to Simpson's "open method" of dropping chloroform on the corner of a towel or handkerchief. The controversy between protagonists of the two methods lasted for the remainder of the century, but Snow was the pioneer in raising the art and practice of English anesthesia and anesthetic apparatus to its subsequent heights.

Simpson's goal had been the prevention of the pangs of childbirth, and he fought valiantly against religious and medical prejudice. Anesthesia, however, became respectable on 7 April 1853, when Snow administered chloroform to Queen Victoria at the birth of Prince Leopold, the so-called "chloroform à la reine." Snow continued his work in anesthesia for the remainder of his short life. He introduced amylene in 1856, and his great book *On Chloroform*, completed a few days before his death, was edited by B. W. Richardson, who added a definitive biography.

During these years Snow was occupied also with investigations of cholera, which many will consider as giving him an even greater claim to recognition as a benefactor of humanity. Since his interest in the disease had been aroused by his earlier work in the colliery near Newcastle, recurrent outbreaks in London gave him opportunity and experience, and in 1849 he wrote the first of many papers and published his book *On the Mode of Communication of Cholera*. Many physicians still believed in the ancient view that infectious diseases such as cholera and smallpox were carried by "miasmas" or evil humors arising from mud, sewage, or other noxious sources. Snow's theory and proof of transmission by water infected with fecal matter was to provoke controversy between supporters of Snow, such as William Budd, and the "miasmatists." Even workers in the Board of Health were slow to alter their ideas.

In the great London epidemic of 1854, Snow's genius as an epidemiologist and statistician reached fruition. By meticulous survey he established that the areas supplied by water from the Southwark and Vauxhall Water Company, obtained from the fecal-contaminated Thames, were infected nine times more fatally than the areas supplied by the Lambeth Company, which supplied water from an upstream source.

Even more dramatic was the affair of the Broad Street pump, which he showed by careful plotting to be in the center of a cholera outbreak in his own parish of Soho. Within a few hundred yards of this pump, some five hundred fatal cases occurred in ten days. Snow found that a sewer pipe passed within a few feet of the well, and his belief that contaminated water was the source of infection was vindicated when he persuaded the parish councillors to remove the pump handle.

Pasteur and Lister had not yet published their work on microorganisms and infection, and the vibrio of cholera was not to be described by Koch till 1884. Snow's reasoned argument was that cholera was propagated by a specific living, waterborne, self-reproducing cell or germ. He recommended sensible precautions such as decontamination of soiled linen, washing hands, and boiling water. In treatment, he believed in the use of saline fluids, given intravenously, although techniques were hardly sufficiently advanced to make full use of this advice, which is now the basis of modern treatment. Snow's writings and practice were a very considerable influence upon the great sanitary reformers such as Sir John Simon and Sir Edwin Chadwick in the later part of the century. He was a founder of the Epidemiological Society.

Tired and worn by overwork, and perhaps undermined by too ascetic a way of life, Snow died of a cerebral hemorrhage at the age of forty-five. He was buried in Brompton churchyard, where his tombstone, originally erected by Richardson, was reconstructed in 1947 by the Association of Anaesthetists of Great Britain and Ireland.

BIBLIOGRAPHY

I. ORIGINAL WORKS. Snow wrote over 30 papers on cholera and matters of public health, and a similar number on ether, chloroform, other anesthetics, and respiratory physiology. Among the most important works on cholera, are *On the Mode of Communication of Cholera* (London, 1849; 2nd ed., 1855); "On the Pathology and Mode of Communication of Cholera," in *London Medical Gazette*, **44** (1849), 730, 745, 923; "On the Communication of Cholera by Impure Thames Water," in *Medical Times and Gazette*, n.s. **9** (1854), 365–366; "On the Chief Cause of the Recent Sickness and Mortality in the Crimea," *ibid.*, n.s. **10** (1855), 457–458; and "Drainage and Water Supply in Connection With the Public Health," *ibid.*, n.s. **16** (1858), 161, 189.

On anesthesia, see "Asphyxia and the Resuscitation of New-born Children," in *London Medical Gazette*, **n.s. I** (1842), 222–227; *On the Inhalation of the Vapour of Ether in Surgical Operations* (London, 1847); "On the Use of Ether as an Anaesthetic . . .," in *London Medical Gazette*, n.s. **4** (1847), 156–157; "On the Inhalation of Chloroform and Ether," in *Lancet* (1848), **1**, 177–180; "On Narcotism by the Inhalation of Vapours," in *London Medical Gazette*, in 16 parts from n.s. **6** (1848) to n.s. **12** (1851); "Death From Inhalation of Chloroform," in *Association Medical Journal*, **1** (1853), 134; "On the Administration of Chloroform During Parturition," *ibid.*, **1** (1853), 500–502; and *On Chloroform and Other Anaesthetics* (London, 1858).

II. SECONDARY LITERATURE. The chief biographical source on Snow is Benjamin W. Richardson's memoir in *On Chloroform and Other Anaesthetics*. An obituary is in *Medical Times and Gazette*, n.s. **16** (1858), 633–634; and reviews (written almost as obituaries) of Snow's posthumous book are in *Lancet* (1858), **1**, 555–556; and in *British Medical Journal* (1858), **11**, 1047–1049.

See also Lord Cohen of Birkenhead, "John Snow—the Autumn Loiterer?" in *Proceedings of the Royal Society of Medicine*, **62** (1969), 99–106; B. Duncum, *The Development of Inhalation Anaesthesia* (Oxford, 1947), with an extensive discussion of Snow's work on anesthesia; J. Edwards, "John Snow, M.D., 1813–1858," in *Anaesthesia*, **14** (1959), 113–126; and K. B. Thomas, "John Snow, 1813–1858," in *Journal of the Royal College of General Practitioners*, **16** (1968), 85–94.

Snow MSS are in the Clover/Snow Collection of the Woodward Biomedical Library, University of British Columbia (annotated by K. B. Thomas, in *Anaesthesia*, **27** [1972], 436–449).

K. BRYN THOMAS

SODDY, FREDERICK (*b.* Eastbourne, England, 2 September 1877; *d.* Brighton, England, 22 September 1956), *radiochemistry, science and society.*

Soddy developed with Lord Rutherford during 1901–1903 the disintegration theory of radioactivity, confirmed with Sir William Ramsay in 1903 the production of helium from radium, advanced in 1910 the *concept* of isotope, proposed in 1911 the alpha-ray rule leading to the full displacement law of 1913, and was the 1921 Nobel laureate in chemistry, principally for his investigations into the origin and nature of isotopes.

The youngest son of a London merchant, Soddy was raised in the Calvinist tradition by his dominant half-sister. He developed a lifelong sense of extreme social independence, as well as a plague-on-both-your-houses attitude toward religious controversy, later extended to social institutions in general. An aspiring scientist from an early age, Soddy was encouraged by his influential science master, R. E. Hughes, at Eastbourne College to study chemistry at Oxford. After an interim year at co-educational Aberystwyth, Soddy in 1895 received a science scholarship to Merton College, Oxford. In 1898, with Ramsay as external examiner, Soddy received a first-class honors degree; he remained at Oxford for two more years, engaged in independent chemical research.

In May 1900, Soddy adventurously followed up an unsuccessful application to Toronto, with a personal visit to Montreal, accepting a position as demonstrator at McGill University. His childless marriage in 1908 to Winifred Beilby (*d.* 1936) was a source of great happiness and stability in his life. Soddy was "an admirable writer and a clear and interesting lecturer,"[1] noted for originality in demonstrations. A fellow of both the Chemical Society (from 1899) and the Royal Society (from 1910), Soddy was also a foreign member of the Swedish, Italian, and Russian academies of science. In 1913 he was awarded the Cannizzaro Prize for his important contributions to the new chemistry.

Profoundly disturbed by World War I and "enraged"[2] by the death of Moseley, Soddy felt that society was not yet sufficiently mature to handle properly the advances of science. He began to concern himself more with the interaction between science and society. In order to ascertain "why so far the progress of science has proved as much a curse as a blessing to humanity,"[3] Soddy studied economics. He considered the free development of science to be the new wealth of nations and advocated the rise of a "scientific civilization."[4] The "curse" he felt arose from constraints, put upon both the progress of science and the distribution of technological productivity, for the self-maintenance of the existing but decadent economic system.[5]

At McGill, Soddy joined with Rutherford in a series of investigations which produced the theoretical explanation of radioactivity. The constant production of a material "emanation" from thorium was shown to be the combined effect of the production of an intermediate, but chemically separable, substance, thorium X, balanced by its decay. The production of one substance was thus the result of the uncontrollable disintegration of another. The "radiation" proved to be both particulate in nature and a direct accompaniment of the process of disintegration. The rate of the process was found in every case to be as the exponential law of a monomolecular chemical reaction. So complete was their 1903 disintegration theory of radioactivity, that in 1909 only an extension to branching series was required.[6]

In March 1903, Soddy elected to join Ramsay in London to examine more fully the gaseous products of decay. Using Giesel's radium preparations, Ramsay and Soddy experimentally confirmed in July 1903 the prediction of Rutherford and Soddy that radium would continuously produce helium. In 1908 Rutherford "settled for good"[7] the long-suspected identity of the helium, so produced, with expelled alpha particles. During the ten-year period following his 1904 appointment to the University of Glasgow, Soddy helped to clarify the relation between the plethora of radioelements and the periodic table.

McCoy and Ross had reported in 1907 that Hahn's 1905 radiothorium was chemically inseparable from thorium. Boltwood, in turn, indicated a similar difficulty with thorium and ionium. From crystal morphology studies, Strömholm and Svedberg in 1909 confirmed a family resemblance between such radioelements as thorium X and radium. In 1910 the chemical inseparability of mesothorium 1 and radium, reported by Marckwald, as well as Soddy's own experimental evidence, that these two radioelements form an inseparable trio with thorium X, convinced Soddy that such cases of chemical inseparability were actually chemical *identities*. Without the unnecessary continuation of the genetic series of radioelements throughout the entire periodic table, postulated by Strömholm and Svedberg, Soddy declared in 1910 that "the recognition that elements of different atomic weight may possess identical chemical properties seems destined to have its most important application in the region of the inactive elements."[8] "Soddy possessed," as Hahn wrote in admiration,[9] "the courage to declare that these were chemically identical elements."

To be able to refer generically to these active and inactive elements with identical chemical properties, Soddy introduced the technical term "isotope" in 1913.[10] While chemically inseparable, active isotopes were distinguishable by their radioactive properties, and all isotopes differed in atomic weight. Soddy suggested that the 1912 metaneon of J. J. Thomson be considered "a case of isotopic elements outside the radioactive sequences."[11] Following Soddy, Aston announced a partial separation in 1913 on this very basis.[12] The connection between chemical properties and the periodic table became increasingly clarified with concurrent developments in the physics and chemistry of the nuclear atom. From the chemical side, Soddy proposed the alpha-ray rule in 1911, the key to the first of two locks. Applying his general principle that the common elements are mixtures of chemically inseparable elements "differing step-wise by whole units of atomic weight"[13] specifically to the case of the radioelements, Soddy recognized that the expulsion of an alpha particle would result in a lighter element chemically inseparable from those occupying the "next but one"[14] position in the periodic table. The second lock to the displacement law involved the beta transitions.

During 1912 Soddy assigned Lord Fleck the task of sorting out the short-lived beta emitters, especially at the complex branching points in the series. Once these experimental results became available, several partially correct generalizations were published, inducing Soddy, therefore, to publish his own complete and correct form of the law in February 1913. "Fajans," Soddy acknowledged, "worked out the Periodic Law Generalization quite independently of me,"[15] although his conclusions were fundamentally different. On electrochemical considerations, Fajans interpreted the changes among the clusters, "plejade,"[16] of radioelements as evidence against the nuclear origin of radio-changes.[17] Soddy, on the other hand, argued for a crucial distinction[18] between radiochange and chemical change, concluding on chemical evidence, as Bohr had done on physical evidence, that beta decay, like alpha decay, was of nuclear origin. As a result, Soddy considered van den Broek's hypothesis, that successive places in the periodic table correspond to unit differences in the net intra-atomic charge (see Figure 1) "practically proved so far as the . . . end of the sequence,

from thallium to uranium, is concerned."[19]

By early 1914 Moseley,[20] using physical methods, had completed his independent extension of this verification throughout the entire periodic table. During the period 1914–1919, in the chair of chemistry at Aberdeen, Soddy, in addition to his war work, examined two predictions of the displacement law. It was commonly accepted that lead was the end product only of the uranium series, and Soddy had predicted by 1913 that a heavier isotope of lead from thorium must also exist. Separate determinations were undertaken in 1914 on lead from Ceylon thorite by Soddy and on lead from uranium ores by T. W. Richards and O. Hönigschmid, thereby confirming the prediction that common lead was indeed a mixture of isotopes.[21] Soddy suggested that the parent of actinium might be an alpha-decaying member of Mendeleev's missing eka-tantalum. An exclusively beta-emitting homologue of tantalum found by Fajans and O. Göhring in 1913 and called "brevium" [UrX_2], however, caused Soddy to begin to investigate the other alternative. But after proving that the parent of actinium could not be a beta-decay product of radium, he reexamined the first alternative with Cranston. In 1918 they found, isotopic with UrX_2, the direct parent of actinium, produced through the rare UrY branch, which was found in 1911 by G. Antonoff and later linked to uranium 235. Protactinium, element 91, was simultaneously and independently found by Hahn and Meitner.

Soddy was called in 1919 to a chair of chemistry at Oxford. During his seventeen-year tenure, he failed to establish the expected school of radiochemistry, devoting himself rather to the improvement of chemistry teaching and to the modernization of the laboratories.[22] He also continued to treat radioactive minerals for their constituents. After the disturbing death of his wife, Soddy retired early. He went exploring for monazite sand, and patented his 1923 process for thorium extraction in 1940. He then turned his attention to mathematics. Looking beyond to the significance of science, Soddy, who had once confidently spoken of the potential peaceful benefits for society given the key to "unlock this great store of energy bound up in the structure of the element,"[23] and, by controlling it, "virtually provide anyone who wanted it with a private sun of his own,"[24] was profoundly concerned by subsequent developments. He zealously endeavored[25] to awaken the conscience of the scientific community to the social relevance of their own research. Soddy urged that "universities and learned societies should no longer evade their

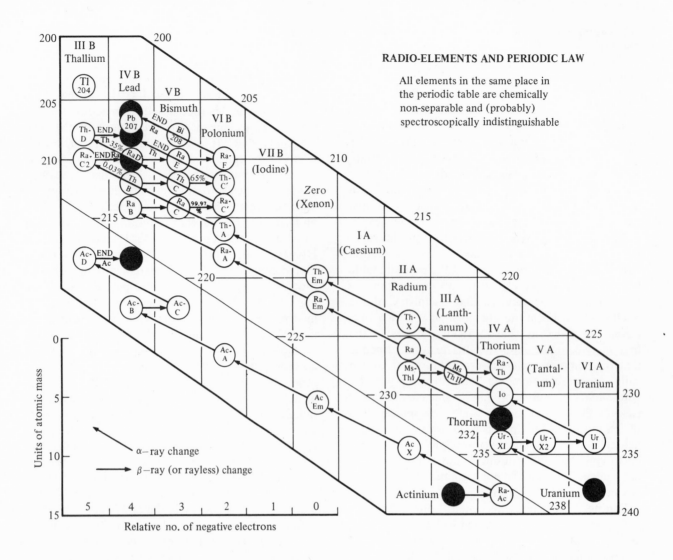

FIGURE 1. Reproduced with the permission of the British Association for the Advancement of Science.

responsibilities and hide under the guise of false humility as the hired servants of the world their work has made possible, but do that for which they are supported in cultured release from routine occupations, and speak the truth though the heavens fall."[26] He was largely unheeded, however, and he judged at the end that the blame for the plight of civilization "must rest on scientific men, equally with others, for being incapable of accepting the responsibility for the profound social upheavals which their own work primarily has brought about in human relationships."[27]

NOTES

1. Rutherford letter, 15 June 1914. Cf. Howorth, *Pioneer Research*, 192. The original is in Bodleian Library, Soddy-Howorth Collection, 75, 95, courtesy Soddy trustees.

2. Soddy, *Memoirs*, I, 274.

3. Fleck, "Soddy," 210, courtesy the Royal Society.

4. Soddy, "Social Relations of Science," in *Nature*, **141** (1938), 784–785.

5. A comprehensive statement of his general view regarding the monetary system preventing modern Western civilization from distributing its scientific and technological abundance by peaceful means appears in an address, February 1950, partially republished in the 24-page *Commemoration to Professor Frederick Soddy* (London, 1958).

6. Soddy, "Multiple Atomic Disintegration: A Suggestion in Radioactive Theory," in *Philosophical Magazine*, **18** (1909), 739–744; this was developed in "Multiple Disintegration," in *Annual Report*, **9** (1912), 311–316.

7. Referring to his joint paper with Royds, *Philosophical Magazine*, **17** (1909), 281, Rutherford further noted in his letter of 14 Feb. 1909 to Elster and Geitel that "you will have seen that the α particle has at last been proved to be helium." Darmstaedter Collection, G 1, 1896 (26), courtesy Staatsbibliothek, Preussischer Kulturbesitz.

8. Soddy, "Radioactivity," in *Annual Report*, **7** (1910), 286. Strikingly similar views regarding mixtures of similar elements of different atomic weight were expressed by D.

Strömholm and T. Svedberg in *Zeitschrift für Anorganische Chemie*, **63** (1909), 206.

9. Fleck, "Soddy," 208. The rare earths had given ample evidence of chemical "inseparability" without identity.

10. Soddy, "Intra-atomic Charge," in *Nature*, **92** (4 Dec. 1913), 400. "The same algebraic sum of the positive and negative charges in the nucleus, when the arithmetic sum is different, gives what I call 'isotopes' . . . because they occupy the same [*iso*] place [*topos*] in the periodic table" (see diagram). Perhaps the first use of "isotope" for the position of elements was W. Preyer, *Das Genetische System der chemischen Elemente* (Berlin, 1893). The stimulus for Soddy's term arose when he "got tired of writing 'elements chemically identical and non-separable by chemical methods' and coined the name *isotope* . . . ," as he said in "Contribution to a Discussion on Isotopes," in *Proceedings of the Royal Society*, **99** (1921), 98.

11. Soddy, "Radioactivity," in *Annual Report*, **10** (1913), 265.

12. Aston, *Isotopes*, 37, 42.

13. Soddy, "The Chemistry of Mesothorium," in *Transactions of the Chemical Society*, **99** (1911), 82; cf. n. 8.

14. Soddy, *The Chemistry of the Radioelements* (1911), 29. For a remarkable partial anticipation of isotopes and the displacement law, see A. T. Cameron, *Radiochemistry* (London, 1910), 141.

15. Soddy letter to F. O. Giesel, *ca.* 1913/14 in Giesel Archives, courtesy Chininfabrik, Buchler & Co., Brunswick. The generalization of A. S. Russell had not only assumed a *discontinuous* series, *Chemical News*, **107** (31 Jan. 1913), 49, but also questioned the chemical identity notion of Soddy; cf. Russell letter to Rutherford, 14 Sept. 1912, Cambridge Univ. Lib., Add. MSS 7653/R106. Russell "knew of Fleck's results," and "through him they got known to Hevesy and Fajans"; cf. *Report of the British Association for the Advancement of Science* (1913), 446; and the Soddy letter to Howorth, 29 Jan. 1953, Bodleian Lib., Soddy Collection, Alton 29, item no. Trenn S-6.

16. K. Fajans, *Radioaktivität und die neueste Entwickelung der Lehre von den chemischen Elementen* (Brunswick, 1919), 35.

17. Fajans' letter to Rutherford, 10 April 1913, Cambridge Univ. Lib. Add. MSS 7653/F5.

18. Soddy's distinction between chemical change and radiochange was originally based upon the disintegration theory, "Radioactive Change," in *Philosophical Magazine*, **5** (1903), 576. With the development of the nuclear atom, however, it became possible to clarify this distinction by defining the actual locus of the radio-changes. Bohr expressed this clarification in his letter to Hevesy, 7 Feb. 1913, L. Rosenfeld, "Introduction" to *On the Constitution of Atoms and Molecules* (Copenhagen, 1963), xxxii.

19. Soddy, "Intra-atomic Charge," 400.

20. H. G. J. Moseley, in *Nature*, **92** (1914), 554. "My work was undertaken for the express purpose of testing [van den] Broek's hypothesis . . . [and] certainly confirms the hypothesis."

21. "Soddy's prediction concerning the atomic weights of leads from uranium and thorium minerals had been triumphantly vindicated by some of his most severe critics." F. W. Aston, "The Story of Isotopes," in *British Association Report* (1935), Presidential Address to Section A, p. 26. The concurrent investigations comparing uranium lead with ordinary lead could neither confirm nor deny the possibility of thorium lead.

22. Brewer, "Chemistry at Oxford," 185.

23. Soddy, "The Internal Energy of Elements," in *Journal of the Proceedings of the Institution of Electrical Engineers, Glasgow*, **37** (1906), 7. An earlier statement on the latent internal energy of the atom is Soddy, "The Disintegration Theory of Radioactivity," in *Times Literary Supplement* (26 June 1903), 201.

24. Soddy, "Advances in the Study of Radio-active Bodies," two lectures to the Royal Institution on 15 May and 18 May 1915, as recorded in *The Royal Institution Friday Evening Lectures 1907–1918* (privately bound at the Royal Institution, London, n.d.). The original MS is in the Bodleian Library, Soddy-Howorth Collection, 58. The quotation is from this MS, page II, 9. The lectures are apparently unpublished but are reviewed in *Engineering*, **99** (1915), 604.

25. Shortly after Soddy's retirement, Joseph Needham pointed out the importance of such efforts, "Social Relations of Science," in *Nature*, **141** (1938), 734.

26. Soddy, *Frustration in Science*, Foreword.

27. Soddy, Typescript-A, 1953, concluding statement, Bodleian Library, Soddy-Howorth Collection 4.

BIBLIOGRAPHY

A nearly complete list of Soddy's main scientific papers, books, lectures, and other contributions is given by Alexander Fleck, "Frederick Soddy," in *Biographical Memoirs of Fellows of the Royal Society*, **3** (1957), 203–216. For comparisons and additions, including his contributions on economics and on science and society, see Muriel Howorth, *Pioneer Research on the Atom* (London, 1958), 281–286. This unusual account is subtitled *Rutherford and Soddy in a Glorious Chapter of Science*, and further subtitled *The Life Story of Frederick Soddy*. In spite of the author's uncritical attempt to glorify Soddy, this remarkable reference source is the fruit of great effort to preserve the existing documents of Soddy. Soddy gave all his papers to Muriel Howorth of Eastbourne, and his will contained the provision: "I give to Muriel Howorth also the copyright of all my published works," cf. *Pioneer Research*, p. 286. The Soddy-Howorth Collection was deposited in the Bodleian Library and a partial reference key thereto is appended to *Pioneer Research*, pp. 333–339. In 1974 J. Alton of the Contemporary Scientific Archives Centre, Oxford, deposited in the Bodleian a 29-page systematic catalogue of the Soddy Collection incorporating the Howorth portion. This collection must be directly consulted for precision in both quotations and other references. Richard Lucas, *Bibliographie der radioaktiven Stoffe* (Leipzig, 1908), 72–73, provides a useful list of Soddy's early works. Consultation of the British Museum General Catalogue of Printed Books, 1964, amplifies the list of works of Soddy. In addition to the scientific contributions collectively listed in Fleck and Howorth, the following should be noted: "The First Quarter-Century of Radioactivity," in *Isotopy* (Westminster, 1954), 1–25. See the obituaries of "Rutherford," in *Nature* (30 October 1937); "Ramsay," *ibid.* (10 August 1916); and of H. Becquerel, "The Founder of Radioactivity," in *Ion: A Journal of Electronics, Atomistics, Ionology, Radioactivity and Raumchemistry*, **1** (1908), 2–4. Soddy was joint editor of this short-lived serial, *Ion*. In this same issue, Soddy completed his series of investigations concerning whether the alpha particle was charged before, during, or after expulsion. Soddy's abstracts of the papers by Russell, Fajans, and Soddy concerning the displacement law are also of interest; see *Abstracts of Chemical Papers Journal of the Chemical Society London*, pt. 2 (1913), 274–278. Soddy's classic call for scientific responsibility appears as the foreword to *Frustration in Science* (London, 1935).

Soddy's nine joint papers with Rutherford (1902–1903) are reproduced in *Collected Papers of Lord Rutherford of Nelson*, Sir James Chadwick, ed., I (London, 1962). Soddy contributed a series of original reports on "Radioactivity" for the *Annual Reports on the Progress of Chemistry* (London, 1904–1920). These articles contain much otherwise unpublished work on isotopes, as well as a running account of the history of radioactivity. These articles have been published in facsimile and edited with commentary by T. J. Trenn, in *Radioactivity and Atomic Theory* (London, 1975). The diagram "Radio-Elements and Periodic Law" first appeared as a supplement to Soddy's paper "The Radio-elements and the Periodic Law," in *Chemical News*, **107** (28 Feb. 1913), 97–99. Essentially the same diagram appeared in *Jahrbuch der Radioaktivität und Elektronik*, **10**, no. 2 (1913), 193. The actinium series was separated and minor additions were included in the version drafted July 1913 for the *British Association Report* (1913), 446, and here reproduced; it also appeared in the *Annual Report*, **10** (1913), 264.

Soddy's most important books are *Radio-Activity: an Elementary Treatise From the Standpoint of the Disintegration Theory* (London–Leipzig, 1904), based upon a series of lectures at the University of London from Oct. 1903 to Feb. 1904, carried concurrently in *The Electrician*, **52** (1903), 7 et. seq.; *The Interpretation of Radium* (London, 1909; 4th ed., 1920), translated into several languages). In the series edited by Alexander Findlay, *Monographs on Inorganic and Physical Chemistry*, Soddy contributed *The Chemistry of the Radio-Elements*, pt. I (London, 1911; Leipzig, 1912); pt. II (1914), containing "Radioelements and the Periodic Law"; and pt. I, 2nd. ed. (1915). See also *The Interpretation of the Atom* (London, 1932).

Soddy's most important lectures were The Wilde Lecture VIII, "The Evolution of Matter as Revealed by the Radioactive Elements," 16 March 1904, in *Memoirs and Proceedings of the Manchester Literary and Philosophical Society*, **48** (1904; Leipzig, 1904); The Nobel Lecture, 12 Dec. 1922, "The Origin of the Conception of Isotopes," in *Les Prix Nobel en 1921–1922* (Stockholm, 1923).

Information concerning the life and work of Soddy can be obtained from *Pioneer Research*. Howorth also edited the *Memoirs* of Soddy, as *Atomic Transmutation, Memoirs of Professor Frederick Soddy*, vol. I (London, 1953), subtitled *The Greatest Discovery Ever Made*. Volume one deals with the period until 1904. There were no further volumes. There are numerous sketches of Soddy's life and work. Alexander Fleck, in *Nature*, **178** (1956), 893, is an interesting personal account. Fleck also contributed the note for the *Dictionary of National*

Biography (1951–1960), 904. Alexander S. Russell, "F. Soddy, Interpreter of Atomic Structure," in *Science*, **124** (1956), provides insights into Soddy the man. Russell published further on Soddy, in *Chemistry and Industry*, no. 47 (1956), 1420–1421, and in Eduard Farber, ed., *Great Chemists* (New York, 1961), 1463–1468. Perhaps the best account is F. Paneth, "A Tribute to Frederick Soddy," in *Nature*, **180** (1957), 1085–1087; repr. in the Paneth Collection, H. Dingle, ed., *Chemistry and Beyond* (London, 1964), 85–89. A more recent sympathetic account is that of A. Kent, "Frederick Soddy," in *Proceedings of the Chemical Society* (November 1963), 327–330. Besides his brief editorial "Frederick Soddy and the Concept of Isotopes," in *Endeavour*, **23** (1964), 54, T. I. Williams wrote the article on Soddy for his *Biographical Dictionary of Scientists* (London, 1969). The account of I. Asimov, *Biographical Encyclopedia of Science and Technology* (New York, 1964), no. 398, is subject to the limitations imposed by this effort. An extremely concise and accurate summary is included in W. A. Tilden and S. Glasstone, *Chemical Discovery and Invention in the Twentieth Century* (London, 1936), 140. There is a supplementary account in Eduard Farber, *Nobel Prize Winners in Chemistry 1901–1961* (London, 1963), 81–85. It is of interest to compare the biographical account in *Nobel Lectures in Chemistry* (Amsterdam, 1966), 400–401, with the original in *Les Prix Nobel en 1921–1922* (Stockholm, 1923), 128–129. See also the account in H. H. Stephenson, *Who's Who in Science* (London, 1914), 535, and *Journal of Chemical Education*, **8** (1931), 1245–1246.

Relevant sketches of Soddy's work are to be found in F. W. Aston, *Isotopes*, 2nd ed., 1924. His work on lead isotopes, pp. 17–19, is particularly valuable. See A. Kent and J. A. Cranston, "The Soddy Box," in *Chemistry and Industry* (1960), 1206, 1411, which describes Soddy's original 1910 preparation, a deliberate mixture of radium and mesothorium, which led him to the concept of the isotope. In Gleditsch, "Contribution to the Study of Isotopes," *Norske Videnskaps-Akademi* I. *Mat.-Natur. Klasse* no. 3 (Oslo, 1925), E. Gleditsch notes, p. 7, that "The theory of isotopes put forward . . . by Soddy in the years 1911–1914 has proved to be fully in accord with our present views on atomic structure." See also Fleck, "Early Work in the Radioactive Elements," in *Proceedings of the Chemical Society* (1963), 330. In this same issue, J. A. Cranston contributed "The Group Displacement Law," pp. 330–331, and an even more detailed documentation in the following issue (1964), 104–107. Soddy's work with Rutherford is considered by A. S. Eve, *Rutherford* (Cambridge, 1939); N. Feather, *Lord Rutherford* (London, 1940); A. Romer, *The Restless Atom* (New York, 1960); Howorth, *Pioneer Research*; and T. J. Trenn, "Rutherford and Soddy: From a Search for Radioactive Constituents to the Disintegration Theory of Radioactivity," in *Rete*, **1** (1971), 51–70. M. W. Travers, *A Life of Sir William Ramsay* (London, 1956), ch. 14, pp. 210–221, deals with his work with Ramsay. At the request of Travers, Soddy contributed a portion of this account. The original transcript is in Soddy-Howorth 4.

In addition to F. M. Brewer, "The Place of Chemistry at Oxford," in *Proceedings of the Chemical Society* (July 1957), 185, Soddy's work at Oxford is considered by Sir Harold Hartley, "The Old Chemical Department," in *Journal of the Royal Institute of Chemistry* (1955), 126. J. A. Cranston's "The Discovery of Isotopes by Soddy and his School in Glasgow," in *Isotopy* (1954), 26–36, and "Concept of Isotope," in *Journal of the Royal Institute of Chemistry*, **18** (1964), 38, provide important historical and scientific distinctions in the use of the term "isotope."

A. Romer, ed., *The Discovery of Radioactivity and Transmutation*, Classics of Science, II (New York, 1964), provides not only some of the papers of Soddy in collaboration both with Rutherford and with Ramsay but also valuable comments on this pre-1904 work. Soddy's hypothesis concerning an isotope of lead as the final product of the thorium series is dealt with in S. I. Levy, *The Rare Earths* (London, 1915), 107–108.

For a partial account of Soddy's work on isotopes, emphasizing the contributions of Fajans and Richards, see O. U. Anders, "The Place of Isotopes in the Periodic Table: the 50th Anniversary of the Fajans-Soddy Displacement Laws," in *Journal of Chemical Education*, **41** (1964), 522–525. Additional information about Soddy as others saw him is in L. Badash, ed., *Rutherford and Boltwood: Letters on Radioactivity* (New Haven, 1969), which exposes Soddy's research on the parent of radium. Soddy as a public figure and social rebel, who ushered in the atomic age, is epitomized in C. Beaton and K. Tynan, *Persona Grata* (London, 1953), 87. Besides the Soddy-Howorth Collection, extensive correspondence exists also at the Cambridge Univ. Library, Add. MSS 7653/S. There is also correspondence with W. H. Bragg at the Royal Institution, with J. Larmor courtesy the Royal Society, and with O. Lodge at University College London. The Soddy Memorial at Glasgow was reported in "Unveiling of the Soddy Memorial," in *Chemistry and Industry* (8 Nov. 1958), 1462–1464. There is one collection of Soddy's apparatus and equipment at the Chemistry Department of the University of Glasgow and another at the Inorganic Chemistry Laboratory of the University of Oxford.

THADDEUS J. TRENN

SOEMMERRING, SAMUEL THOMAS (*b*. Torun, Poland, 18 January 1755; *d*. Frankfurt, Germany, 2 March 1830), *comparative anatomy, human anatomy, anthropology, physiology.*

Soemmerring's maturity coincided with the French Revolution and the subsequent political disorders in Germany. Yet despite the instability of his career, his writings made him the most famous German anatomist of the early nineteenth century. His works were characterized by a fully developed presentation of the text and by scientifically accurate illustrations of considerable artistic merit.

After attending the Gymnasium in Torun (1769–1774), Soemmerring studied medicine from 1774 to 1778 at Göttingen, where he was inspired by the zeal for research of two of his teachers, Heinrich August Wrisberg and Johann Friedrich Blumenbach. While still a student Soemmerring had decided to become an anatomist; the prerequisites for this career were a gift for observation and skill in drawing. Soemmerring's choice of profession did not meet with the approval of his father, Johann Thomas Soemmerring, the municipal physician of Torun. (Soemmerring's mother was the former Regina Geret, a pastor's daughter.) The family was upper middle class; old-fashioned thrift and Lutheran convictions were the foundations of its way of life. By accepting various privations, Soemmerring was able to pursue his plans without his father's assistance and earned the M.D. on 7 April 1778 with a dissertation on the base of the brain and the origin of the cranial nerves. With the aid of his own illustrations he criticized earlier accounts and proposed the order of the twelve cranial nerves that is still taught. Although not the first to adopt this order, Soemmerring provided such solid grounds for it that ultimately it was generally accepted. To complete his training, he traveled in Holland, England, and Scotland. Among the physicians and scientists he met, those who most impressed him were Peter Camper, John Hunter, and Alexander Monro (Secundus).

In April 1779, shortly after his return to Göttingen, Soemmerring became professor of anatomy and surgery at the Collegium Carolinum in Kassel. He remained there until the fall of 1784, when he assumed the professorship of anatomy and physiology at the University of Mainz (until 1797). Both Kassel and Mainz were important cultural centers where the arts and sciences were encouraged by discerning rulers. At Kassel, Soemmerring was permitted to dissect animals that had died in the menagerie and to examine the corpses of members of the city's Negro colony. These investigations resulted in a study on the bodily characteristics of Negroes and Europeans (1784); Soemmerring concluded that despite several differences, both belonged to the same species.

One of Soemmerring's chief fields of research was neuroanatomy. His demonstration of the crossing of the optical nerve fibers (1786) was followed by a publication on the brain and spinal cord (1788), the annotations to which contained a wealth of findings in comparative anatomy. Further evidence of Soemmerring's extensive knowledge can be seen in the footnotes to his translation of Haller's *Primae lineae physiologiae* (1788). Soemmerring no longer considered the spinal cord to be a "great nerve" but, rather, a part of the central nervous system. Further, he gave the hypophysis its current name, replacing the outmoded term *glandula pituitaria*. Soemmerring's interest in the nervous system and the sense organs also resulted in the publication of illustrations and descriptions of several deformities (1791); the frontispiece to the work showed a series of progressive duplications of the face and head.

In 1796 Soemmerring published a work on "the organ of the soul." The anatomical part was well received, especially the assertion that the cranial nerves originate (or, as the case may be, terminate) in the ventricle wall. But the speculative claim—based on the ideas of *Naturphilosophie*—that the intraventricular cerebrospinal fluid is the seat of a *sensorium commune*—was rejected by more perceptive readers. In contrast, the illustrations of the base of the brain (1799) were widely admired. In Mainz, Soemmerring had met Christian Koeck, whom he trained as a scientific draftsman. Koeck enriched the literature with many excellent illustrations, including those of the brain of a three-year-old boy.

Soemmerring presented further anatomical findings in a book on the effect of corsets. He showed that the deformation of the thorax that they produced led to the displacement of the stomach and liver, and consequently he opposed the tight lacing of the waist and the crinoline. His handbook of human anatomy, *Vom Baue des menschlichen Körpers* (1791–1796), was based as far as possible on his own observations and was conceived as a supplement to Haller's *Primae lineae physiologiae*; the work was still in use in expanded form a half century later. The foreword to the first edition reveals Soemmerring's preoccupation with the use of clear, unmistakable terminology. It also contains an impressive list of his anatomical discoveries, although not all of them have proved to be valid. Among those that are still accepted, two of the most remarkable are the observation that arterial trunks always lie on the bent side of the joints and the discovery that the small part of the trigeminal nerve always lies against the third branch. Soemmerring also sought to illustrate the ideal form of a female skeleton (1797) and published a collection of illustrations of the human embryo (1799).

During his last years in Mainz, Soemmerring's life changed in important ways. In March 1792 he married Margaretha Elisabetha Grunelius, who came from a prominent Frankfurt family. Wartime conditions precluded his establishing a permanent residence in Mainz, and he supervised his office from Frankfurt. Soemmerring was offered various posts but accepted none of them because of the low salaries. He sold a portion of his anatomical and anthropological collections, dedicated himself to medical practice in Frankfurt, and completed scientific studies that he had begun earlier. After his wife died in January 1802, he was sought by many universities and in March 1805 finally accepted nomination as member of the Bavarian Academy of Sciences in Munich.

Soemmerring's abiding interest in the anatomy of the sense organs was especially stimulated after his discovery in 1791 of the fovea centralis in the macula lutea. Between 1801 and 1810 he published four groups of illustrations of the human sense organs, with descriptions in German and Latin. The work was greatly enriched by copperplate engravings based on Koeck's drawings. In preparing the drawings Soemmerring was less concerned with correct perspective than with the architectonically correct representation of the material.

Soemmerring translated and commented upon the works of others and did extensive reviewing for the scholarly journals published in Göttingen. In addition he often participated in prize competitions, but the material he submitted was mostly of a clinical nature—except for a paper on the structure of the lung (1808). Of Soemmerring's communications published in the *Denkschriften* of the Bavarian Academy of Sciences the most important by far was one on electric telegraphs (1809–1810).

Soemmerring's rheumatic fever and chest ailments were aggravated by the severe climate of Munich, and in 1820 he returned to Frankfurt, where he practiced medicine for ten years and studied sunspots. Soemmerring was awarded many titles and honors. He became a privy councillor and was named to several orders. As a knight of the Order of the Civil Service of the Bavarian Crown (1808) he was granted personal nobility.

BIBLIOGRAPHY

I. ORIGINAL WORKS. A bibliography of Soemmerring's writings is in Adolph Callisen, *Medicinisches Schriftsteller-Lexicon der jetzt lebenden Verfasser*, supp., XXXII (Altona, 1844), 348–359.

His works include *De basi encephali et originibus nervorum cranio egredientium libri quinque* (Göttingen, 1778); *Ueber die körperliche Verschiedenheit des Mohren vom Europäer* (Mainz, 1784; 2nd ed., slightly different title, Frankfurt–Mainz, 1785); *Vom Hirn und Rückenmark* (Mainz, 1788; 2nd ed., Leipzig, 1792); *Ueber die Schädlichkeit der Schnürbrüste* (Leipzig, 1788; 2nd ed., slightly different title, Berlin, 1793); *Abbildungen und Beschreibungen einiger Missgeburten* (Mainz, 1791); *Vom Baue des menschlichen Körpers*, 5 vols. (Frankfurt, 1791–1796; 2nd ed., 1796–1801), also in Latin, 6 vols. (Leipzig, 1794–1801); *Ueber das Organ der Seele* (Königsberg, 1796); *Tabula sceleti feminini juncta descriptione* (Frankfurt, 1797); "De foramine centrali limbo luteo cincto retinae humanae," in *Commentationes Societatis regiae scientiarum Göttingensis,* **13** (1799), 3–13; *Icones embryonum humanorum* (Frankfurt, 1799); *Tabula baseos encephali* (Frankfurt, 1799); *Abbildungen des menschlichen Auges* (Frankfurt, 1801), also in Latin (Frankfurt, 1804); *Abbildungen des menschlichen Hörorganes* (Frankfurt, 1806), also in Latin (Frankfurt, 1806); *Abbildungen der menschlichen Organe des Geschmackes und der Stimme* (Frankfurt, 1806), also in Latin (Frankfurt, 1808); *Ueber die Structur, die Verrichtung und den Bau der Lungen* (Berlin, 1808), 57–126, written with F. O. Reisseisen; *Abbildungen der menschlichen Organe des Geruches* (Frankfurt, 1809), also in Latin (Frankfurt, 1810); and "Ueber einen elektrischen Telegraphen," in *Denkschriften der Bayerischen Akademie der Wissenschaften zu München* for 1809–1810 (1811), 401–414.

II. SECONDARY LITERATURE. See Gerhard Aumüller, "Zur Geschichte der Anatomischen Institute von Kassel und Mainz (I–III)," in *Medizinhistorisches Journal*, **5** (1970), 59–80, 145–160, 268–288; Ignaz Döllinger, *Gedächtnisrede auf Samuel Thomas Soemmerring* (Munich, 1830); W. Riese, "The 150th Anniversary of S. T. Soemmerring's Organ of the Soul," in *Bulletin of the History of Medicine*, **20** (1946), 310–321; Wilhelm Stricker, *Samuel Thomas Soemmerring nach seinem Leben und Wirken geschildert* (Frankfurt, 1862); and Rudolph Wagner, *Samuel Thomas Soemmerrings Leben und Verkehr mit seinen Zeitgenossen*, 2 vols. (Leipzig, 1844).

ERICH HINTZSCHE

SOHNCKE, LEONHARD (*b.* Halle, Germany, 22 February 1842; *d.* Munich, Germany, 1 November 1897), *crystallography, physics, meteorology.*

Sohncke's chief scientific contribution was the extension of the lattice theory of Bravais to arrive at sixty-five of the 230 possible space groups.

Sohncke's father was professor of mathematics at the University of Halle and was known for his translation into German of Chasles's *Aperçu historique sur l'origine et la développement des méthodes en géométrie.* Sohncke was thus stimulated to study mathematics. He received his early education at the Gymnasium in Halle and then pursued mathematics and physics at the University of Halle and then at the University of Königsberg. There, Franz Neumann, professor of mineralogy and physics, influenced Sohncke greatly and urged him to direct his attention toward theoretical physics. Sohncke received his doctorate in 1866 and taught for a brief period in the Gymnasium in Königsberg before becoming *Privatdozent* at the university.

In 1871, on the recommendation of Kirchhoff, Sohncke was called as professor of physics to the Technische Hochschule in Karlsruhe. In 1883 he moved to the University of Jena in the same capacity, and in 1886 he became professor of physics at the Technische Hochschule in Munich, where he remained until his death. Sohncke acquired a reputation as a fine teacher and instructed many young physicists who later attained success. He also won prominence in educational circles because of his campaign, while in Munich, to break the monopoly held in secondary education by the Gymnasiums and to aid the Realschulen in reaching parity with them.

Early in his career Sohncke was concerned primarily with pure mathematics, particularly series; and he published several short papers in mathematical journals. In the mid-1870's, however, he turned his attention to the internal symmetry of crystals. Working under Neumann at Königsberg, Sohncke had become aware of this field and knew of the previous work of Bravais in determining the fourteen types of space lattices and the thirty-two symmetry classes. He had also followed the investigations of Camille Jordan in group theory. During his research, Sohncke discovered that Hessel, in 1830, had anticipated the work of Bravais; and Sohncke saw to it in his later publications that Hessel's contribution was recognized.

The fourteen Bravais lattices accounted for only seven of the thirty-two classes of external symmetry. In studying internal symmetry, Sohncke realized that previous investigators had looked upon internal symmetry from a completely external orientation. They had imposed, as a condition of symmetry, translational equivalence; and Sohncke saw that this restriction was not justifiable. Inasmuch as symmetry is defined as the equivalence of internal configurations, it is of no consequence whether the direction of one's view has been altered in being transported from one point to another within an object. Thus Sohncke insisted that the view of the system of points is the same from every point and that it need not be a parallel view.

Sohncke eventually arrived at sixty-five different spatial arrangements of points, introducing two new symmetry elements: the screw axis, in which a rotation around an axis is combined with a translation of the system along the axis; and the glide plane, in which the reflection in a mirror plane is combined with a similar translation without rotation along the axis. (Using only simple translation, Bravais had arrived at fourteen lattices.) Sohncke, however, failed to consider two additional symmetry elements of the thirty-two classes of external symmetry: rotation-reflection and rotation-inversion axes. Their inclusion by Fyodorov and almost simultaneously by Arthur Schoenflies and William Barlow in the late 1880's added the additional 165 space groups. Sohncke published his results in his major work, *Die Entwicklung einer Theorie der Krystallstruktur* (1879). He also made models from cigar boxes to demonstrate his derived space groups; and while in Munich, where he became a close friend of the crystallographer Groth, he extended his study of crystal physics.

When Sohncke accepted his post at Karlsruhe he simultaneously took over the direction and administration of the network of meteorological stations in the province of Baden. He also became editor of the *Jahresbericht über die Beobachtungsergebnisse der Badischen meteorologischen Stationen*, and in order to popularize meteorology he published *Über Stürme und Sturmwarnungen* (1875). He also wrote several articles on temperature changes in humid, rising streams of air; the derivation of the formula for barometric height; and the green rays of the sunset. Further, he proposed a theory of the presence of electricity in thunderstorms. Sohncke further conducted research in optics. He determined the thickness of a drop of oil when placed on water after having diffused on its surface.

While in Munich, Sohncke became particularly interested in the flight of aerial balloons, and he directed the activities of a society that encouraged this activity. He organized a number of ascents, and as a reward for his efforts the group named one of its balloons "Sohncke."

BIBLIOGRAPHY

I. ORIGINAL WORKS. Sohncke's chief publications are *Über Stürme und Sturmwarnungen* (Berlin, 1875); *Die Entwicklung einer Theorie der Krystallstruktur* (Leipzig, 1879); *Über Wellenbewegung* (Berlin, 1881); and *Ge-mein Verständliche aus dem Gebiete der Physik* (Jena, 1892), his last publication. He also published more than forty articles in scientific journals.

II. SECONDARY LITERATURE. See S. Günther, "Leonhard Sohncke," in *Allgemeine Deutsche Biographie*, LIV, 377–379; F. Erk, "Leonhard Sohncke," in *Meteorologische Zeitschrift*, **15** (1898), 81–84; and C. Voit, "Leonhard Sohncke," in *Akademie der Wissenschaften (München), Sitzungsberichten*, **28** (1898), 440–449.

JOHN G. BURKE

SOKHOTSKY, YULIAN-KARL VASILIEVICH (*b.* Warsaw, Poland, 5 February 1842; *d.* Leningrad, U.S.S.R., 14 December 1927), *mathematics.*

Sokhotsky was the son of Vasili Sokhotsky, a clerk, and Iozefa Levandovska. After graduating from the Gymnasium in Warsaw, he joined the department of physics and mathematics of St. Petersburg University in 1861 but returned to Poland the following year to study mathematics independently. In 1865 he passed the examinations at the mathematics department of the University of St. Petersburg and received the bachelor of mathematics degree in 1866. After defending his master's thesis in 1868, Sokhotsky began teaching at the university as assistant professor and in 1869–1870 delivered the first course taught there on the theory of functions of a complex variable. He defended his doctoral thesis in 1873 and was elected extraordinary professor, becoming professor in 1883; from 1875 he also taught at the Institute of Civil Engineers. His lectures, especially on higher algebra, the theory of numbers, and the theory of definite integrals, were extremely successful. Sokhotsky was elected vice-president of the Mathematical Society at its founding in St. Petersburg in 1890 and succeeded V. G. Imshenetsky as president in 1892. He taught at the university until 1923.

Sokhotsky belonged to the school of P. L. Chebyshev; and the latter's influence, while not exceptional, is strong throughout his work. Thus, in his master thesis, which was devoted to the theory of special functions, Sokhotsky, besides employing expansions into an infinite series and continued fractions, made wide use of the theory of residues. (Chebyshev avoided the use of functions of a complex variable.) Elaborating the foundations of the theory of residues, Sokhotsky discovered and demonstrated one of the principal theorems of the theory of analytical functions. According to this theorem, a single-valued analytical function assumes in every vicinity of its essential singular point all complex values. This result was simultaneously published by Felice Casorati, but the theorem attracted attention only after its independent formulation and strict demonstration by Weierstrass in 1876. In his doctoral thesis Sokhotsky continued his studies on special functions, particularly on Jacobi polynomials and Lamé functions. One of the first to approach problems of the theory of singular integral equations, Sokhotsky in this work considered important boundary properties of the integrals of the type of Cauchy and, essentially, arrived at the so-called formulas of I. Plemel (1908).

Sokhotsky also gave a brilliant description of E. I. Zolotarev's theory of divisibility of algebraic numbers and wrote several articles on the theory of elliptic functions and theta functions.

BIBLIOGRAPHY

I. ORIGINAL WORKS. There is no complete bibliography of Sokhotsky's writings. His principal works include *Teoria integralnykh vychetov s nekotorymi prilozheniami* ("The Theory of Integral Residues With Some Applications"; St. Petersburg, 1868), his master's thesis; *Ob opredelennykh integralakh i funktsiakh upotreblyaemykh pri razlozheniakh v ryady* ("On Definite Integrals and Functions Used for Serial Expansion"; St. Petersburg, 1873), his doctoral dissertation; and *Nachalo naibolshego delitelia v primenenii k teorii delimosti algebraicheskikh chisel* ("The Application of the Principle of the Greatest Divisor to the Theory of Divisibility of Algebraic Numbers"; St. Petersburg, 1898).

II. SECONDARY LITERATURE. See the following (listed chronologically): S. Dickstein, "Wspomnienie pośmiertne o prof. J. Sochoskim," in *Wiadomości matematyczne*, **30** (1927–1928), 101–108; A. I. Markushevich, "Vklad Y. V. Sokhotskogo v obshchuyu teoriyu analiticheskikh funktsy" ("Y. V. Sokhotsky and the Development of the General Theory of Analytic Functions"), in *Istoriko-matematicheskie issledovaniya*, **3** (1950), 399–406; and *Skizzen zur Geschichte der analytischen Funktionen* (Berlin, 1955)—see index; I. Y. Depman, "S.-Peterburgskoe matematicheskoe obshchestvo" ("The St. Petersburg Mathematical Society"), in *Istoriko-matematicheskie issledovaniya,* **13** (1960), 11–106, esp. 33–38; and I. Z. Shtokalo, ed., *Istoria otechestvennoy matematiki* ("A History of Native Mathematics"), II (Kiev, 1967)—see index.

A. P. YOUSCHKEVITCH

SOKOLOV, DMITRY IVANOVICH (*b.* St. Petersburg, Russia [now Leningrad, U.S.S.R.], 1788; *d.* St. Petersburg, 1 December 1852), *geology.*

Sokolov's father, a locksmith, invented a ma-

chine for turning screws that was used in the fountains of St. Petersburg. After his death in 1796 Sokolov was sent to the preparatory class of the St. Petersburg Mining School, which was reorganized in 1804 as the Mining Cadet Corps and, in 1834, as the Institute of the Corps of Mining Engineers (now the Leningrad Mining Institute). He remained associated with this institution throughout his life.

After graduating in 1805, Sokolov worked in the laboratory of the Mining Cadet Corps as assayer and then began lecturing, first in metallurgy and assaying and later in geognosy and mining. In 1813 he was appointed supervisor of the mineralogical laboratory and from 1818 was also in charge of the collection of models. He continued his chemical research following his appointment as director of the joint laboratory of the Mining Cadet Corps and the Department of Mining and Salt Works. In 1817 he participated in the creation of the Mineralogical Society in St. Petersburg.

In 1822 Sokolov became professor of geognosy and mineralogy at St. Petersburg University, where he taught for more than twenty years while serving at the Mining Cadet Corps as class inspector, from 1826, and as assistant director in charge of teaching (1834–1847). He was also active in the creation in 1825 of *Gorny zhurnal* ("Mining Magazine"), the first specialized periodical in Russian, of which he became editor. In 1839 Sokolov was elected member of the Russian Academy of Sciences and, in 1841, honorary member of the division of language and philology of the St. Petersburg Academy of Sciences for the compilation of a dictionary of Old Church Slavonic and Russian.

Sokolov's marriage to Ekaterina Nikolaevna Prytkova was childless; their adopted daughter took care of him during his old age and illness.

Sokolov's early training as an experimental chemist enabled him to approach the problem of the classification of minerals in a new way. An advocate of the atomistic concept, which was then only beginning to win recognition, he believed that the physical properties of minerals depend upon vectorial atomic forces. Sokolov attached primary importance to chemical composition and classified minerals according to their cations. On the basis of similar properties, he outlined their natural groupings long before Mendeleev's periodic system. Thus his first category included lithophile elements of the first four groups of Mendeleev's periodic table, while his second category of metals comprised only the chalcophile elements.

Sokolov correctly attributed the physical properties of minerals—morphology, shape, color, luster, hardness, cleavage—to their chemical composition and regarded physical features as secondary. Although he did not take them into consideration in his classification, he did stress their importance for determination. Following the traditions of the Russian mineralogical school of Lomonosov and Severgin, Sokolov was especially concerned with paragenesis and, in his textbook of mineralogy, discussed the association of minerals, indicating that some, like cinnabar, have no characteristic paragenesis.

By the late 1820's Sokolov's early neptunist views had been superseded by the plutonist approach; and he came to regard most minerals, rocks, and ores as the result of crystallization from a magmatic melt. In his petrographic descriptions he consistently attempted to give not only a chemical and mineralogical description but also an account of their genesis. He distinguished magmatic from sedimentary rocks, adding in the 1830's the category of metamorphic. His interest in problems of petrology led him to conclude that the comparatively limited variety in rock composition could be explained by affinities of chemical elements. He also emphasized the importance of geological conditions in the physicochemical environment (pressure, temperature, presence of water vapor), assuming that with a variation in these conditions a change in petrology occurs.

In associating the conditions of ore formation with the specific features of geological environment, Sokolov attached decisive importance to processes occurring deep within the earth, and tried to distinguish periods of ore formation and provinces. He considered pneumatolytic and contact deposits the most important genetic types and distinguished the hydrothermal concentration of ore.

Sokolov's papers were also devoted to the problems of metalliferous placers. Contrary to prevalent concepts, he demonstrated that placers are located near the outcrops from the weathering of which they originated; this fact substantially altered methods of prospecting for gold. His distinction of metalliferous zones and belts of varying composition laid the foundation of modern concepts of metallogenetic provinces.

On Sokolov's initiative, work was begun on the geological mapping of Russia, and his suggestions resulted in the undertaking, in 1834, of geological surveys of individual mining regions. These surveys were carried out on his instructions and proceeded under his direct supervision. By 1841 the

first geological maps of European Russia had been published. The development of geological surveying had necessitated detailed stratigraphic subdivision. Of great importance for mapping was the summarized stratigraphic table compiled by Sokolov in 1831 and substantially modified in 1839.

Sokolov's three-volume textbook *Kurs geognosii* ("Course of Geognosy," 1839) contains a large section that would now be described as a history of geology; it gave a detailed description of all the geological systems then known. In this work Sokolov first distinguished an independent system at the top of the Paleozoic deposits, which two years later was named the Permian system and was included in international stratigraphic tables by Murchison. Sokolov also pointed out the essential differences between Lower and Upper Silurian deposits that warranted his describing each as an independent system.

In sedimentology Sokolov asserted that sedimentary masses are originally deposited horizontally and are only later compressed into folds, whereas lamination is an indication of episodic changes in the environment.

As early as 1820 Sokolov began to advocate that current geological phenomena can serve as a prototype for past events reflected in the geological sequence and that geological processes proceeded in the same way throughout history. He stressed this approach even more insistently, especially after the appearance of Lyell's *Principles of Geology* (1830–1833), which contributed to the development of the actualistic method and the worldwide dissemination of uniformitarian concepts, certain elements of which were contained in Sokolov's views.

Here, however, he did not take the position of formal uniformitarianism but systematically stressed that physicochemical conditions in the earth's interior, as well as paleogeographical conditions on its surface, are consistently changing and that, consequently, mineral and petrogenesis are not uniformitarian. In this respect Sokolov developed Lomonosov's views on the continual transformation of the world environment and believed that there is a continuous development process in both organic and inorganic nature. Advocating the existence of transformistic phenomena, which alter the organic world, Sokolov pointed out that this process is directed toward the origin of increasingly more highly organized forms—ideas that contained the rudiments of evolutionary concepts.

Sokolov actively disseminated advanced geological ideas through his textbooks and public lectures, which attracted a broad audience. His highly praised books were awarded three prizes by the St. Petersburg Academy of Sciences. Despite the rapid development of geology, Sokolov's textbooks remained valid; *Kurs mineralogii* ("Course of Mineralogy"), for example, was still in use after his death.

BIBLIOGRAPHY

I. ORIGINAL WORKS. Sokolov's writings include "Kratkoe nachertanie gornykh formatsy po noveyshemu sostoyaniyu geognozii" ("A Brief Outline of Rock Formations According to the Latest State of Geognosy"), in *Gorny zhurnal*, nos. 4–5 (1831); *Rukovodstvo k mineralogii s prisovokupleniem statisticheskikh svedeny o vazhneyshikh solyakh i metallakh* ("Textbook on Mineralogy With Additional Statistical Data on the Most Important Salts and Metals"), 2 vols. (St. Petersburg, 1832) and supplement (St. Petersburg, 1838); *Kurs geognosii* ("Course of Geognosy"), 3 vols. (St. Petersburg, 1839); and *Rukovodstvo k geognozii* ("Handbook of Geognosy"), 2 pts. (St. Petersburg, 1842).

II. SECONDARY LITERATURE. On Sokolov and his work, see E. A. Radkevich, *Dmitry Ivanovich Sokolov 1788–1852* (Moscow, 1959); and V. V. Tikhomirov, "Dmitry Ivanovich Sokolov (k 100-letiyu so dnya smerti" (" . . . on the Centenary of His Death"), in *Byulleten Moskovskogo obshchestva ispytatelei prirody*, Ser. geolog., **27**, no. 6 (1952).

V. V. TIKHOMIROV

SOLANDER, DANIEL CARL (*b*. Piteå, Sweden, 19 February 1733; *d*. London, England, 13 May 1782), *natural history*.

Solander's father, Carl Solander, was a delegate to the Riksdag as well as a Lutheran rector and rural dean for Piteå; his mother, Magdalena Bostadia, was the daughter of a district judge. After spending his formative years in Swedish Lapland, he entered the University of Uppsala on 1 July 1750, apparently to prepare for a legal or clerical career; but his study of natural history with Linnaeus and of chemistry with Wallerius turned his interest toward science.

In 1752 Solander helped Linnaeus classify and index the royal natural history collections at Ulriksdal and Drottningholm, as well as the collection of Count Carl Tessin; the results were published in *Museum Adolphi Frederica, Museum Ludovicae Ulricae*, and *Museum Tessinianum*. In 1756 Solander published *Caroli Linnaei Elementa botanica*, an epitome of Linnaeus' general botany.

Two years later he examined a supposedly parasitic worm and reported his findings in "Furia infernalis, vermis" (1772). In 1758 Solander assisted Linnaeus in examining Patrick Browne's herbarium; his efforts, coupled with his frequent visits to Linnaeus' home, aroused in the latter such esteem for his student that he wanted Solander to be both his successor and son-in-law.

During the 1750's Solander made two botanical expeditions to Lapland. In 1753 he traveled up the Piteå River, crossed the Kjölen Mountains into Norway, botanized in the vicinity of Rörstad, and returned to Uppsala. In 1755 he studied the natural history of the Tornio basin.

Chosen by Linnaeus to help popularize the Linnaean system in England, Solander left Uppsala on 6 April 1759; but a severe attack of epidemic influenza detained him in southern Sweden until 30 May 1760, and he did not arrive in England until 30 June. Solander was readily accepted into English society. Boswell once said of him, "Throw him where you will, he swims." Frances Burney found him "very sociable, full of talk, information, and entertainment, . . . a philosophical gossip." Richard Pulteney wrote that "the urbanity of his manners, and his readiness to afford every assistance in his power, joined to that clearness and energy with which he affected it," made Solander and the Linnaean system popular with naturalists.

A few weeks after his arrival, Solander had firmly established himself as the link between Linnaeus and English naturalists. In this capacity he collected plants for Linnaeus, obtained favors for English naturalists from him, and toured southern and southeastern England. He proved so useful an authority in decisions on Linnaean taxonomy that John Ellis and Peter Collinson worked to secure him a post, which he received in 1763, with the newly established British Museum.

Solander immediately began organizing the natural history collection, and by 1768 he had completed the first-draft descriptions. In the meantime he had described the collections of Gustavus Brander, the duchess of Portland, John Ellis, John Bartram, and Alexander Garden.

In June 1764 Solander became an active member of the Royal Society, and his friendship with Joseph Banks dates from that year. He advised Banks on how to prepare for his voyage in 1766 to Labrador and Newfoundland, and two years later, consulted with him on preparations for the voyage of the *Endeavour*, headed by Captain James Cook (1768–1771). After several days of planning, the Swedish naturalist asked to join the voyage and was accepted. Although Solander and Banks spent their time routinely collecting plant and animal specimens and conducting observations of the natural history and inhabitants, the voyage was not without its dangers: a fierce snowstorm on Tierra del Fuego, the near wreck of the *Endeavour* on the Great Barrier Reef, and an outbreak of malaria followed by dysentery in Batavia, Java.

The published results of their joint efforts are disappointing. Solander and Banks collected an estimated 100 new families and 1,000 new species of plants, in addition to hundreds of new species of animals. Of these new specimens, only 100 plant descriptions, printed by the British Museum (Natural History) in the early 1900's, and 200 insect descriptions by Johann Christian Fabricius, have been published. A lazy streak in Solander has often been blamed for the neglect; but the descriptions were, in fact, finished before Solander's death, and in 1785 Banks wrote that the project was nearing completion. Thus it was Banks who, for his own reasons, did not complete the project.

Solander Island (off the southern coast of South Island, New Zealand) and Cape Solander (the south side of Botany Bay, New South Wales, Australia) were named during the voyage, and Solander devised the Solander case, a book-shaped box that is still used, to guard the manuscript records of the voyage. On 21 November 1771 he was awarded the D.C.L. by Oxford for his part in the voyage.

Solander's manuscript descriptions were used by John Latham in his ornithological studies, by Johann Reinhold Forster for his reports on the second Cook voyage, and by Joseph Gaertner for his studies on plants. Furthermore, Solander's efforts helped establish a precedent: naturalists were subsequently included in government-sponsored voyages of exploration. Charles Darwin held the post aboard H.M.S. *Beagle.* Solander's and Banks's praise of the breadfruit contributed to attempts to introduce it to the West Indies and on the voyage of H.M.S. *Bounty.* Their influence on Cook stimulated his awareness of the importance of human and natural history, which was put to good use on his subsequent voyages.

Solander was part of a team of scientists recruited by Banks for Cook's second voyage. Banks refused to go because of inadequate quarters, and in the summer and fall of 1772 the group went instead on a four-month journey to the western coast of Britain, Iceland, and the Orkneys. Again, the results were never published, but the data were made available through Banks's collection and, later, through the collections of the British Museum.

After returning to London, Solander resumed his busy schedule, regaining his post as assistant keeper at the British Museum and becoming keeper in June 1773. He increased its collection, testified at Parliamentary hearings on the museum, organized and described its collection, and conducted tours. As Banks's private secretary, he was in charge of one of the largest natural history collections; as Banks's librarian, he named all of the new plants received by the Royal Botanical Gardens at Kew and assisted William Aiton in the early planning of *Hortus Kewensis.*

Solander helped several others as well. The duchess of Portland continued to employ him to help with her collection, and he aided Thomas Pennant in his studies in zoology, John Fothergill in his Upton garden, and John Lightfoot with his *Flora scotica.* Descriptions for Ellis' works were also written by Solander, and he participated in experiments by Charles Blagden and Benjamin Franklin. According to Thomas Krok, Solander contributed to sixty-six publications.

An active member of several scientific societies, Solander regularly attended meetings of the Royal Society and dined with the Royal Society Club, of which he was treasurer from 1774 until his death. He also regularly attended the meetings of a nameless society of scientists that met at Jack's Coffee House, an affiliation that led him to visit the Lunar Society of Birmingham. He met with Fothergill's medical society and was a corresponding member of the Académie des Sciences, the Royal Swedish Academy of Sciences, the Gesellschaft Naturforschender Freunde, the Royal Academy of Arts and Sciences of Göteborg, and the Academy of Sciences of Naples.

BIBLIOGRAPHY

I. ORIGINAL WORKS. Solander's MSS and letters are dispersed. The British Museum (Natural History) has a large collection of his biological notes and MSS, as well as his "Memoranda Connected With the Visit to Iceland. . . ." The Linnean Society of London has a collection of Solander's letters, particularly those written to Linnaeus. British Museum MSS Add. 45,874 and 45,875 are Solander's diaries of his work at the museum; MS Add. 29,533 contains some of John Ellis' correspondence with Solander. Many of Solander's letters were included in James Edward Smith, *A Selection of the Correspondence of Linnaeus and Other Naturalists* (London, 1821).

Solander's own publications include *Caroli Linnaei Elementa botanica* (Uppsala, 1756); "An Account of the Gardenia. . . ," in *Philosophical Transactions of the Royal Society*, **52**, pt. 2 (1762), 654–661; and "Furia infernalis, vermis, et ab eo concitari solitus morbus," in *Nova acta Regiae Societatis scientiarum upsaliensis*, **1** (1795), 44–58.

II. SECONDARY LITERATURE. On Solander and his scientific work, see Roy A. Rauschenberg, "A Letter of Sir Joseph Banks Describing the Life of Daniel Solander," in *Isis*, **55** (1964), 62–67; "Daniel Carl Solander, the Naturalist on the *Endeavour* Voyage," *ibid.*, **58** (1967), 367–374; and "Daniel Carl Solander. Naturalist on the 'Endeavour,'" in *Transactions of the American Philosophical Society*, n.s. **58**, pt. 8 (1968), 1–58, with extensive bibliography of primary and secondary sources. Earlier accounts and reminiscences include Frances Burney d'Arblay, *Diary and Letters of Madame d'Arblay*, C. F. Barrett, ed., I (London–New York, 1904), 318; James Boswell, *The Journal of James Boswell*, G. Scott and F. A. Pottle, eds., XIV (Mt. Vernon, N.Y., 1930), 182; and Richard Pulteney, *Historical and Biographical Sketches of the Progress of Botany in Britain*, II (London, 1790), 350–351. See also Thomas Krok, *Bibliotheca botanica suecana* (Uppsala–Stockholm, 1925), 655–660.

ROY A. RAUSCHENBERG

SOLDANI, AMBROGIO (or **Baldo Maria**) (*b.* Pratovecchio, Arezzo, Italy, 15 June 1736; *d.* Florence, Italy, 14 July 1808), *geology.*

The son of Dr. Soldano Soldani and Benedetta Nesterini, Soldani dropped the name Baldo Maria and assumed that of Ambrogio in 1752, when he entered the Camaldolese Congregation. Although an exemplary monk, he was active in the cultural life of Siena, where he spent most of his life. With the economist Sallustio Bandini, he reorganized the celebrated Accademia dei Fisiocritici, and in 1781 he was appointed professor of mathematics at the University of Siena.

Soldani was not only a mathematician, however, but also an ardent naturalist. In his studies of Pliocene marine formations of Tuscany and of preexistent ones bordering the Pliocene sea he proved to be an accomplished geologist, describing with great accuracy the lithological, stratigraphic, and paleontological characteristics of the deposits. Although his emphasis on the study of microscopic fossils (he described and drew hundreds of them, from mollusks to foraminifers) entitles him to be considered a paleontologist, Soldani never approached paleontological research as an end in itself. His desire to study the microfauna of the Mediterranean, which was almost unknown in his time, derived from his conviction that knowledge of present zoological conditions would have decisive consequences for the correct interpretation of the deposits left by the ancient seas.

In deposits of the Pliocene Tuscan sea, especially in those found near Siena and Volterra, Soldani identified three layers: an abyssal, formed by material of marine origin; a littoral, formed by material of terrestrial origin; and an intermediate, formed by both marine and terrestrial material. In addition he showed the presence of lacustrine microfauna in the sediments of the early Pleistocene Tuscan lakes that have since disappeared (such as Valdarno Superiore). Soldani's studies distinguished him as a leader in establishing the interrelation of zoology and paleontology; and he deserves considerable credit for his efforts to derive, from present conditions, material for the study of the geological past. Unfortunately he made no effort to classify systematically the many species that he described and distinguished. The harsh criticism, especially in this respect, of his most important work, the *Testaceographia*, so embittered him that he burned all copies of the work in his possession.

Soldani also studied the celebrated meteorites that fell in the region around Siena in 1794. Reasoning on the basis of eyewitness reports and on lithological study of the meteorites, he excluded any possibility of their terrestrial origin, proposing instead that they originated from a condensation of atmospheric vapor. This fallacious hypothesis, as well as that of their extraterrestrial origin, appeared absurd at the time to scientists; and Soldani was derided in a lively polemic.

An impartial evaluation of Soldani's entire work was not possible until after his death. Charles Lyell assigned him a prominent place among eighteenth-century naturalists, and not merely that of a founder of micropaleontology.

BIBLIOGRAPHY

I. ORIGINAL WORKS. Three basic works by Soldani are *Saggio orittografico, ovvero osservazioni sopra le terre nautiliche ed ammonitiche della Toscana* (Siena, 1780); *Testaceographia ac Zoophitographia parva et microscopica*, 4 vols. (Siena, 1789–1798), very rare, partly because Soldani destroyed copies; and *Sopra una pioggetta di sassi accaduta nella sera de' 16 giugno del MDCCXCIV in Lucignan d'Asso nel Sanese* (Siena, 1794).

II. SECONDARY LITERATURE. See E. Manasse, "Commemorazione di Ambrogio Soldani," in *Atti dell' Accademia dei fisiocritici di Siena*, 4th ser., **20** (1908),

365–376; O. Silvestri, "Ambrogio Soldani e le sue ope-re," in *Atti della Società italiana di scienze naturali*, **15** (1872), 273–289; and F. Rodolico, "Ambrogio Soldani e Ottaviano Targioni Tozzetti; carteggio sulla 'pioggetta di sassi' del 1794," in *Physis*, **12** (1970), 197–210.

FRANCESCO RODOLICO

SOLDNER, JOHANN GEORG VON (*b*. Georgen-hof, near Feuchtwangen, Germany, 16 July 1776; *d*. Bogenhausen, Munich, Germany, 18 May 1833), *geodesy, astronomy.*

Soldner's father, Johann Andreas Soldner, was a farmer in Georgenhof. The boy's schooling began in Banzenweiler and continued in Feuchtwangen and at the Gymnasium in Ansbach, where he was taught by the physicist Julius Yelin. His education was interrupted by periods of work on his father's farm. Soldner's diary indicates that his earliest interest in land surveying was aroused by neighboring farmers and by some geometric notes in an early Ansbach calendar. He was largely self-taught and he devised his own instruments for measuring the altitude of the sun.

Soldner was a pupil of the astronomer Bode and first became known through his contributions to Bode's *Astronomisches Jahrbuch*. In 1805 Frederick William of Prussia made him director of the survey of Ansbach, but the battles of Jena and Auerstedt made this work impossible.

Soldner was patronized by the astronomer Ulrich Schiegg, who in 1808 was appointed technical member of the Tax Rectification Commission. Correct land-tax assessments required an accurate survey of the province, and in 1811 Soldner was appointed to the Bavarian Land Survey. In May 1810 he had published his famous memorandum on the calculation of a triangle network, in recognition of which he was made an ordinary member of the Munich Academy of Sciences. This work was lost until 1873, when Karl Orff published an account of the Bavarian survey.

Soldner's method for calculating the spherical triangles of the main network was an improvement on Delambre's method, which was adequate for degree measurement but was not suitable for land surveying, that is, when the lengths of arcs of spherical triangles must be known. Soldner used a system of coordinates that introduced three points into every mesh of the network plan, accurately aligning it with the land to be surveyed. Thus he was able to measure arcs to an accuracy of one

centimeter. Also, his solution of spherical triangles was more convenient than that of Legendre; Soldner kept two angles of the spherical triangle the same and altered the length of the sides when comparing it to a plane triangle.

In 1813 Soldner prepared a paper on a new method of reducing astronomical azimuths. His method depended on the observation of the maximum east and west displacements from the North Star. This discovery aroused the jealousy of the astronomer and councillor Karl Felix Seyffer, who, in 1815, was removed from office and was succeeded by Soldner as director of the Bogenhausen observatory. Soldner was responsible for supervising the construction and equipping of the new observatory. He also retained his post as consultant to the land-tax commission. In 1820 Delambre defended the originality of Soldner's work in the *Connaissance des temps*.

The observatory was completed in 1818, and instruments from the workshops in Utschneider, Reichenbach, and Fraunhofer were installed. Soldner had previously tested many of these instruments for their accuracy and suitability. By 1820 he had begun to observe the positions of the stars and planets on the meridian circle. With Nicolai, he worked on the measurement of a degree; and, independently, he studied lunar methods for determining longitude.

From 1823 on Soldner confined himself to the administration of the observatory; his assistant, Lamont, who succeeded him as director, undertook the observational work. During these years, Soldner's health deteriorated because of a liver ailment.

Soldner was simple and reserved in manner, and he valued real scholarship for its own sake. His painstaking observational work on the detection of motion among the fixed stars could be of value only to future generations of astronomers and illustrates the unselfish spirit of his work. His writings are clear and concise, and he avoided repetition of what was already common knowledge.

BIBLIOGRAPHY

I. ORIGINAL WORKS. Soldner's papers appeared in many leading astronomical journals. His books include *Théorie et tables d'une nouvelle fonction transcendente* (Munich, 1809); *Bestimmung des Azimuths von Alto-munster* (Munich, 1813); *Neue Methode, Beobachtete Azimuthe zu Reduzieren* (Munich, 1813); and probably *Astronomische Beobachtungen von 1819 bis 1827 auf der Sternwarte zu Bogenhausen,* 3 vols. (Munich, 1833–1835). Hostile colleagues prevented the publication of later volumes of this last work.

II. SECONDARY LITERATURE. Biographical information is given by C. M. Bauernfeind, in *Allgemeine Deutsche Biographie,* XXXIV, 557–563; F. J. Müller, *Lebenslaufe aus Franken,* II (Wurzburg, 1922), 417–427; and *Poggendorff,* II, 955–956.

Studies of Soldner's geodetical work include F. J. Müller, *Johann Georg von Soldner der Geodät* (Munich, 1914); and Gunther Rutz, *Die Alte Bayerische Triangulation von Johann Georg Soldner* (Munich, 1971). Müller and Rutz draw extensively on Bauernfeind. See also R. Sigl, "Johann Georg von Soldner zum Gedächtnis," in *Mitteilungsblatt des Deutsches Landesvermessungswerk, Landesverein Bayern,* no. 2 (1966). Archives relating to Soldner exist at the Bayerisches Landesvermessungsarnt, Munich. Letters between Soldner and Gauss exist at Niedersächsische Staats- und Universitätsbibliothek, Göttingen.

SISTER MAUREEN FARRELL, F.C.J.

SOLEIL, JEAN-BAPTISTE-FRANÇOIS (*b.* Paris, France, 1798; *d.* Paris, 17 November 1878), *optical instruments.*

Soleil learned his craft while working under the engineers Hareing and Palmer. From 1823 to 1827 he was intimately associated with the work of Fresnel. Soleil directed the construction of the annular lenses and the mechanism to rotate them that Fresnel had designed for use in lighthouses. Soleil's first lens was made under the direction of Fresnel and was based on his theory. In 1841 it was presented to the Académie des Sciences by his son, Henri. Soleil constructed most of the apparatus used by Fresnel in his optical research based on the experimental demonstration of the wave theory by Thomas Young. This work brought Soleil into contact with those scientists who, following Fresnel, developed the new optics: François Arago, Jacques Babinet, Charles Delezenne, Fredrik Rudberg, and Johann Nörrenberg. A notable piece of apparatus constructed by Soleil—the diffraction bench—was intended for use in public demonstrations of interference and diffraction phenomena with either sunlight or lamplight.

Soleil produced and sold a wide variety of optical instruments at 35 rue de l'Odéon. His inventions included an apparatus for measuring the interaxial angle in biaxial crystals and an improved model of Biot's saccharimeter. In 1849 he retired from business and was succeeded by his son-in-law and former apprentice Jules Duboscq. In November 1850 Soleil was named chevalier of the Légion d'Honneur.

Soleil received a number of exhibition awards, including a gold medal in 1849; and the physical optics section of the Great Exhibition of 1851 in London was devoted solely to the products and inventions of Duboscq and Soleil. This exhibition won the highest award—a council medal.

BIBLIOGRAPHY

I. ORIGINAL WORKS. Soleil's works include "Appareils pour la production des anneaux colorés à centre noir ou blanc," in *Comptes rendus hebdomadaires des séances de l'Académie des sciences,* **18** (1844), 417–419; "Note sur la structure et la propriété rotatoire du quartz cristallisé," *ibid.,* **20** (1845), 435–438; "Note sur moyen de faciliter les expériences de polarisation rotatoire," *ibid.,* 1805–1807; "Note sur perfectionnement apporté au pointage du saccharimètre," *ibid.,* **24** (1847), 973–975; "Notice sur l'horloge polaire de M. Wheatstone, construite et perfectionnée par M. Soleil," *ibid.,* **28** (1849), 511–513; and "Note sur un nouveau caractère distinctif entre les cristaux à un axe, positifs et négatifs," *ibid.,* **30** (1850), 361–362. Brief notices of apparatus shown to the Academy are also printed in *Comptes rendus hebdomadaires des séances de l'Académie des sciences.*

II. SECONDARY LITERATURE. See *Exhibition of the Works of Industry of All Nations 1851. Reports by the Juries on the Subjects in the Thirty Classes Into Which the Exhibition Was Divided* (London, 1852), 272; and G. Vapereau, *Dictionnaire universel des contemporains* (Paris, 1880).

G. L'E. TURNER

SOLLAS, WILLIAM JOHNSON (*b.* Birmingham, England, 30 May 1849; *d.* Oxford, England, 20 October 1936), *geology, paleontology, anthropology.*

Sollas was educated at the Royal School of Mines, London, where he studied under A. C. Ramsay and T. H. Huxley, and then at St. John's College, Cambridge, where T. G. Bonney, deputy to Adam Sedgwick, was his tutor. For six years he gave university extension courses in geology and biology to adult students in various parts of the country. He was afterward successively professor of geology at Bristol (1880–1883), Trinity College, Dublin (1883–1897), and Oxford (1897–1936). Sollas was a versatile investigator and experimentalist, and in the course of a long and active life he made significant contributions to many branches of the geological sciences and to biological research. He received numerous British and foreign academic awards, including the Royal Medal of the Royal Society of London.

Sollas' early work was on fossil and modern sponges and culminated in a paper on Tetractinellida in the *Report of the Scientific Results of the Voyage of H.M.S. Challenger* (1888). While at Dublin, Sollas carried out petrological and mineralogical investigations of the granites of Ireland. In this work he concluded that the "pleochroic haloes" surrounding the zircon crystals—which are contained in the dark micas of Wicklow granite— were probably caused by an unknown element. Joly, his colleague at Dublin, later proved that this phenomenon resulted from the presence of radioactive elements of the uranium decay series in the zircons.

Sollas published papers on riebeckite and zinnwaldite, and he also studied the intimate architecture of crystals. To form crystalline solids he adapted the methods and ideas of Haüy and approached the subject from the standpoint of the structural arrangement of the atomic units. The structures later revealed by more sophisticated X rays fully supported his contention that the closest packing of atoms does not provide the only style of crystal architecture: in many cases the packing is as open as he had postulated. To obtain a preliminary separation of minerals for chemical analysis, Sollas devised the "diffusion column," in which heavy liquids are superposed in layers of graded density that are indicated by floating markers of known specific gravity. He adapted the method of serial sections, which he had used for his sponge research, to the examination of fossils, thus obtaining data on their internal structure and then constructing models of the skeleton. Using this method, he made important investigations on fossils ranging from Silurian echinoderms to Jurassic reptiles. In some of this work his daughter Igerna was his collaborator. His elder daughter, Hertha, was responsible, under his direction, for the English translation of Eduard Suess's *Das Antlitz der Erde.*

In 1911 Sollas published *Ancient Hunters and Their Modern Representatives.* Thereafter he engaged increasingly in research on various aspects of anthropology and prehistoric archaeology. He excavated the Paviland Cave in South Wales, which had first been explored by a predecessor at Oxford, William Buckland. With Breuil, Sollas showed that the flint implements associated with the skeleton of the "Red Lady" belonged to the Aurignacian age,

and he suggested that the skeleton itself belonged to Cro-Magnon man. This conjecture has been confirmed by isotope dating.

BIBLIOGRAPHY

I. ORIGINAL WORKS. Few of Sollas' MSS survive. They consist mainly of notebooks and lecture notes at the department of geology, University of Oxford. He published some 180 works from 1872 to 1933. His major writings include *The Age of the Earth and Other Geological Studies* (London, 1905); *The Rocks of Cape Colville Peninsula, Auckland, New Zealand,* 2 vols. (Wellington, New Zealand, 1905–1906); and *Ancient Hunters and Their Modern Representatives* (London, 1911; 2nd ed., 1915; 3rd ed., 1924).

II. SECONDARY LITERATURE. Accounts of Sollas' work and life are in *Obituary Notices of Fellows of the Royal Society of London,* 2 (1938), 265–281; and *Proceedings of the Geological Society of America for 1937* (1938), 203–220. Both of these contain a complete list of his publications and a portrait.

J. M. EDMONDS

SOLVAY, ERNEST (*b.* Rebecq-Rognon, near Brussels, Belgium, 16 April 1838; *d.* Brussels, 26 May 1922), *industrial chemistry.*

After a modest education at local schools, Solvay entered the salt-making business owned by his father, Alexandre Solvay. Then, at the age of twenty-one, he joined his uncle Florimond Semet in managing a gasworks in Brussels—his particular concern being the discovery of better methods of concentrating ammoniacal liquors. In 1861 he noted the ease with which ammonia, salt solution, and carbon dioxide react to form sodium bicarbonate, which can be converted easily to the soda ash of commerce. The glass and soap trades had created a demand for this chemical that was met only by the economically unstable and chemically complex Leblanc process. At this time Solvay was unaware that the ammonia-soda reaction had been known for fifty years; that several industrial chemists, including William Gossage and Henry Deacon, had been unsuccessful in employing it for large-scale production; and that James Muspratt had lost £8,000 on unsuccessful experiments.

Solvay's knowledge of the industrial preparation of salt and ammonia was useful when he turned to the problems of the ammonia-soda process: particularly those involving the loss of expensive ammonia and the practical difficulties of mixing liquids and gases on a large scale. With his brother

Alfred, Solvay established (1861) a small works in the Schaerbeek district of Brussels. Following some small success, and supported financially by the family, the Solvay brothers built, in 1863, a factory at Couillet, near Charleroi; production started in 1865. Solvay patented every stage of the process but granted licenses to soda manufacturers in other countries. In 1872 a license was acquired by Mond, who introduced the Solvay process in England and later achieved great success with it. Solvay's key contribution to the soda trade was his invention of a carbonating tower in which ammoniacal brine could be mixed thoroughly with carbon dioxide. By 1890 Solvay had established plants in most European countries, in Russia, and in the United States.

Solvay was a member of the Belgian senate and a minister of state. He founded the Solvay International Institutes of Chemistry, of Physics, and of Sociology. By the terms of Solvay's gift, the institutes held periodical international conferences at which such broad areas of science as electrons and photons (1928), the solid state (1951), and the origin and structure of the universe were discussed. The names of the participants testify to the quality of the contributions. The 1928 physics congress, for example, was addressed by Bragg, de Broglie, Bohr, Born, Heisenberg, and Schrödinger.

BIBLIOGRAPHY

I. ORIGINAL WORKS. Solvay's only descriptions of his process are contained in his patents—the most important are the British patents 3131 of 1863, 1525 of 1872, 2143 of 1876, and 999 of 1904. The Royal Society *Catalogue of Scientific Papers*, XI, 450, XVIII, 845, lists nine papers of only minor importance.

II. SECONDARY LITERATURE. A meticulously detailed description of Solvay's plant and methods appears in G. Lunge, *The Manufacture of Sulphuric Acid and Alkali*, 2nd ed., III (London, 1896), 9–100. Obituaries, with portraits, appear in *Industrial and Engineering Chemistry*, **14** (1922), 1156; *Journal of the Society of Chemical Industry*, **41** (1922), 231–R; and *Revue de métallurgie*, **19** (1922), 696, which contains several errors. See also Jacques Bolle, *Solvay: L'homme, la découverte, l'entreprise industrielle* (Brussels, 1968); E. Farber, *Great Chemists* (New York, 1961), 773–782; and P. Heger and C. Lefebure, *La vie d'Ernest Solvay* (Brussels, 1919).

W. A. CAMPBELL

SOMERVILLE, MARY FAIRFAX GREIG (*b*. Jedburgh, Roxburghshire, Scotland, 26 December 1780; *d*. Naples, Italy, 29 November 1872), *scientific and mathematical exposition, experimentation on the effects of solar radiation.*

One of the foremost women of science of the nineteenth century, Mrs. Somerville was through her writings and example influential in gaining wider acceptance among a literate public for various nineteenth-century scientific ideas and practices and in opening new opportunities to women. Her notable career, spanning more than half a century, brought her in contact with many of the foremost scientific, literary, and political personages of Europe and America. Public recognition accorded her had profound and beneficial effects in advancing the cause of science and of women's education and emancipation.

Through her father, Vice-Admiral Sir William George Fairfax, R.N., a hero of the Battle of Camperdown, she was connected with the distinguished Fairfax family of England that produced the great Cromwellian general Sir Thomas Fairfax and the Fairfaxes of the Virginia Colony. Through her mother, Margaret Charters, his second wife, daughter of Samuel Charters, solicitor of customs for Scotland, she was related to several ancient Scottish houses, among them the Murrays of Philiphaugh, the Douglases of Friarshaw, the Douglases of Springwood Park, the Charterises of Wemyss, and John Knox.

Fifth of their seven children (only three of whom survived to majority), Mary Fairfax was born in the manse at Jedburgh, the home of an aunt, Martha Charters Somerville, who later became her mother-in-law. Her childhood was spent in Burntisland, a small seaport on the Firth of Forth opposite Edinburgh. In a house sold to the Fairfaxes by Samuel Charters and still standing, her easygoing, indulgent mother thriftily reared four children—the eldest surviving son Samuel, Mary, and two younger ones, Margaret and Henry—on slim navy pay. Customarily in the Charters, as in many well-connected Scottish families, sons received excellent educations, attending university and entering the kirk, the legal profession, or service in the East India Company. For daughters, mastery of social and domestic arts and a minimum of formal book learning was considered sufficient. Mary's father, returning from a long period of sea duty, was "shocked to find . . . [his daughter] such a savage," hardly able to read, unable to write, and with no knowledge of language or numbers. He dispatched her, at the age of ten, to a fashionable, expensive boarding school at Musselburgh—a drastic step for a man of such strong Tory convictions. There for twelve months she had the only full-time instruction of her long life, emerging from the experience, she recounts in her autobiography, "like a wild animal escaped out of a cage" but with a taste for reading, some notion of simple arithmetic, a smattering of grammar and French, poor handwriting, and abominable spelling.

Over the next years she had occasional lessons in ballroom dancing, pianoforte playing, fine cookery, drawing and painting (under Alexander Nasmyth), penmanship, needlework, and the use of the globes. A lively and persistent mind, immense curiosity and eagerness to learn, supported by a robust constitution and quiet, unswerving determination, enabled her to take advantage of every opportunity for enlightenment. At Burntisland she had freedom to roam the Scottish countryside and seashore, observing nature at first hand. She read through the small family library, teaching herself enough Latin for Caesar's *Commentaries*. In Edinburgh during the winter months, family position brought her in contact with intellectual and professional circles and the rich artistic life of the Scottish capital. A charmingly shy, petite, and beautiful young woman—Edinburgh society dubbed her the "Rose of Jedburgh"—she delighted in the parties, visits, balls, theaters, concerts, and innocent flirtations that, with domestic and daughterly duties, filled the days of popular Edinburgh belles at the turn of the century.

Another and less conventional interest absorbed her during these years. Between the ages of thirteen and fifteen, the chance glimpse in a ladies' fashion magazine of some strange symbols, said to be "algebra," aroused her curiosity. None of her close relatives or acquaintances could have told her anything of the subject, even had she the courage to ask. Mrs. Somerville, in contrast to other scientific women of the nineteenth century, had no family incentive to investigate science or mathematics and no household exposure to these subjects. Her unguided efforts to learn something of this mysterious but strangely attractive "algebra" were fruitless until, overhearing a casual remark by Nasmyth, she was led to persuade her younger brother's tutor to buy for her copies of Bonnycastle's *Algebra* and Euclid's *Elements*, which she then began to study on her own. Discovering her reading mathematics, her father instantly forbade it, fearing that the strain of abstract thought would injure the tender female frame. This view was widely and long held and shared to a degree by Mrs. Somerville herself: she believed her injudicious encouragement of her oldest daughter's intel-

lectual precocity had been a factor in the child's death at age ten. In the late 1790's Captain Fairfax's strictures against arduous mental effort, combined with outspoken criticism of "unwomanly behavior" by aunts and female cousins, drove Mary Fairfax to secret, intermittent application to mathematics but sharpened her resolve to learn the subject.

In May 1804 she married a cousin, Samuel Greig, commissioner of the Russian navy and Russian consul general in Great Britain. Greig's father, Admiral Sir Samuel Greig, a nephew of her grandfather Charters, had been one of five young British naval officers who, at the request of Empress Catherine II, went to Russia in 1763 to reorganize her navy and had been chiefly responsible for the success of that undertaking. He and his English wife reared their children in Russia: their sons made careers in Russian service, and their daughters married into Russian families, but ties with Britain were never broken. Young Samuel Greig, a captain in the Russian navy, trained aboard Admiral Fairfax's ship and, on his marriage to the admiral's daughter, was given an appointment in London, where he and his bride lived until his death in September 1807, at the age of twenty-nine. For Mary Greig, this period in London—away for the first time from family and Scotland—was a difficult one. She was much alone, and although she could read and study more freely than ever before, her husband had, in her words, "a low opinion of the capacity of . . . [the female] sex, and had neither knowledge of nor interest in science of any kind." After his death she returned with their two young sons to her parents' home in Scotland.

With the newly acquired independence of widowhood and a modestly comfortable fortune, she set out openly to educate herself in mathematics, ignoring the ridicule of relations and acquaintances. The greater part of each day was occupied with her children, and her evenings with social and filial obligations; yet she read Newton's *Principia* and began the study of higher mathematics and physical astronomy. Moreover, she found help and encouragement among Edinburgh intellectuals. John Playfair gave her useful hints on study. A group of young Whigs in her social circle, among them Henry Brougham, Francis Jeffrey, the Horner brothers, and Sydney Smith—who had some years earlier launched the successful *Edinburgh Review* and who urged, as social reforms, widened educational opportunities—became and remained her champions, finding in this pretty, quiet, and liberal-minded young widow the capacity and zest for learning that they asserted for her sex. Mrs. Somerville's most helpful mentor in these days was William Wallace, later professor of mathematics at Edinburgh. Wallace advised her by correspondence and rewarded her efforts with a silver medal for solving, in his *Mathematical Repository*, a prize problem, the first of many awards she would receive over the next sixty years.

In May 1812 Mary Greig married, as his second wife, her first cousin, William Somerville, son of the historian and minister at Jedburgh, Thomas Somerville. A cosmopolitan army doctor who had served in Canada, Sicily, and South Africa, and an affable, generous, and intelligent man of liberal convictions, William Somerville, from the first, staunchly supported his wife's aspirations. Throughout their half century of marriage, until his death in 1860 in his ninetieth year, he was her invaluable aide, taking great pride and satisfaction in her fame. Soon after their marriage she began, at age thirty-three, to continue on her own a rigorous course of readings (laid out by Wallace) in French higher mathematics and astronomical science. At her husband's urging she also devoted an hour each morning to Greek and, when the young naturalist George Finlayson became tutor to her son Woronzow Greig, she commenced the systematic study of botany. Together she and Somerville interested themselves in geology and mineralogy under the casual tutelage of their friends John Playfair, Robert Jameson, and James Hall. Among their other Edinburgh intimates were Sir James Mackintosh, Sir Walter Scott, John Leslie, James Gregory, and David Brewster.

When in 1816 William Somerville was named to the Army Medical Board, the family moved from Edinburgh to London, their chief residence for the next twenty years. Through Scottish friends and connections they were immediately introduced into the best intellectual society of the British capital, where they were soon popular figures. Dr. Somerville became a Fellow of the Royal Society. Mrs. Somerville's mathematical and scientific pursuits made her a minor lioness. In 1817 on their first tour abroad, Biot and Arago, who had been charmed by her in London, introduced them to Laplace, Gay-Lussac, Bouvard, Poisson, Cuvier, Haüy, and other French savants, who received them both as colleagues, entertained them during their stay in Paris, and afterward maintained friendly correspondences with the couple. In Switzerland the Somervilles were welcomed by Candolle, de La Rive, Prevost, and Sismondi; and in

Italy by the English colony and various celebrated Italians. Many of Mrs. Somerville's friendships with scientific, literary, and political personages date from this time.

In London their familiar circle included the Henry Katers, the Thomas Youngs, the Alexander Marcets (Mary Somerville and Jane Marcet always held each other in affectionate esteem), Sir Humphry and Lady Davy (whom Mrs. Somerville had known in Edinburgh as Mrs. Apreece), the poets Thomas Campbell, Samuel Rogers, and Thomas Moore, Maria Edgeworth, John Allen, the Misses Berry, Harriet Martineau, Joanna Baillie and her family, Francis Chantrey, John Saunders Sebright, Henry Warburton, and, above all, William Hyde Wollaston. From such natural philosophers she learned science directly, as they discussed their latest findings, described and demonstrated their newest apparatus, and shared their enthusiasms and ideas with fellow guests at the small, convivial gatherings typical of the day. In an age of gentleman amateurs, Mrs. Somerville's informal apprenticeship to these scientific masters was in many respects identical with the nurture of male scientists.

Her first paper, a report in *Philosophical Transactions* of some experiments she designed and carried out on magnetizing effects of sunlight, appeared in 1826; it was communicated to the Royal Society by her husband. This work, widely praised and accepted for some years, although its conclusions were later disputed and disproved, had a vitalizing effect on investigations of the alleged phenomenon. Ten years later Arago presented to the Académie des Sciences an extract from one of her letters as a paper entitled "Experiments on the Transmission of Chemical Rays of the Solar Spectrum Across Different Media," which appeared in the *Comptes rendus*. Her third and final experimental paper, "On the Action of Rays of the Spectrum on Vegetable Juices" (1845), came out in *Abstracts of the Philosophical Transactions*. All her experimental work is characterized by rationality in approach, delicacy and simplicity in execution, and clarity in presentation. Her only essay for a popular journal was a long one on comets in the December 1835 issue of *Quarterly Review*, soon after Halley's comet had been seen.

Research, writing, and study were always unobtrusively carried on in the midst of a full social life and numerous maternal and domestic responsibilities. In 1824 William Somerville was appointed physician to the Royal Hospital, Chelsea; and, with three children, they moved to Chelsea College, on the outskirts of London. Margaret, their oldest daughter, had died the previous year. In 1814 they had lost two children: the younger Greig boy at the age of nine, and their own only son, an infant. Of Mrs. Somerville's remaining offspring, her son Woronzow Greig, a successful and esteemed barrister, graduate of Trinity College, Cambridge, died in 1865 at the age of sixty, while her two daughters, Martha and Mary Somerville, both unmarried, survived their mother. She herself supervised the education of the girls, determined that they should not lack, as she did, for systematic learning. At the behest of Lady Byron, widow of the poet, Mrs. Somerville directed also the early mathematical studies of Ada Byron, later Lady Lovelace; the Byron and Somerville families were, from the mid-1820's onward, intimate friends.

In 1827 Henry Brougham wrote William Somerville to ask him to persuade his wife to put Laplace's *Mécanique céleste*, which she had studied in Edinburgh, into English for the Library of Brougham's Society for the Diffusion of Useful Knowledge. Unsure of her ability, she finally gave in to their urgings, provided the manuscript, if unsatisfactory, would be destroyed. A rendition rather than mere translation—since full mathematical explanations and diagrams were added to make Laplace's work comprehensible to most of its English readers—her treatise when completed in 1830 was too long for the Library series. Somerville, however, submitted it to their great friend J. F. W. Herschel, who urged the publisher John Murray to bring it out. Dubious of the success of a book on such a subject, Murray printed 750 copies in 1831. To his and Mrs. Somerville's amazement, *The Mechanism of the Heavens* sold well and won praise for her. It was put to use in advanced courses at Cambridge. Its preface—the necessary mathematical background—was reprinted in 1832 as *A Preliminary Dissertation on the Mechanism of the Heavens*; both it and the previous volume were immediately pirated in the United States and were used in Britain as textbooks for almost a century. The Royal Society hailed the work by voting to place a portrait bust of Mrs. Somerville in their Great Hall. Acclaim came also from the younger generation of British scientists, including Babbage, Brewster, Buckland, Faraday, Herschel, Lyell, Murchison, Sedgwick, and Whewell, who gave her the same unstinting admiration, respect, and assistance their elders had bestowed, regarding her as the spokeswoman for science and offering her honors and opportunities unique for a woman.

Thus at age fifty-one Mary Somerville embarked on a professional career as a scientific expositor.

Her gift for clear and cogent explanation, a quick and lively mind, access to the best scientific thought of the times, patience and perseverance, together with a sweet simplicity and charm of manner and a "womanliness," which demonstrated that learning and comfortable domesticity could successfully be combined, sustained this career for the next four decades. Mrs. Somerville was fortunate too in her times: industrialization had popularized notions of self-help, expanding opportunities, changes, and new freedoms. Her second book, *On the Connexion of the Physical Sciences*, a synthetical consideration of the mutual dependence of the physical sciences, came out in 1834 to even greater acclaim. The Royal Astronomical Society (1835) elected her and Caroline Herschel their first female honorary members. Sir Robert Peel awarded her a civil pension of £200 annually (later increased to £300 by Lord Melbourne) in recognition of her work. The Royal Academy of Dublin (1834), the Société de Physique et d'Histoire Naturelle (Geneva, 1834), and the Bristol Philosophical Institution (1835?) voted her honorary memberships. In the ten editions of this work Mrs. Somerville put forward the newest, most penetrating, and authoritative ideas and practices, avoiding fads and gimcrackery. Clerk Maxwell, forty years afterward, classed the work as one important in advancing scientific thought through its insistence on viewing physical science as a whole. J. C. Adams attributed his first notions about the existence of Neptune to a passage he read in its sixth edition.

In the late 1830's her husband's health failed, and the family migrated to Italy, where Mrs. Somerville spent the remaining thirty-six years of her long life, a valued guest and brilliant part of the Italian scene during the Risorgimento. Not only was she offered access to Italian libraries and scientific facilities, but she was given membership in six of the leading Italian scientific societies (1840–1845). Although, as the years passed, it became more and more difficult to stay abreast of British science, she managed through letters, visits, journals, and books to keep in touch with major developments. In 1848, at age sixty-eight, she published her third and most successful book, *Physical Geography*, a subject which had always interested her deeply. Its seven editions brought her numerous honors: the Victoria Gold Medal of the Royal Geographical Society (1870); election to the American Geographical and Statistical Society (1857), to the Italian Geographical Society (1870), and to five additional provincial Italian societies (1853–1857); several medals; and praise from Humboldt. In this book, as in the *Connexion of the Physical Sciences*, Mrs. Somerville strongly endorsed the new geology of Lyell, Murchison, Buckland, and their school—a stand that brought her some public criticism.

Twenty-one years later, when she was eighty-nine, her final work, *On Molecular and Microscopic Science*, appeared in two volumes. It deals with the constitution of matter and the structure of microscopic plants. At this date its science was considered old-fashioned, but young John Murray published it out of loyalty to and affection for its author, on the recommendation of Sir John Herschel, who had also been instrumental in persuading Mrs. Somerville to bring out her *Physical Geography*. The public received it with kindly interest and deference to its venerable creator. In the same year she was made a member of the American Philosophical Society (she had warm regard for Americans) and completed her autobiography—a vivid and spritely account of her life in Scotland, England, and Italy; of her visits to Switzerland, France, and Germany; and of the many interesting personages she had known. After her death her elder surviving daughter, Martha, published parts of this manuscript as *Personal Recollections From Early Life to Old Age of Mary Somerville* (1873).

In her later years Mrs. Somerville gave powerful but always temperate support to the cause of the education and emancipation of women. Hers was the first signature on John Stuart Mill's great petition to Parliament for women's suffrage, solicited by Mill himself. An early advocate of higher education for women, many of her books were given after her death to the new Ladies College at Hitchin (now Girton College, Cambridge). Somerville College (1879), one of the first two colleges for women at Oxford, is named after her. Although frail and deaf in her last years, Mary Somerville's spirit and intelligence, her interest in friends, in the cause of women, and in science never faltered. At the time of her death, at ninety-two, she was revising a paper on quaternions.

BIBLIOGRAPHY

I. ORIGINAL WORKS. The Somerville Collection (MSS, papers, letters, documents, diplomas, and memorabilia owned by Mrs. Somerville's heir) is deposited in the Bodleian Library, Oxford.

Mary Somerville's works are "On the Magnetizing Power of the More Refrangible Solar Rays," in *Philosophical Transactions of the Royal Society*, **116** (1826), 132; *The Mechanism of the Heavens* (London, 1831); *A Preliminary Dissertation on the Mechanism of the Heav-*

ens (London, 1832); *On the Connexion of the Physical Sciences* (London, 1834; 2nd ed., 1835; 3rd ed., 1836; 4th ed., 1840; 5th ed., 1842; 6th ed., 1846; 7th ed., 1848; 9th ed., 1858; 10th ed., A. B. Buckley, ed., 1877); "Art. VII.-1. Ueber den Halleyschen Cometen . . .," in *Quarterly Review*, **105** (1835), 195–233; and "Experiments on the Transmission of Chemical Rays of the Solar Spectrum Across Different Media," in *Comptes rendus hebdomadaires des séances de l'Académie des sciences*, **3** (1836), 473–476.

See also the extract from a letter by Mrs. Somerville to Sir John Herschel, Bart., F.R.S., dated Rome, 20 September 1845, entitled "On the Action of the Rays of the Spectrum on Vegetable Juices," in *Philosophical Transactions of the Royal Society*, **5** (1845), 569; *Physical Geography* (London, 1848; 2nd ed., 1849; 3rd ed., 1851; 4th ed., 1858; 5th ed., 1862; 6th [1870] and 7th [1877] eds. revised by H. W. Bates); and *On Molecular and Microscopic Science* (London, 1869).

II. SECONDARY LITERATURE. On Mary Somerville and her work, see the following works by Elizabeth C. Patterson: "Mary Somerville," in *British Journal for the History of Science*, **4** (1969), 311–339; "A Washington Letter," in *Bodleian Library Record*, **8** (1970), 201–205; and "The Case of Mary Somerville: An Aspect of Nineteenth-Century Science," in *Proceedings of the American Philosophical Society*, **118** (1974), 269–275. See also Martha Somerville, ed., *Personal Recollections From Early Life to Old Age of Mary Somerville, With Selections From Her Correspondence* (London, 1873).

ELIZABETH C. PATTERSON

SOMMERFELD, ARNOLD (JOHANNES WILHELM) (*b.* Königsberg, Prussia [now Kaliningrad, U.S.S.R.], 5 December 1868; *d.* Munich, Germany, 26 April 1951), *theoretical physics.*

Sommerfeld's father, Franz Sommerfeld (1820–1906), had been married to Cäcile Matthias (1839–1902) six years when his son Arnold Johannes Wilhelm was born. Franz Sommerfeld had himself been born and raised in Königsberg, where his father, Friedrich Wilhelm Sommerfeld (1782–1862), had been Hof-Post-Sekretär. The family was Protestant; and although Sommerfeld was not religious, he never renounced his faith. "My father, the practicing physician . . . , was a passionate collector of natural objects (amber, shells, minerals, beetles, etc.) and a great friend of the natural sciences"; he was also a member of the semipopular Physikalisch-Ökonomische Gesellschaft in Königsberg. "To my energetic and intellectually vigorous mother I owe an infinite debt," Sommerfeld also acknowledged in 1917 in his autobiographical sketch.[1] At the humanistic Altstädtisches Gymnasium (Collegium Fridericianum) in 1875–

1886, where Hermann Minkowski and Max and Willy Wien were a few years ahead of Sommerfeld, "I was almost more interested in literature and history than in the exact sciences; I was equally good in all subjects including the classical languages."

Passing the *Abitur* at the end of September 1886, Sommerfeld matriculated immediately at the University of Königsberg. "After some irresolution" he opted for mathematics but heard lectures on philosophy and political economy, as well as natural sciences. Active participation in fraternity life (Burschenschaft Germania), with its compulsory drinking bouts and fencing duels, prevented systematic and concentrated study in his first few years at the university. His instructors in mathematics were David Hilbert, *Privatdozent*; Adolf Hurwitz, *extraordinarius*, and Ferdinand Lindemann, *ordinarius*. To the latter Sommerfeld expressed particular and continuing thanks in his doctoral dissertation, "Die willkürlichen Funktionen in der mathematischen Physik,"[2] which "I conceived and wrote out in a few weeks" during the summer of 1891.

The dissertation was indeed but an exposition of the general mathematical foundation for a harmonic analyzer that Sommerfeld and Emil Wiechert, who in those years served Sommerfeld "as the highest model of a deep mathematical-physical thinker," had conceived and constructed in 1890 at the institute of Paul Volkmann, professor of theoretical physics. Their mechanical instrument was, moreover, only part of a comprehensive attack on the problem of interpreting the earth-thermometer observations at the meteorological station in Königsberg, which had been set as a prize question by the Physikalisch-Ökonomische Gesellschaft. The analyzer would reduce the observed temperature curve (arbitrary function) to a trigonometric series; this same series and these same numerical coefficients must then be shown to result from a solution of the heat conduction equation with the appropriate boundary conditions. Sommerfeld tackled this latter problem alone; and although he was not entirely successful, he developed the methods that were to underlie his most important scientific work in the following decade—the application of the theory of functions of a complex variable to boundary-value problems, especially diffraction phenomena.

Although he hoped for a university career, Sommerfeld, as was customary, spent the following academic year preparing for examinations to qualify as a Gymnasium teacher of mathematics and physics. Then, in the autumn of 1892, not yet

twenty-four, small in stature, and still very youthful in appearance—but with virility attested by a long fencing scar on the forehead—he entered upon his year of obligatory military service, choosing his reserve regiment in Königsberg. Discharged in September 1893, Sommerfeld, at his own option, participated in eight-week military exercises in 1894, 1896, 1898, 1901, and 1903, in the latter three as lieutenant. Despite his squat build, by middle age, with the aid of a turned-up waxed moustache, he managed to give the impression of a colonel of the hussars.

Drawn to Göttingen as "the seat of mathematical high culture," Sommerfeld first obtained, through personal connections, an assistantship in the Mineralogical Institute from October 1893 to September 1894. During the following two years he was Felix Klein's assistant, managing the mathematical reading room and writing out Klein's lectures for the use of the students. "Consciously and systematically Klein sought to enthrall me with the problems of mathematical physics, and to win me over to his conception of these problems as he had developed it in lecture courses in previous years. I have always regarded Klein as my real teacher, not only in things mathematical, but also in mathematical physics and in my conception of mechanics." In particular, although continuing the line of research in mathematical physics that he had begun at Königsberg, Sommerfeld recognized that Klein's program for applying analytical mechanics, and higher mathematics generally, to engineering problems promised manifold mutual advantages.

In March 1895, Sommerfeld became a *Privatdozent* in mathematics at Göttingen, presenting as his *Habilitationsschrift* the first exact solution of a diffraction problem, which he gave as a complex integral in closed form suitable for numerical evaluation. Henri Poincaré immediately adopted "my 'méthode extrêmement ingénieuse,'" and in the following decades the reduction of a problem in mathematical physics to the evaluation of a complex integral became Sommerfeld's hallmark. Sommerfeld gave an account of this work in September at the Lübeck Naturforscher-Versammlung, where he had a ringside seat at the bullfight in which the agile Wilhelm Ostwald was charged by Ludwig Boltzmann; he sided with the Bull.

Sommerfeld lectured on advanced topics at Göttingen for five terms before accepting a full professorship in mathematics at the Bergakademie in Clausthal in October 1897. Although the teaching was elementary, the salary allowed him to marry. His bride, Johanna Höpfner, was the daughter of the new *Kurator* of the University of Göttingen, Ernst Höpfner, a close associate of Friedrich Althoff and an enthusiast for Klein's schemes.[3] The distance between Clausthal and Göttingen was short enough for Sommerfeld to remain in close contact with the university and Klein.

At Clausthal, Sommerfeld applied his extraordinary ingenuity in boundary-value problems to the propagation of electromagnetic waves along wires of finite diameter (obtaining the first rigorous solution) and to the diffraction of X rays by a wedge-shaped slit. Both calculations were of considerable interest to experimental physicists at that time. The collaboration with Klein on *Theorie des Kreisels* (1897–1910), which grew out of Klein's lectures in 1895–1896 and became a thousand-page treatise, continued at Clausthal. Sommerfeld also undertook the editorship of the physics volume of the *Encyklopädie der mathematischen Wissenschaften*, initiated and directed by Klein. The last part of this multivolume "volume" was not issued until 1926.

In April 1900, as the result of Klein's energetic wire-pulling, Sommerfeld became full professor at the Technische Hochschule of Aachen—significantly, however, not in mathematics but in technical mechanics. Sommerfeld was expected to show in his courses, as well as in his research, that even this classical engineering discipline could be developed on a consistent mathematical foundation: "Although my Aachen colleagues and students at first regarded the 'pure mathematician' with suspicion, I soon had the satisfaction of being accepted as a useful member not merely in teaching but also in engineering practice; thus I was requested to render expert opinions and to participate in the Ingenieurverein." There resulted fruitful collaborations with several theoretical engineers—with August Föppl on problems of resonance phenomena in the vibration of bridges, with Otto Schlick on the analogous phenomena in ships, and with August von Borries on problems of locomotive construction. Of fundamental importance, however, were Sommerfeld's investigations of the hydrodynamics of viscous fluids, aiming at an explanation of the onset of turbulence and a theory of the lubrication of machines.

Recognition was not withheld by the engineers. Sommerfeld declined a highly complimentary offer of the chair of mathematics and technical mechanics at the Berlin mining academy. In 1903 the council of the Gesellschaft Deutscher Naturforscher und Ärzte invited him to deliver one of the plenary addresses at the Kassel congress. There he pointed to the felicitous collaboration between engineering and mathematics that he had done so much to initiate and that appeared—characteristically, but erroneously—destined to absorb not merely most of Sommerfeld's future efforts but also much of the attention of physicists and mathematicians in general.

At the same time Sommerfeld, with his tremendous capacity for work, continued in mathematical physics and joined the advancing front of fundamental physical research with a series of extensive papers intended to provide a general dynamics of electrons, with special attention to motion faster than the speed of light. In this area his urgent need of discussion to clarify his thoughts could not be satisfied by technical colleagues; instead two bright engineering students, Peter Debye and Walter Rogowski, were invited to dinner two or three times a week and afterward were talked at for two or three hours in Sommerfeld's study.[4]

Although the electron theory papers of 1904–1905 were soon rendered utterly passé by relativity (regaining some interest and currency only after the discovery of Čerenkov radiation), they made Sommerfeld a name among the most advanced theoretical physicists—Boltzmann, Lorentz, Wilhelm Wien. In the summer of 1906 this growing reputation brought a call to the chair of theoretical physics at the University of Munich. It was only under pressure from Roentgen, then professor of experimental physics at the university, that this chair, one of the very few in the field, had recently been funded after having been defunct for several years. Curiously, Sommerfeld's appointment was opposed by Ferdinand Lindemann, now professor of mathematics at Munich, who was hostile to the electron theory in all its various forms and was disturbed by the want of mathematical rigor in its development.

At Munich an institute was established for Sommerfeld—a dozen rooms were fitted up for collections, seminars, assistants, and experimental work. Determined to check his own theories, Sommerfeld directed a considerable program of experimental research—even experimental doctoral dissertations. In the spring of 1912 his experimental assistant, Walter Friedrich, using covertly the facilities of the institute, discovered the diffraction of X rays by crystals.[5]

Sommerfeld always had a very ambitious conception of what he had to offer in his courses: the most recent results of research. Now, as a professor of theoretical physics, he felt obliged to work his way intensively into all the important problems of modern physics. At the September 1907 *Naturforscherversammlung* he defended Einstein's relativity theory—thus placing himself, after Planck, among the earliest converts. In subsequent publications he cast the theory into vector form (1910) and applied it to various problems. One of the most striking applications was the prediction of a forward shift and narrowing of the direction in which an electron decelerated from relativistic velocities emits the greatest amount of energy (distribution of *Bremsstrahlung*).

Sommerfeld met Einstein for the first time at the September 1909 *Naturforscherversammlung* in Salzburg. Despite the great difference in background and talents of the two men, they felt an immediate attraction—"a magnificent fellow" was Einstein's reaction.[6] At Salzburg the subject of the liveliest and most urgent interest was not, however, relativity but the quantum theory. Einstein pressed his radical view of a radiation field containing discrete atoms of light, while Planck and virtually all his colleagues resisted this revolutionary break with Maxwell's electrodynamics. Sommerfeld, accepting Planck's view that one must proceed as conservatively as possible, had in fact been led to his discovery of the forward shift of the *Bremsstrahlung* maximum while seeking an alternative explanation for a group of phenomena in which Johannes Stark, one of the very few advocates of light quanta, had seen strong evidence for the radical view.

During the year following the Salzburg *Naturforscherversammlung*, however, Sommerfeld gradually became convinced of the fundamental importance of the quantum and spent a full week with Einstein at Zurich "in order to parley over the problem of light and a few questions in the relativity theory. His presence was a real festival for me," Einstein reported, especially pleased at the extensive concessions that Sommerfeld made to his views on quantum statistics.[7] Influential in this reorientation, as in so many other shifts of Sommerfeld's scientific opinion, were the work and enthusiasms of his students and assistants—in this case especially Peter Debye and Ludwig Hopf.

It was, however, only after the announcement of the Compton effect in 1922–1923 that Sommerfeld, or his colleagues, accepted Einstein's literally particulate structure of light even tentatively. Thus in 1910–1912, before the introduction of Bohr's theory, Sommerfeld sought to add to the classical Maxwell-Lorentz theory a formal postulate regulating the interaction of atoms and electromagnetic radiation—a postulate that, although in no way demanded or suggested by the classical theory, was also, in contrast with Einstein's and Bohr's postulates, not inconsistent with it. This postulate, that the "action" (the integral of the energy with respect to the time over the duration of the interaction) is always equal to Planck's constant $h/2\pi$, Sommerfeld applied to the production of *Bremsstrahlung*, and to the inverse phenomenon, the photoelectric effect.

Sommerfeld placed great importance upon this work, and his presentations at the first Solvay Congress (October 1911) and elsewhere attracted considerable attention. Although it led nowhere and had been abandoned by the end of 1913, it had nonetheless most effectively emphasized two points of view that were adopted in the more fruitful efforts of J. W. Nicholson and Bohr: it is the action primarily, and the energy only secondarily, that is quantized; the ubiquity of an *h* in the interactions of atoms and radiation is not to be regarded as a secondary expression of the size, structure, and internal energy of atoms, "but rather the existence of molecules [atoms] is to be regarded as a function and consequence of the existence of an elementary quantum of action."[8]

The breakthrough came then in the summer of 1913, with the appearance of Niels Bohr's first paper on the "Constitution of Atoms and Molecules." Sommerfeld studied the paper immediately and closely, for, as he wrote Bohr early in September, "the problem of expressing the Rydberg-Ritz constant [in the exceedingly precise yet empirical formulas for the frequencies of the spectral lines] by means of Planck's *h* has been with me for a long time. I discussed it with Debye a few years ago. Even though I remain for the present in principle somewhat skeptical toward atomic models still your calculation of that constant is undoubtedly a great contribution."[9] And he closed by courteously announcing that he would like to try applying Bohr's model to the Zeeman effect (the splitting of spectral lines emitted in a magnetic field).

That application, as Bohr himself discovered, was not as simple as it appeared. Sommerfeld found himself obliged first to find a generalization of the various quantization prescriptions that could be applied to mechanical systems with more than one degree of freedom. In the winter semester of 1914–1915 he was already lecturing to his students on the astonishing initial results of this investigation: a quantitative theory of the fine structure of the spectral lines of hydrogen and of the X-ray spectra of the heavy elements, regarded as arising from the relativistic increase in mass of an electron by an amount depending upon the eccentricity of its orbit.[10] It was only in the spring of 1916, however, that Sommerfeld found the definitive formulation of his quantization rules yielding a quantum theory of the normal Zeeman effect and, in the hands of his student Paul S. Epstein, of the Stark effect (the splitting of spectral lines emitted in an electric field).[11] In the course of this work Sommerfeld entered into (and afterward maintained) very close contact with experimental spectroscopists, especially Friedrich Paschen, with whom he exchanged some fifty letters within six months in 1916.

This extraordinary extension, enrichment, and precision of Bohr's theory by Sommerfeld contributed decisively to its rapid and widespread acceptance. Only five years after Bohr's first publication Sommerfeld, recognizing that the mathematical development of this quantum-theoretical atomic model had reached a conclusion of sorts, undertook a comprehensive exposition of the field. His *Atombau und Spektrallinien*, of which the first edition appeared late in 1919, immediately became the bible of atomic physics and its successive editions, appearing almost annually in the early 1920's, chronicled the progress of this field up to the eve of the introduction of quantum mechanics.

In these years, 1919–1926, Sommerfeld remained in the forefront of theoretical atomic physics; but he did so by largely reorienting his method and approach. Persuaded that the detailed structure of the spectra of atoms with more than one electron—and the close contact with current experimental work that he valued so highly—could not be obtained deductively by calculations from first principles, Sommerfeld pioneered a new style of theoretical spectroscopy. In this a posteriori approach, in contrast with the older a priori, the theorist began by immersing himself in the spectroscopic data, and worked back, by means of the combination principle, to the atomic energy levels. These levels he then tried to characterize by quantum numbers and selection rules—on the basis of established mechanical and quantal laws if possible, or, if not, ad hoc. Thus where Sommerfeld had previously spoken of "numerical harmonies" in the quantum theory, he now began to speak of "number mysteries" (1919)—in the first instance, and most particularly, in the Zeeman effect. An adequate understanding of this phenomenon, and of the complex structure of spectral lines which was so intimately connected with it, was then widely regarded as the specific content or contribution of

a satisfactory atomic mechanics. Consequently the success of Sommerfeld and his students in the ordering of X-ray, atomic, and molecular spectra was followed with excitement and widely imitated. This approach did not, however, prove to be what it was then widely supposed to be, namely the highroad to quantum mechanics. Still, the results obtained were taken over with but slight alteration into the post-1925 quantum-mechanical theory of atomic structure.

Although not among the inventors of quantum mechanics, of quantum statistics, or of electron spin, Sommerfeld immediately became one of the most adept in the exploitation of these new concepts and prescriptions for the calculation of energies and rates of atomic processes, and the macroscopic properties of matter resulting from them. It was Schrödinger's form, the wave mechanics, the partial differential equation, that Sommerfeld found most congenial. In 1929 he published one of the first textbooks of wave mechanics, the *Wellenmechanischer Ergänzungsband* to *Atombau und Spektrallinien*. That favorite phenomenon, the relativistic forward shift of the *Bremsstrahlung* maximum, was recalculated with wave mechanics; and the reciprocal phenomenon, the distribution of photoelectrons, was given considerable attention. But in these years, and into the early 1930's, the problem that drew most of Sommerfeld's interest was the joint application of wave mechanics and Fermi statistics to the behavior of electrons in metals. With the aid of his students—especially Hans Bethe—Sommerfeld rehabilitated the electron theory of metals, which, after a promising beginning at the turn of the century, had languished under classical statistics and mechanics.

"What I especially admire about you," Einstein wrote to Sommerfeld in January 1922, "is the way, at a stamp of your foot, a great number of talented young theorists spring up out of the ground."[12] In the twenty-five years following his arrival in Munich—the period in which theoretical physics became a recognized, indeed glamorous, subdiscipline—Sommerfeld had more advanced students and turned out more doctorates than any other theorist. The near-monopoly that he held for the first fifteen of these years was seriously challenged only after Max Born arrived at Göttingen in 1921. The first, prewar, generation of doctorates included (in order of seniority) Peter Debye, Ludwig Hopf, Wilhelm Lenz, P. P. Ewald, Paul S. Epstein, Alfred Landé; the second, early postwar, generation included Erwin Fues, Gregor Wentzel, Wolfgang Pauli, Werner Heisenberg, Helmut Hönl, Otto

Laporte; the third, postquantum-mechanical, generation included Hans Grimm, Albrecht Unsöld, Walter Heitler, Hans Bethe, Herbert Fröhlich. To this latter group must be added the American postdoctoral students then flocking to Germany. Partly in consequence of Sommerfeld's visits to the United States (September 1922–April 1923; January–May 1929, as part of a trip around the world begun in October 1928; June–August 1931), the Americans made a point of spending some time in Munich; and several of them (Carl Eckart, William Houston, N. H. Frank) collaborated in Sommerfeld's work on the electron theory of metals.

Sommerfeld took real pleasure in the company of his students, at least of those who had shown the requisite talent and *Sitzfleisch*. With a disregard of social distance almost unheard of before the war, Sommerfeld took his students on strenuous outings in the Bavarian Alps. These occasions too were used for vigorous discussions of the physics that filled Sommerfeld's life and that he insisted be the exclusive intellectual occupation of his students as well. With them he discussed not merely his own and their own work, but also the news that his extensive correspondence and travels brought him. His liberality and enthusiasm for new results were not always welcomed by Sommerfeld's colleagues, who often saw their brain children nostrified and propagated in his conversations, lectures, and papers, or exploited by his protégés.

Although Sommerfeld never received a Nobel Prize, from 1917 on, a steady stream of honors—prizes, memberships in foreign academies, honorary doctorates—flowed to him. The most valuable of these marks of recognition were the offers of the chairs of theoretical physics at the University of Vienna in 1917 (as successor to Hasenöhrl) and at the University of Berlin in the spring of 1927 (to succeed Planck). The first post brought the title *Geheimrat* and a substantial increase in salary; the second brought a great deal of publicity, a doubling of his institute budget, and a far larger increase in personal income.

In return for the compliment Sommerfeld had paid his university by refusing the call to Berlin, it was anticipated that his colleagues would elect him rector of the university for 1927–1928. But grotesque as it may seem, this native of East Prussia, for whom the "Prussian virtues"—devotion to duty and love of the fatherland—had always been the norms of thought and action, was regarded by his colleagues as insufficiently "national" for this post. Properly patriotic as a Burschenschaftler, a

member of the National Liberal Party while at Aachen, a (moderate) annexationist during the war, disgusted and despairing at the revolution, Sommerfeld nonetheless compromised himself irreparably in the Weimar period by his manifest distaste for anti-Semitism, by openly siding with Einstein, by want of intransigence in international scientific relations, by accepting a visiting professorship at the University of Wisconsin in 1922–1923, and by favoring a political party (Deutsche Demokratische Partei) committed to parliamentary democracy. Right-wing groups put forward an opposition candidate with "reliable, national convictions"; and in the election, 16 July 1927, Sommerfeld was defeated 68–50.

Sommerfeld's progress away from the antidemocratic chauvinism in which the great majority of German academics were mired had begun at age fifty; at sixty-five, after fifteen months of Hitler's regime, he noted in the draft of a letter to Einstein: "Moreover I can assure you that the misuse of the word 'national' by our rulers has thoroughly broken me of the habit of national feeling that was so pronounced in my case. I would now be willing to see Germany disappear as a power and merge into a pacified Europe."[13]

As early as 1915 Johannes Stark had labeled Sommerfeld the "energetic executive secretary" of the "Jewish and philo-Semitic circle" of mathematicians and theoretical physicists,[14] and Stark's enmity grew more intense and more open in the Weimar period as Sommerfeld continued to protect the interests of these circles and to frustrate Stark's ambitions. At the Nazi take-over, Stark immediately attained positions of power and influence; and he sought to use them to extirpate, root and branch, the "Jewish" spirit in German physics. A tug-of-war now developed over Sommerfeld's chair, for in the spring of 1935 he passed the obligatory retirement age and continued to function as professor only provisionally, from semester to semester, pending appointment of a successor. The faculty took the position that only a theorist of first rank, if possible from Sommerfeld's own school, could maintain the tradition and placed Werner Heisenberg at the top of its list. This choice was resisted strenuously by the advocates of a "German" physics. In July 1937 an article in the magazine of the SS labeled Sommerfeld and Heisenberg, among others, "white Jews of science" and "agents of Judaism in German intellectual life" who will have to "disappear just like the Jews themselves."[15]

Stark himself added an unreserved endorsement

of the article, although he was more discreet in his rhetoric and charges. Sommerfeld, and other physicists as well, entered official protests; and as Stark went into eclipse, Heisenberg's appointment seemed assured. But the "German physics" faction won the final round; in 1940 Sommerfeld received, as he himself said, "the worst conceivable successor," Wilhelm Müller, one of the stalwarts of the movement.

Through the war Sommerfeld occupied himself with the preparation for publication of his six-semester cycle of lectures on theoretical physics. At its end, now approaching eighty, he resumed the directorship of the Institute of Theoretical Physics—but not his lectures—for several years. Early in April 1951, while strolling with his grandchildren, he was struck by an automobile and died a few weeks later.

NOTES

1. "Autobiographische Skizze," in *Gesammelte Schriften*, IV, 673–682; unless otherwise indicated, all first-person quotations are from this sketch.
2. *Gesammelte Schriften*, I, 1–76; henceforth, where a bibliographic citation is not given for a piece of scientific work, the publication in question has been reprinted in Sommerfeld's *Gesammelte Schriften*.
3. Karl-Heinz Manegold, *Universität, technische Hochschule und Industrie . . .*, Schriften zur Wirtschafts- und Sozialgeschichte, XVI (Berlin, 1970), 164–165.
4. P. Debye, interviews, 3 and 4 May 1962, at Archive for History of Quantum Physics.
5. Paul Forman, "The Discovery of the Diffraction of X-Rays by Crystals; a Critique of the Myths," in *Archive for History of Exact Sciences*, 6 (1969), 38–71.
6. Einstein to J. J. Laub, 31 Dec. 1909, as quoted by Carl Seelig in *Albert Einstein, Leben und Werk eines Genies unserer Zeit* (Zurich, 1960), 145.
7. Einstein to Laub, Sept. [?] 1910, as quoted *ibid.*, 197.
8. "Das Plancksche Wirkungsquantum und seine allgemeine Bedeutung für die Molekularphysik," address at the Karlsruhe *Naturforscherversammlung*, Sept. 1911 in *Gesammelte Schriften*, III, 19.
9. German original published by L. Rosenfeld in his ed. of Niels Bohr, *On the Constitution of Atoms and Molecules* (Copenhagen–New York, 1963), lii.
10. John L. Heilbron, "The Kossel-Sommerfeld Theory and the Ring Atom," in *Isis*, 58 (1967), 451–485.
11. A. Hermann, ed., *Der Stark-Effekt*, Dokumente der Naturwissenschaft, Abt. Physik, VI (Stuttgart, 1965).
12. Albert Einstein and Arnold Sommerfeld, *Briefwechsel . . .* (1968), 98.
13. *Ibid.*, 114–115.
14. Quoted from the draft of a letter to the Prussian Education Ministry by A. Hermann, in *Sudhoffs Archiv . . .*, 50 (1966), 280.
15. *Das Schwarze Korps* (15 July 1937), 6.

BIBLIOGRAPHY

I. ORIGINAL WORKS. An excellent bibliography of Sommerfeld's publications and also of articles about or

honoring him is included in Sommerfeld's *Gesammelte* [in fact, selected] *Schriften*, F. Sauter, ed. (Brunswick, 1968), IV, 683–728. The following significant omissions have been noted: "Die Überwindung der Erdkrümmung durch die Wellen der drahtlosen Telegraphie," in *Jahrbuch der drahtlosen Telegraphie . . .*, 12 (1917), 2–15; "En Ensartet Opfattelse af Balmers og Deslandres Serieled," in *Fysisk Tidsskrift*, 18 (1920), 33–40, and in the original German in *Arkiv für matematik, astronomi och fysik*, 15 (1921), 1–5; and "Spectroscopic Interpretation of the Magneton Numbers in the Iron Group," in *Physical Review*, 29 (1927), 208. Sommerfeld's printed remarks in discussion at scientific meetings are cited only irregularly, as are his newspaper articles.

Sommerfeld's literary remains—some 2,000 pages of lecture notes and some 1,000 letters, almost all to Sommerfeld—are at the Bibliothek des Deutschen Museums, Munich. Microfilms are available at the Archive for History of Quantum Physics, for which see T. S. Kuhn *et al., Sources for History of Quantum Physics* (Philadelphia, 1967), 87–89, where about 200 letters by Sommerfeld in various other collections are also listed. Sommerfeld's correspondence with Albert Einstein and with Johannes Stark, not listed by Kuhn *et al.*, has now been published: A. Einstein and A. Sommerfeld, *Briefwechsel. Sechzig Briefe aus dem goldenen Zeitalter der modernen Physik*, edited and annotated by A. Hermann (Basel–Stuttgart, 1968); and A. Hermann, "Die frühe Diskussion zwischen Stark und Sommerfeld über die Quantenhypothese," in *Centaurus*, 12 (1967), 38–59. Letters from Sommerfeld to Léon Brillouin and W. F. Meggers are included in the collections of the Niels Bohr Library, American Institute of Physics, New York; letters to Felix Klein are in the Klein-Nachlass, Niedersächsische Staats- und Universitätsbibliothek, Göttingen.

Sommerfeld's "Autobiographische Skizze," prepared in 1917 and supplemented in 1950, has been edited and amplified by Fritz Bopp: "Arnold Sommerfeld," in *Geist und Gestalt. Biographische Beiträge zur Geschichte der Bayerischen Akademie . . .*, II (Munich, 1959), 100–109, repr. in Sommerfeld's *Gesammelte Schriften*, IV 673–682. Sommerfeld also supplied the biographical data for his entry in the *Reichshandbuch der Deutschen Gesellschaft* (Berlin, 1931), 1802. Much additional biographical information has been drawn from the Universitätsarchiv, Munich (Akten des Rektorats, Pers. Akt. EII-N, "Sommerfeld, 1905 bis–   ") and from the Bayerisches Hauptstaatsarchiv, Munich (Abt. I, MK 35736, "Sommerfeld, Dr. Arnold").

II. SECONDARY LITERATURE. Numerous commemorative and obituary notices are cited in *Gesammelte Schriften*, IV, 723–727, of which the most detailed and reliable is Max Born, "Arnold Johannes Wilhelm Sommerfeld," in *Obituary Notices of Fellows of the Royal Society of London*, 8 (1952), 275–296, repr. in Born's *Ausgewählte Abhandlungen*, II (Göttingen, 1963), 647–659. Publications omitted from or issued subsequent to the listing in the *Gesammelte Schriften* are "Arnold

Sommerfeld, Recipient of the 1948 Oersted Medal," in *American Journal of Physics*, **17** (1949), 312–314; Linus Pauling, "Arnold Sommerfeld: 1868–1951," in *Science*, **114** (1951), 383–384; Helmut Hönl, "Memoirs of Research on Zeeman Effect in Munich in Early 1920s," unpublished typescript at the Archive for History of Quantum Physics; P. P. Ewald, "Erinnerungen an die Anfänge des Münchener physikalischen Kolloquiums," in *Physikalische Blätter*, **24** (1968), 538–542; and A. Hermann, "Sommerfeld und die Technik," in *Technikgeschichte*, **34** (1967), 311–322; *Frühgeschichte der Quantentheorie* (Mosbach, 1969), esp. ch. 6; and "Arnold Sommerfeld," in *Die Grossen der Weltgeschichte*, IX (Munich–Zurich, 1970), 702–715.

The addresses at the Sommerfeld Centennial Memorial Meeting, Munich, 10–14 Sept. 1968, have been published in F. Bopp and H. Kleinpoppen, eds., *Physics of One- and Two-Electron Atoms* (Amsterdam–New York, 1969): F. A. Bopp, "Opening Address," 1–7; P. P. Ewald, "Arnold Sommerfeld als Mensch, Lehrer und Freund," 8–16; A. Hermann, "Sommerfeld's Role in the Development of Early Quantum Theory," 17–20; B. L. van der Waerden, "The History of Quantum Theory in the Light of the Successive Editions of Sommerfeld's *Atombau und Spektrallinien*," 21–31; H. Welker, "Impact of Sommerfeld's Work on Solid State Research and Technology," 32–43; and W. Heisenberg, "Significance of Sommerfeld's Work Today," 44–52.

P. Forman, "Alfred Landé and the Anomalous Zeeman Effect, 1919–1921," in *Historical Studies in the Physical Sciences, 2* (1970), 153–261, discusses Sommerfeld's work on the Zeeman effect and includes several letters; and Roger H. Stuewer, "William H. Bragg's Corpuscular Theory of X-Rays and γ-Rays," in *British Journal for the History of Science*, **5** (1971), 258–281, publishes correspondence between Bragg and Sommerfeld.

PAUL FORMAN
ARMIN HERMANN

SOMMERING. See Soemmerring, Samuel Thomas.

SOMMERVILLE, DUNCAN MCLAREN YOUNG (*b*. Beawar, Rajasthan, India, 24 November 1879; *d*. Wellington, New Zealand, 31 January 1934), *mathematics*.

Sommerville, the son of Rev. James Sommerville of Jodhpur, India, was educated in Scotland, first at the Perth Academy, then at the University of St. Andrews, where he was awarded Ramsay and Bruce scholarships and in the mathematics department of which he served as lecturer from 1902 to 1914. During that time he met, and in 1912 married, Louisa Agnes Beveridge, originally

of Belfast, Ireland. From 1915 on Sommerville was professor of pure and applied mathematics at Victoria University College, Wellington, New Zealand. He was active in the Edinburgh Mathematical Society, to whose presidency he was elected in 1911. He helped to found the Royal Astronomical Society of New Zealand and became its first executive secretary. Sommerville presided over the mathematics section at the Adelaide meeting (1924) of the Australasian Association for the Advancement of Science. In 1928 the Institute (Royal Society) of New Zealand awarded him its Hector Medal.

Although primarily a mathematician, Sommerville was interested in other sciences, particularly astronomy, anatomy, and chemistry. Crystallography held special appeal for him, and crystal forms doubtless motivated his investigation of repetitive space-filling geometric patterns. Also, his abstract conceptions called for the construction of clarifying models, which revealed an artistic skill that was even more evident in his many watercolors of New Zealand scenes.

Sommerville contributed to mathematics both as a teacher and as an original researcher. His biographer, H. W. Turnbull, who considered him (in 1935) Scotland's leading geometer of the twentieth century, stated that his pedagogic style was scholarly, unobtrusive, and much appreciated at St. Andrews. One of his most distinguished pupils, A. C. Aitken, revealed that when the New Zealand University of Otago was without a mathematics professor, Sommerville willingly provided a sort of "correspondence course" in higher mathematics. Further evidence of his teaching ability is reflected in his four textbooks, which are models of deep, lucid exposition. Among them are *The Elements of Non-Euclidean Geometry* and *An Introduction to the Geometry of n Dimensions*, books whose titles indicate his two major research specialties and whose contents develop geometric concepts that Sommerville himself created. In addition to his texts, his *Bibliography of Non-Euclidean Geometry* is also a bibliography of *n*-dimensional geometry.

Sommerville wrote over thirty original papers, almost all on geometric topics. Notable exceptions were his 1928 "Analysis of Preferential Voting" (geometrized, however, in his 1928 "Certain Hyperspatial Partitionings Connected With Preferential Voting") and two 1906 papers that gave pure mathematical treatment to statistical questions arising from notions in Karl Pearson's biometric research.

In his texts Sommerville explained how non-

Euclidean geometries arose from the use of alternatives to Euclid's parallel postulate. Thus, in the Lobachevskian or hyperbolic geometry, it is assumed that there exist two parallels to a given line through an outside point. In Riemannian or elliptic geometry, the assumption of no parallels is made. By suitable interpretation Klein, Cayley, and then Sommerville showed that Euclidean and non-Euclidean geometries can all be considered as subgeometries of projective geometry. For Klein any geometry was the study of invariants under a particular transformation group. From his point of view, projective geometry is the invariant theory associated with the group of linear fractional transformations. Those special plane projective transformations leaving invariant a specified conic section, Cayley's "absolute," constitute a subgroup of the plane projective group; and the corresponding geometry is hyperbolic, elliptic, or Euclidean according to whether the conic is real (an ellipse, for example), imaginary, or degenerate. This conception makes it possible in all three geometries to express distance and angle measure in terms of a cross ratio, the fundamental invariant under projective transformation.

Even in two of his earliest investigations, namely, "Networks of the Plane in Absolute Geometry" (1905) and "Semi-Regular Networks of the Plane in Absolute Geometry" (1906), Sommerville used the Cayley-Klein notion of non-Euclidean geometries, in particular the projective measurement of lengths and angles. These two papers indicated a trend that he was to follow in much of his research, namely, the study of tesselations of Euclidean and non-Euclidean spaces, a theme suggested by the repetitive designs on wallpaper or textiles and by the arrangement of atoms in crystals. Sommerville showed that whereas there are only three regular tesselations in the Euclidean plane (its covering by congruent equilateral triangles, squares, or regular hexagons), there are five mosaics of congruent regular polygons of the same kind in the elliptic plane, and an infinite number of such patterns in the hyperbolic plane. In all cases the variety is greater if "semi-regular" networks of regular polygons of different kinds are permitted. Moreover, as Sommerville pointed out, still further variations are attainable because the regular patterns are topologically equivalent, if not aesthetically so, to nonregular designs. In several papers and in his text on n-dimensional geometry, he generalized his earlier results and methods to include honeycombs of polyhedrons in three-dimensional spaces and "honeycombs" of polytopes in spaces (Euclidean and non-Euclidean) of 4, 5, $\cdots$, n dimensions.

Many of Sommerville's geometric concepts have algebraic counterparts in the theory of groups. Thus, since his repetitive patterns can be considered as the result of moving a single basic design to different positions, it is possible to asssociate with each tesselation or honeycomb one or more "crystallographic groups," each a set of motions that displace a fundamental region so that it will cover an entire plane, space, or hyperspace. Thus, if a square (with sides horizontal and vertical) is the fundamental region in a Euclidean plane, one can cover that plane with duplications of the square by two basic motions or their inverses, namely translation of the square one side-length to the right, and a similar translation upward. Those two motions are said to "generate" a crystallographic group corresponding to the network of squares. For that same network a different crystallographic group is generated by three basic motions—the two reflections of the square in its vertical sides, and the translation of the square one side-length upward.

There are also associations with group theory in Sommerville's "On Certain Projective Configurations in Space of n Dimensions and a Related Problem in Arrangements" (1906), in which he showed interrelationships between certain finite groups and the finite projective geometries of Veblen and Bussey. Such groups also played a role in his "On the Relation Between the Rotation-Groups of the Regular Polytopes and Permutation Groups" (1933).

BIBLIOGRAPHY

I. ORIGINAL WORKS. Among Sommerville's many research papers are "Networks of the Plane in Absolute Geometry," in *Proceedings of the Royal Society of Edinburgh*, **25** (1905), 392–394; "Semi-Regular Networks of the Plane in Absolute Geometry" in *Transactions of the Royal Society of Edinburgh*, **41** (1906), 725–747; "On the Distribution of the Proper Fractions," in *Proceedings of the Royal Society of Edinburgh*, **26** (1906), 116–129; "On the Classification of Frequency Ratios," in *Biometrika*, **5** (1906), 179–181; "On Links and Knots in Euclidean Space of n Dimensions," in *Messenger of Mathematics*, 2nd ser., **36** (1906), 139–144; "On Certain Projective Configurations in Space of n Dimensions and a Related Problem in Arrangements," in *Proceedings of the Edinburgh Mathematical Society*, **25** (1906), 80–90; "The Division of Space by Congruent Triangles and Tetrahedra," in *Proceedings of the Royal Society of Edinburgh*, **43** (1923), 85–116; "The Regular Divisions of Space of *n* Dimensions and Their Metrical Constants," in *Rendiconti del Circolo matematico di Palermo*, **48** (1924), 9–22; "The Relations Connecting the Angle-Sums and Volume of a Polytope in Space of *n* Dimensions," in *Proceedings of the Royal Society of London*, **A115** (1927), 103–119; "An Analysis of Preferential Voting," in *Proceedings of the Royal Society of Edinburgh*, **48** (1928), 140–160; "Certain Hyperspatial Partitionings Connected With Preferential Voting," in *Proceedings of the London Mathematical Society*, 2nd ser., **28** (1928), 368–382; "Isohedral and Isogonal Generalizations of the Regular Polyhedra," in *Proceedings of the Royal Society of Edinburgh*, **52** (1932), 251–263; and "On the Relations Between the Rotation-Groups of the Regular Polytopes and Permutation-Groups," in *Proceedings of the London Mathematical Society*, 2nd ser., **35** (1933), 101–115.

Sommerville's books are *Bibliography of Non-Euclidean Geometry* (London, 1911); *The Elements of Non-Euclidean Geometry* (London, 1914, 1919); *Analytical Conics* (London, 1924); *An Introduction to the Geometry of n Dimensions* (London, 1929); and *Analytical Geometry of Three Dimensions* (Cambridge, 1934).

II. SECONDARY LITERATURE. On Sommerville and his work, see H. W. Turnbull, "Professor D. M. Y. Sommerville," in *Proceedings of the Edinburgh Mathematical Society*, 2nd ser., **4** (1935), 57–60.

EDNA E. KRAMER

SOMOV, OSIP IVANOVICH (*b*. Otrada, Moscow gubernia [now Moscow oblast], Russia, 1 June 1815; *d*. St. Petersburg, Russia [now Leningrad, U.S.S.R.], 26 April 1876), *mathematics, mechanics*.

Somov graduated from the Gymnasium in Moscow and enrolled at the Faculty of Physics and Mathematics of Moscow University. After graduating in 1835, he published a work on the theory of determinate algebraic equations of higher degree (1838), in which he manifested not only deep knowledge but also extraordinary skill in presenting the newest achievements of algebraic analysis.

Somov's pedagogic career began in 1839 at the Moscow Commercial College. After defending his master's dissertation in Moscow, he was invited to St. Petersburg University in 1841 and taught various courses in mathematics and mechanics there for the next twenty-five years. Somov defended his doctoral dissertation at St. Petersburg and was awarded the title of professor of applied mathematics.

In 1857 Somov was elected an associate member of the St. Petersburg Academy of Sciences, and in 1862 he succeeded Ostrogradsky as academician.

Turning his attention to problems of theoretical mechanics, Somov applied results obtained in analytical mechanics to specifically geometric problems. He is rightfully considered the originator of the geometrical trend in theoretical mechanics in Russia during the second half of the nineteenth century. In the theory of elliptical functions and their application to mechanics, he completed the solution of the problem concerning the rotation of a solid body around an immobile point in the Euler-Poinsot and Lagrange-Poisson examples.

The first in Russia to deal with the solution of kinematic problems, Somov included a chapter on this topic in his textbook on theoretical mechanics. His other kinematic works include studies of a point in curvilinear coordinates. Somov's theory of higher-order accelerations of a point, and of an unchanging system of points, was a significant contribution. His works were the first special studies in Russia of *n*th-order accelerations of both absolute and relative motions of points. His studies of small oscillations of a system around the position of equilibrium are also important.

BIBLIOGRAPHY

I. ORIGINAL WORKS. In addition to more than fifty papers on mechanics and mathematics, Somov published *Teoria opredelennykh algebraicheskikh uravneny vysshikh stepeny* ("Theory of Determinate Algebraic Equations of Higher Degree"; Moscow, 1838); *Analiticheskaya teoria volnoobraznogo dvizhenia efira* ("Analytic Theory of the Undulatory Motion of the Ether"; St. Petersburg, 1847); *Osnovania teorii ellipticheskikh funktsy* ("Foundations of the Theory of Elliptical Functions"; St. Petersburg, 1850); *Kurs differentsialnogo ischislenia* ("Course in Differential Calculus"; St. Petersburg, 1852); *Analiticheskaya geometria* ("Analytic Geometry"; St. Petersburg, 1857); *Nachalnaya algebra* ("Elementary Algebra"; St. Petersburg, 1860); *Nachertatelnaya geometria* ("Descriptive Geometry"; St. Petersburg, 1862); and *Ratsionalnaya mekhanika* ("Rational Mechanics"), 2 pts. (St. Petersburg, 1872–1874), translated into German by A. Ziwet as *Theoretische Mechanik* (Leipzig, 1878).

II. SECONDARY LITERATURE. Bibliographies of Somov's works are included in Y. L. Geronimus, *Ocherki o rabotakh korifeev russkoy mekhaniki* ("Essays on the Works of Leading Russian Mechanists"; Moscow, 1952), 58–96; T. R. Nikiforova, *Osip Ivanovich Somov* (Moscow–Leningrad, 1964); and E. I. Zolotarev, "Ob uchenykh trudakh akademika O. I. Somova," in *Zapiski Imperatorskoi akademii nauk*, **31** (1878), 248–266.

A. T. GRIGORIAN

SONIN, NIKOLAY YAKOVLEVICH (*b.* Tula, Russia, 22 February 1849; *d.* Petrograd [now Leningrad], Russia, 27 February 1915), *mathematics.*

The son of a state official who later became a lawyer, Sonin received his higher education at the Faculty of Physics and Mathematics of Moscow University (1865–1869). His first scientific work was a report on differentiation with arbitrary complex exponent (1869). After defending his master's thesis in 1871, Sonin was appointed *Dozent* in mathematics at Warsaw University in 1872 and, after defending his doctoral dissertation in 1874, was promoted to professor in 1877. He taught at Warsaw for more than twenty years, was twice elected dean of the Faculty of Physics and Mathematics, and was an organizer of the Society of Natural Scientists. In 1891 Sonin was elected corresponding member of the Russian Academy of Sciences and, in 1893, academician in pure mathematics. In connection with the latter rank he moved to St. Petersburg, where from 1894 to 1899 he was professor at the University for Women, from 1899 to 1901 superintendent of the Petersburg Educational District, and from 1901 to 1915 president of the Scientific Committee of the Ministry of National Education. With A. A. Markov, Sonin prepared a two-volume edition of the works of Chebyshev in Russian and French (1899–1907).

Sonin made a substantial contribution to the theory of special functions; the unifying idea of his researches was to establish a few convenient definitions of initial notions and operations leading to broad and fruitful generalizations of these functions. Especially important were his discoveries in the theory of cylindrical functions, which he enriched both with general principles and with many particular theorems and formulas that he introduced into the contemporary literature. He also wrote on Bernoullian polynomials, and his works on the general theory of orthogonal polynomials were closely interwoven with his research on the approximate computation of definite integrals and on the various integral inequalities; in the latter area he continued Chebyshev's research. Also noteworthy are Sonin's works on the Euler-Maclaurin sum formula and adjacent problems.

BIBLIOGRAPHY

I. ORIGINAL WORKS. Sonin's writings include "O razlozhenii funktsy v beskonechnye ryady" ("On the Expansion of Functions in Infinite Series"), in *Matematicheskii sbornik*, **5** (1871), 271–302, his master's thesis;

"Ob integrirovanii uravneny s chastnymi proizvodnymi vtorogo poryadka" ("On the Integration of Partial Differential Equations of the Second Order"), *ibid.*, **7** (1874), 285–318, translated into German in *Mathematische Annalen*, **49** (1897), 417–447, his doctoral dissertation; "Recherches sur les fonctions cylindriques et le développement des fonctions continues en séries," *ibid.*, **16** (1880), 1–80; "Sur les termes complémentaires de la formule sommatoire d'Euler et de celle de Stirling," in *Annales scientifiques de l'École normale supérieure*, **6** (1889), 257–262; "Sur les polynômes de Bernoulli," in *Journal für die reine und angewandte Mathematik*, **116** (1896), 133–156; "Sur les fonctions cylindriques," in *Mathematische Annalen*, **59** (1904), 529–552; see also *Issledovania o tsilindricheskikh funktsiakh i o spetsialnykh polinomakh* ("Research on Cylindrical Functions and on Special Polynomials"), N. I. Akhiezer, ed. (Moscow, 1954).

II. SECONDARY LITERATURE. See N. I. Akhiezer, "Raboty N. Y. Sonina po priblizhennomu vychisleniyu opredelennykh integralov" ("The Works of N. Y. Sonin on the Approximate Computation of Definite Integrals"), in Sonin's *Issledovania o tsilindricheskikh funktsiakh*, 220–243; A. I. Kropotov, *Nikolay Yakovlevich Sonin* (Leningrad, 1967), with complete bibliography of Sonin's works, pp. 126–130; and G. N. Watson, *A Treatise on the Theory of Bessel Functions* (Cambridge, 1922).

A. P. YOUSCHKEVITCH

SONNERAT, PIERRE (*b.* Lyons, France, 18 August 1748; *d.* Paris, France, 31 March 1814), *natural history.*

Sonnerat started his career as secretary to his godfather and relative, Pierre Poivre, enlightened intendant of Île de France (now Mauritius). Through influential patrons he rose from clerk in the overseas service of the Ministry of Naval Affairs to commissioner of the colonies, ending his career as commandant of the French settlement at Yanam, India, then a center for the manufacture of salt and cotton goods. He would have ended his life in affluence if the French Revolutionary Wars had not broken out; the English invaded the French settlement in 1793 and took Sonnerat to Pondicherry. He remained in captivity there until 1813, when he was repatriated on account of the joint intervention of Joseph Banks and Antoine-Laurent de Jussieu. Soon afterward Sonnerat died in Paris.

Sonnerat's fame rests on his determination to adhere, despite the lack of sympathy of his traditionally oriented bureaucratic superiors, to the enlightened policy initiated by the last naval ministers under the royal government: that of collecting essential scientific information on the overseas territories they administered. Indeed, he insisted on his title of "naturaliste pensionnaire du roi et correspondant de son cabinet."

The right opportunities had been given to Sonnerat by Poivre, who had sent him at the beginning of his career on an expedition to Poelau Gebe, in the Moluccas, in search of the spice plants that he sought to acclimatize in the Mascarenes. This was an auspicious beginning to extensive travels in Asia. The botanical and zoological collections that Sonnerat brought back, mainly from the Philippines and the Moluccas, formed the basis of his first major publication, *Voyage à la Nouvelle Guinée*, and no doubt promoted his admission to the Académie des Sciences, Belles-Lettres et Arts of Lyons as associate member, and his election on 19 January 1774 to the Académie Royale des Sciences as correspondent of the botanist Adanson (communication of December 1773: "Description du coco de mer [*Lodoicea maldivica* Pers.] de l'Isle Praslin"). His accomplishments were well summarized by Adanson: "sachant parfaitement bien le dessin, la peinture et la miniature."

Sonnerat's success with the academies may have been due in great measure to the legend that he created and sedulously fostered: that he had been a student and "disciple" of Philibert Commerson, who was the naturalist on Bougainville's expedition round the world. Sonnerat also claimed to have accompanied Commerson on his explorations of Île de France, Bourbon (Réunion), and Madagascar. Chronological and contemporary evidence disprove this assertion, however; and official documents invariably cite Paul Philippe Sauguin de Jossigny as Commerson's constant companion and draftsman. Sonnerat's awareness of the prestige that science commanded in the Enlightenment is exemplified in his use of his membership in academies to open doors for him. Relying on a chance acquaintance with Joseph Banks in 1771 at the Cape of Good Hope, where Cook's expedition had called on the last lap of the journey round the world, Sonnerat sought to secure election in 1783 as foreign associate of the Royal Society. He confided to Banks that membership would be of great help to him in the travels he proposed to make in Tibet and Central Asia, and would serve as an introduction to British governors in India. Disappointed in London, he was later honored by Revolutionary France by election as correspondent in the Botanical Section (First Class) of the Institut National on 28 November 1803. In 1806 the Société d'Émulation de l'Île de France elected him corresponding associate.

The success of the *Voyage à la Nouvelle Guinée* (1776) was doubtless on account of the very powerful, but anonymous, patronage. In the field of natural history, the work appears to have been a supplement to Brisson's *Ornithologie* (1760) and a link with *Histoire naturelle des oiseaux* of Buffon and Guéneau de Montbéliard.

Heartened by this first success, Sonnerat confidently launched his second publication, the *Voyage aux Indes orientales et à la Chine* (1782), dedicated to his lifelong patron, the Comte d'Angiviller, intendant of the Jardin Royal des Plantes. Severe censure of the frivolity of his observations on the countries he had visited came from many sources: the missionaries of Peking criticized what he had written on China; J. A. B. Law de Lauriston, his account of India; and J. F. Charpentier de Cossigny, his strictures on Île de France. Nevertheless, the success outlasted the criticism, for a second, less lavish edition (that does not seem to have been authorized), with critical notes by C. N. Sonnini de Manoncourt, was published in 1806. The work was probably a prey to literary piracy, for as late as 1816 Jean-Amable Pannelier published anonymously a work entitled *L'Hindoustan, ou religion, moeurs, usages, arts et métiers des Hindous*, with descriptions of crafts literally transcribed from Sonnerat's text of 1782.

Sonnini's edition of the *Voyage* must not be confused with a proposed publication that Sonnerat planned to entitle *Nouveau voyage aux Indes orientales*. He had worked on the manuscript during the latter part of his stay in India; and he intended the publication to be in three, later extended to four volumes. After his death the completed manuscript, brought to France on his last journey, was entrusted by his daughter to Antoine-Laurent de Jussieu, who was requested to edit it. Despite exhaustive searches in the Paris archives, the manuscript has not been traced; and the work is known only from a prospectus that was distributed shortly after 1803.

Sonnerat was an avid, if admittedly indiscriminate, collector. Botanical specimens were sent to Adanson, A.-L. de Jussieu, Linnaeus the younger, and Lamarck; collections of reptiles from India and of tropical fishes were sent to Lacépède; and his notes and drawings were used by Cuvier. Sonnerat had a great interest in tropical fishes—attested by the handsome collection of seventeen undated plates in the collection of *Vélins du roi*; and he seems to have been among the first to study, in a scientific spirit, those fishes from the lagoons of Île de France that were reported to cause poisoning.

Sonnerat was the first to give an account of the indris (*I. brevicaudatus*) and of the aye-aye (*Daubentonia madagascariensis*) from Madagascar. His elegant drawings of exotic birds, if not free from error in attribution or habitat, are fundamental for the study of ornithology. His name is commemorated in the genus *Sonneratia* (mollusk) and in six or eight species of mangrove swamp plants (*Sonneratia* L. *f*) of the eastern tropics.

Unfortunately Sonnerat's fame rests on his achievements as a young man. Little is mentioned of his accomplishments as a skillful administrator, or of his understanding of contrasting cultures and civilizations that made him a forerunner of modern social anthropologists. In his two major publications it is evident that his insight into other civilizations gave a strong impetus in Europe to the spread of a fashionable interest in the religion, arts, and customs of India and the Indian Archipelago; this marked the second part of the eighteenth century in Europe, in contrast to the interest in the arts and civilization of China that had prevailed earlier. Sonnerat was responsible for nurturing in France a taste for the exotic style of painting known in England as "company painting." This style is evident in the collections of prints and drawings preserved in the Bibliothèque Nationale, Paris, dating from the end of the eighteenth century to almost the 1840's, and representing French artistic interest in the racial types and crafts of India and Southeast Asia.

BIBLIOGRAPHY

I. ORIGINAL WORKS. Sonnerat's published writings are *Voyage à la Nouvelle Guinée* . . . (Paris, 1776), also in English ed. (Bury St. Edmunds, 1781); and *Voyage aux Indes orientales et à la Chine fait par ordre du roi, depuis 1774 jusqu'en 1781* . . ., 2 vols. (Paris, 1782); also rev. ed. by C. N. Sonnini de Manoncourt, 4 vols. (Paris, 1806); other eds. are in German (Zurich, 1783), Swedish (Uppsala, 1786), and English (Calcutta, 1788).

There is also abundant archival material preserved in the following institutions: Académie des Sciences, Paris; Muséum National d'Histoire Naturelle, Paris; Archives Nationales, Paris and Depôt des Archives d'Outre-Mer at Les Fenouilères, Aix-en-Provence; Bibliothèque Nationale, Paris; Archives Municipales, Lyons; British Museum, London; Hunt Botanical Library, Pittsburgh; and Archives of the Royal Society of Arts and Sciences of Mauritius.

II. SECONDARY LITERATURE. A short note on Sonnerat appears in *Index biographique des membres et correspondants de l'Académie des sciences, du 22 décembre 1666 au 15 décembre 1967* (Paris, 1968), 509. The basic biographical article is Alfred Lacroix, "Notice historique sur les membres et correspondants de l'Académie des sciences ayant travaillé dans les colonies françaises des Mascareignes et de Madagascar au XVIIIe siècle et au début du XIXe . . .," in *Mémoires de l'Académie des sciences de l'Institut de France*, 2nd ser., **62** (1936), 70–75, also in *Figures de savants*, IV: *L'Académie des sciences et l'etude de la France d'outremer de la fin du XVIIe siècle au début du XIXe* (Paris, 1938), 25–31. M. J. van Steenis-Kruseman has given a factual account in *Cyclopaedia of Collectors* ser. 1 I: *Flora Malesiana: The Botany of Malaya, Indonesia, the Philippines, and New Guinea*, C. G. G. J. van Steenis, ed. (Groningen, 1950). A short, balanced notice is given by Jean Vinson in *Dictionary of Mauritian Biography*, no. 18 (Port Louis, 1945), 561–562.

It should be noted that none of these writers gives any account of the latter part of Sonnerat's life, spent mainly in India. These biographies are based on Sonnerat's testimony or on his published work. Berthe Labernadie, who has done pioneer work in the Pondicherry archives, has written a spirited account of the French Revolution in Yanam in *La révolution et les établissements français dans l'Inde* (Pondicherry, 1929).

See also Madeleine Ly-Tio-Fane, "The Career of Pierre Sonnerat (1748–1814): A Reassessment of His Contribution to the Arts and to the Natural Sciences" (Ph.D. diss., University of London, 1973), which is based on a critical study of all the extant archival material preserved in the above-mentioned institutions.

More general works are *Adanson. The Bicentennial of Michel Adanson's "Familles des Plantes,"* 2 vols. (Pittsburgh, 1963–1964); Mildred Archer, *Company Drawings in the India Office Library* (London, 1972); L. H. Bailey, "Palms of the Seychelles," in *Gentes herbarum*, **6**, fasc. 1 (1942), 9–29; Joseph Banks, *The Banks Letters, a Calendar of the Manuscript Correspondence of Sir Joseph Banks Preserved in the British Museum, the British Museum (Natural History) and Other Collections in Great Britain*, Warren R. Dawson, ed. (London, 1958), 774; Bibliothèque Nationale, Paris, *Trésors d'Orient (Exposition organisée sous l'égide du Comité national des commémorations orientalistes, . . . réalisée avec le concours du 29e Congrès international des Orientalistes)* (Paris, 1973); J. F. Charpentier de Cossigny, *Lettre à M Sonnerat* (Port Louis, 1784); R. Decary, *La faune malgache: Son rôle dans les croyances et les usages indigènes* (Paris, 1950), 19, 26–30; A.-A. Fauvel, "Le cocotier de mer des Îles Seychelles (*Lodoicea Sechellarum*)," in *Annales du Musée colonial de Marseille*, 3rd ser., **1** (1915), 169–307; *The Journals of Captain James Cook*, J. C. Beaglehole, ed., 5 vols. (London, 1961–   ); Berthe Labernadie, *Le vieux Pondichéry (1673–1815)* (Pondicherry, 1936), 175–187; Madeleine Ly-Tio-Fane, *Mauritius and the Spice Trade*: I, *The Odyssey of Pierre Poivre* (Port Louis, 1958), 13, 34, 96–97, II, *The Triumph of Jean Nicolas Céré and His Isle Bourbon Collaborators* (Paris–The

Hague, 1970), 26–28, 178–179, 186; Madeleine Ly-Tio-Fane, "Pierre Poivre et l'expansion française dans l'Indo-Pacifique," in *Bulletin de l'Ecole française d'Extrême-Orient*, **53** (1967), 453–511, with specific reference to Sonnerat on pp. 473–478; S. P. Sen, *The French in India, 1763–1816* (Calcutta, 1958), 486–490; and C. P. Thunberg, *Voyages de C. P. Thunberg au Japon, par le Cap de Bonne Espérance, les Îles de la Sonde, etc.*, I (Paris, 1796), 275–278.

MADELEINE LY-TIO-FANE

SORANUS OF EPHESUS (*fl.* Rome, second century), *medicine.*

Soranus of Ephesus can be considered one of the major Greek physicians in the Roman Empire at the beginning of the second century. According to Suidas he was the son of Meandros and Phoibe, but a second article of the lexicographic *collectaneum*, "Sōranos Ephesios, iatros neōteros," does not justify a belief that two physicians with the same name had historical importance.[1] Scheele's careful research has confirmed this opinion; and even the fact that many other physicians were named Soranus and that in the families of physicians a name often was given to the son or the grandson, is not sufficient reason for new doubts.[2] Some of the statements about his life and sites of activity from late antiquity and from Byzantine literature are legends.[3] But it is certainly correct that he was a member of the methodist sect, that he practiced at Rome during the reigns of Trajan and Hadrian, and that he had studied in Alexandria.[4]

Although there is no direct evidence, priority must be given to Ephesus as the site of Soranus' medical training and scientific development; for in the first two centuries of the Christian era it gradually became necessary to offer the professional studies, as taught at Alexandria, in schools and academies throughout the Roman Empire.[5] And in this respect Ephesus was of special importance for the whole of Asia Minor.[6] Soranus thus was trained primarily at the medical school of Ephesus; and if his references to medical experience in Egypt and Rome are taken as proof for his training and activity there, serious consideration must likewise be given to his remarks concerning Caria.[7] It must be left undecided if he only took his training there—perhaps under Magnus Ephesius, whom he repeatedly cites[8]—or was a lecturer. His numerous textbooks, obviously meant for practical instruction, and the fact that he had pupils are evidence for such a supposition. In any case, he ranks among the important physicians of the Ephesian school.[9]

These statements are not meant to diminish Soranus' merits of the methodist school. The methodist doctrine rejected the theory of humors and, influenced by Epicurus' philosophy and its skepticism, had developed ideas stating that the human body consists of movable and immovable atoms, interlaced by fine pores, the tension of which is responsible for health and sickness. This cellular-pathological structure allowed certain vaguely defined communities of the human organism — τερατώδεις ἐκεῖναι κοινότητες ("communities miraculous," as Galen caustically called them).[10] This type of structure provided the opportunity to classify diseases into three conditions according to the state of the pores: *status laxus* (grossly relaxed), *status strictus* (grossly contracted), and *status mixtus* (mixed).[11] Thus the method basically renounced any etiology and pathology, as well as basic anatomical and physiological knowledge, and was guided in its practice by observing "certain communities of sicknesses."[12] This kind of thinking made it possible for Thessalus of Tralles, Soranus' predecessor, to develop the distinction between acute and chronic illnesses, which proved successful where the old theory of the crasis had failed.[13]

Such a simplified method impressed the Romans—and thus imperial physicians were predominantly representatives of methodism—but this "method" could not satisfy the advanced, highly developed, and occasionally contradictory standard of knowledge attained after the early Alexandrian epoch. It was therefore Soranus' main contribution "to have reestablished the 'method' by ordering its principles," and Caelius Aurelianus called him "methodicorum princeps."[14] From the existing theoretical suppositions he had to direct his attention to consolidating diagnostics, and thus in his work differential diagnostics gained importance for the first time. Soranus also sought to place the vague and extremely hypothetical "communities" on a firm basis and to give them a distinct definition; and the strict separation of acute and chronic diseases was made with remarkable clarity and excellent power of clinical observation in his practical instruction on diseases.[15] In his time the "method" became a genuine alternative to the older theories, especially for those who did not cling slavishly to the details and had a solid medical training.

Soranus retained his own views, which sometimes diverged from those of the methodist school. Even if he considered the science of the healthy body, including anatomical and physiological knowledge, to be useless, as a scholar at Ephesus and Alexandria he frequently used it and declared the former to be necessary.[16] His gynecological works demonstrate to what extent he valued Herophilus' teachings on obstetrics, so that it is incorrect to call him—as did Diepgen—merely a *Vertreter methodischer Gynäkologie* ("representative of methodist gynecology")[17] who added nothing to the development of this specialty. His knowledge comprised the whole of medicine and even extended to philosophy and grammar, fields in which he also was outstanding. Therefore Galen, who expressed contempt for the masters of "method," never attacked Soranus; on the contrary, he recommended some of his prescriptions. Even Tertullian, a theologian not at all on friendly terms with the physicians, characterized him as "methodicae medicinae instructissimus autor."[18]

Soranus' works deal with many fields of medical science and are noted for their clarity and the rigorous treatment of the stated problems; they also give the reader a more comprehensive biological view by using vivid comparisons from zoology and agriculture.[19] Both his manner of citing the sources and his exact observance of their chronological sequence in mentioning the doctrines and theories of older physicians, to whom he gave considerable attention, were remarkable.

Soranus' major extant work, *Gynaecia*, comprised four books.[20] Book I records the necessary qualities of a prospective midwife (integrity, zest for work and strong constitution, smooth hands, good theoretical knowledge and practical experience, refusal to perform a criminal abortion) and her work (gynecological physiology with exact representation of the anatomy; feminine hygiene, including comments on menstruation and conception; how to have healthy children; hygiene during pregnancy and abortion). Book II deals with obstetrics (symptoms of and preparations for delivery, parturition, complications, nursing by women in childbed, the nursing of the baby and the choice of a wet nurse, confinement and infant hygiene, and childhood diseases). Books III and IV deal with women's diseases. In Book III, Soranus concedes that women have diseases ($\pi\acute{\alpha}\vartheta\eta$) that men cannot, a controversial thesis in antiquity, and comments on diseases to be treated dietetically; and Book IV deals with diseases that can be treated surgically and pharmaceutically. Although the *Gynaecia* was a comparatively complete work in the original text, it is necessary to warn against the prevalent view that Soranus was "the" gynecologist of antiquity. His work would have been impossible without the preliminary studies of the Herophileans, however independent and superior his mastery and exposition of the subject; in addition, his knowledge far surpassed this specialty.

A shorter compendium, a sort of catechism for midwives, has been lost in its original edition; but it may be preserved in Muscio's sixth-century translation, as well as in a Greek retranslation that was formerly considered the original edition, by the Greek physician Moschion.[21] $\Pi\epsilon\rho\grave{\iota}$ $\sigma\pi\acute{\epsilon}\rho\mu\alpha\tau\sigma\varsigma$ $\kappa\alpha\grave{\iota}$ $\zeta\omega\sigma\gamma\sigma\nu\acute{\iota}\alpha\varsigma$, on sperm and the genesis of creatures, now lost, counts in the same interrelation.[22] Parts of the work were translated into Latin in a treatise by Vindicianus.[23]

Soranus' magnum opus, $\Pi\epsilon\rho\grave{\iota}$ $\dot{o}\xi\acute{\epsilon}\omega\nu$ $\kappa\alpha\grave{\iota}$ $\chi\rho\sigma\nu\acute{\iota}\omega\nu$ $\pi\alpha\vartheta\tilde{\omega}\nu$, on acute and chronic diseases, also was lost; but there is a sufficient substitute in Caelius Aurelianus' *Celerum sive acutarum passionum*, Books I–III, and *Tardarum sive chronicarum passionum*, Books I–V, because Caelius made a faithful translation into Latin and introduced very few of his own ideas.[24] This work is solidly grounded in the methodist doctrine; and when treating each of the major "internal" diseases, it quite distinctly shows, even in the Latin, the disposition, systematic manner, and wording of Soranus. This work also regularly cites the doctrines of earlier authors, although Soranus nearly always agrees with the views of his own school; and when there are divergencies, he takes a conciliatory standpoint. He is as critical of every sort of medical superstition as he was in the *Gynaecia*, a practice that was no longer a matter of course in science; but when searching for the natural causes of diseases, he reaches beyond both the therapeutic frame of the work and the intentions of his school.

The lost work $A\grave{\iota}\tau\iota\sigma\lambda\sigma\gamma\sigma\acute{\upsilon}\mu\epsilon\nu\alpha$, on causes of diseases, seems to treat that subject exclusively; and $\Pi\epsilon\rho\grave{\iota}$ $\kappa\sigma\iota\nu\acute{o}\tau\eta\tau\omega\nu$, on the "communities," apparently seeks a more distinct definition of that vague concept.[25] Soranus also wrote $\Pi\epsilon\rho\grave{\iota}$ $\pi\upsilon\rho\epsilon\tilde{\omega}\nu$, containing instructions for treating fever, and $\Pi\epsilon\rho\grave{\iota}$ $\beta\sigma\eta\vartheta\eta\mu\acute{\alpha}\tau\omega\nu$, on medical resources, both of which are probably supplements to the work on acute and chronic diseases that have been lost.[26] Caelius Aurelianus often quoted the latter in such a way that one is inclined to consider it as a systematic description of nursing, bloodletting, purgations, and physical therapy.[27]

When prescribing remedies Soranus used only medicaments approved by his teachers and friends—or so Galen said—and recorded them in $\Pi\epsilon\rho\grave{\iota}$ $\varphi\alpha\rho\mu\alpha\kappa\epsilon\acute{\iota}\alpha\varsigma$ ("Instruction on Medicaments") and in a pharmaceutical booklet, $M\sigma\nu\sigma\beta\iota\beta\lambda\acute{\iota}\sigma\nu$

φαρμακευτικόν.[28] He largely agreed with the theories of his school in pharmaceutical practice but disagreed in matters of surgery and the closely related techniques of bandaging. Here the methodist doctrine was unable to support him because it was opposed to anatomy and consequently to surgery as well.[29] Although his great work on surgery, Χειρουργούμενα, is lost, an apparently extant fragment, Περὶ σημείων καταγμάτων ("On the Symptoms of Fractures"), reveals not only an exact knowledge of the normal skeletal anatomy but also a precise conception of the anatomicopathologic misposition of the fragments of bones.[30] It is characteristic that Demetrius, a Herophillean, is the only physician quoted in this fragment.[31] Soranus' completely extant Περὶ ἐπιδεσμάτον ("On Bandages") gives numerous examples of conformity with the pseudo-Galenic instruction on bandages and with that of Heliodorus, as it is presented in Oribasius' work.[32] Two other lost works on medical practice are Ὀφθαλμικόν, on ophthalmology, and Ὑγιεινόν, a general work on hygiene. The latter was also translated by Caelius Aurelianus, but the Latin edition has not survived.[33] In addition to hygiene Soranus was deeply concerned with the human psyche and wrote the four-book Περὶ ψυχῆς βιβλίαδ´, on the human soul.[34] Although this work has not survived, it is possible to obtain an idea of its contents because Tertullian used it as the main source of his De anima.[35] There will always be uncertainty, however, whether Soranus really composed commentaries on Hippocratic writings.

The work on the soul extends into philosophical as well as allied fields of medicine, as do his last two works. The first is Βίοι ἰατρῶν καὶ αἱρέσεις καὶ συντάγματα δέκα, ten books containing biographies of physicians and information on their schools and writings.[36] This biographical work, together with the doxographic description of the existing medical groups and their writings on theoretical and practical problems, is Soranus' main contribution to medical history. An extant fragment is Ἱπποκράτους γένος καὶ βίος κατὰ Σωρανόν ("The Noble Origin and the Life of Hippocrates According to Soranus' Statements").[37] Written many centuries after the death of Hippocrates, Soranus' statement must necessarily contain some traces of legend.[38] Nevertheless, apart from occasional remarks in Plato and later authors, it is the oldest extant complete biography of him. The second work, Περὶ ἐτυμολογιῶν τοῦ σώματος τοῦ ἀνθρώπου, on the origin of bodily terms, concerns the nomenclature for the parts of the human body and its linguistic origin.[39] Its loss is less serious, for later etymologists made extensive use of it; thus a judgment is still possible concerning its conception, range, and quality.[40]

The extent of Soranus' work demonstrates that, with Galen, he was the greatest medical author of late antiquity. That almost all his works were lost, whereas Galen's were widely preserved, is a result of the fact that Galen and his theory of crasis dominated medical thought during the following 1,500 years and deprived the atomistic and cellular-pathological approach of any chance of acceptance. And yet these latter theories exerted a decisive effect. In addition to the works of translators and physicians of the Western Empire, of etymologists, of lexicographers, and of theologians, important chapters of Soranus' works appeared in the compilations of Byzantine medical science;[41] even Galen used parts of them. Soranus' surviving works reveal a physician with an unprejudiced view of the substance of a medical science that was threatened with being swamped by its own abundance of knowledge. Essential parts of his work show that he was a master of "method"—but by no means indoctrinated in a way that might prevent him from looking beyond the limits of his school. His liberal views permitted Soranus to use the Herophileans as a base in obstetrics and osteology and to accept principles of other schools—for instance, in matters of bandaging. This cultivation of a liberated mind was characteristic of the school of Ephesus, and Soranus proves that he belonged to it through his use of terminology: only this school produced such personages as Rufus and, enlarging the circle a bit, Charmides, who wrote the Onomasticon.[42] Galen, on the other hand, deliberately neglected distinct diction in the nomenclature.[43]

Soranus' moral and intellectual freedom also enabled him to write about Hippocrates and his followers in a way that presented an analysis of their doctrines without advocating a return to them. If we knew more about him, we would undoubtedly conclude that Soranus was Galen's only great intellectual antagonist, intellectually his peer—if we are allowed to use Tertullian's De anima—and in character his superior. His pupil Statilius Attalus, unjustly defamed by Galen, held an eminent place at the court of the emperor at Ephesus.[44]

NOTES

1. Suidas, *Lexicon*, T. Gaisford, ed., rev. by G. Bernhardy, II (Halle – Brunswick, 1853), 850.
2. L. Scheele, *De Sorano Ephesio medico etymologo* (Strasbourg, 1886), 3 ff. (Ph.D. diss.); also see R. Fuchs, "Ge-

schichte der Heilkunde bei den Griechen," in T. Puschmann, M. Neuburger, and J. Pagel, eds., *Handbuch der Geschichte der Medizin*, I (Jena, 1902), 340.

3. See F. E. Kind, "Soran," in Pauly-Wissowa, 2nd ser., III A, pt. 1, 1114.

4. For Rome, Suidas, *loc. cit.*; Soranus, *Gynaeciorum libri quattuor*, II, 44, edited by J. Ilberg, in *Corpus medicorum Graecorum*, IV (Leipzig–Berlin, 1927), 85; Caelius Aurelianus, *De morbis acutis*, II, 130, edited and translated by J. E. Drabkin (Chicago, 1950), 218; and M. Albert, "Les médecins grecs à Rome," in *Les grecs à Rome* (Paris, 1894), 197 ff. For Alexandria, see Suidas, *loc. cit.*; Soranus, *op. cit.*, II, 6, Ilberg, ed., p. 55; Caelius Aurelianus, *De morbis chronicis*, V, 30, J. E. Drabkin, ed., 924.

5. See U. Kahrstedt, *Kulturgeschichte der römischen Kaiserzeit*, 2nd ed. (Bern, 1958), 276.

6. Concerning Ephesus at this time see Kahrstedt, *op. cit.*, 169 f. For the medical school and the association of the physicians, see J. Keil, "Ärzteinschriften aus Ephesos," *Jahreshefte des Österreichischen archäologischen Instituts Wien*, **8** (1905) and **23** (1926); and *Forschungen in Ephesos*, IV, pt. 1 (Vienna, 1932).

7. See Kind, *loc. cit.*; and Fuchs, *loc. cit.* Cf. Caelius Aurelianus, *De morbis acutis*, III, 124; and *De morbis chronicis*, V, 30, Drabkin, ed., 378, 924.

8. M. Wellmann, following H. Haeser, placed Magnus, among others, in the Pneumatic school because he was a pupil of Athenaeus; and he has remained uncontradicted. M. Wellmann, "Die pneumatische Schule," in *Philologische Untersuchungen*, A. Kiessling and U. v. Wilamowitz-Moellendorff, eds., XIV (Berlin, 1895), 178 ff., 187; H. Haeser, *Lehrbuch der Geschichte der Medizin und der epidemischen Krankheiten* (Jena, 1875; repr. Hildesheim–New York, 1971), I, 334 ff. At first this view gives the impression that a connection between Magnus and Soranus would be incompatible. There is no doubt that the investigation and intellectual definition performed by the medical schools of late antiquity were important and instructive; but the classic science of antiquity and the historians of medicine of the past century, influenced by Galenic polemics, have attached too much importance to the differences among these schools; and in doing so they have failed entirely to notice the importance of the schools' belonging to the same academy and its physicians' association. Haeser, referring to Athenaeus, the teacher of Magnus, said, "The methodists had made him make so many concessions that they could call him one of theirs." Thus it is not necessary to state that belonging to a school separates more strongly than belonging to an academy can bind. It seems that this statement becomes valid with Magnus, for Galen sees Magnus' view concerning the cause, origin, and importance of the pulse in total contrast with that of Archigenes, who was a faithful follower of the Pneumatic school. Only a few pages later in Galen's work there is this statement: ". . . καὶ αὐτὸς ἀπὸ τῆς πνευματικῆς αἱρέσεως εἶναι προσποιούμενος . . ." (". . . and he himself makes us believe that he is"—or, to put it more distinctly, ". . . and he himself claims to be"—"a member of the Pneumatic school"). Galen, *De pulsuum differentiis* III.1, in Galen's *Opera omnia*, C. G. Kühn, ed., VIII (Leipzig, 1824), 640, 646. Therefore, even if Magnus styled himself a follower of the Pneumatic school, he must have remained much more of a methodist than his master. This view is also proved by the title Περὶ τῶν ἐρευρηγένων μετὰ τοὺς Θεμίσωνος χρόνομς ("[Medical] Discoveries After the Time of the Methodist Themison"), *ibid.*, 640. It seems impossible that in such a work a qualified follower of the Pneumatic school would base his chronology on such a confirmed methodist. Thus it is not astonishing that we find Magnus thoroughly incorporated into the school of the methodists by Caelius Aurelianus in *De morbis acutis*, II, 58, Drabkin, ed., 160.

9. To the list of Rufus of Ephesus, Titus Statilius Kriton, and Statilius Attalus given by J. Benedum in his archaeologically oriented essay "Statilios Attalos," in *Medizinhistorisches Journal*, **6** (1971), 274, we can add from the literature—besides Soranus and Magnus—Heraclides of Ephesus as a traumatologist. See M. Michler, *Die Hellenistische Chirurgie*, I, *Die Alexandrinischen Chirurgen* (Wiesbaden, 1968), 89, 132 ff., 148 f. A recommendation of the school can be seen in the fact that the author Athenaeus of Naucratis makes an Ephesian physician join the discussions in his *Deipnosophistae* ("The Learned Banquet"). From this, G. Kaibel, in his pref. to the Teubner ed. (Stuttgart, 1965), iv, expressed the idea that Athenaeus might have derived the names of the two physicians who had been the interlocutors—Daphnus Ephesius and Rufinus Nicaeensis—from Rufus of Ephesus. In any case, during the discussions about medical problems the two physicians are referred to as "the Ephesians and the like-minded persons": Οἱ μὲν Ἐφέσιοι καὶ οἱ τούτοις ὅμοιοι. Lib. III, sec. 33 (87 c), Kaibel, ed., I, 202.

10. Galen, *De methodo medendi*, I, 4, in his *Opera omnia*, C. G. Kühn, ed., X, 35.

11. See T. Meyer-Steineg, "Das medizinische System der Methodiker," in *Jenaer medizin-historische Beiträge*, nos. 7–8 (1916), 23.

12. See Celsus, *De medicina*, "Prooemium" 54, edited and translated by W. G. Spencer, I, 30.

13. Until then only the acute diseases were distinguished from the rest. See Meyer-Steineg, *op. cit.*, 33.

14. Caelius Aurelianus, *De morbis acutis*, II, 46, Drabkin, ed., 150 f.

15. See Meyer-Steineg, *op. cit.*, 38 ff.; and Fuchs, *op. cit.*, 341 f.

16. Soranus, *Gynaeciorum libri quattuor*, I, 2, 3, p. 4, Ilberg, ed., I, 5, p. 6.

17. See Michler, *op. cit.*, 142 f.; and Wellmann, *op. cit.*, 118. See also P. Diepgen, "Geschichte der Frauenheilkunde. I: Die Frauenheilkunde der Alten Welt," in W. Stoeckel, *Handbuch der Gynäkologie*, XII, pt. 1 (Munich, 1937), 107.

18. Tertullian, *De anima* 6.

19. See J. Ilberg, "Die Überlieferung der Gynäkologie des Soranus von Ephesos," in *Abhandlungen der Königlich-Sächsischen Gesellschaft der Wissenschaften*, Phil.-hist. Kl., **28**, no. 2 (1910), 36, 76 ff.

20. The ed. by J. Ilberg, *Corpus medicorum Graecorum*, IV, 3–152, is still the authoritative one; an English trans. is O. Temkin, *Soranus' Gynecology* (Baltimore, 1956). For a systematic order other than Ilberg's, see Kind, *op. cit.*, 1118 ff.

21. *Gynaecia ex Muscionis ex Graecis Sorani in Latinum translatum sermonem*, Valentin Rose, ed. (Leipzig, 1882); the Greek retrans. is Μοσχίωνος, Περὶ γυναικείων παθῶν. See Ilberg, *op. cit.*, 102 ff.; and Diepgen, *op. cit.*, 108.

22. See Ilberg, *op. cit.*, 38, and n. 1.

23. Bruxellensis, 1342–1350 (12th century).

24. The ed. and trans. by Drabkin is the authoritative publication today, but for reliability of text one should also consult G. Bendz, "Caeliana, Textkritische und sprachliche Studien zu Caelius Aurelianus," in *Acta Universitatis lundensis*, n.s. **38**, no. 4 (1943); and "Emendationen zu Caelius Aurelianus," in *Publications of the New Society of Letters at Lund*, **44** (1954). For Caelius Aurelianus, see M. Wellmann, in Pauly-Wissowa, III, 1257 ff.; and Meyer-Steineg, *op. cit.*, 42 ff. On the treatment of paralysis, see M. Michler, "Die physikalische Behandlung der Paralysis bei Caelius Aurelianus," in *Sudhoffs Archiv . . .*, **48** (1964), 123.

25. On Αἰτιολογούμενα, see Caelius Aurelianus, *De morbis chronicis*, I, 55, Drabkin, ed., 474. To the overcoming doxographic reports from this work, see Kind, *op. cit.*, 1127. Referred to as Περὶ κοινότητων, see Soranus, *Gynaeciorum libri quattuor*, I, 29, 3, Ilberg, ed., 19.

26. See Caelius Aurelianus, *De morbis acutis*, II, 177, Drab-

kin, ed., 254; and Soranus, *Gynaeciorum libri quattuor*, III, 28, 6, Ilberg, ed., 112.

27. See Kind, *op. cit.*, 1128.

28. Galen, *De compositione medicamentorum secundum locos*, in his *Opera omnia*, I, 7, C. G. Kuhn, ed., XII, 493 f.

29. See M. Michler, *Das Spezialisierungsproblem und die antike Chirurgie* (Bern–Stuttgart–Vienna, 1969), 37.

30. Cited from Soranus, *Gynaeciorum libri quattuor*, I, 7, 4 [76], Ilberg, ed., 56. See also Soranus, *De signis fracturarum*, J. Ilberg, ed., in *Corpus medicorum Graecorum*, IV, 155–158.

31. *Ibid.*, §9, p. 156.

32. Soranus, *De fasciis*, J. Ilberg, ed., in *Corpus medicorum Graecorum*, IV, 159–171. See also Pseudo-Galen, *De fasciis*, in Galen's *Opera omnia*, C. G. Kühn, ed., XVIII A (Leipzig, 1829), 768–827; for Heliodorus, see Oribasius, *Collectiones*, XLVIII, J. Raeder, ed., in *Corpus medicorum Graecorum*, VI, 2, 1 (repr. Amsterdam, 1964).

33. Cited from Soranus, *Gynaeciorum libri quattuor*, I, 32, 1, and 40, 4, Ilberg, ed., 21, 28. For the Latin trans. by Caelius Aurelianus, *Salutaria praecepta*, see Wellmann, in Pauly-Wissowa, *loc. cit.*

34. Tertullian, *loc. cit.*

35. See H. Diels, *Doxographi Graeci* (repr. Berlin, 1958), 206 ff.

36. See Suidas, *loc. cit.*

37. *Vita Hippocratis secundum Soranum*, J. Ilberg, ed., in *Corpus medicorum Graecorum*, IV, 175–178; on the origin of this, see the pref. to IV, xiv f.

38. See also H. E. Sigerist, *Anfänge der Medizin* (Zurich, 1963), 697 ff. This is a trans. of *A History of Medicine* (New York, 1955).

39. See Orion, *Etymologicon*, F. W. Sturz, ed. (Leipzig, 1820), 34, ll. 9 f.; also 131, ll. 4 f., and 159, l. 18.

40. Such a judgment is possible from Orion, who cites him some twenty times, occasionally in long and detailed passages; there are also citations from him in *Etymologicum magnum*, Gudianum, and other Greek etymological dictionaries. Fragments are in Pollux, *Onomasticon* II. See also Kind, *op. cit.*, 1117.

41. For instance, in works of Philumenus of Alexandria, Aëtius of Amida, and Paul of Aegina; see Fuchs, *op. cit.*, 341.

42. See Rufus of Ephesus, Περὶ ὀνομασίας τῶν τοῦ σώματος μορίων, Daremberg and Ruelle, eds., (repr. Amsterdam, 1963), 237 ff. For Charmenides and his *Onomasticon*, see J. Benedum, "Charmenides," in Pauly-Wissowa, Supp. XIV (1974), 96.

43. See E. Marchel, *Galens anatomische Nomenklatur* (Bonn, 1951), 117 (M.D. diss.).

44. See J. Benedum, "Statilios Attalos," 264 ff.

MARKWART MICHLER

SORBY, HENRY CLIFTON (*b.* Woodbourne, near Sheffield, England, 10 May 1826; *d.* Sheffield, 10 March 1908), *microscopy, geology, biology, metallurgy.*

Most of Sorby's ancestors since the seventeenth century had been middle-class cutlers in Sheffield. His father, Henry Sorby, owned a small cutlery factory; his mother was the daughter of a London merchant. Sorby attended local schools and at age fifteen he won, as a prize for mathematics, a book entitled *Readings in Science*, published by the Society for Promoting Christian Knowledge (first edition 1833), which set the direction of his life. During the next four years he completed his education with a full-time private tutor, the Rev. Walter Mitchell, a competent scientist who later wrote on crystallography and mechanical philosophy in the popular compendium *Orr's Circle of the Sciences*. Sorby attended no university—he later said that he planned his education "not to pass an examination but to qualify myself for a career of original investigation." Closely tied to his mother, he never married. He inherited a modest fortune after his father's death in 1847 and thereafter devoted himself entirely to science while continuing to live in Sheffield, a flourishing steel manufacturing town with somewhat limited intellectual resources. Sorby became very active in the local Literary and Philosophical Society, which had fortnightly discussions on a wide range of subjects and provided him with diverse intellectual stimulation and the opportunity for both leadership and service that he could not have obtained as a young man in a metropolis.

Isolated from the most active scientific circles, Sorby worked quietly on unfashionable topics in a laboratory in his own house. Cast in much the same mold as many other English country gentlemen whose education, isolation, and leisure enabled them to make original observations, he initiated two major areas of science—and carried neither to the point of maturity. Often called an amateur, he was one only in the sense that he was not working in an institutional environment or at the expense of anyone else. He was, in fact, a full-time independent research scientist at a time when there were few such.

Sorby's most influential scientific work was done between 1849 and 1864 on the application of the microscope to geology and metallurgy. In both fields his work had a certain elegance derived from a mixture, in about equal proportions, of simple quantitative observation, meticulous new experimental technique, and novel interpretation based on the application of elementary physicochemical principles to complex natural phenomena. "My object," he said in his last paper, "is to apply experimental physics to the study of rocks." His most famous achievement is the development of the basic techniques of petrography, using the polarizing microscope to study the structure of thin rock sections. The geological conclusions that Sorby drew from such studies were of utmost importance. He started this work in 1849 with studies of sedimentary rocks. In 1851 he became involved in a widely noticed debate on the origin of slaty cleavage, and in an 1853 paper he showed conclusively that cleavage was a result of the reorientation of particles of mica accompanying the deformation (flow) of the deposit under anisotropic pressure. Sorby later studied organisms in limestone and discovered the presence and significance of microorganisms in chalk. In a paper published just before his death (1908) he returned to sedimentation and summarized his whole approach.

Sorby first studied the rate of settling and angle of repose of sand and silt particles in still and turbulent water, and the transport of grains along the bottom by currents of various velocities; then, observing bedding angles, ripple marks, and the variation of particle size with depth (with porosity measurements to allow correction for compaction, solution, or compression of strata) in actual sandstones, he deduced rather precisely the conditions under which the sediments had been deposited.

From slate Sorby moved to schists and metamorphic rocks in general. Of great importance was his 1858 paper on liquid inclusions in crystals, both natural and artificial. Inclusions in large crystals had been observed by David Brewster and Humphry Davy in the 1820's, but Sorby used the microscope to find abundant smaller ones within the microcrystals in many metamorphic rocks. He measured the size of the bubbles that resulted from liquid shrinkage after the cavity had been sealed, and he performed laboratory experiments to measure the expansion of liquids in sealed tubes under pressure that enabled him to deduce the temperature and pressure at which the rocks had been formed. This information revealed large differences in the temperature of formation of granites from various localities and led Sorby to realize the great role played in rock formation by water-bearing magma at high temperature and pressure. (In 1863, after further experiments, he wrote: "Pressure weakens or strengthens chemical affinity according as it acts against or in favour of the change in volume"—a clear anticipation of Le Chatelier's principle.) The 1858 paper was illustrated with 120 drawings made under the microscope at magnifications between 60 and 1,600, transferred to the lithographer's stones by Sorby himself. He concluded: "There is no necessary connection between the size of an object and the value of a fact, and . . . though the objects I have described are minute the conclusions to be derived from the facts are great."

There were still eminent geologists who saw little good to come from studying mountains with microscopes, and Sorby's work was rather slow to be widely appreciated. He was not one to wring the last shred of meaning from a topic, however; and it was fortunate for geology that while touring

the Rhine valley with his mother before a conference in the summer of 1861, he met the young geology student Ferdinand Zirkel (1838–1912), whom he inspired to take up the new methods. Zirkel did so with Germanic thoroughness, and his two-volume *Lehrbuch der Petrographie* (1866) established petrography as a broad and systematic science.

In 1863–1864 Sorby turned briefly from rocks to metals. Although he began with a general interest in the structure of meteorites (the only metallic bodies to have an easily visible crystalline structure), the principal stimuli seem to have been two evenings at the Literary and Philosophical Society during which ornamental etching and the manufacture of iron and steel were discussed—combined, of course, with the omnipresence of these metals in his native city. On 28 July 1863 he recorded in his diary, "Discover the Widmannstättischm structure in Ⓛ iron." Circle-L was the brand mark of the Swedish wrought iron preferred over all others by Sheffield steelmakers for conversion to blister steel. (Sorby was probably using a piece that had already been converted to steel and had large grains containing easily visible plates of iron carbide. The iron itself, being free from carbon, could not have had a true Widmannstätten structure.) Always somewhat of a showman, Sorby prepared six different samples to display under the microscope at a soirée of the meeting of the British Association at Newcastle in August, by which time he had already identified in steel three separate crystalline compounds that differed in their reaction to nitric acid.

Early in 1864 Sorby recorded his structures by nature printing, an old and simple process in which a relief-etched surface was inked and pressed to paper. A superb print showing the structure in the Elbogen meteorite made by Aloys von Widmannstätten and Karl von Schreibers in 1813 had inspired later ones of which Sorby knew; but before 1863 the etching of terrestrial irons was done only decoratively or to reveal gross texture, not microstructure.

Sorby worked with a local photographer to make several photomicrographs of steel, which he showed and discussed at the British Association meeting in September 1864. This paper was the true foundation of metallography, although it was published only in abstract. Sorby mentions "various mixtures of iron, two or three well-defined compounds of iron and carbon, of graphite and of slag; and these, being present in different proportions, and arranged in various manners give rise to a large number of varieties of iron and steel." Despite considerable interest at the time, no one followed this start. There was no Zirkel of metallurgy, and Sorby himself moved on to other fields, not returning to steel until 1882 and not publishing anything in detail until 1885. By that time interest in metal structure had been aroused by papers by Chernoff (1868, 1879), Martens (beginning in 1878), and Osmond (1885), none of whom knew Sorby's earlier work. Sorby's 1885 paper was circulated in preprint form, but final publication was delayed for two years by a search for suitable photogravure methods.

In the meantime Sorby had shown, by the use of higher magnifications, that the feature that he had earlier called the "pearly constituent" because of its iridescence was an extremely fine duplex lamellar mixture of iron and iron carbide resulting from the decomposition on slow cooling of a constituent that was stable at high temperatures. Earlier he had identified graphite and iron oxide in iron samples and had described the true nature of recrystallization and transformation: "Iron and steel are not analogous to simple minerals, but to complex rocks." The structural origin of many age-old differences between various kinds of iron and steel was now clear. After 1885 people in many countries took up the new field. By 1900 a range of structures had been observed in many alloys and cataloged in relation to composition and heat treatment, and a beginning was being made in the application of thermodynamics to the study of alloys and of the effects of mechanical deformation.

The interest that supplanted metals and meteorites in Sorby's mind in 1864 was spectrum analysis. Four new elements had been discovered by emission spectroscopy since Bunsen and Kirchhoff's announcement of 1860. G. G. Stokes described the use of absorption spectra for identifying organic substances in March 1864, and Sorby at once saw a new application for his favorite instrument. Quickly developing the necessary combination of microscope and spectroscope, he first examined minerals in rock sections, then moved on to study the coloring matter in animal and plant tissues. Carotene was one of his discoveries, and his work on chlorophyll, autumn colors, and blood identification aroused popular interest, the last involving him in a famous murder trial in 1871. Sorby's observation of unrecorded lines in the absorption spectrum of the mineral jargon (jargoon) led him to announce, in March 1869, the discovery of a new element that he named jargonium. He became involved in an unpleasant priority dispute and more embarrassment when, six months later,

he had to retract, for he had found that the lines were due to uranium. Also in 1869 he used his microspectroscope to study the color of borax beads, thus refining an old, and at the time very important, method of mineral analysis.

After his mother's death in 1874 Sorby widened his activities. He frequently traveled to London for scientific meetings, became a member of the Council of the Royal Society, and was elected president of several societies: the Royal Microscopical Society in 1874, the Mineralogical Society (of which he was the first president) in 1876, and, in 1878–1880, the Geological Society of London. Although he continued to conduct his own research on a purely personal basis, he became increasingly concerned with public policy in support of science. Sorby advocated separation of research and teaching, and in the contribution "On Unencumbered Research—A Personal Experience," to *Essays on the Endowment of Research* (1876), edited anonymously by Charles Appleton for a group of scientists at Oxford, he used his own work as an example of the value of unencumbered and undirected—but not isolated—research. In 1871 he had discussed the possibility of endowing a Royal Society professorship in experimental physical research that would be free from teaching duties. In 1874 he planned a marine biological research station that he proposed to endow and direct; but when one was established ten years later by the Royal Society, he was not asked to participate either financially or scientifically. This was apparently the result of a quarrel with Cambridge biologists including Alan Sedgwick (great-nephew of the geologist of the same name), whose intolerant antireligious attitude disgusted him. Though a revolutionary in science, Sorby was a pillar of the Church of England and very conservative in general outlook.

Sorby's public activities thereafter assumed a more local focus. Beginning in 1880, he worked to promote the formation of Firth College in Sheffield and served as its president from 1882 to 1897. In 1897 the University College was formed in Sheffield by the amalgamation of Firth College with the local technical and medical schools. Despite his international reputation, Sorby was not a great enough local figure to be chosen as its president, and he noted in his diary that he was "a trifle disappointed at being thus superseded after so many years of work." He was appointed vice-president of the college, however, and his research continued. He had bought a thirty-five-ton yawl, carrying a crew of five, in 1878 and had equipped it as a floating laboratory. Thereafter he spent five summer months of almost every year until 1903 cruising off the east coast, studying marine biology and geology but also developing new interests, especially architectural history based on a close study of brick dimensions and construction details in Roman, Saxon, and Norman buildings in East Anglia. History and archaeology remained at the level of serious hobbies, however, and Sorby did not carry them to the point of professional publication. He undertook important studies on temperatures and on silt and sewage movements in the Thames estuary for the Royal Commission on the Thames. For some years, marine biology was his dominant interest. This work has not been critically evaluated by historians, but it seems that his only lasting contribution was the technique he developed in 1889 for differentially staining biological tissues and mounting soft-bodied animals as permanent lantern slides for demonstration and study.

Sorby became lame in 1902 and suffered partial paralysis after an accident in 1903 that confined him virtually to his room. For the next five years he worked over the notes that he had accumulated throughout his life, returning to the geology that had begun his career and that resulted in a last major, although retrospective, paper on sedimentary rock formation. It was read at the meeting of the Geological Society of London on 8 January 1908, two months before his death.

In his will Sorby left some journals and £500 to the Literary and Philosophical Society, but his main bequests were to the University of Sheffield for the establishment of a professorship and a research fellowship, the latter under the control of the Royal Society. The bulk of his library also went to the university.

BIBLIOGRAPHY

I. ORIGINAL WORKS. The library of the University of Sheffield has Sorby's diary, containing terse daily entries for 1859–1908 (except for most of 1871–1882, 1894–1895, and 1903–1905) and a 2-vol. bound assembly of his printed papers and notices. A collection of letters to Sorby from many correspondents is in the Sheffield Central Library, Cat. no. SLPS 51. The metallurgy and geology departments of the University of Sheffield have preserved many of Sorby's original microsamples of rock and steel, the earliest bearing the date 1849. Many of his magnificent preparations of marine animals are in the zoology department.

Sorby wrote no book. G. H. Humphries, "A Bibliography of Publications—H. C. Sorby," in C. S. Smith,

ed., The Sorby Centennial Symposium on the History of Metallurgy (New York, 1965), 43–58, contains 233 entries. The most important of these are "On the Origin of Slaty-Cleavage," in Edinburgh New Philosophical Journal, 55 (1853), 137–150; "On the Microscopical Structure of Crystals Indicating the Origin of Minerals and Rocks," in Journal of the Geological Society, 14 (1858), 453–500; "Bakerian Lecture. On the Direct Correlation of Mechanical and Chemical Forces," in Proceedings of the Royal Society, 12 (1863), 538–550; "On a Definite Method of Qualitative Analysis of Animal and Vegetable Colouring Matters by Means of the Spectrum Microscope," ibid., 15 (1867), 433–456; "On Unencumbered Research—A Personal Experience," in Essays on the Endowment of Research (London, 1876), 149–175; "The Application of the Microscope to Geology, etc. Anniversary Address of the President," in Monthly Microscopical Journal, 17 (1877), 113–136; "On the Structure and Origin of Limestone," in Quarterly Journal of the Geological Society of London, 35 (1879), 56–95; "On the Application of Very High Powers to the Study of the Microscopical Structure of Steel," in Journal of the Iron and Steel Institute, 31 (1886), 140–144; "The Microscopical Structure of Iron and Steel," ibid., 33 (1887), 255–288; "On the Preparation of Marine Animals as Lantern Slides to Show the Form and Anatomy," in Transactions of the Liverpool Biological Society, 5 (1891), 269–271; "Fifty Years of Scientific Research," in Annual Report of the Sheffield Literary and Philosophical Society (1898), 13–21; and "On the Application of Quantitative Methods to the Study of the Structure and History of Rocks," in Quarterly Journal of the Geological Society of London, 64 (1908), 171–233.

II. SECONDARY LITERATURE. The only complete biographical study is Norman Higham, A Very Scientific Gentleman. The Major Achievements of Henry Clifton Sorby (Oxford, 1963). Obituary notices with more than usual perception are J. W. Judd, "Henry Clifton Sorby, and the Birth of Microscopical Petrology," in Geological Magazine, 5th ser., 5 (1908), 193–204; and Archibald Geikie, "Henry Clifton Sorby, 1826–1908," in Proceedings of the Royal Society, B80 (1908), lvi–lxvi; and W. J. Sollas, "Anniversary Address of the President," in Proceedings of the Geological Society (London), 65 (1909), 1–lvii. Shortly before Sorby's death Geikie had discussed nineteenth-century achievements in petrology as part of his anniversary address as president of the Geological Society—Transactions of the Geological Society of London, 64 (1908), 104–111—which presents Sorby's great impact on geology from a contemporary viewpoint. See also George P. Merrill, "The Development of Micro-Petrology," in The First One Hundred Years of American Geology (New Haven, 1924), 643–647.

For later analyses, see W. H. Wilcockson, "The Geological Work of Henry Clifton Sorby," in Proceedings of the Yorkshire Geological Society, 27 (1947), 1–22; and G. H. Humphries, "Sorby: The Father of Microscopical

Petrography," in C. S. Smith, ed., *The Sorby Centennial Symposium on the History of Metallurgy* (New York, 1963), 17–41. This centennial volume depicts the changes in metallurgy following Sorby and contains other comments on Sorby himself by the editor (ix–xix) and N. Higham (1–15). Sorby's metallurgical contributions also were analyzed by C. H. Desch in his 20-page pamphlet *The Services of Henry Clifton Sorby to Metallurgy* (Sheffield, 1921); and by C. S. Smith in "Metallography in Sheffield," ch. 13 of his *A History of Metallography* (Chicago, 1960). Records and memorabilia of Sorby are described by A. R. Entwisle, "An Account of the Exhibits Relating to Henry Clifton Sorby . . . ," in *Metallography 1963*, Special Report no. 80, Iron and Steel Institute (London, 1964), 313–326. A rather personal view of the role of microscopic petrography in the broader science of rocks is given by F. Y. Levinson-Lessing, *Vvedenie v istoriyu petrografii* (Leningrad, 1936), English trans. by S. I. Tomkeieff as *A Historical Survey of Petrology* (Edinburgh–London, 1954).

CYRIL STANLEY SMITH

SØRENSEN, SØREN PETER LAURITZ (*b.* Havrebjerg, Slagelse, Denmark, 9 January 1868; *d.* Copenhagen, Denmark, 12 February 1939), *chemistry.*

The son of a farmer, Sørensen was educated at the high school at Sorø and entered the University of Copenhagen at the age of eighteen. He planned to study medicine; but under the influence of S. M. Jorgensen, an important investigator of inorganic complex compounds, he chose chemistry for his career. While at the university Sørensen received two gold medals, the first for a paper on the concept of the chemical radical and the second for a study of strontium compounds. While working for the doctorate he assisted in a geological survey of Denmark, acted as assistant in chemistry at the laboratory of the Danish Polytechnic Institute, and served as a consultant at the royal naval dockyard. His doctoral dissertation (1899) concerned the chemistry of cobaltic oxides. Thus most of his training was in inorganic chemistry.

All this was changed when, in 1901, Sørensen succeeded Johann Kjeldahl as director of the chemical department of the Carlsberg Laboratory in Copenhagen, where he remained for the rest of his life. Kjeldahl had worked on biochemical problems, and Sørensen continued this line of inquiry. His investigations can be divided into four classes: synthesis of amino acids, analytical studies, work on hydrogen ion concentration, and studies on proteins. The first, beginning in 1902, was concerned with synthesis of such amino acids as ornithine,

proline, and arginine. The following year he demonstrated that the Kjeldahl method for determination of amino nitrogen was of much greater generality than its discoverer had claimed. After working out the Formol titration method for analysis of proteins, he turned to a study of the effects of such buffers as borates, citrates, phosphates, and glycine on the behavior of proteins, with especial attention to enzymes.

This work led Sørensen to study the action of quinhydrone electrodes and the effect of ion concentration in the analysis of proteins. His most notable suggestion came from this work. In 1909 he investigated the EMF method for determining hydrogen ion concentration and introduced the concept of pH as an easy and convenient method for expressing this value. He was particularly interested in the effects of changes in pH on precipitation of proteins. After 1910 Sørensen made many studies on the application of thermodynamics to proteins and the quantitative characterization of these substances in terms of laws and constants. In much of this work he was assisted by his wife, Margrethe Høyrup Sørensen. They studied lipoproteins and the complexes of carbon monoxide with hemoglobin and in 1917 succeeded in crystallizing egg albumin for the first time.

Sørensen always encouraged visiting scientists at the Carlsberg Laboratory to work on medical problems. He also was active in chemical technology, contributing to the Danish spirits, yeast, and explosive industries. He received many honors from both scientific and technological societies. Sørensen retired in 1938 after a period of poor health and died the following year.

BIBLIOGRAPHY

I. ORIGINAL WORKS. There is a complete bibliography in *Kolloidzeitschrift*, **88** (1939), 136–139. The pH concept is presented in "Enzymstudien. II. Über die Messung und die Bedeutung der Wasserstoffionkonzentration bei enzymatischen prozessen," in *Biochemische Zeitschrift*, **21** (1909), 131–200. The isolation of crystalline egg albumin is described in "On the Composition and Properties of Egg-Albumin Separated in Crystalline Form by Means of Ammonium Sulphate," in *Comptes rendus du Laboratoire de Carlsberg*, **12** (1917), 164–212.

II. SECONDARY LITERATURE. Biographical sources are the Sørensen memorial lecture by E. K. Rideal, in *Journal of the Chemical Society* (1940), 554–561; K. Linderstrøm-Lang, "S. P. L. Sørensen," in *Kolloidzeitschrift*, **88** (1939), 129–136; and Edwin J. Cohn, "Søren

Peter Lauritz Sørensen," in *Journal of the American Chemical Society*, **61** (1939), 2573–2574.

HENRY M. LEICESTER

SOSIGENES (*fl.* Rome, middle of first century B.C.), *astronomy.*

Sosigenes helped Julius Caesar with his reform of the calendar. Caesar is said to have made use of Egyptian astronomy, but this may mean only that he discussed astronomy with Greeks from Alexandria. It is, in any case, not certain that Sosigenes was an Alexandrian, and he is not the only person whom Caesar consulted. Plutarch (*Caesar*, 59) simply states, without mentioning any names, that Caesar consulted the best philosophers and mathematicians before producing an improved calendar of his own. Caesar's adoption of the 365-1/4-day solar year may have been one result of Sosigenes' advice, and the statesman's seasonal calendar another. The 365-1/4-day year could even have been borrowed directly from Callippus at the suggestion of Sosigenes. All that Pliny says in this connection, however, is that during Caesar's dictatorship Sosigenes helped him to bring the years back into conformity with the sun (*Naturalis historia* 18.211). He adds (*Naturalis historia* 18.212) that Sosigenes wrote three treatises, including corrections of his own statements.

Sosigenes agreed with Cidenas in giving the greatest elongation of Mercury from the sun as 22° (Pliny, *Naturalis historia* 2.39). It is therefore possible, but far from certain, that he made use of Babylonian astronomical knowledge. Lucan (*Pharsalia* 10.187) implies that Caesar tried to improve upon the seasonal calendar of Eudoxus— "nec meus Eudoxi vincetur fastibus annus" ("and my year shall not be found inferior to the calendar of Eudoxus"). Theodor Mommsen maintains that Caesar ". . . with the help of the Greek mathematician Sosigenes introduced the Italian farmer's year regulated according to the Egyptian calendar of Eudoxus, as well as a rational system of intercalation, into religious and official use." Mommsen here alludes to the calendar in the papyrus *Ars Eudoxi*, but there is no proof of any close connection between the ideas of Sosigenes and the doctrines in the *Ars*.

BIBLIOGRAPHY

On Caesar's alleged use of "Egyptian" sources, see Appian, *Bella civilia* 2.154; Dio Cassius, *Hist. Rom.* 43.26; and Macrobius, *Saturnalia* 1.16.39 and 1.14.3. There are useful discussions regarding Caesar and Eudoxus' seasonal calendar in A. Böckh, *Ueber die vierjährige Sonnenkreise der Alten* (Berlin, 1863), 340–342; F. K. Ginzel, *Handbuch der mathematischen und technischen Chronologie*, II (Leipzig, 1911), 274–277; and Pauly-Wissowa, *Real-Encyclopädie*, 2nd ser., III (Stuttgart, 1927), s.v. Sosigenes (b) 1153–1157—compare Theodor Mommsen, *The History of Rome*, IV (London, 1887), 555. The calendar in the *Ars Eudoxi* is discussed in C. Wachsmuth, *Ioannis Laurentii Lydi Liber de ostentis et calendaria Graeca omnia* (Leipzig, 1897), lxviii–lxix, 299–301.

G. L. HUXLEY

SOTO, DOMINGO DE (*b.* Segovia, Spain, 1494 or 1495; *d.* Salamanca, Spain, 15 November 1560), *logic*, *natural philosophy.*

Born to parents of modest means who gave him the baptismal name of Francisco, Soto received his Latin training at Segovia under Juan de Oteo and Sancho de Villaveses. He continued his education in arts at the newly founded University of Alcalá, where he studied logic and natural philosophy under Thomas of Villanova and earned the baccalaureate in 1516. Shortly thereafter he transferred to the College of Santa Barbara at the University of Paris; his preceptors included Juan de Celaya, under whose tutelage he became acquainted with the terminist physics then current in Paris, where he completed the master's degree in arts. He then began the study of theology, while teaching the arts, and came under the influence of the Scottish nominalist John Major, who was then teaching at the Collège de Montaigu (along with two of Soto's fellow Segovians, Luis and Antonio Coronel), and the Spanish Thomist Francisco de Vitoria, who was lecturing at the Dominican priory of Saint-Jacques.

In 1519, however, Soto's longing for Spain and for his close friend Pedro Fernández de Saavedra prompted his return to Alcalá, where he completed the course in theology under Pedro Ciruelo and immediately (October 1520) occupied the chair of philosophy at the College of San Ildefonso. Here he taught logic, physics, and metaphysics until early in 1524, when internal difficulties in the college led him to resign his post. By this time he had received the licentiate in theology at San Ildefonso. He withdrew temporarily to the Benedictine abbey of Montserrat and was advised there to enter the Dominican order. In the summer of 1524 he became a Dominican novice at the priory of San Pablo in Burgos, changing his name to Domingo and being professed on 23 July 1525.

Assigned to the priory of San Esteban in Salamanca, Soto taught theology until 1532, a period of service interrupted only by a stay in Burgos during 1528–1529 while supervising the publication of his first work, the *Summulae*. During the academic year 1531–1532 he substituted for his former mentor, Francisco de Vitoria, who held the "prime chair" of theology at the University of Salamanca. The next year Soto was elected to the "vesper chair" of theology at the same university, a post he held for sixteen years. During this period he prepared a second edition of the *Summulae* (1539), a *Dialectica* (1543), and a commentary and questions on the *Physics* of Aristotle (1545). Immediately adopted at both Salamanca and Alcalá, these works went through many editions in Spain and elsewhere.

The works on the *Physics* are particularly important for the history of science, since in his questions on Book VII Soto was the first to apply the expression "uniformly difform" to the motion of falling bodies, thereby indicating that they accelerate uniformly when they fall and thus adumbrating Galileo's law of falling bodies. Soto accounted for the velocity increase in terms of an accidental impetus built up in the body. He assimilated the "calculatory" techniques developed at Merton College, Oxford, in the fourteenth century and the terminist physics perfected at Paris during the early sixteenth century within a Thomistic framework, and thus dealt with most of the physical problems that interested the nominalists and realists of his day. On this account he is sometimes charged with eclecticism, although he tried to work out a position intermediate between those of Duns Scotus and Ockham and more consistent with Aquinas' teaching. Soto had distinctive views on the nature of motion, time and space, infinity, movement through a vacuum, maxima and minima, and the ratios of velocities. He subscribed to the Ptolemaic theory of the universe and generally defended the Scholastic Aristotelian theses of natural philosophy.

Soto was called to the Council of Trent early in 1545, having just completed his questions and commentary on Book VII of the *Physics*; the incomplete texts were printed immediately but did not include the passages of interest to present-day historians of science. He returned from Trent in 1550 and finished both texts, which were published at Salamanca in 1551. (In all, these works went through nine editions, the penultimate appearing at Venice in 1582, when Galileo was beginning his

studies at Pisa. Soto's questions on the *Physics* are cited by Galileo in his *Juvenilia*, although not in the context of discussions of falling bodies.) While at Trent, Soto was closely associated with the Spanish ambassador to Venice, Diego Hurtado de Mendoza, who had studied the science of weights under Niccolò Tartaglia; Mendoza's correspondence shows him critical of Soto's physics, probably more because of Mendoza's Averroist and classical leanings than because of any particular attachment, on his part, to Archimedean statics.

Soto held various professorial and administrative positions at Salamanca until his death. He achieved renown in this university city for his extensive knowledge of both philosophy and theology, and is best known for his work in political philosophy, *De iure et iustitia* (1553–1554), in which he developed concepts of natural law and a "translation theory" of the origin of political authority. His competence is attested by a saying current in sixteenth-century Spain: "Qui scit Sotum, scit totum" ("Whoever knows Soto, knows everything").

BIBLIOGRAPHY

I. ORIGINAL WORKS. For a complete listing of Soto's writings, see Vicente Beltrán de Heredia, O.P., *Domingo de Soto: Estudio biográfico documentado* (Salamanca, 1960), 515–588. Brief Latin and English texts from Soto's works on the *Physics* are in Marshall Clagett, *The Science of Mechanics in the Middle Ages* (Madison, Wis., 1959), 257, 555–556, 658. Pierre Duhem, *Études sur Léonard de Vinci*, III (Paris, 1913), gives excerpts from the same in French translation.

II. SECONDARY LITERATURE. See William A. Wallace, O.P., "The Concept of Motion in the Sixteenth Century," in *Proceedings of the American Catholic Philosophical Association*, 41 (1967), 184–195: "The Enigma of Domingo de Soto: *Uniformiter difformis* and Falling Bodies in Late Medieval Physics," in *Isis*, 59 (1968), 384–401; and "The 'Calculatores' in Early Sixteenth-Century Physics," in *British Journal for the History of Science*, 4 (1968–1969), 221–232. See also Erika Spivakovsky, "Diego Hurtado de Mendoza and Averroism," in *Journal of the History of Ideas*, 26 (1965), 307–326; Vicente Muñoz Delgado, *La logica nominalista en la Universidad de Salamanca* (1510–1530), Publicaciones del Monasterio de Poyo, XI (Madrid, 1964); *Logica formal y filosofia en Domingo de Soto*, Publicaciones del Monasterio de Poyo, XVI (Madrid, 1964); and W. A. Wallace, "Galileo and the Thomists," in Armand Maurer *et al.*, eds., *St. Thomas Aquinas Commemorative Studies 1274–1974*, II (Toronto, 1974), 293–330.

WILLIAM A. WALLACE, O.P.

SOULAVIE, JEAN-LOUIS GIRAUD (*b*. Largentière, Ardèche, France, 8 July 1752; *d*. Paris, France, 11 March 1813), *geology*.

Ordained in 1776, Soulavie was one of the many philosophical *abbés* and pamphleteers active before the Revolution. He became an early member of the Jacobin Club, supported the Civil Constitution of the Clergy (1790), and served as the diplomatic resident of the First Republic in Geneva (1793–1794). He married in 1792 and was later permitted to return to secular life by Pope Pius VII. After Thermidor (27 July 1794) he devoted himself to the writing and editing of memoirs concerned with the history of France; perhaps best known is his *Mémoires historiques et politiques du règne de Louis XVI* (1801), which, like his other works, remains difficult to evaluate for its accuracy and historical significance.

Soulavie's scientific activities occupied a relatively short period of his life. A self-taught amateur, he was widely read and spent some time during the 1770's exploring the volcanic regions of Vivarais and Velay. On his arrival at Paris in 1778, his geological views had already been formulated; after additional field trips, he returned to Paris in 1780, established permanent residence there, and became a familiar figure at several salons.

Soulavie's major geological publication was the eight-volume *Histoire naturelle de la France méridionale* (1780–1784). Beginning with the then common idea that most sedimentary formations had been deposited by a universal, gradually diminishing ocean, he went on to stress and develop the principle of superposition. Soulavie, however, used superposition not only to determine the relative ages of strata, but he also attempted to correlate age with fossil remains. He argued that the oldest strata also contain the largest proportion of extinct species, while the youngest show a predominance of forms with living analogues.[1] He then attempted to work out a local geochronology for Vivarais by taking note of those sedimentary formations in which volcanic debris could be found.[2] These observations and ideas were expressed on geological maps of his own design, using a combination of symbols, hachures, and color.[3]

Soulavie's geological ideas were actually less clear and consistent than is suggested by any one of his publications. Although he always insisted that volcanic activity was more important and widespread than some contemporaries believed, he was vague and contradictory about the source of volcanic heat. On occasion, he seems to have held Neptunist views of the nature of the earth's core and oldest formations; elsewhere, however, he discussed the probable existence of a central heat within the earth.[4] In different portions of the *Histoire naturelle*, he emphasized both the extinction of species and the likelihood that seemingly extinct species had merely migrated to warmer climates.[5]

Although extravagant claims have been made for Soulavie's originality, his place in the history of geology cannot yet be assessed. Certain of his contemporaries admired his boldness and imagination, while others condemned the very same traits. He himself condemned system-building and was complimented on his "method of philosophizing" by Benjamin Franklin.[6] However, Buffon (to whom Soulavie was indebted for many of his ideas) roundly condemned Soulavie as an observer and thinker. Such negative views were not shared by some members of the Académie Royale des Sciences, which awarded its *privilège* to the first two volumes of Soulavie's *Histoire naturelle*. The conflicting evaluations can be attributed in part to factionalism within the French scientific community, but also, in part, to the fact that naturalists were not wholly in agreement about two of Soulavie's major ideas: the extinction of species and the importance of volcanic activity.[7]

NOTES

1. *Histoire naturelle*, esp. I, 161–163, 317–332. References to this work are to the copy at the Bibliothèque Nationale, *cotes* S. 21194–21200 and Rés. S. 1158. See Bibliography.
2. *Ibid*., esp. II, 362–377; IV, 16, 42–44.
3. *Ibid*., I, 143–149, for his method of constructing maps. A good example of the result is in vol. II, and the same map is in *Géographie* (in color in the copy at the Bibliothèque Nationale).
4. For Neptunism and the recent origins of volcanoes, see *Classes*, 101, 140–141, 149 (table), 157. The role of central heat is treated in *Oeuvres*, 290–297, and *Histoire naturelle*, I, 167.
5. *Ibid*., V, 217–221, and above, n. 1.
6. Carl Van Doren, *Benjamin Franklin* (1938; reissue New York: Viking Press, 1964), 659–660. For Soulavie on system-building, *Oeuvres*, 280–281, 288.
7. *Correspondance inédite de Buffon*, H. Nadault de Buffon, ed., II (Paris, 1860), 109. Also, letter of Faujas de St.-Fond, in Bibliothèque Municipale de Nîmes, MS 94, fols. 59–60. Specific scientific issues separating Buffon and Soulavie are mentioned by Aufrère, p. 38. The copy of *Classes* at the Bibliothèque Nationale includes a prefatory statement by the Imperial Academy that it admires some of Soulavie's ideas and information, but "ne prétend pas autoriser par son suffrage [ses] hypothèses . . . hazardés." The work received a second *accessit* (third prize).

BIBLIOGRAPHY

I. ORIGINAL WORKS. *Géographie de la nature* (Paris, 1780) is a brochure presenting the principal ideas of

Soulavie's *Histoire naturelle de la France Méridionale*, 8 vols. (Paris, 1780–1784). Some sections of the latter work bear different titles and have their own publication history; the order in which parts are bound may vary in different copies. The first 7 vols. deal with "minerals," and another vol. on this subject was apparently planned (see Bibliothèque Nationale, *Catalogue des livres imprimés, s.v.* Soulavie, entry S. 21206). Vol. VIII deals with the plant kingdom. *Prospectus de l' "Histoire naturelle de la France méridionale"* (Nîmes, 1780) was reprinted in the *Histoire naturelle*, I, 3–51. *Oeuvres complettes de M. le Chevalier Hamilton* (Paris, 1781) has extensive notes and commentary by Soulavie; part of the volume consists of Sir William Hamilton's *Campi phlegraei* (Naples, 1776). *Les Classes naturelles des minéraux et les époques de la nature correspondantes à chaque classe* (St. Petersburg, 1786) was written in response to a prize question posed in 1785 by the Imperial Academy of St. Petersburg. He published articles in *Observations sur la physique, sur l'histoire naturelle et sur les arts*, as well as many works on nonscientific subjects. Soulavie's library and other possessions were sold in several lots after his death; of the extant sales catalogs, the one listing his science library is *Notice des principaux articles composant le cabinet de livres, tableaux, gravures, et collection d'estampes* . . . (Paris, 1813), B.N., Δ13478.

II. SECONDARY LITERATURE. See Albin Mazon, *Histoire de Soulavie (naturaliste, diplomate, historien)*, 2 vols. (Paris, 1893), and *Appendice à l' "Histoire de Soulavie"* (Privas, 1901); E.-J.-A. d'Archiac de St.-Simon, *Introduction à l'étude de la paléontologie stratigraphique*, 2 vols. (Paris, 1864), I, 348–354, and *Géologie et paléontologie* (Paris, 1866), 142–145. Mazon relies heavily on Archiac in discussing Soulavie's geology. Léon Aufrère, *De Thalès à Davis. Le relief et la sculpture de la terre. Tome IV. La fin du XVIIIᵉ siècle. I. Soulavie et son secret* (Paris, 1952), 71–83, discusses the "unexpurgated" and "expurgated" versions of vol. I of the *Histoire naturelle*; the final version omitted Soulavie's evidence for the great age of the earth.

RHODA RAPPAPORT

SOULEYET, LOUIS-FRANÇOIS-AUGUSTE (*b.* Besse, Var, France, 8 January 1811; *d.* Martinique, 7 October 1852), *zoology*.

Souleyet is one of several health officers in the French navy who won renown for zoological work connected with a voyage of circumnavigation. Nothing is known about his family and childhood. His entry into the health service of the navy was fairly late; and after some difficulty at the outset of his career, he obtained in 1835 the opportunity to sail on the voyage of the *Bonite* around the globe under the command of August-

Nicholas Vaillant. The main purpose of the voyage was to transport French consular agents to various parts of the world. In conformance with the practice begun on Louis-Claude de Freycinet's voyage of the *Uranie* (1817–1820), all scientific research was to be handled by members of the navy. Fortuné Eydoux, surgeon major of the expedition, was charged with zoology, and Souleyet, as second surgeon, became associated with his research. Souleyet also benefited from the friendship and guidance of Charles Gaudichaud-Beaupré, pharmacist and adjoint to the expedition for research on natural history. Gaudichaud introduced Souleyet to the study of pelagic mollusks, which became his field of specialization. The *Bonite* left Toulon in February 1836, stopped in South America, Hawaii, the Philippines, and various parts of the Indian and Chinese seas, and returned to Brest in November 1837. Because the brevity of the stopovers precluded an investigation of the ecology or anthropology of the areas visited, the naturalists concentrated on collecting new species, particularly microscopic mollusks. The collections were deposited at the Museum of Natural History and cataloged by the professors there.

Eydoux, who after the voyage became physician in chief at Martinique, died there in 1841, leaving Souleyet with most of the work of publishing the zoology of the voyage. Another tour of duty during 1846–1849 interrupted publication. Souleyet finally returned to Paris in January 1850 and completed the work in 1851. Free to pursue his career, he was preparing for the competitive examination to become a professor when he received orders to embark for the Antilles. Leaving France reluctantly, he reached Martinique in July 1852, during an epidemic of yellow fever, and soon fell victim to the disease.

The results of Souleyet's anatomical and physiological investigations of pteropod and gastropod mollusks are contained in the second volume of the zoology of the *Bonite* voyage and in various memoirs. Zoologists had been divided over the composition of the Pteropoda, a group created by Cuvier, and the position of this group among the mollusks. Souleyet reworked its classification, removing the Heteropoda and dividing it into four natural families. Accepting Blainville's ranging of the Pteropoda among the Gastropoda, Souleyet pointed out the analogies between these two groups of mollusks. He demonstrated that the alary expansion of the pteropods is merely the foot of the gastropod in disguise. In 1852 Souleyet completed a monograph on the pteropods begun in 1830 by P.-C.-A.-L. Rang. Besides writing the entire text, which appears to be an abbreviated version of the zoology of the *Bonite*, Souleyet added several plates depicting newly discovered species.

Also important is Souleyet's description of the nervous collar of mollusks, which he believed to correspond to both the brain and the spinal cord of vertebrates. He argued that the apparently anomalous nervous collar of pteropods was merely a modification of the general form of that structure in mollusks.

From 1844 Souleyet was involved in a controversy with Armand de Quatrefages on the subject of "phlebenterism." Quatrefages had established a new order of gastropod mollusks, the Phlebenterata, which he defined as degraded gastropods with no proper respiratory organs and an imperfect or absent circulatory system. He claimed that a system of intestinal canals, a "gastro-vascular apparatus," took over part of the functions of respiration and circulation. Elaborating on the general ideas of his master, Henri Milne-Edwards, Quatrefages believed that the animal kingdom was composed of several series in which the type was effaced at the lower limits. Phlebenterism was a general phenomenon of degeneration among animals.

Souleyet, in a series of memoirs and notes beginning with "Observations sur les mollusques gastéropodes designées sous le nom de *Phlébentérés* par M. de Quatrefages" (*Comptes rendus . . . de l'Académie des sciences*, **19** [1844], 355–362), attacked Quatrefages's position. He argued that the Phlebenterata were not essentially different from other Gastropoda, that they did have a complete circulatory system including veins, and that the "gastro-vascular" canals were in reality hepatic canals not without analogues in other mollusks. The controversy touched on the large questions of whether types degraded, whether exterior and interior conformation can be independent, and whether organs can degenerate and be replaced by other organs developed especially for the purpose. The issues were important enough to merit two commission reports, one by the Academy of Sciences and the other by the Society of Biology. The former report was noncommittal, and the latter declared in favor of Souleyet.

BIBLIOGRAPHY

I. ORIGINAL WORKS. With Fortuné Eydoux, Souleyet published *Voyage autour du monde exécuté pendant les années 1836 et 1837 sur la corvette la Bonite commandée par M. Vaillant, Zoologie*, 2 vols. plus atlas (Paris, 1841–1852). This work contains Blainville's instructions to the zoologists of the voyage in the name of the Academy of Sciences and his report on the zoological results of the voyage. The instructions and report had previously been published in *Comptes rendus . . . de l'Académie des sciences*, **1** (1835), 373–377, and **6** (1838), 445–460, respectively. With P.-C.-A.-L. Rang, Souleyet published *Histoire naturelle des mollusques ptéropodes* (Paris, 1852). A list of Souleyet's memoirs written alone or in conjunction with Eydoux is in the Royal Society *Catalogue of Scientific Papers*, V, 760.

II. SECONDARY LITERATURE. Apparently the only biographical notice on Souleyet is S. Petit, "Louis-François-Auguste Souleyet," in *Journal de conchyliologie*, **4** (1853), 107–111. For a helpful review of Souleyet's second volume of the *Bonite* voyage, see Pierre Gratiolet, "Zoologie du voyage de la *Bonite*, par MM. Eydoux et Souleyet," in *Journal de conchyliologie*, **4** (1853), 93–107. On the phlebenterism controversy, see the commission report of the Academy of Sciences, presented by Isidore Geoffroy Saint-Hilaire in *Comptes rendus . . . de l'Académie des sciences*, **32** (1851), 33–46, and in *Mémoires de l'Académie des sciences . . .*, **23** (1853), 83–104; and the commission report of the Society of Biology, presented by Charles Robin in *Comptes rendus des séances de la Société de biologie*, **3** (1851), 5–132.

TOBY A. APPEL

SOUTH, JAMES (*b*. Southwark, London, England, October 1785; *d*. Campden Hill, Kensington, London, 19 October 1867), *astronomy*.

South's great disappointments in, and severe criticisms of, contemporary scientific institutions often overwhelmed his actual scientific accomplishments. The son of a pharmaceutical chemist, he had studied surgery, become a member of the Royal College of Surgeons, and acquired an extensive practice when, through marriage in 1816, he became sufficiently wealthy to forgo medicine and devote himself to astronomy. He established several observatories, in the environs of London and Paris, where he observed with some of the finest telescopes available. From its inception in 1820 South held various offices in the Astronomical Society of London; barred by a technicality from serving as first president of the chartered Royal Astronomical Society in 1831, he thereupon left the organization. He was knighted in 1831 and awarded an honorary LL.D by Cambridge in 1863; in addition he was a fellow of the Royal Society of London (1821), the Linnean Society, and the Royal Society of Edinburgh, and a member of the Royal Irish Academy, the Académie Royale des Sciences, des Lettres, et des Beaux-Arts Belgique, and the Academia Scientiarum Imperialis Petropolitana.

Double stars, essentially discovered by William Herschel, were of great interest throughout the nineteenth century—new ones being found and position measurements made more precise with each improvement in telescope construction. South, working with John Herschel during the years 1821–1823, reobserved the double stars charted originally by William Herschel, mainly for the purpose of detecting position changes. Their observations helped verify the newly recognized orbital motion of these neighboring stars. Their resulting catalog of 380 double stars, presented to the Royal Society in 1824, earned them the gold medal of the Astronomical Society and the grand prize of the Institut de France. For his second catalog of double stars, two years later, South was awarded the Copley Medal of the Royal Society.

South was concerned, perhaps rightly so, by the decline of science in Britain. In 1822 he published a criticism of the *Nautical Almanac,* alleging its inferiority to Continental ones; and in 1829 he presided over an Astronomical Society committee charged with suggesting improvements in this institution. In 1830 South publicly criticized the Royal Society, but to no avail. His major disappointment, however, came from his quarrel with Edward Troughton. In 1829 South bought a French achromatic objective of 11.7 inches aperture, one of the largest in the world, and contracted with Troughton—who had made many of his other instruments—for an equatorial mount. South's dissatisfaction with Troughton's work led to a court suit that Troughton eventually won, extended and acrimonious debates, and South's public destruction of the mount in 1836.

BIBLIOGRAPHY

South's articles are listed in the Royal Society *Catalogue of Scientific Papers*, V, 761–762; his books, in the British Museum *General Catalogue of Printed Books*.

Secondary literature includes J. C., "Sir James South," in *Monthly Notices of the Royal Astronomical Society*, **28** (1867–1868), 69–72; A. M. C[lerk], "Sir James South," in *Dictionary of National Biography*, LIII, 272–274; and T. R. R., "James South," in *Proceedings of the Royal Society*, **16** (1867–1868), xliv–xlvii.

DEBORAH J. WARNER

SOWERBY, JAMES (*b.* London, England, 21 March 1757; *d.* London, 25 October 1822), *natural history, geology.*

Sowerby, son of John and Arabella Sowerby, was trained as an artist and studied at the Royal Academy of Arts. He married Anne de Carle, of Norwich; and their sons, particularly the eldest, James de Carle Sowerby (1787–1871), and the second, George Brettingham Sowerby (1788–1854), from an early age assisted him with his work. Their children, too, were artists and naturalists, so that throughout the nineteenth century there were Sowerbys illustrating works of natural history.

Sowerby is best known for his illustrations to *English Botany; or Coloured Figures of British Plants, With Their Essential Characters, Synonyms, and Places of Growth* (1790–1814). The text was supplied by James Edward Smith, whose name was at first withheld, at his own request; and the work became widely known as Sowerby's *Botany.* Sowerby's skillful drawings, beautifully colored, and Smith's accurate descriptions made it a highly esteemed work that was frequently reissued, later with supplements.

In 1802 Sowerby began to issue *British Mineralogy,* also with colored plates, in parts and followed it with *Exotic Mineralogy.* More important was his *Mineral Conchology of Great Britain,* illustrating "remains of Testaceous Animals or Shells," issued in parts from 1812 and continued after his death by his son James de Carle. Although lacking any systematic arrangement, it was a valuable aid to collectors and is still important as a reference work. Sowerby also prepared illustrations for many natural history works, including William Smith's *Strata Identified by Organized Fossils.*

Not the least of Sowerby's contributions to natural history was his vast correspondence with naturalists in Britain and abroad, in which he encouraged and advised collectors of plants, birds, insects, fossils, and minerals. Specimens were sent to him for identification, and he sent in return other specimens as well as parts of his publications, thus stimulating further research. His own museum, at 2 Mead Place, Lambeth, was regularly visited by naturalists.

BIBLIOGRAPHY

I. ORIGINAL WORKS. There is a useful, although incomplete, list of Sowerby's publications, with many bibliographical details, in *Catalogue of the Books, Manuscripts, Maps and Drawings in the British Museum (Natural History)*, V (London, 1915), 1981–1983. See also R. J. Cleevely, "A Provisional Bibliography of Natural History Works by the Sowerby Family" in *Journal of the Society for the Bibliography of Natural History*, **6** (1974), 482–559. Sowerby's herbarium and more than 2,500 original watercolor drawings for *English Botany* were purchased in 1859 by the British Museum (Natural History), which also bought his collection of about 5,000 fossils in 1861. A large collection of his correspondence is also in the museum. See Jessie Bell MacDonald, "The Sowerby Collection in the British Museum (Natural History): A Brief Description of Its Holdings . . . ," *ibid.*, **6** (1974), 380–401.

II. SECONDARY LITERATURE. There is no definitive biography, but A. de C. Sowerby *et al.*, *The Sowerby Saga* (Washington, 1952), has much information about the family. An obituary notice appeared in *Gentleman's Magazine*, **92**, pt. 2 (Dec. 1822), 568. See also R. J. Cleevely, "The Sowerbys, the *Mineral Conchology*, and Their Fossil Collection," in *Journal of the Society for the Bibliography of Natural History*, **6** (1974), 418–481.

JOAN M. EYLES

SPALLANZANI, LAZZARO (*b*. Scandiano, Italy, 12 January 1729; *d*. Pavia, Italy, 11 February 1799), *natural history, experimental biology, physiology.*

Among the many dedicated natural philosophers of the eighteenth century, Spallanzani stands preeminent for applying bold and imaginative experimental methods to an extraordinary range of hypotheses and phenomena. His main scientific interests were biological and he acquired a mastery of microscopy; but he probed also into problems of physics, chemistry, geology, and meteorology, and pioneered in volcanology. Acute powers of observation and a broadly trained and logical mind helped him to clarify mysteries as diverse as stone skipping on water; the resuscitation of Rotifera and the regeneration of decapitated snail heads; the migrations of swallows and eels and the flight of bats; the electric discharge of the torpedo fish; and the genesis of thunderclouds or a waterspout. His ingenious and painstaking researches illuminated the physiology of blood circulation and of digestion in man and animals, and also of reproduction and respiration in animals and plants. The relentless thoroughness of his work on the animalcules of infusions discredited the doctrine of spontaneous generation and pointed the way to preservation of foodstuffs by heat.

Spallanzani's father, Gianniccolò, was a successful lawyer. He was of locally established stock; and his wife, Lucia Zigliani, came of good family from Colorno, in the duchy of Parma. The natal house is still preserved in Scandiano, a small town in the province of Emilia, northeast of the Apennines. They had a large, closely knit family, but of Lazzaro's siblings only two sisters and a brother feature in his letters. His younger brother Niccolò, who acquired a doctorate in law and wide knowledge of agronomy, and his sister Marianna, who became a naturalist, shared many of his scientific interests; both survived him.

After attending the local school, Lazzaro went at age fifteen to a Jesuit seminary in Reggio Emilia, seven miles away, where he excelled in rhetoric, philosophy, and languages. The Dominicans wanted him to join their order. Instead, he left Reggio Emilia in 1749 to study jurisprudence at the ancient University of Bologna, where Laura Bassi, a cousin on the paternal side, was professor of physics and mathematics. Under this remarkable woman's influence, Spallanzani liberalized his education. New subjects included mathematics, which impressed him with the significance of quantitative exactitude, while physics, chemistry, and natural history aroused his curiosity and revealed his bent. His classical talents, stimulated and polished, brought lasting advantages in historical awareness and aptness of self-expression; and he acquired an invaluable knowledge of French. For some three years he also worked toward his doctorate in law, a project that familiarized him with logic but otherwise grew distasteful. With Laura Bassi's support, Antonio Vallisneri the younger, professor of natural history at Padua and a fellow Scandianese, secured paternal consent for Lazzaro to abandon jurisprudence and follow his predilections.

In 1753 or 1754 Spallanzani became a doctor of philosophy. Then, having received instruction in metaphysics and theology, he took minor orders. Within a few years he was ordained priest and attached to two congregations in Modena. By 1760 he was designated "l'Abate Spallanzani" and was generally known as such thereafter. His priestly offices were performed irregularly; nevertheless, even in later life he still officiated at mass. Since he had no private income, the financial assistance (and moral protection) of the church facilitated his investigations of natural phenomena.

Apart from casual religious commitments, and despite an insatiable enthusiasm for travel, his career was wholly academic and centered in Lombardy. The main features of his last thirty years (1769–1799) as professor of natural history at Pavia are documented adequately, and his period of tenure in the chair of philosophy at Modena now seems settled as 1763 to 1769; but some aspects of his initial appointments at Reggio Emilia remain unclear. Loss of earlier letters and lack of other records misled biographers into discrepant conjectures. Fortunately, fresh and dependable data are available in his *Bibliografia* (1951) and *Epistolaria* (1958–1964).

Reggio Emilia. Early in 1755 Spallanzani began teaching logic, metaphysics, and Greek at the ancient College of Reggio Emilia. Two years later he was appointed lecturer in applied mathematics at the small, recently founded University of Reggio Emilia. In 1758 he was concurrently professor of both Greek and French at Nuovo Collegio, which, presumably, replaced the old seminary. The university lectureship remained unaltered in title, but in 1760 his chair at the college was designated languages and by 1762 had become Greek.

Spallanzani assisted in the public oral examinations of graduating students, and his first publication was possibly the anonymously compiled booklet of astronomical questions headed *Ex coelestibus corporibus*, and variously titled *Theses philosophicae . . .* and *Propositiones physico-mathematicae . . .* (1757–1759), which served as the basis for interrogating candidates. During this period also, certain literary and philosophic papers read by him to the Accademia degli Ipocondriaci at Reggio Emilia may have appeared anonymously in print. His first acknowledged publication is a critique of A. Salvini's Italian translation of the *Iliad*. This work, *Riflessioni intorno alla traduzione dell'Iliade del Salvini . . .* (1760), comprising three letters addressed to Count Algarotti, chamberlain to Frederick the Great of Prussia, displayed intimate understanding of Greek style and metaphor. In numerous examples Spallanzani showed that the translator's prolixity enfeebled the vigor of the original and that the Italian language, when chosen felicitously, conserved the beauty and pith of Homer.

In the summer of 1761 Spallanzani set out for the Reggian Apennines and Lake Ventasso, on the first of many scientific excursions to various parts of Italy and elsewhere, in the multiple capacities of natural historian in the broadest sense, field investigator of unexplained occurrences, aggressive collector of museum specimens, and observer of humanity. An indefatigable walker and daring climber, his main concern on this journey was the origin of springs and fountains gushing from the mountain slopes. Descartes's contention that the source was seawater, purged of salinity by subterranean fires after reaching the mountain sides through devious channels, was superseded after

1715 by an unconfirmed hypothesis of Antonio Vallisneri the elder, who stated that water precipitated near the summit, whether as snow, rain, or mist, insinuated itself between sloping strata of the mountain and descended by gravity until arrested by an impervious stratum, whereupon it emerged from some hidden reservoir. Spallanzani verified the latter concept by observing such factors as the relationship between the number and size of springs and total precipitation in the area; the water-condensing characteristics of the mountain involved; and the disposition, nature, and water affinity of the constituent strata. Further, he disproved a local belief that a great whirlpool existed in the middle of Lake Ventasso. Embarking on a raft improvised of beech stumps, he sounded the depth of the lake at various points, including its center, afterward tracing its origin to two fountains. His report (1762) appeared in the form of two letters to Vallisneri the younger.

Spallanzani was introduced by Vallisneri in 1761 to works by Buffon and to those by his occasional collaborator, the English priest and microscopist John Turberville Needham. For some twenty years thereafter Spallanzani recurrently focused his attentions upon the fundamental phenomena of vitality and reproduction and on the doctrines of Buffon and Needham concerning them. Buffon had claimed in the second volume (1749) of his *Histoire naturelle* that all plant and animal matter (including seminal fluid) decomposed ultimately into minute motile particles, termed "organic molecules," which served as elementary building blocks for the reconstitution of every form of life. Buffon contended he could identify these particles in Needham's microscopic preparations. Needham, an enthusiastic but erratic experimenter, hurriedly published further surmises in *Nouvelles observations microscopiques . . .* (1750), an expanded French version of a letter to the Royal Society of London on the generation, composition, and decomposition of animal and vegetable substances. Needham described animalcules that developed in many kinds of infusions, despite precautions to exclude external air. These animalcules, and likewise those in spermatic fluid, eventually languished, died, and disintegrated. Their debris, with that of decomposing plants, resolved into filaments yielding "animals of an inferior species." He traced various other fancied modes and sequences of renascence. The agent provoking such spontaneous generation was designated a productive "vegetative force," present in the most minute component of organic matter.

Equipped in 1762 with an adequate microscope, Spallanzani began to repeat Needham's experiments. The work was interrupted by his departure from Reggio Emilia. Supposedly, chairs had been offered him from as far afield as Coimbra and St. Petersburg and also from neighboring Modena and Cesena. In 1763 he went to Modena as professor of philosophy at the university and at the College of Nobles. Here he was still only fourteen miles from the family home at Scandiano.

Modena. Francesco Redi's experiments on fly maggots in 1668 had dispelled the myth of spontaneous generation for complex animals. But the notion was reapplied to lesser forms of life after the pioneer microscopist Leeuwenhoek described the little animals teeming and cavorting in his infusions (1674); he and several of his successors supposed that these animals were of atmospheric origin. Spallanzani verified this surmise experimentally and proved the animalcules did not arise spontaneously. His infusions of vegetables or cereal seeds, whether boiled or unboiled, in plugged or open vessels, yielded various microorganisms, possessing such attributes of animality as definite shape, orderly motion, and ability to withstand certain degrees of heat or cold. Whereas Needham had abandoned as unavailing and superfluous all precautions designed to control these infusoria, Spallanzani redoubled efforts to prevent their appearance. In hundreds of experiments he tested various rituals for rendering infusions permanently barren and finally found that they remained free of microorganisms when put into flasks that were hermetically sealed and the contents boiled for one hour. The entrance of air into the flask through a slight crack in its neck was followed by proliferating infusoria. His masterful essay, dedicated to the Bologna Academy of Sciences, *Saggio di osservazioni microscopiche* . . . (1765), reported no spontaneous generation in strongly heated infusions protected from aerial contamination. Further, the causes of Needham's misinterpretations were analyzed and Buffon's assertions about organic molecules refuted. The work first appeared jointly, under the title *Dissertazioni due* . . . , with a short thesis in Latin about the mechanism of stone skipping on water, *De lapidibus ab aqua resilientibus*. This latter tract, dedicated to Laura Bassi, explained "ducks and drakes" physicomathematically.

Charles Bonnet at Geneva had predicted (unknown to Spallanzani) in his *Considérations sur les corps organisés* (1762) that Needham's claims would prove fallacious. A uniquely constructive and durable friendship developed between Bonnet and Spallanzani following the former's receipt of a copy of the *Saggio*. In 1765, after cutting up thousands of earthworms and exploiting the ability of the aquatic salamander to regrow its tail, Spallanzani resolved to investigate reproductive phenomena in animals and plants. He received encouragement from Bonnet (coupled with a warning against spreading his energy among too many problems) and began to study methodically the regeneration of lost parts in lower animals. This phenomenon, brought to attention twenty years earlier by Trembley's work on regrowth in polyps, had been extended to earthworms by Réaumur and Bonnet himself. Spallanzani found the precise location of those cuts in earthworms that affected the segmental regenerative response. Other species of worms displayed different reactions after being divided. Amputation of the tail of the freshwater boat worm, the young aquatic salamander, and the tadpole was followed by vascularization of the transparent growing stump, observable microscopically. Regenerative capacities of remarkable complexity and repetitiveness were noted in the horns of the slug; in the foot, horns, and head of the land snail; the limbs and jaw of the salamander; and the limbs of the toad and frog. Besides adding to the knowledge of the potentialities of the mechanism, Spallanzani established the general law that in susceptible species an inverse ratio obtains between the regenerative capacity and age of the animal.

Early in 1768 he reported these findings in *Prodromo di un opera da imprimersi sopra le riproduzioni animali*, which he intended as a prelude to a major work on animal reproduction. Reactions ranged from surprised interest to disbelief, particularly as regards the ability of decapitated snails to produce completely new heads. Some of his peers, on attempting to repeat the work, reported deaths or only partial regenerations in such snails; others confirmed his findings, including Bonnet and Senebier at Geneva, Laura Bassi, Lavoisier, and the Danish naturalist Müller. Spallanzani promptly sent a copy of the *Prodromo* to the secretary of the Royal Society of London (who translated it into English), and in that same year he was elected a fellow of the society. He detailed his experiments involving more than 700 decapitated snails in *Resultati di esperienze sopra la riproduzione della testa nelle lumache terrestri* (1782, 1784).

Two other publications appeared in 1768. The first, *Memorie sopra i muli* . . . , was a collection of communications about hybrids by Bonnet and various authors, edited by Spallanzani, who urged that experiments on insect hybridization were a possible means of disentangling the problem of generation. He did not pursue this particular path but later attempted to cross batrachian species and even such diverse animals as cats and dogs. A second booklet, *Dell'azione del cuore ne' vasi sanguini*, outlined his findings on the action of the heart upon the blood vessels and was addressed to the great physiologist Albrecht von Haller.

Haller's microscopic observations of blood movements in his *Deux mémoires sur le mouvement du sang* (1756) had been made by refracted light on medium-sized vessels in the isolated mesentery of the frog. Spallanzani, using P. Lyonet's novel dissecting apparatus, conducted his observations mostly in a darkened room with reflected light from sunbeams impinging upon exposed parts of the aquatic salamander. He systematically noted how the cardiac systolic force motivated the blood circulation. The rhythmic inequality of blood flow in the aorta and large vessels disappeared in medium and small arteries, becoming regular and uniform. The velocity diminished in the smaller vessels, but sinuosities did not retard the flow. In the smallest vessels, individual red corpuscles negotiated acute angles and folds by elastically changing shape. The blood velocity in the venous system increased as the caliber of the vessels enlarged. Haller responded to the many amplifications and corrections of his work by securing Spallanzani's election to the Royal Society of Sciences of Göttingen.

Pavia. His scientific accomplishments and growing renown as an eloquent, informative lecturer brought offers of chairs at Parma and Pavia. The latter city had been in Austrian hands for more than fifty years, and Maria Teresa's government sought to restore some of its ancient dignity by appointing new professors to a reconstituted university. The prospect of higher emoluments and greater distinction proved irresistible, and Spallanzani became professor of natural history at Pavia in November 1769. He had just completed a painstaking Italian translation of Bonnet's philosophic and eloquent *Contemplation de la nature*; and he looked forward to his official duties being confined to natural history—"my dominating passion for several years." A recent French version of the *Saggio*, elaborately annotated by Needham, contended that excessive heat enfeebled or destroyed the vegetative force of infusions and impaired the essential elasticity of air within sealed flasks. Spallanzani had lost patience with his opponent: "Quelle confusion, quelle obscurité règne-t-il dans ses notes à mes observations microscopiques!

Quelles monstruosités dans ses pensées!" he complained to Bonnet. His inaugural address, delivered in Latin and published as *Prolusio . . .* (1770), made clear his intention to settle the dispute with Needham and to rebut the peculiar views of his supporter Buffon. Meanwhile, educated laymen aligned themselves with scientists on each side of the spontaneous generation controversy, as happened a century later over Darwinian theories.

Spallanzani found his daily lectures taxing, and other duties interrupted his researches. He took charge of the public Museum of Natural History of the university, the development of which the court at Vienna supported through its minister plenipotentiary, the governor of Lombardy, Count Carlo di Firmian. The acquisition of exhibits proved congenial to Spallanzani's aggressive instincts and broad vision, so that within a decade the collections of the museum were among the most magnificent in Italy. In the summer of 1772, when the government sent him to visit the mines and collect fossils in the Alps north of Milan, his itinerary included lakes Como and Maggiore, and the towns and villages of Ticino. Less agreeable distractions ranged from the procurement and disposition of new specimens to the preparation of a complete catalogue. Nevertheless, because of his energy, versatility, and enterprise, Spallanzani secured monumental collections for posterity and also made lasting contributions to science in Pavia.

Spallanzani launched countless experiments relating to infusion animalcules and "spermatic worms," with results that soon made a chimera of the vegetative force and undermined the doctrine of organic molecules; but unforeseen complications or fresh ideas demanded further investigation, and publication was postponed. His previous observations on the physiology of circulation were expanded to include species of frogs and lizards. Through a chance discovery in 1771 that the vascular network in the umbilical cord of an embryonated hen's egg could be seen clearly with the Lyonet apparatus, he first established the existence of arteriovenous anastomoses in a warm-blooded animal. He also studied the effects of growth (in the chick embryo and tadpole) upon circulatory mechanisms; the influence of gravity and the consequences of wounds on different parts of the vascular system; and changes in the languid or failing circulation in dying animals. Finally, Spallanzani demonstrated that the arterial pulse is due not to mere cardiac displacements but to lateral pressure upon an expansile wall from cardiac impulses conveyed by the blood column. A total of 337 experiments were outlined and expounded in four dissertations, forming a treatise on the dynamics of circulation that appeared as *De' fenomeni della circolazione* . . . (1773).

Spallanzani's next outstanding publication, *Opuscoli di fisica animale e vegetabile* . . . (1776), contained five reports that displayed unexcelled experimental skill, remarkable powers of observation, and lucid literary talent. The first volume included the long-deferred treatise on infusoria, "Osservazioni e sperienze intorno agli animalculi delle infusioni . . ." This work challenged Needham's concept of a heat-labile vegetative force by comparing the growth-promoting qualities of various infusions preheated to different extents and left in loosely stoppered flasks. After several days infusions that had been boiled for two hours generally showed better growth than corresponding preparations boiled for shorter periods. Profuse growth appeared in infusions made from vegetable seeds reduced to powder in a coffee roaster or burned to a cinder by a blowpipe. Spallanzani concluded that the vegetative force was imaginary. He disposed of Needham's other objection by instantaneously sealing the capillary end of the drawn-out neck of each infusion flask. Thus rarefaction of the enclosed air was avoided, and the sterility of boiled infusions could be attributed no longer to diminished elasticity of air in the sealed flasks.

Spallanzani also found that complex infusoria are more susceptible to heat and cold than the "infinitely minute" germs of lower class, whose relative resistance he ascribed to their eggs. He sought comparisons between such effects and the influence of temperature upon seeds and their respective plants; upon frog spawn, tadpoles, and adult frogs; and upon species of insects and their ova. Finally, he developed a technique for isolating single animalcules in water drops; he then observed their modes of reproduction, whether by transverse division, longitudinal fission, budding, or the peculiar daughter-colony system of *Volvox*, which he followed through thirteen generations.

The main treatise in the second volume of the *Opuscoli* confirmed and extended Leeuwenhoek's observations on spermatozoa (which began in 1677) and refuted Buffon's erroneous concepts of their nature and origin. The latter claimed that both male and female gonads contained a fluid teeming with nonspecific, incorruptible organic molecules, of which all living matter was fundamentally constituted. Tailed spermatic vermiculi, if present, developed in stale semen from mucilaginous and filamentous components and eventually disintegrated into smaller animalcules and organic molecules. Spallanzani always used fresh semen in studying spermatozoal form, size, motion, and reactions to heat, cold, and drying. He even demonstrated their unaltered appearance in the epididymis of live dogs and a ram. Initially he had considered the spermatic vermiculi analogous to infusion animalcules; but he later concluded that the former are distinctive components of the living animal body and that they neither shed their tails nor divide. Buffon's perversity stemmed from poor microscopy, metaphysical confusion, and overconfident eloquence; but since he had a considerable following, Spallanzani (who sincerely admired some of Buffon's accomplishments) at first hesitated to refute him. Five years earlier, however, Bonnet had urged him to overcome such diffidence: "You have cherished no theory, but are satisfied with interrogating nature, and giving the public a faithful account of her responses." Spallanzani therefore minced no words. Describing Buffon's theory as "completely destroyed," he urged him to repeat experiments "with better microscopes, forgetting his beloved organic molecules, and imposing the rule on himself to receive as truth only the images transmitted by the senses, without adding the corrections of his imagination."

The remaining three tracts were of lesser significance. The first concerned the effects of stagnant air upon animals and vegetables, which Spallanzani was led to investigate after observing the proliferation of infusoria and germination of vegetable seeds in sealed vessels. Impaired vitality occurred among his specimens after widely varying exposure periods. Death was accelerated when the volume of the container was diminished or the temperature increased. Since the animals did not die from lack of air, he cautiously postulated a toxic exhalation acting upon the nervous system. Another tract concerned animalcules that "enjoy the advantages of real resurrection after death"—unlike his infusoria, which were nonrevivable after death. This resurgence from the torpid state had been earlier observed in Rotifera found in a roof gutter by Leeuwenhoek (1702) and in the Anguillae of blighted wheat described by Needham (1745). In the latter species, Spallanzani induced eleven revival cycles by alternate humidification and desiccation, without significant casualties, but found its immortality limited. He discovered in roof-tile sand two novel animalcules that had this property, a sloth (Tardigrada) and another Anguilla species. The final communication reported that the black dust on the ripened heads of a mold engendered new moldiness when implanted on moistened bread. Powdered roots, stalks, or unripened heads of the mold were ineffective. The unusually heat-resistant "seeds" would not develop on naturally mold-resistant substrates but their proven germinal power eliminated spontaneous generation as a factor to be considered in mold production.

Late in 1780 another two-volume work appeared, of similar title but altogether different content, *Dissertazioni di fisica animale e vegetabile*. Volume one, a treatise on digestion, comprised six dissertations arranged in 264 sections. The second volume, on the generation of certain animals and plants, partly fulfilled the intention expressed in his *Prodromo*. As in the *Opuscoli*, two letters of analytic comment and constructive suggestions from Bonnet were incorporated. The first work, completed in not more than two years, shows Spallanzani at his best as a thorough, resourceful, and courageous physiologist, dedicated to the scientific investigation and understanding of what he called "a subject of so much beauty and utility as the function of Digestion."

In 1777 he publicly demonstrated the great force exerted by the gizzards of fowls and ducks in pulverizing hollow glass globules, thus confirming Redi's century-old account (1675). The French physicist Réaumur had opened a different line of investigation by persuading a kite to swallow open-ended tubes containing foodstuffs, which when regurgitated showed partial digestion, for which gastric fluid was apparently responsible (1752). Spallanzani greatly extended Réaumur's experiments. He administered food samples, generally in perforated metallic tubes or spherules, to an astonishing variety of animals. The containers were recovered by regurgitation, by passage in the feces, or by sacrificing the animal, and the contents examined for weight loss and other changes. Sometimes pieces of meat were fed, to which string was attached, permitting withdrawal at will. The test animals included many bird species, from turkeys and pigeons to herons, owls, and an eagle, grouped according to stomach wall structure and feeding habits. A miscellaneous category was formed of frogs and newts, water snakes and vipers, fish, and ruminants (sheep, ox, and horse). The final group comprised cats, dogs, and one man. Spallanzani experimented on himself to the limit of endurance. The fate of foodstuffs swallowed in linen bags or wooden tubes was noted, remnants being sought in the voided containers. One piece of resistant membrane was returned twice for further digestion in his alimentary tract before it finally dissolved.

Samples of gastric fluid were procured by inducing himself to vomit on an empty stomach. Crows yielded more liberal samples through sponges placed in the tubes, as described by Réaumur.

The solvent action of this fluid on foodstuffs was determined *in vitro* at different temperatures. Comminuted meats were most readily dissolved; but tendon, cartilage, and soft bone disappeared slowly. Bread, broken grains, and vegetable products were also susceptible. The speed of dissolution of a given food was related to the quantity of available juice, but more particularly to the prevailing temperature. Since body heat gave optimal reactions, Spallanzani sometimes kept the glass tubes containing such mixtures in his axillae. He concluded that the basic factor in digestion is the solvent property of the "gastric juice"—a term introduced by him. Trituration only makes food particles more accessible to this juice. In gizzardless animals, mastication substitutes for trituration. Nor is the digestive process associated with putrefaction; indeed, the gastric juice is strongly antiputrefactive. The acidity that mainly accounts for this property was overlooked by G. A. Scopoli, professor of chemistry and botany at Pavia, on analyzing a specimen of gastric juice from the crow. His nugatory report was capped by Spallanzani's own assertion that the juice "is neither acid nor alkaline, but neutral." Nevertheless, Spallanzani suggested some "latent acid" might account for its milk-curdling properties. These experiments concerned only digestion in the stomach, and he realized secretions of the small intestine might "complete the process." Despite errors and gaps, the work successfully illuminated many phenomena of gastric digestion. Biochemical techniques were not applied to such studies during Spallanzani's lifetime; but he cleared the way for John Richardson Young, whose M.D. thesis for the University of Pennsylvania, "An Experimental Inquiry Into the Principles of Nutrition and the Digestive Process" (1803), emphasized the acidity of gastric juice. Only in 1824 was this reaction identified as due to hydrochloric acid.

The first dissertation in the second volume related detailed observations and original experiments (some carried out many years earlier) on natural generation in four species of frogs and toads and in the water newt. The prolonged amours of the mating season for the frogs and toads culminated in fertilization, shortly after the eggs were extruded from the female cloaca, through semen bedewed upon them by the tightly clasping male. Spallanzani showed that this clasp reflex persisted after severe mutilation, including amputation of limbs or even decapitation. The nuptials of the newt followed a different pattern. Without firm contact, the couple remained in close proximity until the male discharged semen into the water near the female's cloaca, whence fertilized ova soon emerged without intromission. He adduced abundant evidence that, notwithstanding the absence of true copulation in these amphibians, actual contact between eggs and seminal fluid is essential to fecundation. When the hindquarters of the green frog were covered with waxed taffeta breeches—a device used earlier by Réaumur and Nollet—the male's amatory clasp was undiminished, but impregnation was prevented.

The next dissertation reported Spallanzani's recent findings on artificial fecundation. Only slight contact between mature ova and homologous seminal fluid was necessary to achieve fertilization. This fluid was sufficiently prolific to fecundate after being diluted 1:8,000 in water. Admixture with amphibian blood, bile, urine, and various tissue juices, or with human urine, was not inhibitory. But there were no cross-reactions: attempts at artificial hybridization between toads, frogs, and newts were fruitless. Bonnet, who had discovered parthenogenesis in the aphid more than three decades earlier, suggested that an electric current might serve as a nonspecific fertilizing agent. But parthenogenesis could not be induced in frog eggs either by electricity or by various body fluids; and "stimulating agents"—for example, vinegar, and lemon or lime juice—failed to replace the appropriate seminal fluid. Last-minute findings allowed Spallanzani to end this section on a positive note. By impregnating silkworm eggs with seed from male silkworms, he succeeded where Malpighi had failed. Further, Spallanzani recorded the first artificial insemination of a viviparous animal. A spaniel bitch in heat, carefully isolated throughout the experiment, received by vaginal syringe some fresh semen from a dog of the same breed. Two months later, three healthy whelps resembling both parents were born—an event that provoked Spallanzani to aver, "I never received greater pleasure upon any occasion since I cultivated experimental philosophy."

These two dissertations illustrated the indispensability of seminal fluid to the generative process, but Spallanzani obscured rather than elucidated how it functioned. He demonstrated that the *aura seminalis* could not fertilize but left the role of spermatozoa undefined, despite his previous studies of them. Indeed, he apparently welcomed the fallacious results of a single experiment that

yielded tadpoles from eggs touched with droplets of semidried sperm "quite free from worms"; for this permitted him to deride the "vermiculists," followers of Leeuwenhoek's concept that the spermatozoon solely embodies the preformed future individual. Spallanzani thought that this mode of impregnation equally demonstrated "the falsehood of epigenesis, or of that system which has been raised from the dead, protected and caressed by Buffon. . . ." He himself was, in fact, a convinced preformationist, but of the "ovist" persuasion, like Malpighi, Haller, and Bonnet before him. Thus he held that the embryo was already within the ovum: a small, coiled-up tadpole awaiting only vitalization by seminal fluid in order to uncoil and grow. This belief can be traced back to 1767, when he informed Bonnet that by "rigorous comparison" (including microscopic examination) of their external and internal structure, unimpregnated and freshly impregnated eggs of frogs were identical. Since tadpoles visibly unfolded in the fertile spawn, he felt entitled to assert that "the tadpole that becomes a frog preexists fecundation." In the following year his *Prodromo* contained a hint to that effect. Now, with unsubstantial evidence buttressing a fruitless concept, he publicly exemplified those very faults that he condemned in others, particularly his old adversary the archepigenesist Needham. Spallanzani's espousal of this doctrine encouraged much futile disputation and perhaps helped to delay until the mid-nineteenth century the discovery that the spermatozoon fertilizes the ovum by actually penetrating it.

Publication of the whole work was delayed pending completion of a final section on generation in diverse plants. His observations were made principally on common vegetables and flowering plants, during summer and autumn visits to Scandiano. He thought that the striking analogies noted between animal and plant life might include their reproductive arrangements. After removing the anthers from flowering hermaphrodite plants, and safeguarding female from male blossoms in other selected species, he studied their ovaria for seed and embryo development. Again influenced by preformationist leanings, he contended that embryos appeared in all seeds prior to and irrespective of fecundation. In hermaphrodites such as sweet basil and Syrian mallow, and in the female plants of annual mercury, want of pollen rendered their seeds sterile. Here, he compared the role of pollen to the effect of seminal fluid upon dormant embryos in amphibian ova. Productive seeds were borne, without benefit of pollination, by gourds, spinach, and hemp—a claim that Spallanzani anticipated would receive disfavor from "all modern naturalists and botanists." He admitted accumulating experimental data as foundation for a speculative disquisition on generation in plants. Unfortunately, his industrious and novel contribution did little to resolve the prevailing confusion and rancor over this complex problem.

The *Dissertazioni* brought Spallanzani additional recognition at home and abroad. A French version of the *Opuscoli*, translated with unmatched promptitude and accuracy by Senebier, the distinguished naturalist-librarian of Geneva, had expanded the circle of his readers. Followers, competitors, and opponents again increased when the same translator duly produced French editions of the dissertations on digestion and reproduction. Spallanzani's latest publication climaxed a period of such unbounded experimentation that he may have sensed the dangers of overextension. For although during the early 1780's he intermittently decollated snails, observed the breeding habits of his amphibia, and planned a monograph on artificial fecundation, he did not turn to new researches in experimental biology and physiology until the last five years of his life. Other possible reasons for a change of direction included the risk, largely unrecognized or ignored, of antagonizing his Pavian colleagues and even foreign specialists by overconfident pronouncements or trespassings. Tardy and unjustified evidence that he had given this kind of offense came in 1786, when the choleric John Hunter insulted Spallanzani for his work on digestion. Hunter was angered by some mild and gentlemanly criticism in "Digestione" of his vitalistic explanation of digestion of the stomach wall observed in some cases of sudden death, as reported to the Royal Society of London in 1772. A still more delayed reaction was that of a spiteful colleague, G. S. Volta, who alleged in 1795 that experiments on plant generation described in the *Dissertazioni* were never performed. Spallanzani replied effectively, with dignity to Hunter and bitterness to Volta.

More powerful influences were the demands made upon him for teaching, at which he excelled: he was elected rector for the scholastic year 1777–1778. Enrollment in his natural history course had increased each year and in 1780 exceeded 115. Finally, as there were large gaps in the museum collections and he was starved for travel, his curiosity and talents could be exercised on specimen-gathering excursions. His appetite was whetted in 1779, when, after several annual postponements, he enjoyed a month-long summer tour

of Switzerland; during this time, he stayed for several days at Bonnet's villa outside Geneva. There he met Senebier and other naturalists, Abraham Trembley and his nephew Jean, and H. B. de Saussure, all of whom he deeply impressed. On the return journey he called on Haller's widow and son at Bern and visited other Swiss cities. In his letter of thanks to Bonnet, Spallanzani stated that of all the natural history museums he visited in Switzerland, only Zurich possessed one where the collections and curator were not amateurish. A few months later, with self-assurance fully harnessed to new objectives, he wrote that his sole remaining pleasure was to see the Royal Museum enlarge daily under his direction.

During the next five years, beginning in the spring of 1780, Spallanzani made several marine and overland excursions, mostly during summer vacations. He thereby corrected the deficiencies of the museum in marine biology (while he himself developed broad scientific interests in that field) on expeditions to Marseilles and the Genoese gulf in 1781; to Istrian and other northern Adriatic ports in the autumn of 1782; to Portovenere on the Gulf of Spezia in 1783; and to Chioggia, near Venice, in 1784. He also traveled to Genoa and vicinity during Easter vacations in 1780 and 1785; on the latter occasion he was equipped with meteorological instruments. In October 1783 he returned from Portovenere on foot to Scandiano, through the Carrara marble quarries and over the Apuan Alps, collecting many geological and fossil specimens on the way. He wrote happily to Bonnet of this sea and land expedition: "During the whole time I was occupied always in observing and interrogating Nature; I have assembled an astonishing collection of observations and facts, of which several appear to me very interesting and until now unknown."

At Marseilles, Spallanzani collected 150 fish species, many of them large and rare, and in improvised quarters studied and dissected marine fauna. During the visit to Portovenere, he instituted the first marine zoological laboratory and while there described new species of fireflies and conducted studies on deep-sea phosphorescence. He refuted the claim that the torpedo fish was attracted by magnets, intrepidly showing that its greatest shock was delivered when the fish was laid on a glass plate. Excising the heart did not lessen the shock until the circulation began to fail. He showed the animal nature of corals and many other minute marine organisms and assigned several sponges and sea moss to the vegetable kingdom. He also studied marine infusoria, testaceans, and crustaceans. The Adriatic waters proved more plentiful in many species than did the Mediterranean. His intention to write a major work on the natural history of the sea did not materialize; but in open letters to Bonnet he recorded observations on "diverse produzioni marine," from sponges, corals, and sea-mussels, to a freshwater fountain gurgling through the salt water of the Gulf of Spezia. (For further details and an amplified bibliography of his voyages and scientific excursions, G. Pighini's account should be consulted.)

In October 1784 a prominent Venetian patron of science, Girolamo Zulian, conveyed the offer of the chair of natural history at Padua, vacant through the recent death of Vallisneri the younger. Spallanzani informed Count Giuseppe Wilzeck (successor to Firmian) that the humidity in Pavia so aggravated his gout that he must relinquish his teaching post. Although lacking the requisite length of service for a pension, he solicited special consideration because of the arduous expeditions for the museum that were made without recompense. Wilzeck offered financial concessions but overcame Spallanzani's obduracy only by granting a leave of absence for a prolonged visit to Constantinople, in addition to a substantial salary increase. Moreover, Joseph II refused to permit his resignation and granted an ecclesiastical benefice. In August 1785 he sailed from Venice in a gunboat with a flotilla escort, as a guest of Zulian, now the Venetian envoy to the Porte. Two months later they reached Constantinople, where Spallanzani was given quarters in Zulian's palace. Their ship had nearly foundered in a gale off Kíthira, where they refitted; then, having threaded the Cyclades, they reached Tenedos, whence the sultan's emissaries escorted them to the locality that excavators a century later identified as the site of Homer's Troy. Spallanzani never forgot that he was a natural historian, even while exploring territory suffused with classical and Homeric reminders. He recorded a waterspout in the Adriatic; collected medusae in the Sea of Marmara; and, during the last part of his visit, spent on the Bosporus, made elaborate geological studies, described local semiprecious stones, and studied marine fauna. Many of the social and political customs of the country, the apathy, polygamy, and excessive wealth and poverty distressed him. He secured information from a friendly seraglio physician that developed into one of his most popular lectures; collected eudiometer samples at dances to determine the effect of overcrowding on atmospheric vitiation; negotiated for crocodiles and skins of lions and ti-

gers with the British and French ambassadors; and was received in audience and regaled with a sixty-course repast by the sultan.

In August 1786, having dispatched the valuable museum collections by ship, Spallanzani set out with a single attendant on the unimaginably difficult return overland. Despite hazardous mountain passes, floods and torrents, brigands and cutthroats, detours were made to inspect mines and geological structures, and more specimens were collected. Reaching Bucharest through the eastern Balkans, he crossed the Transylvanian Alps to the Hungarian plain and also Buda and Pest. In December, although welcomed in high circles in Vienna and bemedaled by Joseph II, he encountered rumors that he had enriched his personal museum at Scandiano by transferring exhibits from Pavia. In Milan he learned that certain university colleagues had circulated a defamatory letter after a subordinate, Canon Serafino Volta, curator of the Royal Museum, whom Spallanzani had recommended as a suitable temporary substitute during his absence, had visited incognito the Scandiano collection and there discovered specimens missing from the Royal Museum. Spallanzani importuned Wilzeck to establish a judicial enquiry into the calumny.

Notwithstanding the spreading scandal, Spallanzani was welcomed at the gates of Pavia by enthusiastic students, more than 400 of whom attended his first lecture. The conspirators, besides Volta, were identified as Gregorio Fontana; Antonio Scarpa, the distinguished anatomist and surgeon; and Scopoli. In common they envied his fame and resented his authoritarianism: also, each had some personal grudge against "the pasha." Spallanzani submitted his evidence to the Royal Imperial Council, and in August an imperial decree exonerated him completely; Volta was dismissed from the university and banished from Pavia; the other parties were reprimanded and ordered to desist from troublemaking. While Volta nursed his grievances in Mantua, Fontana acknowledged his transgression and Scarpa sought to make amends; Scopoli bore the brunt of a malicious reprisal. Spallanzani considered him a plagiarist and knew that he had signed the libelous letter sent to Bonnet, Senebier, and other well-known scientists. A curious specimen, purportedly excreted by a patient, was sent to Scopoli, who designated it *Physis intestinalis*, a novel species of intestinal worm, and illustrated it in a text, dedicated to Sir Joseph Banks, president of the Royal Society of London. The worm was actually a cunningly teased-out portion of chicken gullet. In 1788 the hoax was revealed in a pseudonymous publication addressed to Scopoli. This work was followed by another volume, of anonymous authorship, disparaging Scopoli's earlier text on natural history.

In 1788 Spallanzani journeyed to the Two Sicilies, mainly in order to correct deficiencies in the volcanic collections of the museum. Southern Italy had suffered for five years from intense eruptive and seismic activities. Messina was still in ruins and the countryside devastated. Vesuvius, near Naples, Stromboli and Vulcano in the Eolian Isles, and Etna on the island of Sicily, remained active. Spallanzani visited them all, undauntedly making several perilous ascents that involved great physical endurance. Vesuvius was tranquil on his first visit, but a later attempt to reach the summit was frustrated by a violent eruption. He went to within five feet of the lava pouring from the rent mountainside and accurately measured its flow rate. Just short of the crater of Etna, toxic gases rendered him unconscious; but later he peered from the rim at the boiling lava. From a cavern near the summit of Stromboli he noted that bellowing gas explosions forced up the red-hot lava and ejected massive rocks—an observation fundamental to the science of volcanology. He descended alone into the crater of Vulcano and retired with burned feet and his staff afire when sulfurous fumes prevented further identification of mineral structures. Field observations were correlated with laboratory analyses and thermal tests on volcanic specimens. A glass furnace and the Wedgwood pyrometer made it possible to determine the composition and fusion temperatures of lava and the identity of gases liberated from the melted igneous rocks.

Throughout these volcanic travels, Spallanzani's attention focused upon innumerable phenomena, from Scylla and Charybdis to the annual passage of swordfish through the Strait of Messina; from the punctuality of migrant birds to the kindness of the stricken peasantry. Becalmed off Laguna di Orbetello, noted for its eels, he went inland to investigate by mass dissection their mysterious mode of propagation. In 1789 and 1790 he climbed the Modenese Apennines carrying chemical apparatus for examining the natural gas fires of Barigazzo and the salses. Two years later he made further studies on eels at Lake Comacchio, south of Venice. The new wonders of the Pavia museum attracted many distinguished visitors, including Joseph II himself in 1791. A fascinating five-volume account of these journeys, *Viaggi alle due Sicilie e in alcune parti dell'Appennino*, appeared in 1792

and was dedicated to Count Wilzeck. A sixth volume was added in 1797.

Although now more than sixty years old, Spallanzani undertook several new researches. In 1794 he reported that blinded bats could fly without striking artificial obstacles. After apparently eliminating other explanations, he reluctantly postulated a sixth sense. Two Italian scientists, and also Senebier, were invited to repeat the work. All confirmed Spallanzani's findings; but a French scientist, L. Jurine, demonstrated that blinded bats blundered helplessly into obstacles after their ears were effectively plugged. Spallanzani promptly accepted the ear hypothesis, but the notion of a chiropteran sixth sense prevailed. The extraordinary sensitivity of the ear of the bat to self-emitted supersonic notes as the basic mechanism in the directional sense of this animal was first clearly demonstrated by D. R. Griffin and R. Galambos in 1941.

Spallanzani had adopted the new chemical doctrines that developed following the discoveries, mainly by British chemists, of carbon dioxide, hydrogen, nitrogen, and oxygen during the period 1755–1774. Contrary to the claim of Johann Göttling of Jena that phosphorus would burn in nitrogen, Spallanzani denied in 1796 that this element would burn in either nitrogen, hydrogen, or carbon dioxide. When plunged into oxygen, however, phosphorus ignited with a luminosity proportional to the amount of that gas present in the eudiometer. In that year, Napoleon's armies were overrunning Lombardy. One of Spallanzani's biographers, the French military surgeon J. Tourdes, found his laboratory full of vessels containing different gases, the effects of which were being tested upon various substances. He was engaged already in researches that, although incomplete, formed a major contribution to the understanding of animal and plant respiration. His last personal report, appearing in 1798, contained the novel observation that whereas plants kept in water and in sunlight furnish oxygen and absorb carbon dioxide, they reverse this exchange in deep shade.

Spallanzani suffered from an enlarged prostate, complicated by a chronic bladder infection. Early in February 1799, shortly after his seventieth birthday, he became anuric and after a restless night fell unconscious. Among the medical attendants were Tourdes and Scarpa. In the ensuing week, during lucid intervals between bouts of uremic coma, he discussed experiments with colleagues, reviewed personal affairs with relatives, and recited passages from the classics. He died peacefully at night, after receiving religious offices.

He was buried in the cemetery at Pavia. The heart was placed by his brother Niccolò in the church at Scandiano, while by his own wish the bladder became an exhibit in the historical museum of the university.

Three manuscript memoirs, translated and assembled by Senebier, were published posthumously in 1803 as *Mémoires sur la respiration*. Lavoisier's suggestion that respiration was a form of slow combustion, with direct oxidation of carbon and hydrogen occurring in the lungs, was disputed by the French mathematician Lagrange. Spallanzani's experimental data resolved this controversy and laid the groundwork for modern conceptions of respiratory physiology. Snails kept in an atmosphere of nitrogen or hydrogen exhaled almost as much carbon dioxide as when breathing air. Even after lung removal, snails absorbed oxygen and gave up carbon dioxide. Excised individual organs, including the stomach, liver, and heart, respired similarly. In concluding that the blood transported carbon dioxide as a product of tissue oxidation, Spallanzani discovered parenchymatous respiration—usually accredited to the biochemist Liebig half a century later. Spallanzani left additional notes on many thousands of experiments concerning the respiratory processes of animals and plants; Senebier again loyally edited these. They appeared as *Rapports de l'air avec les êtres organisés . . .* (1807). The first two volumes comprised fourteen additional memoirs on respiration, which established the basic uniformity of the respiratory process throughout the animal kingdom. The third volume concerned respiration in plants.

Spallanzani received many honors, including membership in the ten most distinguished Italian academies, and foreign associateship in a dozen famous European scientific societies. Frederick the Great personally arranged his election to the Berlin Academy of Sciences in 1776. Spallanzani made fortunate friendships with generous-minded scientists, especially Haller and Bonnet. The latter once assured him, "You have discovered more truths in five years than entire academies in half a century." His fame was commemorated at Scandiano, Reggio Emilia, Modena, Pavia, even at Portovenere—wherever he had lived and labored—by statues, busts, tablets, museums, manuscripts, or other memorabilia.

Of middle stature, with dark eyes and complexion, domed head, aquiline nose, and pensive countenance, Spallanzani had a resonant voice and firm gait. Masterful in personality, his character was complex. He conversed eagerly and forthrightly about scientific problems but avoided political or personal topics. He did not underrate his accomplishments, often resented criticism, and was not above canvasing friends and influential acquaintances to obtain election to learned societies. Although disliking formal restraints, he flattered and cajoled authorities from whom he sought favors. His life-style was frugal, but he enjoyed good food and wine and the company of high-minded women. If his religious vows ever vexed his robust temperament, they spared him many distracting and time-consuming obligations, and perhaps secured him from persecution by church, state, or invading armies. Considerate of relatives and friends, he could become ruthlessly angry when wronged. In unraveling the secrets of nature, every aspect of which intrigued or inspired him, he maimed and slaughtered countless animals. Among his few relaxations were fishing and hunting, and he was expert at chess. Athletic in his youth, he remained vigorous to the end.

About a decade after his death, Spallanzani was portrayed as a genius-wizard in one of E. T. A. Hoffmann's fantastic *Tales*. In more recent times the overspecialized have ignored the rare scope and stature of his accomplishments and have disparaged his prodigious output as dilettantism. Allegations that nothing practical came of his splendid studies on infusorial microorganisms overlook the importance of food canning. Nicolas Appert's . . . *l'Art de conserver pendant plusieurs années toutes les substances animales et végétales* (1810) was made possible through Spallanzani's work on heat sterilization. To suggest that he should have gone further and discovered the germ theory of disease is to forget that 100 years later Pasteur had to repeat Spallanzani's work before he finally laid to rest the specter of spontaneous generation; and only then could he convince a reluctant medical profession and skeptical fellow scientists that man might be brought low and killed by parasites of almost incredible minuteness. Pasteur paid his tribute daily; he commissioned a full-length portrait of Spallanzani, which hung in the dining room of his apartment.

The particular indifference of the English-speaking world to Spallanzani's significance stems partly from linguistic difficulties. Certain translations were made into English, but some were of poor quality and none was widely circulated. There is still no version of his complete works in English. Besides, in Spallanzani's day Britain had a number of brilliant investigators who, collectively, covered his many fields. Stephen Hales, John Hunter, Erasmus Darwin, Joseph Black, Henry Cavendish, and Joseph Priestley were among those whose combined luster outshone the multifaceted achievements of any foreign priest-polymath. Spallanzani's countrymen view him in different perspective. In his birthplace a bust of Spallanzani stands on a marble mantel. Above it is a plaque inscribed: *Natus Scandiani Clarus Ubique*. Even after allowing for local pride, this assertion is surely close to truth.

BIBLIOGRAPHY

I. ORIGINAL WORKS. The only two eds. of Spallanzani's collected writings are in Italian: *Opere di Lazzaro Spallanzani* (Milan, 1825–1826) and *Le opere di Lazzaro Spallanzani* (Milan, 1932–1936), each 6 vols. The latter, compiled by Filippo Bottazzi and ten collaborators under the auspices of the Royal Academy of Italy, was to include Spallanzani's letters, edited by Benedetto Biagi, but World War II intervened and Biagi died. Dino Prandi became coeditor, adding to the collection until 1,475 letters, written to 173 individuals or institutions (and twelve anonymous addressees), appeared as *Lazzaro Spallanzani. Epistolario* (Florence, 1958–1964). Prandi's *Bibliografia delle opere di Lazzaro Spallanzani* (Florence, 1951) is a detailed and generally dependable bibliography. It also cites writings about Spallanzani in various languages.

Several lengthy monographs on natural history and physiology, published in Italian during the thirty-year period 1773–1803, reached wider circles through trans. into French, English, or German. The first of these, *De' fenomeni della circolazione* . . . (Modena, 1773), was translated by J. Tourdes as *Expériences sur la circulation* . . . (Paris, 1800), and by R. Hall as *Experiments Upon the Circulation of the Blood* . . . (London, 1801). The next great treatise, *Opuscoli di fisica, animale e vegetabile* . . . , 2 vols. (Modena, 1776), finalizes his famous work on the animalcules of infusions, "Osservazioni e sperienze intorno agli animalculi delle infusioni . . . ," and records observations and experiments on human and animal spermatozoa, "Osservazioni e sperienze intorno ai vermicelli spermatici . . . ." Also included are two letters to the author from Bonnet about the animalcules and reports on the effects of stagnant air on animal and plant life, the killing and resuscitation of Rotifera, and the origin of moldiness. This work was translated into French by Jean Senebier as *Opuscules de physique, animale, et végétale*, 2 vols. (Geneva, 1777), and into English by T. Beddoes as *Tracts on Animals and Vegetables*, 2 vols. (London, 1784, 1786). Another trans., by J. G. Dalyell, appeared as *Tracts on the Nature of Animals and Vegetables*, 2 vols. (Edinburgh, 1799), the second edition of which, entitled *Tracts on the Natural History of Animals and Vegetables*, 2 vols. (Edinburgh, 1803), was augmented by Dalyell's introductory observations and by "Tracts on Animal Reproduction," which included accounts by Spallanzani and by Bonnet of experimental reproduction of the head of the garden snail.

Another important treatise, *Dissertazioni di fisica animale e vegetabile* . . . , 2 vols. (Modena, 1780), of which a second ed. was entitled *Fisica animale e vegetabile*, 3 vols. (Venice, 1782), contains his experimental enquiries into digestion in various animal species ("Digestione"), reproduction in animals and plants ("Della generazione di alcuni animali . . . di diverse piante"), and artificial fecundation ("Sopra la fecondazione artificiale in alcuni animali"). An English version of the *Dissertazioni*, translated and prefaced by T. Beddoes, is *Dissertations Relative to the Natural History of Animals and Vegetables*, 2 vols. (London, 1784, 1789). The sections on digestion and on reproduction, translated by Senebier, appeared separately as *Expériences sur la digestion de l'homme et de différentes espèces d'animaux* . . . (Geneva, 1783, 1784; facs. ed., Paris, 1956) and as *Expériences pour servir à l'histoire de la génération des animaux et des plantes* . . . (Geneva, 1785). These two dissertations in French, added to the *Opuscules*, were republished as *Oeuvres de M. l'Abbé Spallanzani*, 3 vols. (Pavia–Paris, 1787).

The long account of his travels, *Viaggi alle due Sicilie e in alcune parti dell'Appennino* . . . (Pavia, 1792–1797), became available in French, German, and English under the respective titles *Voyages dans les deux Siciles, et dans quelques parties des Apennins*, 6 vols. (Bern, 1795–1797); *Des Abtes Spallanzani Reisen in beyde Sicilien und in Gegenden der Appenninen*, 5 vols. (Leipzig, 1795–1798); and *Travels in the Two Sicilies, and Some Parts of the Apennines*, 4 vols. (London, 1798).

Spallanzani translated and annotated Bonnet's *Contemplation de la nature*, 2 vols. (Amsterdam, 1764–1765), under the title *Contemplazione della natura del Signor Carlo Bonnet*, 2 vols. (Modena, 1769–1770). Several eds. of this work appeared. Published posthumously and translated by Senebier, were *Mémoires sur la respiration* (Geneva, 1803) and *Rapports de l'air avec les êtres organisés* . . . , 3 vols. (Geneva, 1807). The former appeared in Italian as *Memorie su la respirazione*, 2 vols. (Milan, 1803), and in English as *Memoirs on Respiration* (London, 1804).

Spallanzani's earliest publication, variously titled *Theses philosophicae* . . . (Parma, 1757) and *Propositiones physico-mathematicae* . . . (Reggio Emilia, 1759), probably served as basis for public disputations by university degree candidates. A better-known early work is the essay of classical criticism, *Riflessioni intorno alla traduzione dell'Iliade del Salvini* . . . (Parma, 1760). A short monograph, *Prodromo di un opera da imprimersi sopra le riproduzioni animali* (Modena, 1768), translated by M. Maty as *An Essay on Animal Reproduction* (London, 1769), which included an account of regeneration of the decapitated head of the snail, was the first work of Spallanzani to appear in English.

Many reports in the foregoing vols. were published initially as tracts or booklets; others first appeared as articles in scholarly periodicals, often in the form of letters to well-known personages. Among Spallanzani's characteristic shorter communications are "Lettere due . . ." [to Antonio Vallisneri], in *Nuova raccolta di opuscoli scientifici e filologici* . . . , **9** (1762), 271–298, on the circulation of subterranean waters and the sources of fountains observed during his travels in the Reggian Apennines; and *Dissertazioni due* . . . (Modena, 1765), comprising "Saggio di osservazioni microscopiche concernenti il sistema della generazione dei Signori di Needham e Buffon," and "De lapidibus ab aqua resilientibus" (stone skipping on water). The former appeared in a French trans. by Abbé Regley, with added critical commentary by J. Needham, as *Nouvelles recherches sur les découvertes microscopiques, et la génération des corps organisés* (London–Paris, 1769). In *Prolusio* (Modena, 1770), his University of Pavia inaugural address, given in Latin, Spallanzani again disputed Needham's support of spontaneous generation; and six years later the doctrine received further rebuttals in the *Opuscoli*, I, pp. 3–221.

Meanwhile, Spallanzani reviewed sterility in hybrids, *Memorie sopre i muli* . . . (Modena, 1768), and reported studies on the circulation of the blood, *Dell'azione del cuore* . . . (Modena, 1768). These two short monographs, along with *Dissertazioni due* (1765) and *Prodromo* (1768), were republished in a German trans. as *Herrn Abt Spallanzanis physikalische und mathematische Abhandlungen* (Leipzig, 1769). A pioneering interest in artificial fecundation, revealed by the article "Fecondazione artificiale," in *Prodromo della nuova enciclopedia Italiana* (Siena, 1779), 129–134, culminated in an account of the artificial insemination of a bitch, "Fecondaziona artificiale di una cagna," in *Opuscoli scelti sulle scienze e sulle arti* . . . , **4** (1781), 279–282. Continued investigations of regeneration phenomena, especially of the decapitated head of the snail, are summarized in "Resultati di esperienze sopra la riproduzione della testa nelle lumache terrestri," in *Memorie di matematica e fisica della società Italiana*, **1** (1782), 581–612, and **2** (1784), 506–602.

Spallanzani's range of interests continued undiminished in later life, as witness "Osservazioni sopra alcune trombe di mare formatesi sull' Adriatico," *ibid.*, **4** (1788), 473–479, which describes waterspouts in the Adriatic; "Memoria sopra le meduse fosforiche," *ibid.*, **7** (1794), 271–290, on a phosphorescent jellyfish; *Lettere sopra il sospetto di un nuovo senso nei pipistrelli* . . . (Turin, 1794), and "Lettere sul volo dei pipistrelli acciecati," in *Giornale de letterati*, **13** (1794), 120–186, which record correspondence about his experiments on the sense of direction in bats; *Chimico esame degli esperimenti del Sig. Gottling, professor a Jena, sopra la luce del fosforo di Kunkel* . . . (Modena, 1796), which criticizes Göttling's chemical explanation of the luminosity of phosphorus; and "Lettera . . . sopra le piante chiuse ne' vasi dentro l'acqua e l'aria, ed esposte all'immediato lume solare, e all'ombra," in *Opuscoli scelti sulle scienze e sulle arti* . . . , **20** (1798), 134–146, on exposure to sunlight or shade of plants kept in water or air.

Spallanzani's reply to John Hunter is "Lettera apologetica in risposta alle osservazioni sulla digestione del Sig. Giovanni Hunter . . . ," *ibid.*, **11** (1788), 45–95. Many of his writings contained polemic passages; and vengefulness marked the anonymous letters to G. A. Scopoli, one of four colleagues who had accused him of stealing museum specimens: "Lettere due . . . al Sig. Dottore Gio. Antonio Scopoli . . . ," and "Lettere tre . . . al chiarissimo Signore Gio. Antonio Scopoli, professore di chimica e di botanica . . ." (Modena, 1788 – ostensibly "In Zoopolis").

Details of Spallanzani's journey to the Near East, selected from his letters and diaries, were edited by N. Campanini, *Viaggio in Oriente* (Turin, 1888). At Reggio Emilia, the municipal library has custody of about 200 Spallanzani MSS, many still unpublished, and also correspondence with contemporary scientists. The Natural History Museum contains a unique collection of animal, plant, fossil, and mineral specimens catalogued by A. Jona, *La collezione monumentale di Lazzaro Spallanzani* . . . (Reggio Emilia, 1888), and historically documented by N. Campanini, *Storia documentale del Museo di Lazzaro Spallanzani a Reggio Emilia* (Bologna, 1888). His other great zoological collection, now at the Institute of Zoology, University of Pavia, is described by C. Jucci in *L'Istituto di Zoologia "Lazzaro Spallanzani* . . ." (Pavia, 1939). The Historical Museum of that university exhibits relics of Spallanzani, besides a small MS collection. Additional MSS and memorabilia are in the state archives at Milan.

II. SECONDARY LITERATURE. Short biographical accounts in English, often unevenly selective and containing minor inaccuracies, include A. E. Adams, "Lazzaro Spallanzani (1729–1799)," in *Scientific Monthly*, **29** (1929), 529–537; T. Beddoes, "Translator's Preface," in *Dissertations Relative to the Natural History of Animals and Vegetables* (London, 1784), vii–xl; W. Bulloch, "L'Abbate Spallanzani. 1729–1799," in *Parasitology*, **14** (1922), 409–411; G. E. Burget, "Lazzaro Spallanzani (1729–1799)," in *Annals of Medical History*, **6** (1924), 177–184; B. Cummings, "Spallanzani," in *Science Progress in the Twentieth Century*, **11** (1916), 236–245; G. Franchini, "Lazzaro Spallanzani (1729–1799)," in *Annals of Medical History*, n.s. **2** (1920), 56–62; J. B. Hamilton, "The Shadowed Side of Spallanzani," in *Yale Journal of Biology and Medicine*, **7** (1934–1935), 151–170; P. de Kruif, "Spallanzani," in *Microbe Hunters* (New York, 1926), 25–56; A. Massaglia, "Lazzaro Spallanzani," in *Medical Life*, **32** (1925), 149–169; J. G. M'Kendrick, "Spallanzani: A Physiologist of the Last Century," in *British Medical Journal* (1891), **2**, 888–892; F. Prescott, "Spallanzani on Spontaneous Generation and Digestion," in *Proceedings of the Royal Society of Medicine*, **23** (1930), 495–510; J. G. Rushton, "Lazzaro Spallanzani (1729–1799)," in *Proceedings of Staff Meetings of the Mayo Clinic*, **13**

(1938), 411–415; and W. Stirling, *Some Apostles of Physiology* (London, 1902), 60–64.

Important biographic writings in French range from J. L. Alibert, "Éloge historique de Lazare Spallanzani," in *Mémoires de la société médicale d'émulation*, **3** (1800), i–ccii, to J. Rostand, *Les origines de la biologie expérimentale et l'Abbé Spallanzani* (Paris, 1957). Jean Senebier prefaced his trans. of three major works with lengthy essays, "Des considérations sur sa méthode de faire des expériences et les conséquences pratiques qu'on peut tirer en médecine de ses découvertes," in *Expériences sur la digestion de l'homme et de différentes espèces d'animaux par l'Abbé Spallanzani* (Geneva, 1783), i–cxlix; "Réflexions générales sur les volcans pour servir d'introduction aux voyages volcaniques de M. l'Abbé Spallanzani," in *Voyages dans les deux Siciles et dans quelques parties des Apennins*, I (Bern, 1795), 1–74; and "Notice historique sur la vie et les écrits de Lazare Spallanzani," in *Mémoires sur la respiration par Lazare Spallanzani* (Geneva, 1803), 1–58. Another translator, J. Tourdes, wrote "Notices sur la vie littéraire de Spallanzani," as a preface to *Expériences sur la circulation . . .* (Paris, 1800), 5–112.

Among many biographic contributions in Italian are B. G. De'Brignoli, "Dell'Abate Lazzaro Spallanzani scandianese," in *Notizie biographiche . . .*, IV (Reggio Emilia, 1833–1841), 247–387; P. Capparoni, *Spallanzani* (Turin, 1941, 1948); A. Fabroni, "Elogio di Lazzaro Spallanzani," in *Memorie di matematica e fisica della società Italiana delle scienze*, **9** (1802), xxi–xlviii, which reappeared as "Vita di Lazzaro Spallanzani," in the *Opere*, I (Milan, 1825–1826), vii–xxvi; P. Pavesi, "L'Abate Spallanzani a Pavia," in *Società Italiana di scienze naturali di Milano. Memorie*, **6** (1901), fasc. III; P. Pozzetti, *Elogio di Lazzaro Spallanzani* (Parma, 1800); and L. Salimbeni, *L'Abbate Lazzaro Spallanzani . . .* (Modena, 1879). A short eulogy pronounced two days after Spallanzani's death by the leader of the 1786 "conspiracy," Gregorio Fontana, "Mozione . . . in proposito della morte di Lazzaro Spallanzani," is reproduced in *Memorie e documenti per la storia dell'università di Pavia . . .*, I (Pavia, 1878), 421–422. An account of the final illness and autopsy is given by V. L. Brera, in *Storia della malattia e della morte del Prof. Spallanzani* (Pavia, 1801).

Scopoli's libelous letter of 2 February 1787, conveying the accusations about Spallanzani's museum curatorship, appears in P. Leonardi, *Centenario del Prof. Giovanni Antonio Scopoli . . .* (Venice, 1888). Lazzaro's nephew, G. B. Spallanzani, vigorously defended his late uncle's reputation in *L'ombra di Spallanzani vendicata . . .* (Reggio Emilia, *ca.* 1802), but was rebutted in *Lettera di Giovanni Martinenghi . . .* (Pavia, 1803). Nearly a century later the alleged calumny was reviewed by P. Pavesi, "Il crimine scientifico Spallanzani giudicato," in *Rendiconti del Reale Istituto Lombardo di scienze e lettere*, 2nd ser., **32** (1899), 564–568. A fuller modern account appears in Capparoni's *Spallanzani*, ch. 4, 113–127.

Special appraisals are by E. Franco, "Lazzaro Spallanzani precursore dell' industria delle conserve," in *Atti della reale stazione sperimentale per l'industria delle conserve alimentari* (Parma, 1943); C. Massa, in *Modena a Lazzaro Spallanzani* (Modena, 1888), celebrating the dedication of the monument at Scandiano, 21 October 1888; A. Stefani, "In omaggio a Lazzaro Spallanzani nel centenario della sua morte," in *Atti e memorie della reale accademia di scienze, lettere ed arti in Padova*, n.s. **15** (1899), 209–220; and T. Taramelli, "Ricordo dello Spallanzani come vulcanologo," in *Rendiconti del Reale Istituto Lombardo di scienze e lettere*, **46** (1913), 937–951. Commemorative papers by Italian and foreign scientists honoring the centenary of his death are collected in *Nel primo centenario dalla morte di Lazzaro Spallanzani . . .*, 2 vols. (Reggio Emilia, 1899). A booklet, *Nelle feste centenarie di Lazzaro Spallanzani 1799–1899* (Reggio Emilia, 1899), contains portraits and Italian tributes. The second centenary of his birth also was celebrated by addresses published in *Onoranze a Lazzaro Spallanzani nel II centenario dalla nascità* (Reggio Emilia, 1929), the most notable being a detailed review of his travels by G. Pighini, "Lazzaro Spallanzani viaggiatore," pp. 1–441. In 1939 the University of Pavia was host to a meeting of the Italian Society of Experimental Biology and other organizations honoring Spallanzani. The memorabilia exhibited are listed by A. Lo Vasco, *Catalogo della mostra in onore di Lazzaro Spallanzani, 11 Aprile-18 Maggio 1939* (Pavia, 1939). The scientific communications appear in *Commemorazioni Spallanzaniane. 11–14 Aprile 1939*, 4 vols. (Pavia–Milan, 1939–1940).

Writings that relate Spallanzani to the scientific setting of his century include L. Belloni, "Antonio Vallisneri ed il contagio vivo," in *Il metodo sperimentale in biologia da Vallisneri ad oggi* (Padua, 1962); N. Campanini, "Lazzaro Spallanzani, Voltaire e Federico il grande," in *Rassegna Emiliana di storia, letteratura ed arte*, **1**, fasc. VII (1888), 389–406, reprinted in *Nelle feste centenarie . . .* (Reggio Emilia, 1899); A. Castiglioni, "Eighteenth Century Physiology. Haller, Spallanzani, English School," in *A History of Medicine* (New York, 1946), E. B. Krumbhaar, trans. and ed., 609–614; A. Clark-Kennedy, *Stephen Hales, D.D., F.R.S. An Eighteenth Century Biography* (Cambridge, 1929); C. Dobell, *Antony van Leeuwenhoek and His "Little Animals" . . .* (New York, 1932; 2nd ed., 1958; paperback ed., 1960); M. Foster, *Lectures on the History of Physiology During the Sixteenth, Seventeenth and Eighteenth Centuries* (Cambridge, 1924), 200–254; A. von Haller, *Elementa physiologiae corporis humani*, 8 vols. (Lausanne–Bern, 1757–1764); A. von Muralt, "Lazzaro Spallanzani e Albrecht von Haller," in *Commemorazioni Spallanzaniane . . . 1939*, III (Pavia–Milan, 1939–1940), 116–118; R. Savioz, *Mémoires autobiographiques de Charles Bonnet, de Genève* (Paris, 1948); J. Senebier, *Éloge historique d'Albert de Haller* (Geneva, 1778); P. Vaccari, *Storia della università di Pavia* (2nd ed., Pavia, 1957), ch. 8, pp. 177–218; and G. S. Volta, "Nuove ricerche ed osservazioni sopra il sessualismo di alcune piante," in *Memorie della reale accademia di scienze, belle lettere ed arti, Mantova*, **1** (1795), 225–267.

The following works illustrate the significance of Spallanzani's main scientific contributions. SPONTANEOUS GENERATION: C. Bastian, *The Beginnings of Life*, 2 vols. (London, 1872); L. Belloni, *Le "contagium vivum" avant Pasteur* (Paris, 1961); W. Bulloch, "Spontaneous Generation and Heterogenesis," in *The History of Bacteriology* (London, 1938, repr., 1960), ch. 4, pp. 67–125; H. Dale, *Viruses and Heterogenesis. An Old Problem in a New Form* (London, 1935), the Huxley lecture; J. T. Needham, *Nouvelles observations microscopiques, avec des découvertes intéressantes sur la composition et la décomposition des corps organisés* (Paris, 1750); and G. Pennetier, *Un débat scientifique. Pouchet et Pasteur 1858–1868* (Rouen, 1907). REGENERATION, EMBRYOLOGY AND FECUNDATION: C. Bonnet, "Expériences sur la régéneration de la tête du limaçon terrestre," in *Journal de physique*, **10** (1777), 165–179; Comte de Buffon (G. L. Leclerc), "Histoire des animaux," in *Histoire naturelle*, **2**, pt. 1 (Paris, 1749); A. W. Meyer, *The Rise of Embryology* (Stanford, Calif., 1939), chs. 5, 9–11, pp. 62–85, 132–211; and J. Needham, *A History of Embryology* (Cambridge, 1934), 179–229. DIGESTION: D. G. Bates, "The Background to John Young's Thesis on Digestion," in *Bulletin of the History of Medicine*, **36** (1962), 341–362; J. Hunter, "Some Observations on Digestion," in *Observations on Certain Parts of the Animal Oeconomy* (London, 1786), 147–188; R.-A. F. de Réaumur, "Sur la digestion des oiseaux," in *Académie des sciences* (Paris, 1752), 266–307, 461–495; and J. R. Young, *An Experimental Inquiry into the Principles of Nutrition and the Digestive Process* (Philadelphia, 1803), repr. with intro. essay by W. C. Rose (Urbana, Illinois, 1959). FLIGHT OF BATS: R. Galambos, "The Avoidance of Obstacles by Flying Bats: Spallanzani's Ideas (1794) and Later Theories," in *Isis*, **34** (1942), 132–140; D. R. Griffin, *Echoes of Bats and Men* (New York, 1955), 27–33, 87–88; and L. Jurine, "Experiments on Bats Deprived of Sight," in *Philosophical Magazine*, **1** (1798), 136–140, trans. from *Journal de physique*, **46** (1798), 145–148. Spallanzani's chief monographs were reviewed anonymously at some length in *Giornale de' letterati di Pisa* (1774–1795).

CLAUDE E. DOLMAN

SPEMANN, HANS (*b.* Stuttgart, Germany, 27 June 1869; *d.* Freiburg im Breisgau, Germany, 12 September 1941), *embryology.*

Spemann was the eldest of four children of a well-known book publisher, Johann Wilhelm Spemann, and the former Lisinka Hoffmann. His father's family, of Westphalian peasant stock, had a number of members in the legal profession, and his mother's family contained several doctors. There were three other children in the family, and he grew up in a fairly large house well provided with books, with parents who led an active social and cultural life. Spemann attended the Eberhard-Ludwigs-Gymnasium, where he was particularly attracted by classics. He first decided, however, to study medicine; and for that purpose he attended the University of Heidelberg as soon as he had completed his year of military service in the Kassel hussars.

At Heidelberg, Spemann formed a friendship that without doubt greatly influenced the direction of his life. Gustaf Wolff, a few years older than he, had begun experiments on the embryological development of newts and had shown that if the lens of the eye is removed, a new lens may be formed—not from the tissue that gives rise to the lens in normal development, but from the edge of the retina. This "Wolffian lens regeneration" intrigued Spemann throughout most of his life, and it still retains some of the air of mystery that originally surrounded it. At that time (1892) Wolff interpreted it as strong evidence against Darwin's "selection theory" and as proof of "organic purposiveness." Thus Spemann was introduced, at the beginning of his academic career, to the animal that was to remain his favorite experimental material; acquired an insight into the character of a well-planned and clean experiment; and developed an inclination toward what might now be considered a somewhat mystical conception of the nature of biological processes. He retained strong traces of these influences throughout his life.

As a young biologist Spemann began work in 1894 at Würzburg as a doctoral student and teacher, and was the favorite pupil of Theodor Boveri. It was there, just after taking his doctorate, that he married Clara Binder. After fourteen years at Würzburg, Spemann became professor at Rostock (1908–1914). He spent the years of World War I as director of the Kaiser Wilhelm Institute of Biology in Berlin-Dahlem; and in 1919 he succeeded Weismann as professor at Freiburg im Breisgau. He remained at Freiburg for the rest of his life, retiring in 1938 and dying in his country house nearby in 1941. He was awarded the Nobel Prize for physiology and medicine in 1935.

Spemann combined great persistence, foresight, and careful planning with beautifully precise manipulative skill and an insistence on *Sauberkeit* (cleanliness, in all aspects). His first two major works in biology were fully thought out, before he started writing them, to answer quite clearly defined questions. The time for this creative thinking had been forced on him by a lung illness that necessitated a rest cure in Switzerland.

For one line of work Spemann chose the object about which he had first learned from his friend Wolff—the lens of the amphibian eye—but asked himself a question more basic than any raised by Wolff's work on regeneration: how the lens came to develop in the first place. It is formed from the outer layer of cells in the embryo (the ectoderm, which also gives rise to the skin and the nervous system), and it appears at the point where an outgrowth from the brain reaches the surface. At an early stage of development, the region from which this outgrowth arises is exposed on the surface of the egg, and Spemann was able to kill this group of cells by burning with a minute hot needle. He found that the remainder of the embryo could develop normally without the retina that should have developed from the brain outgrowth and, most important, also without the lens. This discovery strongly suggested that the brain outgrowth, when it reaches the ectoderm, exerts an influence that causes the cells to develop into the lens.

In order to study further the reality of this postulated "induction" of the lens by the retina, Spemann had to perfect his experimental methods. He invented a number of very simple but elegant and refined instruments, mostly made from glass, which made it possible to carry out complicated surgical operations on eggs and embryos only a millimeter or two in diameter. In this way he became almost solely responsible for founding the techniques of microsurgery, certainly one of his greatest contributions to biology. Using such instruments, Spemann could remove the region of ectoderm from which the lens would be expected to form, and substitute some other piece for it before the development of the retina; he found that this foreign ectoderm was induced by the retina to develop into a lens.

Spemann's other early problem did not demand as much technical originality, but led even deeper into the major questions of development. The newt's egg, when laid, is enclosed in an oval capsule of jelly. A thin hair—Spemann maintained that it should be from the head of a blond infant less than nine months old—can be tied around it and pulled tight enough to cut the egg in half or compress it to a dumbbell shape. Spemann found that if this constriction is carried out soon after laying, each separate half of the egg may develop into a complete larva; or, alternatively, one may develop into a whole larva and the other only into a more or less formless mass of cells. If the constriction is

not complete, and produces only a dumbbell, one may obtain an embryo with a single tail and two complete heads.

The important point is that a half egg (or half region) never produces a half embryo, but always either a complete embryo (or organ such as the head) or nothing at all. The production of a complete embryo from half the egg shows clearly that at this early stage the various parts of the egg are not fixed in their "developmental fate" ("Determined"). On the other hand, if the same constriction experiment is carried out considerably later, after gastrulation but still before the first embryonic organs can be recognized, the halves form only half embryos, each part developing exactly as if there had been no constriction. Some process of "fixing the developmental fate of the parts" must have occurred between the early stage and the later; and Spemann called this process "determination."

Spemann was thus led to take two further steps that, in combination, opened a new era in the understanding of biological development. From the constriction experiments it seemed to follow that, long before any particular organs can be recognized in the embryo, some process of "determination" decides, more or less irrevocably, the nature of the end product into which any given region will develop. It might seem obvious to ask what the nature of this process is. But Spemann was too wary to get involved in such philosophical traps and too good an experimentalist. He posed the more restricted but more manageable problem of whether we can discover any causal antecedent that brings about this determination.

Calling on the microsurgical techniques elaborated in his study of the lens, Spemann devised experimental procedures that did indeed reveal a causal sequence of events leading up to the determination of the main organ that appears in early stages of development: the central nervous system. By transferring small fragments of tissue from one location in the embryo to another, he (and some of his student collaborators, particularly Hilde and Otto Mangold) showed that any part of the ectoderm of the embryo, if brought into contact with the mesoderm before or at the time of gastrulation, would be induced to become neural tissue; whereas if it were not allowed to contact the mesoderm, it would not become neural tissue, even if its original location in the embryo would have led one to expect it to develop in that way. By this achievement Spemann had discovered the first known example of a causal mechanism that makes it possible to control precisely the direction in which a part of the embryo will develop; by surgical manipulation of its neighboring cells, it can be determined whether this embryonic part will develop into nerves or into skin.

When a piece of ectoderm is placed in contact with the mesoderm, it is induced to form not a mere mass of neural cells but a part of a neural organ, such as the brain, with a greater or lesser degree of organization. This finding led Spemann to approach the problem of the mechanism of "the induction of determination" with considerable caution. His biological philosophy, while not explicitly vitalist, tended to fall within the "organicist" framework characteristic of German biology at the turn of the century. He seems at first to have felt that the process of induction occurs in cells that are so biologically complex that an attempt to analyze it would necessarily entail an oversimplification. He therefore used, as a name for the region that develops into mesoderm and that induces the neural plate, the word "Organisator", and he stated, "It creates [schafft] an organization field out of the indifferent material in which it lies."

In later experiments, devoted to the study of induction in other regions of the embryo, Spemann again found that what is induced usually is an organ, with its own characteristic shape. But some of these experiments, in which fragments from frogs' eggs were transplanted to newts' eggs, or vice versa, led to what should probably be considered Spemann's second major contribution: the discovery that the character of the induced organ depends much more on its own intrinsic (presumably genetic) constitution than on that of the inducer. Thus a frog inducer, acting on newt tissues, produces a newt organ. The reacting material is by no means indifferent, as he had earlier thought. Further, under the influence of younger, more analytically oriented students, Spemann gradually accepted the importance of experiments designed to discover the extent to which the effects of his "Organisator" can be produced when the cells of it have been killed or chemically extracted. He never seems, however, to have considered induction from the point of view that now seems so natural: as involving the genetic potentialities of the cells. Perhaps only T. H. Morgan, among his contemporaries, would have been tempted to approach the subject from that angle during the period when Spemann was most active. The communication between German experimental embryologists and American geneticists was so slight that the connection was made only toward the end of Spemann's

life. It was, however, the precision and rigor of Spemann's experiments that led him to formulate clear questions concerning the causal sequences of particular and well-defined developmental performances by identifiable groups of cells, and thus to provide the foundations on which the more recent advances have been based.

BIBLIOGRAPHY

I. ORIGINAL WORKS. All but the very last of Spemann's publications were summarized by the author himself in his *Experimentelle Beiträge zu einer Theorie der Entwicklung* (Berlin, 1936), translated into English as *Embryonic Development and Induction* (New Haven, 1938). An autobiography is *Forschung und Leben, Errinerungen* (Stuttgart, 1943).

II. SECONDARY LITERATURE. An extensive discussion by a long-time pupil and collaborator is O. Mangold, *Hans Spemann, ein Meister der Entwicklungsphysiologie, sein Leben und sein Werk* (Stuttgart, 1953). Less extensive surveys of Spemann's work, and discussion of it by authors not so closely associated with him, are in J. Needham, *Biochemistry and Morphogenesis*, 2nd ed. (London, 1969); L. Saxén and S. Toivonen, *Primary Embryonic Induction* (London, 1962); and C. H. Waddington, *Principles of Embryology* (London, 1956).

Biographical writings are F. Baltzer, "Zum Gedächtnis Hans Spemann," in *Naturwissenschaften*, **30** (1942), 229–239; and O. Mangold, "Hans Spemann als Mensch und Wissenschaftler," in *Wilhelm Roux Archiv für Entwicklungs-mechanik der Organismen*, **141** (1942). 385–425; and "Hans Spemann," in *Freiburger Professoren des' 19. und 20. Jahrhunderts* (Freiburg, 1957), 159–182.

C. H. WADDINGTON

SPENCER, HERBERT (*b.* Derby, England, 27 April 1820; *d.* Brighton, England, 8 December 1903), *philosophy, biology, psychology, sociology.*

Spencer was the only surviving child of William George and Catherine Spencer; his father, a private school teacher of very modest means, was inclined to a deist rationalism and frequented Quaker meetings. Spencer was educated privately, first by his father (author of an original system of teaching geometry, by "discovery" methods) and then by his uncle, the Rev. Thomas Spencer, a radical and scientifically inclined parson. He also participated in the Derby Philosophical Society, a coterie of amateur "natural philosophers" founded by Erasmus Darwin in 1783 along the lines of the Birmingham Lunar Society, and thus became an heir to that provincial tradition of political radicalism, religious free thought, and scientific endeavor of which the key figure had been Joseph Priestley. Above fairly elementary levels he was a virtual autodidact, learning his science from casual reading, attending lectures, and, later, associating with working scientists.

In 1837 Spencer took up railway engineering, during the boom period of railway construction in England, and was active in radical, middle-class, dissenting politics. Dissatisfied with engineering, he hovered long over other choices, finally taking a job in London in 1848 as subeditor of the *Economist*. There he moved among leaders of literary and scientific opinion and gradually shaped his career as an independent writer and reviewer. Spencer never married (despite his celebrated affair with Marian Evans [George Eliot]) and from 1855 suffered, despite good physical health, from a neurotic condition that intermittently prevented him from sleeping, working, or being in company. Despite his friendships (notably with T. H. Huxley and with the other scientists who composed the X-Club) and his membership in the Athenaeum, Spencer was socially an isolate and took pride in declining all the many honors that were offered him. His considerable reputation as a proponent of extreme laissez-faire liberalism, of the claims of science against traditional religion, and of evolutionary philosophy was at its height in the late 1870's (most especially in the United States) but had diminished dramatically by the time of his death.

Spencer is important less for specific discoveries or for his contribution to particular sciences (except sociology and psychology) than for his synthesis of so much of the accepted science of his day in the integrating framework of evolution. In an age when natural science was becoming institutionalized and differentiated, both internally and externally, Spencer was the last of the *Naturphilosophen*. This accounts for the vagaries of his reputation among his scientific contemporaries: low among specialist working scientists and high among many of the most original boundary-crossing innovators (Darwin, Galton, A. R. Wallace). Spencer's unified vision of science, expressed in methodological writings as well as in the synthesis itself, contributed greatly to the acceptance of science as a major component in the intellectual culture of industrial society. If the evolutionary totality had many of the attributes of a theology, it was not merely because of its place in the last decisive battle between science and religion, but because its original and enduring motive had been to establish "the secularization of ethics," now that the unanimous hold of religion had been weakened. It was necessary to integrate physical science with social science and ethics in order to invest the latter with the authority that only science could truly claim. The unity of the whole, and the fertile but misleading cross references between the parts, were essential to both Spencer's scientific and his social-ethical interests.

The precise origin of Spencer's evolutionary views is impossible to date, but it is likely that they were imbibed in some form during his youth from the "Darwinians" of Derby. He had become a Lamarckian through his reading of Lyell in 1840, and although critical of the *Vestiges of Creation* (1843), he accepted its basic tenet, "the development hypothesis." *Social Statics* (1850), his first book, is evolutionary; and his long essay "A Theory of Population" (1852), in attempting to show that progress is necessitated by population pressure, comes within an ace of anticipating the main elements of Darwinian natural selection. In the latter Spencer applied Malthusian principles to animal populations, deduced a struggle for survival, and coined the phrase "survival of the fittest"; but the perspective remained Lamarckian. It is clear from his subsequent essay "Progress: Its Law and Cause" (1857) that the goal of his theory was quite distinct from Darwin's: to show how progress or development in all areas of the universe—the solar system, the totality of organic species, the maturation of each organism, the psychic development and socialization of the individual, the evolution of society and culture—consists of one fundamental, determinate motion from an incoherent homogeneity to a complex and interdependent heterogeneity.

The path to this vision had been cleared by Spencer's reading of K. E. von Baer's work on embryology and H. Milne-Edwards' theme of "the physiological division of labor"—a notion that, introduced into biology from political economy, was now to be reapplied by Spencer to the social world, in an extensive use of the organic analogy. *First Principles* (1862), with its doctrine of an ultimate unknowable force, sought to reconcile science and religion, and to lay the metaphysical underpinnings of all evolution. The necessity of differentiation was derived from "the Persistence of Force," the instability of all homogeneous physical conditions, and the tendency of all changes to produce multiple effects, leading to ever more heterogeneous and complex results. He resisted Clerk Maxwell's suggestion that the second law of thermodynamics implied increasing entropy, not increasing heterogeneity, as the cosmic trend.

Starting from a definition of life as "a definite combination of heterogeneous changes, both simultaneous and successive . . . in correspondence with external coexistences and sequences," Spencer saw higher forms emerging from a gradual process of adaptation to the environment. *The Principles of Biology* (1864–1867) analyzes the principal mechanisms by which this occurs and relates them to the specialized structures and functions of plants and animals. Although Darwinian natural selection was easily incorporated into Spencer's system (as "indirect equilibration"), Spencer was always concerned to insist on the inheritance of acquired characteristics as a major mechanism of evolution. Long after most professional biologists had abandoned it, Spencer, in *The Factors of Organic Evolution* (1886), his last important scientific essay, argued that "use-inheritance" was necessary to explain most organized systems of behavior or physiological structure. The fatal weakness in his case was his inability to explain how modifications of organs derived from use and the direct effects of the environment could become embodied in the genetic stock. There was one powerful reason—quite apart from the unresolved difficulties that the neo-Darwinism of Weismann and others had left—why Spencer was unwilling to abandon his Lamarckism. It would have undermined what he most wanted to maintain: the fundamental identity of biological evolution and of psychic and social evolution. This tenet of the unity of evolution also led him to blur differences between processes in which the outcome is in some sense "programmed" at the outset (such as the maturation of the embryo) and those in which it is not (such as the evolution of species or the socialization of children).

The Principles of Psychology (1855) was an important and original work, a real milestone in the history of the subject, marking its transition from a heavily epistemological phase to one in which it was closely dependent on physiology. In it Spencer paved the way for Wundt, William James, and Pavlov. Spencer had in his youth accepted phrenology, which, although abandoned, provided him with a critique of the associationist psychology of Hartley, Jeremy Bentham, and J. S. Mill, on the grounds of its not embracing the fact of species or racial character. Spencer presented this character not as an innate essence, but as the "organized" residue of the past experience of the species, a factor that interacted with present experience. But he could give no firm account of just how fixed or fluid this "character" was; and he never distinguished properly between the (in our terms) racial and cultural components of "character" in man. The end of psychological evolution was the emergence of ever more complex powers of "representation" in response to environmental stimuli. The same basic processes operated at all levels, so that abstract thought and developed moral sympathy differed only in degree from the automatic contractions of microorganisms.

Spencer's social theory rested on his psychology, just as his psychology presupposed his biology, because of his basic principle that the character of any aggregate, whether society or physical substance, is fixed by that of its constituent units. The mental development of man, Spencer argued, lay from egotism to altruism: thus society developed from a "militant" phase, in which rigid coercion was needed to hold men together, to an "industrial" phase, in which altruism and a marked individualism permitted the decline of external control and the complex interdependence of an advanced division of labor. The "social state," or end product of evolution, was the ideal of Spencer's youth: a society with the minimum of state control over its members' activities and associations, in which altruism permitted the harmonious free play of each person's individual interest. His lifework was to try to show that this ideal was uniquely in accord with natural principles.

Spencer failed, yet it was a grand failure. Apart from his major contributions to the nascent fields of sociology and psychology, he performed a major function for the science of his day by drawing out and integrating its principal themes with the general culture of his age. It is a function that no one has performed since.

BIBLIOGRAPHY

I. ORIGINAL WORKS. There is a complete bibliography of Spencer's writings in J. Rumney, *Herbert Spencer's Sociology* (London, 1937), 311–323. His principal works, all published in London, are *Social Statics: Or the Conditions Essential to Human Happiness Specified, and the First of Them Developed* (1850); *The Principles of Psychology* (1855; 2nd ed., enl. and rev., 2 vols., 1870–1872); *Education: Intellectual, Moral and Physical* (1861); *First Principles* (1862); *The Principles of Biology*, 2 vols. (1864–1867); *The Study of Sociology* (1873); *The Principles of Sociology*, 3 vols. (1876–1897); *The Principles of Ethics*, 2 vols. (1879–1893); *The Man Versus the State* (1884); and *An Autobiography* (1904).

Many of his essays were reprinted in his *Essays, Scientific, Political, and Speculative*, 3 vols. (various eds., rev. London, 1890). The principal essays of scientific interest are "A Theory of Population, Deduced From the General Law of Animal Fertility," in *Westminster Review* (1852); "The Development Hypothesis," in *Leader* (1852); "The Genesis of Science," in *British Quarterly Review* (1854); "Progress: Its Law and Cause," in *Westminster Review* (1857); "The Social Organism," *ibid.* (1860); "The Factors of Organic Evolution," in *Nineteenth Century* (1886); and "The Inadequacy of Natural Selection" and further rejoinders, in *Contemporary Review* (1893–1894).

Several selections from Spencer's writings, mostly on sociology, have recently been published: *The Man Versus the State, With Four Essays on Politics and Society*, D. G. MacRae, ed. (Harmondsworth, 1969); *Herbert Spencer: Structure, Function and Evolution*, S. L. Andreski, ed. (London, 1971); and *Herbert Spencer on Social Evolution*, J. D. Y. Peel, ed. (Chicago, 1972).

Original MSS of most of Spencer's books are at the British Museum. The remains of his personal papers (seemingly only a small part) are at the Athenaeum (London). Otherwise his letters are widespread in the collected papers of his correspondents, especially T. H. Huxley (at Imperial College, London) and Beatrice Webb (Passfield Papers, British Library of Political and Economic Science).

II. SECONDARY LITERATURE. The indispensable work is D. Duncan, *Life and Letters of Herbert Spencer* (London, 1908). Among the great volume of contemporary or near-contemporary discussion, criticism, and paraphrase of Spencer's work are F. H. Collins, *An Epitome of the Synthetic Philosophy* (London, 1889); J. Arthur Thompson, *Herbert Spencer* (London, 1906); and William James, *Memories and Studies* (New York, 1911), which contains a judicious obituary assessment. J. Rumney, *Herbert Spencer's Sociology* (London, 1937), stands almost alone in the period when Spencer was all but forgotten. Most present interest is in Spencer as social philosopher and forerunner of sociology. J. D. Y. Peel, *Herbert Spencer: The Evolution of a Sociologist* (London, 1971), gives the fullest account of the social and intellectual background; see also J. W. Burrow, *Evolution and Society* (London, 1966); S. Eisen, "Herbert Spencer and the Spectre of Comte," in *Journal of British Studies*, **7** (1967); and "Frederic Harrison and Herbert Spencer: Embattled Unbelievers," in *Victorian Studies*, **12** (1968); D. Freeman, "The Evolutionary Theories of Charles Darwin and Herbert Spencer," in *Current Anthropology*, **15** (1974); M. Harris, *The Rise of Anthropological Theory* (New York, 1968); J. D. Y. Peel, "Spencer and the Neo-evolutionists," in *Sociology*, **3** (1969); W. H. Simon, "Herbert Spencer and the Social Organism," in *Journal of the History of Ideas*, **21** (1960); and G. W. Stocking, *Race, Culture and Evolution* (New York, 1968). For a greater emphasis on Spencer as natural scientist, see P. B. Medawar, "Herbert Spencer and the General Law of Evolution," in *The Art of the Soluble*

(London, 1967); and R. M. Young, "Malthus and the Evolutionists," in *Past and Present*, **43** (1969); and *Mind, Brain and Adaptation in the Nineteenth Century* (Oxford, 1970).

J. D. Y. PEEL

SPENCER, LEONARD JAMES (*b.* Worcester, England, 7 July 1870; *d.* London, England, 4 April 1959), *mineralogy.*

Spencer was the eldest of the eight children of the former Elizabeth Bonser and James Spencer, for many years headmaster of the school attached to Bradford Technical College, from which the boy won a Royal Exhibition to the Royal College of Science for Ireland, Dublin, in 1886. He graduated in chemistry in 1889 and immediately entered Sidney Sussex College, Cambridge, to read geology, mineralogy, and chemistry. In 1893 Spencer won the coveted Harkness scholarship in geology. From September to December of that year he studied at Munich under Groth, Ernst Weinschenk, and Wilhelm Muthmann. Earlier in 1893 he had been appointed to the staff of the mineral department of the British Museum. When he took up this post on New Year's Day 1894, and the following month joined the Mineralogical Society of Great Britain and Ireland, the course was set for the remainder of Spencer's long life: about these two institutions his professional career, and indeed his whole life, were to revolve. In 1899 he married Edith Mary Close of Mortimer, Berkshire; they had one son and two daughters. Almost all Spencer's time was devoted to mineralogy; he allowed himself the occasional relaxation of gardening in London and at his country cottage.

From the beginning Spencer's curatorial duties involved him in widely ranging descriptive mineralogy, and this is reflected in his original publications. His establishment of the relationship between the three lead antimony sulfides plagionite, heteromorphite, and semseyite is notable, and his description of enargite was a model of its kind. The eight new minerals he named—miersite, tarbuttite, parahopeite, chloroxiphite, diaboleite, schultenite, aramayoite and bismutotantalite—are all nonsilicates. Spencer's interest later turned to meteorites and especially to the origin of tektites, which he thought to be impact products; he was responsible for important additions to the already notable meteorite collection at the British Museum and, in 1934, made an expedition to the silica-glass occurrences in the Great Sand Sea of Egypt but failed to find associated meteorite craters. His meticulous curatorial work was largely responsible for making the British Museum mineral collection the best-documented and best-indexed in the world at the time of his retirement in 1935 as keeper, a post to which he had been appointed in 1927.

While still an undergraduate at Cambridge, Spencer began his long career as an abstractor, probably through financial necessity, by preparing abstracts of patents for H. M. Patent Office. In his first years at the British Museum, he abstracted mineral chemistry for *Journal of the Chemical Society*, reviewed the same field for the annual *Report on the Progress of Chemistry* of the Chemical Society, and compiled and edited the mineralogy volumes of the *International Catalogue of Scientific Literature* from 1901 to 1914. In 1900 he was appointed editor of the *Mineralogical Magazine*, an office he held until 1955, and immediately began to publish a few pages annually of abstracts of significant papers. In 1920 Spencer persuaded the Mineralogical Society to start publication of *Mineralogical Abstracts* with coverage from the expiry of the *International Catalogue* in 1915. He edited twelve volumes of *Mineralogical Abstracts* (1920–1955), contributing two-thirds of the text himself. His triennial lists of new mineral names and obituary notices were features of *Mineralogical Magazine* throughout his long editorship.

Spencer wrote two books, *The World's Minerals* (1911) and *A Key to Precious Stones* (1936); he translated, with his wife's assistance, two important German works, Max Bauer's *Edelsteinkunde* (1904) and R. Braun's *Das Mineralreich* (1908–1912).

Spencer's eminence in mineralogy was not unrecognized in his lifetime. He was elected fellow of the Royal Society in 1925; correspondent in 1926, later honorary fellow, and in 1940 Roebling medalist of the Mineralogical Society of America; Murchison medalist of the Geological Society of London in 1937; and honorary member of the German Mineralogical Society in 1927. At the Mineralogical Society he was president (1936–1939) and foreign secretary (1949–1959).

Spencer's service to mineralogy at the British Museum and in the Mineralogical Society, especially through its publications, was long and outstanding. His deep knowledge of his subject and his untiring energy were remarkable. His brusque manner and his single-minded devotion to his science were allied with a sense of humor and an essential kindness that encouraged others to emulate his high standards of scientific scholarship.

BIBLIOGRAPHY

I. ORIGINAL WORKS. Spencer wrote more than 150 original papers. His two books are *The World's Minerals* (London–Edinburgh, 1911; rev. American ed., New York, 1916); and *A Key to Precious Stones* (London–Glasgow, 1936; 2nd ed., 1946). *Precious Stones* (London, 1904) is his translation, with additions, of M. Bauer, *Edelsteinkunde* (1896); and *The Mineral Kingdom*, 2 vols. (London, 1908–1912), is the translation, with additions, of R. Brauns, *Das Mineralreich* (1903–1904). A useful selected bibliography is in C. E. Tilley, *Biographical Memoirs of Fellows of the Royal Society*, 7 (1961), 243–248.

II. SECONDARY LITERATURE. Detailed accounts of Spencer's curatorial and bibliographical work are W. Campbell Smith, in *Mineralogical Magazine and Journal of the Mineralogical Society*, **29** (1950), 256–270; and J. Phemister, *ibid.*, **31** (1956), 1–4. A critical account of Spencer's scientific contribution is given by Tilley, *loc. cit.*

DUNCAN McKIE

SPENCER JONES, HAROLD (*b.* Kensington, London, England, 29 March 1890; *d.* Greenwich, England, 3 November 1960), *astronomy.*

Spencer Jones was the third child of Henry Charles Jones, an accountant. His early interest in mathematics was fostered at Hammersmith Grammar School, from which he won a scholarship to Jesus College, Cambridge. Thereafter his career followed, with minor modifications, the course usual for men of his abilities and background.

Spencer Jones's scholarly career at Cambridge culminated in his election to a research fellowship of his college in 1913. That year the astronomer royal, F. W. Dyson—following the established pattern for recruiting chief assistants at the Royal Observatory—appointed Spencer Jones to Greenwich as replacement for A. S. Eddington, who returned to Cambridge as Plumian professor; he remained there until 1923, when he was appointed H.M. Astronomer at the Cape of Good Hope. Spencer Jones spent the next decade in South Africa, from which he returned early in 1933 to become astronomer royal—an office he held until his retirement at the end of 1955.

During most of his life Spencer Jones held high positions in the scientific civil service of his country and a number of honorary posts in international professional bodies, including the presidency of the International Astronomical Union in 1944–1948 (to which he succeeded following Eddington's death) and the secretary-generalship of the International Council of Scientific Unions in 1955–

1958. In Britain he received most of the national honors due a man of his station (including knighthood in 1943) and for most of his life was active in the Royal Astronomical Society, of which he was president from 1937 to 1939.

Spencer Jones's scientific interests were connected mainly with the tasks of the observatories with which he was associated: primarily the problems of positional and fundamental astronomy. His outstanding personal contributions were a study of the speed of rotation of the earth, and one of the solar parallax. In his epochal paper "The Rotation of the Earth and the Secular Acceleration of the Sun, Moon, and Planets" (1939) he proved—qualitatively, but quite definitely— that the fluctuations in the observed longitudes of these celestial bodies can be attributed not to any peculiarities of their motions but, rather, to fluctuations in the angular velocity of rotation of the earth.

Spencer Jones devoted several years to a new determination of the mean distance of the earth from the sun through measurements of the parallactic displacement of the asteroid Eros during its favorable opposition in 1930–1931. Still at the Cape of Good Hope, he contributed more than 1,200 photographic observations to this program and later, by international agreement, was entrusted with the reductions of all observations of Eros made in 1930–1931.

The principal result of this work (1941) disclosed that the value of the solar parallax was equal to $8.7904'' \pm 0.0010''$—a considerable improvement over previous results. This figure did not, however, remain unchallenged for long; in 1950 the German astronomer E. K. Rabe, then working in the United States, found from a reduction of all observations made between 1926 and 1945—a feat facilitated by the advent of automatic computers—that a more accurate value was $8.7984'' \pm 0.0004''$, significantly larger than the value deduced by Spencer Jones.

A postscript to the age-long quest for determination of the solar parallax was added after 1961 by a completely different technique, based on the direct measurements by radar of the distance to Venus. The most recent (1967) value of the parallax—$8.79410'' \pm 0.0001''$—rendering the semimajor axis of the terrestrial orbit close to 149,597,890 kilometers (with an uncertainty of a few units of the penultimate digit), is more than ten times as accurate as Spencer Jones's result; and its remaining error hinges, in fact, on limitations of the present knowledge of the velocity of light.

All considered, Spencer Jones's principal original contributions suffered—as did those of many others—from the fact that they were concerned with problems eminently suitable for treatment by automatic computing machinery, but were carried out ten years or so before its advent.

BIBLIOGRAPHY

A complete bibliography of papers published (alone, or jointly) by H. Spencer Jones since 1913 includes 59 separate entries; their sequence terminated rather abruptly in 1945. Many of these papers dealt with subjects of more routine nature (reporting on work carried out at observatories under Spencer Jones's direction). Some of those which should remain of permanent interest for the historian of science are "The Rotation of the Earth and Secular Accelerations of the Sun, Moon, and Planets," in *Monthly Notices of the Royal Astronomical Society*, **99** (1939), 541; and "The Solar Parallax and the Mass of the Moon From Observations of Eros at the Opposition of 1931," in *Memoirs of the Royal Astronomical Society*, **76**, pt. 2 (1941), 11–66. See also his earlier papers on the motion and figure of the moon, in *Monthly Notices of the Royal Astronomical Society*, **97** (1937), 406; and his redetermination of the constant of nutation, *ibid.*, **98** (1938), 440; and **99** (1939), 211.

ZDENĚK KOPAL

SPERRY, ELMER AMBROSE (*b*. Cortland County, New York, 21 October 1860; *d*. Brooklyn, New York, 16 June 1930), *technology, engineering.*

The son of Mary Burst, a schoolteacher, and Stephen Sperry, a farmer, Sperry was raised by his Baptist grandparents after his mother died in childbirth. He later moved from their farm to the village of Cortland and attended the normal school, where the professors interested him in applied science. A visit to the Philadelphia Centennial Exposition, regular reading of *Scientific American* and the patent abstracts in the *Official Gazette*, and the publicity then given to such inventors as Thomas Edison persuaded Sperry to embark upon a career as an inventor and an engineer.

Cortland capitalists with Chicago affiliations helped Sperry to develop a generator and an arc light and, in 1882, to found his own company in Chicago to market them. Among the prominent Chicagoans who backed him was the president of the first University of Chicago. When the company demanded too much routine engineering, Sperry withdrew in 1888 to found his own invention and development company. For the next two decades, in Chicago, Cleveland, Ohio, and Brooklyn, New York, he was successful as an independent inventor concentrating successively upon the electric streetcar, mining machinery, the automobile, and industrial chemistry. Sperry was particularly adept at identifying critical problems, especially those of automatic control, in rapidly expanding areas of technology and in defining with clarity and force his inventive responses—and his patents.

Sperry investigated gyro applications in 1907, stimulated by reports from Germany of Ernst Otto Schlick's gyrostabilizer and Hermann Anschütz's gyrocompass for ships. He committed himself fully to the field after the United States navy adopted his improved gyrocompass, used his gyrostabilizer, and tested his airplane stabilizer. Before World War I, Sperry founded the Sperry Gyroscope Company, which was to become a world-renowned small research and development firm, staffed by resourceful young development engineers and specializing in complex technology and precision manufacture.

During World War I, Sperry, after Edison, was the most active member of the Naval Consulting Board, an early effort to organize science and technology for the military-industrial needs of wartime. Later, Secretary of the Navy Charles Francis Adams said of Sperry, "No one American has contributed so much to our naval technical progress."

During the postwar decade Sperry emerged as a leader in the engineering profession and was elected president of the American Society of Mechanical Engineers, chairman of the Division of Engineering and Industrial Research of the National Research Council, and member of the National Academy of Sciences. He was a major advocate of industrial research, symbolizing for many the transition of America from the era of heroic invention to that of industrial science. Only after his death, and after guidance and automatic control became a major field of science and technology popularized by the concepts of automation and cybernetics, was Sperry's role as a pioneer recognized. The widespread adoption of the Sperry automatic ship pilot, and later the Sperry automatic airplane pilot, further enhanced his reputation. An analysis of his 350 patents reveals his consistent focus upon automatic controls, even in diverse fields of endeavor.

Sperry's sons, Edward, Lawrence, and Elmer, Jr., joined their father at the Sperry Gyroscope Company.

BIBLIOGRAPHY

I. ORIGINAL WORKS. On Sperry's gyrostabilizer, gyrocompass, and automatic ship pilot, see especially his articles in *Transactions of the Society of Naval Architects and Marine Engineers*, **18** (1910), 143–154; **20** (1912), 201–215; **21** (1913), 181–187; **23** (1915), 43–48; **24** (1916), 207–214; **25** (1917), 293–299; **27** (1919), 99–108; and **30** (1922), 53–57. His other articles and patents are listed in the first two references below.

II. SECONDARY LITERATURE. See Thomas Parke Hughes, *Elmer Ambrose Sperry: Inventor and Engineer* (Baltimore, 1971); and J. C. Hunsaker, "Biographical Memoir of Elmer Ambrose Sperry, 1860–1930," in *Biographical Memoirs. National Academy of Sciences*, **28** (1954), 223–260. See also Preston R. Bassett, "Elmer A. Sperry," in *Nassau County Historical Journal*, **21** (Fall 1960).

THOMAS PARKE HUGHES

SPEUSIPPUS (*b.* Athens, *ca.* 408 B.C.; *d.* Athens, 339 B.C.), *philosophy.*

Speusippus' father was Eurymedon, and his mother was Plato's sister Potone. A member of the Academy, he became its head after Plato's death. He was a friend of Dion and supported his political plans. Diogenes Laërtius lists the titles of thirty writings by Speusippus, but his catalog is incomplete. Only scattered fragments have survived. The thirtieth of the so-called letters of the Socratics is presumably from Speusippus to King Philip of Macedonia, in which the writer boasts that his devotion to the king excels that of Isocrates.

Speusippus distinguished several levels of existence, none of which was assigned to the "ideas." The highest level is that of the mathematics, specifically that of the numbers. For the interpreter the main problem is the cohesion of these levels. Aristotle charged that there is no more cohesion among them than between the episodes of a bad tragedy. In spite of this criticism, it has been maintained in recent times that the Neoplatonic conception of a gradual "procession" of being from the absolute One can be traced back, if not to Plato himself, at least to the younger members of the Academy, Speusippus and Xenocrates. That Speusippus was one and possibly the first of the thinkers who conceived of an ontological step-by-step descent without any traces of a dualistic idealism was most impressively argued by Merlan, who supported his claim by information on Speusippus' doctrine, which he had discovered in Iamblichus' *De communi mathematica scientia.*

Regarding Aristotle's criticism of Speusippus as a disjointer, Merlan suggests that it is not aimed at the absence but at the weakness of the vinculum that connects the levels. Not only must any temporal connotation be kept away from this "procession," but the bond that holds together the parts amounts to no more than an analogy (Merlan, p. 118).

Speusippus recognizes two principles of being, which are of unequal rank. The absolutely first principle is the One, which transcends existence like the One of Plotinus, from which it differs, however, in that it is not identical with the Good. Its inferior counterpart is called the Multitude. On each level of existence being is generated by principles that are analogous to the absolute One and its counterpart. In arithmetic, for example, the first principle is the One, in geometry it is the point.

A large proportion of Speusippus fragments comes from his work Ὅμοια ("Similar Things") and deals with zoological classifications. They contain a wealth of detailed information, which has been shown to be very similar to accounts of genera and species of animals in Aristotle's *Historia animalium* (Lang, pp. 9–15). The principle of Speusippus' classifications is a modified form of the Platonic diaeresis. The importance of such classifications can be inferred from Speusippus' assumption that every being is fully determined by the totality of its logical relations to all other beings. This seems to correspond to the doctrine that the concatenation of the levels of existence is constituted by logical relations (analogies).

BIBLIOGRAPHY

I. ORIGINAL WORKS. A collection of fragments is in Paulus Lang, *De Speusippi Academici scriptis. Accedunt fragmenta* (Bonn, 1911; repr., Frankfurt, 1964). A new fragment was discovered by R. Klibansky; see *Parmenides . . . nec non Procli Commentarium in Parmenidem interprete Guillelmo de Moerbeka*, R. Klibansky and C. Labowsky, eds. (London 1953), 38. For the letter to King Philip of Macedonia, see E. Bickermann and J. Sykutris, "Speusipps Brief an König Philipp . . .," in *Berichte. Sächsische Akademie der Wissenschaften*, **80**, fasc. 3 (Leipzig, 1928).

II. SECONDARY LITERATURE. See also the following, listed chronologically: J. Ravaisson, *Speusippi de primis rerum principiis placita* (Paris, 1838); Ernst Hambruch, *Logische Regeln der platonischen Schule in der aristotelischen Topik* (Berlin, 1904); E. Zeller, *Die Philosophie der Griechen*, 5th ed., II, pt. 1 (1922), 986, n. 3, and 996–1010; E. Frank, *Plato und die sogenannten Pythagoreer* (Halle, 1923), 239–261; J. Stenzel, "Speu-

sippos," in Pauly-Wissowa, *Real-Encyclopädie der classischen Altertumswissenschaft*, 2nd ser., III (1929), 1636–1669; H. Cherniss, *Aristotle's Criticism of Plato and the Academy* (Baltimore, 1944), and *The Riddle of the Early Academy* (Berkeley, 1945; repr., New York, 1962), 31–43 and *passim*; H. J. Krämer, *Der Ursprung der Geistesmetaphysik* (Amsterdam, 1964), 207–223; and P. Merlan, in *The Cambridge History of Later Greek and Early Medieval Philosophy* (Cambridge, 1967), 30–32, and esp. *From Platonism to Neoplatonism*, 3rd rev. ed. (The Hague, 1968).

ERNST M. MANASSE

SPHUJIDHVAJA (*fl.* western India, A.D. 269), *astronomy, astrology.*

Sphujidhvaja, who was a Yavanarāja or "official in charge of foreigners," apparently in the kingdom of the Mahākṣatrapas of Ujjayinī in western India, wrote a *Yavanajātaka* in 269, when Rudrasena II (*ca.* 255–277) was reigning. His work was a versification (in *upendravajrā* meter) of a prose translation into Sanskrit of a Greek astrological textbook made by Yavaneśvara in 149. This poem became the foundation of genethlialogy and of interrogational astrology in India, adapting the foreign Greco-Egyptian material for an Indian context; with a lost translation of another Greek text available to Satya (*ca.* 300) it formed the basis of the *Vṛddhayavanajātaka* of Mīnarāja (*ca.* 325–350) and of the *Bṛhajjātaka* of Varāhamihira (*ca.* 550). But besides this Indianized Greek material from Yavaneśvara, Sphujidhvaja drew upon traditional Indian *āyurveda* for his materia medica, and upon the Indian adaptations of Mesopotamian astronomy presented in the *Jyotiṣavedāṅga* of Lagadha (fifth or fourth century B.C.?) and of Greco-Babylonian linear planetary theory in his chapter on astronomical computations (see essay in Supplement). His curious mixture of various traditions indifferently comprehended is characteristic of the exact sciences in India.

BIBLIOGRAPHY

Several passages from the *Yavanajātaka* are discussed by D. Pingree in the following articles: "A Greek Linear Planetary Text in India," in *Journal of the American Oriental Society*, **79** (1959), 282–284; "The Yavanajātaka of Sphujidhvaja," in *Journal of Oriental Research*, **31** (1961–1962), 16–31; "The Indian Iconography of the Decans and Horās," in *Journal of the Warburg and Courtauld Institutes*, **26** (1963), 223–254; and "Representation of the Planets in Indian Astrology," in *Indo-*

Iranian Journal, **8** (1965), 249–267. The text is edited, translated, and furnished with an elaborate commentary by D. Pingree, *The Yavanajātaka of Sphujidhvaja*, *Harvard Oriental Series* (Cambridge, Mass., in press).

DAVID PINGREE

SPIEGEL, ADRIAAN VAN DEN (also **Spieghel, Spigelius, Spiegelius, Adriano Spigeli**) (*b*. Brussels, Belgium, 1578; *d*. Padua, Italy, 7 April 1625), *botany, anatomy, medicine*.

Spiegel was named for his father and his grandfather, both of whom were surgeons; his mother was Barbara Geens. In 1588 his father was appointed inspector general of the military and naval surgeons of the Dutch Republic; he died in 1600, leaving two sons. Adriaan's (probably younger) brother Gijsbertus became a surgeon at the ducal hospital in Florence. Adriaan studied at the universities of Louvain and Leiden, and later at Padua, where he inscribed his name in the register of the Natio Germanica on 28 March 1601. At Padua he studied under Fabrici and Casserio. It is generally believed that he graduated before 1604, but his name has not been found in the registers of the Sacrum Collegium that granted the degrees to Catholic students. (It is possible that he had not yet become a Catholic and therefore graduated privately.)

In 1606 Spiegel was appointed ordinary physician to the students of the Natio Germanica. Probably he assisted Fabrici in his private practice; certainly he accompanied the old man on a trip to Florence and on another to Venice, where Fabrici gave a consultation. During these years Spiegel studied botany and wrote an introduction to the science, *Isagoge in rem herbariam libri duo* (1606), which he dedicated to the students of the Natio Germanica. In 1607 he competed unsuccessfully for the chair of practical medicine at Padua, left vacant by the death of Ercole Sassonia. In 1612 he left Italy for Belgium. He remained there briefly, however, then traveled through Germany and finally settled in Moravia. Soon afterward he became *medicus primarius* of Bohemia.

On 22 December 1616 the Venetian Senate appointed Spiegel professor of anatomy and surgery. He succeeded Casserio, who had replaced Fabrici after the latter's retirement in 1608. On 17 January 1617 Spiegel performed a public anatomy demonstration in the famous theater at Padua, where in the following years he attracted many foreign students to his public performances. On 25 January 1623 he was elected knight of St. Mark.

He died two years later after an illness of some six weeks—according to one version, as a result of an infection resulting from an injury caused by the breaking of a glass at the wedding of his only daughter Anzoletta (7 February 1625); according to another version because, weakened by his studies, he had no resistance to a feverish disease that ended in a liver abscess.

During Spiegel's lifetime only the *Isagoge*, a work on the tapeworm, and one on malaria (*febris semitertiana*) were published. He did, however, leave some important manuscripts. His son-in-law, Liberalis Crema, published a book on embryology (*De formatu foetu*); and Daniel Rindfleisch, better known as Bucretius, edited his great anatomical work, *De humani corporis fabrica*. It is said that Spiegel entrusted the editing of this book to Bucretius on his deathbed or in his will. Since the manuscript lacked illustrations, Bucretius obtained the beautiful plates that Casserio had had made by a German draftsman and engraver named Josias Murerus (Joseph Maurer). Bucretius added ninety-eight of these fine copperplates to Spiegel's work, separately paginated and under the name of Casserio. These splendid engravings contributed much to the success and fame of the work. Some faults in the text have been indicated, however. J. Riolan the younger blamed Bucretius for them, accusing him of having altered the original text. Nevertheless, the work established Spiegel's renown as an anatomist.

Spiegel's name appears in two anatomical terms: the *linea Spigelii* (the semilunar line between the muscle and the aponeurosis of the *transversus abdominis*) and the *lobus caudatus hepatis* (Spigelii), which, however, had already been described by Eustachi and others.

BIBLIOGRAPHY

I. ORIGINAL WORKS. Spiegel's writings include *Isagoge in rem herbariam libri duo* (Padua, 1606, 1608; Leiden, 1633, 1673; Helmstedt, 1667), 1633 ed. with *Catalogus plantarum* of Leiden and the surrounding area; *De lumbrico lato liber, cum notis et ejusdem lumbrici icone* (Padua, 1618), with a letter, *De incerto tempore partus*; *De semitertiana libri quatuor* (Frankfurt, 1624); *De formatu foetu liber singularis, aeneis figuris ornatus. Epistolae duae anatomicae. Tractatus de arthritide, opera posthuma* (Padua, 1626; Frankfurt, 1631), see also Meyer (below); *De humani corporis fabrica libri X, cum tabulis 98 aeri incisis*, Daniel Bucretius, ed. (Venice, 1627; Frankfurt, 1632), also with other works (Venice, 1654); "Consultatio de lithotomia, *sive calculi vesicae sectione*," a letter included in Johan van Beverwijck, *De calculo renum et vesicae* (Leiden, 1638), in all eds. and translations of this book but not in vander Linden; and *Adriani Spigelii Bruxellensis . . . opera quae extant omnia*, edited, with a preface, by J. A. vander Linden, 2 vols. in 3 pts. (Amsterdam, 1645), which includes works by others—such as Harvey's *De motu cordis*—a short biography, and a portrait.

II. SECONDARY LITERATURE. Spiegel's accomplishments as a botanist are evaluated in M. Morren, "Adrien Spiegel," in *Revue de Bruxelles*, **1** (Feb. 1838), 51–79.

The following articles deal with Spiegel's life and his contributions to medicine: C. van Bambeke, in Académie royale . . . de Belgique, *Biographie nationale*, XXIII (1921–1924), 330–334; C. Broeckx, *Essai sur l'histoire de la médecine belge* (Brussels, 1838), 311–312; Pietro Capparoni, "Cinque lettre inedite di Adriaan van den Spiegel (Adriano Spigeli)," in *Bollettino dell'Istituto storico italiano dell'arte sanitaria*, **10** (1930), 248–253; Giuseppe Favaro, "Contributo alla biografia di A. Spigeli (Adriaan van den Spiegel) nel terzo centenario della sua morte (1625–1925)," in *Atti del Istituto veneto di scienze, lettere ed arti*, **85**, pt. 2 (1925–1926), 213–252; J. B. Marinus, "Éloge de van den Spiegel (Adrien)," in *Bulletin de l'Académie royale de médecine*, **5** (1846), 842–860, also issued separately (Brussels, 1846); A. W. Meyer, "The Elusive Human Allantois in Older Literature," in E. Ashworth Underwood, ed., *Science, Medicine and History* (London–New York–Toronto, 1953), 510–520, with an English trans. of Spiegel's work on the allantois in ch. 5 of his *De formatu foetu*, 512–513; and A. Portal, *Histoire de l'anatomie et de la chirurgie*, II (Paris, 1770), 449–455.

G. A. LINDEBOOM

SPIEGELIUS. See **Spiegel, Adriaan van den.**

SPIX, JOHANN BAPTIST VON (*b.* Höchstadt an der Aisch, Germany, 9 February 1781; *d.* Munich, Germany, 15 May 1826), *zoology.*

Spix was the son of a surgeon and *Bürgerrath*. He studied theology at Bamberg and Würzburg, where he decided in 1804 to pursue medicine instead. He graduated M.D. and in 1811 was made an *Adjunkt* of the Munich Academy; he later became a full member and curator of the zoological collections. In 1815 he and K. F. P. Martius were selected by the Bavarian government to take part in an expedition to South America; in April 1817 they left Trieste in the retinue of the Austrian Archduchess Leopoldina, who had just married the crown prince of Brazil (later Emperor Dom Pedro I). Their party, which also included a number of Austrian scientists, reached Rio de Janeiro in July,

and by December of the same year Spix and Martius had set off into the interior to work independently.

Spix and Martius visited the provinces of São Paolo and Minas Gerais, then continued through Minas Novas to Salvador, where they arrived in November 1818, having suffered heat and drought. They sailed to the Amazon estuary by way of Pernambuco, Piauí, and São Luís, at the mouth of the Itapecuru. Spix then left Martius and proceeded upstream as far as the Peruvian frontier, reaching Tabatinga in January 1820. He explored the Rio Negro, then returned to Manaus, where he met Martius. Together they returned in April 1820 to Pará, from which they embarked for Europe two months later. They were back in Munich in December 1820, having accomplished one of the most important scientific expeditions of the nineteenth century.

Spix and Martius were the first European scientists to visit the Amazon after La Condamine. Their collections—including specimens of eighty-five species of mammals, 350 species of birds, nearly 2,700 species of insects, and fifty-seven living animals—provided material for a vast number of works by other scientists. Spix himself was occupied entirely with publishing his findings after his return to Munich. He had planned to expand his study of the skull, published in 1815, and he also had projected a study, for which he had collected a considerable amount of material, of the subterranean zoography and phytography of Bavaria, but he was unable to realize either of these works. Weakened by the fevers that he had suffered on his voyage, he died, leaving other zoologists, including Louis Agassiz, to complete the publication of his works.

BIBLIOGRAPHY

I. ORIGINAL WORKS. *Geschichte und Beurtheilung aller Systeme in der Zoologie nach ihrer Entwicklungsfolge von Aristoteles bis auf die gegenwärtige Zeit* (Nuremberg, 1811) includes a discussion of the difference between "natural" and "artificial" systems. In this book, which follows the German *Naturphilosophen*, Spix differs with Lamarck, who stated that the species was the only natural group. *Cephalogenesis s. capitis ossei structura, formatio et significatio . . .* (Munich, 1815), on the structure of the skull throughout the animal kingdom, lacks importance for zoology. *Reise in Brasilien . . . in den Jahren 1817–20 gemacht und beschrieben von J. B. von Spix und C. Fr. Ph. von Martius.* is in

3 vols. (Munich, 1823–1831), vols. II and III written by Martius. Vol. I was translated into English by H. E. Lloyd, 2 vols. (London, 1824). See also Royal Society, *Catalogue of Scientific Papers*, V, 779.

II. SECONDARY LITERATURE. See *Allgemeine deutsche Biographie*, XXXV (1893), 231–232; and C. F. P. von Martius, *Akademische Denkreden* (Leipzig, 1866), 599–601. On the expedition see Hermann Ross, "Dem Andenken der Forschungsreise von Spix und Martius in Brasilien 1817–1820," in *Berichte der Deutschen botanischen Gesellschaft*, 35 (1917), 119–128.

A. P. M. SANDERS

SPOERER, GUSTAV FRIEDRICH WILHELM (*b.* Berlin, Germany, 23 October 1822; *d.* Giessen, Germany, 7 July 1895), *astronomy.*

Spoerer attended the Friedrich Wilhelm Gymnasium in his native city and in 1840–1843 studied mathematics and astronomy at Berlin University, where he attended the lectures of Encke and Dove. He concluded his studies with the dissertation "De cometa qui a. 1723 apparuit," defended on 14 December 1843. Thereafter Spoerer worked with Encke at the Berlin observatory, performing astronomical computations, and passed the examination for teaching mathematics and sciences in 1846. He taught subsequently at the secondary schools of Bromberg (now Bydgoszcz, Poland) and Prenzlau, and in 1849 moved to Anklam, where he was awarded the title of professor.

In this era such a position afforded an opportunity for scientific work, which was expected by the Ministry of Education. Spoerer gave much more than was customary, especially in his astronomical observations, most of which concerned sunspots. For these efforts in 1868 the crown prince of Prussia presented Spoerer with a parallactic mounted refractor with a five-inch aperture, which made possible more and better observations. In the same year Spoerer participated in an expedition with Friedrich Tietjen and F. W. R. Engelmann to observe a total solar eclipse in India.

In 1874 Spoerer was appointed an observer at the planned astrophysical observatory in Potsdam and moved to that city. Until the building was completed, he continued to make observations of sunspots with his own instrument, mounted on a tower in the city.

Spoerer's main accomplishments were his very careful observations of the sun. He determined the elements of the solar rotation and improved the law for the decrease of the rotation and improved the law for the decrease of the rotation of the sun from the equator to the poles, already derived by Carrington. His statistics for 1879–1893 contain much material on proper motions and on the evolution and distribution of sunspots during a sunspot period.

BIBLIOGRAPHY

Nearly each vol. of *Astronomische Nachrichten* from 55 (1861) to 125 (1890) contains contributions by Spoerer concerning observations of sunspots. Compilations are *Beobachtungen der Sonnenflecken zu Anclam*, 2 vols. (Leipzig, 1874–1876); and "Beobachtungen von Sonnenflecken in den Jahren 1871 bis 1873," *Publikationen des Astrophysikalischen Observatoriums zu Potsdam*, 1, no. 1 (1878); ". . . in den Jahren 1874 bis 1879," ibid., 2, no. 1 (1880); ". . . in den Jahren 1880 bis 1884," ibid., 4, no. 4 (1886); and ". . . in den Jahren 1885 bis 1893," ibid., 10, no. 1 (1894).

There is an obituary by O. Lohse, in *Vierteljahrsschrift der Astronomischen Gesellschaft*, 30 (1895), 208–210.

H.-CHRIST. FREIESLEBEN

SPORUS OF NICAEA (*fl.* second half of third century), *mathematics.*

Little is known of Sporus. The juxtaposition of available historical data makes it likely that he came from Nicaea, was a pupil of Philo of Gadara, and was either the teacher or a slightly older fellow student of Pappus of Alexandria. Our knowledge of Sporus' activities stems only from such secondary sources as the works of Pappus and the writings of various commentators, among them Eutocius and Leontius, a seventh-century engineer.[1] Most historians, with the notable exception of J. L. Heiberg, agree that Sporus was the author of a work entitled Κηρία, noted by Eutocius.[2] They interpret a second reference by Eutocius to an anonymous Κηρία 'Αριστοτελικά[3] as a subsection of Sporus' work, but Heiberg believes this to be a reference to Aristotle's *De sophisticis elenchis.*

From the above sources it appears that Sporus concerned himself intensively with two mathematical problems: that of squaring the circle and that of doubling the cube.[4] Like many Greek mathematicians who attempted to solve them, he was aware that neither has a solution by means of ruler and compass alone. The close relationship of both problems to limiting processes[5] suggests that Sporus was also interested in questions dealing with approximation, since he reportedly criticized Archimedes for having failed to approximate the value of π more accurately.[6]

The value of the ancient Greeks' preoccupation with special mathematical problems of this type clearly lies in the by-products that this study produced. The squaring problem led to the development of special curves, the quadratrix of Hippias, for example; and the doubling-of-the-cube problem resulted in Menaechmus' discovery of the theory of conic sections and produced a refinement of the theory of proportions. Sporus seems to have contributed to the study of these problems chiefly through his constructive criticism of existing solutions. Indeed, his own solution of the doubling-of-the-cube problem essentially coincides with that of Pappus.

Sporus' writings seem to have been a fruitful source of information for Pappus and later scholars. Pappus, in particular, appears to have valued Sporus' reputation and judgment, since he quoted Sporus in support of his own criticism of the use of the quadratrix in the solution of the squaring problem.

Sporus' nonmathematical writings are known essentially only by topics, through references to them in Maass's *Analecta Eratosthenica* and *Commentariorum in Aratum reliquiae*. They consist of scientific essays on subjects such as the polar circle, the size of the sun, and comets. His literary achievements are reported to include a critical edition of the Φαινομενά of Aratus of Soli.

NOTES

1. E. Maass, *Analecta Eratosthenica*, pp. 45, 47–49, 1939, and *Commentariorum in Aratum reliquiae*, p. lxxi.
2. J. L. Heiberg, *Archimedis opera omnia*, 2nd ed., III, p. 258.
3. *Ibid.*, p. 228.
4. T. L. Heath, *A History of Greek Mathematics*, I, pp. 226, 229–230, 234, 266–268.
5. *Ibid.*, pp. 230, 269.
6. J. L. Heiberg, *Archimedis opera omnia*, 2nd ed., III, p. 258.

BIBLIOGRAPHY

See T. L. Heath, *A History of Greek Mathematics*, I (Oxford, 1921), 226, 229–230, 234, 266–268; J. L. Heiberg, ed., *Archimedis opera omnia*, 2nd ed., III (Leipzig, 1915), 228, 258; F. Hultsch, ed., *Pappus, Collectionis quae supersunt*, I (Berlin, 1878), 252; *Lexikon der alten Welt* (Zurich, 1965), 2863; E. Maass, *Analecta Eratosthenica* (Berlin, 1883), 45–49, 139; and *Commentariorum in Aratum reliquiae* (Berlin, 1898), lxxi; Pauly-Wissowa, *Real-Encyclopädie der classischen Altertumswissenschaft*, 2nd ser., III, 1879–1883; G. Sarton, *Introduction to the History of Science*, I (Baltimore, 1927), 331, 338; P. Tannery, "Sur Sporos de Nicée," in *Annales de la Faculté des lettres de Bordeaux*, 4 (1882), 257–261.

MANFRED E. SZABO

SPRAT, THOMAS (*b*. Beaminster, Dorset, England, 1635; *d*. Bromley, Kent, England, 20 May 1713), *history of science.*

Sprat was one of several children born to Thomas Sprat, a poor parish curate who held B.A. and M.A. degrees from Oxford, and his wife, who was the daughter of a Mr. Strode of Parnham, Dorset. From this "obscure birth and education in a far distant country," as he later described it, he entered Wadham College, Oxford, in November 1651, receiving the B.A. in June 1654 and an M.A. three years later. At Wadham, Sprat became a member of the active and soon influential circle that launched him on his surprising and varied career as the historian and defender of the Royal Society and as a man of the church. He became the favorite and protégé of John Wilkins and formed close associations with other members of the scientific group that gathered around Wilkins during those years, especially with Christopher Wren, Seth Ward, and Ralph Bathurst. Although Sprat may possibly have attended their meetings, there is no record of his having done so and no indication that he ever engaged in the sort of scientific work that was their interest.

In 1659 Sprat's first publications appeared. One was a poem, "To the Happy Memory of the Late Lord Protector," dedicated to Wilkins for "having been as it were moulded by your own hands, and formed under your government," and charged with devoted admiration for Cromwell as the great savior who had led his people into the promised land. Sprat's loyalties were always pliable, a fact often noted by his contemporaries, for he later served Charles II, James II, and William and Mary with the same devotion he had expressed for Cromwell. In politics he became a staunch Tory, a defender of the divine rights of kings, and a strong exponent of high church doctrines. He has, not without reason, been called a time-server. In 1659 Sprat also published a poem in praise of the poet Abraham Cowley, written "in imitation of his own Pindaric odes," thus gaining the nickname "Pindaric Sprat." Cowley, who was also known as a promoter of natural philosophy, returned the favor in his "Ode to the Royal Society," prefixed to Sprat's *History of the Royal Society*, when he said that "ne'er did Fortune better yet / Th' Historian to the Story fit."

Sprat's close association with Cowley had important consequences. In accordance with the poet's will, Sprat was charged with the publication of his *English Works*, published in 1668 and often reprinted, for which he wrote "Account of the Life and Writings of Abraham Cowley." Cowley may also have brought Sprat to the attention of George Villiers, second duke of Buckingham, who by the late 1660's was Wilkins' patron. Having been ordained early in 1660, Sprat later that year gained his first ecclesiastical office through the influence of Cowley and the duke, who also helped him to some of his later preferments. During most of the 1660's and perhaps longer, Sprat was the duke's chaplain, and in 1675 he was appointed one of the three trustees for part of Buckingham's estate, a position that may have helped to pay for his well-known love of good living. In August 1676 he became one of the king's chaplains, soon rising steadily to canon of the Chapel Royal, Windsor, near the end of 1680; dean of Westminster in September 1683; and bishop of Rochester in November 1684, holding the last two offices until his death. In 1676 Sprat married Helen, Lady Wolseley, of Ravenstone, Staffordshire, an event that later in that year led Robert Hooke to note in his diary that he "saw fat Tom Sprat joyd him of marriage." Sprat was survived by his wife, who died in February 1726, and by a son, Thomas, archdeacon of Rochester. They were all buried in Westminster Abbey.

Although he was a prominent figure in his time, Sprat's fame today rests entirely on his *History of the Royal Society*, first published in 1667. Its 438 pages constitute a large and puzzling work on an institution barely seven years old when the book appeared. Since its concerns and their implications touched all major aspects of contemporary affairs, not least religion, the infant Royal Society quickly became involved in controversy and detraction, against which even the good fortune of royal patronage proved insufficient. Neither its present position nor its controversial origins during the past twenty years, open to many unwelcome interpretations, was strong enough to allow it to ignore this opposition without risking serious damage to its reputation and success, which depended on wide cooperation and not least on considerable financial support.

It was the first design of the *History* to explain the nature, organization, work, and aims of the Royal Society to the public, thus showing that the promotion of its affairs was a national, even a patriotic, enterprise that promised both a healing of the wounds left by the recent turbulent events and great material benefits. The *History* was a piece of public relations, even of propaganda. The material that went into it was carefully supervised and selected, and its omissions and suppressions are as significant as its contents. It is not an impartial document; and it gave such strong impetus to renewed controversy that it may be doubted whether the Royal Society would not, at least in England, have been better off without this premature piece of justification. The formidable Henry Stubbe said a few years later that Sprat's work was "a nonsensical and illiterate history." It is a curious irony that the early Royal Society has been the center of similar debate in the extensive recent literature on its history.

The *History* is divided into three parts without separate titles. Part one (pp. 1–51) presents a survey of ancient, medieval, and Renaissance philosophy that is meant to show "what is to be expected from these new undertakers, and what moved them to enter upon a way of inquiry different from that on which the former have proceeded." With exaggeration that mars the conciliatory tone, the Royal Society "most unanimously" follows in the footsteps of antiquity except in "matters of fact: for in them we follow the most ancient author of all others, even Nature itself." It proposes to honor the ancients by being their children rather than their pictures. Here, and often in the rest of the work, Sprat's strong words are reserved for "downright enthusiasts" and the "modern dogmatists," whom he compares to the recent "pretenders to public liberty," who became the greatest tyrants themselves. This political theme recurs forcefully throughout the work—for instance, in a later passage eulogizing Charles I as the royal martyr who followed the "divine example of our Saviour." Sprat finds agreement between the growth of learning and of civil government. Already in this first part Bacon is, as it were, the Royal Society's patron saint, "who had the true imagination of the whole extent of this enterprise, as it is now set on foot." Even members and friends of the Society must have known that this respect for Bacon as the sole intellectual ancestor was exaggerated; but it was necessary in order to rule out the thought of any foreign influence or indebtedness, which an impartial judge would readily have admitted. Both Gassendi and Descartes had been read and admired in England.

Part two (pp. 52–319) contains the history

proper and is chronologically divided into three sections. The first (pp. 52–60) relates the prehistory of the Royal Society up to the first regular meeting on 28 November 1660, tracing its origin exclusively to the meetings that were held "some space after the end of the Civil Wars at Oxford, in Dr. Wilkins his lodgings, in Wadham College." Contradicted repeatedly in the seventeenth century, this brief account has dominated most discussions of Sprat's work and has recently formed the center of much fruitless argument. It will be considered more closely below.

The second section (pp. 60–122) covers the period between the first meeting and the granting of the second royal charter in the spring of 1663. At this time Sprat was proposed for membership by Wilkins and was duly elected. When ninety-four original fellows were elected on 20 May, in accordance with the provisions of the new charter, the Royal Society was firmly established with a large and varied membership. This section is not historical. It explains the nature and aspirations of the Society; its organization, membership, meetings, subject matter, and method of inquiry; its careful interpretation of evidence; and "their manner of discourse," a subject that has received more than its fair share of comment in the secondary literature. These pages contain a panegyric on "the general constitution of the minds of the English" and the special prerogative of England, "whereby it may justly lay claim to be the head of a philosophical league above all other nations in Europe," owing to the "unaffected sincerity," "sound simplicity" of speech, and "universal modesty" that characterize the English as a nation.

This section contrasts the need for cooperative labors and shared verification with Descartes's contemplative method, explains that a division between teachers and scholars is not "consistent with a free philosophical consultation," and suggests that the Royal Society seeks to satisfy the same ambition as the one which at Babel was punished by a "universal confusion" because it "was managed with impiety and insolence." But true knowledge cannot be separated from "humility and innocence": since the Society's ambition "is not to brave the Creator of all things, but to admire him the more, it must needs be the utmost perfection of humane nature."

At this point Sprat observed that the preparation of the *History* had been interrupted for more than a year by the plague (which caused the Royal Society to discontinue its meetings from June 1665 to February 1666) and the great fire of London during the first week of September 1666. Thus, although parts of the rest of the work may have been written before, it was not printed until after this date. The third section (pp. 122–319) of part two tells the story of the Royal Society's work since the spring of 1663. Its first division (pp. 122–157) deals with its reputation and correspondence abroad, and with the encouragement it has received at home from professional and social groups and from the royal family. It concludes with epitomes of the charter of 1663 and of the statutes that had been prepared between June and the end of that year. As late as April 1667 Wilkins was, by order of the Council, directed to prepare these epitomes for the *History*.

The second division (pp. 158–319) of the third section of part two presents fourteen instances "of this their way of inquiring and giving rules for direction . . . from whose exactness it may be guessed, how all the rest are performed," interspersed with Sprat's comments. These papers, not in chronological order, were read before the Royal Society between February 1661 and November 1664. Most of them were also printed in other contemporary publications; and they were drawn from the Society's records under the careful supervision chiefly of Wilkins, who received orders regarding their selection between the end of 1664 and April 1667. The choice was clearly designed to be representative and to have wide appeal both to scientific and, not least, to practical and even lucrative interests. At the end of this part, Sprat confidently observes, "If any shall yet think [the Society] have not usefully employed their time, I shall be apt to suspect, that they understand not what is meant by a diligent and profitable laboring about Nature."

Finally, part three (pp. 321–438) is an apology for the Royal Society that tries to meet all conceivable objections to its enterprise, thus giving a telling picture of the Society's conception of itself in relation to contemporary society, thought, and opinion. Among the many points raised, the following are the most important. The Royal Society poses no threat to learning, education, or the universities. This matter obviously caused some concern, for in the brief account of the Wadham meetings Sprat claimed that they had not only armed many young men against "the enchantments of enthusiasm" but also had helped to save the university itself from ruin. The Society is also a great ally of religion, leading man "to admire the wonderful contrivance of the Creation" so that his praises "will be more suitable to the Divine Nature than the blind applauses of the ignorant," unlike the "enthusiast that pollutes his religion with his own passions." Indeed, experiments are necessary to separate true miracles from falsehoods, and they especially support the Church of England by the agreement that exists "between the present design of the Royal Society and that of our Church in its beginning: They both may lay equal claim to the word reformation." It is Sprat's conviction that "The universal disposition of this age is bent upon a rational religion." Finally, the Society offers great benefits to all manual arts, to trade, to "wits and writers," and to "the interests of our nation." The *History* concludes with a list of all present fellows of the Society up to June 1667.

By early summer the *History* was in the press; in mid-August Pepys saw a copy at the booksellers; at the end of September several persons had read it; and on 10 October 1667 it was presented to the Society by Wilkins, hearty thanks being "ordered to the author for his singular respect to the Society shewed in that book." That it did not, although issued by its printers, bear the Royal Society's imprimatur may indicate some hesitancy to grant it, since this procedure was normal for books encouraged by the Society or written by its fellows, in accordance with the provisions of the royal charter. The *History* sold well, for some six months later Oldenburg reported that the first printing—presumably 1,000 copies—was nearly gone. The work was greatly praised in England and immediately gained the somewhat exaggerated reputation for eloquence and style that has been conventional ever since.

For nearly three years Oldenburg had been announcing the work's imminent publication to his correspondents on the Continent, and at last he could satisfy the inquiries that had kept streaming in. He sent out copies with elaborate covering letters inviting cooperation, an effort that soon proved successful in the form of further inquiries about details of experiments and other matters described in the *History*, although several correspondents complained that their poor English would deny full benefit until they had Latin or French translations. The Royal Society immediately tried to supply them, but only an unsanctioned French translation was published, in identical versions at Geneva and Paris in 1669 and 1670. Thus, as a careful exercise in public relations, Sprat's work confirmed his hope that "this learned and inquisitive age will . . . think [the Society's] endeavours worthy of its assistance."

From the seventeenth century to the present day, the main problem raised by Sprat's work has always been its historical reliability. As early as 1756, Thomas Birch explained in the preface to his own *History of the Royal Society* that part two of Sprat's account was less admired than the others; and he could cite well-informed contemporary opinion for his wish that the history of the Royal Society's "institution and progress" had omitted less and given more facts, and that "the order of time in which they occurred had been more exactly marked." At the very least, Birch was certainly thinking of Sprat's silence on the London meetings in 1645 attended by John Wallis, who in the meantime had given two detailed accounts of them. Their relevance to the prehistory of the Society has been denied—at the cost of creating an unconvincing, ad hoc image of the early post-1660 Society, built on interpretations and arguments so bizarre and ill-informed that they disprove themselves.

In addition to Wallis' two accounts, both of which include Wilkins, it is well-known that since the early 1640's Wilkins had taken a strong interest in natural philosophy, was present in London in the mid-1640's, and in other ways was associated with the people he met at those early gatherings. A further piece of information must be accorded high authority, although it seems not to have been previously cited in this context. It occurs in the Royal Society's official memorial on Wilkins' death, read on 27 November 1672, and it plainly says: "He had been one of that assembly of learned men, who met as early as 1645, and continued their meetings at London and Oxford, until they were formed into the Royal Society" (Birch, *History*, III, 68).

Clearly, the *History* is not reliable on matters of fact; it cannot, as has been claimed, be considered an impartial account written under the supervision of those who had all the information. They may have had it but not wished to use it all. And if less than dependable on this point, the *History* may be so on others, where similar interests were at stake. Well aware of French competition that might challenge its priority, and understandably concerned about some prominent members' actions and allegiances during the 1640's, the Society's interests demanded that its official history omit information that cast doubt on its pure Englishness, on its agreement with the Church of England, and on its loyalty to the restored monarchy. The early London meetings were embarrassing on all counts. There is good reason to accept Wallis' statement that they were suggested by Theodore Haak, a foreigner who had received the suggestion from his French connections, especially from Marin Mersenne, with whom he had then for some years been in correspondence on matters of this sort. At the time both Haak and Wallis were active in the Westminster Assembly; and Haak was associated not only with Comenian circles but also with Comenius, who by 1660, if not earlier, had become anathema owing to his strong millenarianism and defense of the apocalyptic prophets—no doubt Sprat's strong words against enthusiasm are also aimed at Comenius. Tracing the Royal Society's origins only to Wilkins' Wadham group and Oxford ensured respectability. But there would seem to have been more involved than this.

Fortunately we have a great deal of information about the composition, supervision, and uncertain progress of Sprat's work. Referring to the two secretaries, Oldenburg and Wilkins, and their authority "to publish whatever shall be agreed upon by the Society," Sprat said that he was not usurping their prerogative, "for it is only my hand that goes, the substance and direction came from one of them." That man undoubtedly was Wilkins, and Oldenburg seems to have had little to do with the project. The records abundantly demonstrate that the historical part was closely supervised, not only by Wilkins but also by several small groups of fellows, from 21 December 1664 until it went to press. That the choice fell on Sprat is perhaps not surprising: young, energetic (although, before it was finished, Oldenburg complained that the *History* was in "lazy hands"), available, an intimate of Wilkins and perhaps also recommended by Cowley, he had the time that others, especially Wilkins, could hardly have spared. But it might also—for the sake of distance—have been thought useful that the writer not have lived through the entire history of the last decades. Given the sort of image the Royal Society needed, Wilkins was safer in the background, unknown to the public, than as the official historian. Capable but busy, Oldenburg was no doubt ruled out by his German origin and perhaps by other considerations as well. Sprat was a useful and willing tool.

The first mention of a history dates from May 1663, immediately after the second charter and the election of the ninety-four additional original fellows, when Robert Moray wrote to Huygens that the Royal Society would soon publish a small treatise about itself. At the end of the year, again in a letter to Huygens, this work was for the first time called the "history of the Society," intended to accompany the statutes when they were printed, which was believed to be soon. Nothing was heard of the project until November 1664, when Olden-

burg wrote to two correspondents that the history was nearly finished and would "we hope, be published soon," and informed Boyle that Sprat intended to give it to the printer in early December. Brouncker, Moray, Wilkins, Evelyn, and others had read it; "but we are troubled," Oldenburg added, "that you cannot have a sight of it, before the publication," for he was worried "whether there be enough said of particulars, or . . . whether there are performances enough for a Royal Society, that has been at work so considerable a time." So far there was indication that the Society had supervised the work; but within a month, and then repeatedly, well before the plague caused the meetings to be discontinued, it began active supervision and selection of suitable materials for Sprat. There is no doubt that this change was caused by the publication, in May 1664, of Samuel Sorbière's *Relation d'un voyage en Angleterre*, addressed to the French king in the form of a letter dated 25 October 1663 (with a dedication dated 12 December). Sorbière had spent three months in England, beginning in early June 1663, seeing several prominent members of the Society, attending a number of its meetings, and becoming a member on the same day as Christiaan Huygens.

The *Relation* was soon answered by Sprat in the form of a long letter addressed to Christopher Wren, dated 1 August 1664 and published in 1665 under the title *Observations on Monsieur de Sorbière's Voyage Into England*. It was an unfair and defamatory pamphlet, in which Evelyn may have had a share, commensurate with the provocation Sprat felt, "for having now under my hands the History of the Royal Society, it will be in vain for me to try to represent its design to be advantageous to the glory of England, if my countrymen shall know that one who calls himself a member of that assembly has escaped unanswered in the public disgraces, which he has cast on our whole nation." A brief view of the reasons for this violent reaction will explain the aim and reliability of Sprat's *History*.

Sorbière was a somewhat unsteady and superficial character with considerable talent and flair. Some unwise political implications of the *Relation* had caused such strong displeasure in both England and Denmark that Louis XIV banished Sorbière to Nantes; but before the end of the year he had been pardoned, partly owing to the intercession of Charles II through diplomatic channels. Having also heard that some members of the Royal Society were preparing an answer, the king ordered them to desist. Thus the issue in fact concerned the Royal Society alone. As was usual in contemporary travel accounts, Sorbière had made some critical observations on individuals and on English history and institutions, but in general the *Relation* gave a very favorable picture of England and especially of the Royal Society. Sprat, however, dealt only with the criticism, often with obvious misrepresentation of his source. He chided Sorbière for reducing the Society to triviality in his account of its meetings, although clearly no such effect was either intended or expressed. He rejected Sorbière's statement that Hobbes was Bacon's follower in natural philosophy, "between whom there is no more likeness than there is between St. Gregory and the Waggoner." Sorbière's intimacy with Hobbes was a strong irritant: they met several times during Sorbière's English visit—in fact, one of his reasons for going to England was to see Hobbes, whose early work he had translated into French in the 1640's. Worst of all, Sprat claimed—again incorrectly—Sorbière had said that the Royal Society relied upon books for its knowledge of nature and that it divided into sects and parties, the mathematicians holding to Descartes and the men of general learning to Gassendi, "whereas neither of these two men bear any sway amongst them." With the exception of Hobbes, wisely not mentioned in that work, these matters were all made prominent in the *History*, which also shared with the *Observations* Sprat's patriotic defense of English politics and religion, about which Sorbière had said much that was now better forgotten.

Sprat's suppressions are equally telling. He does not refer to Sorbière's statements that he went to England to see his friends and to inform himself about the state of science in England; that the Royal Society's history was being prepared (the first public mention); that as secretary of the Montmor Academy in Paris he knew Oldenburg, who while in Paris as tutor to Boyle's nephew Richard Jones had "constantly" attended its meetings from the spring of 1659 to the spring of 1660, a matter easily attested by other sources and well known to the Society, which in fact had very cordial relations with that Academy during the early 1660's; and that the establishment of the Royal Society had been preceded by the establishment of the Montmor Academy. The official beginning of the latter is placed in 1657, but it was known to have its ancestry in Mersenne's meetings during the 1640's, which through Haak connect with the early London meetings in 1645. Sprat's silence on the Montmor Academy is notable also in the *History*, which cites only a single institution akin to the Royal Society, although only as a "modern academy for language"—the French Academy, well-known for its hostility to natural philosophy in those very years. This undoubtedly was the crux of the matter: only by suppressing all mention of the London meetings and of the Montmor Academy in favor of Wilkins' Wadham circle was it possible to preserve priority and originality for the Royal Society, for Bacon, and for England.

There is finally one aspect of Sorbière's *Relation* that could not escape any informed reader. Addressed to Louis XIV, the work clearly had as its primary aim, very cleverly pursued by a judicious balance between praise and criticism, to goad the king into official support and patronage for a French academy of science, an effort Sorbière is known to have begun before he went to England, just as the French king is also known to have sought secret intelligence of the state of learning in England at the same time, the eventful spring of 1663. The publication of Sorbière's *Relation* had created a crisis. Sprat put aside his *History* to write his *Observations*, and the Royal Society intervened with its supervision late in 1664 because it felt that it was now openly in a race with Paris and shared Oldenburg's fears that the *History*, in its late 1664 version, did not say enough about details and accomplishments for a society that had "been at work so considerable a time." Thus Sprat's *History* is thoroughly unreliable as history in our sense of the word. Far from ensuring impartiality and truth, the supervision was designed to suppress known but discomfiting facts. That the work also, in this respect, was transformed into a piece of propaganda shows the Society's sense of its vulnerability.

For these reasons, whatever the truth (which may not now be ascertainable and may not matter much), Sprat's *History* cannot be used to refute such accounts as Gian Domenico Cassini's, in *Recueil d'observations faites en plusieurs voyages* (1693), to the effect that on his return to England in 1660, Oldenburg "gave the occasion for the formation of the Royal Society." The general attitude of the Society to the whole matter may be reflected in its reaction to the suggestion that Sorbière be omitted from the lists of the Society, made and favored on 13 November 1666 in a meeting of the Council—which, however, did not have the power to do so. The following day, a vote taken at a meeting of the Society showed fourteen in favor of continuance, eight against.

Sprat was only thirty-two when the *History* was published but never again took any part in the Society's affairs, although he remained a member until his death. Owing to his increasingly conservative politics and his services to changing monarchs, he soon assumed many high offices in the church, although not so high as he had hoped and others expected; he did not become archbishop of York when that see fell vacant in 1686. During the reign of James II, he was an active member of the "infamous" ecclesiastical commission but ultimately terminated its effectiveness when he resigned in August 1688, refusing to prosecute the clergy who had not read the king's Declaration for Liberty of Conscience, although three months earlier he had himself caused much displeasure in London by insisting that it be read in Westminster Abbey. In May 1685 Sprat brought out a tendentious account of the Rye House Plot, written at the request of the king; but he later evaded James's command to write an account of the Monmouth Rebellion. Only a few years later he assisted at the coronation of William and Mary.

Sprat often preached in London, where Evelyn heard him no fewer than seventeen times between 1676 and 1694, always with the greatest praise for "that great wit Dr. Sprat." The sermons extol the monarchy and reason with as much spirit as they denounce "the Romish tyranny" and "the Anabaptistical Madness and Enthusiastical Phrensies of these last ages."

In May 1692, Sprat was the victim of a fantastic blackmail attempt, complete with a forged incriminating document secretly placed in a vase in his palace, purporting to show that he was involved in a conspiracy to restore James II. It caused him great embarrassment, with house arrest and close examination by his peers, before the forgery was found out. For the rest of his life Sprat celebrated the day of his deliverance. He wrote a vastly entertaining account of the plot and the intriguing characters who perpetrated it. It may be argued that this is his best piece of writing.

Estimates of Sprat's character have not been unanimous, either by his contemporaries or by posterity. Gilbert Burnet was not one of his friends, but on Sprat's death he wrote a sketch for which there is support in other contemporary sources: "His parts were bright in his youth, and gave great hopes: but these were blasted by a lazy, libertine course of life, to which his temper and good nature carried him without considering the duties, or even the decencies of his profession. He was justly esteemed a great master of our language, and one of our correctest writers." Swift said that Burnet's estimate was false. Still, both the

Observations on Sorbière's Voyage and the *History of the Royal Society* show qualities that would seem to have belonged also to the man.

BIBLIOGRAPHY

I. ORIGINAL WORKS. There is a mimeographed bibliography by Harold Whitmore Jones and Adrian Whitworth, "Thomas Sprat 1635–1713, Check List of His Works and Those of Allied Writers" (Queen Mary College, Univ. of London, 1952). The *Observations on Monsieur de Sorbière's Voyage* was reissued in 1668, and again in 1709 in a volume that also contained the first English translation of Sorbière's *Relation* and of François Graverol's "Memoirs for the Life of M. Samuel Sorbière." The *Relation* was published in German and Italian in 1667 and 1670. Sprat's *History* was reissued at London in 1702, 1722, and 1734. It has recently been made available in a facsimile reprint "edited with critical apparatus by Jackson I. Cope and Harold Whitmore Jones" in the series Washington University Studies (St. Louis, Mo., 1958). The introduction and notes are useful also for bibliography, but are weak on the actual *History* itself, paying more attention to contemporary controversy, especially to Joseph Glanvill and Henry Stubbe. Unfortunately, this edition does not supply an adequate table of contents and, astonishingly, has no index. Some of Sprat's sermons were printed during his lifetime, but these are all among the ten printed in *Sermons Preached on Several Occasions* (London, 1722). None of the sermons heard by Evelyn is among them. *A True Account and Declaration of the Horrid Conspiracy to Assassinate the Late King Charles II at the Rye-House* was reissued in 3 vols., Edmund Goldsmid, ed., as Collectanea Adamantaea, XIV (Edinburgh, 1886). *A Relation of the Late Wicked Contrivance of Stephen Blackhead and Robert Young, Against the Lives of Several Persons, by Forging an Association Under Their Hands*, 2 pts. (London, 1692), is in *Harleian Miscellany*, VI (London, 1745), 178–254. Sprat's few poems were often reprinted in various collections during the eighteenth century.

II. SECONDARY LITERATURE. There is no full life of Sprat, and the materials for one hardly exist. There is a very brief life in E. Curll, *Some Account of the Life and Writings of the Right Reverend Father in God, Thomas Sprat, D.D.* (London, 1715); it also contains Sprat's will. Much detail is in H. W. Jones, "Thomas Sprat (1635–1713)," in *Notes and Queries*, **197** (5 Jan. 1952), 10–14 and (15 Mar. 1952), 118–123; this is meant to supplement the entry in the *Dictionary of National Biography*. There is much information about Sprat and his *History* in most of the well-known seventeenth-century sources. The most important are the following. Thomas Birch, *The History of the Royal Society*, 4 vols. (London, 1756–1757), has been reissued in facsimile reprint by A. Rupert and Marie Boas Hall as Sources of Science, no. 44 (New York–London, 1968): there is a very incomplete index of names and subjects at the beginning of vol. I. Since Birch's order is strictly chronological, the information drawn from that work can be readily identified. *The Correspondence of Henry Oldenburg*, A. R. and M. B. Hall, eds., II–VII, covers 1663–1672 (Madison, Wis., 1966–1970). Of comparable importance is the correspondence of Christiaan Huygens, in *Oeuvres complètes de Christiaan Huygens*, 22 vols. (The Hague, 1888–1950), with relevant material in II–VII. Sprat's name occurs often in *The Diary of John Evelyn*, 6 vols. (Oxford, 1955), with much information in the excellent notes by the editor, E. S. de Beer.

Balthasar de Monconys, *Journal des voyages de Monsieur de Monconys*, 3rd ed., 3 vols. in 4 pts. (Paris, 1695), III, 1–170, deals with the six weeks he spent in England, where he often saw Sorbière and attended meetings of the Royal Society; where the two accounts cover the same matters, Monconys agrees with Sorbière. *Parentalia, or Memoirs of the Family of the Wrens*, Christopher and Stephen Wren, eds. (London, 1750), has some information about Sprat. Sprat has an entry in Anthony à Wood, *Athenae Oxonienses*, Philip Bliss, ed., IV (London, 1820), cols. 727–730.

Indispensable for reference is *The Record of the Royal Society*, 4th ed. (London, 1940), which reprints the charters and the statutes. General bibliography for the Royal Society can be found in *Isis Cumulative Bibliography 1913–1965*, Magda Whitrow, ed., 2 vols. (London, 1971), II, 749–751; and in Marie Boas Hall, "Sources for the History of the Royal Society," in *History of Science*, **5** (1966), 62–76. Two relevant studies that have appeared since the Hall work are Charles Webster, "The Origins of the Royal Society," *ibid.*, **6** (1967), 106–128 (a review and critique of Margery Purver, *The Royal Society: Concept and Creation* [London, 1967], which is informed by a doctrinal faith in the historical integrity of Sprat's *History*, but the arguments that support this faith are unbelievable); and Quentin Skinner, "Thomas Hobbes and the Nature of the Early Royal Society," in *Historical Journal*, **12** (1969), 217–239.

Valuable for information and bibliography about French academies is Harcourt Brown, *Scientific Organizations in Seventeenth-Century France (1620–1680)* (Baltimore, 1934), to be supplemented by Albert J. George, "The Genesis of the Académie des Sciences," in *Annals of Science*, **3** (1938), 372–401. To Vincent Guilloton goes the credit for first showing that the cause of the Sorbière-Sprat controversy lay in the Royal Society, although he uses only a few of the available sources: "Autour de la *Relation du voyage de Samuel Sorbière en Angleterre*," in *Smith College Studies in Modern Languages*, **11**, no. 4 (July 1930), 1–29. Important further information is in three studies by André Morize: "Samuel Sorbière et son *Voyage en Angleterre*," in *Revue d'histoire littéraire de la France*, **14** (1907), 231–275; "Samuel Sorbière," in *Zeitschrift für französische Sprache und Literatur*, **33** (1908), 214–265, with bibliography of Sorbière's MSS and printed works on 257–265; and "Thomas Hobbes et Samuel Sorbière. Notes

sur l'introduction de Hobbes en France," in *Revue germanique* (Paris), **4** (1908), 193–204. There is a useful essay on Sorbière's philosophical orientation in A. G. A. Balz, *Cartesian Studies* (New York, 1951), 64–79.

Sprat's *History* and the problem of English prose style have been treated in a number of not very fruitful literary studies. The most significant is Francis Christensen, "John Wilkins and the Royal Society Reform of Prose Style," in *Modern Language Quarterly*, **7** (June 1946), 179–187 and (Sept. 1946) 279–290. For general background there are the relevant chapters in R. F. Jones, *Ancients and Moderns*, 2nd ed. (Berkeley–Los Angeles, 1961; paperback, 1965).

HANS AARSLEFF

SPRENGEL, CHRISTIAN KONRAD (*b.* Brandenburg, Germany, 22 September 1750; *d.* Berlin, Germany, 7 April 1816), *botany.*

Sprengel was the last child of Ernst Victor Sprengel (1686–1759), Archdeacon of St. Gotthardt-Gemeinde, and his second wife, Dorothea Gnadenreich Schaeffer (*d.* 1778); and he was the fifteenth child of two marriages.[1] He entered Halle University in 1770 to study theology and philology. Four years later he began teaching in Berlin at the Friedrichs-Hospital School and at the royal military academy. In 1780 he was appointed rector of the Great Lutheran Town School at Spandau, where he taught languages and natural science. His friend Ernst Ludwig Heim, a physician and mycologist, gave instruction in botany to both Sprengel and Alexander von Humboldt. Sprengel in turn shared his knowledge of the Spandau flora with Carl Willdenow. Sprengel's two brothers, Johann Christian and Joachim Friedrich, also studied theology at Halle.[2] The latter taught for a time at the Realschule in Berlin, specializing in history, botany, and mineralogy, and was the father of the botanist Kurt P. Sprengel.

In the summer of 1787 Sprengel began observing the pollination of *Geranium* flowers. These relationships of flower structure, insect visitors, and pollination mechanisms occupied him for the next six years and culminated in the publication of his great work, *Das entdeckte Geheimniss der Natur im Bau und in der Befruchtung der Blumen*, in 1793.[3] Printed in double-column format, it had twenty-five copperplates crowded with 1,117 drawings of floral parts representing 461 species. The striking title page also served as a plate, since the wide border comprised twenty-eight insect and flower drawings. Although it became a milestone on the road to understanding the biology of flowers, Sprengel was greatly disappointed at the book's reception.

Although J. G. Koelreuter had already noted some of the relationships of floral parts, nectar, and insects to pollination, Sprengel went much further in stating that the structure of the flower can be interpreted only by considering the role of each part in relation to insect visits. He noted that color and scent are attractions; that the corolla markings are guides to the hidden nectar; and that grasses have light pollen and are wind-pollinated. His rediscovery of dichogamy (the maturation of anthers and stigmas at different times in the same flower, such that self-pollination cannot occur) led him to one of his major conclusions: "Nature appears not to have intended that any flower should be fertilized by its own pollen."[4] This doctrine, together with the even more important view of the close integration of floral structures with insect visitation, was the first attempt to explain the origin of organic forms from definite relations to the environment. "Since Darwin breathed new life into these ideas by the theory of selection, Sprengel has been recognized as one of its chief supports."[5]

There are a few early comments on Sprengel's book—including a book review, a 1794 letter by Goethe,[6] and a later commentary by his nephew Kurt P. Sprengel. In England, Robert Brown published an article on pollination in 1833, citing two observations from Sprengel.[7] Furthermore, Charles Darwin noted that it was on Brown's advice in November 1841 that he obtained and read "C. K. Sprengel's wonderful book."[8] Perhaps through the work of Brown (and later of Sprengel), Darwin became interested in pollination by insects with observations that began in the summer of 1838. In the chapter "Natural Selection" of the *Origin of Species* (1859) he refers to these observations, and confirms Sprengel's similar ones, on dichogamy: "These plants have in fact separated sexes, and must habitually be crossed. . . . How simply are these facts explained on the view of an occasional cross with a distinct individual being advantageous or indispensable."[9]

Further comments on Sprengel's work are in Darwin's two botanical works, *Orchids* (1862) and *Cross and Self Fertilization* (1876). In the former he refers to Sprengel's "curious and valuable work," to "Sprengel's Doctrine," and again to Sprengel's work that ". . . until lately was often spoken lightly of. No doubt he was an enthusiast, and perhaps carried some of his ideas to extreme length. But I feel sure, from my own observations, that his work contains an immense body of truth."[10] In the latter book Darwin cites Sprengel's notes on the essential role of insects in the pollination of many plants, and says: "He was in advance of his age, and his discoveries were for a long time neglected." Further, he states that Sprengel, while noting that cross-pollination between flowers of the same species occurred, was not ". . . aware that there was any difference in power between pollen from the same plant and from a distinct plant."[11] It remained for Darwin to assess the importance of this for his theory of natural selection.

Sprengel's difficulties at Spandau with school superintendent D. F. Schulze (noted by R. Mittmann [1893] and by O. Recke [1913]) resulted in his being pensioned, leaving Spandau at age forty-four, and moving to Berlin, where he became a private tutor. A proposed second part of *Das entdeckte Geheimniss* was never published, but a small work on bees appeared in 1811 and a work on philology in 1815.[12] Heinrich Biltz,[13] who studied with Sprengel from 1809 to 1813, published a closely drawn character study (1819) that refers to his botanical excursions, to his work in philology, and to his criticism of Linnaeus and Willdenow for their ignorance of Greek. Sprengel did not marry and died in relative obscurity—but not in poverty.[14] Some archival items are known, including seven letters and notes by Sprengel.[15] He is commemorated by the plant genus *Sprengelia* (Epacridaceae).[16]

Were it not for his remarkable book Sprengel would be forgotten today. This work reached Darwin, and the insect-plant mutualism so elegantly and minutely described there profoundly influenced him. Although the two were poles apart in religious beliefs, the elemental natural processes revealed by their studies provided Darwin with evidence for his theory of evolution.

NOTES

1. D. E. Meyer ("Goethes . . .") has clarified the Sprengel genealogy: the first wife of E. V. Sprengel (1686–1759) was Katharina Elisabeth Krause (1692–1732), whose fourth child was Joachim Friedrich, and his son was Kurt P. Sprengel. Thus, the half brothers Joachim Friedrich and Christian Konrad had different mothers. His second wife was "Dorothea, geb. Hopf . . ." (see *Evangelischen Pfarrerbuch für die Mark Brandenburg*, II, pt. 2 [Berlin, 1941], a letter dated 2 October 1972). The account of Christian's birth has been found in the church record of St. Gotthardtgemeinde in Brandenburg as recorded by his father, the archdeacon, with a later note that this was his fifteenth child (occurring in his sixty-fourth year). A copy of this item is in the Botanical Museum in Berlin (D. E. Meyer, "Biographisches . . .").

  A. Krause states that Sprengel's ancestors on his mother's side included the Grunow and Goedicke families; his grandfather was Peter Schaeffer; that in 1799 he was elected an honorary member of the Königliche Bayerische Botanische Gesellschaft, Regensburg; and that a street in Berlin was named for him.

The large E. V. Sprengel family resulted from two marriages, for Peter Nathanael Sprengel (1737–1814) was a "stepbrother of both J. F. and J. C. G. Sprengel." *Das gelehrte Teutschland*, VII (Lemgo, 1798), 588–589. In publications some confusion exists between C. K. Sprengel and Kurt Polykarp Sprengel when first initials are used (the latter often used the Latin form, Curtius Sprengel); and signing letters just "Sprengel" provides further problems.

2. Joachim Friedrich Sprengel wrote *Vorstellung der Kräuterkunde in Gedächtnisstafeln* (Greifswald, 1754); see G. A. Pritzel, *Thesaurus literaturae botanicae* (Leipzig, 1872), no. 8858, p. 303; he also wrote two other works (1751, 1753); see C. G. Kayser, *Vollständiges Bücher-Lexicon, 1750–1832*, V (Leipzig, 1835), 295; and J. G. Meusel, *Das gelehrte Teutschland*, VII (1798), 582–583.

3. "The Newly Revealed Mystery of Nature in the Structure and Fertilization of Flowers" (Berlin, 1793). The title page at lower left reads "Gezeichnet v. C. K. Sprengel," and at lower right W. Arndt is credited as the engraver. The preface is dated "18 Dec., 1792–C. K. Sprengel, Rektor." The plates were engraved mainly by Johann S. Capieux and bear dates 1791 and 1792; some were by J. Wohlgemuth.

4. Sprengel, *Das entdeckte Geheimniss*, 43.

5. J. von Sachs, *History of Botany*, 415.

6. D. E. Meyer ("Biographisches . . .") noted a letter from Goethe to August Batch (professor of botany, Jena), 26 Feb. 1794. J. W. Goethe, *Goethe's Werke*, edited by order of Grand Duchess Sophie of Saxony, pt. 4, *Goethes Briefe*, X (Weimar, 1892), letter 3044, pp. 143–144. An unsigned book review also has been found in *Göttingische Anzeigen von gelehrten Sachen*, 20 (1793), 1105–1114.

7. R. Brown, "On the Organs and Mode of Fecundation . . .," 687, 717.

8. F. Darwin, ed., *C. Darwin, Life and Letters*, 47. The copy that Brown utilized may be the one now in the library of the Linnean Society of London. Although the copy is not dated or identified (except for a heraldic bookplate transferred from the former binding), the library stamp would indicate the first half of the nineteenth century (letter, 5 Jan. 1973, G. Bridson, Linnean Society of London). Darwin's copy (with his signature) is on permanent deposit in the Cambridge University Library; it contains Darwin's numerous marginal annotations with evidence that he acquired (presumably by purchase) this work in Aug. 1841 and read it on 10 Nov. 1841 (letter, 5 Jan. 1973, P. J. Gautrey, Cambridge University Library).

9. Pp. 98–99.

10. *Orchids* 2, 27, 275.

11. *Cross and Self Fertilization*, 5, 6

12. *Neue Kritik der classischen römischen Dichter* (1815). E. Strasburger (1893) located a copy in the Leipzig University Library and noted that it comprised 142 pp.; Strasburger comments at some length (pp. 116–117); J. D. Fuss (1824) published a refutation of some of Sprengel's emendations of Ovid's works.

13. See biography of Friedrich Heinrich Biltz (d. 1835) in *Archive der pharmazie*, 54 (1835), 1–25. See also Royal Society, *Catalogue of Scientific Papers*, XII, 82.

14. No notice at his death has been found; Landesarchiv, Berlin, searched the newspaper *Berlinische Nachrichten von staats- und gelehrten Sachen* from 7 Apr. 1816 to the end of May 1816, with no results.

Previous accounts indicate the place of burial was unknown; Hoffmann ("Urkundliches . . .") cites the church register of the Werderschen Kirche for burial "auf dem Kirchhof vor dem Oranienburger Thor"; Landesarchiv Berlin notes also that the Sprengel burial ground was "Friedhof der Dorotheenstädtischen und Friedrich-Wer-

derschen Gemeinden, Chausseestrasse 126" (W. von Wohlberedt), destroyed when roads to Hannover were constructed. G. Hintze, "Rundgang," 84–85.

15. One MS source is D. F. Schulze's "Chronicle" (to 1804), which in 1893 existed as a folio vol. of 1,071 handwritten pp. in St. Nicholas Church at Spandau, later edited by O. Recke (1913); the diaries of E. L. Heim are additional sources (G. L. Kessler, *Der alte Heim*; see also D. Meyer).

P. Hoffmann ("Urkundliches . . .") has provided data from a large number of sources and original documents: birth record; matriculation at Halle; first teaching position; note on H. Biltz (and his article of 28–29 Dec. 1819 in *Morgenblatt für gebildete Stände*); the full text of the original draft of the will (30 Jan. 1816) and the will (5 Feb. 1816); the death certificate of 9 Apr. 1816, signed by Dr. Kohlrausch. Hoffmann notes that Kerner von Marilaun (*Pflanzenleben*, 3rd ed., II, 310) states that although Sprengel's pension was only 150 taler, he left the Berlin orphanage 5,000 taler. In addition he furnishes the death entry in the register of the Werderschen Kirche, Sprengel's correct street address, and his burial record. He provides a picture of the memorial tablet in the Berlin-Dahlem Botanical Garden. See an anonymous article, "J. G. Kölreuter et C. K. Sprengel: Souscription pour leur élever des monuments," in *Isis*, 1 (1913), 243–244.

D. Meyer ("Biographisches . . .") examined some sheets from Willdenow's herbarium (of more than 20,000 specimens) in the Berlin-Dahlem Herbarium and noted three sheets (*Carex, Juncus,* and *Stipa*) that bore the full Latin names in Sprengel's writing (reproduced in Fig. 1, p. 121).

Following an inquiry to Friedrich Vieweg and Son, Brunswick (the firm publishing Sprengel's book of 1793), five Sprengel letters dating from 11 Sept. 1794 to 23 July 1803 have been discovered in their archives (letter, V. Schlecht, 11 Oct. 1972); see P. Forman, "The Archive of Friedr. Vieweg et Sohn, Braunschweig . . .," in *Isis*, 60, pt. 3 (1969), 384–385, which notes that the archives contain possibly between 150,000 and 300,000 items representing roughly 5,000 correspondents. Hoffmann ("Urkundliches . . .") quotes in full a Sprengel letter of 18 Nov. 1781 to the magistrate in Spandau (original in the Darmstadt collection, Deutsche Staatsbibliothek, Berlin). A Sprengel letter of 1793 exists in the Archiv der Akademie der Wissenschaften in Göttingen–card catalog indicates C. C. Sprengel, but the letter is signed "Sprengel." Letter (Jäykkä), Niedersächsische Staats- und Universitätsbibliothek, Göttingen, 27 Sept. 1972. A photocopy of this letter reveals that it is not in the handwriting of C. K. Sprengel. It was sent from Halle and is a note of thanks for election to the Academy (at the age of twenty-seven). This letter was probably from Kurt P. Sprengel. C. K. Sprengel was not elected to this Academy.

16. J. E. Smith, "Description of a New Genus . . ."; see also *Index Kewensis* (Oxford, 1905), IV, 970, which cites a Swedish publication of 1794 in which this new genus was first described. A "Biographische Tafel" in honor of Sprengel has been established at the Heimatsmuseums, Bezirksamt Spandau von Berlin, which owns a Sprengel handwritten note of 1784 (letter, E. Blume, 5 July 1973).

BIBLIOGRAPHY

I. ORIGINAL WORKS. Sprengel's books are *Das entdeckte Geheimniss der Natur im Bau und in der Befruchtung der Blumen* (Berlin, 1793), also facs. ed. as Wissenschaftliche Classiker in Facsimile-Drucken, no. 7 (Berlin, 1893) and edited by P. Knuth as Ostwalds Klassiker der Exakten Wissenschaften, nos. 48–51 (Leipzig, 1894), with biographical notes in I, 180–181; *Die*

Nützlichkeit der Bienen und die Nothwendigkeit der Bienenzucht, von einer neuen Seite dargestellt (Berlin, 1811), also edited, with epilogue, by August Krause (Berlin, 1918); *Neue Kritik der classischen römischen Dichter, in Anmerkungen zu Ovid, Virgil und Tibull* (Berlin, 1815). On the last, see W. Engelmann, *Bibliotheca scriptorum classicorum* (Leipzig, 1882), 467. D. E. Meyer ("Goethes . . .") has revealed two journal articles of Sprengel: "Über die Nectarien; Ankündigung," in *Botanisches Magazin,* 4 (1788), 186; and "Versuch die Konstrucktion der Blumen zu erklärung; Ankündigung," in *Botanisches Magazin,* 8 (1790), 160–164.

II. Secondary Literature. See the anonymous "Hermann Müller's 'Fertilisation of Flowers,'" in *Nature,* 27 (1883), 513–514, a book review; P. Ascherson, "Christian Konrad Sprengel als Florist und als Frucht-Biolog," in *Naturwissenschaftliche Wochenschrift,* 8 (1893), 140–141; and "Zur Erinnerung an Chr. K. Sprengel und sein vor 100 Jahren erschienenes Werk: 'Das entdeckte Geheimniss der Natur im Bau und in der Befruchtung der Blumen,'" in *Verhandlungen des Botanischen Vereins der Provinz Brandenburg,* 35 (1894), viii–xiii; H. B., "Erinnerung an Christian Conrad Sprengel, nebst einigen Bemerkungen aus seinem Leben," in *Flora oder Botanische Zeitung,* 2 (1819), 541–552, repr. in *Mitteilungen des Thüringischen botanischen Vereins* (Weimar), 15 (1900), 24–29 (a footnote here states the author is H. Biltz of Erfurt, father of Dr. E. Biltz); J. B. Barnhart, *Biographical Notes Upon Botanists,* III (Boston, 1965), 312; W. Bastine, "Christian Konrad Sprengel, ein vergessener märkischer Botaniker," in *Jahrbuch für brandenburgische Landesgeschichte,* 12 (1961), 121–131; and R. Brown, "On the Organs and Mode of Fecundation in Orchideae and Asclepiadae," in *Transactions of the Linnean Society of London,* 16 (1833), 685–745.

Also of value are Charles Darwin, *On the Origin of Species . . .* (London, 1859); *On The Various Contrivances by Which . . . Orchids Are Fertilized by Insects . . .* (London, 1862; 2nd ed., London, 1877; New York, 1895); and *The Effects of Cross and Self Fertilization in the Vegetable Kingdom* (London, 1876; 2nd ed., New York, 1895); Francis Darwin, *Charles Darwin, His Life Told in an Autobiographical Chapter and in a Selected Series of His Published Letters* (London, 1887; New York, 1893); Francis Darwin and A. C. Seward, eds., *More Letters of Charles Darwin. A Record of His Work in a Series of Hitherto Unpublished Letters,* 2 vols. (New York, 1903), which mentions Sprengel's work in letters to Asa Gray (II, 254) and to Sir Joseph Hooker (I, 446); A. Engler, "Bericht über die Enthüllung des Denksteins für Christian Konrad Sprengel," in *Notizblatt des Botanischen Gartens und Museums zu Berlin,* 7, no. 62 (1917), 417–420; K. Faegri and L. van der Pijl, *The Principles of Pollination Ecology* (London, 1966), 2, 3, 220; K. von Frisch, "Christian Konrad Sprengels Blumentheorie vor 150 Jahren und heute," in *Naturwissenschaften,* 31 (1943), 223–229, repr. in *Chronica botanica,* 12 (1951), 242–245; and J. D. Fuss. *Ad J. B.*

Lycocriticum . . . epistola, in qua loci Metamorphoseon et Fastorum Ovidii, nec non alii nonnulli sive defunduntur . . ., C. C. Sprengel emendationes . . . refutantur (Cologne, 1824)—*British Museum General Catalog of Printed Books to 1955,* compact ed., IX (London, 1967), 1215; and W. Engelmann, *Bibliotheca scriptorum classicorum* (Leipzig, 1882), 462.

Further works that may be consulted are K. Goebel, "The Biology of Flowers," ch. 20 of A. C. Seward, *Darwin and Modern Science* (Cambridge, 1909); H. A. Hagen, "Christian Conrad Sprengel," in *Nature,* 29 (1883), 29, 573; R. J. Harvey-Gibson, *Outlines of the History of Botany* (London, 1919), 60–61, 132, 160; G. Hintze, "Rundgang über die Berliner Friedhöfe," in *Brandenburgia,* 24 (1933), 84–85; P. Hoffmann, "Einiges über Christian Konrad Sprengel," in *Mitteilungen des Vereins für die Geschichte Berlins,* 36 (1919), 37–39; and "Urkundliches von und über Christian Conrad Sprengel," in *Naturwissenschaftliche Wochenschrift,* 19 (1920), 692–695; G. L. Kessler, ed., *Der alte Heim, Leben und Wirken Ernst Ludwig Heims' . . . aus Hinterlassenen Briefen und Tagebuchern . . .* (Leipzig, 1846), 194; O. Kirchner, "Christian Konrad Sprengel, der Begründer der modernen Blumentheorie," in *Naturwissenschaftliche Wochenschrift,* 8 (1893), 101–105, 111–112, which cites (p. 111) "Herrn Forstmeisters Sprengel in Bonn" as a source of oral and written biographical data; O. Kirchner and H. Potonié, *Die Geheimnisse der Blumen. Eine populäre Jubiläumsschrift zum Andenken an Christian Konrad Sprengel* (Berlin, 1893); P. Knuth, "Christian Konrad Sprengel, Das Entdeckte Geheimniss der Natur. Ein kritisches Jubiläums-Referat," in *Botanisch jaarboek* (Ghent), 5 (1893), 42–107; and *Handbook of Flower Pollination Based Upon Hermann Müller's Work,* "The Fertilization of Flowers by Insects," translated by J. R. Ainsworth Davis, 3 vols. (Oxford, 1906–1909); G. Kraus, *Der botanische Garten der Universität Halle* (Leipzig, 1894), no. 2, 57, 59, 60; and A. Krause, "Christian Konrad Sprengel," in *Mitteilungen des Vereins für die Geschichte Berlins,* 36 (1919), 32.

Additional secondary works are R. Lamprecht, "Der Rektor Sprengel (1780–1794)," in *Die grosse Stadtschule von Spandau von ca. 1300 bis 1853* (Spandau, 1903); D. E. Meyer, "Biographisches und Bibliographisches über Christian Conrad Sprengel," in *Willdenowia,* 1 (1953), 118–125; D. E. Meyer, "Goethes botanische Arbeit in Beziehung zu Christian Konrad Sprengel (1750–1816) und Kurt Sprengel (1766–1833) auf Grund neuer Nachforschungen in Briefen und Tagebüchern," in *Berichten Deutschen botanischen Gesellschaft,* 80 (1967), 209–217; R. Mittmann, "Material zu einer Biographie Christian Konrad Sprengel's," in *Naturwissenschaftliche Wochenschrift,* 8 (1893), 124–128, 138–140, 147–149; C. Nissen, *Die botanische Buchillustration, ihre Geschichte und Bibliographie,* II (Stuttgart, 1951), 174, which notes that Sprengel prepared the drawings, and Johann Stephan Capieux (1748–1813) the plates, for *Das entdeckte Geheimniss;*

O. Recke, ed., *Zur Beschreibung und Geschichte von Spandow. Gesammelte Materialien von D. F. Schulze*, 2 vols. (Spandau, 1913), I, 237, 251–252, 256–260, 274–279, 315, 424; J. von Sachs, "Further Developments of the Sexual Theory by Joseph Gottlieb Koelreuter, and Konrad Sprengel, 1761–1793," in his *History of Botany (1530–1860)*, translated by H. E. F. Garnsey, revised by A. C. Bayley Balfour (Oxford, 1890), 406–422; J. E. Smith, "Description of a New Genus of Plants Called *Sprengelia*," in *Tracts Relating to Natural History* (London, 1798), 269–274; Kurt P. Sprengel, "Geheimnis der Natur in Befruchtung der Blumen," in *Repertorium des Neuesten und Wissenwürdigsten aus der gesammten Naturkunde*, **5** (1813), 356–364; and *Geschichte der Botanik* (Altenburg–Leipzig, 1817), 266–267; and E. Strasburger, "Zum hundertjährigen Gedächtnis an 'Das entdeckte Geheimnis der Natur,'" in *Deutsche Rundschau*, **20** (1893), 113–130.

Also see G. Wichler, "Kölreuter, Sprengel, Darwin und die moderne Blütenbiologie," in *Sitzungsberichte der Gesellschaft naturforschender Freunde zu Berlin* for 1935 (1936), 305–341; M. Wieser, "Der märkische Darwin Konrad Sprengel," in *Brandenburgische Jahrbücher*, **3** (1938), 48–57; W. von Wohlberedt, *Verzeichnis der Grabstätten bekannter und berühmter Persönlichkeiten in Gross-Berlin und Potsdam*, pt. 2 (Berlin, 1934), 125–126; and G. Wunschmann, "Christian Konrad Sprengel," in *Allgemeine deutsche Biographie*, LIII (1893), 293–296.

LAWRENCE J. KING

SPRENGEL, KURT POLYCARP JOACHIM (*b.* Boldekow, Germany, 3 August 1766; *d.* Halle, Germany, 15 March 1833), *botany, medicine*.

In Hermann F. Kilian's survey of German universities of 1828, Sprengel was viewed as the most prestigious professor in Germany. His reputation was principally the result of his erudite and detailed publication in medical history and some botanical contributions, especially in phytotomy. At the time of his death, Sprengel was a member of almost fifty German and foreign academies and learned societies, a shining star in the otherwise bleak sky of contemporary medicine in Germany.

Sprengel was born in a small Pomeranian village, the son of a local preacher and nephew of the distinguished botanist Christian K. Sprengel. Under the direction of his father, a former teacher at the Berlin Realschule, Sprengel learned Greek, Latin, and Hebrew, and also received a solid background in the natural sciences. Later he taught himself Arabic and began the study of five modern European languages, which he soon mastered.

Short of funds and barely seventeen years old, Sprengel found employment as a private tutor near Greifswald, studying theology and philology in his spare moments. In 1784 he successfully passed his religious examinations and was allowed to preach. In 1785 Sprengel matriculated at the University of Halle, determined to study medicine (and not theology, as adduced in some accounts). At the end of five semesters under the direction of Phillip F. T. Meckel and Johann F. G. Goldhagen, he graduated in 1787 with a dissertation on nosology.

Two years later Sprengel began to teach legal and historical subjects at the university as an unsalaried instructor. During the same years he successfully established a medical practice in Halle. In 1795, however, he courageously accepted an invitation to become a full-time academician at the University of Halle, thereby terminating his more lucrative private practice and his higher status.

Versatile and talented, Sprengel taught pathology, legal medicine, semeiology, medical history, and botany at the university. He was popular with the students and well-known for his charity to the needy. After 1800 Sprengel devoted more attention to botany than to medicine. This shift possibly reflected his growing dissatisfaction with the prominence of philosophical German medicine. As professor of botany, he was also director of the university's botanical gardens, where he resided with his family. He established an extensive herbarium and conducted research tours in the nearby countryside.

His contemporaries considered Sprengel to be a keen classical scholar and historian. His most important publication was a medical history, *Versuch einer pragmatischen Geschichte der Arzneikunde*. Although it became the standard work on the subject for nearly a century, Sprengel modestly labeled it an "attempt" to portray medicine chronologically in the various historical periods. He deemphasized the strictly biographical aspects, stressing instead the connections between medicine and contemporary cultural and philosophical forces.

Sprengel called his work a "pragmatic" history of medicine written with a definite utilitarian purpose. In this approach he followed the historical conceptions prevalent during the Enlightenment, which raised the hope of a perfected future, if only the shackles of superstition could be unfastened and the path of reason followed. Therefore Sprengel's goal was to present the medical past with all its errors and pitfalls, in the hope that these aberrations would provide valuable lessons and reveal the basic truths on which a more rational medicine could be developed.

591

Sprengel's fame was further enhanced by his numerous translations—many of them from English authors—and his editorship of five journals dealing with medical and botanical subjects. When defending his beliefs or attacking those trends in medicine that he profoundly disliked, he wrote clearly, incisively, and to the point, without allowing petty personal arguments to vitiate his criticism.

Sprengel was a vigorous critic of the emerging speculative currents in German medicine. He opposed Brownianism and its modified *Erregungstheorie*, and wrote a monograph against animal magnetism. Moreover, he disproved Hahnemann's claims of classical roots for homeopathy, thus incurring the wrath of its founder, who sought vindication in the courts. Sprengel's analysis of German medicine during the last decade of the eighteenth century provided an invaluable document, written by a strict adherent of Kant's critical philosophy, who found himself averse to the new *Naturphilosophie*.

Although hampered by inadequate optics and preparation techniques, Sprengel strongly promoted the microscopic examination of plants and studied their structure, developing his own theory of plant-cell formation. Although soon superseded, his ideas about the nature of cells and fibers provided an essential stimulus for further investigations by other notable botanists, such as Heinrich F. Link, Johann J. Bernhardi, and Ludolf C. Treviranus.

BIBLIOGRAPHY

I. ORIGINAL WORKS. A complete list of Sprengel's publications is in Rohlfs (see below), 212–218; and Adolph C. P. Callisen, *Medicinisches Schriftsteller-Lexicon*, XXXII (Altona, 1844), 389–399. His most famous work, *Versuch einer pragmatischen Geschichte der Arzneikunde*, 5 vols. (Halle, 1792–1799), was reprinted with corrections (1800–1803, 1821–1828) and was translated into French (1810) and Italian (1812), running to several eds. Other historical publications include *Geschichte der Medicin im Auszuge* (Halle, 1804) and *Geschichte der Chirurgie*, 2 vols. (Halle, 1805–1819).

Among Sprengel's numerous translations of classical and modern medical authors are *Galen's Fieberlehre* (Breslau–Leipzig, 1788); *Apologie des Hippocrates und seiner Grundsätze* (Leipzig, 1789); and *William Buchan's Hausarzneikunde* (Altenburg, 1792).

Sprengel summarized the contemporary medical knowledge in two textbooks: *Handbuch der Pathologie*, 3 vols. (Leipzig, 1795–1797), and *Handbuch der Semi-*

otik (Halle, 1801). In addition he broadly criticized the medical developments of 1790–1800 in *Kritische Uebersicht des Zustandes der Arzneikunde in dem letzten Jahrzehend* (Halle, 1801).

His principal botanical works are *Anleitung zur Kenntniss der Gewächse*, 3 vols. (Halle, 1802–1804); *Vom Baue und der Natur der Gewächse* (Halle, 1812); and *Geschichte der Botanik* (Altenburg, 1817). One section of the first was translated into English and published as *An Introduction to the Study of Cryptogamous Plants* (London, 1807).

II. SECONDARY LITERATURE. The most extensive treatment of Sprengel's life and writings is in Heinrich Rohlfs, *Geschichte der deutschen Medicin*, II (Stuttgart, 1880), 212–279, under the heading "Kurt Sprengel, der Pragmatiker." An early biography and list of his writings are in Julius Rosenbaum, *Curtii Sprengelii opuscula academica* (Leipzig–Vienna, 1844), xii–xx. Shorter biographical sketches appeared in *Allgemeine deutsche Biographie*, XXXV, 296–299; August Hirsch, *Biographisches Lexikon*, 2nd. ed., V (Munich, 1932), 374–375; and *Neuer Nekrolog der Deutschen*, XI (1833), 200–208.

A discussion of Sprengel's medical historiography is in E. Heischkel, "Die Medizinhistoriographie im XVIII. Jahrhundert," in *Janus*, **25** (1931), 67–151. Goethe's minor relationship with Sprengel is mentioned in D. E. Meyer, "Goethes botanische Arbeit in Beziehung zu Christian Konrad Sprengel (1750–1816) und Kurt Sprengel (1766–1833) auf Grund neuer Nachforschungen in Briefen und Tagebüchern," in *Berichte der Deutschen botanischen Gesellschaft*, **80** (1967), 209–217. A more recent article stressing Sprengel's opposition to the prevailing medical systems is S. Alleori, "Il sistema dottrinario medico di Curzio Sprengel avversario dei sistemi," in *Pagine di storia della medicina. Collana miscellanea*, **19** (1968), 119–131.

Some of Sprengel's botanical contributions are mentioned in Julius von Sachs, *History of Botany (1530–1860)*, translated by H. E. F. Garnsey, 2nd imp. (Oxford, 1906). A more extensive account can be found in Gregor Kraus, *Der Botanische Garten der Universität Halle* (Leipzig, 1894), no. 2: "Kurt Sprengel." See also Hermann F. Kilian, *Die Universitaeten Deutschlands in medicinisch-naturwissenschaftlicher Hinsicht betrachtet* (Heidelberg–Leipzig, 1828), 114, 120.

GUENTER B. RISSE

SPRING, WALTHÈRE VICTOR (*b*. Liège, Belgium, 6 March 1848; *d*. Tilff, Belgium, 17 July 1911), *chemistry, physics*.

Spring was the son of Antoine Spring, professor of physiology at the medical school of the University of Liège, a competent man of science, and author of a body of published work in medicine, botany, and anthropology. The scholarly physician was disappointed by his son's slow progress in school and by the boy's dislike of classical languages, in which the father was proficient. Spring failed his university entrance examination; and rather than endure his father's reproaches, he left home and found employment as a gunsmith. In the workshop his manual dexterity was well-paid and further developed. He repeated his examinations, this time successfully, and in 1867 enrolled at the school of mines of the University of Liège, from which he graduated with a diploma in mining engineering in 1872. This, however, was merely preparation for a career in experimental chemistry, toward which he had been strongly influenced by Jean Stas, an eminent Belgian chemist and friend of the family. Guided by Stas's advice, Spring went to study under Kekulé at the University of Bonn. Here he also worked in physics with Clausius, who impressed on him the need for disciplined patience and the ability to sustain drudgery while in quest of a long-range objective. Kekulé's work in organic chemistry showed Spring the value of intuition and imagination.

In 1875, after two years at Bonn, Spring returned to Liège to teach theoretical physics at the university. He was appointed assistant professor of organic chemistry in 1876 and full professor in 1880, a post that he retained for the rest of his life. Early in his career Spring was concurrently an engineer with the Belgian Bureau of Mines. The Belgian Academy of Sciences elected him a corresponding member in 1877, titular member in 1884, and president in 1899. He was permanent examiner for the Military School of Belgium from 1884 to 1906.

Spring's earliest researches dealt with the molecular structures of the polythionic acids. He followed Kekulé in denying the possibility of more than one valence to an atom. This principle was an erroneous extension to all atoms of Kekulé's productive theory of the linking of carbon atoms—which are almost the only ones to have that property. Kekulé and his followers were therefore required to write formulas for complex radicals in the form of chains—for example, H-O-O-S-O-O-H for sulfuric acid. Spring's early papers on the inorganic chemistry of sulfur are flawed by too slavish an adherence to this spurious principle. He nevertheless produced a valuable series of papers on the oxyacids of sulfur and on the polythionates, in which he synthesized new compounds and found new chemical reactions.

Spring's most important work, however, was in physical chemistry. He was prompted to investi-

gate the effect of high pressure on the compaction of powdered solids by the lively controversy on the flow of glaciers that was then arousing great interest, fanned by such masters of the polemic arts as Tyndall, Tait, and Ruskin. Spring found that sodium nitrate, potassium nitrate, and even sawdust, when subjected to great compression in a screw press, become hard, solid masses of unusually high density. These observations were the beginning of a series of researches in which he cleverly used the same experimental technique to investigate the effects of pressure on phase equilibria, on chemical equilibria, on the chemical reactions of solids, and on the ability or inability of one metal to diffuse into another. In this way he was able to explain the formation of solid solutions in certain alloys. Geologists also were interested by his discoveries that the application of high pressure could transform peat into lignite and that layers of clay between which organic humus is introduced can, by the same means, produce schist rocks.

In 1870 Tyndall created much public interest by his partial explanation of the blue color of the sky. It stimulated Spring to ask a cognate question about the color of water. After much labor he succeeded in observing the actual color of natural and of chemically pure waters, as well as of aqueous solutions and alcohols. These investigations required the exercise of his utmost skill as an experimentalist. By ingenious techniques he produced optically empty water, free from all traces of suspended particles. The water was to be contained in glass tubes fifteen millimeters in diameter and up to twenty-six meters long. The difficulty lay in making a tube of this length coaxial with the beam of light that is required to pass through it. Almost six weeks of work was required for the alignment of the apparatus. Spring succeeded in completing these exacting experiments, and reported that the natural color of water is "a pure cerulean blue similar to that of the sky at its zenith when seen from a high mountain." He discovered that convection currents, caused by differences of temperature as small as 0.6°C., were enough to render a twenty-six-meter column of water opaque to transmitted light. In extensive discussions of the use of a Tyndall beam to detect the presence of colloidal particles in water, Spring supplied ideas and emphasis that contributed significantly to the development of the ultramicroscope of Siedentopf and Zsigmondy.

In another series of researches Spring found that soap solutions perform their detergent action by preferential adsorption of the soap on the particles of dirt, which are thereby detached and suspended in water.

Spring's work was characterized by the selection of problems dealing with entire natural phenomena that had not yet received adequate explanation, by his originality of viewpoint combined with experimental ingenuity and manipulative skills, and by the clarity and force of his writing. The versatility of his interests was also remarkable.

BIBLIOGRAPHY

Most of Spring's papers were published in the *Bulletin de l'Académie royale de Belgique. Classe des sciences.* His *Oeuvres complètes*, comprising more than 100 papers, was published by the Société Chimique de Belgique in 2 vols. (Brussels, 1914–1923).

The memoir by L. Crismer, prefixed to vol. I of the *Oeuvres complètes*, is the principal source of biographical information. Briefer sketches are F. Lionetti and M. Mager, in *Journal of Chemical Education*, **28** (1951), 604–605; and F. Swarts, in *Chemikerzeitung*, **35** (1911), 949–950.

SYDNEY ROSS

SPRUCE, RICHARD (*b.* Ganthorpe, near Malton, England, 10 September 1817; *d.* Coneysthorpe, Castle Howard, near Malton, 28 December 1893), *botany.*

Spruce, the only child of Richard and Etty Spruce, emulated his father by becoming a schoolmaster, first at Haxby and then at the Collegiate School of York. His principal recreation was the study of the local flora, particularly Bryophyta, on which he published several papers. Upon the closing of the school at York in 1844, he resolved to make botany his career.

From April 1845 to April 1846 Spruce collected plants in the Pyrenees, where he discovered bryophytes previously unrecorded in the region. The results of this expedition were published in 1849–1850. In June 1849 he sailed to South America, where he spent the next fifteen years in botanical exploration.

Undeterred by constant ill health and incredible hardships, Spruce studied the rich vegetation of the Amazon valley with characteristic thoroughness, dispatching to England specimens of more than 7,000 species, many of them previously unknown. A commission from the British government sent him to Andean Ecuador in 1860 to collect cinchona plants suitable for cultivation in India. He procured 100,000 seeds and many young plants, which were sent to India for the production of quinine to alleviate malaria. He spent his remaining years in South America exploring the coastal regions of Ecuador and Peru.

On his return to England in 1864, Spruce acquired a modest cottage in Coneysthorpe, in his native Yorkshire. Despite comparative poverty and constant ill health brought about by his years in South America, he worked hard on his immense plant collections. "Palmae Amazonicae" (1869) is a scholarly elucidation of the geographical distribution of the palms of the Amazon, with a new classification of the genera. "Hepaticae Amazonicae et Andinae" (1884) convinced Sir Joseph Hooker that this would be Spruce's enduring monument.

Spruce's sound botanical judgment, his accuracy, and his meticulous detail were widely recognized. The Royal Geographical Society acknowledged his skill as a cartographer by electing him an honorary fellow in 1866, and in the year of his death the Linnean Society of London made him an associate.

BIBLIOGRAPHY

I. ORIGINAL WORKS. Spruce's writings include "The Musci and Hepaticae of the Pyrenees," in *Transactions and Proceedings of the Botanical Society of Edinburgh*, **3** (1850), 103–216; "Palmae Amazonicae . . .," in *Journal of the Linnean Society. Botany,* **11** (1869), 65–183; "Hepaticae Amazonicae et Andinae . . .," in *Transactions and Proceedings of the Botanical Society of Edinburgh*, **15** (1884), 1–588; and *Notes of a Botanist in the Amazon*, A. R. Wallace, ed., 2 vols. (London, 1908).

II. SECONDARY LITERATURE. See V. W. von Hagen, *South America Called Them* (London, 1949), 291–374; C. Sandeman, "Richard Spruce, Portrait of a Great Englishman," in *Journal of the Royal Horticultural Society*, **74** (1949), 531–544; and R. E. Schultes, "Richard Spruce Still Lives," in *Northern Gardener*, **7** (1953), 20–27, 55–61, 87–93, 121–125.

R. G. C. DESMOND

SPRUNG, ADOLF FRIEDRICH WICHARD (*b.* Kleinow, near Perleberg, Germany, 5 June 1848; *d.* Potsdam, Germany, 16 January 1909), *meteorology.*

The son of a schoolteacher, Sprung demonstrated an early inclination for the natural sciences and especially for chemistry, which led him to study pharmacy. He gave up a career as a pharmacist, however, because of a serious illness. Instead, he studied mathematics, physics, and chemistry at Leipzig from 1872 to 1876, in which year he received the doctorate for an experimental investigation on the hydraulic friction of salt solutions. Sprung turned his attention to meteorology when his teacher, the physicist G. Wiedemann, recommended him to the newly established naval observatory in Hamburg, the director of which, G. Neumayer, was seeking qualified young workers. There, in the department of synoptic meteorology, Sprung collaborated closely with Wladimir Köppen, Wilhelm van Bebber, and Louis Grossman from August 1876 until the spring of 1886. In his daily concern with atmospheric conditions, Sprung became the first to apply the theorems of mathematical physics to the interpretation of meteorological processes. He thereby laid the foundations for the theory of the dynamics of the atmosphere, with which meteorology became an exact science.

Sprung's field of study expanded when, on 1 April 1886, he was appointed director of the instrument division of the Prussian Meteorological Institute in Berlin, which had been reorganized by J. F. W. von Bezold. Six years later he became director of the meteorological-magnetic observatory in Potsdam, constructed according to his proposals, which he made into an institute of worldwide importance. Most of Sprung's works on instruments occurred during this period. With the collaboration of R. Fuess, a master maker of fine instruments, he enriched the field with remarkable new designs. In his last years a nervous ailment increasingly crippled his creative powers. He died suddenly in 1909.

Sprung was one of the first to expand meteorology into a physics of the atmosphere. While in Hamburg he applied the laws of statics and of dynamics to atmospheric problems, which express themselves both in aperiodic phenomena and in occurrences subject to daily cycles. He investigated the relationship of wind strength to barometric gradient (1876, 1879) and the influence of frictional resistance of the ground (1880). From the curvature of the inertial path of a particle with respect to rotating surfaces, he derived the influence of the deflecting force of the earth's rotation on atmospheric circulation (1881). Sprung's theorem for the effect of the sun on the direction of the wind provided an explanation for the daily period of the wind (1881, 1884). His law of areas in meteorology (1881), which stems from Kepler's second law of planetary orbits, is still applied. In 1885 Sprung gathered all this data; combined it with ideas of Buys-Ballot, Ferrel, Guldberg and Mohn, Hadley, and others; and presented the whole in his *Lehrbuch der Meteorologie*, the first complete work on dynamic meteorology.

Sprung's work on instruments was equally progressive. As early as 1877 he had developed his steelyard for the precise recording of air pressure; and in 1908 he applied its ingenious principle to the measurement of rain, snow, and humidity. He also employed the conversion of the measuring process into electrical impulses to achieve remote recording of wind and precipitation. Other measuring devices determined snowfall and precipitation intensity. Sprung's formula for ascertaining vapor pressure from observations with the aspiration psychrometer became the basis for the calculation of the psychrometer table, which is indispensable to the networks of meteorological stations. It is still considered sufficient for practical operations, even at subfreezing temperatures.

For the International Cloud Year 1896–1897, Sprung built for the Potsdam observatory an automatic cloud instrument capable of the simultaneous photogrammetric surveying of several points and a reflector for measuring cloud motion. Only with the introduction of electronic structural elements into meteorological measuring techniques were Sprung's designs superseded.

BIBLIOGRAPHY

I. Original Works. Many of Sprung's writings on dynamic meteorology were brought together in his *Lehrbuch der Meteorologie* (Hamburg, 1885). Such works include "Studien über den Wind und seine Beziehungen zum Luftdruck," in *Aus dem Archiv der Deutschen Seewarte*, **2**, nos. 1–2 (1879)—articles on the same topic in *Zeitschrift der Österreichischen Gesellschaft für Meteorologie*, **17** (1882), 161–175, 276–282; and *Meteorologische Zeitschrift*, **11** (1894), 197–200, 384–387; "Zur Theorie der oberen Luftströmungen," in *Zeitschrift der Österreichischen Gesellschaft für Meteorologie*, **15** (1880), 17–21; "Die Anwendung des Prinzips der Flächen in der Meteorologie," *ibid.*, **16** (1881), 57–63; "Über die Bahnlinie eines freien Teilchens auf der rotierenden Erdoberfläche und deren Bedeutung für die Meteorologie," in *Wiedemanns Annalen*, **14** (1881), 128–149—articles on the same subject in *Zeitschrift der Österreichischen Gesellschaft für Meteorologie*, **15** (1880), 1–21; **17** (1882), 75; and *Meteorologische Zeitschrift*, **1** (1884), 250–252; "Eine periodische Erscheinung im täglichen Gang der Windrichtung," in *Zeitschrift der Österreichischen Gesellschaft für Meteorologie*, **16** (1881), 419–424—articles on the same subject in *Meteorologische Zeitschrift*, **1** (1884), 15–22, 65–70; **3**

(1886), 223–225; **11** (1894), 252–262; and "Die vertikale Komponente der ablenkenden Kraft der Erdrotation in ihrer Bedeutung für die Dynamik der Atmosphäre," in *Meteorologische Zeitschrift,* **12** (1895), 449–455.

Sprung's articles on instrumental techniques include "Waagebarograph mit Laufgewicht nach Sprung," in *Zeitschrift der Österreichischen Gesellschaft für Meteorologie,* **12** (1877), 305–308; **16** (1881), 1–4; **17** (1882), 44–48; "Bestimmung der Luftfeuchtigkeit durch Assmanns Aspirationspsychrometer," in *Wetter,* **5** (1888), 105–108; "Über den photogrammetrischen Wolkenautomaten und seine Justierung," in *Zeitschrift für Instrumentenkunde,* **19** (1889), 111–118; **24** (1904), 206–213; "Registrierapparate für Regenfall und Wind mit elektrischer Übertragung," in *Meteorologische Zeitschrift,* **24** (1889), 344–348—also in *Zeitschrift für Instrumentenkunde,* **9** (1889), 90–98; and *Meteorologische Zeitschrift,* **32** (1897), 385–388, written with R. Fuess; "Über die automatische Aufzeichnung der Regenintensität," in *Wetter,* **22** (1905), 56–58, also in *Zeitschrift für Instrumentenkunde,* **27** (1907), 340–343; and "Die registrierende Laufgewichtswaage im Dienste der Schnee-, Regen- und Verdunstungsmessung," in *Meteorologische Zeitschrift,* **25** (1908), 145–154.

Additional publications on climatology and maritime meteorology appeared between 1880 and 1908 in *Meteorologische Zeitschrift, Annalen der Hydrographie und maritimen Meteorologie,* and *Wetter.*

II. SECONDARY LITERATURE. See Richard Assmann, "Professor Dr. Adolf Sprung†," in *Wetter,* **26** (1909), 25–27; and Wladimir Koeppen, "Dr. Adolf Sprung. Nachruf," in *Meteorologische Zeitschrift,* **26** (1909), 215–216.

J. GRUNOW

SPURZHEIM, JOHANN CHRISTOPH (*b.* Longuich, near Trier, Germany, 31 December 1776; *d.* Boston, Massachusetts, 10 November 1832), *psychology, psychiatry, neuroscience.*

Spurzheim's family, who were Lutheran, farmed the land of an abbey in a small town on the Moselle about sixty miles from Koblenz. His early education was intended to prepare him for a clerical career. He studied Greek and Latin in his native village and at the age of fifteen entered the University of Trèves (now Trier), where he studied Hebrew, divinity, and philosophy. Around 1799 he moved to Vienna and was engaged as a private tutor. The following year he met Franz Joseph Gall, with whom he collaborated on neuroanatomical research for the next thirteen years. From 1800 to 1804 Spurzheim completed his medical studies at Vienna, where he was formally awarded his medical degree in 1813, after he and Gall had ceased working together. He received licensure in London from the Royal College of Physicians; was awarded a second degree, possibly a medical one, at Paris around 1821; and received recognition from many learned societies, including honorary membership in the Royal Irish Academy. He remained a theorist all his life, however, for his skepticism regarding medicine as it was then understood led him to avoid private medical practice.

Spurzheim's unique contributions to the behavioral sciences have traditionally been intertwined in those of his mentor Franz Gall, who, although considered the founder of what later came to be known as phrenology, never used that term to describe his own system. Furthermore, Spurzheim was often accused of being a popularizer of Gall's views on cerebral localization of mental functions because he was responsible for making them into a complete system of phrenology and teaching it widely. Spurzheim accepted the basic assumptions of this theory of mind, brain, and behavior—(1) that the brain is the organ of the mind, (2) that the moral and intellectual faculties are innate, (3) that their exercise or manifestation depends on organization, (4) that the brain is composed of a congeries of as many particular organs as there are propensities, sentiments, and faculties that differ from each other, and (5) that the shape and size of the skull faithfully reflect the shape and size of the underlying cerebral mass. Nevertheless, he extended Gall's basic views in a singular way and made them in many respects more utilitarian and also more acceptable to a wider audience. In contrast with the more conservative view that Gall held in regard to his own doctrines, Spurzheim took the position that phrenology was capable of ameliorating most of the social ills of his day.

Shortly after his professional and personal break with Gall in 1813, Spurzheim formalized his views and presented them in his first major publication, *The Physiognomical System of Drs. Gall and Spurzheim: Founded on an Anatomical and Physiological Examination of the Nervous System in General, and of the Brain in Particular; and Indicating the Dispositions and Manifestations of the Mind* (London, 1815). It was from this major effort that Spurzheim later extracted sections, extended them, and published them as separate works. For example, his *Essai philosophique sur la nature morale et intellectuelle de l'homme* (Paris, 1820) elaborated upon his philosophical position. *A View of the Elementary Principles of Education Found-*

ed on the *Study of the Nature of Man* (Edinburgh, 1821) applied phrenology to education, and *Observations on the Deranged Manifestations of the Mind, or Insanity* (London, 1817) applied phrenology to psychiatry. Like many of Spurzheim's works, the latter was published in other languages, including German (Hamburg, 1818) and French (Paris, 1818). The work on insanity influenced the development of early American psychiatry; and when it was first published in America (Boston, 1832), it was edited by the well-known alienist Amariah Brigham.

Spurzheim believed that he had been denied the recognition due him as Gall's collaborator. Moreover, he felt that he was personally responsible for many of the neuroanatomical discoveries traditionally credited to Gall alone—especially those made between 1805 and 1813. He was constantly placed on the defensive, furthermore, because he was seen by his critics as only parroting what Gall had taught. But he did not simply take Gall's position unaltered and present it as his own. He contributed to their joint efforts almost from the beginning, and he placed his unique stamp on the history of that very special nineteenth-century doctrine of brain and mind.

Spurzheim taught that there were no fewer than thirty-five innate faculties of the mind—Gall had claimed to have discovered twenty-seven. He placed great emphasis on individual differences in cerebral organization and held that education had to be individualized. He discarded the view that mental faculties have determinate functions, offering instead a more "dignified" view of man that allowed for a greater emphasis on his more positive traits. Spurzheim separated what he believed to be the combined actions of faculties from what individual faculties were held to do, and added a more theological and philosophical perspective.

As a result of Spurzheim's conviction of phrenology's truthfulness, he convinced a great number of auditors to support it. In this regard he was able, unintentionally, to play a unique historical role. By inducing a wide audience to investigate for itself the truthfulness of his enthusiastically espoused belief, Spurzheim inspired inquiries that in some cases led to the establishment of phrenology's inherent incorrectness. Thus, although much of phrenology and Spurzheim's assumptions were essentially wrong—and were shown to be so as neuroanatomical science advanced in the nineteenth century—they were just right enough to further scientific thought.

BIBLIOGRAPHY

I. ORIGINAL WORKS. The small collection of Spurzheim MSS at Harvard Medical School, Boston, includes fragments of Spurzheim's American journal and his correspondence with his wife around the time they were married. A complete bibliography of the many eds. of his works is not available. A listing of his major works is in A. A. Walsh's intro. to *Observations on the Deranged Manifestations of the Mind, or Insanity, by J. G. Spurzheim* (Gainesville, Fla., 1970).

II. SECONDARY LITERATURE. Two biographies of Spurzheim were prepared by his American publisher, Nahum Capen of Boston: *Reminiscences of Dr. Spurzheim and George Combe: And a Review of the Science of Phrenology, From the Period of Its Discovery by Dr. Gall to the Time of the Visit of George Combe to the United States, 1838, 1840* (Boston, 1881); and "Biography of the Author [Spurzheim]," in J. G. Spurzheim, *Phrenology in Connexion With the Study of Physiognomy* (Boston, 1833), 9–168. Andrew Carmichael has published the only complete book on Spurzheim's life, which, despite its errors, is generally well done: *A Memoir of the Life and Philosophy of Spurzheim* (Boston, 1833). W. M. Williams, *A Vindication of Phrenology* (London, 1894), discusses Spurzheim in England (328–340); and A. A. Walsh discusses Spurzheim in America in "The American Tour of Dr. Spurzheim," in *Journal of the History of Medicine and Allied Sciences*, **27** (1972), 187–205, and in "Johann Christoph Spurzheim and the Rise and Fall of Scientific Phrenology in Boston: 1832–1842" (doctoral diss., University of New Hampshire, 1974). Finally, the reader should consult the many references appended to the article on Franz Joseph Gall in the DSB.

ANTHONY A. WALSH

ŚRĪDHARA (*fl.* India, ninth century), *mathematics.*

Śrīdhara, of whose life nothing is known save that he was a devotee of Śiva, wrote two works on arithmetic, the *Pāṭīgaṇita* and the *Pāṭīgaṇitasāra* or *Triśatikā*, and one work, now lost, on algebra. Since he seems to refer to the views of Mahāvīra (*fl.* ninth century), and was used by Āryabhaṭa II (*fl.* between *ca.* 950 and 1100) and cited by Abhayadeva Sūri (*fl.* 1050), it can be concluded that he flourished in the ninth century.

The *Pāṭīgaṇita* is divided into two sections. The first, after metrological definitions, covers the mathematical operations of addition, subtraction, multiplication, and division; finding squares and square roots; finding cubes and cube roots; fractions; and proportions; the second gives solutions for problems involving mixtures, series, plane fig-

597

ures, volumes, shadows, and zero. The text, preserved in a unique manuscript in Kashmir, breaks off in the middle of the rules for determining the areas of plane figures in the second section. The *Triśatikā* summarizes much of the material in the *Pāṭīgaṇita*, including the parts no longer available to us. In the Kashmir manuscript there is an anonymous commentary on the *Pāṭīgaṇita*, and the *Triśatikā* was commented on by Śrīdhara himself and in Kannaḍa (Kanarese), Telugu (by Vallabha), and Gujarātī; the commentaries on the *Triśatikā* ascribed to Śambhūnātha or Śambhūdāsa (*fl.* 1428; *Gaṇitapañcaviṃśatikā* or *Gaṇitasāra* and to Vṛndāvana Śukla (*Pāṭīsāraṭīkā*) are still uncertain, pending an investigation of the manuscripts.

BIBLIOGRAPHY

The best work on Śrīdhara is the introduction to K. S. Shukla's valuable ed. and trans., *The Patiganita of Sridharacarya* (Lucknow, 1959). There is also a Russian trans. and study of the *Pāṭīgaṇita* by A. I. Volodarsky and O. F. Volkovoy in *Fiziko-matematicheskie nauki v stranakh vostoka* (Moscow, 1966), 141–246. The *Triśatikā* was edited by Sudhākara Dvivedin (Benares, 1899) and was largely translated into English by N. Ramanujacharia and G. R. Kaye, "The *Triśatikā* of Śrīdharācarya," in *Bibliotheca mathematica*, 3rd ser., **13** (1912–1913), 203–217.

DAVID PINGREE

ŚRĪPATI (*fl.* Rohiṇīkhaṇḍa, Mahārāṣṭra, India, 1039–1056), *astronomy, astrology, mathematics.*

Śrīpati, who was the son of Nāgadeva (or Nāmadeva) and the grandson of Keśava of the Kāśyapagotra, is one of the most renowned authorities on astrology in India, although his works on astronomy and mathematics are not negligible; in many he follows the opinions of Lalla (*fl.* eighth century; see essay in Supplement). His numerous works include not only Sanskrit texts but also one of the earliest examples of Marāṭhī prose extant. They include the following:

1. The *Dhīkoṭidakaraṇa*, written in 1039, a work in twenty verses on solar and lunar eclipses. There are commentaries by Harikṛṣṇa (*fl.* 1708–1714 at Delhi) and Dinakara. The *Dhīkoṭidakaraṇa* was edited by N. K. Majumdar in *Calcutta Oriental Journal*, **1** (1934), 286–299—see also his "Dhikoti-Karanam of Śrīpati," in *Journal of the Asiatic Society of Bengal*, n.s. **17** (1921), 273–278—and by K. S. Shukla, in *Ṛtam*, **1** (1969), supp.

2. The *Dhruvamānasa*, written in 1056, is a

short treatise in 105 verses on calculating planetary longitudes, on gnomon problems, on eclipses, on the horns of the moon, and on planetary transits. It is very rare and has not been published.

3. The *Siddhāntaśekhara*, a major work on astronomy in nineteen chapters, follows, in general, *the Brāhmapakṣa*. The chapters are on the following subjects:

1. Fundamentals.
2. Mean motions of the planets.
3. True longitudes of the planets.
4. On the three questions relating to the diurnal rotation.
5. Lunar eclipses.
6. Solar eclipses.
7. On the syzygies.
8. On the *pātas* of the sun and moon.
9. On first and last appearances.
10. On the moon.
11. On transits of the planets.
12. On conjunctions of the planets with the constellations.
13. Arithmetic.
14. Algebra.
15. On the sphere.
16. On the planetary spheres.
17. On the cause of eclipses.
18. On the projection of eclipses.
19. On astronomical instruments.

A commentary on this work, the *Gaṇitabhūṣaṇa*, was composed by Makkibhaṭṭa (*fl.* 1377); unfortunately, only the portion on the first four chapters survives. The *Siddhāntaśekhara*, with Makkibhaṭṭa's commentary on chapters 1–4 and the editor's on chapters 5–19, was edited by Babuāji Miśra, 2 vols. (Calcutta, 1932–1947).

4. The *Gaṇitatilaka* is a mathematical treatise apparently based on the *Pāṭīgaṇita* or *Triśatikā* of Śrīdhara; there is a commentary by Siṃhatilaka Sūri (*fl.* 1269 at Bijāpura, Mysore). Both text and commentary were published by H. R. Kapadia (Baroda, 1937).

5 and 6. The *Jyotiṣaratnamālā*, in twenty chapters, is the most influential work in Sanskrit on *muhūrta* or catarchic astrology, in which the success or failure of an undertaking is determined from the time of its inception. It is based largely on the *Jyotiṣaratnakośa* of Lalla. Śrīpati himself wrote a Marāṭhī commentary on this (edited and studied for its linguistic content by M. G. Panse [Poona, 1957]); but of much greater historical importance is the commentary *Gautamī* composed by Mahādeva in 1263, for it contains numerous citations from lost or little-known astronomical

and astrological texts. There are also commentaries by Dāmodara (*Bālāvabodha*), Paramakāraṇa (*Bālabodhinī* in Prākṛt), Śrīdhara (*Śrīdharīya*), and Vaijā Paṇḍita (*Bālāvabodhinī*). The *Jyotiṣaratnamālā* was published twice with Mahādeva's *Gautamī*: at Bombay in 1884 and by Rasikamohana Caṭṭopādhyāya (2nd ed., Calcutta, 1915). The first six chapters were edited by P. Poucha, "La Jyotiṣaratnamālā ou Guirlande des joyaux d'astrologie de Śrīpatibhaṭṭa," in *Archiv orientální*, **16** (1949), 277–309.

7. The *Jātakapaddhati* or *Śrīpatipaddhati*, in eight chapters, is one of the fundamental textbooks for later Indian genethlialogy, contributing an impressive elaboration to the computation of the strengths of the planets and astrological places. It was enormously popular, as the large number of manuscripts, commentaries, and imitations attests. The more important of these commentaries are Sūryadeva Yajvan (*b.* 1191), *Jātakālaṅkāra*; Parameśvara (*ca.* 1380–1460); Acyuta (*fl.* 1505–1534), *Bhāvārthamañjarī*—see D. Pingree, *Census of the Exact Sciences in Sanskrit*, ser. A, I (Philadelphia, 1970), 36a–36b; Kṛṣṇa (*fl.* 1600–1625), whose *udāharana* was edited by J. B. Chaudhuri (Calcutta, 1955)—see also D. Pingree, *Census*, II (Philadelphia, 1971), 53a–55b; Sumatiharṣa Gaṇi (*fl.* 1615); Mādhava; and Raghunātha. Acyuta Piṣāraṭi (*ca.* 1550–1621; see D. Pingree, *Census*, I, 36b–38b) wrote an imitation, the *Horāsāroccaya*. The *Jātakapaddhati* was edited with an English translation by V. Subrahmanya Sastri (Bombay, 1903; 4th ed., Bangalore, 1957).

8. A *Daivajñavallabha* on astrology, in fifteen chapters, sometimes is attributed to Śrīpati and sometimes to Varāhamihira (*fl. ca.* 550); its real author remains unknown. It was published with the Hindī translation, *Subodhinī*, of Nārāyaṇa (*fl.* 1894) at Bombay in 1905, in 1915–1916, and in 1937.

There is no reliable discussion of Śrīpati or study of his works.

DAVID PINGREE

STÄCKEL, PAUL GUSTAV (*b.* Berlin, Germany, 20 August 1862; *d.* Heidelberg, Germany, 12 December 1919), *mathematics, history of science.*

Stäckel studied at Berlin and defended his dissertation in 1885. He wrote his *Habilitationsschrift* at Halle in 1891 and then held chairs at various German universities, teaching finally at Heidelberg. His interests were varied, for he worked with equal ease in both mathematics and its history. The chief influence was the work of Weierstrass. He specialized in analytical mechanics (particularly in the use of Lagrangians in problems concerning the motion of points in the presence of given fields of force), related questions in geometry, and properties of analytical functions. A linking problem for these fields was the solution of linear differential equations; Stäckel also explored the existence theorems for such solutions. His other interests in mathematics included set theory and, in his later years, problems concerning prime numbers. He was renowned among his students for delivering new sets of lectures every academic year, and he wrote on problems in mathematical education.

In the history of mathematics Stäckel's interests centered on the eighteenth and early nineteenth centuries. He was especially noted for his role in instituting the publication of Euler's *Opera omnia*; and he also published editions of works, manuscripts, and correspondence of J. H. Lambert, F. and J. Bolyai, Gauss, and Jacobi. In addition, he edited several volumes in Ostwald's *Klassiker der Exacten Wissenschaften*. His interpretive articles dealt largely with the history of the theory of functions and of non-Euclidean geometry. From indications in his and others' writings, it seems clear that locating his *Nachlass* is highly desirable.

BIBLIOGRAPHY

The most comprehensive list of Stäckel's works is in Poggendorff, IV, 1427–1428, and V, 1194–1195.

For a sympathetic obituary, see O. Perron, "Paul Stäckel," *Sitzungsberichte der Heidelberger Akademie der Wissenschaften*, Math.-naturwiss. Kl., Abt. A (1920), no. 7.

I. GRATTAN-GUINNESS

STAHL, GEORG ERNST (*b.* Ansbach, Germany, 21 October 1660 [1659?]; *d.* Berlin, Germany, 4 May 1734), *medicine, chemistry.*

Stahl has aroused much controversy. As a physician he was outstanding; he held the highest academic positions, enjoyed a very active practice, and through his writings became vastly influential. As a philosopher he supported the viewpoint known as vitalism and wove that concept into the fabric of his medical system. As a chemist he elaborated and maintained the doctrine of phlogiston, which, until outgrown later in the eighteenth century, provided a reasoned explanation for many chemical phenomena. But his teachings, particularly his stand on vitalism, in large part ran counter to the trend of the times; his chemical theories were overthrown; his vitalist doctrine, in the form that he elaborated it, could not stand up against the onrushing tide of research and experimentation; while his system of medical practice faded away before numerous competitors. Furthermore, his personality was often antagonistic, his style of writing obscure and hard to understand. Yet, even though he seemed to be discredited, Stahl influenced the whole of eighteenth-century medicine; and his imprint is being increasingly appreciated as historians trace his role in the drama of eighteenth-century medical thought.

Although the generally accepted date of Stahl's birth is 21 October 1660, Gottlieb disputes this and claims that the baptismal register, in the parish of St. John in Ansbach, shows 1659. There is little information about Stahl's early life. Even as a youth he had considerable interest in chemistry. He studied medicine at Jena and received his degree in January 1684. He then devoted himself to scientific work and lectured in chemistry at the university, attaining considerable reputation. In 1687 Stahl was invited to become court physician at Weimar, where he remained for seven years. He subsequently joined the medical faculty of the new University of Halle.

Elector Frederick III of Brandenburg (Frederick I of Prussia), eager to surpass his neighbors, decided to establish a new university at Halle. The great liberal jurist Christian Thomasius, who had been expelled from Leipzig, settled at Halle at Frederick's invitation. The elector built his university around Thomasius and attracted such men as August Francke in oriental languages and Friedrich Hoffmann in medicine. In 1693 the university received the imperial privilege and was officially inaugurated in 1694.

Hoffmann, needing help, was instrumental in securing Stahl's appointment as the second professor of medicine. In 1694 Stahl went to Halle, where he remained until 1715, lecturing particularly on the theory of medicine and on chemistry. Hoffmann and Stahl, although different in many respects, formed a very strong faculty, and Halle became a leading medical school. In 1715, at the request of Frederick William I of Prussia, Stahl left Halle and went to Berlin to be court physician. He remained there until his death.

Stahl's personality has received much unfavorable comment. He has been condemned as misan-

thropic and harsh, narrow-minded and intolerant. These qualities also have been contrasted unfavorably with the sunnier and more open disposition of Hoffmann. Much of the evaluation rests on rather slender evidence and stems particularly from the statements of Haller, which many historians have repeated. On the other hand, Stahl had many defenders. The truth is virtually impossible to establish, unless further primary source material should be discovered.

Stahl was a devout Pietist—Halle, in the early days, was the center for Pietism as well as rationalism—and this background undoubtedly colored his doctrines. Many misfortunes attended his personal life. His first wife died in 1696 of puerperal fever and his second wife in 1706, of the same disease. A daughter died in 1708. These were the years of his greatest productivity, and it is only reasonable to see in his outward attitudes some reflection of his personal life. He was a prodigious worker, and pride and self-confidence apparently were notable qualities. Gottlieb quotes Stahl's personal motto as *E rebus quantumcumque dubiis quicquid maxima sententium turba defendit, error est*, for which I suggest the translation, "Where there is doubt, whatever the greatest mass of opinion maintains . . . is wrong."

Stahl's style of writing is prolix and convoluted, and difficult to understand. Perhaps the style is the man himself.

Stahl, who lived well into the eighteenth century, was nevertheless part of the seventeenth-century rebellion against tradition; and his doctrines reflect, in a way, the intense turmoil of that period. The rebellion, of course, involved all phases of intellectual life. In medicine the Galenic theories, which rested largely on Aristotle, had come under severe attack. In astronomy and physics, especially mechanics, new experimental methods had shown how untenable were the older views. In physiology and biology Harvey was the greatest among many investigators who introduced new concepts that were firmly grounded on empirical demonstration. In philosophy Descartes offered new vistas and new methodology, while Gassendi helped to reintroduce atomism. In chemistry the arch-rebel Paracelsus had given great impetus to a movement of which the leading representatives were van Helmont, in the early seventeenth century, and Sylvius and Willis in the later part. At the same time traditional religion remained powerful and entrenched. Piety and orthodoxy were strong values, and atheism and materialism were epithets dreaded by most scientific workers. The new philosophy and the new science, which threatened orthodox religions, had to come to terms with religious tenets.

In the medical world of the later seventeenth century, many different theories competed actively; but no clear victory was in sight for any one. The traditional Galenic theories were in retreat but by no means annihilated. Iatrophysicists tried to explain all medical phenomena on the basis of matter, motion, and the simple laws of mechanics; iatrochemists relied on the chemical "principles" as their explanatory terms. The dichotomy between mind and body had taken deep root and was influencing medical theory, while the close relation between the "mind" of medical doctrine and the "soul" of religious orthodoxy was troublesome indeed.

Although Stahl did not provide any straightforward or systematic exposition of his doctrines, his prolix writing contains certain recurrent themes that serve as a foundation for his more specific discussions. Foremost among his basic concepts is the irreducible difference between the living and the nonliving. Mind and matter are distinct and ultimate. Matter, particulate in its nature, exists as a real entity in its own right and comprises the material aspect of the universe. But equally real and equally deserving of the designation *ens* are the immaterial aspects, of which the *anima* is the key manifestation. While both the living and the nonliving are composed of matter, only living creatures have an *anima*. The immaterial vital principle serves as the ultimate differential feature that distinguishes the living from the nonliving.

A second major principle involves the concept of goal or purpose. The philosopher (or scientist) who tries to describe and explain the phenomena of life must take account of the goal activity. Behavior is not blind or mechanical. Living creatures can be understood only if we pay attention to their striving toward particular ends or purposes. This striving, in turn, implies a directive agency controlling the goal-seeking effort. The agent is the *anima*.

A third principle concerns the place of mechanism in the scheme of things. All nonliving creatures—the inorganic or "mixed"—are entirely mechanical. Living creatures, up to a point, also are mechanical; but the mechanism involved represents only the instrument of the directing agent or *anima*. The agent exerts itself, manifests itself, through mechanical principles.

These major doctrines give rise to certain corollaries: the *anima* that directs the purposive activities of the body acts in an intelligent fashion. It is rational and exhibits foresight to bring about the desired ends. Furthermore, the directing force can be understood only as a process involving a time span. It implies wholes rather than parts, and only a false philosophy will focus exclusively on the parts and neglect the whole.

On this framework Stahl elaborated a rather detailed and intricate, if rambling and untidy, superstructure. The entire doctrine of animism rests on the ultimate distinction between the living and the nonliving. Stahl pointed out certain significant differences—the nonliving, which may be either homogeneous or heterogeneous, is relatively inert, remains stable over an indefinite time span, and is not readily changed or decomposed. Living creatures, however, are always heterogeneous and always have a great tendency to decomposition and putrefaction. Yet the components of the living body, despite this tendency to putrefaction, remain stable over the limited time that life persists. The tendency to decomposition is held in check by a conserving agent. This agent, the essence of life, is the *anima*, which thus preserves the body from corruption.

The living body depends on motion—most obviously the motion of the heart and the circulation of the blood. The *anima* exerts its control over the body through this very property of motion. By using this concept Stahl engages in some remarkable semantic juggling that enables him to construct a formal and orderly system.

He explicitly denies that motion is in any sense a function of matter. Although material objects do exhibit motion, this property is not intrinsic to them. On the contrary, matter—consisting of material particles—is inert; motion is something added, superimposed from outside. For Stahl motion derives from the *anima*. It is in no sense material (this, indeed, follows clearly from the concept that motion is not a property of matter). On the contrary, he considers it to be immaterial. Motion, then, is somehow reified into an immaterial entity representative of the *anima*, which is also immaterial. The immaterial *anima* acts through motion—also immaterial—and in turn affects material particles.

This sequence is Stahl's answer to the problem, how can an immaterial entity act on something material. This difficulty, the crux of Cartesian dualism, had remained a stumbling block. One popular "solution," widely accepted, involved an intermediary—the animal spirits, which were extremely subtle matter. The soul acted on the animal spirits, which, being material, could then act on the coarser material elements. This formulation employs a sort of Neoplatonic maneuver whereby extremely subtle matter seems to mediate the transition between the conceptual realm and the material world.

This "solution," however, simply begs the question. Stahl, by calling motion an immaterial entity subject to control through the *anima*, believed that he had solved the problem. The concept of motion served as a link whereby an immaterial *anima* could act on the body.

The most important motions of the body are primarily the circulation of the blood, and then those motions that activate the processes of excretion and secretion. Without these, life could not exist. Motion, operative on the humors and the solids, maintains life and health. If the motions are impaired, disease occurs. Motion, Stahl emphasized, is not life but merely its instrument. This concept of instrumentality has extreme importance for his system, which centered on the *anima*.

We do not perceive the *anima*, nor can we study it directly. Instead, we perceive and study the bodily activities in health and the changes in disease, that is, physiology and pathology, and from these data we infer the nature of the *anima*. Stahl was not in any sense an obscurantist or mystic but, rather, a hard-headed clinician. He taught that the proper study of medicine involves the functions of the body, and his voluminous writings concerned themselves with physiology, pathology, and clinical medicine. But while emphasizing the importance of these aspects, he placed them in a suitable perspective: that the motions of the body, in health and in disease, are subordinate to a certain directing and integrating force—the *anima*.

The mind acts on the body in various ways. So-called voluntary actions, depending on a deliberate exercise of will, are quite obvious. But more important for Stahl's system are those bodily effects that result from other psychic causes. Stahl repeatedly referred to the effects on the body produced by psychic disturbance, and he offered examples in two major areas. What we today call emotions—anger, fear, disgust, hatred, love—produce certain significant changes in the bodily functions. The alterations in pulse, respiration, or various digestive activities that result from emotional stress were well-known and obviously were quite different from "voluntary" motions that involve skeletal muscle. Stahl's reasoned explanation presupposed an immaterial *ens*, the *anima*, that felt the emotion and reacted on the bodily organs by inducing changes in their motion.

In a second major illustration, used repeatedly, Stahl fell back on the belief that in a pregnant woman the emotions of the mother exert a material effect on the body of the fetus. It was a firm article of belief that a mother could "mark" the baby *in utero*. In emotional states such as fright or desire, the psychic state could have a physical effect upon the baby. Stahl could not explain in detail how this came about; but he did use these examples to bolster his claims that the *anima*, of immaterial psychic character, had power over the body.

The physical effects of emotion provide merely a striking example of a general situation: that primary changes in the mind are, through motion, transferred to the solids and fluids of the body. But this is merely a special case. Actually, according to Stahl, the *anima* affects the body at all times. It is continually exerting regulatory and directing functions over all bodily activities—and these functions are all purposive.

This is the crux of animism. The *anima* regulates all bodily actions in accordance with certain goals. Life is purposeful. The *anima* is the source not merely of motion but also of directive, purposeful motion. Purpose thus involves the deliberate activity of mind, whereas chance concerns the activity of matter alone, without the intervention of mind. Purpose, implying a goal toward which activity is directed, has what we may call a forward reference, comparable with the final cause of Aristotle. Whatever happens by chance depends solely on backward reference, the *vis a tergo*.

Around these ideas Stahl constructed his important distinction between mechanism and organism. Mechanical properties depend only on the configuration, size, position, and movement (or disposition to movement) of the component parts. The movements have purely mechanical causes. In an organism, however, movements are combined toward a specific end, with a responsible agent that regulates and integrates them. To be sure, in any organism the activities involve mechanism, but merely in an instrumental fashion, subordinate to the purpose of the organism. The purpose, goal, or intent constitutes the reason for existence of the organism. A mechanism does not have such a reason for existence.

Stahl provides numerous examples. In a watch, for instance, a skillfully constructed mechanism, the parts act on each other in mechanical fashion. But the watch also has properties of an organism, insofar as it has the goal of keeping time. If, because of defective parts, it fails to keep correct time, it no longer has the properties of an organism but remains a mere mechanism.

In entities that are not man-made, the question

of possible goal or purpose lies beyond human knowledge. Thus, no one can penetrate the ends served by celestial bodies or the existence of so many species of insects. The answers can lie only in the will of God.

The *anima*, Stahl made explicitly clear, exists only in the body, is inseparable from it, and cannot be thought of apart from the body. It is not a religious concept, nor is it an obscurantist or mystical doctrine. It is understood by rational analysis, which discloses that the *anima* is entirely dependent upon the body for perception and ideas. The body is the instrument of the *anima*, which must have sensory organs to aid the intellect and locomotive organs to aid the will.

Stahl rejected the view that bodily action is carried out solely by the motion of particles. The mechanical philosophy, depending on the *vis a tergo*, simply did not explain observed phenomena. For example, a certain noise—a stimulus falling on the ear—may induce a turning of the eyes toward the noise. Mechanists explained this by the activity of certain particles of the body, incited by the sense organs and reaching the motor organs to act upon them directly and to induce movement. In contrast, Stahl gave the example of a miser who hears a noise like a falling coin. He not only turns his eyes (what we would call a simple reflex) but also searches the entire room, with all the complicated associated movements. He does not stop until he finds the object of his search. That such complex behavior should have a simple mechanical explanation in the motion of particles seemed utterly absurd to Stahl.

Stahl propounded some views that may also seem absurd unless we relate them to the Aristotelian background and see the relationship between the *anima* of Stahl and the form of Aristotle (especially as the Aristotelian doctrine is manifest in the sixteenth- and seventeenth-century Galenists). Stahl declared that the body exists only because of the *anima*, and its form and structure are determined through the energy of the mind. More important, there must reside in the *anima* some special knowledge of the organs, knowledge that regulates growth, shape, and function, and keeps the organs in proper proportion and relationship—proper, that is, for undertaking their functions and achieving appropriate goals. This concept of the immaterial entity controlling both growth and other activity ties in with the Galenists' notion of "substantial form." The form of the oak inheres in the acorn and determines its development into an oak rather than into a pine or a dahlia. Because of

an appropriate form, the seed of a radish develops into a radish and not into a chrysanthemum. Stahl's *anima* includes among its many other functions the directive activities that earlier writers had attributed to form.

Stahl met one obvious objection head on. The *anima* is a conscious agent, but many of the activities attributed to it do not appear in consciousness. We are, for example, consciously aware of sensations but not of directing the growth of bodily parts. Stahl disposed of this objection through a verbal distinction. He distinguished *logos* from *logismos*, *ratio* from *ratiocinatio*. *Logos* is simple "intelligence" or "perception," which cannot be the subject of reasoning or memory and can inhere in the *anima* without being perceived. This is quite different from ideas, which, derived from the external senses, serve as the subject of reasoning and memory (*logismos*). Stahl was saying that the soul has ideas and activities of which it is not fully aware.

All this, of course, merely begs the question; but it does maintain the empirical analysis. At work are forces the nature of which can be identified through observation. Stahl drew into a single concept all the forces operative in living organisms and bestowed on this aggregate the name *anima*.

In carrying out a particular activity, the *anima* must regulate all actions necessary to achieve that goal, even those performed unconsciously. Stahl gave the example that in jumping over a ditch, one controls various muscular movements without any awareness of doing so. Although conscious only of the final goal, the *anima* regulates all the activities needed to achieve that end. Similar considerations apply to the efforts of the *anima* in combating disease. For carrying out the proper end—the restoration of health—it performs all functions necessary for the task and for this goal calls into action various mechanical activities. The *anima*, in brief, is an intelligent agent that wills certain ends and therefore must have organs suitable for achieving them. The human body is the organ of the rational *anima* and is formed for its needs.

The goals of medicine are intensely practical: to maintain health, to keep the body free from threatening ailments, and to combat disease. To achieve these goals, practical medicine must rely on established experience, assisted by sound reason. Speculations that deflect medicine from its goal, even if buttressed by skillful arguments and experiments, have no use. Stahl emphasized that many aspects of knowledge are of little or no positive help. For example, he denied the value of detailed anatomical or chemical studies because attention to precise anatomical findings draws attention away from the body as a whole. And, as Stahl repeatedly indicated, medicine has to do with the whole living organism, presided over by the *anima*, rather than with specific actions of specific parts, which are only instruments. He also rejected from the confines of medicine the specific study of chemistry. Although one of the leading chemists of his era, he expressly denied that chemistry was advantageous in the theory or practice of medicine.

In his strictures Stahl was referring specifically to the teaching of the iatrochemists, who explained bodily activity by the use of a small number of concepts—acidity and alkalinity, coagulation and liquefaction, fermentation, volatility, acrimony. He cogently pointed out that a wide range of ailments was being attributed to essentially the same causes, and that the explanations had neither a priori support from assured theory nor confirmation in solid a posteriori experience, such as a concrete demonstration of fermentation or acidity. This type of doctrine he condemned as useless, unscientific, and sterile. The humors in health or disease simply did not show the various chemical changes that were being invoked as explanatory principles.

We need not concern ourselves with specific details of Stahl's physiology or pathology. He stated that free and orderly circulation, secretion, and excretion are necessary in maintaining health. Harmful material must be eliminated, and if refractory to direct elimination, it must be converted into a state suitable for elimination. The basic reactions of the body exemplify the healing power of nature, through which the *anima*, as an intelligent active force, conserves life and restores health. If nature falters, the physician must use appropriate means to aid the natural processes.

In chemistry as in biology, Stahl strongly disavowed the mechanical viewpoint, which in turn opposed the qualitative philosophy of Aristotle. Aristotelian elements, four in number, embodied qualitative properties that served as the "principles" for material objects. In the mechanical philosophy, on the other hand, the particulate elements had quantitative attributes—size and shape, position and motion—while qualities and properties depended on the interaction of atoms. All atoms obeyed the laws of mechanics; but those that were round, for example, would react differently from those that were pointed or angular.

In addition to the Aristotelian and corpuscular philosophies, a third and more specifically chemi-

cal tradition with three principles (salt, sulfur, and mercury) had developed. These principles had a rather ambiguous status, for they represented not only certain qualities or predictable modes of behavior—such as hardness, inflammability, or volatility—but also concrete material substances. This ambiguity—being characteristic objects and at the same time representing properties that, by inhering in many discrete objects, explained the phenomena of change—went unresolved. Nevertheless, the spagyric elements helped to provide an essentially chemical mode of explanation.

Stahl realized that the simple mechanical atomist viewpoint could not adequately explain the phenomena in chemical operations. He was also aware that the atomist viewpoint must be not totally rejected but merely regarded as inadequate. Matter is not infinitely divisible but exists in elementary particles that are indivisible and impenetrable. Simple elementary bodies, however, are not found in isolation. Everything that we observe is composite, and these composites exist in a hierarchy of increasing complexity. Atoms, never existing by themselves, join to form simple molecules. These in turn unite into more complex molecules, to produce visible objects.

Correlative to this aspect of Stahl's philosophy was the need to explain properties or qualities. In order to account for observed phenomena, the atoms must have specific reactive and qualitative characteristics. Stahl's atoms do indeed bestow particular qualities on the various compounds. However, precisely how a particular quality or functional property relates to the size and shape of atoms he could not satisfactorily explain.

In his attempts to find adequate explanations, Stahl relied heavily on the doctrines of Becher, who believed in three elementary principles—air, water, and earth. Air, however, did not enter into combinations, so that water and earth formed the material bases of objects. "Earth," however, was not a unitary principle. It comprehended three different types: the first, having to do with substantiality, rendered bodies solid and vitrifiable; the second, of moist oily character, provided color, odor, and combustibility; the third supplied weight, ductility, and volatility. These three kinds of earth, despite denials, have rather obvious relationship to the spagyric salt, sulfur, and mercury.

Stahl adopted these views from Becher and used the name "phlogiston" to designate the second earth—the principle of combustibility. It differed from the other two earths, for the first and third could not be separated from the bodies in which they existed, whereas phlogiston did not form any such stable compound.

While the concept of three kinds of earth applied to the vegetable and animal kingdoms as well as to the mineral, the experimental bases for phlogiston rested principally on the behavior of minerals and metals. Striking evidence arose from the reversible relationship of metals and their calxes. A metal contained all three kinds of earth. When the metal was heated intensely, the phlogiston was driven off and a calx appeared. However, when phlogiston was reintroduced into the calx, the metallic form reappeared. Here we have a reversible process: calx plus phlogiston yields the metal; the metal minus phlogiston yields the calx. When phlogiston was driven from a substance, the properties of that substance changed very markedly. And, similarly, if a substance lacking phlogiston received this element through appropriate chemical manipulation, the properties would change. This process also applied to nonmetallic minerals. Sulfur, for example, which had lent its name to the spagyric terminology, was deemed a compound consisting of vitriolic acid plus phlogiston. Far from being synonymous with sulfur, phlogiston was merely a constituent of it.

For minerals the expulsion or reception of phlogiston was a reversible process, but this was not the case in the animal or vegetable kingdoms. Plants were particularly rich in phlogiston; but once it was driven out, the original compound could not be reestablished.

Phlogiston was an element or substance and not an abstract quality or property. As a substance it combined with other chemical substances to form compounds. But, unlike other elements, which could not exist in isolated form, phlogiston could exist in relatively pure form. Finely divided carbon or lampblack, obtained, for example, by holding a cold object close to burning turpentine, was relatively pure phlogiston, visible and palpable. But ordinarily the phlogiston was not directly perceptible. From its combined form it was set free and passed into the air. Flame was considered the whirling motion produced by the escape of phlogiston, and air was necessary for the production of this motion. The air did not enter into the compound but was the receptacle for the phlogiston. In the absence of air, phlogiston could not escape and consequently combustion could not occur. This provided a reasonable explanation for the observation that calcination could not take place in a closed vessel.

Stahl recognized the close relationship between phlogiston and air. Where the quantity of air was limited, the amount of combustion was correlatively limited. He explained this phenomenon through the postulate that air could absorb only a limited amount of phlogiston; and when the limit had been reached, no more combustion—no more liberation of phlogiston—could take place. What happened to the phlogiston that was poured into the air? The Stahlian chemistry held a theory of recycling—the phlogiston in the air passed into plants and thence could pass into animal bodies through the ingestion of plant material.

A retrospective analysis can point out innumerable flaws in the phlogiston theory; and the way in which later eighteenth-century chemists quite demolished the theory forms an important chapter in the history of science and of thought. But this should not blind us to its important role as a bridge between the older concepts and the new. It tried to modify an existing intellectual framework in order to explain experimental observations. It succeeded, but only at the expense of ignoring certain other observations. And it proved unable to encompass new observations as scientific ingenuity devised new experiments.

BIBLIOGRAPHY

Stahl was a very prolific writer, and his doctrines form the subject of a vast secondary literature. Only a few of the more important writings can be mentioned here.

I. ORIGINAL WORKS. Three relatively short essays provide a background for Stahl's general medical philosophy. *Disquisitio de mechanismi et organismi diversitate* (Halle, 1706); *Paraenesis, ad aliena a medica doctrina arcendum* (Halle, 1706); and *De vera diversitate corporis mixti et vivi* (Halle, 1707). His greatest single medical work is *Theoria medica vera, physiologiam et pathologiam . . . sistens* (Halle, 1708), which provides in quite massive detail his doctrines of physiology and pathology, and presents his animistic philosophy as incidental to the exposition. The work includes, as intrinsic introductory material, the three essays mentioned above, plus a fourth, *Vindiciae & indicia de scriptis suis*. A further ed. of the *Theoria medica vera* was published at Halle in 1737. A more recent, 3-vol. ed. edited by Ludovicus Choulant was published at Leipzig in 1831–1833. The work has never been translated into English.

A French rendition of Stahl's writings, *Oeuvres médico-philosophiques et pratiques*, translated with commentaries by T. Blondin, II–VI (Paris, 1859–1864), apparently was intended as 6 vols., although vol. I was not published. This ed. is, unfortunately, rare. The translation is fairly good, although sometimes quite verbose and excessively interpretive.

A German text expounding Stahl's doctrines is Karl Wilhelm Ideler, *Georg Ernst Stahl's Theorie der Heilkunde,* 3 vols. (Berlin, 1831–1832). Although often referred to as a translation, it is only an abbreviated paraphrase. At best it can serve as a "finder"—a rapid way of getting an overview and of locating significant passages that must then be studied in the original Latin.

Stahl and his pupils published extensive clinical studies, describing particular problems, that are significant for the light they throw on the medical practice of the times—for instance, *Collegium casuale magnum* (Leipzig, 1733)—but these are not especially relevant here. He also wrote or was coauthor of a considerable number of dissertations, many of which are available at the National Library of Medicine, Bethesda, Md., and are important for any definitive study of Stahl.

A further work that deserves special mention is *Negotium otiosum seu Σκιαμαχια* (Halle, 1720), an attempt to answer some objections that Leibniz had made to Stahl's animistic doctrines.

Stahl's more specific chemical writings are very numerous. Partington, II, 659–662, has devoted almost four pages to the bibliographic listing, taken from an eighteenth-century bibliography prepared by J. C. Goetz.

One of the earliest is *Zymotechnia fundamentalis* (Halle, 1697). Other important works are *Specimen Beccherianum,* appended to Stahl's ed. of Becher's *Physica subterranea* (Leipzig, 1703); and *Zufällige Gedancken . . . über den Streit von den sogenannten Sulphure* (Halle, 1718), which was translated into French by Holbach as *Traité du soufre* (Paris, 1766). *Fundamenta chymiae dogmaticae et experimentalis* (Nuremberg, 1723), prepared by Stahl's pupils, was translated by Peter Shaw as *Philosophical Principles of Universal Chemistry* (London, 1730). *Fundamenta chymiae dogmatico-rationalis & experimentalis* (Nuremberg, 1732) had a 2nd ed. in 1746. Another important work that presents Stahl's doctrines was written by his pupil Johann Juncker: *Conspectus chemiae theoretico-practicae* (Halle, 1730).

II. SECONDARY LITERATURE. Only a few of the more significant secondary sources can be listed. A relatively recent work is Bernward Josef Gottlieb, "Bedeutung und Auswirkungen des Hallischen Professors . . . Georg Ernst Stahl auf den Vitalismus des XVIII Jahrhunderts, insbesondere auf die Schule von Montpellier," in *Nova acta Leopoldina,* n.s. **12,** no. 89 (1943), 423–502, which covers a great amount of literature but does not exhibit any specially penetrating insight and is far too concerned with Teutonic chauvinism. Walter Pagel, "Helmont, Leibniz, Stahl," in *Archiv für Geschichte der Medizin,* **24** (1931), 19–59, is an important contribution. Albert Lemoine, *Le vitalisme et l'animisme de Stahl* (Paris, 1864) is an important nineteenth-century analysis; an older but very helpful discussion is under the heading "Stahlianisme," *Dictionnaire des sciences médicales,* 60 vols. (Paris, 1812–1822), LII, 401–449. Every general history of medicine devotes space to Stahl. Of especial value, and a source for many subsequent but more shallow discussions, is Kurt Sprengel, *Versuch einer pragmatischen Geschichte der Arzneikunde,* 2nd ed., V (Halle, 1803), 9–47. Stahl's animism, especially in relation to Friedrich Hoffmann's mechanistic views, is discussed in two recent articles by Lester S. King: "Stahl and Hoffmann: A Study in Eighteenth Century Animism," in *Journal of the History of Medicine,* **19** (1964), 118–130; and "Basic Concepts of Early Eighteenth Century Animism," in *American Journal of Psychiatry,* **124** (1967), 797–807.

A very important secondary source dealing with Stahl's chemistry is J. R. Partington, *History of Chemistry,* II (London, 1961), 637–690. An indispensable analysis of the chemical doctrines is Hélène Metzger, *Newton, Stahl, Boerhaave et la doctrine chimique* (Paris, 1930).

LESTER S. KING

STALLO, JOHANN BERNHARD (*b.* Sierhausen, Oldenburg, Germany, 16 March 1823; *d.* Florence, Italy, 6 January 1900), *philosophy of science.*

Stallo's father was a teacher, as were his ancestors on both sides for many generations. After a private education, at the age of thirteen he entered the normal school at Vechta and then the Gymnasium. In 1839, when he was ready to enroll at a university, lack of money led him to emigrate to the United States, where he joined the German colony in Cincinnati. At first Stallo taught mainly German in a Catholic parish school; at that time (1840) he published a textbook, *ABC, Buchstabier und Lesebuch, für die deutschen Schulen Amerikas,* which went through several editions and was widely used. While teaching at St. Xavier College from 1841 to 1844, he continued to study Greek and mathematics. From 1844 to 1848 he was a professor of physics, chemistry, and mathematics at St. John's College (now Fordham University), New York City.

In 1847 Stallo returned to Cincinnati and began to study law, a program he pursued until 1849, when he was admitted to the bar. From 1852 to 1855 he was judge of common pleas, before returning to private practice. In 1870, before the superior court at Cincinnati, he defended the Cincinnati School Board against the Protestant clergy who tried to enforce the retention of Bible reading and hymn singing as a part of the curriculum. From 1884 to 1889 he was American ambassador in

Florence, where he remained even after his official period of service had ended.

The development of Stallo's thought can be characterized as a gradual transition from post-Kantian idealism in his youth to his own version of positivistically oriented phenomenalism in his mature years. He studied Leibniz, Kant, Herbart, Schiller, and Goethe while still in Germany. This influence is visible in the poem "Gott in der Natur," published in *Wahrheitsfreund* (Cincinnati, 1841) which enthusiastically proclaims, in Goethe's fashion, the unity of God and nature. In 1848 he published *The General Principles of the Philosophy of Nature, With an Outline of Its Recent Developments Among the Germans*; *Embracing the Philosophical Systems of Schelling and Hegel and Oken's System of Nature*, the title of which indicates Stallo's exclusive commitment to *Naturphilosophie*. The book is now of value only as a document illuminating the early stage of Stallo's philosophical development, and Stallo himself later conceded its worthlessness: "That book was written while I was under the spell of Hegel's ontological reveries—at a time when I was barely of age and still seriously affected with the metaphysical malady which seems to be one of the unavoidable disorders of intellectual infancy" (preface to *The Concepts and Theories of Modern Physics* [New York, 1881]). Realizing that these words may have been too harsh, he added: "The labor expended in writing it was not, perhaps, wholly wasted, and there are things in it of which I am not ashamed, even at this day . . ." (*ibid*).

It is not difficult now to see what those things were in Stallo's first book that he was not ashamed of in his mature years. One idea was common to all phases of his thought: that things are not "insular existences" but complexes of relations. Also, the influence of the book was not as negligible as Stallo believed. There is definite evidence that his "evolutionary idealism" greatly appealed to Ralph Waldo Emerson, who copied passages from Stallo's book into his journals beginning in November 1849; in 1873 he even credited Stallo with having anticipated Darwin's theory of evolution by regarding animals as "foetal forms of man." Even later Thomas Sterry Hunt, the American chemist and geologist, conceded Stallo's influence and dedicated *A New Basis for Chemistry* (Boston, 1887) to him.

In 1855 Stallo wrote a critical essay on materialism, published at Cincinnati in *Atlantis* (pp. 369–386) and then as a separate offprint entitled *Naturphilosophische Untersuchungen. Der Materialismus*. It represents an intermediate stage between Stallo's early Hegelianism and his mature work in the philosophy and epistemology of science. Its main target was materialism, which had been revived in Germany and was becoming popular in the United States, especially among German immigrants. Stallo explicitly mentioned Karl Vogt and Ludwig Feuerbach. His criticism was written in a semipopular style and clearly was directed to a wide audience. It consists of three distinct parts: an analysis of the epistemological assumptions of materialism; a questioning of its scientific adequacy; and a sharp rejection of the materialistic reduction of thoughts to the brain processes.

In the first part Stallo showed the intrinsic inconsistency of the materialistic epistemology that claimed that all knowledge comes from sensory perception and at the same time postulated the existence of atoms that can never be perceived; furthermore, in basing all knowledge on the sensations—that is, on conscious data—it unwittingly conceded their primary character (contrary to its professed reductionism). In the third part Stallo criticized the then famous statement of Karl Vogt, "The brain secretes thought as the kidney does urine . . . ." He concluded by recommending that materialists read Kant's *Critique of Pure Reason* and Hegel's *Phenomenology of Mind*.

Stallo's original idealism is even more apparent in the middle part. His main argument is the alleged inadequacy of the atomistic explanation of chemical phenomena. At that time the distinction between the atom and the molecule was still not clarified, and thus Stallo's doubts about the indivisibility of the atoms appeared plausible. Similarly, chemical formulas were still far from being established (there was, for instance, still a dispute over whether the formula of water was HO or H_2O) and structural formulas were unknown; thus it was easy for him to speak of "the chaos in organic chemistry." Stallo obviously mistook the temporary incompleteness of the atomic theory for its basic inadequacy. That he was still far short of positivism is indicated by the polemical note against Comte's veto of any metaphysics. On the other hand, it contains the idea found in his first book: that every material thing is a network of forces and relations (*das Gewebe von Kraften und Beziehungen*).

The preface to Stallo's *Concepts and Theories of Modern Physics* is dated 1 September 1881. Three years later, in the extensive introduction to the second edition, he stressed that the main purpose of the book was an epistemological criticism of the corpuscular-kinetic theory of nature. In the first eight chapters he restated the basic theses of the "atomo-mechanical theory" (as he called it) and showed its empirical difficulties. These basic theses were the following: (a) The primary elements of all natural phenomena are mass and motion. (b) Mass and motion are disparate. "Mass is indifferent to motion, which may be imparted to it, and of which it may be divested, by a transference of motion from one mass to another. Mass remains the same, whether at rest or in motion." (c) Both mass and motion are independently conserved. From these theses two general corollaries followed: (a) All phenomenal diversity is reducible to quantitative differences in configuration and motion. (b) All apparently qualitative changes are reducible to the quantitative changes of position and configuration. These two corollaries thus imply the absolute homogeneity, hardness, rigidity, and passivity of the basic elements of matter.

In subsequent chapters Stallo showed how all previous propositions followed from the basic principles of the "atomo-mechanical theory" and how they simultaneously contradicted the empirical findings of his own time. Thus the claim that the basic units of matter are homogeneous followed from the qualitative unity of matter assumed by classical atomism, but it was at variance with the irreducible diversity between the atoms of different elements. Stallo believed that the persistent hope of reducing these differences to different configurations of the more basic and truly homogeneous units had been definitively buried by the failure of Prout's hypothesis. Similarly, the classical assumption of absolute hardness and rigidity of the basic material units was contradicted in the area where the triumph of mechanistic explanations seemed to be the most spectacular—in the kinetic theory of gases, based on the very opposite assumption of the elasticity of the bouncing particles. Yet the concept of an elastic (compressible) atom was a contradiction. The passivity of the basic material units implied the denial of action at a distance, and Stallo again emphasized how persistent the tendency is to reduce all dynamic interaction to the direct pressure and impact of bodies. This led him to point out the difficulties of the kinetic explanations of gravitation, of the mechanical models of ether, and of the theory of atoms as "vortex rings" proposed by William Thomson (later Lord Kelvin).

After showing what he regarded as the empirical inadequacies of the corpuscular-kinetic models, Stallo proceeded to trace their shortcomings to "the structural fallacies of the intellect," which he

attributed to the following four assumptions: (a) that to every concept there corresponds a distinct objective entity; (b) that the alleged entities corresponding to more general concepts exist prior to the entities corresponding to less general concepts; (c) that the order of the genesis of concepts is identical with the order of the genesis of things; (d) that things exist independently of and antecedently to their relations. Thus had arisen "the four radical errors of metaphysics," characterizing "the atomo-mechanical theory." The concept of homogeneous matter, devoid of concrete sensory qualities and existing separately from motion and force, was merely a reified abstraction, comparable with the Hegelian "Being," even though Stallo conceded that it was "somehow less hollow." With equal severity he censured Bošković and the dynamists for their reification of the concept of force. The assumption of the absolute solidity of the basic material units was a mere prejudice due to man's psychobiological conditioning: the fact that "the most obtrusive form of matter is the solid," which was first recognized and manipulated by "the infant intellect of mankind," was the basis of man's tendency to interpret every physical phenomenon in corpuscular terms and every physical interaction by direct contacts and impacts of such solid particles. But there was no absolutely solid body, nor was there any absolutely gapless contact between bodies in nature.

The most valuable and most prophetic insights are expounded in this part of the book. Stallo's firm opposition to the fiction of "insular existence," originally motivated by the metaphysical idea of "the relatedness of reality," was placed on a more convincing basis of concrete physical considerations. He pointed out that the concept of the isolated material body, whether on the atomic or the macrophysical scale, as well as the concept of the single isolated force, was physically meaningless. All physical properties were relational and owed their existence to the physical interaction between various parts of the world. Even inertia, which, according to Newton, represented the very core of matter (*vis insita*) was no exception. Stallo demonstrated it in analyzing Carl Neumann's argument (1870) in favor of the Newtonian absolute space. His thesis was a modification of Newton's classical argument: the absolute rotations (the rotations with respect to absolute space) are physically distinguishable from mere relative rotations, since in the first case centrifugal forces arise while in the second case they do not.

Neumann inferred from this that centrifugal

force would appear on an absolutely rotating body even if it were completely alone in space. Against this Stallo claimed that not only the rotation of a solitary body, but even its very existence, would be utterly meaningless if no other bodies existed: "All properties of a body which constitute the elements of its distinguishable presence in space are in their nature relations and imply terms beyond the body itself" (*Concepts and Theories*, p. 215). He clearly anticipated a similar criticism of Newton by Ernst Mach, who concluded that in the principle of inertia there is "an abbreviated reference to the entire universe" and that "the neglecting of the rest of the world is impossible." This passage from Stallo's book had appeared in *Popular Science Monthly* in 1874 and shows that Mach's criticism of Newton was anticipated a full decade before *Mechanik in ihrer Entwickelung* appeared. Stallo arrived at the same conclusion in showing that Newton's third law requires the existence of at least two bodies in the universe. He quoted Maxwell's comment on this law: Action and reaction are two complementary aspects of the same phenomenon—stress; thus the concept of a single, isolated force is as meaningless as that of a solitary body. Such a body would be not only without weight but also without inertia.

The second anticipatory insight in Stallo's book was his epistemological criticism of mechanical models in general. Its basic idea was concisely expressed in his statement that "a phenomenon is not explained by being dwarfed." In other words, to explain the properties of macroscopic matter by postulating the very same properties on the microphysical scale was no explanation at all. Stallo thus raised doubt about the adequacy of the mechanical and, more generally, intuitive models of the microcosmos. It is hardly necessary to stress how prophetic his view proved to be and how bold it was in the era when William Thomson equated the understanding of any physical phenomenon with the possibility of making a mechanical model of it.

On the other hand, Stallo dogmatically excluded non-Euclidean geometries from physics. His position in this respect was not consistent; and his arguments against "transcendental geometries," as he called them, were inconclusive. First, he claimed that the curvature of space implies the absolute finitude of the material universe, which is "a necessary complement of the assumption of its absolute minimum, the atom." This clearly is not true of Lobachevsky's space, which is infinite. Second, he claimed, as Poincaré did later, that no empirical proof can ever be given for a non-Eu-

clidean character of space; even the discovery of a nonzero parallax of very distant stars would not be conclusive, since it would be more natural to explain it by some deviation of the light rays *in* space rather than by some intrinsic curvature *of* space. He dogmatically insisted that by its own nature space must be homogeneous, confusing homogeneity with Euclidean character; he did not realize that Riemannian and Lobachevskian spaces of a constant curvature are also homogeneous. Finally, he claimed that the concept of a straight line, purportedly eliminated by Riemann and others, was surreptitiously reintroduced in the form of "the radius of curvature." Stallo clearly misunderstood the metaphorical nature of this term, which can be taken literally only for two-dimensional illustrative models of non-Euclidean spaces and not for those spaces themselves, for which the term "space constant" is less misleading than "radius of curvature." Thus today we see that it was Helmholtz and Clifford who were on strong ground, rather than Stallo, who criticized them.

In *Essay on the Foundations of Geometry* (1897) Bertrand Russell pointed out the irrelevance of Stallo's criticism of non-Euclidean geometry (p. 88), and his demonstration caught Ernst Mach's attention. While disagreeing with Stallo about non-Euclidean geometry, Mach welcomed his criticism of what he called "mechanistic mythology" and referred to him in the fourth edition of his *Science of Mechanics*. He regretted not having known Stallo's work earlier, and began a correspondence with him. Mach wrote the preface to H. Kleinpeter's German translation of Stallo's *Concepts and Theories of Modern Physics* (Leipzig, 1901), and dedicated his *Principien der Wärmelehre* (1896) to him.

This was not the only recognition that Stallo received, although his influence was greater on philosophers, particularly philosophers of science, than on scientists. Josiah Royce, in his introduction to G. B. Halsted's translation of Poincaré's *Foundation of Space*, recalled how scientific orthodoxy was shocked by the appearance of Stallo's book. Its early translation into French (1884) also attracted considerable attention: it probably inspired Arthur Hannequin's *Essai critique sur l'hypothèse des atomes* (1895); and Bergson, Meyerson, and L. Brunschvicg referred to it in their books. With the mounting crisis of the mechanical models in physics, Stallo's work began to receive increasing attention: Rudolf Carnap referred to him in *Der Raum* (1922) and *Physikalische Begriffsbildung* (1926), and P. W. Bridgman reedited

Concepts and Theories with his own introduction (1960).

In a broader historical perspective Stallo appears as one of the prophets of twentieth-century physics. Like Mach, he correctly recognized the inadequacy of the classical corpuscular-kinetic models on the microphysical scale and questioned the absolutistic assumptions of Newton. But, also like Mach, he failed to appreciate the fruitfulness of the same models on the macrophysical and molecular level. This failure was revealed in Stallo's rejection of the kinetic theory of gases; his comments on this theory, especially his claim that it is simpler to assume "gaseousness" as a primary attribute of matter, are mere historical curiosities today. On the other hand, his lucid analysis of the logical structure of classical atomism is on a par with similar analyses by Kurd Lasswitz and Émile Meyerson, and will remain a lasting contribution to the history of ideas.

BIBLIOGRAPHY

On Stallo and his work, see M. Čapek, "Two Critics of Newton Prior to Mach: Boscovich and Stallo," in *Actes du XII Congrès international des sciences* (Paris, 1968), IV, 35–37; Stillman Drake, "J. B. Stallo and the Critique of Classical Physics," in *Men and Moments in the History of Science* (Seattle, 1959); Lloyd D. Eaton, *Hegel's First American Followers* (Athens, Ohio, 1966); H. Kleinpeter, "Stallo als Erkenntniskritiker," in *Vierteljahrsschrift für wissenschaftliche Philosophie*, **25** (1901), 401–440; and *Die Erkenntnistheorie der Naturforschung der Gegenwart. Unter Zugrundelegung der Anschauungen von Mach, Stallo, Clifford, Kirchhoff, Hertz, Pearson und Ostwald* (Leipzig, 1905); J. H. Rattermann, *Johann Bernard Stallo, deutsch-amerikanischer Philosoph, Jurist und Staatsmann*: . . . (Cincinnati, 1902); and Lancelot Whyte, "Stallo Versus Matter," in *Anglo-German Review*, **1** (1961).

M. Čapek

STAMPIOEN, JAN JANSZ, DE JONGE (*b*. Rotterdam, Netherlands, 1610; *d*. The Hague, Netherlands [?], after 1689), *mathematics*.

Stampioen's father (of the same name, whence the cognomen *de Jonge*) made astronomical instruments and was an official surveyor and gauger until his removal from office in 1660 for breach of trust.[1] The son began his own career in 1632 with an edition of Frans van Schooten the Elder's sine tables, to which Stampioen appended his own fully algebraic treatment of spherical trigonometry.

In 1633, while a mathematics teacher in Rotterdam, Stampioen took part in a public competition, during which he challenged Descartes to resolve a quartic problem involving a triangle with inscribed figures. Descartes derived the correct equation but did not solve it explicitly, and Stampioen rejected the solution as incomplete.[2] The issue was dropped for the moment, but Stampioen had made an enemy of Descartes and would soon feel the effects.

After being named tutor to Prince William (II) in 1638, Stampioen moved to The Hague, where he opened up a printing shop and in 1639 published his *Algebra ofte nieuwe stelregel* (*Algebra, or the New Method*), which he had completed in 1634. Despite the general title, the work focused on a new method of determining the cube root of expressions of the form $a + \sqrt{b}$ and on the method's application to the solution of cubic equations. In order to attract attention to his forthcoming book, he assumed in 1638 the alias Johan Baptista of Antwerp and posed two public challenges, the more difficult of which demanded the calculation of a traversing position for a siege gun (as stated, a cubic problem). Then he immediately published a solution under his own name. Soon thereafter, he presented another challenge requiring the determination of the position of the sun from the condition that three poles of given heights placed vertically in the ground each cast shadows reaching to the feet of the other two.[3]

A young surveyor in Utrecht, Jacob van Waessenaer, also published a solution to the first, or Antwerp, challenge, employing the methods of Descartes's *Geometry*. Stampioen's rejection of this solution prompted Waessenaer to publish a broad-scale critique of Stampioen's mathematics, emphasizing the inadequacies of the "new methods."[4] The exchange of pamphlets lasted two years and soon involved Descartes, who may in fact have been behind Waessenaer from the beginning.[5] With a wager of 600 gulden riding on the outcome, the issue was adjudicated in 1640 by Van Schooten and Jacob Gool, who found in Waessenaer's favor.[6]

Judging from their correspondence, Constantijn Huygens agreed with Descartes that Stampioen behaved badly during the dispute. Nonetheless, in 1644 Huygens engaged Stampioen for a year as mathematics tutor for his two elder sons, Constantijn, Jr., and Christiaan.[7] Thereafter, Stampioen faded from public notice. A brief reprise of the Waessenaer dispute in 1648, a topographical map published in 1650, and a mention of his having served in 1689 as an expert in a test of a method for determining longitude at sea are the only traces left of Stampioen's later life.

NOTES

1. The British Museum Catalogue (Ten-year supplement, XXI, col. 148) lists a copy of the *Sententien, by den Hove van Hollant gearresteert, jegens Ian Ianssz Stampioen en Quirijn Verblas. Gepronuncieert den acht en twintichsten Iulij Anno 1660.* For further details, see Bierens de Haan's "Bouwstoffen," cited in the bibliography.
2. For details, see the letter from Descartes to Stampioen in Charles Adam and Paul Tannery, eds., *Oeuvres de Descartes,* I (Paris, 1897), 275–280, and the editorial note in *ibid.* 573–578.
3. Newton, in his deposited lectures on algebra, published in *Universal Arithmetick* (London, 1707), states the problem as follows: "When, somewhere on Earth, three staves are erected perpendicular to the horizontal plane at points *A, B,* and *C*—that at *A* being 6 feet, that at *B* 18 feet and that at *C* 8 feet, with the line *AB* 33 feet in length—, it happens on a certain day that the tip of stave *A*'s shadow passes through the points *B* and *C,* that of stave *B,* however, through *A* and *C,* and that of stave *C* through the point *A.* What is the sun's declination and the polar elevation? in other words, on what day and at what place do these events occur?" (Derek T. Whiteside, ed., *The Mathematical Papers of Isaac Newton,* V [Cambridge, 1972], 267.) Newton's complete solution of this problem, which involves conic sections, occupies pp. 266–278 of this edition.
4. Waessenaer's two major tracts are *Aanmerckingen op den nieuwen Stel-Regel van J. Stampioen, d'Jonge* (Leiden, 1639); and *Den On-wissen Wis-konstenaer I. I. Stampioen ontdeckt Door sijne ongegronde Weddinge ende mis-lucte Solutien van sijne eygene questien. Midtsgaders Eenen generalen Regel om de Cubic-wortelen ende alle andere te trecken uyt twee-namighe ghetallen: dewelcke voor desen niet bekent en is geweest. Noch De Solutien van twee sware Geometrische Questien door de Algebra: dienstich om alle te leeren ontbinden* (Leiden, 1640).
5. That is the conclusion of Bierens de Haan in his "Bouwstoffen," cited in the bibliography below, 79ff.
6. Stampioen published the judgment, entitling it so as to make himself appear the winner: *Verclaringe over het gevoelen by de E. H. professoren matheseos der Universiteit tot Leyden uyt-ghesproken, nopende den Regel fol. 25 van J. Stampioen, Welcke dese Verclaringhe soodanigh ghetstelt is, dat yeder een daer uyt can oordeelen dat den Regel fol. 25 beschreven van Johan Stampioen de Jonge in sijnen Nieuwen Stel-Regel, seer licht, generael, ende der waerheydt conform is, om daer door den Teerling-wortel te trecken uyt twee-naemighe ghetallen* (The Hague, 1640). Judging by Descartes's complaints to Henricus Regius (Bierens de Haan, "Bouwstoffen," 99), the decision was formulated in a manner vague enough to permit such a contrary reading.
7. See Christiaan Huygens, *Oeuvres complètes,* XXII (The Hague, 1950), 399ff., and *ibid.,* I (The Hague, 1888), 15, for the list of mathematical works suggested by Stampioen as a syllabus for Huygens' sons.

BIBLIOGRAPHY

I. ORIGINAL WORKS. Stampioen's major works include his *Kort byvoeghsel der sphaerische triangulen* appended to his edition of Frans van Schooten, *Tabula sinuum* (Rotterdam, 1632); and his *Algebra, ofte Nieuwe stel-regel, waer door alles ghevonden wordt inde wisconst, wat vindtbaer is . . .* (The Hague, 1639).

The challenges and disputes of 1633 and 1638–1640 gave rise to several polemic pamphlets, a complete listing of which can be found in either of Bierens de Haan's articles listed below. The more important items are "Solutie op alle de questien openbaer angeslagen ende voorgestelt door Ez. de Decker" (Rotterdam, 1634); "Questie aen de Batavische Ingenieurs, Voor-gestelt door Johan Baptista Antwerpiensis. Volghens het spreeckwordt: Laet const blijken, Met goet bewys" (1638; for a more easily accessible statement of the problem, see *Oeuvres de Descartes,* C. Adam and P. Tannery, eds., II [Paris, 1898], 601ff.); "Wiskonstige Ontbinding. Over het Antwerpsch Vraegh-stuck toe-ge-eyghent alle Lief-Hebbers der Wis-Const" (The Hague, 1638); and "Wis-Konstigh Ende Reden-Maetigh Bewijs. Op den Reghel Fol. 25, 26 en 27. Van sijn Boeck ghenaemt den Nieuwen Stel-Regel" (The Hague, 1640).

Bibliographical details of Stampioen's map are given by Bierens de Haan in his "Bouwstoffen" (see below), 114.

II. SECONDARY LITERATURE. The most complete biography is that of Cornelis de Waard in *Nieuw Nederlandsch Biografisch Woordenboek,* II (Leiden, 1912), cols. 1358–1360. See also David Bierens de Haan, "Bouwstoffen voor de geschiedenis der wis- en natuurkundigen weteschappen en de Nederlanden, XXX: Jan Jansz. Stampioen de Jonge en Jacob à Waessenaer," in *Verslagen en Mededeelingen der koninklijke Akademie van Wetenschappen, Afdeeling Natuurkunde,* 3rd ser., III (Amsterdam, 1887), 69–119; and "Quelques lettres inédites de René Descartes et de Constantyn Huygens," in *Zeitschrift für Mathematik und Physik,* 32 (1887), 161–173. Further bibliography can be found in these three articles.

MICHAEL S. MAHONEY

STANNIUS, HERMANN FRIEDRICH (*b.* Hamburg, Germany, 15 March 1808; *d.* Sachsenburg, Germany, 15 January 1883), *comparative anatomy, physiology.*

Stannius was the son of a merchant, Johann Wilhelm Julius Stannius, and the former Johanna Flügge. After attending the Johanneum in Hamburg, he began his medical studies at the Akademisches Gymnasium there (1825). To complete his studies, Stannius went to Berlin in 1828 and then to Breslau, where he finished a doctoral dissertation in comparative anatomy on 26 November 1831. He returned to Berlin, where he became an assistant at the Friedrichstädter-Krankenhaus (1831–1837) while working as a general practitioner. Simultaneously he investigated a great number of questions in entomology and pathological anatomy.

On 3 October 1837, Stannius, then aged twenty-nine, was offered an appointment as full professor of comparative anatomy, physiology, and general pathology at Rostock University and as director of the institute for the same fields. He lectured on these subjects and also taught histology from 1840 to 1862. Although Stannius had been in poor health since 1843, he succeeded to the rectorship of the university in 1850 and carried out much fruitful scientific research until 1854. Beginning in 1855 his illness, a serious nervous disease connected with mental disturbances, grew worse, and in 1862 it obliged him to abandon his work. The last twenty years of his life were spent in a mental hospital at Sachsenburg.

Although his health and his position at the university allowed Stannius to undertake scientific work for only seventeen years, he nevertheless gained a reputation in various fields of research. He first worked in entomology, dealing with the structure of the diptera and with deformities of insects (1835).

In Berlin he dealt with general pathology (1837). His outstanding monograph was the second volume of *Lehrbuch der vergleichenden Anatomie der Wirbeltiere* (1846). He also investigated the nervous systems and the brains of sturgeons and dolphins (1846, 1849), and he conducted pharmacological studies on the effects of strychnine and digitalis (1837, 1851). In a noted work (1852), he ligatured a frog heart and established the location of the stimulus-building center within the *sinus venosus*. This experiment has since been known as "Stannius' experiment." He was a long-time friend of Rudolph Wagner, a physiologist at Göttingen University. Of the contributions he undertook to write for Wagner's *Dictionary of Physiology*, he was able to finish only the article on fever (1842), which he said resulted from a "changed mood" of the nervous system.

BIBLIOGRAPHY

I. ORIGINAL WORKS. A bibliography of forty of Stannius' papers is in Royal Society, *Catalogue of Scientific Papers*, V, 797–798. His works include *De speciebus nonnullis Mycethophila vel novis vel minus cognitis* (Bratislava, 1831), his inaugural dissertation; *Beiträge zur Entomologie, besondere in Bezug auf Schlesien, gemeinschaftlich mit Schummel* (Breslau, 1832); "Über den Einfluss der Nerven auf den Blutumlauf," in *Notizen aus dem Gebiet der Natur- und Heilkunde*, **36** (1833), 246–248; "Ueber einige Missbildungen an Insekten," in *Archiv für Anatomie, Physiologie und wissenschaftliche Medizin* (1835), 295–310; *Allgemeine Pathologie*, I (Berlin, 1837); "Ueber die Einwirkung des Strychnins auf das Nervensystem," in *Archiv für Anatomie . . .* (1837), 223–236; "Ueber Nebennieren bei Knorpelfischen," *ibid.* (1839), 97–101; "Ueber Lymphherzen der Vögel," *ibid.* (1843), 449–452; "Ueber den Bau des Delphingehirns," in *Abhandlungen aus dem Gebiet der Naturwissenschaften* (Hamburg), **1** (1846), 1–16; *Lehrbuch der vergleichenden Anatomie der Wirbelthiere*, 2 vols. (Berlin, 1846; 2nd ed., 1852), of which Carl von Siebold wrote the first, and Stannius the second volume; "Untersuchungen ueber Muskelreizbarkeit," in *Archiv für Anatomie . . .* (1847), 443–462, and (1849), 588–592; *Das peripherische Nervensystem der Fische, anatomisch und physiologisch untersucht* (Rostock, 1849); "Ueber die Wirkung der Digitalis und des Digitalin," in *Archiv für physiologische Heilkunde*, **10** (1851), 177–209; and "Zwei Reihen physiologischer Versuche," in *Archiv für Anatomie . . .* (1852), 85–100.

II. SECONDARY LITERATURE. See J. Pagel, *Biographisches Lexicon der hervorragenden Aerzte*, 2nd ed., V (Berlin–Vienna, 1934), 390; Wilhelm Stieda, "Hermann Stannius und die Universität Rostock 1837–1854," in *Jahrbuch des Vereins für mecklenburgische Geschichte*, **93** (1929), 1–36; Richard N. Wegner, *Zur Geschichte der anatomischen Forschung an der Universität Rostock* (Wiesbaden, 1917), 2, 127–128; and Axel Wilhelmi, *Die mecklenburgischen Ärzte von den ältesten Zeiten bis zur Gegenwart* (Schwerin, 1901), 107–108, with bibliography.

K. E. ROTHSCHUH

STANTON, THOMAS ERNEST (*b.* Atherstone, Warwickshire, England, 12 December 1865; *d.* Pevensey Bay, Sussex, England, 30 August 1931), *engineering.*

Stanton was educated at Atherstone Grammar School, Owens College, Manchester (1884–1891), and University College, Liverpool (D.Sc. 1898). While a student at Owens, he was an articled pupil at Gimson & Co. Engineers, Leicester (1884–1887). He began his academic career as demonstrator in the Whitworth Engineering Laboratory at Owens College (1891–1896), then advanced steadily; senior lecturer in engineering at University College, Liverpool (1896–1899); professor of civil and mechanical engineering, University College, Bristol (1899–1901); and superintendent of the engineering department at the National Physical Laboratory, Teddington (1901–1930). At Owens College, Stanton was assistant to Osborne Reynolds and later experimentally established the latter's theoretical laws of fluid flow in pipes. He was associated with the National Physical Laboratory from its inception in 1901. Now administered by the Department of Trade and Industry it was originally established under the overall control of the Royal Society, to pursue scientific research, particularly for application in industry.

Throughout his career Stanton was occupied with hydrodynamics, strength of materials, heat transmission, and lubrication. His papers on the flow of water in channels of varying cross section (1902), the resistance of thin plates and models in a current of water (1909), the mechanical viscosity of fluids (1911), and comparisons of surface friction and eddy-making resistance in fluids (1912) led to his definitive text *Friction* (1923), in which he postulated the boundary theory. Experiments in alternating stress and impact testing machines (1905–1906) and on hardness testing (1916–1917) resulted in awards by the Institution of Civil Engineers (1899, 1906, 1921) culminating in the Howard Quinquennial Prize for his research and writing on the properties of iron and steel.

Stanton was involved with aerodynamics from the early years of airplane development, the engineering department of the National Physical Laboratory having charge of this work until it was assigned to a separate department. He built a vertical wind tunnel and other equipment for wind velocity investigations; and as late as 1928, although no longer engaged in administration, Stanton made tests for the British Airscrew Panel on airfoils at speeds near the velocity of sound in air. He was elected a Fellow of the Royal Society in 1914 and also served on its Council in 1927–1929. He was a member of the committee for the restoration of St. Paul's Cathedral, London, in the early 1930's. Stanton was awarded the C.B.E. for his service in World War I and knighted in 1928.

BIBLIOGRAPHY

I. ORIGINAL WORKS. Stanton's writings include "Flow of Water in Channels of Varying Cross Section" in *Engineering*, **74** (1902), 664; "Resistance of Thin Plates and Models in a Current of Water," in *Transactions of the Institution of Naval Architects* (1909), 164–169; "Mechanical Viscosity of Fluids as Affected by the Speed and by the Dimensions of the Channel . . .," in *Proceedings of the Royal Society of London, *A85 (1910), 366–376; "Similarity of Motion in Relation to the Surface Friction of Fluids," in *Philosophical Transactions of the Royal Society of London*, A214 (1914), 199–224, written with J. R. Pannell; *Friction* (London, 1923); "Tests Under Conditions of Infinite Aspect Ratio of Four Airfoils in High-Speed Wind Channel" and "Distribution of Pressure Over Symmetrical Joukowski Section at High Speeds," both in *Technical Report of Aeronautical Research Committee of National Physical Laboratory, 1929–1930*, I, Aerodynamics (London, 1931), 290–296; and "Engineering Research," in *Engineer*, **151** (1931), 506; and *Nature*, **127** (1931), 748–749.

II. SECONDARY LITERATURE. See S. H. Hooker, "Compressibility Effects in High Speed Air Flow," in *Journal of the Royal Aeronautical Society*, **35** (1931), 665–674, with illustration of high-speed wind tunnel at 669; and the unsigned "The Late Sir Thomas Stanton," in *Engineering*, **132** (4 Sept. 1931), 280.

P. W. BISHOP

STARK, JOHANNES (*b.* Schickenhof, Upper Palatinate, Germany, 15 April 1874; *d.* Traunstein, Upper Bavaria, Germany, 21 June 1957), *experimental physics.*

Stark, the son of a farmer, entered the University of Munich in 1894 and received the doctorate in May 1897 for a dissertation entitled "Untersuchungen über Russ" ("Investigations on Lampblack"). After passing the two state examinations required for the teaching of mathematics at an advanced level, he began work on 1 October 1897 at the University of Munich, spending most of his time as private assistant to Eugen Lommel. On 1 April 1900 he became assistant to Eduard Riecke at the University of Göttingen, where the following autumn he qualified as lecturer and was appointed *Privatdozent* on 24 October 1900. While noting Stark's highly developed technical and experimental skill and his gift for conceptualization, the Faculty observed in its confidential report to the university curator that "it is accompanied by a definite deficiency in the area of exact mathematical formulation of the problems under consideration."

Stark's main field of interest was electrical conduction in gases, and his first book dealt with this subject. In 1904 he founded *Jahrbuch der Radioaktivität und Elektronik* to publish studies in the newly developing field of particle physics. He rapidly acquired a broad understanding of this field through intensive reading of the literature and his own experiments. This knowledge prompted him to test for the existence of the optical phenomenon known as the Doppler effect in canal rays, which had been recognized as fast-moving particles by Wilhelm Wien. The effect had never been detected in terrestrial light sources; but, as Stark later said, he found it "almost effortlessly" in the hydrogen lines. He made this discovery immediately after moving into the new physics institute at Göttingen.

Seeking to determine the scientific significance

of his discovery, Stark attempted to make the optical Doppler effect a proof of Einstein's theory of special relativity and, a year later (1907), with the quantum hypothesis as well. Stark was thus one of the earliest defenders of the hypothesis, and he remained in the forefront of research until 1913. Curiously, after that year he turned vehemently against both the quantum theory and the general theory of relativity. He therefore is still remembered by older physicists as a conservative, indeed as a reactionary.

In his initial campaign for the quantum hypothesis, Stark, following Einstein, sought new natural phenomena that could be understood in terms of it—and only in those terms. Along with many correct deductions, such as the interpretation of the ultraviolet boundary of X radiation due to electron deceleration, he arrived at a considerable number of erroneous interpretations. At the end of 1909 he initiated a vigorous debate with Arnold Sommerfeld on quantum theory that was conducted in the pages of *Physikalische Zeitschrift* and in their correspondence. Stark sought to understand the distinctive features of the radiation—especially the directional dependence—with the aid of the quantum hypothesis of light; and he tried, virtually by brute force, to wrest agreement from Sommerfeld. "I am so bold as to hope," he wrote, "that just as you changed your position regarding the theory of relativity, so you will modify your stand on the quantum hypothesis and . . . that the differences between us will have been the reason for it." But it was not difficult for Sommerfeld to point out that Stark had made serious errors in physics. The classical electromagnetic theory was already leading to experimentally discovered directional dependence. Thus Sommerfeld wrote: "Nothing is further from my intention than to begin a feud with you. That would be a very unfair match. For you far surpass me in experimental ideas, just as I excel you in theoretical clarity." The discussion eventually veered off into a polemic. Only a few months before, Sommerfeld had supported Stark's appointment to Aachen; the resulting enmity later overshadowed the careers of both men.

On 1 April 1906 Stark had become *Dozent* in applied physics and photography at the Technical College in Hannover, where he also received the associated post of assistant and was named professor. He soon came into conflict with his superior Julius Precht, who repeatedly requested the Ministry of Education to dismiss Stark and finally succeeded in having him temporarily transferred to Greifswald on 1 October 1907. Following Stark's return

the tensions between the two increased until Stark, with the energetic support of Sommerfeld, was appointed full professor at the Technical College in Aachen on 1 April 1909.

With the relatively elaborate equipment available to him in his own laboratory at Aachen, Stark completed his research in progress, chiefly on the dissymmetry of *Bremsstrahlung*, and undertook a new series of experiments on the splitting of spectral lines in an electric field. While at Göttingen he had been encouraged by Woldemar Voigt to investigate this electrical analogy to the magnetic Zeeman effect. Stark's first preparatory experiment, at the beginning of 1906, had been a failure; but he was successful in October 1913. He described the experiment in a short autobiographical account. Having procured all the necessary equipment—"a high-intensity spectrograph of rather large dispersion, high-tension sources, and Gaede pumps"—he looked for the effect "simultaneously in the hydrogen and helium lines." An electric field of between 10,000 and 31,000 volts/cm. was established in the canal-ray tube.

> One afternoon soon after courses resumed in October, I began recording the canal rays in a mixture of hydrogen and helium. About six o'clock I interrupted the exposure and . . . went to the darkroom to start the developing process. I was naturally very excited, and since the plate was still in the fixing bath, I took it out for a short time to look at the spectrum in the faint yellow light of the darkroom. I observed several lines at the position of the blue hydrogen line, whereas the neighboring helium lines appeared to be simple ["Die Entdeckung des Stark-Effekte"].

At the beginning of July 1913, several months before Stark's discovery, Niels Bohr published his concept of a quantum-mechanical model of the atom. This provided, in principle, the possibility of understanding the reason for the Stark effect, which the classical theory was powerless to explain. Stark therefore had an opportunity to be doubly gratified, having also been one of the first, after Max Planck and Einstein, to stress the "fundamental significance" of Planck's elementary law (since 1907), which he had championed in many polemical discussions. Yet, almost incomprehensibly, Stark denied himself the satisfaction of seeing his own experiments confirm a theory for which he had helped prepare the way conceptually, even if he had not directly participated in its creation. Apparently he always had to oppose the accepted point of view. Thus, as Bohr's theory continued to gain adherents in 1914–1916, Stark set out to reverse this inexorable development. From the moment that Eduard Riecke's retirement from his chair at Göttingen was announced in June 1914, Stark hoped to be his successor. The process of selection, however, dragged on for years and ended with a bitter dispute between Stark and the Göttingen faculty. In 1917, therefore, Stark went to Greifswald. While there he received the Nobel Prize for physics in 1919, for the "completeness and reliability" of his measurements.

More than ever Stark claimed to be Germany's leading physicist; and in 1920 he founded, in opposition to the Deutsche Physikalische Gesellschaft, the Fachgemeinschaft der deutschen Hochschullehrer der Physik. The latter remained an essentially insignificant organization, but with its help Stark managed to join the board of physics (Fachausschuss) of the Notgemeinschaft der Deutschen Wissenschaft and the Helmholtz-Gesellschaft, the two most important science foundations of German scientists. Since the members of the physics boards had to be confirmed by vote of the entire membership, Stark was obliged to resign from the Notgemeinschaft in 1922 and from the Helmholtz-Gesellschaft in 1924.

In 1920 Stark was appointed successor to Wilhelm Wien at Würzburg. He soon quarreled with almost all his colleagues, and tensions reached a peak in a fight over the habilitation of a student. Unhappy with his situation at Würzburg, Stark was able, by virtue of the large sum of money he received with the Nobel Prize, to resign and move to his native Upper Palatinate, where he devoted himself to the development of a porcelain industry. In the difficult postwar years, however, he was unable to make his project a financial success. He decided to return to science but could not obtain another teaching post: he had made too many enemies. The only physicist whom he had not alienated was Philipp Lenard, who had become an outsider and whose battle against "Jewish, dogmatic physics" Stark unreservedly supported.

After the Nazi seizure of power, Stark, as a partisan of Hitler, was appointed president of the Physikalisch-technische Reichsanstalt (PTR), effective 1 April 1933. He conceived ambitious—not to say grandiose—plans for the expansion of the institution, which was to be part of a total reorganization of physics in Germany. Further, in accord with the "Führerprinzip" and in his capacity as president of the PTR, he hoped to become permanent president of the Deutsche Physikalische Gesellschaft. At the physics congress at Würzburg, however, he encountered such strong resistance,

crystallized above all by a courageous speech by Max von Laue, that he had to abandon this ambition. Similarly, Laue again intervened successfully against Stark when he was about to be forced upon the Prussian Academy—with Friedrich Paschen, Max Planck, and Karl Willy Wagner proposing his nomination on the ground that the academy had no real alternative to accepting him.

In June 1934 the government appointed Stark president of the Notgemeinschaft der Deutschen Wissenschaft (which was renamed "Deutsche Forschungsgemeinschaft"), replacing Friedrich Schmidt-Ott, who had been dismissed. In his new, powerful position as head of both this organization and the PTR, Stark intensified his fight against modern theoretical physics, designating its proponents, led by Laue, Arnold Sommerfeld, and Werner Heisenberg, as "white Jews in science" and "viceroys of the Einsteinian spirit" in Germany. Stark emphasized that the Nazi seizure of power and the Nuremberg laws had brought only a partial victory in the fight against the Jews. The "viceroys of Judaism in German intellectual life," he insisted, must disappear. The violence of his attacks made Stark increasingly appear pathologically quarrelsome.

Struggles within the hierarchy of the Third Reich compelled Stark to retire from the presidency of the Forschungsgemeinschaft at the end of 1936, and he was subsequently pensioned by the PTR. Shortly before the outbreak of war Stark, on bad terms with virtually everyone, retired to his estate of Eppenstatt, near Traunstein in Upper Bavaria. Even more than Philipp Lenard, Stark has been condemned, even despised, by contemporaries and posterity. Nevertheless, he contributed significantly to the development of physics, especially in his earlier years; and he later exerted a strong, if disastrous, influence.

BIBLIOGRAPHY

I. ORIGINAL WORKS. A complete list of Stark's writings is in Poggendorff, IV, 1430–1431; V, 1196–1198; VI, 2524; VIIa, S–Z, 1, 485–486.

Papers on the Doppler effect include "Der Doppler-Effekt bei den Kanalstrahlen und die Spektra der positiven Atomionen," in *Physikalische Zeitschrift*, **6** (1905), 892–897; and "Über die Lichtemission der Kanalstrahlen in Wasserstoff," in Annalen der Physik, 4th ser., **21** (1906), 401–456.

On the quantum hypothesis, see "Elementarquantum der Energie, Modell der negativen und positiven Elektrizität," in *Physikalische Zeitschrift*, **8** (1907), 881–884;

"Beziehung des Doppler-Effekts bei Kanalstrahlen zur Planckschen Strahlungstheorie," *ibid.*, 913–919; "Zur Energetik und Chemie der Bandenspektra," *ibid.*, **9** (1908), 85–94, 356–358; "Neue Beobachtungen zu Kanalstrahlen in Beziehung zur Lichtquantenhypothese," *ibid.*, 889–900; and "Über Röntgenstrahlen und die atomistische Konstitution der Strahlung," *ibid.*, **10** (1909), 826.

His major work on the Stark effect is "Beobachtungen über den Effekt des elektrischen Feldes auf Spektrallinien. I–VI," in *Annalen der Physik*, 4th ser., **43** (1914), 965–1047, and **48** (1915), 193–235, repr. as *Johannes Stark. Paul S. Epstein, Der Stark-Effekt*, which is vol. 6 of Dokumente der Naturwissenschaft (Stuttgart, 1965).

Among his books are *Die Elektrizität in Gasen* (Leipzig, 1902); *Die Prinzipien der Atomdynamik*, 3 vols. (Leipzig, 1910–1915); *Die gegenwärtige Krisis in der deutschen Physik* (Leipzig, 1922); *Die Axialität der Lichtemission und Atomstruktur* (Berlin, 1927); *Atomstruktur und Atombindung* (Berlin, 1928); *Adolf Hitler und die deutsche Forschung* (Berlin, 1935); and *Jüdische und deutsche Physik* (Leipzig, 1941), written with Wilhelm Müller.

Letters from the Stark estate, including 90 percent of his scientific correspondence up to 1920, are at the Staatsbibliothek der Stiftung Preussischer Kulturbesitz, Handschriften Abteilung, Berlin-Dahlem.

II. SECONDARY LITERATURE. See Armin Hermann, "Die Entdeckung des Stark-Effekte," in *Johannes Stark. Paul S. Epstein, Der Stark-Effekt* (Stuttgart, 1965), 7–16; "Albert Einstein und Johannes Stark. Briefwechsel und Verhältnis der beiden Nobelpreisträger," in *Sudhoffs Archiv für Geschichte der Medizin und Naturwissenschaften*, **50** (1966), 267–285; "H. A. Lorentz–Praeceptor physicae. Sein Briefwechsel mit dem deutschen Nobelpreisträger Johannes Stark," in *Janus*, **53** (1966), 99–114; and "Die frühe Diskussion zwischen Stark und Sommerfeld über die Quantenhypothese," in *Centaurus*, **12** (1967), 38–59; and Kurt Zierold, *Forschungsförderung in drei Epochen. Deutsche Forschungsgemeinschaft . . .* (Wiesbaden, 1968), 173–212.

ARMIN HERMANN

STARKEY, GEORGE (*b.* Bermuda, 1628; *d.* London, England, 1665), *medicine, alchemy.*

Starkey, who used his family name Stirk until adopting the more familiar cognomen found on his title pages, was the son of George Stirk, a Puritan minister in Bermuda, and Elizabeth Painter. During his youth he developed an interest in natural history and devised experiments to test the theory of the spontaneous generation of insects. While a student at Harvard College, he began the study of medicine and alchemy and was soon attracted to Helmont's doctrines. He graduated in 1646, took

the master's degree, and practiced medicine in the Boston area, where he married a daughter of Israel Stoughton. Sometimes relying on his friend John Winthrop, Jr., for books, chemicals, and apparatus, he pursued research along Helmontian lines.

In 1650 Starkey emigrated to England. Associating with Samuel Hartlib's circle of investigators, he engaged in a wide range of experiments, including the production of alchemical metals and the preparation of chemical medicines. Starkey told Hartlib's friends of his contact with an "adept" in New England from whom he supposedly had obtained the secret of transmutation and a number of unpublished alchemical treatises. The account was expanded and clothed in more mystification as part of Starkey's contribution to alchemical verse, *The Marrow of Alchemy* (1654–1655).

With the publication of *Natures Explication and Helmont's Vindication* (1657), Starkey entered the dispute between those physicians who adhered to the "Paracelsian compromise" and those who advocated more frequent use of chemical remedies. Starkey's book, an outspoken defense of Helmontian doctrines, was followed by *Pyrotechny Asserted and Illustrated* (1658), in which he continued the style of rhetoric that won him the friendship of only a small fraternity. Starkey claimed that his books were based on the experimental method and a desire to reform the state of medicine, but only vague processes were given for his medicaments.

After a brief excursion into the polemical exchange accompanying the Restoration, Starkey returned to iatrochemical controversies. He frequently resorted to print to combat fellow chemical practitioners, both to secure priority for his own medicines and to condemn those whose preparations invited censure of the chemical cause. A last exchange with the so-called "Galenists" was cut short by the Plague in 1665. Starkey remained in London to treat victims of the disease, of which he himself died at an unknown date.

During his lifetime, only one of his "American" alchemical manuscripts was published, apparently without his permission, but a number of treatises were printed after his death under the pseudonym Eirenaeus Philalethes. Several of these works on the theory and practice of transmutation and related matters became classics of alchemical literature, especially the *Introitus apertus* (1667), which appeared in English as *Secrets Reveal'd* (1669). Evidence points to Starkey as the probable author of the tracts, although John Winthrop, Jr., may have served as the inspiration for the story of the New England adept.

BIBLIOGRAPHY

I. ORIGINAL WORKS. Starkey's *The Marrow of Alchemy* (London, 1654–1655) was published in 2 pts. under the pseudonym "Eirenaeus Philoponos Philalethes." *Natures Explication and Helmont's Vindication* (London, 1657) and *Pyrotechny Asserted and Illustrated* (London, 1658) were followed by political publications concerning the Restoration. Other polemical tracts were *The Admirable Efficacy, and Almost Incredible Virtue of True Oyl, Which is Made of Sulphur-Vive* (London, 1660); *George Starkeys Pill Vindicated From the Unlearned Alchymist* [London, 1663 or 1664]; *A Brief Examination and Censure of Several Medicines* (London, 1664); and *A Smart Scourge for a Silly, Sawcy Fool* ([London], 1664). Starkey's *An Epistolar Discourse to the Learned and Deserving Author of Galeno-Pale* was printed with George Thomson's ΠΛΑΝΟ-ΠΝΙΓΜΟΣ *or, a Gag for Johnson* (London, 1665). *Liquor Alchahest* (London, 1675), J. Astell, ed., was a posthumous work.

The most influential of the "Philalethes" essays was *Introitus apertus* (Amsterdam, 1667), printed in English as *Secrets Reveal'd* (London, 1669); also important are those collected in W. Cooper, ed., *Ripley Reviv'd* (London, 1678). Others are in M. Birrius, ed., *Tres tractatus de metallorum transmutatione* (Amsterdam, 1668), and in W. Cooper, ed., *Opus tripartitum de philosophorum arcanis* (London, 1678). Philalethes' *The Secret of the Immortal Liquor Called Alkahest* (London, 1683) was advertised as a separate imprint by bookseller William Cooper and was included in his *Collectanea chymica* (London, 1684).

II. SECONDARY LITERATURE. On Starkey, see the following, listed chronologically: John L. Sibley, *Biographical Sketches of Graduates of Harvard University*, I (Cambridge, Mass., 1873), 131–137; John Ferguson, "The Marrow of Alchemy," in *Journal of the Alchemical Society*, **3** (1915), 106–129; George H. Turnbull, "George Stirk, Philosopher by Fire," in *Publications of the Colonial Society of Massachusetts*, **38** (1949), 219–251; Ronald S. Wilkinson, "George Starkey, Physician and Alchemist," in *Ambix*, **11** (1963), 121–152; and "The Problem of the Identity of Eirenaeus Philalethes," *ibid.*, **12** (1964), 24–43; J. W. Hamilton-Jones, "The Identity of Eirenaeus Philalethes," *ibid.*, **13** (1965), 52–53; Ronald S. Wilkinson, "The Hartlib Papers and Seventeenth-Century Chemistry, Part II: George Starkey," *ibid.*, **17** (1970), 85–110; "Further Thoughts on the Identity of Eirenaeus Philalethes," *ibid.*, **19** (1972), 204–208; "Some Bibliographical Puzzles Concerning George Starkey," *ibid.*, **20** (1973), 235–244; and "George Starkey, an Early Seventeenth-Century American Entomologist," in *Great Lakes Entomologist*, **6** (1973), 59–64. The most recent discussion of the Philalethes matter is in Wilkinson, *The Younger John Winthrop and Seventeenth-Century Science* (London, 1975), ch. 6.

RONALD S. WILKINSON

STARLING, ERNEST HENRY (*b.* London, England, 17 April 1866; *d.* Kingston, Jamaica, 2 May 1927), *physiology, education.*

In circulatory physiology the Starling legacy is conceptually one of the most influential in the twentieth century. The "Starling sequence," embracing both central circulatory function and fluid exchange at the capillary level, was and remains the unifying theme of contemporary circulatory theory.

Starling was born into a family of limited financial means and fundamentalist religious belief. His father, Matthew Henry Starling, was a barrister and served for many years as clerk of the crown at Bombay, returning to England once every three years. Starling's mother, the former Ellen Watkins, remained in Britain and had the responsibility of rearing their children, of whom Ernest was the eldest. He received his early education at Islington (1872–1879) and at King's College School (1880–1882). In 1882 he entered Guy's Hospital Medical School (London), where he set a record for scholarship and received his qualifying degree (M.B., Lond.) in 1889.

One of the most influential periods in Starling's formative years was the summer of 1885 spent in Kühne's laboratory at Heidelberg. It probably marked the beginning of his strong rejection of empiricism as the basis for clinical practice, and it played a role in directing him toward physiology as a means of bringing basic science to the bedside. In 1887 he became demonstrator in physiology at Guy's and in 1890 began part-time work in Schäfer's laboratory at University College, where he began a lifelong association with William Maddock Bayliss.

It was a highly productive and complementary union. Bayliss was the learned, methodical, and cautious partner; Starling was the aggressive, impatient, and sometimes incautious visionary. The first of their joint papers appeared in 1891, and in January 1902 they presented a preliminary communication that opened the door to the vast field of hormonal function. Published in full in September 1902, the paper established the existence and role of secretin, a product of the duodenum; and in 1905 Starling coined the word "hormone" to designate the body's "chemical messengers" produced by the endocrine glands.

In 1892 Starling again went to Germany, this time to work with Rudolf Heidenhain at Breslau; and on his return he attacked the problems of lymph production, capillary permeability, and the physiological effects of osmotic forces. On the basis of his findings, he began the synthesis of what came to be called the "Starling equilibrium," referring to the balance between intravascular pressure and osmotic forces at the capillary level.

With his acceptance in 1899 of the Jodrell professorship at University College, Starling finally joined Bayliss full time. It was at University College that he shifted his interest from the peripheral circulation to the heart itself. His career as a scientific investigator reached a peak in the years immediately preceding World War I with the publication of two papers on control of the heart, written with S. W. Patterson, who later became his son-in-law.

Starling's wartime service was turbulent, largely because of his outspoken impatience with the obtuseness, where scientific matters were concerned, of his military superiors. He was ultimately sent to Thessaloniki, Greece, with no specific assignment and little opportunity to apply his extraordinary talents in the service of his country. Paradoxically, the only recognition he ever received from his government (the comparatively minor Companion of the Order of St. Michael and St. George) came for his "services at Salonika."

In 1919 Starling delivered the most significant lecture of his career, correcting some of his earlier oversimplified statements on circulatory control and anticipating many present-day workers. Unfortunately, the lecture received little attention at the time and was published in a journal of very limited circulation. His remaining years were vigorous but somewhat anticlimactic. In 1922 Starling accepted the Royal Society's Foulerton research professorship. Despite deteriorating health, he continued his research work with fellows and students from all over the world. He died aboard ship, while on a Caribbean cruise, and was buried at Kingston, Jamaica.

Starling was elected fellow of the Royal Society in 1899 and was a prominent member of the Physiological Society. He was honorary member of many foreign scientific organizations and delivered the Harvey lecture for 1908 in New York.

Starling influenced several areas of physiology and medicine. His work with Bayliss on capillary function and on hormones would, in itself, guarantee him great prominence. But he is best-known for his work on the heart. Focusing primarily on the intrinsic response of the isolated heart to increased filling, Starling formulated a widely quoted law of the heart and summarized the concept in his Linacre lecture (1915). Unfortunately, in the lecture he attempted rather uncritically to extend his findings

on the isolated heart to the intact organism at rest and under stress. Within the next few years he recognized the inadequacy of his earlier concepts, and in 1919 he extended and refined them, incorporating intrinsic myocardial response as one feature of a highly complex control system. Subsequent work in the field has, in large measure, consisted of extensions and elaborations of the views set out by Starling in 1919.

Starling was astonishingly gifted in synthesizing disparate views and information to produce meaningful and effective generalizations. His experimental work was often of simple design and yielded data that have sometimes been thought inadequate to support his conclusions. But using those data and building on the work of several German physiologists, of whom Otto Frank was the most significant, Starling arrived at an expansive and surprisingly accurate understanding of circulatory function as a whole.

Starling's eloquent, often anguished, and biting comments on education still carry great conviction. He called for ". . . educational reform, or even revolution, for the maintenance of our place in the world," and added that ". . . in matters of urgent necessity [such as education] it is unprofitable to count the cost." Writing soon after the Armistice, he reserved his most forceful words for the great peril into which, in his view, the British educational system had brought the nation. "The astounding and disastrous ignorance [of science] . . . displayed by members of the government in the early days of the war raised some doubts . . . as to the efficiency of the education imparted to . . . the upper classes." Noting that Germany had, since Napoleon's day, laid great emphasis on education as a means of enhancing national power, he said that Britain, against such a force, could oppose only " . . . a kindly, gentlemanly stupidity." He attributed Britain's salvation to the self-sacrifice and bravery of her young people: "The great rally of the nation occurred in spite of an education which taught the ruling classes that their first duty was to their clan, their party, or their service. . ." ("Science in Education," p. 474).

Views like these fill in the gaps left when one limits his attention to Starling's scientific publications. Physiology was his passion, but it was not in itself sufficient. He emerges not only as a great scientist but also as a responsible and pragmatic activist in education. He and his colleagues, notably Bayliss, changed the face of classical physiology more, probably, than any other group since Harvey's time. And in the course of his work on the circulation, Starling succeeded to a remarkable degree in replacing empiricism with scientific understanding as the basis for medical practice at its best. But if his pungent and highly critical attacks on British education affected the system, the results were, at least in his lifetime, very difficult to discern.

BIBLIOGRAPHY

Starling's publications include "The Arris and Gale Lectures on Some Points in the Pathology of Heart Disease. Lecture I. On the Compensatory Mechanisms of the Heart. Lecture II. The Effects of Heart Failure on the Circulation. Lecture III. On the Causation of Dropsy in Heart Disease," in *Lancet* (1897), **1**, 569–572, 652–655, 723–726; "The Mechanism of Pancreatic Secretion," in *Journal of Physiology*, **28** (12 Sept. 1902), 325–353, written with W. M. Bayliss; "On the Chemical Correlation of the Functions of the Body," in *Lancet* (1905), **2**, 339–341, 423–425, 501–503, 579–583; "On the Mechanical Factors Which Determine the Output of the Ventricles," in *Journal of Physiology*, **48** (8 Sept. 1914), 357–379, written with S. W. Patterson; "The Regulation of the Heart Beat," *ibid.* (23 Oct. 1914), 465–513, written with S. W. Patterson and Hans Piper; *The Linacre Lecture on the Law of the Heart* (London, 1918), delivered at St. John's College, Cambridge, in 1915; "Natural Science in Education: Notes on the Position of Natural Sciences in the Educational System of Great Britain," in *Lancet* (1918), **2**, 365–368; "Science in Education," in *Science Progress*, **13** (1918–1919), 466–475; and "On the Circulatory Changes Associated With Exercise," in *Journal of the Royal Army Medical Corps*, **34** (1920), 258–272.

CARLETON B. CHAPMAN

STAS, JEAN-SERVAIS (*b.* Louvain, Belgium, 21 August 1813; *d.* Brussels, Belgium, 13 December 1891), *chemistry.*

Stas was the son of a stovemaker of Louvain. As a boy he was taken to Paris by his elder brother Guillaume, a pupil of the sculptor François Rude, to pose for the statue *Neapolitan Fisherboy Playing With a Tortoise*, now at the Louvre. In 1832 Stas entered the medical faculty of the University of Louvain. After receiving the M.D. in 1835, he became assistant to his former professor of chemistry, Jean-Baptiste Van Mons, an expert in pomology who owned an apple nursery and experimented on fruit trees. When the nursery was displanted, Stas and Van Mons's other assistant,

L. G. De Koninck, were provided with a large supply of fresh roots of apple trees from which they isolated a crystalline glucoside that they named phlorizin. Stas conducted research on this substance in a small laboratory that he had equipped in the attic of his father's house.

In 1837 Stas moved to Paris, to profit from the scientific milieu. As a collaborator of Dumas he performed a complete study of phlorizin, splitting it into phloretin and glucose. Stas published papers with Dumas on the composition of carbonic acid and on chemical types, and worked with him on the composition of water and on the action of potassium hydroxide on alcohols.

Stas's career was markedly influenced by contemporary research on the composition of carbonic acid. Following Dalton's hypothesis that the constant ratio combining weights of elementary substance is in the same ratio of their relative atomic weights, the determination of atomic weight had become an objective of prime importance to chemists.

In September 1840 Stas was appointed to the chair of chemistry at the Military School in Brussels. He began teaching in February 1841 under unfavorable conditions, for he lacked adequate facilities for research. During the next four years he contributed to the determination of the atomic weight of carbon. Proceeding by way of the combustion of carbon monoxide, he deduced the atomic weight as between 75 and 75.06 through comparing the weight of carbon dioxide formed by the reduction of a known weight of copper oxide under the action of carbon monoxide.

Following the publication in 1860 of his "Recherches sur les poids atomiques," Liebig arranged financial help for Stas from the king of Bavaria, a gesture that inspired the Belgian government to grant him a subsidy of 6,000 francs, to cover three years' expenses.

Like Dumas, Stas had been inclined to accept Prout's hypothesis that atomic weights are whole-number multiples of the atomic weight of hydrogen. In 1860 he published his main work, "Recherches sur les rapports réciproques des poids atomiques," a study devoted to a number of elements (nitrogen, chlorine, sulfur, potassium, sodium, lead, and silver) that were considered by Dumas to support Prout's hypothesis. In this work Stas demonstrated that the values of the atomic weights he had determined were neither multiples of unity, nor of one half, as Marignac believed, nor of one quarter, as Dumas maintained. This publication led Marignac to doubt the universality of the law of definite proportions. In three papers collectively entitled "Nouvelles recherches sur les lois des proportions chimiques, sur les poids atomiques et leurs rapports mutuels" (1865), Stas presented the results of an extensive series of experiments devoted to the new demonstration. By painstaking and accurate measurements he established that atomic weights were incommensurable, thereby disproving the facile conclusion that discrepancies with whole-number values were due merely to experimental errors. Prout's hypothesis was thus discredited.

Stas determined atomic weights using indirect methods. To determine the atomic weight of nitrogen, for example, he measured (1) the amount of ammonium chloride required to precipitate the chloride of silver from a silver nitrate solution. The result was $Ag : NH_4Cl = 100 : 49.6$; (2) the weight of potassium nitrate obtained by repeated evaporation of potassium chloride with nitric acid, and the weight of potassium chloride obtained from potassium nitrate by evaporation with hydrochloric acid; the result gave an atomic weight of 14.03; (3) the weight of silver nitrate obtained by the dissolution of silver in nitric acid and by evaporation; the result was that 100 Ag yielded 157.4952 $AgNO_3$ not fused, and 157.484 fused, which gives $AgNO_3$ = 169.99 (Ag = 107.94) $\therefore$ N = 14.05. The mean result of these experiments was N = 14.09, which differs little from the currently accepted value, 14.008, achieved through the refinements introduced by recourse to physical methods.

Stas was also active in toxicology and published several papers on this subject in the early 1850's. For a criminal case in which nicotine had been used he developed a method for detecting the poison in the victim's body. It was later generalized to detect alkaloids in cases of poisoning.

Suffering from a herpetic disorder of the respiratory tract, Stas became professor emeritus in 1868. His pension covered only his living expenses. His modest inheritance was exhausted by the research expenses of the laboratory that he had equipped in his own house, where he accomplished the first part of his work on atomic weights.

In 1872 Stas resigned his post as commissioner of currency at the mint, to which he had been appointed in 1865. His simple way of life, his dedication to his work, his undaunted independence, exemplary tolerance, and commitment to the progress of higher education and research were made manifest in the deep influence he exerted in Belgium, which occasionally earned him disfavor in official circles.

BIBLIOGRAPHY

I. Original Works. Stas's writings were collected in Oeuvres complètes, W. Spring and M. Depaire, eds., 3 vols. (Brussels, 1894).

II. Secondary Literature. On Stas and his work, see R. Delhez, "Jean-Servais Stas, 1813–1891," in Florilège des sciences en Belgique pendant le XIXe siècle et le début du XXe (Brussels, 1968), 285–321; L. Errera, "Jean-Servais Stas," in Revue de Belgique, 2nd ser., 4 (1892), 192–210; L. Henry, "Une page de l'histoire de la chimie générale en Belgique: Stas et la loi des poids," in Bulletin de l'Académie royale de Belgique. Classe des sciences (1899), 815–848; J. W. Mallet, "Stas Memorial Lecture. Jean-Servais Stas and the Measurement of the Relative Masses of the Atom of the Chemical Elements," in Journal of the Chemical Society, 63 (1893), 1–56; and J. R. Partington, A History of Chemistry, IV (London–New York, 1964), 876–878.

See also the following works by W. Spring: "Lecture sur la vie et les travaux de Stas," in Bulletin de l'Académie royale de Belgique, Classe des sciences, 3rd ser., 21 (1878), 736–761; "Notice sur la vie et les travaux de Jean-Servais Stas," in Annuaire de l'Académie royale de Belgique, 59 (1893), 217–376; and Académie Royale de Belgique, Biographie nationale, XXIII (Brussels, 1921–1924), cols. 654–684.

Also useful is Prout's Hypothesis (Edinburgh, 1932), which contains papers by Prout, Stas, and Marignac.

Marcel Florkin

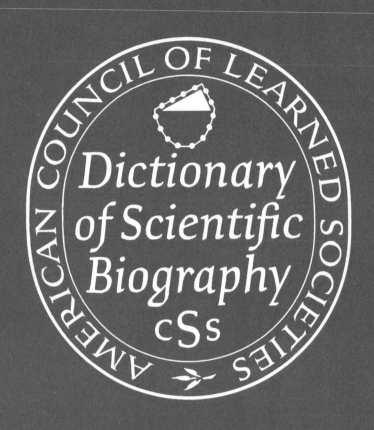

AMERICAN COUNCIL OF LEARNED SOCIETIES

Dictionary
of Scientific
Biography

cSs